ANNUAL REVIEW OF PSYCHOLOGY

ANNUAL REVIEW OF PSYCHOLOGY

VOLUME 38, 1987

MARK R. ROSENZWEIG, *Editor*

University of California, Berkeley

LYMAN W. PORTER, *Editor*

University of California, Irvine

ANNUAL REVIEWS INC.   4139 EL CAMINO WAY   P.O. BOX 10139   PALO ALTO, CALIFORNIA 94303-0897

ANNUAL REVIEWS INC.
Palo Alto, California, USA

International Standard Serial Number: 0066–4308
International Standard Book Number: 0–8243–0238-9
Library of Congress Catalog Card Number: 50-13143

Typesetting by Kachina Typesetting Inc., Tempe, Arizona; John Olson, President
Typesetting coordinator, Janis Hoffman

This volume is dedicated to the memory of

Jean Heavener

Production Editor of Volumes 20–38 of the

Annual Review of Psychology

ANNUAL REVIEWS INC. is a nonprofit scientific publisher established to promote the advancement of the sciences. Beginning in 1932 with the *Annual Review of Biochemistry*, the Company has pursued as its principal function the publication of high quality, reasonably priced *Annual Review* volumes. The volumes are organized by Editors and Editorial Committees who invite qualified authors to contribute critical articles reviewing significant developments within each major discipline. The Editor-in-Chief invites those interested in serving as future Editorial Committee members to communicate directly with him. Annual Reviews Inc. is administered by a Board of Directors, whose members serve without compensation.

ANNUAL REVIEWS OF	Materials Science	SPECIAL PUBLICATIONS
Anthropology	Medicine	
Astronomy and Astrophysics	Microbiology	Annual Reviews Reprints:
Biochemistry	Neuroscience	Cell Membranes, 1975–1977
Biophysics and Biophysical Chemistry	Nuclear and Particle Science	Immunology, 1977–1979
Cell Biology	Nutrition	
Computer Science	Pharmacology and Toxicology	Excitement and Fascination
Earth and Planetary Sciences	Physical Chemistry	of Science, Vols. 1 and 2
Ecology and Systematics	Physiology	
Energy	Phytopathology	Intelligence and Affectivity,
Entomology	Plant Physiology	by Jean Piaget
Fluid Mechanics	Psychology	
Genetics	Public Health	Telescopes for the 1980s
Immunology	Sociology	

For the convenience of readers, a detachable order form/envelope is bound into the back of this volume.

PREFACE

Hans Wallach, author of this year's Prefatory Chapter, has a long history of significant contributions to our field. Dr. Wallach was recently elected to the National Academy of Sciences and also received the Distinguished Scientific Contribution Award from the American Psychological Association in 1983. Readers intrigued with perceptual issues will find his chapter on "Perceiving a Stable Environment When One Moves" of great interest.

This year our special "Timely Topic"—in our series of reviews written with shorter deadlines and covering subjects not included on our regular Master List of topics—is not a solo chapter but a trio. Nancy F. Russo and Florence Denmark provide an overview of "Contributions of Women to Psychology," Hazel Markus and Elissa Wurf analyze "The Dynamic Self-Concept," and David O. Sears reviews current and recent work in the emerging field of "Political Psychology."

The other chapters in the current volume reflect the various categories of the Master List of topics. The Master List undergoes some modification every year, but readers can acquaint themselves with its contents by consulting the cumulative index of chapters on pages 773–76 of this volume.

As usual each year, we must with regret say goodbye to departing members of the Editorial Committee. Norman Garmezy and Bert Green completed their terms on the Committee this past year. With sagacity and wit they have provided excellent input into Committee deliberations through their extensive knowledge of both psychology and psychologists. Also, we wish to acknowledge Bert's special assistance in helping to edit the chapters relating to research methodology.

The Editorial Committee is pleased to welcome as our new members Gordon Bower, whose term began in 1986, and Frances Horowitz, whose term begins in 1987.

We are saddened by the death of Jean Heavener, which occurred when the production of this volume was almost complete. In the Preface to Volume 20 (1969) we acknowledged Jean's cheerful and efficient collaboration in her first year as Assistant Editor. Since then she maintained these qualities, providing invaluable assistance to hundreds of reviewers, as well as faithful collaboration and friendship to the editors, continuing her work even in spite of serious health problems in recent years. Readers and we are in her debt for striving unceasingly to maintain clarity of expression and accuracy of citation in these volumes and for accomplishing marvels to keep their production on time.

L. W. P.
M. R. R.

Annual Review of Psychology
Volume 38, 1987

CONTENTS

SOME RELATED ARTICLES IN OTHER *ANNUAL REVIEWS*

From the *Annual Review of Anthropology*, Volume 15 (1986)

Language Socialization, Bambi Schieffelin and Elinor Ochs
The Changing Role of Women in Models of Human Evolution, Linda M. Fedigan
Acoustic-Phonetic Issues in Speech Perception, Arthur G. Samuel and Vivien Tartter
The Anthropology of Emotions, Catherine Lutz and Geoffrey M. White

From the *Annual Review of Neuroscience*, Volume 10 (1987)

Visual Motion Processing and Sensory-Motor Integration for Smooth Pursuit Eye Movements, Stephen G. Lisberger, E. J. Morris, and L. Tychsen
Visual Processing in Monkey Extrastriate Cortex, John H. R. Maunsell and William T. Newsome
Computational Maps in the Brain, Eric I. Knudsen, Sascha du Lac, and Steven D. Esterly
The Analysis of Visual Motion: From Computational Theory to Neuronal Mechanisms, Ellen C. Hildreth and Cristof Koch
Long-Term Potentiation, Timothy J. Teyler and P. DiScenna
Molecular Mechanisms of Memory: Second Messenger-Induced Modification of Protein Kinases in Neurons, James H. Schwartz and Steven M. Greenberg

From the *Annual Review of Public Health*, Volume 8 (1987)

Alternatives to Using Human Experience in Assessing Health Risks, D. P. Rall, M. D. Hogan, J. E. Huff, B. A. Schwetz, and R. W. Tennant
Health Status Measures, Marilyn Bergner and Margaret L. Rothman
On the Use of Large Data Bases In Health Care Studies, Frederick A. Connell, Paula Diehr, and Gary L. Hart
Graphical Methods in Statistical Analysis, Lincoln E. Moses
Social/Economic Status and Disease, M. G. Marmot, M. Kogevinas, and M. A. Elston
Trends in the Health of the Elderly Population, Jacob A. Brody, Dwight B. Brock, and T. Franklin Williams
The Emergence of Youth Suicide: An Epidemiologic Analysis and Public Health Perspective, Mark L. Rosenberg, Jack C. Smith, Lucy E. Davidson, and Judith M. Conn
Women, Work, and Health, Gloria Sorensen and Lois M. Verbrugge

From the *Annual Review of Pharmacology and Toxicology*, Volume 27 (1987)

From the *Annual Review of Sociology*, Volume 12 (1986)

From the *Annual Review of Medicine*, Volume 38 (1987)

Coming for 1988...

CHAPTERS PLANNED FOR THE NEXT *ANNUAL REVIEW OF PSYCHOLOGY*, Volume 39

Hans Wallach

Ann. Rev. Psychol. 1987. 38:1–27

PERCEIVING A STABLE ENVIRONMENT WHEN ONE MOVES*

Hans Wallach

Department of Psychology, Swarthmore College, Swarthmore, Pennsylvania 19081

CONTENTS

VISUAL STIMULATION CAUSED BY AN OBSERVER'S MOVEMENTS

When we move we produce visual stimulation that could also be caused by motion of the environment. If that stimulation were caused by environmental motion, it would cause us to perceive motion, but when our own movements produce that stimulation, with few exceptions, no perception of motion will result. Turning or nodding head movements, for instance, cause displacements of the environment relative to the eyes that could also have been

---

*This is the eighth in a series of prefatory chapters written by eminent senior psychologists.

brought about by brief rotations of the environment about the subject. Turning the head to the right or moving the environment to the left may bring about the same relative displacement between head and environment and therefore identical visual stimulation. Yet if the environment were moving about us, we would see it move, and when we turn the head we see a stationary scene. The nervous system can distinguish between the two cases because there is sensory information that says, in one case, that the head is moving and, in the other, that it is stationary. Such proprioceptive information has an influence on the outcome of visual stimulation.

There are other circumstances where our own movements evoke from the stationary environment visual stimulation that might have been produced by objective motions, and where only proprioception provides a basis for a distinction. When we move forward, objects which we approach fill larger and larger portions of our visual field. The whole scene in front of us expands. This expansion is not perceived as such. However, if such an expansion were objectively given while we remained stationary, we would either perceive it as such or we would see the scene move toward us. Neither is seen when we cause the expansion by moving forward. Finally, there is the stimulation caused by objects or arrangements of objects that we pass when we move forward. Objects that lie to the side of one's path are successively seen from different directions. This produces the same stimulation that would be caused by turning the object through a small angle. Only rarely is such a rotation perceived. It is sometimes seen when one observes a flat landscape from the window of a rapidly moving train; the landscape seems to turn about a point near the horizon. Yet when one walks, one is mostly not aware of this rotation; the environment appears stationary. We accept this readily, while the rotating landscape seems to present a problem. The reverse should be the case since the rotation is actually given to the eye, whereas not seeing it raises one of the problems we shall have to deal with.

It is hardly surprising that the visual stimulation that results from our own movements is rarely considered. We perceive our environment as rigid and stationary, and we know that the environment in which we move is stable. When perceptual experience agrees with what is known about the physical environment, most people see no problem, but as psychologists, we have to compare perceptual experience with the pattern of stimulation. If we do that, our problem is clear: Sensory inputs that could lead to the perception of motions of the environment will not do so when they are caused by our own movements.

It would be simple if a general mechanism were responsible for the stability of the environment during our movements. Conceivably there could be an arrangement that prevents perception of any motion of the environment during bodily movement, but a series of simple observations shows that this is not so. Not all lateral displacements of the environment during head turning go unperceived. This can be seen when an inverting lens is worn during head turning. Normally, turning the head to the right will cause the environment to move to the left in relation to the head. When the inverting lens reverses this movement to the left into one to the right, one will see the environment move to the right. The environment will appear to swing with each head movement. An analogous demonstration can be made concerning the stimulation received from objects we pass as we move forward. Because it is seen successively from different directions, the scene to the side of one's path slowly rotates relative to one's eyes—counterclockwise when the scene is on one's right—and the same is true of a single object that is actually stationary. If these rotations were not perceived because no such rotations are perceived when one walks, it should not matter if the counterclockwise rotation were reversed, for instance, by looking through a reversing prism, but it does. An object on one's right that is given with clockwise instead of counterclockwise rotation as one passes it *is* perceived to turn.

Processes that Compensate for Such Stimulation

Such observations cannot be explained by a mechanism that prevents perception of environmental motion when we are moving. Rather, we deal here with several compensation processes that evaluate visual inputs by comparing them with proprioceptive data that represent our movements. For instance, when one turns one's head to the right and thereby causes the environment to move relative to the head to the left, the visual stimulus that ordinarily would cause one to perceive a motion to the left will not do so, because it occurs simultaneously with the proprioceptive stimuli that represent the head movement. Since both the visual and the proprioceptive stimulation have the same cause—a turning of the head—the two sets of stimuli stand in a fixed relation to each other. If that is the case, the compensation process prevents the visual stimulation from leading to perceived motion, and immobility results. If it is not the case, as in the two instances just cited, motion will be perceived.

In these instances the given motions are grossly different from the relative motion that the subject's movements produce. We now turn to the question of what happens when the given motions are not as different from the relative motions that are caused by the subject's movements. Are the motions then also perceived? Or more precisely, how much must the given motions be different from the movement-produced motions for some motion to be perceived? This is an important question for it amounts to asking: how accurate are the compensation processes that result in environmental immobility during the subject's movements?

The Accuracy of Compensation

COMPENSATION FOR THE EFFECT OF HEAD TURNING OR NODDING   Turning the head to the right by 20° will result in the environment moving 20° to the left in relation to the head, but what would happen if the environment turned by 25°? This would require an arrangement where the environment can be made to move dependent on the head movement. To achieve the 25° turning of the environment to the left when the head turns right by 20°, the environment must be made to move 5° to the left simultaneously with the head movement. This is done by coupling environmental motion to the head movement so that the environment shifts during every head movement by 5/20 of the head rotation. The total relative displacement is then 25° when the head turns 20°. In such an arrangement, *all* subjects perceive environmental motion. Motion of the surround is also perceived when the environment shifts by 1° during a 20° head turn. In fact, young and healthy subjects regularly detect environmental motions during head turning that amount to 3% of the head movement, whether it is against the head rotation or in the direction with it, that is, whether it is in effect added to or subtracted from the relative motion of the stationary environment. The value of 3% is the result of measurements that determine the range of relative environmental displacements that result in perception of the environment as stationary. We shall call this the *immobility range*. The unit of measurement is the *displacement ratio,* the angle of the real environmental displacement divided by the angle of the head rotation. The range of displacement ratios at which immobility is experienced was found to be between .04 and .06 displacement ratios wide, that is, 2% or 3% on either side of objective immobility. This implies a remarkable precision of the sensory processes that represent the relative environmental displacement and the head movement, and of the compensating process that makes use of them.

A fairly simple apparatus was used to make these measurements. The subject wore a helmet to which a vertical shaft was so attached that it coincided with the head's rotation axis. This shaft was connected to the input shaft of a variable ratio transmission located above the subject's head. The transmission's output shaft, turned vertical, supported a mirror that reflected the beam of a projector on a screen in front of the subject. The beam came to a focus on the screen, and the projected pattern would shift left and right when the subject's head turned and made the mirror turn back and forth. In some experiments the output shaft supported a cylindrical cage of vertical rods with a point source of light in its center. The shadows of the rods fell on a large cylindrical screen that surrounded the subject, and the shadow pattern could be made to rotate to the left or to the right when the subject turned his head from side to side. The variable ratio transmission made it possible to vary the displacement ratio, that is, to vary the extent of the environmental motion that resulted from a particular head rotation. A dial on the transmission provided accurate readings of the displacement ratio for which the transmission was set at a given time (for an illustration see Wallach 1985a, p. 120).

The range of immobility was measured in the following way. The transmission was set so that the pattern seen by the subject moved so much in the direction with each head turn that it was clearly perceived to move. After the displacement ratio had been made smaller by half a percentage point, the subject again sampled the pattern motion by turning his or her head back and forth. If the pattern appeared to move, the transmission setting was changed by another half percentage point and so on until no motion was seen during head turning. At that point one limit of the immobility range was reached. Then the same procedure was used to find the other limit by starting with pattern motion in the direction opposite to the head movement. As mentioned, these limits were 2 or 3% on either side of objective immobility.

COMPENSATION FOR THE RELATIVE ROTATIONS CAUSED BY MOVING FORWARD   The immobility of the scene that we pass when we move forward has hardly ever been understood to be the result of a compensation process. The exception is the work of Wallach et al (1974). It was spurred by rather simple observations that strongly argue for compensation. It is often noticed that the scene in a large painting appears to rotate as we pass by it, or that the head of a portrait seems to turn as if to keep looking at the passing viewer, but this happens only if the painting renders perspective depth realistically. The operation of the compensation process in connection with passing the painting explains this observation. If the scene were real instead of painted, passing it, for instance, on the left would cause it to rotate counterclockwise relative to one's eyes, and compensation would cause this counterclockwise rotation of the scene not to be perceived. Seeing no rotation instead of counterclockwise rotation amounts to perceiving a change in the clockwise direction. In the painting, when the counterclockwise rotation is absent and compensation nevertheless causes the change in the clockwise direction, the nonrotating content of the painting should rotate clockwise. Compensation apparently does operate because the painted scene seems indeed to turn clockwise as we pass it on the left.

The immobility range for the objects that we pass and thereby cause to turn relative to the eyes was measured in a manner analogous to our method of measuring the accuracy of the compensation for the effect of head movements. A variable ratio transmission was suspended from the ceiling; below it and attached to its extended output shaft was the three-dimensional test object. The observer moved back and forth past the object, guided by a handrail. His movement resulted in the object's relative rotation. The changing angle of the observer's position relative to the test object was transmitted to the variable ratio transmission, which in turn could make the test object rotate in either direction and in any proportion of the relative rotation caused by the observer's changing position. It would thereby cause that relative rotation to increase or decrease (for an illustration see Wallach 1985a, p. 121).

The measurements performed with this arrangement showed that the accuracy of the compensation for the relative rotation of objects caused by forward movements is quite low. The mean limits of the range of immobility amounted to about .4 rotation ratios in either direction—that is, the test object had to rotate actually by 40% of its relative rotation before an actual rotation was perceived. Although large, this range of immobility is still compatible with the apparent rotation in paintings of three-dimensional objects or scenes. The paintings present the observer with a failure to rotate that amounts to a rotation ratio of 1.0, well outside the measured .4 limits of the range of immobility.

COMPENSATION FOR DISPLACEMENT OF RETINAL IMAGES DURING EYE MOVEMENT   The compensation process that takes head turning into account and results in immobility of the environment has an analogue that deals with eye movement. A moving object causes displacement of its retinal image in the stationary eye, and this displacement causes perceived motion of the object, but when image displacements are caused by eye movements, they do not lead to perceived motion of the environment. In this compensation process image displacements and registered eye movements are matched up. It has been called position constancy. To differentiate environmental immobility during head movement from it, I have called the latter *constancy of visual direction*.

Mack (1970) did the first experiments that amounted to measuring the range of immobility for image displacements caused by eye movements. She induced saccadic eye movements with light flashes and had them monitored. A visual target, a point of light, moved with varying displacement ratios in the same plane as the eye movement and simultaneously with it. Motions of the target were correctly perceived when they amounted to .2 of the eye movements. Later, William R. Whipple (Whipple & Wallach 1978) made analogous measurements, using a circle subtending 7° of visual angle as a target. Whipple asked his subjects to look from one side of the circle to the other. Again the eye movement was monitored, and the circle was displaced in various amounts as the eye movement took place. He found that target motions amounting to .08 of the simultaneous eye movements were correctly called 80% of the time. When eye movements were vertical a similar threshold for the detection of vertical target motions had a displacement ratio of .09. But even these smaller values are large compared to the .03 displacement ratio at which target motions during head turning are perceived.

The Meaning of the Range of Immobility

These differences in the width of the ranges of immobility are of no consequence where perceiving a stable environment is concerned. It does not matter how wide an immobility range is as long as objective immobility is part of it. On the other hand, a narrow range of immobility favors correct perception of real motions that occur during eye or head movements. Because head movements take more time than saccadic eye movements, it makes sense that compensation for the effect of head movement is more accurate than compensation for the image displacement caused by rapid eye movements; more real motion can take place during head movements. Two conditions transmit to the eyes that an object moves: the direction in which an object is seen gradually changes, and the position of the object changes relative to its background. The first condition is called *subject-relative displacement* and the second *object-relative displacement*. The latter is given to the eye as a changing configuration, and the resulting perceptual process is different in nature from the processes that result from subject-relative displacements (Wallach et al 1982, Wallach 1985b). Our compensation process deals only with the latter, with motion perception that results from displacements relative to the observer. Motion perception that results from object-relative displacement is not subject to the compensation process. Motions of objects that take place during head movements can be correctly perceived because of their displacement in relation to their background, which is perceived as immobile no matter how wide the range of immobility is.

These considerations raise an interesting problem. The motions of most objects are given object-relatively as well as subject-relatively. Only objects that are moving in a homogeneous surround are given solely subject-relatively, and only the perception of their motions is favored by accurate compensation for the effects of head movements. Do we have to assume that accurate compensation develops for the sake of perceiving motions in homogeneous surrounds? If object-relative displacement becomes a stimulus for motion through associative learning (Wallach et al 1978, Wallach 1985b), object-relatively perceived motion may not guide motor responses, and accurate subject-relative motion perception then is needed to guide them.

Dealing with Expansion of a Scene One Approaches

Finally, we come to the perceived stability of a scene that one approaches. The scene appears stable although retinal projection of it expands as it is approached. This case presents a complex problem. Not to see objects grow when their retinal images increase in size as we approach them may not require registering of one's movements and a compensation process. Rather, ordinary size perception may be responsible. The size of an object is correctly perceived even while the size of its retinal image differs greatly because the distance of the object from the eye changes. Under these circumstances, perceived size actually corresponds to the product of the object's image size and its distance as registered by the nervous system. Quite a variety of cues provide the information on which registered distance is based, and under favorable conditions size perception is very accurate. Correct size perception can therefore occur at any point in one's approach to an object, and perceived size may be stable because it is at every instant correctly perceived. A number of distance cues rather than proprioception of one's moving forward would be responsible for the stable size of the objects we approach.

The perceived stability of an approached scene turns out to be not primarily a matter of size perception. Expanding retinal images are stimuli for motion perception also, and compensation for the effect of such stimulation accounts for the stability of the approached scene. This can be shown by a simple experiment in which one's movements do not fit the simultaneously given visual changes. The expansion of the scene in front is here replaced by a contraction, namely, by viewing through a mirror the scene at one's back while taking a few steps forward. The mirror is held at the level of one's head in such a way that one looks backward over one's shoulder. As one walks forward, the scene in the mirror seems to shrink or to recede rapidly. This is in striking contrast to what one sees when the mirror is lowered and one views the scene in front. It will neither appear to expand nor to approach. The nervous system treats the expansion that is normally associated with moving forward differently from a contraction of equal amount, and that suggests that there is a specific effect of moving forward on the perception of expansion. But that does not mean that not seeing objects grow that we approach is entirely the result of a compensation process. Size perception may be involved also. What is needed is a method of testing that is unmistakably a matter of motion perception.

When one looks at a pattern that moves continuously in the same direction for more than 30 sec, two effects of such prolonged exposure can be observed. The apparent speed of the motion becomes slower, and when the motion is stopped, one sees in an objectively stationary pattern a creeping motion in the direction opposite to the motion that had been observed just before. The two effects are manifestations of a quasi-sensory adaptation that developed during the prolonged exposure to the continuous motion.

Flaherty (Wallach & Flaherty 1975) used these quasi-sensory adaptation effects to demonstrate that one's forward movement stops the perception of the expanding motion that is caused by one's forward movement. If the proprioception of forward movement stops the perception of an expanding motion that is associated with such movement, it may also block the motion process caused by a real expansion that is added to the movement-caused expansion, provided that there is room for the added expansion in the immobility range of the compensation process that is here involved. If, during repeated forward movements, the motion perception of a real expansion, along with the expansion caused by the forward movement, were to some degree stopped, the quasi-sensory adaptation effects might be lessened. This was indeed the case and was demonstrated by two experiments.

In one of the experiments, the expanding motion was provided by a spiral that rotated so that the windings appeared to move outward at a standard velocity of 2.25 cm/sec. The perceived speed of expansion of this spiral could be measured by having a subject adjust the rotation velocity of a second spiral until the speed of the two spirals appeared equal. The subjects made such speed matches before and immediately after the exposure period. There were two different exposure conditions, each lasting 10 minutes. In one, the "movement" exposure, the seated subject rocked forward and backward, with the expanding spiral visible only during his forward movements. In the other, the "stationary" exposure, the subject sat still, but here, too, the spiral was alternately visible and invisible. In spite of such intermittent presentation, an effect of prolonged exposure accumulated in the "stationary" condition; after exposure, the average matching speed of expansion was 37% smaller than it had been initially. No such effect was measured after the movement exposure; the mean apparent speed of expansion was exactly the same as it had been before the exposure period. Exposing the expanding spiral only during the subject's forward movements resulted in no accumulation of an effect on perceived speed.

The other experiment made use of the aftereffect of motion; the criterion for the effectiveness of exposure to an expanding spiral was the frequency with which a motion aftereffect, an apparent contraction of a stationary spiral, was reported. The critical exposure conditions were the same as in the previous experiment except that the exposure period was briefer. The result confirmed that of the previous experiment; when the expanding spiral was visible only during forward movements, the frequency of aftereffect reports was strongly diminished. It was also found that backward movements during exposure to contracting motions have no similar effect. Contracting motion paired with backward movements did not diminish the frequency of aftereffect reports. Thus, the combination of moving backwards with contracting retinal images does not initiate compensation, but moving forward does. The reason for this discrepancy may well be that backward movements while one looks forward occur only rarely. Such an influence of frequency would suggest that the compensation operating here is learned.

Limits of the Effect of Compensation

Being unaware of a motion that corresponds to stimulation produced by our own movements does not mean that such stimulation is totally ineffective. The relative rotation of objects we pass is a case in point. The deformations of the retinal images with which objects in relative rotation are given almost certainly give rise to kinetic depth effects, one of the ways by which veridical perception of tridimensional shapes takes place. In fact, the relative rotation of objects we pass during locomotion is the only occasion where the kinetic depth effect comes into play under ordinary circumstances. In experimental demonstrations of the kinetic depth effect (Wallach & O'Connell 1953), the deformations of the retinal images of rotating shapes result in perception of tridimensional objects that rotate. When the image deformations result from the relative rotation of objects that one passes, compensation stops the awareness of rotation but tridimensional form perception is not affected.

Another case where stimulation evoked by our movements has a perceptual effect, although it may not result in awareness of environmental motion, is the expansion of the visual scene when we move forward. Gibson discovered that the center of this expansion serves as visual cue for the direction of one's locomotion (see Gibson 1950, p. 128). The expansion is effective even when it results from walking and is not perceived as such. This was demonstrated by Wallach & Huntington (1973), who obtained adaptation to a laterally displacing wedge prism when the subject, led by the experimenter, was made to walk straight ahead while his or her visual field was laterally displaced. Such an exposure resulted in both visual and proprioceptive adaptation. Proprioceptive adaptation manifested itself in a changed walking direction when after the adaptation period the subject was asked to walk forward in total darkness. Visual adaptation was measured, also in total darkness, by requiring the subject to set a light point in the straight-ahead direction. Since the subject while wearing the prism was, apart from walking, only in visual contact with the environment, discrepancy between the visual and the proprioceptive walking direction caused the adaptation. The visual walking direction, however, was derived from the center of the expansion pattern. Here, too, stimulation evoked by locomotion had an effect, but the subjects were not aware of the motion that resulted from stimulation, although it was effective in another way.

ADAPTATION

Compensation for the Effect of Head Turning or Nodding

The compensation process that keeps the environment stable during head rotation, also called constancy of visual direction, can be altered by perceptual adaptation.[1] The adaptation resembles prismatic adaptation that corrects for the displacement of visual direction caused by wearing wedge prisms. Prismatic adaptation alters the relation between the given and the perceived visual directions so that perception compensates for the displacement of the given directions caused by the prism. Adaptation in the constancy of visual direction corrects for the effect of devices that cause the stationary environment to move optically during head movements so that the environment no longer undergoes the normal relative displacements that are caused by the head movements. Such devices cause the relative displacements of the environment to be larger or smaller than normal relative displacements so that the environment appears to move during each head movement. Such motion will, of course, be perceived only if the added displacement is large enough for the total displacement to fall outside the range of immobility. As adaptation develops, the motion of the environment perceived during every head movement subsides, and the environment becomes again immobile. Such adaptation had been discovered by Stratton (1897), who wore an inverting lens and over days adapted to its effects. Among other effects, such a lens causes a reversal of the motion between the environment and the turning head. While normally a turn of the head to the right causes a relative displacement of the environment to the left, the lens causes the relative displacement to be to the right. Since the compensation process causes the normal displacement in the direction *against* the movement of the head not to be seen, the displacement in the direction *with* the head is perceived as a swinging of the environment with every head movement, with an excursion of roughly twice the angle of the head rotation. Over a period of two days Stratton observed this motion of the environment to subside gradually until the environment remained immobile during head turning. When he took the inverting lens off, he observed still another manifestation of adaptation. He saw a displacement of the environment in the direction opposite to the turning of the head. It had the same direction as the normal relative displacement that results from the head movement but was stronger because adaptation had established an immobility range such that the environment was actually moving in the direction *with* the head movement. This apparent motion subsided rapidly as normal compensation became reestablished.

Stratton's observations were more recently confirmed under conditions where a right-angle prism provided the left-right reversal, but the underlying adaptation process was not investigated in any detail. Only after I designed the method of measuring the immobility range did it become possible to measure partial adaptation instead of having the subject wear the lens or the

---

[1]Perceptual adaptation must be distinguished from sensory adaptation; the latter alters sensitivity to stimulation, while perceptual adaptation alters perceptual processes.

prism until the perceived environment had become stable. This method made it possible to shorten the exposure period from days to hours and eventually to minutes, since partial adaptation of small amounts could be measured accurately. A subject's immobility range, for instance, was measured before the adaptation period and again immediately after it. Ascertaining the adaptation effect then took the form of computing the difference between the midpoints of the two immobility ranges on the displacement ratio scale (DR scale for short).

In our early work on adaptation (Wallach & Kravitz 1965a), no inverting lens or reversing prisms were used because when they are worn an inadvertent tilting of the head causes a tilting of the visual field that nauseates the subject. Instead we used telescopic spectacles of low power. A two-power telescope, for instance, doubles all visual angles and therefore the angle by which a moving object is displaced, and this applies also to the angle of the relative environmental motions caused by head rotation. When this motion is doubled, the environment moves optically with a displacement ratio of 1 in the direction *against* the head rotation. Wallach & Kravitz (1965a) actually used spectacles of .66 power[2] that caused the environment to shift optically with a displacement ratio of .34 in the direction *with* the head rotation. In our first adaptation experiment, 12 subjects wore these spectacles for 6 hr. Their immobility ranges were measured before they put the spectacles on and again immediately after they took them off. All subjects showed adaptation. Since they all saw the environment stationary when it moved to some degree in the direction *with* the head turns, all saw the stationary environment move in the direction *against* the head rotation when they turned their head. What motion of the environment each subject saw as stationary was determined by measuring his or her immobility range after the adaptation period. There were large individual differences in the amount of adaptation achieved. The changes in the midpoint of the immobility ranges after adaptation varied between .10 DR and .345 DR. A change in the displacement ratio of .34 DR meant, of course, that the subject had completely adapted to the spectacles that caused the environment to shift in the amount of .34 DR during each head turn. The mean adaptation measured for all 12 subjects amounted to .175 DR, or one-half of full adaptation.[3]

Adaptation to environmental displacements during head movements could be speeded up by having the subject turn his head continuously during the adaptation period. Since it is the exposure to instances of abnormal dis-

---

[2]These spectacles were constructed in our shop at Swarthmore College according to the scheme of the Galilean telescope.

[3]For a more detailed explication of these experiments, see Wallach & Kravitz 1968, pp. 299–301.

placements of the field content during head movements that causes adaptation, the more frequently such instances occur the faster adaptation should
proceed. Such rapid adaptation can be produced by using the same apparatus
that serves to measure the immobility range. The apparatus is simply set to
some suitable displacement ratio, and the subject keeps turning his head and
observes the shifting environment. When the shifting pattern subtended an
angle of 16° and the displacement amounted to 1.5 DR in the direction *against*
the head movement, 10 min of continuous head turning yielded an adaptation
effect of .137 DR (Wallach & Kravitz 1965b). Much of our subsequent
research employed brief periods of continuous head turning.

We have seen that one manifestation of adaptation to objective horizontal
displacement during head turning consists in an apparent horizontal motion of
the stationary environment during head turning. This motion turned out not to
be merely a matter of experience. Rather, it functions like an objective
displacement. After adaptation to horizontal displacement during head turning, the subjects of Wallach & Frey (1969) pursued a target dot that moved
upward when a subject's head turned to the right and downward during a head
movement to the left. In such a test, the vertical target motion was perceived
to be oblique, the kinematic resultant of the horizontal motion that was the
result of adaptation and the given vertical motion of the target. The authors
obtained estimates of the angle of the sloping motion of the paths and used
them as a measure of adaptation. This slope estimation method of measuring
adaptation had the advantage of requiring only a single trial after adaptation.
It was eventually abandoned, because Bacon (Wallach & Bacon 1977) developed a more accurate method.

In Bacon's method, estimates of the extent of the apparent motion of a
stationary spot were obtained, with the extent of the head movement fixed.
Subjects gave their estimates by marking a distance corresponding to the
extent of the adaptation-caused motion on a paper pad. Before the adaptation
exposure, each subject had given similar estimates for a series of real displacements during head movements of the same fixed extent. This series of
estimates was used to evaluate the subject's postadaptation estimate. This
estimation test was sometimes used along with the test that measured the shift
of the immobility range. The latter was called a compensation test because
those objective environmental motions that after adaptation result in perceived
immobility compensate for the apparent motion of the stationary environment.

The Nature of Adaptation

As stated above, the compensation process that keeps the environment stable
during head movements matches up the stimulation that represents the relative
motion of the environment with proprioceptive stimulation that represents the

head movement. When it comes to explaining adaptation that alters the outcome of this process, three changes may be considered: the outcome of the visual stimulation may be changed; proprioception of the head movement may be changed; or the compensation process itself may be altered.

Wallach & Kravitz (1968) did an experiment that tested whether adaptation consisted of a change in the proprioceptive process that represented the head movement. They demonstrated an auditory analogue to the constancy of visual direction and asked whether adaptation to visual motion during head turning would manifest itself in a shift in the auditory immobility range. If adaptation consists of a change in the representation of the head movement, it should make the auditory immobility range shift in the same direction as it shifts the visual immobility range. The apparatus for measuring the constancy of auditory direction resembled the one for measuring the visual immobility range. The subject's head was attached to a variable ratio transmission whose output shaft turned a rotary switch with 30 contacts that shifted the auditory signal through a row of 30 small speakers in front of the subject. The auditory immobility range was measured before and after an adaptation period lasting an hour, during which the subject wore 1.8 power magnifiers, which caused the visual target to move with a displacement ratio of .8, turned the head frequently, and watched television. While an identical adaptation exposure caused the mean visual range of immobility to shift by .132 DR to target displacements in the direction *against* the head movement, no significant shift of the auditory immobility range was found, and the difference between the two results was significant at the .02 level.[4] This result showed that proprioceptive change does not account for our adaptation.[5]

Wallach & Canal (1976) asked a different question about adaptation. They noted that turning the head to look at another point in the environment involves two kinds of eye movements, a saccade in the direction of the head turn and compensatory eye movements that for moments keep the eyes fixed on a point that together with the whole environment undergoes the relative displacement caused by the head turn. They asked whether perhaps adaptation

[4]Adaptation in the direction *against* the head turning was here deliberately chosen so that a shift in the auditory immobility range would have been in that direction had it occurred. Having the auditory direction move in the direction *with* the head movement to test for an opposite adaptation effect might not have resulted in immobility. A sound direction that moves in the direction *with* the head turn provides the condition of stimulation for perceiving an elevated sound direction (Wallach 1940), and such sound localization would have interfered with our experiment.

[5]This result contradicts a view of Gauthier & Robinson (1975), who studied compensatory eye movements after adaptation to 2.1 power magnifying spectacles lasting 5 days. They attributed the adaptation effects they obtained to a changed evaluation of semicircular canal signals. They found no changes in eye movements when the head was stationary and did not consider changes in the evaluation of eye movements such as Wallach & Bacon (1977) found.

consists in a changed evaluation of these compensatory eye movements. If adaptation is, for instance, to an actual motion of the environment in the direction *with* the head turns, then compensatory eye movements that keep the eyes fixed on a point are diminished, because the point actually moves somewhat in the direction of the head turn. If adaptation takes place and the environment that partially moves with the turns of the head is perceived as stationary, then either one of two changes must have taken place. Either the compensation process had changed so that now a diminished compensatory eye movement results in immobility of the environment, or compensation remained unaltered and the eye movements had become overrated.[6] Fortunately, Wallach & Canal considered, at this point, only the changed evaluation of eye movements, and that turned out to be what happens.

If adaptation consists in changed evaluation of compensatory eye movements, it should not matter how the visual environment moves during the adaptation period so long as the eyes track a mark that undergoes the appropriate head movement–dependent displacements. Wallach & Canal obtained adaptation even when the moving mark was surrounded by a stationary pattern. The latter's immobility indeed did not prevent some adaptation. They also did what seemed to them a control experiment in which motion and rest were reversed. A large pattern representing the visual environment was made to move dependent on head turning while the subject had to fixate a stationary mark, which, because it was stationary, underwent the normal relative displacements caused by the head movements and evoked normal compensatory eye movements. Surprisingly, this condition, too, resulted in some adaptation. It was apparent that the two exposure conditions evoked adaptation processes that were different in nature. The adaptation that resulted from tracking a mark that actually moved during head turning was called "eye movement adaptation," because it presumably consisted in a changed evaluation of compensatory eye movements, and the adaptation that resulted from head movement–dependent motions of a large pattern representing the environment while the eyes performed normal compensatory movements was called "field adaptation."

Wallach & Bacon (1977) compared the two kinds of adaptation with each other. Normal adaptation conditions where the subject looked at the moving pattern freely as in our earlier experiments were included in the comparison. The visual environment was represented by the shadow pattern cast by the cylindrical cage on the curved screen that surrounded the subject and filled his or her visual field. To obtain the conditions for eye movement adaptation, the cage was made immobile and a mirror, connected to the transmission's output

---

[6]For the sake of simplicity, the discussion assumes here complete adaptation, but the consideration fits also partial adaptation.

shaft, reflected the moving mark to the region of the screen in front of the subject. For conditions of normal adaptation and for field adaptation, the output shaft turned the cage so that the movement of the shadow pattern was dependent on the head turns. When conditions for field adaptation were presented, a stationary mark was provided by another lantern. The motion of the shadow pattern or of the mark when it was used for eye movement adaptation amounted to .4 DR and was in the direction *with* the head turns for all adaptation conditions. Exposure lasted always 10 min. Both adaptation tests were used in connection with each of the three adaptation conditions. In the compensation test, the immobility range was measured before and after the adaptation exposure, and in the estimation test, the apparent extent of the motion of the stationary mark was measured as described above.

The results are given in the first two rows of Table 1, which also lists the number of subjects used in each of the experiments. All six adaptation effects listed were significant at the .001 level.

Wallach & Bacon (1977) obtained evidence for Wallach & Canal's proposition that eye movement adaptation consists in a changed evaluation of compensatory eye movements, an overrating when adaptation is to environmental motion in the direction *with* the head turns. There are two ways to show that an overrating of compensatory eye movement can account for this adaptation. In the compensation test, when, after adaptation, actual motion of the test mark in the direction *with* the head turns results in the mark's immobility, compensatory movements that keep the eyes on that mark are shorter than normal. They must be overrated so that the registered extent of the eye movements matches the extent of the head turns and perceived immobility of the mark results, because the compensation process itself is assumed to remain unaltered. Or when, in the estimation test, a stationary mark appears to move in the direction *against* the head turns, the normal

Table 1   Mean adaptation effects of 10 min exposure to three adaptation conditions, in displacement ratio (DR) units and number of subjects (N)

Test	Adaptation Conditions							
	Normal		Eye movement		Field		Field with saccades	
	DR	N	DR	N	DR	N	DR	N
Estimation	.131	16	.055	16	.053	16		
Shift of im- mobility	.098	12	.072	28	.056	28		
Pointing I	.126	12	.133	12	.002	12		
Pointing II			.106	18				
Forward direc- tion	−.004	12	−.013	12	.087	12	.172	12

extent of the eye movements necessary to keep the eye on the stationary mark must be overrated so that the mark appears to undergo this motion.

Wallach & Bacon demonstrated such an overrating of the extent of the eye movements with a simple pointing test (Pointing Test I). In total darkness the subject turned the head to the left by 18°, controlled by a stop. When the stop was reached, a vertical line straight in front of subject's body lit up. The subject had to look at it and point at it. Immediately, the pointing direction was recorded. The subject made three such pointings, and their average direction was computed. The test was repeated after the adaptation exposure. The difference between the two averages became the subject's pointing effect. This test was given in connection with each of the three adaptation conditions.

After eye movement adaptation as well as after normal adaptation, subjects pointed too far to the right, showing that the eye movement to the right that was needed to look at the vertical line was overrated. The mean pointing errors after adaptation were 2.4° and 2.27° respectively and were highly significant. Transformed into DR measures, the pointing effects are listed in the third row of Table 1. No such pointing effect was obtained after field adaptation where the eyes fixated a stationary mark and made normal compensatory movements; and the difference between this result and the results of eye movement and of normal adaptation was also significant (p < .02).

Normal and eye movement adaptation resulted in quite similar pointing effects. Table 1 shows that they were as large as normal adaptation measured with the estimation test. It seems that changed evaluation of eye movements as measured with the pointing test accounts for the normal adaptation that had been obtained. That the adaptation measured after eye movement adaptation conditions was somewhat smaller than the corresponding pointing effect probably resulted from the shadow pattern being stationary during the adaptation exposure. Its normal relative motion provided conflicting information for adaptation, while the result of the pointing test reflected only the abnormal motion of the tracked mark.

We were also able to show that the change in the overrating of eye movements after adaptation did not take place only after the head had just been turned. Eye movement adaptation apparently consists in a changed evaluation of all kinds of eye movements as Pointing Test II showed. This test started with the subject's head locked in normal position and the eyes fixed on a luminous mark straight in front of head and body. When the mark was extinguished, another spot 18° to the right of the mark lit up. The subject had to look at the spot as soon as it appeared and then point at it. The pointing direction was immediately recorded. There were again three such tests before and three after eye movement adaptation. After adaptation, 18 subjects pointed on the average 1.9° farther to the right, a change that was significant at the .001 level. This overrating of the eye movement was equivalent to .106 DR and was not significantly smaller than the result of Pointing Test I.

Another test of visual direction, the forward direction test, that had been used to measure adaptation to a wedge prism (Wallach & Huntington 1973) turned out to show an effect after field adaptation. In that context, the subject, with his head turned to the side by 18°, had to set a luminous mark in the dark to appear to be straight in front of his or her body. The mean settings after the standard field adaptation exposure were 1.6° to the right of the mean pre-adaptation settings, a significant difference at $p < .01$. This effect was equivalent to .087 DR. No such effect was obtained after eye movement adaptation and after normal adaptation. The latter finding suggests that normal adaptation that was produced by 10 min of continuous head movements of moderate extent consisted in eye movement adaptation.

These findings—that the pointing test measured only eye movement adaptation but not field adaptation, and that the forward direction test registered a change only after field adaptation and not after eye movement adaptation—suggests that field adaptation takes place at a level of processing different from the one where eye movement adaptation operates. In field adaptation the eyes fixate a stationary mark and the head movement–dependent actual motions of the environment are given as image displacements. With eye movements corresponding to the normal environmental displacements associated with the head movements, these image displacements are effective at a level of processing where eye positions have been taken into account and where the environment is represented as it is located relative to the head. This higher representation then registers the displacement of the environment relative to the head. When the head is turned under normal conditions, the constancy of visual direction causes this registered displacement to result in environmental immobility. Field adaptation presumably alters the evaluation of displacements represented at this higher level, and the forward direction test that registered only field adaptation is connected with the representation of the environment at this level.

During field adaptation, when the environment is made to move dependent on head turning, the representation of the environment at this higher level registers displacements larger than normal, and the environment is seen to move *with* each head turn. After partial adaptation, displacements somewhat larger than normal are accepted as normal and result in immobility of the environment, while an actually stationary target is perceived to move in the direction *against* the head movements.

The experiment by Wallach & Kravitz (1968), which demonstrated that adaptation in the constancy of visual direction did not transfer to the constancy of auditory direction, eliminated one possible explanation of that adaptation: change in proprioception of the head movement does not account for it. Whether adaptation consists in a changed outcome of visual stimulation or whether the compensation process itself is altered remained an open question. We can now conclude that at least the rapid adaptations that Wallach & Bacon (1977) investigated consist in a changed evaluation of visual stimulation. After eye movement adaptation the pointing tests showed as large an effect of eye movement adaptation as direct measurements. This meant that such adaptation consists in a changed evaluation of eye movements. Similarly, the forward direction test fully measured field adaptation, as the results in Table 1 show, and this made it clear that field adaptation consists in changed evaluation of image displacements.

As stated earlier, compensatory eye movements are not the only eye movements that ordinarily take place during head turning. Saccades in the direction of the head movements also take place. Wallach & Bacon (1977) did an experiment in which such saccades were included in the adaptation conditions. As in their other experiments, a pattern moved during head turns at .4 DR *with* the head turns, but it consisted here of seven columns of groups of three letters. During each head movement to the right the subject had to read a group of three letters in each of two neighboring columns, and that required making a saccade to the right during each right turn of the head. After the 10-min-long adaptation exposure, the forward direction test registered a change of .172 DR. A look at Table 1 shows that this was by far the largest adaptation effect that was obtained under the standard conditions that Wallach & Bacon (1977) employed. If the finding applies, that the forward direction test measures only field adaptation, then the present experiment produces strong field adaptation—a changed evaluation of the representation of the environment after eye position has been taken into account. That the presence of saccades causes adaptation at this level may be an indication that saccades are steered from this level of processing. Inasmuch as the adaptation conditions also evoked compensatory eye movement, eye movement adaptation may also have taken place, and the experiment was likely to have produced adaptation of both kinds. Whether that is the case is worth exploring. It would throw some light on the relationship between the two kinds of compensations involved in the constancy of visual direction.

The two kinds of adaptation strongly suggest that the constancy of visual direction operates at two levels of visual processing. At one, in connection with the operation of compensatory eye movements, eye movements are evaluated; at the other, after eye movements have been taken into account, the visual environment is represented as it is related to the head. It is hard to imagine how one could arrive at this view without knowing about eye movement and field adaptation. Adaptation is an important tool in the investigation of visual processing, and that is an important reason for studying it.

The Secondary Displacement

As Wallach & Kravitz (1965a) pointed out, the relative motion of a visual target depends not only on the head rotation but also on the distance of the target. If that distance is relatively small, the target's displacement is larger than the angle of the rotation of the head would warrant, because the eyes, being located forward of the rotation axis of the head, are laterally shifted during the head rotation. The displacement that depends on this lateral shift of the eyes is additional to the relative target motion caused by the head rotation and has a measurable effect on the target motion up to a distance of two or three meters. Since the distance between the midpoint between the eyes and the head's rotation axis averages 10 cm, the additional displacement of a stationary target caused by head movements amounts to .25 DR when the target distance is 40 cm from the eyes. It amounts to .1 DR when that distance is 1 m, and it is .05 DR when the target is 2 m away. (For the derivation of the formula with which these values were computed see Wallach et al 1972.) This additional displacement caused by the lateral shifting of the eyes will be called secondary displacement.

In our measurements of the immobility range, we used target or pattern distances of 200 cm and 120 cm and found that the midpoint of the immobility range coincided accurately with objective target immobility. At a distance of 120 cm, the average secondary displacement amounts to .083 DR, and compensation for this additional displacement was found to take place. On the other hand, a stationary target 43 cm from the eye was seen to move in the direction against the head turning by half of our subjects. For a group of 10 subjects, the mean midpoint of the immobility range was found to be at .06 DR. Thus, compensation for the secondary displacement was incomplete by this amount. At a distance of 43 cm, the average secondary displacement amounts to .23 DR, but the average compensation amounted only to .17 DR (Wallach et al 1972). Hay & Sawyer (1969), however, measured the immobility range for a target distance of 40 cm using a nodding rather than a turning motion of the head and found that its mean midpoint coincided with objective immobility. We later confirmed their result. Because nodding of the head alters the head position with respect to the gravitational direction, such head movements are probably more sharply represented; this may account for the more accurate compensation during head nodding.

The effect of viewing distance on the constancy of visual direction is best demonstrated by using deceptive distance cues. In the conditions under which the immobility range was measured, only convergence and accommodation served as distance cues. Thus, Wallach et al (1972) had subjects wear spectacles that diminished accommodation by 1.5 diopters and convergence by 5 prism diopters.[7] These spectacles thus caused a target at a distance of 40 cm from the eyes to be viewed with accommodation and convergence for a distance of 1 m.[8] As stated above, the secondary displacement of a stationary target at the distance of 1 m amounts to .1 DR. When the constancy of visual direction takes that distance of 1 m into account, it compensates for a secondary displacement amounting to .1 DR. At the actual target distance of 40 cm, secondary displacement amounts to .25 DR. Since, with the spectacles in place, compensation amounts to .1 DR only, the 40-cm-distant target should be seen to move by .1 DR less than .25 DR. It should therefore appear to move at .15 DR in the direction *with* the head turns. Measurements confirmed this prediction; the mean midpoint of the immobility range for the 40-cm-distant target viewed through the spectacles was found to be .158 DR. The deceptive target distance that the spectacles provided proved fully effective in the compensation process that takes the effect of head movements and the secondary displacements into account.

Wallach et al (1972) also demonstrated an effect of experimentally altered distance perception on the constancy of visual direction. Previously, Wallach & Frey (1972) had found that distance perception based on convergence and accommodation can be altered rapidly when subjects adapt to spectacles like the ones just described. When, for instance, spectacles are worn that have the opposite effect and cause the eyes to be adjusted for distances shorter than the actual distances of the objects viewed, an adaptation develops that partially compensates for the effect of these "near" spectacles. When these spectacles are removed and while this adaptation effect lasts, convergence and accommodation will denote distances larger than normal and target points will appear to be farther away than they really are. Such an adaptation effect, then, changes distance perception in the same direction as wearing the spectacles that were used in the experiment just reported. Therefore, it should change the immobility range in the same direction as did these spectacles. This expectation was confirmed when the immobility range of a target at 40-cm distance was measured twice, once before and again after subjects had adapted to the "near" spectacles for 90 min. It was found that after adaptation the immobility

[7]Such spectacles were much used by Wallach & Frey (1972). They consisted of positive lenses of 1.5 diopters which diminished by that amount the accommodation with which the eye viewed objects at distances of 67 cm or less. The lenses were combined with wedge prisms that diminished the need for convergence of the eyes in corresponding fashion.

[8]Viewing a target at 40 cm distance requires an accommodation amounting to 2.5 diopters. With the spectacles diminishing accommodation by 1.5 diopters and convergence in equivalent amounts, the eyes viewed the target with oculomotor adjustment that corresponded to an accommodation of 1 diopter and to a viewing distance of 1 m.

range had shifted, on the average, by .11 DR. This effect corresponds to 70% of complete adaptation to the "near" spectacles.

These demonstrations of the compensation for the secondary displacement that nearby objects undergo during head movements give a good idea of the complexity of the processes that keep the perceived environment stable during head movements and of the ease with which adaptation can alter them.

Adaptation Unrelated to Existing Compensation

So far I have reported adaptation that altered the constancy of visual direction. Subjects were exposed to objective displacements that either diminished or increased the relative displacements of the stationary environment that are the direct consequence of head turning. The adaptations that developed were modifications of the process that compensates for such relative displacements. Now I am reporting experiments where the head turning–dependent objective displacements were vertical and orthogonal to the relative displacement of the stationary environment that accompanies every head turn. The orthogonal displacements were unrelated to these relative displacements, and any adaptation that developed was unrelated to the constancy of visual directions.

Wallach et al (1969) obtained such adaptation after an exposure period of one hour, during which each of 12 subjects watched a television broadcast through a mirror arrangement that was coupled to their head turning. As the subjects turned their heads back and forth, they saw the TV screen move up and down at .5 DR, that is, at half the angle of their head turns. After the exposure period, a stationary target spot appeared to move down and up. When this effect was measured, it was found that the target spot had to move up and down with a mean displacement ratio of .087 in order to compensate for the apparent motion of the stationary target and to be seen as stationary. A shift of the immobility range amounting to .087 DR means that the exposure resulted in 17.4 percent of complete adaptation.

This kind of adaptation, which was also obtained by Hay (1968), shows that a compensation process can develop from scratch and under completely artificial conditions. Repeated environmental displacement orthogonal to the plane of the head rotation never occurs naturally. If compensation can develop in this case, it follows that the constancy of visual direction can also develop as an adaptation to the relative environmental displacements caused by head movements. But while the constancy of visual direction contributes to the stability of the perceived environment, adaptation to orthogonal displacements occurs only in an artificial situation and is of no advantage. Why does it develop at all? I believe that the central nervous system responds to covariance between proprioceptive information about movements of oneself and stimulation representing environmental motion as a means for identifying those stimuli that represent motions caused by such movements. Since such motion stimuli do not represent genuine environmental events, perceived motion that resulted from such stimulation would have to be disregarded. Instead, the covariance between the representation of our own movements and the stimuli that these movements cause instigates the development of a compensation process. It frees perceptual experience of such uninformative contents. Compensation develops to the point where such covariant visual stimulation no longer results in perception, and that means that the environment becomes stable.

Adaptation to Form Distortions

This interpretation of compensation is supported by two experiments where adaptation developed only when a form distortion caused by spectacles resulted in deformations produced by head movements. In the compensations just discussed, head movements were the causes of the stimulation to which subjects adapted. Whether the head movements caused the stimulation naturally or by means of a mirror arrangement does not matter here. In the experiments to be reported, either the motion that changed the form distortion into deformation could result from head movements and thus be covariant with them, or the motion responsible for deformation could be artificially produced and no head movements made. In the latter case, adaptation did not develop.

Wallach & Barton (1975) adapted subjects to spectacles that caused retinal disparities which in turn caused plane frontal patterns to appear concave instead of flat.[9] The apparent curvature was like an inside view of part of a large cylinder with horizontal axis. During an adaptation period that lasted 20 min, the subjects sat in front of a plane random dot pattern, which they viewed through the spectacles while nodding their heads up and down. When the spectacles were later removed, the pattern appeared to bulge. This adaptation effect was measured by using a test surface with a similar pattern fixed to a flexible metal sheet that could be made to curve. Twice the subject made settings of the flexible surface so that it appeared flat, once before and again after the adaptation period. Because a plane pattern seemed to bulge after adaptation, the flexible surface had to be concave to appear flat. Such measurements made it possible to explore the specific conditions that produce this adaptation. First we demonstrated the need for having the subject see the flat pattern deform: 12 subjects looked at the pattern with the head in a

[9]Viewing a vertical line through a wedge prism with base vertical will cause perception of a small optical curvature of the line. Such a wedge in front of each eye with base toward the temples will cause opposite curvature of the lines in each eye and retinal disparities that make plane patterns concave.

headrest; they saw the pattern as a fixed concave shape.[10] Another group of 12 subjects nodded their heads continuously; the concave shape shifted up and down with the moving heads and caused the pattern to deform. Adaptation occurred only under the latter condition. It caused a curvature that formed a 90-cm-long arc, with a mean height of 2.35 cm (p < .005). At this point the question arose whether the deformation was the only condition necessary for adaptation to develop or whether the head movement was also a necessary condition. In a third adaptation condition, the heads of 16 subjects were stationary and the pattern was made to move up and down continuously. This condition also caused the concave shape produced by the spectacles to shift in relation to the pattern and deform it. No adaptation was here obtained, and this result was significantly different (at the .01 level) from the one obtained with head nodding.

Wallach & Flaherty (1976) did a similar experiment using a different form distortion. It was produced by placing a 30-diopter wedge prism in front of the subject's right eye, with the left eye occluded. The base of the prism was horizontal and downward. In this orientation it caused a distortion in a pattern of evenly spaced horizontal stripes such that the lower part of the pattern looked narrower and its upper part seemed expanded. When the subject nodded his or her head, the prism tilted with the head, and this tilting of the prism caused the distortion to travel up and down with the head movement. After a 10-min adaptation period during which the subject nodded his or her head incessantly, the prism was removed. The stripe pattern then appeared mildly distorted in the opposite manner. This adaptation effect was measured by compensation. A weak wedge prism was selected from a graduated series that would cause the striped pattern to look regular when it was put in front of the eye with base down. For a group of 21 subjects who nodded their heads in the tests, the mean strength of the compensating prism was 2.76 diopters after an adaptation period of 10 min (p < .005).

A further experiment was analogous to the experiments by Wallach & Barton (1975). During the adaptation period the subject either nodded his head or kept it on a biteboard. In that case the pattern was made to deform in the same way as it does during head nodding. The prism that the subject wore during nodding was mounted in front of the subject's eye and was made to undergo the same tilting motions that it underwent when it moved with the nodding head. During the tests, the subject's head was kept immobile by a biteboard. A single group of 16 subjects served in both adaptation conditions, with an interval of 5 days between the two parts of the experiment. Whereas the mean strength of the compensating prism after a 20-min adaptation period

[10]No figural aftereffect (Köhler & Emery 1946) developed, because the subjects did not fixate a stationary point.

of head nodding was 1.91 diopters, there was no adaptation after the subjects observed, for 20 min, the same pattern deformations with the head stationary. The difference between the results was significant at the .01 level.

In both experiments rapid adaptation took place only when the subjects' head movements changed the form distortions caused by the spectacles into deformations of the patterns on which the distortion were visible. But the deformations alone were not sufficient; they had to be caused by head movements, a condition that manifested itself as covariance between the proprioception that represented the head movements and the motions of the distortions visible on the pattern. This covariance is a requisite for the adaptations that were found, and it may be their cause. Because it serves as an indication that the perceived deformations are not genuine environmental facts, the resulting adaptations free perceptual experience of immaterial contents. Covariance, thus, may serve as a general cause for adaptation and may make the existence of a variety of normative tendencies and of specific capacities for developing various compensation processes unnecessary.

APPENDIX: COMPENSATION FOR FIELD ROTATION CAUSED BY HEAD TILTING

So far we have considered the stimulation caused by turning and nodding of the head, horizontal or vertical translatory motions of the environment. A sideways tilting of the head, which amounts to a rotation of the head about a front-back axis, causes rotation of the environment, a change in its orientation relative to the head. The compensation that deals with this relative orientation change was investigated by Wallach & Bacon (1976). The accuracy of this compensation was measured in the same manner as the accuracy of the constancy of visual direction. An apparatus that made it possible to have a tilting of the head cause a pattern in front of the subject to rotate in either direction at a variable ratio to the head rotation was constructed, and the immobility range was measured as before. It turned out to be almost as narrow as the one for the constancy of visual direction—on the average .05 rotation-ratios wide. There was one difference: While, in the case of head turning, the range of immobility was symmetrically located about the point of objective immobility, in the case of head tilting the immobility range comprised, in addition to the point of objective immobility, only objective rotation in the direction *with* the head tilting.

The circular pattern in front of the subject that yielded these results consisted of radial lines that originated from a point in the center of the subjects' visual field. The pattern subtended a visual angle of 40°. Measurements of the range of immobility were taken also for a central portion of the pattern that subtended a visual angle of 5° and for a peripheral region. To obtain the latter, a central portion of the pattern subtending 10° of visual angle was obscured so that only a ring 15° wide was visible. In the latter case, a small lightspot, which the subject had to fixate, marked the invisible center of the radial pattern.

For this ring-shaped peripheral region the range of immobility was somewhat larger than that for the whole pattern; it was .09 rotation-ratios wide. It, too, was asymmetrically located in the *with* direction. A surprising result was obtained for the central region. Its mean immobility range extended from .06 to .184 in the direction *with* the head tilting on the rotation ratio scale. This result means that when the central region was actually stationary, it appeared to turn slightly in the direction *against* the head tilting. Of the 35 subjects who observed the central region 31 saw this motion. Many readers will be able to duplicate this observation when they look through a tube that causes the visible field to subtend only 5° of visual angle or less. When they look at a vertical or horizontal edge through the tube and tilt their heads from side to side, they will see the edge tilt in the direction *against* their head tilting. It appears that in central vision, compensation for field rotation during head tilting is incomplete.

The compensation for field rotation caused by head tilting could be altered by adaptation. Ten minutes of continuous tilting of the head from side to side while the radial pattern in front of the subject turned at a rotation ratio (RR) of .4, either in the direction *with* or *against* the head tilting, yielded measurable adaptation. For the peripheral ring-shaped region it amounted to .064 RR, and for the central region it was .085 RR.

ACKNOWLEDGMENT

This report is an expanded version of the second James J. Gibson Memorial Lecture, which the author delivered at Cornell University in 1982.

Literature Cited

Gauthie, G. M., Robinson, D. A. 1975. Adaptation of the human vestibulo-ocular reflex to magnifying lenses. *Brain Res.* 92:331–35

Gibson, J. J. 1950. *The Perception of the Visual World*. Boston: Houghton Mifflin

Hay, J. C. 1968. Visual adaptation to an altered correlation between eye movement and head movement. *Science* 160:429–30

Hay, J. C., Sawyer, S. 1969. Position constancy and binocular convergence. *Percept. Psychophys.* 5:310–12

Köhler, W., Emery, D. A. 1946. Figural aftereffects in the third dimension of visual space. *Am. J. Psychol.* 40:159–201

Mack, A. 1970. An investigation of the relationship between eye and retinal image

movement in the perception of movement. *Percept. Psychophys.* 8:291–97

Stratton, G. M. 1897. Vision without inversion of the retinal image. *Psychol. Rev.* 4:341–60, 463–81

Wallach, H. 1940. The role of head movements and vestibular and visual cues in sound localization. *J. Exp. Psychol.* 27: 339–68

Wallach, H. 1985a. Perceiving a stable environment. *Sci. Am.* 252(5):118–24

Wallach, H. 1985b. Learned stimulation in space and motion perception. *Am. Psychol.* 40:399–404

Wallach, H., Bacon, J. 1976. The constancy of the orientation of the visual field. *Percept. Psychophys.* 19:492–98

Wallach, H., Bacon, J. 1977. Two kinds of adaptation in the constancy of visual direction and their different effects on the perception of shape and visual direction. *Percept. Psychophys.* 21:227–41

Wallach, H., Bacon, J., Schulman, P. 1978. Adaptation in motion perception: Alteration of induced motion. *Percept. Psychophys.* 24:509–14

Wallach, H., Barton, W. 1975. Adaptation to optically produced curvature of frontal planes. *Percept. Psychophys.* 18:21–25

Wallach, H., Canal, T. 1976. Two kinds of adaptation in the constancy of visual direction. *Percept. Psychophys.* 19:445–49

Wallach, H., Flaherty, E. W. 1975. A compensation for field expansion caused by moving forward. *Percept. Psychophys.* 17:445–49

Wallach, H., Flaherty, E. W. 1976. Rapid adaptation to a prismatic distortion. *Percept. Psychophys.* 19:261–66

Wallach, H., Frey, K. J. 1969. Adaptation in the constancy of visual direction measured by a one-trial method. *Percept. Psychophys.* 5:249–52

Wallach, H., Frey, K. J. 1972. Adaptation in distance perception based on oculomotor cues. *Percept. Psychophys.* 11:77–83

Wallach, H., Frey, K. J., Rommey, G. 1969. Adaptation to field displacement during head movement unrelated to the constancy of visual direction. *Percept. Psychophys.* 5:253–56

Wallach, H., Huntington, D. 1973. Counteradaptation after exposure to displaced visual direction. *Percept. Psychophys.* 13:519–24

Wallach, H., Kravitz, J. 1965a. The measurement of the constancy of visual direction and of its adaptation. *Psychon. Sci.* 2:217–18

Wallach, H., Kravitz, J. 1965b. Rapid adaptation in the constancy of visual direction with active and passive rotation. *Psychon. Sci.* 3:165–66

Wallach, H., Kravitz, J. 1968. Adaptation in the constancy of visual direction tested by measuring the constancy of auditory direction. *Percept. Psychophys.* 4:299–303

Wallach, H., O'Connell, D. N. 1953. The kinetic depth effect. *J. Exp. Psychol.* 45:205–17

Wallach, H., O'Leary, A., McMahon, M. L. 1982. Three stimuli for visual motion perception compared. *Percept. Psychophys.* 32:1–6

Wallach, H., Stanton, L., Becker, D. 1974. The compensation for movement-produced changes in object orientation. *Percept. Psychophys.* 15:339–43

Wallach, H., Yablick, G. S., Smith, A. 1972. Target distance and adaptation in distance perception in the constancy of visual direction. *Percept. Psychophys.* 12:139–45

Whipple, W. R., Wallach, H. 1978. Direction-specific motion thresholds for abnormal image shifts during saccadic eye movement. *Percept. Psychophys.* 24:349–55

Ann. Rev. Psychol. 1987. 38:29–60

NEW DESIGNS IN ANALYSIS OF VARIANCE

Rand R. Wilcox

Department of Psychology, University of Southern California, Los Angeles, California 90089

CONTENTS

INTRODUCTION

As the reader has probably noticed, an overwhelming number of introductory statistics texts intended for psychologists or other social scientists appear each

29

0066-4308/87/0201-0029$02.00

year. In fact, every year I get several new books from publishers who want their text adopted for use in my statistics course. Most of these books are consistent about the advice they give regarding basic hypothesis testing procedures, and so it might seem that developments in this field are fairly static. Occasionally a book will make a recommendation that contradicts other books, but usually the author does not give convincing reasons for adopting a different view. Indeed, for several basic issues, the typical advice in textbooks directly contradicts a number of published journal articles. Of course there is always going to be some lag between results in books and current developments in the literature. One goal in this paper is to review these results and to explain and illustrate why they should be of concern to psychologists. Another general goal is to describe some recent results that are related to testing hypotheses. It should be stressed that this is a selective review, and so many results are not discussed here. For instance, the most complicated experimental design considered is a J by K ANOVA. Repeated measures are discussed briefly, but, for example, split-plot designs are not. Also, the emphasis is on familywise Type I error probabilities as opposed to other concepts of error rate such as those found in Rodger (1974, 1975a,b).

THE ONE-WAY ANOVA

First consider the one-way ANOVA model where $\mu_1, \ldots, \mu_J$ are the means of J independent normal random variables having variances $\sigma_1^2, \ldots, \sigma_J^2$. Of course the typical goal is to test

$$H_0: \mu_1 = \ldots = \mu_J \qquad\qquad 1.$$

and this is usually done with the well-known F test. (For a recent review of results on robustness to nonnormality, see Tan 1982; cf Bradley 1978, 1980.)

The Homogeneity of Variance Assumption

To test Equation 1, typically it is assumed that

$$\sigma_1^2 = \sigma_2^2 = \ldots = \sigma_J^2 \qquad\qquad 2.$$

A basic issue is whether violating Equation 2 can substantially affect the Type I error probability α and power. The answer in both cases is an unequivocal yes (Welch 1937, Hsu 1938, Scheffé 1959, Brown & Forsythe 1974a, Bishop 1976, Rogan & Keselman 1977, Wilcox 1985h). Table 1 illustrates this problem with some monte carlo results reported by Bishop (1976) that were based on 10,000 iterations. For example, if there are $J = 3$ groups, $n = 11$ observations per group, $\alpha = .05$, $\sigma_1 = 1$, $\sigma_2 = 2$, and $\sigma_3 = 3$, then α_a, the actual Type I error probability, is .081. Note that for $J = 4$ the difference between the nominal and actual error probabilities is fairly large even when there are equal sample sizes, in particular for $n = 12$ observations per group and $\alpha_n = .05$, $\alpha_a = .101$. Even with 50 observations per group, $\alpha_a = .088$ can occur (Wilcox et al 1985). For unequal sample sizes, Wilcox et al report practical situations where α_a exceeds .3. It has long been known that equal sample sizes reduce the effect of violating the homogeneity of variance assumption, but equal sample sizes may not eliminate this problem. Also, large sample sizes reduce the effects of unequal variances, but it is difficult to know just how large a sample size is needed. Apparently the answer depends in part on the value of J. For results on this problem for $J = 2$, see Ramsey (1981) and Wilcox (1985h).

With so much evidence that unequal variances can substantially affect Type I error probabilities, why do so many books tell us not to be concerned about unequal variances? Apparently the reason stems from results reported by Box (1954). In an earlier paper Box (1953) pointed to results in Horsnell (1953) in support of the view that equal sample sizes eliminate the need to be concerned about whether the variances are equal.

It might appear that Box's paper contradicts the other papers cited above, but in fact the results they report are consistent. The reason for the different views regarding the importance of homogeneity of variances lies in the interpretation of the results, plus apparent a priori beliefs held about the differences among variances that are likely to occur in practice. To clarify this point, let

$$\sigma_{[1]} \le \sigma_{[2]} \le \ldots \le \sigma_{[J]}$$

be the J standard deviations written in ascending order. That is, $\sigma_{[1]}$ is the smallest of the J variances, while $\sigma_{[J]}$ is the largest. In the papers by Box

Table 1   Type I error rates of the F test

J	Sample sizes $n_j, j=1,\ldots,J$	Standard deviations $\sigma_j, j=1,\ldots,J$	Nominal α level .1	.05	.01
3	6,6,6	1,2,3	.116	.066	.018
		1,1,3	.137	.082	.029
	11,11,11	1,1,3	.129	.081	.030
	6,12,15	3,2,1	.214	.142	.054
4	12,12,12,12	1,1,1,4	.144	.101	.046
		1,1,1,3	.132	.089	.036
	6,10,16,20	1,1,1,4	.050	.026	.009
		3,1,1,1	.289	.221	.125

(1954) and Horsnell (1953), attention was restricted to situations for which θ = $\sigma_{[J]}/\sigma_{[1]} \leq \sqrt{3}$. In contrast, other papers, particularly in recent years, have considered values of θ as large as 4. It may seem odd that Box limited his study to values of $\theta \leq \sqrt{3}$, but in his paper he expressed the ratios in terms of variances rather than standard deviations, and presumably some researchers were willing to believe that $\sigma^2 = \sigma_{[J]}^2/\sigma_{[1]}^2 \leq 3$ was likely to be true in practice. Another important point is that Box's results assume normality, and so even if $\theta \leq \sqrt{3}$, the F test may not be appropriate.

Of course the real issue is how large a θ value can be expected in practice. Unfortunately, it is common for psychologists not to report their sample variances, and so this valuable information is lost forever, or at least is difficult to obtain. However, I went through several years of the *American Educational Research Journal* and examined the sample variances where a one-way ANOVA design was used. Among the 14 studies I found, three reported sample variances with $s_{[k]}^2/s_{[1]}^2 > 16$. That is, the ratio of the largest sample variance to the smallest exceeded 16. It is not being suggested that values as large as 16 are relatively common, but it certainly seems that for practical purposes, equal variances should not be taken for granted. In summary, some violation of the homogeneity of variance assumption is tolerable in terms of maintaining the nominal Type 1 error probability, but all indications are that there are practical limits beyond which this assumption cannot be ignored.

Handling Unequal Variances

Based on the results just described, there are at least three ways in which a researcher might approach the problem of unequal variances:

1. Test $H_0: \sigma_1^2 = \ldots = \sigma_J^2$. If H_0 is not rejected, proceed with the usual F, and if it is rejected, replace the F test with one that is robust to unequal variances;

2. Never use the F test, but instead use some procedure that is robust to unequal variances, or

3. Test $H_0: \theta > \theta_0$, where θ_0 is some appropriately chosen constant. If H_0 is rejected, use the F test, otherwise use a test that is robust to unequal variances.

The last approach apparently has received no consideration in the literature. The idea is, of course, that some inequality of the variances is permissible, but there is the problem of specifying just how much inequality can be allowed. In particular, there is the problem of deciding what θ_0 should be (cf Ramsey 1981). The second approach seems reasonable because tests for equal means that are robust to unequal variances (which are described below) seem to have power levels that are similar to the F test when the variances are equal.

That is, in terms of power, little is lost if the F test is replaced by a procedure that is robust to unequal variances. The first approach certainly appears reasonable, but from Wilcox et al (1985) it seems that tests for equal variances do not have enough power in situations where researchers should replace the F test with a procedure that handles unequal variances. Consequently, the best advice at the moment is to never use the conventional F test—one of the procedures described below should be used instead.

There are numerous tests for equal variances, many of which appear to be sensitive to departures from normality. That is, if the normality assumption is violated, the actual and nominal alpha levels can be quite different. Box (1953) was one of the earliest researchers to point to this problem. Conover et al (1981) list and compare 60 methods for testing the homogeneity of variance assumption, but there is no point in describing all of these procedures here. Instead it is merely pointed out that a test for equal variances proposed by Brown & Forsythe (1974b) seems to be an especially good candidate for general use. One reason is that it is easy to use. In particular, let X_{ij} be the ith observation in the jth group, let M_j be the sample median for the jth group, and let

$$Z_{ij} = |X_{ij} - M_j|.$$

That is, for every treatment group, compute the sample median, subtract this sample median from each observation in the corresponding group, and take the absolute value of this difference. The Brown-Forsythe test consists of simply performing an F test on the Z_{ij}'s. That is, the mean square within and between groups are computed in the usual way, only the Z_{ij}'s are used instead of the X_{ij}'s. A significant F test indicates that the variances are not equal. Moreover, all indications are that for typical departures from normality, the actual Type I error probability will, in most cases, be less than the nominal level. Conover et al describe other tests that are also robust, but their results indicate that none of these procedures is substantially better than the Brown-Forsythe solution. However, the Brown-Forsythe procedure does not have a clear superiority over other procedures listed by Conover et al, and so the emphasis here on the Brown-Forsythe procedure is somewhat arbitrary.

Another robust test is the Box-Scheffé test (see Kirk 1982), but monte carlo studies indicate that the Brown-Forsythe procedure usually has more power (O'Brien 1978, Games et al 1979). O'Brien (1979) proposed another robust test for equal variances, but apparently there are no results on how it compares to the Brown-Forsythe technique. More recently Tiku & Balakrishnan (1984) proposed still another test for equal variances, and although it appears to be robust in some situations, it is far from clear whether it will be robust in other practical situations, and there is no indication that it is a serious competitor of the Brown-Forsythe solution. The important point here is that there seems to be little or no merit in applying the Brown-Forsythe test to determine whether the conventional F test should be used—the F test should be abandoned in favor of one of the procedures described below.

Testing For Equal Means When the Variances Are Unequal

Next suppose the null hypothesis of equal variances has been rejected. Of course this raises the issue of how to test Equation 1. First consider the case $J = 2$. An approximate solution was proposed about 50 years ago by Welch (1937). Fenstad (1983) compared this solution to another approximate solution proposed by Welch. In terms of power and controlling Type I error probabilities, Welch's V test gave the best results. A more extensive study by Wilcox (1985h), that included the effects of nonnormality, suggests that Welch's V is usually best except when the variances are equal. To describe the procedure, let n_1 and n_2 be the sample sizes for the two groups, and let t_j be the $1 - \alpha/2$ quantile of a Student's t distribution with $n_j - 1$ degrees of freedom ($j = 1, 2$). That is, if T_ν is a Student's t random variable with ν degrees of freedom, then for $\nu = n_j - 1$, $\Pr(-t_j \le T_\nu \le t_j) = 1 - \alpha$. Of course t_j can be determined from a table of Student's t distribution. Next compute

$$A = \max \left[\left(\frac{n_1 - 3}{n_1 - 1} \right)^{1/2} t_1, \left(\frac{n_2 - 3}{n_2 - 1} \right)^{1/2} t_2 \right]$$

and

$$B = \left[\frac{(n_1 - 1)s_1^2}{n_1 (n_1 - 3)} + \frac{(n_2 - 1)s_2^2}{n_2 (n_2 - 3)} \right]^{1/2}$$

where s_1^2 and s_2^2 are the usual sample variances. Then Welch's approximate $100(1 - \alpha)\%$ confidence interval for $\mu_1 - \mu_2$ is

$$(\bar{X}_1 - \bar{X}_2) \pm AB.$$

The techniques used by Welch (1937) as well as by Satterthwaite (1941) can be extended to the problem of testing for equal means when there are more than two groups. Brown & Forsythe (1974a) have examined these procedures and found them to give good results when in fact the variances are unequal. Let $\bar{X}_{.j} = \Sigma_i X_{ij}/n_j$ and $\bar{X}_{..} = \Sigma\Sigma X_{ij}/N$, where n_j is the number of observations in the jth group, and $N = \Sigma n_j$, and let s_j^2 be the sample variances for the jth group. For the first procedure compute

$$F^* = \frac{\sum n_j (\bar{X}_{.j} - \bar{X}_{..})^2}{\sum (1 - n_j/N)s_j^2}.$$

When H_0 is true, F^* has approximately an F distribution with $\nu_1 = J - 1$ and

$$\nu_2 = [\Sigma c_j^2/(n_j - 1)]^{-1}$$

degrees of freedom, where

$$c_j = \left(1 - \frac{n_j}{N}\right)s_j^2/\Sigma_k\left(1 - \frac{n_k}{N}\right)s_k^2.$$

If $F > f_{1-\alpha}$ ($f_{1-\alpha}$ being $1 - \alpha$ quantile of the F distribution with ν_1 and ν_2 degrees of freedom), reject H_0.

For the second procedure compute $w_j = n_j/s_j^2$, $u = \Sigma w_j$, $\tilde{X}_{..} = \Sigma w_j \bar{X}_{.j}/u$

$$A = \Sigma w_j(\bar{X}_{.j} - \tilde{X}_{..})^2/(J - 1)$$

$$B = 1 + \frac{2(J - 2)}{J^2 - 1}\Sigma (1 - w_j/u)^2/(n_j - 1)$$

and

$$W = A/B.$$

The degrees of freedom are $J - 1$ and

$$f = [(3/(J^2 - 1))\Sigma_j(1 - w_j/u)^2/(n_j - 1)]^{-1}.$$

Although F^* and W both perform much better than F, Wilcox et al 1985 found practical situations where both F^* and W are not robust to unequal variances. However, for equal sample sizes, W seems to be robust while F^* may be unsatisfactory. The power levels of F^* and W can differ dramatically. Usually W has more power, but the reverse can be true.

MULTIPLE COMPARISON PROCEDURES

Again consider J independent treatment groups, and suppose that all pairwise comparisons of the means are to be made. That is, for all $i < j$, the goal is to test $H_0: \mu_i = \mu_j$ with the property that the familywise Type I error probability (FWI) is to be α. In other words, the probability of at least one Type I error is to be α. There are now many procedures aimed at solving this problem, but before discussing their relative merits, another issue should be discussed.

Applying Multiple Comparison Procedures Only After a Significant F Test

Many books still claim that multiple comparison procedures should be applied only after a significant F test has been obtained. However, following this advice has certain practical consequences that need to be considered. In particular, the actual FWI will, in general, be smaller than the specified α level. This is illustrated with results reported by Bernhardson (1975). Table 2 shows the actual value of α for several well-known multiple comparison procedures when the procedure is used only after a significant F test, and when the procedure is applied regardless of whether the F test is significant. As can be seen, the actual value of FWI is lower when a procedure is applied only after a significant F test, as opposed to applying the procedure regardless of whether the F test is significant. The second facet of the problem is that most multiple comparison procedures are not designed under the assumption that a significant F test has already been obtained. Smith & Han (1981) derived some results on controlling the Type I error probability when testing a single contrast only after a significant F test, but the results are complicated and not yet general enough to be of use in practical situations. The important point here is that in terms of controlling the Type I error probability, most multiple comparison procedures should be used regardless of whether the F test is significant. These include Tukey's, the Tukey-Kramer, Scheffé's, Dunnett's, and the Bonferroni t-test which are discussed below. In fact, if one of these procedures is used, there seems to be little reason for applying the F test at all!

In light of the results just cited, it might seem that the F test could be abandoned completely. However, O'Brien (1983) notes that the procedure actually used should be a function of what an experimenter wants to know and the Type I error probability that can be allowed. If any inequality among the means is of interest, the F test can be used. If several tests are to be performed, such as all pairwise comparisons of means, an appropriate multiple comparison procedure can be used instead.

Table 2 Experimentwise error rates, $\alpha=0.05$[a]

	$J = 2$		$J = 4$		$J = 8$		$J = 10$	
	α_1	α_2	α_1	α_2	α_1	α_2	α_1	α_2
Fisher	.055	.055	.211	.051	.500	.050	.591	.050
Tukey	.055	.055	.053	.046	.049	.034	.049	.034
Scheffé	.055	.055	.025	.025	.003	.003	.003	.003

[a]The quantity α_1 is the experimentwise Type I error rate when the multiple comparison procedure is applied regardless of the outcome of the F test. The second entry, α_2, is the error rate when the multiple comparison procedure is applied only after F is significant at the α level.

Choosing a Multiple Comparison Procedure When Making Pairwise Comparisons of the Means

With so many multiple comparison procedures to choose from, which one should be used? Evidently the answer depends on the situation at hand. For now it is assumed that all pairwise comparisons of the means are to be made.

First assume that all J treatment groups have equal variances and equal sample sizes. A well-known technique is Tukey's Studentized range procedure (e.g. Kirk 1982). If you want the familywise Type I error probability to be α, there seems to be little doubt that Tukey's procedure should be used (Stoline 1981). Some books recommend Scheffé's procedure, but Scheffé (1959) points out that Tukey's procedure is better, i.e. it yields shorter confidence intervals and it guarantees FWI $\leq \alpha$.

If the population variances are equal but the sample sizes are not, Hayter (1984) has shown that a procedure proposed by Tukey (1953) and Kramer (1956) will always give conservative results. That is, it guarantees FWI $\leq \alpha$. To obtain a $100(1 - \alpha)\%$ confidence interval with the Tukey-Kramer procedure, simply compute

$$(\bar{X}_i - \bar{X}_j - T, \bar{X}_i - \bar{X}_j + T),$$

where

$$T = q\sqrt{\text{MSWG}(n_i^{-1} + n_j^{-1})/2}$$

and q is the usual Studentized range statistic used in Tukey's procedure. Competitors of the Tukey-Kramer procedure are the Bonferroni t-test, also known as Dunn's test (see, for example, Kirk 1982), Scheffé's test, the Spjøtvoll & Stoline (1973) procedure, and a procedure proposed by Hunter (1976), but Stoline notes that the Tukey-Kramer procedure yields shorter confidence intervals. Another possibility is the Newman-Keuls procedure, but there is some doubt as to whether this procedure should be used (Hartley 1955, Ramsey 1981).

Begun & Gabriel (1981) have improved the Newman-Keuls procedure, but there seems to be no strong evidence that it should replace the Tukey-Kramer solution. Two other possibilities are Duncan's procedure and Fisher's LSD test, but from the review by Stoline (1981), it seems that neither is a serious competitor of the Tukey-Kramer technique. Assuming equal variances, Felzenbaum et al (1983) show that the Tukey-Kramer procedure is best among a large class of procedures. But despite all the evidence that the Tukey-Kramer procedure is best for pairwise comparison of means, perhaps an even better procedure could be derived. In fact, for $J = 3$ and large imbalance, Spurrier

(1981) describes a procedure that is indeed better (also see Spurrier & Isham 1985).

Unfortunately, the Tukey-Kramer procedure is sensitive to unequal variances (Keselman & Rogan 1978, Dunnett 1980a). Approximate solutions for handling unequal variances have been proposed by Games & Howell (1976), Tamhane (1979) and Dunnett (1980b). For equal sample sizes, the two procedures proposed by Dunnett (1980b) seem to give the shortest confidence intervals, and guarantee FWI $\leq \alpha$. For these reasons, Stoline (1981) recommends Dunnett's procedures. Dunnett's procedures appear to give good results when both the sample sizes and variances are unequal, but Stoline (1981) feels it is too early to recommend which procedure should be used in this case. Another possibility is to use Welch's V test in conjunction with the Bonferroni inequality. That is, $H_0: \mu_j = \mu_k$ is tested with Welch's V test, for all $j < k$, and in an attempt to ensure that FWI $\leq \alpha$, each test would be performed at the α/q level where $q = (J^2 - J)/2$ is the number of tests (pairwise comparisons) being performed. Unfortunately, there are no results on how this procedure compares with Dunnett's.

Another competitor of Dunnett's procedures that deserves serious consideration was proposed by Games & Howell (1976). Their procedure allows FWI $> \alpha$ (Tamhane 1979, Dunnett 1980a), but simulation studies suggest that FWI will not exceed α when there are at least 50 observations in each group. Moreover, for this special case the Games-Howell procedure appears to be superior to Dunnett's T3 or C. For yet another approach to handling unequal variances, see Ury & Wiggins (1971).

As mentioned above, Dunnett actually proposed two tests. For Dunnett's C procedure, the confidence interval for $\mu_k - \mu_j$ is given by

$$(\bar{X}_k - \bar{X}_j) \pm Q_{\alpha,J,\nu}/\sqrt{2}$$

where

$$Q_{\alpha,J,\nu} = \frac{q_{\alpha,J,\nu_k}\, s_k^2/n_k + q_{\alpha,J,\nu_j}\, s_j^2/n_j}{(s_k^2/n_k + s_j^2/n_j)^{1/2}}$$

$\nu_k = n_k - 1$, $\nu_j = n_j - 1$, and q_{α,J,ν_j} is read from a Table of the Studentized range statistic. Note that q is the same critical value used in Tukey's procedure.

As for Dunnett's T3 procedure, the confidence interval is given by

$$\bar{X}_k - \bar{X}_j \pm V_{\alpha,C,\nu_{kj}} \sqrt{s_k^2/n_k + s_j^2/n_j}$$

where V is read from a Table of the Studentized maximum modules distribution,

$C = (J^2 - J)/2$ is the number of comparisons, and the degrees of freedom are

$$\nu_{kj} = \frac{(s_k^2/n_k + s_j^2/n_j)^2}{s_k^4/n^2\nu_k + s_j^4/n_j^2\nu_j}.$$

For a Table of V values, see Bechhofer & Dunnett (1982), or Wilcox (1985i).

The choice between T3 and C depends on whether the degrees of freedom are large or small. For small degrees of freedom, use T3. There are no exact guidelines for deciding whether the degrees of freedom are small, but from Dunnett (1980b), if $J = 4$, a rough guideline is to use T3 when the degrees of freedom are less than 50 for any treatment group; otherwise use Dunnett's C procedure. The same recommendation applies for $J = 8$, but other values of J were not considered in Dunnett's simulation studies. Stoline (1981) recommended that T3 be used whenever $\nu_j < 50$ for any j; otherwise the C procedure should be used. However, for large degrees of freedom, Dunnett's (1980) results suggest that the Games-Howell procedure should be used.

As a final note, the goal in this section was to briefly describe the current status of multiple comparison procedures, but to conserve space, not all of the relevant literature was described or cited. For further details, see the reviews by Jaccard et al (1984), Stoline (1981), and Games et al (1983).

Two-Way Models and Linear Contrasts

Again consider J independent treatment groups having a common variance, σ^2, and let

$$\text{MSWG} = \Sigma_i \Sigma_j (X_{ij} - \overline{X}_{.j})^2/(N - J)$$

be the usual mean square within groups estimate of σ^2 having $\nu = N - J$ degrees of freedom. Also let $\psi_k(k = 1, \ldots, q)$ be q linear contrasts defined by

$$\psi_k = \Sigma_j c_{jk}\mu_j$$

where the c_{jk}'s are known constants specified by the experimenter and satisfying $\Sigma_j c_{jk} = 0$. A common goal is to test

$$H_0: \psi_1 = \psi_2 = \ldots = \psi_q = 0$$

such that FWI $= \alpha$. The ψ_k's are estimated with

$$\hat{\psi}_k = \Sigma_j c_{jk} \overline{X}_j$$

and as is well known, $H_0: \psi_k = 0$ is tested with

$$T_k = \hat{\psi}_k / \sqrt{\text{MSWG} \, (\Sigma_j c^2_{jk}/n_j)} \; .$$

The statistic T_k has a Student's t distribution with $N - J$ degrees of freedom.

The joint distribution of the T_k's is the multivariate t distribution as defined by Dunnett & Sobel (1954), a result that has important implications for practitioners. For example, suppose the $\hat{\psi}_k$'s are independent of one another. From basic results, $\hat{\psi}_k$ and $\hat{\psi}_m$ are independent if $\Sigma_j c_{jk} c_{jm} = 0$, but the T_j's are *not* independent even though their correlations are zero (e.g. Tong 1980). Some books assume the T_j's are independent and state that if each of the null hypotheses is tested at the $1 - (1 - \alpha)^{1/q}$ level, then FWI $= \alpha$, but this is incorrect. In order to ensure FWI $= \alpha$, percentage points of the multivariate t distribution are required, and these can be found in Bechhofer & Dunnett (1982). When the correlations among the $\hat{\psi}_k$'s are all equal to zero, the distribution of $\max_q T_q$ is called the Studentized maximum modulus distribution, and it is these percentage points that are tabled by Bechhofer & Dunnett. As noted in their paper, these critical values guarantee FWI $= \alpha$ when the $\hat{\psi}_k$'s are independent.

The critical values reported by Bechhofer & Dunnett are better than those obtained from the Bonferroni inequality (i.e. they give shorter confidence intervals), and they are uniformly better than the critical values reported by Games (1977). For additional tables of the Studentized maximum modulus, see Hahn & Hendrickson (1971), Stoline & Ury (1979), Ury et al (1980), and Wilcox (1985i).

Next consider the case where the $\hat{\psi}_k$'s are correlated. Again the T_j's have a multivariate t distribution, but except for a few very special cases, critical values are not available for ensuring that FWI $= \alpha$. However, from an inequality derived by Šidák (1967) it can be shown that the critical values reported by Bechhofer & Dunnett (1982) guarantee FWI $\leq \alpha$. Games (1977) used Šidák's inequality in a slightly different fashion to derive conservative critical values, but the Bechhofer and Dunnett critical values are uniformly better. For an improvement on the Bechhofer-Dunnett procedure, see Wilcox (1986a).

Because the c_{jk}'s are known constants, the correlations among the $\hat{\psi}_k$'s are easily determined (e.g. Kirk 1982, p. 92). If the percentage points of the multivariate t distribution could be determined for these particular correlations, even better critical values would be available, and in fact FWI $= \alpha$ could be ensured. Unfortunately, there seems to be no satisfactory way of evaluating the multivariate t distribution for an arbitrary set of correlations. Nelson (1982) derived a solution when the correlations satisfy a certain property, but this property is too restrictive to be of interest here. Wilcox

(1984a) proposed an approximation of the multivariate t distribution, but the resulting critical values will usually yield FWI $> \alpha$. Other approximations were derived by Dunnett & Sobel (1955), but again they do not yield better results. It is noted that Slepian's inequality (e.g. Tong 1980) could be used in conjunction with results in Nelson (1982) to get better critical values and still guarantee FWI $\leq \alpha$. However, without the aid of a computer this approach is not practical, and so further details are not given.

It is noted that for unequal variances, $H_0 : \psi_k = 0$ can be tested with Welch's adjusted degrees of freedom test (e.g. Kirk 1982), and FWI for all q linear contrasts can be controlled with the Bonferroni inequality by testing each hypothesis at the α/q level. For q large, a modification of Scheffé's test for unequal variances can be used (Kaiser & Bowden 1983).

Disordinal Interactions

An important point is that the critical values reported by Bechhofer & Dunnett (1982) are not appropriate for one-tailed tests. Instead the tables in Krishnaiah & Armitage (1966) should be used. Again to ensure FWI $\leq \alpha$, use the critical value in their table that corresponds to having all of the correlations among all of the $\hat{\psi}_k$'s equal to zero. For a more extensive table of critical values, see Wilcox (1985i).

To illustrate where a one-tailed test might be used, consider a 2 by 2 ANOVA. To be more specific, suppose two methods of teaching statistics are being considered, and that gender is to be taken into account. The population means are as shown in the table.

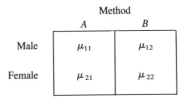

A disordinal interaction is said to exist if, for example, $\mu_{11} > \mu_{12}$ but $\mu_{21} < \mu_{22}$. In this case method A is better than B for males, while for females the reverse is true. Of course, conventional tests for interactions do not distinguish between disordinal interactions and ordinal interactions where an ordinal interaction means that $\mu_{11} - \mu_{21} > \mu_{21} - \mu_{22} > 0$ or $\mu_{11} - \mu_{21} < \mu_{12} - \mu_{22} < 0$. In many situations an experimenter wants to know whether a disordinal interaction exists, which means, for example, that

$$H_0 : \mu_{11} \leq \mu_{12}$$

and

$$H_0 : \mu_{22} \leq \mu_{21}$$

might be tested. Because these are one-tailed tests, the critical values in Bechhofer & Dunnett (1982) are inappropriate. Instead, the critical values reported by Krishnaiah & Armitage (1966) should be used. It should also be noted that again equal variances are assumed.

TESTING LINEAR CONTRASTS IN REPEATED MEASURES DESIGNS

In contrast to the previous section, suppose that $\mu_1, \ldots, \mu_J$ are the means of J dependent treatment groups, and the observations have a multivariate normal distribution with variance-covariance matrix Σ. Again suppose the goal is to test

$$H_0 : \psi_1 = \psi_2 = \ldots = \psi_q = 0.$$

A simple way of testing each of the q hypotheses, and guaranteeing FWI $\leq \alpha$, is to compute

$$T_k = \sqrt{n} \hat{\psi}_k / \hat{\sigma}_k$$

where

$$\hat{\psi}_k = \Sigma_i \, \Sigma_j \, c_{jk} \, X_{ij} / n$$

and

$$\hat{\sigma}_k^2 = \Sigma_i \, [\Sigma_j \, (c_{jk} \, X_{ij}) - \hat{\psi}_k]^2 / (n - 1).$$

If

$$|T_k| > t_{\alpha/2q}$$

where $t_{\alpha/2q}$ is the $\alpha/2q$ quantile of a Student's t distribution with $\nu = n - 1$ degrees of freedom, reject $H_0 : \psi_k = 0$. From the Bonferroni inequality (e.g. Tong 1980), FWI $\leq \alpha$.

It is known that under certain restrictions on Σ, if all pairwise comparisons of the means are to be made, FWI $\leq \alpha$ can be ensured (e.g. Keselman 1982, Kirk 1982). However, when these restrictions are violated, FWI $> \alpha$ can result (Maxwell 1980). Maxwell (1980) compared the Bonferroni solution to four other multiple comparison procedures (for the special case where all pairwise comparisons of the means are to be made), and the conclusion was that the Bonferroni procedure gives the best results. Appropriate critical values can be found in Dunn (1961), Kirk (1982), Dayton & Schafer (1973) and Bailey (1977).

Using results in Halperin (1967), slightly better critical values yielding shorter confidence intervals can be obtained, and a table of these values can be found in Wilcox (1985b).

It has been suggested by some psychologists that even better critical values can be obtained with an inequality derived by Šidák (1967) which states that

$$Pr(\,|X_1|\leq c_1 \ldots,|X_q|\leq c_q) \geq \prod_{i=1}^{q} Pr(\,|X_i|\leq c_i) \qquad\qquad 3.$$

where $X_1, \ldots, X_q$ have a multivariate normal distribution with means all equal to zero, and $c_1, \ldots, c_q$ are constants. Equation 3 suggests the possibility that when H_0 is true

$$Pr(\,|T_1|\leq c, \ldots,|T_q|\leq c) \geq \prod_{i=1}^{q} Pr(\,|T_i|\leq c). \qquad\qquad 4.$$

If Equation 4 is true, even better critical values than those reported in Wilcox (1985b) could be derived. Scott (1967) offered a proof of Equation 4, but Šidák (1971) showed that the proof was incorrect. Equation 4 can be shown to be true when certain restrictions are place on Σ (Šidák 1971), but the general validity of 4 has not yet been established. Consequently, for the moment at least, the best critical values that are justified on analytic grounds are those in Wilcox (1985b). Alberton & Hochberg (1984) have considered an alternative approach to obtaining critical values for pairwise differences, and simulation studies for $J = 3$ suggest that this approach is correct, but an analytic proof has not yet been found. Even if a proof were available, the critical values would need to be approximated, but this could be done with the critical values in Bechhofer & Dunnett (1982). In summary, there is a good chance that the critical values reported by Bechhofer & Dunnett (1982) should replace those reported by Wilcox (1985b) when making all pairwise comparisons of the means, but it seems that more research is needed before the Alberton and Hochberg approach can be recommended.

Relative Efficiency of Repeated Measures Designs Versus Completely Randomized Designs

Vonesh (1983) has studied the relative efficiency of the Bonferroni procedure in repeated measures designs versus designs based on independent treatment groups. It was found that if $n \geq 10$, $J \leq 4$, and the minimum correlation among the treatment groups is at least .25, repeated measures designs are better than having independent groups. However, as J increases, the minimum ρ needed to ensure the superiority of repeated measures designs increases. To complicate matters, the superiority of repeated measures designs also depends on n, the sample size. Unfortunately, Vonesh only considered $J = 4$ and 5, and so general guidelines are difficult. However, when the minimum $\rho \geq .5$, repeated measures designs were considerably better than completely randomized designs, and in fact Vonesh suggests that repeated measures designs should be preferred when the minimum ρ is at least .25. For further details, see Table 3 in Vonesh (1983).

Handling Missing Observations

Next suppose there are $J = 2$ treatment groups, that each subject is observed under both conditions, but that some observations are missing. For convenience, the observations are arranged as follows:

$$X_1, \ldots, X_n; X_{n+1}, \ldots, X_{n+n_1}$$

$$Y_1, \ldots, Y_n; \qquad\qquad Y_{n+1}, \ldots, Y_{n+n_2}.$$

Thus, for the first n subjects there are no missing observations. For the next n_1 subjects the Y's are missing, and for n_2 subjects the X's are missing. The goal is to test

$$H_0 : \mu_1 = \mu_2$$

and the problem is deciding how to handle the missing observations. An obvious solution is to ignore the subjects having missing observations and simply apply the usual correlated t-test to the first n subjects. A general issue is finding a way of improving on this solution that is based on all of the data available.

First assume $\sigma_1^2 = \sigma_2^2$. One approach (Bhoj 1978) is to use

$$T = \sqrt{n}\,(\bar{X} - \bar{Y})/s + \frac{\bar{X}_1 - \bar{Y}_1}{s_1\sqrt{(1/n_1) + (1/n_2)}}$$

where $\bar{X} = \sum_{i=1}^{n} X_i/n, \bar{Y} = \sum_{i=1}^{n} Y_1/n, \bar{X}_1 = \sum_{j=1}^{n_1} X_{n+j}/n_1, \bar{Y}_1 = \sum_{k=1}^{n_2} Y_{n+k}/n_2$ 5.

$$s^2 = \sum_{i=1}^{n} (X_i - Y_i - \bar{X} + \bar{Y})^2/(n - 1),$$

$$s_1^2 = \left[\sum_{j=1}^{n_1} (X_{n+j} - \bar{X}_1)^2 + \sum_{k=1}^{n_2} (Y_{n+k} - \bar{Y}_1)^2 \right]/(n_1 + n_2 - 2).$$

Equation 5 is a special case of a family of statistics suggested by Bhoj (1978) for testing H_0. Notice that the first term of Equation 5, namely, $\sqrt{n}(\bar{X} - \bar{Y})/s$, is just the usual correlated t-test. Also, $\bar{X}_1$ and $\bar{Y}_1$ are independent, and the second term in Equation 5 is the usual t-test for independent groups. (In Bhoj's notation, testing H_0 with T is equivalent to setting $\lambda = \frac{1}{2}$.) If H_0 is true, T is the sum of two independent Student's t random variables having $\nu_1 = n - 1$ and $\nu_2 = n_1 + n_2 - 2$ degrees of freedom, respectively. Thus, H_0 can be tested by determining the percentage points of T. Fisher & Yates (1957) as well as Wilcox (1986b) provide some percentage points of T. Ghosh (1975a) as well as Chaubey & Mudholkar (1982) suggest approximations of the critical values. (When referring to their articles, it might help to note that if T_1 and T_2 are two independent t random variables, the distribution of $T_1 - T_2$ is the same as the distribution of $T_1 + T_2$.) These approximations give very accurate results when $\nu_1 > 5$ and $\nu_2 > 5$, but it is not clear how good the approximations are for extremely small degrees of freedom. For an illustration of how to determine the critical values in Bhoj's procedure, see Wilcox (1985i). Also, Bhoj (1978) notes that it is possible to improve slightly the test of H_0 based on Equation 5, but the procedure is rather difficult to apply.

The Case $\sigma_1^2 \neq \sigma_2^2$

For $\sigma_1^2 \neq \sigma_2^2$, Bhoj (1978) suggests using a slightly different approach. For notational convenience, assume $n_1 \leq n_2$. A test that is a special case of the general approach used by Bhoj is to use

$$T = \sqrt{n}(\bar{X} - \bar{Y})/s + \sqrt{n_1}(\bar{X}_1 - \bar{Y}_1)/s_2 \qquad \qquad 6.$$

where

$$s_2^2 = \sum_{j=1}^{n_1} (W_j - \bar{W})^2, \quad W_j = X_{n+j} - (n_1/n_2)^{1/2} Y_{n+j}, \quad \bar{W} = \sum_{j=1}^{n_1} W_j/n_1$$

and the other notation in Equation 6 is the same as before. Again the critical values can be determined from results in Ghosh (1975a) as well as Chaubey & Mudholkar (1982); further details can be found in Wilcox (1985i).

It should be noted that Lin & Stivers (1974) proposed another approach to handling missing observations that allows $\sigma_1^2 \neq \sigma_2^2$. In terms of controlling Type I error probabilities, Bhoj's procedure works well if $\nu_1 > 5$ and $\nu_2 > 5$, but perhaps the Lin-Stivers procedure does a better job when the degrees of freedom are small, or perhaps it has more power; these are issues that have not been resolved. For still other procedures for handling missing observations, see Ekbohm (1976), Morrison (1974), as well as Mehta & Gurland (1973).

Testing $H_0: \sigma_1^2 = \sigma_2^2$

Because the choice of procedures proposed by Bhoj (1978) depends on whether $\sigma_1^2 \neq \sigma_2^2$, $H_0: \sigma_1^2 = \sigma_2^2$ might be tested, but it is speculated that the best procedure is simply to assume the variances are not equal. Bhoj (1979) proposed a test of this hypothesis that takes into account the missing observations, but when the normality assumption is violated, this undoubtedly has an effect on Bhoj's procedure. Ekbohm (1982) compared several procedures for testing H_0, but again it appears that all of these procedures will be sensitive to departures from normality—at least there is no evidence that they are robust. Sandvik & Olsson (1982) proposed a test that is robust to nonnormality but that does not handle missing observations. To apply their procedure, simply compute

$$Z_i = |X_i - M_x| - |Y_i - M_y|$$

$(i = 1, \ldots, n)$ where M_x and M_y are the sample medians corresponding to the two groups, and then apply the Wilcoxon signed rank test to the Z's. For the moment it seems best to simply ignore the missing observations and apply the Sandvik-Olsson procedure.

As a final note, while the emphasis in this section has been on multiple comparison procedures, there are other issues related to repeated measures designs, but because of space restrictions they are not described here. For some recent results, see Lewis & van Knippenberg (1984), Jensen (1982), and Afsarinejad (1983). Huynh & Feldt (1970) derived conditions under which repeated measurements have an F distribution, and their results have been generalized by Jeyaratnam (1982).

MEASURING TREATMENT EFFECTS

It has long been recognized that testing and rejecting $H_0: \mu_1 = \ldots = \mu_J$ does not give a satisfactory indication of whether the means are substantially different or just significantly different. If H_0 is rejected at the 10^{-6} level, the means might be nearly equal or substantially different. Of course, which is true depends in part on both the sample sizes and the variances. It is often important to establish that there is indeed a difference between two means, and perhaps there are situations where any difference is important, but in many practical situations the size of the difference is a crucial issue that will ultimately determine which of several methods should be chosen when dealing with a particular problem. An interesting illustration of this point was recently provided by a massive study on the benefits of using a drug to lower cholesterol levels. Various experts (see *Nutrition Today*, 1984, 19:22–29) were asked to comment on the findings. Those in favor of using the drug to lower cholesterol pointed out that the number of heart attacks for the control group was significantly lower ($\alpha = .001$) than the group receiving a placebo, but critics of using the drug to lower cholesterol point out that the difference in the number of heart attacks was trivially small. They conclude, therefore, that because of the expense and possible side effects of the drug, there is no compelling evidence, at least so far, that patients with high cholesterol should be put on medication.

Of course, making a judgment about what constitutes a substantial difference is no easy task, but an even more basic issue is deciding how to measure treatment effects, in terms of parameters, and then deriving an appropriate estimate of this quantity. It is these last two problems that are the focus of attention here.

First consider two treatment groups. A simple measure of treatment effects is just

$$\delta = \mu_1 - \mu_2$$

the difference of the population means. A second measure is the standardized difference of the means, namely,

$$\Delta = (\mu_1 - \mu_2)/\sigma$$

where $\sigma_1 = \sigma_2 = \sigma$ is assumed. The quantity Δ has been suggested by Glass (1976) as well as Cohen (1977). Three issues have been raised about the relative merits of δ and Δ. First, Gibbons et al (1977) argue that δ is a measure that is expressed in terms of the original units of the problem, while Δ is unitless. They suggest that, as a result, it is easier to make judgments about δ than Δ when trying to decide whether a treatment effect is large. However, they do not argue that Δ be abandoned. The second difficulty is that Δ is defined under the assumption that $\sigma_1 = \sigma_2$. If $\sigma_1 \neq \sigma_2$, Δ is not defined. In fact, at present if $\sigma_1 \neq \sigma_2$, a unitless or standardized measure of treatment effects comparable to Δ would seem not to exist. A third criticism of Δ is that it implicitly assumes normality and assumes treatment affects all subjects equally (Kraemer & Andrews 1982). They also point out that even though Δ is unitless, rescaling the data can affect the value of Δ. Also note that knowing Δ does not indicate whether δ is large or small. (For a related difficulty with Δ, see Abelson 1985.)

The parameters δ and Δ are easily extended to $J > 2$ treatment groups. For example, δ might be replaced with

$$\delta_1 = \Sigma(\mu_j - \bar{\mu})^2$$

where $\mu = \Sigma\mu_j/J$, or $\sqrt{\delta_1}$ might be preferred since it is a measure in the original units of the problem. As for Δ, a natural extension, assuming equal variances, is

$$\Delta_1 = \Sigma(\mu_j - \bar{\mu})^2/\sigma^2$$

where σ^2 is the common standard deviation of the J groups. Cohen (1977) suggested using

$$\Delta_2 = [\Sigma(\mu_j - \bar{\mu})^2/J]^{1/2}/\sigma.$$

Of course, Δ_1 and Δ_2 are related to Hays' omega squared (Hays 1981) given by

$$\omega^2 = \frac{\Sigma\alpha_j^2/J}{\sigma^2 + \Sigma\alpha_j^2/J},$$

where $\alpha_j = \mu_j - \bar{\mu}$, and again equal variances are assumed. If this assumption is violated, some other measure of treatment effects would seem to be required.

Hedges (1981) examined the problem of estimating Δ. In particular, he notes that

$$(\bar{X}_1 - \bar{X}_2)/\sqrt{\text{MSWG}},$$

where MSWG is the usual mean square within groups, is a biased estimate of Δ, and that a nearly unbiased estimate is

$$A(\bar{X}_1 - \bar{X}_2)/S$$

where

$$A = 1 - 3[4(n_1 + n_2 - 2) - 1]^{-1}$$

and

$$S^2 = \frac{(n_1 - 1)s_1^2 + (n_2 - 1)s_2^2}{n_1 + n_2 - 2}.$$

One other method of measuring treatment effects should be mentioned. It is

$$\eta^2 = \frac{(J - 1)F}{(J - 1)F + N - J}$$

where F is the usual F statistic, and $N = \Sigma n_j$ is the total sample size (e.g. Cohen 1966). Friedman (1968) notes that η^2 is the proportion of variance of the observations X that can be accounted for on the basis of membership in a particular treatment group. For a discussion of other issues related to measuring treatment effects, see O'Grady (1982), Hedges (1982a,b,c,d) and Rosenthal & Rubin (1982).

It is noted that once a measure of treatment effects is settled upon, an issue that arises is whether the effect is large or small. If, for example, there are $J = 2$ treatment groups, $\delta = \mu_1 - \mu_2$ is used to measure treatment effects, an experimenter might specify some constant, say δ_0, and then want to test $H_0: \delta \le \delta_0$. The idea is, of course, that if $\delta \le \delta_0$, the effect is marginal, while if $\delta > \delta_0$, the effect is large. Testing this null hypothesis can be accomplished using well-known procedures. Wilcox (1985c) describes a method of comparing δ to δ_0 that gives an experimenter a precise method of determining whether the sample sizes are large enough so that there will be a high probability of correctly determining whether δ is large or small. If more observations are required, the procedure indicates how many additional observations are needed. Moreover, the population variances need not be equal. Several related solutions were also noted by Wilcox (1985i).

If instead it is desired to compare Δ to a known constant, results in Kraemer (1983) can be used. It is noted that both Kraemer (1983) and Wilcox (1985c) assume that one of the two groups has been designated as a control group. If this is not the case, or if $J > 2$, and the goal is to determine for all $i < j$, whether $|\mu_i - \mu_j|$ is large or small, see Wilcox (1985a, 1985i).

Nonparametric Methods of Measuring Treatment Effects

Brief mention will be made of some nonparametric methods for measuring treatment effects for $J = 2$ groups. The first method is $p = \Pr(X_1 < X_2)$. That is, p is the probability that a randomly sampled subject from the first treatment group will have a value that is less than the value of a subject randomly sampled from the second group. It has long been known (e.g. Hogg & Craig 1970), that an unbiased estimate of p is obtained with the Mann-Whitney U statistic. The variance of this statistic is given in textbooks such as Hays (1981).

Another possibility is to use the difference of the medians rather than the means, and in fact several variations of this approach are possible (Hedges &

Olkin 1984). For related results, see Kraemer & Andrews (1982), Krauth (1983) and Kraemer (1984).

CONTROLLING POWER AND DETERMINING SAMPLE SIZES

A basic issue in any experiment is deciding how many observations should be sampled from each treatment group. The typical approach to this problem is specifying how much power is desired, but first it is necessary to specify some alternative to the null hypothesis that is of interest. This, in turn, means that an appropriate measure of treatment effects must be settled upon. If the variances are equal and treatment effects are expressed in terms of Δ_2, then appropriate sample sizes can be determined using well-known procedures (e.g. Cohen 1977, Kirk 1982). However, as noted in the previous section, a researcher may not want to measure treatment effects with Δ_2, but rather in terms of $\delta_1 = \Sigma \alpha_j^2$.

The goal in this section is to describe procedures that control power in terms of δ_1, or control the length of confidence intervals when performing multiple comparison procedures. The procedures described here have the additional advantage of guaranteeing FWI $= \alpha$ even when the variances are unequal. Many of these procedures were reviewed in Wilcox (1984b), so the emphasis here will be on some related results plus recent developments. For illustrations on how to use these procedures, see Wilcox (1985i).

First, if power is to be reasonably close to one, say greater than or equal to $1 - \beta$, for a given value of β, it is impossible to determine a sample size n prior to collecting the data that guarantees this goal will be satisfied (e.g. Dantzig 1940, Stein 1945, Bishop 1976). Instead a two-stage procedure must be used. This just means that observations are randomly sampled, and some calculations are performed that indicate whether the sample size is large enough. This is the first stage. If the sample sizes are too small, the calculations indicate precisely how many more observations are required. The second stage consists of sampling the additional observations that are required and performing the desired test. Of course, if more observations are needed, obtaining additional observations may be very difficult or perhaps impossible. However, the procedures outlined here might still be of use because if a more conventional procedure fails to reject H_0, it may be that the sample sizes were too small to guarantee that the power will be reasonably high, and two-stage procedures help determine whether this is the case.

The first two-stage procedure was developed by Stein (1945), and nearly all of the two-stage procedures for controlling power that have been developed since are based on his general technique. Stein (1945) was concerned with testing $H_0: \mu = \mu_0$, μ_0 a known constant, and his goal was to devise a test so that the power would be at least $1 - \beta$ for a specified value of $\mu - \mu_0$ and α. The difficulty is that the power depends on the unknown variance, but Stein devised a very clever method of dealing with this problem.

Suppose n_0 observations are randomly sampled, and that the sample variance, s^2, is computed, and let

$$n = \max \{n_0, [s^2/d]^* + 1\} \qquad 7.$$

where $[s^2/d]^*$ is the integer portion of s^2/d, and d is a constant that is chosen by the experimenter. A method for determining d is described momentarily. Stein showed that for any d, if $n - n_0$ additional observations are randomly sampled, and $\bar{X} = \Sigma_{i=1}^n X_i/n$ is computed, then when H_0 is true,

$$\sqrt{n}(\bar{X} - \mu_0)/s \qquad 8.$$

has a Student's t distribution with $n_0 - 1$ degrees of freedom. Note that s in Equation 8 is based on only the first n_0 observations. Thus, if H_0 is rejected whenever

$$|\sqrt{n}(\bar{X} - \mu_0)/s| > t,$$

where t is the $1 - \alpha/2$ quantile of a Student's t distribution with $n_0 - 1$ degrees of freedom, the Type I error probability will be exactly α. The remarkable feature of Stein's procedure is that if d is chosen so that

$$\beta = \Pr[-t + (\mu - \mu_0)/\sqrt{d} \leq T_\nu \leq t + (\mu - \mu_0)/\sqrt{d}], \qquad 9.$$

where T_ν is a Student's t distribution with $\nu = n_0 - 1$ degrees of freedom, the power will be at least $1 - \beta$.

As a simple illustration, suppose $\mu_0 = 50$, $\alpha = .05$, $n_0 = 25$ and the power is to be at least .9 when $\mu = 45$. Then with 24 degrees of freedom, $t = 2.064$, and the constant d must be chosen so that

$$.1 = \Pr\left(-2.065 + \frac{50 - 45}{d^{1/2}} \leq T_{23} \leq 2.064 + \frac{50 - 45}{d^{1/2}}\right).$$

From a table of Student's t distribution, it follows that d is given approximately by the equation

$$-2.064 + (50 - 45)/\sqrt{d} = 1.318$$

which yields $d = 2.186$. If this value of d is used in Equation 7, the power will be at least .9.

Stein proved his result by first showing that it was possible to choose constants $a_1, \ldots, a_n$ such that $(\tilde{X} - \mu_0)\sqrt{d}$ has a Student's t distribution with $\nu = n_0 - 1$ degrees of freedom, where $\tilde{X} = \Sigma a_i X_i$, and that if H_0 is rejected when

$$|(\tilde{X} - \mu_0)/\sqrt{d}| > t,$$

the Type I error probability is exactly α and the power is exactly $1 - \beta$. Again d is given by Equation 9. Stein then showed that the procedure based on $\tilde{X}$ has power greater than or equal to the power of the procedure based on $\bar{X}$.

Stein never gave an explicit method for choosing the a_i's. It was not important in his paper, but in other situations, as will become evident, the a_i's are required. It turns out that the a_i's must satisfy certain properties, but the a_i's are not uniquely determined. One choice for the a_i's was proposed by Chapman (1950), and it is equivalent to setting

$$\tilde{X} = \left[\frac{1 - (n - n_0)b}{n} \right] \sum_{i=1}^{n_0} X_i + b \sum_{i=n_0+1}^{n} X_i \qquad \text{10.}$$

where

$$b = n^{-1} \left\{ 1 + \left[\frac{n_0(nd - s^2)}{(n - n_0)s^2} \right]^{1/2} \right\}.$$

It is noted that Chapman (1950) and Ghosh (1975b) extended Stein's results to the problem of testing $H_0: \mu_1 = \mu_2$; the relative merits of these procedures are discussed in Wilcox (1984b), and critical values for Chapman's procedure can be determined using results in Wilcox (1986b). Here attention is directed to recent results on testing $H_0: \mu_1 = \ldots = \mu_J$ using the technique suggested by Bishop & Dudewicz (1978).

To apply the Bishop-Dudewicz procedure, first randomly sample n_0 observations from each treatment group, compute

$$n_j = \max \{n_0 + 1, [s^2/d]^* + 1\},$$

sample an additional $n_j - n_0$ observations from the jth group, and compute $\tilde{X}_j$, the value of $\tilde{X}$ for the jth group. Next compute

$$\tilde{X} = \Sigma \tilde{X}_j / J$$

and

$$\tilde{F} = \Sigma(\tilde{X}_j - \tilde{X}_.)^2/d$$

where again the constant d controls power.

Percentage points of the null distribution of $\tilde{F}$ are not available, but fairly accurate approximations of the critical value c have been derived. In particular, choose c so that

$$\Pr \left(\frac{n_0 - 1}{n_0 - 3} \chi^2_{J-1} \leq c \right) = 1 - \alpha$$

where χ^2_{J-1} is a chi-square random variable with $J - 1$ degrees of freedom (Bishop & Dudewicz 1978). For example, if $J = 3$, $n_0 = 10$, and $\alpha = 0.05$, then $\Pr(\chi^2_2 \leq 5.99) = .95$, so $c = (9/7)5.99 = 7.70$. For slightly more accurate approximations of c, see Bishop et al (1978) and Wilcox (1984d). If $\tilde{F} > c$, reject H_0.

If the power is to be $1 - \beta$ for a specified value of δ_1, Bishop & Dudewicz (1978) show that the constant d is given by the equation

$$\Pr(\Sigma\{(T_j - \overline{T} - [\mu_j - \overline{\mu}])/\sqrt{d}\}^2 > c) = 1 - \beta \qquad 11.$$

where the T_j's are independent Student's t random variables each having $n_0 - 1$ degrees of freedom. The practical problem is that the left side of Equation 11 is difficult to evaluate, so Bishop & Dudewicz suggested an approximation of d, namely, choose d so that

$$\Pr \left(\frac{n_0 - 1}{n_0 - 3} \chi^2_{J-1}(\delta_1/d) > c \right) = 1 - \beta \qquad 12.$$

where $\chi^2_{J-1}(\delta_1/d)$ is a noncentral chi-square random variable with noncentrality parameter δ_1/d. Tables of the noncentral chi-square distribution are available (Hayman et al 1970), but in all likelihood these tables are not readily available to most readers, and more recent results found that Equation 12 can give an inaccurate approximation of d in certain cases (Wilcox 1985d). A simpler and more accurate approximation is obtained by determining z such that $\Pr(Z \leq z) = \beta$, where Z is a standard normal random variable, computing

$$A = [- z\sqrt{2} + \sqrt{2z^2 + 4(2b - \eta + 1)}]/2$$

where $\eta = J - 1$, $b = (n_0 - 3)c/(n_0 - 1)$, and c is the critical value,

$$B = A^2 - c\,\frac{n_0 - 3}{n_0 - 1}$$

in which case d is approximately equal to

$$\frac{n_0 - 3}{n_0 - 1}\,(\delta_1/B). \qquad\qquad 13.$$

For the accuracy and justification of this approximation see Wilcox (1985d).

Two-Stage Multiple Comparisons

Next suppose all pairwise comparisons of the means are to be made, but in contrast to procedures previously described, suppose the goal is to have, for every $i < j$, a confidence interval for $\mu_i - \mu_j$ having length $2m$ where m is some constant chosen by the experimenter. In single-stage procedures, the length of the confidence interval is a random variable, and relatively inaccurate estimates of $\mu_i - \mu_j$ might be obtained. The goal here is to control the accuracy of the estimate of $\mu_i - \mu_j$, regardless of what the variance might be. Tamhane (1979) derived a solution to this problem that guarantees FWI = α even when the variances are unequal. To apply his procedure, randomly sample n_0 observations from each treatment group, compute the sample variances, s_j^2, ($j = 1, \ldots, J$), and $d = (m/h)^2$ where h is read from the table in Wilcox (1983). When referring to Wilcox's table, the degrees of freedom are $\nu = n_0 - 1$. Next compute

$$n_j = \max\,\{n_0 + 1,\ [s_j^2/d]^* + 1\}$$

where $(s_j^2/d)^*$ is the integer portion of s_j^2/d. The second stage consists of randomly sampling an additional $n_j - n_0$ observations from the jth group, computing $\tilde{X}_j$ for each j ($j = 1, \ldots, J$) using Equation 10 in which case the confidence interval for $\mu_i - \mu_j$ is

$$(\tilde{X}_i - \tilde{X}_j - m,\ \tilde{X}_i - \tilde{X}_j + m).$$

As usual, if the interval does not contain zero, reject $H_0: \mu_i = \mu_j$. For an illustration of the procedure, see Wilcox (1983, 1985i).

Notice that as was the case with the Bishop-Dudewicz ANOVA, at least one additional observation must be sampled in the second stage. To always include the possibility of not having to sample any additional observations, it is perfectly legitimate to use only the first $n_0 - 1$ observations in the first stage, and if only one additional observation is needed, use the n_0th observation to compute $\tilde{X}$.

A practical issue is what to do with an unequal number of observations in the first stage. A method for handling this problem is described and illustrated in Wilcox (1984c).

Tamhane (1977) as well as Hochberg (1975) have proposed two-stage procedures for testing linear contrasts. Again these procedures give an experimenter control over the length of the confidence intervals. The relative merits of these procedures are discussed in Wilcox (1984b). The only point repeated here is that if attention is restricted to pairwise comparison of the means, Tamhane's procedure seems preferable to Hochberg's.

The Equal Variance Case

Assuming that the J treatment groups have a common variance, Stein (1945) proposed an extension of his results to the problem of testing $H_0: \mu_1 = \ldots = \mu_J$, and a table of constants needed to apply Stein's procedure can be found in Rodger (1976).

Again assuming equal variances, Healy (1956) considered the problem of obtaining joint confidence intervals of predetermined length for 1. all of the means, 2. all pairwise differences (a Tukey-type procedure), and 3. linear contrasts $\psi_k = \Sigma_j c_{kj} \mu_j (k = 1, \ldots, q)$ where $\Sigma_j c_{kj}^2 = 1$. When testing $J - 1$ linearly independent contrasts, the procedure and tables in Rodger (1978) can be used. For results on dependent groups having a common variance, see Wilcox (1985f).

While two-stage procedures have important practical advantages, they have the obvious disadvantage of possibly requiring the investigator to collect more observations. Accordingly, it may be important to consider ways in which the expected number of observations in the second stage can be reduced. Of course, if possible, a researcher would like to completely eliminate the need of sampling any additional observations. If equal variances can be assumed, the number of observations may be reduced, and perhaps no additional observations will be required. The reason is that the number of observations in the second stage is a decreasing function of the degrees of freedom. For unequal variances, the degrees of freedom are $n_0 - 1$, while for equal variances the degrees of freedom are $J(n_0 - 1)$. In fact, using a "generalized" sample estimate of the parameters in the general linear model, Bishop (1978) extended Stein's procedure to the general linear model for the case of unequal variances. Wilcox (1985e) noted that if the variances are equal, uniformly better results can be obtained by replacing the generalized estimate used by Bishop with the "usual" estimates. It seems that for unequal variances, it may not be possible to improve upon the procedure that uses the generalized sample estimates, but a proof does not yet exist. The main point here is that if there are equal variances, using the procedures just cited might reduce or possibly eliminate the need for sampling additional observations.

As a final remark, it is customary to arbitrarily set the probability of a Type I error at .05 or .01, but there seems to be no corresponding rule for power. One possibility might be to use a ten percent rule. For instance, when testing $H_0: \mu_1 - \mu_2$ if $\delta = \mu_1 - \mu_2$ is greater than or equal to 10% of the range of possible observed values, determine sample sizes so that the power will be at least .9. For example, if X measures a psychological construct, and the possible values of X are 0 to 15, then if $\delta = 1.5$ (10% of 15), the power should be at least .9. For $J > 2$ the slippage configuration might be considered. That is, for the case $\mu_1 = \mu_2 = , \ldots , \mu_{J-1}$, and $\mu_J - \mu_{J-1} = \delta$, the power should be at least .9. Once δ is specified, the computational steps in Wilcox (1985i) can be followed. Of course there is nothing sacred about this ten percent rule, and there will be situations where considerably different power requirements are more appropriate. However, this rule might be used in situations where it is unclear just what the power requirement should be.

SUMMARY

Perhaps the most striking implication of this review is that all of the conventional hypothesis testing procedures that assume equal variances should be abandoned. At a minimum, approximate solutions for handling unequal variances should be used, and wherever possible, exact two-stage procedures should be employed. Two-stage procedures can be inconvenient if additional observations are needed in the second stage, but this problem can be avoided if n_0 is large or if d is large in Equation 7. Methods for measuring treatment effects have been investigated, but methods for testing hypotheses about treatment effects are nearly nonexistent. Research on this problem is being carried out by the author and others, and perhaps some results will be available in the near future. For instance, the author is working on a method for testing $H_0: |\mu_1 - \mu_2| < \delta_0$, δ_0 a constant specified by the experimenter. If $\delta_0 = 0$, the method reduces to the usual t-test. The idea is that an experimenter can fix α and report the largest δ_0 that yields a significant result. This is in contrast to setting $\delta_0 = 0$ and reporting the smallest α that is significant. It is hoped the results will soon be available.

ACKNOWLEDGMENTS

The author would like to thank R. S. Rodger, Norman Cliff, Ventura Charlin, R. Shavelson, H. Huynh, and Bert Green for their very helpful comments on earlier versions of this paper.

Literature Cited

Abelson, R. P. 1985. A variance explanation paradox: Where a little is a lot. *Psychol. Bull.* 97:129–33

Alberton, Y., Hochberg, Y. 1984. Approximation for the distribution of a maximal pairwise t in some repeated measure designs. *Commun. Stat. Theory & Methods* 13:2847–54

Asfarinejad, K. 1983. Balanced repeated measurement designs. *Biometrika* 70:199–204

Bailey, B. J. R. 1977. Tables of the Bonferroni t statistic. *J. Am. Stat. Assoc.* 72:469–78

Bechhofer, R. E., Dunnett, C. W. 1982. Multiple comparisons for orthogonal contrasts: Examples and tables. *Technometrics* 24:213–22

Begun, J. M., Gabriel, K. R. 1981. Closure of the Newman-Keuls multiple comparison procedure. *J. Am. Stat. Assoc.* 76:241–45

Bernhardson, C. S. 1975. Type I error rates when multiple comparison procedures follow a significant F test of ANOVA. *Biometrics* 31:299–32

Bhoj, D. S. 1978. Testing equality of means of correlated variates with missing observations on both responses. *Biometrika* 65:225–28

Bhoj, D. S. 1979. Testing equality of variances of correlated variates with incomplete data on both responses. *Biometrika* 66:681–83

Bishop, T. A. 1976. *Heteroscedastic ANOVA, MANOVA, and multiple comparisons*. PhD thesis. Ohio State Univ., Columbus. Unpublished

Bishop, T. A. 1978. A Stein two-sample procedure for the general linear model with unequal variances. *Commun. Stat. Theory & Methods A* 7:495–507

Bishop, T. A., Dudewicz, E. J. 1978. Exact analysis of variance with unequal variances: Test procedures and tables. *Technometrics* 20:419–30

Bishop, T. A., Dudewicz, E. J., Juritz, J. M., Stephens, M. A. 1978. Percentage points of a quadratic form in Student's t variates. *Biometrika* 65:435–39

Box, G. E. P. 1953. Nonnormality and tests of variances. *Biometrika* 40:318–35

Box, G. E. P. 1954. Some theorems on quadratic forms applied in the study of analysis of variance problems, I. Effect of inequality of variance in the one-way classification. *Ann. Math. Stat.* 25:290–302

Bradley, J. V. 1978. Robustness? *Br. J. Math. Stat. Psychol.* 31:144–52

Bradley, J. V. 1980. Nonrobustness in Z, t, and F tests at large samples. *Bull. Psychon. Soc.* 16:333–36

Brown, M. B., Forsythe, A. B. 1974a. The small sample behavior of some statistics which test the equality of several means. *Technometrics* 16:129–32

Brown, M. B., Forsythe, A. B. 1974b. The ANOVA and multiple comparisons for data with heterogeneous variances. *Biometrics* 30:719–24

Chapman, D. G. 1950. Some two-sample tests. *Ann. Math. Stat.* 21:601–6

Chaubey, Y. P., Mudholkar, G. S. 1982. A new approximation for the distribution of the difference of two t-variables. *Commun. Stat. Theory & Methods* 11:2335–42

Cohen, J. 1966. Some statistical issues in psychological research. In *Handbook of Clinical Psychology*, ed. B. B. Wolman. New York: McGraw-Hill

Cohen, J. 1977. *Statistical Power Analysis For The Behavioral Sciences*. New York: Academic

Conover, W. J., Johnson, M. E., Johnson, M. M. 1981. A comparative study of tests for homogeneity of variances, with applications to the outer continental shelf bidding data. *Technometrics* 23:351–61

Dantzig, G. B. 1940. On the non-existence of tests of "Student's" hypothesis having power functions independent of σ. *Ann. Math. Stat.* 11:186

Dayton, C. M., Schafer, W. D. 1973. Extended tables of t and chi-square for Bonferroni tests with unequal error allocation. *J. Am. Stat. Assoc.* 68:78–83

Dunn, O. J. 1961. Multiple comparisons among means. *J. Am. Stat. Assoc.* 56:52–64

Dunnett, C. W. 1980a. Pairwise multiple comparisons in the homogeneous variance, unequal sample size case. *J. Am. Stat. Assoc.* 75:789–95

Dunnett, C. W. 1980b. Pairwise multiple comparisons of the unequal variance case. *J. Am. Stat. Assoc.* 75:796–800

Dunnett, C. W., Sobel, M. 1954. A bivariate generalization of Student's t-distribution, with tables for certain special cases. *Biometrika* 41:153–69

Dunnett, C. W., Sobel, M. 1955. Approximations to the probability integral and certain percentage points of a multivariate analogue of Student's t-distribution. *Biometrika* 42:258–60

Ekbohm, G. 1976. On comparing means in the paired case with incomplete data on both responses. *Biometrika* 63:299–304

Ekbohm, G. 1982. On comparing variances in the paired case with incomplete data. *Biometrika* 69:670–73

Felzenbaum, A., Hart, S., Hochberg, Y. 1983. Improving some multiple comparison procedures. *Ann. Stat.* 11:121–28

Fenstad, G. W. 1983. A comparison between U and V tests in the Behrens-Fisher problem. *Biometrika* 70:300–2

Fisher, R. A., Yates, F. 1957. *Statistical Tables*. New York: Hafner

Friedman, H. 1968. Magnitude of experimental effect and a table of its rapid estimation. *Psychol. Bull.* 70:245–51

Games, P. A. 1977. An improved *t* table for simultaneous control on *g* contrasts. *J. Am. Stat. Assoc.* 72:531–34

Games, P. A., Howell, J. F. 1976. Pairwise multiple comparison procedures with unequal *n*'s and/or variances: A monte carlo study. *J. Educ. Stat.* 1:113–25

Games, P. A., Keselman, H. J., Clinch, J. J. 1979. Tests for homogeneity of variance in factorial designs. *Psychol. Bull.* 86:978–84

Games, P. A., Keselman, H. J., Rogan, J. C. 1983. A review of simultaneous pairwise multiple comparisons. *Stat. Neerl.* 37:53–58

Ghosh, B. K. 1975a. On the distribution of the difference of two *t*-variables. *J. Am. Stat. Assoc.* 70:463–67

Ghosh, B. K. 1975b. On the distribution of the difference of two *t*-variables. *J. Am. Stat. Assoc.* 70:457–62

Gibbons, J., Olkin, I., Sobel, M. 1977. *Selecting and Ordering Populations: A New Statistical Methodology*. New York: Wiley

Glass, G. V. 1976. Primary, secondary, and meta-analysis of research. *Educ. Res.* 10:3–8

Hahn, G. J., Hendrickson, R. W. 1971. A table of percentage points of the distribution of the largest absolute value of *k* student *t* variates and its applications. *Biometrika* 58:323–32

Halperin, M. 1967. An inequality on a bivariate Student's *t* distribution. *J. Am. Stat. Assoc.* 62:603–6

Hartley, H. O. 1955. Some recent developments in analysis of variance. *Commun. Pure Appl. Math.* 8:47–72

Hayman, G. E., Govindarajulu, Z., Leone, F. C. 1970. *Selected Tables in Mathematical Statistics*, Vol. I, ed. H. L. Harter, D. B. Brown. Chicago: Markham

Hays, W. L. 1981. *Statistics*. New York: Holt, Rinehart & Winston

Hayter, A. J. 1984. A proof of a conjecture that the Tukey-Kramer multiple comparisons procedure is conservative. *Ann. Stat.* 12:61–75

Healy, W. C. 1956. Two-sample procedures in simultaneous estimation. *Ann. Math. Stat.* 27:687–702

Hedges, L. V. 1981. Distribution theory for Glass' estimator of effect size and related estimators. *J. Educ. Stat.* 6:107–28

Hedges, L. V. 1982a. Estimation and testing for differences in effect size: Comment on Hsu. *Psychol. Bull.* 91:391–93

Hedges, L. V. 1982b. Estimation of effect size

from a series of independent experiments. *Psychol. Bull.* 91:490–99

Hedges, L. V. 1982c. Fitting categorical models to effect size from a series of experiments. *J. Educ. Stat.* 7:119–37

Hedges, L. V. 1982d. Fitting continuous models to effect size from a series of experiments. *J. Educ. Stat.* 7:245–70

Hedges, L. V., Olkin, I. 1984. Nonparametric estimators of effect size in meta-analysis. *Psychol. Bull.* 96:573–80

Hochberg, Y. 1975. Simultaneous inference under Behrens-Fisher conditions—A two sample approach. *Commun. Stat.* 4:1109–19

Hogg, R. W., Craig, A. T. 1970. *Introduction to Mathematical Statistics*. New York: Macmillan

Horsnell, G. 1953. The effect of unequal group variances on the F-test for the homogeneity of group means. *Biometrika* 40:128–36

Hsu, P. L. 1938. Contribution to the theory of "Student's" *t*-test as applied to the problem of two samples. *Stat. Res. Mem.* 2:1–24

Hunter, D. 1976. An upper bound for the probability of a union. *J. Appl. Probab.* 13:597–603

Huynh, H., Feldt, L. A. 1970. Conditions under which mean square ratios in repeated measurements designs have exact F-distributions. *J. Am. Stat. Assoc.* 65:1582–89

Jaccard, J., Bechker, M. A., Wood, G. 1984. Pairwise multiple comparison procedures: A review. *Psychol. Bull.* 96:589–96

Jensen, D. R. 1982. Efficiency and robustness in the use of repeated measurements. *Biometrika* 38:318–25

Jeyaratnam, S. 1982. A sufficient condition on the covariance matrix for F tests in linear models to be valid. *Biometrika* 69:679–80

Kaiser, L. D., Bowden, D. C. 1983. Simultaneous confidence intervals for all linear contrasts of means with heterogeneous variances. *Commun. Stat. Theory & Methods* 12:73–88

Keselman, H. J. 1982. Multiple comparisons for repeated measures means. *Multivar. Behav. Res.* 17:87–92

Keselman, H. J., Rogan, J. C. 1978. A comparison of the modified-Tukey and Scheffé methods of multiple comparisons for pairwise contrasts. *J. Am. Stat. Assoc.* 73:47–51

Kirk, R. E. 1982. *Experimental Design: Procedures for the Behavioral Sciences*. Belmont, CA: Brooks/Cole

Kraemer, H. C. 1983. Theory of estimation and testing effect size: Use in meta-analysis. *J. Educ. Stat.* 8:93–101

Kraemer, H. C. 1984. Nonparametric effect

size estimation: A reply. *Psychol. Bull.* 96:569–72

Kraemer, H. C., Andrews, G. 1982. A nonparametric technique for meta-analysis effect size calculation. *Psychol. Bull.* 91: 404–12

Kramer, C. Y. 1956. Extensions of multiple range tests to group means with unequal numbers of replications. *Biometrics* 12: 307–10

Krauth, J. 1983. Nonparametric effect size estimation: A comment on Kraemer and Andrews. *Psychol. Bull.* 94:190–92

Krishnaiah, P. R., Armitage, P. V. 1966. Table for multivariate *t*-distributions. *Sankhya Ser. B* 28:31–56

Lewis, C., van Knippenberg, C. 1984. Estimation and model comparisons for repeated measures data. *Psychol. Bull.* 96:182–94

Lin, P. E., Stivers, L. E. 1974. On the difference of means with incomplete data. *Biometrika* 61:325–34

Maxwell, S. E. 1980. Pairwise multiple comparisons in repeated measures designs. *J. Educ. Stat.* 5:269–87

Mehta, J. S., Gurland, J. 1973. A test for equality of means in the presence of correlation and missing values. *Biometrika* 60: 211–12

Morrison, D. F. 1974. A test for equality of means in the presence of correlation and missing values. *Biometrika* 60:101–6

Nelson, P. R. 1982. Multivariate normal and *t* distributions with $\rho_{jk} = \alpha_j \alpha_k$. *Commun. Stat. Simulation & Computation* 11:239–48

O'Brien, P. C. 1983. The appropriateness of analysis of variance and multiple comparison procedures. *Biometrika* 39:787–88

O'Brien, R. G. 1978. Robust techniques for testing heterogeneity of variance effects in factorial designs. *Psychometrika* 43:327–42

O'Brien, R. G. 1979. A general ANOVA method for robust tests additive models for variances. *J. Am. Stat. Assoc.* 74:877–80

O'Grady, K. E. 1982. Measures of explained variance: Cautions and limitations. *Psychol. Bull.* 92:766–77

Ramsey, P. H. 1981. Power of univariate pairwise multiple comparison procedures. *Psychol. Bull.* 90:352–66

Rodger, R. S. 1974. Multiple contrasts, factors, error rate and power. *Br. J. Math. Stat. Psychol.* 27:179–98

Rodger, R. S. 1975a. The number of nonzero, post hoc contrasts for ANOVA and error-rate I. *Br. J. Math. Stat. Psychol.* 28:71–78

Rodger, R. S. 1975b. Setting rejection rate for contrasts selected post hoc when some nulls are false. *Br. J. Math. Stat. Psychol.* 28: 214–32

Rodger, R. S. 1976. Tables of Stein's noncentral parameter $D\beta$; ν_1, ν_2 required to set power for numerical alternatives to H_0 tested by two-stage ANOVA. *J. Stat. Computation & Simulation* 5:1–22

Rodger, R. S. 1978. Two-stage sampling to set sample size for post hoc tests in ANOVA with decision-based error rates. *Br. J. Math. Stat. Psychol.* 31:153–78

Rogan, J. C., Keselman, H. J. 1977. Is the ANOVA F-test robust to variance heterogeneity when sample sizes are equal? An investigation via a coefficient of variation. *Am. Educ. Res. J.* 14:493–98

Rosenthal, T., Rubin, D. B. 1982. Comparing effect sizes of independent studies. *Psychol. Bull.* 92:500–4

Sandvik, L., Olsson, B. 1982. A nearly distribution-free test for comparing dispersion in paired samples. *Biometrika* 69:484–85

Satterthwaite, F. E. 1941. Synthesis of variance. *Psychometrika* 6:309–16

Scheffé, H. 1959. *The Analysis of Variance.* New York: Wiley

Scott, A. 1967. A note on conservative confidence regions for the mean of a multivariate normal. *Ann. Math. Stat.* 38:278–80

Šidák, Z. 1967. Rectangular confidence regions for the means of multivariate normal distributions. *J. Am. Stat. Assoc.* 62:626–33

Šidák, Z. 1971. On probabilities of rectangles in multivariate Student distributions: Their dependence on correlations. *Ann. Math. Stat.* 42:169–75

Smith, W. C., Han, C. P. 1981. Error rate for testing a contrast after a significant F test. *Commun. Stat. Simulation & Computation B* 10:546–56

Spjøtvoll, E., Stoline, M. R. 1983. An extension of the T-method of multiple comparisons to include the case with unequal sample size. *J. Am. Stat. Assoc.* 68:975–78

Spurrier, J. D. 1981. An improved GT2 method for simultaneous confidence intervals on pairwise difference. *Technometrics* 23:189–92

Spurrier, J. D., Isham, S. P. 1985. Exact simultaneous confidence intervals for pairwise comparisons of three normal means. *J. Am. Stat. Assoc.* 80:438–42

Stein, C. 1945. A two-sample test for a linear hypothesis whose power is independent of the variance. *Ann. Math. Stat.* 16:243–58

Stoline, M. R. 1981. The status of multiple comparisons: Simultaneous estimation of all pairwise comparisons in one-way ANOVA designs. *Am. Stat.* 35:134–41

Stoline, M. R., Ury, H. K. 1979. Tables of the studentized maximum modulas distribution and an application to multiple comparisons among means. *Technometrics* 21:87–93

Tamhane, A. C. 1977. Multiple comparisons in model I one-way ANOVA with unequal variances. *Commun. Stat. Theory & Methods A* 6:15–32

Tamhane, A. C. 1979. A comparison of procedures for multiple comparisons of means with unequal variances. *J. Am. Stat. Assoc.* 74:471–80

Tan, W. Y. 1982. Sampling distributions and robustness of t, F and variance-ratio in two samples and ANOVA models with respect to departure from normality. *Commun. Stat. Theory & Methods* 11:2485–2511

Tiku, M. L., Balakrishnan, N. 1984. Testing equality of population variances the robust way. *Commun. Stat. Theory & Methods* 13: 2133–42

Tong, Y. L. 1980. *Probability of Inequalities in Multivariate Distributions.* New York: Academic

Tukey, J. W. 1953. *The problem of multiple comparisons.* Princeton, NJ: Princeton Univ. Unpublished report

Ury, H. K., Stoline, M. R., Mitchell, B. T. 1980. Further tables of the Studentized maximum modulus distribution. *Commun. Stat. Simulation & Computation B* 9:167–78

Ury, H. K., Wiggins, A. D. 1971. Large sample and other multiple comparisons among means. *Br. J. Math. Stat. Psychol.* 24:174–94

Vonesh, E. J. 1983. Efficiency of repeated measures designs versus completely randomized designs based on multiple comparisons. *Commun. Stat. Theory & Methods* 12:289–302

Welch, B. L. 1937. The significance of the difference between two means when the population variances are unequal. *Biometrika* 29:350–61

Wilcox, R. R. 1983. A table of percentage points on the range of independent t variables. *Technometrics* 25:201–4

Wilcox, R. R. 1984a. Approximating multivariate distributions. *J. Organ. Behav. Stat.* 1:24–36

Wilcox, R. R. 1984b. A review of exact hypothesis testing procedures (and selection techniques) that control power regardless of the variances. *Br. J. Math. Stat. Psychol.* 37:34–48

Wilcox, R. R. 1984c. On two-stage multiple comparison procedures when there are unequal sample sizes in the first stage. *J. Educ. Stat.* 9:227–36

Wilcox, R. R. 1984d. Simple approximations of percentage points of quadratic forms in Student t variates. *J. Organ. Behav. Stat.* 1:102–8

Wilcox, R. R. 1985a. A multiple comparison procedure for determining which means are substantially different: The unequal variance case. *J. Organ. Behav. Stat.* 2:233–40

Wilcox, R. R. 1985b. An extended and slightly improved table of critical values for testing q linear contrasts in repeated measures designs. *Commun. Stat. Simulation & Computation* 14:55–69

Wilcox, R. R. 1985c. On comparing treatment effects to a standard when the variances are unknown and unequal. *J. Educ. Stat.* 10:45–54

Wilcox, R. R. 1985d. A note on controlling power in the Bishop-Dudewicz heteroscedastic ANOVA procedure. *Br. J. Math. Stat. Psychol.* In press

Wilcox, R. R. 1985e. On a Stein-type two-stage procedure for the general linear model. *Br. J. Math. Stat. Psychol.* 38:222–26

Wilcox, R. R. 1985f. Controlling power and the length of confidence intervals in multivariate normal distributions having a common variance. *J. Organ. Behav. Stat.* In press

Wilcox, R. R. 1985h. On the robustness of Welch's V, Welch's U, and the t-test. Unpublished technical report

Wilcox, R. R. 1985i. *Advances in Basic Statistics,* Vol. 2. Los Angeles: Center for the Study of Evaluation, Univ. Calif.

Wilcox, R. R. 1986a. Improved simultaneous confidence intervals for linear contrasts and regression parameters. *Commun. Stat.* In press

Wilcox, R. R. 1986b. Critical values for the correlated t-test when there are missing observations. *Commun. Stat. Simulation & Computation.* In press

Wilcox, R. R., Charlin, V., Thompson, K. L. 1985. New results on the robustness of the ANOVA F, W and F* statistics. Technical report

Ann. Rev. Psychol. 1987. 38:61–90

PERCEPTION AND INFORMATION

James E. Cutting

Department of Psychology, Cornell University, Ithaca, NY 14853-7601

CONTENTS

How, then, is it, that we receive accurate information, by the eye, of size, and shape, and distance?

James Mill (1829, p. 95)

0066-4308/87/0201/0061$02.00

INTRODUCTION

What is the nature of information; what enables it to inform our perceptual systems? Psychology, particularly in its study of information processing, aspires to an answer; but since perception researchers measure information in different ways, this answer is not definitive. By its focus on processing, psychology has long taken information for granted, usually assuming it to be like text or speech; but if information were actually so constrained, I contend, the bulk of perception would be uninformed. The world rarely presents itself language-like to our senses.

In this review I consider various types of information assumed by perceptual researchers. Assumptions about information constrain our ideas about the relations between perception and cognition. They shape the emerging field of cognitive science. They also form the backdrop to the issue of bottom-up versus top-down processing—the latter a time-worn but far from weary idea; formal syntheses of these two positions are emerging (e.g. McClelland 1985, McClelland & Elman 1986), but here I focus on bottom-up issues.

Historical Roots

Among English writers, Shakespeare may have had priority in linking perception and information in a single statement: "It is the bloody business," says Macbeth, "which informs thus to mine eyes" [*Macbeth* (II, *i*)]. But Mill, as quoted above, was among the first philosophers of mind to conjoin the two. Indeed, perception and information are a natural pair. Both of Latin origin, they appeared in English literature in the 14th and 15th centuries. Information, the older term, signified communication of knowledge, a notion with which modern treatments are still in tune (Machlup & Mansfield 1983). Etymologically, to *inform* means "to instill a form within," and it is a modest step to consider perception as instilling the forms of external objects in the mind of a perceiver.

"Perception" has a more curious etymology. In feudal economics it meant the collection of rents. Its present meaning retains an aspect of its heritage if we recognize perception as the collection of information about the world. For Locke (1690) and Berkeley (1709) perception was broadly associated with thinking. Reid (1785) distinguished it from sensation; yet, to use Hamilton's (1859) terminology, how does one separate presentation by the senses from re-presentation by the mind? One approach is to study the mapping entailed between proximal *information* and distal objects and events.

Mapping, Inference, Structure, and Measurement

Proximal-distal mappings are central to the discussion of perceptual information. Their consideration began in earnest with Koffka (1935), but roots can be found in the causal theory of perception (e.g. Russell 1927). The typical course of perception for a readied organism proceeds 1. from real-world object or event, 2. through a medium, 3. to sensory surfaces and receptors, and then 4. to the central nervous system. One can study information at stage 2. If the mapping from stage 3 back to stage 1 is ruly, then perception can be relatively straightforward; if not, additional elements must be adduced. Doubts about the completeness of these four steps caused many to add 5. a stage of conceptual elaboration and re-presentation (e.g. Descartes 1649, Locke 1690). Berkeley (1733) waffled, but J. S. Mill (1843) finally christened stage 5 with the name *inference*. Helmholtz (1866) then toyed with the term *unconscious inference* but gave it up (Helmholtz 1878) because Schopenhauer had used this term to denote a different concept. Regardless, the idea of unconscious inference remains with us today (e.g. Rock 1983, 1985).

But inferences come in two kinds: They can be deductively valid or inductively strong (e.g. Skyrms 1975). Perception could be *deductive* if all premises came from stimulus information and from design features of a perceptual system. Bottom-up processing is almost by necessity deductive. If the mapping from proximal stimulus back to distal object is assured, then no probabilistic associations need be added; no cognition is required. Richards et al (1982) employed mathematical proof to determine when information is sufficient and deductive perception possible. This is a type of inference with which Gibson (1979), for one, could be happy. If, however, perception is *inductive,* some premises come from memory and cognition; perception must have top-down components with no recourse but to concepts of probabilism and cue-validity. Many modern thinkers have espoused such ideas (Brunswik 1956, Gregory 1974, Neisser 1967, Kolers 1983).

In broad form, however, this view seems on the wane. Part of the reason is an upturn of interest in the work of James Gibson and his ecological approach, an interest registered both by psychologists (Bruce & Green 1985, Shepard 1984, Turvey et al 1981, Warren & Shaw 1984b, Wilcox & Edwards 1982) and philosophers (Fodor & Pylyshyn 1981). Some have tried to improve on Gibson (Bickhard & Richie 1983, Heil 1983, Michaels & Carello 1981, Natsoulas 1984), others have pointed out problems with the ecological approach (Ullman 1980, Cutting 1982b), and still others have broached these problems for all theories of perception (Hochberg 1982, 1984; Cutting 1986).

New support for the idea of bottom-up processing has come from the field of machine vision. Through Marr (1982), Ullman (1979), the work that theirs has fostered (e.g. Brady 1981, Grimson 1981, Pentland 1986, Pinker 1984), and the work from somewhat different traditions (e.g. Ballard & Brown 1982, Binford 1981, McArthur 1982), machine vision has outraced the early lead of the ecological approach in its search for specifiable information on which percepts might be based. An emerging synthesis of methodologies in psychology (Cutting 1986, Proffitt & Bertenthal 1986, Todd 1982, Todd & Mingolla 1983, Warren 1984) and machine vision (Hildreth 1984; Stevens 1981, 1983b; Ullman 1979) has brought a new style of research. Two steps are entailed: 1. mathematical proof of the consistency of information and 2. demonstration that it is perceptually useful.

Approaches to information are many. One could, following Aristotle, Külpe (1895), and Kubovy (1981), look for stimulus dimensions that carry information—extent, time, frequency, and intensity. While such a neat beginning may be suitable for taste, olfaction, kinesthesis, and touch, it is much less so for audition and vision. Instead, another tradition has it that information is in structure (Garner 1962, 1974). Following this lead, I have divided approaches to information into five groups according to potential origins of structure—experience, constraints, statistics, analysis, and geometry. The crux of any information is its *measure*. How it is measured determines what is deemed important to a perceptual system. Each type assumes that perception, typically vision, is *informed* by measures of the stimulus, and that perception is, in part, information measurement (Lappin 1984).

STRUCTURE FROM EXPERIENCE

For James Mill, information existed in association networks and in what twentieth century analytic philosophy calls sense-data. This is the oldest form of information discussed in psychology.

Information in Frequency of Occurrence

The idea that *information exists in the number of times something happens* was at the base of Morton's (1969; Gordon & Caramazza 1985) logogen model, which counted occurrences of words for later recognition; it also has a place in cognitive learning (Estes 1976), in concept formation (Mervis & Rosch 1981), and in memory [Hasher & Zacks 1979; although not in all contexts (Kahneman et al 1982)]. In music perception, Krumhansl (1985) has found that probe tone ratings given by listeners to notes and chords as they fit into a diatonic scale are highly correlated with their frequency of occurrence in pieces of classical music. Such results complement her continued interest in the density of events in space and time (Krumhansl 1978, 1982).

PROBLEMS WITH FREQUENCY   Despite its utility to perception, frequency information is not perceptual; it must be cognitive. It can only be useful to an organism after large amounts of processing, or many logogen ticks, have occurred. It is not information about a current stimulus; it is about similar previous stimuli. Thus, frequency information leaves as a mystery how a stimulus informs for the first time, or how similarity with previous stimuli is determined.

STRUCTURE FROM CONSTRAINTS

A second general approach to information considers constraints. Rather than concentrating on what a stimulus is, this approach focuses on what it is not, considering potential false targets and weeding out alternative percepts.

Information from Bits to Simplicity

Perhaps the most familiar style of information measure comes from electrical engineering and information theory (Shannon & Weaver 1949)—bitwise assessment through logarithmic counts of alternatives. According to this approach *information exists in the set size to which an object or event belongs*. Early applications to perception include those of Attneave (1954) and Garner (1962). Currently, this approach is not so popular in perception as in cognitive science more generally (Dretske 1981, Machlup & Mansfield 1983), but two threads remain: Bits-measure plays a practical role in electronic transmission of images, and it has fostered continuing interest in perceptual economy.

Sperling (1980, Sperling et al 1985a) described techniques for the transmission of American Sign Language (ASL) over telephone lines. Since telephone transmission typically uses a bandwidth about 1/300 that of television, serious compression of the visual signal is necessary. Using many different coding schemes, the most successful entailing reduction and adaptive coding of pixels (picture elements) and reduction of frames transmitted, Sperling et al found it possible to transmit acceptable ASL at near-telephone line capacity. The practical import of these findings is patent; their theoretical implications are discussed below.

The second thread of interest in bits-measure involves the Gestalt concept of simplicity. The importance of design simplicity, or minimality of physical solutions to structural problems in nature, was emphasized by Mach (1886) and later by Köhler (Koffka 1935, Attneave 1982). In perception, good figures, the Gestaltists argued, should also be simple. The task of quantifying minimality began with Hochberg & McAlister (1953) and has been renewed by Hemenway & Palmer (1978) and by Butler (1982). It has also received philosophical attention from Sober (1975) and from Hatfield & Epstein (1985). The natural descendent of the study of perceptual simplicity is the work of Leeuwenberg (1971; Buffart et al 1981, 1983) and what is now called structural information theory. In vision and audition, stimuli are parsed into primitive elements. These are then combined, counted, and demonstrated to predict perceived forms over certain nonperceived forms, which have less parsimonious combinatorics. In the visual perception of motion, Restle

(1979) applied this general scheme to Johansson's (1950) demonstrations, Cutting (1981) adapted it further, and Todd (1982), Cutting & Proffitt (1982), and Proffitt et al (1984) explored constraints.

PROBLEMS WITH BITS AND SIMPLICITY   Among the assumptions in almost any application of information theory to perception is that perceptual objects come in fixed, homogeneous, nonoverlapping sets of known size. Unfortunately, the world around us is not populated with such things. And as with frequency, bits-measure is information only for an organism with substantial personal history.

Sperling's work with ASL sequences suggests further difficulties. Bitwise assessment of images and its assumed psychological relevance rest on two deeper assumptions about aliasing, the distortions found in any quantized signal: That spatial aliasing [or discreteness effects due to receptor packing in the retina (Williams & Collier 1983)] constrains all perception of form and that temporal aliasing [or discreteness effects in stroboscopic motion due to low temporal resolution in the signal (Burr 1981)] constrains all perception of motion. Although both are important to perception and to discussion of high-quality images, neither has psychological preeminence. Multiplying pixels by gray scale by frame rates, seems an inadequate way to measure perceptual information.

The problems with approaches to simplicity are two. First, and appreciated by Goodman (1972) and Sober (1975), is justification of primitives or the stimulus "atoms" underlying percepts. One must have an a priori rationale for their choice; otherwise one's proofs rest only upon shrewd guesses. Restle (1979), in selecting primitives from the mechanics of motions, seems to have justified this approach best. Second, Hochberg (1981, 1982), the originator of this approach, has shown that perceptual economy is easily overridden by other stimulus factors, thus robbing it of central importance.

Information from Group Theory

Where information theory and bitwise assessment left off, interest in mathematical groups picked up. The switch was led by Garner (1970) and his analysis of symmetry: If good patterns have few alternatives, there might be information in counting members of a symmetry group. The idea here is a plea for formalism—*information is constrained through groups of transformations on a stimulus* that follow postulates of closure, association, identity, and inversion. The roots of this idea can be traced to Cassirer (1944), Poincare (1907), and Helmholtz. Promoting what is now known as the "group of displacements," Helmholtz (1894, p. 504) suggested: "Being acquainted with the material form of an object, we are able to represent clearly in our minds all the perspective images we expect to see when we look at it from different sides; and we are startled if an image we actually see does not correspond to our expectations." The group of Euclidean translations (along *x*, *y*, and *z* axes) and rotations (around orthogonal axes oriented in *x*, *y*, and *z*) consists of six dimensions of continous transformations that leave an object's shape invariant (Lévy-Leblond 1971).

Recent applications of group theory to perception are many. Balzano (1980) and M. Jones (1981) applied groups to tonality and rhythm; Dodwell (1983, 1984) has taken W. Hoffman's (1966, 1984) group-theoretic approach as applied to fields of vectors in hopes of revealing the underlying structure of objects in images; Foster (1975), Cooper & Shepard (1984), and Shepard (1981, 1984) discussed application of group theory to paths of apparent motions; Leyton (1984, 1985, 1986) used groups to propose generative factors in object perception; Palmer (1982, 1983) looked at subsymmetries and transformations in visual forms; and Warren & Shaw (1984a) discussed group theory in perception generally.

PROBLEMS WITH GROUPS   Eddington (1939, p. 148) stated that "The starting point of physical science is knowledge of *the group-structure of a set of sensations* in a consciousness." Group theory has much promise in perception, but there are nagging problems (Cutting 1986). For example, although groups can describe perceptual phenomena, their capacity to explain them is less clear. Consider a parallel from another branch of mathematics: Although catastrophe theory (e.g. Zeeman 1976) models equally well the hysteresis effects in stereopsis and in binge/purge eating disorders, it explains neither. So too group theory may model but not explain perception. At the very least, group theory suggests interesting questions about perception.

STRUCTURE FROM STATISTICS

A third approach to information is statistical, and in vision research it roughly divides two ways. The first considers statistics of textures that varicolor a surface; the second considers whole forms and has its roots in signal detection theory. In both, information is in spatial distribution.

Information in Texture Shape

Julesz has developed a theory of textons, or statistical primitives for the visual system (Julesz & Bergen 1983), where *information is measured by the shape of a texture element.* Julesz (1975) began by discussing the probability of two-dimensional (2-D) placement of dots, dipoles (oriented needles), and sequential gray scale (a kind of shading pattern) as first-, second-, and third-order statistics, respectively. His original conjecture was that textures identical in dot and dipole statistics but differing in gray scale could not be discriminated. Interesting variations and counterexamples were found (Diaconis & Freedman 1981, Julesz 1981). Statistical order has faded from central importance, and the universe of textons is now tripartite, comprising elongated blobs, terminators, and the crossing of line segments. Any one of these can be located easily and rapidly on a surface of differing textons. Beck (1982b, 1983; Beck et al 1983b) has followed in this vein, Julesz has continued (Sagi & Julesz 1985), and Caelli (1981, 1985) and Foster (1984) have promoted related schemes.

Perhaps the most important work on texture is that of Treisman (1982, 1985; Treisman & Paterson 1984; Treisman & Souther 1985; see also Prinzmetal 1981). Eschewing statistics, Treisman has proposed a feature-integration theory of perception, where focal attention is necessary to merge separate attributes of a stimulus. As in Julesz's work, empirical results determine features in an experimental task of visual search. Treisman demonstrated that search time is very long for a target among distractors that possess its component features. She found emergent features and search-time asymmetries that are further diagnostics for visual primitives. Her current list includes color, lines, terminators, and closure, matching Julesz's list (and Marr's) rather well.

Other statistical attributes of form are treated by Zusne (1970) and Lord & Wilson (1984). In addition, Pentland (1983) has suggested that fractals may have psychological correlates. Fractals are graphical objects (technically curves) that fill space through recursion (self-similarity at different scales), can have noninteger dimensionality, and can have stochastic character (Mandelbrot 1983).

PROBLEMS WITH TEXTONS AND FEATURES   Texton theory neatly bypasses one problem of structural information theory by basing its selection of primitives upon empirical results. But other difficulties arise. First, texton studies are, in essence, the study of wallpaper. A quick look around an environment without walls reveals that most common textures overlap, interleave, grade, and are differentially shaded. This may not pose insufferable difficulties because textons can be slanted without changing character (Kanade & Kender 1983; but see Beck 1982b). Second and more important, because it studies rapid perception texton theory bears only on static images. Reaction-time and tachistoscopic measures of perception apply primarily to information detectable at a single moment. But much information is revealed to vision through motion, and there is conflicting evidence as to whether form and motion are processed independently (Cutting 1982a, Krumhansl 1984). And third, texton studies do not consider natural textures.

Careful study of Brodatz's (1966) work on such textures will repay anyone.

Information in Dotted Forms

Another statistical approach concerns signal detection, proposing that *information derives from probabilistic relations among signal elements and noise*. In psychology this style of research began as part of an engineering approach to speech perception (Miller et al 1951). In vision, such studies began at the dawn of the application of computer technology to perception: Researchers represented stimuli and noise by means of computer controlled dots; stimulus dots were placed on the surface of or within the form of primary interest. Dots have several physical properties that make them good tools of inquiry (Sperling 1971), and they are also easy to generate. This type of study has been sustained in three areas: 1. stereopsis, most notably studied by Julesz (1971; see also Prazdny 1985a); 2. the microtexture of form; and 3. the perception of motion. Only the latter two areas concern us here, and I discuss the last in a later section.

Glass (1969) discovered that by rotating identical sheets of speckled transparencies, with respect to one another one will see remarkable, global swirling patterns, now known as Glass patterns. Their interest is in what they can tell us about local determinants of global patterns. Recently, Prazdny (1984, 1985b) has shown that spatial distributions of energy rather than of symbolic codes are responsible for the effect, and Zucker (1984, 1985; Zucker et al 1983; see also Stevens 1983a) used such patterns to discriminate two types of form: one of edge detection and the other of global patterning.

Uttal (1983, 1985) has continued his study of dotted forms. Among recent findings he noted two in conflict. In two-dimensional figures the most important attribute for detectability of dotted lines is evenness of spacing; but in three dimensions the detection of a curved surface peppered with dots is better when dots are randomly rather than regularly distributed. Uttal suggested that the latter finding is due to effects of spatial aliasing, the biases that emerge from regular sampling. Under conditions of three points with no noise, however, Lappin & Fuqua (1983) found remarkable sensitivity for even spacing of three dots rotating on a line slanted in depth.

PROBLEMS WITH DOTTED FIGURES   Like textons and features, Glass patterns suggest fundamental processes early in the sequence of visual processing. But how do such processes work in the perception of everyday scenes? Zucker (1985) analyzes this issue, but his distinction relegates all normal perception to global-pattern processes. More importantly, dotted forms were initially used in studies of visual perception for the pragmatic reason that they were easy to generate and easy to control. With the development of better and cheaper computer graphics capabilities, which allow generation of increasingly naturalistic scenes, it is not clear what future role dotted-form research should have in our field. Control is no longer sacrificed in complex displays.

STRUCTURE FROM NEURAL ANALYSIS

One aspect of simplicity and texton/featural approaches to perception is their focus on primitives—decomposition of scenes into discrete building blocks. When confronted with complex stimuli, such approaches cannot always guarantee straightforward decomposition. Some stimulus attributes, for example, may be both bloblike and terminatorlike. Two forms of analysis, however, guarantee complete decomposition. In one, currently called the neural dynamics approach (Cohen & Grossberg 1984; Grossberg & Mingolla 1985a,b), various perceptual phenomena are considered and neural networks proposed to model them (see also Anderson 1983). In the other and more traditional approach, stimuli are decomposed by Fourier analysis.

Information in Fourier Components

Fourier analysis of visual stimuli has burgeoned in the last 20 years. Borrowed from auditory research, this approach assumes that *information lies in distribution, amplitude, and phase of sine wave components* of a visual image. Yellott et al (1984) recently reviewed this work.

Four threads can be traced within the recent literature. First, interesting new data are available on Fourier-like components that pervade underwater environments (MacFarland & Loew 1983). Second, the relation between Fourier channels and attention continues to be explored (Banks et al 1985, Graham 1985, Yager et al 1984); third, new spatiotemporal analyses have been performed (Nakayama & Silverman 1985; van Santen & Sperling 1984, 1985; Sekuler et al 1984; Stromeyer et al 1984), some including Gabor functions (Watson et al 1983); and fourth, parsimonious image analysis and regeneration is now possible through pyramid schemes that provide excellent Fourier approximation (Burt & Adelson 1983a, 1983b).

PROBLEMS WITH SINE WAVES   There is great power in Fourier analysis, and that is its problem. Joseph Fourier guaranteed that any signal could be analyzed into sine waves. Thus, Fourier analysis (or the multilevel zero-crossing analysis of Marr 1982) is unselective: *Everything* in the stimulus is transformed, not merely the most meaningful or important parts. And except in work with faces (e.g. Harmon 1973), Fourier analysis is generally used to look inward at predispositions of the nervous system, rather than outward at the objects and events of the surrounding world. It simply cannot be that our visual system finds informative everything at 8 cycles/degree.

STRUCTURE FROM GEOMETRY

The idea that geometry is the foundation of vision has a long history—from Euclid through Alhazen, Kepler, and Descartes. We have generally ignored those roots, but Euclid (Burton 1945) was much interested in size, the horizon, occlusions, induced motion, and motion parallax. Euclid's *Optics,* an extension of his *Elements* (the foundation of geometry), deals entirely with physical constraints on perception.

Although admonished otherwise, we can fit Gibson (1979) into the Euclidean tradition of classical optics: *Information is geometrized "in the light," measured in visual angles.* For nearly a century the geometry thought relevant to vision has been projective (Russell 1897, Poincaré 1905, Johansson et al 1980). But projections vary [see Carlbom & Paciorek (1978) for an overview of planar projection techniques and Sedgwick (1983) for their application to perception].

Information, Geometry, and Static Form

Geometric information concerns both the static and the moving form. Research on static projections has advanced in three areas: 1. relations of object parts to objects; 2. use of textures on surfaces to derive surface shape, without recourse to textons or features; and 3. use of shading to recover surface shape.

First, consider object recognition and the interpretation of junctions of line segments in recovery of object shape. Ballard & Brown (1982), McArthur (1982), and S. Lee et al (1985) have reviewed work since Guzman's (1969) analysis of intersections—forks, arrows, and tees—and Perkins (1983), Shepard (1981), and Barnard (1985) have considered constraints on the perception of rectangular solids. One basic assumption here—that solids are made up of edges that intersect at right angles—is clearly false for most natural objects.

The most important recent advance in figure-ground segregation is in the study of nonrectilinear contours. Koenderink & van Doorn (1982) and Koenderink (1984b) noted constraints on ending contours of smooth objects, and Hoffman & Richards (1984; Richards & Hoffman 1985) have suggested that six *codons,* or arrangements of maximal and minimal curvature in line segments, can be used to break up objects into parts on the basis of self-occluding contour, or silhouette profile. Codons map onto *geons* [or generalized cones (Binford 1981)] for object recognition. Biederman (1985) estimated that 36 geons can describe 2 million different objects. Nonrigid objects with rigid parts, like animals and people, might be categorized and recognized by such a scheme (Webb & Aggarwal 1982). Implementation of object recognition by such a scheme is probably far into the future, but the idea seems promising.

Second, consider surfaces. Discussion of surface geometry began with Gibson's (1950) analysis of information in texture relations. But after Gibson for a period of 30 years the issue of recovering surface shape from textures was bypassed for discussion of absolute surface slant and texture density, neither of which is an important psychological variable. Slant research continues (Epstein & Lovitts 1985), applied most notably to the practical problem of landing aircraft (Perrone 1984).

Owing to more recent interest in machine vision, the recovery of surface shape from texture geometry has recaptured attention. Orthogonally specifiable measures of textures on surfaces number at least three: density, scaling (or perspective), and foreshortening (or compression). Information about flatness is contained in the scaling measure and that about curvature in foreshortening (Cutting & Millard 1984, Stevens 1984, Todd & Mingolla 1984). Recent work in machine vision (Besl & Jain 1986, Brady et al 1985, Grimson 1983, Kanatani 1984, Ullman & Richards 1984) has concentrated on complex surface shape. But textures, like textons, are too sensitive to spacing considerations to play more than a minor role in the perception of natural surfaces.

Third, and most important, is shading. Studies of illumination have received recent psychological attention (Bergström et al 1984, Flock & Nusinowitz 1984, Gilchrist & Jacobsen 1984, Granrud et al 1985). Assisted by computers, psychological (Todd & Mingolla 1983, Mingolla & Todd 1986) and machine-vision (Pentland 1982, Woodham 1984, C. Lee & Rosenfeld 1985) studies of shaded surfaces are paving the way for a new kind of psychophysics, impossible even a few years ago, in which complex variables of lighting, reflectance, shading, and color can be minutely controlled.

Information, Geometry, and Motion

Ullman (1983) outlined three geometric approaches for the recovery of structure from "unrestricted" motion, which assumes nothing but rigidity (see also Webb & Aggarwal 1981). Rephrased slightly, they are: 1. discrete points and views, 2. discrete points and displacements, and 3. displacement fields. The first two, and often the third, are related to the statistics of dotted forms discussed earlier, but here motion and geometry are paramount.

DISCRETE POINTS AND VIEWS   The first approach considers planar projections of a rigid 3-D array of points at particular times. The projection locations are then used to derive 3-D structure. Following Ternus (1926), Ullman (1979) explored the correspondences among projections of points across different stimulus frames. More recently, Ullman (1984a) and Williams & Sekuler (1984) explored spatial and statistical constraints, respectively. Various stroboscopic effects have also been explored. Petersik (1979) placed dots within a sphere and Lappin et al (1980), Lappin & Kottas (1981), and Doner et al (1984) placed them on its surface in the study of object coherence. Results show a remarkable ability of the human visual system to solve correspondences, considerable susceptibility to noise interference, and increased resistence to disruption with increased numbers of frames presented. Continuing studies of apparent motion also fit into this scheme (e.g. Ramachandran 1985; see also Allik & Dzhafarov 1984, Bregman & Mills 1982, Sperling et al 1985b).

A PROBLEM WITH POINTS AND VIEWS   The drawback of points-and-views analysis is that it sets up a correspondence problem—negotiating which points map onto themselves across frames—that occurs only in phenomena of apparent motion, not in real motion. Todd (1984a, 1985), for example, has argued against points analysis in vision and has shown that correspondence is not necessary for the perception of a moving object.

DISCRETE POINTS AND DISPLACEMENTS   The second approach to motion uses point locations and vectors (lines of particular length, direction, and sometimes curl) to represent relative velocities through 3-D space. This approach started with Johansson (1950) and Wallach & O'Connell (1953), but Green (1961) and Braunstein (1962) paved the way with studies of computer-generated motion. Johansson et al (1980) reviewed much of this work from the 1970s. More recently, Gogel (1978) and Goldberg & Pomerantz (1982) looked at proximity interactions among points of light; Rogers & Graham (1979) and Carpenter & Dugan (1983) studied motion parallax; Mori (1984) explored velocity effects in vector analysis; Shum & Wolford (1983), Wallach et al (1985), and Wallach & O'Leary (1985) decomposed vectors in various ways that Johansson (1985) claimed were consistent with his theory; Poizner (1983) has used the technique to explore information in ASL; Proffitt et al (1983) extended the vector analyses of points to those of shaded areas; and in a related development, Kaiser et al (1985) showed that the intuitive-physics results of McCloskey (1983) are due, in part, to differences between static line drawings and actual presentations of moving objects.

  Within this framework an orthogonal issue has developed. Is information about motion merely kinematic or is it dynamic—i.e. are forces perceived and used? Several different lines of research suggest that forces are derivable from kinematic displays. Todd & Warren (1982) and Kaiser & Proffitt (1984) have shown that the ballistic motions of objects can be correctly determined; Runeson & Frykholm (1983) have shown that point-light displays of human actions reveal information about objects, otherwise unseen, that they interact with; and Freyd (1983), Freyd & Finke (1984), and Finke et al (1986) have shown dynamic effects for static and stroboscopically presented forms.

In the study of machine vision, vector analysis is used to recover object shape. Ballard & Kimball (1983) explored the perception of objects in motion, and Horn & Schunck (1981), Prazdny (1981, 1983a,b), Rieger & Lawton (1985), and Rieger & Toet (1985) have used such analysis in the study of optic flow for a moving observer, a topic I treat below.

PROBLEMS WITH POINTS AND DISPLACEMENTS   This approach continues to have the problem of points, which Hildreth (1984, 1985), for one, circumvented by dealing with the motion of boundary edges and sorting out the possible vector fields generated. There is, however, a more pressing problem with the study of unrestricted object motion. Embedded in Gibson's (1979) invariance, in Johansson's (1978) decoding principles, and in most machine-vision research (but see Bennett & Hoffman 1985) is a rigidity assumption. Only in the domain of growth (Todd et al 1980, Pittenger & Todd 1983) has rigidity been relaxed. But viewers do not always see rigid objects even when such objects are possible interpretations of the stimuli (Braunstein & Andersen 1984a, Hochberg 1986, Schwartz & Sperling 1983, Todd 1984b). Ullman (1984b) suggested that before rejecting the rigidity principle one should be sure 1. that no 3-D structure is perceived in a static display and 2. that motion is not misperceived. But this replaces a reasonable assumption about rigidity with a less reasonable one about veridical measurement and interpretation of motion. Research is needed on the boundary conditions of perceived nonrigidity over rigidity.

DISPLACEMENT FIELDS AND WAYFINDING   A third approach to motion perception involves analysis of fields of vectors. Braunstein & Andersen (1981, 1984b) and Graham & Rogers (1982) explored depth effects through motion parallax in displacement fields, and Nakayama et al (1985) and Ball & Sekuler (1982) explored motion discrimination effects that occur in viewing fields of moving dots. But most researchers have used this approach in attempts to characterize the information available about one's direction of movement during locomotion, a task I call wayfinding. Gibson (1950) and Calvert (1950) characterized the resultant motion of objects, often called optic flow in this context, as a set of vectors (flow lines of position, direction, and length) that point away from a focus of expansion. The location of this focus, they argued, provided the information for wayfinding.

Although the subsidiary effects of divergent motion on wayfinding are of much interest (Andersen & Braunstein 1985, Clocksin 1980, Harrington & Harrington 1981, Keller & Henn 1984, McLeod & Ross 1983, Mori 1985, Owen et al 1981, Probst et al 1984, Riemersma 1981, Stoffregen 1985), empirical support for the focus of expansion was never strong (Llewellyn

1971, Johnston et al 1973). Regan & Beverley (1982) pointed out a reason: In certain environments there is always a focus of expansion where one looks, regardless of where one is going. This focus is due to vector cancellations resulting from eye rotations (Longuet-Higgins & Prazdny 1980, Koenderink & van Doorn 1981). Although Regan & Beverley's analysis has problems (Priest & Cutting 1985), it is unlikely that the focus of expansion can be salvaged. Instead, Cutting (1986) proposed that certain properties of motion parallax and of serial fixations in optokinetic nystagmus can be used for wayfinding accuracy within one degree of visual angle, approximately that needed for running through a cluttered environment.

A PROBLEM FOR FIELDS   It seems likely that the human visual system does analyze displacement fields, employing massively parallel neural systems (Ballard et al 1983). But research that only considers unnatural displacements across a projection surface, probing what the visual system sees (Regan & Beverley 1982, Nakayama et al 1985), deals only with unrepresentative manipulations of a perceptual system and may not apply to real perceptual problems.

Information for Perception and Action

Perception subserves activity. It is a major disappointment of modern psychology that studies of perception and action are rarely linked. The field analyses discussed above are a promise of linkage.

Visual perception tells us where we are within our surrounds, information we can use in changing our location and to get needed feedback. Among the few studies relevant to this area, Thomson (1983) and Elliott (1986) found conflicting results on the necessity of monitoring visual information during locomotion. D. Lee et al (1982, 1983) measured the use of visual information during long jumps and when hitting an accelerating ball, Lee & Reddish (1981) looked at visual information for plummeting gannets, and Warren et al (1986) found that, when moving over irregular ground, an observer adjusted the vertical component of gait, leaving velocity unchanged. The latter result means that information about time to contact (Lee 1980) with objects along the path is generally unchanged by terrain. Recent explorations of sensory-motor adaptations are also relevant to perception and action (Lackner 1985, Shebilske 1981, Shebilske et al 1983).

Information, Topology, and the "Geometry of the Visibles"

Two sidelights on geometry and perception should be considered. One concerns topology, the only kind of geometric information not ultimately couched as visual angles. Koenderink (1984a), Lappin (1984), and particularly Chen (1982, 1985) proposed that the visual system is quite sensitive to the topology of form, segregating those objects with bounded external contour from those that have holes. But Rubin & Kanwisher (1985) suggest that much of Chen's effect may be due to luminance differences in stimuli.

The second sidelight concerns non-Euclidean geometry. Measurement of visual angles in Euclidean systems depends on straight rays of light, or projectors. But following from Reid's (1764) "geometry of the visibles," Helmholtz's (1866) discussion of curved visual space, and Luneburg's (1947) analyses of binocularity, a series of inquiries into Riemannian curvature has ensued, some philosophical (Daniels 1974, Hopkins 1973, Suppes 1977). Psychological efforts have focused on binocularity (Blank 1978) and the alley problem (Indow 1982, Indow & Watanabe 1984), or on illusions (Watson 1978). The major issue was raised by Grünbaum (1973): How do these non-Euclidean models of perceptual data map back onto the Euclidean experience we have of our normal surrounds? A possible resolution lies in whether curvatures measured are within the tolerances of our visual system.

INFORMATION AND ICONIC MEMORY

A series of topics do not handily fit into the structure of my overview but are important to any discussion of information and perception. Iconic memory research is one, and it is in a state of transition. Thorough reviews of an immense literature (Coltheart 1980, Long 1980) have given way less to increased knowledge about the role of persistence in vision than to the mantra of ecological validity (Haber 1983). Rather than synthesizing anything new, let me point out several trends pertinent to my topic.

In a series of studies Loftus (1985; Loftus et al 1983, 1985; Sperling 1986) has shown that holistic information is retained better upon a single glance at a photograph, that featural information is retained better upon multiple glances, that visual persistence is worth about 110 ms of extra stimulus presentation, and that luminance reduces both information available and information extraction rate. Long & Wurst (1984) have shown that complexity in perimeters and areas of figures affects the duration of visible persistence, but in reversed fashion depending on whether the form is filled or not. Di Lollo (1984) and Di Lollo & Hogben (1985) have studied the duration and suppression of persistence, which others have studied in both stroboscopic (Burr 1981, Farrell 1984, Pomerantz 1983b) and apparent (Hogben & Di Lollo 1985) motion. In this connection, the role of abrupt onsets continues to receive attention (Kowler & Sperling 1983, Yantis & Jonides 1984), as do partial report procedures (Bundeson et al 1984, Yeomans & Irwin 1985). In addition, Weichselgartner & Sperling (1985) developed a continuous measure of visual persistence.

INFORMATION IN NONVISUAL MODALITIES

Vision may be the least representative of our senses. Thus, a review of information and perception would ideally devote much effort and space to other modalities. Unfortunately, comparatively few studies on these other modalities are available.

Outside of work in auditory psychophysics, and an occasional foray into ecological acoustics (Jenkins 1984, Warren & Verbrugge 1984), work in audition is focused on speech and music. In speech research a 30-year debate continues on whether information for speech is in the acoustic signal (Blumstein & Stevens 1980) or in the match of gestures to that signal (Liberman & Mattingly 1985). Longstanding interest continues in categorical perception (Massaro & Cohen 1983a, Repp 1984) and it does in selective adaptation (Samuel 1986). In music research, a livelier and more tractable endeavor, investigators study information with respect to tonality (Krumhansl 1985), sequence and contour (Wright & Bregman 1986, Boltz & Jones 1986, Deutsch & Feroe 1981, Dowling 1978, Massaro et al 1980), and rhythm (Handel & Todd 1981, Povel 1981).

For touch and haptic perception Klatsky et al (1985) found, in keeping with Gibson (1966), that exploration and object recognition can be both rapid and accurate. Anstis & Tassinary (1983), Oldfield & Phillips (1983), and Benedetti (1985) explored tactile illusions. In olfaction and taste, soluble chemical compounds inform the perceiver, but we know remarkably little about how these modalities work (Carterette & Friedman 1978, Engen 1982). Natural conditions of tasting (licks, sips, and gulps) and smelling (sniffs) yield optimal conditions (Halpern 1983, Laing 1983); taste is not as sluggish as once thought (Kelling & Halpern 1983); entropy can be measured during adaptation (Norwich 1984); and there is a tight relation between chemosensation and cognition (Rabin & Cain 1984).

INFORMATION USE

Individual sources of information—whether experiential, statistical, or geometric—rarely stand by themselves. Unless all the information needed for a percept is contained in one prepackaged source (unlikely in everyday situations), perceptual information must exist in several forms. The perceiver must choose among or combine these forms.

Equivalence, Cognitive Penetrability, and Choice

Equivalent information has most often been discussed in the contexts of speech perception (Liberman 1982, Repp 1982) and visual perception of objects in depth (Gogel 1984). In both, one "cue"—or physical source of information—can trade off against another, and perception remain unperturbed. In speech and vision, trading relations might be taken as evidence for modularity of perceptual system.

Modular systems (Fodor 1983) are thought to be "cognitively impenetrable" (Pylyshyn 1984), data driven from the bottom up. The perception of different stem lengths in the Müller-Lyer figure, for example, is not altered by knowing that they are identical. Information specifying the percept is thought to be "encapsulated," and that knowledge cannot descend into the guts of the perceptual process. Although the broad strokes of this example are compelling, careful analysis (Peterson & Hochberg 1983, Peterson 1986) of ambiguous line drawings and stereographic displays can show the role of intention on what otherwise might seem to be low-level visual processes. Moreover, some percept-percept couplings (Hochberg 1974, Epstein 1982) demonstrate that higher-level assumptions and interactions may invade a module to determine perceptual outcomes.

But perhaps none of the assumptions made for perception need be cognitively based. Johansson (1970) felt that they were hard-wired. Gibson (1970) objected to Johansson's decoding principles because they seemed to imply insufficient information in the stimulus. But Cutting (1986) has suggested the opposite: When more than one information source is available, a perceptual system must choose between (or combine) them. In two viewing situations, entailing judgments of planar rigidity and of wayfinding as discussed above, different invariants equally specified a perceptual outcome, but the visual system most often chose only one.

Additivity, Integration, and Multimodal Perception

When information is combined, additive models often fit best (Cutting & Millard 1984, Dosher et al 1986). Such additivity, however, is confined only to certain stimulus dimensions. Garner (1974; Lasaga & Garner 1983), Pomerantz (1981, 1983a), and Kemler Nelson (Foard & Kemler Nelson 1984, L. Smith & Kemler 1978, J. Smith & Kemler Nelson 1984) have explored the nature of stimulus dimensions and their interaction in various tasks. Some dimensions are often separable and allow for additivity, others are integral and do not. Garner (1986) now regards integrality as a mandatory, and separability as an optional, secondary process: children often start out classifying stimuli in integral terms and later, as a result of developmental changes, move to strategies of separability. But whereas it is relatively easy to see how integrality might work within a sensory modality, it is more difficult to anticipate such effects across them (but see Algon et al 1986). And more generally,

Ashby & Townsend (1986) provide an overview of the kinds of perceptual independence that provide a backdrop for discussions of stimulus additivity.

Hornbostel (1927, p. 210) suggested that "It matters little through which sense I realize that in the dark I have blundered into a pigsty." This may be true for a folk phenomenologist; but to a psychologist it should matter quite a lot how such a conclusion might be reached, particularly since a single modality is not likely to provide all the information needed for pigsty perception. Marks (1978) gave us a thorough history of views on the unity of the senses, and research has been done on how information from the different senses might fashion unified percepts.

Two modalities are usually considered at a time, and one is almost always vision. The interrelation of vision and kinesthesis has been investigated by Lackner & Taublieb (1984) and Lackner & Shenker (1985); B. Jones & O'Neil (1985) explored bimodal and unimodal responses to texture, finding that visual and haptic information seemed to be additive. The interrelation of vision and audition in speech perception has received much attention since the discovery by McGurk & MacDonald (1976) that simultaneous presentation of an auditory /ba/ and a visual image of the lips forming /ga/ yields a compelling percept of /da/. Summerfield (1979) and Massaro & Cohen (1983b) replicated and extended the result, Dodd (1979) and Kuhl & Meltzoff (1984) explored it with infants, and Green & Miller (1985) looked at the influence of visual rate on the combined percept. The perception by infants of more general visual-auditory combinations has been explored by Spelke (1976; Spelke et al 1983), and discussed by E. Gibson (1984).

Informative Displays

Finally, information in stimuli is important not only in terms of the perceiver but also in practical situations for the researcher. Given the increase in use of computer displays, it is good to see that some attention has been given to how they are perceived (Haber & Wilkinson 1982). Tufte (1983) provides new insights into how we might most effectively present scientific information in graphs and charts.

ACKNOWLEDGMENTS

Preparation of this review was supported by the National Institutes of Mental Health grant MH37467. It is dedicated to the memory of Paul Kolers. I thank Nicola Bruno, Jennifer Freyd, Eleanor Gibson, Bruce Halpern, and Joseph Lappin for discussion and comments.

Literature Cited

Algon, D., Raphaeli, N., Cohen-Raz, L. 1986. Integration of noxious stimuli across somatosensory communication systems: A functional theory of pain. *J. Exper. Psychol.: Hum. Percept. Perform.* 12:92–103

Allik, J., Dzhafarov, E. N. 1984. Motion direction identification in random cinematograms: A general model. *J. Exp. Psychol: Hum. Percept. Perform.* 10:378–93

Andersen, G. J., Braunstein, M. 1985. Induced self-motion in central vision. *J. Exp. Psychol: Hum. Percept. Perform.* 11:122–32

Anderson, J. A. 1983. Cognitive and psychological computation with neural models. *IEEE Trans. Syst. Man Cybern.* SMC-13:799–815

Anstis, S. M., Tassinary, L. 1983. Pouting and smiling distort the tactile perception of facial stimuli. *Percept. Psychophys.* 33:295–97

Ashby, F. G., Townsend, J. T. 1986. Varieties of perceptual independence. *Psychol. Rev.* 93:154–79

Attneave, F. 1954. Some information aspects of visual perception. *Psychol. Rev.* 61:183–93

Attneave, F. 1982. Prägnanz and soap bubble systems: A theoretical exploration. See Beck 1982a, pp. 11–29

Ball, K., Sekuler, R. 1982. A specific and enduring improvement in visual motion discrimination. *Science* 218:697–98

Ballard, D. H., Brown, C. M. 1982. *Computer Vision.* Englewood Cliffs, NJ: Prentice-Hall. 523 pp.

Ballard, D. H., Hinton, G. E., Sejnowski, T. J. 1983. Parallel visual computation. *Nature* 306:21–26

Ballard, D. H., Kimball, O. A. 1983. Rigid body motion from depth and optical flow. *Comput. Vision Graph. Image Proc.* 22:95–115

Balzano, G. J. 1980. The group-theoretic description of 12-fold and microtonal pitch systems. *Comput. Music J.* 4:66–84

Banks, M., Stephens, B., Hartmann, E. 1985. The development of basic mechanisms of pattern vision: Spatial frequency channels. *J. Exp. Child Psychol.* 40:501–27

Barnard, S. T. 1985. Choosing a basis for perceptual space. *Comput. Vision Graph. Image Proc.* 29:87–99

Beck, J., ed. 1982a. *Organization and Representation in Perception.* NY: Erlbaum. 387 pp.

Beck, J. 1982b. Textural segmentation. See Beck 1982a, pp. 285–317

Beck, J. 1983. Textural segmentation, second-order statistics, and textural elements. *Biol. Cybern.* 48:125–30

Beck, J., Hope, B., Rosenfeld, A., ed. 1983a. *Human and Machine Vision.* NY: Academic. 567 pp.

Beck, J., Prazdny, K., Rosenfeld, A. 1983b. A theory of textural segmentation. See Beck et al 1983a, pp. 1–38

Benedetti, F. 1985. Processing of tactile spatial information with crossed fingers. *J. Exp. Psychol: Hum. Percept. Perform.* 11:517–25

Bennett, B., Hoffman, D. 1985. The computation of structure from field-axis motion: Nonrigid structure. *Biol. Cybern.* 51:293–300

Bergström, S. S., Gustafsson, K.-A., Putaansuu, J. 1984. Information about three-dimensional shape and direction of illumination in a sine wave grating. *Perception* 13:129–40

Berkeley, G. 1709. An essay towards a new theory of vision. See Fraser 1871, pp. 25–112

Berkeley, G. 1733. The theory of vision, or visual language, vindicated and explained. See Fraser 1871, pp. 369–400

Besl, P. J., Jain, R. C. 1986. Invariant surface characteristics for 3D object recognition in range images. *Comput. Vision Graph. Image Proc.* 33:1–48

Bickhard, M. H., Richie, D. M. 1983. *On the Nature of Representation.* NY: Praeger. 107 pp.

Biederman, I. 1985. Human image understanding: Recent research and a theory. *Comput. Vision Graph. Image Proc.* 32:29–73

Binford, T. O. 1981. Inferring surfaces from images. *Artif. Intell.* 17:205–44

Blank, A. A. 1978. Metric geometry in human binocular perception: theory and fact. See Leeuwenberg & Buffart 1978, pp. 82–102

Blumstein, S., Stevens, K. N. 1980. Perceptual invariance and onset spectra for stop consonants in different vowel environments. *J. Acoust. Soc. Am.* 67:648–62

Boltz, M., Jones, M. R. 1986. Does rule recursion make melodies easier to reproduce? If not, what does? *Cogn. Psychol.* 18: In press

Brady, M., ed. 1981. *Computer Vision.* Amsterdam: North-Holland. 508 pp.

Brady, M., Ponce, J., Yuille, A., Asada, H. 1985. Describing surfaces. *Comput. Vision Graph. Image Proc.* 32:1–28

Braunstein, M. 1962. Depth perception in rotating dot patterns: Effects of numerosity and perspective. *J. Exp. Psychol.* 64:415–520

Braunstein, M., Andersen, G. 1981. Perceived relative depth from velocity gradients: A model. *Acta Psychol.* 48:195–201

Braunstein, M., Andersen, G. 1984a. A counterexample to the rigidity assumption in the visual perception of structure from motion. *Perception* 13:213–17

Braunstein, M., Andersen, G. 1984b. Shape and depth perception from parallel projections of three-dimensional motion. *J. Exp. Psychol: Hum. Percept. Perform.* 10:749–60

Bregman, A. S., Mills, M. 1982. Perceived movement: The Flintstone constraint. *Perception* 11:201–6

Brodatz, P. 1966. *Textures.* NY: Dover. 112 pp., 112 plates

Bruce, V., Green, P. 1985. *Visual Perception: Physiology, Psychology, and Ecology.* London: Erlbaum. 369 pp.

Brunswik, E. 1956. *Perception and the Representative Design of Psychological Experiments.* Berkeley: Univ. Calif. 154 pp.

Buffart, H., Leeuwenberg, E., Restle, F. 1981. Coding theory of visual pattern completion. *J. Exp. Psychol: Hum. Percept. Perform.* 7:241–74

Buffart, H., Leeuwenberg, E., Restle, F. 1983. Analysis of ambiguity in visual pattern completion. *J. Exp. Psychol: Hum. Percept. Perform.* 9:980–1000

Bundeson, C., Pedersen, L. F., Larsen, A. 1984. Measuring efficiency of selection from briefly exposed visual displays: A model for partial report. *J. Exp. Psychol: Hum. Percept. Perform.* 10:329–39

Burr, D. C. 1981. Temporal summation of moving images by the human visual system. *Proc. R. Soc. London Ser. B* 211:321–30

Burt, P. J., Adelson, E. H. 1983a. The Laplacian pyramid as a compact image code. *IEEE Trans. Commun.* 31:532–39

Burt, P. J., Adelson, E. H. 1983b. A multiresolution spline with application to image mosaics. *ACM Trans. Graph.* 2:217–36

Burton, H. E. 1945. The optics of Euclid. *J. Opt. Soc. Am.* 35:357–72

Butler, D. L. 1982. Predicting the perception of three-dimensional objects from the geometrical information in drawings. *J. Exp. Psychol: Hum. Percept. Perform.* 8: 674–92

Caelli, T. 1981. *Visual Perception: Theory and Practice.* Oxford: Pergamon. 197 pp.

Caelli, T. 1985. Three processing characterists of visual texture segmentation. *Spat. Vision* 1:19–30

Calvert, E. S. 1950. Visual aids for landing in bad visibility with particular reference to the transition from instrument to visual flight. *Trans. Illum. Eng. Soc. London* 15:183–219

Carlbom, I., Paciorek, J. 1978. Planar geometric projections and viewing transformations. *Comp. Surv.* 10:465–502

Carpenter, D. L., Dugan, M. P. 1983. Motion parallax information for direction of rotation in depth: Order and direction components. *Perception* 12:559–69

Carterette, E., Friedman, M., eds. 1978. *Handbook of Perception: Vol. VIA, Tasting and Smelling.* NY: Academic. 321 pp.

Cassirer, E. 1944. The concept of group and the theory of perception. *Philos. Phenom. Res.* 5:1–35

Chen, L. 1982. Topological structure in visual perception. *Science* 218:699–700

Chen, L. 1985. Topological structure in the perception of apparent motion. *Perception* 14:181–92

Clocksin, W. F. 1980. Perception of surface slant and edge labels from optic flow: a computational approach. *Perception* 9:253–70

Cohen, M. A., Grossberg, S. 1984. Neural dynamics of brightness perception: Features, boundaries, diffusions, and resonance. *Percept. Psychophys.* 36:428–56

Coltheart, M. 1980. Iconic memory and visible persistence. *Percept. Psychophys.* 27:183–228

Cooper, L. A., Shepard, R. N. 1984. Turning something over in the mind. *Sci. Am.* 251(6):106–14

Cutting, J. E. 1981. Coding theory adapted to gait perception. *J. Exp. Psychol: Hum. Percept. Perform.* 7:71–87

Cutting, J. E. 1982a. Blowing in the wind: Perceiving structure in trees and bushes. *Cognition* 12:25–44

Cutting, J. E. 1982b. Two ecological perspectives: Gibson vs. Shaw and Turvey. *Am. J. Psychol.* 95:199–222

Cutting, J. E. 1986. *Perception with an Eye for Motion.* Cambridge, Mass: MIT Press. 321 pp.

Cutting, J. E., Millard, R. T. 1984. Three gradients and the perception of flat and curved surfaces. *J. Exp. Psychol: Gen.* 113:198–216

Cutting, J. E., Proffitt, D. R. 1982. The minimum principle and the perception of absolute, common, and relative motions. *Cogn. Psychol.* 14:211–46

Daniels, N. 1974. *Thomas Reid's Inquiry.* NY: Burt Franklin

Descartes, R. 1649. The passions of the soul. In *The Philosophical Works of Descartes,* transl. E. Haldane, 1955, pp. 329–427. NY: Dover

Deutsch, D., Feroe, J. 1981. The internal representation of pitch sequences in tonal music. *Psychol. Rev.* 88:503–22

Diaconis, P., Freedman, D. 1981. On the statistics of vision: the Julesz conjecture. *J. Math. Psychol.* 24:112–38

Di Lollo, V. 1984. On the relationship between stimulus intensity and duration of visible persistence. *J. Exp. Psychol: Hum. Percept. Perform.* 10:144–51

Di Lollo, V., Hogben, J. H. 1985. Suppression of visible persistence. *J. Exp. Psychol: Hum. Percept. Perform.* 11:304–17

Dodd, B. 1979. Lip-reading in infants: Attention to speech presented in- and out-of-synchrony. *Cogn. Psychol.* 11:478–84

Dodwell, P. C. 1983. The Lie transformation group model of visual perception. *Percept. Psychophys.* 23:1–16

Dodwell, P. C. 1984. Local and global factors in figural synthesis. See Dodwell & Caelli 1984, pp. 219–48

Dodwell, P. C., Caelli, T., eds. 1984. *Figural Synthesis.* Hillsdale, NJ: Erlbaum. 310 pp.

Doner, J. F., Lappin, J. S., Perfetto, G. 1984. Detection of three-dimensional structure in moving optical patterns. *J. Exp. Psychol: Hum. Percept. Perform.* 10:1–11

Dosher, B. A., Sperling, G., Wurst, S. A. 1986. Tradeoffs between stereopsis and proximity luminance covariance as determinants of perceived 3D structure. *Vision Res.* 38: In press

Dowling, W. J. 1978. Scale and contour: Two components of a theory of memory for melodies. *Psychol. Rev.* 85:341–54

Dretske, F. I. 1981. *Knowledge and the Flow of Information.* Cambridge, Mass: MIT Press. 273 pp.

Eddington, A. 1939. *The Philosophy of Physical Science.* Cambridge: Cambridge Univ. Press. 230 pp.

Elliott, D. 1986. Continuous visual information may be important after all: A failure to replicate Thomson (1983). *J. Exp. Psychol: Hum. Percept. Perform.* 12: In press

Ellis, W. D., ed. 1938. *Sourcebook of Gestalt Psychology.* London: Kegan Paul, Trench, Trubner. 403 pp.

Engen, T. 1982. *The Perception of Odors.* NY: Academic. 201 pp.

Epstein, W. 1982. Percept-percept couplings. *Perception* 11:75–85

Epstein, W., Lovitts, B. E. 1985. Automatic and attentional components in perception of shape-at-a-slant. *J. Exp. Psychol: Hum. Percept. Perform.* 11:355–66

Estes, W. K. 1976. The cognitive side of probability learning. *Psychol. Rev.* 83:37–64

Farrell, J. E. 1984. Visible persistence of moving objects. *J. Exp. Psychol: Hum. Percept. Perform.* 10:502–11

Finke, R. A., Freyd, J. J., Shyi, G. C.-W. 1986. Implied velocity and acceleration induce transformations of visual memory. *J. Exp. Psychol.: Gen.* 115:175–88

Flock, H., Nusinowitz, S. 1984. Visual structures for achromatic color perception. *Percept. Psychophys.* 36:111–30

Foard, C. F., Kemler Nelson, D. 1984. Holistic and analytic modes of processing: The multiple determinants of perceptual analysis. *J. Exp. Psychol: Gen.* 113:94–111

Fodor, J. A. 1983. *The Modularity of Mind.* Cambridge, Mass: MIT Press. 145 pp.

Fodor, J. A., Pylyshyn, Z. 1981. How direct is perception? Some reflections on Gibson's "ecological approach." *Cognition* 9:139–96

Foster, D. H. 1975. Visual apparent motion and some preferred paths in the rotation group *SO*(3). *Biol. Cybern.* 18:81–89

Foster, D. H. 1984. Local and global computational factors in visual pattern recognition. See Dodwell & Caelli 1984, pp. 83–115

Fraser, W., ed. 1871. *The Works of George Berkeley.* Oxford: Clarendon

Freyd, J. J. 1983. The mental representation of movement when viewing static stimuli. *Percept. Psychophys.* 33:575–81

Freyd, J. J., Finke, R. A. 1984. Representational momentum. *J. Exp. Psychol: Hum. Percept. Perform.* 10:126–32

Garner, W. R. 1962. *Uncertainty and Structure as Psychological Concepts.* NY: Wiley. 369 pp.

Garner, W. R. 1970. Good patterns have few alternatives. *Am. Sci.* 58:34–42

Garner, W. R. 1974. *The Processing of Information and Structure.* Hillsdale, NJ: Erlbaum. 202 pp.

Garner, W. R. 1985. Interaction of stimulus and organism in perception. In *One Hundred Years of Psychology in America*, ed. S. Hulse, B. Green. Baltimore, Md: Johns Hopkins Univ. Press. In press

Gibson, E. J. 1984. Development of knowledge about intermodal unity: Two views. In *Piaget and the Foundations of Knowledge*, ed. S. Liben, pp. 19–41. Hillsdale, NJ: Erlbaum

Gibson, J. J. 1950. *The Perception of the Visual World.* Boston: Houghton Mifflin. 235 pp.

Gibson, J. J. 1966. *The Senses Considered as Perceptual Systems.* Boston: Houghton Mifflin. 335 pp.

Gibson, J. J. 1970. On theories for visual space perception: A reply to Johansson. *Scand. J. Psychol.* 11:75–79

Gibson, J. J. 1979. *The Ecological Approach to Visual Perception.* Boston: Houghton Mifflin. 332 pp.

Gilchrist, A., Jacobsen, A. 1984. Perception of lightness and illumination in a world of one reflectance. *Perception* 13:5–19

Glass, L. 1969. Moire effect from random dots. *Nature* 223:578–80

Gogel, W. C. 1978. The adjacency principle in visual perception. *Sci. Am.* 238(5):126–39

Gogel, W. C. 1984. The role of perceptual interrelations in figural synthesis. See Dodwell & Caelli 1984, pp. 31–80

Goldberg, D. M., Pomerantz, J. R. 1982. Models of illusory pausing and sticking. *J. Exp. Psychol: Hum. Percept. Perform.* 8:547–61

Goodman, N. 1972. *Problems and Projects,* pp. 275–355. Indianapolis, Ind: Bobbs-Merrill

Gordon, B., Caramazza, A. 1985. Lexical access and frequency sensitivity: Frequency saturation and open/closed class equivalence. *Cognition* 21:95–115

Graham, M., Rogers, B. 1982. Simultaneous and successive contrast effects in the perception of depth from motion-parallax and stereoscopic information. *Perception* 11:247–62

Graham, N. 1985. Detection and identification of near-threshold visual patterns. *J. Opt. Soc. Am. A* 2:1468–81

Granrud, C. E., Yonas, A., Opland, E. A. 1985. Infants' sensitivity to the depth cue of shading. *Percept. Psychophys.* 37:415–19

Green, B. F. 1961. Figure coherence in the kinetic depth effect. *J. Exp. Psychol.* 62:272–82

Green, K. P., Miller, J. L. 1985. On the role of visual rate information in phonetic perception. *Percept. Psychophys.* 38:269–76

Gregory, R. H. 1974. *Concepts and Mechanisms in Perception.* NY: Scribners. 669 pp.

Grimson, W. E. 1981. *From Images to Surfaces.* Cambridge, Mass: MIT Press. 274 pp.

Grimson, W. E. 1983. Surface consistency constraints in vision. *Comput. Vision Graph. Image Proc.* 24:28–51

Grossberg, S., Mingolla, E. 1985a. Neural dynamics of form perception: Boundary completion, illusory figures, and neon color spreading. *Psychol. Rev.* 92:173–211

Grossberg, S., Mingolla, E. 1985b. Neural dynamics of form perception: Textures, boundaries, and emergent segmentations. *Percept. Psychophys.* 38:141–71

Grünbaum, A. 1973. *Philosophical Problems of Space and Time.* Boston: Reidel. 884 pp. 2nd ed.

Guzman, A. 1969. Decomposition of a visual scene into three-dimensional bodies. In *Automatic Interpretation and Classification of Images,* ed. A. Grasselli, pp. 243–76. NY: Academic

Haber, R. N. 1983. The impending demise of the icon: A critique of the concept of iconic storage. *Behav. Brain Sci.* 6:1–54; 8:188–92

Haber, R. N., Wilkinson, L. 1982. The perceptual components of computer graphics displays. *IEEE Comp. Graph. Appl.* 2:23–35

Halpern, B. P. 1983. Tasting and smelling as active, exploratory sensory processes. *Am. J. Otolaryngol.* 4:246–49

Hamilton, W. 1859. *Lectures on Metaphysics,* Vol. II. Edinburgh: Blackwood & Sons. 568 pp.

Hamilton, W., ed. 1895. *The Works of Thomas Reid.* Vol. 1. Edinburgh: James Thin. 508 pp. 8th ed.

Handel, S., Todd, P. 1981. Segmentation of sequential patterns. *J. Exp. Psychol: Hum. Percept. Perform.* 7:41–55

Harmon, L. D. 1973. The recognition of faces. *Sci. Am.* 232(2):70–82

Harrington, T. L., Harrington, M. K. 1981. Perception of motion using blur pattern information in the moderate and high-velocity domains of vision. *Acta Psychol.* 48:227–37

Hasher, L., Zacks, R. T. 1979. Automatic and effortful processes in memory. *J. Exp. Psychol: Gen.* 108:356–88

Hatfield, G., Epstein, W. 1985. The status of the minimum principle in the theoretical analysis of visual perception. *Psychol. Bull.* 97:155–86

Heil, J. 1983. *Perception and Cognition.* Berkeley: Univ. Calif. Press. 243 pp.

Helmholtz, H. von. 1866. *Physiological Optics,* Vol. 3. 3rd ed., transl. J. Southall, 1925. Menasha, Wis: Optical Soc. Am. 736 pp.

Helmholtz, H. von. 1878. The facts of perception. See Kahl 1971, pp. 366–407

Helmholtz, H. von. 1894. The origin and correct interpretation of our sense impressions. See Kahl 1971, pp. 501–12

Hemenway, K., Palmer, S. E. 1978. Organizational factors in perceived dimensionality. *J. Exp. Psychol: Hum. Percept. Perform.* 3:388–96

Hildreth, E. C. 1984. *The Measurement of Visual Motion.* Cambridge, Mass: MIT Press. 241 pp.

Hildreth, E. C. 1985. Computation underlying the measurement of visual motion. *Artif. Intell.* 23:309–34

Hochberg, J. 1974. Higher-order stimuli and inter-response coupling in the perception of the visual world. In *Perception: Essays in Honor of J. J. Gibson,* ed. R. MacLoed, H. Pick, pp. 17–39. Ithaca, NY: Cornell Univ. Press

Hochberg, J. 1981. Levels of perceptual organization. See Kubovy & Pomerantz 1981, pp. 255–78

Hochberg, J. 1982. How big is a stimulus? See Beck 1982a, pp. 191–217

Hochberg, J. 1984. Form perception: experience and explanations. See Dodwell & Caelli 1984, pp. 1–30

Hochberg, J. 1986. Visual perception of real and represented objects and events. In *Behavioral and Social Sciences: Fifty Years of*

Discovery, ed. N. Smelser, D. Gerstein. Washington, DC: Natl. Acad. Press. In press

Hochberg, J., McAlister, E. 1953. A quantitative approach to figural "goodness." *J. Exp. Psychol.* 46:361–64

Hoffman, D. D., Richards, W. A. 1984. Parts of recognition. *Cognition* 18:65–96

Hoffman, W. C. 1966. The Lie algebra of visual perception. *J. Math. Psychol.* 3:65–98; errata, 4:348–49

Hoffman, W. C. 1984. Figural synthesis by vectorfields: Geometric neurophysiology. See Dodwell & Caelli, 1984, pp. 249–82

Hogben, J. H., Di Lollo, V. 1985. Suppression of visible persistence in apparent motion. *Percept. Psychophys.* 38:450–60

Hopkins, J. 1973. Visual geometry. *Phil. Rev.* 82:3–34

Horn, B. K., Schunck, B. G. 1981. Determining optic flow. See Brady 1981, pp. 184–204

Hornbostel, E. von. 1927. The unity of the senses. See Ellis, 1938, pp. 210–16

Indow, T. 1982. An approach to geometry of visual space with no a priori mapping functions: Multidimensional mapping according to Riemannian metrics. *J. Math. Psychol.* 26:205–36

Indow, T., Watanabe, T. 1984. Parallel- and distance-alleys with moving points in the horizontal plane. *Percept. Psychophys.* 35:144–54

Jenkins, J. J. 1984. Acoustic information for objects, places, and events. See Warren & Shaw 1984b, pp. 115–38

Johansson, G. 1950. *Configurations in Event Perception*. Uppsala, Sweden: Almqvist & Wiksells. 226 pp.

Johansson, G. 1970. On theories of visual space perception: a letter to Gibson. *Scand. J. Psychol.* 11:67–74

Johansson, G. 1978. About the geometry underlying spontaneous visual decoding of the optical message. See Leeuwenberg & Buffart 1978, pp. 265–76

Johansson, G. 1985. Vector analysis and process combinations in motion perception: a reply to Wallach, Becklen, and Nitzberg (1985). *J. Exp. Psychol: Hum. Percept. Perform.* 11:367–71

Johansson, G., von Hofsten, C., Jansson, G. 1980. Event perception. *Ann. Rev. Psychol.* 31:27–66

Johnston, I. R., White, G. R., Cumming, R. W. 1973. The role of optical expansion patterns in locomotor control. *Am. J. Psychol.* 86:311–24

Jones, B., O'Neil, A. 1985. Combining vision and touch in texture perception. *Percept. Psychophys.* 37:66–72

Jones, M. R. 1981. Music as a stimulus for psychological motion: Part I. Some determinants of expectancies. *Psychomusicology* 1:34–51

Julesz, B. 1971. *Foundations of Cyclopean Perception*. Chicago: Univ. Chicago Press. 405 pp.

Julesz, B. 1975. Experiments in the visual perception of texture. *Sci. Am.* 232(4):34–43

Julesz, B. 1981. Textons, the elements of texture perception and their interactions. *Nature* 290:91–97

Julesz, B., Bergen, J. R. 1983. Textons, the fundamental elements in preattentive vision and perception of textures. *Bell Syst. Tech. J.* 62:1619–45

Kahl, R., ed. 1971. *Selected Writings of Hermann von Helmholtz*. Middletown, Conn: Wesleyan Univ. Press. 542 pp.

Kahneman, D., Slovic, P., Tversky, A. 1982. *Judgment under Uncertainty: Heuristics and Biases*. Cambridge: Cambridge Univ. Press. 555 pp.

Kaiser, M. K., Proffitt, D. R. 1984. The development of sensitivity to causally-relevant dynamic information. *Cogn. Dev.* 55:1614–24

Kaiser, M. K., Proffitt, D. R., Anderson, K. 1985. Judgments of natural and anomalous trajectories in the presence and absence of motion. *J. Exp. Psychol: Learn. Mem. Cogn.* 11:795–803

Kanade, T., Kender, J. 1983. Mapping image properties into shape constraints: Skewed symmetry, affine-transformable patterns, and the shape-from-texture paradigm. See Beck et al 1983a, pp. 237–57

Kanatani, K. 1984. Detection of surface orientation and motion from texture by a stereological technique. *Artif. Intell.* 23:213–37

Keller, G., Henn, V. 1984. Self-motion sensation influenced by visual fixation. *Percept. Psychophys.* 35:279–85

Kelling, S. T., Halpern, B. P. 1983. Taste flashes: Reactions times, intensity, and quality. *Science* 219:412–14

Klatzky, R. L., Lederman, S. J., Metzger, V. A. 1985. Identifying objects by touch: An "expert" system. *Percept. Psychophys.* 37:299–302

Koenderink, J. J. 1984a. The concept of local sign. In *Limits in Perception*, ed. A. J. van Doorn, W. van de Grind, J. J. Koenderink, pp. 495–547. Utrecht, Netherlands: VNU Sci. Press

Koenderink, J. J. 1984b. What does the occluding contour tell us about solid shape? *Perception* 13:321–30

Koenderink, J. J., van Doorn, A. J. 1981. Exterospecific component for the detection of structure and motion in three dimensions. *J. Opt. Soc. Am.* 71:953–57

Koenderink, J. J., van Doorn, A. J. 1982. The shape of smooth objects and the way contours ends. *Perception* 11:129–37

Koffka, K. 1935. *Principles of Gestalt Psychology.* NY: Harcourt. 720 pp.

Kolers, P. A. 1983. Some features of visual form. *Comput. Vision Graph. Image Proc.* 23:15–41

Kowler, E., Sperling, G. 1983. Abrupt onsets do not aid visual search. *Percept. Psychophys.* 34:307–13

Krumhansl, C. L. 1978. Concerning the applicability of geometric models to similarity data: The interrelationship between similarity and spatial density. *Psychol. Rev.* 85:445–63

Krumhansl, C. L. 1982. Density feature weights as predictors of visual identifications: Comment on Appleman and Mayzner. *J. Exp. Psychol: Gen.* 111:101–8

Krumhansl, C. L. 1984. Independent processing of visual form and motion. *Perception* 13:535–46

Krumhansl, C. L. 1985. Perceiving tonal structure in music. *Am. Sci.* 73:371–78

Kubovy, M. 1981. Concurrent-pitch segregation and the theory of indispensible attributes. See Kubovy & Pomerantz 1981, pp. 55–98

Kubovy, M., Pomerantz, J. R., ed. 1981. *Perceptual Organization.* Hillsdale, NJ: Erlbaum. 506 pp.

Kuhl, P. K., Meltzoff, A. N. 1984. The intermodal representation of speech in infants. *Infant Behav. Dev.* 7:361–81

Külpe, O. 1895. *Outlines of Psychology,* transl. E. Titchener. London: Swan Sonnenschein

Lackner, J. R. 1985. Human sensory-motor adaptation to the terrestrial force environment. In *Brain Mechanisms and Spatial Vision,* ed. D. Ingle, M. Jeannerod, D. Lee, pp. 175–209. Boston: Dordrecht

Lackner, J. R., Shenker, B. 1985. Proprioceptive influences on auditory and visual spatial localization. *J. Neurosci.* 5:579–83

Lackner, J. R., Taublieb, A. 1984. Influence of vision on vibration-induced illusions of limb movement. *Exp. Neurol.* 85:97–106

Laing, D. 1983. Natural sniffing gives optimum odour perception for humans. *Perception* 12:99–117

Lappin, J. S. 1984. Reflections on Gunnar Johansson's perspective on the visual measurement of space and time. See Warren & Shaw 1984b, pp. 67–86

Lappin, J. S., Doner, J. F., Kottas, B. L. 1980. Minimal conditions for the detection of structure and motion in three dimensions. *Science* 209:717–19

Lappin, J. S., Fuqua, M. A. 1983. Accurate visual measurement of three-dimensional moving patterns. *Science* 221:480–82

Lappin, J. S., Kottas, B. L. 1981. The perceptual coherence of moving visual patterns. *Acta Psychol.* 48:163–74

Lasaga, M. I., Garner, W. R. 1983. Effect of line orientation on various information-processing tasks. *J. Exp. Psychol: Hum. Percept. Perform.* 9:215–25

Lee, C.-H., Rosenfeld, A. 1985. Improved methods of estimating shape from shading using the light source coordinate system. *Artif. Intell.* 26:125–43

Lee, D. N. 1980. The optic flow field: The foundation of vision. *Philos. Trans. R. Soc. London Ser. B.* 280:169–79

Lee, D. N., Reddish, P. E., Thomson, J. A. 1982. Regulation of gait in long jumping. *J. Exp. Psychol: Hum. Percept. Perform.* 8:448–59

Lee, D. N., Lishman, R., Thomson, J. A. 1981. Plummeting gannets: A paradigm of ecological optics. *Nature* 293:293–94

Lee, D. N., Young, D. S., Reddish, P. E., Lough, S., Clayton, T. M. 1983. Visual timing in hitting an accelerating ball. *Q. J. Exp. Psychol. A* 35:333–46

Lee, S. J., Haralick, R. M., Zhang, M. C. 1985. Understanding objects with curved surfaces from a single perspective view of boundaries. *Artif. Intell.* 26:145–69

Leeuwenberg, E. 1971. A perceptual coding language for visual and auditory patterns. *Am. J. Psychol.* 84:307–47

Leeuwenberg, E., Buffart, H., eds. 1978. *Formal Theories of Visual Perception.* Chichester: Wiley. 345 pp.

Lévy-Leblond, J.-M. 1971. Galilei group and Galilean invariance. In *Group Theory and its Applications,* ed. E. M. Loebl, 2:221–99. NY: Academic

Leyton, M. 1984. Perceptual organization as nested control. *Biol. Cybern.* 51:141–52

Leyton, M. 1985. Generative systems of analyzers. *Comput. Vision Graph. Image Proc.* 31:201–14

Leyton, M. 1986. Principles of information structure common to six levels of the human cognitive system. *Info. Sci.* 38:1–120

Liberman, A. M. 1982. On finding that speech is special. *Am. Psychol.* 37:148–66

Liberman, A. M., Mattingly, I. G. 1985. The motor theory of speech perception revised. *Cognition* 21:1–36

Llewellyn, K. R. 1971. Visual guidance of locomotion. *J. Exp. Psychol.* 91:245–61

Locke, J. 1690. *An Essay Concerning Human Understanding.* Reprinted 1853. Philadelphia: James Kay. 524 pp.

Loftus, G. R. 1985. Picture perception: Effects of luminance on available information and information-extraction rate. *J. Exp. Psychol: Gen.* 114:342–56

Loftus, G. R., Johnson, C. A., Shimamura, A. P. 1985. How much is an icon worth. *J. Exp. Psychol: Hum. Percept. Perform.* 11: 1–13

Loftus, G. R., Nelson, W., Kallman, H. 1983. Differential acquisition rates for different types of information from pictures. *Q. J. Exp. Psychol.* 35A:187–98

Long, G. M. 1980. Icon memory: A review and critique of the study of short-term visual storage. *Psychol. Bull.* 88:785–820

Long, G. M., Wurst, S. A. 1984. Complexity effects on reaction-time measures of visual persistence: Evidence for peripheral and central contributions. *Am. J. Psychol.* 97: 537–61

Lord, E. A., Wilson, C. B. 1984. *The Mathematical Description of Shape and Form.* Chichester: Ellis Horwood

Longuet-Higgins, H. C., Prazdny, K. 1980. The interpretation of moving retinal images. *Proc. R. Soc. London Ser. B* 208:385–97

Luneburg, R. K. 1947. *Mathematical Analysis of Binocular Vision.* Princeton, NJ: Princeton Univ. Press. 104 pp.

MacFarland, W. N., Loew, E. R. 1983. Wave produced changes in underwater light and their relations to vision. *Environ. Biol. Fish.* 8:173–84

Mach, E. 1886. *The Analysis of Sensations.* Transl. S. Waterlow. Reprinted 1959. NY: Dover. 380 pp.

Machlup, F., Mansfield, U., ed. 1983. *The Study of Information.* NY: Wiley. 743 pp.

McArthur, D. J. 1982. Computer vision and perceptual psychology. *Psychol. Bull.* 92: 283–309

McClelland, J. L. 1985. Putting knowledge in its place: A scheme for programming parallel processing structures on the fly. *Cogn. Sci.* 9:113–46

McClelland, J. L., Elman, J. 1986. The TRACE model of speech perception. *Cogn. Psychol.* 18:1–86

McCloskey, M. 1983. Intuitive physics. *Sci. Am.* 248(4):122–30

McGurk, H., MacDonald, J. 1976. Hearing lips and seeing voices. *Nature* 264:746–48

McLeod, R. W., Ross, H. E. 1983. Optic-flow and cognitive factors in time-to-collision estimates. *Perception* 12:417–23

Mandelbrot, B. B. 1983. *The Fractal Geometry of Nature.* NY: Freeman. 468 pp.

Marks, L. E. 1978. *The Unity of the Senses.* NY: Academic. 289 pp.

Marr, D. 1982. *Vision.* San Francisco: Freeman. 397 pp.

Massaro, D. W., Cohen, M. M. 1983a. Categorical or continuous speech perception: A new test. *Speech Commun.* 2:15–35

Massaro, D. W., Cohen, M. M. 1983b. Evaluation and integration of visual and auditory information in speech perception. *J.*

Exp. Psychol: Hum. Percept. Perform. 9: 753–71

Massaro, D. W., Kallman, H., Kelly, J. 1980. The role of tone height, melodic contour, and tone chroma in melody recognition. *J. Exp. Psychol: Hum. Percept. Perform.* 6: 77–90

Mervis, C. B., Rosch, E. 1981. Categorization of natural objects. *Ann. Rev. Psychol.* 32:89–115

Michaels, C. F., Carello, C. 1981. *Direct Perception.* Englewood Cliffs, NJ: Prentice-Hall. 200 pp.

Mill, J. 1829. *Analysis of the Phenomena of the Human Mind,* Vol. I. 2nd ed., 1878. London: Longmans, Green, Reader, & Dyer. 453 pp.

Mill, J. S. 1843. *System of Logic.* 8th ed., 1874. NY: Harper. 659 pp.

Miller, G. A., Heise, G., Lichten, W. 1951. The intelligibility of speech as a function of the context of test materials. *J. Acoust. Soc. Am.* 41:329–55

Mingolla, E., Todd, J. T. 1986. Perception of solid shape from shading. *Biol. Cybern.* In press

Mori, T. 1984. Change of a frame of reference with velocity in visual motion perception. *Percept. Psychophys.* 35:515–18

Mori, T. 1985. An active method of extracting egomotion parameters for optical flow. *Biol. Cybern.* 52:405–7

Morton, J. 1969. Interaction of information in word recognition. *Psychol. Rev.* 76:165–78

Nakayama, K., Silverman, G. 1985. Detection and discrimination of sinusoidal grating displacements. *J. Opt. Soc. Am. A* 2:267–74

Nakayama, K., Silverman, G., MacLeod, D., Mulligan, J. 1985. Sensitivity to shearing and compressive motion in random dots. *Perception* 14:225–38

Natsoulas, T. 1984. Towards the improvement of Gibsonian perception theory. *J. Theory Soc. Behav.* 14:231–58

Neisser, U. 1967. *Cognitive Psychology.* Englewood Cliffs, NJ: Prentice-Hall. 351 pp.

Norwich, K. 1984. The psychophysics of taste from the entropy of the stimulus. *Percept. Psychophys.* 35:269–78

Oldfield, S., Phillips, J. 1983. The spatial characteristics of tactile form perception. *Perception* 12:615–26

Owen, D. H., Warren, R., Jensen, R. S., Mangold, S. J., Hettinger, L. J. 1981. Optical information for detecting loss in one's own forward speed. *Acta Psychol.* 48:203–13

Palmer, S. E. 1982. Symmetry, transformation, and the structure of perceptual systems. See Beck 1982a, pp. 95–144

Palmer, S. E. 1983. The psychology of perceptual organization: A transformational approach. See Beck et al 1983a, pp. 269–339

Pentland, A. P. 1982. Finding the illuminant direction. *J. Opt. Soc. Am.* 72:448–55

Pentland, A. P. 1982. Fractal-based description of natural scenes. *IEEE Pattern Anal. Machine Intell.* 6:661–74

Pentland, A. P., ed. 1986. *From Pixels to Predicates.* Norwood, NJ: Ablex

Perkins, D. N. 1983. Why the human perceiver is a bad machine. See Beck et al 1983, pp. 341–64

Perrone, J. A. 1984. Visual slant misperception and the 'black-hole' landing situation. *Aviat. Space Environ. Med.* 55:1020–25

Petersik, J. T. 1979. Three-dimensional object constancy: Coherence of a simulated rotating sphere in noise. *Percept. Psychophys.* 25:328–35

Peterson, M. A. 1986. Illusory concomittant motion in ambiguous stereograms: Evidence for nonstimulus contributions to perceptual organization. *J. Exp. Psychol: Hum. Percept. Perform.* 12:50–60

Peterson, M. A., Hochberg, J. 1983. Opposed-set measurement procedure: A quantitative analysis of the role of local cues and intention in form perception. *J. Exp. Psychol: Hum. Percept. Perform.* 9:183–93

Pinker, S. 1984. Visual cognition: an introduction. *Cognition* 18:1–63

Pittenger, J. B., Todd, J. T. 1983. Perception of growth from changes in body proportions. *J. Exp. Psychol: Hum. Percept. Perform.* 9:945–54

Poincaré, H. 1905. *Science and Hypothesis.* NY: Dover. 244 pp. Reprinted 1952

Poincaré, H. 1907. *The Value of Science.* NY: Dover. 137 pp. Reprinted 1958

Poizner, H. 1983. Perception of movement in American Sign Language: Effects of linguistic structure and linguistic experience. *Percept. Psychophys.* 33:215–31

Pomerantz, J. R. 1981. Perceptual organization in information processing. See Kubovy & Pomerantz 1981, pp. 141–80

Pomerantz, J. R. 1983a. Global and local precedence: Selective attention in form and motion perception. *J. Exp. Psychol: Gen.* 112:516–40

Pomerantz, J. R. 1983b. The rubber pencil illusion. *Percept. Psychophys.* 33:365–68

Povel, D. 1981. Internal representation of simple temporal patterns. *J. Exp. Psychol: Hum. Percept. Perform.* 7:3–18

Prazdny, K. 1981. Determining the instantaneous direction of motion from optical flow generated by a curvilinearly moving observer. *Comput. Graph. Image Proc.* 17:238–48

Prazdny, K. 1983a. A sketch of a (computational) theory of visual kinesthesis. See Beck et al 1983a, pp. 413–23

Prazdny, K. 1983b. On the information in optic flows. *Comput. Vision Graph. Image Proc.* 22:235–59

Prazdny, K. 1984. On the perception of Glass patterns. *Perception* 13:469–78

Prazdny, K. 1985a. Detection of binocular disparities. *Biol. Cybern.* 52:93–99

Prazdny, K. 1985b. Studies of some new phenomena of motion perception. *Biol. Cybern.* 52:187–94

Priest, H. F., Cutting, J. E. 1985. Visual flow and direction of locomotion. *Science* 227:1063–64

Prinzmetal, W. 1981. Principles of feature integration in visual perception. *Percept. Psychophys.* 30:330–40

Probst, T., Krafczyk, S., Brandt, T., Wist, E. R. 1984. Interaction between perceived self-motion and object-motion impairs vehicle guidance. *Science* 225:536–38

Proffitt, D. R., Bertenthal, B. I. 1986. Recovering connectivity from moving point-light displays. In *Motion Understanding,* ed. J. Aggarwal, W. Martin. Hingham, Mass.: Kluwer. In press

Proffitt, D. R., Bertenthal, B. I., Cutting, J. E. 1984. Infant sensitivity to invariant structure revealed through motion. *J. Exp. Psychol: Hum. Percept. Perform.* 37:213–30

Proffitt, D. R., Thomas, A. M., O'Brien, R. G. 1983. The roles of contour and luminance distribution in determining perceived centers of objects. *Percept. Psychophys.* 33:63–71

Pylyshyn, Z. 1984. *Computation and Cognition.* Cambridge, Mass: MIT Press. 292 pp.

Rabin, M., Cain, W. 1984. Odor recognition: familiarity, identifiability, and encoding consistency. *J. Exp. Psychol: Learn. Mem. Cogn.* 10:316–25

Ramachandran, V., ed. 1985. Human motion perception. *Perception* 14:97–241

Regan, D. M., Beverley, K. I. 1982. How do we avoid confounding the direction we are looking and the direction we are moving? *Science* 215:194–96

Reid, T. 1764. Inquiry into the human mind. See Hamilton 1895, pp. 95–211

Reid, T. 1785. Essays on the intellectual powers of man. See Hamilton 1895, pp. 215–508

Repp, B. H. 1982. Phonetic trading relations and context effects: New experimental evidence for a speech mode of perception. *Psychol. Bull.* 92:81–110

Repp, B. H. 1984. Categorical perception: Issues, methods, findings. In *Speech and Language: Advances in Basic Research and Practice.* ed. N. Lass, 10:243–335. NY: Academic

Restle, F. 1979. Coding theory of the perception of motion configurations. *Psychol. Rev.* 86:1–24

Richards, W. A., Hoffman, D. D. 1985. Codon constraints on closed 2D shapes. *Comput. Vision Graph. Image Proc.* 31: 265–76

Richards, W. A., Rubin, J., Hoffman, D. D. 1982. Equation counting and the interpretation of sensory data. *Perception* 11:557–76

Rieger, J. H., Lawton, D. T. 1985. Processing differential image motion. *J. Opt. Soc. Am. A* 2:354–60

Rieger, J. H., Toet, L. 1985. Human visual navigation in the presence of 3-D motions. *Biol. Cybern.* 52:377–81

Riemersma, J. B. 1981. Visual control during straight road driving. *Acta Psychol.* 48:214–25

Rock, I. 1983. *The Logic of Perception.* Cambridge, Mass: MIT Press. 365 pp.

Rock, I. 1985. Perception and knowledge. *Acta Psychol.* 59:1–20

Rogers, B., Graham, M. 1979. Motion parallax as an independent cue for depth perception. *Perception* 8:125–34

Rubin, J. M., Kanwisher, N. 1985. Topological perception: holes in an experiment. *Percept. Psychophys.* 37:179–80

Runeson, S., Frykholm, G. 1983. Kinematic specification of dynamics as an informational basis for person-and-action sequences. *J. Exp. Psychol: Gen.* 112:585–615

Russell, B. A. 1897. *Essay on the Foundations of Geometry.* Cambridge: Cambridge Univ. Press. 201 pp.

Russell, B. A. 1927. *The Analysis of Matter.* London: Kegan Paul, Trench, Trubner. 407 pp.

Sagi, D., Julesz, B. 1985. Detection versus discrimination of visual orientation. *Perception* 14:619–28

Samuel, A. 1986. Red herring detectors and speech perception: In defense of selective adaptation. *Cogn. Psychol.* 18: In press

Santen, J. van, Sperling, G. 1984. Temporal covariance model of human motion perception. *J. Opt. Soc. Am. A* 1:451–73

Santen, J. van, Sperling, G. 1985. Elaborated Reichardt detectors. *J. Opt. Soc. Am. A* 2: 300–21

Schwartz, B., Sperling, G. 1983. Luminance controls the perceived 3-D structure of dynamic 2-D displays. *Bull. Psychon. Soc.* 21:456–58

Sedgwick, H. 1983. Environment-centered representation of spatial layout: Available visual information from texture and perspective. See Beck et al 1983a, pp. 425–58

Sekuler, R., Wilson, H., Owlsey, C. 1984. Structural modeling of spatial vision. *Vision Res.* 7:689–700

Shannon, C. E., Weaver, W. 1949. *The Mathematical Theory of Communication.* Urbana: Univ. Illinois Press. 117 pp.

Shebilske, W. L. 1981. Visual direction illusions in everyday situations: Implications for sensorimotor and ecological theories. In *Eye Movements: Cognition and Visual Perception,* ed. D. Fisher, R. Monty, J. Senders, pp. 95–110. Hillsdale, NJ: Erlbaum

Shebilske, W. L., Karmiohl, C., Proffitt, D. R. 1983. Induced esophoric shifts in eye convergence and illusory distance in reduced and structured viewing conditions. *J. Exp. Psychol: Hum. Percept. Perform.* 9: 270–77

Shepard, R. N. 1981. Psychophysical complementarity. See Kubovy & Pomerantz 1981, pp. 279–341

Shepard, R. 1984. Ecological constraints on internal representation: Resonant kinematics of perceiving, imagining, thinking, and dreaming. *Psychol. Rev.* 91:417–47

Shum, K., Wolford, G. 1983. A quantitative study of perceptual vector analysis. *Percept. Psychophys.* 34:17–24

Skyrms, B. 1975. *Choice and Chance.* Belmont, Calif: Wadsworth. 165 pp. 2nd ed.

Smith, J. D., Kemler Nelson, D. G. 1984. Overall similarity in adults' classification: The child in all of us. *J. Exp. Psychol: Gen.* 113:137–59

Smith, L. B., Kemler, D. G. 1978. Levels of experienced dimensionality in children and adults. *Cogn. Psychol.* 10:502–32

Sober, E. 1975. *Simplicity.* London: Oxford. 189 pp.

Spelke, E. 1976. Infants' intermodal perception of events. *Cogn. Psychol.* 8:553–60

Spelke, E., Born, W., Chu, F. 1983. Perception of moving, sounding objects by four-month-old infants. *Perception* 12: 719–32

Sperling, G. 1971. The description and luminous calibration of cathode ray oscilloscope visual displays. *Behav. Res. Methods Instrum.* 3:148–50

Sperling, G. 1980. Bandwidth requirements for video transmission of American Sign Language and finger spelling. *Science* 210: 797–99

Sperling, G. 1986. A signal-to-noise theory of the effects of luminance on picture memory: Comment on Loftus. *J. Exp. Psychol.: Gen.* 115:189–92

Sperling, G., Landy, M. S., Cohen, Y., Pavel, M. 1985a. Intelligent encoding of ASL image sequences at extremely low information rates. *Comput. Vision Graph. Image Proc.* 31:335–91

Sperling, G., Santen, J. van, Burt, P. 1985b. Three theories of stroboscopic motion detection. *Spat. Vision* 1:47–57

Stevens, K. A. 1981. The visual interpretation of surface contours. See Brady 1981, pp. 47–73

Stevens, K. A. 1983a. Evidence relating subjective contours and interpretations involving interposition. *Perception* 12:481–500

Stevens, K. A. 1983b. Surface tilt (the direction of slant): a neglected psychological variable. *Percept. Psychophys.* 33:241–50

Stevens, K. A. 1984. On gradients and texture "gradients". *J. Exp. Psychol: Gen.* 113: 221–24

Stoffregen, T. 1985. Flow structure versus retinal location in the optical control of stance. *J. Exp. Psychol: Hum. Percept. Perform.* 11:554–65

Stromeyer, C., Kronauer, R., Madsen, J., Klein, S. 1984. Opponent-movement mechanisms in human vision. *J. Opt. Soc. Am. A* 1:876–84

Summerfield, Q. 1979. Use of visual information for phonetic perception. *Phonetica* 36:314–31

Suppes, P. 1977. Is visual space Euclidean? *Synthese* 35:397–421

Ternus, J. 1926. The problem of phenomenal identity. See Ellis 1938, pp. 149–60

Thomson, J. A. 1983. Is continuous visual monitoring necessary in visually guided locomotion? *J. Exp. Psychol: Hum. Percept. Perform.* 9:427–43

Todd, J. T. 1981. Visual information about moving objects. *J. Exp. Psychol: Hum. Percept. Perform.* 7:795–810

Todd, J. T. 1982. Visual information about rigid and nonrigid motion: A geometric analysis. *J. Exp. Psychol: Hum. Percept. Perform.* 8:238–52

Todd, J. T. 1984a. Formal theories of visual information. See Warren & Shaw 1984b, pp. 87–102

Todd, J. T. 1984b. The perception of three-dimensional structure from rigid and nonrigid motion. *Percept. Psychophys.* 36:97–103

Todd, J. T. 1985. Perception of structure from motion: Is projective correspondence of moving elements a necessary condition? *J. Exp. Psychol: Hum. Percept. Perform.* 11: 689–710

Todd, J. T., Mark, L. S., Shaw, R. E., Pittenger, J. B. 1980. The perception of human growth. *Sci. Am.* 242(2):132–44

Todd, J. T., Mingolla, E. 1983. The perception of surface curvature and direction. of illumination from patterns of shading. *J. Exp. Psychol: Hum. Percept. Perform.* 10: 734–49

Todd, J. T., Mingolla, E. 1984. Simulation of curved surfaces from patterns of optical texture. *J. Exp. Psychol: Hum. Percept. Perform.* 10:734–39

Todd, J. T., Warren, W. H. 1982. Visual perception of relative mass in dynamic events. *Perception* 11:325–35

Treisman, A. 1982. Perceptual grouping and attention in visual search for features and for objects. *J. Exp. Psychol: Hum. Percept. Perform.* 8:194–214

Treisman, A. 1985. Preattentive processing in vision. *Comput. Vision Graph. Image Proc.* 31:167–77

Treisman, A., Paterson, R. 1984. Emergent features, attention, and object perception. *J. Exp. Psychol: Hum. Percept. Perform.* 10: 12–31

Treisman, A., Souther, J. 1985. Search asymmetry: A diagnostic for preattentive processing of separable features. *J. Exp. Psychol: Gen.* 114:285–310

Tufte, E. R. 1983. *The Visual Display of Quantitative Information.* Cheshire, Conn: Graphics Press. 197 pp.

Turvey, M. T., Shaw, R. E., Reed, E. S., Mace, W. M. 1981. Ecological laws of perceiving and acting: In reply to Fodor and Pylyshyn. *Cognition* 9:237–304

Ullman, S. 1979. *The Interpretation of Visual Motion.* Cambridge, Mass: MIT Press. 229 pp.

Ullman, S. 1980. Against direct perception. *Behav. Brain Sci.* 3:373–415

Ullman, S. 1983. Recent computational studies in the interpretation of structure from motion. See Beck et al 1983a, pp. 459–80

Ullman, S. 1984a. Maximizing rigidity: the incremental recovery of 3-D structure from rigid and nonrigid motion. *Perception* 13:255–74

Ullman, S. 1984b. Rigidity and misperceived motion. *Perception* 13:219–20

Ullman, S., Richards, W., eds. 1984. *Image Understanding 1984.* Norwood, NJ: Ablex. 268 pp.

Uttal, W. R. 1983. *Visual Detection of Form.* Hillsdale, NJ: Erlbaum. 163 pp.

Uttal, W. R. 1985. *The Detection of Nonplanar Surfaces in Visual Space.* Hillsdale, NJ: Erlbaum. 172 pp.

Wallach, H., Becklen, R., Nitzberg, D. 1985. Vector analysis and process combination in motion perception. *J. Exp. Psychol: Hum. Percept. Perform.* 11:93–102

Wallach, H., O'Connell, D. N. 1953. The kinetic depth effect. *J. Exp. Psychol.* 45: 205–17

Wallach, H., O'Leary, A. 1985. Vector analysis of rotary motion perception. *Percept. Psychophys.* 38:47–54

Warren, W. H. 1984. Perceiving affordances: Visual guidance of stair climbing. *J. Exp. Psychol: Hum. Percept. Perform.* 10:683–703

Warren, W. H., Shaw, R. E. 1984a. Events and encounters as units of analysis for ecological psychology. See Warren & Shaw 1984b, pp. 1–27

Warren, W. H., Shaw, R. E., eds. 1984b. *Persistence and Change.* Hillsdale, NJ: Erlbaum. 368 pp.

Warren, W. H., Verbrugge, R. R. 1984. Auditory perception of breaking and bouncing events: A case study in ecological acoustics. *J. Exp. Psychol: Hum. Percept. Perform.* 10:704–13

Warren, W. H., Young, D. S., Lee, D. N. 1986. Visual control of step length during running over irregular terrain. *J. Exp. Psychol: Hum. Percept. Perform.* 12: In press

Watson, A. B. 1978. A Riemann geometric explanation of the visual illusions and figural after-effects. See Leeuwenberg & Buffart 1978, pp. 139–69

Watson, A. B., Barlow, H., Robson, J. 1983. What does the eye see best? *Nature* 302: 419–20

Webb, J. A., Aggarwal, J. K. 1981. Visually interpreting the motion of objects in space. *Computer* 14(8):40–46

Webb, J. A., Aggarwal, J. K. 1982. Structure from motion of rigid and jointed objects. *Artif. Intell.* 19:107–30

Weichselgartner, E., Sperling, G. 1985. Continuous measurement of visible persistence. *J. Exp. Psychol: Hum. Percept. Perform.* 11:711–25

Wilcox, S., Edwards, D. A. 1982. Some Gibsonian perspectives on the ways that psychologists use physics. *Acta Psychol.* 52:147–63

Williams, D. R., Collier, R. 1983. Consequences of spatial sampling by a human receptor mosaic. *Science* 221:385–87

Williams, D. W., Sekuler, R. 1984. Coherent global motion percepts from stochastic local motions. *Vision Res.* 24:55–62

Woodham, R. J. 1984. Photometric method for determining shape from shading. See Ullman & Richards 1984, pp. 97–125

Wright, J. K., Bregman, A. S. 1986. Auditory stream segregation and the control of dissonance in polyphonic music. *Contemp. Music Rev.* In press

Yager, D., Kramer, P., Shaw, M., Graham, N. 1984. Detection and identification of spatial frequency: Models and data. *Vision Res.* 24:1021–35

Yantis, S., Jonides, J. 1984. Abrupt visual onsets and selective attention: Evidence from visual search. *J. Exp. Psychol: Hum. Percept. Perform.* 10:601–21

Yellott, J., Wandell, B., Cornsweet, T. 1984. The beginning of visual perception: the retinal image and its initial encoding. In *Handbook of Physiology, The Nervous System III*, ed. J. Brookhard, V. Mountcastle, pp. 257–316. Baltimore, Md: Williams & Wilkins

Yeomans, J. M., Irwin, D. E. 1985. Stimulus duration and partial report procedure. *Percept. Psychophys.* 37:163–69

Zeeman, E. C. 1976. Catastrophe theory. *Sci. Am.* 234(4):65–83

Zucker, S. W. 1984. Two constraints on early orientation selection in dot patterns. See Dodwell & Caelli 1984, pp. 283–300

Zucker, S. W. 1985. Early orientation selection: Target fields and the dimensionality of their support. *Comput. Vision Graph. Image Proc.* 32:74–103

Zucker, S. W., Stevens, K. A., Sander, P. 1983. The relation between proximity and brightness similarity in dot patterns. *Percept. Psychophys.* 34:513–22

Zusne, L. 1970. *Visual Perception of Form.* NY: Academic. 547 pp.

Ann. Rev. Psychol. 1987. 38:91–128
Copyright © 1987 by Annual Reviews Inc. All rights reserved

DEVELOPMENTAL PSYCHOBIOLOGY: Prenatal, Perinatal, and Early Postnatal Aspects of Behavioral Development

W. G. Hall

Department of Psychology, Duke University, Durham, North Carolina 27706

R. W. Oppenheim

Department of Anatomy, Bowman Gray School of Medicine, Wake Forest University, Winston-Salem, North Carolina 27103

CONTENTS

0066-4308/87/0201-0091$02.00

INTRODUCTION

Aims and Scope

From its rather feeble origins, at the turn of the century, as a vague and ill-defined attempt to bridge the gap between psychological (or behavioral) and biological development, developmental psychobiology has grown to its present status as a separate and major research field encompassing, in principle, virtually all developmental research in psychology and neurobiology.

Because of space limitations our review focuses on the analysis of behavior and, to some extent, its neurobiological basis during the early stages of ontogeny before and shortly after the time of birth. Furthermore, we emphasize certain critical concepts in development that represent contemporary research strategies in developmental psychobiology. In our view, these have shifted during the past few years from simply providing demonstrations of the persisting effects of early experience, and a related focus on precursors of adult behavior, to studying the characteristics and organization of early behavior per se and how it is determined and influenced by a variety of factors, intrinsic and extrinsic in origin, ranging from ecology and social interactions to genetics and neurobiological events. Previous concerns with the integration of early experience into adult behavior have not been neglected but, rather, have been partly supplanted by a growing concern with how developing animals sense and respond in their own world and the ways in which these capacities are influenced by and related to those of preceding and subsequent stages in development (Kagen et al 1978).

Thus, we believe that specific behavioral capabilities and their neurobiological substrates are primarily the result of selection pressures operating at a particular stage in ontogeny. According to this view, most early behaviors represent "ontogenetic adaptations" (Oppenheim 1981, 1984; Prechtl 1981, 1984) to one degree or another. Consequently, we must ask, to what extent are such adaptations transient or utilized at other developmental stages? For species that have relatively complex life histories and that undergo considerable postnatal development, the dynamically changing status of the young may have required the evolution of new stage-specific neurobehavioral capacities, many of which are then likely to have been exploited by and integrated into later stages in development. We hope that the developmental work discussed in this review will help illustrate the ontogenetic and phylogenetic role of neurobehavioral adaptations.

History and Definition of Developmental Psychobiology

For most investigators a developmental approach to neurobehavioral development involves both the description and causal analysis of events through time. The primary goal is to specify the intrinsic and extrinsic factors that are responsible for the emergence and maturation of behavior. Because, in the broadest sense, this means understanding the role of genes, cells, tissues, organs, and the interactions of all of these with endogenous and exogenous factors during ontogeny, we consider the field of developmental psychobiology to be a subfield of the parent disciplines of developmental biology, on the one hand, and developmental psychology, on the other. This means that in principle all levels of analysis and all stages of ontogeny comprise the subject matter of developmental psychobiology. Because behavior and its development involve nervous system function, the field of neuroembryology or developmental neurobiology is pertinent to a comprehensive analysis of problems in developmental psychobiology (Oppenheim & Haverkamp 1986).

In a recent review, Gottlieb (1983) has offered a definition of developmental psychobiology that represents our own views and nicely captures the significance and purview of the field as presently conceived: "A psychobiological approach signifies the study of the development of behavior from a broadly biological perspective. A broad biological point of view includes not only some interest in the physiological, biochemical, and anatomical correlates of behavior but also embraces ecological and evolutionary considerations as well" (Gottlieb 1983, p. 1).

We have not made an extensive effort to trace the origins of the term "developmental psychobiology." Although the comparative neuroanatomist C. J. Herrick (1955) has stated that the term "psychobiology" was coined by the pioneer psychiatrist Adolf Meyer in 1915, it is obvious that the term predates this time. The psychologist Knight Dunlap had already published a book in 1914 entitled *An Outline of Psychobiology,* and, in a little-known paper published in 1894, E. Gates used the term "psychobiology" to define the field that, "studies structures from the standpoint of mind, and interprets organic phenomena in psychologic terms" (p. 581). It is clear from reading the literature from the turn of the century that psychobiology was conceived as an emerging new interdisciplinary approach that would attempt to integrate findings in psychology, neurology, and biology in much the same way that neurobiology serves a similar role today. The conceptual and empirical integration of many disciplines that was implied in the early use of the term "psychobiology" provided a useful frame of reference for developmentally oriented pioneers in the field including J. B. Watson, K. Lashley, F. Beach, L. Carmichael, C. L. and C. J. Herrick, G. Coghill, W. Windle, Z. Y. Kuo, T. C. Schneirla, A. Gesell, M. McGraw, J. Piaget, and many others.[1]

---

[1]The term "psychobiology" has no entries in any of the standard English dictionaries we have examined, including the Oxford English Dictionary. There are also no entries for psychobiology in either the 1902 or 1940 editions of J. M. Baldwin's *Dictionary of Psychology and Philosophy* or the 1950 edition of *A History of Experimental Psychology* by E. G. Boring. More recent dictionaries of psychological terms that do include entries for psychobiology provide only brief and vague definitions that fail to capture the real meaning of the term for those working in the field (Drever 1952; Wolman 1973; Harriman 1969). For instance, Drever defines psychobiology as "the investigation of psychological problems in the field of general biology."

Emerging interest in the developmental study of psychobiology at the turn of the century cannot be attributed to the efforts of any single individual but rather represents the expression of a zeitgeist heavily influenced by Darwinism and by a growing interest among psychologists, biologists, neurologists, and psychiatrists in development, behavior, and neuroanatomy. Perhaps no one expressed these new trends more clearly in his own work and writings than the neuroanatomist and embryologist George E. Coghill. As a trained anatomist and embryologist with an abiding interest in behavior, evolution, and the nervous system, Coghill was in a unique position to synthesize the various emerging trends into a biologically valid and psychologically relevant field of developmental psychobiology (Herrick 1949; Oppenheim 1978; Windle 1975). Although Coghill did not live long enough to fully develop and implement his ideas for a discipline of developmental psychobiology, his work and writings (e.g. Coghill 1929) served as an inspiration to a later generation of psychologists and biologists interested in neurobehavioral development and who themselves are the immediate intellectual predecessors of many of us today who continue to carry on the line of work initially foreshadowed by Coghill. Thus, we consider Coghill and the investigation of the development of brain and behavior that he inspired to be one of the most important influences in the establishment of developmental psychobiology in this century.

THE ORGANIZATION OF PRENATAL BEHAVIOR

The Onset of Behavior

A neuroembryological basis for behavior is realized once anatomical connections (synapses) begin to be formed between nerves and muscles as well as between interneurons and motoneurons within the central nervous system (Purves & Lichtman 1984). With the initiation of functionally patent synapses in the developing motor system, the embryo becomes potentially capable of endogenously generated movements. Following the formation of functional connections between sensory receptors and the interneurons and motoneurons that mediate overt movements, the developing embryo can respond to sensory input and thus for the first time is capable of modifying its behavior according to the contingencies of its sheltered, but by no means stimulus-free, prenatal environment.

Although the specific point when these fundamentally important neurobiological events occur in a given animal's life history may vary according to evolutionary and ecological constraints that affect each species differently, the available evidence clearly shows that the embryos of virtually all species (vertebrate and invertebrate) exhibit spontaneous movements and respond to various kinds of sensory stimuli at remarkably early stages (Oppenheim 1982;

Hamburger 1963; Gottlieb 1968, 1973; Provine 1981a, 1986; Bekoff 1981, 1986). Thus, the fact of prenatal neurobehavioral function is no longer an issue. Rather the central concerns of investigators in this field have long been the related issues of (*a*) what role (or roles) this early behavior plays in the survival and well-being of the developing embryo, larva, and fetus (i.e. with ontogenetic adaptations); and (*b*) determining the contribution of prenatal behavior to the normal organization and manifestation of behavior at later stages in life (i.e. ontogenetic precursors or antecedents). To a very large extent, the history of developmental psychobiology in this century has been characterized by an overriding concern with the development of behavior from the perspective of ontogenetic antecedents (Oppenheim 1981). That is to say, investigators have been guided by the central idea that developing behaviors are primarily (or even solely) imperfect or nascent reflections of adult behavior and thus that development is merely a process during which these seemingly deficient forms of immature behavior attain their mature adult state.[2] Although it is certainly true that all adult behavior has a developmental history, it has become increasingly clear in recent years that the pathway from the embryo to the adult is seldom so straightforward as implied in this perspective. Rather, the behavior exhibited by developing animals reflects a balance between meeting the needs of the moment and preparing for later life. Irrespective of which of these two major conceptualizations of ontogeny one chooses as a focus, the fact that the nervous system begins to function long before birth or hatching means that behavioral development must begin with the first feeble and simple movements and responses of the embryo.

Motor Behavior

In the embryos of some animals (e.g. certain fish), spontaneous overt movements can occur without the involvement of the nervous system. This type of activity is the result of endogenous muscle activity, and in some instances (e.g. shark embryos) the behavior can even be as complex as swimming-like movements. In most vertebrates, however, the musculature can initially only be activated by direct mechanical or electrical stimulation, and the resulting movement is a simple, brief local twitch of the stimulated muscle. In both of these cases, we use the term "myogenic" to describe the stage when muscle is capable of contracting prior to innervation. Earlier stages are termed pre-

---

[2]For instance, the biologist Bonner has argued that "the goal of development is the final form and function of the adult" (Bonner 1958, p. 1). In a similar vein the psychologist Marshack has stated that "the cognitive skills of the child are not adaptive. The child's skills are preparatory for the successful strategies of adults" (Marshack 1979, p. 394). Even Piaget fell victim to this mode of thought as indicated by his statement, "There is a continuous progression from spontaneous movements to acquired habits and from the latter to intelligence" (Piaget & Inhelder 1969, p. 6).

myogenic (i.e. the absence of muscle contraction under any condition). Typically, the pre-myogenic and myogenic phases are relatively short and are followed by the neurogenic stage, when direct neural input to muscles assumes control of motility. Neurogenic activity can be subdivided according to whether the neurally mediated movements are initiated (triggered) by stimuli impinging on sensory receptors, in which case they are termed reflexogenic, or whether they occur in the absence of such stimuli, in which case they are referred to as autogenic, or spontaneous. Reflexogenic behavior is mediated over simple or complex reflex arcs [sensory receptor(s), interneurons, motoneurons, muscle], whereas autogenic behavior only involves the activation of the efferent pathways [interneurons, motoneurons, and muscle (Provine 1973)]. In the past, the distinction between reflexogenic and autogenic behavior has been the subject of considerable debate, with some investigators arguing that bona fide autogenic activity, even in the embryo, does not exist. Observations and experiments conducted over the past few years have now resolved this issue in favor of autogenic behavior by showing that in some cases complex behaviors are manifest in the embryo even prior to the completion of the first reflex arcs (Bekoff 1976; Hamburger 1973). In species such as the chick embryo, which exhibits movements prior to reflexes, this period is referred to as the pre-reflexogenic stage. Furthermore, deafferentation experiments have shown that even following the onset of reflexogenic behavior in the embryo and fetus, the removal of the sensory or afferent components of the reflex circuit results in little, if any, perturbation of motor output (Hamburger et al 1966). That is, normal behaviors continue to be spontaneously generated in the absence of sensory input. Thus, autogenic behavior constitutes a primary and fundamental feature of the earliest stages of ontogeny. Many of the complex species–typical motor action patterns that characterize the behavioral repertoire of adult animals (swimming, locomotion, flying, etc) very likely represent the activation of a neuronal circuitry that to a large extent has its origins in a basic neurobiological substrate laid down in the embryo and whose functional manifestation is reflected in spontaneous prenatal behavior (Bekoff 1986; Provine 1980, 1986).

Considerable attention devoted to the study of prenatal behavior has been concerned with what embryos actually do at different stages of development (Carmichael 1954, 1970; Gottlieb 1973). A major focus of these efforts has been to discern the earliest precursors of a behavior and to trace its subsequent perfection and organization. By necessity, much of what is known about the behavior of animals during the prenatal period is derived from those forms that are accessible to observations and experiments under relatively normal conditions. This means that most reliable information has been obtained from fish, amphibians, birds, and a few invertebrates. Nonetheless, a variety of mammalian species have also been investigated and, despite the inherent drawbacks to making reliable observations of the embryos and fetuses of these forms, much valuable information is available (Windle 1940; Hooker 1952; Humphrey 1969; Barcoft & Barron 1939; Smotherman et al 1984; Dawes 1984). The increasing use of real-time ultrasound analyses of human embryos and fetuses has also provided valuable new insights into early behavioral development (both normal and pathological) in our own species (Prechtl 1985; Birnholz et al 1978; Vries et al 1982, 1985; van Vliet et al 1985; Suzuki & Yamamuro 1985; Visser et al 1985).

Owing to a general tendency for neuronal maturation to proceed in a rostral-caudal direction, spontaneous and sensory-evoked movements first appear in the upper body and later spread to progressively more caudal regions, culminating in movements of the tail (Carmichael 1954; Oppenheim 1974). Furthermore, in animals with appendages the limbs become active after the trunk, and within the limb there is a tendency for more proximal regions (e.g. upper arm) to become functional prior to distal regions (e.g. the hand). Although the activation of muscles involves the functioning of excitatory neurons, many movements of the embryo require a balanced activation of both excitatory and inhibitory neurons, and there is now considerable evidence indicating that inhibitory neurons are functional at even the earliest stages of development (Oppenheim & Reitzel 1975; Reitzel et al 1979). Thus, the old notion that excitation precedes inhibition during ontogeny is no longer a valid generalization. In addition to its role in patterned embryonic movements, early inhibition may also suppress entire neuronal circuits and behaviors that are not needed until after birth or hatching (Bekoff 1981, 1986).

In species where detailed observations are available, the movements of the embryo tend to be organized temporally into periods of stereotyped activity and inactivity (Hamburger 1963; Corner & Bot 1967; Corner et al 1979; Robertson et al 1982). That is, the movements occur in rhythmic bursts, during which all or most of the body parts capable of moving are activated. Most vertebrate embryos also exhibit complex waves of trunk contractions that resemble swimming movements. In terrestrial vertebrates this stage is transient, whereas in fish and amphibians it persists into the larval or adult stage as full-blown swimming. As originally shown by Coghill over 75 years ago (Coghill 1929), the behavioral development of fish and amphibian embryos appears to be almost entirely directed towards the gradual perfection and organization of swimming. The early movements of these embryos represent a series of stages in which imperfect fragments of the swimming pattern are gradually and progressively organized into adult-like swimming. By contrast, it is considerably more difficult to discern the origins of equally complex postnatal behavior patterns in the often unorganized movements of the early avian or mammalian embryo. For instance, the movements of the chick embryo have been characterized as "irregular, seemingly uncoordinated twistings of the trunk, jerky flexions, extensions and kicking of the legs, gaping and later clapping of the beak, eye and eyelid movements and occasional wing-flapping in later stages. The movements are performed in un-predictable combinations" (Hamburger 1963). Similarly, in the rat fetus it is reported that "the movements performed during an activity burst give the impression of unintegrated, aimless movements in the sense that the move-ment of different parts, such as head, anterior, posterior trunk and face and hindlimbs, tail and mouth are not related to each other as in clearly integrated action patterns such as walking" (Narayanan et al 1971). Although these early, relatively unorganized motor behaviors persist into later stages, there is a tendency for more complex and highly organized patterns to become manifest at later prenatal stages. Alternating leg movements, wing-flapping, respiratory movements, hatching, grasping, swallowing, suckling, grooming, and organized withdrawal and related reflexes, for example, have all been described in older avian or mammalian fetuses (Carmichael 1954; Kuo 1932; Hamburger & Oppenheim 1967; Bekoff 1981; Gottlieb & Kuo 1965; Hooker 1952; Provine 1980; Smotherman et al 1984). Furthermore, finer levels of analysis have revealed a surprising degree of order in at least certain aspects of even the early, seemingly unorganized embryonic behavior. For instance, the earliest activation of specific muscles (e.g. flexors and extensors) in the hindlimb of chick embryos occurs in a manner quite similar to that seen during postnatal locomotion (Bekoff 1976, 1986; Landmesser & O'Donovan 1985; Landmesser & Morris 1975). Thus, although the neuronal circuitry required for organizing complex, behaviorally relevant movements between different parts of the embryo is not well-developed (or at least is not often activated) until late prenatal stages, the components of the circuitry at the level of a given muscle or set of muscles are, by contrast, highly organized early during ontogeny.

Irrespective of the form or pattern of behavior exhibited by developing embryos, the mere fact of its existence raises questions that are of fun-damental importance in understanding the evolutionary significance of the prenatal period for neurobehavioral development. For instance, is embryonic behavior merely an epiphenomenon of neuroembryological development? Does it represent a kind of early use or practice that is essential for later neurobehavioral development? Or does it serve some unique role for the embryo analogous to the transient role of the extraembryonic membranes and related structures that surround, protect, and nourish the embryo *in utero* or *in ovo?* These and related questions of direct relevance to embryonic activity also apply to many early postnatal behaviors and are discussed in the final section of our review.

Sensory Behavior

For all species for which we have information, some, and in many cases all, of the sensory modalities become functional prior to birth or hatching. For many vertebrates the various sensory modalities appear to begin functioning in a rather stereotyped sequence during development, although exceptions exist (Gottlieb 1971; Bradley & Mistretta 1975). The first sensory modality to become functional is cutaneous, or touch (temperature sensation may become functional at about the same time although the evidence is scanty), followed by proprioception, vestibular function, taste, olfaction, audition, and vision. The extent to which some or all of the modalities are capable of functioning prior to birth or hatching partly defines whether the species is altricial or precocial and may be based on the degree to which a given modality is required for meeting the adaptive needs of the developing organism. For instance, newly hatched amphibians, reptiles, and precocial birds depend upon visually guided independent feeding for their survival, whereas newborn altricial birds and mammals do not. Thus, in most altricial birds and mammals the visual system becomes functional only several days or weeks after birth. Humans as well as other primates are an interesting exception to these trends in that, although they are generally considered altricial, all of their sensory modalities are functional by the time of birth. This apparent dissociation of sensory development from the more typical altricial trend may reflect an important recent evolutionary strategy for gaining access to a variety of sources of sensory information at the earliest possible stages that are compatible with neurobiological development.

The fact that a given sensory modality becomes functional at some early prenatal stage of development does not necessarily mean that this functioning is similar to that of the adult system. In fact, this is probably seldom, if ever, the case. Different components of a sensory system may become functional at different times. Differential emergence of function is generally true whether one is dealing with sensory receptors or with higher order components of the system such as various projection nuclei in the CNS. For instance, in avian embryos the first auditory neurons in the cochlea and cochlear nuclei to become functional respond to low-frequency sounds, and only later do high-frequency components of the system become functional (Konishi 1973; Rubel 1978; Rubel & Ryals 1983; Lippe & Rubel 1983; Saunders et al 1973; Jackson & Rubel 1978). Furthermore, sensory systems appear to differentiate both structurally and functionally in a peripheral-to-central direction starting with the peripheral receptors and ending with the highest projection centers in the CNS.

Although in many instances sensory systems can be shown experimentally to begin to function prior to birth or hatching, the extent to which they are actually activated *in ovo* or *in utero* during normal development is a separate and, in many respects, a more fundamental question. Unlike motor systems in which autogenic, or spontaneous, activity provides compelling evidence for the onset of motor function prenatally, sensory systems must be stimulated or perturbed (e.g. sensory deprivation) in order to demonstrate their functional state as well as to determine whether such function plays any role in normal development. The first question that must be addressed in this regard is whether or not the normal *in ovo* or *in utero* environment provides adequate sources of stimulation for a given sensory modality. Certainly in the case of tactile, proprioceptive, vestibular, and taste receptors, adequate sources of sensory information are very likely available during the prenatal period (Bradley & Mistretta 1975). Temperature and olfactory cues, on the other hand, are probably not sufficient to stimulate these modalities during the prenatal development of most animals, although considerably more work is required before this possibility can be excluded. What about vision and hearing? There is now considerable information indicating that avian and mammalian fetuses (including humans) can respond to sounds that are normally present in the *in ovo* or *in utero* environment (e.g. heartbeats, gastrointestinal sounds, embryonic vocalizations in birds, etc) as well as to sounds that arise from outside the egg or mother (Rubel 1978; Gottlieb 1971, 1976a; Schmidt et al 1985; Birnholz & Benacerraf 1983; Vince et al 1985; Vince 1973, 1979; DeCasper & Fifer 1980). Concerning vision, there is no convincing evidence that either avian or mammalian embryos are normally responsive *in utero* to changes in ambient light. Thus, although the visual system of precocial mammals, humans, and avians has been shown by experimental means to be capable of functioning prior to birth and hatching (Gottlieb 1971; Bradley & Mistretta 1975), it is unlikely that the retina ever receives adequate visual stimuli during this period. The situation may be different, however, for fish and amphibian embryos that develop within a transparent egg *ex utero*. The fact that a sensory system is not subject to adequate sources of stimulation prenatally is not, however, a sufficient basis for concluding that the system is nonfunctional or that function plays no role whatsoever in the differentiation of that system. Many sensory systems exhibit "spontaneous" generation of impulses, and this source of endogenous activity may play an important role in certain aspects of normal sensory differentiation (Archer et al 1982; Harris 1981).

The demonstration that a given sensory modality is in some sense functionally competent prenatally and the observation that adequate sources of sensory stimuli are normally available to the developing embryo are both important achievements in the study of prenatal sensory capacities. But these still do not resolve the more fundamental issue of whether normally occurring sources of sensory stimuli are actually used by the embryo as developmental signals for fostering neurobehavioral ontogeny. The ability of embryos and fetuses to respond to sensory stimuli or to have their behavior altered by them (e.g. learning or conditioning) may only be an illustration of the principle of "anticipatory maturation" (e.g. Carmichael 1954) whereby psychobiological systems become functional prior to their actual use for the survival of the animal (e.g. fetal "breathing"). The demonstrations of prenatal learning or conditioning, if done within a meaningful ethological and ecological context, can provide strong circumstantial evidence for the importance of early experience; but the mere fact that learning or conditioning occurs (e.g. Spelt 1948) is not itself compelling proof that similar processes are part of the normal developmental pathway. Perhaps the strongest evidence in support of the experiential role of normally occurring sensory stimuli as essential developmental signals for the embryo or fetus are several studies in birds involving auditory stimuli (Vince 1979; Gottlieb 1976a; Evans 1973; Impekoven 1976; Tschanz & Hirsbrunner-Scharf 1975). These studies have clearly shown that various species-typical prenatal and postnatal behaviors (e.g. recognition of species or parental vocalizations) depend upon the embryo being exposed to specific kinds of auditory stimulation that are normally present prior to hatching. Conceptually similar results have been reported for sheep and humans, although the ethological relevance of such demonstrations are not as clear as in the case of the avian studies (Vince et al 1985; DeCasper & Fifer 1980).

Several recent studies have reported that chemical (taste?) stimuli presented to rat fetuses *in utero* can alter postnatal taste/odor responses involving pup-maternal interactions (Pedersen et al 1983; Stickrod et al 1982; Smotherman & Robinson 1985; Pedersen & Blass 1982). Although these results must be interpreted cautiously concerning their relevance to normal development (see above), they do indicate that natural associations involving chemical stimuli *in utero* (blood-born or in the amniotic fluid) may, in fact, represent a normal process by which seemingly "innate" postnatal behaviors are acquired or influenced prenatally.

THE ORGANIZATION OF POSTNATAL BEHAVIOR

Birth or hatching represents a marked physical transition for all developing infants. Its obvious demands and repercussions on physiology and behavior are accompanied by numerous, less obvious transitional events. In the development of behavior, the transition from the prenatal to the postnatal period represents a seemingly more striking change for precocial animals than for altricial forms. Within a few hours following birth or hatching, the neonates of precocial species exhibit behaviors that were not present or at least were unrecognizable prenatally. By contrast, much of the behavior of newborn altricial animals appears to be a continuation of prenatal activities, particularly the patterning of activity (Prechtl 1984). In attempting to understand the developmental basis for this difference, as well as the changes that occur in any species between the prenatal and postnatal period, it is essential to carry out such analyses within the context of the adaptive needs of the newborn. In the following sections of this review, we describe the organization of behavior in the immediate postnatal period. We first consider the patterns of activity that shape early response organization. Then perinatal characteristics of motor organization and the developmental processes they reveal are reviewed. These discussions provide a context, in the next section of this paper, for our consideration of specific early adaptive behaviors. All early behavior, adaptive or otherwise, occurs in the context of constraints created by these state and motoric processes found in early patterned activity.

The Patterning of Activity

In the fetus, irregular patterns of spontaneous activity punctuate the general inactive state of hatchlings and mammalian neonates (Corner 1977). Analysis of this activity frequently reveals primitive, embedded, patterns of several types. Microstructural (5–15 sec and 1–5 min) and ultradian (40–90 min) rhythms are typically apparent early, whereas circadian periodicities in activity usually emerge somewhat later in the postnatal period (McGinty & Siegel 1983; Parmelee 1983; Sostek & Anders 1981).

For many species of birds and mammals, there is evidence for continuity of microstructural and ultradian activity rhythms from the fetus to the neonate (Corner 1977). The repeated 5–15 sec periods of spontaneous motility that characterize fetal activity, for example, are readily observed in active sleep and waking activity in infants. Similar bursting patterns are even found within adult active or rapid-eye-movement (REM) sleep (Corner & Kwee 1976). Corner (1977) suggests that these activity bursts represent the continued expression of primordial rhythmic organization that originated during early developmental and evolutionary stages. Slightly longer periodicities of 1–10 min are also observed in mammalian fetuses and neonates (Jouvet-Mounier et al 1970; Robertson et al 1982) and just before and after hatching in chicks (Corner 1977; Oppenheim 1973). Moreover, ultradian activity rhythms of 30–60 min, which have been identified in fetuses, are discernible in the activity patterns of mammalian infants [e.g. rats (Richter 1927; Teicher & Flaum 1979), humans (Parmelee 1974; Sterman 1972)]. Ultradian activity becomes increasingly distinct and regular within a short period after birth (Corner 1977; Teicher & Flaum 1979) and is particularly obvious when infants are studied in isolation from external stimuli. These periodicities in activity and inactivity, termed basic rest-activity cycles (Kleitman 1963), ride on the later appearing sleep/wake cycle and define periods of active (REM) sleep as well as heightened activity during waking (Parmelee 1983). Thus the activity pattern associated with REM sleep emerges before the distinction between sleep and waking (Sterman 1972).

For most species studied, sleep and waking, while somewhat ambiguous and undifferentiated, can be behaviorally identified shortly after birth (e.g. by types of movement). For altricial animals, cortical electrophysiological characteristics are immature and show few between-state differences (Gramsbergen 1974; Jouvet-Mounier et al 1970; McGinty et al 1977; McGinty & Siegel 1983). In part because of immature electrophysiological characteristics, the simple terms "quiet" and "active" are used to distinguish sleep stages in altricial infants. In humans and guinea pigs, electrophysiological activity is more mature, and REM indices (in EEG and EMG) can be traced back to the late fetal period (McGinty & Siegel 1983).

At birth, the relative amount of time spent in sleep is large, and this sleep is primarily active for all species (Sostek & Anders 1981; Parmelee 1983). For example, neonatal rats spend 70–90% of the day in apparent sleep, with about 40% of this sleep period identified as active (Gramsbergen 1974, 1976; Jouvet-Mounier et al 1970). The proportions of both sleep and active sleep rapidly decrease with age (e.g. Sterman 1972), and by two weeks of age, rats sleep only 60% of the day, with 15% of this period being active. This preponderance of sleep leaves neonates with limited time to direct towards other activities. This might be a disadvantage for food-getting, but many mammalian infants, such as rats, maintain suckling while they are sleeping (Shair et al 1984), and much of their day is spent awaiting milk delivery while asleep and attached to a nipple (Lincoln et al 1973). Infants of other species also exhibit coordinated ingestion as well as other motor activities during sleep (e.g. Petre-Quadens 1974; Wolff 1972).

The periodicities in sleep and waking (as for activity) become more distinct as infants move beyond the first few days of age (e.g. Harper et al 1981). It is assumed that events in neural maturation underly these changes and subserve the emergent patterning of activities (Hakamada et al 1981; Parmelee 1983; Prechtl 1977; Tamasy et al 1980). In fact, the development of day-to-day consistency in states (in terms of durations of each type) is indicative of the neurological status of infants and, for humans, is predictive of developmental problems in otherwise apparently normal infants (Prechtl 1981; Thoman et al 1981; Watt & Strongman 1985). Unfortunately, the specific neural substrates of these activity patterns are still poorly understood.

For altricial mammals, there is little evidence of 24-hr periodicities in general activity at birth, particularly when infants are observed in isolation from patterned stimulation (Teicher & Flaum 1979). Despite this absence of overt circadian patterns of activity in early infancy, there is good evidence that circadian neurobiological processes can influence certain behavioral and physiological responses (see Stratton 1982). For example, infant rats and primates possess endogenous neural circadian generators (Davis 1981; Snyder 1968). Such generators were initially shown in biochemical studies and have recently been confirmed by deoxyglucose metabolic mapping of neural activity cycles (Reppert & Schwartz 1983; Reppert 1986). Before birth, activity of the fetal suprachiasmatic nucleus (believed to be a major source of circadian signals) mirrors that of the mother (high activity during the day and low activity at night), and this maternal entrainment continues postnatally. This neural oscillator may partially explain why rats, as young as one day of age, exhibit shorter latencies to attach to a nipple and suckle during the maternal dark period (Dollinger et al 1980) than during the day (note, though, that because of maternal patterns of behavior, pups actually ingest more during the day). Other shifts in the efficacy or strength of behavior may also depend on circadian generators whose effects are not otherwise obvious.

Changes in activity and inactivity and modulation of activity by internal rhythms can also be viewed as changes in "reactivity" to external and internal stimuli, a perspective that relates these processes to the concept of motivational state and arousal (Zucker 1983). Thus, the organization of infant activity is frequently described in terms of the effects of infant state on infant reactivity (Hofer 1981a). Studies from such a perspective indicate complex interaction of state with the effects of particular types of infant stimulation (Prechtl 1977; Parmelee 1983; Rose 1983). For example, attention, orientation, and learning in human infants are related to behavioral state (Field 1981), and the variability in organized infant behavior is also related to shifts in state (Hofer 1981a; Thelen & Fisher 1983). For infant rodents, the latency of nipple attachment behavior and the vigor of sucking appear to be modulated by underlying state changes (Dollinger et al 1980; Henning & Gisel 1980). Moreover, movement towards the nest (homing), early learning, and responses to drugs are all influenced by the circadian pattern of activity (Infurna 1981). Endogenous patterns of activity are thus important factors in modulating the occurrence of behaviors during the perinatal period.

Modulation of Activity Patterns

Although we have focused on the behavioral patterning intrinsic to infants themselves, the normal occurrence of activity episodes and their differentiation into patterns is structured by events over which young organisms have little control. For example, the activity of recently hatched altricial birds and newborn mammals increases with time from feeding and is dramatically stimulated by arrival of a parent at the nest (e.g. Harper et al 1977; Wolff 1972); some mammals and particularly humans also show heightened activity in reaction to several aspects of parental behavior (Sander et al 1979). This activation is most impressive in species such as rabbits that receive only limited attention from the parents (Hudson & Distel 1982).

Parental contributions to organizing the circadian activity of infant rodents provides a good example of the subtle manner in which such entrainment can be accomplished. Although we have noted that isolated rodent infants do not have circadian patterns of general activity, from early ages, rat pups do show circadian patterns in some secondary measures such as food intake (Stern & Levin 1976). The ingestive activity of pups appears to be determined by the mother, since it quickly shifts if the mother is blinded and out of phase with previous patterning of pups. Moreover, even though independent circadian rhythmicities of the young pup are not apparent, the mother appears to be entraining an endogenous oscillator (e.g. the SCN activity noted above). The most important aspect of this entrainment seems to occur during the first 10 days of life, because after this time blind pups are resistant to having their ingestive period reset by mothers on different cycles (Sasaki et al 1984). Indeed, the mother is so important in initiating entrainment that if pups are artificially reared in isolation from the patterns of maternal stimulation they do not show patterned daily activity through 18 days of age, even if provided with normal light cues (Smith & Anderson 1984).

The parents' behavioral contribution to the patterning and regulation of many types of ongoing activity provides considerable structure for emerging behavioral and physiological processes of infants. Thus it is hardly surprising that isolation from such parental stimulation would have profound repercussions on behavior and physiology in neonates of many species (e.g. Hofer 1978; Levine 1983, 1986; Suomi et al 1983; Hoffman & Solomon 1974). These separation effects have attracted considerable attention because of their possible relevance for human development. In contrast to the prevailing interpretation of these effects in terms of infants' emotional responses to separation from an attachment figure, Hofer (1978) has argued that such effects might be better viewed as the effects of removing specific structural and regulatory contributions of the mother from their role in the ongoing function of infant systems. Hofer (1981b) has found that identifiable components of maternal care (behavioral, thermal, nutritive, etc) contribute to separable aspects of the effects of maternal deprivation. For example, increases in activity that occur with maternal deprivation in 2-week-old rats appear to result from deprivation of the mother's tactile stimulation. Heart rate changes, on the other hand, appear to be related to nutritive deprivation. Other findings are also compatible with Hofer's perspective. For instance, metabolically significant biochemical effects of separation in infant rats can be ameliorated with a highly specific form of brisk stroking that may mimic components of normal maternal behavior (Butler et al 1978; Schanberg et al 1979). Maternal stimulation also influences opiate release in infants (Kehoe & Blass 1986). Further, the loss of REM sleep, which occurs in both rats and primates in response to maternal deprivation (Astic & Jouvet-Mounier 1968; Hofer 1976; Reite et al 1974) and which may contribute to increased activity, may also depend on the absence of specific regulatory contributions from the mother.

Hofer has also made another point regarding the regulatory contribution of the mother; namely, the features of maternal stimulation that structure the mammalian infants' organization become increasingly complex during development (and are thus more difficult to identify). Separation effects that are attributable to the loss of simple support stimuli for young organisms are mediated by increasingly complex configurations of stimuli in older animals in which such mediation appears increasingly social. Examples of this progressive complexity of maternal cues is seen in pups' locomotor responses to deprivation (Campbell & Raskin 1978; Hofer 1981b) and in the increasing complexity of determinants of huddling and feeding (Alberts & Brunjes 1978; Johanson & Hall 1981).

Perceptual Capabilities

We noted earlier that sensory systems show differential ontogenies and thus make changing contributions to the activity and experience of the fetus and newborn. As infants begin to move about in the complex postnatal environment, the emergence of perceptual processes becomes a critical determinant of early organized behavior. Sensory/perceptual competence defines and constrains the range of reactivity of young animals. More importantly, in altricial young, such systems change rapidly in both peripheral and central function. Managing such postnatal change in perception must be viewed as a major challenge to altricial infants. Because of the availability of several recent compilations of reviews of sensory and perceptual development in human and nonhuman animals (two volumes edited by Aslin et al 1981; also see Aslin et al 1983; Banks & Salapatek 1983; Pedersen et al 1986), we have not included this topic in our discussion, and we refer the reader to these other informative sources.

Motor Coordination and Behavioral Subcomponents

What do infant organisms do during periods of activity? Analysis of the more specific topography of early behavior during these periods reveals both apparently directed and structured adaptive responses (e.g. those getting infants to the nest and parent, and those involved in feeding) as well as less complete fragments of behavior. The latter, more fragmentary, responses raise questions similar to those provoked by prenatal behavior: Are these behaviors merely anticipatory, or is there some necessity for them to occur or be practiced? As with fetal activity, both types of explanation no doubt apply, though there have been few specific tests. These postnatal behaviors provide information on the dynamics of motor organization and the nature of developmental change in behavioral systems (Fentress & McLeod 1986; Thelen 1985). Sporadic limb movements resembling locomotion, swimming, and grooming are good examples. The emergence of coordination in these sequences is an impressive aspect of development and is a continuation of processes that had their origin in the prenatal period. With the exception of gross body responses of certain species described earlier, coordinated postnatal activity typically proceeds (as *in utero*) in an intralimb to interlimb manner and in a roughly rostral-caudal fashion (Fentress 1981). As local patterns are differentiated, they are then integrated into more global sequences and relationships. The ontogeny of many behavior sequences reflects an obvious integration and recruitment of progressively more components [e.g. initiation of rodent locomotion (Golani et al 1981)].

The postnatal environment, however, strongly structures the expression of early motor sequences and complicates the interpretation of developmental events. These complications are obvious in response patterns related to posture and locomotion, particularly as they interact with different stages of physical development. In rats, for example, righting becomes efficient 2–3 days after birth (Bignall 1974). This early righting is accomplished with a whole body response that gives way to a more specific "corkscrew" movement of the trunk, and later a lateral rotation involving specific orientation of the limbs (Pellis & Teitelbaum 1983). However, this last form can actually be seen at early stages of development. Nonetheless, it is not frequently utilized, probably not because of neural immaturity but because relative sizes and weights of trunk, head, and limbs make it difficult or ineffective.

While locomotion in newborn rats is erratic, patterned limb movements during swimming [patterns closely related to locomotion, but for which many physical restrictions have been removed (Gruner & Altman 1980)] show a progressive coupling between limbs starting shortly after birth (Bekoff & Trainer 1979), with the coupling occurring first in forelimbs, then hindlimbs. The kicking behavior of human infants similarly becomes more coordinated. Interlimb patterning similar to that later used in walking can be observed in kicking (Thelen 1984). Moreover, although infant humans do not walk they will show an early "stepping" response when held erect (Zelazo 1983). "Infantile" stepping disappears during subsequent months, probably due more to increased limb weight and muscle weakness than to neural maturation (Thelen 1984). Thelen, in fact, argues that many of the developmental changes occurring in motor patterns may be functions of the changes in the physical requirements for movement, as well as of neural development, that interact with these changes. Other examples of physical limitations on locomotion can be noted: Young birds lacking muscles and feathered wings do not fly, but if appropriately stimulated (i.e. dropped) they will show coordinated wing-flapping shortly after hatching (Provine 1981b); Infant mice, if propped-up into a sitting position, will make grooming responses that they do not normally emit (Golani & Fentress 1985). These, as well as many other examples that could be cited, underscore the important role of environmental context for assessing the motoric capacities of developing animals. As noted previously, the failure of embryos and fetuses to perform certain coordinated behaviors may reflect the presence of powerful inhibitory mechanisms that are removed or released by the appropriate postnatal environmental context.

Central mechanisms for producing sequences of other complex behaviors exist in infant organisms and can be made manifest with an appropriate manipulation, appropriate in this case being a highly specific experimental context accompanied by a state of high arousal (Wolgin 1982). Such premature appearance of behaviors under high arousal has been demonstrated in birds (Andrew 1974) and mammals (e.g. Szechtman & Hall 1980). It has further been shown that prematurely elicited behaviors, such as those revealed in the behavioral excitement of rats to oral infusions of milk or to electrical stimulation of the medial forebrain bundle, become more coherent and controlled with age (Hall 1979; Moran et al 1983). In this regard, Williams has shown that under appropriate deprivation and temperature conditions, flank-stroking of newborn rats will elicit lordosis and what appears to be ear-wiggling (i.e. components of rodent female sexual responses), responses that are typically not seen until after puberty (Williams & Lorang 1985). Such responses become better coordinated with age but, interestingly, are more easily elicited in females than males and become hormonally modulated. These data provide additional evidence for the anticipatory presence of behavioral systems (see Carmichael 1954). Thus, besides anticipatory functions that can be observed in normal behavior of fetuses or newborns, neural systems for behavior can exist in anticipation of their use, but to observe them, the organism must be stimulated in atypical ways. Here, use or practice clearly is not required for development, since the behaviors are normally not expressed.

Although postnatal motor patterns can often be assigned some putative adaptive significance associated with environmental (i.e. sensory) regulation, the categorization of postnatal motor behavior into autogenic and reflexogenic, as derived from the prenatal period (see section on motor behavior), also continues to be a useful distinction. Despite the increasing importance of environmental cues for initiating and modifying postnatal motor patterns, the neurobiological substrates for many of these behaviors consist of endogenous pattern generators that are often activated spontaneously and play a central role in determining the pattern of the behavior. Similar to the situation with certain well-studied prenatal behaviors [e.g. swimming (see above)], some postnatal motor behaviors also do not appear to depend upon use, practice, or sensory input for their normal development or manifestation [e.g. wingless chick (Provine 1979), armless mice (Fentress 1973), and classic papers on restricted rearing of birds and flight; flight of moths and butterflies after metamorphosis; as well as walking in newborn precocial mammals such as sheep, horses, guinea pigs, etc (Marler & Hamilton 1966; Hinde 1970; Eibl-Eibesfeldt 1975)].

THE ORGANIZATION OF EARLY ADAPTIVE RESPONSES

The ability of animals to benefit from a postnatal period of growth and development is critically dependent on whether they [or, more broadly, the parent-infant unit (e.g. Alberts & Gubernick 1984; Galef 1981)] possess the coherent behavioral strategies needed to create an appropriate environment for development and to obtain the necessary foods and fluids for growth. There are two major adaptive needs related to such delayed postnatal development: (a) the creation of behavioral systems to accommodate the physical and organizational limitation of immature infants; and (b) the organization of this system so that it can adjust to the dynamic and dramatic developmental changes in size, shape, sensation, perception, and changing neural substrate in order to provide continuity in day-to-day function. The solutions that natural selection has provided to these problems define major phyletic lineages (e.g. mammals utilizing suckling/lactation) and, as will be discussed later, have likely contributed early developmental substrates for the evolution of other characteristics.

For many altricial avian species, continuity in the provision of warmth and food is accomplished by highly orchestrated parental behavior, which may or may not involve special physiological adaptations (e.g. crop milk, brood patches). Young are confined to a nest, are kept warm by parents, nest, or down, and their food is provided to them by the parents. These infants respond to a relatively simple visual stimulus associated with parental feeding [e.g. ring doves (Wortis 1969)]. Weaning usually involves a transition to another source of food, but one identified by stimuli in the same modality. Parental care represents an extension of incubation behaviors with addition of food provision, and the parents provide continuity to feeding and protection by maintaining their care for infants despite the infants' physical and behavioral maturation. Thus for birds, much of the burden of delayed development of altricial young is placed on the parent, especially the burden of early feeding.

Mammals, while similar to birds in the burden assumed by the lactating parent (i.e. in their presence at the nest and possession of specialized mechanisms of producing food for the young), are different in at least one significant way. Most infant altricial mammals must locate and identify the mammillary region, attach to the nipple, and withdraw milk. Such accomplishments are particularly striking in marsupial young, which are born at stages of morphological immaturity impressive even for mammalian young (Walker & Berger 1980). Moreover, the mammalian infant must somehow maintain this behavior throughout infancy, appropriately responding to the cues of the mother and nest, despite changes in sensation and perception and shifts in the modalities of relevant cues. Rosenblatt (1983) has reviewed these transitions for a number of species; Leonard (1982) provides an example of the role of neural maturation. In the following sections we discuss some of the contributions of young altricial infants to temperature maintenance and feeding, and we specifically consider systems that are relevant to the mammalian infant's continuity in responding during neural and somatic maturation.

Keeping Warm

There is a great deal of variability in the physiological and behavioral thermoregulatory capabilities of infant birds and mammals (Leon 1986). Both size and developmental rate are relevant factors in determining infant trade-offs between the use of energy for thermogenesis and growth. While most endothermal young do increase metabolic rate in response to cooling (e.g. that resulting from removal from the nest), this response is usually not sufficient to maintain temperature (even for the normal range of temperature variation that would characterize the environment of infants in highly protected environments such as burrows). While altricial infants may show a great physiological tolerance to temperature variation (Adolph 1968), for most species the maintenance of appropriate infant temperature ultimately depends on the nest-building and caretaking activities of the parent.

Nonetheless, behavioral thermoregulatory capabilities of the newborn can and do facilitate temperature regulation. In addition, these thermally mediated responses, while highly variable from species to species, may serve secondary functions and contribute in other fashions to developmental success (e.g. maintaining proximity to the nest). Kittens (Freeman & Rosenblatt 1978), hamsters (Leonard 1974), and rabbits (Hull & Hull 1982; Kleitman & Satinoff 1982) all move on a thermal gradient to regions of warmth if they are placed at sites below nest temperature, and rabbits will, in addition, move away from regions of high temperature. Hamsters are particularly quick to move towards warmth (Leonard 1974), and this response may be related to the fact that they show virtually no thermogenesis in the cold (Leon 1986). Preference for appropriate temperatures in infant rabbits appears to depend on a central thermostatic mechanism. Infants injected with a pyrogen, while not showing increased thermogenesis and fever, do choose to settle at higher temperatures on a thermal gradient (Satinoff et al 1976).

It was initially believed that rat pups did not show thermotaxis until they were 6 days old (Fowler & Kellogg 1975; Johanson 1979), but if given long periods of time and restricted temperature ranges, both neonatal rats and mice will settle at temperatures approximating nest temperature (Kleitman & Satinoff 1982). This active early behavioral response to temperature is consistent with the finding that young rat pups huddle with warm objects, independent of other cues (Alberts 1978a; Brunjes & Alberts 1979).

The thermotaxic response capabilities revealed by isolated infants on a thermal gradient probably contribute to thermoregulation in the nest by influencing the behavior of the huddle. In a cool environment, thermotaxis contributes to keeping the huddle clumped together (Alberts 1978b). Such clumping is very effective in retaining heat in cool environments, since it reduces the surface to volume ratio of the huddle. At warm temperatures, the clump disperses. All pups actively participate in this thermoregulatory behavior of the huddle and are observed to establish flow patterns in the huddle that resemble convection currents, with the direction of "pup flow" being determined by the ambient temperature (Alberts 1978b). The behavioral thermoregulatory system of altricial infants constitutes a significant adaptation that, along with the caretaking behavior of parents, provides the solution to the problem of thermal vulnerability and immaturity. This system, by helping maintain proximity to parents and siblings, helps establish opportunities for other adaptive functioning (e.g. Alberts & Gubernick 1984; Galef 1981; Rosenblatt 1983).

Thermal factors also contribute to the organization of the infant rodent's environment by influencing maternal periods in the nest. In an extensive series of studies, Leon and co-workers have shown that the duration of maternal bouts on the nest is limited by the increase in the mother's temperature that results from being with the litter (Leon et al 1978, 1985). A maternal rat does not directly respond to the litter's temperature, but responds indirectly when an increase in her own temperature becomes sufficient to signal the end to a nursing bout. Pups' temperature also may influence maternal behavior by stimulating ultrasonic vocalizations that serve to attract the mother (Geyer 1979; Noirot 1972; Okon 1972).

Getting Fed

The thermoregulatory capabilities of altricial infants have relatively obvious origins in the behavior of more primitive animals. Yet, success in thermal orientation to the mother and nest establishes the opportunity for a highly novel adaptation by infant mammals—suckling behavior. In species other than primates, the mother provides limited guidance in this process; she identifies her own young (e.g. Gubernick 1981) and makes her nipple region available to them. The lack of guidance is significant, for it highlights an impressive skill of mammalian young: namely, to be able to search out, identify, attach to, and procure food and fluid from the maternal nipple.

The suckling sequence in mammals (which begins with contact with the mother) typically involves searching the mother's ventrum with sweeping or scanning head movements, sometimes referred to as "rooting." When the area of a nipple is located, rooting stops and the infant probes into the ventrum with its mouth or snout. As contact with the nipple is made by the lips and tongue, the nipple is quickly brought into the mouth by a process of licking and grasping (Anokhin & Shuleikina 1977; Blass et al 1979; Distel & Hudson 1984; MacFarlane et al 1983). These responses are initially well-coordinated and become even better directed and more efficient with age (Hall et al 1977). The sequencing of components of suckling, and transitions from one to another, are dependent on the topography of the environment.

For rodents, whose suckling behavior is characteristic of many mammals, nipple search is energized and guided by odors of the nipple region (Hofer et al 1976; Teicher & Blass 1977). These odors are present as a result of the deposition of saliva or amniotic fluid during maternal licking of the ventrum or during pups' previous suckling (Pedersen & Blass 1982), or they are secreted in response to milk ejection (Singh & Hofer 1978). Prenatal chemo-sensory experiences may contribute to the initial responsiveness to the olfac-tory characteristics of these stimuli (Pedersen & Blass 1982) and thus may provide a potentially significant continuity from prenatal features of experi-ence into postnatal behavior (Gottlieb 1976b). Yet, the effects of such experi-ence may be short-lived since, as will be described below, infant rodents show a remarkable ability to learn about olfactory stimuli related to suckling and to adapt to new ingestive cues.

Olfactory stimulation is, as might be expected, only part of the perceptual array relevant to suckling. Direction of the searching response and recognition of the nipple depend on tactile inputs from the orofacial region that are conveyed by the trigeminal system. Disruption of trigeminal input eliminates nipple attachment in a number of species (Distel & Hudson 1985; Hofer et al 1981; Shuleikina-Turpaeva 1986), though in contrast to the disruption of olfactory systems, it does not seem to prevent the initiation of searching.

Once achieved, nipple attachment is maintained by intraoral negative pressure (e.g. Brake et al 1979). There are, however, considerable species differences in the duration of suckling periods, the pattern of suckling, and the behaviors used for milk-withdrawal and ingestion (Blass & Teicher 1980). For instance, some mammals suckle nearly continuously, receiving milk only episodically during this time (e.g. rodents); others suckle for brief periods at long intervals, quickly receiving their nutritive aliquot (e.g. rabbits, tree shrews). What is not clear at this point is the relationship between suckling activities of infants and the very obvious earlier swallowing seen *in utero* (e.g. Vince & Billing 1986). Since it has been suggested that suckling and feeding may have little in common (Hall & Williams 1983), it is possible that fetal activity is more representative of the maturation systems for early feeding than of those used immediately after birth for getting milk during suckling (Hall 1985). The latter are highly specialized responses, at least in rodents, and can themselves, under special conditions, be elicited *in utero* (W. P. Smotherman, personal communication).

Plasticity in Early Adaptive Response Systems

The altricial neonate is remarkably competent in securing vital resources. But these initial accomplishments obscure a second achievement: that of dealing with the constant change in perceived environment. The infant's size and shape are changing, its sensory systems are changing (with new modalities becoming progressively functional), responses required to find the nest and mother are changing, and for most mammalian infants, the brain undergoes postnatal differentiation, growth, and maturation of function that must contribute great flux to perceptual processes and motor organization. Altricial species have, no doubt, evolved means to deal with these instabilities. Conceptually, such solutions either could be based on a preexisting coding of all the readjustments necessary for each stage of development or they could be based on a plasticity of organization that allows transitions from one stage to the next. With respect to some of the adaptive systems we have just described, it would seem that the latter solution in terms of capacity for behavioral plasticity plays a major role in allowing animals to make regular transitions in the coding of stimuli and the organization of responses.

This point is clearly made by demonstrations of the role of experience in the maintenance of suckling. For most altricial species, the ability to suckle from the mother is reduced if suckling is not practiced [e.g. if animals are fed from cups, by gastric intubation, or even from artificial nipples (McKee & Honzik 1964; Blass et al 1979; Dollinger et al 1978; Rosenblatt 1971)]. This vulnerability of suckling can be contrasted to the robustness of feeding behavior, which emerges independent of experience during the preweaning period, and which, as noted above, can be artificially elicited throughout development, and even prenatally (Hall & Williams 1983). The dependence of suckling on experience suggests that the daily transitions in suckling behavior made by infant mammals depend on some form of learning and not on "hard-wired" solutions that anticipate developmental change (see Alberts & Gubernick 1984; Rosenblatt 1983). Indeed, such a perspective on the utility of early learning helps explain why virtually all of the organized maternally oriented behavior of most infant animals can be shown to be heavily influenced by experienced events (Rovee-Collier & Lipsitt 1982).

The impressive learning capabilities of infant altricial animals are clearly revealed in numerous studies using cues that are in some way related to the parents or early ingestion. Hatchlings become increasingly reactive to cues from their parents (e.g. Sieber 1985), learning to recognize those that signal food availability. Human newborns show rapid learning of anticipatory mouthing responses to tactile cues that signal a sugar solution (Blass et al 1984; Lipsitt et al 1977). Rodent infants, as well, quickly come to show conditioned activity to cues (particularly olfactory cues) that are paired with feeding (Johanson et al 1984). This type of conditioned activation may play a normal role in the anticipation of the availability of the mother or food and contribute to more effective attachment on the pups' part and stimulation of lactation on the mother's part [in rabbits (Hudson 1985)]. Such learning appears Pavlovian in the manner that conditioning occurs and may have specific selective advantages for the mother/litter unit (see Hollis 1984).

At the same time that specific anticipatory responses to the mother's arrival are being learned by the mammalian infant, the learned stimuli also acquire new values in terms of infants' preference or orientation (Lipsitt 1977). In neonate rodents this process has been well demonstrated for olfactory stimuli. Novel odors paired with the mother (Brake 1981) or with maternal-like stimulation (Pedersen et al 1982) become preferred in tests of olfactory orientation. Indeed, the conditioning process is so robust that any of the previously described forms of stimulation that produce behavioral arousal appear to support it (e.g. physical stimulation from the mother, oral infusions of milk, brain stimulation, etc). The relationship to arousal suggests a parallel between this impressive form of mammalian learning and more temporally restricted forms of auditory and visual imprinting in birds, which are also influenced by arousal-inducing parental stimulation.

Many of these early learning capabilities were neglected or unnoticed until recent years, when investigators began to attend to the special features of early behavior and environments (Lipsitt 1970; Campbell & Coulter 1976; Spear & Kucharski 1984). The discovery of such capabilities largely depended on studying infants, or at least conceptualizing the methodology, in terms of the natural response repertoire or natural conditions of the young organism. The prevalence of early learning is now seen to provide for a plasticity-based transition through stages of early development.

Research by developmental psychobiologists has also revealed that infant animals are quite capable of learning about unpleasant or aversive events. In fact, aversive conditioning was demonstrated long before appetitive conditioning in infants (see review by Campbell 1984). For instance, a few days after birth, infant rats will learn to withhold movement into an area if shocked there (Nagy 1979) and to avoid odors that have been paired either with shock or illness (Kucharski & Spear 1984; Rudy & Cheatle 1977). Young chicks learn in a single trial to avoid pecking at a bitter target (Cherkin 1969), and this training is being used extensively in the study of mechanisms of learning and memory formation (e.g. Gibbs & Ng 1977). Such rapid aversive learning may also serve transitional functions in allowing infants to adjust rapidly to features of their physical surroundings. Instructively, however, there appear to exist mechanisms that protect infants against certain kinds of aversive conditioning. Infant rats, for example, do not learn aversions to tastes if the tastes are experienced during normal suckling (Martin & Alberts 1979). Learning aversions to mother's milk would, of course, be maladaptive, since even if milk occasionally produces illness, it is still the young infant's only source of nourishment. The mechanism for this block may depend on some perceptual effect of suckling or milk-getting (Martin & Alberts 1979; Gubernick & Alberts 1984), or it may simply result because milk is delivered far back in the mouth in rodent sucking and may not stimulate many taste receptors (Kehoe & Blass 1986).

Even though infants seem to be competent learners, with the exception of certain cues related to later social or sexual behavior, they appear to have poor long-term memory—a phenomenon referred to as "infantile amnesia" (see Campbell 1984). This poor memory can perhaps be better understood in the context of the dilemma of altricial infants: How to maintain a continuity of responding during a dynamic period of development. The neonate has little need for a long memory; in fact, its major learning requirement is simply for mechanisms that allow consistent behavioral accomplishment from one day to the next. Indeed it may benefit from a capacity to forget cues that might activate inappropriate responses. Amnesia for early events may occur because memory processes are immature or because stimulus perception changes and conditioned stimuli are not equivalently decoded at later ages. In fact, it is interesting that long-term memory capacities only appear to mature in rodents at about the time that physical development is fairly complete and infants have adopted the adult mode of feeding and locomotion (Rudy et al 1984). These demonstrations of late maturing memory substrates are instructive. They argue that permanence is not a feature of early learning, nor even desirable; that the fundamental learning capabilities that have evolved to subserve behavioral transitions during maturation do not require long-lasting memory storage.

THE SIGNIFICANCE OF EARLY BEHAVIOR

The goals of developmental psychobiology encompass issues common to the entire field of organismic development and include (*a*) a description of the onset and differentiation of specific behaviors and their neurobiological bases; (*b*) an analysis of the mechanisms by which neurobehavioral events change and become organized into adult forms during ontogeny; and (*c*) attempts to understand neurobehavioral phenomena during development within the broader biological context of evolution, in which questions concerning the adaptiveness or survival value of particular ontogenetic events and strategies are paramount. Having summarized some of the neurobehavioral phenomena that characterize early periods in development, we would like to turn to the issue of the evolutionary context of ontogenetic events and to illustrate it with a discussion of both prenatal and postnatal phenomena. An instructive starting point is to consider the question, What is the adaptive role of early behavior, especially the undifferentiated behavior of the fetus? Examination of this question should provide a framework for thinking about the purpose and significance of early behavior in general.

Considered within the context of postnatal survival value, the occurrence of prenatal behavior is, on the face of it, a paradox. Most embryos are relatively well-protected *in ovo* or *in utero* with their nutritional and other biological needs largely taken care of by "passive" mechanisms requiring little, if any, active behavioral contribution on their part. Enclosed within the egg or uterus there is little, if anything, that the embryo can do behaviorally that would be effective in adaptively responding to environmental stimuli. As we have discussed, after birth or hatching, survival needs become more explicit and can be employed in explaining the putative adaptive value of behavior. By contrast, it is more difficult to appreciate embryonic or fetal behavior in terms of adaptation to immediate needs. We suggest three categories of explanation to help account for the early appearance of behavior. Each relates in a different way to evolutionary processes.

1. For any early behavior (at the time it initially appears or first can be elicited), the initial emergence of a behavior pattern may simply represent an epiphenomenon reflecting the "anticipatory" onset of a function that will only become adaptive at some later age, but which is itself of no immediate adaptive value. Logically, a system cannot be used until it exists, and a formative period is an obvious necessity. Early function would thus be viewed as simply a sign that this process is underway. Some of the most interesting questions regarding this process concern the degree to which a system undergoing construction may be protected from premature use.

2. Early behavior may also represent necessary antecedents to later behavior which, when suppressed, perturbed, or inadequately stimulated, result in the abnormal, maladaptive expression of postnatal behavior and atypical development of its neurobiological substrates. This explanation establishes the value of early behavior in terms of its contribution to a system of later utility.

3. Finally, early behavior may serve some immediate adaptive role for the embryo, fetus, or infant (ontogenetic adaptation).

Before we discuss evidence illustrating these categories, we wish to point out that these possibilities are by no means mutually exclusive. Depending upon the species, the stage of development, the specific behavior in question, or the part of the nervous system involved, early behaviors may occur for each of these reasons. In particular, considerations related to the first explanation are likely to apply to all behaviors at early stages.

The second explanation for early behavior, that it may be an essential antecedent in the emergence of postnatal behaviors, is obviously of great interest for psychobiologists. The evidence for its applicability to prenatal behavior patterns, however, is limited. As discussed previously, by late prenatal stages, many vertebrate embryos exhibit movements, movement patterns (both spatial and temporal), and sensory responses that resemble patterns seen postnatally. In at least some cases these movements appear to be derived from less well-organized movements that occur at even earlier pre-natal stages (Hamburger & Oppenheim 1967; Bekoff 1986; Provine 1980, 1986). However, with only a few exceptions—including the few cases discussed previously, in which certain postnatal behaviors were shown to depend upon exposure to normally occurring sensory stimuli *in ovo* or *in utero*—the causal relationships between the early and later occurring events have not been rigorously explored experimentally.

One instructive exception involves the development of swimming in amphibian embryos. Older as well as more contemporary studies have now shown conclusively that the pharmacological suppression of all impulse activity (and thus of all behavior) in the nervous system of amphibian embryos from the pre-myogenic stage to the time when swimming is well-developed does not impair the ability of the tadpole to exhibit normal swimming behavior when the suppressing drug is removed (Haverkamp & Oppenheim 1986; Harrison 1904; Matthews & Detwiler 1926; Fromme 1941; Carmichael 1926, 1927). Detailed analyses following such treatment have failed to detect any quantitative or qualitative deficits in swimming. Moreover, the anatomical and neurophysiological substrates of swimming have also been examined in these preparations and were found to be indistinguishable from normal tadpoles (Haverkamp 1986). On the basis of these findings it can be concluded that the embryonic behaviors leading up to swimming are not necessary for either the normal emergence of this complex behavior pattern or for the development of its underlying neurobiological substrate. Furthermore, because the experimental treatment used here also produced a functional deafferentation, it can be concluded that sensory input is also unnecessary for the development of this behavior (also see Kahn & Roberts 1982; Stehouwer & Farel 1981). Although analogous experiments with avian embryos have resulted in similar findings (Oppenheim et al 1978; Landmesser et al 1985), it remains to be seen whether or not the prenatal behavior of mammals (or postnatal behavior that is not obviously adaptive) is directly involved either in the development of the nervous system or in the emergence of postnatal behavior. Thus despite the potential value of this explanatory category for understanding early behavior, the findings from amphibians and birds should serve as a cautionary note that neurobehavioral ontogeny does not necessarily represent a series of causally linked events extending back into the embryo. As appealing as such a view may be, it seems clear that what, on the basis of observations, appear to be obvious connections between early ontogenetic events and later behavior may reflect little more than the persistence of common functional substrates that do not require expression at an earlier stage for their maintenance or expression at a later stage of development.

The third explanation of the origins or cause of early behavior is that many early behaviors may represent "ontogenetic adaptations" to the environmental demands of particular developmental stages. One of us has extensively reviewed the literature relevant to ontogenetic adaptations as explanations for prenatal behaviors (Oppenheim 1981, 1984). Briefly, numerous examples exist, ranging from hatching behavior in egg-laying vertebrates and invertebrates and behavioral alterations in fetal position in mammals in preparation for birth, to the role of fetal movements for normal musculoskeletal development (see Oppenheim 1985). In fact, a major role of autogenic or spontaneous movement in many vertebrate embryos appears to be the regulation of musculoskeletal development. Following chronic, experimentally induced paralysis, the skeletal muscles atrophy and fail to develop many of their normal histological, biochemical, and functional properties, and the joints between the bones in the limbs and vertebra fail to form, resulting in severe ankylosis or joint stiffness (Oppenheim et al 1978; Murray & Drachman 1969). Similar defects are observed in mammalian fetuses with naturally occurring (i.e. due to genetic or congenital factors) movement disorders (Pai 1965; Rieger & Pincon-Raymond 1981; Oppenheim et al 1986).

Ontogenetic adaptation as an explanation for unique, age-specific behaviors is even more compelling postnatally, when specialized behavior patterns are required to solve the environmental demands resulting from morphological and physiological immaturity (Oppenheim 1981; Hofer 1981a). Suckling behavior is a good example. It serves the needs (nutritional and otherwise) of infant mammals, yet appears to be completely lost as a response mechanism in the adults of most species (Blass et al 1979). In fact, during the period that suckling is being used by mammals, more adult-like feeding capabilities exist but are not utilized (Hall & Williams 1983) and may even be actively suppressed to prevent ingestion of inappropriate substances (Hall & Browde 1986). Highly specialized ontogenetic adaptations such as suckling become most apparent for species in which birth or hatching has, during the course of evolution (for other selective reasons), moved to earlier stages in which animals are still relatively immature. Rather than relying on the stability of the egg or uterus, infants of such species have evolved

techniques to deal with the phylogenetically novel situation of finding themselves in a challenging environment but not having adult characteristics or
capabilities. Early birth or hatching has, in fact, produced a variety of
strategies, both behavioral and physiological, on the part of parents and
infants. These solutions distinguish both species and phyla.

We call attention to the adaptations of developing animals because we
believe these phenomena have greater evolutionary significance than is immediately apparent. The more obvious ontogenetic adaptations are the ones
that attract our notice by their disappearance. But, it is likely that many early
adaptations persist and, though they may have initially arisen to deal with
early needs, that they are exploited at later stages in development as well.
Indeed, novel ontogenetic adaptations may create special evolutionary opportunities by shifting development towards new capabilities and niches. Expressed in another manner, evolution can proceed by adding new characteristics to the end of the development sequence, by altering the relative rates of
development of different characteristics, or by inserting new characteristics
early in the developmental sequence (Gould 1977). The latter process may be
most relevant when other selection pressures have favored earlier separation
from the prenatal or prehatch environment and thus require the evolution of
ontogenetic adaptations. Recognition of the more striking (though transient)
adaptations of early life should emphasize the possibility of other developmental adaptations that extend to later life, and whose selective advantage might otherwise be mistakenly interpreted in terms of later selection
pressures.

Recent research by developmental psychobiologists has, in fact, revealed
the richness of behavioral capabilities and sensitivities of altricial infants. The
need to solve the problem of thermoregulation in the immature infant may, for
example, have been the origin of systems that could provide neurobehavioral
substrates that later differentiate to subserve social interaction and other
behaviors. The identification of individual response systems in early physiology and behavior (e.g. those that contribute to the effects of maternal separation) represents a step towards identifying the specific initial origins of later
coherent response capabilities and the manner in which such responses may
have initially been based on unique adaptive needs of the immature infant
(Hofer 1981b). Intriguing in a similar regard is the demonstration of a high
degree of behavioral plasticity in infant mammals, along with indications that
this capacity may represent an evolutionary solution to the dynamic perceptual demands of immaturity. The early emerging substrates for such
plasticity may represent the origins of mammalian capabilities for exploitation
of niches requiring great behavioral flexibility. Thus we view the adaptations
of infancy, both those that are transient and those that may be the source of
further adaptive accomplishment, as central to our understanding of de-

velopmental processes. We expect that studies of these adaptations will figure prominently in the work of developmental psychobiologists in the next decades.

ACKNOWLEDGMENTS

We are grateful to S. Coyle, C. O. Eckerman, D. Kucharski, C. B. Phifer, and L. Terry for helpful comments on an earlier version of this review and to K. McCall for assistance in preparation of the manuscript. Portions of our own work described in this review have been supported by NIH grants NS-20402 (RWO) and HD-17457-8 (WGH).

Literature Cited

Adolph, E. F. 1968. *The Origins of Physiological Regulations*. New York: Academic

Alberts, J. R. 1978a. Huddling by rat pups: Multisensory control of contact behavior. *J. Comp. Physiol. Psychol.* 92:220–31

Alberts, J. R. 1978b. Huddling by rat pups: Group behavioral mechanisms of temperature regulation and energy conservation. *J. Comp. Physiol. Psychol.* 92:231–46

Alberts, J. R., Brunjes, P. C. 1978. Ontogeny of thermal and olfactory determinants of huddling in the rat. *J. Comp. Physiol. Psychol.* 92:897–907

Alberts, J. R., Gubernick, D. J. 1983. Reciprocity and resource exchange: A symbiotic model of parent-offspring relations. In *Symbiosis in Parent-Young Interactions*, ed. H. Moltz, L. Rosenblum, pp. 7–44. New York: Plenum

Alberts, J. R., Gubernick, D. J. 1984. Early learning as ontogenetic adaptation for ingestion by rats. *Learn. Motiv.* 15:334–59

Andrew, R. J. 1974. Arousal and the causation of behavior. *Behavior* 51:135–65

Anokhin, P. K., Shuleikina, K. V. 1977. System organization of alimentary behavior in the newborn and the developing cat. *Dev. Psychobiol.* 10:385–419

Archer, S. M., Dubin, M. W., Slavis, L. A. 1982. Abnormal development of kitten retino-geniculate connectivity in the absence of action potentials. *Science* 217:743–45

Aslin, R. N., Alberts, J. R., Petersen, M. R., eds. 1981. *Development of Perception: Psychobiological Perspectives*, Vol. 1, Vol. 2. New York: Academic. 463 pp., 387 pp.

Aslin, R. N., Pisoni, D. B., Jusczyk, P. W. 1983. Auditory development and speech perception in infancy. In *Handbook of Child Psychology, Vol. 2, Infancy and Developmental Psychobiology*, ed. P. H. Mussen, pp. 573–688. New York: Wiley

Astic, L., Jouvet-Mounier, D. 1968. Effets du sevrage en fonction de l'âge sur le cycle veille-sommeil chez le cobaye. *J. Physiol.* 60:389

Baldwin, J. M. 1940. *Dictionary of Psychology and Philosophy*. New York: Macmillan

Banks, M. S., Salapatek, P. 1983. Infant visual perception. See Aslin et al 1983, pp. 435–572

Barcroft, J., Barron, D. H. 1939. The development of behavior in foetal sheep. *J. Comp. Neurol.* 70:477–502

Bekoff, A. 1976. Ontogeny of leg motor output in the chick embryo: A neural analysis. *Brain Res.* 106:271–91

Bekoff, A. 1981. Embryonic development of the neural circuitry underlying motor coordination. In *Studies in Developmental Neurobiology: Essays in Honor of Viktor Hamburger*, ed. W. M. Cowan, pp. 134–70. Oxford/New York: Oxford

Bekoff, A. 1986. Ontogeny of chicken motor behavior: Evidence for multi-use limb pattern generating circuitry. In *Neurobiology of Vertebrate Locomotion*, ed. S. Grillner, P. Stein, R. Herman, P. Wallen. Hampshire, England: Macmillan. In press

Bekoff, A., Trainer, W. 1979. The development of interlimb coordination during swimming in postnatal rats. *J. Exp. Biol.* 83:1–12

Bignall, K. E. 1974. Ontogeny of levels of neural organization: The righting reflex as a model. *Exp. Neurol.* 42:566–73

Birnholz, J. C., Benacerraf, B. R. 1983. The development of human fetal hearing. *Science* 222:516–18

Birnholz, J. C., Stephens, J. C., Furia, M. 1978. Fetal movement patterns: A possible means of defining neurologic developmental milestones *in utero*. *Am. J. Roentgenol.* 130:537–40

Blass, E. M., Ganchrow, J. R., Steiner, J. E. 1984. Classical conditioning in newborn humans 2–48 hours of age. *Infant Behav. Dev.* 7:223–35

Blass, E. M., Hall, W. G., Teicher, M. H. 1979. The ontogeny of suckling and ingestive behaviors. In *Progress in Psychobiology and Physiological Psychology*, Vol. 8, ed. J. M. Sprague, A. N. Epstein, pp. 243–99. New York: Academic

Blass, E. M., Teicher, M. H. 1980. Suckling. *Science* 210:15–22

Bonner, J. T. 1958. *The Evolution of Development*. Cambridge: Univ. Press

Boring, E. G. 1950. *A History of Experimental Psychology*. New York: Appleton-Century-Crofts

Bradley, R. M., Mistretta, C. M. 1975. Fetal sensory receptors. *Physiol. Rev.* 55:352–82

Brake, S. C. 1981. Suckling infant rats learn a preference for a novel olfactory stimulus paired with milk delivery. *Science* 211:506–8

Brake, S. C., Wolfson, V., Hofer, M. A. 1979. Electromyographic patterns associated with nonnutritive sucking in 11–13-day-old rat pups. *J. Comp. Physiol. Psychol.* 93:760–70

Brunjes, P. C., Alberts, J. R. 1979. Olfactory stimulation induces filial preferences for huddling in rat pups. *J. Comp. Physiol. Psychol.* 93:548–55

Butler, S. R., Suskind, M. R., Schanberg, S. M. 1978. Maternal behavior as a regulator of polyamine biosynthesis in brain and heart of the developing rat pup. *Science* 199:445–47

Campbell, B. A. 1984. Reflections on the ontogeny of learning and memory. In *Comparative Perspectives on the Development of Memory*, ed. R. Kail, N. E. Spear, pp. 23–38. Hillsdale, NJ: Erlbaum

Campbell, B. A., Coulter, X. 1976. The ontogenesis of learning and memory. In *Neural Mechanisms of Learning and Memory*, ed. M. R. Rosenzweig, E. L. Bennett, pp. 209–35. Cambridge, MA: MIT Press

Campbell, B. A., Raskin, L. A. 1978. Ontogeny of behavioral arousal: The role of environmental stimuli. *J. Comp. Physiol. Psychol.* 92:176–84

Carmichael, L. 1926. The development of behavior in vertebrates experimentally removed from the influence of external stimulation. *Psychol. Rev.* 33:51–58

Carmichael, L. 1927. A further study of the development of behavior in vertebrates experimentally removed from the influence of external stimulation. *Psychol. Rev.* 34:34–47

Carmichael, L. 1954. The onset and early development of behavior. In *Manual of Child Psychology*, ed. L. Carmichael, pp. 60–214. New York: Wiley

Carmichael, L. 1970. The onset and early development of behavior. In *Carmichael's Manual of Child Psychology*, ed. P. H. Mussen, 1:447–563. New York: Wiley

Cherkin, A. 1969. Kinetics of memory consolidation: Role of amnesic treatment parameters. *Proc. Natl. Acad. Sci. USA* 63:1094–1101

Coghill, G. E. 1929. *Anatomy and the Problem of Behavior*. Cambridge: Univ. Press

Corner, M. A. 1977. Sleep and the beginnings of behavior in the animal kingdom—studies of ultradian motility cycles in early life. *Prog. Neurobiol.* 8:279–95

Corner, M. A., Bot, A. P. C. 1967. Somatic motility during the embryonic period of birds and its relation to behavior after hatching. *Prog. Brain Res.* 26:214–36

Corner, M. A., Bour, H., Mirmiran, M. 1979. Development of spontaneous motility and its physiological interpretation in the rat, chick and frog. In *Neural Growth and Differentiation*, ed. E. Meisami, M. Brazier, pp. 253–67. New York: Raven

Corner, M. A., Kwee, P. 1976. Cyclic EEG and motility patterns during sleep in restrained infant rats. *Electroencephalogr. Clin. Neurophysiol.* 41:64–72

Davis, F. C. 1981. Ontogeny of Circadian Rhythms. In *Handbook of Behavioral Neurobiology*, Vol. 4, *Biological Rhythms*, ed. J. Aschoff, pp. 257–74. New York: Plenum

Dawes, G. S. 1984. Fetal physiology and behavior: Changing direction 1954–1983. *J. Dev. Physiol.* 6:259–65

DeCasper, A. H., Fifer, W. P. 1980. Of human bonding: Newborns prefer their mothers' voices. *Science* 208:1174–76

Distel, H., Hudson, R. 1984. Nipple-search performance by rabbit pups—changes with age and time of day. *Anim. Behav.* 32:501–7

Distel, H., Hudson, R. 1985. The contribution of the olfactory and tactile modalities to the nipple-search behaviour of newborn rabbits. *J. Comp. Physiol. A* 157:599–605

Dollinger, M. J., Holloway, W. R., Denenberg, V. H. 1978. Nipple attachment in rats during the first 24 hours of life. *J. Comp. Physiol. Psychol.* 92:619–27

Dollinger, M. J., Holloway, W. R., Denenberg, V. H. 1980. The development of behavioral competence in the rat. In *Maternal Behavior and Early Influences*, ed. R. W. Bell, W. P. Smotherman, pp. 27–56. New York: Spectrum

Drever, J. 1952. *A Dictionary of Psychology*. Baltimore: Penguin

Dunlap, K. 1914. *An Outline of Psychobiology*. Baltimore: The Johns Hopkins Press

Eibl-Eibesfeldt, I. 1975. *Ethology: The Biology of Behavior*. New York: Holt, Rinehart, Winston

Evans, R. M. 1973. Differential responsiveness of young ring-billed gulls and herring gulls to adult vocalizations of their own and other species. *Can. J. Zool.* 51:759–70

Fentress, J. C. 1973. Development of grooming in mice with amputated forelimbs. *Science* 179:704–5

Fentress, J. C. 1981. Order in ontogeny: Relational dynamics. In *Behavioral Development*, ed. K. Immelmann, G. Barlow, M. Main, L. Petrinovich, pp. 338–71. New York: Cambridge Univ. Press

Fentress, J. C., McLeod, P. J. 1986. Motor patterns in development. In *Handbook of Behavioral Neurobiology, Vol. 8, Developmental Psychobiology and Developmental Neurobiology*, ed. E. M. Blass, pp. 35–97. New York: Plenum

Field, T. 1981. Infant arousal, attention and affect during early interactions. In *Advances in Infancy Research*, ed. L. P. Lipsitt, C. K. Rovee-Collier, 1:57–100. Norwood, NJ: Ablex

Fowler, S. J., Kellogg, C. 1975. Ontogeny of thermoregulatory mechanisms in the rat. *J. Comp. Physiol. Psychol.* 89:738–46

Freeman, N. C. G., Rosenblatt, J. S. 1978. The interrelationship between thermal and olfactory stimulation in the development of home orientation in newborn kittens. *Dev. Psychobiol.* 11:437–57

Fromme, A. 1941. An experimental study of the factors of maturation and practice in the behavioral development of the embryo of the frog *Rama pipiens*. *Genet. Psychol. Monogr.* 24:219–56

Galef, B. G. 1981. The ecology of weaning: Parasitism and the achievement of independence by altricial mammals. See Gubernick 1981, pp. 211–42

Gates, E. 1894. The science of mentation and some new general methods of psychologic research. *The Monist* 5:574–97

Geyer, L. A. 1979. Olfactory and thermal influences on ultrasonic vocalization during development in rodents. *Am. Zool.* 19:421–30

Gibbs, M. E., Ng, K. T. 1977. Psychobiology of memory: Towards a model of memory formation. *Biobehavioral Rev.* 1:113–36

Golani, I., Bronchti, G., Moualem, D., Teitelbaum, P. 1981. "Warm up" along dimensions of movement in the ontogeny of exploratory behavior in the infant rat and other infant mammals. *Proc. Natl. Acad. Sci. USA* 78:7226–29

Golani, I., Fentress, J. C. 1985. Early ontogeny of face grooming in mice. *Dev. Psychobiol.* 18:529–44

Gottlieb, G. 1968. Prenatal behavior of birds. *Q. Rev. Biol.* 43:148–74

Gottlieb, G. 1971. Ontogenesis of sensory function in birds and mammals. In *The Biopsychology of Development*, ed. E. Tobach, L. Avonson, E. Shaw, pp. 67–128. New York: Academic

Gottlieb, G., ed. 1973. *Studies on the Development of Behavior and the Nervous System: Behavioral Embryology*. New York: Academic

Gottlieb, G. 1976a. Early development of species-specific auditory perception in birds. In *Studies on the Development of Behavior and the Nervous System: Neural and Behavioral Specificity*, ed. G. Gottlieb, pp. 237–80. New York: Academic

Gottlieb, G. 1976b. Conceptions of prenatal development: Behavioral embryology. *Psychol. Rev.* 83:215–34

Gottlieb, G. 1983. The psychobiological approach to developmental issues. See Aslin et al 1983, pp. 1–26

Gottlieb, G., Kuo, Z. Y. 1965. Development of behavior in the duck embryo. *J. Comp. Physiol. Psychol.* 59:183–88

Gould, S. J. 1977. *Ontogeny and Phylogeny*. Cambridge, Mass: Belknap

Gramsbergen, A. 1974. Neuro-ontogeny of sleep in the rat. See Petre-Quadens 1974, pp. 339–53

Gramsbergen, A. 1976. The development of EEG in the rat. *Dev. Psychobiol.* 9:501–13

Gruner, J. A., Altman, J. 1980. Swimming in the rat: Analysis of locomotor performance in comparison to stepping. *Exp. Brain Res.* 40:374–82

Gubernick, D. J. 1981. Parent and infant attachment in mammals. In *Parental Care in Mammals*, ed. D. J. Gubernick, P. H. Klopfer, pp. 243–305. New York: Plenum

Gubernick, D. J., Alberts, J. R. 1984. A specialization of taste aversion learning during suckling and its weaning-associated transformation. *Dev. Psychobiol.* 17:613–28

Hakamada, S., Watanabe, K., Hara, K., Miyazaki, S. 1981. Development of the motor behavior during sleep in newborn infants. *Brain Dev.* 3:345–50

Hall, W. G. 1979. The ontogeny of feeding in rats: I. Ingestive and behavioral responses to oral infusions. *J. Comp. Physiol. Psychol.* 93:977–1000

Hall, W. G. 1985. What we know and don't know about the development of independent ingestion in rats. *Appetite* 6:333–56

Hall, W. G., Browde, J. A. Jr. 1986. The ontogeny of independent ingestion in mice: Or, why won't infant mice feed? *Dev. Psychobiol.* 19:211–22

Hall, W. G., Cramer, C. P., Blass, E. M. 1977. The ontogeny of suckling in rats. *J. Comp. Physiol. Psychol.* 91:1141–55

Hall, W. G., Williams, C. L. 1983. Suckling isn't feeding, or is it? A search for developmental continuities. *Adv. Study Behav.* 13:219–55

Hamburger, V. 1963. Some aspects of the embryology of behavior. *Q. Rev. Biol.* 38:342–65

Hamburger, V. 1973. Anatomical and physiological basis of embryonic motility in birds and mammals. See Gottlieb 1973, pp. 52–76

Hamburger, V., Oppenheim, R. W. 1967. Prehatching motility and hatching behavior in the chick. *J. Exp. Zool.* 166:171–204

Hamburger, V., Wenger, E., Oppenheim, R. W. 1966. Motility in the chick and embryo in the absence of sensory input. *J. Exp. Zool.* 162:133–60

Harper, R. M., Hoppenbrouwers, T., Bannett, D., Hodgman, J., Sterman, M. B., McGinty, D. J. 1977. Effects of feeding on state and cardiac regulation in the infant. *Dev. Psychobiol.* 10:507–17

Harper, R. M., Leake, B., Miyahara, L., Mason, J., Hoppenbrouwers, T., et al. 1981. Temporal sequencing in sleep and waking states during the first 6 months of life. *Exp. Neurol.* 72:294–307

Harris, W. A. 1981. Neural activity and development. *Ann. Rev. Physiol.* 43:689–710

Harriman, P. L. 1969. *Handbook of Psychological Terms.* Totowa, NJ: Littlefield, Adams

Harrison, R. G. 1904. An experimental study of the relation of the nervous system to the developing musculature in the embryo of the frog. *Am. J. Anat.* 3:197–220

Haverkamp, L. 1986. Anatomical and physiological development of the *Xenopus* embryonic motor system in the absence of neural activity. *J. Neurosci.* 6:1332–37

Haverkamp, L., Oppenheim, R. W. 1986. Behavioral development in the absence of neural activity: Effects of chronic immobilization on amphibian embryos. *J. Neurosci.* 6:1338–48

Henning, S. J., Gisel, E. G. 1980. Nocturnal feeding behavior in the neonatal rat. *Physiol. Behav.* 25:603–5

Herrick, C. J. 1949. *George Ellett Coghill: Naturalist and Philosopher.* Chicago: Univ. Chicago Press

Herrick, C. J. 1955. Clarence Luther Herrick: Pioneer Naturalist, Teacher and Psychobiologist. *Trans. Am. Philos. Soc.* 45:1–85

Hinde, R. A. 1970. *Animal Behavior.* New York: McGraw-Hill

Hofer, M. A. 1976. The organization of sleep and wakefulness after maternal separation in young rats. *Dev. Psychobiol.* 9:189–205

Hofer, M. A. 1978. Hidden regulatory processes in early social relationships. In *Perspectives in Ethology, Vol. 3,* ed. P. P. G. Bateson, P. H. Klopfer, pp. 135–66. New York: Plenum

Hofer, M. A. 1981a. *The Roots of Human Behavior.* San Francisco: Freeman

Hofer, M. A. 1981b. Parental contributions to the development of their offspring. See Gubernick 1981, pp. 77–115

Hofer, M. A. 1986. Nutrient control of cardiac rate in the infant rat. *Physiol. Behav.* 36:557–65

Hofer, M. A., Fisher, A., Shair, H. 1981. Effects of infraorbital nerve section on survival, growth, and suckling behaviors of developing rats. *J. Comp. Physiol. Psychol.* 95:123–33

Hofer, M. A., Shair, H., Singh, P. 1976. Evidence that maternal ventral skin substances promote suckling in infant rats. *Physiol. Behav.* 17:131–36

Hoffman, H. S., Solomon, R. L. 1974. An opponent-process theory of motivation: III. Some affective dynamics in imprinting. *Learn. Motiv.* 5:149–64

Hollis, K. L. 1984. The biological function of Pavlovian conditioning. *J. Exp. Psychol.* 10:413–25

Hooker, D. 1952. *The Prenatal Origin of Behavior.* Lawrence: Univ. Kansas Press

Hudson, R. 1985. Do newborn rabbits learn the odor stimuli releasing nipple-search behavior? *Dev. Psychobiol.* 18:575–86

Hudson, R., Distel, H. 1982. The pattern of behavior of rabbit pups in the nest. *Behaviour* 79:255–71

Hull, J., Hull, D. 1982. Behavioral thermoregulation in newborn rabbits. *J. Comp. Physiol. Psychol.* 96:143–47

Humphrey, T. 1969. Postnatal repetition of human prenatal activity sequences with some suggestions of their neuroanatomical basis. In *Brain and Early Behavior: Development in the Embryo and Fetus,* ed. R. J. Robinson, pp. 43–84. New York: Academic

Impekoven, M. 1976. Prenatal parent-young interactions in birds and their long-term effects. *Adv. Study Behav.* 7:201–53

Infurna, R. N. 1981. Daily biorhythmicity influences homing behavior, psychopharmacological responsiveness, learning, and retention of suckling rats. *J. Comp. Physiol. Psychol.* 95:896–914

Jackson, H., Rubel, E. W. 1978. Ontogeny of behavioral responsiveness to sound in the chick embryo as indicated by electrical recording of motility. *J. Comp. Physiol.* 92:682–96

Johanson, I. B. 1979. Thermotaxis in neonatal rat pups. *Physiol. Behav.* 23:871–74

Johanson, I. B., Hall, W. G. 1981. The ontogeny of feeding in rats: V. Influence of texture, home odor, and sibling presence on ingestive behavior. *J. Comp. Physiol. Psychol.* 95:837–47

Johanson, I. B., Hall, W. G., Polefrone, J. M. 1984. Appetitive conditioning in neonatal rats: Conditioned ingestive responding to stimuli paired with oral infusions of milk. *Dev. Psychobiol.* 17:357–81

Jouvet-Mounier, D., Astic, L., Lacote, D. 1970. Ontogenesis of the states of sleep in rat, cat and guinea pig during the first postnatal month. *Dev. Psychobiol.* 2:216–39

Kagen, J., Kearsley, R. B., Zelazo, P. R. 1978. *Infancy: Its Place in Human Development.* Cambridge: Harvard Univ. Press

Kahn, J. A., Roberts, A. 1982. The central nervous origin of the swimming motor pattern in embryos of *Xenopus laevis. J. Exp. Biol.* 99:185–96

Kehoe, P., Blass, E. M. 1986. Conditioned aversions and their memories in 5-day-old rats during suckling. *J. Exp. Psychol: Anim. Behav. Process.* 12:40–47

Kehoe, P., Blass, E. M. 1986. Opioid-mediation of separation distress in 10-day-old rats: Reversal of stress with maternal stimuli. *Dev. Psychobiol.* In press

Kleitman, N. 1963. *Sleep and Wakefulness.* Chicago: Univ. Chicago

Kleitman, N., Satinoff, E. 1982. Thermoregulatory behavior in rat pups from birth to weaning. *Physiol. Behav.* 29:537–41

Konishi, M. 1973. Development of auditory neuronal responses in avian embryos. *Proc. Natl. Acad. Sci. USA* 70:1795–98

Kucharski, D., Spear, N. E. 1984. Conditioning of aversion to an odor paired with peripheral shock in the developing rat. *Dev. Psychobiol.* 17:465–79

Kuo, Z. Y. 1932. Ontogeny of embryonic behavior in Aves. IV. The influence of embryonic movements upon the behavior after hatching. *J. Comp. Psychol.* 14:109–22

Landmesser, L., Morris, D. 1975. The development of functional inervation in the hindlimb of the chick embryo. *J. Physiol.* 249:301–26

Landmesser, L., Szente, M., Dahm, L. 1985. The effect of blocking functional activity and motoneuron cell death on the activation patterns of chick lumbosacral motoneurons. *Soc. Neurosci. Abstr.* 11:976

Landmesser, L., O'Donovan, M. 1985. Activation patterns of embryonic chick hindlimb muscles recorded *in ovo* and in an isolated spinal cord preparation. *J. Physiol.* 347:189–204

Leon, M. 1986. Development of thermoregulation. See Fentress & McLeod 1986, pp. 297–321

Leon, M., Adels, L., Coppersmith, R. 1985. Thermal limitation of mother-young contact in Norway rats. *Dev. Psychobiol.* 18:85–106

Leon, M., Croskerry, P. G., Smith, G. K. 1978. Thermal control of mother-young contact in rats. *Physiol. Behav.* 21:793–812

Leonard, C. M. 1974. Thermotaxis in golden hamster pups. *J. Comp. Physiol. Psychol.* 86:458–69

Leonard, C. M. 1982. Shifting strategies for behavioral thermoregulation in developing

golden hamsters. *J. Comp. Physiol. Psychol.* 96:234–43

Levine, S. 1983. A psychobiological approach to the ontogeny of coping. In *Stress, Coping and Development in Children,* ed. N. Garmezy, M. Rutter, pp. 107–31. New York: McGraw-Hill

Levine, S. 1986. Psychobiological consequences of disruption in mother-infant relationships. In *Psychological Aspects of Behavioral Development,* ed. N. A. Krasnegor, W. P. Smotherman, E. M. Blass, M. A. Hofer. New York: Academic. In press

Lincoln, D. W., Hill, A., Wakerly, J. B. 1973. The milk-ejection reflex of the rat: An intermittent function not abolished by surgical levels of anesthesia. *J. Endocrinol.* 57:459–76

Lippe, W., Rubel, E. W. 1983. Development of the place principle: Tonotopic organization. *Science* 219:514–16

Lipsitt, L. P. 1970. Developmental psychology. In *Contemporary Scientific Psychology,* ed. A. R. Gilgen, pp. 147–82. New York: Academic

Lipsitt, L. P. 1977. The study of sensory and learning processes of the newborn. *Clin. Perinatol.* 4:163–86

Lipsitt, L. P., Mustaine, M. G., Zeigler, B. 1977. Effects of experience on the behavior of the young infant. *Neuropaediatrie* 8:107–33

MacFarlane, B. A., Pedersen, P. E., Cornell, C. E., Blass, E. M. 1983. Sensory control of suckling-associated behaviours in the domestic Norway rat, *Rattus norvegicus. Anim. Behav.* 31:462–71

Marler, P., Hamilton, W. J. 1966. *Mechanisms of Animal Behavior.* New York: Wiley

Marshack, A. 1979. Data for a theory of language origins. *Brain Behav. Sci.* 2:394–96

Martin, L. T., Alberts, J. R. 1979. Taste aversions to mother's milk: The age-related role of nursing in acquisition and expression of a learned association. *J. Comp. Physiol. Psychol.* 96:668–75

Matthews, S. A., Detwiler, S. R. 1926. The reaction of *Amblystoma* embryos following prolonged treatment with chloretone. *J. Exp. Zool.* 45:279–92

McGinty, D. J., Siegel, J. M. 1983. Sleep states. In *Handbook of Behavioral Neurobiology, Vol. 6, Motivation,* ed. E. Satinoff, P. Teitelbaum, pp. 105–81. New York: Plenum

McGinty, D. J., Stevenson, M., Hoppenbrouwers, T., Harper, T. M., Sterman, M. B., Hodgman, J. 1977. Polygraphic studies of kitten development: Sleep state patterns. *Dev. Psychobiol.* 10:455–69

McKee, J. P., Honzik, M. P. 1964. The sucking behavior of mammals: An illustration of the nature-nurture question. In *Psychology in the Making,* ed. L. Postman, pp. 585–661. New York: Knopf

Moran, T. H., Schwartz, G. J., Blass, E. M. 1983. Organized behavioral responses to lateral hypothalamic electrical stimulation in infant rats. *J. Neurosci.* 3:10–19

Murray, P. D., Drachman, D. 1969. The role of movement in the development of joints and related structures. *J. Embryol. Exp. Morphol.* 22:339–71

Nagy, Z. M. 1979. Development of learning and memory processes in infant mice. In *Ontogeny of Learning and Memory,* ed. N. E. Spear, B. A. Campbell, pp. 101–34. Hillsdale, NJ: Erlbaum

Narayanan, C. H., Fox, M. W., Hamburger, V. 1971. Prenatal development of spontaneous and evoked activity in the rat. *Behavior* 40:100–34

Noirot, E. 1972. Ultrasounds and maternal behavior in small rodents. *Dev. Psychobiol.* 5:371–87

Okon, E. E. 1972. Factors affecting ultrasound production in infant rodents. *J. Zool.* 168:139–48

Oppenheim, R. W. 1973. Pre-hatching and hatching behavior—a comparative and physiological consideration. See Gottlieb 1973, pp. 164–243

Oppenheim, R. W. 1974. The ontogeny of behavior in the chick embryo. *Adv. Study Behav.* 5:133–72

Oppenheim, R. W. 1978. G. E. Coghill (1872–1941): Pioneer neuroembryologist and developmental psychobiologist. *Perspect. Biol. Med.* 22:45–64

Oppenheim, R. W. 1981. Ontogenetic adaptations and retrogressive processes in the development of the nervous system and behavior: A neuroembryological perspective. See Prechtl 1981, pp. 73–109.

Oppenheim, R. W. 1982. The neuroembryological study of behavior: progress, problems, perspectives. *Curr. Top. Dev. Biol.* 17:257–309

Oppenheim, R. W. 1984. Ontogenetic adaptations in neural development: Toward a more "ecological" developmental psychobiology. See Prechtl 1984, pp. 16–30

Oppenheim, R. W. 1985. Naturally-occurring cell death during neural development. *Trends Neurosci.* 8:487–93

Oppenheim, R. W., Reitzel, J. 1975. Ontogeny of behavioral sensitivity to strychnine in the chick embryo: Evidence for the early onset of CNS inhibition. *Brain Behav. Evol.* 11:130–59

Oppenheim, R. W., Haverkamp, L. 1986. Early development of behavior and the nervous system: an embryological perspective. See Fentress & McLeod 1986, pp. 1–33

Oppenheim, R. W., Pittman, R., Gray, M.,

Maderdrut, J. L. 1978. Embryonic behavior, hatching and neuromuscular development in the chick following a transient reduction of spontaneous motility and sensory input by neuromuscular blocking agents. *J. Comp. Neurol.* 179:619–40

Oppenheim, R. W., Hovenou, L., Pincon-Raymond, M., Powell, J., Reiger, F., Standish, L. 1986. The development of motoneurons in the embryonic spinal cord of the mouse mutant, muscular dysgenesis (*mdg/mdg*): Survival, morphology and biochemical differentiation. *Dev. Biol.* 114:426–36

Pai, A. C. 1965. Developmental genetics of a lethal mutation, muscular dysgenesis (*mdg*), in the mouse: I. General analysis and gross morphology. *Dev. Biol.* 11:82–92

Parmelee, A. H. Jr. 1974. Ontogeny of sleep patterns and associated periodicities in infants. In *Pre- and Postnatal Development of the Human Brain,* ed. S. R. Berenberg, M. Caniaris, N. P. Masse, pp. 298–311. Basel: Karger

Parmelee, A. H. Jr. 1983. Perinatal brain development and behavior. See Aslin et al 1983, pp. 95–155

Pedersen, P. E., Blass, E. M. 1981. Olfactory control over suckling in albino rats. See Aslin et al 1981, 1:359–82

Pedersen, P. E., Blass, E. M. 1982. Prenatal and postnatal determinants of the first suckling episode in albino rats. *Dev. Psychobiol.* 15:349–55

Pedersen, P. E., Greer, C. A., Shepherd, G. M. 1986. Early development of olfactory function. See Fentress & McLeod 1986, pp. 163–203

Pedersen, P. E., Stewart, W. B., Greer, C. A., Shepherd, G. 1983. Evidence for olfactory function in utero. *Science* 221:478–80

Pedersen, P. E., Williams, C. L., Blass, E. M. 1982. Activation and odor conditioning of suckling behavior in 3-day-old albino rats. *J. Exp. Psychol: Anim. Behav. Process.* 8:329–41

Pellis, V. C., Teitelbaum, P. 1983. Qualitative and quantitative changes in the patterns of contact-righting during the ontogeny of the rat. *Int. Soc. Dev. Psychobiol.* Abstr. 63

Petre-Quadens, O. 1974. Sleep in the human newborn. In *Basic Sleep Mechanisms,* ed. O. Petre-Quadens, J. D. Schlag, pp. 355–80. New York: Academic

Piaget, J., Inhelder, B. 1969. *The Psychology of the Child.* London: Routledge & Kegan Paul

Prechtl, H. F. R. 1977. Assessment and significance of behavioral states. In *Brain: Fetal and Infant,* ed. S. R. Berenberg, pp. 79–90. The Hague: Nijoff

Prechtl, H. F. R. 1981. The study of neural

development as a perspective of clinical problems. In *Maturation and Development: Biological and Psychological Perspectives,* ed. K. Connolly, H. F. R. Prechtl, pp. 198–215. Philadelphia: Lippincott

Prechtl, H. F. R. 1984. Continuity and change in early neural development. In *Continuity of Neural Functions from Prenatal to Postnatal Life,* ed. H. F. R. Prechtl, pp. 1–15. Philadelphia: Lippincott

Prechtl, H. F. R. 1985. Ultrasound studies of human fetal behavior. *Early Hum. Dev.* 12:91–98

Provine, R. R. 1973. Neurophysiological aspects of behavior development in the chick embryo. See Gottlieb 1973, pp. 77–102

Provine, R. R. 1979. "Wing-flapping" develops in wingless chicks. *Behav. Neural Biol.* 27:233–37

Provine, R. R. 1980. Development of between-limb movement synchronization in the chick embryo. *Dev. Psychobiol.* 13:151–63

Provine, R. R. 1981a. Embryonic and postembryonic development. In *The American Cockroach,* ed. W. J. Bell, K. G. Akiyodi, pp. 399–423. London: Chapman & Hall

Provine, R. R. 1981b. Wing-flapping during development and evolution. *Am. Sci.* 72:448–55

Provine, R. R. 1986. Behavioral neuroembryology: Motor Perspectives. In *Developmental Neuropsychobiology,* ed. E. Greenough, J. Juraska, pp. 213–39. New York: Academic

Purves, D., Lichtman, J. 1984. *Principles of Neuronal Development.* Sunderland, Mass: Sinauer

Reite, M., Kaufman, I. C., Pauley, J. D., Stynes, A. J. 1974. Depression in infant monkeys: Physiological correlates. *Psychosom. Med.* 36:363–67

Reitzel, J., Maderdrut, J., Oppenheim, R. W. 1979. Behavioral and biochemical analysis of GABA-mediated inhibition in the early chick embryo. *Brain Res.* 172:487–504

Reppert, S. M. 1986. Maternal influences on the fetal biological clock in utero. See Levine 1986

Reppert, S. M., Schwartz, W. J. 1983. Maternal coordination of the fetal biological clock in utero. *Science* 220:969–71

Richter, C. P. 1927. Animal behavior and internal drives. *Q. Rev. Biol.* 2:307–43

Rieger, F., Pincon-Raymond, M. 1981. Muscle and nerve in muscular dysgenesis in the mouse at birth: Sprouting and multiple innervation. *Dev. Biol.* 87:85–101

Robertson, S. S. 1982. Intrinsic temporal patterning in the spontaneous movement of awake neonates. *Child Dev.* 53:1016–121

Robertson, S. S., Dierker, L. J., Sorokin, Y., Rosen, M. G. 1982. Human fetal movement: Spontaneous oscillations near one cycle per minute. *Science* 218:1327–30

Rose, S. A. 1983. Behavioral and psychophysiological sequence of preterm birth: the neonatal period. In *Infants Born at Risk: Physiological, Perceptual, and Cognitive Processes,* ed. T. Field, A. Sostek, pp. 45–68. New York: Grume & Stratton

Rosenblatt, J. S. 1971. Suckling and home orientation in the kitten: A comparative developmental study. See Gottlieb 1971, pp. 345–410

Rosenblatt, J. S. 1983. Olfaction mediates developmental transition in the altricial newborn of selected species of mammals. *Dev. Psychobiol.* 16:347–76

Rovee-Collier, C. K., Lipsitt, L. P. 1982. Learning, adaptation, and memory in the newborn. See Stratton 1982, pp. 147–90

Rubel, E. W. 1978. Ontogeny of structure and function in the vertebrate auditory system. In *Handbook of Sensory Physiology,* ed. J. Jacobson, 9:135–237. Berlin: Springer-Verlag

Rubel, E. W., Ryals, B. M. 1983. Development of the place principle: Acoustic trauma. *Science* 219:512–14

Rudy, J. W., Cheatle, M. D. 1977. Odor-aversion learning in neonatal rats. *Science* 198:845–46

Rudy, J. W., Vogt, M. B., Hyson, R. L. 1984. A developmental analysis of the rat's learned reactions to gustatory and auditory stimulation. See Campbell 1984, pp. 181–208

Sander, L. W., Stechler, G., Burns, P., Lee, A. 1979. Change in infant and caregiver variables over the first two months of life: Integration of action in early development. In *Origins of the Infant's Social Responsiveness,* ed. E. B. Thoman, pp. 349–407. Hillsdale, NJ: Erlbaum

Sasaki, Y., Murakami, N., Yakahaski, K. 1984. Critical period for the entrainment of the circadian rhythm in blinded pups by dams. *Physiol. Behav.* 33:105–10

Satinoff, E., McEwen, G. N. Jr., Williams, B. A. 1976. Behavioral fever in newborn rabbits. *Science* 193:1139–40

Saunders, J. C., Coles, R. B., Gates, G. R. 1973. The development of auditory evoked responses in the cochlea and cochlear nuclei of the chick. *Brain Res.* 63:59–74

Schanberg, S. M., Evonuik, G. E., Kuhn, C. M. 1979. The effect of tactile stimulation on serum growth hormone and tissue ornithine decarboxylase activity during maternal deprivation in rat pups. *Commun. Psychopharm.* 3:363–70

Schmidt, W., Bons, R., Gnirs, J., Aver, L., Schulze, S. 1985. Fetal behavioral status and controlled sound stimulation. *Early Hum. Dev.* 12:145–53

Shair, H., Brake, S., Hofer, M. A. 1984.

Suckling in the rat: Evidence for patterned behavior during sleep. *Behav. Neurosci.* 98:366–70

Shuleikina-Turpaeva, K. V. 1986. Sensory organization of alimentary behavior in the kitten. *Adv. Study Behav.* In press

Sieber, O. J. 1985. Individual recognition of parental calls by bank swallow chicks (Riparia riparia). *Anim. Behav.* 33:107–16

Singh, P. J., Hofer, M. A. 1978. Oxytocin reinstates maternal olfactory cues for nipple orientation and attachment in rat pups. *Physiol. Behav.* 20:385–91

Smith, G. K., Anderson, V. 1984. Effects of maternal isolation on the development of activity rhythms in infant rats. *Physiol. Behav.* 33:751–56

Smotherman, W. P., Richard, L. S., Robinson, S. R. 1984. Techniques for observing fetal behavior *in utero:* A comparison of chemomyelotomy and spinal transection. *Dev. Psychobiol.* 17:661–74

Smotherman, W. P., Robinson, S. R. 1985. The rat fetus in its environment: Behavioral adjustments to novel, familiar, aversive and conditioned stimuli presented *in utero. Behav. Neurosci.* 99:521–30

Snyder, S. H. 1968. Development of enzyme activities and a circadian rhythm in pineal gland serotonin: Evidence for nonretinal pathway of light to the pineal gland of newborn rats. *Adv. Pharmacol.* 6A:301–5

Sostek, A. M., Anders, T. F. 1981. The biosocial importance and environmental sensitivity of infant sleep-wake behaviors. In *Prospective Issues in Infancy Research,* ed. K. Bloom, pp. 99–118. Hillsdale, NJ: Erlbaum

Spear, N. E., Kucharski, D. K. 1984. Ontogenetic differences in stimulus selection during conditioning. See Campbell 1984, pp. 227–52

Spelt, D. K. 1948. The conditioning of the human fetus *in utero. J. Exp. Psychol.* 38:338–46

Stehouwer, D. J., Farel, D. J. 1981. Sensory interactions with a central motor program in Anuran larvae. *Brain Res.* 218:131–40

Sterman, M. B. 1972. The basic rest-activity cycle and sleep: Developmental considerations in man and cats. In *Sleep and the Maturing Nervous System,* ed. C. D. Clemente, D. P. Purpura, F. E. Mayer, pp. 175–97. New York: Academic

Stern, J. M., Levin, R. 1976. Food availability as a determinant of the rats' circadian rhythm in maternal behavior. *Dev. Psychobiol.* 9:137–48

Stickrod, G., Kimble, D., Smotherman, W. P. 1982. In utero taste/odor aversion conditioning in the rat. *Physiol. Behav.* 28:5–7

Stratton, P. 1982. Rhythmic functions in the newborn. In *Psychobiology of the Human*

Newborn, ed. P. Stratton, pp. 119–45. New York: Wiley

Suomi, S. J., Mineka, S., Harlow, H. F. 1983. Social separation in monkeys as viewed from several motivational perspectives. See McGinty & Siegel 1983, pp. 543–83

Suzuki, S., Yamamuro, T. 1985. Fetal movement and fetal presentation. *Early Hum. Dev.* 111:255–63

Szechtman, H., Hall, W. G. 1980. Ontogeny of oral behavior induced by tail pinch and electrical stimulation of the tail in rats. *J. Comp. Physiol. Psychol.* 94:436–45

Tamasy, V., Koranyi, L., Lissak, K. 1980. Early postnatal development of wakefulness—sleep cycle and neuronal responsiveness: A multiunit activity study on freely moving newborn rat. *Electroencephalogr. Clin. Neurophysiol.* 49:102–11

Teicher, M. H., Blass, E. M. 1977. First suckling response of the newborn albino rat: The roles of olfaction and amniotic fluid. *Science* 198:635–36

Teicher, M. H., Flaum, L. E. 1979. Ontogeny of ultradian and nocturnal activity rhythms in the isolated albino rat. *Dev. Psychobiol.* 12:441–55

Thelen, E. 1985. Developmental origins of motor coordination: Leg movements in human infants. *Dev. Psychobiol.* 18:1–22

Thelen, E. 1984. Learning to walk: Ecological demands and phylogenetic constraints. In *Advances in Infancy Research,* ed. L. P. Lipsitt, C. Rovee-Collier, 3:213–50. Norwood, NJ: Ablex

Thelen, E., Fisher, D. M. 1983. The organization of spontaneous leg movements in newborn infants. *J. Motor Behav.* 15:353–77

Thoman, E. B., Denenberg, V. H., Sievel, J., Zeidner, L. P., Becker, P. 1981. State organization in neonates: Developmental inconsistency indicates risk for developmental dysfunction. *Neuropediatrics* 12:45–54

Tschanz, B., Hirsbrunner-Scharf, M. 1975. Adaptations to colony life on cliff ledges: A comparative study of guillemot and razorbill chicks. In *Function and Evolution in Behavior,* ed. G. Baerends, C. Beer, A. Manning, pp. 358–80. Oxford: Clarendon

van Vliet, M. A. T., Martin, C. B., Mijhuis, J. G., Prechtl, H. F. R. 1985. Behavioral states in growth-retarded human fetuses. *Early Hum. Dev.* 12:183–97

Vince, M. A. 1973. Some environmental effects on the activity and development of the avian embryo. See Gottlieb 1973, pp. 285–323

Vince, M. A. 1979. Postnatal effects of prenatal sound stimulation in the guinea pig. *Anim. Behav.* 27:908–18

Vince, M. A., Billing, A. E. 1986. Infancy in the sheep: The part played by sensory stimulation in bonding between the ewe and lamb. In *Advances in Infancy Research*, ed. L. P. Lipsitt, C. K. Rovee-Collier, 4:1–37. Norwood, NJ: Ablex

Vince, M. A., Billing, A. E., Baldwin, B. A., Toner, J. N., Weller, C. 1985. Maternal vocalizations and other sounds in the fetal lamb's sound environment. *Early Hum. Dev.* 11:179–90

Visser, G. H. A., Laurini, R. N., Vries, J. I. P. de, Bekedam, D. J., Prechtl, H. F. R. 1985. Abnormal motor behavior in anencephalic fetuses. *Early Hum. Dev.* 12: 173–82

Vries, J. I. P. de, Visser, G. H. A., Prechtl, H. F. R. 1982. The emergence of fetal behavior: I. Qualitative aspects. *Early Hum. Dev.* 7:301–22

Vries, J. I. P. de, Visser, G. H. A., Prechtl, H. F. R. 1985. The emergence of fetal behavior: II. Quantitative aspects. *Early Hum. Dev.* 12:99–120

Walker, J. M., Berger, R. J. 1980. The ontogenesis of sleep states, thermogenesis, and thermoregulation in the Virginia opossum. *Dev. Psychobiol.* 13:443–55

Watt, J. E., Strongman, K. T. 1985. The organization and stability of sleep states in fullterm, preterm, and small-for-gestational-age infants: A comparative study. *Dev. Psychobiol.* 18:151–62

Williams, C. L., Lorang, D. 1985. Neural control of lordosis and ear wiggling in 6-day-old rats. *Soc. Neurosci. (Abstr.)* 15:161.12

Windle, W. F. 1940. *Physiology of the Fetus.* Philadelphia: Saunders

Windle, W. F. 1975. *The Pioneering Role of Clarence Luther Herrick in American Neuroscience.* Hicksville, NY: Exposition Press

Wolff, P. H. 1972. The interaction of state and non-nutritive sucking. In *Oral Sensation and Perception. The Mouth of the Infant*, ed. J. F. Bosma, pp. 293–310. Springfield: Thomas

Wolgin, D. L. 1982. Motivation, activation, and behavioral integration. In *The Expression of Knowledge: Neurobehavioral Transformations of Information into Action*, ed. R. L. Isaacson, N. E. Spear, pp. 243–90. New York: Plenum

Wolman, B. B., ed. 1973. *Dictionary of Behavioral Science.* New York: Van Nostrand, Reinhold

Wortis, R. P. 1969. The transition from dependent to independent feeding in the young ring dove. *Anim. Behav. Monogr.* 2:3–54

Zelazo, P. R. 1983. The development of walking: New findings and old assumptions. *J. Motor Behav.* 15:99–137

Zucker, I. 1983. Motivation, biological clocks and temporal organization of behavior. See McGinty & Siegel 1983, pp. 3–22

Ann. Rev. Psychol. 1987. 38:129–51

THE ORGANIZATION OF NEOCORTEX IN MAMMALS: Implications for Theories of Brain Function

Jon H. Kaas

Department of Psychology, Vanderbilt University, Nashville, Tennessee 37240

CONTENTS

INTRODUCTION

Over the last several years, microelectrode mapping procedures and highly sensitive methods of revealing anatomical connections, used in conjunction with classical cell and fiber stains and new histochemical protocols for studying cortical architecture, have led to new insights on cortical organization and major revisions of longstanding viewpoints. These revised concepts

129

are outlined here because they can limit and direct theories of brain function. This review is concerned with how cortex is divided into areas or fields, how areas are subdivided into processing modules, how areas are interconnected, how cortical organization develops and is maintained, and how species differ and are similar. We start with the premise that newer procedures have led to an improved understanding of cortical organization.

TRADITIONAL ARCHITECTONIC THEORIES OF CORTICAL ORGANIZATION

Until recently, the main way of subdividing cortex was by architectonic differences. Before and since the extensive reports of Brodmann (1909), many investigators have described regional differences in cortical architecture, and have used such descriptions to subdivide cortex and develop theories of cortical organization (for review, see Kemper & Galaburda 1984). Such investigators have not agreed on how cortex is subdivided, on homologies and differences across species, or even on whether cortical fields are sharply defined or gradually change from one to the other. Largely because of such disagreements, the architectonic method has been subjected to major criticism (e.g. Lashley & Clark 1946). Yet, the comprehensive proposals that have been produced by architectonic studies have continued to influence how we think about cortical organization.

The problem of identifying cortical fields has been a major one in traditional architectonic studies for several reasons. First, for any complex mammal with a large brain, there is the general supposition, not agreed upon by all, that there must be a large number of subdivisions. Yet, the cell and fiber stains reveal only a few obvious subdivisions and most proposed borders and areas have been based on such subtle differences that there is little agreement among investigators. In fact, many researchers have concluded that large expanses of cortex are basically uniform in structure, even though they have been subdivided in various ways in architectonic studies. Another difficulty in architectonic studies is that observed differences usually had uncertain significance. The "clear border" of one investigator could be attributed to random variation, variation within a field, or distortions produced by sulci by another investigator. A third difficulty is that species differ profoundly, not only in amount of cortex, but in the relative differentiation of cortex.

An appreciation of the magnitude of the difficulty of recognizing the same field across species by architectonic criteria alone can be realized by comparing the cytoarchitecture of the primary and secondary visual areas (V-I or area 17 and V-II or area 18) in a hedgehog, which has a small brain and poorly differentiated cortex, and a tree shrew, which has a somewhat larger brain and obviously greater cortical differentiation (Figure 1). The point of using area

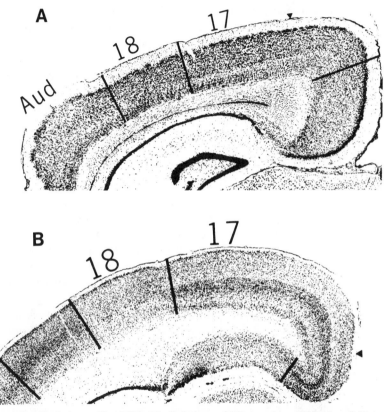

Figure 1. Cortical areas 17 and 18 in (*A*) a hedgehog and (*B*) a tree shrew. While these fields are clearly homologous in these two mammals, they differ considerably in appearance. Lines mark borders, while a small triangle indicates the junction of binocular and monocular portions of area 17. A standard Nissl preparation for cell bodies. Frontal brain sections with medial to the right.

17 as an example is that it is perhaps the most distinctive and easily recognized of neocortical fields, and yet species differences are so great that it is not immediately apparent that the fields designated as area 17 are homologous (the same field). In fact, area 17 was completely misidentified in some early comparative studies (e.g. Mott 1907), and even Brodmann (1909) mistook the less-developed monocular portion of striate cortex as another field (area 18) in some mammals. Several recent investigators have been so impressed with the species differences in cortical structure that they have disagreed with Brodmann's (1909) contention that area 17 is present in hedgehogs, and have concluded instead that hedgehogs have no primary visual or other primary fields (von Bonin & Bailey 1961; Sanides 1972). We now know from other

types of evidence (see Kaas et al 1970) that Brodmann correctly identified area 17 in hedgehogs, but the nature of the difficulty is clear: species differences in cortical structure are so great that homologies can be difficult to recognize even for the most distinctive of fields.

In brief, the traditional proposals of cortical organization, based on architecture, have been unreliable because regional differences in cortical structure are often unimpressive, species differences in cortical differentiation are considerable, and, above all else, there has been little attempt to evaluate the significance of the variation that exists.

DEFINING FIELDS BY MULTIPLE CRITERIA

Brodmann (1909) viewed cortical areas as "organs" of the brain, and this is the way areas are usually considered. Each area, as an "organ" of the brain with a unique function or set of functions, should differ from other areas in a number of ways related to its functional role. The list of potentially useful differences is not necessarily limited, but only a few can be easily revealed by current techniques (for a review of methods of revealing subdivisions, see Kaas 1982).

The early architectonists had stains for cells and fibers. They correctly assumed that functionally distinct fields should have morphological differences, but clearly many fields are not obvious in traditional preparations. Fortunately, traditional stains are now being supplemented with techniques for revealing distributions of cellular enzymes, evoked and resting metabolic levels, and neurotransmitters (Figures 2 and 3; also see Livingstone & Hubel 1984; Tootell et al 1985). In addition, new recipes have greatly improved the usefulness of fiber stains (e.g. Maunsell & Van Essen 1983; Krubitzer et al 1986).

Functionally distinct subdivisions of cortex often contain a systematic representation or map of a sensory surface or a motor map of body movements. Such a map is fairly compelling evidence for a cortical area. Early studies with surface recordings and stimulations resulted in much progress, but these procedures were not accurate enough to reveal important details about where the pattern contained in one map ended and where a new pattern began. Microelectrode mapping methods allow representations to be revealed in great detail, and with considerable accuracy, and large portions of cortex have been found to be devoted to sensory and motor maps (Figure 6). A difficulty is that "higher" sensory and motor areas may be relatively unresponsive under many typical recording and stimulation conditions, and that maps with complex organization may be difficult to discern.

The uniqueness of cortical areas should also be reflected in connections, and today we have a number of sensitive procedures for determining con-

Figure 2. Area 18 and adjoining cortex in a squirrel monkey. The cortex has been separated from the brain, unfolded, flattened, cut parallel to the surface, and reacted for cytochrome oxidase (an enzyme related to levels of neural activity). The plane of section passes from layer IV to layer III in area 17 more caudally (upper figure) and laterally along 17/18 border (right in figure). Note that the 17/18 border (open arrows) is "line-sharp," even in layer III. In addition, a sharp border is apparent over much of the rostral extent of area 18. Area 18 is characterized by alternating light and dark bands, and thus clearly has subunits. Four of the dark bands are marked by thick arrows, which also indicate the rostral border of area 18. Thin arrows mark three of the dense cytochrome oxidase puffs that are distributed in layer III of area 17. The photomicrograph was kindly supplied by L. A. Krubitzer.

nections. Each cortical area should have a systematic pattern of connections with a number of other areas. Once the validity of an area has been established, its connections can reveal the locations and internal topography of other areas.

Other methods of indicating areas are potentially useful, but have not been widely applied. Thus, areas can be distinguished by overall differences in the responses of neurons to sensory stimuli, but such recordings have been used more often to help establish the validity of an area rather than to help discover areas. Likewise, ablation-behavior studies can help demonstrate the functional role of a proposed area, and thus help establish its validity, but ablation studies have not often uncovered the presence of previously unknown fields.

Each experimental approach has its value, but each is also subject to its own problems of interpretation. It follows that errors in identifying cortical

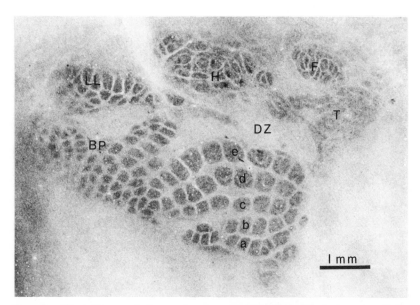

Figure 3.   The architecture of primary somatosensory cortex in the rat. The brain section was cut parallel to the surface of an artificially flattened brain and stained for the enzyme, succinic dehydrogenase. Dense clusters of staining reveal the pattern of dense thalamic inputs. The pattern indicated that S-I is sharply defined and has a precise somatotopic organization. Labels indicate where in S-I various body parts are represented: H = "hand"; F = foot; T = trunk; a-1 = rows of mystacial vibrissae from dorsal to ventral on the face; BP = bucal pad; LL = lower lip; DZ = dysgranular zone. The photomicrograph was kindly supplied by H. P. Killackey and D. R. Dawson. See Kaas 1983 for references on S-I organization in rats.

areas are best avoided by using multiple criteria. It has long been held that potential neurotransmitters are presumptive until a list of defining criteria are met. The evidence for proposed cortical areas varies from weak to very strong, and it must be admitted that most proposed fields in complex brains are now only presumptive. However, much progress has been made, specific proposals have been made for further testing, and the methods are available for rapid progress.

The newer methods have led to a number of conclusions, but one seems particularly relevant for discussion of cortical organization. Theories of cortical organization based solely on the study of architecture have not been supported by the results of newer methods, with the significant and important exceptions of the proper identification of a few fields in some species by some investigators. But even judgments that proved to be correct for some investigators for some species have been confounded by different opinions of other investigators and even by the same investigator in other species. For example, it appears that the proposed somatosensory fields 3a, 3b, 1, and 2 of

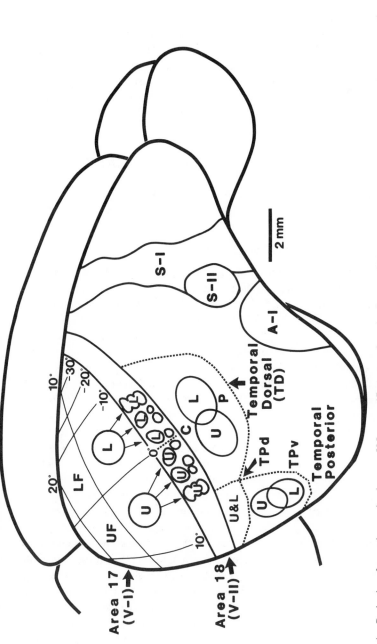

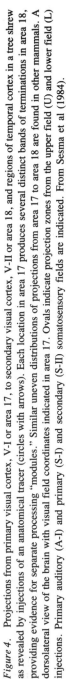

Figure 4. Projections from primary visual cortex, V-I or area 17, to secondary visual cortex, V-II or area 18, and regions of temporal cortex in a tree shrew as revealed by injections of an anatomical tracer (circles with arrows). Each location in area 17 produces several distinct bands of terminations in area 18, providing evidence for separate processing "modules." Similar uneven distributions of projections from area 17 to area 18 are found in other mammals. A dorsolateral view of the brain with visual field coordinates indicated in area 17. Ovals indicate projection zones from the upper field (U) and lower field (L) injections. Primary auditory (A-I) and primary (S-I) and secondary (S-II) somatosensory fields are indicated. From Sesma et al (1984).

Brodmann (1909) and Vogt & Vogt (1919) actually do correspond to functionally distinct areas in macaque monkeys (see Kaas 1983), but these areas have been illustrated as fairly different in extent and exact location in macaque monkeys by other investigators, and they have been combined and misidentified in other monkeys and other primates by Brodmann and other investigators. In non-primates, these architectonic terms have been applied in a number of different ways that do not correspond to the way they are used in macaque monkeys.

CURRENT CONCEPTS OF CORTICAL ORGANIZATION

Evidence has rapidly accumulated to support a number of conclusions about cortical organization. Each of these conclusions has implications for theories of cortical functions.

Cortical Areas Are Sharply Defined

Whether cortical localization is precise or not has been a classical issue of debate. Eliot Smith (1907) concluded that at least 50 fields in the human brain had "exact boundaries," von Economo & Koskinas (1925) extended this list to 107 fields, while von Bonin and coworkers (e.g. von Bonin & Bailey 1961) have emphasized the view that there are fewer fields and that the fields gradually change from one to another. Brodmann (1909) believed in both absolute and relative localization; that is in fields with sharp boundaries and in fields that gradually change to the next. The issue is not completely resolved, but recent evidence that many borders are sharp supports the conclusion that boundaries in general are sharp so that one field changes to the next within 100 μm or so. The evidence comes from microelectrode recordings, reconsiderations of cortical architectonics, and from studies of connections. An example is the second visual area, V-II, or "area 18," which in tissue sections with standard stains for cell bodies is clearly different and sharply separated from primary visual cortex, V-I or area 17, but is often indistinctly separated from other adjoining fields at its rostral boundary. Thus, Brodmann (1909) failed to correctly identify the rostral border of area 18 in Old World monkeys, and included cortex within "area 18" that we now know is occupied by other fields. As can be seen in Figure 2, current histochemical stains indicate that both the caudal and rostral borders of area 18 are sharply defined. Similar conclusions would stem from studies of patterns of retinotopic organization, neural properties, or connections. As an example of an elegant demonstration of the existence of sharp boundaries using microelectrode recordings, Rasmusson et al (1979) recorded from sequences of neurons in microelectrode penetrations passing parallel to the cortical surface and perpendicular to the border between primary somatosensory cortex and the adjoining rostral field

"3a," in cats (see Figure 6 for the location of these fields). In each electrode penetration, the response properties of neurons changed sharply and completely from those activated by noncutaneous receptors (muscle spindles) in area 3a to cutaneous receptors in S-I.

Historically, it has been common to acknowledge sharp borders between fields in advanced species, while suggesting a lack of such borders in primitive species. There is no compelling evidence to support this viewpoint. Borders seem to be just as sharp in the cortex of the hedgehog (Kaas et al 1970) as in advanced primates and carnivores. Certainly anyone who has seen a properly prepared "surface view" tangential section through somatosensory cortex of a rat (Figure 3) will agree that S-I is sharply defined in these rodents.

The evidence for sharp boundaries has accumulated rapidly, while there is no clear evidence for gradual borders between areas. Thus, the conclusion seems warranted that functional boundaries are usually and perhaps always sharp.

Cortical Areas Are Functionally Heterogeneous

Mountcastle (1978) is known for stressing that cortical areas are subdivided into mosaics of functionally distinct "columns" or processing modules. While areas may not contain groups of cells with all of the features of columns as outlined by Mountcastle (1978), a number of cortical areas have now been shown to be heterogeneous in structure and function, and it seems reasonable to postulate from this sample of fields that areas in general are heterogeneous. The best example of a field with clear subdivisions is primary visual cortex of macaque monkeys where occular dominance bands, orientation bands, and cytochrome oxidase dense "puffs" (Figure 2) of neurons that are non-selective for orientation have been demonstrated as subunits (see Livingstone & Hubel 1984). Evidence is also accumulating for subunits within area 18 or V-II. The uneven pattern of projections from V-I to V-II that is found in most mammals is shown in Figure 4. A given location in V-I projects to several locations in V-II, and two nearby locations in V-I project to locations in V-II that are partially separate and partially interdigitated. These observations argue that given locations in V-I send the same information to several spatially separate modules in V-II. The internal organization of V-II is better understood in monkeys, where "thick bands," "thin bands," and "interbands" crossing the width of the field in cytochrome oxidase (Figure 2; also see Livingstone & Hubel 1984; Tootell et al 1985) and fiber stain preparations have been related to neurons and connections mediating different functions (see Hubel & Livingstone 1985). As a third example, primary somatosensory cortex of monkeys (area 3b, see Kaas 1983) is divided into alternating and irregularly shaped strips of neurons that respond in a rapidly adapting (RA) or slowly

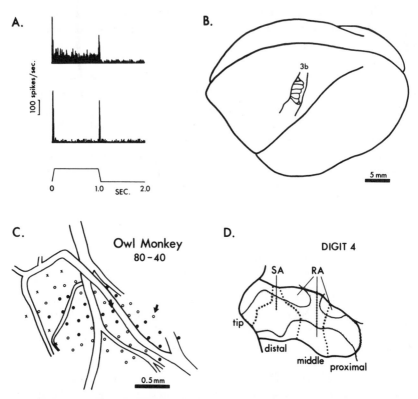

Figure 5. The spatial distribution of neurons that adapt slowly (SA) or rapidly (RA) to maintained skin indentation in primary somatosensory cortex (area 3b) of an owl monkey. The bandlike regions, which are shown only for the representation of a finger, were determined by multiple recordings with microelectrodes. The distinctly separate regions were only apparent in middle layers of cortex. *A.* Peristimulus time histograms of a slowly adapting *(top)* and rapidly adapting *(bottom)* neuron. Trace shows waveform of the skin indentation probe. *B.* The region of the hand representation in area 3b on a dorsolateral view of the brain. *C.* An enlarged view of cortex representing filled circles mark penetrations outside the field. *D.* An enlarged view of the representation of digit 4 with the RA and SA regions. The results support the notion of modular organization in somatosensory cortex. From Sur et al 1981a; also see Sur et al 1984.

adapting (SA) manner to maintained pressure on the skin (Figure 5; Sur et al 1981a, 1984).

Species Vary in Number of Areas

Brodmann (1909) and most other investigators have long contended that mammals with large complex brains, especially humans, have more cortical areas than mammals with small primitive brains, but without compelling evidence it was still possible to argue, as Lashley did, that mammals have few fields, on the order of 10 or so, and that there was no reason to suppose that the number differed in rats and humans (e.g. Lashley & Clark 1946). Figure 6 illustrates current theories of how cortex is divided into areas in hedgehogs, squirrels, cats, and New World monkeys. Some of the fields are well supported, others are tentative, and revisions and additions will undoubtedly occur. Yet, the evidence for enough of the fields is so solid that there is no escaping the conclusion that species differ in numbers of areas. Furthermore, as Brodmann (1909) and Eliot Smith (1907) proposed, advanced mammals have more fields.

All Mammals Have Some Fields in Common

One major conclusion stemming from modern evidence on cortical organization is that a few basic areas of cortex are present in most or all mammals. Hedgehogs, with cortex that is probably not much different from that of the first Eutherian mammals, have primary and secondary visual fields (areas 17 or V-I and 18 or V-II), primary and secondary somatosensory fields (S-I and S-II), a motor field (M-I), a primary auditory (A-I) and perhaps one or two other auditory fields, probably taste cortex, prefrontal cortex related to the mediodorsal nucleus of the thalamus, several subdivisions of limbic cortex related to the anterior and lateral dorsal nuclei of the thalamus, a small region of temporal cortex that is probably visual with input from area 17, and a perirhinal strip of transitional cortex that probably relates other neocortical fields with the amygdala and the hippocampus (see Kaas 1982). These same fields have been identified in a wide range of placental mammals (Figure 6), and they can be considered basic to Eutherian mammals, evolving early in the divergence of mammals and retained in most or all subsequent lines of divergence.

Studies on opossums and other marsupials indicate that these same fields, with the exception of motor cortex, are part of the basic plan of the Metatherian radiation as well. Opossums apparently do not have a primary motor field (M-I), but instead the motor functions of primary somatosensory cortex (S-I) are emphasized (Lende 1963). S-I receives both somatosensory information from the ventroposterior thalamus and cerebellar information, normally projected to motor cortex, from the ventroanterior thalamus (Killackey & Ebner 1973). Much less is known about cortical organization in monotremes, but available evidence (Lende 1964) suggests that they have at least primary visual, auditory, and somatosensory areas, and, as in marsupials, no primary motor field. Hence, a few fields appear to be common to all mammals and undoubtedly were present in reptilian ancestors.

HEDGEHOG

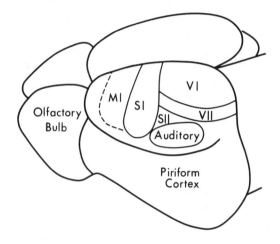

SQUIRREL

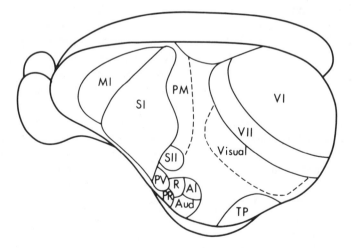

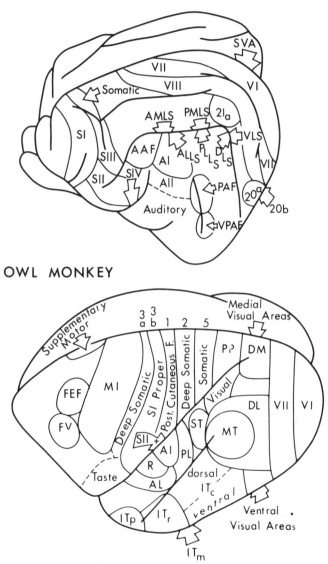

Figure 6. Subdivisions of cortex in a primitive mammal (hedgehog), a mammal with a somewhat advanced brain (squirrel), and two mammals with moderately advanced brains (cat and owl monkey). The primary motor (M-I), primary and secondary somatic (S-I and S-II), and primary and secondary visual areas (V-I and V-II) are present in all. Other fields have been named by location (e.g. anterior auditory field, AAF; middle temporal area, MT) or related to a traditional architectonic field of Brodmann (1909) by various authors (for details and additional references, see Kaas 1982; Krubitzer et al 1986).

Major Advances in Brain Evolution Have Been Marked by Increases in Numbers of Unimodal Sensory Areas

Of the mammals with relatively advanced brains, only monkeys and cats have been studied to an extent where reasonable comparisons can be made. The primate and carnivore lines diverged at a time when brain development was probably not much different from that now found in the hedgehogs, and both of these lines have the basic areas found in hedgehogs. However, both lines have additional somatosensory, visual, and auditory areas. Both cats and monkeys have more than 10 visual areas, and perhaps as many as 15–20. Cats have at least five and monkeys at least eight somatosensory areas, and both lines have on the order of five or more auditory fields. All of the above fields are dominated by one modality and most exclusively code inputs of only one modality. Generalizing from cats and monkeys, it appears that evolutionary advance in brain organization is marked by increases in the numbers of unimodal sensory fields, not by increases in multimodal association cortex, as traditionally thought. Of course, it should be stressed that the lines leading to cats and monkeys, and almost certainly those leading to other advanced brains, independently increased the number of sensory areas, and therefore most sensory fields in these different lines are not homologous.

Areas Are Multiply Interconnected; Connections Are Species-Variable

Some of the demonstrated connections of visual cortex of owl monkeys are shown in Figure 7. Typically, each field is interconnected with 3–6 other fields in the same hemisphere. In addition, each field connects callosally with its counterpart and 1–3 other fields in the opposite hemisphere. Finally, subcortical connections with subdivisions of the pulvinar complex, the lateral geniculate nucleus, the claustrum, the basal ganglia, the superior colliculus, and pontine nuclei add to the complexity of the wiring diagram (see Weller & Kaas 1981; Kaas & Huerta 1987). Thus, neurons in any field are subject to a multitude of influences from other fields. Somatosensory, auditory, and motor areas have connection patterns that are similarly complex, and such complexity is seen across species. It follows that even simple stimuli delivered to a receptor surface would, in advanced mammals, activate an array of interacting locations in the multitude of cortical areas and subcortical nuclei related to that modality. Thus, processing is distributed across a large expanse of the forebrain.

Of course, not all pathways shown in Figure 7 are equivalent. They differ in magnitude and type. The so-called "feedforward" connections terminate most densely on the middle (receiving) layers of cortex, IV and inner III, which contain the stellate neurons that initiate the processing in an area. Connections that terminate in the upper and lower layers largely relate to the

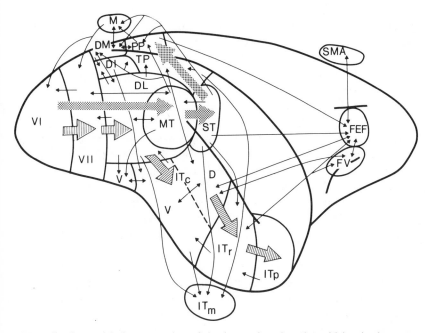

Figure 7. Some of the interconnections of visual cortex in owl monkeys. Major visual process-ing sequences are indicated by the thick arrows. Thin arrows indicate other connections. V-I and V-II, primary and secondary fields; FEF and SMA are the frontal eye field, and the eye movement portion of the supplementary motor area. FV is a frontal visual area of uncertain significance. Other visual areas are named by location (e.g. dorsolateral, DL; dorsomedial, DM; dorsointermediate, DI) or by location in a lobe (e.g. IT$_C$, caudal area of the inferior temporal lobe). See Weller & Kaas (1986) for details. Note that each area is interconnected with several other visual areas. Major processing sequences are directed toward the temporal lobe for object vision (thick hatched arrows) and posterior parietal cortex (thick stippled arrows) for visual attention (see Ungerleider & Mishkin 1982; Kaas 1986).

dendrites of pyramidal cells that project to other structures. These "feedback" connections appear to modulate the outflow of information after much of the local processing has occurred (see Maunsell & Van Essen 1983; Weller & Kaas 1981 for review). Pathways also differ in effectiveness. For example, the neurons in the central nucleus of the inferior pulvinar with visual inputs from striate cortex and the superior colliculus, depend on the striate cortex and not the superior colliculus for activation (Bender 1983).

By considering only the major feedforward projections that presumably provide most of the activation, it is possible to construct the dominant processing streams or hierarchies. Thus, in the visual cortex of owl monkeys, there is a stream from striate cortex to the inferior temporal lobe that appears to mediate form vision, and a stream to the posterior parietal cortex that is important in visual attention (Weller & Kaas 1986; Kaas 1986; see Ungerleider & Mishkin 1982 for "two cortical visual systems"). While the processing hierarchies, such as those in Figure 7, are tempting frameworks for theories of cortical processing, the true complexity of the system should be remembered. Processing has both parallel and hierarchical components, but "later" stations receive inputs from both "intermediate" and "early" stations, confounding simple hierarchical schemes.

It is also important to recognize that species can differ considerably in connections. Both areas 17 and 18 receive major inputs from the lateral geniculate nucleus in cats, for example, while these projections are almost exclusively to area 17 in monkeys. There is also some evidence that a type of "corticalization of function" occurs so that higher stations tend to acquire more direct sensory inputs as an advance in evolution. In anterior parietal cortex of monkeys, information is relayed from the ventroposterior nucleus to area 3b (S-I), from area 3b to area 1, and from area 1 to area 2 (see Kaas 1983). Thus, areas 3b, 1, and 2 can be considered a processing hierarchy. In both New and Old World monkeys, some projections from the ventroposterior nucleus also terminate directly in area 1 of monkeys, but no such projections have been found in prosimians. In Old World monkeys, there is an additional projection from the ventroposterior nucleus to the part of area 2 that represents the hand (Pons & Kaas 1985). Such observations suggest that behavioral advances sometimes are achieved by rerouting relatively unprocessed information to higher stations, rather than completely depending on cortical processing sequences. In some systems this may be more important than others. For example, most of the auditory areas in the cortex of cats receive direct thalamic auditory information in addition to cortically relayed information (see Merzenich & Kaas 1980).

Detailed Organization Is Dynamically Maintained

The excitatory receptive fields of cortical neurons reflect only a portion of their total inputs. Maps of receptor surfaces in cortex can have organization that supercedes that of the anatomical distribution of inputs. Retinotopic organization clearly exists within the overlapping distributions of the terminal arbors of single geniculostriate axons (Blasdel & Lund 1983), and somatotopic organization is found within the distance covered by the arbors of ventroposterior axons that terminate in area 3b (Pons et al 1982). Thus, the axons drive neurons only within a portion of their arbors. In this sense, connections are superabundant, and superabundant connections occur at all levels in sensory systems. Obviously, neurons somehow select inputs from a menu of possibilities. The selection may be based on intrinsic mechanisms that tend to preserve a fairly constant level of synaptic activation, and a favoring of synapses that are active during the firing of the postsynaptic cell, and thereby temporally correlated with the activity of other synapses (see Constantine-Paton 1982 for review).

When the sources of activation for cortical neurons are altered, they rapidly acquire new sources of activation. One way of altering input has been to section a nerve to the skin of part of the hand or some other region (see Kaas et al 1983; Wall & Kaas 1985 for review). Neurons in somatosensory cortex formerly with receptive fields exclusively within the denervated skin rapidly recover new receptive fields in adjoining innervated skin. At first, the new receptive fields are abnormally large, but over weeks they reduce in size to that appropriate for the region of cortex, rather than for the normal representation of the skin field. These results suggest that cortex is constantly in a state of flux, and stability results from a balance of competing factors.

Self-Organization Occurs During Development

As the adult nervous system is characterized by neurons that select a portion of potential inputs from a menu of inputs from widespread axon terminal arbors, an analogous but more extensive selection process takes place during development. Neurons and neural connections in the developing nervous system are superabundant, and the prevailing view is that neurons are in competition with each other for synaptic space and survival (e.g. Killackey & Chalupa 1986; Rakic et al 1986). It is clear from many experiments that the selection process is related to neural activity, and it appears likely that the co-activation of inputs results in a selective increase in synaptic efficacy and survival (for reviews, see Constantine-Paton 1982, Easter et al 1985; Schmidt & Tieman 1985). Such a process would account for at least four features of cortical fields that systematically represent sensory surfaces.

1. A fundamental feature of cortical maps, their topographic organization, may largely be the outcome of selection for receptor surface neighborhood correlations. Simple, two-dimensional arrangements of receptor sheets, such as the cochlea or hemiretina, can be represented in simple topographic maps, having distortions but no splits. However, even representation of the hemiretina can be "split" along the representation of the horizontal meridian in such fields as V-II and DL (Figure 6), apparently due to constraints imposed by form and a long matched border at the representation of the zero vertical meridian. The more complex receptor surface of the contralateral body surface cannot be represented in a cortical sheet without "folds" and "splits." Folds occur when skin regions that are not normally next to each other are represented by adjacent blocks of neurons in cortex. For example, the thumb is commonly represented next to the lower lip in S-I (Kaas 1983). Splits occur when two or more parts of a continuous skin surface are represented in separate cortical locations within a field. As dramatic examples, the upper back is separated from the lower back by the representation of the wing in S-I

of bats (Calford et al 1985), and the upper trunk is separated from the lower trunk by the representation of the hindlimb in tree shrews (Sur et al 1981b). Despite the folds and splits, there is remarkable topography in cortical maps, as if every effort is made to preserve neighborhood relationships. Thus, it is usually possible to trace maze-like lines of continuity throughout cortical maps. For example, there is complete somatotopic continuity along the caudal border of S-I in tree shrews, and other parts of S-I have somatotopic continuity with that border (Sur et al 1981b). It is as if S-I in tree shrews developed from caudal to rostral in cortex with a somatotopic continuity rule that initially could be met due to a large degree of freedom, but soon led to discontinuities based on the constraints of having "used up" some skin surfaces.

The locations of folds and, to a greater extent, splits, are species-variable. Other species variations appear to occur for skin surfaces that are relatively isolated somatotopically in S-I and other fields. For instance, the enlarged representations of the hand and foot in areas 3b of monkeys tend to somatotopically isolate the representation of the trunk from the limbs. Perhaps as a result, the back is represented rostrally in area 3b of some monkeys and caudally in others (Sur et al 1982). The species variability, and the lesser individual variability in the relative locations of parts of receptor surfaces in sensory maps, suggest that details are not genetically specified, but related to other factors, such as the relative sequencing of correlated activity during development.

2. Features related to somatotopic "folds" in cortical maps suggest that a second developmental feature is shaped by activity. Folds result in adjacent groups of neurons with inputs from quite different skin regions, the lower lip and thumb, for example. Apparently, arbors of entering axons select one block of tissue or the other, and avoid a narrow "no-man's land" in between. Thus, the hand-face border in area 3b of monkeys remains stable while the hand representation does not when nerves to the hand are cut (Merzenich et al 1983). Borders between folds are often apparent as narrow, poorly differentiated regions. In the thalamus, such folds are marked by cell-poor zones or laminae that partially separate cell groups in nuclei. Thus, the face, hand, and foot representations are separated in the ventroposterior nucleus (see Kaas et al 1984 for review), and there is a cell-poor zone in the lateral geniculate nucleus separating neurons with inputs from either side of the optic disc of the retina (Kaas et al 1973). In cortex, the "folds" in the map and the resulting narrow zones of poor differentiation (e.g. the dysgranular zones in Figure 3) apparently result in a physically "weaker" zone that favors the development of an actual fold or fissure. Thus, representations of the hand and face, for example, are often separated in cortex by a shallow fissure (e.g. Welker & Campos 1963).

3. In addition, carefully timed selection for correlated activity in develop-

ment could account for many local features of organization such as the sequencing of orientation-selective neurons in cortical modules in area 17 and MT (see Kaas 1986), the variability in the presence of ocular dominance columns in striate cortex of monkeys and other mammals (see Florence et al 1986), the segregation by sublamina or patches of "on center" and "off center" receptive field classes of inputs in area 17 of some mammals (Norton et al 1983; McConnell & LeVay 1984) and classes of geniculate inputs in area 17 of monkeys (see Kaas 1986), and even the specific response properties of cells throughout cortex. The grouping of neurons with similar response properties within areas is a logical outcome of a selection process based on correlated activity.

4. Typically, cortical maps of receptor surfaces are precisely matched at common borders. Visual fields are commonly matched along representations of the zero vertical or portions of the zero horizontal meridians (see Allman & Kaas 1976; Kaas 1980; Van Essen 1985). The match is so precise that receptive fields overlap for neurons slightly displaced from the border in either direction. Similar matches occur between somatosensory fields and between auditory fields. For example, primary and secondary somatosensory fields are aligned along a common representation of the top of the head (e.g. Krubitzer et al 1986), the adjoining maps of the body surface in steplike areas 3b and 1 of monkeys are somatotopically aligned along their complete borders (see Kaas 1983), and auditory fields in cats and monkeys are matched at borders for representing high or low tones (see Merzenich & Kaas 1980). Such matched borders, because of the exactness of the alignment, have been called "congruent" (Allman & Kaas 1975). Such border alignments have no obvious function. They do allow short interconnections between areas at the border region, but other parts of the fields thereby have longer interconnections. Thus, it seems unlikely that border alignments would develop for functional reasons. However, the alignments would be an obvious outcome of selection for correlated activity.

CONCLUSIONS

Current viewpoints on how cortex is organized can usefully restrict and direct theories of brain function. Some of the conclusions that follow from these viewpoints are listed below.

1. Architectonic methods, when used alone, have not reliably determined functionally valid subdivisions of cortex. Subdivisions identified by architecture alone should be treated as hypothetical, subject to evaluation with other techniques. Studies of patterns of connections, topographic organization, neuron response properties, and the behavioral consequences of lesions have been valuable sources of additional information. Cortical subdivisions can be

most reliably identified by multiple criteria. A common practice in studies of cortex has been to refer to regions studied by architectonic terms, even when the architectonic fields have not been shown to be functionally significant, and even when the investigators fail to demonstrate that they have identified the fields by architecture in the experimental animals. This practice, by implying a state of understanding and accuracy that does not exist (see Lashley & Clark 1946, for further discussion), discourages and hinders further efforts to understand cortical organization. It is better to refer to cortical regions by reference to surface landmarks (e.g. posterior parietal cortex) if that is the actual practice.

2. Cortical areas, as functionally distinct divisions of the brain, frequently and perhaps always, are precisely localized. Therefore, restricted lesions can produce very specific and irreversible changes in behavior. However, because many of the details of internal organization within cortical areas are dynamically maintained, brain lesions are followed by a progression of alterations that may effectively compensate for aspects of the damage (see below).

3. Functional heterogeneity within fields permits parallel processing of information, and one field can function as several. However, more complex processing and the resulting behavioral advances have not been achieved by simply increasing the sizes and internal complexity of cortical areas. Thus it seems likely that no more than a few independent channels or types of processing modules coexist within a field. In addition, evidence for processing modules does not necessarily imply that an area mediates more than one function, since an uneven distribution of neurons with certain properties could relate to a single function. For example, neural mechanisms for discrimination of the orientation of line segments may require the grouping for local interactions of orientation-selective cells with similar preferences.

4. Behavioral advances are commonly dependent on increases in number of fields. This mechanism has been used in a number of lines of evolution. As a result, most areas in advanced mammals of different lines have been independently acquired and are not homologous, but they may function in similar ways and be highly analogous. However, because most fields are not homologous, generalizations across major taxonomic groups should be made with great caution.

5. In primitive to at least moderately advanced mammals, most of cortex is occupied by orderly sensory representations. Thus, sensory processing is the dominant cortical function, and most processing is concerned with a single modality.

6. In advanced mammals, perception is based on the coactivation of a number (5–20 for a single modality) of cortical fields. Even simple attributes of stimuli (such as color, motion, form) are unlikely to be based on processing within a single field. However, each activated area undoubtedly makes a field-specific contribution to the resulting perception.

7. Cortical maps function while having a number of different organizations across and even within species. It does not appear that the normal function of a field is seriously limited by the specifics of the internal representation of the receptor surface.

8. The microorganization of cortex is constantly in a state of flux, and stability results from a balance of competing factors. Receptors activate cortical space to an extent that is influenced by competition between inputs and relative use, so that increasing use probably increases cortical space and decreasing use probably decreases cortical space. Such a mechanism could account for the improvements in perceptual and motor skills that occur with practice, and the remarkable recoveries that often follow central nervous system injuries. It also follows that it will be very difficult to study the contribution of specific cortical areas in sensory-perceptual systems by deactivating (ablating) the areas, because reactions to lesions immediately start to alter the synaptic strengths of other connections. A partial solution to this problem may be to determine changes immediately after lesions, but changes can be very rapid.

9. The apparent importance of self-organizing processes in development, based on activity patterns, suggests that some specific features of cortical organization, such as the topographic details of sensory and motor representations, the border alignments of fields, and types of modular grouping of neurons, could be side-products of timing sequences in the building of brains. Thus, specific features of cortical organization may be necessary outcomes of the building process rather than features designed for maximizing function.

Literature Cited

Allman, J. M., Kaas, J. H. 1975. The dorsomedial cortical visual area: A third tier area in the occipital lobe of the owl monkey (*Aotus trivirgatus*). *Brain Res.* 100:473–87

Allman, J. M., Kaas, J. H. 1976. Representation of the visual field on the medial wall of occipital-parietal cortex in the owl monkey. *Science* 191:572–75

Bender, D. B. 1983. Visual activation of neurons in the primate pulvinar depends on cortex but not colliculus. *Brain Res.* 297:258–61

Blasdel, G. G., Lund, J. S. 1983. Terminations of afferent axons in macaque striate cortex. *J. Neurosci.* 3:1384–413

Brodmann, K. 1909. *Vergleichende Lokalisationlehre der Grosshirnrinde.* Leipzig: Barth

Bonin, G. von, Bailey, P. 1961. Pattern of the cerebral isocortex. In *Primatologia, Handbook of Primatology,* ed. H. Hofer, A. H. Schultz, D. Starck, 10:1–42. Basel: Karger

Calford, M. B., Graydon, M. L., Huerta, M.

F., Kaas, J. H., Pettigrew, J. D. 1985. A variant of the mammalian somatotopic map in a bat. *Nature* 313:477–79

Constantine-Paton, M. 1982. The retinotectal hookup: The process of neural mapping. In *Developmental Order: Its Origin and Regulation,* ed. S. Subtelny, pp. 317–49. New York: Liss

Easter, S. S., Purves, D., Rakic, P., Spitzer, N. C. 1985. The changing view of neural specificity. *Science* 230:507–11

Economo, C. von, Koskinas, G. N. 1925. *Die Cytoarchitektonic der Hirnrinde des erwachsenen Menschen.* Berlin: J. Springer. 811 pp.

Florence, S. L., Conley, M., Casagrande, V. A. 1986. Ocular dominance columns and retinal projections in New World spider monkeys (*Ateles ater*). *J. Comp. Neurol.* 243:234–48

Hubel, D. H., Livingstone, M. S. 1985. Complex-unoriented cells in a subregion of primate area 18. *Nature* 315:325–27

Kaas, J. H. 1980. A comparative survey of visual cortex organization in mammals. In *Comparative Neurobiology of the Telencephalon*, ed. S. O. E. Ebbesson, pp. 483–502. New York: Plenum

Kaas, J. H. 1982. The segregation of function in the nervous system: why do sensory systems have so many subdivisions? *Contrib. Sensory Physiol.* 7:201–40

Kaas, J. H. 1983. What, if anything, is S-I? Organization of first somatosensory area of cortex. *Physiol. Rev.* 63:206–31

✓Kaas, J. H. 1986. The structural basis for information processing in the primate visual system. In *Visual Neuroscience*, ed. J. P. Pettigrew, W. R. Levick, K. J. Sanderson. New York: Cambridge Press. In press

Kaas, J. H., Guillery, R. W., Allman, J. M. 1973. Discontinuities in the dorsal lateral geniculate nucleus corresponding to the optic disc: A comparative study. *J. Comp. Neurol.* 147:163–80

Kaas, J. H., Hall, W. C., Diamond, I. T. 1970. Cortical visual areas I and II in the hedgehog: Relation between evoked potential maps and architectonic subdivisions. *J. Neurophysiol.* 33:595–615

✓Kaas, J. H., Huerta, M. F. 1987. The subcortical visual system of primates. In *Comparative Primate Biology*, Vol. 4, *The Neurosciences*, ed. H. D. Steklis. New York: Liss

Kaas, J. H., Merzenich, M. M., Killackey, H. P. 1983. The reorganization of somatosensory cortex following peripheral nerve damage in adult and developing mammals. *Ann. Rev. Neurosci.* 6:325–56

Kaas, J. H., Nelson, R. J., Sur, M., Dykes, R. W., Merzenich, M. M. 1984. The somatotopic organization of the ventroposterior thalamus of the squirrel monkey, *Saimiri sciureus. J. Comp. Neurol.* 226:111–40

Kemper, T. L. B., Galaburda, A. M. 1984. Principles of cytoarchitectonics. In *Cerebral Cortex, Cellular Components of the Cerebral Cortex*, ed. A. Peters, E. G. Jones, 1:35–57. New York: Plenum

Killackey, H. P., Chalupa, L. M. 1986. Ontogenetic change in the distribution of callosal projection neurons in the postcentral gyrus of the fetal rhesus monkey. *J. Comp. Neurol.* 244:331–48

Killackey, H. P., Ebner, F. 1973. Convergent projection of three separate thalamic nuclei onto a single cortical area. *Science* 179:283–85

Krubitzer, L. A., Sesma, M. A., Kaas, J. H. 1986. Microelectrode maps, myeloarchitecture, and cortical connections of three somatotopically organized representations of the body surface in parietal cortex of squirrels. *J. Comp. Neurol.* 250:403–30

Lashley, K. S., Clark, G. 1946. The cytoarchitecture of the cerebral cortex of *Ateles:* A critical examination of architectonic studies. *J. Comp. Neurol.* 85:223–305

Lende, R. A. 1963. Cerebral cortex: A sensorimotor amalgram in the *Marsupial. Science* 141:730–32

Lende, R. A. 1964. Representation in the cerebral cortex of a primitive mammal. *J. Neurophysiol.* 27:37–48

Livingstone, M. S., Hubel, D. H. 1984. Anatomy and physiology of a color system in the primate visual cortex. *J. Neurosci.* 4:309–56

Maunsell, J. H. R., Van Essen, D. C. 1983. The connections of the middle temporal visual area (MT) and their relationship to a cortical hierarchy in the macaque monkey. *J. Neurosci.* 3:2563–86

McConnell, S. K., LeVay, S. 1984. Segregation of ON- and OFF-center afferents in mink visual cortex. *Proc. Natl. Acad. Sci. USA* 81:1590–93

Merzenich, M. M., Kaas, J. H. 1980. Principles of organization of sensory-perceptual systems in mammals. *Prog. Psychobiol. Physiol. Psychol.* 9:1–42

Merzenich, M. M., Kaas, J. H., Wall, J. T., Sur, M., Nelson, R. J., Felleman, D. J. 1983. Progression of change following median nerve sections in the cortical representation of the hand in areas 3b and 1 in adult owl and squirrel monkeys. *Neuroscience* 10:639–65

Mott, F. W. 1907. The progressive evolution of the structure and functions of visual cortex in mammalia. *Arch. Neurol.* 3:1–117

Mountcastle, V. B. 1978. An organizing principle for cerebral function: The unit module and the distributed system. In *The Mindful Brain*, ed. G. M. Edelman, V. B. Mountcastle, pp. 7–50. Cambridge: MIT Press

Norton, T. T., Kretz, R., Roger, G. 1983. ON and OFF regions in layer IV of tree shrew striate cortex. *Invest. Opahthalmol. Suppl.* 24:265

Pons, T. P., Kaas, J. H. 1985. Connections of area 2 of somatosensory cortex with the anterior pulvinar and subdivisions of the ventroposterior complex in macaque monkeys. *J. Comp. Neurol.* 240:16–36

Pons, T. P., Sur, M., Kaas, J. H. 1982. Axonal arborizations in area 3b of somatosensory cortex in the owl monkey, *Aotus trivirgatus. Anat. Rec.* 202:151A

Rakic, P., Bourgeois, J.-P., Eckenhoff, M. F., Zecevic, N., Goldman-Rakic, P. S. 1986. Concurrent overproduction of synapses in diverse regions of the primate cerebral cortex. *Science* 232:232–34

Rasmusson, P. P., Dykes, R. W., Hoeltzell,

P. B. 1979. Segregation of modality and submodality information in S-I cortex of cat. *Brain Res.* 166:409–12

Sanides, F. 1972. Representation in the cerebral cortex and its areal lamination pattern. In *The Structure and Function of Nervous Tissue,* ed. G. H. Bourne, 5:329–53. New York: Academic

Schmidt, J. T., Tieman, S. B. 1985. Eyespecific segregation of optic afferents in mammals, fish, and frogs: The role of activity. *Cell. Mol. Neurobiol.* 5:5–34

Sesma, M. A., Casagrande, V. A., Kaas, J. H. 1984. Cortical connections of area 17 in tree shrews. *J. Comp. Neurol.* 230:337–51

Smith, G. E. 1907. A new topographic survey of the cerebral cortex: Being an account of the distribution of the anatomically distinct cortical areas and their relationship to the cerebral sulci. *J. Anat.* 42:237–54

Sur, M., Nelson, R. J., Kaas, J. H. 1982. Representations of the body surface in cortical areas 3b and 1 of squirrel monkeys: Comparisons with other primates. *J. Comp. Neurol.* 211:177–92

Sur, M., Wall, J. T., Kaas, J. H. 1981a. Modular segregation of functional cell classes within the postcentral somatosensory cortex of monkeys. *Science* 212:1054–61

Sur, M., Wall, J. T., Kaas, J. H. 1984. Modular distribution of neurons with slowly adapting and rapidly adapting responses in area 3b of somatosensory cortex in monkeys. *J. Neurophysiol.* 51:724–44

Sur, M., Weller, R. E., Kaas, J. H. 1981b. Physiological and anatomical evidence for a discontinuous representation of the trunk in S-I of tree shrews. *J. Comp. Neurol.* 210:135–47

Tootell, R. B. H., Hamilton, S. L., Silverman, M. S. 1985. Topography of cytochrome oxidase activity in owl monkey cortex. *J. Neurosci.* 5:2786–800

✓Ungerleider, L. G., Mishkin, M. 1982. Two cortical visual systems. In *Advances in the Analysis of Visual Behavior,* ed. D. J. Ingle, J. W. Mansfield, M. A. Goodale, pp. 459–86. Cambridge: MIT Press

Van Essen, D. C. 1985. Functional organization of primate visual cortex In *Cerebral Cortex,* ed. E. G. Jones, A. A. Peters, 3:259–329. New York: Plenum

Vogt, C., Vogt, O. 1919. Allgemeinere Ergebnisse unserer Hirnforschung. *J. Psychol. Neurol. (Leipzig)* 25:279–462

Wall, J. T., Kaas, J. H. 1985. Cortical reorganization and sensory recovery following nerve damage and regeneration. In *Synaptic Plasticity,* ed. C. W. Cotman, pp. 231–60. New York: Guilford

Welker, W. I., Campos, G. B. 1963. Physiological significance of sulci in somatic sensory cerebral cortex in mammals of the family *Procyonidae. J. Comp. Neurol.* 120:19–36

✓Weller, R. E., Kaas, J. H. 1981. Cortical and subcortical connections of visual cortex in primates. In *Cortical Sensory Organization,* Vol. 2, *Multiple Visual Areas,* ed. C. N. Woolsey, pp. 121–55. Clifton, NJ: Humana

✓Weller, R. E., Kaas, J. H. 1986. Subdivisions and connections of inferior temporal cortex in owl monkeys. *J. Comp. Neurol.* In press

Ann. Rev. Psychol. 1987. 38:153–80

ADULT DEVELOPMENT AND AGING

Nancy Datan, Dean Rodeheaver, and Fergus Hughes

Human Development, University of Wisconsin–Green Bay, Green Bay, Wisconsin 54301-7001

CONTENTS

INTRODUCTION

Life-span development first appeared in the *Annual Review of Psychology* in 1980 (Baltes et al) and appeared for a second time in 1984 (Honzik). This third review presents a narrower focus in age range in order to explore in adequate depth recent significant developments in the field. Increased attention by psychologists to the period of adult development and aging is indicated by the American Psychological Association's "Older Boulder" Conference on Training Psychologists for Work in Aging (Santos & VandenBos 1982) and the new APA journal *Psychology and Aging*.

In the 1970s, Neugarten and Datan observed that historians, biographers, novelists, poets, philosophers, and dramatists had preceded developmental

153

0066-4308/87/0201-0153$02.00

psychologists into the study of the life cycle (Neugarten & Datan 1973; Neugarten 1977). In the 1980s we find that the field of life-span developmental psychology has been broadened by a newly augmented interdisciplinarity: humanists, philosophers, political scientists, economists, sociologists, and historians contribute new perspectives to the study of the life span (Datan et al 1986).

METHODOLOGICAL HERESIES

The diversity of methodologies that have been incorporated into the study of the life span, together with the substantive disciplines that give rise to them, suggests what we term heuristically a growth in *intrapsychic interdisciplinarity*. Meacham (1984) suggests that the field is moving away from testing hypotheses derived from theory, and towards more basic descriptive work, including a more systematic use of autobiography, biography, storytelling and conversation, diaries, literature, clinical case histories, historical fiction, and the like, with a new emphasis upon the person's construction and reconstruction of the "life story," rather than upon what might be considered a more objective account of what happened.

The field of life-span developmental psychology, in particular that portion of the field devoted to adult development and aging, demonstrates an increasing appreciation of the dialectic between researcher and research population, between the individual as object of study and the individual as the maker of the environment (Lerner & Busch-Rossnagel 1981). Personality and cognition, traditionally individualistic areas of research, now look to the social and historical context of individual development.

One illustration of this new synthetic approach is found in the work of Broughton (1984), who rejects the assumption that cognition can be studied in isolation from other developmental processes and from the sociocultural network in which it occurs. He argues that Piagetian psychologists, including those now searching for levels of adult cognition beyond formal operations, have supported a false dichotomy of cognition vs affect. They have practiced a "denial and elimination of critical social, biographical, and historical insight" (1984, p. 409) from their theorizing about adult cognition. The suggestion that a pure form of abstract logic is central to mature cognition leaves little room for the possibility that a person's intuition, judgment, or powers of reflection can influence intellectual functioning. In addition, the model is inappropriate for problem-solving of a psychological or social nature. Broughton (1984) sees the Piagetian model as artificially separating the subject from the object of knowledge, excluding the history of the individual thinker as well as the historical transformations of society.

Datan has proposed that the behavioral sciences disciplines demonstrate increased appreciation of the individuality of the research population as they move toward decreased focus on the individual as subject, as suggested by the following graphic contrast (Datan & Adams-Price 1986):

Discipline	Research Population
Psychology	Subjects
Sociology	Respondents
Anthropology	Informants

As the method of study moves away from the experimental, hypothesis-testing mode and toward the exploratory mode, a corresponding transformation in the posture of the investigator may be seen, from arrogance to humility. With increased interdisciplinarity characterizing the study of the life span, the field has come to embrace as complementary methodologies that were once viewed as mutually exclusive. (One indication of this shift is the recent change in terminology: psychologists now use the term "participants" for people who take part in their experiments.)

The need for greater humility in the study of the life span is also expressed by Rappaport (1985), who uses the autobiography of Fritz Heider to illustrate the inadequacy of normative developmental models for dealing with the life of a creative individual. He suggests a new focus on what he calls the "poetics" of human development and notes "a growing theoretical concern to elucidate the persistent, qualitative, figurative structures of personality (hence the poetics) that would allow us to appreciate an individual life course as a unique project" (1985, p. 140).

Datan employs "poetics" in the study of human development through a critical reconsideration of the "developmental mythologies" manifested by the selective use of Greek tragedy in the construction of developmental theory (Datan 1986a,c). Among these are the focus on Oedipus, the inadvertent parricide, to the exclusion of purposeful murderous parents such as Laius, Medea, and Agave (Datan 1982, 1984), the foreshadowing of the modern midlife crisis of achievement in the myth of Midas (Datan 1980), and the awareness of androgyny as adaptive in The Bacchae (Datan 1984).

In an attempt to understand the individual life course, gerontologists are increasingly adopting biographical techniques for delineating adult lives. In the process they are becoming "storytellers" (Kastenbaum 1985) and humorists (Datan 1986b). Perhaps the best example of this approach is the construction of the "personal narrative" (Cohler 1983, Cohler & Grunebaum 1981, Freeman 1984). The personal narrative is the individual's telling of a life story and the psychologist's interpretation of the story, weaving facts and inferences—derived from interviews, social history, and projective techniques—into a larger narrative to describe the individual's life in social context. The construction of such a narrative demands that the researcher become enmeshed in the story and the storyteller's life, striving for "the 'unity of mine and other' that is historical understanding" (Freeman 1984, p. 16). The researcher also becomes a storyteller, one who embellishes the story with social, cultural, and historical context and interprets the story in those contexts. Ideally, this "unity of mine and other" leads the researcher to an understanding of the future, as well—toward an understanding of the "past-in-the-present . . . [so that] out of retrospection . . . a project, an approximation toward desired ends, can be revealed. The shape that emerges out of the past extends itself into the future" (Freeman 1984, p. 17).

Many gerontologists are becoming dissatisfied with statistical profiles as conceptions of adult personality, profiles Kastenbaum has labelled "phantom cohorts . . . indeterministic statistical zones that construct people who never were and never could be" (1985, p. 7). Longitudinal study of personality traits "yields abundant evidence of the consistency and stability of selected personality dimensions but tells us little about more fundamental issues" (Carlson 1985, p. 390). Questions are being asked about the value of years of empirical work in the study of individual personality development:

> Measures of the relationship between test behavior and other test responses or actual behavior have consistently been reported to account for about 10% of the common variance. Even in those instances where such findings have been demonstrated to be nonrandom or significant at an accepted probability level, these statistically significant relationships provide little information about the manner in which persons interpret their experiences (Cohler & Grunebaum 1981, p. 3).

Increasingly, then, gerontologists are suggesting we surrender abstract notions of linear development and personality and focus on the individual's construction of adulthood (see, for example, Bengtson et al 1985). Much current research on personality argues for a personology of adulthood—an approach to personality development focused on individuals' attempts to order their lives rather than the psychologist's use of variables to order individuals' lives for them (Rodeheaver & Datan 1981, 1985).

Finally, in the study of adult development and aging the basic researcher looks to the practitioner to test the implications of developmental theory, while the practitioner looks to the basic researcher for the broader developmental context of the immediate clinical issue (Datan & Ginsberg 1975, Datan & Lohmann 1980). Investigators find that the individual shapes the social context, a finding that is reflected in recent scholarly emphasis upon the social context of aging and its implications for public policy.

ADULT DEVELOPMENT IN THE FAMILY CONTEXT

The growing interdisciplinarity in the study of adult development is most apparent in the study of the family, where sociological, historical, and cross-cultural research has altered our conceptions of the psychological development of family members (Datan et al 1986). Until the late 1960s, much of the work of developmental psychologists on the family could be described as an epitaph to the extended family, which recorded the destructive path of urbanization and modernization (see Bronfenbrenner 1970). However, recent research on the family suggests some alternate views. First, anthropologists and social historians have demonstrated that the extended family was never as prominent either in American history or in other cultures as popular myth would suggest (Laslett 1976, Nydegger 1983). Second, family relations persist into late life—the elderly are not isolated from family members (Shanas 1968). Gerontologists now accept these findings and are examining their consequences for psychological development.

Variations in family forms are increasingly viewed as inevitable, as adaptations to social and economic change (Datan et al 1984). Gerontologists are examining these adaptations, including, for example, an increasing emphasis on the psychological development and social adaptation of childless elderly, demonstrating that there is no decline in well-being, life satisfaction, or support among those without children in old age (Beckman & Houser 1982; DeJong et al 1984; Keith 1983). Investigators have also considered adult developmental issues among those who never marry. For example, Ward (1979) found never-married women emotionally vulnerable because of the absence of a "ready made confidant represented by a spouse" (p. 868). However, this vulnerability seemed to reflect the absence of social, psychological, legal, and economic support for the life-style of the never married. Thus, social and historical changes may make this life-style a more viable adaptation in future generations.

Other investigators have turned to an examination of the impact of divorce among older adults and their children. Chiriboga (1982), for example, has found the impact of divorce to differ depending on age and sex. "During the period immediately after separation . . . the older respondents were more unhappy and reported fewer positive emotional experiences. Their dealings with the social world appeared more tortured, there were more signs of personal discomfort, and their perceptions of the past and future reflected both greater pessimism and long-term dissatisfaction" (p. 113). This pessimism was especially apparent among men over the age of 50, 77% of whom were unable to project their lives into the future and anticipate what the future might hold. Women, by contrast, seemed to experience a short-term release from a confining marriage, and had expressed dissatisfaction earlier than men.

Older adults also experience some impact from their children's divorce, both psychologically and materially. Johnson (1981) found sorrow, shock, distress, and fury common among women when their children were divorced; and the stress persisted for some time after the divorce. Cicirelli (1983) observed that children experiencing a divorce felt less obligated to help their parents and perceived them as needing less help, at least in part because of changes in the children's economic conditions. These perceptions were accompanied by a real decline in help with transportation, recreation, protection, bureaucracies, and social services.

These studies indicate that the psychological development of adults occurs in the broader context of the life cycle of the family. The impact of changing demography on the social roles and psychological development of adults is most apparent with regard to the status of grandparents. Troll (1983) has suggested that the diversity of grandparenting styles and the number of factors related to grandparenting style—occupation, health, personality, and so on— indicate that grandparenting is not a role in the classic sense at all. There is no clear definition of the role; the status of grandparent is not attained voluntarily; and contact between grandparents and grandchildren is typically mediated by a middle generation. These factors seem to make grandparents particularly vulnerable during family disruptions. Matthews & Sprey (1984) found grandparents' vulnerability exhibited even before family disruptions: Grandparents in their study had not been consulted before their children sought a divorce; even if they had been consulted, they would not have been prepared because they apparently refused to consider such an event possible. This is consistent with what Troll (1983, 1985) has called the "family watchdog" role of grandparents: Grandparents may be seen as monitors of family affairs who are anxious to get on with their own lives and only step in when they see their values threatened or the family in trouble.

Furthermore, contact between grandparents and grandchildren depended for the most part on who got custody—if their own children had custody, grandparents could become significant figures in their grandchildren's lives (Matthews & Sprey 1984). Paternal grandparents, then, were especially likely to lose contact with their grandchildren. Finally, and perhaps most significantly, divorce affected not just the amount of contact between grandparents and grandchildren but the quality of that contact as well. Of the 13 grandparents in this study who labelled their grandparenting style "surrogate parents," 12 had experienced divorce in their families. "Adopting a particular style of grandparenting, then, does not appear to be simply a matter of personal choice but also a function of particular relationships, and it should be conceptualized as a response to circumstances" (Matthews & Sprey 1984, p. 44).

The ambiguous social status of grandparents is mirrored by their ambiguous legal status. Wilson & DeShane (1982) examined legal codes and cases in the United States regarding the rights and responsibilities of grandparents and found that "grandparents . . . are left with a legal history in case law that provides them with very few legal rights and the potential for extensive legal responsibilities" (p. 69). For example, grandparents may be sued for support of grandchildren in 32 states under family responsibility statutes dictating that the care of indigent kin lies with the nearest relative. By contrast, until 1977, the rights of grandparents were limited, usually to cases where the parents could be shown to be negligent or where the grandparent was already contributing significantly to the support of the grandchild. By 1977, 21 states had adopted laws allowing visitation rights for grandparents, regardless of the parents' situation.

Thus demographic and social changes affect the family and individuals within it. One such change that has been particularly important is the increase in longevity and the concomitant increase in the duration of family relations. Family ties, which now last longer than ever and extend over so many generations, require an increasing recognition of both love and hate as they interact to form the texture of intergenerational dynamics (Nydegger 1983, Rodeheaver & Thomas 1986, Troll 1984a). From such a point of view, the nature of the relationship that characterizes the family becomes the focus of attention rather than the individuals in the family (Troll 1985).

Cohler & Grunebaum have suggested that studies of adult relationships in the family have focused exclusively on notions of autonomy and separateness and have ignored other important dimensions of family relations. Their study describes the relationship among three generations of women as developmental interdependence—a complex relationship between personal autonomy and dependence in the developmental tasks of mothers and daughters. Interdependence, they suggest, arises from several conditions in the family lives of women. First, the socialization of women directs them toward relational modes of identity formation and towards dependency. Second, in young adulthood, traditional women's roles, interests, and concerns become increasingly like those of their mothers. Third, role strain and overload in the homemaking role lead women to look for help, often selecting their own mothers whose experience with the same role provides a model. Thus, in the family lives of women in the middle generation, "intimacy between husbands and wives is often less important than the satisfaction the wives seek from continuing close ties with their own mothers" (Cohler & Grunebaum 1981, p. 323). The women in the oldest generation, however, were disturbed by what they saw as the continued dependence of their daughters and often sought emotional distance from them. This may reflect a developmental shift in their lives away from interdependence toward personal autonomy—greater interiority, the desire for more time to themselves. Thus, the developmental needs of each generation put them in conflict but left the successful accomplishment of the developmental tasks of each dependent on the other. However, with an increase in life expectancy, families face a reversal of this interdependent relationship. Cohler & Grunebaum note that women reach a stage of personal autonomy and independence at a point when aging parents are dependent on them for care.

Brody (1985) has written evocatively about this relationship, estimating that at any given time, well over five million people in the United States are involved in parent care. Most are adult daughters, who face a psychological dilemma arising from a combination of popular myths about the family, changing values, and the nature of parent-child relationships. First, the myth persists that children are not taking care of their aging parents the way they used to in "the good old days" (Brody 1985, p. 19). In reality, people are living longer and suffering more chronic illnesses: Children are placed in the position of providing skilled nursing care for which they are not prepared. Thus, Brody concludes, "The irony of the myth is that *nowadays adult children provide more care and more difficult care* to more parents over much longer periods of time than they did in the good old days" (p. 21). This reality notwithstanding, adult caregivers believe that they are not taking care of their parents the way parents used to be taken care of. Adult children also believe that they are not taking care of their parents as well as their parents took care of them, thus compounding the guilt created by the myth. As Brody notes, they cannot match the care their parents provided for them because the dependence of old age is much less total than the dependence of infancy and childhood. Thus, popular fallacies and the developmental dynamics of the life cycle trap adult children in self-perceived hopeless inadequacy.

For the adult daughters of aging parents who need care, changing cultural values add to their frustration. These daughters, whom Brody calls the "women in the middle" (1985, p. 24), are caught between two sets of values—one emphasizing women's roles as family caregivers, the other egalitarianism between the sexes and careers for women. In addition to the stress of providing care for which they are not trained and the guilt from believing they are not providing adequate care, these women in the middle, embracing conflicting values, face a choice between the caregiving career and other careers they have pursued outside the home.

Thus, studies of the family increasingly emphasize constant change in family forms and have begun to examine the impact of such changes on psychological development. This emphasis on the context of adult development is also seen in studies of personality.

PERSONALITY DEVELOPMENT: NEW PERSPECTIVES ON CONTINUITY AND CHANGE

During the 1970s, conceptions of adult personality development could be divided between those suggesting stages of personality change and those suggesting stability of personality despite the life-cycle transitions of adulthood. The study of adult development suddenly became the topic of bestselling books, foremost among which was Gail Sheehy's *Passages: Predictable Crises of Adult Life* (1976). The scholarly works from which *Passages* drew, including Roger Gould's *Transformations* (1978) and Daniel Levinson's *The Seasons of a Man's Life* (1978), examined the same theme of orderly change in adult life. At the same time, Costa & McCrae, in longitudinal studies of personality traits (Costa & McCrea 1980, McCrea & Costa 1984), found no evidence of systematic transformations in adult personality. These contradictory positions led some developmental psychologists to declare that the study of adult personality development was in disarray. Neugarten (1977), for example, suggested that no predictive statements of any kind regarding adult personality development were within reach because of the enormous conceptual and methodological problems within the field. To some extent, this situation persists, with a continued focus on stages of change or stability of traits. Recent research, though, has questioned the generalizability of each of these perspectives. Two examples illustrate this point.

Daniel Levinson has studied the life structure, "the underlying pattern or design of a person's life at a given time" (Levinson 1986, p. 6). Levinson's theory of psychosocial development suggests age-related seasons of development of the life structure—an alternating pattern of structure-building, in which the goal is to "form a life structure and enhance our life with it" (p. 7), and structure-changing, in which the individual reappraises the life structure, explores new possibilities, and moves toward new commitments. The life structure does not change in an orderly fashion, but the seasons in which it changes are predictable and universal.

In contrast to research suggesting developmental stages, some research demonstrates stability in adult personality traits. The Baltimore Longitudinal Studies conducted by Costa & McCrae have demonstrated stable patterns of traits over a series of repeated personality tests that are not attributable to the effects of attrition, practice, social or historical changes, or time of measurement (McCrae et al 1980). Costa & McCrae suggest that although adult personality can change, it typically does not.

However, arguments for the stability of personality are challenged by research suggesting that the social and cultural context must be considered. Some investigators have found that generational differences in social norms affect measures such as achievement motivation (Troll & Schwartz 1984). Furthermore, certain personality traits have been related to differences in mortality, which suggests that our picture of personality in later adulthood is incomplete since some personality types are more likely to survive into old age than others (Siegler 1985). Finally, some research suggests that results from all-male samples in the work of Levinson and Costa & McCrae may be truer of men than women (Chiriboga 1982). Reinke et al (1985) found that the seasons of a woman's life were not age-related but rather changed with the timing of events in the family. Transitions were most frequent during the creation of a family, the launching of the next generation, and the postparental period. Nor were these seasons of change universal. Most women did not experience these family-cycle transitions at all; among those who did, each woman faced an idiosyncratic transition, dealing with her own unique issues and outcomes.

Another challenge to a traditional and perhaps masculine view of women's lives is provided by Datan et al (1981) in a cross-cultural study of women in middle age. Contrary to widely held beliefs, the loss of fertility at menopause was welcomed by women in five Israeli subcultures, despite wide, culturally consistent differences in childbearing histories and marital relationships. This finding suggests a universal developmental stage at midlife that is the reverse of the regret over lost fertility predicted by early psychoanalytical theorists.

Significant conceptual questions about stability and change are raised by the Jerusalem Study of Mid-Adulthood and Aging, a longitudinal study of several subcultures in Israel. Findings have been reported for two independent samples, each followed for seven to eight years from 1967 to 1980 (Shanan 1985) and provide a dialectical perspective on the question of stability versus ordered change. Stability was clearly demonstrated to be a function of the antecedent personality type. Two personality types (active integrated copers and dependent passive copers), to which the majority of the sample belonged, were relatively stable. Two types (failing overcopers and self-negating undercopers), representing about a quarter of the sample, were unstable. Significant changes included attitudes toward work and family, a shrinking time perspective, and increasing passivity. It was suggested that these types differed from the beginning in internal consistency. In addition to antecedent personality type, stability was related to educational and subcultural differences. In accounting for this combination of stability and change Shanan concludes that the personality development of adults is characterized by reorganization toward internal consistency, but that such reorganization is not identical to stability in personality.

A dialectical perspective on adult personality development suggests that previous models were constrained first by the notion that adult development is linear and cumulative, and second by the notion that personality consists of objectively measurable traits. The notion that adult development is linear and cumulative—that is, that certain personalities are more "adult" than others—underlies stage theories of adult development. There is little empirical evidence for such orderly and progressive change, nor is there any agreement on the outcome. That there seems to be no final stage toward which the adult personality evolves has led Neugarten (1983) to suggest that we liberalize the concept of development, free it from the notion of linearity, perhaps even go so far as to say we are not studying life-span development at all but rather the "course of human lives." From this perspective, life-span development becomes individual life history, which in turn becomes a life story—an attempt by the individual to create a narrative given order and predictability only by the choices and decision-making of that individual. The order in the course of lives lies, then, in the minds of the persons experiencing those lives, not in the observer. The goal of this study of the course of human lives "is not to discover universals, not to make predictions that will hold good over time, and certainly not to control; but, instead, to explicate contexts and thereby to achieve new insights and new understandings" (Neugarten 1984, p. 292).

If adult personality demonstrates any order, then, it may not be the result of a developmental trajectory but instead a reflection of the individual's attempts to maintain a sense of continuity. Gerontologists have offered a number of suggestive perspectives on this process. One of the most intriguing is Kastenbaum's notion of aging as habituation, a decreasing attention to repetitive stimuli in one's life: "What we recognize as 'aging' or 'oldness,' " he suggests, "is the emerging tendency to overadapt to one's own routines and expectations rather than to adapt flexibly and resourcefully to the world at large" (1984, p. 113). An individual's life may exhibit inordinate continuity ("hyperhabituation") as in cases when the individual fears change, resists the future, and experiences the present always in the same way: The "past draws the present and future like a magnet, and so rapidly that one may never actually experience the present as present. It is as though the past devours the new moment before it can establish its own unique character" (1980–81, p. 167).

Another view of adaptation to stress among the elderly suggests that it can be seen as a striving toward self-sameness (Fisseni 1985, Tobin 1985): "The adaptive challenge in old age is to maintain self-consistency when confronted with assaults that include not only bodily deterioration but loss of others and whatever it means to confront one's own mortality. [Compared to the young], . . . the very old have had a more extensive past life, have responded over several years to the accumulation of narcissistic assaults, have become aware that their life span has been lived and most likely have accepted their personal finitude. Whereas the task of maintaining the self may be similar, the mechanisms for doing so may be quite different" (Tobin 1985, p. 183). Self-sameness may be maintained through a variety of mechanisms, including reference to the way one is now, reference to specific events in the past that confirm that one has always been as one is now, a generalized notion that one has simply always been this way, or through distortion and wishes. Self-sameness may also be maintained through the process of mythmaking—a form of self-validation involving changing one's past or one's present to justify the self or make vivid to oneself one's uniqueness. Fisseni (1985) reports a similar process whereby individuals come to conceptualize constrictions in life space—due to low income, poor health, or widowhood, for example—by developing a personal life theme premised on the "perceived unchangeability" of life.

Script theory attempts to account for the merger of biology, socialization, and the historical moment in the life of the individual and thus constitutes an approach with particular value for the study of life-span development, emphasizing the individual construction of adult life (see, for example, Carlson 1981, Tomkins 1986). The premise of script theory is simple: "The human being is born a biological entity, whose destiny it is to die a socialized, acculturated advocate or adversary of a civilization at a particular historical moment" (Tomkins 1986). Individuals experience events in their lives as "scenes"—organized wholes combining people, places, time, actions, and, in particular, affects that amplify these experiences and provide a sense of urgency about understanding them. Out of early scenes, the individual develops sets of rules for interpreting, evaluating, producing, predicting, or controlling future scenes. These rules—"scripts"—are initially innate but are supplemented and replaced by learned scripts. Higher-order scripts are created when scenes are combined and instilled with fresh affect—"psychological magnification." These co-assembled scripts develop an enduring importance in the individual's life because of the power of psychological magnification, which involves "recruitment of memories, thoughts, actions, and feelings" (Carlson 1981, p. 503). Thus, the individual constructs his or her own increasingly complex way of comprehending the major happenings in life—a set of co-assembled scripts.

Script theory provides a historical and contextual account of individuals making sense of the course of their lives.

> Personality development is best understood as the formation, growth, or decline of (*a*) scenes that represent important features of an individual's life and (*b*) scripts that enable the person to anticipate, respond to, control, or create events in a meaningful fashion. An essential premise of script theory is that personality development is not plotted as a one-way progression from earlier to later constructions of experience. Instead, there is two-way traffic through time. Constructions of the past may be radically changed in the light of later experience; anticipations of the future may color the present and revise the past; old experiences may return to alter the present (Carlson 1981, p. 503).

The order in personality development, then, derives from the individual's need to impose order—the script—on the critical events, or scenes, in life. And, finally, scripts that initially arise from scenes begin to give rise to scenes instead, as the individual's construction of experience affects experience itself.

McCrae & Costa (1984) have suggested that biographical, interview, and projective techniques invariably contaminate the life story with the subjective influence of the researcher. Furthermore, they argue, since these life stories are told by individuals whose memories are flawed, it would seem that the story must always be fiction. However, as Kastenbaum notes, statistical "stories" about adults might also be seen as fiction. Moreover, while memory may well be distorted, so may so-called objective techniques, since "the investigator's measures may be only a different kind of distortion of psychological reality" (Neugarten 1983, p. 11). Cohler & Grunebaum suggest that the fear of subjectivity is overstated, since the goal of the personal narrative is to present a detailed network of fact, inference, and interpretation concerning an individual's life—a narrative that can be *publicly* evaluated on its own terms. The life narrative is judged on the basis of its consistency, coherence, comprehensiveness, and intelligibility to the reader; "that interpretation is judged most successful which provides the most complete account and which is most capable of integrating additional data into the formulation" (Cohler & Grunebaum 1981, p. 4).

In summary, much of the research on adult personality has been concerned with whether or not personality changes in an orderly fashion. The researcher's goal is prediction, either the prediction of a sequence of changes or the prediction of constancy. But recent studies of adult personality development differ in focusing on continuity as it is created by the individual, not measured by the researcher (Lerner & Busch-Rossnagel 1981).

We suggest that such studies ask the Humpty Dumpty question of adult personality: "Who is to be master?" when it comes to orderliness in adult development—the researcher or the participant? The distinction between stability and reorganization toward internal consistency reflects a new conceptual and methodological unity that seems to be emerging from earlier disarray in the study of adult personality. The adult life span is increasingly seen as a product of the adult's attempts to maintain a sense of continuity. Furthermore, the study of that process demands that the researcher relinquish a measure of conceptual and methodological "objectivity" in exchange for increasing sensitivity to the individual's construction of a life story and the social, historical, and cultural contexts of that story.

The study of adult personality development has moved a long way from the early debate over orderly change versus stability. It is now marked by an increasing attention to the contexts of change and continuity, and to the individual's construction of the life course. As we shall show, the study of cognitive development exhibits similar trends.

COGNITIVE DEVELOPMENT

Growth and Regression in Adult Cognition

An examination of the last 30 years of research on adult cognition yields a fairly consistent pattern. The early research, in the 1950s and 1960s, was characterized by an accumulation of data in many cognitive areas—conditioning, verbal learning, problem-solving, memory, formal reasoning—

and comparisons of the performances of young and elderly adults on identical measures. Conclusions drawn from the early studies were depressingly similar: Negative change was found in virtually all areas of cognition across the span of adult life. As Botwinick (1967) noted in summarizing the findings to date, "The general trend in [adult] cognitive functioning is downhill, and it would be foolhardy to ignore this" (p. 202).

During the 1970s some of the earlier negative perceptions of adult cognition were revised; a newer body of research seemed to indicate that cognitive decline occurs later in life than had been suspected and was restricted to fewer functions (Botwinick 1977, Labouvie-Vief 1985). The issue of adult cognitive decline became at least a controversial one, as a variety of questions were raised about the nature of the circumstances under which regression occurs. These questions were generally addressed in terms of what became known as the competence-performance distinction. Research repeatedly demonstrated that the intellectual performance of the old was hindered by their poor health, lack of education, greater cautiousness, inexperience with tests, slower responses, and so on (Reese & Rodeheaver 1985). These findings suggest that, if these factors were eliminated, young and old adults could perform alike. There is no age difference in intellectual competence, then; the difference lies in performance—how the competence of old and young is demonstrated in measures of intelligence, problem-solving, and memory.

The current trend is toward recognition that existing theoretical models, and most notably the formal operational framework proposed by Piaget (Inhelder & Piaget 1958; Piaget 1983), may not be adequate to explain adult intellectual change. As Labouvie-Vief (1985) observed, the question whether or not age brings with it a cognitive decline may no longer be a useful one. For example, while the competence-performance distinction focuses on demonstrating that old and young are *equally* competent, we might better assume that they are *differently* competent. More pertinent to the study of adult cognition is the question of how intellectual maturity is to be defined, and whether unstated assumptions about optimal intellectual functioning may be distorting our views of the intellectual capacities of older adults.

The current challenge to the Piagetian model of adult cognition has come from two directions. Some who accept the basic Piagetian framework argue that Piaget did not go far enough in describing the richness of adult cognition. Volumes edited by Commons et al (1984, 1986a,b) contain a number of newer perspectives on adult reasoning. Such researchers are attempting to identify stages or modes of thinking that build upon and go beyond formal operations. One example of such a stage is found in the work of Arlin (1975, 1984), who suggests that the problem-solving mode of formal thought is a necessary but insufficient condition for the more advanced mode of "problem-finding." Richards & Commons (1984) have developed instruments to assess the presence of three levels of reasoning beyond formal operations: the systematic, the meta-systematic, and the cross-paradigmatic.

Other critics challenge the very assumptions upon which the Piagetian model is based. Labouvie-Vief (1982, 1984, 1985) points out the inherent bias against late-adulthood modes of thinking that underlies the Piagetian assumptions about the process of development. His theory, she asserts, assumes a progression toward a "pure" state of reasoning, free from subjectivity and cultural contamination and totally objective in its search for truth. For Piaget, the dynamics of individual personality and the sociocultural milieu can be thought of as influences on, and perhaps hindrances to, cognitive growth rather than as essential features of it. Abstract, hypothetical reasoning is the paragon of mature human cognition. In marked contrast is the thinking of the child, which Piaget considers subjective, intuitive, perception-bound and egocentric, and later rational but concrete in its ability to engage in hypothetic-deductive reasoning. It is only when the "final stage of equilibrium" has been reached that the mature mind can engage in dispassionate objective reasoning, free from the subjectivity of earlier stages; this is the transition to formal operational thought. "Mature" reasoning thus involves a denial of subjectivity; it requires what Labouvie-Vief calls a devaluation of the inner life and an increase in the efficiency of thinking at the expense of depth and intensity.

The separation in the realm of cognitive development between a personal, subjective, intuitive mode of knowing on the one hand and a universal, objective, and rational mode on the other has typically carried with it, as in Piaget's view, the assumption that the former mode is developmentally inferior to the latter—a concept of cognition that Labouvie-Vief (1985) refers to as vertical, or hierarchical. The implications of Piaget's and other such vertical models of modes of thinking for the area of adult cognition are especially troublesome. Compared to young adults, older adults typically do not perform as well on measures of formal reasoning ability. Older adults tend to personalize such tasks, to analyze the possible ways in which a question might be interpreted, to consider affective dimensions that might be involved in a problem solution, and to suggest that several answers might be possible, when in fact a pure form of hypothetico-deductive reasoning would suggest that only one correct solution exists. In other words, it appears to be their reliance on intuitive and personal modes of thinking, their tendency to "go beyond the information given," that has resulted in the failure of older adults to demonstrate formal operational skills. If one views dispassionate reasoning ability as the crowning achievement of human cognition, then the subjectivity often seen in the problem-solving of older adults can only be viewed as regression.

Labouvie-Vief's recent work (1982, 1984, 1985, 1986a,b; G. Labouvie-

Vief, C. Adams, J. Hakim-Larson, M. Hayden, and M. DeVoe, submitted for publication) contains the most basic challenge to the Piagetian premise that the intuitive and the rational modes of thinking are arranged hierarchically. She argues that the subjective, intuitive mode, which she calls "mythos," exists in parallel with instead of subordinate to the objective, rational mode, referred to as "logos." Thus the two modes of knowledge balance and enrich each other.

The thinking of older adults would not be characterized as regressive in Labouvie-Vief's view of thinking modes as parallel. A certain degree of subjectivity in reasoning, a reliance on intuition, and a reference to an appropriate social context would indicate a move away from the literal, formal and somewhat rigid thinking of young adulthood. Mature adults progress rather than regress in their attention to the "psychological, social-normative, and metaphoric implications of information" (1986a). They become increasingly autonomous as they dare to bring a sense of their own individuality to the reasoning process. They recognize the limitations of pure forms of reasoning for solving problems; what is logically correct does not always work where reality is ordered from many different perspectives. In fact, complex social reasoning can be seen as a developmental extension of formal reasoning.

Consider, for example, the difference in the ways young and old adults might deal with the logic of complex human relationships. Young adults may try to exercise logic to resolve an ambiguous situation. Older adults, by contrast, may be more likely to apply their experiences to illustrate the ambiguity of such situations. Labouvie-Vief (1985, 1986a) suggests that such a tendency to personalize issues and to reason by intuition rather than principles of formal logic is not an inferior mode of problem-solving. It represents not a failure in reasoning ability, but an effective dialog between intuitive and formal reasoning, between "mythos" and "logos."

Current perspectives on adult cognition do not suggest that age differences and/or age changes are insignificant, or that a reexamination of the yardsticks by which performance is measured will eliminate all age-related signs of cognitive regression. Rather, current research emphasizes that the unidirectional and hierarchical model of development contains an inherent bias against adult cognitive development, and, further, that intellectual performance cannot be separated from its social and cultural context. Assumptions about intellectual maturity are being challenged by new interdisciplinary perspectives on adult cognition.

Social Cognition

As does research on adult cognitive development, research in the area of social cognition (the application of cognitive principles to the social arena) reflects the trends described throughout this chapter: increasing interdisciplinarity in developmental research and the recognition that the sociocultural context cannot be ignored in research on individual development.

Earlier studies of social cognition focused primarily on the childhood years. Interest centered on concepts of empathy and role-taking as well as on the child's understanding of, needs for, and expectations of friendship (Radke-Yarrow et al 1983, Rubin & Ross 1982, Shantz 1983). The framework used in much of the earlier work was the genetic epistemological model of Piaget, a reflection of his influence on the study of childhood cognition. A parallel was noted between the child's move from an egocentric perspective to the ability to engage in role-taking behavior and genuine empathy. As the child moved from the level of concrete to the level of abstract formal reasoning, there was a parallel move from superficial and action-oriented conceptions of friendship to conceptions based on mutual understanding, trust, and shared values. With development, shared actions as the criterion for friendship selection was supplanted by shared psychological characteristics.

While the social cognition research on children and adolescents often lent support to Piagetian theory, a different pattern emerged when social cognition was studied in adulthood. Studies of the cognitive components of adult interpersonal relationships called into question the validity of Piaget's formal operational model as the end point of human cognition—indeed, required the postulation of post-formal reasoning stages.

Formal operational reasoning allows an individual to define key variables in a problem, to consider a matrix of possible outcomes, and to estimate the probabilities of various outcomes (Piaget 1983, Powell 1984). Formal reasoning has a dispassionate quality, however; the subject of knowing is divorced from its object. As Benack (1984) noted, the formal reasoner considers reality to have an independent existence beyond the knower; the knower thus becomes a vessel through which objective reality is passed, with the presumption that all reasonable persons should arrive at identical definitions of truth.

A knowledge of social reality reveals complex social interactions, in which roles and relationships change constantly and depend to a significant degree on the perceptions of the participants in those relationships. Thus social cognition requires an intrusion of the subject into the knowing process, and the dispassionate formal operational model does not suffice. In fact, interpersonal conflict, a failure in the area of social intelligence, is thought to result from formal operational reasoning, in which "pure" knowledge, free from subjectivity and devoid of a social context, is glorified; in the mind of such "dualist" thinking, "what I feel" becomes "what any reasonable person would feel" and consequently "what you must feel" (Benack 1984, Perry 1970). The result is interpersonal tension, or, at a more global level, an intolerance of the beliefs and life-styles of other people (Sinnott 1984).

It is precisely this failure of mature formal reasoning to bring about an equally mature version of adult social reasoning that has led many current researchers of adult development (e.g. Benack 1984, Powell 1984, Sinnott 1984) to question the utility of the Piagetian model. As Sinnott (1984) observed, a different set of operations is needed to organize a person's complex understanding of interpersonal reality. These are relativistic operations, which involve a subjective selection among logically contradictory, but internally consistent, formal-operational subsystems. For example, the formal operational thinker may see a particular type of parent-child relationship as one of a number of possible relationships within the family unit. The post-formal relativistic thinker realizes that a particular parent-child relationship is not just one or another of a range of possibilities; it may actually be many relationships, even contradictory relationships, depending on the particular social circumstances and prevailing moods of the persons involved. The relationship has no existence independent of the persons within it and no existence without a given social context.

Some have also maintained that sophisticated peer interactions involve a component of relativism that goes beyond formal reasoning (e.g. Benack 1984, Powell 1984). To interact effectively with others, to develop a mature sense of empathy, one must realize that any issue can be viewed from many perspectives. Effective social interaction requires an understanding that a search for one absolutely correct course of action is futile because reality and truth depend upon the social context. This perspective stresses that the subject and the object of knowing can never be separated. What a person feels or believes in a particular social context may be different from what others think and feel; contradictory perspectives on any issue may be expressed by flawlessly logical thinkers.

FROM LAB TO LIFE: DEMOGRAPHY AND THE DIALECTIC BETWEEN THEORY AND PRAXIS

The age distribution of the population has been shifting: By the year 2000 the largest age group in the United States will be between the ages of 30 and 44, and significant growth in the over-45 age group will continue (Cross 1981, 1985). The median American age in 1975 was 28.8; by 1990 it will be nearly 33 (Apps 1981). In the CORAD report of 1967, Robert Havighurst proposed that the traditional tripartite division of the life cycle—the first third devoted to learning and apprenticeship, the second to work and productivity, and the third to leisure—was not an optimal pattern for the life course. Rather, periods of productive labor and the refreshment of leisure might be interspersed earlier in the life cycle, and learning be extended throughout the life course. Goals that reason (or idealism) failed to accomplish in the 1960s have become, through the realpolitik of changing demographics, the new developmental opportunities of the 1980s.

Learning and the Life Cycle

A substantial portion of the American adult population, approximately one person in four, is thought to be currently undergoing career transition; mid-career change is becoming increasingly common as economic and social circumstances restrict career mobility (Cross 1981, Meadors 1984). In order to plan for career advancement, make a mid-life change, or simply gain entry into the job market as a mature adult, 60% of those involved in career transition indicate they plan to seek additional education (Cross 1981). The aging of the population and the increased likelihood of mid-career changes have had a significant impact on the world of higher education. "Adult" college students already outnumber students in the traditional age range of 18–22, and there is every indication that this pattern will become even more pronounced in the 1990s and beyond (Chickering 1981, Cross 1985, Meadors 1984). Thus the college classroom is increasingly becoming a social context, a real-life situation, in which adult learning takes place. What is more, the traditional emphasis of psychological research on adult learning (e.g. studies of conditioning, verbal learning, and abstract problem-solving) hardly touches upon the issues faced by adult college students, precisely because so many of the learning challenges faced by these students are framed within a larger social context. Cultural expectations of age or gender, availability of support from friends and family, history of prior academic success or failure, and expectations about self and the demands of the academic world all combine to influence the adult learning experience.

Throughout the 1960s and 1970s, the adult learner was of interest primarily to educators (e.g. Apps 1981; Cross 1971, 1981; Kidd 1973; Knowles 1978; Smith 1982), who compared older learners to traditional students with a view to understanding the special needs and problems of the older learner both within and outside of the classroom. Adult learners were found to be more highly motivated than traditional students, more accustomed to thinking of learning as occurring in both informal and formal settings, and more capable of bringing a rich variety of experiences to the classroom material, despite deficiencies in many skills required for success in the classroom. Moreover, returning adult students lacked self-confidence in formal learning settings (as did their age-mates who were research participants in laboratories) and experienced higher anxiety about learning than their younger counterparts. Adult learners also faced a number of obstacles not usually faced by younger students: conflicting home and/or job responsibilities, lack of transportation, absence of child-care facilities, lack of support from friends and family, and difficulty in accommodating to course schedules designed for traditional full-time students.

Although adult learners have been of interest to educators for the past 20 years, psychological studies of adult learning have until recently been confined to the laboratory. Reviews of research on adult cognition (e.g. Hughes 1980, Wass & Olejnik 1983), have led to the same frustrating conclusions: The link between laboratory research and learning in the larger social context is tenuous at best. As Wass & Olejnik (1983) concluded, laboratory research on adult cognition should be seen as a first step in a process that eventually leads to field research in actual educational settings. Studies of conditioning or paired-associate learning have limited applicability in applied learning environments; memory drums are not found in college classrooms (Datan & Adams-Price 1986).

In the 1980s we find the work of educators at last converging with the work of psychologists interested both in adult cognition and in the complex of social and cultural factors influencing the adult learning experience. Psychologists are becoming increasingly interested in the larger social context of adult learning—in the subjective experience of being a learner and in objective performance on a learning task. Educators, meanwhile, are increasingly likely to apply the methods of the laboratory to the world of adult education. Psychologists are increasingly interested in global noncognitive variables that form the broad sociocultural context of learning.

As an example, studies of younger and older women in college suggest that stereotyped expectations for feminine behavior may inhibit the achievement of younger women (Datan & Hughes 1985, Komarovsky 1985, Troll 1984b); however, while the older woman student comes to college after having discarded some restrictive conceptions of gender, other factors, such as lack of support from family, from friends, and from professors may undermine her. The intellectual challenge of the classroom is embedded in a complex network of cultural expectations.

Adult students, like their younger classmates, are often seen by professors as dependent on authority and in need of direction and control (Schlossberg 1984). But dependency has been outgrown by many adult learners, who have achieved success in other areas of their lives, are not accustomed to such assumptions of dependence and the result may be a bruising of tender egos and a disruption of the learning process (Steitz 1985). This student-faculty tension mirrors broader developmental processes: Professor and adult student may be divided by academic expertise or lack of it, but united by a shared stage in ego development; in Erikson's (1982) framework, both feel a need to achieve generativity, with its related virtues of productivity in one's own life and caring for the younger generation. A professor may fail to recognize that adult students have already been productive in many areas and consider the care provided younger students to be condescending. Indeed, the professor's sense of productivity may be threatened when adult students, who have the real-world expertise to do so, challenge his/her academic material (Steitz 1985). Thus, the developmental needs of both teacher and student interact to influence the learning situation.

Gray America and Public Policy

Andrew Achenbaum's history of aging in America (1978) indicates that until the 1900s the reality and the rhetoric of aging constituted separate histories. When aging became a social problem, rhetoric and reality converged. The rhetoric of aging—especially as expressed through policies and programs designed to solve the problems of the aged—began to shape the reality of aging in America. Given the increasing emphasis on contexts of adult development, then, social policy as a shaper of context becomes an integral part of the study of the course of adult lives. Gerontologists have been generally concerned with the social dilemma created by age entitlement programs, and particularly concerned with the relationship between the rhetoric of policy and the realities of the new elderly poor—a process that has been called "the graying of the feminization of poverty."

Social programs created during this century have improved the social condition of the aged. The number of old people living in poverty, for example, has dropped dramatically in the past few decades. However, not all the elderly have benefited equally from government programs: ". . . when all federal programs are considered together—the direct payments, the in-kind transfers, the tax benefits—it is evident that most of the benefits are going to those older people who are in the top third of the income distribution. Further, if these programs continue in their present direction, they will not only maintain the present inequalities, they will create even further disadvantages for those older persons who are poor" (Neugarten & Neugarten 1986, p. 44). Thus, while only a few decades ago the aged as a group were seen as disadvantaged, evidence suggests that within the older population, a different economic problem is arising: The poor are getting poorer.

The impact of the Reagan administration's economic plan has received considerable attention in relation to the new poverty of aging. Storey (1983) has noted that the Reagan plan was not directed toward the aged specifically but toward improving the living conditions of all by promoting economic growth through tax cuts, reducing federal government control and funding of state and local programs, and limiting federal spending. While programs for the aged have experienced fewer cuts than programs aimed at other age groups, the aged themselves, and in particular the poor aged, have been disproportionally hurt. They gain nothing from tax cuts since most of their income is from nontaxable sources. They are the group most dependent on state and local health and social service programs, those programs for which federal support is being reduced. And attempts to limit spending have led to two strategies of great importance for the low-income aged—increased Medicare premiums and cost sharing and delayed cost of living adjustments in Social Security and other cash benefits. An individual case reveals the impact of these changes: " . . . a food stamp recipient who lived in subsidized housing may have experienced all the following reductions in benefits and services over a span of 1 or 2 years: a rent increase, a reduced food stamp allotment, a decline in public transportation, fewer social services, and reduced access to free medical care" (Storey 1986, p. 29). Perhaps more significant is the suggestion that such an economic and political climate might actually inhibit dealing with recently identified social problems experienced by the aged. For example, Douglass (1983) concludes a review of research on elder abuse with the following pessimistic forecast:

> The early 1980s may be the least opportune time since World War II to "discover" a "new" social problem. The political climate, economic uncertainty and increasingly conservative public spending all suggest that it is unlikely that major government supported programs will be created to combat neglect and abuse of the elderly in ways that even remotely reflect the government's past responses to child abuse and spouse abuse. (p. 401)

The oldest of the old are most affected by current social policies (Storey 1983), and the oldest of the old are predominantly female. Storey's hypothetical food stamp recipient was most likely a woman, since the majority of food stamp recipients and beneficiaries of subsidized housing, social services, and health care programs are women. Thus, attempts to balance the budget are placing an additional burden on elderly women, whose economic condition shows they are already overburdened. Two out of every three elderly poor are female (Warlick 1985). One half of elderly women earned less than $5000 a year in 1980. Poverty rates are particularly high for elderly women living alone and are astronomical for elderly black women, 82% of whom are poor or near poor (Minkler & Stone 1985). The economic vulnerability of women is further aggravated by their poorer health—they experience more injuries, disabilities, and restricted activity days than men—and by their spending more for health care—25% of their median income is spent on out-of-pocket health care costs.

The process Minkler & Stone term "the graying of the feminization of poverty" reflects not merely the impact of aging in a less than hospitable world, but also social roles, choices, and differential opportunities throughout adulthood. First, women are disadvantaged by their work histories. Family and caretaking concerns that produce interrupted or delayed careers result in less retirement income and lower Social Security benefits. Job segregation has restricted many women's employment to small firms in occupations characterized by low unionization and low wages and fringe benefits so that private pensions are small and unreliable (Minkler & Stone 1985). Second, inequities in economic policies and benefits in old age represent a carryover from common law notions of dependency and deservingness—women whose husbands abandon them or are unwilling or unable to support them have long been considered undeserving of public support. Limitations on both Social Security and private pension benefits reflect this notion: Before the recent enactment of legislation such as the Retirement Equity Act, for example, widows had no coverage under their husbands' private pensions unless their husbands decided early in their work lives to reduce their own benefits to take out survivors' annuities (Minkler & Stone 1985, Warlick 1985).

The inherent sexism in some social policies is further reflected in the caretaking dilemmas faced by those Brody calls the "women in the middle" (1985). Women are more likely than men to sacrifice their careers to take care of spouses and, increasingly, parents (Datan 1981, Holt & Datan 1984). As we noted earlier, such women, who sacrifice their jobs during the final stages of a career of caregiving which began with childrearing, experience further frustration because of the pervasive myth that families are no longer taking good care of their oldest members: " . . . social policy echoes, uses, and perpetuates the myth, exerting psychological pressure on adult children, increasing their guilt, and adding to their strains by failing to provide services and facilities that are urgently needed to back up their efforts" (Brody 1985, p. 27).

Furthermore, such guilt may lead some families to avoid in-home care altogether due to concerns about the quality of care, loss of control, the stigma of welfare, and the intrusiveness of the bureacracy of such programs; likewise, families delay seeking long-term care. The cost of avoiding in-home care and delaying long-term care is demonstrated in research which consistently finds that elders are typically admitted to long-term care facilities too late (Troll 1984a). Thus, the new voluntarism benignly suggests that family members take better care of the aged. The reality behind this rhetoric is that adult women are taking care of their aging parents and are often trying to provide help that is beyond their means. As Brody points out, they need help in doing so, not the admonition that they should be doing more.

Gerontologists are also concerned with more general effects of age entitlement programs and with the failure of such programs to address the real problems of aging (Neugarten 1982). Laws and policies based on chronological age—e.g. age entitlement programs like Supplemental Security Income and Medicare—assume a correspondence between age and some other characteristic, such as income or health care needs. Gerontologists are becoming increasingly uncomfortable advocating the needs of the elderly while simultaneously recognizing that the elderly do not exist as a homogeneous group. It has become difficult to distinguish age groups—even among those over age 65—in terms of health status, life events, or any other measure (Neugarten & Neugarten 1986). Several alternatives to age entitlement exist:

eliminating age as a proxy and measuring need and competence directly; redefining old age by using the age of 75 as a consistent criterion; or moving toward viewing old age as "an earned status that should provide special rewards and benefits" (Neugarten 1981, p. 820); but each alternative is associated with a problem of its own.

The dilemma of this conflict between age entitlement and need-based policies is discussed by Neugarten & Neugarten (1986). On the one hand, until age-based programs targeted the old, their social problems went largely ignored. If age-based programs are abandoned in favor of need-based programs, will the social progress made by the aged be abandoned as well? On the other hand, while targeting the aged identifies them as a social problem, it may likewise contribute to age segregation and stereotyping since age-based policies ignore the diversity of the aged. That social policies for the aged are based on ageist assumptions was noted in 1970 by Neugarten and has been reiterated by Binstock (1983), who further suggests that ageist social policies have led to a scapegoating of the aged as the primary reason for current budget deficits. In truth, while entitlements to the aged represent 26% of federal outlays, the proportion of outlays spent on entitlements to the aged has not changed since 1980. Defense spending, rising interest rates, and tax cuts are primarily responsible for budget deficits. This scapegoating suggests, however, the possibility that social programs for the aged have aggravated their social condition by erroneously identifying them as a homogeneous target group.

Thus, an increasing emphasis on the contexts of adulthood and the resulting diversity in adult development lead to the dialectic between theory and practice in the study of adulthood. The economic conditions of aged women must be understood in terms of the relational and familial contexts of women's adult lives and in terms of the social policies that inequitably distribute both the benefits and the burdens of economic recovery. Furthermore, an understanding of the relationship between rhetoric and reality should inspire gerontologists not to take the role of objective outsider but to recognize that the lives of the aged are increasingly shaped by social perceptions that take the form of policy.

ADULT DEVELOPMENT AND AGING: NEW FRONTIERS IN THE SOCIOLOGY OF KNOWLEDGE

This review of adult development and aging has suggested that the study of the life cycle has been broadened by new intellectual perspectives and new social realities. With the graying of America has come increased attention to the older population, manifest through a greater appreciation of the individual as active in the construction of knowledge, in the creation of consistency in personality development, and in the shaping of the broader social context of the life course.

Literature Cited

Achenbaum, W. A. 1978. *Old Age in the New Land: The American Experience Since 1790.* Baltimore: Johns Hopkins Univ. Press

Apps, J. W. 1981. *The Adult Learner on Campus.* Chicago: Follet

Arlin, P. K. 1975. Cognitive development in adulthood: A fifth stage. *Dev. Psychol.* 11:602–6

Arlin, P. K. 1984. Adolescent and adult thought: A structural interpretation. See Commons et al 1984, pp. 258–71

Baltes, P. B., Reese, H. W., Lipsitt, L. P. 1980. Life-span developmental psychology. *Ann. Rev. Psychol.* 31:65–110

Beckman, L. J., Houser, B. B. 1982. The consequences of childlessness on the social-psychological well-being of older women. *J. Gerontol.* 37:243–50

Benack, S. 1984. Postformal epistemologies and the growth of empathy. See Commons et al 1984, pp. 340–56

Bengtson, V. L., Reedy, M. N., Gordon, C. 1985. Aging and self-conceptions: Personality processes and social contexts. See Labouvie-Vief 1985, pp. 544–93

Binstock, R. H. 1983. The aged as scapegoat. *Gerontologist* 23:136–43

Botwinick, J. 1967. *Cognitive Processes in Maturity and Old Age.* New York: Springer

Botwinick, J. 1977. *Aging and Behavior.* New York: Springer. 2nd ed.

Brody, E. M. 1985. Parent care as a normative family stress. *Gerontologist* 25:19–29

Bronfenbrenner, U. 1970. *Two Worlds of Childhood.* New York: Simon & Schuster

Broughton, J. M. 1984. Not beyond formal operations but beyond Piaget. See Commons et al 1984, pp. 395–411

Carlson, R. 1981. Studies in script theory: I. Adult analogs of a childhood nuclear scene. *J. Pers. Soc. Psychol.* 40:501–10

Carlson, R. 1985. Masculine/feminine: A personological perspective. *J. Pers.* 53:384–99

Chickering, A. W., and Associates. 1981. *The Modern American College.* San Francisco: Jossey-Bass

Chiriboga, D. A. 1982. Adaptation to marital separation in later and earlier life. *J. Gerontol.* 37:109–14

Cicirelli, V. G. 1983. A comparison of help-ing behavior to elderly parents of adult children with intact and disrupted marriages. *Gerontologist* 23:619–25

Cohler, B. J. 1983. Autonomy and interdependence in the family of adulthood: A psychological perspective. *Gerontologist* 23:33–39

Cohler, B. J., Grunebaum, H. 1981. *Mothers, Grandmothers, and Daughters: Personality and Child Care in Three-Generation Families.* New York: Wiley

Commons, M. L., Richards, F. A., Armon, C., eds. 1984. *Beyond Formal Operations: Late Adolescent and Adult Cognitive Development.* New York: Praeger

Commons, M. L., Sinnott, J., Richards, F. A., Armon, C., eds. 1986a. *Beyond Formal Operations 2: Comparisons and Applications of Adolescent and Adult Developmental Models.* New York: Praeger.

Commons, M. L., Kohlberg, L., Richards, F. A., Sinnott, J., eds. 1986b. *Beyond Formal Operations 3: Models and Methods in the Study of Adult and Adolescent Thought.* New York: Praeger. In press

Costa, P. T. Jr., McCrae, R. R. 1980. Still stable after all these years: Personality as a key to some issues in adulthood and old age. In *Life-Span Development and Behavior,* ed. P. B. Baltes, O. G. Brim Jr., 3:65–102. New York: Academic

Cross, K. P. 1971. *Beyond the Open Door: New Students to Higher Education.* San Francisco: Jossey-Bass

Cross, K. P. 1981. *Adults as Learners.* San Francisco: Jossey-Bass

Cross, K. P. 1985. The changing role of higher education in the learning society. *Continuum* 49:101–10

Datan, N. 1980. Midas and other mid-life crises. In *Mid-Life: Developmental and Clinical Issues,* ed. W. H. Norman, T. J. Scaramella, pp. 3–19. New York: Brunner/Mazel

Datan, N. 1981. The lost cause: The aging woman in American feminism. In *Towards the Second Decade: The Impact of the Women's Movement on American Institutions,* ed. B. Justice, R. Pore, pp. 119–25. Westport, Conn: Greenwood Press

Datan, N. 1982. After Oedipus: Laius,

Medea, and other parental myths. *J. Mind Behav.* 3:17–26

Datan, N. 1984. Androgyny and the life cycle: the Bacchae of Euripides. *J. Imag. Cog. Pers. Sci. Stud. Consciousness* 4:405–13

Datan, N. 1986a. Oedipal conflict, Platonic love: Centrifugal forces in intergenerational relations. See Datan et al 1986

Datan, N. 1986b. The last minority: Humor, old age, and marginal identity. In *Humor and Aging*, ed. L. Nahemow, K. A. McCluskey-Fawcett, P. E. McGhee, pp. 161–71. New York: Academic

Datan, N. 1986c. The Oedipus cycle: Developmental mythology, Greek tragedy, and the sociology of knowledge. *Int. J. Aging Hum. Dev.* In press

Datan, N., Adams-Price, C. 1986. We get too soon old and too late smart—Or do we? Developmental perspectives on intelligence and aging. In *Handbook of Applied Gerontology*, ed. G. Lesnoff-Caravaglia. New York: Human Sciences Press. In press

Datan, N., Antonovsky, A., Maoz, B. 1981. *A Time to Reap: The Middle Age of Women in Five Israeli Subcultures.* Baltimore: Johns Hopkins Univ. Press

Datan, N., Antonovsky, A., Maoz, B. 1984. Love, war, and the life cycle of the family. In *Life-Span Developmental Psychology: Historical and Generational Effects on Life-Span Human Development*, ed. K. A. McCluskey, H. W. Reese, pp. 143–59. New York: Academic

Datan, N., Ginsberg, L. H., eds. 1975. *Life-Span Developmental Psychology: Normative Life Crises.* New York: Academic

Datan, N., Hughes, F. 1985. Burning books and briefcases: Agency, communion and the social context of learning in adulthood. *Acad. Psychol. Bull.* 7:175–86

Datan, N., Greene, A., Reese, H. W. 1986. *Life-Span Developmental Psychology: Intergenerational Relations.* Hillsdale, NJ: Erlbaum

Datan, N., Lohmann, N., eds. 1980. *Transitions of Aging.* New York: Academic

DeJong, G. F., Cornwell, G. T., Hanson, S. L., Stokes, C. S. 1984. Childless and one child, but not by choice: A note on some long-term consequences for life-satisfaction of rural-reared married women. *Rur. Sociol.* 49:441–51

Douglass, R. L. 1983. Domestic neglect and abuse of the elderly: Implications for research and service. *Fam. Relat.* 32:393–402

Erikson, E. 1982. *The Life Cycle Completed: A Review.* New York: W. W. Norton

Fisseni, H. J. 1985. Perceived unchangeability of life and some biographical correlates. In *Life-Span and Change in a Gerontological Perspective*, ed. J. M. A. Munnichs, P. Mussen, E. Olbrich, P. G. Coleman, pp. 103–31. New York: Academic

Freeman, M. 1984. History, narrative, and life-span developmental knowledge. *Hum. Dev.* 27:1–19

Gould, R. L. 1978. *Transformations.* New York: Simon & Schuster

Holt, L., Datan, N. 1984. Senescence, sex roles, and stress: Shepherding resources into old age. In *Sex Roles and Psychopathology*, ed. C. S. Widom, pp. 339–52. New York: Plenum

Honzik, M. P. 1984. Life-span development. *Ann. Rev. Psychol.* 35:309–31

Hughes, F. P. 1980. Review of research in selected areas of adult cognitive development: Implications for adult education. *Resources in Educ.* ERIC clearinghouse on adult, career, and vocational education, ED 203, 078, July. (Unpublished)

Inhelder, B., Piaget, J. 1958. *The Growth of Logical Thinking from Childhood to Adolescence.* New York: Basic Books

Johnson, E. S. 1981. Older mothers' perceptions of their child's divorce. *Gerontologist* 21:395–401

Kastenbaum, R. J. 1980–81. Habituation as a model of human aging. *Int. J. Aging Hum. Dev.* 12:159–70

Kastenbaum, R. J. 1984. When aging begins: A lifespan developmental approach. *Res. Aging* 6:105–17

Kastenbaum, R. J. 1985. *The life history work of Barbara Myerhoff: A critical appraisal.* Presented at Ann. Meet. Gerontol. Soc. Am., 38th, New Orleans

Keith, P. M. 1983. A comparison of the resources of parents and childless men and women in very old age. *Fam. Relat.* 32:403–9

Kidd, J. R. 1973. *How Adults Learn.* New York: Assoc. Press

Knowles, M. S. 1978. *The Adult Learner: A Neglected Species.* Houston: Gulf. 2nd ed.

Komarovsky, M. 1985. *Women in College: Shaping New Feminine Identities.* New York: Basic Books

Labouvie-Vief, G. 1982. Dynamic development and mature autonomy: A theoretical prologue. *Hum. Dev.* 25:161–91

Labouvie-Vief, G. 1984. Logic and self regulation from youth to maturity. See Commons et al 1984, pp. 158–79

Labouvie-Vief, G. 1985. Intelligence and cognition. In *Handbook of the Psychology of Aging*, ed. J. E. Birren, K. W. Schaie, pp. 500–30. New York: Van Nostrand Reinhold. 2nd ed.

Labouvie-Vief, G. 1986a. Modes of knowledge and the organization of development. See Commons et al 1986b

Labouvie-Vief, G. 1986b. Towards adult autonomy: A theoretical sketch. In *Adult Development*, ed. E. Langer, C. Alexander. Cambridge, Mass: Oxford Univ. Press. In press

Laslett, P. 1976. Societal development and aging. In *Handbook of Aging and the Social Sciences*, ed. R. H. Binstock, E. Shanas, pp. 87–116. New York: Van Nostrand Reinhold

Lerner, R. M., Busch-Rossnagel, N., eds. 1981. *Individuals as Producers of Their Own Development*. New York: Academic

Levinson, D. J. 1986. A conception of adult development. *Am. Psychol.* 41:3–13

Levinson, D. J., and Assoc. 1978. *The Seasons of a Man's Life*. New York: Knopf

Matthews, S. H., Sprey, J. 1984. The impact of divorce on grandparenthood: An exploratory study. *Gerontologist* 24:41–47

McCrae, R. R., Costa, P. T. 1984. *Emerging Lives, Enduring Dispositions: Personality in Adulthood*. Boston: Little, Brown

McCrae, R. R., Costa, P. T., Arenberg, D. 1980. Constancy of adult personality structure in males: Longitudinal, cross-sectional and time-of-measurement analyses. *J. Gerontol.* 35:877–83

Meacham, J. A. 1984. The individual as consumer and producer of historical change. See Datan et al 1984

Meadors, A. C. 1984. Non-traditional education: A slowly developing giant. *Educ. Res. Q.* 9:5–9

Minkler, M., Stone, R. 1985. The feminization of poverty and older women. *Gerontologist* 25:351–57

Neugarten, B. L. 1970. The old and the young in modern societies. *Am. Behav. Sci.* 14:13–24

Neugarten, B. L. 1977. Personality and aging. In *Handbook of the Psychology of Aging*, ed. J. E. Birren, K. W. Schaie, pp. 626–49. New York: Van Nostrand Reinhold

Neugarten, B. L. 1981. Age distinctions and their social functions. *Chicago Kent Law Rev.* 57:809–25

Neugarten, B. L., ed. 1982. *Age or Need? Public Policies for Older People*. Beverly Hills: Sage

Neugarten, B. L. 1983. *The study of aging and human development*. Presented at Conf. Race, Class, Socialization, Life Cycle, Univ. Chicago, Chicago

Neugarten, B. L. 1984. Interpretive social science and research on aging. In *Gender and the Life Course*, ed. A. Rossi, pp. 291–300. Chicago: Aldine

Neugarten, B. L., Datan, N. 1973. Sociological perspectives on the life cycle. In *Life-Span Developmental Psychology: Personality and Socialization*, ed. P. B. Baltes,

K. W. Schaie, pp. 53–69. New York: Academic

Neugarten, B. L., Neugarten, D. A. 1986. Age in the aging society. *Daedalus* 115:31–49

Nydegger, C. N. 1983. Family ties of the aged in cross-cultural perspective. *Gerontologist* 23:26–32

Perry, W. G. 1970. *Forms of Intellectual and Ethical Development in the College Years*. New York: Holt, Rinehart & Winston. 2nd ed.

Piaget, J. 1983. Piaget's theory. In *Handbook of Child Psychology*: Vol. 1. *History, Theory, and Methods*, ed. W. H. Kessen; series ed. P. H. Mussen, pp. 103–28. New York: Wiley

Powell, P. M. 1984. Stage 4A: Category operations and interactive empathy. See Commons et al 1984, pp. 326–39

Radke-Yarrow, M., Zahn-Waxler, C., Chapman, M. 1983. Children's prosocial dispositions and behaviors. In *Handbook of Child Psychology*: Vol. 4. *Socialization, Personality, and Social Development*, ed. E. M. Hetherington; series ed. P. H. Mussen, pp. 469–545. New York: Wiley

Rappaport, L. 1985. Scholarly creativity and the poetry of human development: The life of Fritz Heider. *Hum. Dev.* 28:131–40

Reese, H. W., Rodeheaver, D. 1985. Problem solving and complex decision making. See Labouvie-Vief 1985, pp. 474–99

Reinke, B. J., Ellicott, A. M., Harris, R. L., Hancock, E. 1985. Timing of psychosocial changes in women's lives. *Hum. Dev.* 28:259–80

Richards, F. A., Commons, M. L. 1984. Systematic, metasystematic, and cross-paradigmatic reasoning: A case for stages of reasoning beyond formal operations. See Commons et al 1984, pp. 92–119

Rodeheaver, D., Datan, N. 1981. Making it: The dialectics of middle age. See Lerner & Busch-Rossnagel 1981, pp. 183–96

Rodeheaver, D., Datan, N. 1985. Gender and the vicissitudes of motivation in adult life. In *Advances in Motivation and Achievement*, Vol. 4, *Motivation and Adulthood*, ed. D. A. Kleiber, M. L. Maehr, pp. 169–87. Greenwich, Conn: JAI Press

Rodeheaver, D., Thomas, J. 1986. Family and community networks in Appalachia. See Datan et al 1986

Rubin, K. H., Ross, H. S., eds. 1982. *Peer Relationships and Social Skills in Childhood*. New York: Springer-Verlag

Santos, J. F., VandenBos, G. R., eds. 1982. *Psychology and the Older Adult: Challenges for Training in the 1980s*. Washington, DC: Am. Psychol. Assoc.

Schlossberg, N. K. 1984. Caught in a dilemma: Adults as learners. In *New Perspectives on Counseling Adult Learners,* ed. H. B. Gelatt, N. K. Schlossberg, E. L. Herr, A. Q. Lynch, A. W. Chickering, G. R. Walz, L. Benjamin, pp. 15–26. Ann Arbor, Mich: ERIC Couns. Personnel Serv. Clearinghouse

Shanan, J. 1985. Personality types and culture in later adulthood. *Contrib. Hum. Dev.* Vol. 12. Basel: Karger (Monograph)

Shanas, E. 1968. Family help patterns and social class in three countries. In *Middle Age and Aging,* ed. B. L. Neugarten, pp. 296–305. Chicago: Univ. Chicago Press

Shantz, C. U. 1983. Social cognition. In *Handbook of Child Psychology, Vol. 3. Cognitive Development,* ed. J. H. Flavell, E. M. Markman; series ed. P. H. Mussen, pp. 495–555. New York: Wiley

Sheehy, G. 1976. *Passages: Predictable Crises of Adult Life.* New York: E. P. Dutton

Siegler, I. C. 1985. *Facets of adulthood: towards a developmental health psychology.* Presented at Ann. Meet. Am. Psychol. Assoc., 93rd, Los Angeles

Sinnott, J. D. 1984. Postformal reasoning: the relativistic stage. See Commons et al 1984, pp. 298–325

Smith, R. M. 1982. *Learning How to Learn: Applied Theory for Adults.* Chicago: Follett

Steitz, J. A. 1985. Issues of adult development within the academic environment. *Lifelong Learn.* 8:15–17

Storey, J. R. 1983. *Older Americans in the Reagan Era.* Washington, DC: Urban Inst. Press

Storey, J. R. 1986. Policy changes affecting older Americans during the first Reagan administration. *Gerontologist* 26:27–31

Tobin, S. S. 1985. Psychological adaptation to

stress by the elderly. In *Homeostatic Function and the Aged,* ed. B. B. Davis, W. G. Wood, pp. 181–95. New York: Raven

Tomkins, S. S. 1986. Script theory. In *Structuring Personality,* ed. J. Aronoff, R. A. Zucker, A. I. Rabin. Orlando, Fla: Academic. In press

Troll, L. E. 1983. *The contingencies of grandparenting.* Presented at Wingspread Conf. Grandparenting and Family Connections, Racine, Wis.

Troll, L. E. 1984a. *Old ways in new bodies: handing down kinkeeping.* Presented at Ann. Meet. Gerontol. Soc. Am., 37th, San Antonio

Troll, L. E. 1984b. *Old women: "Poor, dumb, and ugly."* Presented at Ann. Meet. Am. Psychol. Assoc., 92nd, Toronto, Canada

Troll, L. E. 1985. *Parent-child relationships over the life span.* Presented at Univ. Wis., Madison

Troll, L. E., Schwartz, L. 1984. A three-generational analysis of changes in women's achievement motivation and power. In *Social Power and Dominance in Women: Interdisciplinary Perspectives on Women's Contexts for Exerting Control and Influence,* ed. L. S. Auerbach, C. D. Ruff, pp. 81–98. Washington, DC: AAAS

Ward, R. L. 1979. The never married in later life. *J. Gerontol.* 34:861–69

Warlick, J. L. 1985. Why is poverty after 65 a women's problem? *J. Gerontol.* 40:751–57

Wass, H., Olejnik, S. F. 1983. An analysis and evaluation of research in cognition and learning among older adults. *Educ. Gerontol.* 9:323–37

Wilson, K. B., DeShane, M. R. 1982. The legal rights of grandparents: A preliminary discussion. *Gerontologist* 22:67–71

Ann. Rev. Psychol. 1987. 38:181–202
Copyright © 1987 by Annual Reviews Inc. All rights reserved

AUDITORY PSYCHOPHYSICS:
Spectrotemporal Representation of Signals

E. de Boer and W. A. Dreschler[1]

Academic Medical Center, Laboratory of Auditory Physics, University of Amsterdam, Amsterdam, The Netherlands

CONTENTS

INTRODUCTION

Selecting papers for a review chapter is a difficult task, the more so since we feel it is better to discuss just a few subjects at some length rather than going through the literature on a "random walk" with no more than a walking stick to point at landmarks. As a result, the list of contemporary papers referenced in this chapter is restricted. Many good and important papers will be missing from that list, and work is omitted in several fields far from central hearing theory (e.g. noise and noise annoyance, fatigue, adaptation, TTS, au-

---

[1] In the chapter's table of contents the section marked with an asterisk was written by W. A. Dreschler and E. de Boer, the others by E. de Boer.

181

0066-4308/87/0201-0181-$02.00

diometry, and other purely clinical applications). Also omitted are tactile communication and psychophysical testing of people equipped with a cochlear implant. Because of the growing importance of these fields we mention one review paper on tactile communication (Verrillo 1985), and two books on cochlear implants (Schindler & Merzenich 1985, Gray 1985).

One general line of research in auditory psychophysics—one might well call it conservative—is directed at consolidation of what has been achieved previously. Another line is directed at better understanding the nature of impaired hearing. As a consequence of the first line the reader will find in the present chapter sections on spectral analysis, temporal phenomena, binaural hearing, and pitch perception. These topics all entail spectrotemporal analysis of sounds. Examples of the (straightforward) application of the techniques developed to the testing of hearing-impaired subjects will be found in these sections as well.

Determination of thresholds—of detection or of discrimination—forms a central tool in most studies. The methodology of threshold determination is conservative, Levitt's classical (1971) paper being perhaps the most-cited in the literature scanned. Hall (1983) improved the usefulness of adaptive up-down methods, Jesteadt (1980) proposed successfully the use of two interleaving sequences of trials, and de Boer & van Breugel (1984) extended the class of adaptive measuring procedures. A procedure that would be suitable for use in clinical testing has been developed by Stelmachowicz & Jesteadt (1984). Their procedure is a variation of the so-called PEST method (cf Taylor et al 1983). Note that the theory behind many types of adaptive procedure has not been worked out at all.

So much for the conservative side. Several new effects have been discovered. In a general sense these all demonstrate interactions between excitations in different frequency bands, often far wider apart than one critical band. They are reviewed below under the appropriate headings. One effect not easily categorized is profile analysis. A brief description of this concept follows. Two types of experiment are possible to measure discrimination of auditory intensity. In one, the traditional successive method, two stimuli with different intensities (tones, for instance) are presented in succession. In the other method, two complex stimulus bursts are presented and the tone under consideration, the signal, is made stronger in one of them. It turns out that in the second type of experiment the detection threshold can be significantly lower than in the first (Green et al 1983). The auditory system appears to carry out a "profile analysis," as it is called, to detect the component that is "sticking out" of the background formed by the remaining components. In later studies remarkable properties of the effect have been found such as the virtual absence of phase influences (Green and Mason, 1985). Surprisingly enough, demonstration of the effect requires much experience on the part of the subject. Appealing as the concept of profile analysis might be for auditory theory, it probably does not play an important part in everyday sound analysis.

The second line of research is directed at pathological hearing. McFadden & Wightman's (1983) *Annual Review of Psychology* paper was devoted entirely to that theme. Here we describe mainly psychophysical findings in this field, especially those concerned with speech reception. The relations among the various data obtained are complex. One section of this chapter reviews the problem of finding the underlying structure of these relations.

SPECTRAL RESOLUTION AND INTEGRATION

Why is such a large part of psychophysical research in audition devoted to spectral analysis? Evidently not everything has been discovered yet, and one reason is that in psychophysics the excitation of the auditory system can be measured only indirectly, usually via masking. Masking itself is a nonlinear phenomenon (one sound overriding another one, a thing that can never happen in a linear system), but excitation is also highly nonlinear. Therefore, one has to be careful in choosing the appropriate measuring technique, and because a unique interpretation of the results is often impossible one has to be equally careful in explaining the results. Verschuure (1981a,b) presented a concise classification of types of experiments to outline auditory frequency selectivity. An "extension pattern" is measured when the frequency of the masker is kept constant and the excitation evoked by that masker is mapped via the use of a variable-frequency probe tone. In measuring a "filter pattern" the situation is reversed: the frequency of the probe tone is fixed and that of the masker is varied. Experimental paradigms can differ also in that either the input or the output level is kept constant. This is described by referring to an "input extension pattern," etc; a clearer designation would be "constant-input extension pattern," etc. Wegel & Lane's (1924) classical study of frequency selectivity actually reports a constant-input extension pattern. The measurement of a psychophysical tuning curve (PTC) is a technique to determine a constant-output filter pattern. This method is used to seek all combinations of masker level and frequency that produce a constant amount of excitation in the frequency region of the probe tone. Because of the nonlinearity, the two patterns are not equivalent.

Measurement of PTCs was initiated by Chistovich (1957) and Small (1959), was restarted by Zwicker (1974), and has continued into the present (e.g. Stelmachowicz & Jesteadt 1984). However simple the technique looks, it has many pitfalls. Two varieties are used: simultaneous masking and forward masking. In the former, the probe tone occurs while the masker is on, providing ample opportunity for direct interaction of the two signals. In forward masking, the probe is presented after the masker has ceased. Direct interaction of masker and probe signals is then absent or negligible.

A great problem in interpreting the data is that PTCs measured with simultaneous and with forward masking are different. Moore (1978) described the differences in detail. Tips of PTCs measured with forward masking are sharper and they become even sharper when the level of the probe tone is increased. Just the opposite occurs in simultaneous masking. What part is played by suppression? According to the results of Weber (1983), suppression may be minimal in simultaneous-masking PTC situations. Then what other effects are contributing? And which of the two types of PTC really represents physiological tuning? Moore et al (1984) made a rather successful attempt to solve this problem. Off-frequency listening constitutes an important problem in both types of PTC measurement. The major component of off-frequency listening is traceable to the fact that the excitations of masker and probe spread over certain frequency regions. Hence the auditory system may well utilize the point where the signal-to-noise ratio is largest. This component can be countered by using an additional masker in the form of a noise band (cf Johnson-Davies & Patterson 1979).

A peculiar effect to which Moore and his associates have often called attention concerns a perceptual cue in forward masking. When masker and probe frequencies are similar, the probe sounds as a continuation of the masker, and as such it is difficult to detect. When the two frequencies are dissimilar, this effect does not occur. The net effect of this cue is that a PTC measured with a nonsimultaneous masker lies at too low levels around its tip and thus looks artificially sharpened. The influence of this perceptual cue can be eliminated or reduced by giving the listener an additional cue to the cessation of the masker. A wide-band noise signal presented contralaterally has proved effective (Moore & Glasberg 1982) but in their 1984 paper Moore et al have presented the cueing noise to the ipsilateral ear, gating it on and off with the masker burst. To serve both as a timing cue and as a means to avoid off-frequency detection, that additional masker noise is composed of two frequency bands: for a 1-kHz probe one band goes from 0.6 to 0.925 Hz and the other from 1.075 to 1.4 kHz. The notch in the center exposes the probe. The noise level is adjusted to just mask the probe at 10 dB above its threshold in quiet; after that adjustment the probe is made 10 dB stronger.

Results of PTC experiments with this method in simultaneous and forward masking are impressive. The tips of the two PTCs have almost the same shape and indicate a degree of frequency selectivity fully compatible with that measured by other methods, notably the notched-noise method advocated by Patterson (1976). Thus a satisfactory method of measuring PTCs has now been found, and it has become a matter of convenience whether the measurement is made with simultaneous or with forward masking. However, the stimulus presentation is quite complex, and this may preclude extensive application.

A subject that is not at all clear concerns interaction between critical bands. Work reported by Hall et al (1984) illustrates that interaction exists under conditions of coherent modulation. One of the methods to determine the width of the critical band is that of Fletcher (1940) where the tone threshold is measured as the width of the masking-noise band, centered at the frequency of the tone, is varied. From a certain bandwidth on, the tone threshold is constant because increasing the bandwidth further produces components that do not mask the tone. Hall et al (1984) did the same experiment in a situation where the noise signal was amplitude modulated by a 0–50-Hz low-pass noise. In that situation they found the tone threshold to decrease when the width of the modulated noise exceeded the critical bandwidth. The maximum unmasking at 1 kHz due to the modulation amounted to ~10 dB. In further experiments the authors found that ~4 dB should be attributed to temporal phenomena associated with fluctuations, but the remaining effect is clear. Under conditions of "co-modulation"—i.e. where adjacent frequency bands are modulated coherently—a cooperation between critical bands results in unmasking.

The foregoing has reviewed what might be called classical work in auditory research. This concerns particularly the measurement of PTCs. Often PTCs are measured in hearing-impaired listeners with the aim of assessing the patients' power of frequency resolution. Factors other than those discussed above also turn up as important. One is a disturbance in the detection of beats (affecting the tip region of the tuning curve) and the other, more or less unique to normal hearing, concerns the detection of combination tones (Carney & Nelson, 1983). All studies reviewed here emphasize the unique importance of frequency selectivity, and it is not surprising that a symposium dedicated to this theme was held in 1986 (Moore & Patterson 1986). The proceedings, not available when this chapter was written, should contain answers to many of the problems that have remained unsolved. More puzzles were undoubtedly uncovered as well.

TEMPORAL RESOLUTION AND INTEGRATION

The auditory system is adapted to detecting and analyzing temporal variations of sounds. Human beings and animals have learned to use this facility in communication. In humans, communication occurs with especially shaped and modulated sounds, speech sounds. Several fields of auditory psychophysics concern the perception of human speech, especially the ability to follow temporal variations of speech signals. As in the study of frequency analysis, there is a tradition in research on temporal phenomena. Major aspects that have been studied extensively include (a) temporal integration and (b) temporal resolution (for general reviews see Green 1985 and de Boer 1985). Both are described by time constants of ~ 200 ms. A third aspect is (*c*) temporal acuity (Green 1971). The question involved is how fast the auditory system can react in processing a brief acoustical event. The time constant involved is of the order of 1–2 ms and appears to be independent of frequency (Green 1973). Many other temporal effects merit review but these do not bear upon spectrotemporal analysis.

Hall & Fernandes (1983a) studied frequency resolution and temporal integration in normally hearing and cochlear-impaired listeners. In their experiments tone bursts were used as signals and bands of noise as maskers; the tone frequency was 1 kHz and the bandwidth ranged from 25 to 600 Hz. The effect of temporal integration is that the threshold of a tone burst decreases when the duration increases (up to $\sim$ 200 ms). Accordingly, in this study temporal integration was expressed as the threshold difference for tones of 20- and 200-ms duration. Integration in normal listeners was found to be constant for bandwidths above 100 Hz (as expected) but to be smaller than normal for bandwidths of 25–100 Hz. The pattern obtained in hearing-impaired listeners was completely different. At the smaller bandwidths their temporal integration seemed better than that of normal listeners whereas the converse was true for larger bandwidths. These findings should be attributed in part to effects of frequency splatter. Apparently, in experiments of this kind precautions should be taken against such artifacts. At any rate, abnormal temporal integration was once more confirmed to be possible in cases of impaired hearing.

Another classical experiment directed at temporal resolution concerns gap detection. That a temporal gap in an ongoing sound cannot be detected when it is shorter than a certain limit is attributable partly to "persistence of sensation" and partly to ringing effects of the peripheral filter. As regards the former effect, the influence of the preceding sound seems to persist for a while, and it decays slowly. The persistence of sensation has unique properties: For all levels of the stimulus the sensation appears to decay over the same period, $\sim$200 msec (Plomp 1964), a phenomenon independent of frequency. For the persistence component the minimum detectable gap length will thus be independent of frequency; the component due to ringing, on the other hand, is clearly related to the critical bandwidth.

Fitzgibbons (1983) measured the minimum detectable gap length (MDG) for band-limited noise stimuli over a large set of experimental conditions. The variable that most affected MDG was found to be frequency (0.6–6 kHz). A simple algebraic expression summarizes his asymptotic (i.e. high-level) values:

$$T = 1.88 + 800/\Delta f,$$

where T is the MDG in ms and Δf is the critical bandwidth at the appropriate frequency in Hz. The second term describes the component due to ringing of the peripheral filter. It is remarkable that the MDG appears to be the sum of two terms, each representing one contributing factor. From this work it can be concluded that the ringing effect of the peripheral auditory filter—the main temporal feature that is frequency-dependent—plays an important part in gap detection. De Boer (1985) questions the apparent absence of such an influence on the detection of short increments instead of gaps in the intensity of sounds.

In his work Fitzgibbons (1983) used a notched-noise masker signal in order to reduce the influence of spectral splatter components. The spectra of signal and masker were complementary; the level of the masker noise in its pass band was 25 dB below that of the signal in its own pass band. Shailer & Moore (1983, 1985) used the same expedient but raised the noise level to 5 dB below that of the signal (measured in the appropriate pass bands) to have a better safeguard against artifacts. They found that asymptotic MDGs decreased with increasing bandwidth and suggested two reasons for this finding: (*a*) Excitation in the spectral gap is not zero and (*b*) audible fluctuations may hamper detection of a silent gap. These authors also suggested that listeners may combine information from different frequency regions. Shailer & Moore drew an important conclusion: The finding of larger than normal MDGs at high frequencies may be taken as a sign of impaired neural functioning, but only if the pattern of hearing loss is taken into account.

A comprehensive study of gap detection has been published by Buus & Florentine (1985). They describe a model in which the first stage is the peripheral auditory filter. During the temporal gap the amplitude of the filter's output signal will decrease; it is assumed that the amplitude is integrated by the (leaky) temporal-integration mechanism. Whether or not the gap is detected depends on (internal and external) noise; the decision process is modelled after signal-detection theory. The resulting expressions describe asymptotic performance for high levels, but numerical calculations were carried out as well with the aim of describing more realistic situations. In general, the model predictions fit the data well. The actual frequency effect due to the ringing of the filter is somewhat larger than predicted. Another well-predicted effect is that it takes 10–15 dB of masking before an asymptote is reached.

A considerable part of Buus & Florentine's (1985) study is devoted to data obtained in hearing-impaired listeners. To eliminate all possible artifacts, they used in all experiments a notched-noise masker but adjusted its level to an even higher value than Shailer & Moore (1983) had. Hearing-impaired listeners were compared with normally hearing people under conditions where the latter had comparable pure-tone hearing thresholds (this was accomplished by masking with spectrally shaped noise). The conclusion was reached that elevated pure-tone thresholds are primarily responsible for abnormal MDG values. MDG tests therefore should be done at levels above 85 dB SPL (see also Fitzgibbons 1984) and even then the findings must be interpreted with considerable caution. In terms of the model described, MDG data primarily reflect the state of the short-term integrator, not that of the peripheral auditory filter.

Gap detection can be viewed as a special case of a more general test where it is attempted to measure the temporal course of excitation as a function of time. Detailed temporal tracking is possible when stimuli have exactly repeating waveforms. An introductory study by Patterson et al (1983) revealed clear phase effects when masking tests were carried out with "frozen" masker-noise waveforms and sinusoidal signals. Inverting the phase of the signal in every other noise burst produced the temporal analogue of a binaural masking level difference (BMLD) test: Instead of being presented to the two ears the stimuli were alternated in time. The temporal MLD effect was small, however, and it remained unexplained why thresholds in nonrepeating (i.e. random) noise bursts were lower than in repeating noise bursts. Hanna & Robinson (1985) developed a vector model to account for the phase effects found when a sinusoid of adjustable starting phase is masked by a reproducible noise signal. The model appears to fit the data well; the authors claim that tests with reproducible stimuli will yield more quantitative information from an experiment, the reason being that many of the assumptions normally needed for interpretation are not necessary. The present author remains somewhat skeptical because the vector model implies a comparable number of assumptions.

A most specific type of temporal interaction has been described by Wakefield & Viemeister (1985). They used the combination of two signals: (a) a pure tone of, say, 100 Hz and (b) a 3-kHz-wide band of noise centred at 10 kHz and amplitude-modulated by (the same) 100 Hz. They varied the phase of the tone with respect to that of the modulation and found that the threshold of modulation clearly depended upon this phase. A most remarkable feature is that under the conditions of the experiment the high-frequency signal was not masked by the low-frequency tone. This property distinguished the interaction effect found from other effects that seem similar (cf McFadden 1975 and the masking-period pattern described by Zwicker 1976). From the available data Wakefield & Viemeister could not decide whether to explain their findings in terms of an additive or a multiplicative interaction. At any rate, the absence of masking under the conditions used makes the results intriguing.

BINAURAL HEARING

We are seldom aware of the many tasks the binaural hearing mechanism performs for us: localization of sounds, selection of wanted sounds, decoloration (i.e. removal of audible effects caused by reflections), suppression of interference and reverberation influences, etc (not to mention its help at the legendary cocktail party). Under laboratory conditions we measure such properties as lateralization, the binaural masking level difference, the precedence effect, binaural pitches, and so on [For a review see the new edition of Blauert's book (1983)]. From this review we learn that just-noticeable time differences between the ears are of the order of tens of microseconds, two orders of magnitude smaller than the smallest time constants in monaural listening (see the section on temporal phenomena). Time constants involved in temporal integration are still two orders of magnitude larger.

As in other fields of audition we start with frequency selectivity. Reports comparing binaural with monaural critical bandwidth have long been contradictory, but a way out of the problem seems to have been found. Most studies report thresholds of tones masked by noise; the noise is usually presented in phase at the two ears (N0), the tone (signal) can be presented monaurally (Sm), in phase (S0) or in opposite phase at the two ears (Sπ). Thresholds under condition N0S0 are, in general, equivalent to monaural thresholds (NmSm), but those under condition N0Sπ may be lower. This effect is one form of what is known as the binaural masking level difference. Critical bandwidths can be measured according to the classical method introduced by Fletcher (1940): The tone threshold is measured as a function of masker-noise bandwidth, keeping the noise power density constant. It has been found repeatedly that the way the N0Sπ threshold depends on bandwidth indicates that the critical bandwidth for the binaural system would be larger than that for the monaural one (e.g. Sever & Small 1979).

A different view on the subject was gained when Yama & Small (1983) used masking by a combination of a tone and a noise band and found that most of the deviant behavior of the N0Sπ threshold that causes a BMLD is really a narrow-band phenomenon. A more consistent view on the binaural critical bandwidth is possible after the experiments done by Hall et al (1983). These authors used masking-noise signals in which a band of components around the tone frequency was removed. When the notch width was varied, the N0S0 and N0Sπ thresholds exhibited the same variations. Apparently, the weighting of frequencies that participate in the formation of the N0Sπ threshold occurs according to the same auditory filter as in the case of the N0S0 threshold.

However, we are left with another paradox. Hall & Fernandes (1984) refined the experiment of Hall et al (1983), using dichotic presentation of the masking noise and monaural presentation of the tone (Sm); furthermore, they introduced the notch only in the noise to the nonsignal ear. When the notch width was varied from 0 to 50 Hz (about the *monaural* critical bandwidth at the signal frequency of 500 Hz), the BMLD was found to vary as expected from its maximal value to zero. However, Hall & Fernandes also used another condition in which the noise signal at the nonsignal ear was band-pass filtered around the signal frequency (in the pass band the noise components were in

N0 phase). For a bandwidth of 50 Hz the BMLD was, surprisingly enough, zero. It attained substantial values only when the bandwidth was increased by a factor of 3–5. This finding illustrates once more than an N0Sm or N0Sπ condition entails very special properties; the detection of a tone in one of these cases is quite different from the simple monaural detection of a tone in noise (cf Yost 1985). Stated in general terms, the "receiver" (the subject's binaural system) should be steered toward a certain operation in order to cope with its task.

Hall & Fernandes (1983b) investigated the influence of temporal variations by introducing deliberate amplitude variations in wide-band stimuli. In a general sense N0Sπ thresholds were found to be less susceptible to fluctuations than N0S0 thresholds (we forego the subtler conclusions in the paper cited). Thus, there is a release from masking whenever interaural conditions allow it, and the binaural system is relatively resistant to fluctuations. Meanwhile we have turned away from the spectral to the temporal domain. A study of the BMLD with reproducible samples ("frozen waveforms") of wide-band noise was done by Gilkey et al (1985). The technique allows measurement of the effect of signal phase. As expected, the phase effect was substantial in the N0S0 condition and, in line with earlier observations, it was very small in the N0Sπ condition. This finding almost rules out the applicability of the vector model (Jeffress 1972) for binaural hearing in this case. Most remarkable was that the subject's performance for individual noise samples under the N0S0 condition was highly correlated with that under the N0Sπ condition. By modifying the equalization and cancellation model (Durlach 1963) the authors were able to account for this finding.

The precedence effect (originally called the Haas effect) illustrates in a different way the capability of the binaural system to process temporal information. The classical view is that the localization of a sound is predominantly determined by the times of arrival of the first waves at the ears—hence the alternative name, the law of the first wavefront. Gaskell (1983) studied the precedence effect using an interaural intensity difference instead of a time difference as the cue for lateralization. If the first click of a pair (with an interclick interval of, for example, 0.6 ms, so that the pair was actually heard as a single click) was presented with such an intensity difference, the lateralization of the sound was always determined by the first click. If, however, the interaural difference was in the second click, lateralization was anomalous over a range of inter-click intervals around 0.4 ms. Yost & Soderquist (1984) studied the case where the two clicks give opposite cues. Their results are consistent with the view that the first click of the pair makes the system less sensitive to the cue provided by the second click. One cue may be partly offset by the other, but there is no trading in the sense that the image can always be centered on the midline. The idea of a reduction of sensitivity has led to an inhibition model, which is being developed by Lindemann (1984, 1985). That model also explains anomalous lateralization, as described above, and works well for larger time differences between pulses such as occur in practical situations.

In a simple formulation, lateralization is described by stating that interaural time differences (ITDs) are lateralization cues for low-frequency sounds and interaural intensity differences (IIDs) for high-frequency sounds. This must, of course, be extended: The binaural system is also sensitive to ITDs of envelopes of high-frequency stimuli (e.g. Henning 1980). An important question is whether listeners can lateralize on the basis of similar envelope ITDs for low-frequency stimuli. In a study with transient signals Henning (1983) came to the definite conclusion that the answer is negative. Of late, the problem is taken up again by Bernstein & Trahiotis (1985) with the reasoning that Henning's stimuli, being transients, were probably too short to let the disparity between the envelopes be processed. They found, in short, that envelope delays can indeed induce lateralization for low-frequency signals but that this cue is easily overridden by other interaural differences (phase differences, for instance).

Work that addresses the capabilities of the binaural system in the temporal domain in an original way was presented by Hafter & Dye (1983). They used a succession of a limited number (n) of high-frequency clicks, presented dichotically. In the experiments the just-noticeable difference for ITD was determined as a function of n. For an inter-click interval (ICI) of 10 ms most of the subjects showed thresholds that improve with the factor $\sqrt{n}$, in agreement with statistical theory. For shorter ICIs the improvement was definitely smaller. Various explanations of this property were tried, but most of these yielded the $\sqrt{n}$ law. The only mechanism consistent with the data is one involving "saturation," where the neural information evoked by n clicks is a compressive function of n. It should be noted that an adaptation mechanism whereby later clicks produce progressively less neural activity gives similar results. In a later study Hafter & Buell (1984) presented evidence that the saturation occurs in the monaural channels feeding the binaural system. For the relation of this study with other research in binaural hearing see Hafter & Buell (1985).

PITCH PERCEPTION

Pitch perception has long been a major topic in auditory research, and it continues to interest students today. Pitch perception is important when it concerns the pitch of complex stimuli such as speech sounds or musical notes. Particularly important is the case of periodic stimuli where pitch usually corresponds to the frequency of repetition. For a periodic stimulus the pitch usually remains the same when the fundamental component (the one with the corresponding frequency) is absent from the complex; this is known as the "case of the missing fundamental." Originally, this component of pitch was thought to be determined in the time domain and to result from incomplete frequency resolution, hence the names "periodicity pitch" and "residue pitch" (Schouten 1940). In the 1970s it became clear that residue pitch is determined by a feature-extracting mechanism that operates on the spectrum. For reviews of this development see de Boer (1976) or Wightman & Green (1974).

Goldstein (1973) developed a comprehensive theory that appears to encompass most psychophysical features of residue pitch perception. In what follows we refer to elements of that theory, so we first outline its structure briefly. As the first stage, Goldstein postulates that the peripheral filtering mechanism isolates the components of the sound stimulus and measures their frequencies with a certain finite accuracy. In the next stage a "central pitch processor" tries to determine the most likely fundamental frequency f_0 of which the harmonics $n_i f_0$ agree best with the component frequencies. The frequency f_0 then determines the residue pitch. In this operation the rank numbers n_i of the components are assumed to be unknown; it is one of the tasks of the central pitch processor to estimate them. The basic point of the theory is that there is one function $\sigma(f)$, solely dependent upon frequency f, that describes the standard deviation of the frequency measurement of a component with frequency f. The beauty of the theory is that with this sole assumption it is possible to explain virtually all psychophysical data on pitch perception. It should be noted well that $\sigma(f)$ must be chosen as large as 5–7 times the jnd for frequency of an isolated pure tone with frequency f. Furthermore, components either participate in the process of pitch determination or not; there is no gradation.

Goldstein's theory has obtained a firmer basis from the central spectrum model presented by Srulovicz & Goldstein (1983), a model that gives a quantitative description of the first stage of processing, the isolation of components. It is assumed that this is done on the basis of the temporal firing patterns of auditory-nerve fibers. More specifically, the interval histogram of the firings of a fiber is determined, and this histogram is subsequently processed by a filter tuned to the characteristic frequency (CF) of the fiber. The (integrated) output of the filter contains two terms: one component representing the average rate of firing and another representing the temporal coherence of the firings. It is mainly the second component that is responsible for providing the necessary frequency information to the central pitch processor. This model thus provides a link between what we know about the physiology of the cochlea and the psychophysics of pitch perception.

In this author's opinion, however, the model has a few weak points. Frequency jnds for single pure tones are well predicted by the model, as regards their dependences on frequency, duration, and amplitude. To accomplish this, the model operates on information provided by fibers with CFs over a range of ~30 Hz, for all frequencies. The precision with which frequency information is used for the pitch of complex signals is, as we saw above, 5–7 times lower than that for single pure tones. In the Srulowicz/Goldstein model this property is accounted for by arbitrarily reducing the 30-Hz band to 5 Hz. However, such a restriction runs counter to intuition: An equivalent effect would have been obtained by introducing noise at this stage. Furthermore, the model does not satisfactorily explain why frequency discrimination deteriorates rapidly when the available components are so close together that they are resolved only partially. It is important, though, that the model contains an operational mechanism for extracting frequency information from the temporal firing patterns of auditory-nerve fibers.

In its original form Goldstein's (1973) model is difficult to handle. Duifhuis et al (1982) brought it to a more manageable form, with the intent to realize it eventually in a form that operates in real time. The resulting procedure is commonly known as the DWS pitch meter (after the names of the authors involved). Scheffers (1983) modified this procedure so that it can be used for stimuli in which just a few components are detectable above the noise, a situation all too common in everyday speech communication. The improvements concerned the representation of peripheral filtering, the recognition of spectral peaks, and the properties of the "harmonic sieve"—i.e. the part of the central pitch processor that selects which components to use as harmonics. The modified DWS pitch meter was found to replicate the classical findings in inharmonic signals (cf de Boer 1976) well, including the prediction of multiple pitches. It also worked well with artificial speech sounds partially masked by noise. Another improvement of the DWS pitch meter was briefly reported by Allik et al (1984). Remarkably enough, many algorithms that are used to extract pitch from speech signal waveforms (Hess 1983) are not related to a psychophysical theory of pitch.

Our ability to estimate the pitch of an individual component of a complex sound was studied by Peters et al (1983). The match to a mistuned component was found to be accurate over mistunings of up to approximately ±3% of the frequency; this tallies with the 30-Hz width of the central spectrum that is handled in the Srulowicz/Goldstein model and the width of the harmonic sieve (±4%) in the DWS pitch meter. Related topics are treated by Moore et al (1985a,b), who asked: (a) when is a mistuned component detected as such, and (b) what happens to a component that is not passed by the harmonic sieve? A mistuned component is detected when the sound is judged to be inharmonic. The threshold for inharmonicity was found to lie within the width of the harmonic sieve. The range over which a mistuned component "stands out" and can be followed in pitch (with reduced accuracy) is larger and extends to over 8%.

CONSEQUENCES OF INCOMPLETE SPECTRO-
TEMPORAL REPRESENTATION OF SIGNALS FOR THE
RECEPTION OF SPEECH

This section deals with the reception of speech by hearing-impaired subjects. Reduced auditory sensitivity is one factor that causes poor speech intelligibility in pathological ears. However, speech intelligibility is also impaired by other auditory defects. Especially serious is the finding that where interfering noise is present the perception of speech may be more disturbed than under quiet conditions (cf Kryter et al 1962).

Speech is one of the most difficult signals to describe, and we still do not understand exactly how human listeners recognize it. Several of the problems involved were recently outlined by Pisoni (1985): lack of acoustic-phonetic invariance, uncertainty about the internal representation of speech sounds, influence of differences between talkers, and knowledge of the structure of the language spoken. On the other hand, we know that spectral and temporal information are decisive factors in speech recognition because utterances can be recognized from speech spectrograms by experienced spectrogram readers (Cole 1980).

In reducing the observations to a small set of explanatory concepts, Plomp (1978) pointed out that speech-reception thresholds in quiet and in noise can be described by a two-component model. Speech-reception thresholds in quiet then depend mainly on the "attenuation" component, whereas speech-reception thresholds in noise are mainly determined by the "distortion" component. Because of this duality, predictive formulas for speech intelligibility from the pure-tone audiogram have only a limited value. The question now is, on which auditory properties does the distortion component depend?

We are pretty certain that good frequency resolution is indispensable for speech perception and analysis. During the last few years it was confirmed that sensorineural hearing loss is often accompanied by reduced frequency resolution or discrimination (Zurek & Formby 1981; Carney & Nelson 1983; Tyler et al 1983, 1984; Glasberg & Moore 1986; Moore & Glasberg 1986). Most studies show a rather strong relation between frequency resolution and audiometric loss. However, that result is not simply due to the higher presentation levels used (e.g. McFadden & Pasanen 1980, Carney & Nelson 1983, Festen & Plomp 1983). As described in a preceding section, auditory frequency selectivity can be measured in various ways. Results obtained with the various methods are in good agreement (Florentine et al 1980). One factor contributing to reduced spectral resolution may be that lateral supression is absent in cases of moderate hearing loss (Festen & Plomp 1983, Dreschler & Festen 1986).

The impact of spectral representation upon speech reception is evident from results of several correlational studies. Horst (1982) found 'a significant correlation between the sharpness of simultaneous psychophysical tuning curves (PTCs) at 2000 Hz and speech-reception thresholds in (SRTs) in noise. Lyregaard (1982) found the best correlation between speech intelligibility in noise and the critical ratio (CR) (averaged over 500, 1000, 2000, and 4000 Hz). Stelmachowicz et al (1985) pointed out that in broadband masking noise, speech reception is related to the sharpness of the PTC; in low-pass masking noise, however, especially the low-frequency side of the PTC is important. A broadened PTC was found to affect maximum word discrimination scores (Ritsma et al 1980) and consonant-intelligibility scores (Preminger & Wiley 1985), but it is not the only factor involved. Hannley & Dorman (1983) and Gordon-Salant (1984) confirmed the negative influence of upward spread of masking on phoneme perception by hearing-impaired subjects.

As a consequence of incomplete spectral representation the perception of loudness may be affected too. Especially in cochlear impairment the dynamic range of the ear can be reduced considerably, there can be an abnormally rapid increase of loudness as a function of intensity (recruitment). Smits & Duifhuis (1982) showed by means of a partial-masking experiment that the dynamic range of hearing in hearing-impaired subjects can be reduced even more under conditions of masking, and this may also occur in frequency regions with almost normal hearing sensitivity. For many years excessive spread of excitation due to reduced spectral resolution was considered to be responsible for recruitment. Moore et al (1985c) recently questioned this relationship and hypothesized the coexistence of impaired "low-threshold" fibers and normal "high-threshold" fibers to be the cause of recruitment. Anyway, a reduced dynamic range will certainly result in the occurrence of either inaudibly weak or uncomfortably loud portions in current speech.

Some temporal properties have also been shown to be degraded in hearing-impaired subjects (Hall & Fernandes 1983a, Kidd et al 1984, Bacon & Viemeister 1985, Buus & Florentine 1985). Additional information about the causes of poor speech reception was obtained by means of studies with isolated speech-like stimuli in which the effect of specific acoustical manipulations was tried out. Confusions in the detection of voicing can be explained by increased discrimination thresholds for differences in voice-onset-time (Tyler et al 1982a). Older listeners proved to be extremely sensitive to shortening the initial, high-frequency fricative segment in CVCV-words (Ginzel et al 1982). This may reflect deterioration in high-frequency temporal resolution, but age is a confounding factor. The confusions of consonants have also been studied (Gutnick 1982, Gordon-Salant 1985, Dreschler 1986), and the data show the importance of different acoustical features for consonant perception by the hearing impaired.

So far we have discussed only single features that may or may not affect reception of speech by hearing-impaired listeners. Experimentally, any single relation is found in the form of a correlation value. In practical situations combinations of these features will be active and more than one correlation value will be significantly different from zero. We certainly need a method that can provide insight into the structure of the set of correlation values. This goal can be reached via the multivariate approach, which can be applied to sets of results from several psychophysical tests in a test battery, measured in a fixed group of subjects. After the early work (Mullins & Bangs 1957, Ross et al 1965) this approach seemed forgotten, but the groups of Plomp (Amsterdam) and Tyler (Nottingham) have recently revived interest in it.

In this kind of study interindividual differences are used as sources of information. (This contrasts with measurements in normally hearing listeners.) For that reason it is essential to measure all auditory parameters with an error that is small relative to the inter-individual spread. Provided this is the case, the multivariate approach has two advantages: (a) the interaction between test results can be evaluated, and (b) possible shifts in perceptual strategy can be brought into view.

It is logical that tests on spectral as well as temporal resolution were included in the test battery. Frequency-resolution parameters have been chosen as special characteristics rather than frequency-discrimination parameters (e.g. Festen & Plomp 1983, Tyler et al 1982b). In order to address temporal characteristics a variety of tests was applied, including tests on temporal integration, forward and backward masking, gap detection, and just-noticeable differences for duration and gap width (Tyler et al 1982a, Dreschler & Plomp 1985). Some authors included tests on auditory nonlinearity (Festen & Plomp 1981) and loudness perception (Dreschler & Plomp 1985). In most studies speech reception was studied both in quiet and in noise. Some studies also incorporated tests on an intermediate level—e.g. on the discrimination of voice-onset time (Tyler et al 1982a) or on the perception of phonemes by means of an analysis of confusions (Dreschler & Plomp 1985).

In normally hearing listeners such a test battery yielded only low correlations (Festen & Plomp 1981). These results prove that the lack of significant correlations was not due to measurement error. However, in hearing-impaired listeners a much greater inter-individual spread may be expected, and significant correlations may be revealed.

In hearing-impaired subjects these studies show clear relations between reduced frequency resolution and poor temporal resolution (Tyler et al 1982a, Festen & Plomp 1983, Dreschler & Plomp 1985). These results contradict the reciprocal relation between spectral and temporal resolution predicted by simple linear-filter models. Concerning the relations with speech reception Festen & Plomp (1983) concluded on the basis of a battery of tests at 1 kHz that particularly the reception of speech in noise is related to frequency resolution. With partly different tests at more than one measuring frequency Tyler et al (1982b) and Dreschler & Plomp (1985) pointed out that especially frequency resolution at 2 and 4 kHz is important for speech reception in noise. Likewise, the effect of impaired temporal representation upon speech reception is illustrated well by results of these studies. Tyler et al (1982a) found that temporal integration, especially at 4 kHz, is significant for the reception of speech in noise. In addition, they showed abnormally large gap-detection thresholds to affect speech reception both in quiet and in noise. In the study of Dreschler & Plomp (1985) the relation between temporal-resolution parameters and speech reception showed the following pattern: Forward and backward masking affects mostly speech hearing loss in quiet; gap detection appears more to affect speech hearing loss in noise.

The basic question in the multivariate approach is whether fundamental auditory phenomena are expressed in the various aspects of pathological hearing. A principal-components analysis can be applied to the data in order to reveal basic factors underlying the pattern of relations. In doing this, Festen & Plomp (1983) found two principal factors. One expresses the property that speech reception in quiet is predominantly determined by audiometric loss at 1 kHz; in a similar way the other relates speech reception in noise to frequency resolution at 1 kHz. Compared to these factors, other influences are certainly not independent but they are less important. In a similar analysis Dreschler & Plomp (1985) found that tone-perception tests on the one side, and phoneme-perception tests on the other, seem to be almost independent. The dichotomy makes us believe that different perceptual mechanisms are involved in the two tasks. Auditory functions at higher frequencies proved to be the most important for speech reception in noise, auditory functions at lower frequencies to speech reception in quiet. Dreschler & Plomp's data suggested that the role of loudness perception was completely independent.

SUMMARY

The study of audition has widened: Having been concentrated in the 1960s on a few topics like pitch perception, binaural hearing, and fatigue, it now spans many more subjects. In the present paper we have emphasized the following topics:

1. frequency analysis—this topic includes spectral integration and resolution, auditory excitation patterns, and processing of spectral information;
2. temporal analysis—this topic refers mainly to studies in which abstract and stylized temporal variations in stimuli are used;
3. binaural hearing—a subfield that still attracts a great deal of attention because of its unique character;
4. pitch perception—of particular interest is this field for the perception of prosodic features of speech, but it also addresses fundamental questions of how the auditory system works; and

5.pathology of hearing—in particular the effects of impaired hearing on speech perception and the relations among various hearing-test results. (This section was written in collaboration with W. A. Dreschler.)

Many of the topics discussed have a direct relation to the capabilities of the auditory system in analyzing sounds—in particular, speech sounds. Experimentally, the problem can be approached from two sides: in one the stimuli are generated in a stylized form, and in the other they are taken as distorted versions of actual speech elements. In this paper we have described mainly the first category of experiments. Whereas we know for certain that the auditory system operates in the frequency-temporal domain, it is remarkable that the distinction between fields 1 and 2 (above) can still be made. Temporal effects in frequency analysis are often considered as perturbations, and the same is true for spectral effects in the study of temporal resolution. A true integration of time and frequency is often sought but seldom achieved as the focus of study.

Of the many subjects that would ideally have received more coverage we mention two: the use of additional stimulation pathways to help patients with large hearing loss or deaf-blind people, and the use of a cochlear prosthesis ("cochlear implant"). Because we lacked space to cover these topics adequately, we omitted them completely. This indicates no undervaluation of these subjects of study or of the benefits they can provide to hearing-impaired people.

ACKNOWLEDGMENTS

E. de Boer wishes to acknowledge with great gratitude the wise comments and constructive criticism from Drs. E. R. Hafter and P. Kuyper. It would have been impossible to review the material on speech reception and multivariate studies had Dr. W. A. Dreschler not taken the major share in writing the section dedicated to these fields. Dr. Dreschler also suggested improvements to the readability of the other sections.

Literature Cited

Allik, J., Mihkla, M., Ross, J. 1984. Comment on "Measurement of pitch in speech: An implementation of Goldstein's theory of pitch perception" [J. Acoust. Soc. Am. 71:1568 (1982)]. *J. Acoust. Soc. Am.* 75:1855–57

Bacon, S. P., Viemeister, N. F. 1985. Temporal modulation transfer functions in normal-hearing and hearing-impaired listeners. *Audiology* 24:117–34

Bernstein, L. R., Trahiotis, C. 1985. Lateralization of low-frequency, complex waveforms: The use of envelope-based temporal disparities. *J. Acoust. Soc. Am.* 77:1868–80

Blauert, J. 1983. *Spatial Hearing—The Psychophysics of Human Sound Localization.* Cambridge, Mass: MIT Press

Buus, S., Florentine, M. 1985. Gap detection in normal and impaired listeners: The effect of level and frequency. In *Time Resolution in Auditory Systems,* ed. A. Michelsen, pp. 159–79. Berlin: Springer-Verlag

Carney, A. E., Nelson, D. A. 1983. An

analysis of psychophysical tuning curves in normal and pathological ears. *J. Acoust. Soc. Am.* 73:268–78

Chistovich, L. A. 1957. Frequency characteristics of masking effect. *Biofizika* 2:249–55

Cole, R. A., ed. 1980. *Perception and Production of Fluent Speech.* Hillsdale, NJ: Erlbaum

Darwin, C. J. 1984. Perceiving vowels in the presence of another sound: Constraints on formant perception. *J. Acoust. Soc. Am.* 76:1636–47

de Boer, E. 1976. On the "residue" and auditory pitch perception. In *Handbook of Sensory Physiology,* ed. W. D. Keidel, W. D. Neff, 5(3):481–583. Berlin: Springer-Verlag

de Boer, E. 1985. Auditory time constants: A paradox? See Buus & Florentine 1985, pp. 141–58

de Boer, E., van Breugel, H. 1984. Distribution of judgements in adaptive testing. *Biol. Cybern.* 50:343–55

Dreschler, W. A. 1986. Phonemic confusions in quiet and noise for the hearing-impaired. *Audiology* 25:19–28

Dreschler, W. A., Festen, J. M. 1986. The effect of hearing-impairment on auditory filter shapes in simultaneous and forward masking. In *Auditory Frequency Selectivity,* ed. B. C. J. Moore, R. D. Patterson. New York: Plenum

Dreschler, W. A., Plomp, R. 1985. Relations between psychophysical data and speech perception for hearing-impaired subjects. II. *J. Acoust. Soc. Am.* 78:1261–70

Duifhuis, H., Willems, L. F., Sluyter, R. J. 1982. Measurement of pitch in speech: An implementation of Goldstein's theory of pitch perception. *J. Acoust. Soc. Am.* 71:1568–80

Durlach, N. 1963. Equalization and cancellation theory of binaural masking-level differences. *J. Acoust. Soc. Am.* 35:1206–18

Festen, J. M., Plomp, R. 1981. Relations between auditory functions in normal hearing. *J. Acoust. Soc. Am.* 70:356–69

Festen, J. M., Plomp, R. 1983. Relations between auditory functions in impaired hearing. *J. Acoust. Soc. Am.* 73:652–62

Fitzgibbons, P. J. 1983. Temporal gap detection in noise as a function of frequency, bandwidth, and level. *J. Acoust. Soc. Am.* 74:67–72

Fitzgibbons, P. J. 1984. Temporal gap resolution in masked normal ears as a function of masker level. *J. Acoust. Soc. Am.* 76:67–70

Fletcher, H. 1940. Auditory patterns. *Rev. Mod. Phys.* 12:47–65

Florentine, M., Buus, S., Scharf, B., Zwicker, E. 1980. Frequency selectivity in normally-hearing and hearing-impaired observers. *J. Speech Hear. Res.* 23:646–69

Gaskell, H. 1983. The precedence effect. *Hear. Res.* 11:227–303

Gilkey, R. H., Robinson, D. E., Hanna, T. E. 1985. Effects of masker waveform and signal-to-masker phase relation on diotic and dichotic masking by reproducible noise. *J. Acoust. Soc. Am.* 78:1207–19

Ginzel, A., Pedersen, C. B., Spliid, P. E., Andersen, E. 1982. The role of temporal factors in auditory perception of consonants and vowels. *Scand. Audiol.* 11:93–100

Glasberg, B. R., Moore, B. C. J. 1986. Auditory filter shapes in subjects with unilateral and bilateral cochlear impairments. *J. Acoust. Soc. Am.* 79:1020–33

Goldstein, J. L. 1973. An optimum processor theory for the central formation of the pitch of complex tones. *J. Acoust. Soc. Am.* 54:1496–1516

Gordon-Salant, S. 1984. Effects of reducing low-frequency amplification on consonant perception in quiet and noise. *J. Speech Hear. Res.* 27:483–93

Gordon-Salant, S. 1985. Phoneme feature perception in noise by normal-hearing and hearing-impaired subjects. *J. Acoust. Soc. Am.* 28:87–95

Gray, R. F., ed. 1985. *Cochlear Implants.* London: Croom Helm

Green, D. M. 1971. Temporal auditory acuity. *Psychol. Rev.* 78:540–51

Green, D. M. 1973. Temporal acuity as a function of frequency. *J. Acoust. Soc. Am.* 54:373–79

Green, D. M. 1985. Temporal factors in psychoacoustics. See Buus & Florentine 1985, pp. 122–38

Green, D. M., Mason, C. R. 1985. Auditory profile analysis: Frequency, phase, and Weber's law. *J. Acoust. Soc. Am.* 77:1155–61

Green, D. M., Kidd, G. Jr., Picardi, M. C. 1983. Successive versus simultaneous comparison in auditory intensity discrimination. *J. Acoust. Soc. Am.* 73:539–43

Gutnick, H. N. 1982. Consonant-feature transmission as a function of presentation level in hearing-impaired listeners. *J. Acoust. Soc. Am.* 72:1124–30

Hafter, E. R., Buell, T. N. 1984. Onset effects in lateralization denote a monaural mechanism. *J. Acoust. Soc. Am. Suppl.* 76(S):91 (Abstr.)

Hafter, E. R., Buell, T. N. 1985. The importance of transients for maintaining separation of signals in space. In *Attention and Performance,* ed. M. Posner, O. Martin, 11:337–54. Hillsdale, NJ: Erlbaum

Hafter, E. R., Dye, R. H. 1983. Detection of interaural differences of time in trains of high-frequency clicks as a function of interclick interval and number. *J. Acoust. Soc. Am.* 73:644–51

Hall, J. L. 1983. A procedure for detecting variability of psychophysical thresholds. *J. Acoust. Soc. Am.* 73:663–67

Hall, J. W., Fernandes, M. A. 1983a. Temporal integration, frequency resolution, and off-frequency listening in normal-hearing and cochlear-impaired listeners. *J. Acoust. Soc. Am.* 74:1172–77

Hall, J. W., Fernandes, M. A. 1983b. The effect of random intensity fluctuation on monaural and binaural detection. *J. Acoust. Soc. Am.* 74:1200–3

Hall, J. W., Fernandes, M. A. 1984. The role of monaural frequency selectivity in binaural analysis. *J. Acoust. Soc. Am.* 76:435–39

Hall, J. W., Tyler, R. S., Fernandes, M. A. 1983. Monaural and binaural auditory frequency resolution measured using band-limited noise and notched-noise masking. *J. Acoust. Soc. Am.* 73:894–98

Hall, J. W., Haggard, M. P., Fernandes, M. A. 1984. Detection in noise by spectrotemporal pattern analysis. *J. Acoust. Soc. Am.* 73:50–56

Hanna, T. E., Robinson, D. E. 1985. Phase effects for a sine wave masked by reproducible noise. *J. Acoust. Soc. Am.* 77:1129–40

Hannley, M., Dorman, M. F. 1983. Susceptibility to intraspeech spread of masking in listeners with sensorineural hearing loss. *J. Acoust. Soc. Am.* 74:40–51

Henning, G. B. 1980. Some observations on the lateralization of complex waveforms. *J. Acoust. Soc. Am.* 68:446–54

Henning, G. B. 1983. Lateralization of low-frequency transients. *Hear. Res.* 9:153–72

Hess, W. 1983. *Pitch Determination of Speech Signals: Algorithms and Devices.* Berlin: Springer-Verlag

Horst, J. W. 1982. *Discrimination of complex signals in hearing.* Doctoral thesis. Univ. Groningen, The Netherlands

Jeffress, L. A. 1972. Binaural signal detection: Vector theory. In *Foundations of Modern Auditory Theory*, ed. J. V. Tobias, 2:349–68. New York: Academic

Jesteadt, W. 1980. An adaptive procedure for subjective judgments. *Percept. Psychophys.* 28:85–88

Johnson-Davies, D., Patterson, R. D. 1979. Psychophysical tuning curves: Restricting the listening band to the signal region. *J. Acoust. Soc. Am.* 65:765–70

Kidd, G. Jr., Mason, C. R., Feth, L. L. 1984. Temporal integration of forward masking in listeners having sensorineural hearing loss. *J. Acoust. Soc. Am.* 75:937–44

Kryter, K. D., Williams, C., Green, D. M. 1962. Auditory acuity and the perception of speech. *J. Acoust. Soc. Am.* 34:1217–23

Levitt, H. 1971. Transformed up-down methods in psychoacoustics. *J. Acoust. Soc. Am.* 49:467–77

Lindemann, W. 1984. Ein Mechanismus lateraler Inhibition zur Erweiterung eines Modells der binauralen Kreuzkorrelation. In Fortsch. Akust. *Dtsch. Arbeitsgem. Akust.* 1984, pp. 727–30

Lindemann, W. 1985. Hörversuche zur Aufdeckung von Inhibitionsmechanismen bei der binauralen Signalverarbeitung. In Fortschr. Akust. *Dtsch. Arbeitsgem. Akust.* 1985, pp. 491–94

Lyregaard, P. E. 1982. Frequency selectivity and speech intelligibility in noise. *Scand. Audiol. Suppl.* 15:113–22

McFadden, D. 1975. Beat-like interactions between periodic waveforms. *J. Acoust. Soc. Am.* 57:983

McFadden, D., Pasanen, E. G. 1980. Altered psychophysical tuning curves following exposure to a noise band with steep spectral skirts. In *Psychophysical, Physiological, and Behavioural Studies in Hearing*, ed. G. van den Brink, F. A. Bilsen, pp. 136–39. Delft: Delft Univ. Press

McFadden, D., Wightman, F. L. 1983. Audition: Some relations between normal and pathological hearing. *Ann. Rev. Psychol.* 34:95–128

Moore, B. C. J. 1978. Psychophysical tuning curves measured in simultaneous and forward masking. *J. Acoust. Soc. Am.* 63:524–32

Moore, B. C. J., Glasberg, B. R. 1982. Contralateral and ipsilateral cueing in forward masking. *J. Acoust. Soc. Am.* 71:942–45

Moore, B. C. J., Glasberg, B. R. 1986. Comparisons of frequency selectivity in simultaneous and forward masking for subjects with unilateral cochlear impairments. *J. Acoust. Soc. Am.* In press

Moore, B. C. J., Patterson, R. D., eds. 1986. *Auditory Frequency Selectivity.* New York: Plenum

Moore, B. C. J., Glasberg, B. R., Roberts, B. 1984. Refining the measurement of psychophysical tuning curves. *J. Acoust. Soc. Am.* 76:1057–66

Moore, B. C. J., Glasberg, B. R., Peters, R. W. 1985a. Relative dominance of individual partials in determining the pitch of complex tones. *J. Acoust. Soc. Am.* 77:1853–60

Moore, B. C. J., Peters, R. W., Glasberg, B. R. 1985b. Thresholds for the detection of inharmonicity in complex tones. *J. Acoust. Soc. Am.* 77:1861–67

Moore, B. C. J., Glasberg, B. R., Hess, R. F., Birchall, J. P. 1985c. Effects of flanking noise bands on the rate of growth of loudness of tones in normal and recruiting ears. *J. Acoust. Soc. Am.* 77:1505–13

Mullins, C. J., Bangs, J. L. 1957. Relationships between speech discrimination and other audiometric data. *Acta Otolaryngol.* 47:149–57

Patterson, R. D. 1976. Auditory filter shapes derived with noise stimuli. *J. Acoust. Soc. Am.* 59:640–54

Patterson, R. D., Milroy, R., Lutfi, R. A. 1983. Detecting a repeated tone burst in repeated noise. *J. Acoust. Soc. Am.* 73:951–54

Peters, R. W., Moore, B. C. J., Glasberg, B. R. 1983. Pitch of components of complex tones. *J. Acoust. Soc. Am.* 73:924–29

Pisoni, D. B. 1985. Speech perception: Some new directions in research and theory. *J. Acoust. Soc. Am.* 78:381–88

Plomp, R. 1964. Rate of decay of auditory sensation. *J. Acoust. Soc. Am.* 36:277–82

Plomp, R. 1978. Auditory handicap of hearing impairment and the limited benefit of hearing aids. *J. Acoust. Soc. Am.* 63:533–49

Preminger, J., Wiley, T. L. 1985. Frequency selectivity and consonant intelligibility in sensorineural hearing loss. *J. Speech Hear. Res.* 28:197–206

Ritsma, R. J., Wit, H. P., van der Lans, W. P. 1980. Relations between hearing loss, maximal word discrimination score and width of psychophysical tuning curves. See McFadden & Pasanen 1980, pp. 472–76

Ross, M., Huntington, D. A., Newby, H. A., Dixon, R. F. 1965. Speech discrimination of hearing-impaired individuals in noise. *J. Acoust. Soc. Am.* 5:47–72

Scheffers, M. T. M. 1983. Simulation of auditory analysis of pitch: An elaboration on the DWS pitch meter. *J. Acoust. Soc. Am.* 74:1716–25

Schindler, R. A., Merzenich, M. M., eds. 1985. *Cochlear Implants.* New York: Raven

Schouten, J. F. 1940. The residue, a new component in subjective sound analysis. *Proc. K. Ned. Akad. Wet.* 43:991–99

Sever, J. C. Jr., Small, A. M. Jr. 1979. Binaural critical masking bands. *J. Acoust. Soc. Am.* 66:1343–50

Shailer, M. J., Moore, B. C. J. 1983. Gap detection as a function of frequency, bandwidth, and level. *J. Acoust. Soc. Am.* 74:467–73

Shailer, M. J., Moore, B. C. J. 1985. Detection of temporal gaps in bandlimited noise: Effects of variations in bandwidth and signal-to-masker ratio. *J. Acoust. Soc. Am.* 77:635–39

Small, A. M. 1959. Pure tone masking. *J. Acoust. Soc. Am.* 31:1619–25

Smits, J. T. S., Duifhuis, H. 1982. Masking and partial masking in listeners with a high-frequency hearing loss. *Audiology* 21:310–24

Srulovicz, P., Goldstein, J. L. 1983. A central spectrum model: A synthesis of auditory-nerve timing and place cues in monaural communication of frequency spectrum. *J. Acoust. Soc. Am.* 73:1266–76

Stelmachowicz, P. G., Jesteadt, W. 1984. Psychophysical tuning curves in normal-hearing listeners: Test reliability and probe level effects. *J. Speech Hear. Res.* 27:396–402

Stelmachowicz, P. G., Jesteadt, W., Gorga, M. P., Mott, J. 1985. Speech perception ability and psychophysical tuning curves in hearing-impaired listeners. *J. Acoust. Soc. Am.* 77:620–27

Taylor, M. M., Forbes, S. M., Creelman, C. D. 1983. PEST reduces bias in forced choice psychophysics. *J. Acoust. Soc. Am.* 74:1367–74

Tyler, R. S., Summerfield, A. Q., Wood, E. J., Fernandes, M. A. 1982a. Psychoacoustic and phonetic temporal processing in normal and hearing-impaired listeners. *J. Acoust. Soc. Am.* 72:740–52

Tyler, R. S., Wood, E. J., Fernandes, M. 1982b. Frequency resolution and hearing loss. *Br. J. Audiol.* 16:45–83

Tyler, R. S., Wood, E. J., Fernandes, M. 1983. Frequency resolution and discrimination of constant and dynamic tones in normal and hearing-impaired listeners. *J. Acoust. Soc. Am.* 74:1190–99

Tyler, R. S., Hall, J. W., Glasberg, B. R., Moore, B. C. J., Patterson, R. D. 1984. Auditory filter asymmetry in the hearing impaired. *J. Acoust. Soc. Am.* 76:1363–68

Verrillo, R. T. 1985. Psychophysics of vibrotactile stimulation. *J. Acoust. Soc. Am.* 77:225–32

Verschuure, J. 1981a. Pulsation patterns and nonlinearity of auditory tuning. I. Psychophysical results. *Acustica* 49:288–95

Verschuure, J. 1981b. Pulsation patterns and nonlinearity of auditory tuning. II. Analysis of psychophysical results. *Acustica* 49:296–306

Wakefield, G. H., Viemeister, N. F. 1985. Temporal interactions between pure tones and amplitude-modulated noise. *J. Acoust. Soc. Am.* 77:1535–42

Weber, D. L. 1983. Do off-frequency simultaneous maskers suppress the signal? *J. Acoust. Soc. Am.* 73:887–93

Wegel, R. L., Lane, C. E. 1924. The auditory masking of one pure tone by another and its probable relation to the dynamics of the inner ear. *Physiol. Rev.* 23:266–85

Wightman, F. L., Green, D. M. 1974. The perception of pitch. *Am. Sci.* 62:208–15

Yama, M. F., Small, A. M. Jr. 1983. Tonal masking and frequency selectivity for the monaural and binaural hearing systems. *J. Acoust. Soc. Am.* 73:285–90

Yost, W. A. 1985. Prior stimulation and the masking-level difference. *J. Acoust. Soc. Am.* 78:901–7

Yost, W. A., Soderquist, D. R. 1984. The precedence effect: Revisited. *J. Acoust.* *Soc. Am.* 76:1377–83

Zurek, P. M., Formby, C. 1981. Frequency-discrimination ability of hearing-impaired listeners. *J. Speech Hear. Res.* 46:108–12

Zwicker, E. 1974. On a psychoacoustical equivalent of tuning curves. In *Facts and Models in Hearing,* ed. E. Zwicker, E. Ter-hardt, pp. 132–40. Berlin: Springer-Verlag

Zwicker, E. 1976. A psychoacoustic equiv-alent of period histograms. *J. Acoust. Soc. Am.* 59:166–75

Ann. Rev. Psychol. 1987. 38:203–27

CONCEPT, KNOWLEDGE, AND THOUGHT

Gregg C. Oden

Department of Psychology, University of Wisconsin, Madison, Wisconsin 53706

CONTENTS

Thinking, broadly defined, is nearly all of psychology; narrowly defined it seems to be none of it. Every specific kind of thought process is more commonly known by some other name: pattern recognition, language comprehension, memory retrieval, and the like. What, then, is a review of thinking to be about? Traditionally, the term "thinking" has been used with a scope between the narrow and the broad to refer to a loose collection of topics at the heart of psychology. Over the 15 years that thinking has been a triennial topic for the *Review,* it has been a catchall category that has included, at various times, areas as unrelated as Gestalt approaches to problem solving, learning-theoretic approaches to concept identification, and Bayesian approaches to decision making.

    This is an odd state of affairs. One might suppose that the development of psychology would require that there first be a coherent, detailed account of

203

0066-4308/87/0201-0203$02.00

general thought mechanisms to serve as a core around which the study of specific mental subcomponents, such as perception or memory, would be built. Instead, we have begun at the periphery and worked toward the center, leaving psychology with well-developed subfields on all sides surrounding a sparsely developed middle. The reasons for this are clear: even without the long-term subjugation of psychology by behaviorism with its obsession for sticking to observable phenomena, we would have followed this course simply because it is easier and safer to stay close to external reality where the relevant variables are readily accessible and their means of measurement are determined by our colleagues in the physical sciences.

Nevertheless, over the past decade or so, there has been considerable research activity in this previously largely neglected area. In part, no doubt, this upsurgence (or, more accurately, resurgence) has been due to the loosening of the final bonds of the behavioral view, in part due to the unrelenting pressure for fresh research topics for the exploding population of experimental psychologists, and in no small part due to inroads toward the center resulting from advances made in other areas of cognitive psychology and artificial intelligence (AI).

As past reviews have documented, the area is now immensely active but also fractionated into what can be a bewildering assortment of unrelated or even apparently incompatible research questions and paradigms. This contrasts with the early days of modern interest in these issues when there was a fairly unified view of things with alternative models being variations on the common theme. One way to look at the current state of affairs is that the separate approaches are the splinterings of the formerly monolithic theoretical viewpoint. Indeed, it is easiest to make sense out of the field by considering where each such approach lies with respect to the now largely unrepresented central locus. Accordingly, we will begin by setting at least a minimal historical context.

THE BEGINNINGS OF THE MODERN ERA

"Dass de way de world go—modern time, mon." (Matthiessen 1975).

Mindful of the injustice inherent in attributing credit or blame for ideas to individuals, it nevertheless seems clear in retrospect as it did, indeed, at the time, that Ross Quillian's (1966) development of the semantic network is largely responsible for getting this area going. Although often thought of as originally being a piece of computer science (partly, no doubt, because his dissertation was included in Minsky's 1968 widely read collection of AI theses), Quillian's theory was actually part of the work done toward his degree in psychology under the guidance of Herbert Simon. In fact, it can readily be seen as a natural outgrowth of Newell, Shaw, and Simon's own pioneering research on list processing (Newell et al 1958) that began as psychological modeling but eventually led to what is now a major component of basic computer science.

No significant part of Quillian's network model of semantic memory was unique or novel in itself. Its influence was a result of (*a*) the impact of having a complete, working system and (*b*) the fact that he consistently made smart choices about which old ideas to use; the system encapsulated a number of principles that have proven to be of enduring importance. Chief among these are the principles of *propositionality, cognitive economy, default reasoning,* and *distributed meaning:*

1. Concepts are represented by nodes that are connected by labeled links corresponding to properties and relations. The result is equivalent to a collection of propositional expressions with complex concepts being composed of simpler ones combined with various operators.
2. Things true of a class of items are stored with the representation of the class rather than separately for each item.
3. Properties of a class are taken to be true of its instances unless they are explicitly marked to the contrary.
4. The meaning of a concept is given by its relationships, indirect as well as direct, to all other concepts in the network.

In addition, the notion of *intersection search* was central to the working of Quillian's system. Intersection search is an important alternative to the two traditional computational search methods: depth-first search (follow a single path through a search space as far as possible before considering alternatives) and breadth-first search (follow all viable paths simultaneously a step at a time). Intersection search is used to find the shortest path between two specified nodes in a network by performing simultaneous breadth-first searches from each original node until a common node is reached. This process is often conceptualized as "activation spreading" from the nodes by analogy to neural functioning (invited by the network character of the semantic memory model).

Quillian's model was elaborated and tested in work in collaboration with Collins (Collins & Quillian 1969, 1972), and later in the work of Collins in collaboration with Loftus (Collins & Loftus 1975). In addition, it led directly to important work on knowledge representation both in psychology and in AI (see particularly Findler 1979, Miller & Johnson-Laird 1976, Norman, Rumelhart & the LNR Research Group 1975). In AI, research in this tradition has progressed in an incremental fashion up to the present, with current influential work (e.g. Brachman & Schmolze 1985, Fikes & Kehler 1985) being clearly traceable to conceptual beginnings in Quillian's semantic nets.

For a time, the same seemed to be the case in psychology, but for various reasons, not all entirely clear, the main track of this area was largely abandoned (with the important exception of Anderson 1983) in favor of the pursuit of more peripheral issues heading off in different directions from the common base.

In delving through the leavings of 20th century cognitive psychology, future historians will, no doubt, venture hypotheses to account for the deflection of the field at what seemed to be a time of glory. Perhaps it was that the team approach required for large-scale simulations was too greatly incompatible with our tradition of "cottage industry" research. Almost certainly, the importance of Rosch's (1973, 1978) insights combined with her nonanalytic style distracted people from integrating category structure ideas with network formalism. It may even be that the headlessness of the field when both Rosch and Quillian dropped out of the enterprise soon after having had an enormous impact contributed to the drifting that has since characterized the area. (This is at least preferable to that of related fields that achieve their coherency at the expense of domination by central figures). My own pet account is that the semantic network approach was abandoned because it provided the clarity that made the complexity of human cognition apparent—"It couldn't possibly be that complicated" was (and, to some extent, still is) a common reaction. The irony, if this is the case, is that in many instances the replacements have been weaker formalisms subsumed by network theories.

A SAMPLER OF CURRENT TRENDS

The most recent review of thinking (Medin & Smith 1984) undertook the heroic task of providing a catalog of differing approaches to the part of the area having to do with concepts and concept formation. A major difficulty with any such attempt, no matter how carefully done, is the degree of arbitrariness that must be imposed in order to fit instances within whatever organizational scheme is chosen. Nearly all theoretical viewpoints hold that natural concepts are resistant to simple partitioning and this principle applies no less to the theories themselves.

Consequently, the present review will take the alternative tack of describing some of the recently emerging important trends in the field and relating one to another without attempting to arrange them within an overall organization of the field. Indeed, as will become apparent, very few of the trends represent competing positions aimed at one another from opposite ends of common theoretical dimensions; rather, most are concerned with sometimes complementary and sometimes completely orthogonal issues.

Distributed Representations of Knowledge

ON NOT KEEPING MEMORIES IN THEIR PLACE   One important trend is the return to an interest in distributed knowledge and intelligence by both psychologists and AIists. In this regard, a point of some confusion is that "distributed" can mean several different things within the knowledge representation domain. First, *meaning* is distributed in a semantic memory model over the entire network in the sense that the individual nodes themselves have no inherent meaning (they do not "contain" meaning) but rather attain meaning as a result of the particular relations that they hold to other concepts in the system.

Second, *processing* may be distributed in that the computation involved in performing a mental operation may be broken up into separate, relatively independent components allowing for parallel execution and, in some cases, for doing without monitor processes (which to many researchers smack of homunculi). This line of thought can be traced back to the intersection search notion and through later generalizations of spreading activation to other forms of computation. This approach was pioneered by Levin (1976), and continues to be important (e.g. Feldman & Ballard 1982, Rumelhart & McClelland 1982; see also Hillis 1985).

It is with yet a third sense of distribution that the present section is concerned. This notion is closely related to the first two senses, but it runs back to distinctly different roots (although roots that clearly also inspired Quillian) in early neural net modeling (Hebb 1949, McCulloch & Pitts 1943, Rosenblatt 1962). In this case, it is the *representations* that are distributed across the network. Such models are termed "superpositional" by Rumelhart & Norman (1986) because "each storage element contains information from many different memories *superimposed* upon one another." As such, these models contrast with the "positional" character of other memory models in which each distinct item of memory resides in a given conceptual place or location in the system.

Like semantic networks, superpositional models (e.g. Ackley et al 1985, Grossberg & Stone 1986, Fahlman et al 1983, Hinton 1981, Rumelhart & Zipser 1985) have nodes interconnected by links. However, in these models, instead of being represented by individual nodes, concepts are represented by patterns of activation over the entire system of nodes. Each concept involves a unique pattern of activation over the same node space, hence, the sense in which concepts are superimposed. The links connecting the nodes are not labeled (sometimes leading people to call these systems nonsymbolic; see Kosslyn & Hatfield 1984; but see also Newell 1983, Pylyshyn 1984). However, the links have weights that determine the degree (and polarity) of the activation that spreads to connected nodes as a result of activation of the nodes connected from. Collectively, the configuration of node weights determines what pattern of activation, and hence what activated concept, results from any particular prior activation pattern. In this way, relationships between concepts are represented. There are many variations on this basic approach (with some models formulated in terms of filters, convolutions, holograms, and matrixes) with resulting differences that seem more important to some researchers than to others (e.g. Anderson et al 1977, Eich 1982, Murdock 1982, Pike 1984).

Much work on superpositional models involves showing how they can accomplish many of the things that more directly intuitive models can do, such as forming arbitrary connections between concepts, categorizing input patterns, and retrieving stored knowledge. In addition, many aspects of the way superpositional models perform these functions are argued to be superior to those of their more traditional counterparts. For example, the distributed character of both concepts and relationships means that, given adequate redundancy in the whole system, a certain degree of noise can be tolerated without seriously degrading performance and that the injection of more noise leads only to graceful deterioration in performance. Indeed, it is even argued that this property of invariance of response over perturbations in input can be interpreted as the basis for some types of desirable stimulus generalization. Hinton (1984) gives a particularly lucid account of the power of such "coarse coding" in perceptual systems.

An even more important attraction of these models is that they are incrementally modifiable. New linkages between concepts (and, in some sense, even new concepts) gradually emerge within the system as a consequence of appropriately changing the relevant weights in small steps after each additional learning episode. Not only does this seem to reflect the dynamics of many kinds of learning (especially perceptual and motor learning, but also arguably much of the conceptual learning that happens automatically as a result of exposure to one's environment), but it also removes the requirement for an explicit, discrete decision to add or modify a relationship between concepts. Advocates of the superpositional approach sometimes describe the way changes are made in traditional network models as involving "someone reaching in to solder in a new link."

Because of the incremental nature of learning in superpositional models, interest in them seems to have gone hand in hand (as both cause and effect) with a renewal of interest in learning more generally. This is another parallel of current work with its intellectual forebears: much of the interest and excitement for this type of model when originally proposed in the form of the Perceptron (Rosenblatt 1962) was due to the convergence theorem that established the existence of a procedure for adjusting the weights that was guaranteed to lead in a finite number of steps to the appropriate values for mapping all input patterns onto the respective output patterns if such was possible. At the start, this theoretical result led to wild optimism, but the euphoria was abruptly terminated by Minsky & Papert's (1969) demonstration that Perceptrons were seriously limited in terms of the kinds of functions they could compute, that is, in the kinds of associations between input and output they could represent.

Proponents of the superpositional approach now believe that the impact of Minsky & Papert's book was unfair, not because the claims made were incorrect, but because it discouraged extending the Perceptron model to overcome its limitations. The current work is self-consciously a resurrection of this enterprise, specifically in allowing for arbitrarily many layers of intermediate nodes between the input and output. That is, current Perceptron-like models differ from the original in exactly the way that cognitive models generally differ from strictly behavioral ones: in making use of internal representations. As always, this move also increases complexity and reduces tractability. In this light, a recent result of Rumelhart, Hinton & Williams (1986) generalizing the Perceptron learning algorithm to work with multilayer superpositional systems, appears to be monumental. Their algorithm works in two stages: first, the effects of the input vector propagate forward through the multiple levels. Then the discrepancy between the produced and desired responses is propagated backwards through the levels allowing incremental weight changes that yield a proportional descent along the response surface to the configuration of values that ultimately satisfies the requirements.

While there is much about superpositional models that is exciting and attractive, some of their properties are decidedly problematic. The fact that all concepts are represented as patterns of activation over a single set of nodes makes it impossible for more than one concept to be active at a time. Thus, there can be no form of distributed processing requiring simultaneous activity over multiple concepts. All search from concept to concept would have to be serial; neither parallel breadth-first search nor intersection search will work. There have been attempts to alleviate the consequences of this limitation (such as proposing independent subsets of nodes—this is, of course, a "regressive" step towards positionality), but it remains a formidable challenge to this approach.

SUBSTITUTE OR SUBSTRATE?   This work has considerable promise to advance our understanding of the workings of knowledge and thought. However, the contrast between superpositional and positional models is misleading. Instead, as Hinton (1981, 1984; see also Rueckl 1986, Touretsky & Hinton 1985, Wickelgren 1981) argues, superpositional models are best thought of as the substrate on which more "ordinary" positional models are built, i.e. the machine language into which concepts and relations are compiled. This is favored because propositional descriptions are appropriate for the cognitive or functional level whereas distributed descriptions are neurally more realistic. The combination of the two in a bistratal system can potentially provide (a) the structural richness and naturalness sufficient for modeling cognitive processes, (b) the insusceptibility to noise and local insult characteristic of the brain, (c) a principled basis for incremental modification, and (d) an account of primitive net operations that are otherwise "magical." In a pragmatic sense, the resulting system crosses the mind-body gap in a way analogous to how a grammar relates sound to meaning—in each case, a bridging between incommensurable domains. ". . . brain *functions* are *brain* functions . . . the fact that human psychological functions are realized by the brain affords an exciting opportunity for deriving additional empirical constraints on the nature of the functions themselves" (Kosslyn & Hatfield 1984).

However, not everyone in this area takes this view. For example, Rumelhart & McClelland (1985) argue that there may be no cognitive level to which distributed models are the substrate. The neural level may be the one and only level of psychological reality. It is true that computers have machine language underlying their high-level language programs but not necessarily vice versa: there are many machine language programs for which there is no direct high-level language equivalent. If we limit ourselves to looking for only those neural organizations that could underlie hypothesized cognitive functions, we may fail to see the system the way it really is at either level.

However, I believe that this overstates the case. The computer analogy appealed to is accurate, of course, if we limit ourselves to extant high-level languages. If SNOBOL had never been invented, then the sequence of instructions that is the result of compiling a SNOBOL program would not be describable in any existing high-level language. But it does not follow that there is any machine language program that cannot, in principle, be described by a high-level language, at least if we limit ourselves to programs that do something reasonable. Indeed, it can be counterargued that behaving in a systematic way can only be the result of a well-structured process, one describable in computational terms such as loops, branches, routines, and the like. Furthermore, no computational process can be understood without invoking this level of analysis. Even a program written in assembly language is understood by its programmer in terms of higher-level structures. Psychological science has the same need if it is to achieve anything that can be considered to be understanding. Even if the "true facts" differ from our resulting account to some degree, it is better (that is, counts more as scientific knowledge) to have an understandable description that approximates reality than an exact description that is as incomprehensible as the world itself.

Knowledge of Particulars

ON GIVING THE SPECIFIC ITS DUE   A viewpoint that is similar in some respects to the superpositional approach is the exemplar view. In exemplar models, most or all knowledge is encoded in terms of the representation of individual objects and events. The sense in which this relates to superpositionality is that what is known about a category of things is distributed across all of the specific things that belong to the category. However, there is a crucial difference between these two approaches. In the superpositional account, both specific and abstract concepts have the same sort of representation: as patterns of activation over uninterpreted nodes. In contrast, exemplar models discriminate between the psychological realities of instances and abstractions in that, by and large, only specific instances are explicitly represented at any level.

In extreme versions of this approach, e.g. Hintzman (1986), there are no abstract categories stored in memory at all; rather, abstractions are derived when needed, as at retrieval time. Not all exemplar models go to this extreme, but all emphasize the "priority of the specific" as the title of a recent conference on these ideas put it. Indeed, an apparent motivation for the development of many of these models is as an antidote to the excessive emphasis on abstraction that is seen to characterize "standard" propositional models. However, to a large extent, this view of propositional models is a misconception of the role of cognitive economy, namely, that it is enforced to such an extent as to drive out all specific knowledge, even that which is specifying. This was explicitly disavowed early on by semantic networkers. For example: Collins & Quillian (1969) observed that knowing the general fact that trees have leaves does not preclude our knowing quite specifically what maple leaves are like.

At some point, the contrasting models become isomorphic, representing exactly the same knowledge and differing only in terms of what is explicit and what implicit. One might suppose that ease of retrieval would be a basis for discrimination between such alternatives and, indeed, the well-known recognition advantage for prototypes favors the abstraction position. However, Hintzman has shown how this result can fall out of an exemplar-based system as well. Nevertheless, his further argument that there is some sort of theoretical privilege for the exemplar view, that is, that the introduction of abstractions can only be warranted if they cannot be done without, seems entirely unjustified. On the contrary, accounting for knowledge in terms of abstract categories and concepts is familiar and intuitive—features we should not sacrifice if avoidable.

Ironically, one of the inventors of what has become the prototypical exemplar model (Medin & Schaffer 1978) has recently coauthored a paper

(Murphy & Medin 1985) that argues persuasively against such approaches and, indeed, against all models for which category membership is based on similarity measures (see also Oden & Lopes 1982 on this point). Instead, Murphy & Medin claim that categorization involves, at heart, the development and application of "theories," by which they mean coherent, integrated systems of knowledge and belief, a considerably abstract view.

In a very thoughtful pro-specifics paper, Brooks (1986) presents a more tempered view than that of the extreme versions of exemplar models. Brooks pleads a compelling case for the importance of specific knowledge not being overlooked, but he does not urge the abandonment of abstractions (Posner 1986 takes a similar position). Brooks gives a number of convincing demonstrations that people do encode a considerable amount of the mundane detail of their experience even when they are also developing and using abstract categories and even when the task nominally requires only the abstract information. As he says, it is reasonable to make use of what we know about specifics so that "the meanings of complex everyday events are not perpetually synthesized anew from semantic components and cognitive models every time a minor variant is encountered." Rather, we can rely on the fact that "ecologically, most conceptual neighborhoods contain more friends than enemies, more useful than misleading analogies among stimuli that are very similar." Nevertheless, we surely do also exploit regularities and form useful abstractions: "we are continually specializing general principles into context-specific understandings on the one hand and disciplining this drift into new generalities on the other." Brooks concludes that "sometimes we make the decisions we do because of overall policy, sometimes because of local expedience, and sometimes because all our friends seem to be doing it."

Intensional Representations

ON HAVING GOOD INTENSIONS   In the last review (Medin & Smith 1984), there was considerable discussion of the arguments of Osherson & Smith (1981) against the viability of fuzzy set theory[1] as a model of concepts and categorization. Since then, Cohen & Murphy (1984) and Oden (1984a) have shown that the problem is not with the fuzzy part of fuzzy set theory but rather with the set part. These recent papers (see also Hampton 1983, 1985) conclude that the representations of concepts must be based on their intensions, which may well necessarily be fuzzy.

The notion of intensional meaning as developed by philosophers and used by linguists is of that which one must know in order to know what an object is; more technically, a function that determines for any possible world what the

---

[1]A theory of sets to which objects may belong to varying degrees (Zadeh 1965).

concept refers to. In contrast, extensional meaning is simply a listing of which things are instances of the concept; that is, that which the concept happens to refer to in this particular world. Thus, meaning by extension is represented by sets of exemplars, whereas meaning by intension is represented by proposition and rule. In the former case, as Osherson & Smith formulated it, conceptual combination is limited to operations upon sets: union, intersection, and so on. In the latter, conceptual combination includes elaboration, specification, individuation, and other powerful forms of semantic modification. In the extensional view, to use the famous example, it is paradoxical that an apple that is striped is more truly an instance of striped apples than of apples since the one set must be contained within the other. In the intensional view, this is a natural consequence of the fact that "striped" modifies "apple": a striped apple has all of the features of apples generally except that whereas apples are ordinarily red, green, or yellow, a striped apple is striped and, as a result, strange for an apple. (For further details, see Oden 1984a,b, Oden & Lopes 1982).

While providing a compelling argument for the need for intensional models of concepts, the sort of modification involved in adjective-noun phrases is but a simple instance of a general property of concepts that is becoming increasingly clear, namely, that they are not static structures with fixed referents and permanent linkages to the world they represent. Rather, the intensional basis of concepts allows them to be constructed, amended, and tuned "on the fly" as the needs of the concept-holder and the demands of the task require. This modifiability includes that which must underlie the comprehension of the rather extraordinary transformations in Ovid's *Metamorphoses,* which Kelly & Keil (1985) found, nevertheless, to be rule-governed. It also includes the less fantastic case studied by Roth & Shoben (1983), who demonstrated that the category structure of a concept's extension may be drastically changed by its context, so that, for example, what counts as a bird (and to what degree) is very different in the context of "The bird crossed the barnyard" than in the context of "The hunter shot at the bird overhead." Likewise, Barsalou (1983) has shown that many natural categories (such as the set of things to take on a camping trip) are "ad hoc" in that the extension must be computed at the time the concept is used rather than being the basis for specifying the meaning of the concept a priori. Barsalou & Medin (1986) argue from such results against the classical view of concepts (including the core-concept-plus-identification-procedure idea appealed to by Osherson & Smith 1981) and for a view of concepts as dynamic and context-dependent.

All of these recent results corroborate the need to represent concepts intensionally—intensions allow for sufficiently powerful semantic operations and also provide for the computation of extensions as needed. Indeed, in a more recent paper, even Smith & Osherson (1984) adopt a position largely in agreement with this view, saying ". . . it is time to explore an approach to conceptual combination that starts with the prototype representations themselves." Thus, within this corner of the field, there appears to be converging agreement.

WHITHER FUZZINESS?   With respect to the original issue, it is still a very open question whether the required intensional theories may not actually be fuzzy. There have been fewer direct attacks on the premises of the fuzzy view recently, and there are a gradually increasing number of people who are working within the fuzzy framework or doing work that is in the same spirit. For example, Newstead & Griggs (1984) showed that part of subjects' supposed errors in set inclusion problems may be due to their interpreting "all" fuzzily, that is, to mean "almost all." Zimmer (1982) applied a fuzzy theoretical analysis to the use of color terms with one result being that "turquoise is neither a mere convention of communication nor a superfluous ornamental color name in the blue-green area, but a distinctive best-fitting term for a part of the color spectrum." Forsyth (1986), following up on Oden (1981) who followed up on Labov (1973), examined the knowledge structures underlying the degree to which pieces of dishware are categorized as cups or bowls. Hollan & Hutchins (1984) argued for the importance of tuned ballpark estimates and other forms of "quasi-quantitative" reasoning in problems confronted by automated tutorial systems. Wallsten et al (1986) used a pair-comparison procedure to establish fuzzy membership functions of vague probability terms such as "doubtful," "good chance," and "tossup." Oden (1983) showed how semantic constraints may act as fuzzy restrictions to determine the degree of sensibleness of sentence interpretations. Hampton (1985) performed a thorough analysis of naturally conjunctive concepts such as "sports which are games," and found that people overextend them in systematic ways that are largely consistent with certain formulations of fuzzy conjunction. On the applied front, the first expert system on a chip was developed by Bell Lab's Machine Perception and Robot Intelligence Department using a fuzzy inference system (Togai & Watanabe 1985).

Much of the remaining disagreement over the fuzziness issue seems to arise not from what the data are nor what they mean but rather about what such data could mean, that is, about how the world could possibly be. On the one hand are people who are eager to embrace nontraditional ("deviant") logics of various sorts as coming closer to being realistic models of people's representation of and reasoning about the world. On the other hand are researchers who believe that traditional logic is universal and that the only plausible possibility is that people's thought processes at least approximately follow its dictates. The former camp often appears to believe that penguins really are sort of birds and sort of not. The latter camp sometimes seems a little embarrassed to participate in a science whose subjects may act as if they do.

Penguins, of course, really are birds biologically speaking, although it is not clear why we should be willing to give biologists the last word on the matter. Indeed, in many cases, biological reality has changed over the years depending on the criteria and theories in biological vogue.[2] Furthermore, with regard to many fundamental categorical issues, reality as even biologists know it is by no means clear-cut. This is a point that is prominent in the recent writings of Stephen Jay Gould, an outspoken champion of taxonomy, which he calls "the Cinderella of the sciences" (Gould 1985). In discussing one classic "hard case" (whether Siamese twins are one person or two), Gould says "We inhabit a complex world. Some boundaries are sharp and permit clean and definite distinctions. But nature also includes continua that cannot be neatly parceled into two piles of unambiguous yeses and noes." And on the nature of species (the prototypical prototypicality question) and whether Portugese man-of-wars and like entities are one critter or collections of cooperative ones, Gould says "when an inquiry becomes so convoluted, we must suspect that we are proceeding in the wrong way. We must . . . not pursue every new iota of information or nuance of argument in the old style, hoping all the time that our elusive solution awaits a crucial item, yet undiscovered. Nature, in some respects, comes to us as continua, not as discrete objects with clear boundaries." Thus, even from eminent biologists, the final word seems to be that if we shed our naïve views of biology, we may find our subjects not to be so naïve as intuitive biologists after all.[3]

Natural Reasoning

ON RATIONALITY UNBOUNDED   For a number of years, one focus of the limited amount of work that continues to be done on inference and reasoning has been on logical errors made by subjects in many experimental tasks. This focus has paralleled that which has dominated the related area of decision making (formerly part of the domain covered by this chapter series on thinking). In both areas (reasoning is covered here; for decision making, see Hogarth 1981, Lopes 1982, Thorngate 1980) there are signs of a healthy emerging countertrend under which subjects' behavior is reevaluated in light of the broader context of the situations people ordinarily face outside the experimental psychology lab.

The work in this area has largely been organized around a handful of

---

[2]Presently, tricky cases are resolved by recourse to the similarity of DNA structure, which is obviously of little direct relevance to the reality in which most of us live our lives. In addition, like all similarity-based measures, it ultimately depends on judgments of how to specify the metric.

[3]Of course, this point is not intended to be limited only to intuitive knowledge of the biological sort.

specific reasoning tasks, with the research on each being ". . . somewhat of a small industry, spawning a host of variations, dozens of studies, and more than its share of interpretational controversies" (Tweney & Doherty 1983). Among the most popular of such tasks are two devised by Peter Wason in the 1960s. In one task, called the "selection problem" or the "four card problem" (Wason 1966), subjects are given a rule such as "if a card has a vowel on one side then it will have an even number on the other side." Subjects are then shown four cards displaying an E, a K, a 4, and a 7 (one instance of each respective logical type), and are asked which cards they need to turn over to determine if the rule is, in fact, correct for the set of cards. The other task, the "2,4,6 problem" (Wason 1960), requires subjects to formulate the rule that completely describes a set of number triples. As in concept formation tasks (Bourne 1970), subjects can ask whether particular candidate triples belong to the set until confident of what the rule must be. Subjects are started out (on the wrong foot, as it turns out) by being told that 2,4,6 is in the set.

In both tasks, subjects' typical responses have been taken to reflect deficiencies in reasoning. In the former case, subjects almost always correctly check the E card, often check the irrelevant K card, and seldom check the critical 7 card. In the case of the 2,4,6 task, subjects mostly stick to queries about triples that satisfy their own hypothesized rule. By failing to seek to "falsify" their hypotheses, they do not discover that the rule the ever-devious experimenter has in mind, three ascending numbers, is more general than they would have imagined. Both of these findings have been taken to reflect a "confirmation bias" on the part of subjects in focusing on establishing that their tentative rule is right rather than that it could not be wrong.

In each case, the standard result has often been replicated but also shown to be sensitive to a variety of additional factors. For example, numerous studies have documented a "semantic facilitation effect" in which the bias in the selection task is obviated (subjects do check the negative consequent card) when the if-then rule is meaningful or familiar, e.g. "if someone is drinking beer, then he must be 19 years or older." For some (e.g. Griggs & Cox 1982), this suggests that it is not that people do not use logical rules properly, but that they often do not use them at all, relying instead on retrieved experiences with specific cases. Other researchers (e.g. Hoch & Tschirgi 1983; see also Griggs & Cox 1983, Rips 1986a) take such results to mean that people have adequate logical skills but need the familiar setting to recognize the appropriate logical structure. In fact, Wason himself has recently taken such a position, arguing that the revised tasks "may do more justice to the individual's logical competence than the standard selection task, . . . [since] in everyday reasoning logical form is intrinsically related to the content in which it is expressed" (Wason & Green 1984). Ordinary people are neither well-practiced at nor particularly motivated to reason about things out of context. Nor is there any very compelling reason (other than intellectual chauvinism on the part of those of us who have mastered, perhaps after grueling effort, the formal procedures) why we should expect them to be.

Indeed, Klayman & Ha (1986) have shown through detailed analysis of the structure of these tasks considered broadly, that even the supposedly biased pattern of responding can be seen to be optimally efficient when coping with exceptions—arguably the kind of situation most often encountered not only by ordinary people but by scientists and professional diagnosticians as well. That is, whenever the consequent of a rule describes an uncommon state of affairs (e.g. when most of the people at a party are under the drinking age), one is more likely to gain information through disconfirmation by checking the antecedent than by checking the negative of the consequent. In a related vein, Tukey (1986) argues that when analyzed according to alternative philosophies of science, what has been interpreted as evidence of faulty reasoning under Popperian logic may be seen as well-founded (even sophisticated) means to knowing.

An additional consideration from work involving learning in simulated novel physical environments (Mynatt et al 1978) is that with respect to the encompassing issue of how best to learn about the world in which we find ourselves, coming up with reasonable hypotheses is at least as important as being able to evaluate them validly. Further, accomplishing this seems to depend on being undeterred by initial disconfirmations, at least until the hypothesis is fairly well-defined as a result of sufficient confirmations. The importance of this has been shown through case study as well as lab work: Faraday's discovery of electrical induction strikingly follows this pattern (Tweney 1986). Similarly, Klayman (1985) found that to achieve a useful understanding of naturally perplexing environments depends on making a systematic attempt to build a model of the situation rather than doggedly trying to test hypotheses incrementally in a traditional data-driven manner. Thus, not only is people's reasoning such as to most often be efficient, it also mirrors that practiced by great scientists, and may, in fact, be the only possible course to follow except within the narrow, artificial exercise of the abstract puzzles of logicians and experimental psychologists.

Mental Models

ON MODELING MODELS   For some time now, researchers have realized that much of what people know is structured in terms of explicit internal models of aspects of the world they experience. This has played a particularly important role in psycholinguistics where it has become clear that what goes on in a conversation can be understood only in terms of the models that speaker and listener have about each other (see Clark & Marshall 1978 for an elaborate analysis in these terms; see Gibbs 1986 for a recent example). Lately, these notions have come to be popularly applied in the study of the development of expertise. An excellent sampling of such work is the collection of papers edited by Gentner & Stevens (1983) titled *Mental Models*. The chapters in this volume include discussions of the models that people have of how their electronic calculators work (Young 1983), the changes in models as expertise is acquired (Greeno 1983, Larkin 1983; see also Means & Voss 1985), the effect of alternative models of electricity (Gentner & Gentner 1983), the models of physical motion held by people without serious physics training (McCloskey 1983), and the model of position and movement used by Micronesians in accurately navigating between distant South Pacific islands "without recourse to mechanical or electrical or even magnetic devices" (Hutchins 1983).

In each case, the appeal to the use of a mental model is based on people's abilities to "run internal simulations" of what would be expected to happen under various hypothetical situations as a means of evaluating alternative problem solutions and making reliable predictions of outcomes in the world. Being able to perform this obviously powerful thinking procedure requires having a systematic body of knowledge about properties of relevant objects and operations. However, people's models by no means need to be complete or even consistent in order to be effective—a reasonably large and reasonably coherent interconnected set of facts and hypotheses can be workably robust. This is part of the reason why technically incorrect models may be resistant to change. In fact, in some instances, naïve models outperform more sophisticated ones. Kempton (1986), for example, discovered that believing furnace thermostats to work as valves rather than as feedback systems more reliably leads people to the correct conclusion that reduced nighttime settings conserve heat. (The more technically correct feedback model often fails to include an adequate consideration of the critical factor of heat dissipation.)

In other instances, concrete mental models allow the performance of complex tasks that might be supposed to require abstract formal reasoning procedures. For example, Denny (1986) found that Ojibway and Inuit hunters successfully accomplish environmentally relevant quantitative reasoning even though their concepts of number and arithmetical operations are completely tied to the particular objects to which they are applied. Strikingly similar results were obtained in a very different setting by Scribner (1984) in a study of preloaders in an American dairy who accomplish the equivalent of mixed-base arithmetic by visualization of partial case lots without having to resort to counting. In both instances, the situational context, through the mediation of appropriate mental models, supports the accomplishment of tasks that would require much more sophisticated and difficult procedures to do out of context.

USER MODELS   While it is inadvisable to persuade people to put much effort into devising more accurate models (for each individual person, the cost of improving each of his individual models of real-world phenomena is unlikely to be compensated by anything like a corresponding amount of improvement in performance), it is undoubtably worthwhile for designers of artificial systems to have a better understanding of the models that people begin with for each task. For example, it is generally acknowledged (Norman 1983) that computer software should be designed to be consistent in behavior rather than, as is often the case, simply the result of "creeping featurism".[4] However, it is also a truism within the computer software community that apparent inconsistency often results from the fact that even expert users may develop substantially different models from what the designer had in mind (and, more than likely, thought would be obvious). Part of this difficulty arises simply because people are different. For example, everyone wonders why developers of text editors fail to use the "natural" names for editing operations, but studies of preferences for command names (Landauer et al 1983) reveal little consistency between people (beyond the fact that naïve users prefer the term "change" for nearly every operation). The ultimate solution to this problem may require systems that are smart enough to adapt to the individual user's individual model (Rich 1983).

On the other hand, in many other cases, the problem does not have to do with differences among users (who may predictably rely on particular models for understanding task operations), but rather with the difference between users and software designers, who almost certainly have very different assumptions about the structure of the system and the problem. In this case, significant help can be provided if we can develop an adequate psychological characterization of the users' models (Carroll & Mack 1985, Good et al 1984, Gould & Lewis 1985). Interesting work along these lines is being done on a wide variety of problems. Eisenstadt (1983) presents the rationale behind a programming environment for cognitive psychology students doing AI projects at remote study centers. Perlman (1984) and Hutchins et al (1985) discuss new approaches to user interfaces for complex software systems. Levin et al (1983) describe how grade school students can become intensely involved with developing writing skills when text processing software is made more understandable from a child's point of view. Williams (1984) illustrates how an information retrieval system can be devised to match much more

---

[4]Having evolved through the addition of one unrelated feature after another, where a feature is either something useful whether or not intended or something intended whether or not useful (Steele et al 1983).

closely the strategies people use in retrieving information from their own memories.

This is likely to be an increasingly important area of psychological study, both for theoretical and practical reasons. Indeed, industry appears more than ready to learn from what psychologists can uncover for them. Nowhere has this been more clear than in the case of microcomputer manufacturers who have in recent years invested hundreds of millions of dollars in trying to significantly raise the degree to which the operation of their machines matches the models users bring to them. As the software development guidelines of the leader in this movement puts it "The Macintosh is designed to appeal to an audience of nonprogrammers, including people who have previously feared and distrusted computers . . . Applications should build on skills that people already have, not force them to learn new ones. . . . The user should be able to accomplish what needs to be done spontaneously and intuitively . . ." (Apple Computer, Inc. 1985).

More Mental Models

ON MUDDLING MODELS?   Somewhat ironically, a second book was published in 1983 with the same name as the Gentner & Stevens volume. This other *Mental Models* was written by Phillip Johnson-Laird as a fleshing out of ideas that he has advocated over the past several years (Johnson-Laird 1980, 1981). Like the previously discussed researchers, Johnson-Laird believes that much of human reasoning involves constructing and running internal models of some portion of the external world. For example, in one particularly well-chosen illustration, he shows how reasoning about the "right of" relation between people seated at a table cannot be done on the basis of general purpose ("syntactic") inference rules but rather has to involve a fairly precise representation of the details of the situation including the size and shape of the table and the number and arrangement of the people around it. Otherwise, inferences, such as transitivity of "right of"-hood, that are valid in some cases (for a small subset of many people at a table or even a few people all together at one side of a large table) will be applied in cases (three people evenly spaced around a small, round table) where they are not valid. When the reasoning processes are construed to be mental operations applied to models of the world, then the constraints that govern the corresponding operations in the modeled world will ensure valid conclusions (if the mental model is accurate). This is an instance of a representation intrinsically capturing the relations among its represented objects (Palmer 1978).

However, unlike other mental model advocates, Johnson-Laird does not devote himself to working out the details of such models for particular domains. As Ford (1985) observes, even with syllogistic reasoning, which is

Johnson-Laird's most fully developed example and that which originally inspired him to pursue these arguments, his system is not explicit enough to determine how it could actually be made to work. Instead, his work focuses on the claim that the use of mental models is an argument against the adequacy of propositional representations. That is, Johnson-Laird believes that his conception of the mental models that people use is, in principle, incompatible with the strictly propositional approach to knowledge, and that, indeed, it is because of what mental models in this sense can do and propositional representations cannot that we need to postulate the existence and use of such models.

Examining the specifics of this claim, we find, once again, that an argument turns on the distinction between intensions and extensions. Johnson-Laird claims that his notion of mental model is demanded because of the inadequacy of strictly intensional accounts of meaning. Such accounts are inadequate, he believes, because (*a*) some mental operations, as we have seen, must be applied directly to the specific instantiations of concepts, and (*b*) intensional representations have no meaning without a specification of what they refer to. The latter contention is what Rips (1986b) calls the "model-theory-in-the-head idea" that mental models, as Johnson-Laird envisions them, are somehow literal representations of the world and may thereby provide the sort of referential semantics that model-theoretic logicians believe is necessary for any account of meaning.

All of this seems more than slightly odd in at least three respects. First, it is odd to argue that intensional representations are incomplete without explicit extensional components since the former is usually considered to subsume the knowledge of the latter. That is, as you will recall, intensions have traditionally been defined to be that which is required in order to determine a concept's extension for any specific situation to which it might be applied (e.g. who "the President of the United States" refers to in the world of 1987, what "the morning star" refers to in the celestial world as we experience it, or what "to the right of" refers to for a particular seating arrangement).

Second, in a paper titled "Mental muddles," Rips (1986b) argues that mental models, no matter how literal, being nevertheless mental, can no more provide a referential semantics than any other representation system. At best, mental models allow us to map from one representation system to another, but they provide a model-theoretic basis of meaning for neither. As Rips puts it, "Although it might be possible to construct a theory of what it means for one mental representation (e.g. mental propositions) to be true in relation to another (e.g. mental models), this clearly wouldn't fulfill the goal of connecting mental representations to the external world. . . . Fans of reference-and-truth are unlikely to find internal models to be fair substitutes."

Third, Johnson-Laird's claims seem particularly surprising given that the proponents of propositional approaches have, over the years, been the most active and enduring supporters of the need to talk in terms of mental models. There seems no principled reason why the relationships among specific real-world objects that are captured in Johnson-Laird's mental models might not as well be represented in a semantic network (see, once again, Rips 1986b). Indeed, Johnson-Laird is fully aware that the notion of propositional representations held by many scholars can subsume his current approach. His own book with Miller (Miller & Johnson-Laird 1976) provided an outstanding demonstration of the power and universality of propositional language. Thus, in arguing that propositional models are inadequate, he is quite explicitly claiming that we should limit what gets called propositional to a more restricted sense of "language-like" or "close to language in form." His rationale is that this restriction is required to preserve the falsifiability of the claim that mental representations are propositional (see also Johnson-Laird et al 1984). I believe this to be a confusing of the representation language used to express a theory of knowledge with the theoretical claims expressed within that language. This is a general issue that applies to other debates in the field and so will be considered here in some detail.

REPRESENTATION AND IMPLEMENTATION   The representation language in which a theory is expressed provides a vocabulary along with semantic interpretations that allow us to formulate specific theoretical accounts of knowledge content, organization, and use. It can be considered analogous to the computer language that a researcher chooses for implementing a simulation of a cognitive process (indeed, AI can be seen, in part, as the use of computer languages as representation languages with the advantage of direct executability and the disadvantage of opacity—although see Perlman 1984). Just as the details of the chosen implementation language (e.g. LISP, Pascal, or C) are not ordinarily taken to be part of the theory embodied by a simulation, so too we should not mix up aspects of the representation language (e.g. propositions) with theoretical statements about what is represented. On the other hand, just as the limitations of a poorly chosen implementation language may prevent a simulation from being successful, so too can an inadequate representation language significantly handicap a theory of knowledge.

In sum, a knowledge representation account requires, first, an adequate representation language—one capable of expressing what we need to express regardless of what that might be—and then, an accurate description within the language. Many controversies seem to be arguments about details of description within a woefully lacking language, as if we were playing a game of how high one can jump with a 40-pound weight when the real question is whether we can jump high enough by any means.

CONCLUDING (BUT NOT CONCLUSIVE) REMARKS

The history of knowledge representation (and of cognitive psychology more generally), has been one of theoretical contrasts artificially (and disruptingly—see Newell 1973, 1983) intensified:

- serial versus parallel
- analog versus propositional
- procedural versus declarative

Some of the recent trends documented here may seem to include a new series of such contrasts:

- distributed versus positional
- specific versus abstract
- mental models versus propositions

Certainly, many researchers feel strongly that one or another (or perhaps several or all) of these contrasts reflects a fundamental division between alternative possible psychological realities, and that posing such stark yes/no questions promotes the advancement of the science. The present discussion has disputed this view and stressed instead isomorphism in concept where there is apparent conflict in the theoretical language. Clearly there are many people working here[5] heading in seemingly different directions after certainly different goals. It would be foolhardy to pretend to know where it is going and where it will end up. Still, the field has the decided appearance of one in need of unification.

As always with perception, if one looks hard enough it is possible to discern a pattern, to see suggestions of common ideas emerging from quite different sources. It may be that we are heading toward a re-coalescence of our splintered views. The work on the construction of a superpositional substrate for semantic memory, the development of intensional representations capable of accounting for graded category membership, the examination of the psycho-logical basis of concepts and reasoning, and the specification of

---

[5]The present review treats only a small, necessarily highly selected sample of the field. For additional coverage, see the excellent chapters by Rumelhart & Norman (1986) on knowledge representation and by Greeno & Simon (1986) on problem solving and reasoning.

the structure of mental models, together with the future work of psychologists who are bound to be inspired by advances in AI on knowledge representation, all seem to be pointing toward a new agreement on the need to return to the conceptual framework provided by propositional models. Certainly no other single unified approach has had a like potential to handle problems ranging from language comprehension to pattern identification to categorization to memory and learning. Perhaps after having indulged itself with specialized models for limited ("toy") problems, the field is ready once again to undertake the development of an adequate, coherent, encompassing account of concept, knowledge, and thought that may serve as the core, the heart for psychology.

ACKNOWLEDGMENTS

I want to thank Lola Lopes for her helpful comments and the members of the CALM group at Wisconsin (especially Jay Rueckl, Pete Sandon, Seng-Beng Ho, Tom Sanocki, Len Uhr, and David Neves) for valuable discussions of the issues considered here. Preparation of this manuscript was supported by the National Science Foundation through grant BNS83-10870.

Literature Cited

Ackley, D. H., Hinton, G. E., Sejnowski, T. J. 1985. A learning algorithm for Boltzman machines. *Cognit. Sci.* 9:147–69

Anderson, J. A., Silverstein, J. W., Ritz, S. R., Jones, R. S. 1977. Distinctive features, categorical perception, and probability learning: Some applications of a neural model. *Psychol. Rev.* 84:413–51

Anderson, J. R. 1983. *The Architecture of Cognition.* Cambridge, Mass: Harvard

Apple Computer, Inc. 1985. *Inside Macintosh.* Reading, Mass: Addison-Wesley

Atkinson, R. C., Herrnstein, R. J., Lindzey, G., Luce, R. D. 1986. *Handbook of Experimental Psychology.* New York: Wiley. In press

Barsalou, L. W. 1983. Ad hoc categories. *Mem. Cognit.* 11:211–27

Barsalou, L. W., Medin, D. L. 1986. Concepts: Fixed definitions or context-dependent representations? *Cah. Psychol. Cognit.* In press

Bourne, L. E. Jr. 1970. Knowing and using concepts. *Psychol. Rev.* 77:546–56

Brachman, R. J., Schmolze, J. G. 1985. An overview of the KL-ONE knowledge representation system. *Cognit. Sci.* 9:171–216

Brooks, L. R. 1986. Decentralized control of categorization: The role of prior processing episodes. In *Categories Reconsidered: The Ecological and Intellectual Bases of Categories,* ed. U. Neisser. Cambridge: Cambridge Univ. Press. In press

Carroll, J. M., Mack, R. L. 1985. Metaphor, computing systems, and active learning. *Int. J. Man-Machine Stud.* 22:39–57

Clark, H. H., Marshall, C. 1978. Reference diaries. In *Theoretical Issues in Natural Language Processing-2,* ed. D. L. Waltz, pp. 57–63. New York: Assoc. Comput. Mach.

Cohen, B., Murphy, G. L. 1984. Models of concepts. *Cognit. Sci.* 8:27–58

Collins, A. M., Loftus, E. F. 1975. A spreading activation theory of semantic processing. *Psychol. Rev.* 82:407–28

Collins, A. M., Quillian, M. R. 1969. Retrieval time from semantic memory. *J. Verb. Learn. Verb. Behav.* 8:240–47

Collins, A. M., Quillian, M. R. 1972. Experiments on semantic memory and language comprehension. In *Cognition in Learning and Memory,* ed. L. W. Gregg, pp. 117–37. New York: Wiley

Denny, J. P. 1986. Cultural ecology of mathematics: Ojibway and Inuit hunters. In *Native American Mathematics,* ed. M. Closs. Austin: Univ. Texas Press. In press

Eich, J. M. 1982. A composite holographic associative recall model. *Psychol. Rev.* 89:627–61

Eisenstadt, M. 1983. A user-friendly software environment for the novice programmer. *Commun. ACM* 26:1058–64

Fahlman, S. E., Hinton, G. E., Sejnowski, T. J. 1983. Massively parallel architectures for AI: NETL, Thistle, and Boltzmann machines. *Proc. Meet. Am. Assoc. Artif. Intell., 3rd, Washington, DC*, pp. 109–13

Feldman, J. A., Ballard, D. H. 1982. Connectionist models and their properties. *Cognit. Sci.* 6:205–54

Fikes, R., Kehler, T. 1985. The role of frame-based representation in reasoning. *Commun. ACM* 28:904–20

Findler, N. V., ed. 1979. *Associative Networks: Representation and Use of Knowledge by Computers.* New York: Academic

Ford, M. 1985. Review of *Mental Models* by P. N. Johnson-Laird. *Language* 61:897–903

Forsyth, B. H. 1986. The subjective attributes of natural categories: An application of a constrained generalized Euclidean model. In *Multidimensional Scaling: Theory and Application*, ed. F. W. Young, R. M. Hamer. Hillsdale, NJ: Erlbaum. In press

Gentner, D., Gentner, D. R. 1983. Flowing waters or teeming crowds: Mental models of electricity. See Gentner & Stevens 1983, pp. 99–129

Gentner, D., Stevens, A. L. 1983. *Mental Models.* Hillsdale, NJ: Erlbaum

Gibbs, R. W. Jr. 1986. On the psycholinguistics of sarcasm. *J. Exp. Psychol: Gen.* 115:3–15

Good, M. D., Whiteside, J. A., Wixon, D. R., Jones, S. J. 1984. Building a user-derived interface. *Commun. ACM* 27:1032–43

Gould, J. D., Lewis, C. 1985. Designing for usability: Key principles and what designers think. *Commun. ACM* 28:300–11

Gould, S. J. 1985. *The Flamingo's Smile.* New York: Norton

Greeno, J. G. 1983. Conceptual entities. See Gentner & Stevens, 1983, pp. 227–52

Greeno, J. G., Simon, H. A. 1986. Problem solving and reasoning. See Atkinson et al 1986

Griggs, R. A., Cox, J. R. 1982. The elusive thematic-materials effect in Wason's selection task. *Br. J. Psychol.* 73:407–20

Griggs, R. A., Cox, J. R. 1983. The effect of problem content on strategies in Wason's selection task. *Q. J. Exp. Psychol.* 35A:519–33

Grossberg, S., Stone, G. 1986. Neural dynamics of word recognition and recall: Attentional priming, learning, and resonance. *Psychol. Rev.* 93:46–74

Hampton, J. A. 1983. *A composite prototype model of conceptual conjunction.* The City Univ., London

Hampton, J. A. 1985. *Overextension of conjunctive concepts: Evidence for a unitary model of concept typicality and class inclusion.* The City University, London

Hebb, D. O. 1949. *The Organization of Behavior.* New York: Wiley

Hillis, W. D. 1985. *The Connection Machine.* Cambridge, Mass: MIT

Hinton, G. E. 1981. Implementing semantic networks in parallel hardware. In *Parallel Models of Associative Memory*, ed. G. E. Hinton, J. A. Anderson, pp. 161–87. Hillsdale, NJ: Erlbaum

Hinton, G. E. 1984. *Distributed representations. Tech. Rep. CMU-CS-84-157.* Carnegie-Mellon Univ., Pittsburgh, Pa.

Hintzman, D. L. 1986. "Schema abstraction" in a multiple-trace memory model. *Psychol. Rev.* In press

Hoch, S. J., Tschirgi, J. E. 1983. Cue redundancy and extra logical inference in a deductive reasoning task. *Mem. Cognit.* 11:200–9

Hogarth, R. M. 1981. Beyond discrete biases: Functional and dysfunctional aspects of judgmental heuristics. *Psychol. Bull.* 90:197–217

Hollan, J. D., Hutchins, E. L. 1984. Reservations about qualitative models. *Proc. Meet. Cognit. Sci. Soc., 6th,* Boulder, Colo., pp. 183–87

Hutchins, E. 1983. Understanding Micronesian navigation. See Gentner & Stevens 1983, pp. 191–225

Hutchins, E., Hollan, J. D., Norman, D. A. 1985. Direct manipulation interfaces. In *User Centered System Design: New Perspectives on Human-Computer Interaction*, ed. D. A. Norman, S. W. Draper. Hillsdale, NJ: Erlbaum

Johnson-Laird, P. N. 1980. Mental models in cognitive science. *Cognit. Sci.* 4:71–115

Johnson-Laird, P. N. 1981. Mental models of meaning. In *Elements of Discourse Understanding*, ed. A. K. Joshi, B. L. Weber, I. A. Sag, pp. 106–26. Cambridge: Cambridge Univ. Press

Johnson-Laird, P. N. 1983. *Mental Models: Towards a Cognitive Science of Language, Inference, and Consciousness.* Cambridge, Mass: Harvard

Johnson-Laird, P. N., Herrmann, D. J., Chaffin, R. 1984. Only connections: A critique of semantic networks. *Psychol. Bull.* 96:292–315

Kelly, M. H., Keil, F. C. 1985. The more things change . . .: Metamorphoses and conceptual structure. *Cognit. Sci.* 9:403–16

Kempton, W. 1986. Two theories of home heat control. *Cognit. Sci.* 10:75–90

Klayman, J. 1985. *Experimentation, observation and learning in probabilistic environments.* Work. Pap. 117. Cent. Decision Res., Univ. Chicago

Klayman, J., Ha, Y.-W. 1986. Confirmation, disconfirmation, and information in hypothesis-testing. *Psychol. Rev.* In press

Kosslyn, S. M., Hatfield, G. 1984. Representation without symbol systems. *Soc. Res.* 51:1019–45

Labov, W. 1973. The boundaries of words and their meanings. In *New Ways of Analyzing Variation in English,* ed. C.-J. N. Bailey, R. W. Shuy, pp. 340–73. Washington, DC: Georgetown

Landauer, T. K., Galotti, K. M., Hartwell, S. 1983. Natural command names and initial learning: A study of text editing terms. *Commun. ACM* 26:495–503

Larkin, J. H. 1983. The role of problem representation in physics. See Gentner & Stevens, 1983, pp. 75–98

Levin, J. A. 1976. *Proteus: An activation framework for cognitive process models.* ISI Work. Pap. 2. Inf. Sci. Inst., Marina del Rey, Calif.

Levin, J. A., Boruta, M. J., Vasconcellos, M. T. 1983. Microcomputer-based environments for writing: A writer's assistant. In *Classroom Computers and Cognitive Science,* ed. A. C. Wilkinson. New York: Academic

Lopes, L. L. 1982. Doing the impossible: A note on induction and the experience of randomness. *J. Exp. Psychol: Learn. Mem. Cognit.* 8:626–36

Matthiessen, P. 1975. *Far Tortuga.* New York: Random House

McCloskey, M. 1983. Naive theories of motion. See Gentner & Stevens 1983, pp. 299–324

McCulloch, W. S., Pitts, W. H. 1943. A logical calculus of the ideas immanent in nervous activity. *Bull. Math. Biophys.* 5:115–33

Means, M. L., Voss, J. F. 1985. Star Wars: A developmental study of expert and novice knowledge structures. *J. Mem. Lang.* 24:746–57

Medin, D. L., Schaffer, M. M. 1978. Context theory of classification learning. *Psychol. Rev.* 85:207–38

Medin, D. L., Smith, E. E. 1984. Concepts and concept formation. *Ann. Rev. Psychol.* 35:113–38

Miller, G. A., Johnson-Laird, P. N. 1976. *Language and Perception.* Cambridge, Mass: Harvard

Minsky, M., ed. 1968. *Semantic Information Processing.* Cambridge, Mass: MIT

Minsky, M., Papert, S. 1969. *Perceptrons.* Cambridge, Mass: MIT

Murdock, B. B. Jr. 1982. A theory for the storage and retrieval of item and associative information. *Psychol. Rev.* 89:609–26

Murphy, G. L., Medin, D. L. 1985. The role of theories in conceptual coherence. *Psychol. Rev.* 92:289–316

Mynatt, C. R., Doherty, M. E., Tweney, R. D. 1978. Consequences of confirmation and disconfirmation in a simulated research environment. *Q. J. Exp. Psychol.* 30:395–406

Newell, A. 1973. You can't play twenty questions with nature and win: Projective comments on the papers of this symposium. In *Visual Information Processing,* ed. W. G. Chase, pp. 283–308. New York: Academic

Newell, A. 1983. Intellectual issues in the history of artificial intelligence. In *The Study of Information: Interdisciplinary Messages,* ed. F. Machlup, U. Mansfield, pp. 187–227. New York: Wiley

Newell, A., Shaw, J. C., Simon, H. A. 1958. Elements of a theory of human problem solving. *Psychol. Rev.* 65:151–66

Newstead, S. E., Griggs, R. A. 1984. Fuzzy quantifiers as an explanation of set inclusion performance. *Psychol. Res.* 46:377–88

Norman, D. A. 1983. Design rules based on analyses of human error. *Commun. ACM* 26:254–58

Norman, D. A., Rumelhart, D. E. and the LNR Research Group. 1975. *Explorations in Cognition.* San Francisco: Freeman

Oden, G. C. 1981. A fuzzy propositional model of concept structure and use. In *Applied Systems Research and Cybernetics,* ed. G. W. Lasker, pp. 2890–97. Elmsford, NY: Pergamon

Oden, G. C. 1983. On the use of semantic constraints in guiding syntactic analysis. *Int. J. Man-Machine Stud.* 19:335–57

Oden, G. C. 1984a. *Everything is a good example of something, and other endorsements of the adequacy of a fuzzy theory of concepts.* WHIPP 21, Wis. Hum. Inf. Process. Prog., Madison, Wis.

Oden, G. C. 1984b. Integration of fuzzy linguistic information in language processing. *Fuzzy Sets Sys.* 14:29–41

Oden, G. C., Lopes, L. L. 1982. On the internal structure of fuzzy subjective categories. In *Recent Developments in Fuzzy Set and Possibility Theory,* ed. R. R. Yager, pp. 75–88. Elmsford, NY: Pergamon

Osherson, D. W., Smith, E. E. 1981. On the adequacy of prototype theory as a theory of concepts. *Cognition* 9:35–58

Palmer, S. E. 1978. Fundamental aspects of cognitive representation. See Rosch & Lloyd 1978, pp. 259–303

Perlman, G. 1984. Natural artificial languages: low level processes. *Int. J. Man-Machine Stud.* 20:373–419

Pike, R. 1984. Comparison of convolution and matrix distributed memory systems for associative recall and recognition. *Psychol. Rev.* 91:281–94

Posner, M. I. 1986. Empirical studies of prototypes. In *Noun Classification and Cate-*

gorization, ed. C. Craig. Amsterdam: Benjamins. In press

Pylyshyn, Z. 1984. *Computation and Cognition: Toward a Foundation for Cognitive Science.* Cambridge, Mass: MIT

Quillian, M. R. 1966. *Semantic Memory.* Carnegie Inst. Tech., Pittsburgh, Pa. Unpublished doctoral dissertation

Rich, E. 1983. Users are individuals: individualizing user models. *Int. J. Man-Machine Stud.* 18:199–214

Rips, L. J. 1986a. Deduction. In *The Psychology of Human Thought*, ed. R. J. Sternberg, E. E. Smith. Cambridge: Cambridge. In press

Rips, L. J. 1986b. Mental muddles. In *Problems in the Representation of Knowledge and Belief*, ed. M. Brand, R. M. Harnish. Tucson: Arizona Univ. Press. In press

Rosch, E. H. 1973. On the internal structure of perceptual and semantic categories. In *Cognitive Development and the Acquisition of Language*, ed. T. E. Moore. New York: Academic

Rosch, E. 1978. Principles of categorization. See Rosch & Lloyd 1978, pp. 27–48

Rosch, E., Lloyd, B. B. 1978. *Cognition and Categorization.* Hillsdale, NJ: Erlbaum

Rosenblatt, F. 1962. *Principles of Neurodynamics.* New York: Spartan

Roth, E. M., Shoben, E. J. 1983. The effect of context on the structure of categories. *Cognit. Psychol.* 15:346–78

Rueckl, J. G. 1986. *A distributed connectionist account of the repetition effect in word and letter identification.* PhD thesis. Univ. Wis., Madison

Rumelhart, D. E., Hinton, G. E., Williams, R. J. 1986. Learning internal representations by error propagation. In *Parallel Distributed Processing: Explorations in the Microstructure of Cognition*, Vol. 1, ed. D. E. Rumelhart, J. L. McClelland. pp. 318–61. Cambridge, Mass: Bradford

Rumelhart, D. E., McClelland, J. L. 1982. An interactive activation model of context effects in letter perception, Part 2. The contextual enhancement effect and some tests and extensions of the model. *Psychol. Rev.* 89:60–94

Rumelhart, D. E., McClelland, J. L. 1985. Levels indeed! A response to Broadbent. *J. Exp. Psychol: Gen.* 114:193–97

Rumelhart, D. E., Norman, D. A. 1986. Representation in memory. See Atkinson et al 1986. In press

Rumelhart, D. E., Zipser, D. 1985. Feature discovery by competitive learning. *Cognit. Sci.* 9:75–112

Scribner, S. 1984. Studying working intelligence. In *Everyday Cognition: Its Development in Social Context*, ed. B. Rogoff, J. Lave, pp. 9–40. Cambridge, Mass: Harvard

Smith, E. E., Osherson, D. N. 1984. Conceptual combination with prototype concepts. *Cognit. Sci.* 8:337–61

Steele, G. L. Jr., Woods, D. R., Finkel, R. A., Crispin, R. M., Stallman, R. M., et al. 1983. *The Hacker's Dictionary.* New York: Harper & Row

Thorngate, W. 1980. Efficient decision heuristics. *Behav. Sci.* 25:219–25

Togai, M., Watanabe, H. 1985. A VLSI implementation of a fuzzy-inference engine: Toward an expert system on a chip. *Inf. Sci.* 37:1–17

Touretsky, D. S., Hinton, G. E. 1985. Symbols among the neurons: Details of a connectionist inference architecture. *Proc. Int. Joint Conf. Artif. Intell. 9th, Los Angeles*, pp. 238–43

Tukey, D. D. 1986. A philosophical and empirical analysis of subjects' modes of inquiry in Wason's 2-4-6 task. *Q. J. Exp. Psychol.* 38A:5–33

Tweney, R. D. 1986. How did Faraday discover induction? In *Faraday Rediscovered*, ed. D. Gooding, F. James. London: MacMillan. In press

Tweney, R. D., Doherty, M. E. 1983. Rationality and the psychology of inference. *Synthese* 57:139–61

Wallsten, T. S., Budescu, D. V., Rapoport, A., Zwick, R., Forsyth, B. 1986. Measuring the vague meanings of probability terms. *J. Exp. Psychol: Gen.* In press

Wason, P. C. 1960. On the failure to eliminate hypotheses in a conceptual task. *Q. J. Exp. Psychol.* 12:129–40

Wason, P. C. 1966. Reasoning. In *New Horizons in Psychology*, ed. B. M. Foss, pp. 135–51. Harondsworth, Middlesex, England: Penguin

Wason, P. C., Green, D. W. 1984. Reasoning and mental representation. *Q. J. Exp. Psychol.* 36A:597–610

Wickelgren, W. A. 1981. Human learning and memory. *Ann. Rev. Psychol.* 32:21–52

Williams, M. D. 1984. What makes RABBIT run? *Int. J. Man-Machine Stud.* 21:333–52

Young, R. M. 1983. Surrogates and mappings: Two kinds of conceptual models for interactive devices. See Gentner & Stevens 1983, pp. 35–52

Zadeh, L. 1965. Fuzzy sets. *Inf. Control* 8: 338–53

Zimmer, A. C. 1982. What really is turquoise? A note on the evolution of color terms. *Psychol. Res.* 44:213–30

Ann. Rev. Psychol. 1987. 38:229–55

POLITICAL PSYCHOLOGY

David O. Sears

Departments of Psychology and Political Science, University of California, Los Angeles, California 90024

CONTENTS

Political psychology has become a self-conscious, if small, academic specialty in its own right. The International Society of Political Psychology is a professional organization with over 500 members and its own journal, *Political Psychology*. There are a few textbooks (Stone 1974, Freedman & Freedman 1975, Elms 1976, Segall 1976, Barner-Barry & Rosenwein 1985) though

0066-4308/87/0201/0229$02.00

none has yet received wide acceptance. Two editions of *Handbook of Political Psychology* have been published (Knutson 1973a, Hermann 1986).

Nevertheless, political psychology is primarily an interdisciplinary field. It has mainly attracted psychologists (social, personality, and clinical), political scientists (in politics and international relations), historians, and psychiatrists, with a smattering of sociologists, anthropologists, lawyers, and educators. The dominant outlets for work in political psychology have thus far been the disciplinary journals and associations (especially the Society for the Psychological Study of Social Issues); there are extensive handbook chapters in the disciplinary handbooks of social psychology and political science. And while two political science departments have explicitly offered doctoral specializations in political psychology (Yale and SUNY-Stony Brook), by and large, political psychologists have been trained in regular disciplinary specialties, with Yale, Michigan, UC Berkeley, and UCLA being particularly active in this regard.

In general, political psychology has very much been stimulated by the urgent political problems of the day, especially those with actually or potentially devastating human consequences, whether maniacs in high office, the rise of totalitarianism, anti-Semitism, the radical right, the Cold War, Arab-Israeli conflict, the specter of nuclear war, or the transitional problems in postcolonial nations. Whether or not these concerns result in basic research (and many of them do), the field of political psychology tends to reflect the headlines; it also reflects the continuing influence of a few basic theoretical traditions—most notably psychoanalytic and Lewinian field theories.

PERSONALITY AND POLITICS

Perhaps the first major work in the field was *Human Nature in Politics* by Graham Wallas (1921). Consistent with the prevailing views of the day, this work was characterized by a strong Darwinian emphasis on instinct, natural selection, and thus irrationality; mob rule and irrational elite decision making were staples of political life (Stone & Smith 1983).

The dominant influence over political psychology in the next three decades, however, was psychoanalytic theory. The psychobiographical tradition began with Freud's study of Leonardo da Vinci. The psychoanalytic macrolevel analysis of society was introduced by Freud in his two monographs, *The Future of an Illusion* and *Civilization and its Discontents*. Given the fundamental data base of psychoanalytic research, its main legacy became the psychobiographical analysis of specific individuals in politics.

To many, a "psychological" approach to politics has simply meant looking at the effects of personality in politics. While this is obviously too narrow, the topic has always been an important one. For useful reviews of this literature, see Greenstein (1975), Elms (1976), and Hermann (1977).

The Role of Personality

A focus on personality raises a number of conceptual and methodological questions. The larger context is the situation versus disposition question that preoccupies both personality and attribution theorists. When applied to politics, this turns into the "man versus the times" question of leadership. Simonton (1985), for example, raises it explicitly in the case of vice-presidential succession to the presidency, and concludes that success results more from situational than personal factors.

Most psychologists presumably would define personality in terms of generalized predispositions to behave in a particular way, regardless of time, situation, role, etc. The focus on such personality predispositions drew great strength in the first half of the century from the psychoanalytic and psychometric traditions. More recently it has come under attack with the complaint that empirical research does not reveal the tight consistency of behavior with personality in varying situations as had been claimed by personality theorists. As a result, political psychologists have more recently looked at a wider variety of personal predispositions, including attitudes, motives, decision style, modes of interpersonal interaction, stress responses, and expertise (Greenstein 1975).

Despite this broadening of focus, it remains important to assess the impact of personality per se. Only a limited set of assessment techniques are available, each with its own well-known assets and liabilities: questionnaires and interviews, observation, archival content analyses, biographical data, and experiments or simulations (Hermann 1977, Tetlock 1983a). Most of these techniques have even more severe liabilities in the study of political leaders than in the study of ordinary people because of the greater self-presentational pressures on persons in public life. Efforts to trace personality to earlier life confront the problem of lack of evidence; one cannot identify political leaders until it is too late to observe formative experiences directly, which has led to some unfortunate examples of excess speculation. Moreover, the person of interest is often dead, which adds even greater limitations.

Another quasi-methodological question is how personality explanations differ from others that emphasize demographic variables, situations, or roles, etc. Greenstein (1975) has made an extraordinarily careful and discerning analysis, which can be commended even to those with no particular interest in politics per se.

Substantive Questions

A major substantive interest has been in political recruitment: Who becomes a political leader? In his well-known formula, Lasswell (1930) asserted that in politics, private conflicts become displaced onto public objects and then are rationalized in terms of the public interest. People are recruited to political life for neurotic personal reasons, by this account. He later (1948) argued that a compensatory need for power was a particularly strong motive. Lane (1959) later argued the contrary, that to be a successful democratic politician one needed to have a healthy, well-balanced personality. Such disagreement concerning the mental health of those recruited to politics recurs throughout the personality-and-politics literature.

A second major area of interest is the impact of personality upon the behavior of political elites. Lasswell's early work provided numerous examples of the deleterious effects of neurotic patterns. Rogow's (1963) biography of Forrestal, the first U.S. Secretary of Defense, argued that his suicide was brought on by progressive paranoia, a possibly dangerous quality for someone in that high position. The Georges' (1956) excellent biography of Woodrow Wilson depicts his identification with, along with his repressed hostility toward, his stern and demanding father. When Wilson became frustrated, this conflict could be expressed by rage and rigidity. The Georges suggest that this aspect of Wilson's personality was partly responsible for his failure to have the United States join the League of Nations. Mazlish's (1972) biography of Richard Nixon described Nixon's need to risk failure to prove himself and his need to create crises in order to cope with his fear of death, along with such potentially hazardous characteristics as suspiciousness, social isolation, difficulty in decision making, and a need for an emotional enemy. Some more recent examples of this approach include Rintala's (1984) analysis of the childhood origins of Churchill's need for power, and the continuing conflict over whether Woodrow Wilson's root problems were physical or mental [See also Post (1983) and others in the same issue].

Various multidimensional typologies of political actors have been proposed to capture major differences in political orientation. Lasswell (1930) suggested agitators, administrators, and theorists; Barber (1965) proposed four types of state legislators; Stewart (1977) discussed several types of Soviet politicians, and so on. Barber's (1985) typology of American presidents is perhaps the best known. In his scheme, the most dangerous are the "active negatives," such as Woodrow Wilson, Herbert Hoover, Lyndon Johnson, and Richard Nixon. This type is characterized by unusual self-concern, perfectionism, an all-or-nothing quality in self-perception, denial of self-gratification, and great concern with controlling aggression. When threatened, the active-negative type has a tendency to rigidify. One consequence is that he may focus anger on a personal enemy; another is to cling tightly to a failing policy, to stand and fight, and even to order others to die for him.

Certain specific needs or motives have been thought to have special driving force for political leaders, Power has been especially salient (Lasswell 1930, Rintala 1984, Rothman 1984). The projective testing tradition had promoted the use of fantasy to measure personality, and was applied to power motivation in politics (e.g. Winter 1973). Maslow's (1954) hierarchy of needs has had some influence in political psychology, especially in Davies's (1963) and Knutson's (1973b) suggestions that political activism is likely only when more basic needs have been satisfied. Following in that line, Inglehart (1981) has suggested that postwar affluence has generated postmaterialist values and political values, since basic subsistence needs have been satisfied. Rothman (1984), on the other hand, has suggested that the leftist activists of the 1960s have strong narcissistic needs today.

In studying the role of personality in mass political behavior, two approaches have been most common. The first has correlated self-report questionnaire or interview measures of various personality traits with political attitudes. The most obvious examples are the role of authoritarianism and dogmatism in intolerance (Adorno et al 1950, Sanford 1973, Sullivan et al 1982), machiavellianism (Christie & Geis 1970), or the cluster including paranoia, hostility, rigidity, etc, behind conservatism and isolationism (McClosky 1958, 1967). Two more positive dimensions are self-esteem (see Sniderman 1975) and a sense of personal control (Renshon 1974). The life history or idiographic approach is a second alternative that looks at individuals in greater detail to understand their idiosyncratic functioning (Smith et al 1956, Lane 1962).

PUBLIC OPINION AND VOTING

A second major influence was the development of survey research, especially its application to public opinion and voting behavior. Sociologists introduced it with their community studies in the 1940s. Lazarsfeld et al (1948) at first emphasized the origins of the vote in large social groupings (class, religion, etc) and then shifted to an emphasis upon direct interpersonal influence (Berelson et al 1954). However, the desire for more representative samples, and the development of increased technological capability, resulted (beginning in 1952) in a long series of voting studies that have been conducted in even-numbered years by the Survey Research Center at the University of Michigan, and are now called the American National Election Studies. These studies led to an individual decision-making analysis best developed in *The American Voter* (Campbell et al 1960). The relevant chapters include those by Lipset et al (1954), Sears (1969), Converse (1975), Kinder & Sears (1985).

Party Identification

In this pivotal book Campbell et al used simple Lewinian field theory to argue that voters, largely nonideological and minimally informed, used their underlying, stable party identifications, which had been developed early in their lives, to organize partisan attitudes toward the various major elements of an election campaign. *The American Voter* has been challenged from a number of perspectives in the years since it was published. Much of the criticism has contended that the key factors are political and economic realities rather than longstanding psychological dispositions. The underlying issue has usually been one that is at the heart of the political psychological approach: Is *homo politicus* informed, consistent, sensible, and rational, operating from a set of stable preferences and values, and responsive to external reality—or is he/she uninformed, inconsistent, irrational, operating from anachronistic preferences and prejudices that are out of touch with current reality?

Not surprisingly, specialists in political psychology and political economy often arrive at opposing answers to this question. For useful contrasts, see Converse (1975) and proponents of a "symbolic politics" approach (Edelman 1971, Sears & Citrin 1985), on the one hand, who emphasize the power of early learning, myths, and symbols, and Fiorina (1981), Nie et al (1979), and Mann & Wolfinger (1980), on the other hand, who emphasize consistency, rationality, and responsiveness to current economic and political realities (whether in voters' personal economic situations, the actual competence of incumbents, their service to their constituents, etc).

At an empirical level, the role of party identification has been a focal point. The authors of *The American Voter* contended that voters are ill-informed and thus vote on the basis of party because it is a simplifying cue, especially in Congressional elections. Its critics instead emphasize the role of constituency service (Mann & Wolfinger 1980) and hence incumbency. Others suggest that voters both vote on the basis of reasonable judgments of the incumbent's performance in office and actually adjust their party identification accordingly (Kinder & Kiewiet 1979, Fiorina 1981), and that policy preferences affect the vote and even party identification (Markus 1979) when the parties and candidates differ unmistakably in policy positions.

At the macro level, this challenge focuses on the dynamics of voting that result from an apparent decline in the strength and power of party identification; "party dealignment" is indicated in the declining intensity of party commitments and increased defection and split-ticket voting (Wattenberg 1984).

Economic Realities

A central area of contention is the role of current economic realities. Kramer (1971) argued that macroeconomic conditions play a major role in determining the outcome of elections. Kinder & Kiewiet (1979) observed that the voters' "sociotropic" judgments of the incumbent's management of the economy were the deciding factor rather than more egocentric, self-interested judgments about their own financial situations.

This explanation of macro political changes generated some contention, but not much modification, of the basic psychological point that material self-interest plays a relatively minor role in the individual's vote. That was the judgment also of a series of studies showing minimal effects of self-interest on such policy preferences as busing (Kinder & Sears 1981, Sears & Allen 1984), national health insurance (Sears et al 1980), or tax and spending policies (Sears & Citrin 1985). Even unemployment has surprisingly few direct political effects on the individual (Schlozman & Verba 1979). Predispositions such as party identification and racial intolerance seem to play a much stronger role. Strong self-interest effects do seem to occur when the positive stakes are high and clear or when the threat is high and ambiguous, and the political remedy is clear and certain (Sears & Allen 1984, Sears & Citrin 1985), but these prove to be rather rare circumstances in the political world of the ordinary citizen.

Consistency and Ideology

Another question that has drawn much attention is the degree of consistency and ideological thinking in public opinion. At first this discussion centered on whether or not the public mirrored the standard abstract ideological categories used by political elites to organize political life cognitively (Campbell et al 1960, Converse 1964). This quickly raised issues of consistency, since Converse (1964) suggested that the low level of "constraint" in the average individual's belief system (i.e. functional interdependence among elements as indexed by correlations across attitudes on issues) indicated a low level of ideological thinking in the mass public.

A number of key areas of public opinion also have been marked by logical inconsistencies that coexist with some reasonable degree of affective consistency. For example, inconsistencies have frequently been noted between tolerance in the abstract and intolerance in concrete situations, both in terms of such civil liberties issues as freedom of speech and in terms of racial integration (Sullivan et al 1982, Sears & Allen 1984). The general resistance to higher taxes and a desire in the abstract for smaller government, on the one hand, also is widely believed to be inconsistent with broad-based support for maintaining specific government social programs, on the other hand (Sears & Citrin 1985).

This view of the public as inconsistent and illogical has been extensively challenged. Much of the argument again concerns whether or not citizens are responding in a rational way to political realities. On the reality-oriented side, it is argued that the public will think ideologically only when political elites offer genuinely different ideological alternatives, as they did in the mid-1960s and early 1970s (Nie et al 1979); that freedom of speech for national enemies such as Communists is denied only when they are perceived as being dangerous, as in the early 1950s (Stouffer 1955, Sullivan et al 1982); that the white public supports integration, but not busing, which is perceived to be in-effective; and that it supports radical tax cuts but not cuts in essential government services because of high levels of waste in government, the many "frills" in these services, or a willingness to pay user fees.

This conflict has stimulated much methodological controversy. One question is whether consistency is more properly reflected in uniform patterning of attitudes across individuals or in idiosyncratic patterns within the individual (Lane 1962, 1973). Over the years, changes in item wording in time-series surveys may have given rise to artifactual increases in consistency (Sullivan et al 1978). Changes in the groups thought to pose danger to the nation may have given rise to illusory increases in tolerance, as tolerance items were not revised to focus on the newest enemies (Sullivan et al 1982). And social desirability pressures may have given rise to deceptively high levels of racial tolerance in the abstract (McConahay et al 1981, Jackman & Muha 1984).

One new approach centers on "political cognition," which applies innovations in social cognition to politics. In particular, political schemas and various cognitive representations of political candidates are emphasized [see the various articles in Lau & Sears (1986); also Lane's contrast of market and political cognition (1983); Hamill et al (1985) on schemata]. A major challenge here is to explain the relatively high level of affect and emotionality associated with politics while using cognitive theories that normally ignore affect.

Racial Conflict

Though social and political groups were emphasized by the early voting studies, they tended not to be given such close attention in later work. Recently they have staged a comeback. Part of the reason is a renewed interest in racial conflict in politics. Three general problem areas seem to have sparked the most recent interest.

A major new theoretical approach has grown out of various cognitive theories. Kluegel & Smith (1986) have developed attributional models of the theories people have about racial differences. And a wide variety of interesting insights have emerged from Tajfel's (1981) theorizing and experiments on the effects of social categorization on in-group biases [see Stephan (1985) and Worchel & Austin (1986) for a comprehensive treatment of the range of these cognitive approaches].

Racial attitudes have liberalized markedly over time (McConahay 1982, Schuman et al 1985), leading to the question of what form politically potent racial attitudes now take. Racial attitudes clearly play an important role in determining racial policy preferences and evaluations of black political candidates (see Kinder & Sears 1981, Sears & Allen 1984). Some argue that the key content of racial attitudes is "symbolic racism," a blend of antiblack affect and traditional values (Kinder & Sears 1981, McConahay 1982). Others disagree (Bobo 1983) and see group conflict or racial threat at work. Realistic racial threats generally have a much weaker effect than does symbolic racism, but the role of group conflict is still not clear (Vanneman & Pettigrew 1972, Sears & Allen 1984). Social desirability biases may also threaten measurement validity of old-fashioned racism (McConahay et al 1981, Jackman & Muha 1984).

A second important applied area concerns the effects of interracial contact, and desegregation, upon the reduction of prejudice. There is much experimental evidence that such contact does reduce prejudice under the right conditions, which include cooperative task interdependence, mutual competence, successful task performance, etc (Aronson et al 1978, Cook 1984). Unfortunately, these conditions are infrequently found when desegregation is implemented (Stephan 1985).

Gender

The women's movement and the many postwar changes in women's roles in society have prompted renewed attention to women's roles in politics. The conventional wisdom in the early days of political behavior research was that women had lower levels of political involvement than men, which was reflected in lower interest, opinionation, sense of efficacy, and turnout, presumably because of a female sex role that made women dependent on men, uninterested in power, and distasteful of conflict (Lane 1959, Campbell et al 1960, Sears 1969, Shapiro & Mahajan 1986). Presumably, few gender differences in attitudes existed except in matters of morality, such as sex and prohibition.

Today, registration and turnout now seem to be quite similar for men and women (Wolfinger & Rosenstone 1980, Poole & Zeigler 1985), and women are nearly as opinionated as men (Shapiro & Mahajan 1986). There is the well-heralded evidence of a "gender gap" in attitudes, especially in women's greater opposition to Ronald Reagan, which, since 1980, accompanies gender differences in party identification (Frankovic 1982).

An interesting line of research has begun to look for the effects of changes in women's social roles upon their group consciousness, and thus upon their political attitudes (Klein 1984). Women today are much more likely to be working, highly educated, unmarried, and free of caretaking for small children. This new reality clearly has the potential for increasing sensitivity to discrimination against women and, in turn, converting those perceptions into potent partisan instruments, whether through a sense of self-interest, group consciousness, or through conversion to feminist ideology by the women's movement.

The evidence is mixed. Young, single women are clearly the most liberal (Frankovic 1982). But women's private lives have rather little spillover into their political lives (Sapiro 1983), and the findings generally do not follow a simple self-interest pattern. Evidence that women voters place extra weight on women's issues is mixed (Klein 1984, Mansbridge 1985). Women's sense of group consciousness, though increasing, remains relatively weak, and so is not believed to be strong enough to explain women's political attitudes (Gurin 1985). Rather, the best evidence is that the "gender gap" is better explained by women's longstanding greater aversion to force (Smith 1984) than by gender differences on such gender issues as ERA or affirmative action for women, which in any case are very small (Frankovic 1982, Mansbridge 1985). In that sense, despite clear polarization of the two parties in the 1980s on women's issues, the "gender gap" does not seem to depend very strongly on self- or group-interest.

Another possibility is that differential sex role socialization promotes greater concern about compassion, violence, and risk to people, because women are taught to be more responsible for others (Gilligan 1982). While this is consistent with gender differences in policy preferences, no such direct links have yet been demonstrated, and indeed women showing the greatest departure from men's political attitudes generally were reared in the least traditionally feminine manner.

POLITICAL PARTICIPATION

The form and level of participation in political life represent another important category of dependent variables. Economic, sociological, and political explanations always must be given their due, and have much to recommend them. Still, psychological explanations have a clear role. Much of the relevant literature has been reviewed elsewhere by Lane (1959), Nie & Verba (1975), Milbrath & Goel (1977), and Kinder & Sears (1985).

Political participation differs widely in its form—from such mainstream behavior as voting, the main activity of ordinary citizens, to engaging in protest or revolutionary behavior, or serving as an official in a legitimate government. Voting turnout has been analyzed principally by social psychologists, in terms of citizenship attitudes (especially "citizen duty," the norm of an obligation. to vote, and "political efficacy," the sense that one's vote counts), attitudes about the election itself (whether or not the contenders differ very much), interpersonal pressures (such as being contacted by a party worker, interviewed in a survey, or driven to vote by a neighbor), and the political context (e.g. how easy it is to register) (see Kinder & Sears 1985).

Early analyses of participation in mass movements were inspired by Freud's analysis of group psychology, perhaps most notably Fromm's *Escape from Freedom* (1941). More sociological treatments focused particularly on the rootlessness or alienation produced by migration and the disintegration of primary group ties (Kornhauser 1959), the consequences of working class life (Lipset 1981), or the costs associated with an open, mobile society (Bettelheim & Janowitz 1964).

Protest and revolutionary activity have been analyzed recently in more sociopsychological terms. Such attitudes as political disaffection, relative deprivation (especially fraternal, rather than egoistic, deprivation), and realistic grievances all play a part (see Vanneman & Pettigrew 1972, Lipset & Raab 1978, Seeman 1984). In recent years, analyses of black, feminist, student, and antiwar protest in the United States have emphasized the role of political socialization, or resocialization, particularly of social and political values, and have in turn traced outbreaks of protest to prior changes in social and economic conditions. Black protest is partly linked to rising expectations stemming from the widespread migration by blacks from the rural South to Northern and Western metropolises (Sears & McConahay 1973); feminism is associated with a rising sense of discrimination against women among the better-educated, working women of recent decades who are less burdened by child care or economic dependency on a male (Klein 1984); and youth or student protest has been linked to the early family learning of liberal values in an affluent society (Flacks 1967, Inglehart 1981).

Personality explanations have been employed to some degree. Contrary to the early views of Lasswell (1930), most data on the mass public tend to show that political participation is associated with such indicators of a healthy personality as high self-esteem, a strong sense of personal efficacy, and satisfaction of basic physical, safety, and social needs (Lane 1959, Knutson 1973b, Renshon 1974, Sniderman 1975). In contrast, case studies of political leaders frequently turn up pervasive feelings of insecurity, low self-esteem, early deprivation, and ungratified social and personal needs (see Chapter 3 of Burns 1978; see also Lasswell 1948, Wolfenstein 1967, Mazlish 1972, Glad 1973, Elms 1976, Barber 1985). These findings have supported Lasswell's view that political participation compensates for personal disabilities in at least these cases.

Psychobiographical studies of political leaders are, of course, vulnerable to criticism in terms of the availability of data and the intrusion of the biographers' own motives (Glad 1973, Falk 1985). But these contradictory findings are also likely to be due to the much more detailed examination of the inner lives of the elite, especially their particular conflicts and anxieties. Surely according to standardized personality tests, or other relatively superficial instruments, such individuals as Nixon, Lenin, Wilson, Lincoln, and Eleanor Roosevelt would, relative to humanity at large, appear to be strikingly strong, confident, effective human beings. It would seem more pertinent to ask how particular disabilities interact with specific political tasks or roles rather than attempt to gauge the overall level of mental health among the politically active.

POLITICAL SOCIALIZATION

The psychoanalytic emphasis on personality development, and research on such predispositions as party identification, racial prejudice, and disaffection, led to an early interest in preadult political socialization. So did studies that attempted to account for variability in the strength of democratic traditions across countries (Almond & Verba 1963; for other reviews see Sears 1975, Dawson et al 1977, Renshon 1977, Kinder & Sears 1985).

Diffuse System Support

One major focus has been on preadult socialization that results in "proper" citizenship attitudes, loyalty to the regime, law-abiding behavior, and compliance with the political rules of the game. According to Easton & Dennis (1969), the major theorists in this area, these are key elements in the development of "diffuse system support," the tendency to support the regime in general, which in turn is a regime's ability to maintain order and authority, an orderly succession of political leadership, the legitimacy of authority, a willingness to fight external enemies, and other such contributors to its persistence. Easton & Dennis (1969), in developing this theory, distinguished diffuse system support from "specific support," or support for the current incumbents and their policies. A regime could persist over many years with the former, even in the absence of the latter.

Their early evidence persuaded them that preadult socialization was crucial in determining diffuse support. They and others observed that young children tend to have extraordinarily positive views of the President and to be aware of very little else in the political arena (Greenstein 1965, Hess & Torney 1967). They theorized that children idealize the President as a result of transferring affect from their fathers and/or such proximal quasi-political figures as the local policeman. As the child matured, he/she began to recognize other more impersonal political objects such as the Congress and practice of voting, to which that positive affect was generalized, thus producing support of the diffuse system.

But later research challenged both the psychological basis of this early idealization and its impact on later regime support. Adelson (1971), Tapp & Kohlberg (1971), and other cognitive developmentalists documented the fact that such positive affects toward authority represented a predictable but usually transitory developmental stage in late childhood and early adolescence, which might therefore have little lasting impact in adulthood. Second, much research indicated that such early idealization was quite specific to the place, samples, and era; such idealized views were not so characteristic in other nations or minority groups, or toward later presidents, and there was no noticeable cost in terms of regime persistence. Hence social learning explanations, rather than psychoanalytic, seemed most appropriate. Third, the distinction between diffuse support and specific support proved extremely difficult to make empirically; evaluations of the most general procedures and institutions seem to be strongly influenced by evaluations of specific current incumbents and their practices (for a review on these points, see Sears 1975). Finally, indices of systemic support, such as they were, proved to have relatively little stability across the life span (Jennings & Niemi 1981) or little impact on such indicators of regime support as support for energy conservation in the 1974 energy crisis (Sears et al 1978) or participation in ghetto riots (Sears & McConahay 1973). Thus the outcome is unfortunately somewhat murky, the problems perhaps methodological and perhaps substantive.

Partisanship

The second major issue concerns the persisting divisions within any polity—those based on party, ideology, class, ethnicity, race, religion, and region. Early empirical research demonstrated that such divisions were the most powerful factors in voting behavior (Lazarsfeld et al 1948, Campbell et al 1960). Attitudes toward them seemed to be acquired early in life, within the family (Hyman 1959, Campbell et al 1960), pointing again to the political socialization process.

This view contained several propositions that lent themselves to more detailed testing. One is the assertion of persistence of such predispositions across a life span. This has been investigated with several research paradigms: the individual's retrospections, longitudinal studies, cohort analyses, and tests of the effects of environmental changes. Each has its strengths and weaknesses (see Kinder & Sears 1985). Persistence clearly varies considerably by attitude object and life stage; it is quite high for party identification and racial attitudes, is quite low for system attitudes (Jennings & Niemi 1981, Jennings & Markus 1984), and it is lower in early adulthood than in later life (Glenn 1980, Sears 1983). Political events such as wars, racial conflict, or poor performance by one's party when it is in power can disrupt it, especially early in adulthood (Markus 1979, Fiorina 1981), as can major changes in social environment, again especially in early adulthood (Brown 1986). And of course times change; party identification has not been socialized as strongly in early life in recent years as in earlier times (Wattenberg 1984). Overall, the emphasis among researchers has probably shifted away from childhood and early adolescence toward early adulthood as a possibly formative period with lasting effects (see Jennings & Niemi 1981, Jennings & Markus 1984). There is a greater appreciation for how people adjust their preferences (even if only modestly) later in life to accommodate changed realities.

The effects of events occurring in formative life stages are of considerable interest. The long-term consequences of affluence, and consequent value changes (Abramson & Inglehart 1986), or of the introduction of new democratic institutions (Barnes et al 1985), tend to follow a generational model. Some research has been done on the effects of war experiences in childhood or of military service (Jennings & Markus 1977) or the possibly traumatic effects upon children of the assassination of a president (Wolfenstein & Kliman 1965). Considerable work has been done on socialization experiences during the adult years, especially on occupation and workplace, status and social mobility, and other environmental events (Sigel & Hoskin 1977, Elden 1981).

Parents were thought to be the central socializing agents, a view based largely on individual retrospections and consistent with the psychoanalytic and learning views of the postwar era. Later research (Jennings & Niemi 1981), based on more thorough measurement of both parents' and children's attitudes, cast doubt on this assumption (though see Dalton 1980). Limits on the parents' role are due especially to lack of political communication in the family (Tedin 1974). There also was much interest in the role of schools as socializing agents, but with some disappointing results (Torney-Purta 1984). Newcomb and colleagues' (1967) study of attending Bennington College as a politically socializing experience is very well known, but it likely is an exceptional case. Recent research has reviewed the role of the military and specially prepared curricula that deal with issues such as value clarification and peace (Jennings & Markus 1977). The role of the media in children's political socialization, always an interesting topic, continues to be somewhat uncertain (see Chaffee 1977).

THE MASS MEDIA

Social scientists' views of the mass media have undergone some cycling since the widespread use of the electronic media, but recurrent themes can be recognized in each era. The invention of the radio coincident with its creative use in the 1930s by demagogues such as Hitler, Goebbels, Huey Long, and Father Coughlin gave rise to the belief that the mass public was a vast, captive, and gullible audience, easy prey for these demagogues' "tricks of the trade" (Institute for Propaganda Analysis, 1939). Inferences of massive effects rested on no particular empirical data other than some loose estimates of audience size and informal content analyses.

A second era followed the introduction of mass survey techniques. Early voting studies found campaign propaganda and the mass media not to be especially influential (Lazarsfeld et al 1948). Early media research led to a general view that might be described as the "minimal effects model"; mass communications normally reinforced prior attitudes, rather than producing converts, except under some special circumstances (Hovland 1959, Klapper 1960).

Most of this research was conducted prior to the sophisticated political uses of television that began to appear in the 1960s. Hence a third era of studies portrayed television as particularly powerful, and with socially dangerous effects.

Concerns about television's ill effects took several forms. One focused on the President's ability to gain prime-time coverage for essentially uncontested defenses of Administration policy (Minow et al 1973). Network news was criticized for attacking mainstream institutions and thus producing "videomalaise" (Robinson 1976), or for taking a stance of "belligerent neutrality" that produced confusion and partisan dealignment (Schultz 1986). Television commentators were criticized for being biased toward the left, or for emphasizing "hoopla" and failing to educate voters about the issues (Patterson & McClure 1976). Subtle nonverbal techniques were used by media consultants to artificially enhance candidates' popularity.

As in the 1930s, these observations of persuasive power were often based on little more than loose estimates of audience size. Audience exposure estimates often were based on the large number of television sets in use and on evidence about the amount of time they were turned on (see Minow et al 1973). Disregarded were more discouraging data about widespread inattention, poor learning, and even the substantial fraction of time that television sets are turned on but with no humans watching or even in the same room (Neuman 1976, Comstock et al 1978, Sears & Chaffee 1979).

Persuasive Effects

The current era thus is marked by the search for the effects of television viewing. Graber (1984a), Comstock et al (1978) and Kraus & Davis (1976) have provided useful overviews. Nevertheless, much of this literature indicates, in my judgment, that partisan communications still have "minimal effects." The clearest examples are perhaps presidential debates (Sears & Chaffee 1979), but other political and entertainment programs seem to follow suit (Kinder & Sears 1985). Hence some researchers have looked for persuasive effects under conditions that are considered to be exceptions by the minimal effects model, e.g. conventions, primary elections, nonpartisan elections, etc (Kraus & Davis 1976), though even then the effects have often not been very powerful. Perhaps the most creative explorers for persuasive effects have been the Langs (1983, 1984), who have investigated the effects of conventions, debates, early announcements of voting returns, and, most extensively, the Watergate episode.

Insofar as money spent on media in a political campaign indexes media effort, its association with the vote might indirectly reflect a persuasive effect. More money spent in a political campaign does not, on the average, produce more votes. So increasingly, analyses have tried to define the conditions under which it does affect voting, e.g. with several obscure candidates for open seats, or in districts with weak party organizations (Grush et al 1978, Wattenberg 1982). The "belligerent neutrality" hypothesis is particularly interesting because it predicts that the most media-attentive will become the most confused, least partisan, most volatile and unstable elements of the electorate. Schultz (1986) provides surprisingly strong evidence for this effect from the 1980 campaign. This is quite a shift from past views of the effects of information flow (Klapper 1960, Sears 1969). Finally, if verbal communications normally do not have major effects, it has been thought that subtle nonverbal cues might. Various facial displays influence emotional and attitudinal responses to televised news coverage of political leaders (though usually in interaction with prior attitudes; see Lanzetta et al 1985).

Agenda-Setting

Some feel the media's main role may be in "agenda-setting": media coverage can place a particular issue or problem foremost on the public's agenda, where it can become the central determinant of the public's evaluations of incumbent performance and/or voting behavior. This phenomenon has now been investigated with experiments (Iyengar & Kinder 1985), surveys (McCombs & Shaw 1972), and time-series analyses of aggregate data (Mac-Kuen 1981). The research raises interesting questions, especially about the magnitude and duration of coverage required to produce an effect, the role of steady coverage versus vivid single cases, and impact on political judgments. An especially important case is the massive attention, and thus boost in popularity, given to early front-runners during the American presidential primary season (Patterson 1980).

The central implication of the agenda-setting approach is that the media can make certain political symbols salient, and in that way determine which predispositions form the basis of voter choice. Edelman (1971) argues that this is a prime technique by which elites control public opinion. For some, a symbolic politics approach focuses particularly on the learning of appropriate feelings about regime symbols (Baas 1984, Feldman 1985), and for others, the learning of values of any kind (Sears & Citrin 1985).

Brief mention, at least, should also be given to more cognitive approaches to media effects. The role of schemata as filters of media messages has begun to be explored in considerable depth (Graber 1984b, Lau & Sears 1986). And, finally, others have conceded that most of the public is not likely to be massively politically persuaded by the media because they use the media for entertainment, not as sources of information; this has generated considerable work under the "uses and gratifications" rubric (Garramone 1985).

INTERNATIONAL CONFLICT

A third major influence on political psychology has been international conflict; initially the Cold War and later international tensions in and around the Mideast. A comprehensive psychological approach to international conflict would require consideration of mutual perceptions of contending parties, attitudes toward each other (such as nationalism and outgroup antagonisms), economics, social roles, organizational behavior and group dynamics within decision making groups, and bargaining and negotiation (e.g. Stagner 1967). Most recent work has taken up these factors in a more piecemeal fashion.

Images and Misperception

A convenient starting point is the images that contending adversaries hold about themselves and each other. Whether focusing on nations, political leaders, or populaces, these images can be held by elites or the public. This point is sufficiently central that about half of the major handbook in this area was devoted to the nature and determinants of international images (see Kelman 1965).

The first priority has been to identify patterns of misperception. Finlay et al (1967) described the delights of perceiving another country as an enemy. White (1970) described a number of other common misperceptions, such as "the diabolical enemy," "the moral self," and "the virile self." He described a mutual pattern of distortion as "the mirror image," in which each side believes it has peaceful intentions, is afraid of the other side because the latter is perceived as aggressive and threatening (at least the rulers are, if not the common people), and endorses its own militarism as self-defense. He has carefully applied these general biases to the cases of Soviet-American relations and the Vietnam conflict (White 1965, 1970). Tetlock (1983b) has contrasted the "spiral" and "deterrence" images of Soviet-American relations, and Herrmann (1985) has dealt with "communist expansionism," "real politik expansionism," and "real politik defensive." These authors, in addition, make heroic efforts to evaluate the accuracy of these images.

These misperceptions need to be described in basic cognitive terms. Most analyses have particularly emphasized black-and-white, oversimplified thinking and egocentric perceptions that satisfy self-serving motives. Jervis (1976) has rooted elites' misperceptions in international relations most clearly and coherently in psychological theory. He particularly emphasizes overestimations of the unity and planfulness of behavior, wishful thinking, egocentricity, and dissonance-reducing defense of prior commitments.

A third line of analysis has focused on the more distal psychological determinants of international images. These have rounded up the usual suspects. The several chapters on this point in the Kelman (1965) handbook emphasize cultural socialization, education and propaganda, political events, cross-national contact, and such personal predispositions as values and personality (personal security, aggressiveness, etc). When applied to concrete cases, these result in excessive loyalty to one's own nation and conformity to its norms, overly enthusiastic adherence to social roles (e.g. in the military), unconsciously expressed motives such as hostility, and the oversimplification and intolerance of ambiguity that personal insecurity is presumed to produce (White 1970). Etheredge (1978) has particularly emphasized the role of male machismo, or the "male narcissism syndrome," in producing leaders that like to "play hardball" or threaten force; they excessively perceive international relations in competitive, coercive, combative, and adversarial terms. In common with the current drift of psychology toward the cognitive, Jervis (1976, 1986) emphasizes the tendency to minimize cognitive effort through theory-driven inference from belief systems (or schemas).

Public Opinion

In dealing with international relations, it is even more important than usual to distinguish leaders' perceptions from those of the mass public. Public opinion proves particularly responsive to bold international acts by national leaders, demonstrated most dramatically by Mueller (1973) in the support given American presidents when they attacked the enemy in the Vietnam and Korean wars. There is a similar "rally round the flag" effect when some disaster occurs (such as the Bay of Pigs or Tet invasions, or the Russian shooting down of the American U-2 plane), which is evidenced in a strong tendency to support presidents in foreign policy (Sears 1969). Mueller goes further and identifies the well-educated and the young as the "followers" who follow most.

Numerous efforts have been made to uncover simple dimensions of public opinion on foreign policy, e.g. interventionism/isolationism, or hawk/dove. They generally find more complex patterns, even toward such apparently well-known issues as the Vietnam War (see Modigliani 1972) or nuclear war (Fiske et al 1983). Part of the problem is that political candidates often do not take distinctive positions, thus preventing simple links to voting preferences.

Elite Decision Making

Political psychologists, like many other social scientists, have tried to develop comprehensive theories of elite decision making. Janis & Mann's (1977) conflict theory of decision making centers upon emotion-laden decisional conflicts, the various patterns of coping behavior that are common in such conflicts, the antecedents of such coping patterns, and their various consequences for decisional rationality. The authors attempt to develop a unique but comprehensive theory of decision making, and they draw examples (or evidence) from a wide variety of arenas. At the other extreme is George's (1980) eclectic theory of presidential decision making; George explains specifically presidential behavior with theories drawn from wherever required: e.g. information processing, belief systems, small group behavior, and organizational behavior. Etheredge (1985) makes a similar attempt in the case of American foreign policy toward Central America.

Political psychologists have developed some insights that seem unique to the psychological approach. One point is that decisional conflicts are inherently emotional and thus stressful (Janis & Mann 1977). Stress can have a number of negative effects, e.g. it can reduce the complexity of information processing (Tetlock 1983a), and it can lead to defensive avoidance and wishful thinking. Various techniques, primarily relying on vigilance, are offered by Janis & Mann for coping constructively with stress.

Some personality characteristics may be particularly relevant to and dangerous in foreign policy decision-making. The "male narcissism" or machismo syndrome described by Etheredge (1978) is an example. Even that humble individual difference variable, birth order, may have considerable consequence. Stewart (1977) believes that first-borns and only children tend to lead us into crisis, war, and civil conflict. The "Machiavellian" personality (Christie & Geis 1970), who demonstrates a lack of interpersonal affect, ideological commitment, and concern with conventional morality, may be highly appropriate for foreign minister positions (such as those held with great effect by Bismarck and Kissinger), but may be utterly unsuited for head of state (Elms 1976).

Cognitive consistency theories generate numerous examples of decision-makers' biases in favor of decisions consistent with their predispositions and images; e.g. in their treatment of their enemies (Finlay et al 1967). An especially important notion is that of a leader's "operational code" (Leites 1951, George 1969), his beliefs about the nature of politics, political conflict, historical developments, and strategy and tactics. Leites suggests that the beliefs of Bolshevik leaders were quite different from those of contemporary American leaders; they were willing to engage in high-risk activities as long as subsequent events could be controlled, so that the sequence could be aborted in the event of failure (for other analyses of operational codes of heads of state and U.S. statesmen, see Johnson 1977).

Recent information processing theories in psychology offer similar insights. Most of these fall under the rubric of social cognition (Fischer &

Johnson 1986, Lau & Sears 1986). One central tenet is that information processing tends to be "theory-driven" rather than "data-driven." Some of the most interesting implications involve elite decision-makers' "learning from history" (Jervis 1976); too often those lessons are learned too early and hence prove to be anachronistic when applied, or are overly responsive to firsthand or especially vivid experiences, or are too responsive to successes—even accidental successes.

Most foreign policy decisions arise from extensive small group delibera- tion, so it is perhaps not surprising that one of the most influential efforts by a political psychologist involves "groupthink"—factors inherent in highly cohe- sive small groups that can produce terrible foreign policy fiascoes (Janis 1982). High group cohesiveness produces pressures toward conformity, and thus suppression of dissent and of one's own doubts, as well as illusions of unanimity and invulnerability. Janis persuasively argues for the critical role of group-think in generating such American fiascoes as the Bay of Pigs, Pearl Harbor, Watergate, and Vietnam (for critiques, see Longley & Pruitt 1980, Tetlock 1983a).

Interactive Processes

A final area of application focuses on relations between adversaries or those in conflict. A considerable sociopsychological literature deals with the issues of interdependence, influence, bargaining, negotiation, escalation, and conflict resolution. Space limitations prevent detailed discussion. Some of the most influential work is by Deutsch (e.g. 1973), who uses extrapolations from simulation and experimental games. The "deterrence" and "spiral" models are central (Jervis 1976). An early innovation was the gradual unilateral initia- tives (Osgood 1962), which Etzioni (1967) believed were employed by President Kennedy in unilaterally stopping atmospheric nuclear testing. For a useful recent collection in this area, see White (1985); also see Tetlock (1983a, pp. 69–71). Those working in this field also have a proclivity for action, so numerous workshops and training programs in negotiation, media- tion, and conflict management are offered (Kelman & Cohen 1986). The best early overview of this distinctively psychological perspective is by Kelman (1965, Chapters 9–15).

DEATH AND HORROR

All historical eras must confront the horrible acts committed in the quest for political power. Our era is no exception. We live under the nuclear cloud as well, arguably a new element (though the plagues, pestilences, and wars of the past may hardly have seemed less devastating and all-encompassing). Economists are obviously uncomfortable with the irrational, and political scientists with the disorderly and impractical. Many psychologists, on the other hand, seek out the extremes—the irrational, the deep, the mysterious, the sense of horror and despair—and even, from another perspective, the astonishing ability of the human being to weather, adapt to, and even ultimately find some small pleasures in many intrinsically quite unpleasant situations.

Americans' responses to the assassination of President Kennedy were examined in great detail (Greenberg & Parker 1965, Wolfenstein & Kliman 1965), in terms of their emotionality, grieving, and overidealization of the dead president; particular attention was given to the impact on children. Reactions to the Nazi Holocaust have become a matter of great interest—for example, the apparent passivity of so many Jews (e.g. Zuckerman 1984). The mass suicide of residents of Jonestown raises questions both about individual charisma (of Jones himself) and collective action, perhaps in terms of collective regression (Ulman & Abse 1983). Terrorism has provoked much analysis of the personalities and motives of terrorists themselves, of course, but also of its effects on the population it attempts to influence. So far, it seems indeed to inspire fear and anxiety (among Israelis), but a hardening of attitude against the terrorists' causes (see Friedland & Merari 1985).

The nuclear stalemate has inspired considerable research as well. The relative lack of public concern, despite some realistic estimates of nuclear effects, has been a source of puzzlement (Fiske et al 1983). Adolescents' perceptions, and efforts at public education and media presentations, have been assessed (Goodman et al 1983, Zweigenhaft 1985). All these matters heighten the salience of death of oneself or others, but the political consequences of this variable have generally not been considered explicitly (though see Peterson 1985).

CONCLUSIONS

Political psychology as an emerging self-conscious specialty has now attracted a fairly stable cadre of workers. Like most interdisciplinary ventures, it is difficult to do well because it requires a sophisticated understanding of two (or more) quite different disciplines. To date understanding of the second discipline has mostly been self-taught. One of the charms of the field is its relative looseness, which provides for more original and imaginative flights of fancy than are usually permitted in the more staid and methodologically proper basic disciplines. Concomitantly, this leads to the unavoidable hazard of mixing sound analyses in with the naive and poorly informed.

As an identifiable specialty, political psychology has drawn together a variety of intellectual strands previously located solely in the traditional social science disciplines. It has done so partly because it does offer a unique perspective on politics, one emphasizing such familiar psychological concerns as emotion and stress, mechanisms of information processing, interpersonal relationships, and the irrational, among others. The coalescence of these strands seems to me particularly valuable at this time because of the surging popularity within the discipline of political science of political economy, which offers a strikingly different account of human behavior.

One of the necessary consequences of this focus upon individuals and their irrationalities is a strong normative undercurrent that usually leads to a caring, understanding, good-hearted empathy for them. The political reformist impulse that follows close behind can produce a soft-headed science. The tension between this impulse and scientific tough-mindedness is but one of the several that promise to keep political psychology lively and provocative in the years to come.

Literature Cited

Abramson, P., Inglehart, R. 1986. Generational replacement and value change in six West European societies. *Am. J. Polit. Sci.* 30:1–25

Adelson, J. 1971. The political imagination of the young adolescent. In *12 to 16: Early Adolescence,* ed. J. Kagan, R. Coles. New York: Norton

Adorno, T. W., Frenkel-Brunswik, E., Levinson, D. J., Sanford, R. N. 1950. *The Authoritarian Personality.* New York: Harper & Row

Almond, G. A., Verba, S. 1963. *The Civic Culture.* Princeton: Princeton Univ. Press

Aronson, E., Stephan, C. W., Sikes, J., Blaney, N., Snapp, M. 1978. *The Jigsaw Classroom.* Beverly Hills, CA: Sage

Baas, L. 1984. The primary sources of meaning of a secondary symbol: The case of the Constitution and Mrs. Murphy. *Polit. Psychol.* 5:687–705

Barber, J. D. 1965. *The Lawmakers.* New Haven: Yale Univ. Press

Barber, J. D. 1985. *The Presidential Character: Predicting Performance in the White House.* Englewood Cliffs, NJ: Prentice-Hall. 3rd ed.

Barner-Barry, C., Rosenwein, R. 1985. *Psychological Perspectives on Politics.* Englewood Cliffs, NJ: Prentice-Hall

Barnes, S. H., McDonough, P., Pina, A. L. 1985. The development of partisanship in new democracies: The case of Spain. *Am. J. Polit. Sci.* 29:695–720

Berelson, B. R., Lazarsfeld, P. F., McPhee, W. N. 1954. *Voting: A Study of Opinion Formation in a Presidential Campaign.* Chicago: Univ. Chicago Press

Bettelheim, B., Janowitz, M. 1964. *Social Change and Prejudice.* New York: Free Press

Bobo, L. 1983. Whites' opposition to busing: Symbolic racism or realistic group conflict? *J. Per. Soc. Psychol.* 45:1196–1210

Brown, T. A. 1986. *Migration and Politics in America.* Chapel Hill: Univ. North Carolina Press

Burns, J. M. 1978. *Leadership.* New York: Harper & Row

Campbell, A., Converse, P. E., Miller, W. E., Stokes, D. E. 1960. *The American Voter.* New York: Wiley

Chaffee, S. H. 1977. Mass communication in political socialization. See Renshon 1977, pp. 223–58

Christie, R., Geis, F. L. 1970. *Studies in Machiavellianism.* New York: Academic

Comstock, G., Chaffee, S., Katzman, N., McCombs, M., Roberts, D. 1978. *Television and Human Behavior.* New York: Columbia Univ. Press

Converse, P. E. 1964. The nature of belief systems in mass publics. In *Ideology and Discontent,* ed. D. E. Apter, pp. 206–61. New York: Free Press

Converse, P. E. 1975. Public opinion and voting behavior. In *Handbook of Political Science,* ed. F. I. Greenstein, N. W. Polsby, 4:75–170. Reading, MA: Addison-Wesley

Cook, S. W. 1984. Cooperative interaction in multiethnic contexts. In *Groups in Contact: The Psychology of Desegregation,* ed. N. Miller, M. Brewer, pp. 156–86. New York: Academic

Dalton, R. J. 1980. Reassessing parental socialization: Indicator unreliability versus generational transfer. *Am. Polit. Sci. Rev.* 74:421–31

Davies, J. C. 1963. *Human Nature in Politics: The Dynamics of Political Behavior.* New York: Wiley

Dawson, R. E., Prewitt, K., Dawson, K. S. 1977. *Political Socialization.* Boston: Little, Brown. 2nd ed.

Deutsch, M. 1973. *The Resolution of Conflict.* New Haven: Yale Univ. Press

Easton, D., Dennis, J. 1969. *Children in the Political System: Origins of Political Legitimacy.* New York: McGraw-Hill

Edelman, M. 1971. *Politics as Symbolic Action: Mass Arousal and Quiescence.* Chicago: Markham

Elden, J. M. 1981. Political efficacy at work: The connection between more autonomous forms of workplace organization and a more participatory politics. *Am. Polit. Sci. Rev.* 75:43–58

Elms, A. C. 1976. *Personality in Politics.* New York: Harcourt, Brace Jovanovich

Etheredge, L. S. 1978. *A World of Men: The Private Sources of American Foreign Policy.* Cambridge, MA: MIT Press

Etheredge, L. S. 1985. *Can Governments Learn?: American Foreign Policy and Central American Revolutions.* New York: Pergamon

Etzioni, A. 1967. The Kennedy experiment. *West. Polit. Q.* 20:361–80

Falk, A. 1985. Aspects of political psychobiography. *Polit. Psychol.* 6:605–19

Feldman, D. L. 1985. Ideology and the manipulation of symbols: Leadership perceptions of science, education, and art in the People's Republic of China, 1961–1974. *Polit. Psychol.* 6:441–60

Finlay, D. J., Holsti, O. R., Fagen, R. R. 1967. *Enemies in Politics.* Chicago: Rand-McNally

Fiorina, M. P. 1981. *Retrospective Voting in American National Elections.* New Haven: Yale Univ. Press

Fischer, G. W., Johnson, E. J. 1986. Behavioral decision theory and political decision making. See Lau & Sears 1986, pp. 55–65

Fiske, S. T., Fischhoff, B., Milburn, M. A., eds. 1983. Images of nuclear war. *J. Soc. Issues* 39(1):41–65

Flacks, R. 1967. The liberated generation: An exploration of the roots of student protest. *J. Soc. Issues* 23:53–75

Frankovic, K. A. 1982. Sex and politics—new alignments, old issues. *PS* 15:439–48

Freedman, A. E., Freedman, P. E. 1975. *The Psychology of Political Control.* New York: St. Martin's Press

Friedland, N., Merari, A. 1985. The psychological impact of terrorism: A double-edged sword. *Polit. Psychol.* 6:591–604

Fromm, E. 1941. *Escape from Freedom.* New York: Holt

Garramone, G. M. 1985. Motivation and political information processing: Extending the gratifications approach. See Kraus & Perloff 1985, pp. 201–19

George, A. L. 1969. The "operational code": A neglected approach to the study of political leaders and decision making. *Int. Stud. Q.* 13:190–222

George, A. L. 1980. *Presidential Decision-making in Foreign Policy: The Effective Use of Information and Advice.* Boulder, CO: Westview

George, A. L., George, J. L. 1956. *Woodrow Wilson and Colonel House: A Personality Study.* New York: Day

Gilligan, C. 1982. *In A Different Voice.* Cambridge, MA: Harvard Univ. Press

Glad, B. 1973. Contributions of psychobiography. See Knutson 1973a, pp. 296–321

Glenn, N. D. 1980. Values, attitudes, and beliefs. In *Constancy and Change in Human Development,* ed. O. G. Brim Jr., J. Kagan, pp. 596–640. Cambridge, MA: Harvard Univ. Press

Goodman, L. A., Mack, J. E., Beardslee, W. R., Snow, R. M. 1983. The threat of nuclear war and the nuclear arms race: Adolescent experience and perceptions. *Polit. Psychol.* 4:501–30

Graber, D. A. 1984a. *Mass Media and American Politics.* Washington, DC: Congressional Quarterly. 2nd ed.

Graber, D. A. 1984b. *Processing the News: How People Tame the Information Tide.* New York: Longman

Greenberg, B. S., Parker, E. B. 1965. Summary: Social research on the assassination. In *The Kennedy Assassination and the American Public,* ed. B. S. Greenberg, E. B. Parker, pp. 361–82. Stanford, CA: Stanford Univ. Press

Greenstein, F. I. 1965. *Children and Politics.* New Haven: Yale Univ. Press

Greenstein, F. I. 1975. Personality and politics. In *Handbook of Political Science,* ed. F. I. Greenstein, N. W. Polsby, 2:1–92. Reading, MA: Addison-Wesley. 2nd ed.

Grush, J. E., McKeough, K. L., Ahlering, R. C. 1978. Extrapolating laboratory exposure research to actual political elections. *J. Pers. Soc. Psychol.* 36:257–70

Gurin, P. 1985. Women's gender consciousness. *Public Opin. Q.* 49:142–63

Hamill, R. C., Lodge, M., Blake, F. 1985. The breadth, depth, and utility of class, partisan, and ideological schemata. *Am. J. Polit. Sci.* 29:850–70

Hermann, M. G., ed. 1986. *Political Psychology: Contemporary Problems and Issues.* San Francisco: Jossey-Bass

Hermann, M. G., ed. 1977. *A Psychological Examination of Political Leaders.* New York: Free Press

Herrmann, R. K. 1985. American perceptions of Soviet foreign policy: Reconsidering three competing perspectives. *Polit. Psychol.* 6:375–411

Hess, R. D., Torney, J. V. 1967. *The Development of Political Attitudes in Children.* Chicago: Aldine

Hovland, C. I. 1959. Reconciling conflicting results derived from experimental and survey studies of attitude change. *Am. Psychol.* 14:8–17

Hyman, H. 1959. *Political Socialization.* Glencoe, IL: Free Press

Inglehart, R. 1981. Post-materialism in an environment of insecurity. *Am. Polit. Sci. Rev.* 75:880–900

Institute for Propaganda Analysis. 1939. *The Fine Art of Propaganda: A Study of Father Coughlin's Speeches.* New York: Harcourt & Brace

Iyengar, S., Kinder, D. R. 1985. Psychological accounts of agenda-setting. See Kraus & Perloff 1985, pp. 117–40

Jackman, M. R., Muha, M. J. 1984. Education and inter-group attitudes: Moral enlightment, superficial democratic commitment, or ideological refinement. *Am. Sociol. Rev.* 49:751–69

Janis, I. L. 1982. *Victims of Groupthink.* Boston: Houghton-Mifflin. 2nd ed.

Janis, I. L., Mann, L. 1977. *Decision Making.* New York: Free Press

Jennings, M. K., Markus, G. B. 1977. The effect of military service on political attitudes: A panel study. *Am. Polit. Sci. Rev.* 71:131–47

Jennings, M. K., Markus, G. B. 1984. Partisan orientations over the long haul: Results from the three-wave political socialization panel study. *Am. Polit. Sci. Rev.* 78:1000–18

Jennings, M. K., Niemi, R. G. 1981. *Generations and Politics.* Princeton: Princeton Univ. Press

Jervis, R. 1976. *Perception and Misperception in International Politics.* Princeton: Princeton Univ. Press

Jervis, R. 1986. Cognition and political behavior. See Lau & Sears 1986, pp. 319–36

Johnson, L. K. 1977. Operational codes and the prediction of leadership behavior: Senator Frank Church at midcareer. In *A Psychological Examination of Political Leaders,* ed. M. G. Hermann, pp. 80–119. New York: Free Press

Kelman, H. C. 1965. *International Behavior: A Social-Psychological Analysis.* New York: Holt, Rinehart, & Winston

Kelman, H. C., Cohen, S. P. 1986. Resolution of international conflict: An interactional approach. In *Psychology of Intergroup Relations,* ed. S. Worchel, W. G. Austin. Chicago: Nelson-Hall. 2nd ed.

Kinder, D. R., Kiewiet, D. R. 1979. Economic discontent and political behavior: The role of personal grievances and collective economic judgments in congressional voting. *Am. J. Polit. Sci.* 23:495–527

Kinder, D. R., Sears, D. O. 1981. Prejudice and politics: Symbolic racism versus racial threats to the good life. *J. Pers. Soc. Psychol.* 40:414–31

Kinder, D. R., Sears, D. O. 1985. Public opinion and political action. In *Handbook of Social Psychology,* ed. G. Lindzey, E. Aronson, 2:659–741. New York: Random House. 3rd ed.

Klapper, J. T. 1960. *The Effects of Mass Communications.* Glencoe, IL: Free Press

Klein, E. 1984. *Gender politics: From Consciousness to Mass Politics.* Cambridge, MA: Harvard Univ. Press

Kluegel, J. R., Smith, E. R. 1986. *Beliefs about Inequality.* New York: Aldine

Knutson, J. N., ed. 1973a. *Handbook of Political Psychology.* San Francisco: Jossey-Bass

Knutson, J. N. 1973b. *The Human Basis of the Polity: A Psychological Study of Political Man.* Chicago: Aldine

Kornhauser, W. 1959. *The Politics of Mass Society.* Glencoe, IL: Free Press

Kramer, G. H. 1971. Short-term fluctuations in U.S. voting behavior, 1896–1964. *Am. Polit. Sci. Rev.* 65:131–43

Kraus, S., Davis, D. 1976. *The Effects of Mass Communication on Political Behavior.* University Park, PA: Penn. State Univ. Press

Kraus, S. A., Perloff, R. M., eds. 1985. *Mass Media and Political Thought: An Information-Processing Approach.* Beverly Hills, CA: Sage

Lane, R. E. 1959. *Political Life: Why People Get Involved in Politics.* Glencoe, IL: Free Press

Lane, R. E. 1962. *Political Ideology: Why the American Common Man Believes What He Does.* New York: Free Press

Lane, R. E. 1973. Patterns of political belief. See Knutson 1973a, pp. 83–116

Lane, R. E. 1983. Political observers and market participants: The effect on cognition. *Polit. Psychol.* 4:455–82

Lang, G. E., Lang, K. 1983. *The Battle for Public Opinion: The President, the Press, and the Polls During Watergate.* New York: Columbia Univ. Press

Lang, G. E., Lang, K. 1984. *Politics and Television Re-viewed.* Beverly Hills, CA: Sage

Lanzetta, J. T., Sullivan, D. G., Masters, R. D., McHugo, G. J. 1985. Emotional and cognitive responses to televised images of political leaders. See Kraus & Perloff 1985, pp. 85–116.

Lasswell, H. D. 1930. *Psychopathology and Politics.* New York: Viking

Lasswell, H. D. 1948. *Power and Personality.* New York: Norton

Lau, R. R., Sears, D. O., eds. 1986. *Political Cognition: The 19th Annual Carnegie Symposium on Cognition.* Hillsdale, NJ: Erlbaum

Lazarsfeld, P. F., Berelson, B., Gaudet, H. 1948. *The People's Choice.* New York: Columbia Univ. Press. 2nd ed.

Leites, N. 1951. *The Operational Code of the Politburo.* New York: McGraw-Hill

Lipset, S. M. 1981. *Political Man: The Social Bases of Politics.* Baltimore, MD: Johns Hopkins Univ. Press (expanded ed.)

Lipset, S. M., Lazarsfeld, P. F., Barton, A. H., Linz, J. 1954. The psychology of voting: An analysis of political behavior. In *Handbook of Social Psychology,* ed. G. Lindzey, 2:1124–75. Reading, MA: Addison-Wesley

Lipset, S. M., Raab, E. 1978. *The Politics of Unreason.* Chicago: Univ. Chicago Press. 2nd ed.

Longley, J., Pruitt, D. 1980. Groupthink: A critique of Janis's theory. In *Review of Personality and Social Psychology,* Vol. 1, ed. L. Wheeler. Beverly Hills, CA: Sage

MacKuen, M. B. 1981. Social communication and the mass policy agenda. In *More than News: Media Power in Public Affairs,* ed. M. B. MacKuen, S. L. Coombs, pp. 19–144. Beverly Hills, CA: Sage

Mann, T. E., Wolfinger, R. E. 1980. Candidates and parties in congressional elections. *Am. Polit. Sci. Rev.* 74:617–32

Mansbridge, J. J. 1985. Myth and reality: The ERA and the gender gap in the 1980 election. *Public Opin. Q.* 49:164–78

Markus, G. B. 1979. The political environment and the dynamics of public attitudes: A panel study. *Am. J. Polit. Sci.* 23:338–59

Maslow, A. H. 1954. *Motivation and Personality.* New York: Harper

Mazlish, B. 1972. *In Search of Nixon: A Psychohistorical Inquiry.* New York: Basic Books

McClosky, H. 1958. Conservatism and personality. *Am. Polit. Sci. Rev.* 52:27–45

McClosky, H. 1967. Personality and attitude correlates of foreign policy orientations. In *Domestic Sources of Foreign Policy,* ed. J. Rosenau, pp. 51–109. New York: Free Press

McCombs, M. E., Shaw, D. L. 1972. The agenda-setting function of the media. *Public Opin. Q.* 36:176–87

McConahay, J. B. 1982. Self-interest versus racial attitudes as correlates of anti-busing attitudes in Louisville: Is it the buses or the blacks? *J. Polit.* 44:692–720

McConahay, J. B., Hardee, B. B., Batts, V. 1981. Has racism declined in America? *J. Confl. Resolut.* 25:563–79

Milbrath, L. W., Goel, M. L. 1977. *Political Participation.* Chicago: Rand McNally

Minow, N. N., Martin, J. B., Mitchell, L. M. 1973. *Presidential Television.* New York: Basic Books

Modigliani, A. 1972. Hawks and doves, isolationism and political distrust: An analysis of public opinion on military policy. *Am. Polit. Sci. Rev.* 66:960–78

Mueller, J. E. 1973. *War, Presidents, and Public Opinion.* New York: Wiley

Neuman, W. R. 1976. Patterns of recall among television news viewers. *Public Opin. Q.* 40:115–23

Newcomb, T. M., Koenig, K. E., Flacks, R., Warwick, D. P. 1967. *Persistence and Change: Bennington College and its Students After 25 Years.* New York: Wiley

Nie, N. H., Verba, S. 1975. Political participation. See Greenstein & Polsby 1975, 4:1–74

Nie, N. H., Verba, S., Petrocik, J. R. 1979. *The Changing American Voter.* Cambridge, MA: Harvard Univ. Press. (enlarged ed.)

Osgood, C. 1962. *An Alternative to War or Surrender.* Urbana, IL: Univ. Illinois Press

Patterson, T. E. 1980. *The Mass Media Election: How Americans Choose Their President.* New York: Praeger

Patterson, T. E., McClure, R. D. 1976. *The Unseeing Eye.* New York: Putnam's

Peterson, S. A. 1985. Death experience and politics: A research note. *Polit. Psychol.* 6:19–27

Poole, K. T., Zeigler, L. H. 1985. *Women, Public Opinion and Politics: The Changing Political Attitudes of American Women.* New York: Longman

Post, J. M. 1983. Woodrow Wilson reexamined: The mind-body controversy redux and other disputations. *Polit. Psychol.* 4:289–306

Renshon, S. A. 1974. *Psychological Needs and Political Behavior: A Theory of Personality and Political Efficacy.* New York: Free Press

Renshon, S. A., ed. 1977. *Handbook of Political Socialization: Theory and Research.* New York: Free Press

Rintala, M. 1984. The love of power and the power of love: Churchill's childhood. *Polit. Psychol.* 5:375–90

Robinson, M. J. 1976. Public affairs television and the growth of political malaise: The case of "the selling of the pentagon." *Am. Polit. Sci. Rev.* 70:409–32

Rogow, A. A. 1963. *James Forrestal: A Study of Personality, Politics, and Policy.* New York: Macmillan

Rothman, S. 1984. Ideology, authoritarianism and mental health. *Polit. Psychol.* 5:341–63

Sanford, N. 1973. Authoritarian personality in contemporary perspective. See Knutson 1973a, pp. 139–70

Sapiro, V. 1983. *The Political Integration of Women.* Urbana, IL: Univ. Illinois Press

Schlozman, K. L., Verba, S. 1979. *Injury to Insult: Unemployment, Class, and Political Response.* Cambridge, MA: Harvard Univ. Press

Schultz, C. K. 1986. *The belligerent neutrality of the news: Creating an environment of informed confusion.* Unpublished doctoral dissertation. Univ. Calif., Los Angeles

Schuman, H., Steeh, C., Bobo, L. 1985. *Racial Attitudes in America: Trends and Interpretation.* Cambridge, MA: Harvard Univ. Press

Sears, D. O. 1969. Political behavior. In *Handbook of Social Psychology,* ed. G. Lindzey, E. Aronson, 5:315–458. Reading, MA: Addison-Wesley. 2nd ed.

Sears, D. O. 1975. Political socialization. See Greenstein & Polsby 1975, 2:96–136

Sears, D. O. 1983. The persistence of early political predispositions: The roles of attitude object and life stage. In *Review of Personality and Social Psychology,* ed. L. Wheeler, P. Shaver, 4:79–116. Beverly Hills, CA: Sage

Sears, D. O., Allen, H. M. Jr. 1984. The trajectory of local desegregation controversies and whites' opposition to busing. In *Groups in Contact: The Psychology of Desegregation,* ed. N. Miller, M. B. Brewer, pp. 123–51. New York: Academic

Sears, D. O., Chaffee, S. H. 1979. Uses and effects of the 1976 debates: An overview of empirical studies. In *The Great Debates, 1976: Ford vs. Carter,* pp. 223–61. Bloomington: Indiana Univ. Press

Sears, D. O., Citrin, J. 1985. *Tax Revolt: Something for Nothing in California.* Cambridge, MA: Harvard Univ. Press (enlarged ed.)

Sears, D. O., Lau, R. R., Tyler, T. R., Allen, H. M. Jr. 1980. Self-interest vs. symbolic politics in policy attitudes and presidential voting. *Am. Polit. Sci. Rev.* 74:670–84

Sears, D. O., McConahay, J. B. 1973. *The Politics of Violence: The New Urban Blacks and the Watts Riot.* Boston: Houghton-Mifflin

Sears, D. O., Tyler, T. R., Citrin, J., Kinder, D. R. 1978. Political system support and public response to the 1974 energy crisis. *Am. J. Polit. Sci.* 22:56–82

Seeman, M. 1984. A legacy of protest: The

"Events of May" in retrospect. *Polit. Psychol.* 5:437–64

Segall, M. H. 1976. *Human Behavior and Public Policy: A Political Psychology.* New York: Pergamon

Shapiro, R. Y., Mahajan, H. 1986. Gender differences in policy preferences: A summary of trends from the 1960s to the 1980s. *Public Opin. Q.* 50:42–61

Sigel, R. S., Hoskin, M. B. 1977. Perspectives on adult political socialization—areas of research. See Renshon 1977, pp. 259–93

Simonton, D. K. 1985. The vice-presidential succession effect: Individual or situational basis? *Polit. Behav.* 7:79–99

Smith, M. B., Bruner, J. S., White, R. W. 1956. *Opinions and Personality.* New York: Wiley

Smith, T. W. 1984. The polls: Gender and attitudes toward violence. *Public Opin. Q.* 48:384–96

Sniderman, P. M. 1975. *Personality and Democratic Politics.* Berkeley: Univ. Calif. Press

Stagner, R. 1967. *Psychological Aspects of International Conflict.* Belmont, CA: Brooks/Cole

Stephan, W. G. 1985. Intergroup relations. In *Handbook of Social Psychology,* ed. G. Lindzey, E. Aronson, 2:599–658. New York: Random House. 3rd ed.

Stewart, L. H. 1977. Birth order and political leadership. See Hermann 1977, pp. 205–36

Stone, W. F. 1974. *The Psychology of Politics.* New York: Free Press

Stone, W. F., Smith, D. C. 1983. Human nature in politics: Graham Wallas and the Fabians. *Polit. Psychol.* 4:693–712

Stouffer, S. A. 1955. *Communism, Conformity, and Civil Liberties.* New York: Doubleday

Sullivan, J. L., Piereson, J. E., Marcus, G. E. 1978. Ideological constraint in the mass public: A methodological critique and some new findings. *Am. J. Polit. Sci.* 22:233–49

Sullivan, J. L., Piereson, J., Marcus, G. E. 1982. *Political Tolerance and American Democracy.* Chicago: Univ. Chicago Press

Tajfel, H. 1981. *Human Groups and Social Categories.* Cambridge, MA: Cambridge Univ. Press

Tapp, J. L., Kohlberg, L. 1971. Developing senses of law and legal justice. *J. Soc. Issues* 27:65–92

Tedin, K. L. 1974. The influence of parents on the political attitudes of adolescents. *Am. Polit. Sci. Rev.* 68:1579–92

Tetlock, P. E. 1983a. Policymakers' images of international conflict. *J. Soc. Issues* 39:67–86

Tetlock, P. E. 1983b. Psychological research on foreign policy: A methodological overview. In *Review of Personality and Social Psychology*, ed. L. Wheeler, P. Shaver, 4:45–78. Beverly Hills, CA: Sage

Torney-Purta, J. 1984. Political socialization and policy: The United States in a crossnational context. In *Child Development and Social Policy*, Vol. 1, ed. H. W. Stevenson, A. E. Siegel. Chicago: Univ. Chicago Press

Ulman, R. B., Abse, D. W. 1983. The group psychology of mass madness: Jonestown. *Polit. Psychol.* 4:637–61

Vanneman, R. D., Pettigrew, T. F. 1972. Race and relative deprivation in the urban United States. *Race* 13:461–86

Wallas, G. 1921. *Human Nature in Politics*. New York: Knopf. Originally published 1908

Wattenberg, M. P. 1982. From parties to candidates: Examining the role of the media. *Public Opin. Q.* 46:216–27

Wattenberg, M. P. 1984. *The Decline of American Political Parties, 1952–1980*. Cambridge, MA: Harvard Univ. Press

White, R. K. 1965. Images in the context of international conflict: Soviet perceptions of the U.S. and the U.S.S.R. In *International Behavior: A Social-Psychological Analysis*,

ed. H. C. Kelman, pp. 236–76. New York: Holt, Rinehart & Winston

White, R. K. 1970. *Nobody Wanted War: Misperception in Vietnam and Other Wars*. Garden City, NY: Doubleday

White, R. K., ed. 1985. *Psychology and the Prevention of Nuclear War: A Book of Readings*. New York: New York Univ. Press

Winter, D. G. 1973. *The Power Motive*. New York: Free Press

Wolfenstein, E. V. 1967. *The Revolutionary Personality*. Princeton: Princeton Univ. Press

Wolfenstein, M., Kliman, G., eds. 1965. *Children and the Death of a President*. Garden City, NY: Doubleday

Wolfinger, R. E., Rosenstone, S. J. 1980. *Who Votes?* New Haven: Yale Univ. Press

Worchel, S., Austin, W. G., eds. 1986. *Psychology of Intergroup Relations*. Chicago: Nelson-Hall. 2nd ed.

Zuckerman, A. S. 1984. The limits of political behavior: Individual calculations and survival during the Holocaust. *Polit. Psychol.* 5:37–52

Zweigenhaft, R. L. 1985. Providing information and shaping attitudes about nuclear dangers: Implications for public education. *Polit. Psychol.* 6:461–80

Ann. Rev. Psychol. 1987. 38:257–78

COUNSELING PSYCHOLOGY: THEORY, RESEARCH, AND PRACTICE IN CAREER COUNSELING

Samuel H. Osipow

Department of Psychology, Ohio State University, Columbus, Ohio 43210

CONTENTS

The psychology of career development as well as the procedures used to enable people to identify and implement their career objectives effectively are growing in sophistication and impact. Increasingly, research and methods dealing with career counseling are in the mainstream of applied psychology. Whereas at one time career counseling efforts seemed to be an activity almost exclusively in the province of counseling psychologists, applied psychologists in clinical, industrial/organizational, and social psychology settings now find career development issues of interest. This is illustrated by the publication in the last decade of books such as Manuso's *Occupational Clinical Psychology*

257

0066-4308/87/0201-0257$02.00

(1983). The importance of work in psychology is further highlighted by the devotion of the 1985 Master Lectures in Psychology Series presented at the American Psychological Association convention to the topic of psychology and work (Pallak & Perloff 1986). Because of its relevance to issues such as occupational stress and adjustment, the feminist movement, and in life-span issues, the research of career psychologists is becoming increasingly important.

This review addresses some of the major issues now being investigated by career psychologists. Emphasis is given to new theoretical developments and their empirical validation. In addition, the review identifies recent findings regarding the effects of various kinds of interventions on career development, advances in vocational assessment, and career issues that pertain to the special problems of subgroups within our society, especially women.

No attempt is made to review the entire literature dealing with career counseling because it has become extraordinarily extensive. For broader and deeper coverage, the reader is referred to some recent review articles and books such as, but not limited to, the last two chapters in the *Annual Review of Psychology* devoted to counseling psychology (Holland et al 1981, Borgen 1984). In addition, the *Journal of Vocational Behavior* annually publishes a review of research in vocational behavior. Since the last *Annual Review of Psychology* coverage of counseling psychology in 1984, the *Journal of Vocational Behavior* has published reviews of vocational psychology by Tinsley & Heesacker (1984) and by Borgen et al (1985). The latter authors identified five problems frequently occurring in the vocational behavior and career development literature: lack of research investigations conducted in a theoretical context; survey return rates which were undesirably low, thus limiting possible generalization; failure to follow correct procedures in data analysis; the use of statistical procedures that maximize results of exploratory studies without subsequent appropriate cross-validation procedures; and the failure to consider the practical as well as the statistical significance of research findings. In addition, Cairo (1983) published a selected review of the literature describing how career counseling is used in industry.

The following list of recent books that address some important issues of career counseling should be perused by the interested reader but are not extensively reviewed here: Brown & Brooks (1984), Brown & Lent (1984), Dawis & Lofquist (1984), Gilbert (1985a), Gordon (1984), Osipow (1983), and Walsh & Osipow (1983).

THEORY: NEW DEVELOPMENTS

Super's Theory

Among Super's most recent theoretical writing is a 1980 article dealing with a life-span, life-space approach to career development. Using a descriptive approach, Super proposes numerous roles people play throughout the life cycle which define their careers in the broadest sense. These roles are played in a variety of so-called theaters, e.g. home, community, school, and workplace, which are more or less common to all people, and a number of other theaters, e.g. church, union, and club, which are not necessarily common to all people. It is the arrangement of and participation in these various so-called theaters that defines the context within which a career occurs. In addition, a variety of the roles that people play to some degree cut across these theaters. For example, some roles change with age, so there are the child, adolescent, and adult roles; there are also certain activity-defined roles, such as the student, the leisurite, and the worker; and there are also a variety of familially defined roles such as the child, spouse, homemaker, or parent. Super has tried to describe how these various roles interweave as well as wax and wane in idiosyncratic yet generalizable fashions that define the occupational tasks individuals must successfully negotiate. While this conception is an interesting and useful description of life-span career issues, it is not an approach that one would expect to lead to a high volume of research because of its descriptive rather than predictive nature.

Other ideas related to Super's theory, however, have continued to be tested empirically. For example, Crook et al (1984) found that self-esteem and career maturity are correlated as self-concept theory used by Super would predict. Crook et al speculate that self-esteem facilitates career maturity, which, in turn, acts to promote achievement. In another study, Adler & Aranya (1984) looked at career stages in accountants to assess the degree to which Holland personality type remained congruent across the life span. Their results indicate that at different life stages accountants differ significantly in their needs and work attitudes and thus in the extent to which they fit the conventional Holland type. Since Holland's theory would predict that occupational congruence is important not only in the initial selection but in the maintenance of and persistence of an occupational direction, this finding is curious. It raises some questions about the long-term predictive validity of Holland types, and highlights the importance of awareness of Super's life stage issues in the prediction of career persistence.

Kidd (1984), in studying the self-concepts of British school children found that self-concept theory applies more adequately to highly talented youngsters and to those youngsters who generally seem to be higher in self-esteem than to those who are somewhat lower in self-esteem. Kidd also found that occupational preferences and ideal self-concepts are more closely related to each other than are self-concepts and occupational preferences, a finding that again suggests that occupational preferences probably operate with fewer constraints than occupational selections. Kidd interpreted the results as generally supporting Super's theory. Some refinements in the theory are suggested by the findings, however, since Kidd found that occupational aspirations seem to be more heavily influenced by the anticipation of the future self than by the present self concept. Given that children know they will be changing as they grow older, that expectation is not unreasonable.

Career maturity is an essential aspect of Super's theory. A number of studies have been conducted dealing with career maturity. Savickas et al (1984) found that students' time perspective is a component in two of three career maturity factors, i.e. attitudinal vocational maturity and career decision making. Time perspectives were found to be related to planfulness as well as to the degree of indecision that students express. In another study, Kahn & Alvi (1983) found that high school students' Career Maturity Inventory scores correlate with educational and occupational aspirations, self-estimates of general ability, and self-estimates of classroom performance, as well as parental educational level and parental educational and occupational aspirations. In addition, they found that higher Career Maturity Inventory scores are correlated with higher self-esteem, with more internal degree of locus of control, and with greater intrinsic as opposed to extrinsic work values. The authors concluded that these findings suggest that programmatic interventions facilitating career development should be aimed at further developing positive self-concepts and increasing levels of aspirations, understanding personal strengths and weaknesses, developing skills in decision making and problem solving, and in fostering appropriate work values. One might question whether or not increased levels of aspirations, however, are necessarily relevant for those individuals who do not have general abilities that match those increased levels of aspirations. In another methodological study dealing with the Crites' Career Maturity Inventory, Alvi & Kahn (1983) found that correlations between the CMI attitudes and the CMI competence tests were more consistent with the Crites model than has been reported by other investigators.

Holland's Theory

Holland's theory has probably driven more empirical research since its initial appearance in the 1950s than any other career behavior theory. Holland has recently published a revised version of his theory and its current status (Holland 1985a) which reflects a number of significant refinements and improvements over previous statements of the theory. These refinements and improvements include a better explanation of how the types develop and more discussion of how organizational and environmental variables interact with individual variables. It is likely that these refinements will produce another generation of empirical studies testing the theoretical hypotheses that naturally grow out of those discussions. The 1985 publication insures yet another long period of research influenced by the Holland model.

One of the most useful papers dealing with the Holland theory published recently is a review by Spokane (1985) in which the voluminous research results studying person-environment congruence based on Holland's theory were analyzed. In his review, Spokane concludes that the many correlational studies of congruence between person and environment show significant and positive relationships between congruence and a large number of pertinent variables related to career development such as persistence, career choice, stability, and job satisfaction. However, nonsignificant relationships tend to be found between congruence and variables like self-concept and sociability. Spokane criticized the general research methodology as being somewhat simplistic in design and called for more complex research designs involving moderator variables, studies of degrees of congruence over time, and experimental studies that will better help us understand the construct of person-environment congruence. The issue of studying congruence over time is reminiscent of the study by Adler & Aranya (1984), cited earlier, in which it was found that the congruence of accountants to their environment seems to be related to life stage. Finally, Spokane suggests that the person-environment research should be designed with an eye toward developing useful applications to practice.

As always, other studies of the empirical aspects of Holland's theory have been published. Rose (1984) analyzed some of the implications of Holland's hexagon. The correlations observed around the rim of the hexagon are ordinarily presumed to be bidirectional. It is assumed that the first choice of a realistic type should relate in a predictable way to the probability of a second choice in the Enterprising field. Rose suggests, however, that the relationship is not necessarily reciprocal in that the first choice of an Enterprising person does not necessarily relate to the same degree to the second choice of a Realistic individual. Such a rationale has important potential for career planning, particularly with respect to generating potential preference "trees."

Schneider & Overton (1983) tested the hypothesis that Investigative and Social students would be the highest academic achievers and Enterprising and Realistic the lowest academic achievers. To test this hypothesis they classified more than 300 male and 300 female freshmen students by Holland type and analyzed their academic performance in terms of grade point average as well as their scholastic aptitude test scores. They found that there were significant differences in the grade point averages earned by males according to type, but not those that had been predicted. Post hoc analysis indicated that Artistic and Conventional males earned higher grades than did Realistic or Enterprising males; the Investigative and Social male students were in the middle. Of course, such a finding could be confounded by differences in the academic rigor of the disciplines reflected in each of these typologies. The scholastic aptitude findings show significant relationships for both males and females. Here it was found that Investigative and Artistic males have higher *Scholastic Aptitude Test* scores than Social or Enterprising males, while Investigative females scored significantly higher than other females on the *Scholastic Aptitude Test*. Grade point average results for females did not differ significantly across types. The interpretation of this finding, however, should be tempered by the knowledge that the women were not represented equally across all six Holland types.

Slaney & Brown (1983) examined the effects of race and socioeconomic status on career choice in college men using the Holland typology. In a comparison of 48 black and white college men matched on socioeconomic indicators, they found that there were differences in *Vocational Preference Inventory* types related to race and socioeconomic status, particularly with respect to differences in preferences for Artistic, Realistic, and Investigative environments. They also found a racial difference on career indecision as reflected by *My Vocational Identity Scale* and in socioeconomic status on the *Career Decision Scale*. Walsh et al (1983) found that on the *Self-Directed Search* (see Holland 1985b) black and white women in the same occupation tended to be more similar to each other than they are different, but on the *Vocational Preference Inventory,* black and white women in the same occupation looked more different than similar. This result suggests some significant differences between the two instruments usually used to measure Holland types.

Bolton (1985) analyzed 69 occupational groups using the 16 PF profile based on Holland's six types. Three discriminant functions were identified which enabled the correct classifications of 75 percent of the groups into the Holland types. The profiles for the six types were consistent with Holland's characterization; a two-dimensional plot of the group centroids corresponded exactly to Holland's hypothesized ordering of the types. Wiggins et al (1983) tested the predicted adequacy of the *Vocational Preference Inventory* in anticipating teacher job satisfaction. They found that personality, environmental congruence, and differentiation were related to the prediction of job satisfaction for teachers in five subject matter areas. This finding supports Holland's theory and further demonstrates the utility of assessment of person-environment congruence to help counsel individuals about career choices.

In another study of the hexagon, Wigington (1983) found that the hexagonal model is useful in explaining the relationships in the occupational interest themes found in a sample of individuals who sought career counseling in college settings. Such a finding is reassuring since the hexagon is frequently used in just such a manner.

Finally, Iachan (1984) developed a measure to evaluate the agreement of the *Self-Directed Search* with occupational preference that he believes is superior to the current method.

Holland's work continues to be an active stimulus to research. Most of the findings point to the theory's vitality and validity for the purposes for which it was designed.

Developmental Approaches

The concept of human development is one that has been central to theory development and practice in career counseling. Super's theory, mentioned earlier (Super et al 1963), is the foremost example of currently active developmental theories that are applied to career behavior. More recently Gottfredson (1981) developed a theory focusing on stages of human development. Other developmental approaches to the study of careers have also been put forth.

Vondracek et al (1983) criticized the manner in which human development has been applied to understanding careers. According to Vondracek and his associates, a number of shortcomings exist including the inappropriate adaptation of key concepts from developmental to career development theory. There is an apparent unawareness on the part of career development theorists of significant changes in developmental theory in recent years. Too few well-designed, contextually sensitive longitudinal studies dealing with career development have been conducted; and finally, too often inadvertent misrepresentation of well-established empirical findings in developmental research as applied to career development has occurred. Vondracek et al conclude that vocational interventions should be viewed as successive procedures designed to enable people to improve vocational functioning through the life span and to adapt their vocational function to changing personal, economic, and other contextual situations. Vondracek et al (1986) have tried to develop an alternative approach to combine human development and career development thinking in a more adequate way.

Vondracek et al's view criticizing career development theory (1983) was taken to task by Gottfredson (1983), who takes issue with the shortcomings Vondracek and his associates have mentioned. Gottfredson asserts that Vondracek's approach fails to possess the qualities needed to guide us to improved research and theory.

Stonewater & Daniels (1983) developed a career decision making course based on Chickering's theory (1969), and compared student outcomes with those of an introductory psychology course and a career information course that was not based on developmental theory. They found that the students in the developmental theory and career information courses grew more in their sense of purpose than those in the introductory psychology courses. Differences in autonomy were also seen between the students in the theory course as compared with the introductory psychology course. Unfortunately, there were apparent differences before assignments to instructional groups that indicated that the students enrolled in the developmental theory based course and the career information course were not as well informed or autonomous to begin with. The results thus could be interpreted to mean that the career courses enabled the students to "catch up" to an appropriate developmental stage.

Career Issues for Special Populations

One of the aspects of career counseling and development that is perhaps most distinctive is its close connection with life-span issues and with issues relating to particular kinds of subgroups in the population who experience different kinds of career development opportunities and problems. Thus, it should be no surprise that some of the most interesting research dealing with career counseling and development has to do with that topic. Much of the research done with adolescents concerns career decision and indecision and the career choice process. That literature has been covered earlier in this review. Other life-span issues concern concepts in research dealing with what happens after career entry. Some of that research has been conducted in the context of women's career development and is discussed in that section of this review.

In a study of career stages, Slocum & Cron (1985) tested a model by studying 675 salespersons between the ages of 21 and 60. The results indicated three distinct stages exist, e.g. trial, stabilization, and maintenance. These stages can be further divided into substages. The results indicate support for a career stage model in that people in each stage displayed different attitudes and behaviors from those in other stages, all of which predicted their performance in sales work.

Increasing attention has also been paid to the older adult approaching retirement. Dobson & Morrow (1984) studied a university population regarding retirement attitudes. Their results indicate that career orientation variables are stronger predictors of attitudes toward retirement than demographic variables, although demographic variables are more adequate in predicting retirement age and level of preparation for retirement. These results suggest differential counseling emphasis as a function of both demographics and preretirement career orientation.

Finally, in a 1985 study, Osipow et al found that older workers report less occupational stress and greater coping resources than younger workers.

Psychoanalytic Developments

Watkins (1984) integrated the literature based on Alfred Adler's theory with the results of some empirical studies in order to develop a set of hypotheses and corollaries derived from the substantive base of Adler's individual psychology to career development theory. While no new empirical data are presented, the effort represents one of the first new psychoanalytic-based theory efforts to understand career developmental processes in recent years.

The time must be right to apply Adler's theory to career development: in another study, Hafner & Fakouri (1984) tested the early recollections of students in clinical psychology, dentistry, and law using Adler's individual psychology as a guide. The investigation explored differences in life-style themes. When the early recollections of 30 students in each of the professional programs were compared, it was found that the three groups differed in the nature of their early recollection. The authors tentatively conclude that the content of early recollections has potential utility for distinguishing among occupational groups. Clearly, however, more investigation is necessary before this can be viewed as a significant finding.

Finally, Markham (1983) has proposed understanding career development in terms of the context of life style and in particular on the basis of Heider's (1958) theory describing the psychology of action. In this approach, action is seen to be a function of trying, ability, task difficulty, and luck. Markham's synthesis describes, in very broad terms, how context variables can be important in understanding and developing theory in career development. One positive aspect of Markham's approach is its emphasis on cognitive processing variables and orienting strategies such as job choice, adaptation, and career interventions. However, it is not clear how the hypotheses that Markham developed in his article actually derive from the theoretical model he proposes. Nonetheless, this is an important development because it is one of the few cognitive models of career development which includes life-style parameters. However, others have proposed some cognitive-based career interventions that will be reviewed later.

INTERVENTIONS

One of the major focus points of career development theory is career counseling and intervention. The potential interventions can be examined along two dimensions: the first is the nature of the targeted behavior to be changed, e.g. vocational adjustment, vocational decision making and its implementation, and vocational productivity; the other dimension deals with the nature of the interventions themselves, e.g. group versus individual, cognitive versus affective in nature. Shortcomings in the approach to studying career counseling outcomes have been carefully analyzed and solutions proposed by a number of writers in recent years, e.g. Fretz (1981), Oliver (1979), Osipow (1982). Most of the studies that have been conducted dealing with the outcomes of career counseling and various interventions in the period since the last article in the *Annual Review of Psychology* dealing with this topic have not significantly addressed the criticisms raised by Oliver, Fretz, and Osipow. Nevertheless, to some degree these studies represent an advance in our understanding of variables associated with career counseling events and should be read in the context of Spokane & Oliver's (1983) discussion of the effects of career counseling interventions as analyzed by a meta analysis procedure. Spokane and Oliver found that career counseling has a rather powerful effect on behaviors of interest.

Career Indecision

Perhaps a disproportionate amount of the attention of career counseling has been focused on working effectively with college students who are undecided about their career directions. One of the studies focused toward that end was done by Raymon et al (1983), who examined the effects of a career course for college students who were undecided about their major fields or careers. They found that career course treatments have a desirable effect on the resulting vocational identity of the students enrolled in the courses that is not significantly affected by specific instruction or student characteristics. The course content is similarly encouraging in that it incorporates many techniques that are very widely used such as training modules dealing with "tips" on how to engage in career planning, interest inventory assessment and feedback to students, clarification of values, information gathering about various academic areas, and an interview with two people employed in a career of potential interest to the student and a written summary of each interview. The results suggest that such a set of interventions can be very powerful and can have an important effect on some significant aspects of vocational identity.

Trebilco (1984) found that career maturity of younger students can also be positively affected as a function of career education programming. The study by Trebilco is one of the few based on a large-scale sample of students in Australia. Similarly, Remer et al (1984) found that a life-planning course produced participants who are more rational and less intuitive and dependent in their decision making styles after the course; it also increased their certainty of major and career choices and produced more crystalized vocational self concepts. Students enrolled in such a life-planning course were found to have fewer vocational identity problems and more career information as a consequence of the instruction.

Other techniques have been used to promote improved career decision making in students. Pinder & Fitzgerald (1984) studied the effect of a computerized guidance system entitled "Choices" on student decision making. Using the *Career Decision Scale* and the Occupational Scale of the *Assessment of Career Decision Making* as outcome measures, they found that improved career decision making resulted as a result of computer interaction with the "Choices" system.

Taylor & Betz (1983) studied the relationship of career indecision and career decision making self-efficacy expectations. They found that students high on self-efficacy expectations were less likely to have high scores reflecting career indecision on the Career Decision Scale. Furthermore, they found that ability level relationships to self-efficacy are minimal, leading them to speculate that self-efficacy expectations can be helpful in structuring the nature of the interventions to be used with career undecided students because the measure of self-efficacy they used has the potential to identify specific problem behaviors needing attention.

Slaney (1983) examined levels of career indecision among undergraduate college women by studying the effects of three different treatments. One group was given a vocational card sort treatment, the second was given the Strong-Campbell Interest Inventory and interpretation, and the third was a no-treatment control group. Each group consisted of 20 women participants. Some treatment effects were found suggesting a relationship between the importance of career indecision to the individual and the impact of the particular intervention.

Berger-Gross et al (1983) found that students who completed a career-planning questionnaire based on Harren's *Assessment of Career Decision Making* scored higher in post-test anxiety than did those students who completed a consumer preference marketing questionnaire. These differences were based on comparisons of pre- and post-scores within groups; that is, the treatment group that was the Harren test group showed greater differences (increased anxiety) after testing than did the control group, which scored about the same in anxiety in both pre- and post-testing measures. Berger-Gross et al interpret this to mean that anxiety is yet another indicator of student progress in the career planning process. However, while understanding student anxiety in the decision making process is clearly an important aspect of developing career counseling approaches, this study raises the question about whether or not decision making styles contribute to anxiety levels or whether anxiety levels contribute to decision making styles.

Phillips & Strohmer (1983) performed a canonical analysis of 174 undergraduate students with respect to vocational coping strategies and progress on career decision making tasks. The results indicated that the employment of a planning orientation either helps or hurts movement beyond the exploratory phase of decision making about occupation; secondly, people who engage in decisions about college majors or occupations without good decision making skills seem to devote more effort to prechoice portions of the decision making process than other students. The results support the importance of planning orientations and development of career decision making skills at an early time.

Noeth (1983) studied almost 2000 high school juniors longitudinally and categorized their subsequent career choices and later occupations into Holland type job clusters on the basis of selected scales of the assessment of career development produced by the American College Testing Program. Based on a criterion of what occupation was held two years after high school, the results indicated that the scales did not contribute to an accurate prediction of vocational choice. High-scoring students on the ACT did not predict their future occupations better than low-scoring students. Taylor & Pryor (1985) studied the process of compromise in career decision making. Their results indicate that interests, prestige, and sex exert a significant influence on the kinds of compromise choices people make. Occupational prestige is likely to moderate the relationship between interests and course choice in that people who make choices that are incongruent with their interests may do so on the basis of occupational prestige. This is reminiscent of the findings of an earlier study by Leonard et al (1973). The Taylor and Pryor study revealed sex differences in occupational interest and prestige, indicating that women may choose courses that are more like their interests but with lower prestige while males seem more willing to compromise their interests in order to engage in higher level prestige activities. Their findings indicate three major compromise styles: the refusal to compromise and an effort to try again, a compromise resulting in the choice of an activity in the same interest area but at a lower level of prestige, or the selection of occupations in a commercial field.

INSTRUMENTATION   Instrument development studies are important in career counseling. Manuele (1983) developed a measure to assess vocational maturity in adults displaying delayed career development. This instrument has potential applications for use with segments of the population not normally given high quality career counseling. Stumps et al (1983) developed a system to examine variables associated with career exploration in adults. Finally, Hartman et al (1985) studied the predictive validity of the *Career Decision Scale* finding that factor 1 of the scale does a reasonably good job of identifying high school students who will ultimately have a stable career direction from those who will not.

Cognitive Approaches to Career Counseling

Cognitive variables have begun to take an increasingly important position in understanding career development and career counseling. Cesari et al (1984) randomly assigned decided versus undecided students to four types of occupational information packets. The dependent measure in the study was cognitive complexity. They found no differences between decided and undecided students with respect to cognitive complexity as a function of the occupational information received, but a significant main effect was found for the *kind* of information that was received. Positive information was associated with relatively greater cognitive simplicity scores and negative information with relatively greater cognitive complexity scores.

M. S. Taylor (1985) predicted that college students' school-to-work transition difficulties would be related to level of occupational knowledge and crystalization of vocational self concept. She found that occupational knowledge that was measured before a job search began predicted whether students received at least one job offer before graduation as well as the total number of offers. Similarly, self-concept crystalization measured before the search predicted the receipt of at least an offer as well as confidence in the ultimate job decision and job satisfaction. This finding is interesting because most previous studies have not examined job knowledge or occupational knowledge, but have rather looked at occupational information. Furthermore, most of the former studies have found little utility regarding career development as a function of occupational information. The Taylor approach, which measures occupational knowledge more than just occupational information, is promising because it appears to deal with targeted information. Accumulating information about careers is insufficient; knowledge may be more significant.

Bihm & Winer (1983) studied occupational information giving aspects of career counseling based on impression theory. Their subjects were 120 students who listened to occupational information and then were asked to describe the occupations in one case either immediately or in the other a week later. The various groups were compared in their accuracy of recall. False positives were taken as evidence of thematic intrusion. Their results supported the hypothesis that over time there would be more thematic intrusions for information about occupations. The second hypothesis that there would be more thematic intrusions for familiar occupations as opposed to unfamiliar occupations was not supported. The findings suggest that people may rely less on information and more on thematically organized impressions about careers in analyzing information about careers to clients. Information itself seems to have little impact in reshaping the stereotypes people have about occupations. Thematically organized impressions about careers may reflect the same processes as Taylor's (1985) career knowledge noted above.

Waas (1984) studied the assumption that occupational information has substantial utility in the process of making occupational choices. According to Waas, cognitive differentiation has been shown to be related to appropriate career choice. In this study the author presented Holland personality characteristics as occupational information and compared the impact of that information on 150 college freshmen who had not yet declared their major. These students were further assigned to one of three groups: objective information, personality information, and no information. Based on the responses to the *Career Decision Scale* and the *Cognitive Differentiation Grid,* the results indicated that students who receive personality information display greater differentiation among careers than those receiving objective information.

In a final study of cognitive structures, Neimeyer et al (1985) found that vocational decision making skills, career exploration, and career planning are all a function of cognitive structures.

Harpaz (1983) studied the concept that cerebral hemisphere functions are related to occupational behavior. More specifically, Harpaz assumed that the right hemisphere specializes in different cognitive processes than the left hemisphere of the brain. As a result, she proposed that occupational jobs and tasks would relate to differences in specific hemispheric abilities. Personnel who perform in a sphere in the relevant hemisphere should be more proficient in their work than those who do not. In an Israeli university, 119 graduate students in economics and accounting were compared with 65 undergraduates in the creative arts field. They were given a special test battery to measure hemispheric functioning. Significant differences in mean performance on the measures as predicted were found. Harpaz tentatively interprets this as suggesting that individual patterns of hemispheric specialization may have some utility for helping match people's abilities and jobs. Actual follow-up of employed people is necessary before such a conclusion can be reached with confidence.

VOCATIONAL ASSESSMENT

Over the years one of the most significant areas of career counseling assessment has been interest measurement. The last few years have seen very important developments in that regard. Notably, the publication of a new edition of the *Strong-Campbell Interest Inventory* (Hanson & Campbell 1985), a new edition of the *Kuder Occupational Interest Survey* (Zytowski 1985), and a new edition of the *Self-Directed Search* (Holland 1985b). These advances and others have been reviewed by Walsh & Osipow (1986).

Another notable publication during this period is a book by Walsh & Betz (1985), which is of particular potential utility to career counselors because it takes an environmental approach to examining the principles and methods involved in a variety of aspects of assessment.

The volume and variety of instruments to assess instruments of relevance to career development and career counseling have become so great as to be nearly impossible to organize. To that end, the recent edition of the *Mental Measurements Yearbook* (Mitchell 1985) and two new publications by Sweetland & Keyser called *Tests* (1983) and *Tests Supplement* (1984) are especially valuable. The *Mental Measurements Yearbook* is a well-established publication containing critical evaluations and reviews of tests. *Tests* lists publications by potential function and population. That same publisher has also begun publishing a critical review of tests which can be useful to prospective users not only to identify appropriate instruments for their career counseling purposes but to evaluate their appropriateness. These two publications help relieve some of the burden on individuals to organize and use the large number of tests that exists. In addition, 1985 saw the publication of a new edition of *Standards for Educational and Psychological Tests* (American Educational Research Association et al 1985). This publication updates information about the responsibilities of test developers, publishers, and users with respect to the standards that should be maintained. Criteria for using tests in counseling in general and career counseling in particular are discussed in this new edition. Furthermore, the topic of computerized testing is discussed and the evolving ethical standards for the use of computerized tests are touched upon. Since career counseling has used computerized interactions for many years, these are issues of central importance to the field.

EMPIRICAL FINDINGS REGARDING INTERESTS AND CHOICES   A number of investigators have continued to look at issues related to how interests develop, what they mean, and how they affect careers. Laing et al (1984) examined the relationship between expressed choices, measured interests, and persistence in expressed choice in a large sample of college students and employed persons over a period of time. The results indicate that the persistence in a field of expressed choice increases as one observes increased congruence between the choice itself and interests. This finding validates the congruence hypothesis as well as the general underpinnings of prediction of the relationship between interests and career pathways.

Mossholder et al (1985) studied the general notion that has been presented in the literature by Zytowski & Hay (1984) regarding the degree to which intraoccupational differences may be underemphasized while we overemphasize the interoccupational differences in career interests. The Mossholder et al study of accountants examined perceived work climate and outcome preferences. They found that intraoccupational differences can be measured and exist for both males and females with respect to perceived work climate and outcome preferences. The Zytowski & Hay (1984) study analyzed the "birds of a feather" hypothesis, which is an old and comfortable one in understanding career interests. In the Zytowski and Hay study, two sets of 40 women each representing five different occupations were studied using hierarchal cluster analysis based on the Kuder Occupational Interest Survey. The results were interpreted by the authors as suggesting that important differences in interests of people in the same occupation may in fact exist. This has obvious important implications for interest inventories, for theories of career development, and for career counseling, even though the findings do not entirely refute the notion that there is more similarity within occupations than between occupations, because the results did not support the assumption that there are few important differences within occupations. As has been concluded earlier by other investigators such as Dolliver & Nelson (1975), important differences within occupations exist, and the interoccupational similarities may be overemphasized in occupational interest inventory development.

Finally, an article by Gati (1984) focused on the development and testing of a theoretical model designed to compare the hierarchical and hexagonal models of occupational classification as hypothesized structures for understanding occupational interests. Based on Gati's interpretation of his results, the hierarchical model has an advantage over the circular model (such as the hexagonal model of Holland).

In summary, recent work in understanding how career interests operate has continued to emphasize the long-standing trends and to refine and consolidate earlier directions.

SEX ROLES

Several overarching publications regarding sex role issues have been published. The most ambitious of these is by Astin (1985), who proposed a sociopsychological model of career choice and work behavior. The model proposes personal characteristics and social forces as the two major forces that shape behavior in general and work behavior in particular. Astin describes work behavior as motivated largely to satisfy the three basic needs of survival, pleasure, and contribution. She assumes that career choices thus reflect expectations of both the access to various work opportunities and the perception of the relative need satisfaction capacity of work of various kinds. Expectations that lead to these career choices are seen to be shaped through early socialization, but they can be modified by opportunity structure changes. When this happens, changes in career choice and behavior in work also change. The theory goes into considerable detail in describing the sex role socialization process that occurs in a variety of contexts and the variables that affect the opportunity structures available to women and presumably also to men.

As is often unfortunately the case, the model does not lead directly to empirical tests since it is very descriptive in nature. Criticisms have been posed by reactors to the theory such as Harmon (1984), who suggests that the model does not lead investigators to define and operationalize the constructs in a way that will result in conclusive findings. Since other models of a similar sort have been posed, it is easy to predict the pitfalls that this model will be likely to experience. Gilbert (1985b) also raises questions about whether the model sufficiently deals with what really happens to women in their career development, particularly in the area of structure and opportunities. Perhaps the harshest criticism is by Fitzgerald & Betz (1985), who do not believe that the Astin model fulfills the criteria ordinarily considered important in evaluating the adequacy of a theory. It remains to be seen whether Astin's model will significantly influence the direction of research on career development and counseling related to women.

Farmer (1985) also proposed a model of career achievement for women as well as for men. Like Astin's, hers is also a multidimensional model that focuses on background, personal variables, and environmental variables with respect to motivational dimensions involving aspirations, mastery, and career commitment. She put her model to the test, examining nearly 2000 high school men and women. Using hierarchical set multiple regressional analyses, she found that the motivational influences of aspiration, mastery, and career commitment are significantly related to the background, personal, and environmental dimensions. Farmer's findings lead her to conclude that the environmental change that is occurring in our society has a powerful effect on career and achievement motivation and that the career models used heretofore to influence career counseling have not taken environmental variables sufficiently into account. In another study, Farmer (1983) found that high school females have higher career aspirations than boys; that boys endorse a life plan reflecting an expectation that they will share parenting and career roles with their spouses; and that more girls than boys endorse statements suggesting that their future careers will be central to their adult roles. However, this finding is not consistent with what really happens and may reflect a lack of realism in high school students.

Another multidimensional model was proposed by Fassinger (1985), who developed a causal model to describe the career choice of women college students. She used a multivariate analysis with latent variables to test the hypothesis that variables such as previous work experience, academic success, the influence of role models, and the perceived encouragement of others have an important effect on work attitude, self attitude, and sex role attitude. Her findings suggest that variables such as ability, achievement orientation, and feminist orientation affect dependent variables involving family and career orientation which in turn affect the career choice variable.

Fitzgerald & Cherpas (1985) examined the relationship between gender and occupation, examining masculine career behavior as an extension of the male sex role. In their study they exposed 122 graduate students, 65 females and 57 males, to stimulus materials related to strongly sex-stereotyped occupations, e.g. physician and nurse. The respondents were exposed to scripts describing a brief segment of a career-counseling interview, one of which showed a client displaying a high degree of scholastic aptitude in which the counselor suggests that medicine is the appropriate choice, while the second version of the tape depicts a client with high academic ability and shows nursing as the favored choice. These tapes were played for respondents in audiotape. The respondents were asked to describe the counselor effectiveness after having listened to this brief audio segment. Subjects were assigned at random to one of four groups depicting a female in each of the two sex-stereotyped counseling sessions and a male in each of the two. Findings indicate that male clients' nontraditional vocational choices were seen as less appropriate than traditional choices, but this was not so for female clients.

Brooks et al (1985) found that a five-week intervention teaching nontraditional career occupations to middle and high school age girls did not significantly change preferences for nontraditional occupations. Post-Kammer & Smith (1985) compared male and female eighth and ninth grade college-bound students on the relationship between self-efficacy interests and the degree to which they would consider ten traditionally male and female occupations. Their findings show that as usual, interests play a very major role in the consideration of male and female traditional occupations in a manner that is related to gender. Sex differences exist in preferences for occupations of dental hygenist, secretary, and social worker, and for drafting and engineering. Differences in self-efficacy for drafting and engineering are higher for males than for females and differences in self-efficacy for dental hygienists, secretaries, and social workers were higher for females than males. It would seem that any influence counselors want to have on consideration of career aspirations related to self-efficacy or related to personal academic aptitude attributes must start earlier than the junior high school years. One study supporting this notion was reported by Waddell (1983), who examined factors that seem to affect the career choices and satisfaction and success of female entrepreneurs. He found that six variables discriminated among three groups of women: female owners, female managers, and female secretaries. Owners scored higher than did secretaries in achieving motivation, locus of control, internality, and sex role "masculinity," though there were no differences between managers on these variables. Of particular interest, however, is the fact that women owners had more parental models, both mothers and fathers, who had engaged in occupational ownership than did either the managers or secretaries. This suggests that very early experience may be significant in determining important career behaviors that are seen later in life.

Finally, Tittle (1983), interested in career interest inventories and ways to make them more useful to women, makes the case that outcome measures related to role types need to be developed in addition to decisions that result. Tittle describes role types in terms of vocational, marital, and parental areas defined in terms of occupation, marriage, and parenting. She believes that these measures added to the traditional measurement procedure should make it possible to increase the relationship between career intervention and outcomes for women.

CONCLUSION

As Borgen pointed out in his 1984 *Annual Review of Psychology* article, the vocational development sector of counseling psychology in general, and the interest measurement part in particular, represent some of the best developed research areas in counseling psychology.

Because of space limitations, some research and theoretical developments have necessarily been omitted from this review. The need to omit some of the work dealing with career development and counseling is itself a testimony to the growth and vigor of the specialty. Promising new directions continue to emerge which have increasing relevance to the discipline of psychology.

Literature Cited

Adler, S., Aranya, N. 1984. A comparison of the work needs, attitudes, and preferences of professional accountants at different career stages. *J. Vocat. Behav.* 25:45–57

Alvi, S. A., Kahn, S. B. 1983. An investigation into the construct validity of Crites' career maturity model. *J. Vocat. Behav.* 22:174–81

American Educational Research Association, American Psychological Association, National Council on Measurement in Education. 1985. *Standards for Educational and Psychological Testing.* Washington, DC: Am. Psychol. Assoc. 100 pp.

Astin, H. S. 1985. The meaning of work in women's lives: A sociopsychological model of career choice and work behavior. *Couns. Psychol.* 12(4):117–26

Berger-Gross, V., Kahn, M. W., Weare, C. R. 1983. The role of anxiety in the career decision-making of liberal arts students. *J. Vocat. Behav.* 22:312–23

Bihm, E. M., Winer, J. L. 1983. The distortion of memory for careers: The influence of thematic organization of occupational information. *J. Vocat. Behav.* 23:356–66

Bolton, B. 1985. Discriminant analysis of Holland's occupational types using the 16 personality factor questionnaire. *J. Vocat. Behav.* 27:210–27

Borgen, F. H. 1984. Counseling psychology. *Ann. Rev. Psychol.* 35:579–604

Borgen, F. H., Layton, W. L., Veenhuizen, D. L., Johnson, D. J. 1985. Vocational behavior and career development, 1984: A review. *J. Vocat. Behav.* 27:218–69

Brooks, L., Holahan, W., Galligan, J. 1985. The effects of a nontraditional role-modeling intervention on sex-typing of occupational preferences in career salience in adolescent females. *J. Vocat. Behav.* 26:264–76

Brown, D., Brooks, L. 1984. *Career Choice and Development: Applying Contemporary Theories to Practice.* San Francisco: Jossey-Bass. 524 pp.

Brown, S. D., Lent, R. W., eds. 1984. *Handbook of Counseling Psychology.* New York: Wiley. 982 pp.

Cairo, P. C. 1983. Counseling in industry: A selected review of literature. *Personnel Psychol.* 36:1–18

Cesari, J. P., Winer, J. L., Piper, K. R. 1984. Vocational decision status and the effect of four types of occupational information on cognitive complexity. *J. Vocat. Behav.* 25:215–24

Chickering, A. W. 1969. *Education and Identity.* San Francisco: Jossey-Bass. 367 pp.

Crook, R. H., Healy, C. C., O'Shay, D. W. 1984. The linkage of work achievement to self-esteem, career maturity, and college achievement. *J. Vocat. Behav.* 25:70–79

Davis, R., Lofquist, L. 1984. *A Psychological Theory of Work Adjustment.* Minneapolis: Univ. Minn. 245 pp.

Dobson, C., Morrow, P. C. 1984. Effects of career orientation on retirement attitudes and retirement planning. *J. Vocat. Behav.* 24:73–83

Dolliver, R. H., Nelson, R. E. 1975. Assumptions regarding vocational counseling. *Vocat. Guid. Q.* 24:12–19

Farmer, H. S. 1983. Career and homemaking plans for high school youth. *J. Couns. Psychol.* 30:40–45

Farmer, H. S. 1985. Model of career and achievement motivation for women and men. *J. Couns. Psychol.* 32:363–90

Fassinger, R. E. 1985. A causal model of college women's career choice. *J. Vocat. Behav.* 27:123–53

Fitzgerald, L. F., Betz, N. E. 1985. Astin's model in theory and practice: A technical and philosophical critique. *Couns. Psychol.* 12(4):135–38

Fitzgerald, L. F., Cherpas, C. C. 1985. On the reciprocal relationship between gender and occupation: Rethinking the assumptions concerning masculine career development. *J. Vocat. Behav.* 27:109–22

Fretz, B. 1981. Evaluating the effectiveness of career interventions. *J. Couns. Psychol.* 28:77–90

Gati, I. 1984. On the perceived structure of occupations. *J. Vocat. Behav.* 25:1–29

Gilbert, L. A. 1985a. *Men in Dual Career Families.* Hillsdale, NJ: Erlbaum. 185 pp.

Gilbert, L. A. 1985b. Comments on the meaning of work in women's lives. *Couns. Psychol.* 12(4):129–30

Gordon, V. N. 1984. *The Undecided College Student.* Springfield, IL: Thomas. 125 pp.

Gottfredson, L. S. 1981. Circumscription and compromise: A developmental theory of occupational aspirations. *J. Couns. Psychol.* 28:545–79

Gottfredson, L. S. 1983. Creating and criticizing theory. *J. Vocat. Behav.* 23:203–12

Hafner, J. L., Fakouri, M. E. 1984. Early recollections of individuals preparing for careers in clinical psychology, dentistry, and law. *J. Vocat. Behav.* 23:236–41

Hanson, J. C., Campbell, D. P. 1985. *Manual for the SVIB-SCII.* Stanford, CA: Stanford Univ. Press. 178 pp. 4th ed.

Harmon, L. W. 1984. What's new? A response to Astin. *Couns. Psychol.* 12(4):127–28

Harpaz, I. 1983. Asymmetry of cognitive functioning as a possible predictor for vocational counseling and personnel classification. *J. Vocat. Behav.* 23:305–17

Hartman, B. W., Fuqua, D. R., Blum, C. R., Hartman, P. T. 1985. A study of the predictability of the Career Decision Scale in identifying longitudinal patterns of career indecision. *J. Vocat. Behav.* 27:202–9

Heider, F. 1958. *The Psychology of Interpersonal Relations.* New York: Wiley. 322 pp.

Holland, J. L. 1985a. *Making Vocational Choices.* Englewood Cliffs, NJ: Prentice-Hall. 211 pp. 2nd ed.

Holland, J. L. 1985b. *The Self-Directed Search, Professional Manual.* Odessa, FL: Psychol. Assess. Resourc. 96 pp.

Holland, J. L., Magoon, T., Spokane, A. R. 1981. Counseling psychology: Career intervention and related research and theory. *Ann. Rev. Psychol.* 32:279–305

Iachan, R. 1984. A measure of agreement for use with the Holland classification system. *J. Vocat. Behav.* 24:133–41

Kahn, S. B., Alvi, S. A. 1983. Educational, social, and psychological correlates of vocational maturity. *J. Vocat. Behav.* 22:357–64

Kidd, J. M. 1984. The relationship of self and occupational concepts to the occupational preferences of adolescents. *J. Vocat. Behav.* 24:48–65

Laing, J., Swaney, K., Prediger, D. J. 1984. Integrating vocational interest inventory results and expressed choices. *J. Vocat. Behav.* 25:304–15

Leonard, R. L., Walsh, W. B., Osipow, S. H. 1973. Self-esteem, self-consistency, and second vocational choice. *J. Couns. Psychol.* 20:91–93

Manuele, C. A. 1983. Development of a measure to assess vocational maturity in adults with delayed career development. *J. Vocat. Behav.* 23:45–63

Manuso, J. S. J. 1983. *Occupational Clinical Psychology.* New York: Praeger. 336 pp.

Markham, S. 1983. I can be a bum: Knowledge about abilities and life style in behavior. *J. Vocat. Behav.* 23:72–86

Mitchell, J. V. 1985. *Mental Measurements Yearbook*, Vols. 1, 2. Lincoln: Univ. Nebraska Press. 713 pp.; 1288 pp. 2nd ed.

Mossholder, K. W., Bedeian, A. G., Touliatos, J., Barkman, A. I. 1985. An examination of intra-occupational differences: Personality, perceived work climate, and occupation preferences. *J. Vocat. Behav.* 26:164–76

Neimeyer, G. J., Nevill, D. D., Probert, B., Fukuyama, M. 1985. Cognitive structures in vocational development. *J. Vocat. Behav.* 27:191–201

Noeth, R. J. 1983. The effects of enhancing expressed vocational choice with career development measures to predict occupational field. *J. Vocat. Behav.* 22:365–75

Oliver, L. W. 1979. Outcome measures in career counseling research. *J. Couns. Psychol.* 25:217–26

Osipow, S. H. 1982. Research in career counseling: An analysis of issues and problems. *Couns. Psychol.* 10(4):27–34

Osipow, S. H. 1983. *Theories of Career Development.* Englewood Cliffs, NJ: Prentice-Hall. 339 pp. 3rd ed.

Osipow, S. H., Doty, R. E., Spokane, A. R. 1985. Occupational stress, strain, and coping across the life span. *J. Vocat. Behav.* 27:98–108

Pallak, M. S., Perloff, R. O., eds. 1986. *Psychology and Work: Productivity, Change, and Employment.* Master Lectures in Psychology. Washington, DC: Am. Psychol. Assoc.

Phillips, S. D., Strohmer, D. C. 1983. Vocationally mature coping strategies and progress in the decision making process: A canonical analysis. *J. Couns. Psychol.* 30:395–402

Pinder, F. A., Fitzgerald, P. W. 1984. The effectiveness of a computerized guidance system in promoting career decision making. *J. Vocat. Behav.* 24:123–31

Post-Kammer, P., Smith, P. L. 1985. Sex differences in career self-efficacy, consideration, and interests of eighth and ninth graders. *J. Couns. Psychol.* 32:551–59

Raymon, J. R., Bernard, C. B., Holland, J. L., Barnett, D. C. 1983. The effects of a career course on undecided college students. *J. Vocat. Behav.* 23:346–55

Remer, P., O'Neill, C. D., Goas, D. C. 1984. Multiple outcome evaluation of a life career development course. *J. Couns. Psychol.* 31:532–40

Rose, R. G. 1984. The use of conditional probabilities in applications of Holland's theory. *J. Vocat. Behav.* 25:284–89

Savickas, M. L., Silling, S. M., Schwartz, S. 1984. Time perspective in vocational maturity and career decision making. *J. Vocat. Behav.* 25:258–69

Schneider, L. J., Overton, T. D. 1983. Holland personality types and academic achievement. *J. Couns. Psychol.* 30:287–89

Slaney, R. B. 1983. Influence of career indecision on treatments exploring the vocational interests of women. *J. Couns. Psychol.* 30:55–63

Slaney, R. B., Brown, M. T. 1983. Effects of race and social economic status on career choice among college men. *J. Vocat. Behav.* 23:257–69

Slocum, J. W. Jr., Cron, W. L. 1985. Job attitudes and performance during three career stages. *J. Vocat. Behav.* 26:126–45

Spokane, A. R. 1985. A review of research on person-environment congruence in Holland's theory of careers. *J. Vocat. Behav.* 26:306–43

Spokane, A. R., Oliver, L. W. 1983. The outcomes of vocational intervention. In *Handbook of Vocational Psychology,* Vol. 1: *Foundations,* ed. W. B. Walsh, S. H. Osipow, pp. 99–136. Hillsdale, NJ: Erlbaum. 369 pp.

Stonewater, J. K., Daniels, M. H. 1983. Psychosocial and cognitive development in a career decision making course. *J. Coll. Student Personnel* 24:403–10

Stumps, S. A., Colarelli, S. M., Hartman, K. 1983. Development of the Career Exploration Survey. *J. Vocat. Behav.* 22:191–226

Super, D. E. 1980. A life-span, life-space approach to career development. *J. Vocat. Behav.* 16:282–98

Super, D. E., Starishevsky, R., Matlin, N., Jordaan, J. P. 1963. *Career Development: Self-Concept Theory.* New York: Coll. Entrance Examination Board Res. Monogr. 4. 95 pp.

Sweetland, R. C., Keyser, D. J. 1983. *Tests.* Kansas City, KS: Test Corp. Am. 890 pp.

Sweetland, R. C., Keyser, D. J. 1984. *Tests: A Supplement.* Kansas City, KS: Test Corp. Am. 426 pp.

Taylor, K. M., Betz, N. E. 1983. Applications of self-efficacy theory to the understanding and treatment of career indecision. *J. Vocat. Behav.* 22:63–81

Taylor, M. S. 1985. The roles of occupational knowledge and vocational self-concept crystalization in students' school-to-work transition. *J. Couns. Psychol.* 32:539–50

Taylor, N. B., Pryor, R. G. L. 1985. Exploring processes of compromise in career decision making. *J. Vocat. Behav.* 27:171–90

Tinsley, H. E. A., Heesacker, M. 1984. Vocational behavior and career development, 1984: A review. *J. Vocat. Behav.* 25:139–90

Tittle, C. K. 1983. Studies of the effects of career interest inventories: Expanding outcome criteria to include women's experiences. *J. Vocat. Behav.* 22:148–58

Trebilco, G. R. 1984. Career education and career maturity. *J. Vocat. Behav.* 25:191–202

Vondracek, F. W., Lerner, R. M., Schulenberg, J. E. 1983. The concept of development in vocational theory and intervention. *J. Vocat. Behav.* 23:179–202

Vondracek, F. W., Lerner, R. M., Schulenberg, J. E. 1986. *Career Development: A Lifespan Developmental Approach.* Hillsdale, NJ: Erlbaum.

Waas, G. A. 1984. Cognitive differentiation as a function of information type and its relation to career choice. *J. Vocat. Behav.* 24:66–72

Waddell, F. T. 1983. Factors affecting choice, satisfaction, and success in the female self-employed. *J. Vocat. Behav.* 23:294–304

Walsh, W. B., Betz, N. E. 1985. *Tests and Assessment.* Englewood Cliffs, NJ: Prentice-Hall. 427 pp.

Walsh, W. B., Hildebrand, J. O., Ward, C. M., Matthews, D. F. 1983. Holland's theory and non-college degreed working black and white women. *J. Vocat. Behav.* 22:182–90

Walsh, W. B., Osipow, S. H., eds. 1983. *Handbook of Vocational Psychology,* Vols. 1, 2. Hillsdale, NJ: Erlbaum. 369 pp.; 271 pp. 2nd ed.

Walsh, W. B., Osipow, S. H. 1986. *Advances in Vocational Psychology, Vol. 1: The Assessment of Interests.* Hillsdale, NJ: Erlbaum.

Watkins, C. E. Jr. 1984. The individual psychology of Alfred Adler: Toward an Adlerian vocational theory. *J. Vocat. Behav.* 24:28–47

Wiggins, J. D., Lederer, D. A., Salkowe, A., Rys, G. S. 1983. Job satisfaction related to tested congruence and differentiation. *J. Vocat. Behav.* 23:112–21

Wigington, J. H. 1983. The applicability of Holland's typology to clients. *J. Vocat. Behav.* 23:286–93

Zytowski, D. G. 1985. *Kuder Occupational Interest Survey Form DD Manual Supplement.* Chicago: Sci. Res. Assoc. 13 pp.

Zytowski, D. G., Hay, R. 1984. Do birds of a feather flock together? A test of the similarities within and the differences between five occupations. *J. Vocat. Behav.* 24:242–48

Ann. Rev. Psychol. 1987. 38:279–98

CONTRIBUTIONS OF WOMEN TO PSYCHOLOGY

Nancy Felipe Russo

Department of Psychology, Arizona State University, Tempe, Arizona 85287

Florence L. Denmark

Hunter College and The Graduate Center, City University of New York, New York, New York 10021

CONTENTS

Until recently, the history of psychology has been virtually equivalent to the history of male psychology. The contributions of women psychologists have been largely unrecognized, undervalued, and invisible in historical accounts. New generations of psychologists have been denied the opportunity to acquire a full picture of their intellectual roots. By understanding how the view of psychology's history has been distorted, we can develop a new, broader vision of what psychology has been, is, and can be.

In a 1976 review of biographies and autobiographies of persons contributing to psychology, only 9 out of 255 books identified (3.5%) dealt with the lives of women (Benjamin & Heider 1976). In an expanded listing of 700

279

0066-4308/87/0201-0279$02.00

short biographical and autobiographical references, only 33 references to female psychologists were uncovered (Benjamin 1974). In 1980, an extensive search of the literature identified approximately 100 sources of biographical and autobiographical material on female contributors to the discipline (Benjamin 1980). The number of women mentioned in recently published texts in the history of psychology remains small (Goodman 1983).

In response to the historical neglect of women's roles and contributions, a subfield of "women's history in psychology" has begun to evolve—a subfield that in many respects mirrors the development of the field of women's history in general (cf Lerner 1979, 1981). The first step—compensating for the omission of women in historical accounts—is well under way. Women neglected in psychology's history books have begun to be identified, and their contributions are beginning to receive long overdue recognition.

Women's history in psychology has gone beyond the level of identifying "missing women," and has begun to preserve history as defined and interpreted by women in psychology. The impact of the social context and societal institutions on the evolution of psychology and the contributions of women psychologists has begun to be analyzed, and the contributions of psychologists who have challenged sex bias in psychological research and theory have begun to receive attention. Psychology's institutions are changing as a result of these contributions.

In this chapter we summarize the literature of women's contributions to psychology, provide an overview of women's participation and status in the discipline, and focus on some major female contributors. We also discuss how the social context has affected the contributions of women psychologists and examine the current status and prospects of contemporary women in the field.

WOMEN'S PARTICIPATION IN PSYCHOLOGY

An overview of studies of women's participation in psychology provides a picture of inequities in education and training, career development, employment, compensation, achievements, and professional recognition (Over 1983). Nonetheless, women have been involved in psychology from the field's beginnings, have made critical contributions to the discipline, and have risen to positions of unquestioned leadership and distinction.

Some of the work on women's participation in and contributions to psychology has focused on countries outside of the U.S. (cf Canziani 1975, Gold Fein 1973, Harper et al 1985), particularly in the countries of Australia, Canada, Great Britain, and New Zealand (Over 1983). Most of the literature, however, deals with psychology and psychologists in the U.S., a partial reflection of where the majority of psychologists, male and female, have trained and/or spent a considerable proportion of their careers.

At least 20 women obtained U.S. doctorates in psychology prior to 1901 (Eells 1957). Of the 186 individuals identified as psychologists in the first edition of the misnamed *American Men of Science* (Cattell 1906), 22 (12%) were women. Not included in that volume were five women who held membership in the newly formed American Psychological Association (APA) (Furumoto & Scarborough 1986).

Despite widespread barriers to education and employment, the numbers of women in psychology have steadily climbed. In 1920, 62 women in America held PhDs in psychology (Rossiter 1974). From 1920–1974, as psychology grew, so did the numbers of women in the field. Of the 32,855 American doctorates awarded in psychology during this period, 7464 went to women.

Women were pursuing degrees in psychology in Europe as well. For example, Bluma Zeigarnik, whose dissertation reported the "Zeigarnik effect," received her PhD from the University of Berlin in 1927. Maria Rickers-Ovsiankina and Tamara Dembo, two of the women who later became associated with Kurt Lewin, earned their degrees from the University of Giessen in 1928 and from the University of Berlin in 1930, respectively. Marie Jahoda was awarded her degree from the University of Vienna in 1932 (Stevens & Gardner 1982a).

At the end of the nineteenth century, women could be found in all subfields of psychology (Furumoto & Scarborough 1986). Over time, however, they became concentrated in applied subfields that reflected societal stereotypes of the "women's sphere." Women's history in psychology has identified some of the complex forces that created and maintained sex segregation in American psychology. Historical opportunities for women's employment in women's colleges, state colleges, schools, and guidance clinics are important factors. In the United States, the progressive education and child welfare movements at the turn of the century interacted with stereotypes about women at that time, creating employment settings hospitable to women. In addition, concern about the quality of draftees in World War I stimulated interest in child development and mental testing (Russo 1983).

From 1920 to 1974, 48% of U.S. PhDs in developmental and gerontological psychology and 32% of PhDs in school psychology went to women. In contrast, 6% of PhDs in industrial, 14% in psychometrics, 15% in comparative, 18% in experimental, 20% in physiological, and 23% in social psychology went to women. During this same period, the proportions of women in the field of clinical, counseling and guidance, and general psychology were similar: 24%. For educational psychology the figure was 25%. The year 1974 is used as an end point to include graduates who began their doctoral training in 1970. This assumes a four-year period for graduate study (Russo 1984).

During the 1970s, along with the changes in American society that evolved with the growth of the women's movement, dramatic changes occurred in psychology's enrollment picture. In 1974, women were 31% of the 2598 U.S. doctoral recipients in psychology. In 1983, ten years later, that figure was nearly 48%. In 1985–86, women were 56% of the 17,562 full-time doctoral students in U.S. departments of psychology: 12% of these 9854 women were identified as members of minority groups (Pion et al 1985).

Sex segregation in psychology's subfields has been reduced. Increases in the proportion of women enrolled in doctoral programs are found in both research and practice specialties, although the proportions of women students are still slightly higher in the applied fields: 58% of full-time doctoral enrollments in clinical, counseling, and school psychology are female, compared to 55% of such enrollments in research specialties. Although an increasing number of developmental psychologists work in applied settings, developmental psychology is still a research specialty. That field continues to have the highest proportion of women receiving doctorates—75% in 1983 (Russo 1984).

Although the numbers are small, the largest *rate* of increase over the decade 1973–1983 is found in the male-dominated field of industrial/organizational (I/O) psychology. In 1973, 6 women comprised 8% of the doctorates awarded in I/O psychology. In 1984, 40 women comprised 38% of the doctorates awarded in that field (CEHR 1985).

While the proportions of women in all subfields of psychology have increased, the concentration of women psychologists in traditionally "female" fields has also increased, partially because these fields were also expanding during the 1970s. However, men are entering these expanding fields as well. In 1973, 46% of psychology doctorates granted to men were in the fields of clinical, counseling, school, or developmental psychology, compared to 53% of doctorates granted to women (National Science Foundation 1983)—a ratio of .87. In 1983 the figures were 57% vs 62% (National Research Council 1983)—a ratio of .92. The more rapid increase of men compared to women over this period is bringing a more equal balance of numbers of women and men in these fields. (Note that NSF figures only consider research doctorates and do not include Doctors of Education or Doctors of Psychology).

While the educational barriers in graduate school have lessened, the legacy of sex discrimination in academic employment has been more difficult to overcome, even with expanding opportunities in the decade of the 1970s. In 1944, 26% of psychologists employed in departments of psychology were women (Bryan & Boring 1946). In 1984, 25% of psychologists employed in U.S. departments of psychology (full- and part-time) were women. Higher proportions of women were still found in part-time positions (41%) compared to full-time positions (22%). Considering only doctoral departments, 21% of the full-time faculty and 39% of the part-time faculty were female (Pion et al 1985). Women are concentrated in lower ranks, and salary differentials favoring men persist, even when years of experience are controlled (Russo et al 1981).

The membership of the American Psychological Association is divided into divisions that can be considered professional networks for psychology's subfields. Membership in these networks continues to be largely male dominated. In 1985, only one of APA's 42 divisions had a membership that was less than 50% male (Division 35, the Psychology of Women, had a membership that was 5.3% male). Thirteen divisions had a membership that was more than 80% male, including Experimental (84.8%), Physiological and Comparative (84.6%), I/O (84.8%), Military (90.5%), and Applied Experimental and Engineering (91.8%). The divisions with between 50–60% male membership were: Developmental Psychology (54.2%), Counseling Psychology (57%), Child, Youth, and Family Services (59.4%), Psychoanalysis (57.1%), and the Society for the Psychological Study of Gay and Lesbian Issues (50.9%) (APA 1985). The first three of these clearly fall into areas that can be considered traditionally female.

Minority Women

Unfortunately, historical information about minority women in psychology continues to be scarce. It was not until 1933, 71 years after the first blacks received college degrees (Mary Jane Patterson and John Brown Russworm, Oberlin; Edward Jones, Amherst), that a black woman, Inez Prosser, received an EdD in educational psychology from the University of Cincinnati (Guthrie 1976). Guthrie (1976) has described the context of the time and how the need for teachers, preachers, and trade workers profoundly affected the development of curricula in the black colleges. Psychology in these schools was limited to its applied aspects and associated with departments of education. As late as 1940 an undergraduate major in the field was only offered in four black colleges. Thirty-two doctorates in psychology (PhD) and education (EdD) went to blacks in the years between 1920–1950, eight of them earned by black women.

The participation of Hispanic, Asian, and Native American women in psychology has received even less attention than that of blacks. Statistical reports rarely present breakdowns by race/ethnicity and sex so that monitoring the changing status of women in the various ethnic minority groups is difficult. In 1984, the National Science Foundation reported that of the total population of approximately 11,900 employed female psychologists holding research doctorates in 1982, 400 (3.4%) were black, 200 (1.7%) were Asian, and 100 (.8%) were Native American. Similarly, 100 (.8%) were Hispanic. Since the National Science Foundation rounds its figures to the nearest 100, these figures are only approximations (National Science Foundation 1984).

WOMEN IN PSYCHOLOGY: SOME MAJOR CONTRIBUTORS

A critical element for studying the history of women in psychology is to identify the contributions of women psychologists that have been historically neglected. Considerable work has been expended toward that end (Bernstein & Russo 1974, Benjamin 1980, Denmark 1980, 1983, Furumoto & Scarborough 1986, Gavin 1983, Gold Fein 1973, 1985, Kimmel 1976, O'Connell & Russo 1980, 1983, Over 1983, Sexton 1969, Stevens & Gardner 1982a,b). Women contributors to psychology are also identified by historians interested in women's history in general (Crovitz & Buford 1978, James et al 1971, Sicherman & Green 1980, Tinker 1983) and women's history in science in particular (Rossiter 1982).

The work has varied in quality and depth, some authors relying on second- and third-hand sources whose accuracy may be suspect (Ross 1985). As a body of literature, however, it irrefutably documents the extensive involvement and invaluable contributions of female psychologists. The autobiographies of the female pioneers, told in their own words, matter-of-factly, with surprisingly little bitterness or recrimination, provide a human complement to the participation statistics. It is impossible in the brief space alloted here to describe or even mention all of the women identified in these publications. Only a few major contributors can be highlighted.

As early as 1903, three women—Mary Whiton Calkins, Christine Ladd-Franklin, and Margaret Floy Washburn—were cited among the 50 most famous U.S. psychologists by James McKeen Cattell, founder of *American Men of Science* (Sexton 1969). In the fifth edition of that volume, 22% of the 539 psychologists recognized were women. Looking at the first seven editions of that work, of the 127 names starred for distinction, eight (6.3%) were women: Mary Whiton Calkins, Christine Ladd-Franklin, Margaret Floy Washburn, Ethel Puffer Howes, Lillien Jane Martin, Helen Thompson Woolley, June Etta Downey, and Florence Goodenough (Bryan & Boring 1944).

These early women exhibited a variety of interests. Mary Whiton Calkins, who founded the psychological laboratory at Wellesley College in 1891 and invented the paired associate technique, created a theoretical system of self psychology that brought her recognition in both psychology and philosophy (Furumoto 1980). Christine Ladd-Franklin developed a widely influential theory of color vision besides making contributions to logic that resulted in her being compared to Aristotle (Stevens & Gardner 1982a). Margaret Floy Washburn became the first woman to earn a PhD in psychology. Her landmark work, *The Animal Mind,* was a precursor and impetus to behaviorism (Goodman 1980). Ethel Puffer Howes focused on esthetics and published her book, *The Psychology of Beauty,* in 1905 (Furumoto & Scarborough 1986).

Lillien Jane Martin, a major contributor to work in psychophysics, esthetics, and imagery, was the first woman to become a department head at Stanford University. After retiring from that post in 1916, she founded the first mental hygiene clinic for "normal" preschoolers. In 1929, at age 78, she started the Old Age Center, the first counseling center for senior citizens (Stevens & Gardner 1982a). Helen Thompson Woolley was a leader in rebutting myths about women's alleged inferiority in mental abilities. A major figure in child development, she, along with Helen Cleveland, developed the Merrill-Palmer Scales which became a widely used tool for testing the mental abilities of children (Rosenberg 1982).

June Etta Downey, a pioneer in the study of traits and developer of the Downey Will-Temperament Test, in 1915 became the first woman to head a department of psychology in a state university, the University of Wyoming (Stevens & Gardner 1982a). Florence Goodenough developed the Draw-a-Man Test. She was also an innovator in the development of observational methods of child development and designed a method of episode-sampling used in research on children's social behavior (Sicherman & Green 1980). Her work, *Anger in Young Children,* continues to be cited frequently in developmental textbooks (Thompson 1983).

Thus, although concentrated in applied fields, women nonetheless have been major contributors to basic research in psychology. Some of these achievements have received recognition. Table 1 contains the names of women receiving awards given by the American Psychological Association and the American Psychological Foundation, along with the reference to the biographical descriptions that accompanied the award announcements appearing in the *American Psychologist.*

As seen in Table 1, from 1956–1985 the American Psychological Association has presented Distinguished Scientific Contribution Awards to five women. In 1966, Nancy Bayley, who pioneered in studies of the measurement and meaning of intelligence, and whose longitudinal studies of infant development evolved into landmark studies of aging, became the first woman to receive this prestigious award. Eleanor J. Gibson, the second woman to receive the award [1968], made major contributions to the understanding of perceptual learning and development and experimental research on reading. Dorothea Jameson [1972, shared with Leo Hurvich], advanced scientific knowledge in the area of color vision. Brenda Milner [1973] contributed to understanding of relationships of brain structure to functioning, particularly with regard to localization of speech, pattern perception, and memory. Beatrice C. Lacey (shared with John I. Lacey) made outstanding contributions to understanding the relationship between the autonomic nervous system and behavior.

Using an international panel of psychologists, Watson (1974) developed a

Table 1 Women receiving awards from the American Psychological Association and American Psychological Foundation by award area, to 1985

Year of award	Name of winner	Reference to award citation in *American Psychologist*	
	AMERICAN PSYCHOLOGICAL ASSOCIATION		
Distinguished Scientific Contributions			
1976	Beatrice C. Lacey (with John Lacey)	32 (1) Jan. 11, 1977	54–61
1973	Brenda Milner	29 (1) Jan. 19, 1974	36–38
1972	Dorothea Jameson (with Leo Hurvich)	28 (1) Jan. 19, 1973	55–74
1968	Eleanor J. Gibson	23 (12) Dec. 19, 1968	857–867
1966	Nancy Bayley	21 (12) Dec. 19, 1966	1190–1200
Distinguished Applications in Psychology			
1981	Anne Anastasi	37 (1) Jan. 1982	52–29
Distinguished Professional Contributions			
1982	Carolyn R. Payton	38 (1) Jan. 1983	32–33
1981	Jane W. Kessler	37 (1) Jan. 1982	65
Distinguished Contributions to Psychology in the Public Interest			
1979	Marie Jahoda	35 (1) Jan. 1980	74–81
Distinguished Scientific Awards for an Early Career Contribution to Psychology			
1984	Marta Kutas	40 (3) Mar. 1985	309–312
1983	Carol L. Krumhansl	39 (3) Mar. 1984	284–286
1982	Martha McClintock	38 (1) Jan. 1983	57–60
1981	Lyn Abramson	37 (1) Jan. 1982	79–83
1980	Lynn Cooper	36 (1) Jan. 1981	78–81
	Shelley Taylor	''	81–84
	Camille Wortman	''	84–87
1977	Judith Rodin	33 (1) Jan. 1978	75–83
1976	Sandra Bem	32 (1) Jan. 1977	88–97
	Rochel S. Gelman	''	
	AMERICAN PSYCHOLOGICAL FOUNDATION		
Gold Medal Award			
1984	Anne Anastasi	40 (3) Mar. 1985	340–341
1982	Nancy Bayley	38 (1) Jan. 1983	61–63
1980	Pauline Snedden Sears (with Robert Sears)	36 (1) Jan. 1981	88–91
Distinguished Teaching in Psychology			
1982	Carolyn Wood Sheriff	38 (1) Jan. 1983	64–65
1975	Bernice L. Neugarten	31 (1) Jan. 1976	83–86
1970	Freda Rebelsky	26 (1) Jan. 1971	91–95

listing of persons living between 1600 and 1967 who were recognized as eminent contributors to psychology. Of the 538 contributors, 228 were identified as psychologists while the others reflected psychology's links to other sciences, philosophy, and medicine.

Eight of the psychologists identified were women: Augusta Bronner, Mary Whiton Calkins, June Etta Downey, Else Frenkel-Brunswick, Florence Goodenough, Leta Stetter Hollingworth, Christine Ladd-Franklin, and Margaret Floy Washburn. There were also three psychoanalysts (Frieda Fromm-Reichmann, Karen Horney, Melanie Klein), one anthropologist (Ruth Benedict), the first Italian woman to earn an M.D. (Maria Montessori), and one layperson (Dorothea Dix) (Russo & O'Connell 1980).

Prior to 1970, only one woman who can be "claimed" as a contributor to psychology was elected to membership in the National Academy of Sciences: Margaret Floy Washburn [1931]. Since 1970, psychologists Eleanor J. Gibson [1971] and Dorothea Jameson [1975] have joined the membership of that prestigious body. Women in related fields who have contributed to the psychological literature include anthropologists Frederica DeLaguna and Margaret Mead [1975] and Elizabeth Colson [1977], and linguist Mary K. Haas [1978].

Two women, Mary Whiton Calkins [1905] and Margaret Floy Washburn [1921], served as President of APA between 1892 and 1970. Since that time, five women have achieved the distinction of that office: Anne Anastasi [1972], Leona Tyler [1973], Florence L. Denmark [1980], Janet Taylor Spence [1984], and Bonnie R. Strickland [1987].

In 1984, 22.9% of the individuals elected to Fellow status in the American Psychological Association were women, up from 8.0% of those elected in 1970. It will take time for such increases to change the overall statistics. Thus in 1985, women were 33.8% of the membership of the American Psychological Association, but only 16.3% of APA members holding Fellow status (APA 1985).

Although women have been underrepresented in I/O psychology, they have been involved in the field from its inception and have made significant contributions both in Europe and the U.S. For example, Franziska Baumgarten-Tramer, who received her PhD from the University of Berlin in 1917, was one of the first industrial psychologists, and made major contributions to the understanding of job satisfaction and personnel selection. In the U.S., Lillian Moller Gilbreth, who received her PhD in Industrial Psychology from Brown University in 1915, became an internationally recognized efficiency expert for time and motion studies. She also made pioneering contributions to kitchen design, including the foot-pedal trash can and storage shelves on refrigerator doors. As a consultant to the Institute of Rehabilitation Medicine at New York University Medical Center, she designed a kitchen to serve the needs of handicapped persons that became an internationally known training center (Sicherman & Green 1980). On February 24, 1985, she became the first psychologist to be featured on a U.S. postage stamp.

Minority Women

The emphasis on women's history in psychology came in time to preserve the autobiographies of some of the minority women who were pioneers in the discipline, including Ruth Howard (Beckham), the first black woman to receive a PhD in psychology (Howard 1983), and Mamie Phipps Clark, whose coauthored research (with her husband Kenneth Clark) cited in *Brown v. the Board of Education,* was instrumental in the United State's Supreme Court ruling to desegregate the Nation's schools (Clark 1983). Such stories offer sources of information as well as inspiration to future generations of psychologists.

The contributions of Hispanic, Asian, and Native American women to psychology have yet to receive adequate attention. However, the autobiography of Martha Bernal (1984), the first Chicana to earn a PhD in psychology, who went on to become a highly cited contributor to the behavior therapy and parenting literatures, has been recorded.

THE SOCIETAL CONTEXT: ITS IMPACT ON WOMEN'S CONTRIBUTIONS

Women's history in psychology has begun to analyze the relationship of the societal context to women psychologists' careers and contributions (Lewin 1984, Rossiter 1982, Rosenberg 1982, Russo & O'Connell 1980, Russo 1983, Shields 1975a,b).

Psychology in the United States began its growth at the end of the 19th century, at a time of great economic and social change in America. It was a time when belief in women's innate moral superiority had become a truism of American life, and women were called upon to use their "superior" qualities to reform society (Hymowitz & Weissman 1978). Attending to the needs of the "young, helpless and distressed" (Terman & Miles 1936) was considered an extension of "true womanhood" (Welter 1966), a reflection of women's "biological destiny."

It was also a time in America when women demanded equal political rights and better conditions of employment. These goals became justified as a means to enable women to reform society. Women's rights were particularly linked with child welfare (Sears 1975). Motherhood was reified, and the "mother's heart" was even used to justify women's fight for suffrage (Ehenreich & English 1978).

The aspirations and interests of women in psychology were shaped and limited by the societal context. Psychology itself was used to justify the exclusion of women from higher education—helping to perpetuate the belief that developing one's intellectual capabilities was incompatible with the female qualities needed to fulfill the obligations of the "women's sphere" and attain "true womanhood" (Lewin 1984, Rosenberg 1982, Welter 1966). Thus, in order to gain the education needed to become a psychologist, women had to face myths perpetuated by psychology itself.

Past luminaries of psychology such as G. Stanley Hall, the founder of the American Psychological Association, proclaimed that the educated woman who selfishly aspired to work rather than to marriage violated her biological ethic—to the detriment of her mammary function, among other evils (Ehrenreich & English 1978). Stephanie Shields (1975a) has developed a classic summary of the stereotypes and prejudices pervading psychology at the turn of the century that should be required reading for all persons who aspire to work in the discipline.

Hall warned that coeducation in adolescence would disrupt the "normalization" of the menstrual period, and that educating women to compete with men "in the world" would cause "race suicide" as maternal urges would become neglected (Shields 1975a,b). The warnings of Hall and other "experts" against the dangers of education for women were not without effect. For example, Martha Carey Thomas, President of Bryn Mawr College, reported that as a young woman, after reading Hall's pronouncements on the female sex, that she had been "terror struck lest she and every other woman . . . were doomed to live as pathological invalids . . . as a result of their education" (Ehrenreich & English 1978, p. 117).

The first women in psychology had to face barriers justified by these stereotypes, and many used their professional knowledge and skills to refute them. The first psychologist (male or female) to receive a PhD from the University of Chicago was Helen Thompson (Woolley), who obtained it in 1903 through the department of philosophy (Heidbreder 1933). Helen Thompson Woolley deserves special mention here because she was the first of these early "greats" of psychology to successfully integrate her interest in science with her commitment to social reform and use her scientific skill to rebut myths about sex differences (Rosenberg 1982).

Influenced by the work of Woolley, Leta Stetter Hollingworth also stands out as a role model *par excellence* for individuals who wish to combine a commitment to scientific excellence with work in the public interest. Leta Hollingworth, who received her PhD in education from Columbia in 1916, came to eminence in psychology primarily because of her contributions to child psychology and education, particularly for her innovative work on exceptional children. She was the first to use the term "gifted," and her book on adolescence became a classic (Benjamin 1975). However, it was her pioneering work on the psychology of women that gives her a special place in any discussion of women's history in psychology.

Leta Hollingworth demanded that psychology apply scientific rigor in research on women. She proceeded to refute the myths of the time through empirical research on mental and physical performance during the menstrual cycle, on the variability hypothesis (which erroneously explained men's higher status due to greater male variability), and women's sex roles (Shields 1975b).

Since psychology has been an academic enterprise (Rossiter 1974), the status of women in academia has affected women's ability to fulfill their scientific potential in psychology. It took independence and a strong will to overcome the social, educational, and employment barriers facing women. By 1900, less than one-fifth of all educational degrees, and only 6% of the doctorates (or equivalent) went to women (Mandel 1981). Even the most talented women were not exempt from the institutional discrimination of our educational systems. Mary Whiton Calkins was denied a degree for her work at Harvard (Furumoto 1980). The fact that the distinguished William James judged her his brightest student was not persuasive to the Harvard trustees (Sexton 1973/1974). Margaret Floy Washburn left Columbia University for Cornell because there were no fellowships even for the brightest women. Cornell was unusual because it both admitted women and considered them eligible for fellowships (Furumoto & Scarborough 1986).

Once women psychologists overcame educational hurdles and obtained their degrees, they faced barriers to employment in the major universities. Employment was to be found in women's colleges and normal schools, where women could pursue interests that spanned all areas of psychology (Furumoto & Scarborough 1986).

Antinepotism rules were particularly hard on the large number of married couples in psychology. Again, even the most distinguished women were not exempt. For example, National Academy of Sciences member Eleanor Gibson and her psychologist husband James J. Gibson were both able to participate fully in Koffka's faculty at Smith; but when Koffka died and they moved to Cornell in 1949, Eleanor Gibson found that she was no longer allowed to teach (Gibson 1966).

In 1976, a study by the American Association of University Women found that one out of every four institutions still had antinepotism policies. Such policies were more likely to be found in large coeducational and public institutions where larger numbers of psychologists were likely to be employed (Howard 1978).

The Emergence of Sex Segregation in Psychology

With the turn of the century came a change in attitudes toward children and a "professional approach to child care." Never before had children's welfare played such a significant role in the nation's political agenda. The role of "mother" became viewed as "a scientific vocation that required intelligence and training" (Filene 1975). This view of motherhood provided a "legitimate" sphere for women in the world of work and a rationale for their higher education.

Society's interest in child welfare stimulated psychological research on child development, mental retardation, and mental testing. The use of mental tests exploded, and many women became pioneers in the testing movement (Denmark 1980, Russo & O'Connell 1980, Sexton 1969, 1973/1974).

The first psychological clinic, established by Lightner Witmer at the University of Pennsylvania in 1896, was founded "for the study and treatment of children who were mentally or morally retarded and of those who had physical defects that slowed development or progress" (French 1984, p. 976). In 1900, Witmer graduated his first PhD student, Anna Jane McKeag. Of Witmer's first 25 students to receive the PhD, 8 were women (French 1984).

In 1909, the Juvenile Psychopathic Institute, considered to be the first mental health clinic, was established in Chicago by psychiatrist William Healy and psychologists Augusta F. Bronner and Grace Fernald. Child guidance clinics spread in the 1920s, and in 1924, child guidance clinicians founded the American Orthopsychiatric Association. In 1931, Augusta Bronner was elected to its presidency (Reisman 1976). Concern with child welfare also led to an expansion of the juvenile court system, where the work of women psychologists can be seen as precursor to what later emerged as the subfield of law and psychology (Russo & O'Connell 1980).

Thus, during the first three decades of the 20th Century the child guidance and progressive education movements provided a place for women psychologists to apply their talents in a way congruent with society's conceptions of women's interests and abilities. Milton Senn (1975) has provided an excellent account of the child development movement in the United States. Although there are other historical treatments of the field (e.g. Anderson 1956, Sears 1975), his is the only one that gives visibility to women.

In the 1930s, as the child guidance movement declined, interest in psychoanalysis increased. Numerous women were involved in the early psychoanalytic circle that had an impact on the development of clinical and child psychology. Early greats such as Frieda Fromm-Reichmann, Karen Horney, Melanie Klein, and Clara Thompson challenged the givens of the Freudian psychoanalytic scheme that so contributed to the myths held about women at the time (Russo & O'Connell 1980).

Other eminent figures include Susan Isaacs, who was a cofounder of the British Psychoanalytic Society. Studies of children based on psychoanalytic perceptions of Anna Freud, Melanie Klein, and Susan Isaacs are considered to have been particularly important in stimulating child development researchers to go beyond the question of *how* to the question of *why* (Senn 1975). Then there was Charlotte Buhler, who was one of the first to begin to look at age and class variables in her research on children, and who is regarded as the first "humanistic psychologist" (Krippner 1977).

In the 1920s, the Laura Spelman Rockefeller Memorial funded institutes for child study that provided supportive employment settings for women to work in the area of child development in the U.S. We might argue that the institutes contributed to the separation of the worlds of work for men and women, a trend fostered by the rapidly growing "female" science of home economics. At that time, there was some tension between the women who chose to pursue careers in male-dominated "scientific" fields and those who pursued the more "feminine" applied fields of child development and education. Nonetheless, the institutes created a source of employment for women that provided access to stimulating colleagues and research facilities. The list of women associated with them reads like a *Who's Who* of women psychologists (Russo & O'Connell 1980).

During the 1930s the depression had an impact on all psychologists. Employment opportunities were limited and salaries small, but women continued to enter psychology: 1 out of 4 psychology doctorates granted from 1933–1937 went to women. Little has been written about women psychologists in the decade of the 1930s, which included the beginning of the immigration of European Jewish contributors to psychology, such as Therese Benedek, Hedda Bolgar, Else Frenkel-Brunswick, Eugenia Hanfmann, Marie Jahoda, and Margaret Mahler, who came to the U.S. to escape Nazism. In her autobiography, Mary Henle talks about the anti-Semitism in the United States that has affected the careers of Jewish psychologists (Henle 1983).

In 1940, although women comprised 30% of psychologists, they held 51% of psychology positions in schools, educational systems, clinics, guidance centers, hospitals, and custodial institutions (Bryan & Boring 1946). A small 1941 study of employment opportunities for black psychologists found a similar pattern of concentration in women's fields. Eleven out of the 76 black psychologists identified were women. One was unemployed and 3 were in applied fields (school, consulting, and social work). The 7 employed in colleges or normal schools were described as concerned "for the most part with the teaching of Educational Psychology, Child Psychology, and the Psychology of Adolescence, with nursery school supervision and work as Dean of Women" (Brunschwig 1941, p. 676).

World War II contributed to sex segregation in psychology. It created opportunities for men by employing them in the war effort directly and by stimulating the growth of male-oriented subfields, particularly in industrial and personnel psychology. Of 1006 psychologists entering the armed forces, only 33 were women (Marquis 1944b).

The military provided intensive training and research experiences for civilian psychologists as well as enlisted personnel. In 1943, the army established a course in Advanced Personnel Psychology in the Army Specialized Training Program. According to Marquis (1944a), "approximately 1,300 enlisted *men* completed the intensive six-month course at 11 selected universities" (p. 472, italics ours). Psychologists became involved in devising personnel selection and training methods, human factors research, and civilian morale studies. This wartime experience stimulated male-dominated subfields of industrial and personnel psychology and created predominently male social networks among researchers that shaped the postwar development of psychology.

The American Psychological Association (APA) played an active role in organizing psychologists during the war, but its initial efforts reflected the interests of male psychologists. During the 1939 convention, the APA authorized the creation of an Emergency Committee in Psychology, without representation of women psychologists. In response, a New York group of women psychologists organized what became the National Council of Women Psychologists (NCWP) "to promote and develop emergency services that women psychologists could render their communities as larger numbers of their male colleagues were drawn into military services" (Portenier, n.d., p. 15). Florence Goodenough served as its first President, with Helen Peak as Vice President, Gladys C. Schwesinger as Secretary, and Theodora M. Abel as Treasurer.

There have been a number of summaries of the research and service of women psychologists during the war years (Finison & Furumoto 1978, Murphy 1943, Portenier, n.d.). These activities reflected the sex segregation of psychology's subfields and focused on problems of civilian morale, relocation, refugees, children, and families in wartime.

This is not to say that women were not involved in every facet of psychology's wartime effort. Barbara Burks worked with Gordon Allport and Gardner Murphy to help settle refugee psychologists, who included Egon Brunswick and Else Frenkel. In the Office of Strategic Services (OSS), Edward Tolman, Donald MacKinnon, James G. Miller, Urie Bronfenbrenner, Donald Fiske, Eugenia Hanfmann, and Ruth Tolman, among others, assessed secret service candidates for assignment overseas. Rensis Likert headed the Morale Division of the U.S. Strategic Bombing Survey, where such persons as Daniel Katz, Eugene Hartley, Helen Peak, David Krech, and Richard Crutchfield worked on various aspects of civilian morale. In England, Heinz Ansbacher, Jerome Bruner, and Hazel Gaudet worked as part of a survey team (Russo & O'Connell 1980). In her autobiography, Eugenia Hanfmann (1983) communicates the excitement as well as the frustration of working as a psychologist for the OSS when it was necessary to burn all records and notes at the end of the war.

After World War II, the nation prepared for the return of its men. The war had created new and highly desirable positions in business and industry for male psychologists. Given the military's stimulation of training and personnel psychology and the expectation that opportunities in business and industry were open to "men" (Marquis 1944b, p. 661), it is not surprising that I/O psychology remained the subfield of psychology with the highest proportion of men through the decade of the 1970s (Russo 1984).

The needs of male-oriented employment settings shaped the knowledge base of psychology, even in those cases where women psychologists have traditionally participated. There were 16 million veterans of World War II and 4 million veterans of previous wars. The Veterans Administration (VA) cooperated with the United States Public Health Service to create funds for clinical training to serve the predominately male population of patients in need of mental health services. Experience in working with outpatients and women and children was neglected (Reisman 1976). In 1944, women psychologists had a higher *un*employment rate than they had at the beginning of the war (Walsh 1986).

The National Council of Women Psychologists continued after the war, developing a number of projects to promote the careers of women psychologists, including a newsletter that gave recognition to the accomplishments of women in the field and announced job opportunities. They also organized career-oriented sessions at APA's annual meetings and published a 1950 handbook on career issues (Walsh 1986).

These women psychologists were operating at a time when there was little societal support for such activities. After the war, in the hopes of raising the status of women in psychology by becoming affiliated with the American Psychological Association, the NCWP voted to change its name and purpose. In 1947, the International Council of Women Psychologists was born, with Gertrude Hildreth as President, and the purpose of the group was now to "further international understanding by promoting intercultural relations to practical applications of psychology" (Portenier n.d.). When subsequently told that APA would not admit a single sex organization, males were admitted to membership and the group was renamed the International Council of Psychologists (Portenier n.d.). Nonetheless, efforts to affiliate with APA were rejected. They were told it was inappropriate to have an international group affiliate with a national organization (Walsh 1986).

The repressive climate for American women in the 1950s eventually gave way to social reform. In 1961, President John F. Kennedy established the first President's Commission on the Status of Women which called attention to sex bias in education, including vocational and guidance counseling, and identified the need to rebut myths and stereotypes about women (Peterson 1983). Concern about women's rights received an expected boost from the civil rights movement when legal prohibition against sex discrimination in employment was included in the 1965 Civil Rights Act in an attempt to kill that legislation. During this period careers of women in psychology once again began to receive attention and were the subject of workshops organized at APA's annual meetings (Sexton 1973/1974).

The 1970s brought new opportunities for women in all areas of American society, and psychology was no exception. Although recognition of the accomplishments of female psychologists has continued to lag behind their performance, substantial changes began to occur.

In 1970, psychologist Bernice Sandler, who had experienced sex discrimination in her search for an academic position, began to file class-action suits under the aegis of the Women's Equity Action League. Complaints were filed at over 250 colleges and universities and helped lead to the passage of Title IX of the Education Amendments of 1972, which prohibited sex discrimination in educational institutions receiving federal financial assistance. Sandler continued her leadership in the area of sex equity in education, helping to draft the Women's Educational Equity Act of 1972 and heading the Project on the Status and Education of Women of the Association of American Colleges (Millsap 1983).

In the late 1960s, women again organized in psychology, this time in a more supportive climate. In 1969 the Association for Women in Psychology dramatically communicated their concern with inequities in the field at the annual convention of the APA. In response, in October of 1970, APA established a task force charged with preparing a paper on the status of women in psychology, with Helen Astin as Chair (Task Force 1973). When the Task Force was discharged in 1972, an ad hoc Committee on the Status of Women was formed, chaired by Martha Mednick, which became a continuing Committee on Women in Psychology (CWP) under Mednick's leadership in 1973. The mission of the committee was to "function as a catalyst, by means of interacting with and making recommendations to the various parts of the Association's governing structure. . . ." (Russo 1984).

CWP recommended the establishment of the Division of the Psychology of Women (Division 35), which was formed in 1973 "to promote the research and study of women . . . to encourage the integration of this information about women with current psychological knowledge and beliefs in order to apply the gained knowledge to the society and its institutions" (Russo 1984). For a description of the history of the Division and the evolution of the field, see Mednick (1978) and Denmark (1977). In addition to having an impact on increasing women's participation in nearly all areas of APA's complex governance structure (Russo 1984), both Division 35 and CWP have played major roles in encouraging attention to the history of women in psychology (O'Connell et al 1978, O'Connell & Russo 1980, 1983).

CURRENT STATUS AND PROSPECTS

Women's history in psychology has focused attention on how the societal context affects the evolution of psychology and shapes women's contributions to the discipline. This historical perspective can help to build broader understanding of the societal factors that underlie the changing demographic trends in the discipline. From this historical perspective, the increasing proportion of women in psychology reflects an expansion of traditionally female applied fields as much as it does a change in women's career patterns.

The more we study women's history, the more we appreciate the power of society's norms and institutions to affect the development of psychology as well as the career paths of individual psychologists. This knowledge is having an effect on the discipline. Led by women, both women and men are working to eliminate sex bias in psychology and to legitimize the study of women's experiences.

Women psychologists can gain inspiration from the lessons of women's history and recognize that disappointments and setbacks are not necessarily defeat. All psychologists can take pride in the excellence and perseverance of women psychologists revealed by women's history in psychology. We look forward to a synthesis of the new scholarship on women and a reconstruction of psychology's history so that we have an enriched understanding of the works of all psychologists—past, present, and future.

ACKNOWLEDGMENTS

The authors would like to thank Allen Meyer, Bonnie Strickland, and Robert Wesner for their comments on the manuscript, and acknowledge the assistance of Michelle Marquand in assembling materials and tracking down references. This work was supported by the Minigrant Program of the College of Liberal Arts, Arizona State University.

Literature Cited

American Psychological Association. 1985. *Membership Directory*. Washington, DC: Am. Psychol. Assoc.

Anderson, J. E. 1956. Child development: An historical perspective. *Child Dev.* 27:181–96

Benjamin, L. T. Jr. 1974. Prominent psychologists: A selected bibliography of biographical sources. *JSAS Cat. Sel. Doc. Psychol.* 4:1. MS. 535. 33 pp.

Benjamin, L. T. Jr. 1975. The pioneering work of Leta Hollingworth in the psychology of women. *Nebr. Hist.* 56:493–505

Benjamin, L. T. Jr. 1980. Women in psychology: Biography and autobiography. *Psychol. Women Q.* 5:140–44

Benjamin, L. T. Jr., Heider, K. L. 1976.

History of psychology in biography: A bibliography. *JSAS Cat. Sel. Doc. Psychol.* 6:61. MS. 1276. 21 pp.

Bernal, M. 1984. *The life of a Chicana psychologist*. Presented at Ann. Meet. Am. Psychol. Assoc., Anaheim, CA

Bernstein, M., Russo, N. F. 1974. The history of psychology revisited: Or, up with our foremothers. *Am. Psychol.* 29:130–34

Brunschwig, L. 1941. Opportunities for Negroes in the field of psychology. *J. Negro Educ.* 10:664–76

Bryan, A. I., Boring, E. G. 1944. Women in American psychology: Prolegomenon. *Psychol. Bull.* 41:447–54

Bryan, A. I., Boring, E. G. 1946. Women in American psychology: Statistics from the

OPP Questionnaire. *Am. Psychol.* 1:71–79

Canziani, W. 1975. Contributions to the history of psychology: XXIII. I. Franziska Baumgarten-Tramer. *Percept. Mot. Skills* 41:479–86

Cattell, J. M., ed. 1906. *American Men of Science: A Biographical Directory.* New York: Science

Clark, M. 1983. Mamie Phipps Clark. See O'Connell & Russo 1983, pp. 267–78

Committee on Employment and Human Resources. 1985. *The Changing Face of American Psychology.* Washington, DC: Am. Psychol. Assoc.

Crovitz, E., Buford, E. 1978. *Courage Knows No Sex.* North Quincy, MA: Christopher. 186 pp.

Denmark, F. L. 1977. The psychology of women: An overview of an emerging field. *Pers. Soc. Psychol. Bull.* 3:356–67

Denmark, F. L. 1980. Psyche: From rocking the cradle to rocking the boat. *Am. Psychol.* 35:1057–65

Denmark, F. L. 1983. Integrating the psychology of women into introductory psychology. *The G. Stanley Hall Lecture Series,* ed. C. J. Scheier, A. Rogers, 3:33–75. Washington, DC: Am. Psychol. Assoc.

Eells, W. C. 1957. Doctoral dissertations by women in the nineteenth century. *Am. Psychol.* 12:230–31

Ehrenreich, B., English, D. 1978. *For Her Own Good.* NU: Anchor. 325 pp.

Filene, P. G. 1975. *Him/Her/Self: Sex Roles in Modern America.* New York: Harcourt, Brace Jovanovich

Finison, L., Furumoto, L. 1978. *An historical perspective on psychology, social action, and women's rights.* Presented at Ann. Meet. Am. Psychol. Assoc., Toronto

French, J. L. 1984. On the conception, birth, and early development of school psychology. *Am. Psychol.* 39:976–87

Furumoto, L. 1980. Mary Whiton Calkins (1863–1930). *Psychol. Women Q.* 5:55–68

Furumoto, L., Scarborough, E. 1986. Placing women in the history of psychology: The first American women psychologists. *Am. Psychol.* 41:35–42

Gavin, E. 1983. *Prominent women in psychology as determined by ratings of distinguished peers.* Presented at Ann. Meet. Am. Psychol. Assoc.

Gibson, J. J. 1966. James J. Gibson. In *History of Psychology in Autobiography,* ed. E. G. Boring, G. Lindzey, 5:124–44. New York: Appleton-Century-Crofts

Gold Fein, L., ed. 1973. Women in national and international psychology. *Int. Understanding* 10:63–114

Gold Fein, L. 1985. *Changing status of women in psychology over past half century.* Invited address, Ann. Meet. Am. Psychol. Assoc.

Goodman, E. 1980. Margaret Floy Washburn (1871-1939): First woman Ph.D. in psychology. *Psychol. Women. Q.* 5:69–80

Goodman, E. 1983. History's choices. *Contemp. Psychoanal.* 28:667–69

Guthrie, R. V. 1976. *Even the Rat Was White.* New York: Harper & Row

Hanfmann, E. 1983. Eugenia Hanfmann. See O'Connell & Russo, pp. 141–54

Harper, R. S., Newman, E. B., Schab, F. R. 1985. Gabriele Gräfin von Wartensleben and the birth of *Gestaltpsychologie. J. Hist. Behav. Sci.* 21:118–23

Heidbreder, E. 1933. *Seven Psychologies.* New York: Appleton-Century

Henle, M. 1983. Mary Henle. See O'Connell & Russo, pp. 220–32

Howard, R. W. 1983. Ruth W. Howard. See O'Connell & Russo, pp. 55–68

Howard, S. 1978. *But We Will Persist. A Comparative Research Report on the Status of Women in Academe.* Washington, DC: Am. Assoc. Univ. Women

Hymowitz, C., Weissman, M. 1978. *A History of Women in America.* New York: Bantam. 400 pp.

James, E. T., James, J. W., Boyer, P. W., eds. 1971. *Notable American Women, 1607–1950: A Biographical Dictionary,* Vols. 1–3. Cambridge, MA/London, Engl: Belknap Press of Harvard Univ. Press

Kimmel, E. 1976. Contributions to the history of psychology: XXIV. Role of women psychologists in the history of psychology in the South. *Psychol. Rep.* 38:611–18

Krippner, S. 1977. Humanistic psychology: Its history and contributions. *J. Am. Soc. Psychosom. Med.* 24:15–20

Lerner, G. 1979. *The Majority Finds Its Past.* New York: Oxford. 217 pp.

Lerner, G. 1981. *Teaching Women's History.* Washington, DC: Am. Historical Assoc. 88 pp.

Lewin, M., ed. 1984. *In the Shadow of the Past: Psychology Portrays the Sexes.* New York: Columbia Univ. 337 pp.

Mandel, J. D. 1981. *Women and Social Change in America.* Princeton, NJ: Princeton Univ. Press

Marquis, D. G. 1944a. The mobilization of psychologists for war service. *Psychol. Bull.* 41:469–73

Marquis, D. G. 1944b. Post-war reemployment prospects in psychology. *Psychol. Bull.* 41:653–63

Mednick, M. T. S. 1978. Now we are four: What should we be when we grow up? *Psychol. Women Q.* 3:123–38

Millsap, M. 1983. Sex equity in education. See Tinker 1983, pp. 91–119

Murphy, G. 1943. Service of women psychologists to the war: Foreward. *J. Consult. Psychol.* 7:249–51

National Research Council. 1983. *Summary*

Report: 1983 Doctorate Recipients from United States Universities. Washington, DC: Natl. Acad. Press

National Science Foundation. 1978. Increasing the Participation of Women in Scientific Research. Washington, DC: Natl. Sci. Found.

National Science Foundation. 1983. Science and Engineering Doctorates: 1960–1983. Washington, DC: Natl. Sci. Found.

National Science Foundation. 1984. Women and Minorities in Science and Engineering. Washington, DC: Natl. Sci. Found.

O'Connell, A. N., Alpert, J., Richardson, M. S., Rotter, N., Ruble, D. N., et al. 1978. Gender-specific barriers to research in psychology: Report of the Task Force on Women Doing Research—APA Division 35. JSAS Cat. Sel. Doc. Psychol. MS. 1753, 8:1–10

O'Connell, A. N., Russo, N. F., eds. 1980. Eminent Women in Psychology: Models of Achievement. New York: Human Sci. Press. 144 pp.

O'Connell, A. N., Russo, N. F., eds. 1983. Models of Achievement: Reflections of Eminent Women in Psychology. New York: Columbia Univ. 338 pp.

Over, R. 1983. Representation, status, and contributions of women in psychology: A bibliography. Psychol. Doc. 13:1–25

Peterson, E. 1983. The Kennedy Commission. See Tinker 1983, pp. 21–34

Pion, G., Bramblett, P., Wicherski, M., Stapp, J. 1985. Summary Report of the 1984–85 Survey of Graduate Departments of Psychology. Washington, DC: Am. Psychol. Assoc. 36 pp.

Portenier, L. G., ed. (n.d.) International Council of Psychologists, Inc.: The First Quarter-Century, 1942–1967. Int. Counc. Psychol. 48 pp.

Reisman, J. 1976. A History of Clinical Psychology. New York: Irvington

Rosenberg, R. 1982. Beyond Separate Spheres: Intellectual Roots of Modern Feminism. New Haven: Yale Univ., 288 pp.

Ross, B. 1985. Scholars, status and social context. Contemp. Psychoanal. 30:853–60

Rossiter, M. W. 1974. Women scientists in America before 1920. Am. Sci. 62:312–23

Rossiter, M. W. 1982. Women Scientists in America: Struggles and Strategies to 1940. Baltimore: Johns Hopkins. 439 pp.

Russo, N. F. 1983. Psychology's foremothers: Their achievements in context. See O'Connell & Russo 1983, pp. 9–24

Russo, N. F. 1984. Women in the American Psychological Association. Washington, DC: Women's Programs Off., Am. Psychol. Assoc.

Russo, N. F., O'Connell, A. N. 1980. Models from our past: Psychology's foremothers. Psychol. Women Q. 5:11–54

Russo, N. F., Olmedo, S., Stapp, J., Fulcher, R. 1981. Women and minorities in psychology. Am. Psychol. 36:1315–63

Scarborough, E., Furumoto, L. 1986. Untold Lives: The First Generation of Women Psychologists. New York: Columbia Univ. In press

Sears, R. R. 1975. Your Ancients Revisited: A History of Child Development. Chicago: Univer. Chicago Press

Senn, M. 1975. Insights on the child development movement in the United States. Monogr. Soc. Res. Child Dev. 40 (3–4, Ser. 16):1–106

Sexton, V. S. 1969. Women's accomplishments in American psychology: A brief survey. Pak. J. Psychol. 2:29–35

Sexton, V. S. 1973/1974. Women in American psychology: An overview. Int. Understanding 10:66–77

Shields, S. A. 1975a. Functionalism, Darwinism, and the psychology of women: A study of social myth. Am. Psychol. 30:739–54

Shields, S. A. 1975b. Ms. Pilgrim's progress: The contributions of Leta Stetter Hollingworth to the psychology of women. Am. Psychol. 30:852–57

Sicherman, B., Green, C. H., with Kantrov, I., Walker, H., eds. 1980. Notable American Women: The Modern Period. Cambridge, MA: Belknap. 773 pp.

Stevens, G., Gardner, S. 1982a. The Women of Psychology: Pioneers and Innovators, Vol. I. Cambridge, MA: Schenkman. 240 pp.

Stevens, G., Gardner, S. 1982b. The Women of Psychology: Expansion and Refinement, Vol. II. Cambridge, MA: Schenkman. 273 pp.

Task Force on the Status of Women in Psychology. 1973. Report of the Task Force on the Status of Women in Psychology. Am. Psychol. 28:611–16

Terman, L. M., Miles, C. C. 1936. Sex and Personality. New Haven: Yale Univ. Press

Thompson, D. 1983. Psychological classics: Older works in developmental psychology frequently cited today. J. Genet. Psychol. 143:169–74

Tinker, I. 1983. Women in Washington: Advocates for Public Policy. Beverly Hills, CA: Sage. 327 pp.

Walsh, M. R. 1986. Academic professional women organizing for change: The struggle in psychology. J. Soc. Issues 41:17–27

Watson, R. I. 1974. Eminent Contributors to Psychology: A Bibliography of Primary References, Vol. I. New York: Springer. 470 pp.

Welter, B. 1966. The cult of True Womanhood: 1820–1860. Am. Q. 18:151–74

Ann. Rev. Psychol. 1987. 38:299–337
Copyright © 1986 by Annual Reviews Inc. All rights reserved

THE DYNAMIC SELF-CONCEPT: A
Social Psychological Perspective

Hazel Markus and Elissa Wurf

Institute for Social Research, University of Michigan, Ann Arbor, Michigan 48106

CONTENTS

The unifying premise of the last decade's research on the self is that the self-concept does not just reflect on-going behavior but instead mediates and regulates this behavior. In this sense the self-concept has been viewed as dynamic—as active, forceful, and capable of change. It interprets and organizes self-relevant actions and experiences; it has motivational consequences, providing the incentives, standards, plans, rules, and scripts for behavior; and

299

it adjusts in response to challenges from the social environment. Virtually all of the early theoretical statements on the self-concept accord it this dynamic role (see Gordon & Gergen 1968), yet until very recently the empirical work lagged far behind these sophisticated conceptions of how the self-system functions. Indeed, the majority of self-concept research could best be described as an attempt to relate very complex global behavior, such as delinquency, marital satisfaction, or school achievement, to a single aspect of the self-concept, typically self-esteem.

In 1974, Wylie reviewed the literature and concluded that the self-concept simply could not be powerfully implicated in directing behavior. In the last decade, however, researchers have redoubled their efforts to understand the self-concept as one of the most significant regulators of behavior (see Suls 1982, Suls & Greenwald 1983, Schlenker 1985a). They have been sustained by their faith in the importance of the self-concept, by a number of compelling theoretical accounts of self-concept functioning, and by the poor showing of those approaches that ignore the self (e.g. theories that focus solely on life events or social structural features of the environment). In this review, we focus primarily on research that views the self-concept as a dynamic interpretive structure that mediates most significant *intrapersonal* processes (including information processing, affect, and motivation) and a wide variety of *interpersonal* processes (including social perception; choice of situation, partner, and interaction strategy; and reaction to feedback).

Progress in research on the self-concept came as a result of three advances. The first was the realization that the self-concept can no longer be explored as if it were a unitary, monolithic entity. The second was the understanding that the functioning of the self-concept depends on both the self-motives being served (e.g. self-enhancement, consistency maintenance, or self-actualization) and on the configuration of the immediate social situation. The third advance was a consequence of observing more fine-grained behavior. Overt, complex actions may not always be the appropriate dependent variables. An individual's behavior is constrained by many factors other than the self-concept. As a consequence, the influence of the self-concept will not always be directly revealed in one's overt actions. Instead its impact will often be manifest more subtly, in mood changes, in variations in what aspects of the self-concept are accessible and dominant, in shifts in self-esteem, in social comparison choices, in the nature of self-presentation, in choice of social setting, and in the construction or definition of one's situation.

CONTENT AND STRUCTURE

The Multifaceted Self-Concept

The most dramatic change in the last decade of research on the self-concept can be found in work on its structure and content. One of the formidable stumbling blocks to linking the self-concept to behavioral regulation has been the view of the self-concept as a stable, generalized, or average view of the self. How could this crude, undifferentiated structure sensitively mediate and reflect the diversity of behavior to which it was supposedly related? The solution has been to view the self-concept as a multifaceted phenomenon, as a set or collection of images, schemas, conceptions, prototypes, theories, goals, or tasks (Epstein 1980, Schlenker 1980, Carver & Scheier 1981, Rogers 1981, Greenwald 1982, Markus & Sentis 1982, Markus 1983, Greenwald & Pratkanis 1984, Kihlstrom & Cantor 1984). These representations of the self have been described as being arrayed in a space (McGuire & McGuire 1982, Markus & Nurius 1986), a confederation (Greenwald & Pratkanis 1984), or a system (Martindale 1980).

Self theorists have abandoned as somewhat premature efforts to describe the active, "I" aspects of the self, and have been temporarily content to elaborate the structural features of the self-concept. Many recent models focus on the nature of cognitive representations of the self (see Greenwald & Pratkanis 1984, Kihlstrom & Cantor 1984 for reviews). The simplest of these models suggests that the self is just one node among many in an associative memory network. Based on network models of memory such as HAM (Anderson & Bower 1973) and ACT (Anderson 1976), such a model assumes that information about the self is stored in the form of propositions (Bower & Gilligan 1979). Others characterize the self-concept as either a hierarchical category structure whose elements are traits, values, and memories of specific behaviors (e.g. Carver & Scheier 1981, Rogers 1981, Kihlstrom & Cantor 1984) or as a multidimensional meaning space (Greenwald & Pratkanis 1984, Hoelter 1985). Another view of the self-concept is as a system of self-schemas or generalizations about the self derived from past social experiences. A schema is hypothesized to have a dual nature: to be at once a structure and a process (Neisser 1976, Rumelhart & Norman 1978, Markus & Sentis 1982). As such, it may have the capacity to represent the self as that which is both known and knower.

Whether researchers define the self-concept in terms of hierarchies, prototypes, networks, spaces, or schemas, they generally agree that the self-structure is an active one. What began as an apparently singular, static, lump-like entity has become a multidimensional, multifaceted dynamic structure that is systematically implicated in all aspects of social information processing. Among sociologists there has been a similar movement, and it is now commonplace to refer to the multiplicity of identity (Burke 1980, Martindale 1980, Stryker 1980, Rowan 1983, Weigert 1983, Lester 1984). Identity is described as including personal characteristics, feelings, and images (e.g. Burke 1980, Stryker 1980, Schlenker 1985b), as well as roles and social status. With this development, psychologists and sociologists are achieving a complete convergence in how they think about the self.

Types of Self-Representations

Not all of the self-representations that comprise the self-concept are alike. Some are more important and more elaborated with behavioral evidence than others. Some are positive, some negative; some refer to the individual's here-and-now experience, while others refer to past or future experiences. Moreover, some are representations of what the self actually is, while others are of what the self would like to be, could be, ought to be, or is afraid of being. Self-representations that can be the subject of conscious reflection are usually termed self-conceptions.

The most apparent difference among self-representations is in their centrality or importance. Some self-conceptions are core conceptions (Gergen 1968) or salient identities (Stryker 1980, 1986), while others are more peripheral. Central conceptions of the self are generally the most well elaborated and are presumed to affect information processing and behavior most powerfully. Yet, more peripheral or less well-elaborated conceptions may still wield behavioral influence.

Self-representations also differ in whether or not they have actually been achieved. Some selves are not actual, but are possible for the person; other selves are hoped-for ideals. Markus & Nurius (1986) theorize that among one's set of self-conceptions are possible selves—the selves one would like to be or is afraid of becoming. These selves function as incentives for behavior, providing images of the future self in desired or undesired end-states. They also function to provide an evaluative and interpretive context for the current view of self. Representations of potential have also been explored by Schlenker (1985b) and Levinson (1978).

Building on earlier notions of the ego ideal (Freud 1925, Horney 1950, Rogers 1951), Rosenberg (1979) discusses ideal self-conceptions, distinguishing those ideal self-conceptions that are likely to be realized from those that are glorified images of the self. Higgins (1983) extends this work and hypothesizes that there are at least three classes of self-conceptions: those that reflect the "actual" self, those that represent the "ideal" self or the attributes the person would like to possess, and those that represent the "ought" self, which are representations of characteristics that someone, self or other, believes the person should possess. A discrepancy between any two of these self-concepts can induce a state of discomfort; and different kinds of discrepancy produce different types of discomfort. For example, Higgins et al (1985, 1986) find that a discrepancy between actual and ideal selves is associated with depression, while a discrepancy between actual and ought selves is related to anxiety.

A third difference in self-representations is whether they refer to past, present, or future views of the self—what Schutz (1964) calls the tense of the self-conception and what Nuttin (1984) refers to as its temporal sign. Images of the self in the past or future may be as significant as the here-and-now aspects of self (Markus & Nurius 1986, Nuttin & Lens 1986).

A final difference among self-representations is in their positivity or negativity. Most work focuses on positive self-conceptions, but there has been some focus on what Sullivan (1953) called the "bad me," or the individual's negative self-conceptions. The majority of this work attempts to understand the "I'm no good, I'm useless or worthless" thinking that seems to predominate in the selves of many depressed individuals. Beck (1967) has postulated that depressives carry with them a depressive self-schema that continually distorts self-relevant thoughts. A large variety of studies now demonstrate that depressed individuals do indeed think more negatively about themselves than about others, and that this negativity pervades all aspects of their information processing (Derry & Kuiper 1981, Kuiper & Derry 1981, Kuiper & MacDonald 1982, Ingram et al 1983, Kuiper & Higgins 1985, Pietromonaco 1985). Currently, investigators disagree as to whether this negativity is a function of a fixed schema that distorts thinking, or whether the thinking of depressives is a fairly accurate reflection and integration of their life experiences.

There has been little attention to negativity in the self-concepts of people who are not depressed. Rosenberg & Gara (1985), following Erikson (1950), talk about the importance of negative identities, but little empirical work focuses on peoples' negative self-views. Indeed, many self-concept theorists (e.g. Tesser & Campbell 1984) give the impression that individuals do virtually everything within their power to avoid forming negative self-conceptions; yet work by Wurf & Markus (1983) suggests that even nonde-pressed, high self-esteem individuals can have negative self-conceptions that may be elaborated into self-schemas. Thus they find, for example, individuals who describe themselves as shy, lazy, or fat; who feel bad about these characteristics; who feel these are important aspects of their self-definition; yet who maintain overall high self-esteem. They suggest that negative self-conceptions are critical in initiating the process of self-concept change. Moreover, Wurf (1986) hypothesizes that these negative self-schemas may function to help individuals cope with the negativity in their lives, ensuring that negative experiences do not swamp the entire self-concept.

In the work on self-representations, several important concerns remain untouched. First, there has been relatively little attention paid to the representation of affect in the self-concept, beyond the assumption that self-conceptions vary in their valence. Some (Guntrip 1971; Kernberg 1977) assume that each self-representation contains both an affective and a cognitive component. Greenwald & Pratkanis (1984) suggest that affect functions as a heuristic that guides how various self-relevant experiences are organized, assigning them either to a positive class or a negative class. Similarly, Fast

(1985) argues that affect plays a major role in determining the connections among our experiences; it defines the similarity of our actions and thus provides the basis of the initial organization of the self-concept. Still others (e.g. Salovey & Rodin 1985) view affect as a consequence of the set of self-conceptions that are currently active.

A second missing element is speculation about how representations of the self differ in form and function depending on when, how, and why they were formed. Some representations may be derived from straightforward perception and organization of one's own behavior. These representations may be directly accessible to conscious awareness; or, they may not be accessible because they are so well rehearsed they have become automatic. Self-representations can assume a variety of forms—neural, motor, and sensory as well as verbal. Nonverbal representations may be inaccessible to conscious awareness. Finally, some self-representations may be actively repressed and kept from consciousness because they are based in certain defenses or desires (Singer & Salovey 1985, Silverman & Weinberger 1985). Representations of the self that derive from wishes or needs may have a very different form and function than representations that derive from straightforward organization of one's behavior.

A third important issue has to do with the structure and organization of self-representations. What happens when two self-conceptions are incompatible? Higgins (1983; Higgins et al 1985, 1986) has attempted to relate different types of self-concept discrepancy to emotional disorders, and Linville (1982) suggests that a complex self-structure can protect the individual from emotional turmoil. Similarly, a variety of studies from a sociological perspective suggest that the more identities individuals have, the better their mental health (Kessler & McRae 1982, Coleman & Antonucci 1983). However, this may only be true if the identities can be successfully integrated with each other (Thoits 1983, Pietromonaco et al 1986). In general, the relationship between variation in the configuration of the self-structure and differential behavior is largely unexplored.

Sources of Self-Representations

Self-representations differ in their origins. Some self-representations result from inferences that people make about their attitudes and dispositions while watching their own actions. People also make inferences from their internal physiological (arousal) reactions (Bandura 1977), and their cognitions, emotions, and motivations (Harter 1983, Anderson 1984, Anderson & Ross 1984). Anderson finds that people's thoughts and feelings have even greater weight in determining self-perceptions than do behaviors. In fact, when observers are given information about the actor's thoughts and feelings, they come to see the actor very much as that person views him- or herself; whereas when they are given information about the actor's behaviors, they may see him or her quite differently (Anderson 1984).

Representations of the self also derive from direct attempts at self-assessment. Trope (1983, 1986) presents a formal model of self-assessment that describes the diagnosticity of a task, based on the person's uncertainty about his or her ability level and the probabilities of success and failure. In research drawing on this model, Trope and his associates find that people prefer to do tasks that are maximally diagnostic of their abilities, particularly when they are uncertain about those abilities (Trope 1983). People may differ in their willingness to seek out potentially threatening information about the self (Sorrentino & Short 1986). In certain situations they may be more willing to seek out or accept potentially threatening information—for example, during life transitions (Cantor et al 1985) or when making decisions with long-term consequences (Trope 1986).

People also learn about themselves from others, both through social comparisons and direct interactions. McGuire and his colleagues (McGuire 1984, McGuire & McGuire 1982) find that one of the most powerful determinants of currently available self-conceptions is the configuration of the immediate social environment. Individuals will focus on whatever aspects of themselves are most distinctive in a particular social setting: for example, short children will notice their height when in classroom of taller children. Social comparison can be a potent source of self-knowledge (Suls & Miller 1977, Schoeneman 1981). Children learn how to use social comparison to evaluate themselves and become progressively more skilled at doing this during their school years (Frey & Ruble 1985). People compare with superior others to evaluate themselves and with inferior others to make themselves feel good; the comparison others may be chosen to satisfy one or both motives (Brickman & Janoff-Bulman 1977, Gruder 1977, Taylor et al 1983). Finally, direct interaction with others also provides information about the self (see the section below on interpersonal processes). Symbolic interactionists in fact suggest that all self-knowledge derives from social interaction (Baldwin 1897, Cooley 1902, Mead 1934; for a historical review, see Scheibe 1985; for a review of symbolic interactionism, see Stryker 1980).

The growth of self-structures is determined by both the information the person receives about the self (through self-perception, social comparison, and reflected appraisals) and by the individual's ability to cognitively process self-conceptions. Harter's (1983) model of the development of self-conceptions posits a tendency for self-descriptions to become increasingly abstract, incorporating first behaviors (e.g. "good at doing sums"), then traits ("smart"), then single abstractions ("scientific"), then higher order abstractions ("intellectual"). Within each of the phases, there is an alternating sequence of first overgeneralizing self-conceptions and then differentiating and reintegrating them (e.g. first the child thinks of herself as "all smart," and then later as "smart in English, but dumb in math"). Thus, conceptions of the self within different domains may be at different developmental stages.

The Working Self-Concept

Among both psychologists and sociologists, an emphasis on the multiplicity or multidimensionality of the self-concept or identity has led to the realization that it is no longer feasible to refer to *the* self-concept. Instead it is necessary to refer to the working, on-line, or accessible self-concept (Schlenker 1985b, Cantor & Kihlstrom 1986, Markus & Nurius 1986, Rhodewalt 1986, Rhodewalte & Agustsdottir 1986). The idea is simply that not all self-representations or identities that are part of the complete self-concept will be accessible at any one time. The working self-concept, or the self-concept of the moment, is best viewed as a continually active, shifting array of accessible self-knowledge.

This approach to the self-concept is welcomed now for several reasons. First, it flows naturally out of an increasingly large volume of research indicating that individuals are heavily influenced in all aspects of judgment, memory, and overt behavior by their currently accessible pool of thoughts, attitudes, and beliefs (Nisbett & Ross 1980, Higgins & King 1981, Sherman et al 1981, Snyder 1982). Second, this view of the self-concept moves much closer to that implied by the symbolic interactionists (Mead 1934, Stryker 1980). There is not a fixed or static self, but only a current self-concept constructed from one's social experiences. Third, this formulation allows for a self-concept that can be at once both stable and malleable. Core aspects of self (one's self-schemas) may be relatively unresponsive to changes in one's social circumstances. Because of their importance in defining the self and their extensive elaboration, they may be chronically accessible (Higgins et al 1982). Many other self-conceptions in the individual's system, however, will vary in accessibility depending on the individual's motivational state or on the prevailing social conditions. The working self-concept thus consists of the core self-conceptions embedded in a context of more tentative self-conceptions that are tied to the prevailing circumstances.

Results that are taken to reveal the malleability of the self (Gergen 1965, 1968, Morse & Gergen 1970, Fazio et al 1981, Jones et al 1981, McGuire & McGuire 1982) can be explained by assuming that the contents of working self-concept have changed. That is, the circumstances surrounding the experimental manipulation make certain self-conceptions, and not others, accessible in thought and memory. For example, if after responding to questions about extroversion, subjects appear to view themselves as more extroverted than do subjects who have responded to questions about introversion (see Fazio et al 1981), it is because most individuals can be assumed to have conceptions of themselves as both introverts and extroverts. The extrovert manipulation makes salient one's extrovert self-representations and the individual is likely to see the self at that moment as relatively more extroverted. Temporary change that occurs in the self-concept when one set of self-conceptions is activated and accessible in working memory rather than another is only one type of self-concept malleability. It is to be distinguished from change of a more enduring nature, the type that occurs when new self-conceptions are added to the set, when self-conceptions change in meaning, or when the relationship among self-components changes.

Self-concept and identity theorists appear to be converging on a notion of the self-concept as containing a *variety* of representations—representations that are not just verbal propositions or depictions of traits and demographic characteristics. Rather, representations of self may be cognitive and/or affective; they may be in verbal, image, neural, or sensorimotor form; they represent the self in the past and future as well as the here-and-now; and they are of the actual self and of the possible self. Some are organized into structures that contain both a well-elaborated knowledge base and production rules for how to behave when certain conditions are met. Other self-conceptions may be more tentative, constructed on the spot for a particular social interaction. At any one time, only some subset of these various representations is accessed and invoked to regulate or accompany the individual's behavior. The important remaining task is systematically to implicate these diverse representations of the self and the various organizations they can assume in the regulation of behavior; and conversely, to delineate how actions in turn influence these various self-representations.

SELF-REGULATION

While some self theorists grapple with the content and structure of the self-concept, others focus on the problem of self-regulatory processes: how individuals control and direct their own actions. Research on self-structure and on self-regulation would appear to have direct relevance for each other, but they are pursued in two virtually nonoverlapping literatures. Self-regulation theorists are concerned with the very general problem of the individual's involvement in controlling his or her own behavior. By self-regulation, some theorists mean how the person, as opposed to the environment, controls behavior, but they do not focus specifically on representations of the self as regulators (e.g. Kanfer 1970). In this section, we review those approaches to self-regulation that at least implicitly involve the self-concept.

The self-concept, of course, is only one of numerous factors, including culture, the social environment, individual need or tension states, and non-self-relevant cognitions, that may directly influence behavior. Although behavior is not exclusively controlled by self representations, it has become increasingly apparent that the representations of what individuals think, feel, or believe about themselves are among the most powerful regulators of many important behaviors.

Several component processes are involved in the process of self-regulation. These include goal setting, cognitive preparation for action (e.g. planning, rehearsal, strategy selection), and a cybernetic cycle of behavior, which includes monitoring, judgment, and self-evaluation. Different theorists stress different components in their theories, and theorists who focus on the same components may disagree about the conditions under which these processes function most optimally. In the following section, we first review the recent literature on some of these processes, pointing out areas of contention; and then we turn to an examination of the role of self-structures in the self-regulation process.

Goal Setting

Self-regulation theorists agree that self-controlled behavior is done in the service of some goal. However, they disagree about the determinants of the goals people set for themselves, and on how goals should be construed to be maximally effective. In general, three types of factors are seen as determining, either singly or jointly, goal selection. These three factors include expectations; affective factors such as needs, motives, or values; and desired self-conceptions derived from the individual's personal and social history.

Various sorts of expectations have been proposed as determinants of goal choice. These include expectations about the self's abilities and control over behavior (efficacy expectations) and expectations about what the outcomes will be if a certain behavior is performed. Bandura (1977, 1982, 1986) is the major proponent of the role of self-efficacy expectations in determining behavior. He has used the term both as a generalized perception of controllability over behavior and as a specialized perception of ability to execute a particular task. The actions that a person attempts, the effort expended at them, the persistence in the face of failure, and the thoughts and feelings experienced while engaging in behavior are presumed to be determined by these percepts of efficacy (see Bandura 1982, 1986 for summaries of research findings). For example, in studies with phobics, the behaviors (e.g. handling a snake) that the subject attempted during a test phase, and the anxiety experienced during execution, were shown to be a function of self-efficacy percepts (Bandura et al 1982).

Research on self-efficacy has demonstrated an impressive array of effects. Kirsch (1985) points out that both ability and willingness to perform an activity may independently contribute to the subject's expectancy for performance, and that these two factors cannot be untangled in some of Bandura's operationalizations of self-efficacy expectations. In addition, both types of expectations are probably influenced by environmental contingencies and by generalized perceptions of control (e.g. Ajzen 1985). Expectations—whether for the self's ability or willingness to execute a particular behavior, or for the probability that the behavior will achieve the desired outcome, or for a generalized sense of controllability over one's actions and outcomes—clearly play an important role in determining what goals the person will select. People generally select goals that they have some expectations of being able to achieve (though they also often have fantasies about unachievable, or low probability, attainments). However, this selection of goals is also influenced by affective factors that determine which of the many possible behaviors the individual will prefer.

Three different affective components have been postulated to influence goal selection—needs, motives, and values. Needs are generally conceived of as internal, organic motivators of behavior (Murray 1938) that inspire interaction between person and environment (Nuttin 1984). Although needs are "required," what satisfies them is not; instead, what satisfies needs is determined by the person's values, experiences, and self-conceptions. This conception of need is fairly similar to McClelland's (1951) concept of motive. The primary difference between the constructs is that needs are diffuse and innate, while motives are more specific and are learned. Thus Nuttin (1984) suggests that motives are "channelized needs." A third affective determinant of which goals the person will select is values. Values, or incentives, are similar to motives in that they are fairly specific. McClelland (1985), however, suggests that values and motives are critically different: values are conscious and related to the behaviors people choose to do, while motives are unconscious and related to spontaneous behavior. Values are seen as directing the form that motivated behavior will take; for example, in a study by Constantian (1981), subjects who had a high motive for affiliation but who valued solitude were particularly likely to spend time writing letters. Thus, while motives are seen as more specific than needs, values are seen as more specific yet.

What is the relationship of needs, motives, and values to self-conceptions? This relationship is rarely discussed in the literature. However, it might be inferred that needs, motives, and values contribute to which self-conceptions are formed or activated in the working self-concept as a behavior is enacted. For example, a person high in need for achievement is likely to seek out challenging achievement situations; as the person engages in these behaviors, he or she is likely to develop a self-concept of being a high achiever. In turn, the activated self-conceptions may call up certain needs, motives, or values. Thus a person who has a "high achiever" self activated in the working self-concept may be particularly motivated to achieve. In this way (and jointly with expectations) the affective factors of needs, motives, and values determine the particular goals for which an individual strives.

Finally, self-conceptions may also become an important source of motivation in themselves. The person may select goals that represent not just achievements, but enduring self-definitions. Thus the person who spends an entire day in the kitchen preparing dinner may be striving not just to cook a delicious meal, but also to demonstrate to self and others that he or she is a gourmet cook. A variety of theorists stress this motivational function of self-conceptions, particularly Wicklund & Gollwitzer (1982) and Markus & Nurius (1986). Similarly, several theories discuss the motivating function of more general life goals derived from the individual's past experience, way of seeing the world, and developmental pressures (e.g. see Cantor & Kihlstrom 1986 on life tasks, Schank & Abelson 1977 on life themes, Little 1983 on personal projects). In these theories, general life goals become personalized into desired self-conceptions that in turn motivate selection of particular goals and behavior (e.g. see Cantor et al 1986). Theories about desired self-conceptions and life goals are further reviewed in the section below on intrapersonal processes.

Although theories agree that goals are important in the regulation of behavior, they disagree on what is the optimal way for the person to construe the goal. Some researchers (e.g. Bandura & Schunk 1981) demonstrate that proximal goals produce the best performance and the most increase in intrinsic motivation. Others, however, find that more distal goals produce maximum results (e.g. Kirschenbaum et al 1981, 1982, De Volder & Lens 1982). Some researchers even question whether focusing on goals at all promotes self-regulation: Kuhl (1984) suggests that too much attention to the end goal can distract attention from acting to achieve it (see also Mischel 1981). One possible resolution to this controversy is that proximal goals may work best for refractory behaviors, while distal goals may work best for nonproblematic behaviors. In support of this interpretation, Manderlink & Harackiewicz (1984) find that distal goals are superior to proximal goals for inspiring performance on an intrinsically motivated task. Similarly, Hyams & Graham (1984) found that specific goals improved performance for subjects low in initiative, while high initiative subjects performed better with the global instruction to do their best.

Cognitive Preparation for Action

The next step in the self-regulation process (and a step that does not always occur) is planning and strategy selection. The cognitive processes engaged in here draw on both the person's repertoire of procedural knowledge or strategies and on the person's metacognitive knowledge about what strategies will be useful in which situations or to meet which goals (Flavell 1979, 1981,

Mischel 1981, Sternberg 1984). Metacognitive knowledge can be used to plan effective behavior. For example, Mischel's work on delay of gratification (summarized in Mischel 1981) shows that children's ability to delay gratification depends on their metacognitive knowledge about which strategies are effective when. Similarly, Rosenbaum (1980) shows that ability to withstand pain in a cold pressor task depends not just on the person's available coping strategies, but on the ability to choose among them effectively. And Kuhl (1985) shows that "action-oriented" subjects use more effective self-regulatory strategies and hence are more likely to achieve their goals. Clinicians are beginning to develop techniques to teach clients metacognitive skills, which suggests that the key to successful behavior management is not just having the right strategies, but knowing when to use each (Meichenbaum & Asarnow 1979, Turk & Salovey 1985).

Besides being able to choose among strategies, the person must have an appropriate repertoire from which to choose. The repertoire of readily available strategies may be represented as some form of procedural knowledge—for example, production rules (Anderson 1982) or scripts (Schank & Abelson 1977) that may be automatically executed in the appropriate situation, and that may be linked to particular knowledge structures. Thus the restaurant script is linked to declarative knowledge about restaurants; similarly, a wall-flower script may be attached to a person's shy self-schema. Such links between declarative and procedural knowledge may be crucial for tying cognitive structures about the self to behavior. Links between self-schemas and scripts are likely to be well developed and automatically executed in the appropriate circumstances, which suggests that the self may be involved even in nonconscious self-regulation. When no script is available, or when the person is consciously trying to change his or her behavior, the person may construct novel plans using metacognitive knowledge to combine lower order strategies in the service of particular goals (Sternberg 1984).

Cybernetic Cycle: Behavior, Monitoring, Judgment, Self-Evaluation

The next step in self-regulation is to attempt performance execution. Most self-regulation theorists talk about a cycle of self-regulation that typically includes monitoring behavior, making a judgment about how well the behavior is being executed, and evaluating or reinforcing the self. Both Bandura (1978) and Kanfer (1970) propose such three-stage cycles. During the self-monitoring phase, people attend to various aspects of their behavior, such as its quality or frequency. The observed behavior is then judged against a criterion derived from one's own standards or the standards of significant others. Finally, the person rewards (or punishes) the self via feelings of approval or disapproval and tangible rewards. Both Bandura and Kanfer see these processes as consciously engaged in and essential for helping people change their own behavior.

Carver & Scheier (1981, 1982) have developed a control theory of self-regulation also based upon a cyclic feedback process. Carver & Scheier's model consists of the cycling of three basic stages: attending to the self, comparing the self to a standard, and attempting to reduce the discrepancy between the way one is behaving and the way one wants to behave. This model is elaborated into an interconnected hierarchy of control systems, each at a progressively higher level of abstraction. For example, at the very highest level of control, the person is concerned with fulfilling self-motives such as self-enrichment; at the next highest level, the person may be concerned with being a good student; at the next level, the person is concerned with studying for a test, and, five levels later, the person is engaged in the various muscle movements involved in writing up a set of notes. This theory differs from Bandura's and Kanfer's theories in three ways. First, the theory posits an interconnecting hierarchy of self-regulatory processes, rather than a single system. Second, the theory attempts to explain the regulation of all behavior, rather than just conscious attempts to behave in a certain manner. Thus Carver & Scheier use control theory to explain nonconscious and automatic processing, as well as conscious control of behavior. Finally, whereas Bandura and Kanfer posit some sort of self-reinforcement as critical for self-regulatory success, Carver & Scheier consider information rather than reward as the critical determinant of attempts at change.

The Involvement of the Self-Concept in Self-Regulation

Self-regulation operates with varying degrees of efficiency. Sometimes the person attempts to regulate her behavior, and she is able to do so effectively: all phases of self-regulation flow naturally one after another. Other times, however, the person attempts to regulate her behavior, but cannot do so. She cannot decide between which of multiple salient goals to pursue; she ends up mulling over her goals, rather than acting to achieve them; she lacks the appropriate procedural knowledge and doesn't know what to do; or she tries but repeatedly fails. There are any number of ways in which the self-regulatory process can go wrong. The involvement of the self-concept has been suggested as a critical variable in how smoothly self-regulatory processes function. The nature and effects of this involvement, however, are unclear.

Some authors suggest that self-regulation will operate most efficiently when the person is self-focused. Carver & Scheier (1981) are the primary proponents of this position. Their theory claims that when a behavioral standard is salient and the person is focused on the self, attention to the self will lead to a comparison between the current state and the standard. The discrepancy between where the person is and where he wants to be is presumed to motivate attempts at behavior (provided the person expects that he can reach the standard; if he expects not to be able to reach it, then he is predicted to withdraw, physically or mentally, from attempts at change). Carver & Scheier use a variety of manipulations (mirrors, audiences, cameras, or dispositional differences in self-consciousness) to demonstrate that self-focused individuals regulate themselves more effectively (i.e. more in line with standards) than do non-self-focused individuals (see Carver & Scheier 1981 for a summary of this research). Greenwald (1982, Breckler & Greenwald 1986) suggests that what is really being affected by self-awareness manipulations is the person's ego involvement; if the manipulation calls up one of the person's "ego tasks," then the person will be ego-involved and will regulate behavior more effectively.

In opposition to these formulations, other authors seem to imply that focusing on the self (implicating the self-concept) can interfere with the smooth operation of self-regulation. Kuhl (1985), for example, suggests that focusing on "states" (internal states or external goals), rather than on actions, impairs effective self-regulation. Similarly, Wicklund (1986) suggests that people who are dynamically oriented (attending to the environment), rather than statically oriented (attending to personal characteristics), will best regulate themselves. Further, the dynamically oriented person is focused on his or her relationship to the environment, and while behaving, experiences a loss of self (cf Csikszentmihalyi 1975). The role of the self in such theories is unclear, because there are circumstances under which these authors claim that self-involvement aids self-regulation. Kuhl (1984), for example, suggests that "the *full* repertoire of volitional strategies is provided only if the current intention is a self-related one" (p. 127). And Wicklund (1986) suggests that a focus on one's own standards for performance may aid dynamically oriented functioning.

Clearly, there is a need for further theorizing to reconcile these approaches. The existence of such disparate theories suggests that there are ways in which the self-concept can both facilitate and interfere with self-regulation. For example, all the theories seem to agree that a focus on discrepancies between where the self is and where it wants to be may effectively motivate behavior (provided the discrepancy is not too large). In contrast, a focus either solely on where the self is or on where it wants to be, without any attention to the discrepancy between the two, is unlikely to motivate behavior change. Consistent with this, research on "self-regulatory failure" (Tomarken & Kirschenbaum 1982) demonstrates that monitoring one's successes (on well-learned behaviors) leads to decreased performance, while monitoring one's failures (i.e. discrepancies) leads to increased performance. For new behaviors (which are characterized by a discrepancy between where one is and where one wants to be), monitoring successes is either superior to or equal to monitoring failure in increasing performance.

A further reconcilation might involve distinguishing between the self as "me" and the self as "I." While theories of self-structure focus on the content of the self, on the "me," theories of self-regulation implicitly focus on dynamic, process-oriented aspects of self—the "I." The subjective experience of loss of self during peak experiences (Privette 1983) or effective self-regulation may reflect a lack of attention to the "me." This does not mean, however, that the self is not involved. The person may experience a subjective loss of self when performing behaviors that are "ego syntonic," that is, congruent with the ego ideal. Instead of expressing a loss of self, these behaviors may reflect the fullest involvement of self, experienced as a merging of the "I" with the behavior it enacts.

THE DYNAMIC SELF-CONCEPT

In the developing model of the dynamic self-concept (see Figure 1), the self-concept is viewed as a collection of self-representations, and the working self-concept is that subset of representations which is accessible at a given moment. These representations vary in their structure and function and have been given a variety of labels. They are activated depending on the prevailing social circumstances and on the individual's motivational state. Some self-representations are more or less automatically activated as a result of salient situational stimuli. Many others, however, are willfully recruited or invoked in response to whatever motives the individual is striving to fulfill. The person may, as we discuss below, seek to develop or maintain a positive affective state about the self—a motive frequently referred to as self-enhancement. Alternatively, or simultaneously, the person may seek to maintain a sense of coherence and continuity, fulfilling a self-consistency motive. Yet another important motive is what Maslow (1954) referred to as self-actualization, the desire to improve or change the self, to develop, grow, and fulfill one's potential. These various self-motives, in conjuction with social circumstance, determine the contents of the working self-concept.

As shown in Figure 1, the affective-cognitive system is distinguished as one feature of the person, and the self-concept is defined as one aspect of this system. In turn, the working self-concept is the particular configuration of representations drawn from the self-concept that regulates the individual's on-going actions and reactions. Thus the individual's behavior is regulated according to whatever set of dynamic structures (self-schemas, possible selves, prototypes, scripts, ego-tasks, standards, strategies, or productions) are currently activated in the working self-concept.

The structures active in the working self-concept are the basis on which the individual initiates actions and also the basis for the observation, judgment,

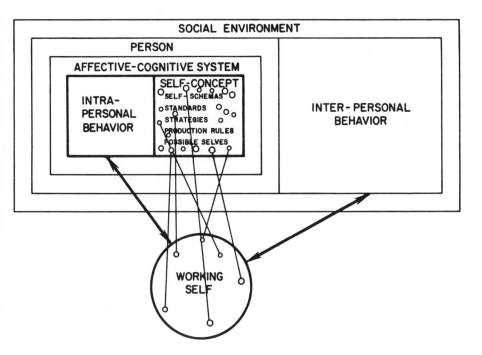

THE DYNAMIC SELF-CONCEPT

Figure 1   The currently active set of dynamic self-structures comprises the working self-concept, which regulates both intrapersonal and interpersonal behavior.

and evaluation of these actions. The influence of the working self-concept in the shaping and controlling of behavior can be seen in two broad classes of behaviors: *intrapersonal processes,* which include self-relevant information processing, affect regulation, and motivational processes; and *interpersonal processes,* which include social perception, social comparison, and seeking out and shaping interaction with others. The outcomes of one's intrapersonal and interpersonal behavior determine the current motivational state and the salient social conditions for the next cycle of self-regulation. In the remainder of the chapter we review the nature of the self-concept's influence on intrapersonal and interpersonal processes.

INTRAPERSONAL PROCESSES MEDIATED BY THE SELF-CONCEPT

In defending the importance of the self-system, early self theorists devoted a significant amount of their theorizing to identifying the crucial functions that the self performed (Allport 1955, Erikson 1950). Several major functions were specified. These included providing the individual with a sense of continuity in time and space, providing an integrating and organizing function for the individual's self-relevant experiences, regulating the individual's affective state, and providing a source of incentive or motivation for the individual.

The first general function, providing a sense of continuity, has received little empirical attention and has been accepted largely as a matter of faith. Recently, however, some theorists have focused specifically on the related question of how individuals weave together various self-conceptions. Most people appear to construct a current autobiography or narrative (Bruner 1986; Dennett 1982; Gergen & Gergen 1983)—a story that makes the most coherent or harmonious integration of one's various experiences. This narrative is a superstructure to which individuals attach their current set of life experiences. This personal narrative is a particularly intriguing type of self-representation because it is very often revised. The flexibility and malleability of self-structure organization is further supported by research suggesting that individuals often rewrite their personal histories to support a current self-view (Ross & Conway 1986, Greenwald 1980).

The other intrapersonal functions of the self have been the source of a burgeoning experimental literature. As the cognitive approach and the information processing model took root in all areas of psychology, it became evident that some empirical underpinnings could be given to the phenomenal or cognitive theories of Rogers (1951), Kelly (1955), Combs & Snygg (1959), and Allport (1955). Long-standing assumptions about the selecting, filtering, or distorting functions of the self-concept could now be assessed using the methods and models provided by cognitive psychology. With the self-concept operationalized as a set of cognitive structures, it became obvious that the self-concept can influence every aspect of the processing of self-relevant information. Individuals appear to be differentially sensitive to stimuli that are self-relevant and to privilege the processing of these stimuli. Such selective processing seems to occur even outside of the subject's awareness.

Information Processing

Research on the information processing consequences of the self-structure continues to grow, and some of the relationships between the self and various cognitive functions are much better documented than others. Extensive reviews of this research can be found in Kihlstrom & Cantor (1984), Greenwald & Pratkanis (1984), Greenwald (1980), Markus & Sentis (1982), Singer & Salovey (1985). Summarized briefly, these consequences include:

1. Individuals show a heightened sensitivity to self-relevant stimuli. Bargh (1982) for example, noted that self-relevant adjectives (trait terms that were very descriptive of the individual) interfered with performance when they

were presented in the unattended ear during a dichotic listening task. Performance was impaired during the presentation of the self-relevant words, yet following the task subjects reported no awareness of the words being presented. More recently, J. M. Nuttin Jr. (1985) has described the name-letter effect, or the tendency to prefer the letters of one's own name. Subjects were presented with a pair of letters, each pair containing a letter from either their first or last name. Asked to choose as quickly as they could which letter they preferred, subjects reliably chose the letter from their own name. Subjects given a chance to study the letter pairs carefully had no awareness that their name was embedded among the pairs of letters.

2. Self-congruent stimuli are efficiently processed. Numerous studies have found that stimulus materials that are highly self-descriptive are processed quickly and confidently (e.g. Markus 1977, Kuiper & Rogers 1979, Mueller 1982). Druian & Catrambone (1986) found that individuals scoring high on the Machiavellianism scale were significantly faster in reading a story congruent with high Machiavellianism than when reading a story congruent with low Machiavellianism. Parallel results were obtained for subjects scoring low on Machiavellianism. Other aspects of efficient processing include more accurate discrimination in self-relevant domains. Thus, Hamill (1980) found higher hit rates in a recognition task for faces that had been judged for independence by those subjects for whom independence was self-descriptive than for subjects for whom it was not.

3. Self-relevant stimuli show enhanced recall and recognition. This effect has been extremely well demonstrated; memory for all aspects of one's behavior is enhanced relative to memory about others or to nonsocial information (Wallen 1942, Cartwright 1956, Jarvella & Collars 1974, Bower & Gilligan 1979, Hull & Levy 1979, Keenan & Baillet 1979, Kuiper & Rogers 1979, Ross & Sicoly 1979, Greenwald 1980, Markus 1980, Brenner 1983, Mills 1983, Mueller et al 1984, Nasby 1985, Strube et al 1986).

4. Individuals make confident behavioral predictions, attributions, and inferences in self-relevant domains (e.g. Markus et al 1982, Anderson 1984, Anderson & Ross 1984).

5. Individuals are resistant to information that is incongruent with the self-structure. They often appear to reject those accounts of their behavior that differ from their own accounts (e.g. Markus 1977, Swann & Read 1981a,b, Swann & Hill 1982, Tesser & Campbell 1983). In addition, they are likely to make situational attributions for any behavior they enact that is inconsistent with their self-view (Kulik et al 1986).

Affect Regulation

One of the most important intrapersonal functions that the self-concept serves is the regulation of affect. Most affective states implicate the self. Giving special attention to the processing of self-relevant information is one method of regulating affect; but individuals engage in a variety of behaviors that have this effect. The regulation of affect typically involves defending one's self against negative emotional states. This is accomplished by maintaining consistency with one's previous views of self (most of which are usually positive), and by enhancing and promoting the self whenever possible.

When individuals receive information that challenges a prevailing conception of the self (e.g. being told that they are not as dominant as they thought, or that they are not academically competent), the structure of the self-concept is threatened and thus their affective state is disturbed. The most obvious choice of action in this situation is to reaffirm the self—to recruit into the working self-concept conceptions of the self that verify the prevailing conception (e.g. Markus & Kunda 1986), or to interact with others who provide support for one's prevailing view of self (Swann & Hill 1982, Swann 1985). In this way, maintaining the stability of the self is one way to regulate affect. It appears that the impressive stability accorded the self (Markus 1977, Greenwald 1980, Mortimer & Lorence 1981, Swann & Read 1981a,b, Swann & Hill 1982, Swann 1983) and the perseverance of certain beliefs about self (Ross et al 1975, Lepper et al 1986) may not be achieved by a flat-out denial of inconsistent information, but rather by an elaborate process in which the individual evaluates the information and then attempts to integrate the self-conceptions offered by the environment with existing ones (e.g. through the process of self-confirmatory attribution, Kulik et al 1986). In many cases this will involve a great deal of work that may not be revealed by global self-descriptive measures. The stability of the self that is implied by such measures may belie significant malleability or fluidity that occurs as individuals respond to information that challenges their view of themselves.

It has been popular to contrast the self-consistency and self-enhancement motives (for reviews, see Moreland & Sweeney 1984, Shrauger 1975). These studies have focused on how people with negative self-conceptions or low self-esteem react to positive (and hence inconsistent) feedback. The results of numerous studies have been equivocal, and various interpretations of the apparent conflict have been offered (Swann 1983, Schlenker 1985b, Raynor & McFarlin 1986, Trope 1986). Currently, most researchers view the two motives as quite interdependent (Epstein 1973, Rosenberg 1979, Greenwald 1980, Trope 1986). If we assume that affect is the primary basis for determining which self-representations are organized together in the self-concept (Greenwald & Pratkanis 1984, Fast 1985), then maintaining the structure of the self is essential for a positive affective state and, conversely, maintaining this affective state is essential for maintaining the structure of the self.

In the absence of a direct challenge or threat to the self, people are generally self-enhancing; that is, they prefer and seek out positive information about themselves. People may structure their activities to enhance the probability that they will receive positive feedback; and, when the feedback is negative, they will selectively interpret information in such a way as to minimize the threat to their positive self-conceptions. Reviews of self-enhancement research can be found in Greenwald (1980), C. R. Snyder et al (1983), and Taylor & Brown (1986).

Tesser's self-evaluation maintenance theory (1986; Tesser & Campbell 1983) suggests that people vary their self-definitions so that an individual claims as most personally relevant those activities he or she is best at. However, he qualifies this statement by suggesting that it is *relative* performance in comparison to similar others, rather than absolute level of performance, that is critical. Tesser posits that people can maintain positive self-evaluations in one of two ways: by being better than similar others on personally relevant dimensions, or by "basking in the reflected glory" (cf Cialdini et al 1976) of a superior other on irrelevant dimensions. Data from a variety of studies by Tesser and his colleagues (Tesser & Campbell 1980, 1982, Tesser & Smith 1980, Tesser & Paulus 1983, Tesser et al 1984) support the idea that people will vary personal relevance and activity choice or the perceived closeness of interaction partners in a manner that enhances their self-evaluations, particularly relative to others.

Similarly, a variety of other work suggests that people can maintain or enhance their self-evaluations through selective social comparisons. Lewicki (1983), for example, demonstrates that people choose to judge others on dimensions that are personally relevant; this enhances the probability that the self will be seen as superior to the other (see also Taylor et al 1983). Work on downward social comparisons (Wills 1981, Wood et al 1985) demonstrates that such selective comparisons are frequently used to enhance self-evaluations and subjective well-being, particularly under conditions of threat to the self. Such downward comparisons are not only sought, but are achieved through biases in perception of others [e.g. false consensus effects (Sherman et al 1984, Campbell 1986) or attributive projection (Sherwood 1981)], and through the active construction of standards in comparison to which the person fares well (Taylor et al 1983). For example, Campbell (1986) finds that people underestimate consensus for domains in which they have high abilities, which lets them see themselves as even better relative to others. People also overestimate consensus for their opinions and for domains in which they lack ability, helping them see the self positively in these domains.

Yet another way in which people are self-enhancing is in their selective interpretation of events. For example, research on biases in memory shows that people selectively remember their successes and revise their memories to support positive self-conceptions (for reviews of this literature, see Greenwald 1980 or Ross & Conway 1986). The existence of self-serving biases in attributions is well-documented (e.g. Miller & Ross 1975, Bradley 1978), and evidence is mounting that these attributions may, at least at times, be motivated (Snyder et al 1978, Zuckerman 1979). Similarly, C. R. Snyder and his colleagues (1983, Snyder 1985) review literature on excuse-making, documenting a variety of ways actors can avoid the implications of their negative performances. Another strategy for handling challenges to the self in one domain is to bolster the self in another domain ("I may not be smart, but I sure am nice"). This process has been termed compensatory self-inflation by Greenberg & Pyszczynski (1985) and self-affirmation by Steele & Liu (1983). It may be one of the most efficient methods of handling a short-term challenge to the self. Finally, people may regulate negative affect by reducing their self-awareness; for example, Hull (1981, Hull et al 1983, Hull & Young 1983) demonstrates that people may drink following negative experiences because alcohol decreases self-awareness and the associated negative affective state.

People are positively biased not only about their pasts, but also about their futures. Taylor & Brown (1986) review literature showing that people maintain illusory perception of control (e.g. Langer 1975) and are unrealistically optimistic about their futures (e.g. Weinstein 1980). Similarly, Kunda (1985) demonstrates self-serving biases in inferential processes which may mediate this unrealistic optimism. Optimism about the future is related to defensiveness about the past: Norem & Cantor (1986) show that optimists had high expectations and perceptions of control before a performance; and, if they failed, they used self-serving attributions to cope with this.

People may even be self-denigrating in the service of self-enhancement. Avoiding self-esteem loss or threats to more valued self-perceptions may lead people to engage in self-handicapping (Berglas & Jones 1978; Jones & Berglas 1978), engaging in self-defeating actions prior to a performance to provide a ready-made excuse for failure. Shyness (Snyder et al 1985), test anxiety (Smith et al 1982), drinking and drug use (Berglas & Jones 1978, Jones & Berglas 1978), and hypochondriasis (Smith et al 1983) have all been shown to have this ultimately self-protecting function.

A controversial issue is how aware people are of various attempts to regulate affect. Generally, people are not presumed to be aware of engaging in self-enhancement, although in some conditions they can be (e.g. Snyder et al 1983, Taylor & Brown 1986, Tesser 1986). However, researchers differ on how motivated this lack of awareness is presumed to be. Some believe that self-enhancement strategies can be motivated self-deceptions (Sackheim & Gur 1978, Gur & Sackheim 1979, Lazarus 1983, Snyder et al 1983, Taylor & Brown 1986). In contrast, others (e.g. Greenwald 1984) suggest that the basis for lack of awareness is in the structure of the cognitive system, with its capacity for automatic processing, and that defensive motivation is not necessary to explain this lack of awareness.

Motivation

A third important function performed by the self is that of motivating individuals, of moving them to action. In the section on self-regulation we discussed how goals are generally assumed to control behavior. In this section we are concerned with the interface between the individual's goals and the self-concept. The question here is how goals, aspirations, motives, fears, and threats are represented in the self-concept.

Nuttin (1984) has noted the need to understand how abstract, nebulous, sometimes unconscious motives are transformed into very personal and concrete intentions and plans. Several theorists have begun to personalize motivation and have framed the question of motivation directly in terms of self-conceptions. These approaches include Markus & Nurius's (1986) conception of possible selves, Wicklund & Gollwitzer's (1982) symbolic self-completion theory, and Schlenker's (1985b) discussion of desired self-images. Markus & Nurius (1986) define possible selves as self-conceptions of the person's perceived potential (either feared or desired), and suggest that they function to individualize global motives and thus can be viewed as the cognitive component of motivation. Possible selves are images of the person having actually achieved a goal; as such, they are both specific and personalized, qualities which may enable them to regulate behavior. Possible selves have been shown to relate systematically to a person's current self-conceptions, especially in domains for which the person has a self-schema (Wurf & Markus 1986a), to mediate feelings about the current self (Markus & Nurius 1986), to regulate effort and task persistence (Ruvolo & Markus 1986), and to be related to coping outcomes (Porter et al 1984).

Schlenker (1985b) also discusses motivation in terms of achieving particular self-conceptions, or desired selves. Desired selves are "what the person would *like to be* and thinks he or she *really can be*" (p. 74). Thus desired selves concentrate on positive and realistic possibility, and are a particularly important subset of the person's possible selves. Schlenker hypothesizes that the desired selves brought to mind at a given time are determined both by situational constraints and by the anticipated audience for the behavior (which can include the self). These available desired selves are presumed to mediate behavior by acting as the cognitive structures that process information in the setting, and by acting as relevant standards for behavior.

Wicklund & Gollwitzer (1982) provide yet another approach to the relationship of self-conceptions to motivation and behavior. These authors stress the importance of commitment to self-definitions. According to their theory, people who are committed to a self-definition strive to achieve "completeness"; that is, they are concerned with establishing that the self-definition in question is an enduring and unquestioned aspect of self. People who are "incomplete" (have not yet achieved, or are interrupted in the process of displaying or enacting relevant behaviors) with regard to a particular committed self-definition feel a psychological tension that causes them to seek alternative *symbolic* routes to achieving the self-definition. These symbolic routes substitute for the achievement of the self-definition by establishing the person as having actually achieved the definition in the eyes of others. Experiments on symbolic self-completion (summarized in Wicklund & Gollwitzer 1982) show that subjects who were committed to a self-definition but who were incomplete in achieving it, described themselves more in terms of the self-definition, were more likely to attempt to influence or proselytize people to endorse the relevant opinion or activity, were unwilling to admit to mistakes made in the activity, and were more likely to display visible symbols (e.g. wearing crucifixes for a religious self-definition), compared to complete or noncommitted subjects. Thus, people committed to an as-yet-unachieved self-relevant goal use multiple paths, symbolic as well as direct, and expend great effort to achieve desired self-definitions.

Recent approaches to motivation developed by personality and clinical psychologists (see Sorrentino & Higgins 1986) also concentrate on the personalization of motivation, discussing how the person's individuality gets played out as they approach their life tasks (Cantor & Kihlstrom 1986), personal projects (Little 1983), current concerns (Klinger 1975), or psychological career (Raynor & McFarlin 1986). While only some of these theories explicitly discuss the relationship to self-conceptions, for all of them the links could be drawn.

Cantor & Kihlstrom (1986) are the most explicit in tying their motivational framework to self-conceptions. These authors posit the notion of "life tasks," or the problems that an individual sees the self as working on at a particular time of life. Life tasks are thus fairly broad units that integrate and give meaning to a wide variety of activities that the individual may undertake. The individual's idiosyncratic construal of a life task is presumed to be importantly determined by his or her self-knowledge. Furthermore, how the task is framed determines what strategies the person will use for dealing with it. Thus, Cantor & Kihlstrom attempt, through the life task conception, to tie self-knowledge to self-regulation. Research on life tasks is beginning to demonstrate these links. For example, Cantor et al (1985) looked at how college freshmen dealt with life tasks such as making friends, establishing an identity, and getting good grades. Subjects were asked to rate each life task on dimensions such as difficulty and enjoyment and to specify plans for dealing with hypothetical problems within each task category. Individuals judged life tasks quite differently, presumably based on their available self-knowledge. These differences in judgments had important implications for self-regulation. Life tasks perceived as more difficult also had more well-elaborated plans; furthermore, the elaboration of these plans was associated with outcomes such as grade point average and perceived stress.

INTERPERSONAL PROCESSES MEDIATED BY
THE SELF-CONCEPT

As the person strives to carry out such personally motivated behavior, he or she is inevitably swept up in social interaction. Other people often serve as the means for achieving one's goals, requiring the person to have skills for successful negotiation. Further, these interactions—a cup of coffee with a friend or an intimate moment with a lover—are very often ends in themselves. Because of these dependencies on others, people both shape and are shaped by their social interactions. The self-concept provides a framework that guides the interpretation of one's social experiences but that also regulates one's participation in these experiences. A great deal of social behavior, sometimes quite consciously and sometimes unwittingly, is in the service of various self-concept requirements. The relevant research questions include how the self-concept influences social perception, how the self-concept guides the selection of situations and interaction partners, what strategies the individual uses to shape and interpret interactions with others, and how the person reacts to feedback from others that is incongruent with the self-concept.

Social Perception

Researchers interested in self-structures have extended their investigations from studying how these structures influence processing information about the self to how these structures influence the processing of information about other people (see Markus & Smith 1981, Markus et al 1985, for reviews). Studies generally find that people tend to judge others on dimensions that are personally important to themselves (Fong & Markus 1982, Lewicki 1983, 1984). Further, when making judgments about others on dimensions that are not only self-relevant, but for which the person also has a well-elaborated self-schema, people encode the information in larger chunks (Markus et al 1985), process it more deeply (Kuiper & Rogers 1979, Hamill 1980, Kuiper 1981), draw a greater number of and more extreme inferences and are more confident about these (Fong & Markus 1982, Markus et al 1985), and are more responsive to processing goals (Markus et al 1985) than are people who lack a self-schema in the domain. The use of the self as a reference point depends on whether the person is primarily focused on the self or on the other, and on relative amount of information about each (Smith 1982, Holyoak & Gordon 1983, Srull & Gaelick 1983, Markus et al 1985): people are more likely to use the self as a basis for judging others when they are focused more on the self than on the other, and when they have much information about the self, but little about the other.

Although most research on how the self influences social perception finds that people are inclined to see others as similar to the self, there are conditions under which the person will see the self as being very different: when the characteristic of concern is a trait rather than an opinion (Marks 1984); when the person has a committed self-definition (Wurf & Markus 1986b); when the person has a high need for uniqueness (Snyder & Fromkin 1980, Kernis 1984); when, because only a moderate level of similarity is preferred, the similarity of others is too high (Snyder & Fromkin 1980, Markus & Kunda 1986); or when the person is motivated to make the self feel better about a negative self-conception by seeing others as being in a worse condition (Wills 1981, Taylor et al 1983, Wood et al 1985). Both cognitive and motivational factors thus seem important in determining the effects of the self on social perception (see Holmes 1978, Sherwood 1981, Sherman et al 1983, 1984, Lewicki 1984).

Situation and Partner Choice

People have knowledge of situations (Cantor et al 1981) as well as of themselves. Both types of knowledge, as well as individual goals, importantly determine that person's situational choices. For example, Snyder (1979) suggests that low self-monitors, who are concerned with being consistent with themselves, have well-elaborated conceptions of themselves in different situations, while high self-monitors, who care about being consistent with the situation, have well-elaborated conceptions of prototypical persons in situations. Accordingly, Snyder & Gangestad (1982) find that low self-monitors preferred situations that let them express their own dispositions, while high self-monitors preferred well-structured situations. Similarly, Lord (1982) demonstrates that similarities in people's conceptions of situations predict whether their behavior will be consistent between different situations. A field study on college students' housing choices (Niedenthal et al 1985) demonstrates that self-knowledge can influence choice in actual, important situations: students, particularly those who were low self-monitors or who saw their housing choice as reflecting personal rather than financial concerns, used a self-to-prototype matching strategy to guide them in their decisions.

Self-conceptions and goals also determine choice of and behavior in personal relationships. Cantor et al (1984) find that people's choice of interaction partners is determined both by the appropriateness of the partner for the activity and by how comfortable the person feels in various situations: people who differentiated more between the comfort of different situations were also more exacting in their partner choice. Similarly, Snyder et al (1983) find that people's choice of partner for casual activities was determined by personal dispositions for low self-monitors and by perceived appropriateness of partner for high self-monitors. High and low self-monitors differ similarly in attention to pragmatic versus personal goals in their intimate relationships (Snyder & Simpson 1984). The interrelationship of self-conceptions may be a critical factor in relationship satisfaction. For example, Swann (1985) suggests that relationship satisfaction depends on partners' confirming each other's self-conceptions; similarly, Schlenker (1984) suggests that satisfaction depends on the partners validating each other's desired self.

Interaction Strategies

The self functions not only to perceive and set the stage for interactions, but also to direct them once the scene is in motion. Much of the work done on the role of the self in social interaction has been done by researchers studying self-presentation, or impression management. The focus of these theories is on how a person tries to shape a particular identity in the mind of his or her audience during an interaction, using a variety of strategies and tactics to fulfill one or more of several possible motives.

An identity is an image of the self that one tries to convey to others; it exists both as a cognitive structure in the mind of the person trying to convey it (see the section on self-structure) and as an entity out in the world. Conceived of as an entity in the world, the situated identity (Alexander & Wiley 1981) is a "joint construction" of the person, the audience, and the situation (Schlenker 1985b) that functions for both the individual and the interaction. Identities are presented to an audience. While early developments in the impression management literature (e.g. Goffman 1959) focused on presentation to external audiences, the recent literature focuses on self-presentation to an internal audience as well (e.g. Baumeister 1982, Tetlock 1985). In fact, two different types of internal audiences have been posited: the self and an internalized reference group (Baldwin 1984, Greenwald & Breckler 1985, Schlenker 1985b).

Different audiences inspire different goals or motives in social interaction. A focus on an external audience may whet the desire for approval and attention (Cheek & Hogan 1983, Hogan 1982) or for social power and influence (Jones & Pittman 1982, Tedeschi & Norman 1985). A focus on an internal audience may lead the person to desire predictability and consistency (Cheek & Hogan 1983, Swann 1985) or to seek signs that one is achieving a desired or ideal self (Baumeister 1982, Wicklund & Gollwitzer 1982, Schlenker 1985b). In turn, the responsiveness of an external audience to the actor's goal has a significant impact on the quality of the relationship (Swann & Giuliano 1982, Schlenker 1984, Swann 1985); and the satisfaction of the internal audience has important consequences for global self-esteem (Greenwald & Breckler 1985) and more specific affects (Higgins et al 1985, 1986).

Depending on the goal and on the audience, the person will try to construct a different identity, using one or more impression management techniques (see Jones & Pittman 1982 or Tedeschi & Norman 1985 for taxonomies of strategies). The use of impression management techniques is seen by most theorists as being potentially either conscious or unconscious (Cheek & Hogan 1983, Paulhus 1984, Schlenker 1985b, Tetlock & Manstead 1985). The effective use of conscious impression management may rely on the person's level of self-awareness (Cheek & Hogan 1983, Buss & Briggs 1984, Schlenker 1985b), while unconscious impression management is usually conceived of as an automatized process. Discussions about the effective management of self-presentation have begun to lead to links with the literature on self-regulation (e.g. Swann 1983, Schlenker 1985b, Tedeschi & Norman 1985).

Reactions to Feedback

A person acting in a situation attends to both the reactions of others and to his or her own behaviors (Darley & Fazio 1980). Both self-perceptions and others' reactions thus constitute feedback to the self-system. This feedback may be either congruent or incongruent with current or with desired self-images. The congruence, affective valence, and personal importance of this feedback, and the goals and interrelationship of the actors (Swann 1984) determine the person's cognitive, affective, and behavioral reactions.

People may bias their chances of receiving congruent feedback by the way they seek information in an interaction. The literature on hypothesis testing in social interactions suggests that people may be biased to seek, and hence to receive, confirmatory feedback (Snyder & Swann 1978a,b, Shrauger & Schoeneman 1979, Nisbett & Ross 1980, Snyder & Gangestad 1981, Darley & Gross 1983; see also Semin & Strack 1980, Trope & Bassok 1982, Fiske & Taylor 1984, Swann 1984, Trope et al 1984 for discussions on limitations to this effect). People seek confirmation about themselves as well as about other people (Snyder & Skrypnek 1981, Swann & Read 1981a,b). Feedback that is congruent with one's self-conceptions is self-affirming and can have positive affective consequences (Schlenker 1985b, Swann 1985).

When a person receives feedback that is incongruent with self-conceptions, he or she may (*a*) cognitively reconcile the discrepancy (*b*) act against it, or (*c*) act in accordance with it. If the person acts in accordance with incongruent feedback, this may or may not lead to the person's accepting the new identity (see Snyder & Swann 1978b, Fazio et al 1981 for two examples of people internalizing others' perceptions; see Swann 1984 for a more general discussion of when this will occur).

The cognitive strategies people use to cope with disconfirming feedback include selective attention, selective memory, and selective interpretation (Swann 1983). These strategies enable the person to reinterpret the disconfirming feedback to see it as irrelevant or as not disconfirming. Although little research has directly addressed the cognitive strategies used in response to self-disconfirming feedback (see Swann 1983, Miller & Turnbull 1986 for reviews), research on biases in social memory and social inference suggests that a variety of biases support confirming over disconfirming information (see Fiske & Taylor 1984 for a review).

Behavioral reactions to self-disconfirming information are discussed in the literature on self-fulfilling prophecies, or interpersonal expectancy effects (for general reviews, see Darley & Fazio 1980, Jussim 1986, Miller & Turnbull 1986, Rosenthal & Rubin 1978). Researchers initially focused on how people behaved to confirm others' perceptions of them; more recently, researchers have turned to exploring the limits of the effect. Whether a person acts to dispel or to confirm another's expectations depends on whether the expectancy is positive or negative (Miller & Turnbull 1986) and on how big the discrepancy is (Fiske & Taylor 1984). In addition, reactions to feedback depend on whether the person is aware of the other's expectation (Hilton & Darley 1985) and whether the person believes that others will learn of it (Baumeister & Jones 1978). Finally, the person's reaction depends on dispositional factors such as (a) whether the disconfirmed self-view is one that the person is highly certain of (Swann & Ely 1984), has a self-schema for (Markus 1977, Wurf & Markus 1983, Jussim 1986), or considers highly important (Fiske & Taylor 1984); (b) situational factors such as the status equality with the other (Jussim 1986); (c) the perceived costs and rewards of reacting (Miller & Turnbull 1986); and (d) the opportunities for doing so (Miller & Turnbull 1986; see also Darley et al 1986).

Recent research and theorizing promises further progress in research on the role of the self-concept in interpersonal interaction. Advances include, first, the suggestion that the nature of the relationship may critically influence the strategies the self will use in social interaction (Jussim 1986; Tedeschi & Norman 1985); and second, the demonstration that the person's interaction goals influence his or her behavior toward others (Darley et al 1986). A third advance in the literature is the attention to reactions of "targets" as well as of perceivers (Hilton & Darley 1985; Swann & Ely 1984). Fourth, several theorists suggest that in order to study self-presentation effectively, the process will have to be studied over time. While there is theorizing about how the self acts in interaction over time (e.g. Darley & Fazio 1980), little research actually undertakes such a process analysis. A fifth promising direction is the examination of how self-conceptions, desired or possible as well as actual, impact on and are affected by the process (e.g. see Wicklund & Gollwitzer 1982, Schlenker 1985b).

CONCLUSION

In this chapter we have reviewed the recent research in social psychology that emphasizes the dynamic nature of the self-concept. The view of the self-concept as an active, interpretive structure that is continually involved in the regulation of on-going behavior is also receiving attention in clinical psychology (e.g. Goldfried & Robins 1982, 1983; Horowitz 1979), sociology (e.g. Gecas 1982), and anthropology (Shweder & LeVine 1984). The self-concept emerges in all of this work as a critical component of the individual's affective and cognitive system. When stimuli, experiences, or events cross the threshold of self-concept such that they achieve self-relevant meaning, they become special. Yet exactly how the self-concept functions in relation to various affective and cognitive processes, and how it can be differentiated from them, remains to be explored.

With respect to the content and structure of the self-concept, we can ask many more questions about the nature of self-representations, about the principles that guide their organization, and about how this organization can be threatened or disrupted. The work reviewed here has yet to confront the perenially thorny issue of what it is that is represented in self-representations (see Shevrin 1986) or, who is this "I" that is asking what is this "me"? The question of individual differences in the structure and organization of the self-concept has barely been broached. How do self-concepts differ in elaboration, integration, and differentiation, and how is this related to the significant experiences of one's social and developmental history? Do individuals differ in which types of self-representations predominate in their self-concepts? What do self-concepts in crisis or conflict look like? These types of questions, of course, lead to the speculation that self-concepts differing in their form may also differ in how they function. Are some self-concepts more centrally involved in regulating behavior than others? Is the self-concept of the individual who is generally less self-reflective and self-focused perhaps less elaborated and hence less likely to mediate on-going behavior?

A significant gap in our understanding concerns when and how self-representations will control behavior. What distinguishes those instances in which one sits in a chair in front of the television and thinks "I shouldn't be eating this ice cream" and "I should be writing my paper" from those instances where one resists the ice cream, doesn't turn on the television, and continues working? Certainly the role of a variety of self-conceptions, standards, behavioral rules, and strategies are critical here, but when and how do they impel behavior? Toward this end, the research on general self-regulatory processes (reviewed above) should be integrated with those studies focusing specifically on how the self regulates intrapersonal behavior. In particular, the place of affect regulation in the behavioral regulation cycle should be drawn out.

The role of the self in interpersonal interaction has been explored in a variety of creative studies. Most of these studies examine how the self guides behavior in interaction; relatively few examine how these interpersonal events in turn have an effect on the structures and organization of self-conceptions. The self guides self-presentation, but what is the impact of making these presentations on the self? When will the person treat self-presentations as unrepresentative acts, and when will the person take these actions to heart and incorporate them into the self-concept? How does the presentation of the self in one situation influence how the person acts in other situations or with other people? Are particular others important in providing feedback to the self, or will any audience do? How are these audiences represented with respect to the self-concept? Such questions remain to be explored and may have important implications for the study of topics such as social support (e.g. Swann & Predmore 1985).

The research summarized here has focused primarily on how the self-concept may guide and control behavior. The reciprocal relation is assumed, but it is much less often addressed. How is the self-concept adjusted and calibrated as a consequence of one's actions? What happens to the self-concept of the individual who keeps changing what is personally relevant to maintain self-esteem? And finally, what is the relationship between momentary variations in which self-conceptions are active and more long-term, enduring changes in the self-concept? It should be possible to develop a model of the self-concept that reveals its relatively continuous and stable nature but at the same time reflects the fact that the self-concept is dynamic and capable of change, as it reflects and mediates the actions of individuals who are negotiating a variety of social circumstances.

ACKNOWLEDGMENTS

We would like to thank Diane Crane for her invaluable assistance with the references and Deborah Francis for preparation of the manuscript. Research for this chapter was supported by a NSF grant to Hazel Markus (BNS-8408057). The second author was supported by a National Science Foundation Graduate Fellowship.

Literature Cited

Ajzen, I. 1985. From intentions to actions: A theory of planned behavior. See Kuhl & Beckmann 1985, pp. 11–39

Alexander, C. N. Jr., Wiley, M. G. 1981. Situated activity and identity formation. In *Social Psychology: Sociological Perspectives*, ed. M. Rosenberg, R. H. Turner, pp. 269–89. New York: Basic Books

Allport, G. 1955. *Becoming: Basic Considerations for a Psychology of Personality*. New Haven: Yale Univ. Press

Anderson, J. R. 1976. *Language, M mory, and Thought*. Hillsdale, NJ: Erlbaum

Anderson, J. R. 1982. Acquisition of cognitive skill. *Psychol. Rev.* 89:369–406

Anderson, J. R., Bower, G. H. 1973. *Human Associative Memory*. Washington, DC: Winston

Anderson, S. M. 1984. Self-knowledge and social inference: II. The diagnosticity of cognitive/affective and behavioral data. *J. Pers. Soc. Psychol.* 46:294–307

Anderson, S. M., Ross, L. 1984. Self-knowledge and social inference: I. The impact of cognitive/affective and behavioral data. *J. Pers. Soc. Psychol.* 46:280–93

Baldwin, J. M. 1897. *Social and Ethical Interpretations*. New York: MacMillan

Baldwin, M. 1984. *Private audiences*. PhD thesis. Univ. Waterloo, Ontario

Bandura, A. 1977. Self-efficacy: Toward a unifying theory of behavioral change. *Psychol. Rev.* 84:191–215

Bandura, A. 1978. The self system in reciprocal determinism. *Am. Psychol.* 33:344–58

Bandura, A. 1982. Self-efficacy mechanism in human agency. *Am. Psychol.* 37:122–47

Bandura, A. 1986. *Social Foundations of Thought and Action: A Social Cognitive Theory*. Englewood Cliffs, NJ: Prentice-Hall

Bandura, A., Reese, L., Adams, N. E. 1982. Microanalysis of action and fear arousal as a function of differential levels of perceived self-efficacy. *J. Pers. Soc. Psychol.* 43:5–21

Bandura, A., Schunk, D. H. 1981. Cultivating competence, self-efficacy, and intrinsic interest through proximal self-motivation. *J. Pers. Soc. Psychol.* 41:586–98

Bargh, J. A. 1982. Attention and automaticity in the processing of self-relevant information. *J. Pers. Soc. Psychol.* 43:425–36

Baumeister, R. F. 1982. A self-presentational view of social phenomena. *Psychol. Bull.* 91:3–26

Baumeister, R. F., Jones, E. E. 1978. When self-presentation is constrained by the target's knowledge: Consistency and compensation. *J. Pers. Soc. Psychol.* 36:608–18

Beck, A. T. 1967. *Depression: Causes and Treatment*. Philadelphia: Univ. Pa. Press

Berglas, S., Jones, E. E. 1978. Drug choice as a self-handicapping strategy in response to noncontingent success. *J. Pers. Soc. Psychol.* 36:405–17

Bower, G. H., Gilligan, S. G. 1979. Remembering information related to one's self. *J. Res. Pers.* 13:420–32

Bradley, G. W. 1978. Self-serving biases in the attribution process: A reexamination of the fact and fiction question. *J. Pers. Soc. Psychol.* 36:56–71

Breckler, S. J., Greenwald, A. G. 1986. Motivational facets of the self. See Sorrentino & Higgins 1986, pp. 145–64

Brenner, M. 1983. The next-in-line effect. *J. Verb. Learn. Verb. Behav.* 12:320–23

Brickman, P., Janoff-Bulman, R. 1977. Pleasure and pain in social comparison. See Suls & Miller 1977, pp. 149–86

Bruner, J. 1986. *Actual Minds, Possible Worlds*. New York: Plenum

Burke, P. J. 1980. The self: Measurement requirements from an interactionist perspective. *Psychol. Q.* 43:18–29

Buss, A. H., Briggs, S. R. 1984. Drama and the self in social interaction. *J. Pers. Soc. Psychol.* 47:1310–24

Campbell, J. D. 1986. Similarity and uniqueness: The effects of attribute type, relevance, and individual differences in self-esteem and depression. *J. Pers. Soc. Psychol.* 50:281–94

Cantor, N., Kihlstrom, J. 1986. *Personality and Social Intelligence*. Englewood Cliffs, NJ: Prentice Hall

Cantor, N., Mackie, D., Lord, C. G. 1984. Choosing partners and activities: The social perceiver decides to mix it up. *Soc. Cognit.* 3:256–72

Cantor, N., Markus, H., Niedenthal, P., Nurius, P. 1986. On motivation and the self-concept. See Sorrentino & Higgins 1986, pp. 96–121

Cantor, N., Mischel, W., Schwartz, J. A. 1981. A prototype analysis of psychological situations. *Cognit. Psychol.* 14:45–77

Cantor, N., Niedenthal, P. M., Brower, A. 1985. *Life task problem-solving in the transition to college*. Presented at Ann. Meet. Soc. Exp. Soc. Psychol., Evanston, IL

Cartwright, D. 1956. Self-consistency as a factor affecting immediate recall. *J. Abnorm. Soc. Psychol.* 52:212–19

Carver, C. S., Scheier, M. F. 1981. *Attention and Self-Regulation: A Control Theory Approach to Human Behavior*. New York: Springer-Verlag. 403 pp.

Carver, C. S., Scheier, M. F. 1982. Control theory: A useful conceptual framework for personality-social, clinical, and health psychology. *Psychol. Bull.* 92:111–35

Cheek, J. M., Hogan, R. 1983. Self-concepts, self-presentations, and moral judgments. See Suls & Greenwald 1983, pp. 249–73

Cialdini, R. B., Borden, R. J., Thorne, A., Walker, M. R., Freeman, S., Sloan, L. R. 1976. Basking in reflected glory: Three (football) field studies. *J. Pers. Soc. Psychol.* 34:366–75

Coleman, L. M., Antonucci, T. C. 1983. Impact of work on women at midlife. *Dev. Psychol.* 19:290–94

Combs, A., Snygg, D. 1959. *Individual Behavior*. New York: Harper. 2nd ed.

Constantian, C. A. 1981. *Attitudes, beliefs, and behavior in regard to spending time alone*. PhD thesis. Harvard Univ., Cambridge, MA

Cooley, D. H. 1902. *Human Nature and the Social Order*. New York: Scribners

Csikszentmihalyi, M. 1975. *Beyond Boredom and Anxiety*. San Francisco: Jossey-Bass

Darley, J. M., Fazio, R. H. 1980. Expectancy confirmation processes arising in the social interaction sequence. *Am. Psychol.* 35:867–81

Darley, J. M., Fleming, J. H., Hilton, J. L.,

Swann, W. B. Jr. 1986. Dispelling negative expectancies: The impact of interaction goals and target characteristics on the expectancy confirmation process. Princeton Univ. Unpublished

Darley, J. M., Gross, P. 1983. A hypothesis confirming bias in labeling effects. *J. Pers. Soc. Psychol.* 44:20–33

√Dennett, D. 1982. Why do we think what we do about why we think what we do? *Cognition* 12:219–37

Derry, P. A., Kuiper, N. A. 1981. Schematic processing and self-reference in clinical depression. *J. Abnorm. Psychol.* 90:286–97

De Volder, M. L., Lens, W. 1982. Academic achievement and future time perspective as a cognitive motivational concept. *J. Pers. Soc. Psychol.* 42:566–71

Druian, P., Catrambone, R. 1986. Cognitive accessibility of the self-concept in person perception. Behav. Sci. Res. Found. Unpublished

Epstein, S. 1973. The self-concept revisited. *Am. Psychol.* 28:404–16

Epstein, S. 1980. The self-concept: A review and the proposal of an integrated theory of personality. In *Personality: Basic Issues and Current Research*, ed. E. Staub. Englewood Cliffs, NJ: Prentice-Hall

Erikson, E. H. 1946. Ego development and historical change. *The Psychoanalytic Study of the Child* 2:359–96. New York: Int. Univ. Press

Erikson, E. H. 1950. Identification as the basis for a theory of motivation. *Am. Psychol. Rev.* 26:14–21

Erikson, E. H. 1959. *Identity and the Life Cycle.* New York: Int. Univ. Press

Fast, I. 1985. *Event Theory: A Piaget-Freud Integration.* Hillsdale, NJ: Erlbaum

Fazio, R. H., Effrein, E. A., Falender, V. J. 1981. Self-perceptions following social interaction. *J. Pers. Soc. Psychol.* 41:232–42

Fiske, S. T., Taylor, S. E. 1984. *Social Cognition.* Reading, MA: Addison-Wesley

Flavell, J. H. 1979. Metacognition and cognitive monitoring: A new area of psychological inquiry. *Am. Psychol.* 34:906–11

Flavell, J. H. 1981. Monitoring social cognitive enterprises: Something else that may develop in the area of social cognition. See Flavell & Ross 1981, pp. 272–87

Flavell, J. H., Ross, L. 1981. *Social Cognitive Development: Frontiers and Possible Futures.* New York: Cambridge Univ. Press

Fong, G. T., Markus, H. 1982. Self-schemas and judgments about others. *Soc. Cognit.* 1:191–204

Freud, S. 1925. *Collected Papers.* London: Hogarth

Frey, K. S., Ruble, D. N. 1985. What children say when the teacher is not around:

Conflicting goals in social comparison and performance assessment in the classroom. *J. Pers. Soc. Psychol.* 48:550–62

Gecas, V. 1982. The self-concept. *Ann. Rev. Soc.* 8:1–33

Gergen, K. J. 1965. Interaction goals and personalistic feedback as factors affecting the presentation of self. *J. Pers. Soc. Psychol.* 1:413–24

Gergen, K. J. 1968. Personal consistency and the presentation of self. See Gordon & Gergen 1968, pp. 299–308

Gergen, K. J., Gergen, M. M. 1983. Narratives of the self. In *Studies in Social Identity*, ed. T. R. Sarbin, K. E. Scheibe. New York: Praeger

Goffman, E. 1959. *The Presentation of Self in Everyday Life.* New York: Doubleday

Goldfried, M. R., Robins, C. 1982. On the facilitation of self-efficacy. *Cognit. Ther. Res.* 6:361–79

Goldfried, M. R., Robins, C. 1983. Self-schema, cognitive bias, and the processing of therapeutic experiences. In *Advances in Cognitive-Behavior Research and Therapy*, ed. P. C. Kendall. New York: Academic

Gordon, C., Gergen, K. J. 1968. *The Self in Social Interaction*, Vol. 1. New York: Wiley. 473 pp.

Greenberg, J., Pyszczynski, T. 1985. Compensatory self-inflation: A response to the threat to self regard of public failure. *J. Pers. Soc. Psychol.* 49:273–80

Greenwald, A. G. 1980. The totalitarian ego: Fabrication and revision of personal history. *Am. Psychol.* 35:603–18

Greenwald, A. G. 1982. Ego task analysis: An integration of research on ego-involvement and self-awareness. In *Cognitive Social Psychology*, ed. A. Hastorf, A. Isen. New York: Elsevier

Greenwald, A. G. 1984. *Self-knowledge and self-deception.* Presented at Ann. Meet. Am. Psychol. Assoc., 92nd, Toronto

Greenwald, A. G., Breckler, S. J. 1985. To whom is the self presented? See Schlenker 1985a, pp. 126–46

Greenwald, A. G., Pratkanis, A. R. 1984. The self. In *Handbook of Social Cognition*, Vol. 3, ed. R. S. Wyer, T. K. Srull. Hillsdale, NJ: Erlbaum

Gruder, C. L. 1977. Choice of comparison persons in evaluating oneself. See Suls & Miller 1977, pp. 21–41

Guntrip, H. 1971. *Psychoanalytic Theory, Therapy, and the Self.* New York: Basic Books

Gur, R. C., Sackeim, H. A. 1979. Self-deception: A concept in search of a phenomenon. *J. Pers. Soc. Psychol.* 37:147–69

Hamill, R. 1980. Self-schemas and face recognition: Effects of cognitive structures on social perception and memory. PhD thesis. Univ. Mich.

Harter, S. 1983. Developmental perspectives on the self-system. In *Carmichael's Manual of Child Psychology*, Vol. 4, ed. P. H. Mussen. New York: Wiley

Higgins, E. T. 1983. A theory of discrepant self-concepts. New York Univ. Unpublished

Higgins, E. T., King, G. A. 1981. Accessibility of social constructs: Information processing consequences of individual and contextual variability. See Cantor & Kihlstrom 1981, pp. 69–122

Higgins, E. T., King, G. A., Mavin, G. H. 1982. Individual construct accessibility and subjective impressions and recall. *J. Pers. Soc. Psychol.* 43:35–47

Higgins, E. T., Klein, R., Strauman, T. 1985. Self-concept discrepancy theory: A psychological model for distinguishing among different aspects of depression and anxiety. *Soc. Cognit.* 3:51–76

Higgins, E. T., Strauman, T., Klein, R. 1986. Standards and the process of self-evaluation: Multiple affects from multiple stages. See Sorrentino & Higgins 1986, pp. 23–63

Hilton, J. L., Darley, J. M. 1985. Constructing other persons: A limit on the effect. *J. Exp. Soc. Psychol.* 21:1–18

Hoelter, J. W. 1985. The structure of self-conception: Conceptualization and measurement. *J. Pers. Soc. Psychol.* 49:1392–1407

Hogan, R. 1982. A socioanalytic theory of personality. *Nebr. Symp. Motiv.* 29:55–89

Holmes, D. S. 1978. Projection as a defense mechanism. *Psychol. Bull.* 85:677–88

Holyoak, K. J., Gordon, P. C. 1983. Social reference points. *J. Pers. Soc. Psychol.* 44:881–87

Horney, K. 1950. *Neurosis and Human Growth*. New York: Norton

Horowitz, M. J. 1979. *States of Mind*. New York: Plenum

Hull, J. G. 1981. A self-awareness model of the causes and effects of alcohol consumption. *J. Abnorm. Psychol.* 44:461–73

Hull, J. G., Levenson, R. W., Young, R. D., Sher, K. J. 1983. Self-awareness—reducing effects of alcohol consumption. *J. Pers. Soc. Psychol.* 44:461–73

Hull, J. G., Levy, A. S. 1979. The organizational functions of the self: An alternative to the Duval and Wicklund model of self-awareness. *J. Pers. Soc. Psychol.* 37:756–68

Hull, J. G., Young, R. D. 1983. Self consciousness, self-esteem, and success-failure as determinants of alcohol consumption in male social drinkers. *J. Pers. Soc. Psychol.* 44:1097–1109

Hyams, N. B., Graham, W. K. 1984. Effects of goal setting and initiative on individual brainstorming. *J. Soc. Psychol.* 123:283–84

Ingram, R. E., Smith, T. W., Brehm, S. S. 1983. Depression and information processing: Self-schemata and the encoding of self-relevant information. *J. Pers. Soc. Psychol.* 45:412–22

Jarvella, R. J., Collars, J. G. 1974. Memory for the intentions of sentences. *Memory Cognit.* 2:185–88

Jones, E. E., Berglas, S. 1978. Control of attributions about the self through self-handicapping strategies: The appeal of alcohol and the role of underachievement. *Pers. Soc. Psychol. Bull.* 4:200–6

Jones, E. E., Pittman, T. S. 1982. Toward a general theory of strategic self-presentation. See Suls 1982, pp. 231–62

Jones, E. E., Rhodewalt, F., Berglas, S., Skelton, J. A. 1981. Effects of strategic self-presentation on subsequent self-esteem. *J. Pers. Soc. Psychol.* 41:407–21

Jussim, L. 1986. Self-fulfilling prophecies: A theoretical and integrative review. *Psychol. Rev.* In press

Kanfer, F. H. 1970. Self-regulation: Research, issues, and speculations. In *Behavior Modification in Clinical Psychology*, ed. C. Neuringer, J. L. Michael. New York: Appleton-Century-Crofts

Keenan, J. M., Baillet, S. D. 1979. Memory for personally and socially significant events. In *Attention and Performance*, Vol. 8, ed. R. S. Nickerson. Hillsdale, NJ: Erlbaum

Kelly, G. A. 1955. *A Theory of Personality: The Psychology of Personal Constructs*. New York: Norton. 190 pp.

Kernberg, O. 1977. *Borderline Conditions in Pathological Narcissism*. Int. Univ. Press

Kernis, M. 1984. Need for uniqueness, self-schemas, and thought as moderators of the false-consensus effect. *J. Exp. Soc. Psychol.* 20:350–62

Kessler, R. C., McRae, J. A. 1982. The effect of wives' employment on the mental health of married men and women. *Am. Soc. Rev.* 47:216–27

Kihlstrom, J. F., Cantor, N. 1984. Mental representations of the self. *Adv. Exp. Soc. Psychol.* 17:1–47

Kirsch, I. 1985. Self-efficacy and expectancy: Old wine with new labels. *J. Pers. Soc. Psychol.* 49:824–30

Kirschenbaum, D. S., Humphrey, L. L., Malett, S. D. 1981. Specificity of planning in adult self-control: An applied investigation. *J. Pers. Soc. Psychol.* 40:941–50

Kirschenbaum, D. S., Tomarken, A. J., Ordman, A. M. 1982. Specificity of planning and choice applied to adult self-control. *J. Pers. Soc. Psychol.* 42:576–85

Klinger, E. 1975. Consequences of commitment to and disengagement from incentives. *Psychol. Rev.* 82:1–25

Kuhl, J. 1984. Volitional aspects of achievement motivation and learned helplessness: Toward a comprehensive theory of action control. *Prog. Exp. Pers. Res.* 13:99–171

Kuhl, J. 1985. Volitional mediators of cognition-behavior consistency: Self-regulatory processes and action versus state orientation. See Kuhl & Beckmann 1985, pp. 101–28

Kuhl, J., Beckmann, J., eds. 1985. *Action Control: From Cognition to Behavior.* New York: Springer-Verlag

Kuiper, N. A. 1981. Convergent evidence for the self as a prototype: The "inverted-URT effect" for self and other judgments. *Pers. Soc. Psychol. Bull.* 7:438–43

Kuiper, N. A., Derry, P. A. 1981. The self as a cognitive prototype: An application to person perception and depression. See Cantor & Kihlstrom 1981, pp. 215–32

Kuiper, N. A., Higgins, E. T. 1985. Social cognition and depression: A general integrative perspective. *Soc. Cognit.* 3:1–15

Kuiper, N. A., MacDonald, M. R. 1982. Self and other perception in mild depressives. *Soc. Cognit.* 1:223–39

Kuiper, N. A., Rogers, T. B. 1979. Encoding of personal information: Self-other differences. *J. Pers. Soc. Psychol.* 37:499–514

Kulik, J. A., Sledge, P., Mahler, H. I. M. 1986. Self-confirmatory attribution, egocentrism, and the perpetration of self-beliefs. *J. Pers. Soc. Psychol.* 50:587–94

Kunda, Z. 1985. *Motivation and inference: Self-serving generation and evaluation of causal theories.* PhD thesis. Univ. Mich.

Langer, E. J. 1975. The illusion of control. *J. Pers. Soc. Psychol.* 32:311–28

Lazarus, R. S. 1983. The costs and benefits of denial. In *Denial of Stress,* ed. S. Greznity. New York: Int. Univ. Press

Lepper, M. R., Ross, L., Lau, R. R. 1986. Persistence of inaccurate beliefs about the self: Perseverance effects in the classroom. *J. Pers. Soc. Psychol.* 50:482–91

Lester, M. 1984. Self: Sociological portraits. In *The Existential Self in Society,* ed. J. A. Kotarbu, A. Fontana. Chicago: Univ. Chicago Press

Levinson, D. J. 1978. *The Seasons of a Man's Life.* New York: Ballantine

Lewicki, P. 1983. Self-image bias in person perception. *J. Pers. Soc. Psychol.* 45:384–93

Lewicki, P. 1984. Self-schema and social information processing. *J. Pers. Soc. Psychol.* 47:1177–90

Linville, P. W. 1982. Affective consequences of complexity regarding the self and others. In *Affect and Cognition,* ed. M. S. Clark, S. T. Fiske. Hillsdale, NJ: Erlbaum

Little, B. R. 1983. Personal projects: A rationale and method for investigation. *Environ. Behav.* 15:273–309

Lord, C. G. 1982. Predicting behavioral consistency from an individual's perception of situational similarities. *J. Pers. Soc. Psychol.* 42:1076–88

Manderlink, G., Harackiewicz, J. M. 1984. Proximal versus distal goal setting and intrinsic motivation. *J. Pers. Soc. Psychol.* 47:918–28

Marks, G. 1984. Thinking one's abilities are unique and one's opinions are common. *Pers. Soc. Psychol. Bull.* 10:203–8

Markus, H. 1977. Self-schemata and processing information about the self. *J. Pers. Soc. Psychol.* 35:63–78

Markus, H. 1980. The self in thought and memory. In *The Self in Social Psychology,* ed. D. M. Wegner, R. R. Vallacher. New York: Oxford Univ. Press

Markus, H. 1983. Self-knowledge: An expanded view. *J. Pers.* 51:543–65

Markus, H., Crane, M., Bernstein, S., Siladi, M. 1982. Self-schemas and gender. *J. Pers. Soc. Psychol.* 42:38–50

Markus, H., Kunda, Z. 1986. Stability and malleability of the self-concept. *J. Pers. Soc. Psychol.* 51:858–66

Markus, H., Nurius, P. 1986. Possible selves. *Am. Psychol.* 41:954–69

Markus, H., Sentis, K. 1982. The self in social information processing. See Suls 1982, pp. 41–70

Markus, H., Smith, J. 1981. The influence of self-schemata on the perception of others. See Cantor & Kihlstrom 1981, pp. 233–62

Markus, H., Smith, J., Moreland, R. L. 1985. Role of the self-concept in the perception of others. *J. Pers. Soc. Psychol.* 49:1494–512

Martindale, C. 1980. Subselves: The internal representation of situational and personal dispositions. In *Review of Personality and Social Psychology,* ed. L. Wheeler, 1:193–218. Beverly Hills, CA: Sage

Maslow, A. H. 1954. *Motivation and Personality.* New York: Harper

McClelland, D. C. 1951. *Personality.* New York: Dryden

McClelland, D. C. 1985. How motives, skills, and values determine what people do. *Am. Psychol.* 40:812–25

McGuire, W. J. 1984. Search for the self: Going beyond self-esteem and the reactive self. In *Personality and the Prediction of*

Behavior, ed. R. A. Zucker, J. Aronoff, A. I. Rabin. New York: Academic

McGuire, W. J., McGuire, C. V. 1982. Significant others in self-space: Sex differences and developmental trends in the social self. See Suls 1982, pp. 71–96

Mead, G. H. 1934. *Mind, Self, and Society.* Chicago: Univ. Chicago Press

Meichenbaum, D., Asarnow, J. 1979. Cognitive-behavior modification and metacognitive development: Implications for the classroom. In *Cognitive-Behavioral Interventions: Theory, Research, and Procedures*, ed. P. C. Kendall, S. D. Hollon. New York: Academic

Miller, D. T., Ross, M. 1975. Self-serving biases in the attribution of causality: Fact or fiction? *Psychol. Bull.* 82:213–25

Miller, D. T., Turnbull, W. 1986. Expectancies and interpersonal processes. *Ann. Rev. Psychol.* 37:233–56

Mills, C. J. 1983. Sex-typing and self-schemata effects on memory and response latency. *J. Pers. Soc. Psychol.* 45:163–72

Mischel, W. 1981. Metacognition and the rules of delay. See Flavell & Ross 1981, pp. 240–71

Moreland, R. L., Sweeney, P. D. 1984. Self-expectancies and reactions to evaluations of personal performance. *J. Pers.* 52:156–76

Morse, S., Gergen, K. J. 1970. Social comparison, self-consistency, and the concept of self. *J. Pers. Soc. Psychol.* 16:148–56

Mortimer, J., Lorence, J. 1981. Self-concept, stability and change from late adolescence to early adulthood. *Res. Community Mental Health* 2:5–42

Mueller, J. H. 1982. Self-awareness and access to material rated as self-descriptive or nondescriptive. *Bull. Psychonomic Soc.* 19:323–26

Mueller, J. H., Heesacker, M., Ross, M. J. 1984. Body-image consciousness and self-reference effects in face recognition. *Br. J. Soc. Psychol.* 23:277–79

Murray, H. A. 1938. *Explorations in Personality.* New York: Oxford Press

Nasby, W. 1985. Private self-consciousness, articulation of the self-schema, and recognition memory of trait adjectives. *J. Pers. Soc. Psychol.* 49:704–9

Neisser, U. 1976. *Cognition and Reality.* San Francisco: Freeman

Niedenthal, P. M., Cantor, N., Kihlstrom, J. F. 1985. Prototype matching: A strategy for social decision making. *J. Pers. Soc. Psychol.* 48:575–84

Nisbett, R., Ross, L. 1980. *Human Inference: Strategies and Shortcomings of Social Judgment.* Englewood Cliffs, NJ: Prentice-Hall

Norem, J. K., Cantor, N. 1986. Anticipatory and post hoc cushioning strategies: Optimism and defensive pessimism in "risky" situations. *Cognit. Ther. Res.* 10:347–62

Nuttin, J. 1984. *Motivation, Planning, and Action: A Relational Theory of Behavior Dynamics.* Hillsdale, NJ: Erlbaum

Nuttin, J., Lens, W. 1986. *Future Time Perspective and Motivation.* Hillsdale, NJ: Erlbaum

Nuttin, J. M. Jr. 1985. Narcissism beyond Gestalt and awareness: The name-letter effect. *Eur. J. Soc. Psychol.* 15:353–61

Paulhus, D. L. 1984. Two-component models of socially desirable responding. *J. Pers. Soc. Psychol.* 46:598–609

Pietromonaco, P. 1985. The influence of affect on self-perception. *Soc. Cognit.* 3: 121–34

Pietromonaco, P. R., Manis, J., Markus, H. 1986. The relationship of employment to self-perception and well-being in women: A cognitive analysis. *Sex Roles.* In press

Porter, C., Markus, H., Nurius, P. 1984. Possible selves and coping with crises. Univ. Mich. Unpublished

Privette, G. 1983. Peak experience, peak performance, and flow: A comparative analysis of positive human experiences. *J. Pers. Soc. Psychol.* 45:1361–68

Raynor, J. O., McFarlin, D. B. 1986. Motivation and the self-system. See Sorrentino & Higgins, pp. 315–49

Rhodewalt, F. 1986. Self-presentation and the phenomenal self: On the stability and malleability of self-conceptions. In *Private and Public Selves*, ed. R. Baumeister. New York: Springer-Verlag.

Rhodewalt, F., Agustsdottir, S. 1986. The effects of self-presentation on the phenomenal self. *J. Pers. Soc. Psychol.* 50:47–55

Rogers, C. R. 1951. *Client-Centered Therapy.* Boston: Houghton Mifflin

Rogers, T. B. 1981. A model of the self as an aspect of the human information processing system. See Cantor & Kihlstrom 1981, pp. 193–214

Rosenbaum, M. 1980. Individual differences in self-control behaviors and tolerance of painful stimulation. *J. Abnorm. Psychol.* 29:581–90

Rosenberg, M. 1979. *Conceiving the Self.* New York: Basic Books. 318 pp.

Rosenberg, S., Gara, M. A. 1985. The multiplicity of personal identity. In *Review of Personality and Social Psychology*, ed. P. Shaver. 6:87–113 Beverly Hills, CA: Sage

Rosenthal, R., Rubin, D. B. 1978. Interpersonal expectancy effects: The first 345 studies. *Behav. Brain Sci.* 3:377–415

Ross, L., Lepper, M. K., Hubbard, M. 1975. Perseverance in self-perception and social perception: Biased attributional processes in the debriefing paradigm. *J. Pers. Soc. Psychol.* 32:880–92

Ross, M., Conway, M. 1986. Remembering one's own past: The construction of personal histories. See Sorrentino & Higgins 1986, pp. 122–44

Ross, M., Sicoly, F. 1979. Egocentric biases in availability and attribution. *J. Pers. Soc. Psychol.* 37:322–37

Rowan, J. 1983. Person as group. In *Small Groups and Social Interaction*, Vol. 2, ed. H. H. Blumberg, A. P. Hare, J. Kent, M. Davies. London: Wiley

Rumelhart, D. E., Norman, D. 1978. Accretion, tuning, and restructuring: Three modes of learning. In *Semantic Factors in Cognition*, ed. J. Cotton, R. Klatsky. Hillsdale, NJ: Erlbaum

Ruvolo, A. P., Markus, H. 1986. *Possible selves and motivation*. Presented at Ann. Meet. Am. Psychol. Assoc., 94th, Washington, DC

Sackheim, H. A., Gur, R. C. 1978. Self-deception, self-confrontation, and consciousness. In *Consciousness and Self-Regulation: Advances in Research*, Vol. 2, ed. G. E. Schwartz, D. Shapiro. New York: Plenum

Salovey, P., Rodin, J. 1985. Cognitions about the self: Connecting feeling states and social behavior. In *Review of Personality and Social Psychology*, ed, L. Wheeler, 6:143–67. Beverly Hills, CA: Sage

Schank, R. C., Abelson, R. P. 1977. *Scripts, Plans, Goals and Understanding*. Hillsdale, NJ: Erlbaum

Scheibe, K. E. 1985. Historical perspectives on the presented self. See Schlenker 1985a, pp. 33–65

Schlenker, B. R. 1980. *Impression Management: The Self-Concept, Social Identity, and Interpersonal Relations*. Monterey, CA: Brooks/Cole

Schlenker, B. R. 1984. Identities, identifications, and relationships. In *Communication, Intimacy and Close Relationships*, ed. V. Derlega. New York: Academic

Schlenker, B. R., ed. 1985a. *The Self and Social Life*. New York: McGraw-Hill. 399 pp.

Schlenker, B. R. 1985b. Identity and self-identification. See Schlenker 1985a, pp. 65–100

Schoeneman, T. J. 1981. Reports of the sources of self-knowledge. *J. Pers.* 49:284–94

Schutz, A. 1964. On multiple realities. In *Collected Papers of Alfred Schutz*, Vol. 1, ed. M. Natunson. The Hague: Martinus Nijhoff

Semin, G. R., Strack, F. 1980. The plausibility of the implausible: A critique of Snyder and Swann. *Eur. J. Soc. Psychol.* 1:379–88

Sherman, S. J., Presson, C. C., Chassin, L., Corty, E., Olshavsky, R. 1983. The false consensus effect in estimates of smoking prevalence: Underlying mechanisms. *Pers. Soc. Psychol. Bull.* 9:197–207

Sherman, S. J., Presson, C. C., Chassin, L. 1984. Mechanisms underlying the false consensus effect: The special role of threats to the self. *Pers. Soc. Psychol. Bull.* 10:127–38

Sherman, S. J., Skov, R. B., Herritz, E. F., Stock, C. B. 1981. The effects of explaining hypothetical future events: From possibility to probability to actuality and beyond. *J. Exp. Soc. Psychol.* 17:142–58

Sherwood, G. G. 1981. Self-serving biases in person perception: A reexamination of projection as a mechanism of defense. *Psychol. Bull.* 90:445–59

Shevrin, H. 1986. *The role of consciousness, motivation and level of organization in person schemata*. Presented at Program on Conscious and Unconscious Mental Processes of the John O. and Katherine T. MacArthur Found., Cent. Adv. Study Behav. Sci., Stanford, CA

Shrauger, J. S. 1975. Responses to evaluation as a function of initial self-perceptions. *Psychol. Bull.* 82:581–96

Shrauger, J. S., Schoeneman, T. J. 1979. Symbolic interactionist view of self-concept: Through the looking glass darkly. *Psychol. Bull.* 86:549–73

Shweder, R. A., LeVine, R. A. 1984. *Culture Theory; Essays on Mind, Self, and Emotion*. New York: Cambridge Univ. Press

Silverman, L. H., Weinberger, J. 1985. Mommy and I are one. *Am. Psychol.* 40:1296–1308

Singer, J. L., Salovey, P. 1985. *Organized knowledge structures and personality: Schemas, self-schemas, protypes, and scripts*. Presented at Program on Conscious and Unconscious Mental Processes of the John O. and Katherine T. MacArthur Found., Cent. Adv. Study Behav. Sci., Stanford, CA

Smith, J. M. 1982. *Self-relevance and the perception of ongoing behavior: The effects of involvement and knowledge*. PhD. thesis. Univ. Mich.

Smith, T. W., Snyder, C. R., Handelsman, M. M. 1982. On the self-serving function of an academic wooden leg: Test anxiety as a self-handicapping strategy. *J. Pers. Soc. Psychol.* 42:314–21

Smith, T. W., Snyder, C. R., Perkins, S. C. 1983. The self-serving function of hypochondriachal complaints: Physical symptoms as self-handicapping strategies. *J. Pers. Soc. Psychol.* 44:787–97

Snyder, C. R. 1985. The excuse: An amazing grace? See Schlenker 1985a, pp. 235–61

Snyder, C. R., Fromkin, H. L. 1980. *Unique-

ness: The Human Pursuit of Difference.
New York: Plenum

Snyder, C. R., Higgins, R. L., Stucky, R. J. 1983. *Excuses: Masquerades in Search of Grace.* New York: Wiley. 327 pp.

Snyder, C. R., Smith, T. W., Augelli, R. W., Ingram, R. E. 1985. On the self-serving function of social anxiety: Shyness as a self-handicapping strategy. *J. Pers. Soc. Psychol.* 48:970–80

Snyder, M. 1979. Self-monitoring processes. *Adv. Exp. Soc. Psychol.* 12:85–128

Snyder, M. 1982. When believing means doing: Creating links between attitudes and behavior. In *The Ontario Symposium,* Vol. 2: *Consistency in Social Behavior,* ed. M. P. Zanna, E. T. Higgins, C. P. Herman, pp. 105–30. Hillsdale, NJ: Erlbaum

Snyder, M., Gangestad, S. 1981. Hypothesis-testing processes. In *New Directions in Attribution Research,* ed. J. H. Harvey, W. Ickes, R. F. Kidd, 3:171–98. Hillsdale, NJ: Erlbaum

Snyder, M., Gangestad, S. 1982. Choosing social situations: Two investigations of self-monitoring processes. *J. Pers. Soc. Psychol.* 43:123–35

Snyder, M., Gangestad, S., Simpson, J. A. 1983. Choosing friends as activity partners: The role of self monitoring. *J. Pers. Soc. Psychol.* 45:1061–72

Snyder, M., Simpson, J. A. 1984. Self-monitoring and dating relationships. *J. Pers. Soc. Psychol.* 47:1281–91

Snyder, M., Skrypnek, B. J. 1981. Testing hypotheses about the self: Assessments of job suitability. *J. Pers.* 49:193–211

Snyder, M., Swann, W. B. Jr. 1978a. Behavioral confirmation in social interaction: From social perception to social reality. *J. Exp. Soc. Psychol.* 14:148–62

Snyder, M., Swann, W. B. Jr. 1978b. Hypothesis testing processes in social interaction. *J. Pers. Soc. Psychol.* 36:1202–12

Snyder, M. L., Stephan, W. G., Rosenfield, D. 1978. Attributional egotism. In *New Directions in Attribution Research,* ed. J. H. Harvey, W. Ickes, R. F. Kidd, 2:91–120. Hillsdale, NJ: Erlbaum

Sorrentino, R. M., Higgins, E. T. 1986. *Handbook of Motivation and Cognition: Foundations of Social Behavior.* New York: Guilford

Sorrentino, R. M., Short, J. A. C. 1986. Uncertainty orientation, motivation, and cognition. See Sorrentino & Higgins, pp. 379–403

Srull, T. K., Gaelick, L. 1983. General principles and individual differences in the self as a habitual reference point: An examination of self- other judgments of similarity. *Soc. Cognit.* 2:108–21

Steele, C. M., Liu, T. J. 1983. Dissonance

processes as self-affirmation. *J. Pers. Soc. Psychol.* 45:5–19

Sternberg, R. J. 1984. Toward a triarchic theory of human intelligence. *Behav. Brain Sci.* 7:269–315

Strube, M. J., Berry, J. M., Lott, C. L., Fogelman, R., Steinhart, G., et al. 1986. Self-schematic representations of the Type A and Type B behavior patterns. *J. Pers. Soc. Psychol.* 51:170–80

Stryker, S. 1980. *Symbolic Interactionism.* Menlo Park, CA: Benjamin/Cummings

Stryker, S. 1986. Identity theory: Developments and extensions. In *Self and Identity,* ed. K. Yardley, T. Honess. New York: Wiley

Sullivan, H. S. 1953. *The Interpersonal Theory of Psychiatry.* New York: Norton

Suls, J., ed. 1982. *Psychological Perspectives on the Self,* Vol. 1. Hillsdale, NJ: Erlbaum. 273 pp.

Suls, J., Greenwald, A. G., eds. 1983. *Psychological Perspectives on the Self,* Vol. 2. Hillsdale, NJ: Erlbaum. 287 pp.

Suls, J. M., Miller, R. L. K., eds. 1977. *Social Comparison Processes.* Washington, DC: Hemisphere

Swann, W. B. Jr. 1983. Self-verification: Bringing social reality into harmony with the self. See Suls & Greenwald, 1983, pp. 33–66

Swann, W. B. Jr. 1984. Quest for accuracy in person perception: A matter of pragmatics. *Psychol. Rev.* 91:457–77

Swann, W. B. Jr. 1985. The self as architect of social reality. See Schlenker 1985a, pp. 100–26

Swann, W. B. Jr., Ely, R. J. 1984. A battle of wills: Self-verification versus behavioral confirmation. *J. Pers. Soc. Psychol.* 46:1287–1302

Swann, W. B. Jr., Giuliano, T. 1982. *How our intimates stabilize our self-views.* Presented at Ann. Meet. Am. Psychol. Assoc., 90th, Washington, DC

Swann, W. B. Jr., Hill, C. A. 1982. When our identities are mistaken: Reaffirming self-conceptions through social interaction. *J. Pers. Soc. Psychol.* 43:59–66

Swann, W. B. Jr., Predmore, S. C. 1985. Intimates as agents of social support: Sources of consolation or despair? *J. Pers. Soc. Psychol.* 49:1609–17

Swann, W. B. Jr., Read, S. J. 1981a. Acquiring self-knowledge: The search for feedback that fits. *J. Pers. Soc. Psychol.* 41:1119–28

Swann, W. B. Jr., Read, S. J. 1981b. Self-verification processes: How we sustain our self-conceptions. *J. Exp. Soc. Psychol.* 17:351–72

Taylor, S. E., Brown, J. 1986. Illusion and well-being: Social psychological contributions to a theory of mental health. Univ. Calif., Los Angeles. Unpublished

Taylor, S. E., Wood, J. V., Lichtman, R. R. 1983. It could be worse: Selective evaluation as a response to victimization. *J. Soc. Issues* 39:19–40

Tedeschi, J. T., Norman, N. 1985. Social power, self-presentation, and the self. See Schlenker 1985a, pp. 293–323

Tesser, A. 1986. Some effects of self evaluation maintenance on cognition and action. See Sorrentino & Higgins 1986, pp. 435–64

Tesser, A., Campbell, J. 1984. Friendship choice and performance: Self-evaluation maintenance in children. *J. Pers. Soc. Psychol.* 46:561–74

Tesser, A., Campbell, J. 1983. Self-definition and self-evaluation maintenance. See Suls & Greenwald 1983, pp. 1–31

Tesser, A., Campbell, J. 1980. Self-definition: The impact of the relative performance and similarity of others. *Soc. Psychol. Q.* 43:341–46

Tesser, A., Campbell, J. 1982. Self-evaluation maintenance and the perception of friends and strangers. *J. Pers.* 50:261–79

Tesser, A., Campbell, J., Smith, M. 1984. Friendship choice and performance: Self-evaluation maintenance in children. *J. Pers. Soc. Psychol.* 46:561–74

Tesser, A., Paulus, D. 1983. The definition of self: Private and public self-evaluation management strategies. *J. Pers. Soc. Psychol.* 44:672–82

Tesser, A., Smith, J. 1980. Some effects of friendship and task relevance on helping: You don't always help the one you like. *J. Exp. Soc. Psychol.* 16:582–90

Tetlock, P. E. 1985. Toward an intuitive politician model of attribution processes. See Schlenker 1985a, pp. 203–35

Tetlock, P. E., Manstead, A. S. R. 1985. Impression management versus intrapsychic explanations in social psychology: A useful dichotomy? *Psychol. Rev.* 92:59–77

Thoits, P. A. 1983. Multiple identities and psychological well-being: A reformulation and test of the social isolation hypothesis. *Am. Soc. Rev.* 48:174–87

Tomarken, A. J., Kirschenbaum, D. S. 1982. Self-regulatory failure: Accentuate the positive? *J. Pers. Soc. Psychol.* 43:584–97

Trope, Y. 1983. Self-assessment in achievement behavior. See Suls & Greenwald 1983, pp. 93–121

Trope, Y. 1986. Self-enhancement and self-assessment in achievement behavior. See Sorrentino & Higgins 1986, pp. 350–78

Trope, Y., Bassok, M. 1982. Confirmatory and diagnosing strategies in social information gathering. *J. Pers. Soc. Psychol.* 43:22–34

Trope, Y., Bassok, M., Alon, E. 1984. The questions lay interviewers ask. *J. Pers.* 52:90–106

Turk, D. C., Salovey, P. 1985. Cognitive Structures, cognitive processes, and cognitive-behavior modification: I. Client issues. *Cognit. Ther. Res.* 9:1–17

Wallen, R. 1942. Ego-involvement as a determinant of selective forgetting. *J. Abnorm. Soc. Psychol.* 37:20–39

Weigert, A. 1983. Identity: Its emergence within sociological psychology. *Symbol. Interaction* 6:183–206

Weinstein, N. D. 1980. Unrealistic optimism about future life events. *J. Pers. Soc. Psychol.* 39:806–20

Wicklund, R. A. 1986. Orientation to the environment versus preoccupation with human potential. See Sorrentino & Higgins 1986, pp. 64–95

Wicklund, R. A., Gollwitzer, P. M. 1982. *Symbolic Self-Completion.* Hillsdale, NJ: Erlbaum. 243 pp.

Wills, T. A. 1981. Downward comparison principles in social psychology. *Psychol. Bull.* 90:245–71

Wood, J. V., Taylor, S. E., Lichtman, R. R. 1985. Social comparison in adjustment to breast cancer. *J. Pers. Soc. Psychol.* 49:1169–83

Wurf, E. 1986. The critical role of the self in the coping process. Univ. Mich., Unpublished

Wurf, E., Markus, H. 1983. *Cognitive consequences of the negative self.* Presented at Ann. Meet. Am. Psychol. Assoc., 91st, Anaheim, CA

Wurf, E., Markus, H. 1986a. Self-schemas and possible selves. In *Perspectives on Personality,* ed. D. J. Ozer, J. M. Healy, A. J. Stewart. Greenwich, Conn: JAI Press

Wurf, E., Markus, H. 1986b. Self-schemas and self-definition: The importance of being different. Univ. Mich. Unpublished

Wylie, R. C. 1974. *The Self Concept.* Lincoln: Univ. Nebr. Press

Zuckerman, M. 1979. Attribution of success and failure revisited, or: The motivational bias is alive and well in attribution theory. *J. Pers.* 47:245–87

Ann. Rev. Psychol. 1987. 38:339–67

ORGANIZATION CHANGE AND DEVELOPMENT

Michael Beer and Anna Elise Walton

Graduate School of Business Administration, Harvard University, Boston, Massachusetts 02163

CONTENTS

Applying theory from psychology and organizational behavior, organization development (OD) comprises a set of actions undertaken to improve organizational effectiveness and employee well-being. These actions, or "inter-

339

0066-4308/87/0201-0339$02.00

ventions," are typically designed and sequenced by an OD consultant following his/her diagnosis of an organization's needs and shortcomings. The tool kit these practitioners draw on ranges broadly from organization-wide changes in structure and systems to psychotherapeutic counseling sessions with groups and individuals. OD, measured as something that professional OD consultants do, appears to be growing moderately.

The application of OD by managers rather than OD consultants has grown even further. In the past five years, general management literature and practice have absorbed many of the concepts, values, and methods OD propounds. This can be seen in the widespread application, and in some cases institutionalization, of innovative plant designs, participative management approaches, collaborative approaches to union–management relations, the use of task forces and other organizational overlays to identify and solve problems, and the frequent practice of off-site team-building or mission-building sessions (Beer & Spector 1985). We see OD concepts strongly emerging in the burgeoning general management literature, specifically via culture and leadership concepts. OD concepts can also be seen in the increasingly common view of organizations as open systems.

Major environmental changes have focused management attention on managing discontinuities in organizations' lives. Revitalization, turnaround, innovation, and the management of decline are becoming major topics in both general management and OD literature. Human-resource management has also absorbed many of OD's precepts, and organizations increasingly realize human resources can be critical strategic and competitive factors.

As the knowledge base of organizational behavior and psychology filters into general management literature, we believe OD must broaden itself. Theorists and practitioners must move away from programs in which the consultant orchestrates interventions to programs in which general managers, staff groups, and consultants work together to manage change, to redirect organizational efforts and performance. The OD practitioner may have specialized behavioral-science expertise but will also need expertise in understanding and interpreting environmental changes. The OD consultant will support changes initiated by general managers.

Thus as a field, organization development will have to become concerned with the theory and practice of managing the continual adaptation of internal organizational arrangements to changes in the external environment. In this capacity, intervention methods become episodes in a long-term process, and consultants become actors in a process orchestrated by general managers. This conception of the field has profound implications for research methodology, theory building, and practice. As its techniques have become staples of modern corporate management, the status of OD becomes more difficult to ascertain. This broader definition makes it impossible to state how widely OD is practiced, since the field no longer has professional boundaries.

Here we review: the status of OD as consultant-centered intervention, the traditional focus of OD; OD-related trends in general management literature; recent literature on organizational adaptation and realignment; trends in human-resource management and their OD implications; and finally, the implementation of change.

OD AS CONSULTANT-CENTERED INTERVENTION

There have been no new breakthroughs in intervention methodologies. Rather, variations on the basic idea of surfacing information and feeding it back for discussion by organizational members continue to be developed. Survey and questionnaire methodologies appear to be growing in popularity. New surveys have been introduced (Kilmann 1984, Sashkin 1985) and established ones are still being utilized (Kleiner 1983, Levine 1983, Gavin 1984). Various forms of team building and the use of collateral organizations are also widely employed (Kanter 1983, Beer & Spector 1985). Process consultation appears in the literature less frequently than the above. We suspect it is a less bounded intervention and therefore more difficult to research with traditional methodologies.

Sashkin et al (1984) note that some types of OD, specifically structural interventions according to contingency theory, third-party consultation, and sociotechnical systems changes have not become as popular. They believe the popular approaches have clear goals and are highly structured. The client knows what the consultant will be doing at any given time.

We do not review new applications of traditional intervention methods because we do not regard extentions of intervention methodology as the frontier of progress in the practice or theory of OD. Moreover, as we discuss in the section on managing change, the manager and/or consultant, their assumptions about organizations and their skills in managing an organic change process, are probably more important than methodology in the final analysis. It is probably because effective change managers or consultants are in such short supply that Sashkin finds more structured methods in greater use.

Recent Research and Evaluation of OD Efforts

In the past five years, several articles (Nicholas 1982, Roberts & Porras 1982, Vicars & Hartke 1984, Nicholas & Katz 1985, Guzzo et al 1985, Macy et al 1986) have reviewed the OD and organization change literature to assess the relative effectiveness of typical interventions. These researchers looked at studies of team building, laboratory training, survey feedback, technostructural interventions, and process consultation.

Vicars & Hartke (1984) evaluated 15 recent studies relative to an earlier study (Morrison 1978) and noted an increase in validity criteria and noticeably more controls. They also noted that OD evaluations often encountered several rival hypotheses: Change results from maturation, history, self selection, and so forth.

Nicholas (1982) reviewed 64 studies and assessed the comparative impact of the interventions on "hard criteria," which ranged from costs and productivity to quality and absenteeism. He noted limitations in the research findings—e.g. outcomes could be the result of intervention duration or the time of posttest (immediately following the intervention or several years later). Nicholas concluded that "The single most apparent finding of this research is that no one change technique or class of techniques works well in all situations" (p. 540).

Katzell & Guzzo (1983) in a literature review of 207 psychologically based productivity experiments reported that 87% found evidence of some productivity improvement. Guzzo et al (1985) performed a meta-analysis of 98 of these experiments and found worker productivity increased by nearly one half standard deviation.

Macy et al (1986) meta-analyzed 56 empirical organization change and work innovation experiments and found an across-study positive and significant relationship with productivity. They found that reward system changes had no significant relationship with productivity and had significant negative relationships with leadership and work involvement measures. Autonomous and semiautonomous work groups, team building, and training related positively and significantly to productivity but were negatively associated with 11 dependent variables (including leadership, work involvement, general attitude, and satisfaction measures).

Both Guzzo et al (1985) and Macy et al (1986) note that most published reports lack the quantitative data necessary for meta-analysis. Both also qualify their findings by recognizing the bias toward publishing positive outcomes.

Measuring attitudinal change has proved tricky. A fair amount of research (Roberts & Porras 1982, Porras 1985, Van de Vliert et al 1985) is going into investigating the types of change: alpha (or "real" change, but no conceptual shift), beta ("scale recalibration," or shift due to changes in expectations), and gamma (a complete conceptual redefinition of the phenomena). These distinctions derive from a study (Golembwiewski et al 1976) that observed rating declines after an intervention. The study argued that these declines occurred because participants had undergone a conceptual shift; their standards of evaluation had changed. Armenakis et al (1983) claimed that this is now the focus of OD research, displacing earlier concerns about experimental design and statistical methods.

In sum, investigators have felt the need for, and have begun to use, quantitative data, sophisticated research designs, and statistical procedures aimed at accurate measurement of change. Nicholas & Katz (1985) and Armenakis et al (1983) call for more longitudinal measures, and Armenakis et al (1983) add that more frequent measurements are needed. Seashore et al (1983) published a major text cataloging current methods and techniques. Researchers of this bent argue that in future lean times OD practitioners will need hard data to justify their projects to management by bottom-line criteria.

Despite more sophisticated research methods, OD research results are still inconclusive. One can find support for many different conclusions, among the results reported in the studies. Why should this be so?

Problems in Research on Intervention Methods

This research suffers from four problems. First, the research aims to isolate causation. By relying on normal science, this research tries to identify the results of a single intervention (though the intervention may combine technologies of team building, technostructural change, etc) and overlooks the systemic nature of organizations. Exogenous variables and intervening events will always prevent any powerful conclusions. For example, influential figures change (Roberts & King 1985), or management changes production methods or makes material changes (Passmore & Friedlander 1982, Fiedler et al 1984). Even worse, normal science methodology can damage the experiment itself. Blumberg & Pringle (1983) describe a sociotechnical intervention, including job redesign and worker participation in a unionized mine, in which the "control" group found out about the experimental group. The "control" miners so resented the experimental group's advantage that they voted to prevent further changes in the workplace.

Traditional research methods make assumptions that may be entirely inappropriate for field research. For example, the concept of control groups or uninformed subjects may diminish the value of the information (survey responses may be more "thoughtless") or halt the experiment altogether (via control-group hostility). Normal science rests on replication, something unquestionably impossible in field research. Finally, events may be multicausal, the constellation of causes being of significance. Thus, it would be impossible to identify the precise effect of a given action.

Second, much of the research overlooks time and is not sufficiently longitudinal. By assessing the events and their impact at only one nearly contemporaneous moment, the research cannot discuss how permanent the changes are. As noted above, different posttest times may support different experimental conclusions.

Third, the research is "flat." While being precise about methodology and instruments, it is often imprecise in depth and description of the intervention and situation. The nature and history of the occupational groups involved are often not explored. The environmental context is overlooked. Notably, one study compares two interventions eight years apart. The environmental context may have changed, thus affecting the intervention's effects. Quantitative description may not be the best method for understanding a multi-causal phenomenon.

Fourth, the research does not fit the needs of its user. This is surprising given the action research tradition of OD. Noting that research knowledge has been slow to transfer to practice, the "crisis in utilization" is increasingly coming under scrutiny (Lindblom & Cohen 1979, Legge 1984, Lawler et al 1985, Kilmann et al 1983). Good science may be antithetical to good action. More complex statistical techniques and more complex quasi-experimental designs, in attempts to achieve more precision and tighter scientific "proof," neglect the "social construction" of knowledge in the social sciences. The complexity of the subject material and the existence of nonrational responses to data will inhibit acceptance of even the most tightly controlled experiments. As Legge (1984) notes, the best predictor of utilized knowledge is the "personal factor," the interest the users have in the evaluation study. Beer (1980) argued that managers make decisions about OD based not on evaluation research but on suitability to their agenda. Rather than create increasingly esoteric designs and increasingly narrow inferences, OD might do better to aim research at needs identified by managers and utilize language managers can understand.

OD research seems to be at a turning point. As long as OD researchers emulate traditional science methodology, they will confine themselves to isolated episodes of change. By evaluating a specific intervention, they neglect the interrelatedness of elements in a system; and because the organization is a system, exogenous variables will prevent any powerful conclusions.

Rather than attempt to find the perfect quantitative methodology and "scientifically" prove its value, OD should attempt to build a different model of knowledge. Argyris et al (1985) proposed action science. Critiquing traditional science methods, they argued for the combination of action and thinking to achieve double-loop, or self-corrective learning. Schon (1983) called for similar methodology. The call for rejection of typical positivistic assumptions is growing (Carnall 1982, Morgan 1983, Legge 1984, Peters & Robinson 1984). This would require a new format of journal reporting as well. What we are recommending is a return to the action research traditions of OD with full participation of the client in the research but with much longer time frames and the inclusion of rich descriptions of context and system dynamics.

Pettigrew provided a persuasive critique and useful counterexample of mainstream OD research and literature. Reviewing the history of and research on OD, he concluded that "theory and practice of change in organisations would continue to remain as circumscribed and ill developed as long as change is studied and thought about as episodes and projects separate from the ongoing processes of continuity and change of which those change projects are a part" (p. 26). His book, *The Awakening Giant: Continuity and Change in ICI,* provides an in-depth look at the history from 1960 to 1983 of Imperial Chemical Industries and four OD groups operating in it. Pettigrew, too, concluded that more longitudinal studies must be conducted.

Our critique of OD research is, of course, also a critique of OD's preoccupation with consultant-centered intervention methods. If research designs that define change too narrowly can be misleading, defining change as a single intervention at a given point in time is too confining. We have therefore decided not to review new intervention methods in depth and instead turn now to the general manager's problem of developing organizations to improve competitiveness and employee well-being.

OD AS GENERAL MANAGEMENT

Managers are learning that they must manage change. Increasing international competition, deregulation, the decline of manufacturing, the changing values of workers, and the growth of information technology have changed the concepts and approaches managers must use. As Beckhard (1969) and Bennis (1969) argued early on, these changes require adaptive, flexible organizations, and skilled managers to manage these changes.

Many OD concepts have filtered into the management literature, and OD techniques are being addressed to the manager (Dyer 1983, Kirkpatrick 1985). Specifically, OD's concept of explicitly intervening to manage norms and culture is emerging in management journals. OD's views on leadership and managing "soft" (style versus systems) change are emerging in the leadership literature. The systemic view of organizations has also received attention.

Culture

OD has long recognized the importance of culture and considered culture management to be within its purview, but it has never developed the concept. Almost completely separate from the OD literature, a group of writings on organizational culture has sprung up. Much of it asserts a positive correlation between type of organizational culture and organizational effectiveness (Ouchi 1981, Deal & Kennedy 1982, Denison 1984). Not surprisingly, these cultures look much like Beckhard's (1969) definition of a healthy organization. Delegating, results-oriented, information-sharing, developmental, egalitarian, employee-centered cultures are believed to enhance adaptiveness, productivity, innovation, and performance (Kanter 1983, Denison 1984, Walton 1985). This view was brought to the practicing public in Peters &

Waterman's popular book, *In Search of Excellence* (1982). Reviewing the characteristics of excellent companies, Peters & Waterman cited the elements of these companies' shared values—achieving productivity through people, the importance of people as individuals, tolerance of failure, and informality to promote communication. Performance is achieved via expectations and peer review rather than management direction and sophisticated control systems.

Surveying several companies, and relying on extensive field experience, Kanter (1983) found certain companies more adaptive and innovative. These companies engendered a culture of pride and encouraged their employees to take risks. Innovators were not separated from the mainstream organization (as some earlier literature had recommended) but integrated their ideas and proposals into the organization by involving the important stakeholders. The innovative organization promotes high levels of collaboration between functions.

In addition to type of culture, the strength of culture can be important. Wilkins & Ouchi (1983) suggested that strong cultures (clan mechanisms) may enhance organizational efficiency only under conditions of uncertainty and ambiguity (hence high "transactions" costs), stability of membership, and reasonably equitable and inescapable reward systems. If these conditions do not exist, markets or hierarchies may better meet the firm's need for internal integration.

A flood of literature on managing corporate culture resulted from the popularizing of culture as a competitive advantage. Current theory suggests that managers spread culture through stories, symbolic acts, and other "soft" techniques (Peters & Waterman 1982, Kanter 1983, Kilmann 1984, Sathe 1985, Schein 1985), much as Barnard (1938) and Selznick (1957) said long ago. The literature offers managers a "culture audit" (Wilkins 1983), which can identify problems and actionable areas for management. The Kilmann-Saxton Culture Gap Survey (Kilmann et al 1985) identifies differences between desired and actual culture and lays out a five-track program for redirecting the culture. Kilmann (1984) claims that any effort to manage change without such a comprehensive program is an ill-fated attempt at a quick fix.

Efforts directed at managing culture alert us to the problem of defining culture. Schein (1985) argued that popular notions of culture reflect culture rather than describe its essence (norms, observed behavioral regularities, dominant values, philosophy, climate, etc). He argued that culture is multilayered: The essence of culture may be found in the organization's embedded, preconscious, basic assumptions and beliefs about human nature, the nature of the world, and so forth. On a second, observable level, culture manifests itself as values, which are testable only by social consensus. Values are about how things ought to be done, or what works. When a value is agreed upon by a group, the group begins the process of cognitive transformation, in which the value becomes a belief or assumption, taken for granted rather than debatable. On the surface layer are artifacts and creations, which include things like art, technology, and behavioral patterns; these have meaning but are often not decipherable.

But how manageable is culture? Can a five-track program like Kilmann's (1984) enable managers to gain control of corporate culture? Or, is culture more powerful than managers, so that "culture controls the manager more than the manager controls the culture" (Schein 1985, p. 315)? It has been argued that cultural change cannot be managed and that special events that trigger change require managers to be temporarily out of control (Deal 1985). Changing and managing are incompatible. We suspect (as we will argue below in more depth) that the idea of planned change, long advocated by OD, requires reexamination and reformation. Preprogrammed approaches such as the five-track Culture Gap Survey are not likely to accord with how managers think and act (Kotter 1982) any more than Grid OD did.

Research suggests that culture may be more resilient than implied by the exhortations to manage it. Researchers examining the "cultural relativity" of change programs have generally found that interventions and technology that suit the host culture are most effective. In their earlier OD review, Faucheux et al (1982) noted that different cultures (US, European, Latin American) have developed different change technologies and that cross-cultural transfers of change technology have proved difficult and slow. Established change techniques used to intervene in culture directly have failed to overcome cultural resistance, suggesting that culture may be a lag rather than a lead variable.

Schein pointed out that the role of culture tends to vary with an organization's life cycle stage. For the youthful company, culture is often seen as a competitive advantage to be nurtured. For the mature company, culture may be a barrier to innovation; it may diminish integration and be a phenomenon to be managed and turned around. Change methods differ in appropriateness depending on the organization's life-cycle stage. For example, revolutionary change through outsiders may help an organization move from early growth to midlife, planned change and organization development may be most useful during organizational midlife, while coercive persuasion may suit a mature organization facing destruction or a turnaround. We believe that a theory of OD relevant to the general manager will only achieve usefulness if change problems, strategy, and tactics are tied to a life-cycle framework.

Leadership

OD has long recognized the importance of leadership in managing change. A vision, a new model for managing (Beer 1980), a "picture of the future"

(Beckhard & Harris 1977) have been considered powerful means by which leaders might motivate behavior change.

Management literature has focused recently on the role of leadership in managing major corporate transformations. In line with OD ideas, this research has found the envisioning skills of the executives to be critical in managing change. Anderson et al (1985) studied 17 companies that had undergone revitalization; each company had transformed itself from a substandard into a superior performer in a period of 5–10 years. A key factor in these change efforts was the existence of a "championing" leader. Such leaders fight persistently for their ideas, are more ideological than their business-as-usual counterparts, manage by symbols, set an example of championing leadership for potential leaders throughout the corporation, and use rewards and interchampion competition as motivators.

Bennis & Nanus (1985) interviewed 90 renowned figures in business, government, labor, academics, and the arts. They found little commonality in behavior, dress, or speech but identified four themes in action. First, leaders got their followers' attention through a vision, agenda, or focus; second, they gave meaning to events and actions through communication, thus developing "shared meanings" among their followers; they engendered trust through positioning, being reliable, and sticking to their goals; and they used their own optimism and positive self-regard to inspire others. Followers benefited through feelings of significance, competence, community, and enjoyment.

These formulations share several themes. First, the leaders articulate and propagate a vision or agenda. Second, the leader assigns meaning and significance to events, expectations, and the vision, and in so doing, structures a cognitive world. In this sense, the leader achieves results not through formal structure or formalized control systems but by creating an understanding of reality that then motivates behavior. Much as OD has argued, the manager creates a set of expectations that powerfully influence behavior in the organization.

Key to these formulations is the notion that leaders empower others, a value long held by OD (Kanter 1983, Burke 1985). Bennis & Nanus's leaders "empower others to translate intention into reality and sustain it" (p. 80). Sashkin (1985) noted that "research is consistent in suggesting that effective leaders involve subordinates rather than dominating and . . . give away power . . . leaders achieve goals through others, and unless others have the power to do what the leader wants done, such achievements are not likely" (p. 5).

The implication of this research is clear. Managers' leadership, not OD consultants', is central to managing major cultural transformations. Unfortunately, none of the research on leadership has specified the skills required of transformational leaders. This specification is required before managers can be helped to develop them, if indeed they are developable. A beginning has been made by Sashkin (1985) and Burke (1985) in profiling leadership style via a questionnaire. Research is also required on the role OD consultants can play in helping managers lead or in symbolically representing the leaders' desire for change.

Open Systems Analysis

OD maintains that the organization is an open system, that it interacts with its environment to maintain a state of fit between internal arrangements and the environment (Katz & Kahn 1966, Lawrence & Lorsch 1967, Beer 1980, Burke 1982). Based on this view, OD has asserted the organization's need for "environmental mapping" or "mapping the demand system" (Beckhard & Harris 1977). Here the organization looks at the transactions that occur across the organization/environment interface and assesses the importance of those transactions.

Popular management books are now arguing that organization effectiveness is a state of fit or congruence between business strategy and several internal organizational arrangements such as systems, structure, management style, skills, staff, and shared values (Pascale & Athos 1981, Peters & Waterman 1982).

The open-systems view receives ever greater attention through stakeholder and network concepts. Recent writings have recognized the importance of stakeholder relationships to management strategy. Freeman (1984) explicitly described techniques for identifying important stakeholders and managing stakeholder relationships. He included specific OD programs as one tool for supporting stakeholder relationships (p. 130). Stakeholder input is achieved via the inclusion of "boundary spanners" in the strategic planning process (Freeman 1984, p. 79). Freeman considered proactive stakeholder management capability critical to managing organizational change. Others have argued for formal inclusion of stakeholders in the corporate governance processes (Auerbach 1984).

OD practitioners are expanding open-systems theory and applying stakeholder concepts in diagnosis and action planning (Roberts & King 1985, Porras 1985). Golembiewski (1985) has found it important to involve stakeholders in major public projects. Kilmann (1983) has used stakeholder analysis to formulate theories and test assumptions in research. The concept of networks has received greater attention. Mandrell (1984) found network analysis valuable in developing roles for managers in a public project.

Senge (1985) has used systems-dynamics thinking and computer technology, previously applied to the creation of a microeconomic model, to the development of a systems-dynamic model of organizations. Based on interviews with managers of innovative, adaptive organizations, he constructed a computer model that specifies system characteristics crucial for creating and maintaining an adaptive organization, one in which information for decision making is widely shared. This model supports much of OD's assumptions about adaptive organizations. With a computer model he plans to train executives in systems dynamics so that they can manage organizations more effectively. This line of research promises to make some breakthroughs in how general managers learn to develop organizations.

OD AS CREATING ADAPTIVE ORGANIZATIONS

OD has long been concerned with fostering organizational adaptation to environmental changes. Management literature is increasingly interested in the organization/environment interface as well. The literature has expanded its focus to deal with issues of revitalization and decline.

Designing Innovative Organizations

Stimulated by the competitive crisis, an emerging stream of research (Tushman & Katz 1980, Kanter 1983, Lawrence & Dyer 1983, Nord & Tucker 1986) on innovation and entrepreneurship speaks to the question of adaptation and revitalization. While this research notes the importance of cultural factors, it also considers the key dilemma of integration and differentiation in developing innovative organizations (Lawrence & Lorsch 1967, Lawrence & Dyer 1983).

Early ideas on innovation suggested that product-planning groups be separated and "protected" from the organization at large. Kanter (1983) suggested more recently that such segmentation may be counterproductive and create barriers to innovations. Innovators must sell ideas into the organization for them to be successful.

Rubenstein & Woodman (1984) accorded critical importance to the boundary-spanner role. Boundary-spanning roles, such as territorial sales person or public relations representative, are considered conducive to innovation since these employees bring environmental information into the firm. While the boundary spanner may be a useful source of information, innovation may be more successful if all members are boundary spanners (Tushman & Katz 1980).

Research on innovation has also focused on the introduction of new technology. Graham & Rosenthal (1986) studied the implementation of flexible machining centers (FMCs) in eight companies. They found those sites that built flexibility into their human systems to be satisfied with results. Specifically, organizations need human flexibility in the composition and organization of product teams; the relations between in-house and vendor teams; and the selection, compensation, and organization of the FMC workforce. Flexibility indicators included broad skill mixes, cross-training, cross-functional cooperation, team building, and so forth. Zuboff (1985) distinguished between technologies that "informate"—bring together information so as to enhance workers' ability to think and act—and technologies that automate—technologies that minimize required skills and remove the need for thinking workers. Informating technologies are said to enhance organizational flexibility. Thus, Zuboff alerts us to the opportunities provided by new information technology for extending decisions down the hierarchy (creating a healthy and adaptive organization).

Nord & Tucker (1986) examine the implementation of an "administrative innovation," the offering of NOW accounts both in large and small banks and in savings and loans. They find that successful implementations shared four characteristics: (a) flexibility with regard to roles, decision making, and communication routes; (b) power concentrated somewhere (high or low); (c) technical readiness and access to technical and social competence (talent for pulling together people to solve problems); and (d) attention to the views of those directly responsible for implementation. These characteristics of successful implementations, except perhaps for the findings about power, might easily have been OD prescriptions.

The above findings suggest that some OD technology may be on target, some not. For example, getting input from those involved in implementation sounds like OD, while a particular cultural style is not requisite for implementation. In fact, it may be that technology and technological readiness are lead variables, while style may be a lag variable. The value of this type of research is that it translates general principles from OD into situation-specific prescriptions while clarifying the role of power in managing change, an area neglected by OD. Much more of such research is needed.

In order to achieve faster, more flexible internal communication routes, some organizations are restructuring, becoming flatter. These organizations have fewer power differentials (fewer titles, levels, status distinctions, reward differentials, etc) and rely on teams to accomplish tasks. Autonomous work groups responsible for a whole task have become popular. This trend parallels OD's precepts that decision making should occur at the level closest to the information (Beckhard 1969). There is continuing interest in organizational overlays: matrix organizations, parallel organizations, and collateral organizations (Zand 1974). The overlaps enhance the permeability at the organization's boundaries and thus allow the corporation to become more adaptive.

Rubenstein & Woodman (1984) noted the advantages of the collateral organization for individuals in the form of fulfillment, heightened perceptions, and connections to senior management. The organization benefits from enhanced disaster preparedness, decision-making ability at lower levels, the receipt of better information, and transmission of the ethos of senior management down to lower levels of the organization.

Interorganizational Relations

In their efforts to adapt to competitive forces organizations are increasingly looking to joint ventures and other interorganizational arrangements. These arrangements are subject to problems of intergroup relationships that OD has been concerned with for a long time. Gray (1985) has begun investigating conditions that enhance interorganizational collaboration. Van de Ven & Walker (1984) have looked at the dynamics of interorganizational cooperation and found that increased communications promote positive feelings and resource exchanges but also increase resource dependence. Johnson et al (1983) have described the innovative linkage model used between university, government, and the criminal justice system.

Buono et al (1985) looked at the pre- and postmerger attitudes in two savings banks. Owing to changes in the industry, most employees recognized the need for the merger, though there was evidence for postmerger ethnocentrism and irrational resistance. They note that management "managed" the hard factors more than the soft factors. Though the merger was between equals, one culture eventually dominated. Buono found that attitudes towards hard factors (compensation, hours of work, training policies, etc) changed less than attitudes toward organizational commitment and top management style.

Sales & Mirvis (1984) analyzed the features of managing an acquisition. They identified phases of cultural adjustment: first, employees feel anger, grief, dread, or anxiety; second, cross-cultural contact promotes change; third, acculturation occurs when the two cultures come to terms with each other. Sales & Mirvis anticipated conflict due to power differences, a one-directional flow from the buyer, and resistance from the subdominant group.

Organizational Decline

The 1974–1975 and 1981–1982 recessions and the declining performance of major US industries have focused the attention of managers and consultants on the task of managing decline. Decline, too, is organization development, possibly as natural as growth or revitalization. Research and theory on decline have grown substantially, though some argue more needs to be done (Nicoll 1982).

Undoubtedly, decline creates high organizational stress, and management is likely to observe irrational responses (Sutton 1983; Krantz 1985). While hostility, denial, and anger may be part of the emotional climate, depression, sadness, fear, and embarrassment may be the more powerful factors. Sutton (1983) notes, too, that lack of acceptance may be rational if possibilities for saving the company exist. Managers face many dilemmas: how to handle blaming (place it on external environment, accept it themselves, scapegoat others); which activities to sustain and which to disband; what and how much advance information to give to customers and employees, offering hope or taking it away (Sutton 1983). The results of different strategies are still unclear, though some generalizations seem possible. Management will need to spend more time on employees' personal concerns. It may be hard to contain information and rumors. Management may be unable to divert all blame from itself. Performance can decline but may well improve, due to increased management effort to deal with the feelings and perceptions of employees.

Cummings et al (1983) identified transorganizational systems as one positive response to managing decline. Conditions likely to facilitate the development of transorganizational systems included environmental turbulence, interdependence, lack of exit options, altruism, or mandates. Cummings et al reviewed transorganizational systems between similar organizations (such as the Microelectronics and Computer Technology company formed by semiconductor companies) or between dissimilar organizations (such as the Jamestown Labor-Management-Government system). They outlined strategies for setting up and running transorganizational systems. Trist (1983) suggested that interorganizational collaboration may be required to handle some of the complex problems facing organizations today. Cummings (1984) has begun exploring the opportunities for transorganizational development.

This research could bear fruit if it helps managers and consultants guide organizations through business or industry changes. It follows our general predisposition toward the development of OD theory that can help general managers manage major transitions or transformations in the life cycles of their organizations.

OD AS HUMAN-RESOURCE MANAGEMENT

As organizations have struggled in an increasingly competitive economy, superior human resources are increasingly seen as a competitive advantage. This has culminated in substantial interest in developing high-commitment work systems that will attract, motivate, and retain superior employees. Indeed the term human resources is coming to represent an integration of personnel administration, labor relations, and organization development, with OD the senior partner. The human-resource function and the practice of human-resources management (HRM) are absorbing the values and often the practices of OD (Beer & Spector 1984).

Human-resource managers have been struggling to define a new change-oriented function for their departments. There is an increasing tendency for human-resources personnel to be consultative, aiding with problem solving on key issues and helping management identify new trends (Finlay 1984, Harris & Harris 1983, Lippitt et al 1983). Many are noting that human-resource managers must model nondefensive behavior (Argyris 1985b) and implement change in the human-resource function to demonstrate that they, as part of the organization, must change.

Human-resource managers with an OD orientation have gained power as organizations attempt to change labor relations from adversarial to collaborative. OD technology has been applied in "relationship by objectives," or in third-party consultation directed at mediating grievance and arbitration disputes (Goldberg & Brett 1983). Solberg (1985) described GM's Black Lake experience, in which labor and management got together to sanction, discuss, and discover quality-of-work-life objectives. He described a deeply emotional and personal experience brought about by close interaction between union leaders and managers. This event had dramatic impact on the rest of the organization. Isolated experiments with job enrichment, sociotechnical designs, and quality of work life have given way to concerted efforts by corporations to change the nature of their relationship with employees and unions. Much of this work draws on OD values and technology.

Quality-of-work-life programs, reviewed extensively in the last *Annual Review* chapter, continue to flourish, although the name is not as much in vogue. Walton (1985) estimates that over 1000 plants in the United States may now be involved in major system redesign. These include special efforts to recruit, select, orient, and train employees so that they fit into an organization that requires higher levels of involvement, responsibility, and interpersonal competence. That requirement comes from the design of autonomous work groups and/or the use of special problem-solving groups. Skill-based compensation systems are also being designed to support the employee growth and development so critical for the functioning of work teams in which individuals rotate jobs and perform vertical tasks. In our view a false distinction has arisen between quality-of-work-life programs, as these plant innovations are sometimes called, and OD. Both the design of a high-commitment work system in a new plant and the transformation of an older plant employ OD concepts, values, intervention methods, and practitioners. Both are organization development.

Through an examination of six cases in which he was a consultant Walton (1980) was able to identify the dynamics of developing innovative green field plants. He found that in the early stages these plants face a human-resource gap. The employees lack the technical or interpersonal skills demanded by the new work system. Training and stress reduction are the key organization development tasks. In later stages there is a human-resource surplus where maintaining challenge and excitement are the key organization development tasks. More research that specifies the dynamics of organization development is needed.

Compensation systems are increasingly being used by management to revitalize organizations. Lawler (1981) has argued that changes in compensation systems can be a lead variable in OD. Scanlon plans and skill-based pay systems are used as examples. Beer et al (1984) argued that in most instances pay system redesign should not be used to lead change, that better management and leadership can often accomplish the same thing without incurring some of the problems that result from rising expectations.

Employee ownership through Employee Stock Ownership Plans (ESOPs) has been tried as a means of increasing employee commitment and of helping failing companies (Simmons & Mares 1983, Kuttner 1985). By making employees owners, ESOPs are expected to achieve greater productivity, greater interest in the business, and heightened flexibility on both management and union sides. (Some ESOPs have been undertaken merely for the tax advantage associated with them.) Research shows that ownership without a climate of participation is unlikely to have a dramatic impact on performance (Long 1982, Bradley 1983). Indeed only when employee ownership or gains sharing is preceded or accompanied by extensive organization development are basic relationships between management and labor likely to change. Much more research is needed on the role of pay, gains sharing, and ownership in organization development, an area of research pioneered by Lawler (1981) and Frost et al (1974) but not continued by others.

OD AS IMPLEMENTING CHANGE

What does the research and practice tell us about managing change? What precursors can indicate change opportunities? The introduction of new business strategies, technology, and administrative practices in response to specific changes in the environment demand that general managers become more competent in these matters. Below, we consider what we have learned about managing change.

Where Does Change Start?

Argyris (1985a) argues it starts with the individual. He offers a five-phase model for bringing about individual changes. Organizations do not develop self-corrective learning because they do not distinguish between espoused theories and theories in use. Though managers may espouse new, adaptive dictates (take risks, communicate openly), their behavior gives contraindications (failure and honesty are punished). This creates mixed messages, which are undiscussable. Because they are undiscussable, they cannot be changed. Only by confronting individuals with their inconsistencies will organizations develop the ability to critique current practice and develop double-loop, or self-corrective learning. To do this, Argyris suggests consultants start small and at the top. Many others have focused on individual change, particularly on trying to change the behavior of leaders and managers, claiming that this is where OD change starts.

Others disagree, and suggest that organization change comes about from change in systems and structures (Greenbaum et al 1983, Macy et al 1986). The argument here is that systemic change is needed to support changes in individual behavior. For example, Tainio & Santalainen (1984) compared the results of Grid OD training and found that it was less successful in Finland, where it fit poorly with organization structure and culture, than in the United States. Even in the United States individual approaches to organization change, most notably the T group movement of the 1960s, have failed.

Yet even system-wide efforts have failed. Researchers note that sociotech and other interventions are often not institutionalized and fade out after two years (Walton 1978, Beer 1979, Goodman & Dean 1982). This has led some to argue that change needs to start at the industry level. For example, Sandeberg (1983) consulted to unions about technology introduction and noted the need for workers and unions alike to be better informed so as to approach industry-wide new technology implementation proactively, rather than have the circumstance defined by management. Related are the findings of Roggemma (1983), who concluded that despite intensive efforts to change practices in the shipping industry, inertia and existing industry structure and institutional forces made lasting change impossible.

Obviously change must occur at the individual, organizational, and industry level for it to be institutionalized. More research is needed, however, on the problems and opportunities created by starting at one or the other of these levels and the most effective sequencing of change once it starts at each of these levels.

Can Change be Planned?

This question strikes at the very heart of OD assumptions. In increasing numbers, researchers and practitioners are expressing doubt (Lippitt et al 1985). Management literature parallels this emerging consensus. Quinn's (1980) study of strategic planning at 10 large companies led him to call the process "logical incrementalism." In this conception, managers make plans, which work imperfectly and attract a great deal of attention, disagreement, and support. The response of the system then affects and redirects the plan. Even managers have a hard time following grand plans (Pettigrew 1985) and must sometimes be out of control. Change is not brought about by following a grand master plan but by continually readjusting direction and goals. Research is needed on the structures and processes organizations must develop to allow an organic planning process to take place.

What Causes Change?

If change cannot be planned, then what causes change? While this question has no simple answer, it seems possible that OD has focused too narrowly on planned, internal efforts and neglected the role of environmental factors. Yet environmental factors may play a critical role in actual change. In a history of General Motors, Fox (1984) suggested that although Dupont placed several of GM's senior managers, had substantial equity in the firm, and continually pressed for changes, GM did not change until environmental contingencies forced change upon it. Dyer's (1985) research suggests that external events and crises precipitate changes far more than planned events. Precipitating events may often be anticipated but not controlled by managers.

Some (Anderson et al 1985, Fry & Killing 1985) are suggesting a taxonomy of change based on environmental factors. For example, a turnaround may occur after the organization has performed poorly over a long period. In this situation, where dissatisfaction and the perceived need to change are likely to be high and thus resistance lower, change may proceed quickly. In a revitalization situation, performance is mediocre and expected to decline. However, the perceived need to change is less acute; hence, slower change must be planned around likely resistance. In the case where mediocre performance has not yet occurred but is anticipated, change is likely to be even more difficult and must proceed at an even slower pace.

What Are the Roles in Change?

The faster pace of change is highlighting the centrality of the manager in managing change. Increasingly, OD practitioners are realizing the limitations on consultants' power and recognizing that it is best to have the manager center stage. Pettigrew (1985) noted that when consultants take greater control of process than management, or when the consultant has a highly visible role, the change process meets management resistance. Dyer (1983) argued that "Organization Development specialists (both internal and external) can assist in the process, but it should be managed by those who are ultimately responsible for all organizational consequences" (p. xiv). Cole (1982) pointed out that change has been better institutionalized in Japan and Sweden, countries in which managers drive the change with little assistance from external consultants.

Our view is that the manager must be central to change management and that OD must become a general management skill. The leader is more an architect than a director. He or she creates the environment (systems, strategy, models, symbols, etc) in which motivation for change will flourish. In this formulation, the leader/manager of an adaptive organization develops a vision of the future and attempts to infuse the organization with that vision, thereby motivating action and change. The manager must be flexible, willing to redraw plans and policies based on new information and system reactions. The manager needs a sense of timing, the ability to seize opportunities for change from the inevitable crises that occur in a firm's life. The leader must be able to pick consultants who will help him or her, particularly those who can provide strengths where he or she is weak. As yet, relatively little empirical research has been done on the leadership function in managing change. We also have focused on the titular head of the organization and neglected to investigate a broad set of leaders and the roles they play in change.

Role of "Change Targets"

The individuals to be affected by organizational change have been involved with some success in planning and implementing that change. Elden (1983) used a diagonal slice of the organization to assess internal relationships, and argued that those at the lower levels identify more system variables and describe more complex interrelationships between them than do employees higher in the organization. Levine (1983) described a self-developed quality-of-work-life (QWL) measure whose items reflected the most common statements by organization members about their work life. Levine demonstrated that this instrument had more criterion and convergent validity when compared with the Job Diagnostic Survey and saw distinct advantages to using the self-developed measure. This survey did not take job constructs as givens and was therefore less likely than the JDS to imply technological determinism.

Interventions are increasingly using teams for data gathering, analysis, and intervention. Friedlander & Schott (1981) described the use of groups as the intervention agent. In this model, the consultant's role is to help group members define tasks and roles, help with data collection, help develop team skills, and aid in understanding the larger organization in systems terms. Lundberg & Glassman (1983) used internal experts, relying on an informant panel for an organizational diagnosis. This is a promising approach to organization interventions, one that takes the consultant out of the limelight.

The Role of the Consultant

The consultant facilitates the managers' actions, providing them with data, skills, and suggestions. The consultant must be an expert in identifying opportunities for motivating change and clarifying visions. Consultants must help managers and staff learn. Naturally occurring events may be more educative and significant than the traditional interventions (laboratory, survey).

This suggests consultants must develop a better sense of what enables learning. In his study of how managers think, Isenberg (1984) found that acting and thinking may not be separable events. He argued that managers do not follow a classical rational problem-solving model but work on several problems at a time and may act on a problem before thinking about it. This again suggests that learning must be integrated with action. Certainly readiness is a key ingredient.

OD needs a new concept of the consultant's role. We believe it must become less purist, less programmed, and less value-laden. Current conceptions of consulting roles and plans are often too grandiose, developing research, knowledge, and practice that empower the consultant rather than the client.

Less Purist

OD practitioners often describe their role as neutral, as consulting to the entire "system," and as antithetical to the power politics that pervade organizations. Recent research is critiquing this concept of OD, noting vast differences between OD as written and as practiced (Lovelady 1984). Mendenhall & Oddou (1983) noted that many programs try to teach Theory-Y principles but use a Theory-X style themselves.

McLean et al (1982) noted that many reports of OD projects may be misrepresentative. Their study of OD consultants' practices identified numerous actions, ranging from overt "power plays" to unconsciously "acting like an expert," that directly contradicted consulting norms presented in the literature. They also concluded that change does not occur in the linear, planned phases of typical OD, and that the best consultants are able to take advantage of events, identifying opportunities to foster change. They identified two types of consultants: the centered consultant, who is opportunistic, takes a long-range view, has high tolerance for ambiguity, realizes organizations are messy, and is gratified with small successes; and the unintegrated consultant, who controls the client's definition of situations and events, is reluctant to exploit natural opportunities, and uses theory as a blueprint for truth.

Many (Carnall 1982, Pettigrew 1985) criticize OD's naiveté in the field of politics. Margulies & Raia (1984) argued that OD has neglected politics, yet politics are a key to success in consulting. Arguing that the consultant cannot be neutral, they outlined how consultants can help clients with the political aspects of problems. Jones (1984) cautioned consultants to look at politics skeptically and to question their clients' perceptions of organizational politics. Brown (1982) noted the difficulty of consulting to a group embroiled in internal conflict and described how politics can undermine the consultant's efforts.

Less Programmed

Research on change clearly argues that change does not obey the linear, phased plan of manager or consultant. Change does not occur in single episodes or interventions. Preprogrammed phase models may be unrealistic. McLean et al (1982) noted that the planned-change model is still used but often breaks down in four typical ways: The cycle (contracting, data collection, analysis, and feedback) results in insufficient data for action and cycles back to data collection; an educational program is set up as a precursor to change activities but detracts from objectives and becomes an end rather than a means; and a steering group may get bogged down analyzing its own process and neglect the problem it was formed to solve (p. 87–89). This raises questions about the more programmed (Blake & Mouton 1981, Kilmann 1984) approaches.

McLean et al (1982) pointed out that the opportunities for powerful interventions arise irregularly and unannounced. The skillful practitioner uses naturally occurring events to enhance the pressure for change. This suggests, too, that consultants need to be opportunistic and develop political skills.

Programs must consider the environment and the situation. In a fast-changing environment, managers learn primarily by doing (Boulden & Lawlor 1982, Eisenstat 1984). A flexible consultant working with managers to solve problems on the job might thus stimulate more of what Eisenstat has called behavioral learning (through doing) as opposed to representational learning (through language) typically delivered by standardized training programs.

These findings suggest that managers and consultants must design interventions that are embedded in the work situation and tailored to it. Such interventions demand that consultants become effective in diagnosing problems and designing and managing experiences that permit inductive learning. The field will have to develop guidelines for designing and managing learning experiences. These would be the equivalent of a contingency theory of intervention.

Plans must also suit the readiness of the client system. Readiness refers to the social, technological, or systemic ability of a group or organization to change or try new things. Programs need to identify where change is possible, rather than attempt to impose change on a highly resistant, unready system. Schlesinger & Oshry (1984) and Jick & Ashkenas (1985) have argued that in order to effect long-term changes, planners must start small, exploit early successes, and seek to tie the elements of change to existing systems and structures.

In assessing a program's impact on a client system, OD consultants must also consider the magnitude of change. Organizations are constantly changing, adding new products, reorganizing, modifying strategy, in a sense fine tuning the existing organization. Tushman et al (in press) observed two basic types of organizational change: converging change, which consists of iterative improvements toward an essentially unchanged goal; and framebreaking change, in which the system drastically reorganizes and redirects itself. They argued that major redirections must be undertaken quickly and powerfully to avoid getting bogged down in politics. Converging change may be managed in a more consensual process.

Throughout our discussion, we have raised the question of lead versus lag variables. Change methods and organizational values appropriate for one organizational situation may be dysfunctional at another phase in the life cycle. Interventions effective in a stable environment may be inefficient in unstable environments. An organization with a powerful culture may use a technological change as a lead intervention, and follow with cultural change. This variability suggests a problem for advocates of a one-best-way approach.

Each consultant may need to specialize in what fits his or her style and experience. Schon (1983) maintained that the best professionals know more than they can put into words. To meet the challenges of their work, they rely less on graduate school theory than on their experience in responding to problems that arise in practice. This suggests that OD consultants, or for that matter managers concerned with knowing what they have learned, need to spend time in reflection to develop their own theory of change.

Less Value-Laden

Some practitioners believe that a return to the simple value of democratic management would create organizational effectiveness, yet evidence suggests that such management may be neither universally advantageous nor universally desired.

Even OD interventions designed to create more open and participative organizations may have negative outcomes for individuals. Walters (1984) points out that OD may reduce an individual's freedom, privacy, or self esteem. For example, consultants may not inform survey respondents of possible negative outcomes (a powerful manager may retaliate after receiving negative feedback); team building or confrontation may dragoon people into revealing private or interpersonal information, imposing on their freedom and privacy for the presumed advantage of improved team performance. These interventions may benefit the organization but harm the individual (Gavin 1984).

The evidence that certain organizational forms or styles foster organizational effectiveness is inconclusive. Though many advocate the open, participative organization, others have found that these attributes do not always correlate with success. Some situations simply may not allow integration of employee and organizational needs. The best organizational style and form is contingent on the organization's task, what it needs to do to succeed in its environment. Moreover, advocacy of values by OD practitioners has not worked well, as evidenced by the rise and decline of many corporate OD efforts. If corporations today are adopting OD values in their efforts to revitalize, they are doing so because environmental pressures are pushing them to do so.

IN CONCLUSION

In the introduction we said our conception of the field involves a reconsideration of its research methodology, theory building, practice, and values. Here we return to a brief discussion of this conception.

Theory building in the field has always been weak. We believe this stems from the traditional focus of the field. Rather than cataloging the technology of organizational change, we need to catalog how external forces create the opportunities for change. Rather than assume that there is a single way to change organizations, a way consistent with our technology and values, we should develop a contingency theory of organization change. Such a theory would specify alternative change strategies appropriate to an organization's stage of development. It would highlight the skills required of the leader, OD consultant, and other supporting change agents as well as their relationship to each other and the task of change, with particular emphasis on what they must know about the business of the organization and its politics. The theory would deal with time frames more explicitly than current theories, and it would specify how continuity of leadership and consultation relate to effective adaptation. In short, we need a theory of organizational adaptation that incorporates *all* types of interventions, applying them to the management of the numerous crises all organizations face. Such a theory could benefit from the general-management orientation of business policy and could contribute to that field ideas about leadership, organizational culture, and change.

The primary research methodology appropriate to this orientation would not be that of normal science, which attempts to answer little questions precisely. Instead we would be more concerned with broader longitudinal designs, creating knowledge that could be used. We suggest a return to the action research traditions of the field but with a longer time frame and a more thorough investigation of the context in which episodes occur. OD need not become lax in its search for knowledge, but we must recognize that our sphere of inquiry is fundamentally different from that of normal science. We cannot borrow the tools and techniques of another paradigm; we must develop our own.

The practice of OD must also change. We suggest the focus should move away from structured and preprogrammed consultant-centered interventions. The general manager is the central character in the drama of organization development. OD practitioners must therefore be more concerned with the selection and development of these leaders. They must also adopt the perspective of the general manager. This means knowledge of the business and task; understanding of the competitive environment and the opportunities for change and development it provides; and much more sophistication in diagnosis, politics, and intervention design suited to the situation. All of this raises serious questions about the source and development of OD consultants and their relationship to general managers and the human-resource function. Tension has always existed in the field between a concern for effectiveness and a concern for the well-being of employees. Our review suggests that in some ways this tension has been eased by the natural evolution of organizations, pushed by competitive forces, toward the values of OD. But, we do not believe this evolution has come about because OD practitioners have been successful in imposing their values on organizations nor that future evolution toward the healthy organization will come from OD practitioners who advocate humanistic values. OD practitioners—general managers and consultants alike—would be well advised to retain a normative vision for long-term guidance while adopting a situational perspective in diagnosing organizational problems and taking action to improve them. As with many human endeavors, managing this paradox is the critical skill.

Literature Cited

Anderson, D. G., Phillips, J. R., Kaible, N. 1985. *Revitalizing Large Companies.*, *Work. Pap.* Cambridge, MA: Mass. Inst. Technol. 35 pp.

Argyris, C. 1985a. *Strategy, Change and Defensive Routines.* Boston: Pitman. 368 pp.

Argyris, C. 1985b. *Reinforcing Defensive Routines: An Unintended Human Resources Activity.* Draft. 24 pp.

Argyris, C., Putnam, R., Smith, D. M. 1985. *Action Science.* San Francisco/London: Jossey-Bass. 480 pp.

Armenakis, A. A., Bedian, A. G., Pond, S. B. III. 1983. Research issues in OD evaluation: past, present and future. *Acad. Manage. Rev.* 8:320–28

Auerbach, J. 1984. *The Now and Future Business Corporation.* Work. pap. Boston: President & Fellows Harvard College

Barnard, C. I. 1938. *The Functions of the Executive.* Cambridge, MA: Harvard Univ. Press. 334 pp.

Beckhard, R. 1969. *Organization Development: Strategies and Models.* Reading, MA: Addison-Wesley. 119 pp.

Beckhard, R., Harris, R. T. 1977. *Organizational Transitions: Managing Complex Change.* Reading, MA: Addison-Wesley. 110 pp.

Beer, M. 1979. The longevity of organization development. In *Organization Change Sourcebook I: Cases in Organization Development,* ed. B. Lubin, L. D. Goodstein, A. W. Lubin, pp. 62–65. La Jolla, CA: Univ. Assoc.

Beer, M. 1980. *Organization Change and Development: A Systems View.* Santa Monica: Goodyear. 367 pp.

Beer, M., Spector, B. 1984. Human resource management: the integration of industrial relations and organization development. In *Research in Personnel and Human Resources Management,* ed. K. M. Rowland, G. R. Ferris, pp. 261–97. San Francisco: JAI Press

Beer, M. Spector, B. 1985. Corporate-wide transformations: In *HRM Trends and Challenges,* ed. R. Walton, P. Lawrence. Boston: Harvard Bus. Sch. Press

Beer, M., Spector, B., Lawrence, P. R., Mills, D. Q., Walton, R. E. 1984. *Managing Human Assets.* New York: The Free Press. 209 pp.

Bennis, W. 1969. *Organization Development: Its Nature, Origins, and Prospects.* Reading, MA: Addison-Wesley. 87 pp.

Bennis, W., Nanus, B. 1985. *Leaders.* New York: Harper & Row. 244 pp.

Blake, R. R., Mouton, J. S. 1981. *The New Managerial Grid.* Houston: Gulf. 329 pp.

Blumberg, M., Pringle, C. D. 1983. How control groups can cause loss of control in action research: the case of Rushton Coal Mine. *J. Appl. Behav. Sci.* 19:409–25

Boulden, G., Lawlor, A. 1982. Surviving in a changing world: the nature of change and its application. *Leadership Organ. Dev. J.* 3:3–9

Bradley, K. 1983. *Worker Capitalism: The New Industrial Relations.* Boston: MIT Press. 192 pp.

Brown, C. M. 1982. Administrative succession and organizational performance: the succession effect. *Admin. Sci. Q.* 27:1–16

Buono, A., Bowditch, J. L., Lewis, J. W. III.

1985. When cultures collide: the anatomy of a merger. *Hum. Relat.* 38:477–500

Burke, W. W. 1982. *Organization Development, Principles and Practices.* Boston/Toronto: Little, Brown. 402 pp.

Burke, W. W. 1985. *Leadership as Empowering Others.* New York: W. Warner Burke Assoc. 31 pp.

Carnall, C. A. 1982. *The Evaluation of Organizational Change.* Brookfield, VT: Gower. 130 pp.

Cole, R. E. 1982. Diffusion of participatory work structures in Japan, Sweden, and the United States. In *Change in Organizations,* ed. P. Goodman and Associates, pp. 166–225. San Francisco/London: Jossey-Bass

Cummings, T. G. 1984. Trans-organization development. *Res. Organ. Behav.* 6:

Cummings, T. G., Blumenthal, J., Greiner, L. 1983. Managing organizational decline: the case for transorganizational systems. *Hum. Resour. Manage.* 22(4):377–90

Deal, T. E. 1985. Cultural change: opportunity, silent killer, or metamorphosis? In *Gaining Control of the Corporate Culture,* ed. R. H. Kilmann, M. J. Saxon, R. Serpa. pp. 292–331. San Francisco/London: Jossey-Bass

Deal, T., Kennedy, A. 1982. *Corporate Cultures.* Reading, MA: Addison-Wesley. 232 pp.

Denison, D. R. 1984. Bringing corporate culture to the bottom line. *Organ. Dyn.* 13:4–22

Dyer, W. G. 1983. *Contemporary Issues in Management and Organization Development.* Reading, MA: Addison-Wesley. 231 pp.

Dyer, W. G. 1985. The cycle of cultural evolution in organizations. See Kilmann et al 1985, pp. 200–29

Eisenstat, R. A. 1984. *Organizational learning in the creation of an industrial setting.* PhD thesis. Yale Univ., New Haven, CT. 240 pp.

Elden, M. 1983. Democratization and participative research in developing local theory. *J. Occup. Behav.* 4:21–33

Faucheux, C., Amado, G., Laurent, A. 1982. Organizational development and change. *Ann. Rev. Psychol.* 33:343–70

Fiedler, F. E., Bell, C., Chemers, M., Patrick, D. 1984. Increasing mine productivity and safety through management training and organization development: a comparative study. *Basic Appl. Soc. Psychol.* 5:1–18

Finlay, J. S. 1984. Diagnose your HRD problems away. *Train. Dev. J.* 38:50–52

Fox, W. 1984. General Motors: Dupont's tough OD case. *Group Organ. Stud.* 9:71–80

Freeman, R. E. 1984. *Strategic Management:* *A Stakeholder Approach.* Boston: Pitman. 276 pp.

Friedlander, F., Schott, B. 1981. The use of task groups and task forces in organizational change. In *Groups At Work,* ed. R. Payne, C. Cooper, pp. 191–218. New York: Wiley

Frost, C. F., Wakeley, J. H., Ruh, R. A. 1974. *The Scanlon Plan for Organization Development: Identity, Participation, and Equity.* East Lansing, MI: Mich. State Univ. Press. 197 pp.

Fry, J. N., Killing, J. P. 1985. *Strategic Analysis and Action.* Englewood Cliffs, NJ: Prentice-Hall

Gavin, J. F. 1984. Survey feedback: the perspectives of science and practice. *Group Organ. Stud.* 9(1):29–70

Goldberg, S. B., Brett, J. M. 1983. An experiment in the mediation of grievance. *Monthly Labor Rev.* 106:23–29

Golembiewski, R. T. 1983. Lessons from a fast-paced public project: perspectives on doing better the next time around. *Public Admin. Rev.* 43:547–56

Golembiewski, R. T., Billingsley, K., Yeager, S. 1976. Measuring change and persistence in human affairs: types of change generated by OD designs. *J. Appl. Behav. Sci.* 12:133–57

Goodman, P., Dean, J. W. 1982. Creating long term change in organizations. In *Change in Organizations,* ed. P. Goodman and Associates, pp. 226–79. San Francisco/London: Jossey-Bass

Graham, M. B. W., Rosenthal, S. R. 1986. Flexible manufacturing systems require flexible people. In *Human Systems Management.* In press

Gray, B. 1985. Conditions facilitating interorganization collaboration. *Hum. Relat.* 38(10):911–86

Greenbaum, H. H., Holden, E. J. Jr., Spartaro, L. 1983. Organizational structure and communications processes: a study of change. *Group Organ. Stud.* 8(1):61–82

Guzzo, R. A., Jette, R. D., Katzell, R. A. 1985. The effects of psychologically based intervention programs on worker productivity: a meta-analysis. *Personnel Psychol.* 38:275–92

Hackman, R., Oldham, G. R. 1975. Development of the job diagnostic survey. *J. Appl. Psychol.* 60:159–170

Harris, P. R., Harris, D. L. 1983. Twelve trends you and your CEO should be monitoring. *Train. Dev. J.* 37:62–69

Isenberg, D. J. 1984. How senior managers think. *Harv. Bus. Rev.* 62:80–90

Jick, T. D., Ashkenas, R. N. 1985. Involving employees in productivity and QWL improvements: what OD can learn from the manager's perspective. In *Contemporary*

Organization Development: Current Thinking and Applications, ed. D. D. Warrick, pp. 218–30. Glenview, IL: Scott, Foresman

Johnson, K. W., Frazier, W. D., Riddick, M. R. 1983. A change strategy for linking the worlds of academia and practice. *J. Appl. Behav. Sci.* 19:439–60

Jones, S. 1984. The politics of problems: intersubjectivity in defining powerful others. *Hum. Relat.* 37:881–94

Kanter, R. M. 1983. *The Change Masters: Innovation and Entrepreneurship in the American Corporation.* New York: Simon & Schuster. 432 pp.

Katz, D., Kahn, R. L. 1966. *The Social Psychology of Organizing.* New York: Wiley. 838 pp.

Katzell, R. A., Guzzo, R. A. 1983. Psychological approaches to productivity improvement. *Am. Psychol.* 38:468–72

Kilmann, R. 1984. *Beyond the Quick Fix: Managing Five Tracks to Organizational Success.* San Francisco/London: Jossey-Bass. 300 pp.

Kilmann, R., Saxton, M. J., Serpa, R., eds. 1985. *Gaining Control of the Corporate Culture.* San Francisco/London: Jossey-Bass. 451 pp.

Kilmann, R. H. 1983. A dialectic approach to formulating and testing social science theories: assumptional analysis. *Hum. Relat.* 36(1):1–22

Kilmann, R. H., Thomas, K. W., Slevin, D. P., Nath, R., Jerrell, L., eds. 1983. *Producing Useful Knowledge for Organizations.* New York: Praeger. 731 pp.

Kirkpatrick, D. 1985. *How to Manage Change Effectively.* San Francisco/London: Jossey Bass. 280 pp.

Kleiner, B. 1983. The interrelationship of Jungian modes of mental functioning with organizational factors: implications for management development. *Hum. Relat.* 36(11):997–1012

Kotter, J. P. 1982. *The General Managers.* New York/London: Free Press. 221 pp.

Krantz, J. 1985. Group process under conditions of organization decline. *J. Appl. Behav. Sci.* 21:1–18

Kuttner, R. 1985. Sharing power at Eastern Air Lines. *Harv. Bus. Rev.* 6:91–101

Lawler, E. E. 1981. *Pay and Organization Development.* Reading, MA: Addison-Wesley

Lawler, E. E., Mohrman, A. M. Jr., Mohrman, S. A., Ledford, G. E. Jr., Cummings, T. G., eds. 1985. *Doing Research That Is Useful for Theory and Practice.* San Francisco/London: Jossey-Bass. 371 pp.

Lawrence, P. R., Lorsch, J. W. 1967. *Organizations and Environment: Managing Differentiation and Integration.* Homewood, IL: Irwin. 279 pp.

Lawrence, P. R., Dyer, D. 1983. *Renewing American Industry.* New York: The Free Press. 384 pp.

Legge, K. 1984. *Evaluating Planned Organizational Change.* Orlando: Academic. 243 pp.

Levine, M. F. 1983. Self-developed QWL measures. *J. Occup. Behav.* 4:35–46

Lindblom, C. E., Cohen, D. K. 1979. *Usable Knowledge: Social Science and Social Problem Solving.* New Haven: Yale Univ. Press. 129 pp.

Lippett, G., Lippett, R., Lafferty, C. 1983. Cutting edge trends in organizational development. *Train. Dev. J.* 38:59–62

Lippitt, G. L., Langseth, P., Mossop, J. 1985. *Implementing Organizational Change.* San Francisco/London: Jossey-Bass. 185 pp.

Long, R. J. 1982. Worker ownership and job attitudes: a field study. *Ind. Relat.* 21:196–215

Lovelady, L. 1984. Change strategies and the use of OD consultants to facilitate change. II. The role of the internal consultant in OD. *Leadership Organ. Dev. J.* 5:2–12

Lundberg, C. C., Glassman, A. M. 1983. The informant panel: a retrospective methodology for guiding organizational change. *Group Organ. Stud.* 3(2):249–64

Macy, B. A., Hurts, C. C. M., Izumi, H., Norton, L. W., Smith, R. R. 1986. Presented at Natl. Acad. Manage., 46th Ann. Meet., Chicago, IL. 101 pp. 52

Mandrell, M. 1984. Application of network analysis to the implementation of a complex project. *Hum. Relat.* 37:659–79

Margulies, N., Raia, A. P. 1984. The politics of OD. *Train. Dev. J.* 38:20–23

McLean, A. J., Sims, D. B. P., Mangan, I. L., Tuffield, D. 1982. *Organization Development in Transition: Evidence of an Evolving Profession.* New York: Wiley. 131 pp.

Mendenhall, M., Oddou, G. 1983. The integrative approach to OD: McGregor revisited. *Group Organ. Stud.* 8:291–301

Morgan, G., ed. 1983. *Beyond Method: Strategies for Social Research.* Beverly Hills, CA: Sage. 424 pp.

Morrison, P. 1978. Evaluation in OD: A review and assessment. *Group Organ. Stud.* 3:42–70

Nicholas, J. 1982. The comparative impact of organization development interventions on hard criteria measures. *Acad. Manage. Rev.* 9:531–43

Nicholas, J., Katz, M. 1985. Research methods and reporting practices in organization development: a review and some guidelines. *Acad. Manage. Rev.* 10:737–49

Nicoll, D. 1982. Organization declines as an OD issue. *Group. Organ. Stud.* 7:165–78

Nord, W. R., Tucker, S. 1986. *Implementing Radical and Routine Innovation.* Lexington, MA: Lexington Books. 416 pp.

Ouchi, W. G. 1981. *Theory Z: How American Business Can Meet the Japanese Challenge.* Reading, MA: Addison-Wesley. 283 pp.

Pascale, R. T., Athos, A. G. 1981. *The Art of Japanese Management.* New York: Simon & Schuster. 221 pp.

Passmore, W., Friedlander, F. 1982. An action research program for increasing employee involvement in problem solving. *Admin. Sci. Q.* 27:343–62

Peters, M., Robinson, V. 1984. The origins and status of action research. *J. Appl. Behav. Sci.* 20:113–24

Peters, T., Waterman, R. H. 1982. *In Search of Excellence.* New York: Harper & Row. 360 pp.

Pettigrew, A. 1985. *The Awakening Giant: Continuity and Change in ICI.* Oxford/New York: Blackwell. 542 pp.

Porras, J. I. 1985. *OD Research Paper #802,* March

Quinn, J. B. 1980. *Strategies for Change: Logical Incrementalism.* Homewood, IL: Irwin. 222 pp.

Roberts, N., King, P. 1985. *The Stakeholder Audit: A Key Political Tool in the Change Process.* Draft

Roberts, N. C., Porras, J. I. 1982. Progress in OD research. *Group Organ. Stud.* 7(1):91–116

Roggemma, J., Smith, M. H. 1983. Organizational change in the shipping industry: issues in the transformation of the basic assumptions. *Hum. Relat.* 8:765–90

Rubenstein, D., Woodman, R. W. 1984. Spiderman and the Burma Raiders: collateral organization theory in action. *J. Appl. Behav. Sci.* 20:1–21

Sales, A. L., Mirvis, P. H. 1984. When cultures collide: issues in acquisition. In *Managing Organizational Transitions,* ed. J. R. Kimberly, R. E. Quinn, pp. 107–33. Homewood, IL: Irwin

Sandeberg, A. 1983. Trade union-orientated research for democratization of planning in work life—problems and pitfalls. *J. Occup. Behav.* 4:59–71

Sashkin, M. 1985. *Visionary Leadership: A New Look at Executive Leadership.* Washington, DC: Off. Educ. Res. Improve. 9 pp.

Sashkin, M., Burke, R. J., Lawrence, P. R., Pasmore, W. A. 1984. Organization development approaches: analysis and application. In *Contemporary Organization Development, Current Thinking and Applications,* ed. D. D. Warrick. Glenview, IL: Scott, Foresman. 502 pp.

Sathe, V. 1985. *Culture and Related Corporate Realities.* Homewood, IL: Irwin. 579 pp.

Schein, E. 1985. *Organizational Culture and Leadership.* San Francisco: Jossey-Bass. 357 pp.

Schlesinger, L. A., Oshry, B. 1984. Quality of work life and the manager: muddle in the middle. *Organ. Dyn.* 13:4–19

Schon, D. E. 1983. *The Reflective Practitioner: How Professionals Think in Action.* New York: Basic Books. 374 pp.

Seashore, S. E., Lawler, E. E., Mirvis, P. H., Camman, C., eds. 1983. *Assessing Organizational Change: A Guide to Methods, Measures and Practices.* New York: Wiley

Selznick, P. 1957. *Leadership in Administration.* White Plains, NY: Row, Peterson. 162 pp.

Senge, P. M. 1985. *System dynamics, mental models and the development of management intuition.* Presented at the 1985 Int. Syst. Dyn. Conf., Keystone, CO

Simmons, J., Mares, W. 1983. *Working Together.* New York: Knopf. 319 pp.

Solberg, S. L. 1985. Changing culture through ceremony: an example from GM. *Hum. Resour. Manage.* 24:329–40

Sutton, R. I. 1983. Managing organizational death. *Hum. Resour. Manage.* 22:391–412

Tainio, R., Santalainen, T. 1984. Some evidence for the cultural relativity of organization development programs. *J. Appl. Behav. Sci.* 20(2):93–111

Terpstra, D. E. 1982. Evaluating selected OD interventions: the state of the art. *Group Organ. Stud.* 7(4):402–17

Trist, E. 1983. Referent-organizations and the development of inter-organization domains. *Hum. Relat.* 36(3):269–84

Tushman, M., Katz, R. 1980. External communication and project performance: an investigation into the role of gatekeepers. *Manage. Sci.* 26:1071–85

Tushman, M., Newman, W. H., Romanelli, E. 1986. Convergence and upheavals: managing the unsteady pace of organizational evolution. *Calif. Manage. Rev.* 28: In press

Van de Ven, A., Walker, G. 1984. The dynamics of interorganizational coordination. *Admin. Sci. Q.* 29:598–621

Van de Vliert, E., Huismans, S. E., Stok, J. J. L. 1985. The criterion approach to unraveling beta and alpha change. *Acad. Manage. Rev.* 10:269–74

Vicars, W. M., Hartke, D. D. 1984. Evaluating OD evaluations: a status report. *Group Organ. Stud.* 9(2):177–88

Walters, G. A. 1984. Organizational development and individual rights. *J. Appl. Behav. Sci.* 20:423–39 (Special issue)

Walton, R. E. 1978. The Topeka story: part II. *Wharton Mag.* 3:36–41

Walton, R. E. 1980. Establishing and maintaining high commitment work systems. In *The Organizational Life Cycle: Issues in the Creation, Transformation and Decline of Organizations,* ed. J. R. Kimberly, R. H. Miles, and Associates. San Francisco/ London: Jossey-Bass

Walton, R. E. 1985. From control to commitment in the workplace. *Harv. Bus. Rev.* 63:76–84

Wilkins, A. L. 1983. The culture audit: a tool for understanding organizations. *Organ. Dyn.* 12:24–38

Wilkins, A. L., Ouchi, W. G. 1983. Efficient cultures: exploring the relationship between culture and organizational performance. *Admin. Sci. Q.* 28:468–81

Zand, D. E. 1974. Collateral organizations: a new change strategy. *J. Appl. Behav. Sci.* 10(1):63–89

Zuboff, S. 1985. Technologies that informate: implications for human resource management in the computerized industrial workplace. In *HRM Trends and Challenges,* ed. R. E. Walton, P. R. Lawrence, pp. 103–40. Boston: Harv. Bus. Sch. Press

Ann. Rev. Psychol. 1987. 38:369–425

SOCIAL COGNITION AND SOCIAL PERCEPTION

E. Tory Higgins and John A. Bargh

Department of Psychology, New York University, New York, New York 10003

CONTENTS

0066-4308/87/0201-0369$02.00

INTRODUCTION

The "modern" trend focuses upon the *processes* of perceiving and judging; the "early" studies concentrated upon the *accuracy* of perception or judgment. (Bruner & Tagiuri 1954, p. 640; original italics).

Over a quarter of a century has passed since this characterization of the major concerns of those studying "social cognition" or the "knowing of people." As will be evident from our review of the recent literature in social cognition and social perception, progress is not noticeable if one measures it solely by trends. Indeed, the "early" trend of focusing on *accuracy* or "correctness" has simply regained its status as "modern" along with the focus on *processes* of perception and judgment. But doggedness in attacking fundamental problems is a healthy feature of any mature science. Progress depends more on how successful a field is in selecting, reconceptualizing, and investigating key aspects of their fundamental problems. Has social cognition obtained some preliminary answers to some important questions?

The purpose of the present chapter is not to provide a general historical review of social cognition (e.g. Landman & Manis 1983, Ostrom 1984, Markus & Zajonc 1985) but to review recent progress. In selecting issues to review, we attempted to find a set that together would cover a sufficient range of theoretical proposals and research findings to provide the reader a fair representation of recent developments in the field. The issues were also selected to permit discussion of some methodological and conceptual problems of general significance. In addition, the issues had to have been investigated sufficiently to permit empirically based conclusions and be nonredundant with issues discussed in recent *Annual Review of Psychology* chapters (e.g. Hastie 1983, Showers & Cantor 1985). We have intentionally framed the four major questions we selected in their most provocative form in order to highlight their challenging and stimulating nature.

DO PEOPLE EVEN CARE ABOUT THE INFORMATION GIVEN?

Social perception and cognition traditionally have been associated with the proposition that people perceive and think about the social world differently from what would be expected based solely on the stimulus information and principles of formal logic. Social perception was founded on the idea that internal factors such as values, needs, and expectancies influence the outcome of perception, so that it could not be accounted for entirely in terms of stimulus qualities (e.g. Postman et al 1948). And social cognition presented evidence that people typically did not reason about social information by weighting and combining available evidence in a rational and judicious manner (e.g. Heider 1958, Mischel 1968, Kahneman & Tversky 1973).

Accordingly, social perception and cognition researchers have tended to take as their domain of inquiry the study of the ways in which people go *beyond* the information given. There has been relatively little emphasis on the ways in which people stay *within* the bounds of the given data.

Because the focus of the field has been on the "theory-driven" rather than the "data-driven" aspect of perception and cognition, there is a danger that we as researchers may suffer from our own "availability heuristic" bias (Kahneman & Tversky 1973) in assuming people are overwhelmingly "theory-driven." It sometimes appears as though the burden of proof is on demonstrating that people take environmental information into account, rather than on showing that they dismiss, discount, or distort it in line with their prior theories. Studies by Hastie & Kumar (1979) and Locksley et al (1980), for example, engendered considerable controversy in part because they appeared to show that subjects were influenced primarily by characteristics of the stimulus information!

Passive Intrusions in Episodic Memory

One method of demonstrating "theory-driven" influences on the processing of social stimuli is to show that the episodic memory trace for that information contains conceptually related information that was not actually presented. Intrusions of unpresented but highly related information from memory have been found to occur during sentence and story comprehension (e.g. Bartlett 1932, Bransford & Franks 1971, Spiro 1977, Bower et al 1979) and in visual memory for common scenarios (e.g. Brewer & Treyens 1981). In a highly influential paper, Cantor & Mischel (1977) posited the existence of prototypical memory structures that represent dimensions of personality and serve to organize social behavioral input. Subjects in their study were presented with target persons who were described by sets of personality traits consisting of either traits mainly related to extraversion or traits mainly related to introversion. There were also control targets described by either traits unrelated to extraversion or traits unrelated to introversion.

After subjects read about each of the targets, they were given a recognition test containing some of the presented trait terms along with new, unpresented trait terms, which were either highly related, moderately related, or unrelated to either extraversion or introversion. Subjects rated each item on a four-point bipolar (certain item was presented vs certain item was not presented) scale as to how confident they were that that item had been presented in the original target descriptions. Results showed that for the prototypical targets, the prototype-related unpresented items had higher recognition confidence ratings than did the prototype-unrelated unpresented items. This pattern did not occur for the control targets. Cantor & Mischel (1977) concluded that for the prototype-related targets, subjects had shown a memory bias consistent with the prototype.

The results of this study and similar ones (Tsujimoto 1978, Tsujimoto et al 1978) have been broadly interpreted as showing that people falsely recognize prototype-consistent stimuli as having been presented when they were not part of the original input (e.g. Nisbett & Ross 1980, Taylor & Crocker 1981, Fiske & Taylor 1984, Markus & Zajonc 1985, Stephan 1985). Subjects in the Cantor & Mischel (1977) and Tsujimoto (1978, Tsujimoto et al 1978) studies, however, did not believe that prototype-consistent unpresented information had been presented. As noted by Hastie (1981), all recognition confidence means for the unpresented items were on the half of the scale indicating the belief that the item had *not* been presented, whereas all of the presented-item means were well on the half of the scale indicating confidence that the item had been presented. Moreover, the bias toward the prototype-related un-presented items may have been the result of a guessing strategy favoring items semantically similar to the input items (Wyer & Gordon 1982). Response biases in recognition memory tests can be ruled out only by taking both hit and false alarm rates for the individual subject into account (Bellezza & Bower 1981, Alba & Hasher 1983, Locksley et al 1984).

When free recall is used to measure memory instead of recognition tests, there is even less evidence for structurally or expectancy driven intrusions in episodic memory (Cantor & Mischel 1979, Hastie & Kumar 1979, Srull 1981, Srull & Brand 1983, Srull & Wyer 1983, Bargh & Thein 1985). Free recall measures the *accessibility* of information stored in memory—that is, how easily it can be retrieved—whereas recognition tests are more sensitive indicators of what information was stored and thus is *available* for retrieval (Tulving & Pearlstone 1966). The lack of intrusions in free recall, therefore, is not conclusive evidence that intrusions do not occur. But if they do occur, they are relatively inaccessible and thus unlikely to have much impact. Moreover, when recognition hit rates and false alarm rates are considered jointly, there is little evidence for belief-congruent intrusions in episodic memory (Locksley et al 1984).

Thus, although prototypical or schematic memory structures may influence social-information processing, they need not alter the encoding such that people believe they have seen something that was not there. Externally and internally generated sources of information may coexist in memory without becoming tangled up with each other. Johnson & Raye (1981) present considerable evidence to this effect, along with a "reality monitoring" model of how people are able to tell the difference between reality and imagination.

A nice example of how memory schemata influence the encoding of social information without necessarily producing intrusions in episodic memory is provided by Picek et al (1975). If social schemata were to cause intrusions in memory to fill in missing information, the balance schema (Heider 1958) would appear to be a prime candidate to show such an effect as it exercises a strong organizational influence on memory for social relationships (e.g. Sentis & Burnstein 1979). Picek et al (1975) presented subjects with four-person relationships in which not all of the possible two-person relations (like or dislike) were indicated. Some of these four-person relationships were balanceable, whereas others were not. In later recalling these relationships, unpresented relationships were rarely remembered as having been presented. Furthermore, of the errors that were made, there was no general trend toward balance. Picek et al (1975) concluded that subjects appeared to be encoding the stories as either balanced or imbalanced and then using this abstract summary as a basis for guessing when they weren't sure of the direction of the relationship.

Automatic Activation of Abstract Representations

Thus, people apparently encode environmental information fairly accurately without supplementing the original information with previous knowledge. But it also appears that some kind of abstract summary representation of the data may be encoded along with the data themselves, and this summary may influence subsequent processing and decisions. The formation of such an abstract summary may have been responsible for the guessing strategies shown by subjects in previous studies (e.g. Picek et al 1975, Cantor & Mischel 1977, Tsujimoto 1978). Questions concerning the extent and nature of these abstract encodings, their impact on subsequent processing, and the conditions under which such encodings do and do not occur have generated considerable research.

Higgins et al (1977) had subjects hold single trait adjectives in memory while naming the color in which a different word was presented. These trait terms varied across different experimental conditions as to whether they were positively or negatively valenced and as to their relevance to subsequently presented information about a target's behaviors. Subjects read about the target in the context of what they thought to be an experiment unrelated to the concerns of the earlier, color-naming study. The description of the target consisted of behaviors that were ambiguous as to which of two traits, differing in social desirability, they indicated. For example, the statement that the target person "was well aware of his ability to do many things well" could be alternatively interpreted as self-confident or as conceited. After reading the behavior description, subjects evaluated the target person as to his overall desirability or characterized him with a single trait term or did both.

Subjects' characterizations and evaluations of the target were influenced by the desirability of the trait terms to which they had been exposed in the unrelated first experiment, but *only* when those trait terms were applicable to interpreting the target's behaviors. Higgins et al (1977) concluded that the "memory words" of the first experiment had activated specific mental representations or categories of trait-related behavior. These activated constructs were then more accessible or likely to be used in subjects' later interpretation of the ambiguous target behaviors than were equally relevant but less accessible constructs.

Four aspects of findings of this study are especially germane here: one is that trait adjectives appear automatically to activate trait constructs related to them, as subjects processed the trait adjectives in the color-naming task for purposes unrelated to person perception, yet this processing still resulted in the activation of the trait constructs. Secondly, when one has the goal of forming an impression of someone based on that person's behavior, those behaviors will spontaneously activate abstract categories relevant to them. Thirdly, such categorization of behaviors occurs even when the behavioral data are only ambiguously diagnostic with regard to the trait category if that category is relatively accessible in memory. Fourthly, such categorization effects did *not* occur if the activated trait constructs were not applicable to the behavioral data.

In a series of studies, Srull & Wyer (1979, 1980) extended these findings on social construct accessibility in a number of important ways. Most relevant to the present discussion is their demonstration that clearly diagnostic behavioral descriptions, not just trait adjectives, automatically activate trait constructs relevant to them. Consistent with Higgins et al's (1977) findings, processing trait-relevant behaviors in one context (allegedly a study of sentence construction) resulted in a greater likelihood that the abstract trait construct relevant to those behaviors would be used subsequently to interpret trait-related ambiguous target behaviors.

The relative accessibility of trait constructs would therefore seem to be a major determinant of social perception, especially as most social information is at least somewhat ambiguous and open to multiple interpretations (e.g. Bruner 1958). The Higgins et al (1977) and Srull & Wyer (1979, 1980) findings suggest a powerful contextual force in the interpretation of social events that is at once both data-driven and theory-driven in nature. Features of the current environment would appear to activate or "prime" automatically the abstract constructs that represent them, no matter what the person's processing goals during priming. Bargh & Pietromonaco (1982, Bargh et al 1986) showed that trait adjectives prime relevant trait constructs even when those adjectives are presented subliminally so that subjects are unaware of even the presence of the priming stimuli. Once a social construct is activated by environmental data, however, it constitutes a theory-driven influence on the interpretation of subsequent environmental events. But the accessible construct will only have this influence if it is applicable (i.e. related) to the data.

Increases in the accessibility of available constructs in memory can also be the result of internal sources, such as one's current goals or needs (Bruner 1957, Higgins & King 1981, Wyer & Srull 1981, Srull & Wyer 1986).

Potentially the most influential of these "top-down" determinants of accessibility is the frequency with which one has used a certain construct to process social input (Higgins et al 1982, Higgins et al 1985, Bargh et al 1986, Wyer & Srull 1986). Frequent and consistent use of a construct, perhaps in response to constancies in one's particular social environment, appears to result in a chronic likelihood of using that construct across all situations. Higgins et al (1982) and Bargh and Thein (1985) have demonstrated that when people form an impression of a target person, they are more sensitive to information that is relevant to their chronically accessible constructs than that which is relevant to other available constructs. Moreover, people's greater sensitivity to stimuli related to chronically accessible constructs does not depend on that construct being primed or preactivated (Higgins et al 1982, Bargh et al 1986). And such stimuli are more likely than others to be detected in the environment in the first place (Bargh 1982, Bargh & Pratto 1986).

Salience effects are a related example of the interplay between data-driven and theory-driven influences. Features of the current environmental context may activate certain temporary expectancies for the situation, so that people or events that do not fit these expectancies are more distinctive or salient and receive greater attention. Moreover, the resultant focus of attention on those particular features that make the person or event salient appears to result in the activation of other abstract representations in memory of which those features are a component, such as stereotypes. Such easily discriminated features as a person's sex, race, or age are particularly likely to be salient features of a social situation, especially when those features are in the contextual minority (Taylor et al 1978, Hamilton 1979, Ashmore & DelBoca 1981, Deaux & Lewis 1984, McCann et al 1985). McArthur & Friedman (1980), for example, varied the age, sex, and race composition of groups of stimulus persons and found that subjects' stereotypic beliefs influenced the overall positivity of their trait ratings for a group member only when that target person was in the contextual minority (see also Hamilton & Rose 1980).

It would seem, therefore, that theory-driven influences on the encoding and interpretation of social information can themselves be determined by data-driven means (see Higgins & Lurie 1983, Bargh 1984). The interpretation and meaning given to a person's behavior and to social events are in large part a function of the relative accessibilities of relevant social constructs and stereotypes, which in turn are partly a function of features of the recent and current social environment. Moreover, there is evidence suggesting that stereotype activation by the contextual salience of stereotype-consistent information occurs under memory set conditions (Mills & Tyrrell 1983). The effects of salient information on the likelihood of stereotypic influences on encoding, therefore, is apparently not limited to occasions in which people have the goal of understanding the behavior of others. As Fiske et al (1982) conclude from their experiments, salient stimuli attract attention, but relevant schemas guide their processing.

What do these findings mean for the issue of the relative influence of the perceiver's theories versus the input data? Principally that social perceivers are continually directed in their interpretation of information by features of the current or recent situational context that activates particular constructs. In addition, these influences on interpretation are automatic and uncontrollable. On the other hand, it should be emphasized that in both the construct accessibility and salience research, the social construct that is automatically activated is clearly related to both the data that activated it and the data to which it is applied. For example, McCann et al (1985) found that with stereotypically neutral stimulus information, the within-group salience of an individual's racial or sexual identity may actually lead to *less* stereotyping, because the attentional focus on the individual that results fosters the development of a more accurate memory organization of his or her attributes. Thus, it is the *relation* between input data and stored constructs that is critical.

Furthermore, the activated structure generally influences only the interpretation of relatively *ambiguous* information for which it is relevant (see Locksley et al 1980, 1982, Ashmore 1981, Deaux & Lewis 1984, Bargh & Thein 1985), although stereotypes and other schemata may well have a simultaneous influence on other judgments for which the input information is irrelevant (Gilovich 1981, Deaux & Lewis 1984, Bodenhausen & Wyer 1985). Thus, even the passive, automatic effects of activated social constructs on the interpretation of subsequent information are sensitive to the nature of the input.

Are Causal Attributions Out of Control?

Another form of intrusion that has been hypothesized to occur during the processing of social information is the automatic generation and storage of inferences based on that information. Smith & Miller (1979) employed a paradigm developed by Pryor & Kriss (1977) in which social behaviors are presented in sentence form, and the order of the actor (e.g. Tom) and the object (e.g. the chemistry exam) within the sentence is varied. Whichever sentence part appears first in the sentence is more likely to be considered the cause of the event. Smith & Miller (1979) elaborated on this paradigm by instructing some subjects to generate causal explanations for each event and to consider these explanations carefully before responding to the attribution measures. The amount of thought subjects were instructed to give to the attributions did not moderate the effects of the sentence order manipulation. On the basis of these findings and those of two additional experiments, Smith & Miller (1983) concluded that causal judgments are made and stored as part of the normal process of sentence comprehension.

This conclusion may be justified by their findings (cf Fiske et al 1982), but aspects of their procedure limit its generalizability. Specifically, subjects in all but one of the Smith & Miller (1979, 1983) experiments understood that their purpose in reading the sentences was to be able to answer subsequent questions regarding the cause of each event. In the one study in which subjects did not have the intent of inferring the cause of each event (Smith & Miller 1979, Study 2), the impact of the sentence order manipulation of salient causes was considerably weaker. On the whole, these results suggest that attributions are made during the encoding of event information when subjects are actively trying to understand why the events occurred. When subjects do not have this purpose, however, they show little evidence of making such attributions spontaneously.

A series of experiments by Winter and Uleman (Winter & Uleman 1984, Winter et al 1985) also focused on whether attributions are made automatically during encoding. In a novel paradigm, subjects read a series of sentences in which various actors, denoted by their occupations, performed actions preselected to be clearly indicative of specific trait constructs (e.g. "The carpenter stops his car and motions the pedestrians to cross"). Subjects were instructed to remember the sentences as best they could. Each sentence was constructed so that the sentence actor, verb, object, and preposition appeared in that order. Following a distractor task, subjects' memory for each sentence was tested under one of three recall conditions: with a semantic associate to the actor (e.g. *wood*) or to the verb (e.g. *brakes*) presented as a cue, with a "dispositional" cue to the action (i.e. the trait term to which the action was related; e.g. *considerate*), or with no recall cue (i.e. free recall). Winter, Uleman, and their associates hypothesized that if subjects spontaneously generate dispositional attributions about the sentence actor from the sentence action, these inferences should be stored along with the representation of the sentence actor or entire sentence (see Tulving & Thomson 1973). They proposed that to the extent that the dispositional cue later facilitated the recall of the sentence actor or entire sentence, one could infer that a dispositional attribution to the actor had been made and encoded along with the sentence at the time of its comprehension.

Because the dispositional cue was reliably more effective than the semantic cues or no cues in retrieving the entire sentence (i.e. actor, verb, and behavior), Winter & Uleman (1984) concluded that their hypothesis was supported. In their studies, however, as well as in a replication by Bassili & Smith (1986), disposition-cued recall of the actor was worse than disposition-cued recall of the other parts of the sentence. And the disposition cue accounted for a greater proportion of the recall of the behavior alone than of the recall of the entire sentence (actor with behavior). Apparently, then, the improvement in the recall of the complete sentence was the result of an increased likelihood of retrieving the behavioral portion, rather than for the actor as would be expected if the actor's disposition had been inferred.

Although these findings do not permit unambiguous conclusions about whether trait inferences about the actor are automatically made at encoding, they do suggest that an abstract summary of the behavior itself is encoded during sentence comprehension, which aids the later recall of the behavioral portion of the sentence. Indeed, Winter et al (1985) found that a cue for the gist of the action of the sentence that had no implications for personality had the same effect on improving the recall of the behavioral part of the sentence as did the dispositional cue.

As noted earlier, the results of the Smith & Miller (1979, 1983) studies suggest that people make attributions spontaneously during sentence comprehension only when they have the intent of doing so. Bassili & Smith (1986) replicated the Winter & Uleman (1984) study with the addition of an impression set condition, and found that disposition-cued recall of all parts of the sentences was nearly twice as much in the impression set as in the memory set condition.

Taken together, the results of these studies suggest that causal or dispositional attributions are not made in an automatic, uncontrollable fashion. If they were, the particular instructions given to subjects in the Smith & Miller (1979) and Bassili & Smith (1986) studies should not have influenced whether or not a causal inference was encoded with the behavioral stimulus itself. Other studies have found that social judgments are not automatically made during the acquisition of the information but depend on the subject having the goal of making them (Sherman et al 1983, Lichtenstein & Srull 1985) as well as having sufficient attentional resources available to do so (Bargh & Thein 1985).

Is Consistent or Inconsistent Information Better Remembered?

People's expectancies or hypotheses about what is likely to happen in a social situation play a critical role in the selection of information from the environment to be encoded, as well as in how that information will be encoded into memory. Cognitive organizations of previous experience in particular environment domains, commonly referred to as schemata, frames, or scripts, have been hypothesized to guide the selection and interpretation process (e.g. Minsky 1975, Neisser 1976, Rumelhart & Ortony 1977, Schank & Abelson 1977). When these structures are actively involved in the comprehension of related information, they facilitate the understanding of material that might otherwise be quite unintelligible (e.g. Bransford & Johnson 1972).

Several studies have shown that the encoding of information is markedly affected by the framework used to process it, and that retrieval of this information is largely determined by the way in which it was encoded (e.g.

Zadny & Gerard 1974, Lingle et al 1979, Cohen 1981, Wyer et al 1982; for reviews see Showers & Cantor 1985, Srull & Wyer 1986, Zukier 1986). Rothbart et al (1979), for example, presented subjects with information concerning a group of 50 men, each of whom performed a single behavior. Of these behaviors, 17 indicated friendliness, 17 intelligence, 3 nonintelligence, 3 unfriendliness, and 10 were unrelated to personality (e.g. "chopped some wood for the fireplace"). Some subjects were told prior to reading the behaviors that the group as a whole was considered to be friendly and sociable, whereas others were informed that the group was considered to be intelligent and scholarly. Recall of the behaviors that were consistent with the initial trait description (e.g. friendly) was better than recall of behaviors that were irrelevant to that description (e.g. intelligent behaviors).

Thus, information consistent with one's expectancies would appear to be preferentially encoded and better remembered than other information. Such findings fit well with the well-known characteristic of impressions and stereotypes to resist change (e.g. Taft 1954) and the tendency of even weakly held beliefs to persevere in the face of disconfirming evidence (e.g. Ross et al 1975). Several researchers have argued that beliefs are resistant to change in part because belief-inconsistent information is poorly remembered (e.g. Cantor & Mischel 1977, Markus 1977, Hamilton 1979).

It was in this historical context that the results of a study by Hastie & Kumar (1979) were surprising. Hastie & Kumar (1979) first gave their subjects a description of a target person containing several adjectives related to the same personality trait (e.g. honest). Next, subjects read a series of behaviors performed by the target that were either clearly consistent with the initial trait description, inconsistent with it, or irrelevant to it. The number of consistent and inconsistent behaviors varied across experimental conditions; for example, some subjects read about a target who performed 13 trait-consistent behaviors and 1 inconsistent behavior, whereas other subjects read about a target who performed 9 consistent and 5 inconsistent behaviors. This same procedure was replicated across several different trait dimensions, both socially desirable and undesirable. The results showed better recall of the behaviors that were inconsistent with the initial trait description than those that were consistent with it, with the irrelevant behaviors being the least well recalled. Hastie (1980) proposed an associative network model to account for these results, arguing that inconsistent behaviors were better recalled because subjects create a greater number of associative linkages in memory among them and the other behaviors when attempting to integrate all of the behaviors into a unitary impression. Consistent behaviors were argued to be better recalled than irrelevant information because they are associated with a well-organized cognitive structure.

Subsequent research has been largely supportive of the Hastie (1980) model, as elaborated and extended by Srull (1981) and by Wyer (e.g. Wyer & Gordon 1982, Wyer et al 1984a). For example, the effect of better recall of expectancy-inconsistent information should hold for behaviors associated with individual members of a group only when subjects expect that the group members would behave similarly, just as an individual target person is expected to behave consistently. This prediction has been upheld (Srull 1981; Srull et al 1985, Experiment 7; Stern et al 1984, Wyer & Gordon 1982, Wyer et al 1984a). In addition, as the model assumes that inconsistent items are better recalled because they have a greater number of associative links with other behaviors, manipulations that prevent the formation of these links or memory tests that bypass them should eliminate the effect. This prediction has also been consistently confirmed. Loading the subject's attentional capacity while reading the behaviors (Srull 1981, Experiment 4; Bargh & Thein 1985) and giving subjects a memory set instead of an impression set (Srull 1981, Wyer & Gordon 1982, Wyer et al 1984a) remove the advantage of inconsistent behaviors.

At first glance, the Hastie & Kumar (1979) results seem to contradict the evidence of better recall of expectancy-consistent information. Some of the apparent differences, however, are attributable to terminology. For example, in the Rothbart et al (1979) study described earlier it was concluded that expected behaviors were better remembered than unexpected behaviors. But the intelligence-related behaviors were not inconsistent with the expectation for friendliness but *irrelevant* to it, and vice versa. As Hastie (1981) pointed out, there is an important difference between information that is "not expected" because it is irrelevant to the expectancy, and information that is "not expected" because it actually violates the expectancy.

Another important clarification was made by Wyer & Gordon (1982). They noted that the inconsistent behaviors in the Hastie & Kumar (1979) study were both evaluatively and denotatively inconsistent with the expectancy and the consistent behaviors. For example, unfriendly behaviors are different from friendly ones not only because they imply the opposite type of behavior, but because they are socially undesirable instead of desirable. Wyer & Gordon (1982) manipulated the two types of inconsistency as a factor in their design and found evaluative inconsistency to be the more important determinant of enhanced free recall for behavioral information. It should be noted, however, that the relative impact of the two forms of inconsistency is at least partly dependent on how powerfully each is manipulated within the experimental design (see Fiske & Pavelchak 1986).

The extent of people's knowledge or expertise in a given domain of social information (see Fiske & Dyer 1985) may also determine whether or not they will notice inconsistent information. Fiske et al (1983), in a study of expertise in politics, found that experts were more likely than nonexperts to notice and make use of the inconsistencies within a fictitious country's political system when making judgments about the country. Bargh & Thein (1985) have obtained parallel results in a different paradigm. Under information overload conditions, subjects with a chronically accessible construct for honesty were able to notice the inconsistent honest or dishonest behaviors of a target person and these inconsistencies influenced their judgments of the target. Subjects without a relevant accessible construct did not show these effects.

Thus, although research has generally supported the associative network model of person memory, it has also underscored the limits on its range of applicability. For inconsistent information to be better remembered than consistent information, the subject must have the goal of forming an impression of the target person as well as adequate time to consider the implications of each behavior. In addition, in all of the supportive research, the behaviors were either clearly consistent or clearly inconsistent with the expectancy. Less diagnostic inconsistent behaviors would be more likely to be interpreted in terms of the expectancy (e.g. Bruner 1957, Higgins et al 1977).

Better recall of inconsistent information may also depend on subjects' attributional options in explaining the inconsistencies. Crocker et al (1983, Experiment 1) found that providing subjects with a situational attribution for an inconsistent behavior resulted in its being recalled at the same rate as the other behaviors. It was only when a dispositional attribution to the target was provided for the behavior that it was better recalled. Though subjects in the Crocker et al (1983) study did not remember the situationally attributed inconsistent behaviors any better than the other behaviors, this may be because those subjects did not generate the explanation themselves. Hastie (1984) has found that spontaneous generation of an explanation for a behavior is positively correlated with the probability of recalling that behavior. Moreover, in another experiment, subjects were instructed to explain some behaviors and elaborate in different ways upon other behaviors. Those behaviors that were explained by the subject were best recalled, *whether they were consistent or inconsistent with the initial expectancy.*

Perhaps the most important limiting condition for the superior recall of inconsistent information is that studies employing the Hastie & Kumar (1979) paradigm were not studying how people *test* already formed impressions or beliefs, as Hastie (1980) argued, but how people *form* beliefs in the first place. The reason for this misunderstanding has to do with the strength of the initial expectancy manipulation. Giving subjects a trait description was intended to instill in them an impression of the target, which they would then test against the behavioral information (Hastie 1980). In the Hastie & Kumar (1979) study, however, the initial expectancy manipulation was confounded with set size. The relative advantage of the expectancy-inconsistent behaviors was almost entirely a function of set size—the smaller the proportion of minority behaviors presented, the greater the proportion of them recalled. Later studies unconfounded set size and initial expectancy by including conditions in which the majority behavior type was inconsistent with the initial expectancy. Hemsley & Marmurek (1982) and Bargh & Thein (1985) found that the minority behavior type was still better recalled, even though it was consistent with the initial trait description (but see Srull 1981). Several other studies have found initial trait descriptions of the type employed by Hastie & Kumar (1979) to be relatively inconsequential compared to the actual target information in determining memory for the target person (Cantor & Mischel 1977, Woll & Graesser 1982, Jones et al 1984). And the initial trait expectancy given to subjects in the Rothbart et al (1979) study did not alter the number of minority behaviors recalled.

Given that subjects appear to be basing their expectancies for the target's behavior on the behavioral data itself and not on the initial trait description provided by the experimenter (Bargh & Thein 1985), the Hastie & Kumar (1979) studies and subsequent research in their paradigm concern *impression formation and not impression testing*. The findings therefore should not be interpreted as showing that information inconsistent with a well-formed prior belief is better recalled. They must be understood in the context of other research that demonstrates the greater attention and processing given to relatively infrequent behaviors during impression formation, and their resultant increased accessibility in memory (e.g. Hamilton & Gifford 1976, Fiske 1980, Hamilton et al 1985, Ruble & Stangor 1986). Thus, there is no contradiction between the results of this line of research and earlier evidence that belief-consistent information is better recalled. It also does not contradict evidence, considered next, that memory of judged stimulus information tends to be consistent with the judgment.

Effects of Stored Judgments on Subsequent Processing

Once a social judgment is made it has pervasive effects on the processing of relevant information, which mainly serves to perpetuate the belief. O'Sullivan & Durso (1984), for example, gave subjects a stereotypic "campus type" label for a target person along with two facts about that person that were highly consistent with the label. Subjects then made judgments of how typical the target was of students at the subjects' university, prior to hearing biographical information about the stimulus person that varied as to how consistent it was with the stereotype. In contrast to Hastie & Kumar's (1979) procedure, therefore, O'Sullivan & Durso (1984) used an established stereotypic belief as the expectancy and had subjects make judgments about the target before the critical information was presented. O'Sullivan & Durso (1984) found better recall of the stereotype-consistent than the stereotype-inconsistent biographical information. These findings support the argument that when an established belief is being tested, it is consistent and not inconsistent information that is better remembered.

One mechanism by which belief-consistent information is better remembered is through the discounting of inconsistent information as irrelevant to the belief. Ruble & Stangor (1986) concluded from their review of developmental research on the processing of gender-related information that as the child develops a well-formed gender schema, and as gender becomes an increasingly more important aspect of his or her identity, information consistent with gender stereotypes becomes increasingly better remembered than inconsistent information. The tendency to discount contradictory evidence has also been found to play a contributing role in the belief-perseverance effect (Ross et al 1975). Lord et al (1979) presented subjects who either favored or opposed capital punishment with descriptions of two studies bearing on the efficacy of the death penalty as a crime deterrent. Even though the study designs were counterbalanced across subjects, subjects tended to discount the study whose results were inconsistent with their own position and believed that the study supporting their position was methodologically more sound. Moreover, the ultimate effect of being exposed to the contradictory evidence was that subjects believed even *more* strongly in their original position! Subsequent research suggests that the strengthening of beliefs following exposure to contradictory information results from the reasoning used by people to explain the apparent inconsistency (Anderson et al 1980, Anderson 1983, Hirt & Sherman 1985). Not only may such reasoning transform the inconsistent information to be consistent with the prior belief (e.g. Crocker 1981, Kulik 1983), the reprocessing of the evidential items comprising the original belief may also strengthen the associative links among them (Srull 1981, Wyer et al 1982, O'Sullivan & Durso 1984).

Another consequence of belief formation is that the belief may influence subsequent reconstruction of information from memory (see Wyer & Carlston 1979, Wyer & Srull 1981, Higgins & Lurie 1983). Higgins & Rholes (1978), for example, had subjects describe a stimulus person to another person who purportedly either liked or disliked the stimulus person. Subjects shaded their communication of the target's behavior in the direction of the other person's opinion. More importantly, subjects' later memory of the original information was found to be distorted in the same direction as their communication of the information to the other person, despite the fact that subjects were instructed to reproduce the original target description word-for-word. For example, the fact that the target had participated in three sports in high school might become "Donald excelled in three sports" in the favorable-audience condition and "Donald participated in a few sports" in the unfavorable-audience condition. In addition, the effect of subjects' communications on their later reproductions increased substantially over time. Higgins & Rholes (1978; see also

Higgins & Lurie 1983) concluded that abstract judgmental summaries are stored along with a representation of the stimulus information, and that people increasingly rely on the judgment to reconstruct the original stimulus information, because the stimulus trace decays quickly over time.

Several lines of research support this proposal. Although subjects may base their initial trait judgments of a target person on the original information, later judgments along different personality dimensions are based on the initial judgments even though the original information itself might suggest a different conclusion (Lingle & Ostrom 1979, Carlston 1980, McCann & Hancock 1983, Wyer et al 1984b). This holds true even if the original information is made available for subjects to use at the time of the later judgment (Schul & Burnstein 1985). Similarly, social judgments made in relation to one context may be used at a later time to reconstruct the stimulus information without taking the original context of judgment sufficiently into account (Higgins & Lurie 1983). For example, one of us is convinced that it doesn't snow as much these winters as it did during his childhood, when the snow consistently came up above his knees.

Varieties of Expectancies

Not all beliefs or expectancies are created equal. They vary in strength and in the person's commitment to them. Manipulations of a subject's expectancy through a reputation-based trait ensemble (e.g. "His friends consider him to be intelligent and trustworthy"), for example, result in a weakly held expectancy. Jones et al (1984) found that subjects placed less stock in such reputational expectancies than in claim-based expectancies in which the target describes him or herself. And expectancies based on target claims have an impact on later target judgments even in the face of contradictory target behavior, unlike reputation-based expectancies.

There has been a growing recognition that there are a variety of different types of expectancies (Jones & McGillis 1976, Darley & Fazio 1980, Higgins & King 1981, Berman et al 1983, Bargh & Thein 1985). The distinction has usually been between long-term expectancies such as stereotypes and temporary expectancies or sets for certain people or events. However, with few exceptions (Jones & McGillis 1976, Higgins & King 1981, Darley & Gross 1983, Jones et al 1984), there has been little work on the relation between the source or type of expectancy and its strength relative to the available data.

When one considers studies that bear on the theory-data interaction in terms of the strength of the theory versus the strength of the data (see Bruner 1951, Postman 1951), it becomes clearer why some experiments show powerful data-driven effects (e.g. Hastie & Kumar 1979, Locksley et al 1980) whereas others indicate that prior theories predominate (e.g. Grant & Holmes 1981, Deaux & Lewis 1984). The former studies are characterized by informational input that is highly diagnostic of a certain trait dimension and dependent measures that tap how that input is encoded in terms of that dimension (cf Zukier 1982). The latter studies show long-term stereotypic beliefs to have an effect in the absence of any other information and also an effect on judgments beyond those directly related to the informational input.

In research bearing directly on this issue, Fiske, Beattie & Milberg (unpublished; see Fiske & Pavelchak 1986) varied the informativeness of both a role-category label and personal attributes describing a target person and found subjects' target likability ratings were influenced more by the category label (i.e. prior theory) when the attributes (i.e. data) were neutral or consistent with the label. Subjects were influenced more by the attribute data when they were inconsistent with the label and when the label was uninformative. Thus the extent to which subjects relied on prior beliefs versus informational input in making their likability judgments depended on the relative diagnosticity of the two sources of information. Bodenhausen & Wyer (1985) similarly developed and tested specific hypotheses regarding the interaction of stereotypes and behavioral information. In addition, Reeder & Brewer (1979) identified differences between trait dimensions as to the range of disconfirming behaviors they permit, Allen & Ebbesen (1981) distinguished between trait categories that can be instantiated by a single unambiguous behavior (e.g. helpful) and more abstract trait categories that require many occasions of related behavior (e.g. resourceful), and Rothbart & Park (1986) have identified several factors that differentiate traits as to how easily behavioral data will confirm or disconfirm them, such as their imageability. Much more research following the lead of these investigators is needed.

A convincing demonstration of the importance of taking the strengths of expectancies into account has been provided recently by Swann & Ely (1984). Previous research had shown that perceivers' expectancies can cause the person being perceived to act in a way that confirms those expectancies (e.g. Word et al 1974, Snyder et al 1977, Snyder & Swann 1978)—a powerful "theory-driven" influence. Swann & Ely (1984) manipulated both the strength of the perceiver's expectancies about a target *and* the strength of the target's self-concept in the domain of the expectancy. The perceiver's expectancy and the target's self-concept were always inconsistent with each other. It was found that the target's self-concept was a stronger determinant than the perceiver's expectancy, as the perceivers' impressions of the target after the interaction were in line with the target's self-concept rather than their initial expectancy. Earlier studies indicating a self-fulfilling prophecy effect of expectations did not demonstrate that a perceiver's expectancies result in a person acting in a way counter to his or her self-concept (Swann & Ely 1984; see also Hilton & Darley 1985, Miller & Turnbull 1986).

When Will Beliefs Change?

There are a variety of reasons why people's beliefs are maintained. Some of these are passive outcomes of cognitive processing, such as the automatic pickup of construct-consistent data, the use of such constructs to interpret ambiguous data, the strong effect of beliefs on future judgments and on reconstructing memory for past events. Other belief-preserving mechanisms are more active: we may create subtypes within stereotypes (e.g. career woman) to account for people who do not fit the overarching belief, which then may remain intact (Taylor 1981, Weber & Crocker 1983). Or people may make situational attributions for belief-disconfirming evidence and dispositional attributions for confirming evidence (Crocker et al 1983, Kulik 1983, Bodenhausen & Wyer 1985), or otherwise generate an explanation for the inconsistency that permits it to be integrated with the other stored information (Hastie 1984). There are other strategies as well that people employ in order to attain a consistent and unified impression of another person at some level (see Asch & Zukier 1984).

All of this may paint a fairly bleak picture of the prospects for belief change in the face of environmental disconfirmation. What is actually happening, however, when a person integrates discrepant information with previous knowledge is that he or she is *modifying* that knowledge structure. Situational attributions or other causal explanations incorporate into a belief conditions under which the belief does not hold. Both assimilation and accommodation (e.g. Piaget 1952) are operative in the interaction of theory and data. To the extent that inconsistent information is better remembered, for example, it is because the inconsistency has been resolved with the expectancy (Hastie 1984). As it is the *original information* that is better recalled, it cannot be said to have been completely assimilated into the prior expectancy. Rather, the resolution must have involved both a change in the meaning of the inconsistency *and* an accommodating change in the belief structure to encompass this exception. In this way, the coherence and stability that social knowledge structures provide to one's understanding and experience of the social world is preserved, while at the same time permitting a gradual change and adjustment to new environmental contingencies (see Crocker et al 1984). Moreover, when people are motivated to be accurate or to understand and predict the behavior of another person, they will expend the effort to modify their beliefs to suit the data (see Langer et al 1978, Chaiken 1980, Petty et al 1981, Borgida & Howard-Pitney 1983, Erber & Fiske 1984).

Concluding Comments

The need for action often requires us to make judgments on the basis of very little evidence, even when we are fully aware of the deficiencies of that evidence (Rothbart 1981). The storage of even these weakly held and poorly justified beliefs alongside the original information in memory has important information-processing consequences. Yet, when people need to be accurate, they seem to be able to reduce the influence of such prior beliefs.

Social perception and cognition are fueled by environmental input; for example, social judgments are much more influenced by what people *do* than by what they *fail* to do (e.g. Fazio et al 1982). In the absence of specific processing goals, the default bias in information pick-up is for information that is clearly related to efficient processing structures (e.g. Higgins et al 1982, Schneider & Fisk 1984, Bargh & Pratto 1986). The automatic use of stored information that reflects the regularities of the environment frees attention to be allocated to input that is salient or inconsistent with these long-term expectancies (e.g. McArthur 1981, Bargh 1984). Moreover, temporary expectancies are automatically driven by the data present in the current situational context, so that our interpretation of the data is tuned to the types of data recently present in the environment (Higgins & King 1981, Wyer & Srull 1981). And information that is salient through its inconsistency with the current context also receives greater attention (Taylor & Fiske 1978). These default processes allow the social perceiver automatically to maintain appropriate contact with the environment, while at the same time focus attention on the potentially informative features of that environment.

The relative impact of theory and data when a specific processing goal *is* operative depends on the nature of that goal. We have noted that people are much more responsive to the characteristics of the environmental data when they have the goal of forming a belief than when they have the goal of testing an already existent belief. But "theories" are present in *both* cases; during belief formation, a temporary expectancy is generated by the stimulus information itself, and more general, pre-established normative expectancies (which, of course, are themselves summaries of past data) also come into play. Thus, the issue of whether processing will be predominately theory-driven or data-driven is not reduceable to the question of whether *any* expectancy is or is not operating, because the source and strength of the particular expectancy(ies) make a dramatic difference as to whether and to what extent the environmental data will be influential.

In summary, if we acknowledge that human perception and cognition are functional and adaptive systems, it is difficult to see why people would be as theory-driven and out of touch with reality as we sometimes make them out to be (see Neisser 1976, Gilovich 1981, Johnson & Raye 1981, McArthur & Baron 1983). People are neither largely "theory-driven" nor predominately "data-driven"; rather, they are continually compelled by the relation *between* knowledge and events.

IS THE SELF A UNIQUE COGNITIVE STRUCTURE?

No one loses their fascination in the self for long. For 20 years or so, it seemed as if experimental social psychologists no longer considered the self to be a major issue. Whether this was because they felt that the major conceptual problems had already been solved or that the questions that remained were not amenable to experimental test is not clear. In any case, other issues took center stage. In the late 1970s, however, the Self leaped back into the limelight. Symbolic of this renewed interest, and highly influential in creating further interest, were two papers that appeared in the same year—Markus (1977) and Rogers et al (1977).

The experimental paradigm used by Rogers et al (1977) was especially influential in generating subsequent research. Adopting Craik & Tulving's (1975) procedure for examining incidental recall as a function of type of orientation to input, Rogers et al (1977) had undergraduates rate a set of trait adjectives in one of a variety of ways—structurally (e.g. long or short word?), phonemically (e.g. rhymes or does not rhyme with another word XXX?), semantically (e.g. is a synonym of or unrelated to another word YYY?), and self-referentially (does the word describe you or not?). After the rating or orientation task, all subjects were asked to recall, in any order, the adjectives they had rated. In the first experiment, Rogers et al (1977) replicated Craik & Tulving's (1975) finding that the semantic orientation task yielded better recall than either the structural or phonemic orientation tasks. In both experiments, however, the self-reference orientation task produced better recall than even the semantic orientation task.

Taking a "depth-of-processing" perspective (Craik & Lockhart 1972), Rogers et al (1977) concluded that the self-reference task must involve deep and semantically rich encoding that produces strong, elaborated and integrated memory traces, which in turn facilitate memory. They also concluded that "for self-reference to be such a useful encoding process, the self must be a uniform, well-structured concept" (p. 686) and that "it is difficult to conceive of an encoding device that carries more potential for the rich embellishment of stimulus input than does self-reference" (p. 687).

The finding that processing input in relation to the self produced superior memory intrigued many psychologists because it suggested that there was a "deeper" level of processing than even semantic processing provided. But the major impact of Rogers et al's (1977) article as well as Markus's (1977) article and some influential contemporary proposals (e.g. Epstein 1973, Beck et al 1979) arose from the suggestion that self-knowledge had a major influence on information processing because it was a cognitive structure of interconnected self-related concepts. One could, therefore, assume that it would have the same impact on information processing that had been described for schemata or cognitive structures in general (e.g. Bartlett 1932, Piaget 1952, Posner 1969, Norman & Bobrow 1975, Neisser 1976), including organizing, integrating, and elaborating input information. Thus, if self-related information is better remembered, one need not assume that this is because of its *motivational* significance. It could be because it is being processed in relation to self-knowledge whose schematic nature produces a strong memory trace.

This "cognitive" interpretation of the effects of self-relatedness fit in nicely with the general Weltanschauung that emerged in the 1970s. Various social phenomena that had been previously interpreted in "hot" motivational terms were now being reinterpreted in relatively "cold" cognitive terms (e.g. Abelson 1974, Erdelyi 1974, Tversky & Kahneman 1974, Miller & Ross 1975, Dawes 1976). In that era of "information processlytizing," the proposal that the effects of self-relatedness were traceable to the cognitive-structural properties of the self was readily accepted.

To argue that cognitive-structural properties of the self have information-processing consequences was not enough. After all, the motivational perspective had always emphasized that the self had special effects. And, indeed, Rogers et al's (1977) findings suggested that self-reference was *especially* effective in facilitating memory. Thus, it is not surprising that Rogers et al (1977) concluded that the self was a special or unique cognitive structure, a sentiment that has been expressed in general terms by others as well (Kendzierski 1980, Markus & Sentis 1982, Greenwald & Pratkanis 1984).

Although not everyone has been led to the conclusion that the self as a cognitive structure is unique in its effects (e.g. Bower & Gilligan 1979, Smith 1982, Fiske & Taylor 1984, Kihlstrom & Cantor 1984) or even that it is necessarily a cognitive structure at all (e.g. Hamilton 1981a, Ferguson et al 1983, Bellezza 1984, Smith 1984, Klein & Kihlstrom 1986), the dominant position in the literature has been that the self is an unusually rich and highly organized cognitive structure. Both the argument that the self is a cognitive structure and that this cognitive structure is special have been based on experimental evidence of information-processing effects of the self. The predominant and most often cited evidence is the "self-referent" effect first described by Rogers et al (1977), and so we begin this part of our review by examining this evidence.

Is There a "Self-referent" Effect?

The basic finding of Rogers et al (1977)—that a self-referent orientation task to trait adjectives as input (i.e. Describes you?) yields superior memory than even a semantic orientation task (as measured by free recall, cued recall, or recognition)—has been replicated in many studies (e.g. Bower & Gilligan 1979, Kuiper & Rogers 1979, Keenan & Baillet 1980, Kendzierski 1980,

Klein & Kihlstrom 1986). It has also been demonstrated that a self-referent orientation task yields superior memory to that of an other-referent orientation task when the other person is not a highly significant or familiar other (e.g. Bower & Gilligan 1979; Ferguson et al 1983; Ganellen & Carver 1985; Keenan & Baillet 1980; Kuiper & Rogers 1979; Lord 1980; Wells et al 1984). A self-referent orientation facilitates memory for videotaped information about a target person as well (Alicke et al 1985).

The results of these studies clearly demonstrate that the "self-referent" orientation task can have a significant facilitating effect on memory for input. To this extent one could conclude that there is a reliable "self-referent" phenomenon. It is not clear, however, that the facilitating effects of the "self-referent" orientation task are due to the input being processed in relation to the self per se. Variables associated with the "self-referent" task *other than its self-reference* have been proposed as being responsible for the facilitating effects of this task. Ferguson et al (1983), for example, found that an orientation task in which subjects rated the trait adjectives in terms of their social desirability facilitated memory as much as did the "self-referent" task. They concluded, therefore, that the "self-referent" orientation task, which may also involve an evaluative judgment, could not be used to draw un-ambiguous conclusions about the effects on information processing of relating input to self-knowledge.

Additional potential confoundings of the "self-referent" effect have been pointed out by Klein & Kihlstrom (1986) and by Wells et al (1984). Klein & Kihlstrom (1986) note that the "self-referent" task requires organizing the input into two categories ("Describes me" or "Does not describe me") where-as the semantic tasks have not required binary organization, and that such categorical organization (see Mandler 1977) by itself facilitates memory for list words. They present some impressive evidence of the facilitating effect of organization, as well as evidence that when the amount of organization encouraged by an orientation task is equated, the advantage of the "self-referent" over the semantic orientation task disappears.

Wells et al (1984) suggest that when the input is trait adjectives, as has typically been the case, subject-generated retrieval cues are likely to involve self-knowledge. If so, then the advantage of the "self-referent" task may not derive from the input being encoded more deeply by relating it to a self structure, but from its being the only orientation task that assures a match between encoding context and retrieval context, which has been shown to improve memory (see Tulving 1983). They found that when an explicit other-referent cue was given at retrieval, the "self-referent" task no longer produced superior memory in comparison to an other-referent orientation task.

Do the results of these latter studies mean that the "self-referent" effect is "nothing but" an effect of evaluative orientation, organization, or an encoding context/retrieval context match on memory? With respect to evaluative orientation, Rogers (1981) and McCaul & Maki (1984), using within-subjects designs rather than Ferguson et al's (1983) between-subjects design, report that when the "self-reference" task is directly compared to desirability/ affective tasks, the "self-reference" task produces superior memory. Moreover, Ganellen & Carver (1985) attempted to test directly the relation between subjects' expressions of their personal affective reactions to a set of trait adjectives and their recall of the traits following the "self-reference" task. The correlation was essentially zero.

Considering the factor of organization, when the studies described earlier compared the effect of reference to self to the effect of reference to a nonsignificant other, the organization encouraged by these tasks has been equivalent, and yet the "self-referent" task still produced superior memory. Organization was also equated in a study by Bellezza (1984) where the "self-reference" task involved subjects describing a different personal experience for each trait word, and the alternative task involved subjects relating each trait word to a different body part. Nevertheless, the trait words were better recalled in the "self-reference" condition. And with regard to the encoding context/retrieval context match, Wells et al (1984) found that the self-referent encoding/self-referent retrieval condition produced better memory than the other-referent encoding/other-referent retrieval condition.

Although the "self-reference" effect cannot be fully explained in terms of these alternative variables, it is certainly possible that these variables have contributed to the strength of the effect. And, at minimum, the results of these studies set boundary conditions for the "self-reference" effect and raise serious issues of interpretation. The results of other studies do so as well.

First, there are a number of studies that have found orientation tasks that are *as effective* in facilitating recall (compared to either semantic or structural tasks) as the self-reference task. Bower & Gilligan (1979) found that subjects' memory was as facilitated by responding to traits in terms of whether or not they could access an incident in which their mother exemplified the trait as whether or not they could access an incident in which they themselves exemplified the trait. Kuiper & Rogers (1979) and Keenan & Baillet (1980) also found that an orientation task involving familiar others as referent (even a lab instructor) was equivalent to the self-referent task in producing better memory than a semantic task. Keenan & Baillet (1980) found further that asking subjects to respond to traits in terms of whether or not they described a familiar city yielded as good memory for the traits as the self-referent task.

There are an additional set of studies in which the "self-referent" effect is not found at all. Lord (1980) found that when subjects were asked to form a mental image relating the concrete nouns in the input to different referents, subjects' memory of the input was *poorest* when the referent was the self. Similarly, a comparison of the results of Bellezza's (1984) Experiment 1 and Experiment 2 indicates that when the input is switched from trait adjectives to concrete nouns, the superiority of self-reference in comparison to body parts as a memory cue disappears. This is so even though memory, if anything, is higher for concrete nouns in both cueing conditions. The "self-referent" effect also was not found under certain conditions in Klein and Kihlstrom's (1986) studies. For example, in one experiment subjects were presented with a list of words in which half referred to external body parts and half to internal body parts. In the semantic/organized condition subjects were asked to decide whether or not the target word (e.g. "hair?") was an external body part. In the self/unorganized condition subjects were asked whether the target word (e.g. "hair?") in combination with a presented sentence frame (e.g. "I prefer to keep my ____ short") created a true statement. Memory for the target words was actually superior with the semantic orientation task than with the self-referent orientation task. Rogers (1977) used personality items as target stimuli in which the items were phrased in the third person (e.g. "most people," "everyone") and found that subjects given self-referent instructions had *poorer* memory for the input than subjects given no orientation instructions at all.

Other studies have found no "self-referent" advantage when the trait terms are negative rather than positive (e.g. Derry & Kuiper 1981, Ferguson et al 1983). And Hull & Levy (1979) did not find the "self-referent" effect when subjects were low in dispositional self-consciousness (Fenigstein et al 1975) even though these subjects rated more of the traits as self-descriptive than did the high self-conscious subjects.

In sum, the "self-referent" effect is a reliable phenomenon under certain conditions. But there are a variety of other conditions where processing input in reference to the self does not have a unique facilitating effect on memory or even fails to facilitate at all. Although it is no simple task to account for all of these findings, one thing is clear—they cannot be explained in terms of a unique memory advantage of self-reference. In brief, *self-reference is neither necessary nor sufficient for memory of input to be facilitated in comparison to a semantic orientation task.*

What Determines When Enhanced Memory Occurs?

What then determines when self-reference, or any other orientation task, will facilitate memory for input? Beginning with Rogers et al (1977), most of the literature in this area has suggested that it is the depth of processing that occurs during encoding in relation to the self or some other rich knowledge area that enhances memory by producing a strong memory trace. But, as already evident from our review of the literature, "deep" encoding of the input by relating it to rich self-knowledge is not by itself sufficient to enhance memory. Moreover, Wells et al's (1984) study demonstrated that memory was affected by the nature of the retrieval cue and not the encoding cue alone.

Perhaps, then, one could account for the results in the literature, as Bower & Gilligan (1979) suggested, in terms of the self and other knowledge areas being especially effective retrieval cues. But if the results were due to the "self-referent" task being an effective retrieval cue, one would expect that the advantage would be greater for traits that did describe a subject than for traits that did not (i.e. for "Yes"-rated vs "No"-rated traits). Yet the great majority of studies have found that the "self-referent" effect is independent of whether the target traits are self-descriptive or not (e.g. Rogers et al 1977, Kuiper & Rogers 1979, Keenan & Baillet 1980, Kendzierski 1980, Lord 1980, Ferguson et al 1983, McCaul & Maki 1984). In addition, Wells et al (1984) found an advantage for self-referent encoding over other-referent encoding even when a self-referent retrieval cue was given in both conditions, and Klein & Kihlstrom (1986) found that providing an effective cue at retrieval (i.e. cued recall) did not make up for the advantage afforded by providing the cue at encoding. Nor can the results be explained by the greater memorability of self-referent cues, as Bellezza (1984) found that even though subjects remembered the body part cues better than the self-referent cues, they nevertheless remembered the target stimuli better in the self-referent condition.

We believe that the best explanation for when orientation tasks will or will not facilitate memory of input is in terms of the relation between encoding and retrieval. But such an account must go beyond simply whether there is or is not a match between the encoding context and the retrieval context, and need not assume that subject-generated retrieval cues center on the self (e.g. Wells et al 1984). Although it is not possible given present space constraints to marshall support for it here, we propose a "synergistic ecphory" account of the literature. This model assumes that both recall and recognition are reconstructive processes that are influenced jointly by the information stored at encoding (i.e. the trace or engram) and the retrieval information, with memory being a function of the number of features that the encoding and retrieval cue representations have in common (see Tulving 1983). Neither properties of the encoding alone nor of the retrieval information alone determine memory, any more than length alone or width alone can produce a rectangle—the combination of variables is essential.

Specifically, the synergistic ecphory model assumes that the orientation task influences memory by affecting both the encoding and retrieval representations and the relation between them. A mismatch of encoding context and retrieval context is likely to impair memory because it is likely to reduce the extent to which the encoding and retrieval representations have features in common, but a match in context will not necessarily facilitate memory unless the contexts actually produce similar representations. In general, the richer the encoding representation the better the memory, but only if the retrieval representation has similar features. Relating input to self-knowledge can lead to an encoding representation that is rich in features, but it will not invariably do so. Moreover, rich representations can also be produced at encoding by relating the input to other kinds of knowledge. And memory will only be facilitated if the retrieval representation contains similar features. Thus, the "self-referent" effect occurs when the self-referent orientation task happens to interact with the input such that both the encoding and retrieval representations contain similar rich features. Otherwise it does not occur. And other orientation tasks will be equally or more effective if they happen to interact with the input such that both the encoding and retrieval representations contain similar rich features.

Is There Other Evidence for the Self's Unique, Structural Nature?

If the findings from the "self-referent" literature do not permit unambiguous conclusions about either the "uniqueness" or the "structural" nature of self-knowledge, is there other evidence that does? Other kinds of evidence have been discussed as support for these conclusions. It has been suggested, for example, that if the number of recognition test false alarms was found to increase with degree of self-reference of the trait stimuli, then this would indicate that the self functions as a cognitive prototype. Rogers et al (1979) found some evidence to this effect, but in previous studies, Rogers (1977) had found that self-reference instructions produced *fewer* false alarms than did no instructions. Thus, the "false alarms" effect does not provide the necessary support for the "self as structure" conclusion.

It has also been suggested that the self is special or a cognitive structure or both because of its extensive use as a point of reference in interpreting social information (e.g. Kuiper & Derry 1981, Markus & Smith 1981, Rogers 1981). Certainly, the effects of "self as reference point" on social evaluation are an important consequence of self-knowledge. But as the literature on social comparison, reference groups, and the use of consensus information testifies, there are many kinds of social knowledge that serve as reference points, even for self-evaluation (see Higgins et al 1986b for a review). The process of role-taking in judging others, moreover, requires the *inhibition* of self-knowledge (see Chandler 1977, Higgins 1981). And the fact that judgments of self and others are often similar need not arise from the common use of the self as a reference point. It could be because each individual has particular constructs available and accessible that are used to process information about both self and others (see Kelly 1955, Higgins et al 1982). As significant as the self is as a reference point, then, this function does not provide strong support for its uniqueness or its structural nature.

There is little question that self-knowledge can have information-processing consequences. For example, it has been demonstrated that self-knowledge is associated with quick decisions, easily retrievable evidence, confident self-prediction, and resistance to contrary evidence (e.g. Markus 1977, Bem 1981, Markus et al 1982). What is less clear is whether self-knowledge has these properties because it is a cognitive "structure." Any belief that a person is committed to or has confidence in would have similar properties (see, for example, Cantril 1932, Kiesler 1971, Fazio & Zanna 1981, Howard-Pitney et al 1986). Thus, evidence of these properties is not strong support for the cognitive-structural nature of self-knowledge as opposed to its motivational nature or simple accessibility. The significance of the motivational nature of self-beliefs is reflected in the dual criteria used by Markus (1977) to measure individuals' self-schemata—a self-descriptive component *and* an importance component. Although this dual-component definition better represents the nature of the self, it makes it difficult to draw unambiguous conclusions about the effects of any structural property of the self per se.

Among the arguments for the special "cognitive" nature of the self, probably the most difficult to evaluate center around the notion of *self-relevance*. A variety of interesting information-processing effects of hedonic relevance, self-serving biases, defensiveness, and personal values and orientation have been discussed in terms of the self being a cognitive structure (e.g. Bem 1981, Cacioppo et al 1982, Markus & Sentis 1982, Mills 1983). But these effects could be produced by motivational factors or the chronic accessibility of individual self-constructs or both. It is not necessary to assume that the information was processed in reference to organized and interconnected elements of self-knowledge. It has also been proposed that self-generation effects and self-involvement effects reflect the cognitive properties of the self system (e.g. Greenwald 1981, Greenwald & Pratkanis 1984). But both of these effects can occur even though the material is not processed *in reference to* self-knowledge. The former effect is a function of various differences between actively generating information versus simply receiving information, and the latter effect is a function of the goal-relevance of material. The "self" part of the label need only signify that the information production and the goal is associated with oneself rather than someone else—not that self-knowledge or a self-system is involved.

Individuals' memory of the past events they have experienced have also been described as a unique "cognitive" property of the self (see Gergen 1971, Greenwald 1981). Episodic memory does indeed reflect personal experience (see Tulving 1983). Is it useful, however, to consider all of episodic memory as part of the self regardless of whether or not self-knowledge was involved in encoding the event (i.e. contributed to the memory trace)? More generally, individuals' procedural knowledge for efficient and effective action that is acquired from personal experience (i.e. "How best to do it?") must be distinguished from the use of self-knowledge to guide action (i.e. "What would be the best way for *me* to do it?"). We believe that progress in understanding the information-processing consequences of self-knowledge would be enhanced by clearly distinguishing among *self-reference* (i.e. processing input in reference to self-knowledge), *self-relevance* (i.e. processing events that have consequences for the processor), and *personal experience*.

It is also necessary to distinguish between self-referent effects that are consistent with the self being a cognitive structure and effects that directly reflect the presence of a cognitive structure. The most popular measures in the social-cognitive literature do not require the presence of interconnected self-elements in order for the predicted effects to occur. It would be useful if more direct measures of structure were used, such as release from proactive inhibition (see Wickens 1972, Mills & Tyrrell 1983), intrusions of nonpresented information in free recall (see Bartlett 1932, Spiro 1977), or semantic priming (Warren 1972). In the latter paradigm, subjects are given a memory load word that functions as a "prime" prior to being shown a slide of a colored target word whose color they are asked to name as quickly as possible. The critical manipulation is the relation between the prime word and the target word. Warren (1972) demonstrated that when the prime was semantically related to the target, color naming was slower, suggesting that the prime and target concepts had a pre-established interconnection in long-term memory. A couple of recent studies using this "Stroop" paradigm found evidence suggesting that "problematic" self-descriptive attributes are structurally interconnected but "nonproblematic" self-descriptive attributes are not (Higgins et al, unpublished; Zindell et al, unpublished).

Concluding Comments

Although the question of whether the self is a unique structure is still open, it would be useful in future research to address some additional issues. For example, *which* aspects of self-knowledge are structurally interconnected and *how* are they structured (see Linville 1985)? Are the information-processing consequences of the self different for different aspects of the self, such as personal identity attributes (e.g. friendly; sensitive) versus group identity attributes (e.g. female; American; Jewish)? And if self-reference is not unique in its cognitive properties, might it have a unique relation to motivation? It has been suggested that self-knowledge has special emotional significance because of the motivational consequences of the relation between people's beliefs about their current self-state and their beliefs about their potential self-states (e.g. Cooley 1902, James 1890, Higgins et al 1986a, Markus & Nurius 1986). The social-cognitive consequences of these motivationally significant *interrelations* among self-beliefs have only begun to be explored.

DO PEOPLE NEVER SEEK THE TRUTH?

Just as one cannot pay attention to everything, one cannot gather all the information relevant to any issue. The question, then, is not whether people generally obtain all the relevant information prior to making a judgment on some issue, but what strategy was used to seek the information that was obtained. One strategy would be to gather as much relevant evidence as possible independently of the implications of the evidence for the final judgment: that is, "seek the truth." Another strategy would be to gather information as a function of its consistency with a particular judgment, such as a positive self-judgment. A traditional notion in psychology has been that people are oriented to "seek the truth" but other motivations can take precedence, such as self-esteem maintenance (for reviews see Raynor & McFarlin 1986, Trope 1986a).

From the traditional perspective, then, a failure to gather the most "truth-related" evidence is attributed to motivational factors. The assumption that, in the absence of interfering motivational factors, people basically follow the tenets of science for gathering evidence is consistent with many classic descriptions of people as lay scientists following logical procedures (e.g. Kelly 1955, Heider 1958, Jones & Davis 1965, Kelley 1967, 1973, McGuire 1969, Fishbein & Ajzen 1974). This assumption was seriously questioned in the 1970s, however. A new view of people began to take hold—a view of people as "faulty computers" or "biased information processors" rather than as lay scientists. Not only did people have information-processing limitations that influenced performance (e.g. Simon 1957, Fitts & Posner 1967, Newell & Simon 1972, Kahneman 1973) but they also did not perform like rational scientists (e.g. Slovic et al 1974, Tversky & Kahneman 1974, Dawes 1976, Nisbett et al 1976, Ross 1977).

The "faulty computer" perspective proposed that deviations from scientific tenets need not be interpreted in terms of motivational interference. Rather, deviations could arise from limitations in people's information-processing capabilities. And what could be more compelling support for this proposal than if people's strategies for hypothesis testing itself were found to be faulty? For hypothesis testing is, after all, the bread and butter of science. Studies by Snyder & Swann (1978) were generally considered to provide evidence that people's hypothesis-testing strategies were faulty.

The basic paradigm of Snyder & Swann's (1978) studies involved asking subjects to find out how well a profile they were given described another person that they would later be interviewing. The subjects were given a personality profile that described either the attributes of an extravert or the attributes of an introvert. They were then given a set of questions that either were neutral with respect to extroversion/introversion or would characteristically be asked of individuals already known to be extraverts or would characteristically be asked of individuals already known to be introverts. In preparation for the supposed interview to follow, subjects then selected a subset of these questions.

Snyder and Swann found that subject-interviewers tended to select questions that asked about attributes matching those contained in the profile they had been given. Because an additional study indicated that actual answers to these questions by an additional sample of respondents also tended to match the attributes contained in the profile, Snyder and Swann concluded that the subjects had confirmatory strategies for testing hypotheses about people, where "confirmatory" questions are nondiagnostic in that they do not allow answers that disconfirm the hypothesis. Although Snyder & Swann (1978) drew no conclusions about the validity of confirmatory strategies (see also Snyder & Gangestad 1982, Snyder 1984, Swann 1984), the results of their studies have been generally accepted as evidence for a problematic "confirmatory bias" in people's hypothesis-testing (e.g. Nisbett & Ross 1980, Fiske & Taylor 1984, Sherman & Corty 1984; cf Markus & Zajonc 1985).

Is There a "Confirmatory Bias" in Hypothesis-testing?

The usual explanation for the "confirmatory bias" is that people have a preference for conceptually positive information, for thinking about the presence rather than the absence of properties (e.g. Snyder & Swann 1978, Nisbett & Ross 1980, Snyder 1981, Sherman & Corty 1984). To evaluate this explanation for the "confirmatory bias," as well as to evaluate whether there is, in fact, a confirmatory bias, it is first necessary to distinguish among some alternative variables. For this purpose, as well as for the sake of some issues to be raised later, let us briefly discuss a well-known phenomenon described by Wason & Johnson-Laird (1972) that is often mentioned when the notion of a "confirmatory bias" in social cognition is raised.

Subjects are presented with four cards. Each card has a number on one side and a letter on the other side. When the cards are presented one card has a consonant showing, one card has a vowel showing, one card has an even number showing, and the final card has an odd number showing. Subjects are asked to test the following hypothesis that refers only to the four cards: *If a card has a vowel on one side, then it has an even number on the other side.* Subjects are asked which cards they would turn over to test the hypothesis. Most subjects do not turn over the card with the odd number showing, which, if it had a vowel on the other side, could disconfirm the hypothesis.

Now imagine that subjects had to select questions rather than select cards to be turned over. And let us assume that the "same" results were found—that most subjects did not select the question, "Does the card with the odd number showing have a vowel on the other side?", where an affirmative answer would disconfirm the hypothesis. Instead, subjects preferred to ask, "Does the card with the vowel showing have an even number on the other side?", where an affirmative answer would support the hypothesis. How can this preference in question selection be described? It *cannot* be described as a preference for confirmatory questions because the respondent could just as easily have answered the question negatively, which would have *disconfirmed* the hypothesis. It also cannot be described as a preference for thinking about the presence of properties because the presence of a property does not distinguish the preferred question, "having an even number on the other side," from the nonpreferred question, "having a vowel on the other side." The preference is best described as a tendency to select a question whose features match the features of the formulated hypothesis.

With these distinctions in mind, let us now review the evidence in the social-cognitive literature concerning the following questions: 1. When people seek information concerning an hypothesis, do they prefer hypothesis-matching questions? 2. When people show a preference for hypothesis-matching questions, is this a confirmatory strategy? Does it reflect a limitation or nonscientific bias in the processes underlying people's hypothesis-testing strategies?

The basic results of Snyder & Swann (1978) have been replicated in a number of studies (e.g. Snyder & Campbell 1980, Lord et al 1984). In addition, preference for hypothesis-matching questions has been found for a variety of different kinds of hypotheses, such as hypotheses about the self (e.g. Swann & Read 1981), hypotheses about others as being similar to the self (e.g. Fong & Markus 1982), and hypotheses about social stereotypes (e.g. Snyder et al 1982).

The particular studies cited, however, have one common procedural feature that creates problems of interpretation. As in the original Snyder & Swann (1978) studies, the questions provided to subjects were constructed to be characteristic of the type of question that would be asked of people *already known* to possess the attribute in question (e.g. "In what situations are you most talkative?"). Such questions cannot be used to test an hypothesis because they *presuppose* an affirmative answer. In order to test a hypothesis, a question must at least permit both an affirmative and a negative response even when it favors the hypothesis (e.g. "Are you talkative in some situations?"). Subjects in these studies, therefore, were not given an opportunity to engage in actual hypothesis testing (see Trope & Bassok 1982). Under such circumstances subjects may believe that the only reasonable strategy is to hypothesis-match, especially when they are also given an hypothesis-matching profile prior to question selection.

It is not the case, however, that the preference for hypothesis-matching questions only occurs for leading questions. Even when the questions provided subjects permit both "Yes" and "No" answers, subjects show a preference for hypothesis-matching questions (e.g. Trope & Bassok 1982, 1983, Bassok & Trope 1984, Skov & Sherman 1986, Kruglanski & Mayseless, unpublished). Thus, the initial answer to the question, "Do people prefer hypothesis-matching questions?", is affirmative. But it would be misleading to end the answer there.

First, there is considerable evidence that when subjects have a choice between hypothesis-matching questions and hypothesis-mismatching questions that vary in their diagnosticity (i.e. that vary in the extent to which they produce different responses as a function of whether the hypothesis is true or false), they prefer highly diagnostic, hypothesis-mismatching questions over slightly diagnostic, hypothesis-matching questions (e.g. Trope & Bassok 1982, 1983, Bassok & Trope 1984, Skov & Sherman 1986, Kruglanski & Mayseless, unpublished). Thus, *although there is a preference for hypothesis-matching questions over hypothesis-mismatching questions, there is a greater preference for highly diagnostic questions over slightly diagnostic questions.* Second, when given an opportunity to formulate their own questions (e.g. Clark & Taylor 1983, Trope et al 1984), *people almost never spontaneously construct leading questions.* Nor apparently is there a special preference for hypothesis-matching questions. Instead, subjects produce diagnostic open-ended questions (e.g. "How do you usually spend your Friday nights?") or bidirectional questions (e.g. "Do you prefer big or small parties?").

What Determines When Hypothesis-matching Questions are Preferred?

Perhaps the most important factor determining *when* a preference for hypothesis-matching questions will be found is the accessibility of an alternative competing hypothesis. A number of studies have found that when an alternative hypothesis is explicitly provided, *no* clear preference for hypothesis-matching questions is found (e.g. Trope & Bassok 1982, 1983, Bassok & Trope 1984, Lord et al 1984, Skov & Sherman 1985, Kruglanski & Mayseless, unpublished). But an explicit alternative hypothesis must be provided; it is not enough to mention alternative attributes only as negative attributes associated with the hypothesis to be tested (e.g. Snyder & Campbell 1980). This could be either because such negative attributes are transformed to positive attributes (see Huttenlocher & Higgins 1971) or because they are simply accepted as negative defining features of the hypothesis (just as "without sleeves" is a negative defining feature of "vest").

Another general factor that may determine preference for hypothesis-matching questions is people's a priori or experimenter-induced beliefs about the distribution of attribute instances associated with the hypothesis versus the alternative. As Trope et al (1984) point out, people often have a priori beliefs about the relative likelihood that the hypothesis versus the alternative is true (see also Snyder 1984). Most people, for example, have a priori beliefs about whether someone else would find them likable or dislikable. These self-beliefs have been shown to influence the social feedback that people seek (e.g. Swann & Read 1981). Presumably, this is because belief-consistent information is judged to be more credible than belief-inconsistent information, and *appropriately* so (see Lord et al 1979).

In hypothesis-testing studies the experimenter asks the subjects to test a particular hypothesis. Because the hypothesis mentions only one alternative, exposure to and thinking about the hypothesis are likely to prime or activate those attributes that are highly associated with that alternative (see Higgins & King 1981). In addition, given the rules of communication (see, for example, Swann et al 1981, Kraut & Higgins 1984), when only one alternative is mentioned by the experimenter it is quite possible that subjects infer that this is so because only this alternative is likely. In fact, such an inference by subjects is especially likely when the communication concerns an extreme trait, such as "extravert," as extreme traits involve especially strong pre-suppositions (see Huttenlocher & Higgins 1971). Experimenter-induced beliefs in the likelihood of an extreme hypothesis are resistant to change, at least by some sources of additional information, as when subjects in a study by Snyder & Swann (1978, Study 3) thought the target was still likely to be an extravert even after they received base rate information that made this unlikely.

Consistent with this proposal, Trope & Bassok (1983) found that when subjects were asked to test an extreme hypothesis (e.g. "extreme politeness;" "extravert") they displayed a preference for hypothesis-matching questions, but when they were asked to test a nonextreme hypothesis (e.g. "on the polite side") they showed no preference. And when Snyder & White (1981) reversed the usual presuppositional nature of the hypothesis by telling subjects to determine the extent to which the person *was not* the type of person in the profile, subjects showed a preference for hypothesis-mismatching questions. Finally, it should be noted that if subjects do believe that the only alternative mentioned by the experimenter is more likely to be true than false, it would be *appropriate* for them to select hypothesis-matching questions as the expected diagnostic value of these questions would be higher (Trope et al 1984).

Thus, the social-cognitive literature on hypothesis-testing suggests that, when given the opportunity, people select diagnostic questions over nondiagnostic questions (i.e. they "seek the truth") but will display a preference for hypothesis-matching questions when the hypothesis under consideration is the only accessible alternative and is believed to be true. The literature does *not* permit any clear conclusions concerning whether there are cognitive limitations in *processing* evidence or whether preferred questions tend to *confirm* the hypothesis. In fact, the two major contingency factors—beliefs concerning the likelihood that the hypothesis is true, and accessibility of alternative competing hypotheses—reflect the *availability and accessibility of social knowledge* rather than the actual process of hypothesis-testing. And except for some studies using leading questions, there is no direct evidence on whether preference for hypothesis-matching questions when it occurs leads to confirmation of the hypothesis. Logically, it need not.

Is Selection of Hypothesis-matching Questions Problematic?

Because the conditions under which people do show a preference for hypothesis-matching questions commonly occur in everyday life, it is worth considering whether this preference is problematic or inappropriate. To the extent that there are reasonable competing hypotheses that are not being considered and people's beliefs concerning the probable validity of their hypothesis are wrong, the evidence that is sought and gathered will not provide the information needed to draw errorless conclusions. It should be noted, however, that this is often the usual state in science (Kuhn 1962), and is mostly problematic when a clearly superior alternative hypothesis is being overlooked (see Greenwald et al 1986). It is not irrational or nonscientific to believe in one's hypothesis and not be aware of all the possible alternative hypotheses (see Mynatt et al 1978). And it is fine to consider only one's own hypothesis as long as the method for gathering evidence permits its negation (i.e. permits acceptance of the null hypothesis).

To consider whether preference for hypothesis-matching questions is an inappropriate or nonoptimal strategy, let us return to the Wason & Johnson-Laird (1972) task described earlier. The hypothesis to be tested can be restated as "All cards with a vowel on one side have an even number on the other side," or more generally, "All A's have X." For this level of exclusiveness, only questions about A and questions about non-X can yield the diagnostic disconfirming datum "A and non-X." Questions about the alternative non-A cannot do so (see Trope & Bassok 1983). Of course, other hypotheses varying in exclusiveness could be tested. In order to determine whether an hypothesis-matching preference is optimal it is necessary to know which level of exclusiveness is being tested. For example, if the hypothesis were "All A's *and only* A's have X" then the optimal strategy would be to search for evidence of A's that have X, A's that have non-X, *and* non-A's that have X, but if the hypothesis were "Some A's have X" then the optimal strategy would be to search for evidence of A's that have X (i.e. an hypothesis-matching preference).

Unfortunately, the social-cognitive literature on hypothesis-testing has rarely been explicit about the level of exclusiveness of their hypothesis. Consider, for example, studies on people's search of their memory for evidence concerning the suitability of a target person (self or other) for a particular job (e.g. Snyder & Cantor 1979, Snyder & Skrypnek 1981). These studies found that people preferred to gather evidence that matched the attributes in the job profile. But this strategy is appropriate given that job suitability is a question of whether the target can do the job, which is equivalent to a "Some A's have X" hypothesis (i.e. some of the target's behaviors indicate a capability to perform the job). Indeed, when a job suitability hypothesis is more exclusive—whether the target would be a "complete success" in the job (i.e. all of the target's behaviors indicate a capability to perform the job or "All A's have X")—subjects search memory for evidence that might contradict the hypothesis (Lingle et al 1983).

With regard to job suitability, it has also been suggested that the tendency to describe only hypothesis-matching attributes in job advertisements is surprising (e.g. Snyder & Cantor 1979). But there are so many possible disqualifying attributes that it is not reasonable to consider all of them. More generally, because there are typically many fewer attributes associated with the specific hypothesis than with the alternatives, it is often more diagnostic to ask hypothesis-matching questions (see Trope & Bassok 1983). Moreover, evidence for an alternative hypothesis, such as suitability for an alternative job (e.g. cook), is often irrelevant to the focal hypothesis (e.g. suitability as a lawyer). If the hypothesis being tested were different, such as "A is especially suited to be a lawyer," then both hypothesis-matching and hypothesis-mismatching questions would be required.

Other studies test other levels of hypotheses, such as studies testing social category stereotypes in which the hypothesis is typically "Most A's have X" (e.g. Snyder et al 1982). For this level of hypothesis a preference for hypothesis-matching questions is appropriate because a negative answer would provide support for the null hypothesis (i.e. some falsification) whereas affirmative answers to questions matching alternative hypotheses (e.g. "Most non-A's have X" or "Most A's have Y") would be irrelevant. If the hypothesis were "A's have X more than B's have X," a social distinctiveness hypothesis, then both hypothesis-matching and hypothesis-mismatching questions would be necessary.

The appropriateness of a question-selection strategy also depends on whether it is assumed that one and only one of the alternative hypotheses is true or that both can be true or that both can be false. Indeed, it has been suggested that scientific discovery is facilitated when hypothesis-testers assume that competing hypotheses are both true (Tweney et al 1980). Again, the literature has rarely been explicit about which of these cases is being tested.

An interesting question for future research is whether people vary their hypothesis-testing strategies as a function of the *exclusiveness of the hypothesis,* and whether this depends upon the accessibility of alternative hypotheses or on beliefs about the likely truth of the hypothesis or both.

In sum, although there is evidence suggesting that "cognitive" variables (i.e. beliefs in the hypothesis and accessibility of alternatives) can influence hypothesis-testing strategies, the social-cognitive literature does not permit any conclusions about people being nonscientific or inappropriate in their strategies because of limitations in their processing abilities or procedural rules.

Concluding Comments

Even when information-seeking strategies are influenced by motivational factors it is not clear whether the strategies are inappropriate. Individual's personal orientations can clearly influence their mode of information seeking, such as individual's self-monitoring orientation (e.g. Snyder et al 1986), dispositional self-consciousness (e.g. Carver et al 1985), need for control (e.g. Swann et al 1981, Taylor 1983), repression-sensitization coping style (e.g. Olson & Zanna 1979), uncertainty orientation (e.g. Sorrentino & Short 1986), and achievement motivation (e.g. Trope 1980). The personal relevance of the evidence can also influence information seeking (e.g. Lord et al 1979, Snyder et al 1982, Petty & Cacioppo 1986). To assess the appropriateness of the various modes of information seeking identified in this literature, it would be necessary to know what hypotheses are being tested. It is possible that motivational factors influence the level of hypothesis selected, as well as the accessibility of alternative hypotheses and beliefs about whether the hypothesis is likely to be true.

Gathering information about others' attributes for the purpose of self-evaluation (i.e. social comparison processes) is also influenced by motivational factors (see Frey & Ruble 1985, Raynor & McFarlin 1986, Tesser 1986, Trope 1986a). But the validity of social comparison processes also depends on what level of hypothesis about the self is being tested. For example, the information needed to test whether one could perform a particular behavior is different than the information needed to test whether one has a distinctive ability to perform the behavior. That is, *which* "truth" is being sought?

Surely there are times when people neither want nor seek the "truth." But there are other times when people do seek the "truth" but it is a different "truth" than others (including experimenters) assume that they are seeking. An area for future research would be to focus on the interface of motivation and cognition in identifying the different kinds and levels of "truth" that people seek. Do these vary depending on whether the target is self or other, or whether the other is an in-group versus an out-group member? Do motivational factors influence which "truth" individuals seek? What is the impact of social knowledge availability and accessibility on which "truth" is sought?

IS NONTARGET PERSON DATA UNDERUTILIZED IN SOCIAL INFERENCE?

It would appear from the perspective of "people as biased information processors" that input data have a minor role in people's judgments and inferences about the social world. After all, people presumably are "theory-driven" rather than "data-driven" to begin with, and when they seek out and gather information they use strategies that simply confirm the theories they already hold. If this were not enough, the literature also suggests that when people are finally confronted with data and told to use it to make a judgment, they do not maximally use all the available information. Instead, they underutilize all nontarget person sources of information.

As discussed earlier, the traditional perspective of "people as lay scientists" assumed that people appropriately integrated multiple sources of information when making judgments (e.g. Jones & Davis 1965, Kelley 1967, Wyer & Goldberg 1970, Bem 1972, Fishbein & Ajzen 1974). Indeed, adults' ability to interrelate simultaneously multiple elements (in contrast to young children's "centration" on only one element at a time) is considered a major developmental milestone (Piaget 1960; for a review see Higgins 1981). In addition, theories of referential categorization have traditionally proposed that adults take into account the context of alternative stimuli in which a target stimulus appears when judging the target, and there is substantial evidence to support this proposal (e.g. Rosenberg & Cohen 1966, Olson 1970, Glucksberg et al 1975, Higgins & Lurie 1983). However, in the 1970s this assumption as well began to be seriously questioned in the social-psychological literature. It had already been suggested that people did not integrate information appropriately (see Hoffman et al 1968, Einhorn 1972) and could not even keep two distinct dimensions in mind at the same time (e.g. Shepard 1964), but it was papers by Jones & Nisbett (1972), McArthur (1972), and, especially, Kahneman & Tversky (1973) and Ross (1977), that brought the issue of "biased data integration" to the forefront in social psychology.

In Kahneman & Tversky's (1973) now classic study, subjects in one condition were told that a panel of psychologists had interviewed and tested a total group of 100 professionals, comprised of 30 engineers and 70 lawyers, and that profiles of each person had been written based on this information. Subjects were told that one of these profiles had been randomly selected from the 100 available. Subjects then read this profile, which included some features that most people associate more with engineers than with lawyers, such as "he shows no interest in political issues" and "his hobbies include home carpentry and mathematical puzzles." Subjects were asked to judge the probability that this target person was "one of the 30 engineers in the sample of 100." Subjects in another condition were given the identical problem except that they were told that the sample consisted of 70 engineers and 30 lawyers. Although the base rate or sample-based prior probability information had a significant effect on subjects' inferences, it was underutilized from a Bayesian normative perspective. Instead, subjects apparently based their inference mostly on the target person information they were given (i.e. its "representativeness" of the predicted category).

Other phenomena suggesting that people underutilize nontarget person information have been described in the literature. For example, there is a substantial literature on people's apparent underutilization of consensus information (i.e. information about the responses of individuals other than the target person) when making causal attributions (see Kassin 1979a, and Nisbett & Ross 1980 for reviews). There is also evidence of people's apparent insensitivity to additional, nontarget person information that totally discredits prior information they received about a target person (i.e. the "perseverance effect" following debriefing; see Ross 1977).

The other major phenomenon of this kind that most captured social psychologists' interest was the "observer bias" (Jones & Nisbett 1972), "correspondence bias" (Gilbert & Jones 1986), or, in its most vivid characterization, the "fundamental attribution error" (Ross 1977). The attributional phenomenon denoted by these labels is the general tendency of people to overestimate the importance of personal or dispositional forces relative to environmental forces when interpreting social behavior. The classic example of this hypothesized bias is Jones & Harris's (1967) finding that observers inferred a correspondence between the attitude reflected in communicators' pro-Castro speech or anti-Castro speech and the communicators' true personal attitude toward Castro even when the observers knew that the experimenter had assigned the communicators to the position they advocated as part of a debate. Such findings were once again taken as evidence that people underutilized nontarget person information or underestimated its significance or both when making inferences.

The evidence across these literatures for an apparent "bias against nontarget person data" is quite remarkable. What does it mean? It does not mean that people cannot or do not use nontarget person sources of data. There is substantial evidence that people can and do use such nonperson information as base rates (for a recent review, see Trope & Ginossar 1986), consensus information (see Kassin 1979a), debriefing/discrediting information (see Ross & Lepper 1980, Anderson 1982), and information about behavioral circumstances (see Quattrone 1982, Trope 1986b; see also Jones & Harris 1967). As a clue to what the "bias against nontarget person data" might mean, let us consider the factors that influence when nontarget person information is or is not underutilized with regard to normative information and information about behavioral circumstances.

When is Normative Information Utilized?

The most detailed consideration of factors that influence when nontarget person information is utilized has been provided with respect to the utilization of base rates and consensus information (see Kassin 1979a, Bar-Hillel 1980, Borgida & Brekke 1981, Sherman & Corty 1984, Trope & Ginossar 1986). In addition, general approaches to accounting for variation in the utilization of such information have been proposed, such as a problem-solving approach (see Trope & Ginossar 1986), a lay-epistemic approach (see Kruglanski & Ajzen 1983, Kruglanski 1986), and a modes of processing (i.e. paradigmatic vs narrative) approach (see Zukier 1986). These accounts, together with a review of the literature, suggest the following general contingent factors:

1. Knowledge Availability: In order to apply a statistical rule or "statistical heuristic" (see Nisbett et al 1983) a person must first possess it. But there are some people who simply do not possess the necessary knowledge (see Ginossar & Trope 1980, Nisbett et al 1983, Kruglanski et al 1984, Trope & Ginossar 1986). Thus, training or cultural factors that lead to the acquisition of the knowledge will increase its utilization (e.g. Nisbett et al 1983, Zukier & Pepitone 1984, Fong et al 1986).[1]

2. Knowledge Accessibility: Once the necessary knowledge to use normative information is available to people, there are a variety of momentary and prolonged factors that could influence the accessibility of that knowledge and thus its utilization (for a review of such factors, see Higgins & King 1981). For example, Trope & Ginossar (1986) showed that recent activation of procedural knowledge for using base rates on one type of problem increased the likelihood that base rates would be used subsequently on Kahneman & Tversky's (1973) engineer-lawyer problem. Ferguson & Wells (1980) demon-

---

[1]"Knowledge availability" refers to knowledge that is stored in memory and could be used, whereas "knowledge accessibility" refers to the readiness with which stored knowledge is utilized (see Bruner 1957, Tulving & Pearlstone 1966, Higgins & King 1981). There has been some confusion over the use of these terms because Tversky & Kahneman (1973) used the term "availability" (as in "availability heuristic") to mean ease with which knowledge could be brought to mind and assessment of that ease. Their usage of "availability" is closer in meaning to accessibility than to availability, although it is, strictly speaking, distinct from both. Distinguishing "availability" from "accessibility" is useful precisely because it permits consideration of how a heuristic, such as the "availability heuristic," could be made available through instruction and how it could then be made more accessible through practice.

strated that priming consensus information increased its utilization in causal attribution. It might be useful in future training studies, such as those conducted by Fong et al (1986), to distinguish between training procedures that make a statistical heuristic available to individuals versus procedures that make an available heuristic more accessible. And just as there are individual differences in the availability of statistical heuristics, there are probably chronic individual differences in their accessibility.

3. Salience/Visual Access: The properties of the normative sources themselves and their contextual presentation in relation to the processor can also influence the likelihood that they will be used. Especially important are variables that affect the relative attention that processors pay to the normative information, such as the salience of and visual access to the data (see Ruble & Feldman 1976, Fischhoff et al 1979, Nisbett & Ross 1980, Borgida & Brekke 1981, Taylor & Thompson 1982, Kruglanski & Ajzen 1983). For example, both Feldman et al (1976) and Manis et al (1980) found that sequentially presented normative information was especially likely to be used. In a demonstration of the importance of mode of presentation, Trope & Ginossar (1986) found that base rates had powerful effects on subjects' probability estimates in the engineer-lawyer problem when they were presented along with the personality data in a list format.

4. Perceived Applicability: Another general factor that can influence whether normative information is used is the extent to which people perceive the information as being relevant or applicable to the inferential task (see Ajzen 1977, Kassin 1979a, Bar-Hillel 1980, Fiske & Taylor 1984, Kruglanski et al 1984, Sherman & Corty 1984). Variables that influence perceived applicability include apparent causal significance (e.g. Ajzen 1977), how the problem is framed (see Einhorn & Hogarth 1981, Sherman & Corty 1984, Trope & Ginossar 1986, Zukier 1986), and perceived reliability and representativeness of the normative sample (see Hansen & Donoghue 1977, Wells & Harvey 1977, Zuckerman 1978, Kassin 1979b, Kulik & Taylor 1980, Trope & Ginossar 1986; cf Borgida & Brekke 1981). For example, Kassin (1979b) found that subjects were more likely to use base rates when the sample was large than small, and Zukier & Pepitone (1984) found that when base-rate information can be interpreted as a measure of the strength of a phenomenon (e.g. the likelihood of getting divorced) it is much more likely to be used.

In an early study, Feldman et al (1976) found that consensus information was more likely to be used when subjects could not question the representativeness of the experimenter-provided sample by comparing it to self-generated normativeness. It is also more likely to be used when the target person is a member of an out-group than when he or she is a member of an in-group (Higgins & Bryant 1982). These results suggest that other kinds of knowledge availability, such as the extent of one's prior knowledge about particular subpopulations, can influence the use of normative information by influencing perceived applicability of experimenter-provided information.

5. Motivational Significance: When people have alternative sources of information available to them, their selection of which to use is often dictated by the relative desirability of the conclusions that the alternative sources afford (see Kruglanski 1980, 1986, Kuhl 1986, Raynor & McFarlin 1986, Tesser 1986, Trope & Ginossar 1986, Zukier 1986). For example, Trope & Ginossar (1986) showed that when use of base-rate information fulfilled a particular goal, such as helping a subject-lawyer to win his or her case, subjects were much more likely to use it. In a remarkable demonstration of the importance of role-associated goals on information use, Zukier & Pepitone (1984) found that when subjects were placed in the role of a personality psychologist when solving the engineer-lawyer problem they displayed the typical underutilization of base rates, but when they were placed in the role of scientist they did not. Zukier (1986) has suggested that when subjects are in the role of personologist, which may have been the case in the original Kahneman & Tversky (1973) study, they may process the information in a narrative mode (i.e. try to construct a meaningful story about the target), but when they are in the role of scientist they may process the information in a categorical mode (i.e. try to identify the target's probable category membership). What this suggests is that perceived applicability of the problem (e.g. framing) is itself affected by motivational factors, as indeed are the other general contingent factors.

When Is Situational Information Utilized?

A review of the attribution literature concerning when information about the situation or behavioral circumstances is utilized in social inference suggests that the same contingency factors are involved:

1. Knowledge Availability: There is evidence of both developmental and cultural variability in the strength of the "correspondence bias" (see Ruble et al 1979, Higgins & Bryant 1982, Miller 1984). Miller (1984), for example, reports that whereas there is a developmental increase in reference to dispositional factors in America (see also Higgins & Bryant 1982), there is a developmental increase in reference to contextual factors in India. These differences are said to reflect contrasting cultural conceptions of the person that are acquired during development. Developmental changes in the knowledge available about in-groups and out-groups are also related to when a correspondence bias appears (Higgins & Bryant 1982). Differences in knowledge availability may underlie the greater tendency to use situational factors as an explanation of the performance of similar than dissimilar targets (e.g. Banks 1976). Also, people are more likely to consider situational constraints on a target's behavior when the behavior is inconsistent with recently acquired knowledge about the target's dispositions (Jones et al 1971).

2. Knowledge Accessibility: As described earlier, there is considerable evidence that making a trait construct more accessible by recent and frequent priming increases the likelihood that subsequent exposure to a related, ambiguous behavior will result in a correspondent inference being made (e.g. Higgins et al 1977, 1985; Srull & Wyer 1979, 1980). There is also evidence that increasing the accessibility of situational constructs by priming increases the likelihood that situational forces will be considered in explaining a target's behavior (Rholes & Pryor 1982).

3. Salience/Visual Access: The importance of salience and visual perspective for the phenomenon of "correspondence bias" has long been noted (e.g. Heider 1958, Jones & Nisbett 1972, Taylor & Fiske 1978; cf Gilbert & Jones 1986). Storms (1973), for example, used videotaped presentations of target persons to manipulate visual access and found that situational features had a greater impact on subjects' inferences when the target's situation was the focus of the presentation. In another well-known set of studies, McArthur & Post (1977) showed that increasing the relative salience of the environment (e.g. brightness, motion) increased the likelihood that situational attributions would be made.

4. Perceived Applicability: There has been relatively little research on the effects of perceived applicability on the use of information about behavioral circumstances. There are some studies, however, that could be interpreted in terms of this factor. For example, in a study by Quattrone (1982) subjects were given instructions to consider the features of the target's situation, and the dependent measures on which subjects were asked to make situational attributions for the target's behavior were worded to describe the behavior in situationally relevant terms (e.g. "pressure toward opposing legalization" and "pressure toward favoring legalization" as scale endpoints). By thus making information about behavioral circumstances clearly applicable, Quattrone (1982) found that subjects *underutilized the target person information!*

5. Motivational Significance: There is substantial evidence that processors' use of information about behaviorial circumstances is influenced by its motivational significance (see, for example, Monson & Snyder 1977, Miller et al 1978, Snyder et al 1978, Weary & Arkin 1981). Regan et al (1974), for example, found that bad actions by liked target persons were more likely to be interpreted in terms of situational factors than bad actions by disliked target persons.

Why Might Nontarget Person Data Be Underutilized? And Is It?

Various explanations have been offered for the apparent underutilization of information about behavioral circumstances (e.g. Ross 1977, Jones 1979, Higgins & Bryant 1982, Quattrone 1982, Gilbert & Jones 1986). The most frequent explanation is that the actor and his or her act forms a more natural, primitive Gestalt than the act and the circumstances, a Gestalt that is automatically perceived (e.g. Heider 1958, Jones 1979, Johnson et al 1984, Gilbert & Jones 1986). But how does this explanation account for cultural and developmental differences (see Higgins & Bryant 1982) or the fact that correspondence bias is found for symbolic behavioral descriptions as well as observed behavior (see Quattrone 1982)? And given that an apparent "bias against nontarget person data" is found for nonbehavioral cases as well, there is a need for a more general explanation.

A general concept that seems to capture the phenomena and reflect many of the contingency factors is *"aboutness."* Given that subjects are typically asked to make an inference "about" some target person (cf Quattrone 1982), it would make sense for them to concentrate on information "about" that person. Whereas the personality profile in the engineer-lawyer problem is "about" the target person, the base-rate information is not. Whereas consistency and distinctiveness information is "about" the target person, consensus information is not. Whereas behavior is "about" the target person, the circumstances of the behavior are not.[2]

Cultural and developmental differences in conceptions of the person and beliefs about individual variability may be associated with differences in what kinds of information are considered to be "about" a target person. Data may be treated as information "about" the person when the target person is an in-group member but not when he or she is an out-group member (e.g. it reflects his or her group membership, not his or her individuality). Actors are more likely than observers to possess additional information "about" the target person (e.g. their own past behaviors) to which they can relate the current behavior. People may consider information that is not "about" the target person only when it has motivational significance or obvious applicability.

Any interpretation of the apparent "bias against nontarget person data," however, will always be highly tentative as the extent to which the bias exists will always be in doubt. This is because the notion of nontarget person data being "underutilized" is meaningful only in relation to some statistical or psychological model of its optimal or appropriate use. But one can never be certain that the currently accepted models are correct. For example, if observers of a target child's expressive reaction to receiving a birthday gift made as strong inferences about the child's dispositional happiness as when the child had the same reaction to a neutral event, the observers would traditionally be

---

[2]It has also been suggested that to the extent that there is a hypothesis-matching bias in information seeking, it may be because matching questions are perceived as being more "about" the hypothesis than mismatching questions, and that there is a preference for questions "about" the hypothesis (Trope, personal communication). If so, then there may be a very general preference for information "about" the topic or focus of the processing.

described as underutilizing the situational information (e.g. Heider 1958). But in an important paper, Trope (1986b) has recently pointed out that prior to causally interpreting a behavior it must be identified, and that situational information may influence this stage of the process as well as the later attributional stage. For instance, the observers in our example are more likely to identify the target child's expressive reaction as a smile when the situation involves receiving a birthday gift than when the situation is neutral. Thus, situational information may appear to have little effect only because it has actually had effects at two or more stages in opposite directions!

In traditional attribution models (e.g. Heider 1958, Jones & Davis 1965), the influence of situational factors on behavior is "subtracted" when dispositional inferences from the behavior are made. Application of this model has generally been restricted to momentary situational factors. What happens when the situational factors are *prolonged?* Supposedly the same "subtractive" logic should apply. Indeed, it has been applied to cases where the prolonged circumstances derive from category membership, such as growing up in the North versus the South. But subjects' dispositional inferences are not lessened by such information about target persons' prolonged circumstances (see Jones & McGillis 1976). Does this mean that information about prolonged circumstances is underutilized? In a recent paper, Higgins and Winter (unpublished) have suggested that when the situational factors are prolonged people may use a different, *"acquisition logic."* Higgins and Winter propose that people are naive "Thorndikians" who assume that prolonged circumstances which either reward a behavior or provide the opportunity to practice a behavior lead to the acquisition of a disposition to perform the behavior. Their data suggest that although momentary situational factors promoting a behavior are subtracted from the dispositional inference, prolonged situational factors are *added* to it.

Concluding Comments

Considerable progress has been made in identifying the factors that influence the extent to which nontarget person data are used in making inferences, but we need to learn more. We need to consider the potential impact of nontarget person data at each of the multiple stages of social evaluation. We also need to consider the influence on evaluation of information other than just attributionally relevant information, such as norms and standards (e.g. Higgins et al 1986b, Kahneman & Miller 1986) and prior beliefs about specific properties of the distribution of traits and behaviors in the population and subpopulations (e.g. Quattrone & Jones 1980, Park & Rothbart 1982, Nisbett & Kunda 1985, Higgins & Winter, unpublished). Only then can we know to what extent the "bias against nontarget person data" is in people's inferential processes or in our current conceptions of those processes.

More generally, whether studying people's information seeking or their use of input information, we need to consider that there may be different "truths" of concern to them (e.g. universal vs conditional; narrative vs paradigmatic; internal vs external). And variables such as knowledge availability and accessibility, salience, and "aboutness" may temporarily or chronically promote one "truth" over another. Rather than focusing on prescribed normative processes that are contrasted with nonstandard, "problematic" processes, the determinants of the various "truths" people seek and how they are sought need to be investigated. Depending on which "truth" people seek, and indeed whether people seek the "truth" or have some other goal (see below), what information is sought and used and how it is used will vary (see Kraut & Higgins 1984, Sorrentino & Hewitt 1984, Swann 1984, Kruglanski 1986, Zukier 1986).

GENERAL DISCUSSION AND CONCLUSIONS

In reviewing the issues addressed in this paper, as well as other issues in social cognition, some general features of the "information processlytizing" that began in the 1970s were conspicuous. First, there has been a tendency to propose that a particular kind of information has "special" information-processing qualities. For example, it has been proposed both that schema-congruent information is special and that schema-incongruent information is special. Individuals' information about their self has been said to be special as has been information about target persons. Our review of each of these kinds of "special" information, however, suggests that any "specialness" that they might have is contingent on a variety of other factors. One might argue, in fact, that it is the contingency factors, such as knowledge availability and accessibility, that are special and not any particular kind of information. A certain type of information, such as information about the self, may appear to be inherently special because it tends to have a value on each of the contingency factors that is associated with distinct kinds of information processing, but this would be a probabilistic feature of that particular kind of information and not some absolute, inherent quality. Again, it would be the set of contingency factors rather than the particular kind of information that would be critical.

There has also been a tendency to locate the source of some phenomena at a particular stage of information processing. For example, results suggesting better memory for schema-congruent information, schema-incongruent information, and self-referent information have generally been interpreted in terms of variables associated with encoding processes. Results suggesting the underutilization of nontarget person information have generally been interpreted in terms of variables associated with reasoning processes. Our review of the contingencies of these phenomena suggests that their occurrence is a function of many stages of information processing as well as the relation among these stages. Thus, it is not always possible to identify the specific stage of information processing that is the source of a phenomenon. For example, when a failure in decision-making occurs it is often not clear whether its source is something that happened at the reasoning stage or something that happened at some earlier stage (e.g. representation of the problem) or later stage (e.g. output strategies). As we suggested for the effects of self-referent orientation tasks, it may often be the relation among different stages that is critical.

A third general tendency of "information processlytizing" has been to propose that the "specialness" of particular kinds of information, as discussed earlier, derives from cognitive rather than motivational factors. Typically it has been assumed uncritically that people are motivated to be accurate and correct in their judgments, inferences, and memory (cf Einhorn & Hogarth 1981, Miller & Cantor 1982, White 1984). Interestingly, this is the one major assumption that the perspective of "people as biased information processors" has shared with the traditional perspective of "people as lay scientists," and maintaining this assumption has contributed to the "surprise" value of some of the prominent phenomena. After all, it is only surprising when people are inaccurate or incorrect if they are *trying* to be accurate or correct.

It may be that people are not motivated solely to be accurate or correct. Indeed, people are likely to have multiple *and conflicting* motivations when processing information such that not all of them can be fully satisfied. Accuracy would then have to be sacrificed to some extent in order that other motivations (e.g. self-esteem maintenance; interpersonal goals) receive some satisfaction.

The assumption that people are motivated to be accurate or correct is an important feature of "information processlytizing" because it supports the position that inaccurate or biased information processing must be due to "cognitive" limitations rather than motivational factors. If one abandons this assumption, then an alternative perspective of people as "creatures of compromise" may be considered, a perspective suggesting that people's judgments and inferences must be understood in terms of the competing motivations that they are trying to satisfy. Indeed, even identifying what is "accurate" or "valid" becomes more difficult when this perspective is taken (see Einhorn & Hogarth 1981, Miller & Cantor 1982, Kruglanski & Ajzen 1983, White 1984). But this perspective need not compete with the perspective of people as "faulty computers." In fact, both perspectives assume that people have limitations—either limitations on how much of their motivational set they can satisfy or on how much of the relevant information they can consider.

Understanding other people's limitations is critical for designing educational curricula and for formulating strategies to maximize performance in various domains. Further, recognizing that one's own beliefs, inferences, and memory are limited promotes the realization, "I could be wrong"—a first step in tolerance, open-mindedness, and prudence. It is useful to remember that, as for the properties of all species, a property that is limiting in one situation may be optimal in most others (e.g. automaticity). Many of the cognitive properties of people that can cause problems (e.g. knowledge accessibility) cannot be removed by the kind of training suggested for faulty reasoning.

Thus, future research should not be restricted to identifying people's limitations. There is a need to explore how effectively people function *within* these limitations. To the extent that information processing is determined by variables such as accessibility, encoding specificity, salience, and so on, which in turn are associated with potentially random contextual variables, how do people master their social cognitions? Just how good is the person-social environment fit? Social cognition has progressed sufficiently in the last ten years that we are now ready to turn to these exciting, next generation questions.

ACKNOWLEDGMENTS

Preparation of this chapter was supported, in part, by Grant MH39429 from the National Institute of Mental Health to E. Tory Higgins, and by Grant BNS-8404181 from the National Science Foundation to John A. Bargh. The authors thank Shelly Chaiken, Susan Fiske, Arie Kruglanski, Charles Lord, Diane Ruble, Yaacov Trope, Robert Wyer, and Henri Zukier for their helpful criticisms of an earlier version of the manuscript, and also the many other members of the Society for Experimental Social Psychology who kindly furnished us with copies of their papers.

Literature Cited

Abelson, R. P. 1974. Social psychology's rational man. In *The Concept of Rationality in the Social Sciences*, ed. G. W. Mortimore, S. I. Benn. Boston: Routledge & Kegan Paul

Ajzen, I. 1977. Intuitive theories of events and the effects of base rate information on prediction. *J. Pers. Soc. Psychol.* 35:303–14

Alba, J. W., Hasher, L. 1983. Is memory schematic? *Psych. Bull.* 93:203–31

Alicke, M. D., Klotz, M. L., Schopler, J. 1985. Relative efficacy of different encoding structures and judgment topics in a cued-recall task. *J. Res. Pers.* 19:261–70

Allen, R. B., Ebbesen, E. B. 1981. Cognitive processes in person perception: Retrieval of personality trait and behavioral information. *J. Exp. Soc. Psychol.* 17:119–41

Anderson, C. A. 1982. Inoculation and counterexplanation: Debiasing techniques in the perseverance of social theories. *Soc. Cognit.* 1:126–39

Anderson, C. A. 1983. Abstract and concrete data in the perseverance of social theories: When weak data lead to unshakeable beliefs. *J. Exp. Soc. Psychol.* 19:93–108

Anderson, C. A., Lepper, M. R., Ross, L. 1980. Perseverance of social theories: The role of explanation in the persistence of discredited information. *J. Pers. Soc. Psychol.* 39:1037–1049

Asch, S. E., Zukier, H. 1984. Thinking about

persons. *J. Pers. Soc. Psychol.* 46:1230–40

Ashmore, R. D. 1981. Sex stereotypes and implicit personality theory. See Hamilton 1981b, pp. 37–81

Ashmore, R. D., DelBoca, F. K. 1981. Conceptual approaches to stereotypes and stereotyping. See Hamilton 1981b, pp. 1–35

Banks, W. C. 1976. The effects of perceived similarity upon the use of reward and punishment. *J. Exp. Soc. Psychol.* 12:131–38

Bargh, J. A. 1982. Attention and automaticity in the processing of self-relevant information. *J. Pers. Soc. Psychol.* 43:425–36

Bargh, J. A. 1984. Automatic and conscious processing of social information. See Wyer & Srull 1984, 3:1–43

Bargh, J. A., Bond, R. N., Lombardi, W. L., Tota, M. E. 1986. The additive nature of chronic and temporary sources of construct accessibility. *J. Pers. Soc. Psychol.* 50: 869–78

Bargh, J. A., Pietromonaco, P. 1982. Automatic information processing and social perception: The influence of trait information presented outside of conscious awareness on impression formation. *J. Pers. Soc. Psychol.* 43:437–49

Bargh, J. A., Pratto, F. 1986. Individual construct accessibility and perceptual selection. *J. Exp. Soc. Psychol.* 22: In press

Bargh, J. A., Thein, R. D. 1985. Individual construct accessibility, person memory, and the recall-judgment link: The case of information overload. *J. Pers. Soc. Psychol.* 49:1129–46

Bar-Hillel, M. 1980. The base-rate fallacy in probability judgments. *Acta Psychologica* 44:211–33

Bartlett, F. C. 1932. *Remembering*. Cambridge: Cambridge Univ. Press

Bassili, J. N., Smith, M. C. 1986. On the spontaneity of trait attribution: Converging evidence for the role of cognitive strategy. *J. Pers. Soc. Psychol.* 50:239–45

Bassok, M., Trope, Y. 1984. People's strategies for testing hypotheses about another's personality: Confirmatory or diagnostic? *Soc. Cognit.* 2:199–216

Beck, A. T., Rush, A. J., Shaw, B. F., Emery, G. 1979. *Cognitive Therapy of Depression*. New York: Guilford

Bellezza, F. S. 1984. The self as a mnemonic device: The role of internal cues. *J. Pers. Soc. Psychol.* 47:506–16

Bellezza, F. S., Bower, G. H. 1981. Person stereotypes and memory for people. *J. Pers. Soc. Psychol.* 41:856–65

Bem, D. J. 1972. Self-perception theory. *Adv. Exp. Soc. Psychol.* 6:1–62

Bem, S. L. 1981. Gender schema theory: A cognitive account of sex typing. *Psychol. Rev.* 88:354–64

Berman, J. S., Read, S. J., Kenny, D. A. 1983. Processing inconsistent social information. *J. Pers. Soc. Psychol.* 45:1211–24

Bodenhausen, G. V., Wyer, R. S. Jr. 1985. Effects of stereotypes on decision making and information-processing strategies. *J. Pers. Soc. Psychol.* 48:267–82

Borgida, E., Brekke, N. 1981. The baserate fallacy in attribution and prediction. See Harvey et al 1981, pp. 63–95

Borgida, E., Howard-Pitney, B. 1983. Personal involvement and the robustness of perceptual salience effects. *J. Pers. Soc. Psychol.* 45:560–70

Bower, G. H., Black, J. B., Turner, T. J. 1979. Scripts in memory for text. *Cognit. Psychol.* 11:177–220

Bower, G. H., Gilligan, S. G. 1979. Remembering information related to one's self. *J. Res. Pers.* 13:420–61

Bransford, J. D., Franks, J. J. 1971. The abstraction of linguistic ideas. *Cognit. Psychol.* 2:331–50

Bransford, J. D., Johnson, M. K. 1972. Contextual prerequisites for understanding: Some investigations of comprehension and recall. *J. Verb. Learn. Verb. Behav.* 11: 717–26

Brewer, W. F., Treyens, J. C. 1981. Role of schemata in memory for places. *Cognit. Psychol.* 13:207–30

Bruner, J. S. 1951. Personality dynamics and the process of perceiving. In *Perception: An Approach to Personality*, ed. R. R. Blake, G. V. Ramsey. New York: Ronald Press

Bruner, J. S. 1957. On perceptual readiness. *Psychol. Rev.* 64:123–52

Bruner, J. S. 1958. Social psychology and perception. In *Readings in Social Psychology*, ed. E. E. Maccoby, T. M. Newcomb, E. L. Hartley, pp. 85–94. New York: Holt, Rinehart & Winston. 3rd ed.

Bruner, J. S., Tagiuri, R. 1954. The perceptions of people. In *Handbook of Social Psychology*, ed. G. Lindzey, pp. 634–54. Cambridge: Addison-Wesley

Cacioppo, J. T., Petty, R. E., Sidera, J. A. 1982. The effects of a salient self-schema on the evaluation of proattitudinal editorials: Top-down versus bottom-up message processing. *J. Exp. Soc. Psychol.* 18:324–28

Cantor, N., Kihlstrom, J. F., eds. 1981. *Personality, Cognition, and Social Interaction*. Hillsdale, NJ: Erlbaum

Cantor, N., Mischel, W. 1977. Traits as prototypes: Effects on recognition memory. *J. Pers. Soc. Psychol.* 35:38–48

Cantor, N., Mischel, W. 1979. Prototypicality

and personality: Effects on free recall and personality impressions. *J. Res. Pers.* 13: 187–205

Cantril, H. 1932. General and specific attitudes. *Psychol. Monogr.* 192

Carlston, D. E. 1980. The recall and use of traits and events in social inference processes. *J. Exp. Soc. Psychol.* 16:303–29

Carroll, J. S., Payne, J. W., eds. 1976. *Cognition and Social Behavior.* Hillsdale, NJ: Erlbaum

Carver, C. S., Antoni, M., Scheier, M. F. 1985. Self-consciousness and self-assessment. *J. Pers. Soc. Psychol.* 48:117–24

Chaiken, S. 1980. Heuristic versus systematic information processing and the use of source versus message cues in persuasion. *J. Pers. Soc. Psychol.* 39:752–66

Chandler, M. J. 1977. Social cognition: A selective review of current research. In *Knowledge and Development,* ed. W. F. Overton, J. J. Gallagher. New York: Plenum

Clark, L. F., Taylor, S. E. 1983. *Hypothesis-testing under Different Interaction Conditions: The Questions People Ask.* Presented at Ann. Meet. Am. Psychol. Assoc., Anaheim, CA

Cohen, C. E. 1981. Person categories and social perception: Testing some boundaries of the processing effects of prior knowledge. *J. Pers. Soc. Psychol.* 40:441–52

Cooley, C. H. 1902. *Human Nature and the Social Order.* New York: Scribner's

Craik, F. I. M., Lockhart, R. S. 1972. Levels of processing: A framework for memory research. *J. Verb. Learn. Verb. Behav.* 11:671–84

Craik, F. I. M., Tulving, E. 1975. Depth of processing and the retention of words in episodic memory. *J. Exp. Psychol: Gen.* 104:268–94

Crocker, J. 1981. Judgment of covariation by social perceivers. *Psych. Bull.* 90:272–92

Crocker, J., Fiske, S. T., Taylor, S. E. 1984. Schematic bases of belief change. In *Attitudinal Judgment,* ed. R. Eiser, pp. 197–226. New York: Springer-Verlag

Crocker, J., Hannah, D. B., Weber, R. 1983. Person memory and causal attributions. *J. Pers. Soc. Psychol.* 44:55–66

Darley, J. M., Fazio, R. H. 1980. Expectancy confirmation processes arising in the social interaction sequence. *Am. Psychol.* 35:867–81

Darley, J. M., Gross, P. H. 1983. A hypothesis-confirming bias in labeling effects. *J. Pers. Soc. Psychol.* 44:20–33

Dawes, R. M. 1976. Shallow psychology. See Carroll & Payne 1976, pp. 3–11

Deaux, K., Lewis, L. L. 1984. Structure of gender stereotypes: Interrelationships among components and gender label. *J. Pers. Soc. Psychol.* 46:991–1004

Derry, P. A., Kuiper, N. A. 1981. Schematic processing and self-reference in clinical depression. *J. Abnorm. Psychol.* 90:286–97

Einhorn, H. J. 1972. Expert measurement and mechanical combination. *Organ. Behav. Hum. Perform.* 7:86–106

Einhorn, H. J., Hogarth, R. M. 1981. Behavioral decision theory: Processes of judgment and choice. *Ann. Rev. Psychol.* 32:53–88

Epstein, S. 1973. The self-concept revisited: Or a theory of a theory. *Am. Psychol.* 28:404–16

Erber, R., Fiske, S. T. 1984. Outcome dependency and attention to inconsistent information. *J. Pers. Soc. Psychol.* 47:709–26

Erdelyi, M. H. 1974. A new look at the new look: Perceptual defense and vigilance. *Psychol. Rev.* 81:1–25

Fazio, R. H., Sherman, S. J., Herr, P. M. 1982. The feature-positive effect in the self-perception process: Does not doing matter as much as doing? *J. Pers. Soc. Psychol.* 42:404–11

Fazio, R. H., Zanna, M. P. 1981. Direct experience and attitude-behavior consistency. *Adv. Exp. Soc. Psychol.* 14:161–202

Feldman, N. S., Higgins, E. T., Karlovac, M., Ruble, D. N. 1976. Use of consensus information in causal attributions as a function of temporal presentation and availability of direct information. *J. Pers. Soc. Psychol.* 34:694–98

Fenigstein, A., Scheier, M. F., Buss, A. H. 1975. Public and private self-consciousness: Assessment and theory. *J. Consult. Clin. Psychol.* 43:522–27

Ferguson, T. J., Rule, G. R., Carlson, D. 1983. Memory for personally relevant information. *J. Pers. Soc. Psychol.* 44:251–61

Ferguson, T. J., Wells, G. L. 1980. Priming of mediators in causal attribution. *J. Pers. Soc. Psychol.* 38:461–70

Fishbein, M., Ajzen, I. 1974. Attitudes toward objects as predictors of single and multiple behavioral criteria. *Psychol. Rev.* 81:59–74

Fischhoff, B., Slovic, P., Lichtenstein, S. 1979. Subjective sensitivity analysis. *Organ. Behav. Hum. Perform.* 23:339–59

Fiske, S. T. 1980. Attention and weight in person perception: The impact of negative and extreme behavior. *J. Pers. Soc. Psychol.* 38:889–906

Fiske, S. T., Dyer, L. M. 1985. Structure and development of social schemata: Evidence from positive and negative transfer effects. *J. Pers. Soc. Psychol.* 48:839–52

Fiske, S. T., Kenny, D. A., Taylor, S. E. 1982. Structural models for the mediation of salience effects on attribution. *J. Exp. Soc. Psychol.* 18:105–27

Fiske, S. T., Kinder, D. R., Larter, W. M. 1983. The novice and the expert: Knowledge-based strategies in political cognition. *J. Exp. Soc. Psychol.* 19:381–400

Fiske, S. T., Pavelchak, M. A. 1986. See Sorrentino & Higgins 1986

Fiske, S. T., Taylor, S. E. 1984. *Social Cognition.* Reading, MA: Addison-Wesley

Fitts, P. M., Posner, M. I. 1967. *Human Performance.* Belmont, CA: Brooks/Cole

Fong, G. T., Krantz, D. H., Nisbett, R. E. 1986. The effects of statistical training on thinking about everyday problems. *Cognit. Psychol.* 18:253–92

Fong, G. T., Markus, H. 1982. Self-schemas and judgments about others. *Soc. Cognit.* 1:191–205

Frey, K. S., Ruble, D. N. 1985. What children say when the teacher is not around: Conflicting goals in social comparison and performance assessment in the classroom. *J. Pers. Soc. Psychol.* 48:550–62

Ganellen, R. J., Carver, C. S. 1985. Why does self-reference promote incidental encoding? *J. Exp. Soc. Psychol.* 21:284–300

Gergen, K. J. 1971. *The Concept of Self.* New York: Holt, Rinehart & Winston

Gilbert, D. T., Jones, E. E. 1986. Perceiver-induced constraint: Interpretations of self-generated reality. *J. Pers. Soc. Psychol.* 50:269–80

Gilovich, T. 1981. Seeing the past in the present: The effect of associations to familiar events on judgments and decisions. *J. Pers. Soc. Psychol.* 40:797–808

Glucksberg, S., Krauss, R., Higgins, E. T. 1975. The development of referential communication skills. In *Review of Child Development Research,* ed. F. Horowitz, E. Hetherington, S. Scarr-Salapatek, G. Siegel, 4:305–45. Chicago: Univ. Chicago Press

Grant, P. R., Holmes, J. G. 1981. The integration of implicit personality theory schemas and stereotype images. *Soc. Psychol. Quar.* 44:107–15

Greenwald, A. G. 1981. Self and memory. In *The Psychology of Learning and Motivation,* ed. G. H. Bower, 15:201–36. New York: Academic

Greenwald, A. G., Pratkanis, A. R. 1984. The self. See Wyer & Srull 1984, pp. 129–78

Greenwald, A. G., Pratkanis, A. R., Leippe, M. R., Baumgardner, M. H. 1986. Under what conditions does theory obstruct research progress? *Psychol. Rev.* 93:216–29

Hamilton, D. L. 1979. A cognitive-attributional analysis of stereotyping. *Adv. Exp. Soc. Psychol.* 12:53–84

Hamilton, D. L. 1981a. Cognitive representations of persons. See Higgins et al 1981, pp. 135–59

Hamilton, D. L., ed. 1981b. *Cognitive Processes in Stereotyping and Intergroup Behavior.* Hillsdale, NJ: Erlbaum

Hamilton, D. L., Dugan, P. M., Trolier, T. K. 1985. The formation of stereotypic beliefs: Further evidence for distinctiveness-based illusory correlations. *J. Pers. Soc. Psychol.* 48:5–17

Hamilton, D. L., Gifford, R. K. 1976. Illusory correlation in interpersonal perception: A cognitive basis of stereotypic judgments. *J. Exp. Soc. Psychol.* 13:392–407

Hamilton, D. L., Rose, T. 1980. Illusory correlation and the maintenance of stereotypic beliefs. *J. Pers. Soc. Psychol.* 39:832–45

Hansen, R. D., Donoghue, J. M. 1977. The power of consensus: Information derived from one's own and others' behavior. *J. Pers. Soc. Psychol.* 35:294–302

Harvey, J. H., Ickes, W. J., Kidd, R. F., eds. 1981. *New Directions in Attribution Research,* Vol. 3. Hillsdale, NJ: Erlbaum

Hastie, R. 1980. Memory for information that confirms or contradicts a personality impression. In *Person Memory: The Cognitive Basis of Social Perception,* ed. R. Hastie et al, pp. 155–77. Hillsdale, NJ: Erlbaum

Hastie, R. 1981. Schematic principles in human memory. See Higgins et al 1981, pp. 39–88

Hastie, R. 1983. Social inference. *Ann. Rev. Psychol.* 34:511–42

Hastie, R. 1984. Causes and effects of causal attribution. *J. Pers. Soc. Psychol.* 46:44–56

Hastie, R., Kumar, P. 1979. Person memory: Personality traits as organizing principles in memory for behaviors. *J. Pers. Soc. Psychol.* 37:25–38

Heider, F. 1958. *The Psychology of Interpersonal Relations.* New York: Wiley

Hemsley, G. D., Marmurek, H. H. C. 1982. Person memory: The processing of consistent and inconsistent person information. *Pers. Soc. Psychol. Bull.* 8:433–38

Higgins, E. T. 1981. Role taking and social judgment: Alternative developmental perspectives and processes. In *Social Cognitive Development: Frontiers and Possible Futures,* ed. J. H. Flavell, L. Ross, pp. 119–53. New York: Cambridge Univ. Press

Higgins, E. T., Bargh, J. A., Lombardi, W. 1985. The nature of priming effects on categorization. *J. Exp. Psychol: Learn. Mem. Cognit.* 11:59–69

Higgins, E. T., Bond, R. N., Klein, R., Strauman, T. 1986a. Self-discrepancies and emotional vulnerability: How magnitude, accessibility, and type of discrepancy influence affect. *J. Pers. Soc. Psychol.* 51:5–15

Higgins, E. T., Bryant, S. 1982. Consensus information and the "fundamental attribution error": The role of development and in-group versus out-group knowledge. *J. Pers. Soc. Psychol.* 43:889–900

Higgins, E. T., Herman, C. P., Zanna, M. P., eds. 1981. *Social Cognition: The Ontario Symposium*, Vol. 1. Hillsdale, NJ: Erlbaum

Higgins, E. T., King, G. 1981. Accessibility of social constructs: Information-processing consequences of individual and contextual variability. See Cantor & Kihlstrom 1981, pp. 69–121

Higgins, E. T., King, G. A., Mavin, G. H. 1982. Individual construct accessibility and subjective impressions and recall. *J. Pers. Soc. Psychol.* 43:35–47

Higgins, E. T., Lurie, L. 1983. Context, categorization, and memory: The "change-of-standard" effect. *Cognit. Psychol.* 15: 525–47

Higgins, E. T., Rholes, W. S. 1978. "Saying is believing": Effects of message modification on memory and liking for the person described. *J. Exp. Soc. Psychol.* 14:363–78

Higgins, E. T., Rholes, W. S., Jones, C. R. 1977. Category accessibility and impression formation. *J. Exp. Soc. Psychol.* 13:141–54

Higgins, E. T., Strauman, T., Klein, R. 1986b. Standards and the process of self-evaluation: Multiple affects from multiple stages. See Sorrentino & Higgins 1986, pp. 23–63

Hilton, J. L., Darley, J. M. 1985. Constructing other persons: A limit on the effect. *J. Exp. Soc. Psychol.* 21:1–18

Hirt, E. R., Sherman, S. J. 1985. The role of prior knowledge in explaining hypothetical events. *J. Exp. Soc. Psychol.* 21:519–43

Hoffman, P. J., Slovic, P., Rorer, L. G. 1968. An analysis-of-variance model for the assessment of configural cue utilization in clinical judgment. *Psychol. Bull.* 69:338–49

Howard-Pitney, B., Borgida, E., Omoto, A. M. 1986. Personal involvement: An examination of processing differences. *Soc. Cognit.* 4:39–57

Hull, J. G., Levy, A. S. 1979. The organizational functions of the self: An alternative to the Duval and Wicklund model of self-awareness. *J. Pers. Soc. Psychol.* 37:756–68

Huttenlocher, J., Higgins, E. T. 1971. Adjectives, comparatives, and syllogisms. *Psychol. Rev.* 78:487–504

James, W. 1890. *The Principles of Psychology.* New York: Holt

Johnson, J. T., Jemmott, J. B., Pettigrew, T. F. 1984. Casual attribution and dispositional inference: Evidence of inconsistent judgments. *J. Exp. Soc. Psychol.* 20:567–85

Johnson, M. K., Raye, C. L. 1981. Reality monitoring. *Psychol. Rev.* 88:67–85

Jones, E. E. 1979. The rocky road from acts to dispositions. *Am. Psychol.* 34:107–17

Jones, E. E., Davis, K. E. 1965. From acts to dispositions: The attribution process in person perception. *Adv. Exp. Soc. Psychol.* 2:219–66

Jones, E. E., Harris, V. A. 1967. The attribution of attitudes. *J. Exp. Soc. Psychol.* 3:1–24

Jones, E. E., McGillis, D. 1976. Correspondent inferences and the attribution cube: A comparative reappraisal. In *New Directions in Attribution Research*, ed. J. H. Harvey, W. J. Ickes, R. F. Kidd, 1:389–420. Hillsdale, NJ: Erlbaum

Jones, E. E., Nisbett, R. E. 1972. The actor and the observer: Divergent perceptions of the causes of behavior. In *Attribution: Perceiving the Causes of Behavior*, ed. E. E. Jones, et al. Morristown, NJ: General Learning Press

Jones, E. E., Schwartz, J., Gilbert, D. T. 1984. Perceptions of moral expectancy violation: The role of expectancy source. *Soc. Cognit.* 2:273–93

Jones, E. E., Worchel, S., Goethals, G. R., Grumet, J. F. 1971. Prior expectancy and behavioral extremity as determinants of attitude attribution. *J. Exp. Soc. Psychol.* 7: 59–80

Kahneman, D. 1973. *Attention and Effort.* Englewood Cliffs, NJ: Prentice-Hall

Kahneman, D., Miller, D. T. 1986. Norm theory: Comparing reality to its alternatives. *Psychol. Rev.* 93:136–53

Kahneman, D., Tversky, A. 1973. On the psychology of prediction. *Psychol. Rev.* 80:237–51

Kassin, S. M. 1979a. Consensus information, prediction, and causal attribution: A review of the literature and issues. *J. Pers. Soc. Psychol.* 37:1966–81

Kassin, S. M. 1979b. Base rates and prediction: The role of sample size. *Pers. Soc. Psychol. Bull.* 5:210–13

Keenan, J. M., Baillet, S. D. 1980. Memory for personally and socially significant events. In *Attention and Performance*, ed. R. S. Nickerson, 8:651–69. Hillsdale, NJ: Erlbaum

Kelley, H. H. 1967. Attribution theory in social psychology. *Nebr. Symp. Motiv.* 15: 192–238

Kelley, H. H. 1973. The process of causal attribution. *Am. Psychol.* 28:107–28

Kelly, G. A. 1955. *The Psychology of Personal Constructs*. New York: Norton

Kendzierski, D. 1980. Self-schemata and scripts: The recall of self-referent and scriptal information. *Pers. Soc. Psychol. Bull.* 6:23–29

Kiesler, C. A. 1971. *The Psychology of Commitment: Experiments Linking Behavior to Belief*. New York: Academic

Kihlstrom, J. F., Cantor, N. 1984. Mental representations of the self. *Adv. Exp. Soc. Psychol.* 17:1–47

Klein, S. B., Kihlstrom, J. F. 1986. Elaboration, organization and the self-reference effect in memory. *J. Exp. Psychol: Gen.* 115:26–38

Kraut, R. E., Higgins, E. T. 1984. Communication and social cognition. See Wyer & Srull 1984, 3:87–127

Kruglanski, A. W. 1980. Lay epistemologic—process and contents: Another look at attribution theory. *Psychol. Rev.* 87:70–87

Kruglanski, A. W. 1986. *Basic Processes in Social Cognition: A Theory of Lay Epistemology*. New York: Plenum. In press

Kruglanski, A. W., Ajzen, I. 1983. Bias and error in human judgment. *Eur. J. Soc. Psychol.* 13:1–44

Kruglanski, A. W., Friedland, N., Farkash, E. 1984. Laypersons' sensitivity to statistical information: The case of high perceived applicability. *J. Pers. Soc. Psychol.* 46:503–18

Kuhl, J. 1986. Motivation and information processing: A new look at decision making, dynamic change, and action control. See Sorrentino & Higgins 1986, pp. 404–34

Kuhn, T. S. 1962. *The Structure of Scientific Revolutions*. Chicago: Univ. Chicago Press

Kuiper, N. A., Derry, P. A. 1981. The self as a cognitive prototype: An application to person perception and depression. See Cantor & Kihlstrom 1981, pp. 215–32

Kuiper, N. A., Rogers, T. B. 1979. Encoding of personal information: Self-other differences. *J. Pers. Soc. Psychol.* 37:499–514

Kulik, J. A. 1983. Confirmatory attribution and the perpetuation of social beliefs. *J. Pers. Soc. Psychol.* 44:1171–81

Kulik, J. A., Taylor, S. E. 1980. Premature consensus on consensus? Effects of sample-based versus self-based consensus information. *J. Pers. Soc. Psychol.* 38:871–78

Landman, J., Manis, M. 1983. Social cognition: Some historical and theoretical perspectives. *Adv. Exp. Soc. Psychol.* 16:49–123

Langer, E. J., Blank, A., Chanowitz, B. 1978. The mindlessness of ostensibly thoughtful action: The role of "placebic" information in interpersonal interaction. *J. Pers. Soc. Psychol.* 36:635–42

Lichtenstein, M., Srull, T. K. 1985. Conceptual and methodological issues in examining the relationship between consumer memory and judgment. In *Psychological Processes and Advertising Effects: Theory, Research, and Application*, ed. L. F. Alwitt, A. A. Mitchell, pp. 113–28. Hillsdale, NJ: Erlbaum

Lindzey, G., Aronson, E., eds. 1985. *Handbook of Social Psychology*, Vols. 1, 2. New York: Random House. 3rd ed.

Lingle, J. H., Dukerich, J. M., Ostrom, T. M. 1983. Accessing information in memory-based impression judgments: Incongruity versus negativity in retrieval selectivity. *J. Pers. Soc. Psychol.* 44:262–72

Lingle, J. H., Geva, N., Ostrom, T. M., Leippe, M. R., Baumgardner, M. H. 1979. Thematic effects of person judgments on impression organization. *J. Pers. Soc. Psychol.* 37:674–87

Lingle, J. H., Ostrom, T. M. 1979. Retrieval selectivity in memory-based impression judgments. *J. Pers. Soc. Psychol.* 37:180–94

Linville, P. W. 1985. Self-complexity and affective extremity: Don't put all of your eggs in one cognitive basket. *Soc. Cognit.* 3:94–120

Locksley, A., Borgida, E., Brekke, N., Hepburn, C. 1980. Sex stereotypes and social judgment. *J. Pers. Soc. Psychol.* 39:821–31

Locksley, A., Hepburn, C., Ortiz, V. 1982. Social stereotypes and judgments of individuals: An instance of the base-rate fallacy. *J. Exp. Soc. Psychol.* 18:23–42

Locksley, A., Stangor, C., Hepburn, C., Grosovsky, E., Hochstrasser, M. 1984. The ambiguity of recognition memory tests of schema theories. *Cognit. Psychol.* 16:421–48

Lord, C. G. 1980. Schemas and images as memory aids: Two modes of processing social information. *J. Pers. Soc. Psychol.* 38:257–69

Lord, C. G., Lepper, M. R., Preston, E. 1984. Considering the opposite: A corrective strategy for social judgment. *J. Pers. Soc. Psychol.* 47:1231–43

Lord, C. G., Ross, L., Lepper, M. R. 1979. Biased assimilation and attitude polarization: The effects of prior theories on subsequently considered evidence. *J. Pers. Soc. Psychol.* 37:2098–2109

Mandler, G. 1977. Commentary on "Organization and Memory." In *Human Memory: Basic Processes*, ed. G. H. Bower, pp. 297–308. New York: Academic

Manis, M., Dovalina, I., Avis, N. E., Cardoze, S. 1980. Base rates can affect individual predictions. *J. Pers. Soc. Psychol.* 38:231–48

Markus, H. 1977. Self-schemata and processing information about the self. *J. Pers. Soc. Psychol.* 35:63–78

Markus, H., Crane, M., Bernstein, S., Siladi, M. 1982. Self-schemas and gender. *J. Pers. Soc. Psychol.* 42:38–50

Markus, H., Nurius, P. 1986. Possible selves: The interface between motivation and the self-concept. In *Self and Identity: Psychosocial Perspectives*, ed. K. Yardley, T. Honess. New York: Wiley. In press

Markus, H., Sentis, K. 1982. The self in social information processing. In *Psychological Perspectives on the Self*, Vol. 1, ed. J. Suls. Hillsdale, NJ: Erlbaum

Markus, H., Smith, J. 1981. The influence of self-schema on the perception of others. See Cantor & Kihlstrom 1981, pp. 233–62

Markus, H., Zajonc, R. B. 1985. The cognitive perspective in social psychology. See Lindzey & Aronson 1985, pp. 137–230

McArthur, L. Z. 1972. The how and what of why: Some determinants and consequences of causal attribution. *J. Pers. Soc. Psychol.* 22:171–93

McArthur, L. Z. 1981. What grabs you? The role of attention in impression formation and causal attribution. See Higgins et al 1981, pp. 201–46

McArthur, L. Z., Baron, R. M. 1983. Toward an ecological theory of social perception. *Psychol. Rev.* 90:215–38

McArthur, L. Z., Friedman, S. 1980. Illusory correlation in impression formation: Variations in the shared distinctiveness effect as a function of the distinctive person's age, race, and sex. *J. Pers. Soc. Psychol.* 39:615–24

McArthur, L. Z., Post, D. L. 1977. Figural emphasis and person perception. *J. Exp. Soc. Psychol.* 13:520–35

McCann, C. D., Hancock, R. D. 1983. Self-monitoring in communicative interactions: Social cognitive consequences of goal-directed message modifications. *J. Exp. Soc. Psychol.* 19:109–21

McCann, C. D., Ostrom, T. M., Tyner, L. K., Mitchell, M. L. 1985. Person perception in heterogeneous groups. *J. Pers. Soc. Psychol.* 49:1449–59

McCaul, K. D., Maki, R. H. 1984. Self-reference versus desirability ratings and memory for traits. *J. Pers. Soc. Psychol.* 47:953–55

McGuire, W. J. 1969. The nature of attitudes and attitude change. In *The Handbook of Social Psychology*, ed. G. Lindzey, E. Aronson, 3:136–314. Reading, MA: Addison-Wesley. 2nd ed.

Miller, D. T., Norman, S. A., Wright, E.

1978. Distortion in person perceptions as a consequence of the need for effective control. *J. Pers. Soc. Psychol.* 35:598–602

Miller, D. T., Ross, M. 1975. Self-serving biases in the attribution of causality: Fact or fiction? *Psychol. Bull.* 82:213–25

Miller, D. T., Turnbull, W. 1986. Expectancies and interpersonal processes. *Ann. Rev. Psychol.* 37:233–56

Miller, G. A., Cantor, N. 1982. Review: Human Inference by Nisbett & Ross. *Soc. Cognit.* 1:78–93

Miller, J. G. 1984. Culture and the development of everyday social explanation. *J. Pers. Soc. Psychol.* 46:961–78

Mills, C. J. 1983. Sex-typing and self-schemata effects on memory and response latency. *J. Pers. Soc. Psychol.* 45:163–72

Mills, C. J., Tyrrell, D. J. 1983. Sex-stereotypic encoding and release from proactive interference. *J. Pers. Soc. Psychol.* 45:772–81

Minsky, M. 1975. A framework for representing knowledge. In *The Psychology of Computer Vision*, ed. P. H. Winston. New York: McGraw-Hill

Mischel, W. 1968. *Personality and Assessment*. New York: Wiley

Monson, T. C., Snyder, M. 1977. Actors, observers, and the attribution process: Toward a reconceptualization. *J. Exp. Soc. Psychol.* 13:89–111

Mynatt, C. R., Doherty, M. E., Tweney, R. D. 1978. Consequences of confirmation and disconfirmation in a simulated research environment. *Q. J. Exp. Psychol.* 30:395–406

Neisser, U. 1976. *Cognition and Reality*. San Francisco: Freeman

Newell, A., Simon, H. A. 1972. *Human Problem Solving*. Englewood Cliffs, NJ: Prentice-Hall

Nisbett, R. E., Borgida, E., Crandall, R., Reed, H. 1976. Popular induction: Information is not necessarily informative. See Carroll & Payne 1976, pp. 113–33

Nisbett, R. E., Krantz, D. H., Jepson, C., Kunda, Z. 1983. The use of statistical heuristics in everyday inductive reasoning. *Psychol. Rev.* 90:339–63

Nisbett, R. E., Kunda, Z. 1985. Perception of social distributions. *J. Pers. Soc. Psychol.* 48:297–311

Nisbett, R., Ross, L. 1980. *Human Inference: Strategies and Shortcomings of Social Judgment*. Englewood Cliffs, NJ: Prentice-Hall

Norman, D. A., Bobrow, D. G. 1975. On data-limited and resource-limited processes. *Cognit. Psychol.* 7:44–64

Olson, D. R. 1970. Language and thought: Aspects of a cognitive theory of semantics. *Psychol. Rev.* 77:257–73

Olson, J. M., Zanna, M. P. 1979. A new look

at selective exposure. *J. Exp. Soc. Psychol.* 15:1–15

Ostrom, T. M. 1984. The sovereignty of social cognition. See Wyer & Srull 1984, 1:1–38

O'Sullivan, C. S., Durso, F. T. 1984. Effect of schema-incongruent information on memory for stereotypical attributes. *J. Pers. Soc. Psychol.* 47:55–70

Park, B., Rothbart, M. 1982. Perception of out-group homogeneity and levels of social categorization: Memory for the subordinate attributes of in-group and out-group members. *J. Pers. Soc. Psychol.* 42:1051–1968

Petty, R. E., Cacioppo, J. T. 1986. The elaboration likelihood model of persuasion. *Adv. Exp. Soc. Psychol.* 19:125–207

Petty, R. E., Cacioppo, J. T., Goldman, R. 1981. Personal involvement as a determinant of argument-based persuasion. *J. Pers. Soc. Psychol.* 41:847–55

Piaget, J. 1952. *The Origins of Intelligence in Children.* New York: Norton

Piaget, J. 1960. *The Moral Judgment of the Child.* New York: Free Press

Picek, J. S., Sherman, S. J., Shiffrin, R. M. 1975. Cognitive organization and coding of social structures. *J. Pers. Soc. Psychol.* 31:758–68

Posner, M. I. 1969. Abstraction and the process of recognition. In *Psychology of Learning and Motivation,* Vol. 3, ed. G. H. Bower, J. T. Spence. New York: Academic

Postman, L. 1951. Toward a general theory of cognition. In *Social Psychology at the Crossroads,* ed. J. H. Rohrer, M. Sherif. New York: Harper

Postman, L., Bruner, J. S., McGinnies, E. 1948. Personal values as selective factors in perception. *J. Abnorm. Soc. Psychol.* 43:142–54

Pryor, J. B., Kriss, M. 1977. The cognitive dynamics of salience in the attribution process. *J. Pers. Soc. Psychol.* 35:49–55

Quattrone, G. A. 1982. Overattribution and unit formation: When behavior engulfs the person. *J. Pers. Soc. Psychol.* 42:593–607

Quattrone, G. A., Jones, E. E. 1980. The perception of variability within ingroups and outgroups: Implications for the Law of Small Numbers. *J. Pers. Soc. Psychol.* 38:141–52

Raynor, J. O., McFarlin, D. B. 1986. Motivation and the self-system. See Sorrentino & Higgins 1986, pp. 315–49

Reeder, G. D., Brewer, M. B. 1979. A schematic model of dispositional attribution in interpersonal perception. *Psychol. Rev.* 86:61–79

Regan, D. T., Straus, E., Fazio, R. 1974. Liking and the attributional process. *J. Exp. Soc. Psychol.* 10:385–97

Rholes, W. S., Pryor, J. B. 1982. Cognitive accessibility and causal attributions. *Pers. Soc. Psychol. Bull.* 8:719–27

Rogers, T. B. 1977. Self-reference in memory: Recognition of personality items. *J. Res. Pers.* 11:295–305

Rogers, T. B. 1981. A model of the self as an aspect of the human information processing system. See Cantor & Kihlstrom 1981, pp. 193–214

Rogers, T. B., Kuiper, N. A., Kirker, W. S. 1977. Self-reference and the encoding of personal information. *J. Pers. Soc. Psychol.* 35:677–88

Rogers, T. B., Rogers, P. J., Kuiper, N. A. 1979. Evidence for the self as a cognitive prototype: The "false alarms effect." *Pers. Soc. Psychol. Bull.* 5:53–56

Rosenberg, S., Cohen, B. D. 1966. Referential processes of speakers and listeners. *Psychol. Rev.* 73:208–31

Ross, L. 1977. The intuitive psychologist and his shortcomings: Distortions in the attribution process. *Adv. Exp. Soc. Psychol.* 10:173–220

Ross, L., Lepper, M. R. 1980. The perseverance of beliefs: Empirical and normative considerations. *New Dir. Method. Soc. Behav. Sci.* 4:17–36

Ross, L., Lepper, M. R., Hubbard, M. 1975. Perseverance in self perception and social perception: Biased attributional processes in the debriefing paradigm. *J. Pers. Soc. Psychol.* 32:880–92

Rothbart, M. 1981. Memory processes and social beliefs. See Hamilton 1981b, pp. 145–81

Rothbart, M., Evans, M., Fulero, S. 1979. Recall for confirming events: Memory processes and the maintenance of social stereotypes. *J. Exp. Soc. Psychol.* 15:343–55

Rothbart, M., Park, B. 1986. On the confirmability and disconfirmability of trait concepts. *J. Pers. Soc. Psychol.* 50:131–42

Ruble, D. N., Feldman, N. S. 1976. Order of consensus, distinctiveness, and consistency information and causal attributions. *J. Pers. Soc. Psychol.* 34:930–37

Ruble, D. N., Feldman, N. S., Higgins, E. T., Karlovac, M. 1979. Locus of causality and use of information in the development of causal attributions. *J. Pers.* 47:595–614

Ruble, D. N., Stangor, C. 1986. Stalking the elusive schema: Insights from developmental and social psychological analyses of gender schemas. *Soc. Cognit.* 4:227–61

Rumelhart, D. E., Ortony, A. 1977. The representation of knowledge in memory. In *Schooling and the Acquisition of Knowl-*

edge, ed. R. C. Anderson, R. J. Spiro, W. E. Montague. Hillsdale, NJ: Erlbaum

Schank, R. C., Abelson, R. P. 1977. *Scripts, Plans, Goals, and Understanding*. Hillsdale, NJ: Erlbaum

Schneider, W., Fisk, A. D. 1984. Automatic category search and its transfer. *J. Exp. Psychol: Learn. Mem. Cognit.* 10:1–15

Schul, Y., Burnstein, E. 1985. The informational basis of social judgments: Using past impression rather than the trait description in forming a new impression. *J. Exp. Soc. Psychol.* 21:421–39

Sentis, K. P., Burnstein, E. 1979. Remembering schema-consistent information: Effects of a balance schema on recognition memory. *J. Pers. Soc. Psychol.* 37:2200–2211

Shepard, R. N. 1964. On subjectively optimum selection among multi-attribute alternatives. In *Human Judgments and Optimality*, ed. M. W. Shelley, G. L. Bryan, pp. 257–81. New York: Wiley

Sherman, S. J., Corty, E. 1984. Cognitive heuristics. See Wyer & Srull 1984, pp. 189–286

Sherman, S. J., Zehner, K. S., Johnson, J., Hirt, E. R. 1983. Social explanation: The role of timing, set, and recall on subjective likelihood estimates. *J. Pers. Soc. Psychol.* 44:1127–43

Showers, C., Cantor, N. 1985. Social cognition: A look at motivated strategies. *Ann. Rev. Psychol.* 36:275–305

Simon, H. A. 1957. *Models of Man*. New York: Wiley

Skov, R. B., Sherman, S. J. 1986. Information-gathering processes: Diagnosticity, hypothesis confirmatory strategies, and perceived hypothesis confirmation. *J. Exp. Soc. Psychol.* In press

Slovic, P., Kunreuther, H., White, G. F. 1974. Decision processes, rationality, and adjustment to natural hazards. In *Natural Hazards: Local, National, Global*, ed. G. F. White, pp. 187–205. New York: Oxford Univ. Press

Smith, E. R. 1984. Attributions and other inferences: Processing information about the self versus others. *J. Exp. Soc. Psychol.* 20:97–115

Smith, E. R., Miller, F. D. 1979. Salience and the cognitive mediation of attribution. *J. Pers. Soc. Psychol.* 37:2240–52

Smith, E. R., Miller, F. D. 1983. Mediation among attributional inferences and comprehension processes: Initial findings and a general method. *J. Pers. Soc. Psychol.* 44:492–505

Smith, J. M. 1982. *Self-relevance and the Perception of Ongoing Behavior: The Effects of Involvement and Knowledge*. PhD thesis. Univ. Mich.

Snyder, M. 1981. Seek, and ye shall find: Testing hypotheses about other people. See Higgins et al 1981, pp. 277–303

Snyder, M. 1984. When belief creates reality. *Adv. Exp. Soc. Psychol.* 18:247–305

Snyder, M., Berscheid, E., Glick, P. 1986. Focusing on the exterior and the interior: Two investigations of the initiation of personal relationships. *J. Pers. Soc. Psychol.* In press

Snyder, M., Campbell, B. H. 1980. Testing hypotheses about other people: The role of the hypothesis. *Pers. Soc. Psychol. Bull.* 6:421–26

Snyder, M., Campbell, B., Preston, E. 1982. Testing hypotheses about human nature: Assessing the accuracy of social stereotypes. *Soc. Cognit.* 1:256–72

Snyder, M., Cantor, N. 1979. Testing hypotheses about other people: The use of historical knowledge. *J. Exp. Soc. Psychol.* 15: 330–42

Snyder, M., Gangestad, S. 1982. Choosing social situations: Two investigations of self-monitoring processes. *J. Pers. Soc. Psychol.* 43:123–35

Snyder, M., Skrypnek, B. J. 1981. Testing hypotheses about the self: Assessments of job suitability. *J. Pers.* 49:193–211

Snyder, M., Swann, W. B. 1978. Hypothesis-testing processes in social interaction. *J. Pers. Soc. Psychol.* 36:1202–1212

Snyder, M., Tanke, E. D., Berscheid, E. 1977. Social perception and interpersonal behavior: On the self-fulfilling nature of social stereotypes. *J. Pers. Soc. Psychol.* 35:656–66

Snyder, M., White, P. 1981. Testing hypotheses about other people: Strategies of verification and falsification. *Pers. Soc. Psychol. Bull.* 7:39–43

Snyder, M. L., Stephan, W. G., Rosenfield, D. 1978. Attributional egotism. In *New Directions in Attribution Research*, ed. J. H. Harvey, W. Ickes, R. F. Kidd, 2:91–117. Hillsdale, NJ: Erlbaum

Sorrentino, R. M., Hewitt, E. C. 1984. The uncertainty reducing properties of achievement tasks revisited. *J. Pers. Soc. Psychol.* 47:884–99

Sorrentino, R. M., Higgins, E. T., eds. 1986. *Handbook of Motivation and Cognition: Foundations of Social Behavior*. New York: Guilford

Sorrentino, R. M., Short, J. C. 1986. Uncertainty orientation, motivation, and cognition. See Sorrentino & Higgins 1986, pp. 379–403

Spiro, R. J. 1977. Remembering information from text: The state of the "schema" approach. In *Schooling and the Acquisition of Knowledge*, ed. R. C. Anderson, R. J.

Spiro, W. E. Montague. Hillsdale, NJ: Erlbaum

Srull, T. K. 1981. Person memory: Some tests of associative storage and retrieval models. *J. Exp. Psychol: Hum. Learn. Mem.* 7:440–63

Srull, T. K., Brand, J. F. 1983. Memory for information about persons: The effect of encoding operations on subsequent retrieval. *J. Verb. Learn. Verb. Behav.* 22:219–30

Srull, T. K., Lichtenstein, M., Rothbart, M. 1985. Associative storage and retrieval processes in person memory. *J. Exp. Psychol: Learn. Mem. Cognit.* 11:316–45

Srull, T. K., Wyer, R. S. Jr. 1979. The role of category accessibility in the interpretation of information about persons: Some determinants and implications. *J. Pers. Soc. Psychol.* 37:1660–72

Srull, T. K., Wyer, R. S. Jr. 1980. Category accessibility and social perception: Some implications for the study of person memory and interpersonal judgments. *J. Pers. Soc. Psychol.* 38:841–56

Srull, T. K., Wyer, R. S. Jr. 1983. The role of control processes and structural constraints in models of memory and social judgment. *J. Exp. Soc. Psychol.* 19:497–521

Srull, T. K., Wyer, R. S. Jr. 1986. The role of chronic and temporary goals in social information processing. See Sorrentino & Higgins 1986, pp. 503–49

Stephan, W. G. 1985. Intergroup relations. See Lindzey & Aronson 1985, 2:599–658

Stern, L. D., Marrs, S., Millar, M. G., Cole, E. 1984. Processing time and the recall of inconsistent and consistent behaviors of individuals and groups. *J. Pers. Soc. Psychol.* 47:253–62

Storms, M. 1973. Videotape and the attribution process: Reversing actors and observers' points of view. *J. Pers. Soc. Psychol.* 27:165–75

Swann, W. B. Jr. 1984. Quest for accuracy in person perception: A matter of pragmatics. *Psychol. Rev.* 91:457–77

Swann, W. B. Jr., Ely, R. J. 1984. A battle of wills: Self-verification versus behavioral confirmation. *J. Pers. Soc. Psychol.* 46:1287–1302

Swann, W. B. Jr., Read, S. J. 1981. Acquiring self-knowledge: The search for feedback that fits. *J. Pers. Soc. Psychol.* 41:1119–1128

Swann, W. B. Jr., Stephenson, B., Pittman, T. S. 1981. Curiosity and control: On the determinants of the search for social knowledge. *J. Pers. Soc. Psychol.* 40:635–42

Taft, R. 1954. Selective recall and memory distortion of favorable and unfavorable material. *J. Abnorm. Soc. Psychol.* 49:23–29

Taylor, S. E. 1981. A categorization approach to stereotyping. See Hamilton 1981b, pp. 83–114

Taylor, S. E. 1983. Adjustment to threatening events: A theory of cognitive adaption. *Am. Psychol.* 38:1161–73

Taylor, S. E., Crocker, J. 1981. Schematic bases of social information processing. See Higgins et al 1981, pp. 89–134

Taylor, S. E., Fiske, S. T. 1978. Salience, attention, and attribution: Top of the head phenomena. *Adv. Exp. Soc. Psychol.* 11:249–88

Taylor, S. E., Fiske, S. T., Etcoff, N. L., Ruderman, A. J. 1978. The categorical and contextual bases of person memory and stereotyping. *J. Pers. Soc. Psychol.* 36:778–93

Taylor, S. E., Thompson, S. C. 1982. Stalking the elusive "vividness" effect. *Psychol. Rev.* 89:155–81

Tesser, A. 1986. Some effects of self-evaluation maintenance on cognition and action. See Sorrentino & Higgins 1986, pp. 435–64

Trope, Y. 1980. Self-assessment, self-enhancement, and task preference. *J. Exp. Soc. Psychol.* 16:116–29

Trope, Y. 1986a. Self-enhancement and self-assessment in achievement behavior. See Sorrentino & Higgins 1986, pp. 350–78

Trope, Y. 1986b. Identification and inferential processes in dispositional attribution. *Psychol. Rev.* 93:239–57

Trope, Y., Bassok, M. 1982. Confirmatory and diagnostic strategies in social information gathering. *J. Pers. Soc. Psychol.* 43:22–34

Trope, Y., Bassok, M. 1983. Information gathering strategies in hypothesis testing. *J. Exp. Soc. Psychol.* 19:560–76

Trope, Y., Bassok, M., Alon, E. 1984. The questions lay interviewers ask. *J. Pers.* 52:90–106

Trope, Y., Ginossar, Z. 1986. On the use of statistical and nonstatistical knowledge: A problem-solving approach. In *The Social Psychology of Knowledge*, ed. D. Bar-Tal, A. W. Kruglanski. New York: Cambridge Univ. Press

Tsujimoto, R. N. 1978. Memory bias toward normative and novel trait prototypes. *J. Pers. Soc. Psychol.* 36:1391–1401

Tsujimoto, R. N., Wilde, J., Robertson, D. R. 1978. Distorted memory for exemplars of a social structure: Evidence for schematic memory processes. *J. Pers. Soc. Psychol.* 36:1402–1414

Tulving, E. 1983. *Elements of Episodic Memory*. New York: Oxford Univ. Press

Tulving, E., Pearlstone, Z. 1966. Availability versus accessibility of information in memory for words. *J. Verb. Learn. Verb. Behav.* 5:381–91

Tulving, E., Thomson, D. M. 1973. Encoding specificity and retrieval processes in episodic memory. *Psychol. Rev.* 80:352–73

Tversky, A., Kahneman, D. 1973. Availability: A heuristic for judging frequency and probability. *Cognit. Psychol.* 5:207–32

Tversky, A., Kahneman, D. 1974. Judgment under uncertainty: Heuristics and biases. *Science* 85:1124–31

Tweney, R. D., Doherty, M. E., Warner, W. J., Pliske, D. B., Mynatt, C. R. 1980. Strategies of rule discovery in an inference task. *Q. J. Exp. Psychol.* 32:109–23

Warren, R. E. 1972. Stimulus encoding and memory. *J. Exp. Psychol.* 94:90–100

Wason, P. C., Johnson-Laird, P. N. 1972. *Psychology of Reasoning: Structure and Content.* London: Batsford

Weary, G., Arkin, R. M. 1981. Attributional self-presentation. See Harvey et al 1981, pp. 223–46

Weber, R., Crocker, J. 1983. Cognitive processes in the revision of stereotypic beliefs. *J. Pers. Soc. Psychol.* 45:961–77

Wells, G. L., Harvey, J. H. 1977. Do people use consensus information in making causal attributions? *J. Pers. Soc. Psychol.* 35:279–93

Wells, G. L., Hoffman, C., Enzle, M. E. 1984. Self-versus other-referent processing at encoding and retrieval. *Pers. Soc. Psychol. Bull.* 10:574–84

White, P. 1984. A model of the layperson as pragmatist. *Pers. Soc. Psychol. Bull.* 10: 333–48

Wickens, D. D. 1972. Characteristics of good encoding. In *Coding Processes in Human Memory,* ed. A. W. Melton, E. Martin, pp. 191–215. Washington, DC: Winston

Winter, L., Uleman, J. S. 1984. When are social judgments made? Evidence for the spontaneousness of trait inferences. *J. Pers. Soc. Psychol.* 47:237–52

Winter, L., Uleman, J. S., Cunniff, C. 1985. How automatic are social judgments? *J. Pers. Soc. Psychol.* 49:904–17

Woll, S. B., Graesser, A. C. 1982. Memory discrimination for information typical or atypical of person schemata. *Soc. Cognit.* 1:287–310

Word, C. O., Zanna, M. P., Cooper, J. 1974. The nonverbal mediation of self-fulfilling prophecies in interracial interaction. *J. Exp. Soc. Psychol.* 10:109–20

Wyer, R. S. Jr., Bodenhausen, G. V., Srull, T. K. 1984a. The cognitive representation of persons and groups and its effect on recall and recognition memory. *J. Exp. Soc. Psychol.* 20:445–69

Wyer, R. S. Jr., Carlston, D. E. 1979. *Social Cognition, Inference, and Attribution.* Hillsdale, NJ: Erlbaum

Wyer, R. S. Jr., Goldberg, L. 1970. A probabilistic analysis of the relationships between beliefs and attitudes. *Psychol. Rev.* 77:100–20

Wyer, R. S. Jr., Gordon, S. E. 1982. The recall of information about persons and groups. *J. Exp. Soc. Psychol.* 18:128–64

Wyer, R. S. Jr., Srull, T. K. 1981. Category accessibility: Some theoretical and empirical issues concerning the processing of social stimulus information. See Higgins et al 1981, pp. 161–97

Wyer, R. S. Jr., Srull, T. K., eds. 1984. *Handbook of Social Cognition,* Vols. 1–3. Hillsdale, NJ: Erlbaum

Wyer, R. S. Jr., Srull, T. K. 1986. Human cognition in its social context. *Psychol. Rev.* 93:322–59

Wyer, R. S. Jr., Srull, T. K., Gordon, S. E. 1984b. The effects of predicting a person's behavior on subsequent trait judgments. *J. Exp. Soc. Psychol.* 20:29–46

Wyer, R. S. Jr., Srull, T. K., Gordon, S. E., Hartwick, J. 1982. Effects of processing objectives on the recall of prose material. *J. Pers. Soc. Psychol.* 43:674–88

Zadny, J., Gerard, H. B. 1974. Attributed intentions and informational selectivity. *J. Exp. Soc. Psychol.* 10:34–52

Zuckerman, M. 1978. Actions and occurrences in Kelley's cube. *J. Pers. Soc. Psychol.* 36:647–56

Zukier, H. 1982. The dilution effect: The role of the correlation and the dispersion of predictor variables in the use of nondiagnostic information. *J. Pers. Soc. Psychol.* 43: 1163–1174

Zukier, H. 1986. The paradigmatic and narrative modes in goal-guided inference. See Sorrentino & Higgins 1986, pp. 465–502

Zukier, H., Pepitone, A. 1984. Social roles and strategies in prediction: Some determinants of the use of base-rate information. *J. Pers. Soc. Psychol.* 47:349–60

Ann. Rev. Psychol. 1987. 38:427–60

SOCIAL AND COMMUNITY INTERVENTIONS

Ellis L. Gesten

Department of Psychology, University of South Florida, Tampa, Florida 33620

Leonard A. Jason

Department of Psychology, De Paul University, Chicago, Illinois 60614

CONTENTS

INTRODUCTION

This chapter examines recent efforts by psychologists and others to enhance the well-being of groups and communities. The origins of psychology's systematic involvement in such activities is fairly recent, traceable in many respects to both critical events and the overall Zeitgeist of the 1960s. At the opening of the decade the Joint Commission on Mental Health and Illness (1961) suggested new mental health interventions and institutions were

427

0066-4308/87/0201-0427$02.00

needed. This came at a point in history when the federal government had both the will and resources to respond. Influenced by the politics and climate of the times, mental illness was seen as a social problem with intrapsychic manifestations but environmental underpinnings susceptible to influence through planned intervention. At the decade's close, in his 1969 presidential address to the American Psychological Association, George Miller (1969) urged its membership to "give psychology away" not through psychotherapy, but by translating research into applied strategies to help people help themselves (Chavis et al 1983).

The 1965 Swampscott Conference (Bennett et al 1966) represents another marker event of that era which helped to both energize and structure new intervention-related roles for psychologists. Organized around dissatisfaction among clinical psychologists with the scope and efficacy of traditional mental health treatment models, one key result of those deliberations was the emergence of community psychology as a new discipline, blending applied science and an abiding commitment to promoting human welfare. Though rooted historically in the service delivery traditions of clinical psychology, community psychology was to overcome those influences and create new prevention-oriented paradigms targeted to groups and the development or enhancement of social systems. Related to this was a commitment to examine the nature of communities in which we intervene and the linkages and reciprocal influences between persons and settings.

We began this review during the 20th anniversary of Swampscott, a time of self-conscious reflection on its legacy and the status and achievements of its offspring. In this context, the extent to which preventively oriented community concepts, values, and technologies have both affected and been incorporated into other fields has been viewed by some with a mixture of pride and alarm (Bloom 1984, Felner 1985, Shinn 1987). Others, by contrast, remind us of how far we must go and overcome to realize the ideals of the discipline (Sarason 1983, Elias 1987). Altman (1987) views the field as entering its adolescence needing both to validate its accomplishments and make necessary mid-course adjustments before moving forward. He also provides a helpful set of guidelines to assist in this process.

Whereas one-to-one therapeutic encounters can and do take place anywhere, between and among a wide variety of persons, the design and implementation of social and community interventions (SCIs) generally require more resources, a special tenacity, and a larger research team. Despite the strong support of the National Mental Health Association (1986), securing necessary funding is made especially difficult by the lack of a natural constituency for prevention services (Hollister 1982). On a positive note, the recent establishment of five NIMH-sponsored Preventive Intervention Research Centers (PIRCs) has created a type of research setting well suited for such larger scale, interdisciplinary, long-term intervention efforts. Governmental commitment to prevention funding, never very strong or consistent, is now threatened further in the current national budget crisis, dimming prospects that all twelve originally planned PIRCs will eventually be funded.

For this fifth review of social and community interventions we have chosen to feature programs with a primary or early secondary preventive—rather than restorative—focus, which offer as well some empirical data regarding impact. In some newly developing areas these criteria were more flexibly applied. Areas chosen for review are: *Primary Prevention: An Overview; Competence Building; Social Support; Empowerment; Mutual Help; Behavioral Community Psychology; Diverse Cultures and Groups; Research;* and *Public Policy.* These topics, while distinct in some ways, clearly overlap in others. Moreover, some may take exception with the decision to classify certain multifaceted SCIs in one as opposed to another category.

PRIMARY PREVENTION: AN OVERVIEW

Bower (1977), in a chapter written for the first of many fine volumes to emerge from the Annual Vermont Conference on Primary Prevention of Psychopathology, described primary prevention as a field of "unstructured spaciousness [in which] one searches eagerly for places to grab or stand . . . a friendly and virtuous territory of high abstraction and low practicality" (p. 24). Kessler & Albee (1975), in a more colorful, if sinister, view of the field, likened primary prevention to the great Okefenokee Swamp. "Attractive from a distance and especially from the air; it lures the unwary into quagmires, into uncharted and impenetrable byways" (p. 558). Both analogies capture something of the essence of primary prevention in the late 1960s and 1970s during which time much of its literature centered upon issues of turf, definition, and its legitimacy as a framework for conceptualizing mental health problems and delivering services.

In the 13 years since these observations were made, modest but significant progress has been made in our understanding and implementation of primary prevention programs. We are, for example, closer to agreement about primary prevention's essential definition and goals. Although Cowen's (1983) description of primary prevention as "group or mass targeted before-the-fact efforts to promote competence or prevent psychological dysfunction in essentially well people" may appear overly restrictive to some (Joffe 1982), this concept offers a clear challenge to mental health's traditional underlying assumptions and practices.

Although no major psychological condition from the *Diagnostic and Statistical Manual of Mental Disorders (DSM III)* has been thus far eliminated, the quality and quantity of documented primary preventive interventions have grown rapidly in the past four years. At least three comprehensive reviews of the field can be cited. Despite rigorous application criteria, Cowen received 49 abstracts which eventually yielded nine intervention studies constituting the *American Journal of Community Psychology's* Special Issue on Primary Prevention (Cowen 1982). Buckner et al (1985) compiled an annotated bibliography of 1008 published references on primary prevention in mental health spanning the past three decades. A critical comparative evaluation of primary prevention programs is currently being conducted by an APA task force seeking to identify some 15 exemplary, research documented programs from among 318 submissions. Finally, at least five significant volumes have appeared summarizing and evaluating both seminal and new research in the field. From the Vermont Conferences comes a book of readings (Joffee et al 1984) and a review of the past decade of progress in prevention (Kessler & Goldston 1986). Three edited volumes by Felner et al (1983b), Roberts & Peterson (1984), and Edelstein & Michelson (1986), though not limited in focus to primary prevention, provide a wealth of information regarding prevention theory, practice, and research.

Controversy continues over: 1. whether prevention should (or can) be disorder-specific or targeted more globally to the prevention of any psychopathology (Bloom 1985); 2. the extent to which psychopathologies to be prevented should be limited to *DSM III* "mental illnesses" as opposed to psychological conditions that do not meet those criteria. These and related issues were discussed in a provocative debate—*"Primary Prevention: Fact or Fallacy"*—among leaders in mental health who were both supportive and antagonistic toward primary prevention (Marlowe & Weinberg 1985).

Those who would tie prevention to specific disorders seemingly ignore the fact that most psychological disorders are associated with multiple causes and any given "cause" may yield multiple outcomes. A second set of concerns resides in the very nature of *DSM III* type disorders, many of which are neither enduring nor reliable, well-defined entities. We find ourselves sympathetic to a position outlined by Muñoz, who points out that while the prevalence rates of (for example) severe affective disorders are relatively small (6%), mild to moderate levels of depressive symptomatology are quite prevalent (9–26%). It thus seems reasonable to hypothesize that the prevention of depressive symptomatology would ultimately lead to decreased incidence of full-blown depression (Muñoz 1982, 1987).

In a field that continues to suffer from the lack of broad integrative theories, one notable exception is provided by the work of life stress researchers. According to Dohrenwend's (1978) model, stressful life events are associated with psychopathology with the degree of relationship moderated by risk and protective variables residing in both the individual and the environment.

Felner and others (1983a) adopting a life-span perspective have emphasized the role of critical life events both anticipatable and nonanticipatable for development of psychopathology or positive, adaptive outcomes. Applying a public health perspective to this model yields at least three generic primary preventive strategies: (*a*) modifying the *environmental surround* in which these events occur to, for example, increase social support and reduce the effects of stress; (*b*) eliminating the *agent* as, for example, reducing the incidence of abuse via legislative, religious, or psychological intervention; or (*c*) strengthening the competence of the *host* to deal with specific stressors or classes of stress. Although these goals may be pursued via intervention targeted at various levels to either persons or social systems, much of the published research reviewed for this chapter was person centered (Cowen 1985).

Both the quality and quantity of primary preventive SCIs continue to improve along with accumulating evidence of their impact. Although "our places to stand have not moved the earth" (Rappaport et al 1975), they have provided a clear vantage point from which to venture forward.

COMPETENCE BUILDING

Many person-centered interventions either explicitly or implicitly embrace a competence building model. In such approaches clusters of personal and/or social skills are taught systematically, followed typically by an assessment of skill acquisition and/or related mental health outcome(s). What follows is an overview of programs designed to enhance the competence of: (*a*) individuals in high risk family or community environments, (*b*) persons experiencing a significant life crisis or transition, and (*c*) groups of well individuals for whom the program is most clearly a preventive innoculation or enhancement opportunity.

Several interventions designed to increase young children's cognitive skills and social adjustment were identified (Slaughter 1983, Berrueta-Clement 1984, Pierson et al 1984, Jordan et al 1985). The Houston Parent-Child Development Center program for Mexican-American children ages 1–3 and their parents (Johnson & Breckenridge 1982) is representative of this class of studies targeted to families at risk because of their low socioeconomic and minority status. Via a 500+ hour intervention spread over two years, mothers were trained in a variety of personal and child-rearing competencies with special emphasis upon promoting language and cognitive development. Results of 1–4 year follow-ups indicate gains in cognitive development, mother-child interaction, and decreased aggressive behavior for boys. Recent 5–8 year follow-up teacher ratings reflect a continued pattern of improvement, this time for girls as well as boys (Johnson & Walker 1985). Notwithstanding limitations of this and similar studies because of subject attrition (Jordan et al 1985), this pattern of results is encouraging in light of the costs and obstacles associated with such multifaceted interventions. Fifteen-year follow-ups of first generation programs such as Head Start now also reveal measurable effects on achievement and adjustment despite the erosion of initial IQ gains (Lazar & Darlington 1982, Consortium for Longitudinal Studies 1983).

Children of chronically disturbed parents represent a high risk group that has been the focus of considerable descriptive, longitudinal research (Barocas et al 1985), but few well-designed preventive interventions (Goodman 1984a). One exception is the Family Support Project (Lyons-Ruth et al 1984) which compared the effectiveness of professional and paraprofessional staff in delivering home-based comprehensive support services to multirisk families. Mothers of infants in the project had experienced psychiatric hospitalization (31%), major depression (47%), and/or spouse abuse (55%). Competence targets related to infant-mother interaction and attachment as well as infant developmental quotient. Preliminary analyses indicate that although both groups evidenced gains in attachment and IQ, the drop-out rate for the professional program was more than double (32% vs 14%) that of the paraprofessional program. This finding is consistent with a substantial body of literature supporting the equivalence (or superiority) of paraprofessionals vs professionals for a wide variety of helping roles (Hattie et al 1984).

A related project still underway (Goodman 1984b) uses a competence building approach emphasizing social problem-solving and reality testing with severely disturbed inner city mothers. Impressive in terms of the number of intervention components included, this project illustrates the trade-offs involved in multifactorial "total push" (Rolf 1985) interventions, e.g. maximizing ecological validity and reach makes it difficult to isolate the most critical treatment component(s). Lack of such information may critically restrict the potential for generalizing program benefits to less well resourced settings.

Conducting and evaluating programs for children and families of divorce has been a productive primary prevention arena in recent years. Incidence statistics combined with an enormous body of findings documenting its short and longer term adverse effects for many (Wallerstein 1983) suggest that divorce is part of the fabric of American life that envelops us all directly or indirectly. Training designed for couples prior to or shortly after marriage to prevent break-up by enhancing problem solving and communication skills is a clear example of primary prevention strategy. Cognitive behavioral relationship enhancement programs which teach specific communication skills (e.g. expressive, empathic, discussion/negotiation, problem/conflict resolution, etc) via highly structured videotape and modeling based exercises, hold much potential in this area (Giblin et al 1985, Guerney 1987, Markman et al 1986).

Two problems associated with such interventions, however, are the low levels of motivation to enter and complete such training during early ("honeymoon") stages of the relationship life cycle plus the need for long-term follow-up. Increased use of court-ordered mediation provides an opportunity for preventionists at another stage of the marriage/divorce process. Slaikeu & Culler (1986) describe a pilot coding system developed to discriminate between successful and unsuccessful mediation strategies.

By far the most promising divorce interventions have been with parents and/or their children subsequent to separation or the filing of a formal court petition. Bloom et al (1985) report a 30 and 48 month follow-up of their 6 month intervention with recently separated adults, designed to promote competence and provide social support in five areas found to correlate with postdivorce adjustment. Significant self-reported adjustment benefits were obtained as long as four years later. A somewhat similar program conducted by Warren and her associates (1984) included direct assessment of child benefits and a more comprehensive initial screening and recruitment of subjects through the use of family court records. Efforts of those investigators made to assess systematically parent-child interactions were unique among divorce interventions reviewed. Postprogram adjustment gains for both children and parents which disappeared at one year follow-up highlight both the advisability of longer term evaluations and the need to strengthen skill-building technologies utilized.

Rarely, it seems, are programs replicated and refined by cross-setting collaboration among investigators. One notable exception is the school-based Divorce Adjustment Project (DAP). Stolberg & Garrison (1985) used a quasi-experimental design to compare the differential impact of: (a) a 12-session structured children's support group for 7–13 year olds, (b) a single parents' group, (c) their combination, and (d) a no-treatment control group. Children in the support group alone condition improved in self-concept, but made only limited other adjustment gains, whereas the parent group alone forestalled the adjustment deterioration found in the other groups at post-testing. The absence of positive outcomes for the combined groups is attributed to matching problems, illustrating one unfortunate consequence of non-random assignment in this type of research design.

The Children of Divorce Intervention Program (CODIP) is a 10-week small group intervention for 9–12 year olds which, while dropping the parent group, added an affective component to the DAP and strengthened its skill-building units (Pedro-Carroll & Cowen 1985). Converging evidence of program benefits were derived from improved parent, teacher, and child ratings of various adjustment indices. These initial positive results were further enhanced by confirmatory findings from a replication study (Pedro-Carroll et al 1986). As the authors point out, however, parents had been separated for two and four years respectively in these studies. Moreover, children in the second study were functioning initially significantly less well than a matched control group from intact families. Whether CODIP or any other model is properly seen as primary or secondary prevention thus depends in part upon the length of time between onset of the stress and program entry.

In a very different arena, Muñoz et al's (1982) skill-building approach to preventing depression in the general population via a two-week television mini-series and a structured eight-session course with medical outpatients (Muñoz 1987) is important both in terms of substantive findings and research design issues posed. Postintervention surveys of television viewers indicated no reduction in depression among the general population, but significant reduction was reported (secondary preventive) among symptomatic subjects. Muñoz argues that to demonstrate preventive outcomes requires not only that the incidence of the targeted disorder be above certain thresholds, but that risk groups, and even higher risk subgroups, be identified using documented markers. By so doing the intervention is effectively pushed closer to the borderline point on the primary/secondary prevention continuum. To maximize generalizability of program findings Muñoz cautions us to specify more clearly the potential pool from which our randomized samples are drawn and points to inconsistencies with which this is currently done.

For a society that considers itself child-oriented, our inability to contain and ultimately eliminate child abuse is a particularly wrenching concern. Rosenberg & Reppucci (1985) describe competence-building prevention efforts in this area, the most comprehensive of which (Olds 1984) appears promising. Arguably the most unique competence-oriented approach uncovered is reflected by the work of Illusion Theater, a theatrical company in Minneapolis, to educate children about sexual abuse (Harvey 1985). Plays and other outreach efforts teach children the difference between good and bad touching and model specific behavioral strategies for dealing with various abuse situations. Whether this unusual approach alone or in combination with other intervention components can reduce the 25–34% incidence of child victimization (Swift 1987) is as yet unknown. Attempts by social and community researchers to participate collaboratively in such natural experiments would provide the empirical data needed to strengthen program practices over time and possibly secure more stable funding.

Social problem-solving training represents a competence building approach which has been systematically evaluated and adapted to a wide variety of target groups and settings. Beginning with the seminal studies of Spivack & Shure (1974) at Hahnemann in the early 1970s, more than 50 child- and adolescent-focused interventions have been conducted based upon the premise that social-cognitive problem solving skills mediate adjustment (Weissberg 1985). Results from the Hahnemann group's early studies with inner-city preschoolers demonstrated that: (a) A relationship existed between certain cognitive problem-solving skills and teacher-rated adjustment; (b) these problem-solving skills could be taught by teachers and mothers, and their acquisition would improve children's adjustment; and (c) program benefits are retained up to two years (Shure & Spivack 1982). While numerous studies report relationships between SPS skills and adjustment (Richard & Dodge 1982, Rubin et al 1984), Durlak's recent review (1983) cites failed intervention replications and concludes on a discouraging note.

The current status of this competence-building approach is neither as negative as Durlak suggests nor as positive as might have been hoped for based upon earlier reports. At least two successful (Mannarino et al 1982, Feis & Simons 1985), and one unsuccessful replication (Sharp 1981) of Shure and Spivack's intervention were published in this last review cycle. Additionally, results from recent meta-analyses (Denham & Almeida 1987) support a link between social problem-solving and adjustment, provide evidence of observation-based problem-solving skill gains, and significant but less strong evidence of teacher-rated adjustment benefits. It has been hypothesized that adjustment gain depends in part upon the extent to which problem-solving interventions and activities are incorporated by teachers into the ongoing classroom routine (Shure 1985).

Recent efforts to modify and extend SPS training to 7–12 year old children have led to significant problem-solving and adjustment improvement (Weissberg et al 1981, Gesten et al 1982). Producing benefits for older children has required a more intensified program with: (a) greater emphasis upon *behavioral* and *affective* as well as *cognitive* problem-solving components, and (b) more explicit attention given to issues of generalization. Results from one, two, and three-year follow-up studies indicated that some, but not all, program benefits were retained. Moreover, pre to postprogram SPS skill acquisition was significantly correlated with pre to follow-up improvements in 5 of 13 blind teacher and peer adjustment ratings (Liebenstein 1981).

Consistent with Durlak's advocacy of task specific rather than generic problem-solving training, Elias and his associates (1986) have embarked on a large-scale effort to prepare preadolescents for the transition to middle school. The *"Improving Social Awareness"* (ISA) project is a classroom-based two year curriculum with an instructional phase followed by a creative application phase designed to integrate problem solving into the broader school curriculum and facilitate generalization. Attention given to the impact of broader system and school climate variables, plus precautions taken to insure the fidelity of replication, add special interest to reports emanating from this ongoing project.

Further developments necessary to clarify findings in this area include: (a) improvements in the psychometric qualities of SPS measures; (b) integration of social skills and problem-solving training models; (c) expansion of a narrow competence-building approach to include intervention at the school or systems level; (d) efforts to understand prior implementation failures, including delineation and evaluation of any required "informal" training activities; and (e) work in progress to conduct training on a larger scale basis and to place problem solving in the context of a more comprehensive competence and coping model of adjustment (G. Spivack, personal communication).

A wide variety of preventively oriented competence building technologies are now available. Future efforts will be strengthened by clear specification of training activities (and costs), as well as examination of the extent to which specific program components and acquired competencies relate to measured adjustment gain. Assessing outcomes in terms of well-being or positive affect as well as reduction in psychopathology also merit consideration in light of the nonclinical nature of participants, and partial independence of these adjustment dimensions.

SOCIAL SUPPORT

The largest body of research reviewed for this chapter was related to social support. A staggering 450 studies have been published in psychology alone in the two years since "Social Support Networks" was entered as an index term in *Psychological Abstracts* (Brownell & Shumaker 1984a). Enthusiasm for the construct over the past two decades derives researchwise from its presumed relationship to life stress and adjustment (Bloom 1985), the activities of informal caregivers (Gottlieb 1983), and communitywise, from a growing sense of isolation associated in part with fragmentation of the family. The enormity of the social support literature base, spread across multiple journals representing diverse disciplines, makes it possible for unwary readers to reach contradictory conclusions, depending on the specific materials reviewed.

The manner in which social support affects functioning has important implications for designing preventive SCIs. Evidence for direct effects encourages the development of programs for entire (normal) populations; by contrast, confirmation of the "buffering hypothesis" (i.e. that social support serves a health protective function only under stressful conditions) would make groups at risk more appropriate, impactful targets. In fact, evidence in support of both positions has been reported (Mitchell et al 1982), with the percentage of variance in psychological functioning accounted for by social support ranging from 2–17% (Rook 1984b). These contradictory findings appear to result from both methodological issues and variations in how social support is measured and conceptualized. Nonetheless, with the publication of several recent edited books (Cohen & Syme 1985, Sarason & Sarason 1985), review articles and chapters (Cohen & Wills 1985, Kessler et al 1985), and special journal issues (Brownell & Shumaker 1984b, Shumaker & Brownell 1985, Heller 1986) a more coherent, albeit complex, understanding of social support is beginning to emerge.

Efforts to measure social support have been hampered by disagreements about how the construct is best conceptualized. Recent taxonomies have been distinctly multidimensional, embracing a variety of potentially useful interpersonal resources that can be shared (Gottlieb 1987), including four common support contents or functions: emotional, instrumental, information, and appraisal or feedback (House 1981). Tardy (1985) reviewed the underlying conceptualizations of support and the psychometric properties of eight frequently utilized measures. Although each has unique strengths and weaknesses, no single questionnaire, with acceptable reliability and validity, measures all or even most of the key support components associated with positive health outcomes.

Whereas some measures, e.g. the Inventory of Socially Supportive Behaviors (ISSB) (Stokes & Wilson 1984), assess supportive *behaviors,* others focus on *qualitative* dimensions such as perception (Procidano & Heller 1983, Oritt et al 1985, Vaux et al 1986) or satisfaction with support (Sandler & Barrera 1984), and still others stress *structural* characteristics of the social network (Wellman 1981). Some of the strongest stress-buffering findings, as for example among highly stressed caregivers of Alzheimer's victims (Fiore et al 1986), have been associated with qualitative or subjective measures of support. Support like beauty appears to reside in the eyes of the beholder. Moreover, that subjective view does not correlate perfectly with support assessed by objective methods. Shinn et al (1984) consider problems associated with structural measures that ignore the quality of interactions (e.g. network size, density). Studies of elderly widows (Rook 1984a,b) and adult cancer patients (Dunkel-Schetter 1984) indicate that members of one's intimate network may, not surprisingly, be a source of stress and thus contribute to negative as well as positive outcomes.

Cohen & Wills' (1985) detailed, well-integrated review concludes that one's concept of social support is an important determinant of the type of support effects obtained. Whereas evidence favoring a buffering model is found when support is measured qualitatively from the perspective of the recipient, when structural measures of support are used, the evidence is better explained by the main effect model. Although being part of a social network may be beneficial generally, it is not necessarily helpful in the face of stress except under certain conditions. The preceding pattern of results has been fairly consistent even in the face of such methodological problems as: heavy reliance upon cross-sectional vs longitudinal designs; confounds among measures of stress, support, and psychopathology; and differences in how interactions are computed (Dohrenwend et al 1984, Cohen & Wills 1985, Depue & Monroe 1986).

Whether social support is seen as an environmental or individual variable has important implications for intervention (Rook & Dooley 1985). Conceptualized as a resource outside the individual, support can be increased by promoting group membership and other vehicles for meaningful social interaction. Such an approach has been used with adolescent mothers, among other target groups, with positive outcomes in several adjustment domains (Henninger & Nelson 1984, Unger & Wandersman 1985a). Felner et al (1982) increased social support among adolescents entering high school using a system intervention that: (a) changed roles of selected school personnel, and (b) modified the social ecology of the environment. The adjustment and school performance benefits reported by those authors are particularly impressive in light of the inherent simplicity and cost-effectiveness of the intervention. Wright & Cowen (1985) attempted to promote cooperative social interactions in 5th grade classrooms using a peer teaching or jigsaw technique. Improvements in classroom climate, teacher-rated adjustment, and academic performance were reported, but not in self-esteem or sociometric status.

Roskin (1982), also conceptualizing social support as primarily a environmental variable, described a support program for adults who had experienced multiple life crises. Interestingly, in addition to overall group benefits, those who had experienced the death of a family member or close friend improved most. Those findings highlight the need to consider characteristics of the context (Bowers & Gesten 1986) in which support interventions are designed in order to maximize person-environment fit (Shinn et al 1984). Cohen & McKay (1984) go even further in hypothesizing that persons under stress can best be helped by providing stressor-specific supportive resources.

Recognizing the active role that people play in the perception and construction of their social environment in general, and in their supportive interactions specifically, helps identify alternative intervention strategies. Rather than providing support directly by modifying the environmental surround, groups can be trained by using the types of social competence building approaches mentioned earlier, among others (Danish et al 1983), to construct their own support system.

Two pilot support interventions are of special interest paradigmatically because of their unique methodologies. Guerney (1985) describes the "Phone Friend Child Helpline" designed to serve varied support functions for children under 13 responsible for their own care after school—a critical social problem. Thirty to forty calls were received weekly; 44% of the callers reported feelings of loneliness or boredom. Unfortunately, difficulties in evaluating this potentially useful service limit the consumer feedback and effectiveness data needed for program dissemination.

"Friends Can Be Good Medicine" (Taylor et al 1984) is a multimedia mental health promotion campaign conducted statewide in California in 1982. The program's main goals were (*a*) to educate people about the links between supportive personal relationships and lowered rates of both disease and psychopathology, and (*b*) to encourage the development of supportive ties. Millions were exposed to the basic message and thousands to the 1300 specific "Friends" activities generated. Those who participated in a program activity or read program literature reported greater gains in knowledge, attitudes, and socializing intentions than controls which were maintained at one year follow-up. Efforts like this to make use of the mass media in preventive programming would benefit from incorporation of validated procedures to translate heightened community awareness into meaningful behavior change. The highly structured follow-up interventions used in the Stanford Heart Disease Project provide a useful model for this process (Farquhar et al 1985).

As the "Friends" project well illustrates, many preventive interventions combine both social support and competence building components. Evaluations which tease apart their separate and interactive contributions would be helpful. The provision and receipt of social support is a dynamic, interactive process whose health protective impact is mediated by context and source of assistance, as well as the conceptual stance and measurement strategy used. More complex research design and assessment strategies will be required to disaggregate these effects in the next generation of support-based SCIs.

EMPOWERMENT

Empowerment theorists view most mental health interventions as typically utilizing "top-down" approaches in which persons with specialized training provide "expert" help to those less fortunate, seen variously as patients, clients, or subjects. This model, described as paternalistic (Swift 1984), often fails to acknowledge the unique strengths and diversities of persons and communities we seek to help. Proponents of this new movement argue that empowerment strategies that enhance justice and peoples' sense of control over their own destinies are preferable to prevention or treatment approaches to strengthen individuals (Rappaport 1981). Moreover, by understanding how persons and groups solve their problems and meet their needs naturally, it is argued we will be in a far better position to leverage our own helping potential.

The imagery of empowerment implies a more symmetrical relationship or alliance with those with whom we work than has traditionally been the case. In this context, the credit that professionals take for outcomes is de-emphasized as we explicitly acknowledge and foster a sense of competence and control (i.e. empowerment) among others. According to Rappaport

(1985a), who has written eloquently and provocatively on the topic, empowerment may or may not turn out to prevent diagnosable mental illness and should not be evaluated solely on that basis. The empowerment view is based on a somewhat different set of values about optimal actions and interventions for SCIs, and indeed about appropriate criteria for evaluating their efficacy.

A concept as new and in some ways as difficult to define as empowerment can best be understood in terms of specific research and program exemplars. One of the best recent resources is the *Studies in Empowerment* special journal issue (Rappaport et al 1984), which includes eight diverse descriptive, theoretical, and intervention efforts based on the concept of empowerment. As a whole this collection should encourage those who believe that complex problems cannot be ignored simply because they don't easily fit our standard designs. Authors in this series of articles used varied research strategies, e.g. participant observation, including some from anthropology and other disciplines. Maton & Rappaport (1984) identified the correlates of empowerment in a religious setting while Fawcett et al (1984) described seven separate studies of empowerment technologies used to assist diverse community groups, e.g. welfare families and community boards, to gain better control of their lives. In each of the latter cases behavioral principles were employed in the design, conduct, and evaluation of individual interventions. One of the most unique empowerment interventions reviewed was reported by Glidewell (1986), who in a five-year program trained members of a community in negotiation skills. Among the observed program outcomes were increased influence attempts in school board meetings and higher self esteem.

Roberts & Thorsheim (1986) report a longitudinal effort, the "Bottled Pain Project," combining social support and empowerment technologies to prevent alcohol abuse. Nearly 10,000 people participated as 24 Lutheran congregations were randomly assigned to receive alcohol abuse information, information plus social support oriented activities, or to a no-treatment control condition. The empowerment component derived from multiple strategies was used to develop program resources and ownership from within each congregation. The authors assumed a consultative role helping leadership teams in each setting generate program activities and involvement among congregates. Alcohol abuse and emotional distress decreased for both treatment groups compared to controls. The fact that increased social support from family members was associated with positive outcomes, whereas increased support from friends had the opposite effect, highlights the importance of unpacking the social support construct. These at first puzzling findings became much clearer as a consequence of formal post hoc interviews with congregates "at risk" which revealed strong associations among stress, help-seeking, friends who *themselves* drink heavily, and alcohol use. Such followup discussion with participants in our interventions has much to commend it.

While the goal of empowerment is ambitious, results from initial studies in this arena are encouraging. For the moment, however, it is too early to tell whether the impact of the empowerment thrust will be the development of methodologically distinctive interventions, or instead a conceptual framework and set of process guidelines that can inform a wide variety of SCIs. Further elaboration of the empowerment construct will also benefit from agreement on the specific variables or classes of variables used to assess outcomes.

MUTUAL HELP

One of the most potentially impactful clusters of SCIs has developed largely independently of professional input. The mutual help movement has grown enormously over the past decade to include over 500,000 groups and 15 million people (Riessman 1985). A National Self-Help Clearinghouse and many others operating at the state and local levels offer information about available support groups and networks and, in some cases, provide training for indigenous leaders. Interest in such groups derives from the potential benefits to members as well as society's unwillingness in the economic and political climate of the 1980s to finance major new mental health initiatives. In the face of this growing "revolution" (Gartner & Riessman 1984; Riessman 1985), questions have been raised about both the efficacy of mutual help and the proper role for community researchers regarding such organizations.

Whereas social support interventions are conceived and run primarily by professionals, most mutual help groups are autonomous or represent a hybrid of professional and grass roots collaboration (Powell 1985). Attempts to evaluate outcomes associated with "pure" mutual help organizations have yielded generally positive results. Illustratively, parents confronted with the early death of a child who participated in a Compassionate Friends group exhibited less depression than those who did not (Videka-Sherman 1982a). Similarly, scoliosis peer support group membership yielded several positive psychosocial outcomes for the most severely disabled adults (Hinrichsen et al 1985). The absence of positive results for adolescent group members however, reinforces the need to be sensitive to person-by-environment interactions and avoid the assumption that participation will have uniformly positive results. The potential benefits to be derived from mutual help may be negated by the threat such groups pose for adolescents who seek a sense of identity and approval from their non-scoliotic peer group.

In those instances where professionals play a more active role in group design, leadership training, and/or assist in the running of groups, the research design may improve, although questions can be raised concerning whether such groups truly represent self-help (Powell 1985). One such issue relates to whether random assignment is equivalent to voluntary association and, if not, what implications this may have for results obtained. Such questions notwithstanding, Edmunson et al (1984) assigned recently discharged patients to a professionally supported mutual aid network featuring a wide variety of social and recreational activities in which emotional and instrumental support were exchanged. At ten month follow-up network members as opposed to controls required 50% fewer rehospitalizations, a one-third shorter average length of stay, and were half as likely to have required professional help. George & Gwyther (1985), working in a more preventive mode with at-risk caregivers for memory-impaired elderly, report similar results. In this case, group membership was associated with greater knowledge of Alzheimer's disease and more importantly, less loneliness.

Mutual help groups embody the themes of empowerment both in terms of process and goals. For this and other reasons, Rappaport (1985a) advocates that community researchers serve and build a constituency among the membership of these organizations. Future efforts to achieve that goal may be informed by the outcome of longitudinal collaboration underway between GROW, a mutual help organization for former mental patients, and researchers at the University of Illinois (Rappaport et al 1985). With the active cooperation of GROW leaders and members, a comprehensive research design is being used to examine process and outcome variables relating to social ties, symptoms, and competencies, as well as organizational development and dissemination issues. Participant observers using a continuous coding procedure during group sessions are collecting unique information not previously available about the basic nature of these groups and interactions among members. Preliminary analyses indicate that high percentages of helping behavior occur in groups consistent with GROW ideology. As Riessman's helper-therapy principle (1965) predicts, it is hypothesized that relationships will be found between help giving and positive outcomes. Evidence from groups as diverse as Weight Management (Wallston et al 1983) and Compassionate Friends (Videka-Sherman 1982b), indicate that more active members who both give as well as receive help achieve the best outcomes. This finding holds important implications for the design of a wide range of helping interventions.

The emerging strength and scope of the mutual help movement poses both an opportunity and a dilemma for the community researcher. Effective alliance with such grassroots efforts may strengthen their impact and broaden the base of support for mental health services. To do so requires an uncommon sharing of control and degree of collaboration. Also needed are research designs that respect the voluntaristic essence of the phenomenon being studied. Tampering in the name of training may also diminish the spontaneity and intimacy critical to such groups' functioning. Finally, pro-

fessional support for mutual help may have the unintended consequences of accelerating governmental cutbacks in mental health budgets (Pilisuk & Minkler 1985) and providing an excuse for "blaming the victim" (Ryan 1971).

BEHAVIORAL COMMUNITY PSYCHOLOGY

The term "behavioral community psychology" refers to the combination of the methodology of behaviorism— its utilization of objective, reliable measures and its careful investigation of functional relationships—with the conceptual framework and goals of community psychology (Jason & Glenwick 1984). Although some behavioral community interventions have targeted mental health outcomes (Klingman 1985), most seek to modify a wide range of personal and interpersonal behaviors whose connections to mental health are neither spelled out nor obviously relevant (e.g. increasing blood donations, Ferrari et al 1986; promoting recycling, Jacobs et al 1984). Behavioral community interventions include some of the best large-scale behavior change efforts (Greene & Neistat 1983) directed at community-level problems (e.g. increasing inoculation rates among preschoolers, Yokley & Glenwick 1984).

One serious problem with important mental health implications facing our planet is that more than a half billion people don't have adequate food. Reductions in the world population as well as more equitable and efficient distribution of food supplies are needed to resolve this issue (Willems & McIntire 1982). Limited efforts toward those goals by behavioral community psychologists have been directed at alleviating malnutrition. Guthrie et al (1982) rewarded Philippine mothers with lottery tickets for engaging in a variety of steps designed to insure adequate weight gain in their infants (e.g. supplementing breast milk adequately, planting green leafy vegetables near their home, etc). Although the program reduced the percent of malnourished infants, reactions among mothers were mixed because some had acquired many coupons but won nothing, whereas others had earned only a few coupons and won major prizes. Thus, an unintended but unfortunate consequence of this ingenious study was that the lottery actually reinforced learned helplessness in many mothers. When this procedure was replaced with a trading stamp approach, mothers' participation and enthusiasm increased.

Shortages in petroleum and energy supplies is another nonmental health problem that behavioral community psychologists have addressed imaginatively (Winkler & Winett 1982). Pavlovich & Greene (1984), for example, successfully trained boy scouts in step-by-step procedures for weatherizing homes. At the community level, Winett et al (1985) showed families a 20-minute home-based energy conservation television program that led to an 11% reduction in energy use. Shippee & Gregory (1982) gave small commercial-industrial firms newspaper publicity for participating in an energy conservation program; that feedback led to moderate reductions in natural gas usage.

Another area receiving increasing attention among behavioral community investigators is accidents, the number one cause of child morbidity and mortality in the United States (Rivara 1985, National Center for Health Statistics 1985). Examples of this work include Peterson & Mori's (1985) use of paraprofessional volunteers to train children in diverse safety responses (e.g. responding to fires, serious cuts, etc), and Tertinger et al's (1984) use of parent instructions, feedback, and demonstrations to decrease home hazards. Other behavioral community research teams have documented ways of reducing highway accidents, motivated by the shocking statistic that 2¼ million people are injured or killed in motor vehicle accidents each year. Thus, Van Houten & Nau (1983) found that the combination of signs (feedback), warning tickets, and informational feedback markedly reduced vehicular speeding (Van Houten et al 1985). Geller and colleagues have been effective in increasing the percentage of drivers wearing seat belts by using lottery tickets as reinforcers (Geller 1984, Rudd & Geller 1985) while Roberts & Turner (1986) increased use of safety restraints with children at day care centers. Geller's suggestion that buckle-up programs must be reintroduced intermittently over long time periods to produce enduring behavior change has been supported by data from Jonah & Grant (1985). Assessing the impact of higher order interventions (e.g. legislation) to improve child safety restraints is another effective strategy used by behavioral community psychologists (Fawcett et al 1986).

Other large-scale behavioral community interventions include Stunkard et al's (1985) and Elder et al's (1986) community-wide projects to reduce cardiovascular risk factors (hypertension, smoking, nutrition). Both projects attempted to maximize public participation by offering inexpensive behavioral technologies couched in local terms and modeled by key community members (Elder et al 1985). Jason et al (1986) distributed 50,000 behavioral self-help manuals concurrent with a 20-day behavioral smoking cessation program televised on the evening news of a major network-affiliated station. Adding biweekly support groups at worksites to accompany the media campaign doubled smoking quit rates of participants (41% vs 21%).

The behavioral community interventions reviewed have provided investigators a methodology for analyzing environments and evaluating program outcomes systematically (Glenwick & Jason 1980). It remains unclear, however, whether these programs can provide a more "ecologically" valid view of human behavior, i.e. one that studies environment-behavior relations over extended time periods, analyzes simultaneously sources of reinforcement, and recognizes that contingency control may not always be a productive way to view the influence of environment on behavior (Epling & Pierce 1983). Nor is it yet clear whether local-level agencies can effectively manage such programs or whether they can be widely disseminated (Kazdin 1980, Backer et al 1986). Interventions that are less expensive to maintain and less demanding of peoples' time have greater likelihood of being accepted and adopted. Unfortunately, at this time few behavioral community projects involve laypersons in program design or implementation; such involvements can lead to a stronger sense of "ownership" and thus more enduring changes (Jason & Glenwick 1984). Consultation with relevant policymakers in designing intervention techniques can also increase the application of research findings.

Behavioral community programs must consider carefully what values underlie an intervention. Failure to do so, as in the Guthrie et al (1982) study (cf above), may inadvertently damage the resiliency and coping of the target population (Fodor 1983). Put another way, the norms and traditions of the community and family must be considered carefully in planning behavioral community interventions; programs that undermine those values can produce long-term detrimental effects including loss of meaning, isolation, and alienation (Woolfolk & Richardson 1984).

Behavioral community psychologists as suggested in several prior program citations frequently target interventions toward lifestyle change. Many such behavioral patterns (e.g. smoking, alcohol and drug use, lack of exercise, accidents) now claim more lives in this country than infectious diseases (Lau et al 1980). Lifestyle factors now account for 43% of all deaths (Milsum 1980).

Increasingly health psychologists have also become interested in studying the social and psychological contributions to health and life-style patterns (Baum et al 1984, Rosen & Solomon 1985). Whereas behavioral community psychologists and health psychologists are both interested in life-style patterns, the former have been oriented more to prevention and large-scale interventions. Although health psychology has embraced several key concepts of community psychology (e.g. stress and coping, social support, and self-help), most of its programs and research are conducted within the framework of social and clinical psychology models, emphasizing individual differences and individual-level interventions (Albino 1983, Revenson 1985). It seems apparent, however, that a one-to-one treatment model will not be sufficient to improve the health of the general population let alone the health of undereducated, unemployed, and at-risk populations.

Some health-oriented psychologists have included prevention in an expanded conceptual framework at both the theoretical and intervention level. Space limitations permit only brief mention of several clusters of studies.

Interventions to prevent smoking and drug abuse, no less than delinquency prevention programs, must rely on more than the fear appeals used in many public health campaigns. The most effective approaches are embedded in an understanding of how, ecologically, target behaviors are acquired and maintained by people in general, particularly among high risk groups (Chassin & Presson 1985). Skill-building programs conducted without such information may be less than effective. Illustratively, teaching adolescents skills to refuse a drink or cigarette while at the same time not understanding that some adolescents seeking the approval of their peers may not wish to say "no" (Leventhal & Cleary 1980) can weaken an otherwise potent strategy.

With 1.1 million teenage pregnancies and over half a million births in the United States annually (National Center for Health Statistics 1983), leaders from all sectors, including minority communities, are searching for ways to prevent adolescent pregnancy. The psychological and health risk for many mothers and children in these circumstances are documented elsewhere (Chilman 1983). Successful recent efforts to modify contraceptive attitudes and behavior (Gerrard et al 1983) address one aspect of this national dilemma. A large-scale study by Hilton and her associates (1983), however, points to the important psychological and survival needs met in many cases by pregnancy, a recognition of which needs must form the foundation of any truly large-scale prevention effort in this arena. Moreover, as Levine (1985) points out, the nature of such programs belies the fact that the choice of which competencies (e.g. sex education, contraception, "saying no," etc) to promote both reflects and has implications for our values—in this case, that of privacy and our liberty to choose.

The downward trend for cardiovascular deaths in the United States since 1968 seems attributable to the American public engaging in preventive, health-protective practices. For example, from 1963 to 1975, butter consumption decreased 32%, animal fats and oils decreased by 57%, and cigarette consumption decreased by 22% (Arnold 1981). Most individuals who have initiated, completed, and maintained reductions in risk factors have done so on their own. Unfortunately, many health programs developed by psychologists have not succeeded in maintaining changes over long periods of time (Glasgow & Klesges 1985). Krantz et al (1985) posit two major obstacles in attempts by health psychologists to bring about lifestyle modification: (a) the fact that immediate rewards are more effective than delayed ones (i.e. the health threats posed by smoking are long-term whereas smoking frequently yields immediate gratification), and (b) that potent social and economic pressures strongly influence the adoption of unhealthy behaviors (e.g. peer pressure and advertisements that lead teenagers to smoke). Program effectiveness is also limited by the lack of knowledge about basic processes in health development and maintenance. For example, we do not know how such factors as age or duration of poor health habits relate to intervention outcome (Leventhal et al 1985).

Regulatory means, such as citizen-initiated change efforts to get government to protect at-risk families from toxic chemical dumps (Hess & Wandersman 1985) and to motivate lawmakers to pass laws to eliminate the production of unsafe products and foods (Laskin & Pilot 1982), have much potential for promoting health (Mechanic 1985). Illustratively, based upon the elasticity of demand for cigarettes, a 10% increase in cigarette prices will lead to a 4% decrease in consumption (Warner & Murt 1985). A fourfold increase in the 1982 excise tax of $.08 per pack could decrease teenage consumption by more than 50% and adult consumption by 15%. Although such strategies are both intriguing and hold promise for comprehensive health promotion programs, they require roles for which psychologists are unprepared. Negotiating with community leaders and politicians, mobilizing support for legislative initiatives, and introducing data-based studies into the political arena represent a few of the new roles which might need to be considered.

While behavioral community psychologists have made considerable progress in understanding how lifestyle practices are learned and maintained, only rarely have they involved community groups and public officials in the design and conduct of their interventions. Such collaboration can make the next generation of these SCIs more sensitive to local values and norms, more likely to produce enduring behavioral gains, and more capable of supporting higher order change.

DIVERSE CULTURES AND GROUPS

The study of different cultures and minority groups offers unique perspectives for understanding how mores, norms, and values affect patterns of adjustment and adaptive and nonadaptive responses to life stressors. Unfortunately, such studies, particularly those of empirically based SCIs focusing on minorities or special groups, have been underrepresented in the literature. Loo et al's (1986) analysis of published research in the community psychology journals revealed only 5% of the articles focused exclusively on ethnic minorities while such groups represent 20% of the U.S. population. Lefley (1984) described a successful program to sensitize professionals to stressors, support systems, and copying styles of minorities. After trainees returned to their agencies, minority use of services increased and significant reductions occurred in overall dropout rates.

Procidano & Glenwick (1985) described *Unitas,* an innovative ongoing intervention combining peer support and a "mentoring" model. Older teenagers and adults served as surrogate parents or mentors for high risk inner-city Hispanic youngsters. Groups of 10–15 youth were formed around each older mentor, creating a surrogate family providing nurturance, discipline, and a sense of belonging. Through regularly held meetings as well as informal interactions, "family" members discussed problems and generated alternatives. Program participation led to significant increases in social support satisfaction, an important finding in light of the high level of disorganization among the youngsters' natural families.

By the year 2030, people who are 65 or older will comprise 20% of the population; and approximately 86% of that age group, living in the community, will have one or more chronic diseases (Gatz 1985). Knight et al (1982) described an interdisciplinary effort to keep seniors from being institutionalized unnecessarily and to make mental health services more accessible to them. Consultation programs were established with agencies serving seniors, self-help groups were established, a minority task force for seniors was formed, and an additional bilingual staff person was hired. As a result of these comprehensive efforts, the percent of seniors seen in area outpatient clinics rose from 2% to 6.4%; simultaneously, the numbers of seniors in a local state hospital decreased.

Women in our society face unique social and psychological problems which need to be carefully analyzed in order to develop ecologically sound interventions. Rickel et al's (1984) recent volume describes a variety of empowering preventive and community strategies and interventions. As an example, Shure (1984) over a two-year period trained 40 black inner-city mothers in interpersonal problem-solving skills. The parents were able to improve problem-solving skills in their children in only three months, and improvements in behavior were observed by their teachers in school.

The articles reviewed sample only a few of the most promising SCI interventions increasingly being implemented with special populations. Other preventive interventions, reviewed in Gonzales et al (1983), indicate that barriers to working with such groups can be overcome. This is best accomplished when needs and interventions have been defined and articulated by the intended recipients of services.

RESEARCH

The design, implementation, evaluation, and dissemination of preventive SCIs often requires the use of flexible and nontraditional research designs. Price & Smith (1985) and Lorion (1983) present guides to many evaluation and design issues, the former including examples of a variety of quasi-experimental methods derived from the recent literature. Models being used include time series analyses (Steiner & Mark 1985), nonequivalent group designs, and social impact assessment (Meissen & Cipriani 1984) among others. Lawler et al (1985) challenge traditional research assumptions in their book based upon a unique conference on research which meets both conventional standards of theoretical excellence and practitioner standards of usefulness. Susskind & Klein (1985) present alternative methods for studying community phenomena from both qualitative and quantitative perspectives.

While there has been a recent proliferation of prevention demonstration projects, most such community interventions are targeted to persons and groups (Cowen 1983) and largely neglect the community or context in which they are embedded. Innovative interventions are essentially grafted onto existing social structures with limited attention to issues of process sufficient to secure permission and cooperation with program conduct. As a result, these SCIs are "in" but not "of" the community. To paraphrase Elias (1987), such interventions may be efficacious to a degree, but are rarely durable or enduring.

In contrast, the theoretical writings and interventions of Kelly, Trickett, and their associates (Kelly 1986a–c, Trickett et al 1985) reflect a steadfast commitment to social systems and person-environment issues consistent with the ideals of the Swampscott conference (Bennett et al 1966). Borrowing the concept of ecology from biology with its focus upon complex interactions among interdependent "community" members and structures, they have sought to develop a new paradigm for community assessment and intervention. The ecological paradigm informs us *how* to analyze and "take the environment into account" (Trickett 1984) and also restructures the nature of the relationship between subject and researcher. In contrast to the positivist's emphasis on keeping subjects uninformed (and thus presumably unbiased), the alternative contextualist approach attempts to integrate objective and subjective views of the environment and behavior. Subjects to a real degree thus become collaborators in the research process (Chavis et al 1983).

Recent descriptions of the emergent ecological paradigm (Kelly 1986a) provide concrete illustrations of how its principles can be applied to strengthen current research areas via attention to the *process* of research and the manner in which setting or situation variables support or undermine program goals (Trickett 1984, Trickett et al 1985). Case examples of preventive consultation guided by this research model are provided in a special issue of *Prevention in Human Services* (Kelly 1986b). The contribution by Roberts & Thorsheim (1986) illustrates well how the requirements of science and an ecological approach to conceptualizing problems and structuring solutions can be combined.

In a quest for universal interventions, investigations have often neglected setting and person variables and their interaction (Rolf 1985). Illustratively, the Jordan et al (1985) study (cf above) found positive follow-up effects for boys but not girls. Anecdotal evidence suggests this may be due to teacher discomfort with girls' increased curiosity and demands for participation.

Moos's (1984) attempt to combine context and coping in a unified conceptual framework suggests strategies to minimize such tensions between person- and environment-centered approaches. Intervention assessments that go beyond an exclusive focus on person-centered competencies to include person-environment transactions, though complex, hold much potential for illuminating change processes in preventive interventions.

Outcome assessments based on meta-analysis appeared in the SCI literature for the first time during this review period. That there are now (arguably) enough preventive interventions to make use of this technology is at one level a positive sign. Illustratively, effect sizes for consultation—representative of those obtained in other areas, e.g. primary prevention (Baker et al 1984), secondary prevention (Stein & Polyson 1984), social problem-solving training (Denham & Almeida 1987), and couple/family enrichment (Giblin et al 1985)—indicate that consultees and clients showed improvement greater than 71% and 66% of untreated comparison groups (Medway & Updyke 1985). These findings, while not overwhelming, are positive and encouraging.

Unfortunately, the availability of these data has led to inevitable, and we think inappropriate, comparisons with effect sizes from psychotherapy outcome research (Smith et al 1980). The latter are in some cases 50% or more larger. Such comparisons overlook the facts that: 1. psychotherapy is older and more established than the field of social and community intervention, 2. clinical groups may by their very nature have more room for improvement, and 3. direct treatment might be expected to have more impact than that mediated by a third party (Medway & Updyke 1985).

The ecological paradigm holds much promise for the design of more durable interventions. Its underlying values are consonant with those of empowerment and mutual help methodologies. Future interventions undertaken in the ecological spirit should describe advantages as well as strategies for overcoming dilemmas or limitations posed by the intimate involvement of setting inhabitants in the design, conduct, and evaluation of SCIs.

PUBLIC POLICY

Kiesler (1985) estimated that 15–35% of the population needs mental health services at any one time. In addition, contrary to popular opinion, the rate of psychiatric hospitalizations has been increasing in a linear fashion for the last 15 years. Despite the intent of deinstitutionalization, more patients are now treated in institutions than ever before if one includes nursing homes, which presently house about 350,000 mental patients (Shadish 1984). Even though evidence indicates more favorable outcomes for alternative treatment in the community, 70% of funds for mental health care are still directed to hospital treatment (Kiesler 1982). Other stark mental health epidemiological data reported by Zigler & Finn (1982) include these facts: 30% of children in the United States receive inadequate medical care; 2 out of 5 children are not immunized against childhood diseases, 500,000 children are adrift in the foster care system, 2000 children die yearly from abuse or neglect; and two million children age 7–13 come home after school to an empty home. Although 3.2 million children evidence major emotional problems, more than 90% will receive no treatment (Alpert 1985). Half of the seven million children with major learning problems will not receive any help.

Statistics such as these highlight the need for community psychologists to become involved at some level in public policy. The development of small effective pilot programs such as those reviewed in this chapter represents a first step, but one which is bound to prove inadequate if unaccompanied by efforts to accomplish change at a higher order system level. A special issue of the *American Journal of Community Psychology* devoted to training (Lorion & Stenmark 1984) includes several articles which examine historical reasons and current resistances to psychologist involvement in public policy matters. Levine (1981) argues convincingly for training psychologists with greater sophistication in the political process. Continuing to view ourselves as disinterested scientist-professionals *outside and apart from* the political and economic system will leave us ill prepared for the tasks of the future.

A look at that future can help social and community psychologists identify mental health related issues that are likely to soon require our attention. If the incidence and prevalence of mental health disorders is the same in 2005 as in 1980, the number of people with mental health disorders will increase from 33 million to 40 million (Kramer 1982). This extraordinary increase reflects the number of people who will be in age groups at high risk, as well as the prolonged duration of chronic diseases because of the successful application of techniques for lengthening the lives of affected individuals. Also forecast are increased numbers of dependent elderly, single-parent households, and households with a working mother. Sundberg (1985) suggests that a future involving high technology and high population density could produce information overload, increased unemployment, and a loss of privacy and autonomy. Future social and community interventions will need to deal with the mental health implications associated with these changes.

On a more positive note, the future might also be a time when traditions are rediscovered and revalued (Berkowitz 1982), when neighborhoods and neighboring take on new interest (Unger & Wandersman 1985b), and when new interactive communication modalities provide quicker access to emotional exchanges and a broader network of community participants (Turkat 1983). Such prospective trends also offer roles and opportunities for the design of SCIs.

Psychologists in the past have largely avoided participation in public policy matters. The concerns of the future may render such involvement on the

part of a significant subgroup far more essential. We seem nonetheless
uncertain about how or whether to prepare for the attendant new roles.

FINAL THOUGHTS

There are at least two standards against which progress in the loosely organized "field" of social and community interventions can be viewed. Seen in
relation to the limited reach and social impact of traditional mental health
services, considerable progress has been made in the decade and a half since
the first review of this area was undertaken (Cowen 1973). A wide variety of
prevention program models, targeted to groups numbering at times into the
thousands, now exist; these have demonstrated short, and in some cases
longer term effectiveness.

Measured in relation to the full complexity and magnitude of social problems many SCIs seek to address, or the ambitious agenda established at
Swampscott, progress has been understandably more modest. Creating or
modifying social systems—indeed, simply evaluating the long-term impact of
more limited interventions—requires longitudinal, programmatic commitment to settings and issues, plus levels of organization, both *intra* and
*inter*disciplinary cooperation, and resources difficult to secure, particularly in
the current economic and political era.

Needed for the next generation of SCIs are fewer individual and more
collective efforts designed in concert with the groups and communities we
seek to assist. Designing and conducting such programs with greater ecological sensitivity to issues of process and context will help insure that effective
interventions endure after initial results have been published. We are encouraged by signs that some steps in this direction are being taken.

ACKNOWLEDGMENTS

The assistance provided by many colleagues who shared their work with us
was much appreciated. We regret only that space limitations did not permit
the inclusion of more material. We gratefully and warmly acknowledge
constructive feedback received from Emory Cowen, Maurice Elias, Jim
Kelly, George Spivack, David Stenmark, Steve Walfish, Roger Weissberg,
and Richard Winett. This chapter is the better for their reviews. We also thank
Nita Desai, our typist, and Lynda Scalf-McIver, who aided in the search for
materials. Their patience, competence, and good humor helped enormously.
Finally, we thank the Department of Psychology at the University of South
Florida and De Paul University and the Florida Mental Health Institute
through Hewitt B. ("Rusty") Clark for their support.

Literature Cited

Albino, J. 1983. Health psychology and primary prevention: National allies. See Felner et al 1983b, pp. 221–33

Alpert, J. L. 1985. Change within a profession: Change, future, prevention, and school psychology. *Am. Psychol.* 40:1112–1121

Altman, I. 1987. Community psychology 20 years later: Still another crisis in psychology? *Am. J. Community Psychol.* In press

Arnold, C. B. 1981. Clinical strategies for chronic disease prevention. In *Advances in Diseases Prevention,* ed. C. B. Arnold, L. H. Kuller, M. R. Greenlick, 1:1–28. New York: Springer. 306 pp.

Backer, T. E., Liberman, R. P., Kuehnel, T. G. 1986. Dissemination and adoption of innovative psychosocial interventions. *J. Consult. Clin. Psychol.* 54:111–18

Baker, S. B., Swisher, J. D., Nadenichek, P. E., Popowicz, C. L. 1984. Measured effects of primary prevention strategies. *Pers. Guid. J.* 62:459–63

Barocas, R., Seifer, R., Sameroff, A. J. 1985. Defining environmental risk: Multiple dimensions of psychological vulnerability. *Am. J. Community Psychol.* 13:433–47

Baum, A., Singer, J. E., Taylor, S. E., eds. 1984. *Handbook of Psychology and Health: Social Psychological Aspects of Health,* Vol. 24. Hillsdale, NJ: Erlbaum. 376 pp.

Bennett, C. C., Anderson, L. S., Cooper, S., Hassol, L., Klein, D. C., Rosenblum, G., eds. 1966. *Community Psychology: A Report of the Boston Conference on the Education of Psychologists for Community Mental Health.* Boston: Boston Univ. Press

Berkowitz, W. R. 1982. *Community Impact: Creating Grassroots Change in Hard Times.* Cambridge, MA: Schenkman. 297 pp.

Berrueta-Clement, J. R., Schweinhart, L. J., Barnett, M. W., Epstein, A. S., Weikart, D. P. 1984. *Changed Lives: The Effects of the Perry Preschool Program on Youths through Age 19.* Ypsilanti, MI: High/Scope Educ. Res. Found.

Bloom, B. L. 1984. Community mental health training. *Am. J. Community Psychol.* 12:217–26

Bloom, B. 1985. *Primary prevention: An overview.* Presented at Ann. Meet. Am. Psychiatric Assoc., Dallas

Bloom, B. L. 1985. *Stressful life event theory and research: Implications for primary prevention.* DHHS Publ. (ADM) 85–1385. Washington, DC: GPO. 110 pp.

Bloom, B. L., Hodges, W. F., Kern, M. B., McFaddin, S. C. 1985. A prevention program for the newly separated: Final evaluations. *Am. J. Orthopsychiatry* 55:9–26

Bower, E. 1977. Mythologies, realities, and possibilities. In *Primary Prevention of Psychopathology,* Vol. 1: *The Issues,* ed. G. W. Albee, J. M. Joffe, pp. 18–41. Hanover, NH: Univ. Press New Engl.

Bowers, C. A., Gesten, E. L. 1986. Social support as a buffer of anxiety: An experimental analogue. *Am. J. Community Psychol.* 14:447–51

Brownell, A., Shumaker, S. A. 1984a. Social support: An introduction to a complex phenomenon. *J. Soc. Issues* 40:1–9

Brownell, A., Shumaker, S. A., eds. 1984b. Social support: New directions in theory, research, and intervention. Part I: Theory and research. *J. Soc. Issues* 40:1–144

Buckner, J. C., Trickett, E. J., Corse, S. J. 1985. *Primary prevention in mental health: An annotated bibliography.* DHHS Publ. (ADM) 85–1405. Washington, DC: GPO. 425 pp.

Chassin, L. A., Presson, C. C., Sherman, S. J. 1985. Stepping backward in order to step forward: An acquisition-oriented approach to primary prevention. *J. Consult. Clin. Psychol.* 53:612–22

Chavis, D. M., Stucky, P. E., Wandersman, A. 1983. Returning basic research to the community: A relationship between scientist and citizen. *Am. Psychol.* 38:424–34

Chilman, C. 1983. *Adolescent Sexuality in a Changing American Society.* New York: Wiley

Cohen, S., McKay, G. 1984. Social support, stress, and the buffering hypothesis: A theoretical analysis. See Baum et al 1984, pp. 253–67

Cohen, S., Syme, L., eds. 1985. *Social Support and Health.* New York: Academic. 390 pp.

Cohen, S., Wills, T. A. 1985. Stress, social support, and the buffering hypothesis. *Psychol. Bull.* 98:310–57

Consortium for Longitudinal Studies. 1983. *As the Twig is Bent: Lasting Effects of Preschool Programs.* Hillsdale, NJ: Erlbaum

Cowen, E. L. 1973. Social and community interventions. *Ann. Rev. Psychol.* 24:423–72

Cowen, E. L., ed. 1982. Special issue: Research in primary prevention in mental health. *Am. J. Community Psychol.* 10:239–367

Cowen, E. L. 1983. Primary prevention in mental health: Past, present, and future. See Felner et al 1983b, pp. 11–30

Cowen, E. L. 1985. Person-centered approaches to primary prevention in mental health: Situation-focused and competence enhancement. *Am. J. Community Psychol.* 13:31–48

454   GESTEN & JASON

Danish, S. J., Galambos, N. L., Laquatra, I. 1983. Life development intervention: Skill training for personal competence. See Felner et al 1983b, pp. 49–61

Denham, S. A., Almeida, M. C. 1987. Children's social problem-solving skills, behavioral adjustment, and interventions: A meta-analysis evaluating theory and practice. *J. Appl. Dev. Psychol.* In press

Depue, R. A., Monroe, S. M. 1986. Conceptualization and measurement of human disorder in life stress research: The problem of chronic disturbance. *Psychol. Bull.* 99:36–51

Dohrenwend, B. S. 1978. Social stress and community psychology. *Am. J. Community Psychol.* 6:1–15

Dohrenwend, B. S., Dohrenwend, B. P., Dodson, M., Shrout, P. E. 1984. Symptoms, hassles, social supports, and life events: Problem of confounded measures. *J. Abnorm. Psychol.* 93:222–30

Dunkel-Schetter, C. 1984. Social support and cancer. Findings based on patient interviews and their implications. *J. Soc. Issues* 40:77–98

Durlak, J. A. 1983. Social problem-solving as a primary prevention strategy. See Felner et al 1983b, pp. 31–48

Edelstein, B. A., Michelson, L., eds. 1986. *Handbook of Prevention.* New York: Plenum. 383 pp.

Edmunson, E., Bedell, J. R., Gordon, R. 1984. See Gartner & Riessman 1984, pp. 195–204

Elder, J. P., Howell, M. F., Lasater, T. M., Wells, B. L., Carleton, R. A. 1985. Applications of behavior modification to community health education: The case of heart disease prevention. *Health Educ. Q.* 12:151–68

Elder, J. P., McGraw, S. A., Abrams, D. B., Ferreira, A., Lasater, T. M., et al. 1986. Organizational and community approaches to community-wide prevention of heart disease: the first two years of the Pawtucket heart health program. *Prev. Med.* 15:107–17

Elias, M. 1987. Considerations in establishing durable, efficacious prevention programs. *Am. J. Community Psychol.* In press

Elias, M. J., Gara, M., Ubriaco, M., Rothbaum, P. A., Clabby, J. F., Schuyler, T. 1986. Impact of a preventive social problem solving intervention on children's coping with middle-school stressors. *Am. J. Community Psychol.* 14:259–76

Epling, W. F., Pierce, W. D. 1983. Applied behavior analysis: New directions from the laboratory. *Behav. Anal.* 6:27–37

Farquhar, J. W., Fortman, S. P., Maccoby, N. et al 1985. The Stanford five-city project: Design and methods. *Am. J. Epidemiol.* 63:171–82

Fawcett, S. B., Seekins, T., Cohen, S., Elder, J., Jason, L. A., et al. 1986. *Child passenger legislation evaluation project.* Unpublished

Fawcett, S. B., Seekins, T., Whang, P. L., Muiu, C., Suarez de Balcazar, Y. 1984. Creating and using social technologies for community empowerment. See Rappaport et al 1984, pp. 145–71

Feis, C. L., Simons, C. 1985. Training preschool children in interpersonal cognitive problem-solving skills: A replication. *Prev. Hum. Serv.* 4:59–70

Felner, R. D. 1985. Prevention. *Community Psychol.* 19:30–34

Felner, R. D., Farber, S. S., Primavera, J. 1983a. Transition and stressful events: A model for primary prevention. See Felner et al 1983b, pp. 199–215

Felner, R. D., Ginter, M., Primavera, J. 1982. Primary prevention during school transitions: Social support and environmental structure. *Am. J. Community Psychol.* 10:277–90

Felner, R. D., Jason, L. A., Moritsugu, J. N., Farber, S. S. 1983b. *Preventive Psychology: Theory, Research and Practice.* New York: Pergamon. 341 pp.

Ferrari, J. R., Barone, R. C., Jason, L. A., Rose, T. 1986. The use of incentives to increase blood donations. *J. Soc. Psychol.* 125:791–93

Fiore, J., Coppel, D. B., Becker, J., Cox, G. B. 1986. Social support as a multifaceted concept: Examination of important dimensions for adjustment. *Am. J. Community Psychol.* 14:93–111

Fodor, I. E. 1983. Behavior therapy for the overweight woman: A time for reappraisal. See Rosenbaum et al 1983, pp. 378–94

Gartner, A., Riessman, F., eds. 1984. *The Self-Help Revolution.* New York: Hum. Sci. Press. 266 pp.

Gatz, M. 1985. *Prevention and aging: Community programs.* Presented at the NMHA commission on the prevention of mental and emotional disability. Alexandria, VA

Geller, E. S. 1984. A delayed reward strategy for large-scale motivation of safety belt use: A test of long-term impact. *Accident Anal. Prev.* 16:457–63

George, L. K., Gwyther, L. P. 1985. *Support groups for caregivers of memory impaired elderly: Easing caregiver burden.* Presented at Ann. Vermont Conf. Primary Prev., Burlington, VT

Gerrard, M., McCann, L., Fortini, M. E. 1983. Prevention of unwanted pregnancy. *Am. J. Community Psychol.* 11:153–68

Gesten, E. L., Rains, M. H., Rapkin, B. D., Weissberg, R. P., Flores de Apodaca, R., et al. 1982. Training children in social problem-solving competencies: A first and second look. *Am. J. Community Psychol.* 10:95–115

Giblin, P., Sprenkle, D. H., Sheehan, R. 1985. Enrichment outcome research: A meta-analysis of premarital, marital, and family interventions. *J. Marital Fam. Ther.* 11:257–71

Glasgow, R. E., Klesges, R. C. 1985. Smoking intervention programs in the workplace. In *Health consequences of smoking, cancer and chronic lung disease in the workplace.* A report of the Surgeon General, US Dept. of Health and Human Services, Public Health Services, Off. Smoking and Health. Rockville, MD

Glenwick, D. S., Jason, L. A., eds. 1980. *Behavioral Community Psychology: Progress and Prospects.* New York: Praeger

Glidewell, J. C. 1986. *Psychosocial empowerment in community action.* Vanderbilt Univ. Unpublished

Gonzales, L. R., Hays, R. B., Bond, M. A., Kelly, J. G. 1983. Community mental health. In *The Clinical Psychology Handbook,* ed. M. Hersen, A. E. Kazdin, A. S. Bellack, pp. 735–58. New York: Pergamon

Goodman, S. H. 1984a. Children of disturbed parents: The interface between research and intervention. *Am. J. Community Psychol.* 12:663–87

Goodman, S. H. 1984b. Children of disturbed parents: A research based model for intervention. In *Intervention with Psychiatrically Disabled Parents and their Young Children,* ed. B. Cohler, J. Musick, pp. 33–51. San Francisco: Jossey-Bass

Gottlieb, B. 1983. Social support as a focus for integrative research in psychology. *Am. Psychol.* 38:278–87

Gottlieb, B. 1987. Using social support to protect and promote health. *J. Primary Prev.* In press

Greene, B. F., Neistat, M. D. 1983. Behavior analysis in consumer affairs: Encouraging dental professionals to provide consumers with shielding from unnecessary x-ray exposure. *J. Appl. Behav. Anal.* 16:13–27

Guerney, B. G. 1987. Family relationship enhancement: A skill training approach. In *Families in Transition: Primary Prevention Programs that Work,* eds. L. Bond, B. Wagner. Beverly Hills, CA: Sage. In press

Guerney, L. F. 1985. *Phone friend child helpline: A community primary prevention service.* Presented at Ann. Vermont Conf. Primary Prev., Burlington, VT

Guthrie, G. M., Guthrie, H. A., Fernandez, T. L., Estrora, N. D. 1982. Cultural influences and reinforcement strategies. *Behav. Ther.* 13:624–37

Harvey, M. R. 1985. *Exemplary rape crisis programs: A cross-site analysis and case studies.* DHHS Publ. (ADM) 85–1423. Washington, DC: GPO. 195 pp.

Hattie, J. A., Sharpley, C. F., Rogers, H. J. 1984. Comparative effectiveness of professional and paraprofessional helpers. *Psychol. Bull.* 95:534–41

Heller, K. ed. 1986. Special Series: Disaggregating the process of social support. *J. Consult. Clin. Psychol.* 54:415–70

Henninger, D. G., Nelson, G. 1984. Evaluation of a social support program for young unwed mothers. *J. Primary Prev.* 5:3–16

Hess, R. E., Wandersman, A. 1985. What can we learn from Love Canal? A conversation with Lois Gibbs and Richard Valensky. In *Beyond the Individual: Environmental Approaches to Prevention,* ed. A. Wandersman, R. Hess, pp. 111–23. New York: Haworth. 211 pp.

Hilton, I., Abrons, P., Dye-Holmes, T., Fishler-Hedgepeth, P., Kunkes, C. 1983. *Teenage pregnancy: Causes, effects, and alternatives—implications for social policy.* Presented at 91st Ann. Meet. Am. Psychol. Assoc., Anaheim

Hinrichsen, G. A., Revenson, T. A., Shinn, M. 1985. Does self-help help? An empirical investigation of scoliosis peer support groups. *J. Soc. Issues* 41:65–87

Hobbs, N., Dokecki, P. R., Hoover-Dempsey, K. V., Moroney, R. M., Shayne, M. W., Weeks, K. H. 1984. *Strengthening Families.* San Francisco: Jossey-Bass. 365 pp.

Hollister, W. G. 1982. Fiscal myopia or constituency building. *J. Primary Prev.* 3:3–5

House, J. S. 1981. *Work, Stress, and Social Support.* Reading, MA: Addison-Wesley

Jacobs, H. E., Bailey, J. S., Crews, J. I. 1984. Development and analysis of a community-based resource recovery program. *J. Appl. Behav. Anal.* 17:127–45

Jason, L. A., Glenwick, D. S. 1984. Behavioral community psychology: A review of recent research and applications. In *Progress in Behavior Modification,* Vol. 18, ed. M. Hersen, R. M. Eisler, P. M. Miller. New York: Academic. 277 pp.

Jason, L. A., Gruder, C. L., Martino, S., Flay, B. R., Warnecke, R., Thomas, N. 1986. Worksite group meetings and the effectiveness of a televised smoking cessation intervention. *Am. J. Community Psychol.* In press

Joffe, J. M. 1982. Let a thousand flowers bloom? *J. Primary Prev.* 3:52–55

Joffe, J. M., Albee, G. W., Kelly, L. D., eds.

1984. *Readings in Primary Prevention of Psychopathology*. Hanover, NH: Univ. Press. New Engl. 493 pp.

Johnson, D. L., Breckenridge, J. N. 1982. The Houston parent-child development center and the primary prevention of behavior problems in young children. *Am. J. Community Psychol.* 10:305–16

Johnson, D. L., Walker, T. 1985. *The primary prevention of behavior problems in Mexican-American children*. Presented at Soc. Res. Child Dev., Toronto

Joint Commission on Mental Illness. 1961. *Action for Mental Health*. New York: Basic Books

Jonah, B. A., Grant, B. A. 1985. Long-term effectiveness of selective traffic enforcement programs for increasing seat belt use. *J. Appl. Psychol.* 70:257–63

Jordan, T. J., Grallo, R., Deutsch, M., Deutsch, C. P. 1985. Long-term effects of early enrichment. A 20-year perspective on persistence and change. *Am. J. Community Psychol.* 13:393–416

Kazdin, A. E. 1980. Implications and obstacles for community extensions of behavioral techniques. See Glenwick & Jason 1980, pp. 465–70

Kelly, J. G. 1986a. Context and process: An ecological view of the interdependence of practice and research. *Am. J. Community Psychol.* 14: In press

Kelly, J. G. 1986b. An ecological paradigm: Defining mental health consultation as a preventive service. In *The Ecology of Prevention: Illustrating Mental Health Consultation*, *Prev. Hum. Serv.*, eds. J. G. Kelly, R. Hess. New York: Haworth. In press

Kelly, J. G. 1986c. Seven criteria when conducting community based prevention research: A research agenda and commentary. In *Community Based Prevention Research*, *Natl. Inst. Ment. Health*. Washington, DC: GPO

Kessler, M., Albee, G. W. 1975. Primary prevention. *Ann. Rev. Psychol.* 26:557–91

Kessler, M., Goldston, S., eds. 1986. *Decade of Progress in Primary Prevention*. Beverly Hills: Sage. In press

Kessler, R. C., Price, R. H., Wortman, C. B. 1985. Social factors in psychopathology: Stress, social support, and coping processes. *Ann. Rev. Psychol.* 36:531–72

Kiesler, C. A. 1982. Mental hospitals and alternative care. *Am. Psychol.* 27:349–60

Kiesler, C. A. 1985. Prevention and public policy. See Rosen & Solomon 1985, pp. 401–13

Klingman, A. 1985. Mass inoculation in a community. The effect of primary prevention of stress reactions. *Am. J. Community Psychol.* 13:323–32

Knight, B., Reinhart, R., Field, P. 1982.

Senior outreach services: A treatment-oriented outreach than in community mental health. *Gerontologist* 22:544–47

Kramer, M. 1982. The continuing challenge: The rising prevalence of mental disorders, associated chronic diseases, and disabling conditions. In *Public Mental Health*, ed. M. O. Wagenfeld, P. V. Lemkau, B. Justice, pp. 103–30. Beverly Hills: Sage

Krantz, D. S., Grunberg, N. E., Baum, A. 1985. Health psychology. *Ann. Rev. Psychol.* 36:349–83

Laskin, C. R., Pilot, L. J. 1982. Defective infant formula: The neo-mull-say-cho-free incident. In *Prevention in Human Services*, ed., H. A. Moss, R. Hess, C. Swift, pp. 97–106. New York: Haworth. 122 pp.

Lau, K., Kane, R., Berry, S., Ware, J., Roy, D. 1980. Channeling health: A review of the evaluation of televised health campaigns. *Health Educ. Q.* 7:56–89

Lawler, E. E., Mohrman, A. M., Mohrman, S. A., Ledford, G. E., Cummings, T. C., and Assoc., eds. 1985. *Doing Research that is Useful for Theory and Practice*. San Francisco: Jossey-Bass. 371 pp.

Lazar, I., Darlington, R. 1982. Lasting effects of early education: A report from the consortium for longitudinal studies. *Monogr. Soc. Res. Child Dev.* 47(2–3):1–151

Lefley, H. P. 1984. Cross-cultural training for mental health professionals: Effects on the delivery of services. *Hosp. Community Psychol.* 3:1227–29

Leventhal, H., Cleary, P. D. 1980. The smoking problem: A review of the research and theory in behavioral risk modification. *Psychol. Bull.* 88:370–405

Leventhal, H., Prohaska, T. R., Hirschman, R. S. 1985. Preventive health behavior across the life span. See Rosen & Solomon 1985, pp. 191–235

Levine, M. 1981. *The History and Politics of Community Mental Health*. New York: Oxford Univ. Press

Levine, M. 1985. A comment on the debate on primary prevention. *J. Primary Prev.* 5: 276–83

Liebenstein, N. 1981. *Social Problem-solving competence building in elementary school classrooms: A follow-up evaluation of three program years*. Univ. Rochester. Unpublished

Loo, C. M., Fong, K. T., Iwamsa, G. 1986. Ethnicity and cultural diversity: An analysis of work published in community psychology journals, 1965–1985. *Community Psychol.* 19:4

Lorion, R. P. 1983. Evaluating preventive interventions: Guidelines for the serious social change-agent. See Felner et al 1983b, pp. 251–68

Lorion, R. P., Stenmark, D. E., eds. 1984. Special Issue: Training in community psychology. *Am. J. Community Psychol.* 12: 133–259

Lyons-Ruth, K., Botein, S., Grunebaum, H. U. 1984. Reaching the hard-to-reach: Serving isolated and depressed mothers with infants in the community. See Goodman 1984b, pp. 95–122

Mannarino, A. P., Christy, M., Durlak, J. A., Magnussen, M. G. 1982. Evaluation of social competence training in the schools. *J. Sch. Psychol.* 20:11–19

Markman, H. J., Floyd, F., Stanley, S., Jamieson, K. 1986. A cognitive behavioral program for the prevention of marital and family distress: Issues in program development and delivery. In *Marital Interaction: Analysis and Modification*, ed. N. Jacobson, K. Hahlweg. New York: Guilford

Marlowe, H. A., Weinberg, R. B., eds. 1985. Is mental illness preventable? Pros and cons. *J. Primary Prev.* 5:207–312

Maton, K. I., Rappaport, J. 1984. Empowerment in a religious setting: A multivariate investigation. See Rappaport et al 1984, pp. 37–72

Mechanic, D. 1985. Health and behavior: Perspectives on risk prevention. See Rosen & Solomon 1985, pp. 6–17

Medway, F. J., Updyke, J. F. 1985. Meta-analysis of consultation outcome studies. *Am. J. Community Psychol.* 13:489–505

Meissen, G. J., Cipriani, J. A. 1984. Community psychology and social impact assessment: An action model. *Am. J. Community Psychol.* 12:369–86

Miller, G. A. 1969. Psychology as a means of promoting human welfare. *Am. Psychol.* 24:1063–1075

Milsum, J. H. 1980. Lifestyle changes for the whole person: Stimulation through health hazard appraisal. In *Behavioral Medicine: Changing Health Lifestyles*, ed. P. A. Davidson, S. M. Davidson, pp. 116–50. New York: Brunner/Mazel. 474 pp.

Mitchell, R. E., Billings, A. G., Moos, R. H. 1982. Social support and well-being: Implications for prevention programs. *J. Primary Prev.* 3:77–98

Moos, R. H. 1984. Context and coping: Toward a unifying conceptual framework. *Am. J. Community Psychol.* 12:1–36

Muñoz, R. F., ed. 1987. *Depression Prevention: Research Directions.* New York: Hemisphere. In press

Muñoz, R. F., Glish, M., Soo-Hoo, T., Robertson, J. 1982. The San Francisco mood survey project: Preliminary work toward the prevention of depression. *Am. J. Community Psychol.* 10:317–29

National Center for Health Statistics. 1985. *Persons Injured and Disability Days Due to Injuries: United States, 1980–81. Vital and Health Statistics.* Ser. 10, No. 149. DHHS Publ. (PHS) 85–1577. Public Health Service, Washington, DC

National Mental Health Association. 1986. *The Prevention of Mental-Emotional Disabilities.* Report of the National Mental Health Association Commission on the Prevention of Mental-Emotional Disabilities. Alexandria: NMHA. 42 pp.

Olds, D. L. 1984. *Final report: Prenatal/early infancy project.* Maternal and Child Health Research, NIMH. Washington, DC

Oritt, E. J., Paul, S. C., Behrman, J. A. 1985. The perceived support network inventory. *Am. J. Community Psychol.* 13:565–82

Pavlovich, M., Greene, B. F. 1984. A self-instructional manual for installing low-cost/no-cost weatherization material: Experimental validation with scouts. *J. Appl. Behav. Anal.* 17:105–9

Pedro-Carroll, J. L., Cowen, E. L. 1985. The children of divorce intervention program: An investigation of the efficacy of a school-based prevention program. *J. Consult. Clin. Psychol.* 53:603–11

Pedro-Carroll, J. L., Cowen, E. L., Hightower, A. D., Guare, J. C. 1986. Preventive intervention with latency-aged children of divorce: A replication study. *Am. J. Community Psychol.* 14:277–90

Peterson, L., Mori, L. 1985. Prevention of child injury: An overview of targets, methods, and tactics for psychologists. *J. Consult. Clin. Psychol.* 53:586–95

Pierson, D. E., Walker, D. K., Tivnan, T. 1984. A school-based program from infancy to kindergarten for children and their parents. *Pers. Guid. J.* 62:448–54

Pilisuk, M., Minkler, M. 1985. Social support: Economic and political considerations. *Soc. Policy* 15:6–11

Powell, T. J. 1985. Improving the effectiveness of self-help. *Soc. Policy* 16:22–29

Price, R. H., Smith, S. S. 1985. *A Guide to Evaluating Prevention Programs in Mental Health.* DHHS Publ. (ADM) 85–1365. Washington, DC: GPO. 135 pp.

Procidano, M. E., Glenwick, D. S. 1985. *Unitas: Evaluating a Prevention Program for Hispanic and Black Youth.* Bronx, NY: Hispanic Res. Cent. 80 pp.

Procidano, M. E., Heller, K. 1983. Measures of perceived social support from friends and family: Three validation studies. *Am. J. Community Psychol.* 11:1–24

Rappaport, J. 1981. In praise of paradox: A social policy of empowerment over prevention. *Am. J. Community Psychol.* 9:1–25

Rappaport, J. 1985a. *The death and resurrection of community mental health.* Presented at 93rd Ann. Meet. Am. Psychol. Assoc., Los Angeles

Rappaport, J. 1985b. The power of empowerment language. *Soc. Policy* 16:15–21

Rappaport, J., Davidson, W. S., Wilson, M. N., Mitchell, A. 1975. Alternatives to blaming the victim or the environment: Our places to stand have not moved the earth. *Am. Psychol.* 30:525–28

Rappaport, J., Seidman, E., Toro, P. A., McFadden, L. S., Reischl, T. M., et al. 1985. Collaborative research with a mutual help organization. *Soc. Policy* 15:12–24

Rappaport, J., Swift, C., Hess, R., eds. 1984. Studies in empowerment: Steps toward understanding and action. *Prev. Hum. Serv.* 3:1–230

Revenson, T. A. 1985. The alliance between community and health psychology: Through the looking glass, again. *Community Psychol.* 19:34–36

Richard, B. A., Dodge, K. A. 1982. Social maladjustment and problem-solving in school-aged children. *J. Consult. Clin. Psychol.* 50:226–33

Rickel, A. U., Gerrard, M., Iscoe, I., eds. 1984. *Social and Psychological Problems of Women: Prevention and Crisis Intervention.* Washington, DC: Hemisphere. 322 pp.

Riessman, F. 1965. The 'helper-therapy' principle. *Social Work* 10:27–32

Riessman, F. 1985. New dimensions in self-help. *Soc. Policy* 15:2–5

Rivara, F. P. 1985. Traumatic deaths of children in the United States: currently available prevention strategies. *Pediatrics* 75:456–62

Roberts, M. C., Peterson, L., eds. 1984. *Prevention of Problems in Childhood.* New York: Wiley. 450 pp.

Roberts, B. B., Thorsheim, H. I. 1986. A partnership approach to consultation: The process and results of a major primary prevention field experiment. See Kelly 1986b

Roberts, M. C., Turner, D. S. 1986. Rewarding parents for their children's use of safety seats. *J. Ped. Psychol.* 11:25–36

Rolf, J. E. 1985. Evolving adaptive theories and methods for prevention research with children. *J. Consult. Clin. Psychol.* 53:631–46

Rook, K. S. 1984a. *Loneliness, Social Support and Social Isolation.* Off. Prev., NIMH. Washington, DC: GPO

Rook, K. S. 1984b. The negative side of social interaction: Impact on psychological well-being. *J. Pers. Soc. Psychol.* 46:1097–1108

Rook, K. S., Dooley, D. 1985. Applying social support research: Theoretical problems and future directions. *J. Soc. Issues* 41:5–28

Rosen, J. C., Solomon, L. J., eds. 1985. *Pre-vention in Health Psychology.* Hanover, NH: Univ. Press New Engl. 441 pp.

Rosenbaum, M., Franks, C. M., Jaffe, Y., eds. 1983. *Perspective on Behavior Therapy in the Eighties.* New York: Springer. 464 pp.

Rosenberg, M. S., Reppucci, N. D. 1985. Primary prevention of child abuse. *J. Consult. Clin. Psychol.* 53:576–85

Roskin, M. 1982. Coping with life changes: A preventive social work approach. *Am. J. Community Psychol.* 10:331–40

Rubin, K. H., Daniels-Beirness, T., Bream, L. 1984. Social isolation and social problem-solving: A longitudinal study. *J. Consult. Clin. Psychol.* 52:17–25

Rudd, J. R., Geller, E. S. 1985. A university-based incentive program to increase safety belt use: Toward cost-effective institutionalization. *J. Appl. Behav. Anal.* 18:215–26

Ryan, W. 1971. *Blaming the Victim.* New York: Random House

Sandler, I. N., Barrera, M. 1984. Toward a multimethod approach to assessing the effects of social support. *Am. J. Community Psychol.* 12:37–52

Sarason, S. B. 1983. Community psychology and public policy: Missed opportunity. See Felner et al 1983b, pp. 245–50

Sarason, I. G., Sarason, B. R., eds. 1985. *Social Support: Theory, Research, and Application.* Boston: Martinus Nijhoff

Shadish, W. R. 1984. Policy research: Lessons from the implementation of deinstitutionalization. *Am. Psychol.* 39:725–38

Sharp, K. C. 1981. Impact of interpersonal problem-solving training on preschoolers' social competency. *J. Appl. Dev. Psychol.* 2:129–43

Shinn, M. B. 1987. Expanding community psychology's domain. *Am. J. Community Psychol.* In press

Shinn, M., Lehmann, S., Wong, N. W. 1984. Social interaction and social support. *J. Soc. Issues* 40:55–76

Shippee, G., Gregory, W. L. 1982. Public commitment and energy conservation. *Am. J. Community Psychol.* 10:81–93

Shumaker, S. A., Brownell, A., eds. 1985. Social support: New perspectives in theory, research, and intervention. Part II: Intervention and policy. *J. Soc. Issues* 41:1–171

Shure, M. B. 1984. Enhancing child-rearing skills in lower income women. See Rickel et al 1984, pp. 121–38

Shure, M. B. 1985. *Mass-targeted competence building approach to intervention with preadolescents.* Presented at Soc. Res. Child Dev., Toronto

Shure, M. B., Spivack, G. 1982. Interpersonal problem-solving in young children: A cognitive approach to prevention. *Am. J. Community Psychol.* 10:341–56

Slaikeu, K. A., Culler, R. 1985. Process and outcome in divorce mediation. *Mediation Q.* In press

Slaughter, D. T. 1983. Early intervention and its effects on maternal and child development. *Monogr. Soc. Res. Child Dev.* 48(4):1–83

Smith, M. L., Glass, G. V., Miller, T. I. 1980. *The Benefits of Psychotherapy.* Baltimore: Johns Hopkins Press

Spivack, G., Shure, M. B. 1974. *Social Adjustment of Young Children.* San Francisco: Jossey-Bass

Stein, D. M., Polyson, J. 1984. The Primary Mental Health Project reconsidered. *J. Consult. Clin. Psychol.* 52:940–45

Steiner, D. D., Mark, M. M. 1985. The impact of a community action group: An illustration of the potential of time series analysis for the study of community groups. *Am. J. Community Psychol.* 13:13–30

Stokes, J. P., Wilson, D. G. 1984. The Inventory of Socially Supportive Behaviors: Dimensionality, prediction, and gender differences. *Am. J. Community Psychol.* 12:53–69

Stolberg, A. L., Garrison, K. M. 1985. Evaluating a primary prevention program for children of divorce: The divorce adjustment project. *Am. J. Community Psychol.* 13:111–24

Stunkard, A. J., Felix, M. R., Cohen, R. Y. 1985. Mobilizing a community to promote health. The Pennsylvania County Health Improvement Program. See Rosen & Solomon 1985, pp. 143–90

Sundberg, N. D. 1985. The use of future studies in training for prevention and promotion in mental health. *J. Primary Prev.* 6:98–114

Susskind, E. C., Klein, D. C., eds. 1985. *Community Research: Methods, Paradigms, and Applications.* New York: Praeger. 523 pp.

Swift, C. 1984. Empowerment: An antidote for folly. *Prev. Hum. Serv.* 3:xi–xv

Swift, C. 1987. Preventing family violence: Family focused programs. In *Families in Transition: Primary Prevention Programs that Work,* eds. L. Bond, B. Wagner. Beverly Hills: Sage. In press

Tardy, C. H. 1985. Social support measurement. *Am. J. Community Psychol.* 13:187–202

Taylor, R. L., Lam, D. J., Roppel, C. E., Barter, J. J. 1984. Friends can be good medicine: An excursion into mental health promotion. *Community Ment. Health J.* 20:294–303

Tertinger, D. A., Greene, B. F., Lutzker, J.

R. 1984. Home safety: Development and validation of one component of an ecobehavioral treatment program for abused and neglected children. *J. Appl. Behav. Anal.* 7:159–74

Trickett, E. J. 1984. Toward a distinctive community psychology: An ecological metaphor for the conduct of community research and the nature of training. *Am. J. Community Psychol.* 12:261–80

Trickett, E. J., Kelly, J. G., Vincent, T. A. 1985. The spirit of ecological inquiry in community research. See Susskind & Klein 1985, pp. 283–333

Turkat, D. 1983. Cable television and psychology: Bringing peace to the planet. *Clin. Psychol.* 36:40–43

Unger, D. G., Wandersman, L. P. 1985a. Social support and adolescent mothers: Action research contributions to theory and application. *J. Soc. Issues.* 41:29–45

Unger, D. G., Wandersman, A. 1985b. The importance of neighbors: The social, cognitive, and affective components of neighboring. *Am. J. Community Psychol.* 13:139–69

Van Houten, R., Nau, P. A. 1983. Feedback interventions and driving speed: A parametric and comparative analysis. *J. Appl. Behav. Anal.* 16:253–81

Van Houten, R., Rolder, A., Nau, P. A., Friedman, R., Becker, M., et al. 1985. Large-scale reductions in speeding and accidents in Canada and Israel: A behavioral ecological perspective. *J. Appl. Behav. Anal.* 18:87–93

Vaux, A., Phillips, J., Holly, L., et al. 1986. The social support appraisals (SS-A) scale: Studies of reliability and validity. *Am. J. Community Psychol.* 14:195–220

Videka-Sherman, L. 1982a. Coping with the death of a child: A study over time. *Am. J. Orthopsychiatry* 52:688–98

Videka-Sherman, L. 1982b. Effects of participation in a self-help group for bereaved parents: Compassionate friends. *Prev. Hum. Serv.* 1:69–78

Wallerstein, J. S. 1983. Children of divorce: Stress and developmental tasks. In *Stress, Coping, and Development in Children,* ed. N. Garmezy, M. Rutter, pp. 265–302. New York: McGraw-Hill

Wallston, K. A., McMinn, M., Pleas, J., Katahn, M. 1983. The 'Helper-Therapy' principle applied to weight management specialists. *J. Community Psychol.* 11:58–66

Warner, K. E., Murt, H. A. 1985. Economic incentives and health behavior. See Rosen & Solomon 1985, pp. 236–74

Warren, N. J., Grew, R. S., Ilgen, E. R., Konanc, J. T., Van Bourgondien, M. E., et al. 1984. *Parenting after divorce: Preventive measures for divorcing families.* Synopsis of research prepared for NIMH Conf., "Children and Divorce," Washington, DC

Weissberg, R. P. 1985. Developing effective social problem-solving programs for the classroom. In *Peer Relationships and Social Skills in Childhood,* ed. B. Schneider, K. H. Rubin, J. Ledingham, 2:225–42. New York: Springer-Verlag

Weissberg, R. P., Gesten, E. L., Carnrike, C. L., Toro, P. A., Rapkin, B. D. et al. 1981. Social problem-solving skills training: A competence building intervention with second to fourth grade children. *Am. J. Community Psychol.* 9:411–23

Wellman, B. 1981. Applying network analysis to the study of support. In *Social Networks and Social Support,* ed. B. Gottlieb, pp. 97–115. Beverly Hills: Sage

Willems, E. P., McIntire, J. D. 1982. A review of preserving the environment: New strategies for behavior change. *Behav. Anal.* 5:191–97

Winett, R. A., Leckliter, I. N., Chinn, D. E., Stahl, B., Love, S. Q. 1985. Effects of television modeling on residential energy conservation. *J. Appl. Behav. Anal.* 18:33–44

Winkler, R. C., Winett, R. A. 1982. Behavioral interventions in resource conservation: A systems approach based on behavioral economics. *Am. Psychol.* 37:421–35

Woolfolk, R. L., Richardson, F. C. 1984. Behavior therapy and the ideology of modernity. *Am. Psychol.* 39:777–86

Wright, S., Cowen, E. L. 1985. The effects of peer teaching on student perceptions of class environment, adjustment, and academic performance. *Am. J. Community Psychol.* 13:417–31

Yokley, J. M., Glenwick, D. S. 1984. Increasing the immunization of preschool children: An evaluation of applied community interventions. *J. Appl. Behav. Anal.* 17:313–25

Zigler, E., Finn, M. 1982. A vision of child care in the 1980s. In *Facilitating Infant and Early Childhood Development,* ed. L. A. Bond, J. M. Joffe, pp. 443–65. Hanover, NH: Univ. Press New Engl. 576 pp.

Ann. Rev. Psychol. 1987. 38:461–89

SOCIAL MOTIVATION

Thane S. Pittman

Department of Psychology, Gettysburg College, Gettysburg, Pennsylvania 17325

Jack F. Heller

Department of Psychology, Franklin and Marshall College, Lancaster, Pennsylvania 17604

CONTENTS

INTRODUCTION

In the current climate of an emphasis on, if not an obsession with, the study of social cognition, it is easy for a reviewer of the research to wonder what ever happened to motivation. However, while interest in social motivation did wane in favor of an emphasis on cold cognition during the last decade and a half (Jones 1985), we see signs of renewed interest in some areas in linking motivational and cognitive processes. These interests have to do, in various ways, with a variety of perspectives on control motivation and on homeostatic and feedback aspects of motivation. First we review an area of research that

461

0066-4308/87/0201-0461$02.00

has grown steadily over the previous 15 years out of a classic view of motivation that emphasizes the role of inherent or intrinsic motives in human behavior, such as effectance, and the role of self-perceived motivation. We then review recent research on *when* the cognitive activity involved in making attributional analyses will be initiated, emphasizing a homeostatic version of control motivation and connecting that research with the literature on hypothesis testing. Finally, we discuss some of the recent interest in the study of affect, and how cognitive and affective views might be merged.

INTRINSIC AND EXTRINSIC MOTIVATIONAL ORIENTATIONS

An early issue faced by students of motivation was whether motives beyond those having to do with tissue deficits (e.g. hunger, thirst) needed to be specified. In contrast to the position that a satiated organism would have no reason to engage in action, the inclusion of additional internal motives or sources of impetus to behave was advocated. Woodworth (1958) argued that organisms not only could behave, they also needed or wanted to do so. This idea was developed by White (1959) in the form of effectance motivation, the desire to have effective interaction with and control over the external environment. On another dimension, the work of Harlow and his colleagues (1950) and Berlyne (1960) on curiosity suggested a need to seek stimulation in specific forms of sensory input acquired through exploration of the environment. Hunt (1965), citing a number of these and other examples of what came to be called intrinsic motives, put forward the idea of optimal levels of stimulation, a homeostatic view in which organisms seek to avoid both too much and too little stimulation in favor of their preferred nonzero level of stimulation.

These theoretical positions were in sharp contrast to Skinner's (1953) attempt to explain behavior without reference to internal motives, a view that placed control over behavior in the external environment. The intrinsic motivation position could be described as one that argued for control over behavior as the product of an interaction between an organism with a variety of internal or intrinsic needs, desires, and preferences in addition to drives produced by tissue deficits, and an external environment with contingencies that could shape or influence behavior. One can see that from this way of viewing behavior, the impetus for action could sometimes be seen as primarily internal or intrinsic, and sometimes primarily external or extrinsic. While theoreticians may argue over the logical status and tactical superiority of these positions, it became clear that individuals do embrace both of these kinds of explanations, sometimes explaining their behavior in internal or personally caused terms, and sometimes utilizing external causal explanations (Rotter 1966; Kelley 1967).

DeCharmes (1968), in his work on personal causation, pointed out that agents in the social environment, by the nature of their exertion of control over others and the kinds of external contingencies they established, could strongly affect whether persons viewed their behavior as internally or externally caused. This analysis set the stage for the recent work on intrinsic and extrinsic motivational orientations.

There are, of course, a large variety of activities that might be chosen for their ability to satisfy intrinsic motives such as curiosity, desire for stimulation, or effectance. Any of these activities might also, however, come to be engaged in under the control of external reinforcement contingencies. A particular activity can, therefore, be approached with either an intrinsic or an extrinsic motivational orientation (Pittman et al 1983). When an intrinsic motivational orientation is adopted, the satisfaction of internal desires is salient, the selection of activities is guided by their ability to satisfy motives such as curiosity and effectance, and the form of actual engagement in the activity will be guided by those motives. When an extrinsic motivational orientation is taken, the selection of activities will instead be guided or controlled by the nature of the contingency in effect, and the form of actual engagement in the activity will be guided by a focus on the external contingency. The research on intrinsic and extrinsic motivational orientations has focused on why a particular orientation is taken and on the kinds of behaviors associated with the two different orientations.

Reward-Produced Shifts in Motivational Orientation

Working in separate laboratories and from somewhat different theoretical perspectives, Deci (1971) and Lepper et al (1973) demonstrated what Lepper called the "overjustification effect." Beginning with an activity of high initial interest (solving puzzles or, for children, drawing pictures), these investigators found that the experience of engaging in the activity in order to obtain a reward (payment or a prize) decreased subsequent intrinsic motivation when compared with a no-reward control group; intrinsic motivation was operationally defined as the likelihood of choosing the activity in a free-choice period.

These were the first of what has become a very large number of studies demonstrating decreased intrinsic motivation following reward (see Deci 1975, Lepper & Greene 1978, and Deci & Ryan 1985, for reviews of much of this research). The basic explanation for this phenomenon has emphasized a shift in the subject's self-perceived motivation from intrinsic to extrinsic. An activity that was originally approached as an "end in itself" comes to be seen as a "means to an end" (Kruglanski 1975) after the experience of engaging in the activity in order to obtain a reward. As a result, the approach toward the activity shifts from an intrinsic motivational orientation, where features of the activity that satisfied intrinsic motives were paramount, to an extrinsic motivational orientation, where aquisition of contingent outcomes becomes the focus. Since in free-choice or leisure time periods no externally contingent rewards are available, a person viewing the activity as one that is extrinsically motivated or controlled would be unlikely to choose it. This analysis suggests that only when rewards are delivered in a way that would produce this shift in motivational orientation will subsequent decreases in intrinsic motivation be seen. Furthermore, any other kind of external constraint that would produce such a shift in motivational orientation should also produce decreases in subsequent intrinsic interest. These predictions have been upheld in studies varying the nature of the reward contingency and other kinds of extrinsic constraints such as deadlines, surveillance, and choice (Lepper et al 1973; Lepper & Greene 1975; Ross 1975; Amabile et al 1976; Karniol & Ross 1977; Swann & Pittman 1977; Zuckerman et al 1978; Reader & Dollinger 1982). Perhaps most convincing in this regard, when one activity is arbitrarily made to be the means to another, the "end" becomes more preferred than the "means" (Lepper et al 1982; Boggiano & Main 1986).

COGNITIVE EVALUATION THEORY   From the beginning of this line of research it was apparent that rewards did not always reduce subsequent intrinsic interest. Deci (1971) found, for example, that verbal reward or praise tended to increase rather than decrease intrinsic motivation. In proposing his *cognitive evaluation theory,* Deci (1975) pointed out that rewards serve two functions. The *informational* function conveys information to the person concerning competence; attainment of rewards often tells us that we have done well, enhancing feelings of competence and self-determination that are central to intrinsic motivational concerns. The *controlling* function makes salient to the person that his or her behavior has been influenced or shaped by the reward. To the extent that the informational properties of reward are most salient, the theory leads us to expect maintenance of or increases in intrinsic motivation; the intrinsic motivational orientation toward the activity should be maintained. To the extent that the controlling properties of reward are most salient, features of the contingency and the extrinsic reward rather than intrinsic motivational concerns are emphasized, and we should expect a shift to an extrinsic motivational orientation.

Cognitive evaluation theory thus emphasizes both cognitive changes in self-perceived motivation and the role of feelings of competence and self-determination as they are affected by informational feedback in making predictions about the subsequent nature of motivation. Many tests of these predictions have generally upheld cognitive evaluation theory. Controlling rewards and environmental constraints decrease subsequent intrinsic interest, and informational rewards or rewards accompanied by positive competence information maintain or increase interest (e.g. Pittman et al 1977, 1980; Enzle & Ross 1978; Boggiano & Ruble 1979; Boggiano et al 1982, 1985; Pallak et al 1982; Ryan 1982; Ryan et al 1983; Koestner et al 1984). Using this theoretical position as the analytic base, researchers have turned to studying other aspects of intrinsic and extrinsic motivational orientations and have been developing applications in several areas.

EXTRINSIC MOTIVATION AND THE SHIFT TO EXPEDIENCY   The studies reviewed so far focused on changes in free-choice behavior following an initial engagement with the target activity. Studies of performance while reward contingencies are still in effect have shown that the shift from an intrinsic to an extrinsic motivational orientation also changes the way in which the activity is approached, both during and after rewarded or otherwise externally constrained performance. McGraw's (1978) review of the reward and performance literature documents a number of cases in which the addition of reward interfered with creative problem solving. Some of these effects seem to be due to a decrease in cognitive flexibility when solving problems (McGraw & McCullers 1979). Other investigators have found that the introduction of extrinsic contingencies changes the nature of task engagement so that individuals shift their preferences toward simpler, more predictable forms of the activity while the reward contingencies are in effect (Shapira 1976; Harter 1978). This shift in preference for complexity has also been found to carry over into subsequent interactions with the activity (Pittman et al 1982).

These results are consistent with the assumptions inherent in the distinction between intrinsic and extrinsic motivational orientations. When approaching an activity with an intrinsic motivational orientation, features that might satisfy intrinsic motives, such as a challenging but not impossible level of difficulty or a level of complexity that contains some interesting surprises and novel or entertaining effects, would be desirable. On the other hand, when approaching an activity with an extrinsic motivational orientation, since the focus is on expedient extrinsic goal attainment, task features that would not interfere with progress such as predictability or a low level of difficulty would be desirable.

The adoption of an expedient task orientation when taking an extrinsic motivational orientation is clearly seen in Amabile's work on creativity. Using a consensual assessment procedure for measuring creativity (Amabile 1982a), she showed that a variety of inductions of an extrinsic orientation (e.g. reward, choice, set) lead to decreases in artistic and verbal creativity (Amabile 1982b, 1985; Amabile & Gitomer 1984; Amabile et al 1986) with both novice and expert and adult and child subjects.

CONTINGENCY, COMPETENCE, AND INTRINSIC MOTIVATION   The way in which extrinsic rewards are contingent on task engagement affects motivational orientation. In many of the studies previously cited, receipt of the offered reward was contingent only on task engagement, not on quality of performance. Under these circumstances, the reward has its controlling feature salient, with little or no competence information being conveyed, and decreases in intrinsic motivation are typically found. However, when the reward is contingent on performance so that its attainment implies competence, then informational features are present. In performance-contingent reward, then, subsequent intrinsic motivation depends on the relative balance of informational and controlling aspects of the reward. Several explicit studies of the nature of reward contingency yielded results consistent with this analysis (Boggiano & Ruble 1979; Boggiano et al 1982; Ryan 1982; Ryan et al 1983; Harackiewicz et al 1984). However, the complete relationship among feelings of competence, intrinsic motivation, and other aspects of reward in performance settings is considerably more complicated, as several recent studies indicate (Harackiewicz & Manderlink 1984; Manderlink & Harackiewicz 1984). For example, Harackiewicz and her colleagues (1985) presented data indicating that anticipation of evaluation is another important component of performance-contingent reward; they have also begun to establish some links between the intrinsic motivation literature and Bandura's (1982) theory of self-efficacy.

INTRINSIC AND EXTRINSIC MOTIVATIONAL ORIENTATIONS IN INTERPERSONAL RELATIONS   Interacting with another person is an activity that can be approached from either an intrinsic or an extrinsic motivational orientation (Pittman 1982). There are several studies in which the kinds of effects seen with inanimate activities have also been found in the context of interpersonal interaction. Garbarino (1975) found that cross-age primary-school tutoring sessions were degraded by the introduction of extrinsic reward. Paid tutors were more critical and demanding, and their students learned less than students of unpaid tutors. Seligman et al (1980) found that when couples had the rewards that are mediated by their partners made salient, they reported less love than when intrinsic concerns were emphasized. Kunda & Schwartz (1983) found that payment for a helpful act reduced subsequent feelings of moral obligation on that dimension of helping. Boggiano et al (1986) found that children's interest in continued interaction with a peer was enhanced when internal attributions for their initial interaction were encouraged. Pittman (1982) showed that subjects who had been paid for talking with each other talked less in a subsequent free-choice session that those who had not been paid. Together these results indicate that the intrinsic-extrinsic motivational orientation analysis can be employed to understand some interesting aspects of human interaction.

Understanding the erosion of intrinsic motivation in interpersonal relations is obviously important. Clark & Mills (1979; Mills & Clark 1982) distinguish between *communal relationships,* such as friendships, in which the participants could be seen as having primarily intrinsic motivational orientations toward each other, and *exchange relationships,* such as business interactions, in which the orientation is primarily extrinsic. Their data indicate that the norms developed for the exchange of benefits in these two kinds of relationships are quite different. In communal relationships, the kinds of immediate repayments for favors that are accepted in exchange relationships are disliked (Clark & Mills 1979), and people either in or anticipating being in communal relationships are less likely to keep track of their inputs in cooperative ventures (Clark 1984). Rempel et al (1985) reported that couples who trust each other also see their partners as primarily intrinsically motivated in the relationship. Together these data indicate that pursuit of the study of intrinsic motivation in close relationships may be productive.

CONTROL MOTIVATION AND COGNITIVE ACTIVITY

Homeostatic Processes

The homeostatic approach to motivation was clearly evident in early theories of animal learning that were concerned with how organisms interacted with the environment (learned) in order to satisfy certain biological needs (Hull 1943; Spence 1956). In the broadest sense, this approach attempted to define what conditions produced and directed behavior in ways that increased the organism's ability to survive. These self-regulation processes functioned through negative feedback mechanisms that acted to reduce the difference between some preferred internal state and the organism's current state. One of the distinguishing features of classic motivational approaches was a concern for the strong impetus-to-action that pushed other psychological processes— in fact, this motivational impetus was regarded as the *sine qua non* for specific behaviors; arousal of a given motivation energized and directed classes of behavior with known goals. Theorists that argued for a variety of intrinsic motives not connected to tissue deficits also had this homeostatic view (e.g. Hunt 1965); curiosity, for example, was assumed to vary as a function of sensory deprivation.

A number of direct descendants of these positions in social psychology have focused on socially relevant internal preferred states such as consistency (Festinger 1957; Heider 1958) and perceptions of freedom (Brehm 1966). These theories attempted to specify preconditions that arouse motivational states and direct the individual to act to restore a sort of cognitive homeostasis. Most such approaches associate specific motivational arousal states with particular cognitive and behavioral responses designed to restore the preferred internal conditions: the negative psychological tension caused by cognitive dissonance produces pressures for consistency, and the reactance produced by threats to freedom leads to efforts to restore freedom. While they differ in the specific goal state they address, these motivational states share the common theoretical function of directing interpersonal and intrapersonal processes in service of fundamental needs to maintain or restore some sort of psychological equilibrium.

Motivational Antecedents of Cognitive Activity

With the rise of attribution theory (Jones 1985), the focus of social psychological research shifted away from motivational issues in favor of exploring *what* attributions would be made given various sets of information. The issue of *when* or *whether* attributions would be made was largely bypassed by including instructions to make attributions in the experimental procedures. It is clear, however, both intuitively and from a variety of research findings (e.g. Kiesler et al 1969; Berscheid et al 1976; Pittman et al 1977; Enzle & Schopflocher 1978; Miller et al 1978; Bassili & Smith 1986) that we do not always engage in an attributional analysis of every available event. A motivational approach to this issue would ask the largely ignored question "Why do people make attributions?"

CONTROL MOTIVATION AND ATTRIBUTIONAL ACTIVITY   Inherent in the original formulations of attribution theory was the assumption that attributions were made in order to render the social world predictable and controllable (Heider 1958; Jones & Davis 1965; Kelley 1967). As we have already seen, the assumption of a general motive to have and exert control has been a common theme in motivational theory (e.g. White 1959), and in the form of competence concerns, has been identified as an important aspect of intrinsic and extrinsic motivational orientations.

Prior motivational state   One explanation for variation in the likelihood that individuals will engage in attributional analyses, then, is that control motivation varies from time to time, functioning in a homeostatic manner so that deprivation of control leads to increases in control-directed behavior such as the generation of attributional explanations for events. Pittman & Pittman (1980) tested this hypothesis by exposing subjects in one experiment to varying degrees of control deprivation and then observing the extent to which their attributions were affected by variations in an available information set in a second unrelated experiment. In general, subjects' attributions were more influenced by informational variations in the available stimulus information when they had previously been deprived of control. McCaul (1983) replicated these findings with the same attribution materials using naturally occurring variations in level of depression as the control deprivation manipulation.

These results are consistent with the assumption that the basic underlying motive for engaging in attributional analyses is control motivation, since increases in control motivation trigger generalized increases in the desire to engage in attributional analyses.

Control-deprived subjects also exhibit more curiosity about interaction partners when given an opportunity to obtain diagnostic information about them (Swann et al 1981). Further research using control deprivation pre-treatments indicates that control-deprived persons are subsequently more likely to make effortful (D'Agostino & Pittman 1982) and accurate attributional analyses, characterized by a careful information-processing style that can be described as relatively more data-driven, "bottom-up," or systematic than that employed by non-control-deprived baseline subjects (Pittman & D'Agostino 1985).

Characteristics of the stimulus information   One variable affecting the likelihood that an attributional analysis of available information will be made is the person's previously established level of control motivation at the time the information is encountered. A second source of change in control motivation lies in the information itself. Information containing stimuli that raise control concerns should be more likely to be subjected to careful and extensive analysis. Two sets of research findings fit with this expectation. Unexpected information has been shown to trigger attributional analysis (Pyszczynski & Greenberg 1981; Wong & Weiner 1981; Clary & Tesser 1983; Hastie 1984). Another set of studies indicates that unusually negative events, both for self and others, increase attributional analysis (Diener & Dweck 1978; Harvey et al 1980; Wong & Weiner 1981). Unexpected information and negative information are both obvious candidates for explanation by a control-motivated organism.

Personal involvement   A third source of control-motivated attributional activity is personal involvement or concern with outcomes, a topic Jones & Davis (1965) addressed in their treatment of hedonic relevance and attributions. Most of the data that are consistent with this argument come from research on the effects of expectations of future interaction. Expected future interaction has been shown to cause increased interest in and processing of information about an interaction partner (Berscheid et al 1976; Miller et al 1978; Elliott 1979; Harvey et al 1980; Monson et al 1982; Harkness et al 1985). Increased personal involvement in the issue involved in a communication has also been shown to instigate attributional processing (Heller 1972; Pittman et al 1977). When personal concerns about issues and outcomes are raised, we would also expect control-motivated information processing to increase.

Hypothesis Testing and the Issue of Accuracy

The research on control deprivation suggests that as the motivation to control increases, individuals increase the extent and care with which they process information. Such findings are consistent with the notion inherent in many cognitive perspectives that individuals seek information about the nature of the environment in service of a motivation to control (e.g. Kelley 1967; Fiske & Taylor 1984). A concern for control suggests a connection between motivational concerns and information-processing perspectives—people are motivated to control their outcomes, and increased attributional accuracy is one functional means of doing so. Presumably, the more accurate the understanding that individuals have of the causal nature of the world, the more effectively they can direct control efforts and reach their goals. Attribution theories have focused primarily on how individuals make causal inferences and have provided a number of useful models for moving from information about the environment and behavior to inferences about causality. Such theories, however, have been relatively silent on two important concomitants of a concern for control: How do such attributions or inferences relate to the actions of individuals, and how do attributions change once they have been made?

HYPOTHESIS-TESTING PROCESSES   Individuals' ability to control their outcomes should increase to the extent that they are able to treat an initial dispositional or causal attribution as a hypothesis and engage in additional activities that test the viability of the inference, since this should lead to a more accurate understanding of the social environment. If such socially directed actions produce additional information consistent with the hypothesis, then confidence should increase about where to direct efforts to control. New information that is inconsistent with a hypothesis should lead to reformulation and retesting of that hypothesis, again in the interest of accuracy.

However, the bulk of the early work done in this area by Snyder and others (e.g. Snyder 1980; Snyder & Gangestad 1981; Swann 1983) seems inconsistent with this functional view of hypothesis testing. By and large, that research suggested that an erroneous or inaccurate hypothesis, once formed, was not very likely to be disconfirmed. In fact, the hypothesis seemed to lead only to processing of information that was consistent with it, serving as something like a homeostatic set point in that it directed behavior and information gathering in ways that preserved the relevant hypotheses and reduced the likelihood of replacing it with a more accurate view. Quattrone (1982), in one of the few studies exploring the influence of attributions on subsequent behavior, showed that individuals with erroneously held hypotheses behaved as if they were true and acted in ways that elicited information consistent with the hypotheses. Once an initial hypothesis existed, subjects seemed firmly set on the path of finding only information that confirmed that initial hypothesis and of acting toward target subjects in ways that were consistent with the existing hypothesis. Snyder (1980) suggested that the consequence for the perceiver is a self-fulfilling prophecy because the hypothesis being "tested" directs the individual's actions in ways that are presumptive of the hypothesis and that tend to evoke behaviors consistent with the hypothesis.

These data imply that instead of hypothesis testing, individuals seem to engage in rather ubiquitous self-confirmatory processes and self-fulfilling behavior patterns. For example, Snyder et al (1977) had males talk on the telephone to females they had never met. When they believed the female was physically attractive, the males were friendlier and acted more interested in their conversation partners. As a result of the males' behavior, the females (regardless of actual physical attractiveness) were warmer and acted in ways that were more sociable and outgoing. The males' initial behavior created actions in the women that were consistent with their stereotyped views of attractive women. Other studies have demonstrated erroneous hypothesis confirmation through selective recognition of confirming information, question-asking strategies that erroneously confirmed personality types, behaviors that induced previously expected aggressiveness in others, teaching strategies that confirmed expectancies, and diagnostic efforts that biased clinical judgments (Snyder & Uranowitz 1978; Snyder & Swann 1978a,b; Arkes & Harkness 1980; Swann & Snyder 1980; Riggs & Cantor 1984).

In addition, more recent work suggests that similar self-confirming processes occur in testing hypotheses about others' and one's own ability (Snyder & White 1981; Darley & Gross 1983; Langer 1983). There is some suggestion that subjects will even refute disconfirming information if they are given the opportunity (Swann & Hill 1982), and that some hypotheses, even about oneself, are likely to persist even if existing supporting information is refuted (Anderson et al 1985; Lepper et al 1986). Thus, while Snyder (1984) suggests a few circumstances that might produce disconfirmation, one major position on hypothesis testing seems to be that interaction with the environment is for purposes of self-confirmation rather than for increased accuracy of information.

However, there are both commonsense and empirical reasons to believe that there are severe limits to such self-confirmatory processes. For example, it would simply be dysfunctional for individuals to guide their social actions entirely by initial hypotheses. Social actions based on erroneous inferences would eventually, in all likelihood, lead individuals to make serious and painful mistakes, mistakes that would clearly expose the inaccuracies in the initial impression of the situation. The extreme position on the self-confirming nature of initial hypotheses also implies an autism in social interactions and interpersonal communications that is typically not borne out by experience. For example, it is clear that individuals do change their attitudes, impressions, and values over time. People do not always continue to act without periodically reevaluating the social situations in which they seek to be effective. Such changes must come about by awareness of a mismatch between existing hypotheses or expectations and some aspect of experience. Perhaps most interesting from our perspective is that such strong commitment to initial hypotheses would be dysfunctional in individuals' efforts to control their outcomes. Effective control requires relative accuracy in persons' perceptions of the causal nature of the environment. We might reasonably expect that individuals seek information sufficient for their current control needs. In fact, the control deprivation literature reviewed above suggests that increased control motivation increases the care and accuracy of information processing.

A growing body of empirical research is certainly consistent with the notion that there are rather severe limits on self-confirmatory and self-fulfilling processes. Trope & Bassok (1982, 1983), for example, found no evidence that subjects used self-confirming information-gathering strategies. Their subjects showed strong and consistent efforts to ask diagnostic questions that provided the maximum discrimination between alternate hypotheses. Trope & Bassok suggest that the early hypothesis-testing studies that found confirmation biases did so because those subjects were not provided alternative hypotheses or information-gathering strategies. They argue that once such alternatives are available, subjects clearly prefer accuracy over simply confirmatory information.

Darley & Gross (1983) found that while subjects did engage in self-confirmatory processes, they resisted accepting any particular hypothesis until they had an opportunity to obtain some (admittedly ambiguous) information potentially relevant to the hypothesis being tested. Subjects appeared to need some information, however flawed, before confirming an initial hypothesis. Schul & Burnstein (1985) investigated the conditions that lead to changes in hypotheses and found that subjects would maintain an old impression until they were confronted with new information that clearly did not fit that impression. Interestingly, subjects would then process that information and add a new impression rather than replacing the old. Both of these studies suggest much more functionality to hypothesis-testing processes than earlier work implied.

Hilton & Darley (1985) investigated self-confirming processes and found that it was possible to eliminate any self-confirming effects by simply informing the target subject of the perceiver's expectations. To the extent that the target has any awareness of the perceiver's evaluation, these findings clearly suggest that disconfirmation is likely to be more typical than atypical in real-world situations. Erber & Fiske (1984) move fairly close to our own concerns when they suggest that subjects' motivation to control their outcomes might lead them to attend to and utilize disconfirming information to the extent that their own goals are mediated by the target individual. In their study, subjects who were dependent on the target for money attended to and utilized information that led to a change in their initial impression. Such results certainly fit with the evidence from control deprivation studies that increasing control motivation increases accuracy of information processing.

This last group of studies adds balance to the emerging view of hypothesis-testing and suggests an interpretation of its role in outcome control. It appears that subjects do not always seek and process information that might disconfirm their initial hypotheses. In the absence of alternative hypotheses to test (Trope & Bassok 1982, 1983) or incentives for accuracy (Erber & Fiske 1984), subjects will use a minimal information-gathering strategy, testing to see if there is *any* support for their hypothesis (e.g. Snyder & Campbell 1980). This strategy is functional to the extent that it requires little effort yet assures at least some correspondence between others' actual characteristics and the individual's belief about those others.

Although it does appear that individuals sometimes seek maximal information in the service of accuracy concerns, much of the existing data tends to be characterized by a hypothesis-testing strategy that Simon (1976) has labeled "satisficing," an approach in which individuals seek just sufficient information to meet the minimal demands of their current goal or need to take action. Maximum information is assumed to be too cognitively demanding and not necessary for acceptable levels of outcome control. In the experimental situations represented in the studies showing hypothesis confirmation, subjects have had a limited need to process information: they needed to do no more than find that the person before them did have the hypothesized trait to some modest degree. Note, also, that subjects do seek *some* information (Darley & Gross 1983). Subjects do as much processing as they must in order to maintain some minimal expectation of controlling what happens to them. As incentives increase or the task becomes more complex, they increase their processing activities accordingly. These increases reflect increased needs to control induced by the particular situation.

MOTIVATIONAL FEATURES OF HYPOTHESIS TESTING   In this chapter, we are arguing for a broader view of social motivation that would include phenomena such as hypothesis-testing processes. This view is based on a more functional approach to motivational processes. That is to say, if some psychological processes that have been viewed in cognitive terms serve the same purpose of activating and directing behavior as was previously relegated to the domain of motivational models, then we might do well to examine more closely the details of both processes.

The hypothesis-testing topic is a particularly good case in point because it has been viewed primarily as a cognitive process relatively devoid of motivational features. Consider, however, the distinguishing features of both motivation and hypothesis testing: both are negative feedback mechanisms that aid an individual to act on the environment so as to create a match between some internal standard and the external world. As Darley & Fazio (1980) point out, the self-fulfilling quality of hypothesis testing functions very much in this way. The hypothesis or expectancy that an individual holds serves as an internal reference value, and the individual acts to bring the environment (target's behavior) into a match with that internal standard. The unexpected persistence of some hypotheses suggests that they are, indeed, guiding behavior rather than simply being subjected to scrutiny. Individuals seem unwilling to replace these internal representations as long as they can find some viable support for them, and as long as no stronger incentives or alternative hypotheses motivate more careful information gathering. We suggest that viewing hypothesis testing as a control-related process and adding motivational features such as varying momentary levels of strength of control motivation may allow us to predict when optimizing or "satisficing" strategies will be employed.

DEVELOPING THEORIES OF AFFECT AND COGNITION

Affect: Heating Up Cold Cognition

While the predominant cognitive approach to studying hypothesis testing certainly has some control features similar to those of motivation theories, by itself the self-confirmation and self-fulfilling prophecy framework is decidedly "cold" compared to traditional views of motivation. It lacks any appropriate mechanism that would account for variability in the intensity or urgency of an individual's actions, the very characteristic that makes motivation "hot." While these cognitive processes clearly aid individuals in controlling their interpersonal outcomes, and while they may fit some of the critical features of homeostatic processes, they currently lack connection with the visceral drive mechanisms most often associated with motivational theories. We have suggested that the addition of control motivation is one remedy. Another way to heat up cold cognitive processes generally may lie in recent approaches to the study of affect.

Zajonc's (1980b) paper on affect has renewed both theoretical (Iran-Nejad et al 1984; Zajonc 1984) and empirical investigations into the role of affect. Along with concepts of a systems approach to control theory (see below), explication of an emerging view of affect provides some interesting new perspectives on social cognition and motivation. We have found a number of issues relevant to social motivation in this work, and we treat them in the context of two general questions: First, what distinction, if any, should be made between affect and cognition? Perhaps the most important thing to consider in this question is not whether each has a separate or independent epistemological status, but rather what the relationship among cognition and affect might be. Second, what is the relationship among motivation, affect, mood, and arousal? Current research has not been clear on the commonalities and distinctions among these phenomena.

AFFECT AND COGNITION: TWO SYSTEMS   Zajonc's (1980b) paper reintroduced affect as an important concern in social psychology. As he pointed out, affect was the major topic ignored by the cognitive revolution in social psychology. Zajonc's paper suggests that it might again be time to turn attention to a range of topics that were deemphasized in light of burgeoning interest in social cognition.

Zajonc (1980b) argued that there are two fundamental psychological systems largely independent of each other. Based on both physiological and behavioral considerations, his proposal included an affective system that reacted independently of and prior to cognitive reactions. Whatever the eventual outcome of the ensuing debate (Zajonc 1984; Lazarus 1984; Epstein 1984) over how reasonable these notions of independence and primacy may be, the treatment of affect has struck a responsive cord, and the research on affective topics is growing (e.g. Levenson & Gottman 1983; Chaiken & Yates 1985; Andersen & Williams 1985).

THE AFFECTIVE SYSTEM   One consequence of the growing interest in affect has been to raise questions about the specific "affective" topics that belonged in an affective system and about what the distinguishing characteristics of affect are. Motivation, affect, arousal, and mood all seemed to be candidates at one level or another for grouping within the "independent system" Zajonc suggested. Some researchers have treated affect within a primarily cognitive framework and have focused on how individuals process information about affect (e.g. Fiske 1981) or how mood states, sometimes defined in ways that are distinct from affect (Isen 1984), influence information processing. Such research (e.g. O'Malley & Davies 1984; Isen & Daubman 1984; Shaffer & Smith 1985) often fails to explicate the differences among variables like motivation, affect, arousal, and mood. However, it seems potentially quite useful to explain in detail the basic nature of these variables and their relationship to social motivation.

Buck's (1985) recent theoretical review of the relationship of motivation and emotion suggests one way to clarify the theoretical status of the above concepts and their ultimate relation to social behavior. Buck suggests that motivations and emotions are hierarchically ordered: biologically necessary, homeostatic motives are at a low level in the hierarchy, followed by acquired drives, and then by primary affects. Together with instincts, reflexes, and a generalized effectance or control motivation, these form the fundamental motivational systems. All of these systems are viewed as intrinsic to the nature of the nervous system, with their primary function being to guide the organism in manipulating its internal states and external environment in order to maximize control.

In accord with a number of other affect researchers (Izard 1977; Tomkins, 1981), Buck suggests that the primary affects include fear, anger, surprise, happiness, sadness, and disgust. These are also viewed as hard-wired neural systems with the potential for modification through learning. Emotions are viewed as subjective states that are functional in that they provide the individual a relatively direct "read-out" on the status of motivational systems. In addition, these emotional read-outs may be expressed socially and thus mediate social gratification of the underlying motivational states.

The critical aspect of this analysis is that it provides one justification for viewing affect, motivation, arousal, and mood as simply different levels of a single underlying hierarchy. Thus, rather than requiring separate formulations for the relation of each "affective state" to cognitive functions and social action, it becomes possible to begin by considering all such "affective states" to be different reflections of a larger affective/motivational system. When we consider the motivational system in the remainder of this review, therefore, we are speaking of it as the kind of multilevel hierarchy Buck has suggested. Specifically, we use the terms *affect* and *motivation* as largely interchangeable, and we explore some of the implications of treating the affective system as partially separate from the cognitive system.

Control Theory: A Cognitive Model of Homeostatic Processes

Perhaps one of the most theoretically interesting developments relevant to motivation has been Carver & Scheier's (1981, 1982) application of systems analysis to social-psychological topics. Carver & Scheier (1982) attempted to create a model of the cognitive mechanisms that guide individuals' attempts to control their outcomes and to gain desirable goal states. These authors focused attention on two of the distinguishing features of almost all motivational approaches mentioned earlier—their homeostatic nature and the role that negative feedback plays in maintaining that homeostasis.

Specification of these feedback processes made explicit some of the mechanisms that underlie individuals' efforts to control interactions in their social world and the source of their reactions when such control efforts fail. While control theory is certainly not a motivational theory, it does specify cognitive mechanisms that might well be common to a wide variety of phenomena regarded as fundamentally motivational, and it suggests how different motivational processes might relate to one another. The theory describes how individuals draw information from the environment, how that information is processed to initiate social behavior, and what mechanism controls the termination of the behavior taken.

The feedback component of control theory that accomplishes these functions is very similar to the TOTE (test-operate-test) model of Miller et al (1960). Operation of a basic "feedback unit" determines when action begins, the direction it takes, and the goal that must be achieved to terminate action. The process begins with *perception* of some feature of the environment. That perception is matched to some internal *reference value* that specifies the preferred or goal state of the individual. When this *comparator function* determines that a mismatch exists between the perceived state of the environment and the goal, *behavior* takes place to change the environment so that subsequent perception matches the reference value. Finally, *evaluation* occurs when the newly created environmental state reenters the feedback cycle for assessment. Action ceases when a match is created with the reference value. Thus, the feedback unit is the primary device by which individuals achieve and maintain both control of their environment and their internal states.

This basic feedback unit is functionally identical to the homeostatic mechanisms of classic motivational theories in that the cybernetic system functions to reduce discrepancies between some internal need state or standard and current environmental or experiential perceptions. The resulting view of self-regulatory processes is entirely consistent with early motivational theories such as dissonance (e.g. Festinger 1957; Aronson 1980), reactance (e.g. Brehm 1966; Wicklund 1974), equity (e.g. Walster et al 1978), and achievement theories (Heckhausen et al 1985).

Control theory may prove to be a useful feature of new motivational formulations because it addresses an important issue not typically considered. Carver & Scheier (1982) suggest that feedback units are hierarchically arranged. That is, the standard that guides behavior at one hierarchical level is the output of a higher level feedback unit. The hierarchical nature of this system provides greater flexibility and some insight into how the mechanisms controlling moment-to-moment actions of individuals are related to higher level goals and aspirations. Control theory specifies the linkage of specific actions both to interpersonal perceptions and to intrapersonal cognitive factors. An example of these hierarchical levels derives from some early concerns with cognitive dissonance theory. As we discuss below, this systems approach makes it possible to relate motivational and cognitive processes that had previously lacked any clear connections.

Consider the person induced to act in a way that is inconsistent with some internal standard (e.g. an existing attitude). As Aronson (1968) points out, there are several levels of analysis to consider. At one level, the cognitions such as "this is a dull task" and "I told someone it was interesting" (see Festinger & Carlsmith 1959) are, indeed, inconsistent and should lead to dissonance arousal. However, there is an implicit standard or "reference value" involved, namely one that specifies that a person *should* display consistency between beliefs and actions. From a control theory perspective, this "be consistent" standard is itself the output of a higher level feedback unit that deals with a more abstract specification of parameters relevant to lower levels in the control hierarchy. To break Aronson's analysis down further, this next higher level feedback unit might incorporate a more general reference value that specifies that one should "be rational/intelligent" in one's social actions. One specific output of this level happens to be the more narrow reference value for the next lower feedback unit, "be consistent." Finally, it seems entirely reasonable to assume that some fundamental conception of self such as, "I should be a good person" lies at the highest level of such a hierarchy. Thus, the analysis derived from control theory provides an important tool for conceptually linking specific cognitive outcomes to more abstract levels of cognition. In this example, it also suggests how the notion of self might explicitly link to a wide range of lower level cognitive processes. While other reviews in this volume focus on the self (Markus & Wurf 1987), it is worth briefly noting its impact on the feedback nature of social motivation.

While theoretical ideas about self have always been important in social speculation (James 1890; Cooley 1902; Mead 1934), recent approaches to the area have provided an empirical lever for the concept that promises a renewed emphasis on the nature and function of the self (e.g. Markus & Smith 1980; Jones & Pittman 1982; Kuiper et al 1983; Greenwald & Pratkanis 1984; Gangestad & Snyder 1985; Bannister 1985; Hale 1985). As others already have, we would argue that notions of self or selfhood are involved in most interpersonal action. Since we have taken the position that motivational processes underlie such actions, it seems reasonable that social motivation typically involves implicit or explicit functioning of the self (Markus & Zajonc 1985; Zajonc 1980a). The advantage of control theory as a partial framework for social motivational processes is that it suggests how abstract notions of self are ultimately connected to specific social behaviors. Understanding the mechanisms that create, change, and maintain self-perceptions should be a central concern for those interested in social motivation.

RESEARCH FINDINGS RELEVANT TO CONTROL THEORY   There are a number of recent studies that demonstrate the potential usefulness of control theory by either implicitly or explicitly relying on the notion of hierarchical structures. Most relevant are Steele & Liu's (1981, 1983) rather direct tests of the analysis of the self in dissonance situations presented above. Steele & Liu (1983) suggest that freely choosing to engage in counter-attitudinal activities constitutes a threat to a person's self-conception that he or she is intelligent, since intelligent people should not do inconsistent things. One indirect way to reaffirm that aspect of self is to make the lower level cognitions consistent, as specified in cognitive dissonance theory. However, another way is to reaffirm directly the higher level part of the self-concept that serves as the reference value for cognitive consistency. Steele & Liu found that when subjects were given a chance to reaffirm their self-concept, cognitive change toward consistency did not occur, presumably because satisfaction of the higher level reference value eliminated the need for a more specific kind of reaffirmation. Cooper & Fazio (1984) have suggested other hierarchical values relevant to the consequences of the act and evaluations of personal responsibility that may also function in free-choice situations.

Swann & Ely (1984) studied an interesting situation in which the tendency of perceivers to evoke confirming behaviors from targets was pitted against the targets' tendency to confirm their own self-concepts. Their findings suggest that the conflict between target's self-verification behaviors and perceiver's hypothesis confirmation tendencies will typically be resolved in favor of self-verification. Targets resisted acting to confirm perceiver's expectations when their view of some aspect of their self was at stake. Self-conceptions seemed to take hierarchical precedence over interpersonal processes. Frey & Ruble (1985) examined a different type of conflict and suggested that one important developmental problem relates to working through the hierarchical priorities of the conflicting goals of competence display and social harmony. In both cases, the concepts of control theory seem at least relevant and potentially useful for understanding the nature and outcome of conflicting tendencies within individuals.

The Relationship of Affective and Cognitive Systems

We have discussed examples of both the current interest in cognitive process and an emerging concern with the potential of a hypothesized affective system. With regard to cognition, control theory suggested a view of cognitive control consisting of hierarchical feedback units. With regard to affect, an affective system has been hypothesized that includes sources of motivation, affect, arousal, and mood, and that functions to energize behavior. We submit that these two systems, both sharing homeostatic and hierarchical properties, interact in ways that determine individuals' control-motivated efforts to direct social actions. However, while current trends in cognitive research and the revival of affective topics naturally turn our thoughts to how such systems might interact, the theoretical mechanism for that interaction is not clear from the nature of the separate positions.

Tomkins (1981) suggests that there are several primary sources of motivation for an organism, ranging from drives that satisfy biological necessities to affective responses such as anger, surprise, and happiness. Tomkins argues that affective responses function as basic motives in that they provide a component of urgency that increases the impetus-to-action of a wide variety of specific responses. This view of the role of affect and Buck's (1985) seem to be quite compatible.

Perhaps the most important aspect of Tomkins position for the current analysis is the connection that he proposes for affective responses and cognitive processes. He suggests that affective reactions "co-assemble" with cognitive systems and amplify their actions. Thus one way to view the interaction of affective and cognitive systems is that the former, under certain conditions, can join with and intensify the action of the latter. We suggest that there is a relatively nice fit between Tomkin's view of affect and the control mechanism described by control theory. Together they provide a more detailed explication of the hierarchical cognitive structure and the impetus-to-action feature of what has previously been viewed as a unitary psychological mechanism.

IMPLICATIONS OF THE CO-ASSEMBLY OF AFFECTIVE AND COGNITIVE PROCESSES   There are several interesting implications of viewing social behaviors as the combined result of two separate psychological systems. The first is a view of social motivation that is flexible and adaptive. Previous approaches to motivation have linked specific cognitive processes to the arousal of specific motivational states. For example, dissonance arousal led to inconsistency reduction and reactance arousal led to efforts to reestablish freedom. Such theories were very useful but also had somewhat limited boundary conditions that placed restrictions of their range of applicability. The notion that a variety of affective, motivational, and arousal reactions can join with and affect a variety of cognitive processes is appealing.

We would expect limits to this flexibility, just as Parkinson (1985) has suggested there are limits on certain misattribution processes. Simple contiguity between arousal and its source will often tend to tie sources of affect and particular cognitive processes together. As Buck (1985) points out, affect sometimes serves as a warning signal and also as a source of experiential readout so that affect and particular kinds of related cognitive processes that can accomplish the person's homeostatic goals will usually go together. Within these limits of flexibility, the possibility of coupling the impetus-to-action available in the kind of affective system suggested by Buck (1985) has the appeal of providing a way to "warm up" existing models of cold cognition without the need to alter our current understanding of the underlying cognitive mechanisms.

Another implication has to do with the ability indirectly to investigate the usefulness of a "two system" view of social motivation. For example, if there is some flexibility in the ability to join affective impetus-to-action to a variety of cognitive processes, then it should also be possible to "disconnect" that affect. Thus, there are two complementary ways to address empirically the relation of cognition and affect. The first is to examine research that has attempted to channel increases in affective levels into a specific cognitive mechanism and see if there is a resulting increase in cognitive activity. The second is to attempt to misdirect affect out of existing cognitive mechanisms and look for a decrease in the level of cognitive work done. The ability to manipulate cognitive processes in this way would provide a means to investigate the relationship of cognition and affect. If the cognitive processes investigated in this way were not normally seen as motivational in nature, then we would need to consider the activity of motivational influences on these cognitive phenomena.

RESEARCH FINDINGS ON SEPARATE SYSTEMS AND THEIR INTERACTION   A primary example of efforts to direct motivational arousal into existing cognitive processes is found in the control deprivation literature reviewed earlier. The studies reviewed clearly suggest that cognitive processing can be and is influenced by activation of motivational processes. An important aspect of those studies was the fact that manipulations of motivation occurred in a situation *independent* of the situation in which cognitive activity was investigated. The finding that such motivational manipulations affected a variety of different cognitive processes is consistent with the notion that some motivational processes are not tied to a particular cognitive mechanism but are somewhat flexible with regard to the cognitive processes that they can energize.

While the above studies suggest how motivation might be joined to and influence very different cognitive processes, there are a number of studies that attempt to uncouple motivation and arousal from some existing cognitive activities. Misattribution of arousal (Schachter & Singer 1962) to an irrelevant source has been the most typical procedure used to accomplish such uncoupling. The logic of such experiments is straightforward: If arousal is necessary to drive some psychological activity, misattribution of that arousal to an irrelevant source should alter the level of output of that cognitive process. Obtaining such decreases would suggest that there was some involvement of the affective system.

Several studies following the misattribution paradigm began with efforts to determine if there were arousal components to processes initiated by freedom of choice. While intended to apply to the dissonance/self-perception debate, the studies are directly relevant to the point under consideration. For example, Zanna & Cooper (1974) found that subjects provided with an alternative explanation for any arousal they were experiencing did not display the differences in final attitudes found when no such misattribution manipulation was used. Pittman (1975) demonstrated that dissonance arousal could be misattributed to another actual source of dissonance-irrelevant arousal, which also eliminated the usual attitude change effects; conversely, when irrelevant arousal was misattributed to the dissonance, the typical attitude change effects were magnified. Cooper et al (1978) later used a barbiturate to eliminate possible physiological arousal in a similar free-choice situation and found similar results—while control subjects evidenced final opinions affected by the choice manipulation, barbiturate subjects showed no such change. Most recently, Croyle & Cooper (1983) found physiological arousal in those free-choice conditions that led to differential attitudes and no arousal where attitudes were not influenced. A consistent interpretation of these results is that some activity of the affective system is necessary for certain attitude change processes to occur, and cognitive or physiological uncoupling of that arousal short-circuits the cognitive processes that normally take place.

In another area of research, Manucia et al (1984) applied a misattribution manipulation to experimental conditions designed to create a mood state that normally led to altruistic behavior. The misattribution manipulation produced a decrease in helping behavior, which suggests the involvement of the affective system described above. Uncoupling of arousal by a misattribution manipulation decreased helping and suggests that it might be useful to consider in more detail the role of the entire affective system in helping.

Pretty & Seligman (1984) report results in the area of intrinsic motivation that are consistent with this analysis. They suggested that negative affect generated by an extrinsic motivational orientation in overjustification experiments might be a basic mediator of the decrease in intrinsic motivation; they further found that, when positive affect was explicitly enhanced, the typical overjustification effect was eliminated. Boggiano & Hertel (1983) also reported data indicating that an intrinsic motivational orientation was associated with a relatively positive mood, while an extrinsic motivational orientation produced a relatively negative mood; again affect seems bound up with motivational orientations.

Thornton's (1984) analysis suggests that the attributional bias in defensive attributions of responsibility is based on control motivation. Typically, responsibility is overattributed to individuals suffering an accident when the nature of the accident arouses fear that a similar fate might befall the observer. In order to protect oneself from such fear, undue blame is attributed to the person suffering the accident. Such an attribution allows the observer to discount the possibility that he or she might suffer a similar fate. Thornton reasoned that if this attributional bias were indeed motivationally based, misattribution of the arousal might well reduce the attributional processes that produced the bias. Results did, in fact, show that the amount of responsibility assigned to the victim was decreased in conditions where any possible arousal would be attributed to an irrelevant source. Although the relationship between control motivation and attributional biases involves some complexities (Pittman & D'Agostino 1985), in this experiment, as in the previous ones, we can see that uncoupling arousal from cognitive processes reduces the amount of cognitive work done. It seems possible to couple and uncouple a variety of affective system sources of arousal with a wide variety of cognitive processes.

CONCLUSION

Historically, specific theories of social motivation have not seemed to capture very well the diversity and pervasiveness of the motivational phenomena that our personal experience assures us exist, perhaps because such theoretical positions tended to focus on a single motive that gave rise to a single psychological process. The resulting fragmentation made it difficult to conceive of unified intrapersonal processes and created theories of somewhat limited scope that either eventually ran out of questions (Jones 1985) or produced a great deal of research on relatively limited issues (e.g. reactance theory). We have tried to suggest in this review that several emerging trends suggest a reconceptualization of motivational processes in general and social motivation in particular. In overview, a hierarchically structured affective system has been hypothesized to serve as a source of potential impetus-to-action. Those affective processes are relatively flexible in their ability to co-assemble with cognitive processes that guide individuals' control efforts in the social environment. Control theory suggests that these cognitive processes operate as negative feedback units to monitor the environment and direct action intended to bring the social environment more into line with individuals' hierarchical goal structure.

The research on shifts between intrinsic and extrinsic motivational orientations can be viewed as switching from one set of homeostatic feedback systems (such as competence, stimulation, and novelty) to another (such as goal attainment and minimization of effort). The research on control motivation and cognitive activity focuses on the flexible energizing effects of variations in level of control motivation on a variety of cognitive processes involved in forming attributions and testing hypotheses.

There is a fundamental theoretical advantage to a social motivational approach that separates the feedback features of motivation from the impetus-to-action features. Division into two systems that together define motivational processes makes it possible to overcome the cumbersomeness inherent in many "mini-motivational" theories. It would be possible to go beyond a simple catalogue of specific motivations and their specific effects, each with independently defined, homeostatically oriented cognitive processes. The approach that we see as inherent in the reviewed literature makes it possible to model a wide variety of underlying psychological processes and "energize" them with the impetus-to-action from hierarchically arranged sources of affect, discomfort, or biological need. Combine this with the hierarchical arrangement of different levels of cognitive processes and we believe that there is a possible framework for integrating a great deal of research on psychological phenomena that now seems unrelated.

Literature Cited

Amabile, T. M. 1982a. Social psychology of creativity: A consensual assessment technique. *J. Pers. Soc. Psychol.* 43:997–1013

Amabile, T. M. 1982b. Children's artistic creativity: Detrimental effects of competition in a field setting. *Pers. Soc. Psychol. Bull.* 8:573–78

Amabile, T. M. 1985. Motivation and creativity: Effects of motivational orientation on creative writers. *J. Pers. Soc. Psychol.* 48:393–99

Amabile, T. M., De Jong, W., Lepper, M. R. 1976. Effects of externally imposed deadlines on subsequent intrinsic motivation. *J. Pers. Soc. Psychol.* 34:92–98

Amabile, T. M., Gitomer, J. 1984. Children's artistic creativity: Effects of choice in task materials. *Pers. Soc. Psychol. Bull.* 10:209–15

Amabile, T. M., Hennessey, B. A., Grossman, B. S. 1986. Social influences on creativity: The effects of contracted-for reward. *J. Pers. Soc. Psychol.* 50:14–23

Andersen, S. M., Williams, M. 1985. Cognitive/affective reactions in the improvement of self-esteem: When thoughts and feelings make a difference. *J. Pers. Soc. Psychol.* 49:1086–97

Anderson, C. A., New, B. L., Speer, J. R. 1985. Argument availability as a mediator of social theory perseverance. *Soc. Cognit.* 3:235–49

Arkes, H. R., Harkness, A. R. 1980. Effect of making a diagnosis on subsequent recognition of symptoms. *J. Exp. Psychol: Hum. Learn. Mem.* 6:568–75

Aronson, E. 1968. Dissonance theory: Progress and problems. In *Theories of Cognitive Consistency: A Sourcebook*, ed. R. A. Abelson, E. Aronson, W. J. McGuire, T. M. Newcomb, M. J. Rosenberg, et al, pp. 5–27. Chicago: Rand McNally

Aronson, E. 1980. Persuasion via self-justification: Large commitments for small rewards. See Festinger 1980, pp. 3–21

Bandura, A. 1982. Self-efficacy mechanism in human agency. *Am. Psychol.* 37:122–47

Bannister, D., ed. 1985. *Issues and Approaches in Personal Construct Theory.* New York: Academic

Bassili, J. N., Smith, M. C. 1986. On the spontaneity of trait attribution: Converging evidence for the role of cognitive strategy. *J. Pers. Soc. Psychol.* 50:239–45

Berlyne, D. D. 1960. *Conflict, Arousal, and Curiosity.* New York: McGraw-Hill

Berscheid, E., Graziano, W., Monson, T., Dermer, M. 1976. Outcome dependency: Attention, attribution, and attraction. *J. Pers. Soc. Psychol.* 34:978–89

Boggiano, A. K., Harackiewicz, J. M., Bessette, J. M., Main, D. S. 1985. Increasing children's interest through performance-contingent reward. *Soc. Cognit.* 3:400–11

Boggiano, A. K., Hertel, P. T. 1983. Bonuses and bribes: Mood effects in memory. *Soc. Cognit.* 2:49–61

Boggiano, A. K., Klinger, C., Main, D. S. 1986. Enhancing interest in peer interaction: A developmental analysis. *Child Dev.* 57:852–61

Boggiano, A. K., Main, D. S. 1986. Enhancing children's interest in activities used as rewards: The bonus effect. *J. Pers. Soc. Psychol.* In press

Boggiano, A. K., Ruble, D. N. 1979. Competence and the overjustification effect: a developmental study. *J. Pers. Soc. Psychol.* 37:1462–68

Boggiano, A. K., Ruble, D. N., Pittman, T. S. 1982. The mastery hypothesis and the overjustification effect. *Soc. Cognit.* 1:38–49

Brehm, J. H. 1966. *A Theory of Psychological Reactance.* New York: Academic

Buck, R. 1985. Prime theory: An integrated view of motivation and emotion. *Psychol. Rev.* 92:389–413

Carver, C. S., Scheier, M. F. 1981. A control-systems approach to behavioral self-regulation. *Rev. Pers. Soc. Psychol.* 2:189–216

Carver, C. S., Scheier, M. F. 1982. Control theory: A useful conceptual framework for personality-social, clinical, and health psychology. *Psychol. Bull.* 92:111–35

Chaiken, S., Yates, S. 1985. Affective-cognitive consistency and thought-induced attitude polarization. *J. Pers. Soc. Psychol.* 49:1470–81

Clark, M. S. 1984. Record keeping in two

types of relationships. *J. Pers. Soc. Psychol.* 47:549–57

Clark, M. S., Mills, J. 1979. Interpersonal attraction in exchange and communal relationships. *J. Pers. Soc. Psychol.* 37:12–24

Clary, E. G., Tesser, A. 1983. Reactions to unexpected events: The naive scientist and interpretive activity. *Pers. Soc. Psychol. Bull.* 9:609–20

Cooley, C. H. 1902. *Human Nature and the Social Order.* New York: Scribner

Cooper, J., Fazio, R. H. 1984. A new look at dissonance theory. *Adv. Exp. Soc. Psychol.* 17:229–62

Cooper, J., Zanna, M., Taves, P. A. 1978. Arousal as a necessary condition for attitude change following induced compliance. *J. Pers. Soc. Psychol.* 36:1101–6

Croyle, R. T., Cooper, J. 1983. Dissonance arousal: Physiological evidence. *J. Pers. Soc. Psychol.* 45:782–91

D'Agostino, P. R., Pittman, T. S. 1982. Effort expenditure following control deprivation. *Bull. Psychon. Soc.* 19:282–83

Darley, J. M., Fazio, R. H. 1980. Expectancy confirmation processes arising in the social interaction sequence. *Am. Psychol.* 35:867–81

Darley, J. M., Gross, P. H. 1983. A hypothesis-confirming bias in labeling effects. *J. Pers. Soc. Psychol.* 44:20–33

deCharmes, R. 1968. *Personal Causation.* New York: Academic

Deci, E. L. 1971. Effects of externally mediated rewards on intrinsic motivation. *J. Pers. Soc. Psychol.* 18:105–15

Deci, E. L. 1975. *Intrinsic Motivation.* New York: Plenum

Deci, E. L., Ryan, R. M. 1985. *Intrinsic Motivation and Self-Determination in Human Behavior.* New York: Plenum

Diener, C. T., Dweck, C. S. 1978. An analysis of learned helplessness: Continuous changes in performance, strategy, and achievement cognitions following failure. *J. Pers. Soc. Psychol.* 36:451–62

Elliott, G. C. 1979. Some effects of deception and level of self-monitoring on planning and reacting to a self-presentation. *J. Pers. Soc. Psychol.* 37:1282–92

Enzle, M. E., Ross, J. M. 1978. Increasing and decreasing intrinsic interest with contingent rewards: A test of cognitive evaluation theory. *J. Exp. Soc. Psychol.* 14:588–97

Enzle, M. E., Schopflocher, D. 1978. Instigation of attribution processes by attribution questions. *Pers. Soc. Psychol. Bull.* 4:595–99

Epstein, S. 1984. Controversial issues in emotion theory. *Rev. Pers. Soc. Psychol.* 5:64–88

Erber, R., Fiske, S. T. 1984. Outcome dependency and attention to inconsistent information. *J. Pers. Soc. Psychol.* 47:709–26

Festinger, L. 1957. *A Theory of Cognitive Dissonance.* New York: Harper & Row

Festinger, L., ed. 1980. *Retrospections on Social Psychology.* New York: Oxford Univ. Press

Festinger, L., Carlsmith, J. M. 1959. Cognitive consequences of forced compliance. *J. Abnorm. Soc. Psychol.* 58:203–11

Fiske, S. T. 1981. Social cognition and affect. In *Cognition, Social Behavior, and the Environment,* ed. J. H. Harvey, pp. 227–64. Hillsdale, NJ: Erlbaum

Fiske, S. T., Taylor, S. E. 1984. *Social Cognition.* Reading, MA.: Addison-Wesley

Frey, K. S., Ruble, D. N. 1985. What children say when the teacher is not around: Conflicting goals in social comparison and performance assessment in the classroom. *J. Pers. Soc. Psychol.* 48:550–62

Gangestad, S., Snyder, M. 1985. On the nature of self-monitoring: An examination of latent causal structure. *Rev. Pers. Soc. Psychol.* 3:65–86

Garbarino, J. 1975. The impact of anticipated reward upon cross-age tutoring. *J. Pers. Soc. Psychol.* 32:421–28

Greenwald, A. G., Pratkanis, A. R. 1984. The self. See Isen 1984, 3:129–78

Hale, S. 1985. The rediscovery of self in social psychology: Theoretical and methodological implications. *J. Theory Soc. Behav.* 15:227–82

Harackiewicz, J. M., Manderlink, G. 1984. A process analysis of the effects of performance-contingent rewards on intrinsic motivation. *J. Exp. Soc. Psychol.* 20:531–51

Harackiewicz, J. M., Manderlink, G., Sansone, C. 1984. Rewarding pinball wizardry: Effects of evaluation and cue value on intrinsic motivation. *J. Pers. Soc. Psychol.* 47:287–300

Harackiewicz, J. M., Sansone, C., Manderlink, G. 1985. Competence, achievement orientation, and intrinsic motivation: A process analysis. *J. Pers. Soc. Psychol.* 48:493–508

Harkness, A. R., DeBono, K. G., Borgida, E. 1985. Personal involvement and strategies for making contingency judgements: A stake in the dating game makes a difference. *J. Pers. Soc. Psychol.* 49:22–32

Harlow, H. F., Harlow, M. K., Meyer, D. R. 1950. Learning motivated by a manipulation drive. *J. Exp. Psychol.* 40:228–34

Harter, S. 1978. Pleasure derived from challenge and the effects of receiving grades on children's difficulty level choices. *Child Dev.* 49:788–99

Harvey, J. H., Yarkin, K. L., Lightner, J. M., Town, J. P. 1980. Unsolicited attribution and recall of interpersonal events. *J. Pers. Soc. Psychol.* 38:551–68

Hastie, R. 1984. Causes and effects of causal attribution. *J. Pers. Soc. Psychol.* 46:44–56

Heckhausen, H., Schmalt, H., Schneider, K. 1985. *Achievement Motivation in Perspective.* Transl. M. Woodruff, R. Wicklund. New York: Academic

Heider, F. 1958. *The Psychology of Interpersonal Relations.* New York: Wiley

Heller, J. F. 1972. *Attribution theory: self and other attributions as a determinant of attitude change.* PhD thesis. Univ. Iowa

Hilton, J. L., Darley, J. M. 1985. Constructing other persons: A limit on the effect. *J. Exp. Soc. Psychol.* 21:1–18

Hull, C. L. 1943. *Principles of Behavior.* New York: Appleton-Century-Croft

Hunt, J. M. 1965. Intrinsic motivation and its role in psychological development. *Nebr. Symp. Motiv.* 13:189–282

Iran-Nejad, A., Clore, G. L., Vondruska, R. J. 1984. Affect: A functional perspective. *J. Mind Behav.* 5:279–310

Isen, A. M. 1984. Toward understanding the role of affect in cognition. In *Handbook of Social Cognition,* ed. R. S. Wyer Jr., T. K. Srull, 3:179–236. Hillsdale, NJ: Erlbaum

Isen, A. M., Daubman, K. A. 1984. The influence of affect on categorization. *J. Pers. Soc. Psychol.* 47:1206–17

Izard, C. E. 1977. *Human Emotion.* New York: Plenum

James, W. 1890. *The Principles of Psychology.* New York: Holt

Jones, E. E. 1985. Major developments in social psychology during the past five decades. See Lindsay & Aronson 1985, pp. 47–108

Jones, E. E., Davis, K. E. 1965. From acts to dispositions: The attribution process in person perception. *Adv. Exp. Soc. Psychol.* 2:220–66

Jones, E. E., Pittman, T. S. 1982. Toward a general theory of strategic self-presentation. In *Psychological Perspectives on the Self,* ed. J. Suls, 1:231–62. Hillsdale, NJ: Erlbaum

Karniol, R., Ross, M. 1977. The effect of performance-relevant and performance-irrelevant rewards on children's intrinsic motivation. *Child Dev.* 48:482–87

Kelley, H. H. 1967. Attribution theory in social psychology. *Nebr. Symp. Motiv.* 15: 192–240

Kiesler, C. A., Nisbett, R. E., Zanna, M. 1969. On inferring one's beliefs from one's behavior. *J. Pers. Soc. Psychol.* 11:321–27

Koestner, R., Ryan, R. M., Bernieri, F., Holt, K. 1984. Setting limits in children's behavior: The differential effects of controlling versus informational styles on intrinsic motivation and creativity. *J. Pers.* 52:233–48

Kruglanski, A. W. 1975. The endogenous-exogenous partition in attribution theory. *Psychol. Rev.* 83:387–406

Kuiper, N. A., MacDonald, M. R., Derry, P. A. 1983. Parameters of a depressive self-schema. In *Psychological Perspectives on the Self,* ed. J. Suls, A. G. Greenwald, 2:191–218. Hillsdale, NJ: Erlbaum

Kunda, Z., Schwartz, S. H. 1983. Undermining intrinsic moral motivation: External reward and self-presentation. *J. Pers. Soc. Psychol.* 45:763–71

Langer, E. J. 1983. *The Psychology of Control.* Beverly Hills: Sage

Lazarus, R. S. 1984. On the primacy of cognition. *Am. Psychol.* 39:124–29

Lepper, M. R., Greene, D. 1975. Turning play into work: Effects of adult surveillance and extrinsic rewards on children's intrinsic motivation. *J. Pers. Soc. Psychol.* 31:479–86

Lepper, M. R., Greene, D. 1978. *The Hidden Costs of Rewards.* Hillsdale, NJ: Erlbaum

Lepper, M. R., Greene, D., Nisbett, R. E. 1973. Undermining children's intrinsic interest with extrinsic reward: a test of the overjustification hypothesis. *J. Pers. Soc. Psychol.* 28:129–37

Lepper, M. R., Ross, L., Lau, R. R. 1986. Persistence of inaccurate beliefs about the self: Perseverance effect in the classroom. *J. Pers. Soc. Psychol.* 50:482–91

Lepper, M. R., Sagotsky, G., Dafoe, J. L., Greene, D. 1982. Consequences of superfluous social constraints: Effects on young children's social inferences and subsequent intrinsic interest. *J. Pers. Soc. Psychol.* 42:51–65

Levenson, R. W., Gottman, J. M. 1983. Marital interaction: Physiological linkage and affective exchange. *J. Pers. Soc. Psychol.* 45:587–97

Lindsay, G., Aronson, E. 1985. *The Handbook of Social Psychology,* Vol. 1. New York: Random

Manderlink, G., Harackiewicz, J. M. 1984. Proximal versus distal goal setting and intrinsic motivation. *J. Pers. Soc. Psychol.* 47:918–28

Manucia, G. K., Baumann, D. J., Cialdini, R. B. 1984. Mood influences on helping: direct effects or side effects? *J. Pers. Soc. Psychol.* 46:357–64

Markus, H., Smith, J. 1980. The influence of self-schemas on the perception of others.

Personality and Cognition, ed. N. Cantor, J. Kihlstrom. Hillsdale, NJ: Erlbaum

Markus, H., Wurf, E. 1987. The dynamic self-concept. *Ann. Rev. Psychol.* 38:299–337

Markus, H., Zajonc, R. B. 1985. The cognitive perspective in social psychology. See Lindsay & Aronson 1985, pp. 137–230

McCaul, K. D. 1983. Observer attributions of depressed students. *Pers. Soc. Psychol. Bull.* 9:74–82

McGraw, K. 1978. The detrimental effects of reward on performance: A literature review and a prediction model. See Lepper & Greene 1978, pp. 31–60

McGraw, K., McCullers, J. 1979. Evidence of a detrimental effect of extrinsic incentives on breaking a mental set. *J. Exp. Soc. Psychol.* 15:285–94

Mead, G. H. 1934. *Mind, Self, and Society.* Chicago: Univ. Chicago Press

Miller, D. T., Norman, S. A., Wright, E. 1978. Distortion in person perception as a consequence of the need for effective control. *J. Pers. Soc. Psychol.* 36:598–607

Miller, G. A., Galanter, E., Pribram, K. H. 1960. *Plans and the Structure of Behavior.* New York: Holt

Mills, J., Clark, M. S. 1982. Communal and exchange relationships. *Rev. Pers. Soc. Psychol.* 3:121–44

Monson, T. C., Keel, R., Stephens, D., Genung, V. 1982. Trait attributions: relative validity, covariation with behavior, and prospect of future interaction. *J. Pers. Soc. Psychol.* 42:1014–24

O'Malley, M. N., Davies, D. K. 1984. Equity and affect: The effects of relative performance and moods on resource allocation. *Basic Appl. Soc. Psychol.* 5:273–82

Pallak, S. R., Costimiris, S., Sroka, S., Pittman, T. S. 1982. School experience, reward characteristics, and intrinsic motivation. *Child Dev.* 53:1382–91

Parkinson, B. 1985. Emotional effects of false autonomic feedback. *Psychol. Bull.* 98:471–94

Pittman, T. S. 1982. *Intrinsic and extrinsic motivational orientations toward others.* Ann. Meet. Am. Psychol. Assoc., 90th, Washington, DC

Pittman, T. S. 1975. Attribution of arousal as a mediator in dissonance reduction. *J. Exp. Soc. Psychol.* 11:53–63

Pittman, T. S., Boggiano, A. K., Ruble, D. N. 1983. Intrinsic and extrinsic motivational orientations: limiting conditions on the undermining and enhancing effects of reward on intrinsic motivation. In *Teacher and Student Perceptions: Implications for Learning,* ed. J. Levine, M. Wang, pp. 319–40. Hillsdale, NJ: Erlbaum

Pittman, T. S., Cooper, E. E., Smith, T. W. 1977. Attribution of causality and the overjustification effect. *Pers. Soc. Psychol. Bull.* 3:280–83

Pittman, T. S., D'Agostino, P. R. 1985. Motivation and attribution: The effects of control deprivation on subsequent information processing. In *Attribution: Basic Issues and Applications,* ed. G. Weary, J. Harvey, pp. 117–41. New York: Academic

Pittman, T. S., Davey, M. E., Alafat, K. A., Wetherill, K. V., Kramer, N. A. 1980. Informational versus controlling verbal rewards. *Pers. Soc. Psychol. Bull.* 6:228–33

Pittman, T. S., Emery, J., Boggiano, A. K. 1982. Intrinsic and extrinsic motivational orientations: Reward-induced changes in preference for complexity. *J. Pers. Soc. Psychol.* 42:789–97

Pittman, T. S., Pittman, N. L. 1980. Deprivation of control and the attribution process. *J. Pers. Soc. Psychol.* 39:377–89

Pittman, T. S., Scherrer, F. W., Wright, J. B. 1977. The effect of commitment on information utilization in the attribution process. *Pers. Soc. Psychol. Bull.* 3:276–79

Pretty, G. H., Seligman, C. 1984. Affect and the overjustification effect. *J. Pers. Soc. Psychol.* 46:1241–53

Pyszczynski, T. A., Greenberg, J. 1981. Role of disconfirmed expectancies in the instigation of attributional processing. *J. Pers. Soc. Psychol.* 40:31–38

Quattrone, G. A. 1982. Behavioral consequences of attributional bias. *Soc. Cognit.* 4:358–78

Reader, M. J., Dollinger, S. J. 1982. Deadlines, self-perceptions, and intrinsic motivation. *Pers. Soc. Psychol. Bull.* 8:742–47

Rempel, J. K., Holmes, J. G., Zanna, M. P. 1985. Trust in close relationships. *J. Pers. Soc. Psychol.* 49:95–112

Riggs, J. M., Cantor, N. 1984. Getting acquainted: The role of the self-concept and preconditions. *Pers. Soc. Psychol. Bull.* 10:432–45

Ross, M. 1975. Salience of reward and intrinsic motivation. *J. Pers. Soc. Psychol.* 32:245–54

Rotter, J. B. 1966. Generalized expectancies for internal versus external control of reinforcement. *Psychol. Monogr.* 80:1

Ryan, R. M. 1982. Control and information in the intrapersonal sphere: An extension of cognitive evaluation theory. *J. Pers. Soc. Psychol.* 43:450–61

Ryan, R. M., Mims, V., Koestner, R. 1983. Relation of reward contingency and interpersonal context to intrinsic motivation: A review and test using cognitive evaluation theory. *J. Pers. Soc. Psychol.* 45:736–50

Schachter, S., Singer, J. E. 1962. Cognitive, social, and physiological determinants of emotional state. *Psychol. Rev.* 69:379–99

Schul, Y., Burnstein, E. 1985. The informational basis of social judgments: Using past impression rather than the trait description in forming a new impression. *J. Exp. Soc. Psychol.* 21:421–39

Shaffer, D. R., Smith, J. E. 1985. Effects of preexisting moods on observers' reactions to helpful and nonhelpful models. *Motiv. Emotions* 9:101–6

Seligman, C., Fazio, R. H., Zanna, M. P. 1980. Effects of salience of extrinsic rewards on liking and loving. *J. Pers. Soc. Psychol.* 38:453–60

Shapira, Z. 1976. Expectancy determinants of intrinsically motivated behavior. *J. Pers. Soc. Psychol.* 34:1235–44

Simon, H. A. 1976. *Administrative Behavior.* New York: The Free Press

Skinner, B. F. 1953. *Science and Human Behavior.* New York: Macmillan

Snyder, M. 1980. Seek, and ye shall find: Testing hypotheses about other people. *The Ontario Symposium on Personality and Social Psychology,* ed. E. T. Higgins, C. P. Herman, M. Zanna, 2:106–30. Hillsdale, NJ: Erlbaum

Snyder, M. 1984. When belief creates reality. *Adv. Exp. Soc. Psychol.* 18:248–99

Snyder, M., Campbell, B. 1980. Testing hypotheses about other people: The role of the hypothesis. *Pers. Soc. Psychol. Bull.* 6:421–26

Snyder, M., Gangestad, S. 1981. Hypothesis-testing processes. *New Directions in Attribution Research,* ed. J. H. Harvey, W. Ickes, R. F. Kidd, 3:171–98. Hillsdale, NJ: Erlbaum

Snyder, M., Swann, W. B. 1978a. Hypothesis-testing processes in social interaction. *J. Pers. Soc. Psychol.* 36:1202–12

Snyder, M., Swann, W. B. 1978b. Behavioral confirmation in social interaction: From social perception to social reality. *J. Exp. Soc. Psychol.* 14:148–62

Snyder, M., Tanke, E. D., Berscheid, E. 1977. Social perception and interpersonal behavior: On the self-fulfilling nature of social stereotypes. *J. Pers. Soc. Psychol.* 35:656–66

Snyder, M., White, P. 1981. Testing hypotheses about other people: Strategies of verification and falsification. *Pers. Soc. Psychol. Bull.* 7:39–43

Snyder, M., Uranowitz, S. W. 1978. Reconstructing the past: Some cognitive consequences of person perception. *J. Pers. Soc. Psychol.* 36:941–50

Spence, K. W. 1956. *Behavior Theory and Conditioning.* New Haven, CT: Yale Univ. Press

Steele, C. M., Liu, T. J. 1981. Making dissonance act in reflection of self: Dissonance avoidance and the expectancy of a value-affirming response. *Pers. Soc. Psychol. Bull.* 7:393–97

Steele, C. M., Liu, T. J. 1983. Dissonance processes as self-affirmation. *J. Pers. Soc. Psychol.* 45:5–19

Swann, W. B. 1983. Self-verification: Bringing social reality into harmony with self. In *Psychological Perspectives on the Self,* ed. J. Suls, A. G. Greenwald, 2:33–66. Hillsdale, NJ: Erlbaum

Swann, W. B., Ely, R. J. 1984. A battle of wills: Self-verification versus behavioral confirmation. *J. Pers. Soc. Psychol.* 46:1287–1302

Swann, W. B., Guiliano, T., Wegner, D. M. 1982. Where leading questions can lead: The power of conjecture in social interaction. *J. Pers. Soc. Psychol.* 42:1025–1035

Swann, W. B., Hill, C. A. 1982. When our identities are mistaken: Reaffirming self-conceptions through social interaction. *J. Pers. Soc. Psychol.* 43:59–66

Swann, W. B., Pittman, T. S. 1977. Initiating play activity of children: The moderating influence of verbal cues on intrinsic motivation. *Child Dev.* 48:1128–1132

Swann, W. B., Snyder, M. 1980. On translating beliefs into action: Theories of ability and their application in an instructional setting. *J. Pers. Soc. Psychol.* 38:879–88

Swann, W. B., Stephenson, B., Pittman, T. S. 1981. Curiosity and control: On the determinants of the search for social knowledge. *J. Pers. Soc. Psychol.* 40:635–42

Thornton, B. 1984. Defensive attribution of responsibility: evidence for an arousal-based motivational bias. *J. Pers. Soc. Psychol.* 46:721–34

Tomkins, S. S. 1981. The quest for primary motives: Biography and autobiography of an idea. *J. Pers. Soc. Psychol.* 41:306–29

Trope, Y., Bassok, M. 1982. Confirmatory and diagnosing strategies in social information gathering. *J. Pers. Soc. Psychol.* 43:22–34

Trope, Y., Bassok, M. 1983. Information-gathering strategies in hypothesis-testing. *J. Exp. Soc. Psychol.* 19:560–76

Walster, E., Walster, G. W., Berscheid, E. 1978. *Equity: Theory and Research.* Boston: Allyn & Bacon

White, R. W. 1959. Motivation reconsidered: The concept of competence. *Psychol. Rev.* 66:297–333

Wicklund, R. A. 1974. *Freedom and Reactance.* New York: Wiley

Wong, P. T. P., Weiner, B. 1981. When people ask "why" questions, and the heuristics of attributional search. *J. Pers. Soc. Psychol.* 40:650–63

Woodworth, R. S. 1958. *Dynamics of Behavior*. New York: Holt

Zajonc, R. B. 1980a. Cognition and social cognition: A historical perspective. See Festinger 1980, pp. 180–204

Zajonc, R. B. 1980b. Feeling and thinking: Preferences need no inferences. *Am. Psychol.* 35:151–75

Zajonc, R. B. 1984. On the primacy of affect. *Am. Psychol.* 39:117–23

Zanna, M., Cooper, J. 1974. Dissonance and the pill: An attribution approach to studying the arousal properties of dissonance. *J. Pers. Soc. Psychol.* 29:703–70

Zuckerman, M., Porac, J., Lathin, D., Smith, R., Deci, E. L. 1978. On the importance of self-determination for intrinsically motivated behavior. *Pers. Soc. Psychol. Bull.* 4:443–46

Ann. Rev. Psychol. 1987. 38:491–532

PSYCHOPATHOLOGY OF CHILDHOOD: From Description to Validation

Herbert C. Quay, Donald K. Routh, and Steven K. Shapiro

Department of Psychology, University of Miami, Coral Gables, Florida 33124

CONTENTS

0066-4308/87/0201-0491$02.00

INTRODUCTION

Taxonomies of psychopathology historically have been derived by means of the observations of clinicians working with disordered individuals. Since most of these clinicians were physicians, it was natural that they followed the traditional methods of clinical medicine in attempting to describe symptoms (phenomena subjectively experienced by the patient, such as pain) and signs (phenomena observed by the clinicians, such as abnormal reflexes) and to decipher the underlying disorders. The multitude of examples which were already provided by clinical medicine were very encouraging.

What was not so obvious was that most physical disorders or diseases are manifested by very few symptoms and signs. One needs only to hear the patient complain of nausea and pain in the lower abdomen and then to find an elevated white blood count and tenderness over McBurney's point to have a strong suspicion that appendicitis is present (Carbone et al 1980). It was perhaps a source of undue optimism for the student of psychopathology that so many clinically derived physical disorders were so rapidly found to have specific etiologies, prognoses, response to treatment, and clear bases of differential diagnosis from related but distinct conditions.

When the clinical student of abnormal behavior was faced with a far wider array of symptoms (and relatively few signs), the descriptive problems were much more difficult, and disagreement as to what disorders did or did not exist, or should or should not be admitted to the taxonomy became the order of the day. The problems were compounded when the search for causes, consequences, specific treatments, and points of differential diagnosis proved to be such a slow process.

The second approach to taxonomy building grew out of a very different tradition. Recognizing the problems associated with trying to bring coherence out of hundreds, perhaps thousands of potential descriptors of human behavior, psychologically trained and mathematically inclined students of personality elected to derive their taxonomies through multivariate statistical techniques, usually factor analysis. The raw material for these analyses was the obtained intercorrelations among the descriptors of normal personality.

This approach, by the very nature of its methods, did not provide the discrete categories derived by the clinical psychopathologists but resulted in continuous dimensions along which all individuals varied. What was also produced was considerable disagreement over the nature and number of dimensions required for an adequate description of human personality, a disagreement not unlike that relative to the number and nature of disorders to be admitted to the taxonomy of abnormal behavior.

These two fundamentally different approaches are both still at work with respect to the classification of child and adolescent personality and psychopathology and have been so for at least 40 years, without any real resolution on what constitutes *the* taxonomy.

How can the differences in these two approaches be reconciled? First, we need to recognize that the description of its elements is only the first step in the process of developing a useful taxonomy. While it is likely that some taxons are composed of co-varying characteristics and are thus amenable to confirmation (if not discovery) by statistical methods such as factor analysis, the actual magnitude of the intercorrelations of the elements may be very low. We need to recognize that some taxons may be adequately described by only *one* positive sign or symptom (e.g. profound alexia may occur in the absence of agraphia or any other symptoms of language dysfunction, though it is true that the condition is generally accompanied by a visual field defect; Dejerine 1891, 1892). But if the correlation matrix did not include a specific evaluation of right homonymous hemianopsia, the existence of pure alexia without agraphia could likely not be either discovered or confirmed by factor analysis.

On the other hand, we need to be aware that clinical observation unchecked by careful validation procedures can also result in a multitude of categories whose existence may be seriously questioned.

To continue the debate as to what is the most fruitful method for the discovery of syndromes (taxons) is unlikely to be productive. We now need to base judgment as to the admissability to a taxonomy of either a clinically derived category or a dimension derived from multivariate statistical procedures on other grounds. We are certainly not the first to advocate the need for establishing the reliability and validity of disorders and dimensions. What we are advocating, however, is that the time has come to move from description to validation in child psychopathology. Given that DSM-III (American Psychiatric Association 1980) contains such a large number of disorders directly applicable to childhood and adolescence and that there are at least 100 multivariate statistical studies of deviant behavior of the same age group (see Achenbach & Edelbrock 1978, Dreger 1982, and Quay 1986a for reviews), our most pressing need is clearly not for more hypotheses about disorders *or* dimensions.

We suggest that future admissability to the status of syndrome (a construct which can subsume both disorders and dimensions) be limited to those categories or dimensions that (*a*) can be discriminated from other syndromes and thus reliably diagnosed or measured; and also meet one or more of the following criteria: (*b*) are associated with different causes, (*c*) have different outcomes, or (*d*) respond to different interventions.

The application of these criteria would seem to rule out many of the categories of DSM-III and not a few of the empirically derived dimensions as well. The remainder of this chapter will be devoted to an examination of a number of putative syndromes of child and adolescent psychopathology relative to these criteria. The hypothesized syndromes to be examined include Attention Deficit Disorder, Unsocialized Aggressive Conduct Disorder, Socialized Conduct Disorder, Infantile Autism, and Depression. These particular hypothesized syndromes have been chosen for review because of the present high level of interest in the field in the study of each of them.

ATTENTION DEFICIT DISORDER (ADD)

Definition

The concept of ADD as a syndrome (apart from conduct disorder) has aroused considerable controversy over the last several years. The definition of ADD given by DSM-III (American Psychiatric Association 1980) specifies that the child must display inattention and impulsivity and may or may not show hyperactivity as well. The onset of the problem must be before age seven, duration at least six months, and the condition must not be due to schizophrenia, affective disorder, or severe or profound mental retardation.

The particular operational criteria given for inattention, impulsivity, and hyperactivity by DSM-III were a product of committee discussion and have not yet been independently validated. For example, to be regarded as showing inattention, the child must have "at least three of the following: 1. often fails to finish things he or she starts, 2. often doesn't seem to listen, 3. is easily distracted, 4. has difficulty concentrating on schoolwork or other tasks requiring sustained attention, 5. has difficulty sticking to a play activity" (pp. 43–44). Similar lists given for impulsivity and hyperactivity are detailed below.

Johnston et al (1985) have reported on the development of a teacher rating scale (the SNAP) based directly on DSM-III criteria and have stated that the validity of the SNAP is evidenced by its reflection of the DSM-III diagnostic criteria and also its high correlation with the Conners Abbreviated Teacher Rating Scale (ATRS, unpublished data). The SNAP may have promise as an operational measure of ADD.

Attempts to operationalize the measurement of inattention have taken mainly three forms: rating scales (especially teacher rating scales), direct behavioral observations, and laboratory tasks. In the past, the teacher rating scales most frequently used in evaluating hyperactivity or ADD were those developed by Conners (e.g. Conners 1969). However, Ullmann et al (1985) have recently suggested that the Conners scales be abandoned in research on ADD because these scales overemphasize conduct problem behavior and overactivity and fail to select homogeneous samples of children with attention deficits. If the Conners scales were no longer used, what teacher rating scales might replace them? Among the possibilities are the teacher version of the Child Behavior Profile (Edelbrock & Achenbach 1984), the ACTeRS scale

(Ullmann et al 1984), or the Revised Behavior Problem Checklist (RBPC; Quay 1983, Quay & Peterson 1983), all of which have scales directed at the measurement of inattention. Or the Conners scales might be reincarnated with the relatively homogeneous Inattention/Overactivity and Aggression subscales introduced by Loney & Milich (1982) and recently validated against observation data (Milich & Fitzgerald 1985).

Direct observation of hyperactive and comparison children in the classroom has been carried out by Abikoff & coworkers (1977), who found that their principal behavioral measure of attention ("Off task") significantly discriminated the two groups; a finding cross-validated in a second study by Abikoff et al (1980) where "Off task" was found to be one of the two most discriminating behaviors observed. Roberts et al (1984) also observed off-task behavior in a standardized playroom and found that this significantly distinguished hyperactive from control boys.

The laboratory task most commonly used in studying attention with hyperactive children is the Continuous Performance Test (e.g. Sykes et al 1972). More recent research (e.g. O'Dougherty et al 1984, Sergeant & Scholten 1985a,b) has asked more refined questions about process deficits. It may turn out that the problem presented by this task to ADD children is not so much attentional per se as it is one of inhibiting impulsive responses or "false alarms."

The criteria given in the DSM-III for impulsivity are "at least three of the following: (1) often acts before thinking, (2) shifts excessively from one activity to another, (3) has difficulty organizing work (this not being due to cognitive impairment), (4) needs a lot of supervision, (5) frequently calls out in class, (6) has difficulty awaiting turn in games or group situations" (American Psychiatric Association 1980, p. 44). Less has been done to operationalize the assessment of impulsivity than to measure inattention. Other than the SNAP checklist, the existing teacher rating scales do not yet have separate subscales for impulsivity.

The Abikoff et al (1977) classroom observation system does include two codes that seem relevant to impulsivity. One of these is labeled "interference" ("calling out, interruption of others during work periods, and clowning"). The other is labeled as "solicitation," which "reflects how often the child seeks out the teacher's attention (e.g. calling out to the teacher, going up to the teacher's desk)" (p. 775). Both of these were found to distinguish hyperactive and control children significantly in the original and replication studies. In fact, interference was found to be one of the two most discriminating behaviors in the second study.

The laboratory task most often used as a measure of impulsivity has been Kagan's Matching Familiar Figures (MFF) test (e.g. Campbell et al 1971). Hyperactive children clearly differ from others in their performance on this task, but serious questions have arisen as to whether the task can be regarded as a measure of impulsivity as it is described in the DSM-III criteria for ADD. Block et al (1974) have argued that children with fast/inaccurate scores on this task were not really impulsive at all but were anxious, hypersensitive, vulnerable, and structure seeking. Bentler & McClain (1976) studied peer, teacher, and self-rating measures of several personality variables including impulsivity and showed that although these other measures met validity criteria in terms of a multitrait-multimethod analysis, only one isolated personality measure correlated highly with any MFF variable. At this point the MFF does not seem suitable as a way to operationalize impulsivity in assessing ADD.

The DSM-III criteria for the symptom of hyperactivity have been more thorough. The criteria for hyperactivity are: "at least two of the following: 1. runs about or climbs on things excessively, 2. has difficulty sitting still or fidgets excessively, 3. has difficulty staying seated, 4. moves about excessively during sleep, 5. is always 'on the go' or acts as if 'driven by a motor' " (American Psychiatric Association 1980, p. 44). In this case, the operational criteria seem to be quite adequate. Several of the teacher rating scales already mentioned have separate hyperactivity factors. For example, the RBPC (Quay 1983) now has a Motor Excess Scale. The Abikoff et al (1977, 1980) studies found that hyperactive children were significantly higher than controls in minor motor movement, gross motor-standing, gross motor-vigorous, and out-of-chair behaviors.

Porrino et al (1983) directly measured the motor activity of 12 hyperactive and normal boys continuously for one week with a portable electronic monitor. The hyperactives exhibited significantly higher levels of motor activity regardless of the time of day, including during sleep. The greatest differences between the groups were found, as expected, during structured school activities. In terms of the discussion of criteria for a syndrome used in this chapter, it is interesting to note that within the hyperactive group in the Porrino et al study, activity did not correlate significantly with attention measures such as the Continuous Performance Test.

Reliability

The inter-rater reliabilities of Attention Deficit Disorder obtained in various studies have been summarized by Quay (1986a). The Kappa coefficients reported for ADD as defined by DSM-III ranged from .50 to .76. For Hyperkinetic Syndrome of Childhood as defined by ICD-9, a Kappa of .63 was reported. For the Achenbach Child Behavior Checklist Hyperactive scale, the inter-rater reliability was reported as .65. For the Revised Behavior Problem Checklist, inter-rater reliabilities of .53 and .58 were reported for Attention Problems and Motor Excess, respectively. These all appear to be adequate at least for research purposes. The above studies were, however, concerned with the inter-rater reliability of ADD in comparison to all varieties of other disorders.

Distinguishing ADD from Other Disorders

The main issue of discriminant validity of ADD concerns whether it can be acceptably distinguished from Unsocialized Aggressive Conduct Disorder. In this research, the influential model has been the fourfold classification of aggressive and hyperactive children by Loney and her colleagues (1978). Using this approach, Roberts (1979) found that the hyperactives and the aggressive-hyperactive children were off task frequently in a standard play-room restrictive academic task, while the pure aggressive children were indistinguishable from normals in this respect. Milich et al (1982) have recently confirmed this distinction in a classroom observation study. The development of the IOWA Conners teacher rating scale (*I*nattention *O*veractivity *W*ith *A*ggression scale) by Loney & Milich (1982) promises to bring about a burst of research relevant to the differential characteristics of aggressive vs hyperactive children.

Causes

In reviewing research on the etiology of a syndrome, one usually expects to be able to report new findings which indicate increasing knowledge about it. Reviews of ADD research in the recent past (e.g. Ross & Ross 1982, Routh 1978, 1983, Rutter 1983) have indeed outlined the evidence for a number of antecedents, including "brain damage," familial/genetic factors, temperamental characteristics or behavior disorders in preschool children at risk for later ADD, exposure to environmental lead, and so on. For each of these hypothesized antecedents, however, knowledge now appears to be less certain than in the recent past rather than more so for the principal reason that hardly any of the past research attempted to distinguish systematically between ADD and Conduct Disorder. Therefore, we cannot be sure whether the putative antecedents were associated with one of these or with the other. For example, Gittelman & Eskenazi (1983) reported finding that hyperactive children had higher chelated urine lead levels than their own siblings. However, the hyperactive children studied were selected using the ATRS, which, as noted above, would actually be as likely to select children with conduct disorder as those with ADD. Future research needs to make a careful distinction between these conditions in order to resolve the ambiguity. Research on antecedents of ADD thus now has to take two steps backward before it can move forward once more.

Outcome

The same ambiguity just discussed also affects research on the outcome of ADD. Thorley (1984a) recently reviewed 24 studies that addressed the outcome of ADD children, but these generally did not take the distinction between ADD and Undersocialized Aggressive Conduct Disorder into account.

Undersocialized Aggressive Conduct Disorder is well known among types of psychopathology for its long-term stability (e.g. Robins 1966). The Milich & Loney (1979) study showing that among hyperactive children, those who were more aggressive had the worst social outcome, was a pathbreaker in suggesting the importance of differential diagnosis in follow-up studies. In fact, this study found that aggressive children were even more hyperactive at follow-up than the purely hyperactive children. The pure hyperactives did have worse academic achievement at follow-up than others. The specific association of ADD with poor academic achievement was confirmed in recent longitudinal research in New Zealand (McGee et al 1984a), where it was also found that ADD children were more likely to have speech articulation problems and a general verbal deficit in addition to reading and spelling problems as compared to the purely aggressive children.

Treatment Response

Part of the impetus to the identification of ADD as a disorder separate from both learning disabilities and Undersocialized Aggressive Conduct Disorder has been the fact that stimulant medications seem to have a specific beneficial effect on inattentive or impulsive behavior (and not so much on academic performance or aggressive, destructive, or "delinquent" behavior). However, the fact that Rapoport et al (1978) found stimulant drugs to have similar effects in normal children took away some of the previously impressive specificity of this finding.

UNDERSOCIALIZED AGGRESSIVE CONDUCT DISORDER (CD)

Definition and Reliability

DSM-III (American Psychiatric Association 1980) characterizes CD as a "repetitive and persistent pattern of aggressive conduct in which the basic rights of others are violated, as manifested by . . . physical violence against persons or property" (and/or) thefts outside the home involving confrontation with the victim." In addition, there is "a failure to establish a normal degree of affection, empathy or bond with others . . ." (pp. 47–48).

Numerous multivariate studies have provided consistent evidence for the appropriateness of the characteristics of CD (see Quay 1986a for a recent review). The Child Behavior Checklist (CBCL; Achenbach & Edelbrock 1979) and the RBPC are two of the more widely used multidimensional rating scales measuring CD.

Although not directly applied to a DSM-III-defined CD population, the work of Patterson et al (1969) has provided an instrument that reliably assesses aggressive behavior in natural settings. The Behavior Coding System (BCS) has been particularly useful because of its specific operational definition of noxious behavior/aggression at home and at school (Harris et al 1977). Reid (1978) obtained interobserver reliabilities for code categories ranging from .96 to .30 with a median of .70. Content validity was indirectly obtained for the code categories by Johnson & Bolstad (1973), who found that mother ratings of degree of deviancy confirmed the aversiveness behavior coded in the BCS. In the same study, concurrent validity was demonstrated by a significant (.69) correlation between Total Deviant scores for the BCS and the parents' daily reports of the occurrence of referral symptoms. Harris & Reid (1981) showed that the hierarchy of coercive responses was similar across situations.

As noted above, DSM-III describes poor interpersonal relationships as a principal characteristic of CD. Deluty (1981a) found a significant negative correlation between levels of aggressiveness and peer-related popularity as well as significantly lower popularity ratings in highly aggressive children compared to a highly assertive and/or submissive group. Similar results have been obtained by Anderson et al (1985). Konstantareas & Homatidis (1985) studied the formation of dominance hierarchies that were derived on the basis of resolution of episodes of physical and verbal aggression. A significantly lower degree of stability in hierarchies as well as increased aggressive episodes were noted for CD children. Panella & Henggeler (1986) found that black CD boys, compared to well-adjusted black controls, showed a lower degree of social competence. Overall, these and other studies have provided consistent evidence that aggression is indeed a valid and in fact the cardinal symptom of CD which affects or coexists with impaired interpersonal relationships and low popularity.

Distinguishing CD from Other Disorders

Much of the research studying the distinct characteristics of CD has used ADD children as a comparison group, or vice versa, often in response to the controversy regarding the independence of these two disorders at a descriptive level noted earlier (see also Lahey et al 1980, Prinz et al 1981, Milich et al 1982). As was previously mentioned in the discussion regarding the discriminant validity for ADD, Loney & Milich (1982) have developed a fourfold classification model of aggression and hyperactivity with concurrent and subsequent work suggesting the partial independence of these two behaviors (Milich et al 1982, Roberts et al 1984, McGee et al 1985). Early research attempting to differentiate hyperactive from CD children has provided useful although sometimes disparate comparative results on both criterion and noncriterion variables for both diagnostic groups.

BIOPSYCHOSOCIAL INDICES   Sandberg et al (1980) found no significant differences in psychosocial, pre- or perinatal complications or neurodevelopmental abnormalities between hyperactive and CD children. While some studies have also found no significant differences regarding familial/social disadvantages (Loney & Milich 1982, Koriath et al 1985), others have reported a greater prevalence in CD children (August & Stewart 1982, Stewart & Behar 1983, McGee et al 1984a, Thorley 1984b). Robins (1979) stated that once the effects of presence of an antisocial parent were statistically controlled, socioeconomic status was not a significant predictor of children's conduct problems.

BEHAVIORAL INDICES   Stewart et al (1981) found a significantly higher level of antisocial behavior (lying, stealing, firesetting, and vandalism) in CD children compared to hyperactives. In addition, while children meeting criteria for both diagnoses showed more antisocial behavior than the "pure" hyperactive group, the 'addition' of hyperactivity to the CD group did not significantly increase antisocial behavior. Similar findings were noted on measures of egocentricity. August & Stewart (1982) reported a higher level of aggression, noncompliance, antisocial behavior, and inadequate social relationships in a mixed group of children compared to a pure hyperactive group. Thorley (1984b) subsequently reported a higher frequency of fighting, bullying, aggression, and stealing in a CD group compared to a hyperkinetic group. However, these studies are somewhat circular as the dependent variables entered into the selection of cases in the first place.

Stein & O'Donnell (1985) applied a discriminant function to ratings of DSM-III diagnostic groups of CD and ADD in order to determine which variables accounted for between-group differences. Accurate classification of 67% of the cases was obtained only when CD and ADD subjects were combined. The authors suggested that ADD should be viewed as part of a broader CD. Werry and his colleagues have provided a review (Werry et al 1986) as well as an impressive multimeasure comparative study (Reeves et al 1986) on diagnostic features of Anxiety, ADD, and CD. Since the occurrence of "pure" CD was so rare in their sample, this group was combined with those in the ADD group who did not show CD. Reeves et al (1986) demonstrated that the mixed diagnostic group showed higher levels of family adversity compared to the ADD and Anxious group. Ratings obtained from the RBPC revealed the mixed group to be equal to the ADD group on the RBPC of Conduct Disorder, Attentional Problems, and Motor Excess subscales. Interestingly, these three groups, including those who were diagnosed as having an Anxiety Disorder, did not significantly differ on ratings of Anxiety-Withdrawal. Slightly different results were obtained from the Conners Teacher Questionnaire (CTRS; Conners 1969) which showed the mixed group to have higher ratings of Conduct Problems and Hyperactivity compared to the Hyperkinetic group. However, the two groups showed equal levels of Inattentive-Passive ratings.

Many of the comparative studies attempting to establish discriminant validity show a useful trend toward adopting a multimethod/multimeasure strategy. Conflicting results, rather than being interpreted as muddling the field, seem to highlight the effects of the different normative samples and the different theoretical notions from which instruments were derived. Certainly, methodological problems accounting for the different results should be considered. Furthermore, large-scale epidemiological studies using current diagnostic criteria are necessary so that diagnostic categories need not be combined because of statistical constraints. If a combinatory strategy is necessary, then accompanying multivariate statistics which address the issue of variance accounted for are essential.

Causes

Biochemical and physiological research has been part of a broadening perspective which seeks to relate peripheral measures of physiological responsivity and neurochemical indices to aggressiveness. Methodological precision as well as a clearer understanding of the relationship between central "arousal" (Claridge 1981) and peripheral measures will assist in better understanding the mechanisms involved.

PHYSIOLOGICAL INDICES   A common approach has been to use heart rate and electrodermal (GSR) responding as physiological measures. Although Raine & Venables (1984a) replicated earlier studies which suggest a lower tonic (resting/basal) heart rate level in antisocial subjects, more homogeneous sample selection which would control for other physical attributes is necessary to examine this relationship in a more unbiased way.

Studies of the relationship between antisocial behavior and GSR measures have been in the literature for over 30 years (Lykken 1957, Borkovec 1970, Siddle et al 1973). Recently, Raine & Venables (1984b) found a significant negative correlation between ratings of antisocial behavior and GSR amplitudes. Compared to a prosocial group, the antisocial group showed a significantly lower level of response to an orienting stimulus. These authors concluded that the antisocial group may be characterized by "a passive/sustained attention deficit marked by a narrowed processing of environmental events" (p. 430) which may in turn represent a biological predispositional factor.

Delamater & Lahey (1983) also demonstrated lower skin conductance levels during a continuous performance task for preadolescents rated high on conduct problems using the CTRS. Applying DSM-III criteria to select CD children, Schmidt et al (1985) found a lower GSR responsivity to a loud bell in the CD group as compared to age, sex, and race-matched normals and suggested that lower reactivity ("lessened inhibition") to situations that would normally arouse fear or aversion in others may play a role in facilitating antisocial behavior.

Many of these results are consistent with a framework described by Gray (1979, 1982) and elaborated by Fowles (1980, 1983) in which behavior is under the control of a behavioral inhibition system (indexed by the GSR) and a reward system (indexed by heart rate). Quay (1985) has suggested that CD might primarily involve an overactive reward system with a concomitantly underactive behavioral inhibition system.

BIOCHEMICAL INDICES   Rogeness and his colleagues (Rogeness et al 1982, 1984) have provided data that can also be interpreted as providing evidence for Quay's derivations from Gray's theory. Rogeness et al (1984) found that children meeting the DSM-III criteria for CD when compared to a normal group show significantly lower levels of dopamine beta hydroxylase (DBH) which converts dopamine (DA) to noradrenaline (NE). Gray (1979, 1982) has suggested that NE (as well as serotonin) is a principal neurotransmitter involved in the activation of the behavioral inhibition system while DA seems to be the principal transmitter in the reward system pathway (see Quay 1985, 1986b). Findings that CD children show lower levels of the essential enzyme responsible for DA to NE conversion are consonant with the notion of possible overactivity of reward mechanisms as a physiologic predisposition in CD.

COGNITIVE INDICES   Cognitive factors have been the object of recent interest in an attempt to understand better the mechanisms of aggressive behaviors. On the basis of their review, Hogan & Quay (1984) suggested that higher-order cognitive deficits may be responsible for search strategy constraints, limited response alternatives, and inaccurate perceptions of environmental stimuli. This latter tendency to misconstrue the environment has been part of recent interests in "social cognition" of aggressive children. For example, Dodge (1980) selected aggressive and nonaggressive boys from each of three grades on the basis of peer nomination and teacher assessments. Three conditions of intent (hostile, benign, and ambiguous) by an unknown peer were used as part of presenting a frustrating negative outcome. Despite the actual content of the peers' statements, aggressive boys tended to infer a hostile intention, suggesting a possible mechanism by which defensive aggressive behavior perpetuates itself (Dodge 1980). Similar tendencies to infer hostility were found by Nasby et al (1980) among CD boys selected by teacher ratings. Both studies showed no difference in the *abilities* of each group to identify hostile and nonhostile social stimuli.

Deluty (1981b) has demonstrated a significantly higher tendency for aggressive boys to verbalize aggressive responses in an attempt to resolve conflict situations. Milich & Dodge (1984) found a higher hostile social attribution in aggressive children compared to normal controls. However, it was shown that this attribution was nonspecific to aggression since the hyperactive group was equal to the aggressive group. These studies suggest a consistent tendency for aggression to carry with it a characteristic tendency to infer hostility from a relatively neutral situation. Although these may be considered antecedent factors, a causal link cannot be assumed without longitudinal studies specifically designed to assess this cognitive tendency.

FAMILIAL INDICES   Of particular interest here is research by Patterson and his colleagues. Since 1980, Patterson has extended his familial determinants model of childhood antisocial behavior (Patterson 1980, 1982, Patterson et al 1984, Patterson & Dishion 1985, Patterson 1986). Most recently, Patterson & Bank (1986) have hypothesized a theoretical relationship among variables involved in the "basic training for antisocial behavior" where inept discipline is seen as the most common deficit in child-rearing skills. It has been commonly noted that parents of antisocial boys use significantly more extreme forms of physical punishment (Reid & Kavanaugh 1986), explosive discipline, and physical abuse (Reid et al 1981). Eron (1982) and Parke & Slaby (1983) have reported consistent correlations between parental use of physical punishment and higher rates of antisocial child behavior. In other studies, failure by the parent to provide adequate monitoring of antisocial episodes occurring outside the home has been shown to result in the escalation of such behaviors. Immediate reinforcers available for antisocial behavior then lead to a rapid increase in antisocial behavior (Patterson & Stouthamer-Loeber 1984, Dishion & Loeber 1987).

A key component in the above model is Patterson's work (1982) on the role of the coercive child. The process of coercion is a clear case of avoidance conditioning in which the child reacts in a manner aversive to the parent in response to an (aversive) behavior by the parent. The child's behavior results in the termination (for him/her) of the aversive stimuli, thereby reinforcing noncompliance and increasing its subsequent amplitude and frequency.

BIOPSYCHOSOCIAL INDICES   McGee et al (1984a) have addressed the issue of perinatal, background, and psychosocial characteristics of children showing aggression and/or hyperactivity. Although earlier studies have assumed a lower socioeconomic level in families with aggressive children, many have not recognized this as a confound and not simply an antecedent. McGee et al (1984a) found that the disadvantaged home backgrounds of the deviant child arose from more primary factors such as impaired parenting skills associated with low maternal mental ability, poor maternal psychological health, parental separation, solo parenting, and poor family relationships. In addition (as already noted above), Robins (1979) indicated that social class as such makes a minimal contribution in the prediction of serious adult antisocial behavior, i.e. when the presence of an antisocial parent is controlled for statistically, social class is not an independent predictor of antisocial behavior in the offspring.

In summary, in light of the diversity of antecedent situations which have been implicated in aggression, an integrative strategy seems most useful. Consistent with this approach, studies have suggested that simple observational and reinforcement models are simply not adequate (Eron et al 1971, Lefkowitz et al 1977, Huesmann et al 1984). Instead, the convergence of environmental, familial, and child characteristics, including those of a biologic nature, seems to be a necessary or sufficient condition for aggression.

Outcome

Longitudinal studies have provided consistent findings regarding the stability of aggressive behavior. Olweus (1979) reported that the stability of aggressive behavior found in studies from 1935 to 1978 was comparable to that found for intelligence. He concluded that stability coefficients were negatively correlated with the length of the follow-up interval and that stability increased with the age of the child at initial measurement. In a later review, Loeber (1982) concluded that compared to nonchronic delinquents, chronic delinquents showed an earlier onset of delinquent behaviors and that the level of antisocial behaviors tended to escalate instead of diminish with age. Furthermore, the frequency of overt antisocial acts (e.g. aggression, excessive quarreling, disobedience, and fighting) declined from childhood up to age 16 with a concurrent increase in covert acts (e.g. lying, stealing, "conning," truancy, drug use, and vandalism).

Recent research by Moskowitz et al (1985) found moderately high stability of aggression regardless of gender or age at time of initial assessment. This pattern differed from a withdrawn group which, although showing comparable stability, showed a late onset of stability. Other researchers have noted differential stability with respect to gender. Richman et al (1982) found that behavioral characteristics of CD (being difficult to control, displaying temper tantrums, having poor peer and sibling relationships, and attention-seeking behavior) at age 4 were strongly associated with disturbance at age 8. This was particularly true for boys but less so for girls. Fagot (1984) also found that problem behavior in toddler boys was strongly associated with a continuation of the pattern whereas the behaviors were unpredictable in girls at follow-up.

Along with clear evidence that aggressive behaviors persist from the early years, August et al (1983) and Loney et al (1981) have also noted the poor prognosis associated with early aggressive behavior even when other problems (e.g. ADD) are presented as the principal complaint. As already noted, Milich & Loney (1979) also found a clearly poorer prognosis for aggression compared to that of hyperactivity.

Early research by Robins (1966) indicated that childhood antisocial behavior is an excellent predictor of adult sociopathy, particularly when evidence is present for sociopathy in the father. More recently, Huesmann et al (1984) found that early aggressiveness was predictive of later criminal behavior, spouse abuse, traffic violations, and self-reported physical aggression. The stability was shown to be consistent across time, situations, and generations within a family.

Clearly, then, the temporal pattern of childhood CD includes antisocial behavior persisting into adulthood. Therefore, aggression carries with it a poor prognosis that transcends situations and generations, suggesting a persistent trait-like feature to it. As will be discussed later, this stability is in contrast to the lower degree of persistence found in socialized aggressive conduct disorder.

Response to Treatment

Intervention with CD children has been largely carried out within a behavior modification paradigm; nonetheless, a variety of techniques have been found to be useful. Patterson (1976), in a child management program following a social-learning model, emphasized the parents' role in accurately defining deviant and prosocial child behavior to aid in subsequent implementation of reinforcement, withdrawal, and positive contingencies. Training sessions to terminate the child's coercive behavior instead of reinforcing it resulted in significant decreases in deviant behavior. Blue et al (1982) likewise concentrated on increasing the coping behavior of aggressive children via methods of contingent reward, modeling, and rehearsal. Instituting a cognitive-behavioral treatment program for aggressive children, Kettlewell & Kausch (1983) found improved interpersonal problem solving skills, but no significant decrease in physical or verbal aggression. On the other hand, Lochman et al (1984) found reduced disruptive and aggressive behavior in both classroom and home as a result of anger coping training alone and in combination with goal-setting training. Konstantareas & Homatidis (1984) reported on an intervention that incorporated elements of psychodynamic theory, social-learning theory, and educational theory, all of which were aimed at improving peer interaction and cooperation, frustration tolerance and self-esteem, and reduction in aggressive behavior. Physical but not verbal aggression was shown to decrease across two age groups.

Pharmacological studies have been very limited in number. Amery et al (1984) reported a double-blind placebo-controlled, crossover study of diagnosed ADD boys in which aggression, particularly that observed in the playroom, was reduced on low doses of D-amphetamine. Campbell & associates (1982, 1984) have pointed out the clear need for well-defined treatment groups and for study designs including combinations of drugs (particularly lithium and haloperidol) with psychosocial treatment in the pharmacotherapy of aggression.

Overall, some studies have shown a significant decrease in target behavior as a result of treatment using some form of behavioral management, whether focused on the child's coping skills or the parents' management skills. However, CD is also very resistant to many forms of treatment (Meeks 1980). Feldman (1983) noted that traditional psychotherapy has been consistently unsuccessful with aggressive children, but that a shift from intervention to prevention, by reducing opportunities for crime and enhancing the skills in those connected with the child, might yield promising results. Few studies have assessed the longitudinal effectiveness of early intervention. Until such time as this occurs, various treatments can only be presumed to provide short-term reduction of what is likely to be a stable behavior problem.

SOCIALIZED AGGRESSIVE CONDUCT DISORDER (SCD)

Definition and Reliability

DSM-III (American Psychiatric Association 1980) characterizes this disorder as a "repetitive and persistent pattern of aggressive conduct in which the basic rights of others are violated, as manifested by . . . physical violence against persons or property . . . (and/or) thefts outside the home involving confrontation with a victim" as well as "evidence of social attachments to others." It is the latter criterion that distinguishes the SCD from the CD pattern. Aggression need not be present for the diagnosis of SCD, but is not excluded as a possible significant feature.

Validating evidence for these "socialized" features is well established. In findings that have stood the test of time, Hewitt & Jenkins (1946) labeled a group as "socialized delinquents" who showed many features that are currently considered to be characteristic of SCD. Most subsequent studies, while reflecting various methodological refinements, have replicated the early findings (see Quay 1986a for a review). Both the CBCL and the RBPC have subscales measuring this syndrome.

Distinguishing SCD from Other Disorders

Much research on SCD has focused on how this subtype can/should be discriminated from CD. Recent studies have recognized that this strategy should also be extended to comparisons with other disorders not subsumed under the general category of conduct disorder. However, because of (*a*) inappropriate sampling procedures, (*b*) low base rates for the disorders in clinic populations, or (*c*) preconceived biases against the subtypes' discriminability, recent validity studies have not directly compared SCD with other disorders (Stein & O'Donnell 1985, Reeves et al 1986).

However, many earlier studies of Socialized Conduct Disorder have directly compared SCD and CD groups on presumed criterion variables and have provided consistent findings. Jurkovic & Prentice (1977) found that those classified as SCD did not differ from normals and were better skilled in taking the perspective of others and more able to use abstract reasoning than CD subjects. Ellis (1982) also found that socialized delinquents were more empathic than an undersocialized group. In studying the relationship between adolescent psychopathology and response to social reinforcement, Stewart (1972) used a sentence building, verbal reasoning task preceded by a frustrating condition (working on an unsolvable puzzle) or by a neutral condition. CD, SCD, and anxious-withdrawn institutionalized delinquents were socially reinforced for the use of aggressive or dependent verbs. The SCD group significantly increased the use of reinforced verbs whereas the CD group significantly decreased the use of reinforced verbs. When conditioning was preceded by the neutral condition, the SCD group did not significantly increase the use of reinforced verbs but the CD group significantly decreased such use. Overall, SCD children were more socially responsive, a finding that certainly would have implications in intervention strategies.

A recent series of articles has introduced the labels "fighters" versus "stealers" to describe the two groups. Loeber et al (1983) studied family interactions of adolescent chronic offenders apprehended for assaultive crimes compared to a matched group of adolescents apprehended for stealing. Assaultive boys showed more aversive behavior in the family setting and were significantly higher in the frequency of such behavior than either the "stealers" or a nondelinquent group. Further studies by Loeber & Schmalling (1985a,b) confirmed the utility of differentiating between "fighters," whom they described as representing an overt pattern of antisocial conduct problems, and "stealers," who show covert antisocial conduct problems. Through a meta-analysis technique and a multimethod-multirespondent descriptive study, they found that "stealers" were much more involved in delinquent acts, whereas "fighters" were less prone to be involved in similar delinquency. In addition, adolescents displaying both stealing and fighting tendencies scored the highest on virtually all types of overt and covert antisocial behavior.

Although the above studies are useful as research representing the validity of the distinction between "fighters" and "stealers," there is a need for these investigations to define their groups less idiosyncratically using DSM-III criteria or one of the more commonly used dimensional measures.

Causes

Few consistent precursors to SCD have been identified. This lack of identified antecedents may result in part from the difficulty in finding adequately large samples amenable to investigation, or, as mentioned before, the failure to treat it as a distinct subtype in need of research and not simply one to be subsumed under a general category of Conduct Disorder. Hetherington et al (1971) have, however, provided some insight into family interaction patterns among SCD boys. Parents of SCD boys tended to be more permissive than did those with CD children. Among SCD boys, fathers tended to be dominant, while mothers were characterized as passively resistant. Although the SCD boys were unable to compromise with their father's decision, they showed a higher participation rate in family interactions. Megargee & Golden (1973), who obtained parent attitude ratings from SCD offenders, found more negative attitudes toward fathers but not mothers. Loeber & Schmalling (1985a,b) found that rejection and lack of parental monitoring by mothers as assessed by home observation ratings were common among adolescents displaying *both* "stealing" and "fighting."

Outcome

A number of studies have indicated a more hopeful prognosis for the SCD than for the CD individual, although SCD seems more predictive of future *legally defined* adolescent delinquency than is CD. Mitchell & Rosa (1981) obtained parental and teacher reports as well as subsequent court records of indictable offenses from a large random sample of boys and girls who ranged in age from 5 to 15. Characteristics that are generally found in the SCD group (i.e. stealing, destructiveness, wandering from home, and lying) were associated with criminality and recidivism. Moore et al (1979) found that children identified as "stealers" had a higher rate of court-recorded offenses and therefore more "official delinquency" than an aggressive or a normal control group. More recently, Hanson et al (1984) similarly found ratings of SCD to be the most powerful predictor of subsequent serious and repeated arrests. Younger age was the second best predictor of future arrests, while family-relationship measures were less predictive. Therefore, as noted by Quay (1986b), "CD persists into late childhood and adolescence, but it does not seem to foretell legally defined delinquency, especially property offenses, as well as does behavior related to socialized conduct disorder." However, CD adolescents who *are* institutionalized for delinquent activities are likely to show poorer adult outcome in terms of more subsequent arrests (Henn et al 1980). The worst prognosis of all may be for "versatile" offenders who combine the characteristics of both syndromes (Loeber & Schmalling 1985b).

Treatment Response

Few, if any, studies have appropriately addressed the issue of effective intervention for the SCD. In part, this is understandable as the result of a lack of real evidence regarding the etiological factors involved. Loeber & Schmalling (1985a), in discussing their conception of a unidimensional and bipolar model of antisocial behavior, point to the necessity of identifying "keystone" behaviors from which intervention plans can be developed.

INFANTILE AUTISM

Definition and Reliability

Infantile autism is characterized by DSM-III (American Psychiatric Association 1980) as a pervasive developmental disorder involving distortions of several basic psychological functions. Specific diagnostic criteria include "*a*) onset prior to 30 months of age; *b*) pervasive lack of responsiveness to other people; *c*) gross deficits in language development; *d*) if speech is present, peculiar speech patterns such as immediate and delayed echolalia, metaphorical language, pronominal reversal; *e*) . . . resistance to change, peculiar interest in or attachment to animate or inanimate objects; *f*) absence of delusions, hallucinations, loosening of association, and incoherence as in Schizophrenia" (pp. 89–90).

Although the criteria used by DSM-III for infantile autism in many ways are similar to those proposed by Kanner (1943), this current conceptualization is an improvement over the earlier descriptions (see Volkmar et al 1986). However, these criteria are by far not universally accepted. There have been consistent problems in operationalizing the DSM-III criteria, although recent advances in this area are encouraging. In addition, valid and reliable measures generally remain specific to the concepts of those who developed instruments (Prior & Werry 1986). Freeman et al (1981) highlight the necessity for using appropriate control groups, particularly ones matched for IQ, so specific characteristics of autism and not mental retardation can be delineated.

Volkmar et al (1986) investigated the diagnostic criteria of infantile autism using 50 children and young adults who had been so diagnosed by Kanner's (1943) criteria or those of Rutter (1976). Parents provided a history of their child's development and behavior before age six. Volkmar et al (1986) pointed out that there were many problems regarding reliability of information and criteria that seem either overly stringent (e.g. age of onset) or weakly specified (language deficit). Reliability of information concerning age of onset was poor. Parents of older subjects tended to report a later age of onset; the later-onset cases, in comparison to an early-onset group, showed less head banging and restlessness, were more responsive to sounds, and were less likely to use another person's hand to indicate a desired object. In terms of social responsiveness, unrelatedness did not seem to be pervasive as suggested in DSM-III, with only 36% appearing to show a considerable deficit in this area, which was not related to IQ or other behaviors reported by the parent. Language development, which was related to IQ, was significantly impaired or absent. For those who had developed speech, most manifested deviant speech tone or rhythm, confusion of personal pronouns, and echolalia. However, such language problems are not in the least specific to autism. Consistent with DSM-III criteria, all of the subjects exhibited some abnormal responsiveness to the environment. Particularly, parents reported that before age six, their children ignored sounds that other children would notice, ignored toys, were excessively preoccupied with spinning and whirling objects, exhibited bizarre use of toys, or were attached to an unusual object. Finally, Volkmar et al (1986) pointed out the difficulty in applying the DSM-III exclusionary criteria of lack of delusions/hallucinations, especially since communication is frequently difficult with the autistic child.

Fein et al (1986; see also Wing & Gould 1979) have argued that the social symptoms should be seen as the primary deficit in autism. Fein et al (1986) suggested, with corroborating thoughts from Rutter (1983), that "a comprehensive model of autism should elaborate the specific ways in which a primary disorder of social affect or relatedness could retard, distort, or accelerate different aspects of cognitive development, and should relate those to the variety of observed cognitive outcomes in autism . . . while functions such as sensorimotor and visual-spatial processes, which are more variable in samples of autistic children, may be more autonomous for social motivation" (page 209).

Schopler (1983) pointed out that definitional differences in autism have been influenced by the interplay between scientific and political purposes as is exemplified in the differences between Rutter (1978) and the National Society for Autistic Children (NSAC 1978; see also Ritvo & Freeman 1978). Both agree on the criteria of impaired social development, language, and cognitive skills, and early onset. Rutter has maintained a scientific perspective and has outlined his main criteria for autism to be insistence on sameness, exemplified by stereotypic play patterns, abnormal preoccupation, or resistence to change. Although the NSAC definition includes these under its criterion of inability to relate to people, events, and objects, the NSAC definition "is intended to help NSAC members to realize their objectives for political and social actions" (Schopler 1983).

Attempts to construct valid and reliable instruments for the classification of autism have been problematic. Rimland (1971) was the first to attempt the development of a rating scale reflecting Kanner's (1943) definition of autism. The Childhood Autism Rating Scale (CARS; Schopler et al 1980) is comprised of 15 scales which include essential features from definitions proposed by Rutter (1978), Ritvo & Freeman (1978), and Rimland (1971). The distribution of the CARS scores delineated three groups—a moderate to severe group, a mild to moderate group, and a communication handicap group without the autistic syndrome. Age of onset was significantly lower for the autistic group compared to the nonautistic group. It was also found that the level of intellectual retardation was associated with the severity of autism. Schopler et al (1980) then compared subgroups of autistic children (based on the CARS) with those who would be classified by Rimland (1971) and Ritvo & Freeman (1978). There was little overlap with the Rimland criteria, which may reflect the differences between ratings obtained through behavioral observations (i.e. CARS) and parental recollection (i.e. Rimland). A significant overlap of the Rutter and Ritvo & Freeman criteria was found using the CARS. Furthermore, the greater frequency of autistic children in the CARS sample also showing sensory peculiarities (lack of eye contact, visual avoidance of toys and educational material) as outlined by Ritvo & Freeman suggested that this should be a primary diagnostic feature in autism.

Overall, the two most commonly used (and seemingly valid) sets of criteria for autism seem to be those of the DSM-III and of Rutter (1978), which overlap with each other. Empirical studies and alternate conceptual models (Fein et al 1986, Volkmar et al 1986) are just beginning to appear which will, it is hoped, generate continued interest in differentiating between the primary and associated features of Infantile Autism.

Quay (1986a) was able to cite but a single study of the reliability of the DSM-III diagnosis of infantile autism, which had 100% inter-rater agreement. A Kappa of .85 was reported from field trials on the reliability of the diagnosis of Pervasive Developmental Disorder.

Distinguishing Autism from Related Conditions

Three main areas of comparative research have provided additional information concerning differential diagnoses and/or discriminating characteristics, namely those concerned with mental retardation, schizophrenia, and language disorders.

MENTAL RETARDATION   Kanner (1943) originally considered the autistic child to be of normal intelligence. This was partly because autistic children frequently show particular peak skills in music (Applebaum et al 1979), in the manipulation of numbers (Park & Youderian 1974), or unusual drawing skills (Park 1978, Selfe 1977). However, sample bias, inadequate evaluation of multiple cognitive abilities, and Kanner's observation that his autistic children lacked any particular physical stigmata, all contributed to this erroneous presumption of normal intelligence. Hermelin & O'Connor (1970) found specific cognitive deficits in autistic children when mental functions were assessed systematically. Autistic children, compared to a matched group of retarded children, made less use of meaning in their memory processes, showed impaired concept use, and exhibited particular deficits in coding and categorizing. Rutter & Lockyer (1967) found autistic children did poorly on verbal tasks requiring abstract thought and logic but relatively well on puzzle-type tests as assessed on the WISC. Contrary to Kanner's first formulation, numerous studies have subsequently reported that over 50% of the autistic subjects had IQ scores below 50. From the North Carolina TEACCH program, Schopler et al (1979) have corroborated this finding.

Therefore, an intellectual deficit emerges when standardized intelligence tests are used, and profile differences are found when studies compare an autistic group with an appropriately matched MR group. Rutter (1982) cited his earlier studies which provide evidence that "mental subnormality as a concept is insufficient to account for autism" (p. 989). The use of an overall IQ score is of little use in planning educational programs, since the autistic child commonly exhibits a widely scattered profile. Mental retardation is a common correlate of autism, but not a defining feature, since various differences in abilities and behavioral characteristics appear between autistic and mentally retarded children. DeMyer et al (1981) aptly point out that "the goal should not be to diagnose mental retardation versus infantile autism, but to judge the degree of intellectual retardation or inadequacy in the various facets of intelligence" (p. 402) "which would impinge on program development and outcome" (see below and also Bartak & Rutter 1976).

CHILDHOOD SCHIZOPHRENIA   Early studies considered schizophrenia and autism to be the same disorder (Creak 1964) and thus did not represent a necessary differentiation (Bender 1947, Goldfarb 1961). Kanner's (1943) conceptualization that autism represented an early form of schizophrenia has received little empirical support. Much of the evidence against this presumption comes from follow-up studies of infantile autism in relation to criteria for adult schizophrenia. Numerous differentiating characteristics exist between these two disorders. Sex ratios appear equal for schizophrenia whereas there is a preponderance of male autistics (Rutter 1967). Even with referral policies of clinics controlled for, some epidemiological studies have confirmed that a higher proportion of parents of autistic children are of above average intelligence and show a higher SES (Lotter 1966, 1967; Dahl et al 1986). An adequate explanation for this familial feature has not yet been developed. A third discriminating characteristic for autism is that schizophrenia is rare in the immediate family of autistic children (Rutter 1967), but there is a clear genetic component in families of schizophrenics (Brown 1967; Shields 1967). Mental deficiency or characteristic profiles on IQ tests are not evident with schizophrenics (Pollack 1960) but, as mentioned earlier, is a common correlate to autism. Rutter (1970) showed that autistic children rarely develop delusions and hallucinations when they reach adulthood, which is in contrast to schizophrenia (Mayer-Gross et al 1955). Finally, the course of the two conditions appears much different, with autism showing a steady course (Rutter et al 1967) and fluctuations being common in schizophrenia.

RECEPTIVE LANGUAGE DISORDERS   As a result of research implemented by Bartak and colleagues (Bartak et al 1975, Cantwell et al 1978) in which direct comparisons were made between autistic children with language deficits and receptive dysphasic children, a refinement resulted from an earlier belief that language disorders found in autistic children were similar to those found in the developmental disorders of receptive language (Rutter 1968). Bartak et al (1975) found that the two groups showed different social and behavioral characteristics and that dysphasic children do not necessarily show autistic behavior despite extreme difficulty in receptive language. Furthermore, similarities between the two groups in nonverbal intelligence, visuospatial perceptual function (Bartak et al 1975), and syntax (Cantwell et al 1978) were found. This suggests that the autistic child's social behavior and language impairments more fully explain the presentation of the autistic syndrome than do the language impairments alone. Marked differences indicate that autism is associated with language *and* cognitive deficits showing greater severity, pervasiveness, and different patterns which clearly differentiate the language-impaired autistic child from the dysphasic child. Rutter (1982) pointed out the necessity for studying some underlying reason for the lack of appropriate language use and its application to social communication.

Causes

Numerous etiologies have been proposed for infantile autism, none of which have provided consistent evidence or have been able to account for more than small subgroups of autistic children. One difficulty in attributing etiologic significance to any one variable is that autism may co-exist with diseases and other syndromes which do not have any causal relationship to infantile autism. Nonetheless, many hypotheses have been generated from diverse methodologies. The reader is directed to a review by DeMyer et al (1981) for a comprehensive discussion regarding causal theories of autism.

CEREBRAL DYSFUNCTION   Mounting evidence suggests that autism is associated with a variety of brain pathologies, although if taken as a group, they represent a heterogeneous collection. Bartak & Rutter (1976) found that mentally retarded autistic children frequently develop epilepsy. The frequency of infantile spasms in autistic children also suggests a neurological basis for autism (Taft & Cohen 1971). Congenital rubella has been shown to be present in 8–10% of autistic cases (Chess 1976, Chess et al 1971). Fein et al (1984) concluded that a left hemisphere dysfunction hypothesis to account for language abnormalities in autism is inadequate. They also concluded that EEG abnormalities are not present in most autistic children. Tsai et al (1985) suggested the unlikely usefulness of EEG in providing subgroup typologies. If abnormalities do exist, they appear bilaterally. It is apparent from this, together with the nature of major cognitive, language, and behavioral abnormalities, that autism cannot be attributed to left hemispheric dysfunction alone.

NEUROCHEMICAL ANTECEDENTS   Young et al (1982) provided consistent evidence that there is a disturbance in serotonin release and turnover as indexed by lower levels of CSF 5-hydroxyindoleacetic acid (5-HIAA). Hyperserotonemia in blood has been consistently found in one-third of autistic children (Campbell et al 1975). However, this is not specific to autism and may be related to the degree of mental retardation (Hanley et al 1977). Increased dopaminergic transmission as indexed by higher levels of homovanillic acid has been found in a subgroup of severely impaired autistic children with increased locomotor activity and stereotypies (Cohen et al 1977). Deutsch et al (1985) found a 30% incidence of blunted plasma growth hormone responses following l-dopa administration, possibly identifying an autistic subgroup with blunted hypothalamic dopamine receptor sensitivity.

FAMILY BACKGROUND   Genetic disorders such as phenylketonuria (PKU) and the Fragile-X syndrome have been reported in autistic patients (Benezech et al 1983; Friedman 1969; Gillberg 1983; Levitas et al 1983; Lowe et al 1980; see also Pueschel et al 1985). Ritvo & Freeman (1984) suggested that the recessive gene which transmits a specific enzymatic defect like PKU could directly provide structural brain abnormalities or other types of neuropathology. It is likely, however, that these genetic conditions at best represent a specific etiology of or simply an associated feature in a subgroup of children with infantile autism. A further confound seems to be that PKU and Fragile-X syndrome may have a closer causal relationship to MR, which appears frequently in infantile autism.

Studies of heredity, i.e. comparing monozygotic and dizygotic twins and siblings with autism, have appeared with greater frequency since 1963 (Vaillant 1963). Rutter (1968) reported a higher incidence of autism among siblings of autistic probands than in the general population. Folstein & Rutter (1977) compared 11 monozygotic and 10 dizygotic twin pairs. The pairwise concordance rate with MZ pairs was 36% versus 0% in DZ pairs. Cognitive abnormalities showed an 82% concordance rate with MZ and 10% with DZ. This suggested the presence of hereditary influences leading to a cognitive deficit which included but was not restricted to autism. August et al (1981) and Ritvo et al (1982) found multiple incidences of autism and cognitive disabilities among relatives of autistic persons. Subdividing a group of biological siblings of 29 autistic probands on the basis of IQ, Baird & August (1985) found a significant clustering of autism and nonspecific intellectual retardation in the siblings of severely retarded autistic probands. The fact that this clustering was not present in siblings of a higher functioning autistic group suggests etiologic differences depending on the degree of associated MR. Once again, we see the importance of MR as a possible subgrouping factor when attempting to delineate etiological factors in autism, since it appears that a genetic factor is related to only a specific subgroup of autistic individuals.

Theories of parental psychogenesis have been presented as a causal factor in autism, but have not been accompanied by empirical evidence (Cantwell et al 1978). Schopler (1983) noted that a variety of "pejorative epithets" have been used to describe the parents of autistic children, including "cold, refrigerator mothers, undemonstrative, introverted, obsessive, overprotective, symbiotic, indecisive, lacking dominance, showing perplexity resulting in lack of spontaneity, psychic paralysis, and double bind" (page 97). This variety could result from scapegoating techniques directed toward parents of psychotic children (Schopler 1971).

The association between autism and socioeconomic status has long been debated. Overall, research suggesting that a higher than expected incidence of high SES families have autistic children can be accounted for by a number of selection factors (Schopler et al 1979, Wing 1980, Schopler 1983). These factors, although not representing an exhaustive list, include: (a) the level of parental education and availability of resources affected the early recognition and identification of autistic symptoms; (b) parents who traveled a greater distance for treatment would have more knowledge and greater financial resources if from a higher SES than those coming for treatment from short distances; (c) a higher SES group resulted from the previous private funding of programs for autistic children and their subsequent funding as public programs. Confounds regarding social class membership still appear in the literature (see Steinhausen et al 1986), and will require that availability of resources be taken into account and that epidemiological studies be performed with unbiased samples.

Outcome

Prognosis for the autistic child is, at best, guarded. Lotter (1978) found that over 25% of autistic children who were not epileptic in childhood developed seizures between the ages of 15 and 29. The likelihood of seizures developing appears to be associated with IQ, with proportions being relatively high in severely retarded autistic children.

In fact, IQ clearly is the most potent prognostic factor in later cognitive and social development in autistic children. Schopler (1983) indicated that when IQ deficits are in the moderate to severe range (IQ less than 50), outcome is particularly poor. Nonverbal IQs above 70 usually predict good adjustment through adult life in 50% of the cases (Rutter 1977). Even with intelligent autistic children, language impairment is another poor prognostic sign, particularly if language comprehension is severely impaired in preschool or gainful use of speech is not obtained by age 5 (Ornitz 1973, Rutter 1977). Rutter (1978) indicated that autistic children without constructive, symbolic play also have a poor prognosis.

Overall, childhood autism is a disorder from which recovery rarely occurs, and may continue to be manifested in a residual state (see DSM-III, American Psychiatric Association 1980). The degree of impairment in language or IQ is clearly associated with lower employability, lack of the kind of interpersonal relationships leading to marriage, and the need for institutional care. However, treatment can reduce the potentially debilitating symptoms (particularly when mental retardation is not an associated problem), allowing for development of better social adjustment and perhaps of gainful employment (Rutter 1977).

Treatment Response

Approaches in treating the autistic child have undergone considerable change in the past 20 years. Many have proved to be ineffective because of unsubstantiated evidence regarding the etiology of autism as an emotional disorder, for which traditional psychotherapy was usually attempted, and/or parental psychogenesis, for which removal from the home was commonly carried out. Since autism is now considered to be a developmental disorder, pharmacotherapy or behavioral/educational treatment programs utilizing such techniques in a developmental context (Lansing & Schopler 1978) have been the focus.

BEHAVIORAL/EDUCATIONAL PROGRAMS   Many programs have emphasized the application of behavioral methods to develop language skills. Lovaas et al (1973) were able to develop spontaneous speech in autistic children through an intensive shaping procedure. However, follow-up studies (Lovaas et al 1974, 1977), have often failed to find maintenance and further development of verbal gains once the training and reinforcement contingencies have stopped. Harris et al (1981) found that autistic children maintained their gains in verbal skills, but no improvement beyond that point was noted at a one-year followup. This suggests that autistic children fail to generalize from the intensive training. Ornitz (1973) reflected the feeling of many by stating that the response to treatment is determined primarily by the degree of impairment and only secondarily by the type of treatment in the individual case (p. 38).

Behavioral methods applied in the developmental context with parents as co-therapists have been part of a strong movement to provide a highly structured psychoeducational teaching approach exemplified by the North Carolina TEACCH program (Schopler & Reichler 1971). Evaluation of the TEACCH program (Schopler et al 1982) indicates: (*a*) parental perception of effectiveness was very high; (*b*) the program increased family adaptiveness and reduced stress; and (*c*) institutionalization rates of 8% at followup were significantly lower than figures from earlier studies reporting rates of between 39% to 74% (Lotter 1978). However, a study of the immediate outcome as a result of the TEACCH program (Short 1984) indicates that treatment effects were not shown for inappropriate child behavior and family stress and adaptive measures. A significant treatment effect was found for appropriate child behavior and parental involvement. This suggests the necessity for further research to determine the particular aspects of the program which contribute to therapeutic change.

PHARMACOTHERAPY   Haloperidol, a high-potency dopamine antagonist, has been found to have facilitating effects on learning in an enriched social environment (Campbell et al 1978). In an attempt to assess whether the positive learning effects resulted from change in attentional mechanisms or reduction of stereotypies and withdrawal symptoms, Anderson et al (1984) assessed 40 autistic children in a double-blind, placebo-controlled study with an ABA design. Overall, haloperidol administration resulted in a significant decrease in hyperactivity, fidgeting, and stereotypies in addition to greater facilitation of discriminant learning. This provides pharmacological evidence that autism may involve excessive dopaminergic activity (also reflected in the fact that some retarded autistic children show high levels of HVA in the CSF).

Consistent with the report that some autistic children are hyperserotonemic, fenfluramine (usually employed as an appetite suppressant), has also shown to be effective in the treatment of infantile autism. Geller et al (1982) found that fenfluramine decreased platelet serotonin, which resulted in increases in IQ scores and decreases in certain clinical symptoms. August et al (1985) found a significant reduction in motor disturbance, hyperactivity, and distractibility in response to fenfluramine which was associated with a 60% reduction of serotonin "without apparent adverse effects."

Haloperidol and fenfluramine provide a promising approach to the amelioration of at least some behavioral symptoms associated with autism. Further studies, however, must assess the frequency of side effects and long-term effects of these agents, since cessation of fenfluramine results in the return of the behavioral symptoms associated with autism. Since traditional behavioral management programs have shown a relatively poor outcome, well-controlled, multimeasure studies may assist in the development of a more effective approach which might incorporate behavioral management and pharmacological techniques.

DEPRESSION

Definition and Reliability

Affective disorders, i.e. depressions and manias, among adults are among the best established syndromes in the field of psychopathology (Cantwell & Carlson 1983a). Although there is hardly perfect agreement on how to define the various subcategories of depression in adulthood, there is certainly consensus on the importance of distinctions such as that between bipolar (manic-depressive) and unipolar depression, and between syndromes of greater and lesser severity within unipolar depression. Some of the distinct varieties of depression in adulthood have been demonstrated to be familial. Over 200 double-blind, placebo-controlled studies exist validating the efficacy of tricyclic antidepressant medications for the treatment of depressed adults (Cantwell 1983), and the efficacy of lithium for bipolar conditions is also well documented. The dexamethasone suppression test (DST) has been found to be a reliable biological marker of the more severe depressive states in adults (Puig-Antich 1983). It is thus not surprising that researchers and clinicians have wished to know to what extent all of these findings can be generalized to childhood and adolescence.

The question much debated over the last several years is whether any of these clinical syndromes of depression occur in prepubertal children. In fact, the authors of this chapter do not agree among themselves about this matter. It is obvious that even very young children do experience sadness and various other "depressive" symptoms, but are there any identifiable clinical syndromes of depression in childhood?

When psychoanalytic theory held a more dominant position among students of child psychopathology, the prevalent view (e.g. Rie 1966) was that children could not be depressed because of the immaturity of their superego functioning (depression being viewed as an attack on the ego by the superego).

In the 1970s the hypothesis of "masked depression" was put forward. The idea was that depression manifested itself differently in children, in the form of various "depressive equivalents." Thus, symptoms of hyperactivity or conduct problems might be viewed as evidence of an underlying depressive condition. It is certainly plausible that what is seen as irritability or agitation in an adult depressed person might be revealed as aggressive behavior or overt motor activity in a depressed child. This hypothesis was difficult to investigate, however, because it was unclear how one was to go about identifying the supposed underlying depressed state. If the depressed state could be identified by explicit criteria, it was not useful to describe it as "masked." If certain subtle criteria are to be used, these must be specified before one can test the hypothesis of masked depression in children.

An influential theoretical paper by Lefkowitz & Burton (1978) questioned whether a clinical syndrome of depression existed in childhood, primarily on the basis of the transience of depressive symptoms in children. Lefkowitz and his colleagues certainly seemed to believe in the existence of depressive symptoms (if not of a depression syndrome) in children, to judge by their subsequent high level of research activity in this area.

The authors of the DSM-III (American Psychiatric Association 1980) at least implicitly took the position that clinical depression does exist in childhood (and adolescence) and that the same general criteria could be used to identify it as are used in adults. In other words, even though there were admitted to be some age differences in how depression manifested itself, the basic phenomena were judged to be the same in children and adults.

Epidemiological data suggest that the prevalence of treated depression is relatively low in children, increases during adolescence, and continues to increase over the adult years (e.g. U.S. Department of Health, Education, and Welfare 1977a,b). Using DSM-III criteria, Kashani et al (1983) estimated the point prevalence of major depression to be 1.8% and that of minor depression to be 2.5% in a sample of 9-year-old children from the general population.

Since the DSM-III appeared, there has been some movement toward accepting its views as to the existence of depressive syndrome(s) in childhood (e.g. Cantwell & Carlson 1983b). As far as we can see, the primary evidence for this is the fact that children reliably can be shown to meet some established criteria for depression. These could be for one of the DSM-III syndromes of depression or other criteria such as the Weinberg et al (1973) or the RDC criteria.

Puig-Antich et al (1978) identified a group of 13 prepubertal children (5 girls and 8 boys) who met unmodified Research Diagnostic Criteria for major depressive disorder. In this study, it is interesting to note that all 13 children had the symptom of separation anxiety as well as depression (onset of separation anxiety followed the onset of depressive mood in every case), and all five boys who were over 10 years old also presented conduct disturbances. Carlson & Cantwell (1979) found that of a series of 102 children evaluated at a psychiatric facility, 28 met DSM-III criteria for some type of affective disorder. Fourteen of these had a primary affective disorder in that no other preexisting psychiatric disorder was identified. Lobovits & Handal (1985) evaluated a series of 50 children age 8–12 seen at two psychology outpatient centers. They found that two independent clinicians listening to audiotaped interviews and using DSM-III criteria for a major depressive episode agreed 90% of the time on the diagnosis. The prevalence of depression defined in this way was 34% based on child interview data but only 22% based on parent interview. Kashani & Carlson (1985) even reported a preschool age child (2 years, 11 months, 25 days of age) who met DSM-III criteria for a major depressive disorder. All of these studies agree that a significant number of children meet the DSM-III criteria for depression. As Kashani & Carlson (1985) commented, however, it is not always clear that for a child to have all the symptoms on a list designed to evaluate adults is the same as having the syndrome of depression. It would be more convincing to validate the syndrome with evidence concerning etiology, outcome, or treatment response obtained from samples of children.

The DSM-III (1980) criteria for a major depressive episode are as follows:

A. Dysphoric mood or loss of interest or pleasure in all or almost all usual activities and pastimes. The dysphoric mood is characterized by symptoms such as the following: depressed, sad, blue, hopeless, low, down in the dumps, irritable. The mood disturbance must be prominent and relatively persistent, but not necessarily the most dominant symptom, and does not include momentary shifts from one dysphoric mood to another dysphoric mood, e.g. anxiety to depression to anger, such as are seen in states of acute psychotic turmoil. (For children under six, dysphoric mood may have to be inferred from a persistently sad facial expression).

B. At least four of the following symptoms have each been present nearly every day for a period of at least two weeks (in children under six, at least three of the first four).

    1. poor appetite or significant weight loss (when not dieting) or increased appetite or significant weight gain (in children under six, consider failure to make expected weight gains)
    2. insomnia or hypersomnia
    3. psychomotor agitation or retardation (but not merely subjective feelings of restlessness or being slowed down) (in children under six, hypoactivity)
    4. loss of interest or pleasure in usual activities or decrease in sexual drive not limited to a period when delusional or hallucinating (in children under six, signs of apathy)
    5. loss of energy; fatigue
    6. feelings of worthlessness, self-reproach, or excessive or inappropriate guilt (either may be delusional)
    7. complaints or evidence of diminished ability to think or concentrate, such as slowed thinking, or indecisiveness not associated with marked loosening of associations or incoherence

8. recurrent thoughts of death, suicidal ideation, wishes to be dead, or suicide attempt.
C. Neither of the following dominates the clinical picture when an affective syndrome is absent (i.e. symptoms in criteria A and B above):
   1. preoccupation with a mood-incongruent delusion or hallucination
   2. bizarre behavior
D. Not superimposed on schizophrenia, schizophreniform disorder, or a paranoid disorder
E. Not due to any organic mental disorder or uncomplicated bereavement (pp. 213–14).

Research on the assessment of depressive symptoms in children has been actively pursued during the last several years. However, its focus has not been upon validating particular symptoms from a list such as the one quoted above. Rather, researchers have concentrated their efforts upon the development and validation of various psychometric measures of depressive symptoms. For example, Kovacs & Beck (1977) developed a self-report questionnaire known as the Children's Depression Inventory (CDI); it is essentially a downward extension of the Beck Depression Inventory (Beck 1967), one of the scales most commonly used with adults. Similarly, Poznanski et al (1979) developed a rating scale to be used by clinicians called the Children's Depression Rating Scale; it is an adaptation of the Hamilton (1960) scale used with adults. Lefkowitz & Tesiny (1980) developed a sociometric measure known as the Peer Nomination Inventory of Depression (PNID). Finally, various standardized psychiatric interview procedures for children and their parents include questions concerning a child's depression. Puig-Antich et al (1983) stated an emerging consensus view that "in the assessment of . . . symptoms which are manifested mostly intrapsychically and which reflect subjective phenomena (emotions, feelings, ideas), information obtained from the child is essential" (p. 162). Several studies in recent years have confirmed the ability of prepubertal children to give accurate information (Rutter & Graham 1968, Herjanic et al 1975, Herjanic & Campbell 1977).

Kazdin and his colleagues (1985) have published research on the relation of direct behavioral observations to depression among child psychiatric patients. It would be useful if, on the one hand, developers of criteria for a depression syndrome would be more explicit about how the symptoms in the list are to be measured operationally. It would likewise be useful if the developers of psychometric measures of depression would try to coordinate their research with that on the issue of putative child depression syndrome(s).

One of the more interesting areas of research on affective disorders in recent years has been the development of the dexamethasone suppression test as a "state marker" for severe depressive episodes in adults. These individuals hypersecrete cortisol, and when an attempt is made to suppress cortisol production by dexamethasone, they tend to escape the suppression within a 24-hour period. Recent research with depressed children has indicated that a certain number of them also have these abnormal reactions to the DST. Unfortunately, this reaction does not appear to be unique to depressive states in children. Recent research showed that the DST was also often abnormal among children with autism (Jensen et al 1985). Physiological tests such as the DST have a special interest because of their potential for assessing depressive or other states in nonverbal humans. Along these lines, Pirodsky et al (1985), for example, used the DST with a sample of 39 mentally retarded adults. Individuals manifesting any two or more of three particular types of deviant behaviors (unprovoked aggression/assault, self-injurious behavior, or severe withdrawal) were significantly more likely to have abnormal findings on the DST. More research is needed, however, investigating the reliability of the DST in child populations.

Causes

Among adults, depression may occur not only as a primary problem but also may be secondary to a wide variety of physical and mental disorders, including rheumatoid arthritis, Cushing's disease, alcoholism, and anxiety disorders (Cantwell & Carlson 1983b). Such secondary depressive states have not yet received much systematic study in childhood and adolescence, however.

Also, various depression syndromes among adults have been shown to be familial. Once criteria for a syndrome of depression among children have been tentatively identified, one naturally wonders whether it is predictive of affective disorders in the child's relatives as compared to an appropriate control group.

There are certain existing studies that look at the offspring of depressed adults. For example, Klein et al (1985) found that the adolescents whose parents had bipolar affective disorder were more likely to have affective disorders, in particular, cyclothymia than the offspring of adults in a control group. Another study by Cytryn et al (1982) compared 19 children of manic-depressive parents with 21 children of normal parents. Significantly more of the children of manic-depressive parents met criteria for childhood depression, and this was true whether Weinberg or DSM-III criteria were used.

Distinguishing Depression from Related Disorders

Regardless of whether childhood syndrome(s) of depression exist, it is clear that dysphoric affect in children covaries with anxiety and social withdrawal to make up the ubiquitous "internalizing" dimension (Quay 1986a). It would be well for those who are trying to devise relatively "pure" measures of depression to assure themselves that they have not inadvertently included items measuring other constructs in their questionnaires and rating scales. Saylor and her colleagues (Saylor et al 1984a,b) have done empirical research documenting the relatively high degree of overlap between child depression, as measured by the CDI, and the related negative affects of anger and anxiety, respectively. In general, this area of research suffers from a lack of differential validity studies of depression vs anxiety, social withdrawal, and other related disorders.

Outcome

Since criteria for a depression syndrome have been identified only very recently in children, there has not been sufficient time for much longitudinal research to be carried out with this population. In the future it would be of interest to see whether affective disorders in childhood place a child at higher risk than the general population for similar types of affective disorders in adulthood.

One recent investigation that does bear on the outcome of childhood depression was that of Puig-Antich (1982). He found that one-third of a group of children with conduct disorders also met the DSM-III criteria for major depression. Interestingly, in 14 out of 16 of these cases, the onset of the depression was prior to the onset of the conduct problems. Also, in 11 out of 13 boys, the conduct problem disorder abated after the depression terminated. This is the same kind of relationship between depression and conduct disorder postulated by the old masked depression hypothesis, except that here the depression was overt rather than masked. If this research is confirmed by other studies, conduct problems may be established as one possible sequel to depression.

Tesiny & Lefkowitz (1982) carried out a 6-month follow-up study of depressive symptoms in fourth and fifth-grade children as measured by self-reports (a modified version of the CDI), peer nominations (the PNID), and teacher ratings. The Pearson rs over the 6-month interval for these three different measures were .44, .70, and .60, respectively, suggesting that the children's depressive symptoms were relatively stable over time. This would seem to be evidence against Lefkowitz & Burton's (1978) earlier argument that such depressive symptoms were too transient in children to be regarded as evidence of psychopathology.

Another well-known consequence of depression in adulthood is suicide. Suicide has not been linked so closely to depression in childhood and adolescence. Indeed, suicide in adolescence seems to be more closely linked to substance abuse and conduct problems than to depression. But it is nevertheless interesting that like the rate of identified depression, suicide rates are quite low before puberty and rise rather strikingly from age 15 onward (Shaffer & Fisher 1981).

Treatment Response

Controlled studies of the effects of antidepressant medications upon child depression are beginning to appear (e.g. the Puig-Antich 1982 study already mentioned, in which the evidence most suggestive of a drug effect was a significant correlation between plasma levels of imipramine in clinical response). Unfortunately, at this point, the results of such research are equivocal. Certainly, antidepressant drugs do not seem to have as dramatic an effect on child depression as upon the adult variety.

Status of Child Depression as a Syndrome

At present, the strongest argument that can be made for the existence of clinical depression in children is that many different studies, using reliable assessment methods, have found a significant number of children who fit rigorous adult-oriented criteria for depression. The skeptic can argue that the concept of a depression syndrome in childhood should rest on evidence gathered using a child subject population, or at least be supported by longitudinal data showing depressed children to be at higher risk for adult affective disorders. Few such data exist at present.

CONCLUSIONS

As noted in the introduction, we elected to discuss only those major disorders/dimensions that are the focus of the greatest current interest in the field. The five chosen meet our criteria for a syndrome to varying degrees. With respect to these major disorders, the field is clearly further along in its ability to describe and identify them reliably and to make prognostic statements than it is to provide solid information as to etiology and treatment. Many problems of distinguishing one syndrome from related ones also remain.

There are, of course, many other putative disorders in DSM-III and elsewhere which we did not review. Because most of these other disorders have been the focus of less research, it might be inferred that the majority of these are even less likely to meet our criteria.

Our review leaves us even more convinced that validation is now much more in order than is further taxonomy-building. We clearly need fewer studies comparing disordered children to normal ones and more studies comparing the syndromes to one another. There is even less reason to lump children with different disorders together into a single group given some generic label such as "emotionally disturbed." Also needed are more longitudinal studies of carefully selected groups of youngsters in which biological, family, and other environmental influences are all assessed so that their joint contributions to outcome can be determined.

Literature Cited

Abikoff, H., Gittelman, R., Klein, D. F. 1980. Classroom observation code for hyperactive children: A replication of validity. *J. Consult. Clin. Psychol.* 48(5):555–65

Abikoff, H., Gittelman-Klein, R., Klein, D. F. 1977. Validation of a classroom observational code for hyperactive children. *J. Consult. Clin. Psychol.* 45:772–83

Achenbach, T. M., Edelbrock, C. S. 1978. The classification of child psychopathology. *J. Am. Acad. Child Psychiatry* 85:1275–1301

Achenbach, T. M., Edelbrock, C. S. 1979. The Child Behavior Profile. II. Boys aged 12–16 and girls aged 6–11 and 12–16. *J. Consult. Clin. Psychol.* 47:223–33

American Psychiatric Association. 1980. *DSM-III: Diagnostic and Statistical Manual of Mental Disorders.* Washington, DC: APA. 3rd ed.

Amery, B., Minichiello, M. D., Brown, G. L. 1984. Aggression in hyperactive boys: Response to d-amphetamine. *J. Am. Acad. Child Psychiatry* 23:291–94

Anderson, J. C., Williams, S., McGee, R., Silva, P. A. 1985. Cognitive and social correlates of DSM-III disorders identified in a sample of 11 year old children from the general population. Unpublished ms

Anderson, L. T., Campbell, M., Grega, D. M., Perry, R., Small, A. M., et al. 1984. Haloperidol in the treatment of infantile autism: Effects on learning and behavioral symptoms. *Am. J. Psychiatry* 141:1195–1202

Applebaum, E., Egel, A. L., Koegel, R. L., Imhoff, B. 1979. Measuring musical abilities of autistic children. *J. Autism Dev. Dis.* 9:279–85

August, G. R., Raz, N., Baird, T. D. 1985. Affects of fenfluramine on behavioral, cognitive, and affective disturbances in autistic children. *J. Autism Dev. Dis.* 15:97–107

August, G. R., Stewart, M. A. 1982. Is there a syndrome of pure hyperactivity? *Br. J. Psychiatry* 140:305–11

August, G. R., Stewart, M. A., Holmes, C. S. 1983. A Four-year follow-up of hyperactive boys with and without conduct disorder. *Br. J. Psychiatry* 143:192–98

August, G. R., Stewart, M. A., Tsai, L. 1981. The incidence of cognitive abilities of autistic children. *Br. J. Psychiatry* 138:416–22

Baird, T. D., August, G. R. 1985. Familial heterogeneity in infantile autism. *J. Autism Dev. Dis.* 15:315–21

Bartak, L., Rutter, M. 1976. Differences between mentally retarded and normally intelligent autistic children. *J. Autism Child. Schizophr.* 6:109–20

Bartak, L., Rutter, M., Cox, A. 1975. A comparative study of infantile autism and specific developmental receptive language; I. The children. *Br. J. Psychiatry* 126:127–45

Beck, A. T. 1967. *Depression: Causes and Treatment.* Philadelphia: Univ. Penn. Press

Bender, L. 1947. Childhood schizophrenia: Clinical study of one hundred schizophrenic children. *Am. J. Orthopsychiatry* 17:40–56

Benezech, M., Noel, B., Noel, L., Bourgeois, M. 1983. Fragile X chromosome and autistic mental retardation. Apropos of 23 cases. *Ann. Med. Psychol. Paris* 141:1006–11

Bentler, P. M., McClain, J. 1976. A multitrait-multimethod analysis of reflection-impulsivity. *Child Dev.* 47:218–26

Block, J., Block, J. H., Harrington, D. M. 1974. Some misgivings about the Matching Familiar Figures Test as a Measure of reflection-impulsivity. *Dev. Psychol.* 10:611–32

Blue, S. W., Madsen, C. H., Heimberg, R. G. 1982. Increasing coping behavior in children with aggressive behavior: Evaluation of the relative efficacy of the components of a treatment package. *Child Behav. Ther.* 3:51–60

Borkovec, T. D. 1970. Autonomic reactivity to sensory stimulation in psychopathic, neurotic and normal delinquents. *J. Consult. Clin. Psychol.* 35:217–22

Brown, G. W. 1967. The family of the schizophrenic patient. In *Recent Developments in Schizophrenia: A Symposium*, ed. A. J. Coppen, A. Walk. London: Royal Medico-Psychol. Assoc.

Campbell, M., Anderson, L. T., Meier, M., Cohen, I. L., Small, A. M., et al. 1978. A comparison of haloperidol and behavior therapy and their interaction in autistic children. *J. Am. Acad. Child Psychiatry* 17:640–55

Campbell, M., Cohen, I. L., Small, A. M. 1982. Drugs in aggressive behavior *J. Am. Acad. Child Psychiatry* 21:107–17

Campbell, M., Friedman, E., Green, W. H., Collins, P. J., Small, A. M., Breuer, H. 1975. Blood serotonin in schizophrenic children: A preliminary study. *Int. Pharmacopsychiatry* 10:213–21

Campbell, M., Small, A. M., Green, W. H., Jennings, S. J., Perry, R., et al. 1984. Behavioral efficacy of haloperidol and lithium carbonate. *Arch. Gen. Psychiatry* 41:650–56

Campbell, S. B., Douglas, V. I., Morgenstern, G. 1971. Cognitive styles in hyperactive children and the effect of methylphenidate. *J. Child Psychol. Psychiatry* 12:55–67

Cantwell, D. P. 1983. Issues in the management of childhood depression. See Cantwell & Carlson 1983a, pp. 354–62

Cantwell, D. P., Bartak, L., Rutter, M. 1978. A comparative study of infantile autism and specific developmental receptive language disorder. IV: Analysis of syntax and language function. *J. Child Psychol. Psychiatry* 19:351–62

Cantwell, D. P., Carlson, G. A. 1983a. Preface. In *Affective Disorders in Childhood and Adolescence: An Update*, ed. D. P. Cantwell, G. A. Carlson. New York: SP Medical/Scientific Books

Cantwell, D. P., Carlson, G. A. 1983b. Depression in childhood: Clinical picture and diagnostic criteria. See Cantwell & Carlson 1983a, pp. 3–18

Carbone, J. V., Brandborg, L. L., Silverman, S. Jr. 1980. Alimentary tract and liver. In *Current Medical Diagnosis and Treatment*, ed. M. A. Krupp, M. J. Chatton. Los Altos, CA: Lange Medical

Carlson, G. A., Cantwell, D. P. 1979. Unmasking masked depression in children and adolescents. *Am. J. Psychiatry* 137:445–49

Chess, S. 1976. Autism in children with congenital rubella. *J. Autism Child. Schizophr.* 1:33–47

Chess, S., Korn, S. J., Fernandez, P. B. 1971. *Psychiatric Disorders of Children with Congenital Rubella*. New York: Brunner/Mazel

Claridge, G. 1981. Arousal. In *Aspects of Consciousness*, ed. G. Underwood, R. Stevens, 2:119–47. New York: Academic

Cohen, D. J., Caparulo, B. K., Shaywitz, B. A., Bowers, M. B. 1977. Dopamine and serotonin metabolism in neuropsychiatrically disturbed children: CSF homovanillic acid and 5-hydroxyindoleacetic acid. *Arch. Gen. Psychiatry* 34:545–50

Conners, C. K. 1969. A teacher rating scale for use in drug studies with children. *Am. J. Psychiatry* 126:884–88

Creak, M. 1964. Schizophrenic syndrome in childhood: Further progress report of a working party. *Dev. Med. Child Neurol.* 6:530–35

Cytryn, L., McKnew, D. H. Jr., Bartko, J. J., Lamour, M., Hamovitt, J. 1982. Offspring of patients with affective disorders: II. *J. Am. Acad. Child Psychiatry* 21:389–91

Dahl, E. K., Cohen, D. J., Provence, S. 1986. Clinical and multivariate approaches to the nosology of pervasive developmental disorders. *J. Am. Acad. Child Psychiatry* 25:170–80

Dejerine, J. 1891. Sur un cas de cecite berbale avec agraphie, suivi d'autopsie. *C. R. Mem. Soc. Biol.* 3:197–201

Dejerine, J. 1892. Contribution a l'etude anatomopathologique et clinique des dif-

ferentes varietes de cecite verbale. *C. R. Mem. Soc. Biol.* 4:61–90

Delamater, A. M., Lahey, B. B. 1983. Physiologic correlates of conduct problems and anxiety in hyperactive and learning-disabled children. *J. Abnorm. Child Psychol.* 11:85–100

Deluty, R. H. 1981a. Adaptiveness of aggressive, assertive, and submissive behavior for children. *J. Clin. Child Psychol.* 10(2):155–58

Deluty, R. H. 1981b. Alternative-thinking ability of aggressive, assertive and submissive children. *Cognit. Ther. Res.* 5:309–12

DeMyer, M. K., Hingtgen, J. N., Jackson, R. K. 1981. Infantile Autism reviewed: A decade of research. *Schizophr. Bull.* 7:388–451

Deutsch, S. I., Campbell, M., Sachar, E. J., Green, W. H., David, R. 1985. Plasma growth hormone release to oral L-dopa in infantile autism. *J. Autism Dev. Dis.* 15:205–12

Dishion, T. J., Loeber, R. 1987. Adolescent marijuana and alcohol use: The role of parents and peers revisited. *Res. Crime Delinq.* In press

Dodge, K. A. 1980. Social Cognition and children's aggressive behavior. *Child Dev.* 51:162–70

Dreger, R. M. 1982. The classification of children and their emotional problems: An overview—II. *Clin. Psychol. Rev.* 2:349–85

Edelbrock, C., Achenbach, T. M. 1984. The teacher version of the Child Behavior Profile: I. Boys aged 6–11. *J. Consult. Clin. Psychol.* 52:207–17

Ellis, P. L. 1982. Empathy: A factor in antisocial personality. *J. Abnorm. Child Psychol.* 10:123–34

Eron, L. D. 1982. Parent-child interaction, television violence, and aggression of children. *Am. Psychol.* 37:197–211

Eron, L. D., Walder, L. O., Lefkowitz, M. M. 1971. *Learning of Aggression in Children*. Boston: Little, Brown

Fagot, B. I. 1984. The consequences of problem behavior in toddler children. *J. Abnorm. Child Psychol.* 12:385–96

Fein, D., Humes, M., Kaplan, E., Lucci, D., Waterhouse, L. 1984. The question of left hemisphere dysfunction in autistic children. *Psychol. Bull.* 95:258–81

Fein, D., Pennington, B., Markowitz, P., Brayerman, M., Waterhouse, L. 1986. Toward a neuropsychological model of infantile autism: Are the social deficits primary? *J. Am. Acad. Child Psychiatry* 25:198–212

Feldman, P. 1983. Juvenile offending: Behavioral approaches to prevention and intervention. *Child Fam. Behav. Ther.* 5(1): 37–50

Folstein, S., Rutter, M. 1977. Infantile Autism: A genetic study of 21 twin pairs. *J. Child Psychol. Psychiatry* 18:297–321

Fowles, D. C. 1980. The Three Arousal Model: Implications of Gray's two-factor learning theory for heart rate, electrodermal activity, and psychopathy. *Psychophysiology* 17:87–104

Fowles, D. C. 1983. Motivational effects on heart rate and electrodermal activity: Implications for research in personality and psychopathology. *J. Res. Pers.* 17:48–71

Freeman, B. J., Ritvo, E. R., Schroth, P. C., Tonick, I., Guthrie, D., Wake, L. 1981. Beharioral characteristics of high- and low-IQ autistic children. *Am. J. Psychiatry* 138:25–29

Friedman, E. 1969. The autistic syndrome of phenylketonuria. *Schizophrenia* 1:249–61

Geller, E., Ritvo, E. R., Freeman, B. J., Yuwiler, A. 1982. Preliminary observations on the effect of fenfluramine on blood serotonin and symptoms in three autistic boys. *N. Engl. J. Med.* 307:165–69

Gillberg, C. 1983. Identical triplets with infantile autism and the fragile X syndrome. *Br. J. Psychiatry* 143:256–60

Gittelman, R., Eskenazi, B. 1983. Lead and hyperactivity revisited: An investigation of nondisadvantaged children. *Arch. Gen. Psychiatry* 40:827–33

Goldfarb, W. 1961. *Childhood Schizophrenia.* Cambridge, MA: Harvard Univ. Press

Gray, J. A. 1979. A neuropsychological theory of anxiety. In *Emotions in Personality and Psychopathology*, ed. C. E. Izard. New York: Plenum

Gray, J. A. 1982. *The Neuropsychology of Anxiety: An Enquiry into the Functions of the Septo-Hippocampal System.* New York: Oxford Univ. Press

Hamilton, M. 1960. A rating scale for depression. *J. Neurol. Neurosurg. Psychiatry* 23:56–62

Hanley, H. G., Stahl, S. M., Friedman, D. X. 1977. Hyperserotonemia and amine metabolites in autistic and retarded children. *Arch. Gen. Psychiatry* 34:521–31

Hanson, C. L., Henggeler, S. W., Haefele, W. F., Rodick, J. D. 1984. Demographic, Individual and family relationship correlates of serious and repeated crime among adolescents and their siblings. *J. Consult. Clin. Psychol.* 52:528–38

Harris, A., Kreil, D., Orpet, R. 1977. The modification and validation of the Behavior Coding System for school settings. *Educ. Psychol. Meas.* 37:1121–26

Harris, A., Reid, J. B. 1981. The consistency of a class of coercive child behaviors across school settings for individual subjects. *J. Abnorm. Child Psychol.* 9:219–27

Harris, S. L., Wolchick, S. A., Weitz, S. 1981. The acquisition of language skills by autistic children: Can parents do the job? *J. Autism Dev. Dis.* 11:373–84

Henn, F. A., Bardwell, R., Jenkins, R. L. 1980. Juvenile delinquents revisited. *Arch. Gen. Psychiatry* 37:1160–63

Herjanic, B., Campbell, W. 1977. Differentiating psychiatrically disturbed children on the basis of a structured interview. *J. Child Psychol. Psychiatry* 5:127–34

Herjanic, B., Herjanic, M., Brown, F., Wheatt, T. 1975. Are children reliable reporters? *J. Child Psychol. Psychiatry* 3:41–48

Hermelin, B., O'Connor, N. 1970. *Psychological Experiments with Autistic Children.* New York: Pergamon

Hetherington, E. M., Stouwie, R., Ridberg, E. H. 1971. Patterns of family interaction and child rearing attitudes to three dimensions of juvenile delinquency. *J. Abnorm. Child Psychol.* 77:160–76

Hewitt, L. E., Jenkins, R. L. 1946. *Fundamental Patterns of Maladjustment, the Dynamics of Their Origin.* Springfield: State of IL

Hogan, A. E., Quay, H. C. 1984. Cognition in child and adolescent behavior disorders. In *Advances in Clinical Child Psychology*, ed. B. B. Lahey, A. E. Kazdin. New York: Plenum

Huesmann, L. R., Eron, L. D., Lefkowitz, M. M., Walder, L. O. 1984. Stability of aggression over time and generations. *Dev. Psychol.* 20:1120–34

Jensen, J. B., Realmuto, G. M., Garfinkel, B. D. 1985. The dexamethasone suppression test in infantile autism. *J. Am. Acad. Child Psychiatry* 24:263–65

Johnson, S. M., Bolstad, O. D. 1973. Methodologic Issues in Naturalistic Observation: Some problems and solutions for field research. In *Behavior Change: Methodology Concepts and Practice*, ed. L. A. Hammerlynck, L. C. Handy, E. J. Mash. Champaign, IL: Research Press

Johnston, C., Pelham, W. E., Murphy, H. A. 1985. Peer relationships in ADDH and normal children: A developmental analysis of peer and teacher ratings. *J. Abnorm. Child Psychol.* 13:89–100

Jurkovic, G. J., Prentice, N. M. 1977. Relation of moral and cognitive development to dimensions of juvenile delinquency. *J. Abnorm. Psychol.* 86:414–20

Kanner, L. 1943. Autistic disturbances of affective contact. *Nerv. Child.* 2:217–50

Kashani, J. H., Carlson, G. A. 1985. Major

depressive disorder in a preschooler. *J. Am. Acad. Child Psychiatry* 24:490–94

Kashani, J. H., McGee, R. O., Clarkson, S. E., Anderson, J. C., Walton, L. A., et al. 1983. Depression in a sample of 9-year-old children: Prevalence and associated characteristics. *Arch. Gen. Psychiatry* 40:1217–23

Kazdin, A. E., Esveldt-Dawson, K., Sherick, R. B., Colbus, D. 1985. Assessment of overt behavior and childhood depression among psychiatrically disturbed children. *J. Consult. Clin. Psychol.* 53(2):201–10

Kettlewell, P. W., Kausch, D. F. 1983. The generalization of the effects of a cognitive-behavioral treatment program for aggressive children. *J. Abnorm. Child Psychol.* 11:101–14

Klein, D. N., Depue, R. A., Slater, J. F. 1985. Cyclothymia in the adolescent offspring of parents with bipolar affective disorder. *J. Abnorm. Psychol.* 94:115–27

Konstantareas, M. M., Homatidis, S. 1984. Aggressive and prosocial behaviours before and after treatment in conduct-disordered children and in matched controls. *J. Child Psychol. Psychiatry* 25:607–20

Konstantareas, M. M., Homatidis, S. 1985. Dominance hierarchies in normal and conduct-disordered children. *J. Abnorm. Child Psychol.* 13:259–67

Koriath, U., Gualtieri, C. T., Van Bourgondien, M. E., Quade, D., Werry, J. S. 1985. Construct validity of clinical diagnosis in pediatric psychiatry: relationships among measures. *J. Am. Acad. Child Psychiatry* 24:429–36

Kovacs, M., Beck, A. T. 1977. An empirical clinical approach toward a definition of childhood depression. In *Depression in Childhood: Diagnosis, Treatment, and Conceptual Models,* ed. J. G. Schulterbrandt. New York: Raven

Lahey, B. B., Green, K. D., Forehand, R. 1980. On the independence of ratings of hyperactivity, conduct problems, and attention deficits in children: A multiple regression analysis. *J. Consult. Clin. Psychol.* 48:566–74

Lansing, M. D., Schopler, E. 1978. Individualized education: A public school model. In *Autism: A Reappraisal of Concepts and Treatment,* ed. M. Rutter, E. Schopler. New York: Plenum

Lefkowitz, M. M., Burton, N. 1978. Childhood depression: A critique of the concept. *Psychol. Bull.* 85:716–26

Lefkowitz, M. M., Eron, L. D., Walder, L. O., Huesmann, L. R. 1977. *Growing up to be Violent: A Longitudinal Study of the Development of Aggression.* New York: Pergamon

Lefkowitz, M. M., Tesiny, E. P. 1980.

Assessment of childhood depression. *J. Consult. Clin. Psychol.* 48:43–50

Levitas, A., Hagerman, R. J., Braden, M., Rimland, B., McBogg, P., et al. 1983. Autism and the fragile X syndrome. *J. Dev. Behav. Pediat.* 4:151–58

Lobovits, D. A., Handal, P. J. 1985. Childhood depression: Prevalence using DSM-III criteria and validity of parent and child depression scales. *J. Pediatr. Psychol.* 10:45–54

Lochman, J. E., Burch, P. R., Curry, J. F., Lampron, L. B. 1984. Treatment and generalization effects of cognitive-behavioral and goal-setting interventions with aggressive-boys. *J. Consult. Clin. Psychol.* 52:915–16

Loeber, R. 1982. The stability of antisocial and delinquent child behavior: A review. *Child Dev.* 53:1431–46

Loeber, R., Schmalling, K. B. 1985a. Empirical evidence for overt and covert patterns of antisocial conduct problems: A metaanalysis. *J. Abnorm. Child Psychol.* 13:337–52

Loeber, R., Schmalling, K. B. 1985b. The utility of differentiating between mixed and pure forms of antisocial child behavior. *J. Abnorm. Child Psychol.* 13:315–36

Loeber, R., Weissman, W., Reid, J. B. 1983. Family interactions of assaultive adolescents, stealers, and nondelinquents. *J. Abnorm. Child Psychol.* 11:1–14

Loney, J., Langhorne, J. E. Jr., Paternite, C. E. 1978. An empirical basis for subgrouping the hyperkinetic/minimal brain dysfunction syndrome. *J. Abnorm. Psychol.* 87:431–41

Loney, J., Milich, R. 1982. Hyperactivity, inattention, and aggression in clinical practice. In *Advances in Developmental and Behavioral Pediatrics,* ed. M. Wolraich, D. K. Routh, 3:113–47. Greenwich, CT: JAI

Loney, J., Whaley-Klahn, M. A., Kosier, T., Conboy, J. 1981. *Hyperactive boys and their brothers at 21: Predictors of aggressive and antisocial outcomes.* Presented at Meet. Soc. Life History Res., Monterey, CA

Lotter, V. 1966. Epidemiology of autistic conditions in young children. I. Prevalence. *Soc. Psychiatry* 1:124–37

Lotter, V. 1967. Epidemiology of autistic conditions in young children. II. Some characteristics of the parents and children. *Soc. Psychiatry* 1:163–73

Lotter, V. 1978. Follow-up studies. In *Autism: A Reappraisal of Concepts and Treatment,* ed. M. Rutter, E. Schopler. New York: Plenum

Lovaas, O. I., Koegel, R. L., Simmons, J. Q., Long, J. S. 1973. Some generalization and followup measures on autistic children in behavior therapy. *J. Appl. Behav. Anal.* 6:131-66

Lovaas, O. I., Schriebman, L., Koegel, R. L. 1974. A behavior modification approach to treatment of autistic children. *J. Autism Child. Schizophr.* 4:111-29

Lovaas, O. I., Varni, J. W., Koegel, R. L., Lorsch, N. 1977. Some observations on the extinguishability of children's speech. *Child Dev.* 48:1121-27

Lowe, T. L., Tanaka, K., Seashore, M. R., Young, J. G., Cohen, D. J. 1980. Detection of phenylketonuria in autistic and psychiatric children. *J. Am. Med. Assoc.* 243:126-28

Lykken, D. T. 1957. A study of anxiety in the sociopathic personality. *J. Abnorm. Soc. Psychol.* 55:6-10

Mayer-Gross, W., Slater, E., Roth, M. 1955. *Clinical Psychiatry.* London: Cassell

McGee, R., Williams, S., Silva, P. A. 1984a. Behavioral and developmental characteristics of aggressive, hyperactive and aggressive-hyperactive boys. *J. Am. Acad. Child Psychiatry* 23:270-79

McGee, R., Williams, S., Silva, P. A. 1984b. Background characteristics of aggressive, hyperactive, and aggressive-hyperactive boys. *J. Am. Acad. Child Psychiatry* 23:280-84

McGee, R., Williams, S., Silva, P. A. 1985. The factor structure and correlates of ratings of inattention, hyperactivity, and antisocial behavior in a large sample of nine year old children from the general population. *J. Consult. Clin. Psychol.* 53:480-90

Meeks, J. E. 1980. Conduct disorders. In *Comprehensive Textbook in Psychiatry,* ed. H. Kaplan, A. M. Friedman, B. J. Sadock. Baltimore: Williams & Wilkins

Megargee, E. I., Golden, R. E. 1973. Parental attitudes of psychopathic and subcultural delinquents. *Criminology* Feb., pp. 427-39

Milich, R., Dodge, K. A. 1984. Social information processing in child psychiatric populations. *J. Abnorm. Child Psychol.* 12:471-90

Milich, R., Fitzgerald, G. 1985. Validation of Inattention/Overactivity and Aggression ratings with classroom observations. *J. Consult. Clin. Psychol.* 53:139-40

Milich, R., Loney, J. 1979. The role of hyperactive and aggressive symptomatology in predicting adolescent outcome among hyperactive children. *J. Ped. Psychol.* 4:93-112

Milich, R., Loney, J., Landau, S. 1982. Independent dimensions of hyperactivity and aggression: A validation with playroom observation data. *J. Abnorm. Psychol.* 91:183-98

Mitchell, S., Rosa, P. 1981. Boyhood behaviour problems as precursors of criminality: A fifteen-year follow-up study. *J. Child Psychiatry* 22:1933

Moore, D. R., Chamberlain, P., Mukai, L. H. 1979. Children at risk for delinquency: A follow-up comparison of aggressive children and children who steal. *J. Abnorm. Child Psychol.* 7:345-55

Moskowitz, D. S., Schwartzman, A. E., Ledingham, J. E. 1985. Stability of change in aggression and withdrawal in middle childhood and early adolescence. *J. Abnorm. Psychol.* 94:30-41

Nasby, W., Hayden, B., DePaulo, B. M. 1980. Attributional bias among aggressive boys to interpret unambiguous social stimuli as displays of hostility. *J. Abnorm. Psychol.* 89:459-68

National Society for Autistic Children. 1978. National Society for Autistic Children definition of the syndrome of autism. *J. Autism Dev. Dis.* 8:162-67

O'Dougherty, M., Neuchterlein, K. H., Drew, B. 1984. Hyperactive and hypoxic children: Signal detection, sustained attention, and behavior. *J. Abnorm. Psychol.* 93:178-91

Olweus, D. 1979. Stability of aggressive reaction patterns in males: A review. *Psychol. Bull.* 86:852-75

Ornitz, E. M. 1973. Childhood autism: A review of the clinical and experimental literature. *West. J. Med.* 118:21-47

Panella, D., Henggeler, S. W. 1986. The peer interactions of conduct disordered, anxious-withdrawn, and well adjusted black adolescents. *J. Abnorm. Child Psychol.* 14:1-12

Park, C. 1978. Review of Nadia: A case of extraordinary drawing ability in an autistic child. *J. Autism Child. Schizophr.* 8:457-72

Park, C., Youderian, P. 1974. Light and number. Ordering principles in the world of an autistic child. *J. Autism Child. Schizophr.* 4:313-23

Parke, R. D., Slaby, R. G. 1983. The development of aggression. In *Handbook of Child Psychology: Socialization, Personality and Social Development,* Vol. 4, ed. E. M. Hetherington. New York: Wiley

Patterson, G. R. 1976. The aggressive child: Victim and architect of a coercive system. In *Behavior Modification and Families,* ed. E. J. Mash, L. A. Hammerlynck, L. C. Handy. New York: Brunner/Mazel

Patterson, G. R. 1980. Mothers: The unacknowledged victims. *Monogr. Soc. Res. Child Dev.* Vol. 45, No. 5

Patterson, G. R. 1982. *Coercive Family Processes.* Eugene, OR: Castilia

Patterson, G. R. 1986. Performance models for antisocial boys. *Am. Psychol.* 41(4):432-44

Patterson, G. R., Bank, L. 1986. Bootstrapping your way in the nomological thicket. *Behav. Assess.* 8:49–73

Patterson, G. R., Dishion, T. J. 1985. Contributions of families and peers to delinquency. *Criminology* 23:63–79

Patterson, G. R., Dishion, T. J., Bank, L. 1984. Family interaction: A process· model of deviancy training. *Aggressive Behav.* 10:253–67 (Special issue)

Patterson, G. R., Ray, R. S., Shaw, D. A., Cobb, J. A. 1969. *A Manual for Coding Family Interactions.* Doc. #01234. Available from ASIS, Natl. Aux. Publ. Serv., c/o CMM Inf. Serv., Inc., 90 Third Ave., New York, New York 10022 (Rev. ed.)

Patterson, G. R., Stouthamer-Loeber, M. 1984. The correlation of family management practices and delinquency. *Child Dev.* 55:1299–1307

Pirodsky, D. M., Gibbs, J. W., Hesse, R. A., Hsieh, M. C., Krause, R. B., Rodriguez, W. H. 1985. Use of the dexamethasone suppression test to detect depressive disorders of mentally retarded individuals. *Am. J. Ment. Defic.* 90:245–52

Pollack, M. 1960. Comparison of childhood, adolescent, and adult schizophrenia. *Arch. Gen. Psychiatry* 2:556–60

Porrino, L. J., Rapoport, J. L., Behar, D., Sceery, W., Ismond, D. R., Bunney, W. E. Jr. 1983. A naturalistic assessment of the motor activity of hyperactive boys. *Arch. Gen. Psychiatry* 40:681–87

Poznanski, E. O., Cook, S. C., Carroll, B. J. 1979. A depression rating scale for children. *Pediatrics* 64:442–50

Prinz, R. J., Connor, P. A., Wilson, C. C. 1981. Hyperactive and aggressive behaviors in childhood: Intertwined dimensions. *J. Abnorm. Child Psychol.* 9:107–44

Prior, M., Werry, J. 1986. Non-organic psychoses: Autism, schizophrenia, and allied disorders. See Quay 1986a, pp. 156–210

Pueschel, S. M., Herman, R., Groden, G. 1985. Screening children with autism for fragile-X syndrome and phenylketonuria. *J. Autism Dev. Dis.* 15:335–38

Puig-Antich, J. 1982. Major depression and conduct disorder in prepuberty. *J. Am. Acad. Child Psychiatry* 21:118–28

Puig-Antich, J. 1983. Neuroendocrine and sleep correlates of prepubertal majoridepressive disorder: Current status of the evidence. See Cantwell & Carlson 1983a, pp. 211–27

Puig-Antich, J., Blau, S., Marx, N., Greenhill, L. L., Chambers, W. 1978. Prepubertal major depressive disorder: A pilot study. *J. Am. Acad. Child Psychiatry* 17:695–707

Puig-Antich, J., Chambers, W. J., Tabrizi, M. A. 1983. The clinical assessment of current depressive episodes in children and adolescents: Interviews with parents and children. See Cantwell & Carlson 1983a, pp. 157–79

Quay, H. C. 1983. A dimensional approach to children's behavior disorder: The Revised Behavior Problem Checklist. *Sch. Psychol. Rev.* 12:244–49

Quay, H. C. 1985. *Attention Deficit Disorder and the Behavioral Inhibition System: The Relevence of the Neuropsychological Theory of Jeffrey A. Gray.* Presented at Conf. Hyperactivity as a Scientific Challenge, Univ. Groningen, The Netherlands

Quay, H. C. 1986a. Classification. In *Psychopathological Disorders of Childhood,* ed. H. C. Quay, J. S. Werry, pp. 1–34. New York: Wiley. 3rd ed.

Quay, H. C. 1986b. Conduct disorders. See Quay 1986a, pp. 35–62

Quay, H. C., Peterson, D. R. 1983. *Interim Manual for the Revised Behavior Problem Checklist.* Coral Gables, FL: Univ. Miami

Raine, A., Venables, P. H. 1984a. Tonic heart rate level, social class and antisocial behavior in adolescents. *Biol. Psychol.* 18: 123–32

Raine, A., Venables, P. H. 1984b. Electrodermal nonresponding, antisocial behavior, and schizoid tendencies in adolescents. *Psychophysiology* 21:424–33

Rapoport, J. I., Buchsbaum, M. S., Zahn, T. P., Weingartner, H., Ludlow, C., Mikkelsen, E. J. 1978. Dextroamphetamine: Cognitive and behavioral effects in normal prepubertal boys. *Science* 199:560–63

Reeves, J. C., Werry, J. S., Elkind, G. S., Zametkin, A. 1986. Attention Deficit, Conduct, Oppositional & Anxiety disorders in children: Clinical characteristics. *J. Am. Acad. Child Psychiatry.* In press

Reid, J. B. 1978. *A social learning approach to family interaction,* Vol. 2: *A Manual for Coding Family Interactions.* Eugene, OR: Castalia

Reid, J. B., Kavanaugh, K. 1986. A social interactional approach to the treatment of abusive families. In *Anger and Hostility in Behavioral and Cardiovascular Disorders,* ed. M. A. Chesney, R. H. Rosenman. Washington, DC: Hemisphere

Reid, J. B., Taplin, P. S., Lorber, R. 1981. A social interactional approach to the treatment of abusive families. In *Violent Behaviors: Social Learning Approaches to Prediction, Management and Treatment.* New York: Brunner/Mazel

Richman, N., Stevenson, J., Graham, P. J. 1982. *Preschool to School: A Behavioral Study.* London: Academic

Rie, H. E. 1966. Depression in childhood: A survey of some pertinent contributors. *J. Am. Acad. Child Psychiatry* 5:653–85

Rimland, B. 1971. The differentiation of infantile autism from other forms of childhood psychosis. *J. Autism Child. Schizophr.* 1: 161–74

Ritvo, E. R., Freeman, B. J. 1978. National Society for Autistic Children definition of the syndrome of autism. *J. Autism Dev. Dis.* 8:162–69

Ritvo, E. R., Freeman, B. J. 1984. A medical model of autism: Etiology, pathology, and treatment. *Pediatr. Ann.* 13(4):298–305

Ritvo, E. R., Ritvo, E. C., Brothers, A. M. 1982. Genetic and immunohematologic factors in autism. *J. Autism Dev. Dis.* 12:109–14

Roberts, M. A. 1979. *A behavioral method for differentiating hyperactive, aggressive, and hyperactive plus aggressive children.* PhD thesis. Univ. Wisconsin-Madison. Unpublished

Roberts, M. A., Ray, R. S., Roberts, R. J. 1984. A playroom observational procedure for assessing hyperactive boys. *J. Pediatr. Psychol.* 9:177–91

Robins, L. N. 1966. *Deviant Children Grown Up.* Baltimore: Williams & Wilkins

Robins, L. N. 1979. Sturdy childhood predictors of adult outcome: replication from longitidinal studies. In *Stress and Mental Disorder,* ed. J. E. Barrett, R. M. Rose, G. L. Klerman. New York: Raven

Rogeness, G. A., Hernandez, J. M., Macedo, C. A., Amrung, S. A., Hoppe, S. K. 1984. *Dopamine-beta-hydroxylase and conduct disorder in emotionally disturbed boys.* Univ. Texas Health Sci. Cent., Dep. Psychiatry, San Antonio

Rogeness, G. A., Hernandez, J. M., Macedo, C. A., Mitchell, E. L. 1982. Biochemical differences in children with conduct disorder socialized and undersocialized. *Am. J. Psychiatry* 139:307–11

Ross, D. M., Ross, S. A. 1982. *Hyperactivity: Current Issues, Research, and Theory.* New York: Wiley

Routh, D. K. 1978. Hyperactivity. In *Psychological Management of Pediatric Problems,* Vol. 2: *Sensorineural Conditions and Social Concerns,* ed. P. Magrab. Baltimore: University Park Press

Routh, D. K. 1983. Attention deficit disorder: Its relationship with activity, aggression, and achievement. In *Advances in Developmental and Behavioral Pediatrics,* Vol. 4, ed. M. Wolraich, D. K. Routh. Greenwich, CT: JAI

Rutter, M. 1967. Psychotic disorders in childhood. In *Recent Developments In Schizophrenia,* ed. A. Coppen, A. Walk. London: RMPA

Rutter, M. 1968. Concepts of autism: A review of research. *J. Child Psychol. Psychiatry* 9:1–25

Rutter, M. 1970. Autistic children: Infancy to adulthood. *Semin. Psychiatry* 2:435–50

Rutter, M. 1976. Infantile autism and other child psychoses. In *Child Psychiatry—Modern Approaches,* ed. M. Rutter, L. Hersov. Oxford: Blackwell

Rutter, M. 1977. Brain damage syndromes in childhood: Concepts and findings. *J. Child Psychol. Psychiatry* 9:1–25

Rutter, M. 1978. Diagnosis and definition. In *Autism: A Reappraisal of Concepts and Treatment,* ed. M. Rutter, E. Schopler. New York: Plenum

Rutter, M. 1982. Concepts of autism: A Review of research. *New Directions in Childhood Psychopathology,* Vol. 2, ed. S. I. Harrison, J. F. McDermott. New York: Int. Univ. Press

Rutter, M., ed. 1983. *Developmental Neuropsychiatry.* New York: Guilford

Rutter, M., Graham, P. 1968. The reliability and validity of the psychiatric assessment of the child: The interview with the child. *Br. J. Psychiatry* 114:563–79

Rutter, M., Greenfeld, D., Lockyer, L. 1967. A five to fifteen year followup study of infantile psychosis II. Social and behavioral outcome. *Br. J. Psychiatry* 113:1183–99

Rutter, M., Lockyer, L. 1967. A five to fifteen year followup study of infantile psychosis I. Description of sample. *Br. J. Psychiatry* 113:1169–82

Sandberg, S. J., Wieselberg, M., Shaffer, D. 1980. Hyperkinetic and conduct problem children in a primary school population: Some epidemiological considerations. *J. Child Psychol. Psychiatry* 21:293–311

Saylor, C. F., Finch, A. J. Jr., Baskin, C. H., Furey, W., Kelly, M. M. 1984a. Construct validity for measures of childhood depression: Application of multitrait-multimethod methodology. *J. Consult. Clin. Psychol.* 52:977–85

Saylor, C. F., Finch, A. J. Jr., Spirito, A., Bennett, B. 1984b. The Children's Depression Inventory: A systematic evaluation of psychometric properties. *J. Consult. Clin. Psychol.* 52:955–67

Schmidt, K., Solanto, M. V., Bridger, W. H. 1985. Electrodermal activity of undersocialized aggressive children. *J. Abnorm. Child Psychol.* 26:653–60

Schopler, E. 1971. Parents of psychotic children as scapegoats. *J. Contemp. Psychother.* 4:17–22

Schopler, E. 1983. New developments in the definition and diagnosis of autism. In *Advances in Clinical Child Psychology,* Vol. 6, ed. B. B. Lahey, A. E. Kazdin. New York: Plenum

Schopler, E., Andrews, L. E., Strupp, K. 1979. Do autistic children come from upper middle-class parents? *J. Autism Dev. Dis.* 9:139–52

Schopler, E., Mesibov, G., Baker, A. 1982. Evaluation of Treatment for autistic children and their parents. *J. Am. Acad. Child Psychiatry* 21:262–67

Schopler, E., Reichler, R. 1971. Parents as co-therapists in the treatment of psychotic children. *J. Autism Child. Schizophr.* 1:87–102

Schopler, E., Reichler, R. J., Develis, R. F., Daly, K. 1980. Toward objective classification of childhood autism: Childhood Autism Rating Scale (CARS) *J. Autism Dev. Dis.* 10:91–103

Selfe, L. 1977. *A Case of Extraordinary Drawing Ability in an Autistic Child.* New York: Academic

Sergeant, J. A., Scholten, C. A. 1985a. On resource strategy limitations in hyperactivity: Cognitive impulsivity reconsidered. *J. Child Psychol. Psychiatry* 26:97–109

Sergeant, J. A., Scholten, C. A. 1985b. On data limitations in hyperactivity. *J. Child Psychol. Psychiatry* 26:111–24

Shaffer, D., Fisher, P. 1981. The epidemiology of suicide in children and young adults. *J. Am. Acad. Child Psychiatry* 20:545–65

Shields, J. 1967. The genetics of schizophrenia in historical context. See Brown 1967

Short, A. B. 1984. Short-term treatment outcome using parents as co-therapists for their own autistic children. *J. Child Psychol. Psychiatry* 25(3):443–58

Siddle, D. A. T., Nicol, A. R., Foggitt, R. H. 1973. Habituation and overextinction of the GSR component of the orienting response in antisocial adolescents. *Br. J. Soc. Clin. Psychol.* 12:303–8

Stein, M. A., O'Donnell, J. P. 1985. Classification of children's behavior problems: Clinical and quantitative approaches. *J. Abnorm. Child Psychol.* 13:269–80

Steinhausen, H., Gobel, D., Breinlinger, M., Wohleben, B. 1986. A community survey of infantile autism. *J. Am. Acad. Child Psychiatry* 25:186–89

Stewart, D. J. 1972. Effects of social reinforcement on dependency and aggressive responses of psychopathic, neurotic, and subcultural delinquents. *J. Abnorm. Psychol.* 79:76–83

Stewart, M. A., Behar, D. 1983. Subtypes of aggressive conduct disorder. *Acta Psychiatr. Scand.* 63:178–85

Stewart, M. A., Cummings, C., Singer, S., DeBlois, C. S. 1981. The overlap between hyperactive and unsocialized aggressive children. *J. Child Psychol. Psychiatry* 22:35–45

Sykes, D. H., Douglas, V. I., Morgenstern, G. 1972. The effect of methylphenidate (Ritalin) on sustained attention in hyperactive children. *Psychopharmacologia* 25:262–74

Taft, L. T., Cohen, H. J. 1971. Hypsarrhythmia and infantile autism: A clinical report. *J. Autism Child. Schizophr.* 1:327–36

Tesiny, E. P., Lefkowitz, M. M. 1982. Childhood depression: A 6-month follow-up study. *J. Consult. Clin. Psychol.* 50(5):778–80

Thorley, G. 1984a. Review of follow-up and follow-back studies of childhood hyperactivity. *Psychol. Bull.* 96:116–32

Thorley, G. 1984b. Hyperkinetic syndrome of childhood: Clinical characteristics. *Br. J. Psychiatry* 144:16–24

Tsai, L. Y., Tsai, M. C., August, G. R. 1985. Implications of EEG diagnosis in the subclassification of infantile autism. *J. Autism Dev. Dis.* 15:339–44

Ullmann, R. K., Sleator, E. K., Sprague, R. L. 1984. A new rating scale for diagnosis and monitoring of ADD children. *Psychopharmacol. Bull.* 20:160–64

Ullmann, R. K., Sleator, E. K., Sprague, R. L. 1985. A change of mind: The Conners Abbreviated Rating Scales reconsidered. *J. Abnorm. Child Psychol.* 13:553–65

U.S. Dep. Health, Education, and Welfare. 1977a. *Primary diagnosis of discharges from non-federal general hospital psychiatric inpatient units, United States—1975.* Mental Health Stat. Note No. 137

U.S. Dep. Health, Education, and Welfare. 1977b. *Diagnostic distribution of admissions to inpatient services of state and county mental hospitals, United States—1975.* Mental Health Statistical Note No. 138

Vaillant, G. E. 1963. Twins discordant for infantile autism. *Arch. Gen. Psychiatry* 9:163–67

Volkmar, F. R., Cohen, D. J., Paul, R. 1986. An evaluation of DSM-III criteria for infantile autism. *J. Am. Acad. Child Psychiatry* 25(2):190–97

Weinberg, W. A., Rutman, J., Sullivan, L., Penick, E. C., Dietz, S. G., et al. 1973. Depression in children referred to an educational diagnostic center: Diagnosis and treatment. *J. Pediatr.* 83:1065–1072

Werry, J. S., Reeves, J. C., Elkind, G. S. 1986. Attention deficit, conduct, oppositional and anxiety disorders in children: I. A review of research on differentiating characteristics. *J. Am. Acad. Child Psychiatry.* In press

Wing, L. 1980. Childhood autism and social class—a question of selection? *Br. J. Psychiatry* 137:410–17

Wing, L., Gould, J. 1979. Severe impairments of social interaction and associated abnormalities in children: Epidemiology and classification. *J. Autism Dev. Dis.* 9:11–30

Young, J. G., Kavanaugh, M. E., Anderson, G. M., Shaywitz, A., Cohen, D. J. 1982. Clinical neurochemistry of autism and associated disorders. *J. Autism Dev. Dis.* 12:177–86

Ann. Rev. Psychol. 1987. 38:533–74

PERSONALITY: Developments in the Study of Private Experience

Jerome L. Singer and John Kolligian, Jr.

Department of Psychology, Yale University, Box 11A Yale Station, New Haven, Connecticut 06520

CONTENTS

INTRODUCTION: PERSONALITY THEORIES, RESEARCH, AND SCIENTIFIC PSYCHOLOGY

A recurrent characteristic of chapters on personality that have appeared in the *Annual Review of Psychology* in the past 15 years has been a tone of "viewing

0066-4308/87/0201-0533$02.00

with alarm" (Sechrest 1976; Phares & Lamiell 1977; Loevinger & Knoll 1983). Carlson (1984) has cogently suggested that not only has the person been lost in personality research but that society has been dropped out of social psychology. Feshbach (1984) has noted that some of the emerging problems can be attributed to disillusion with "grand theories." He also pointed to (a) the materialism of clinical psychology that has absorbed many of the issues in personality research, (b) the growth of social psychology, which has emphasized situationalism and social cognition with general disregard for individual differences and personality variations, and finally (c) a kind of general dissatisfaction with the necessity of hypothesizing "unobservable" processes within the individual (Feshbach 1984, pp. 446–47). Pervin (1983) has argued that we lack adequate research paradigms, a concern also evident in a paper by Tomkins (1981b) and in a number of the *Annual Review* chapters cited above.

One can find a more hopeful prospect by overlooking the scene from a somewhat different vantage point. The formation of the Society for Personology reflects a case in point. From one perspective it can be viewed as a small group of aging, embattled academics still searching for research paradigms that encompass the total personality across the life span in the tradition of Henry Murray, Robert White, Silvan Tomkins, and the Harvard Psychological Clinic or the Berkeley studies. Yet the study of the person across time continues to be reflected in imaginative and challenging research such as the recent work of Helson et al (1984) on "adherence to the social clock" in women, the continuing active work of Jack Block (Block & Block 1980), the studies of power and intimacy by McAdams (1985), and the emergent field of health psychology, where personality variables prove to be predictive of long-term health behavior (Kobasa et al 1982b; Williams et al 1985). Indeed the very great significance now being assigned by psychologists and behavioral medicine specialists to health psychology suggests a revival of interest in the whole person. Such an interest is reflected in the MacArthur Foundation's establishment of a network of institutions carrying out research on health-threatening and health-enhancing behaviors.

A stimulating paper by Blass (1984) has shown that one can document an impressive and increasing convergence of social psychology and personality research. Blass points to the use of personality variables ranging from empathic fantasy ability to measures of Machiavellianism, dogmatism, introversion-extraversion, self-monitoring, self-esteem, repression-sensitization as critical variables in the area of counterattitudinal advocacy experiments in social psychology. Indeed the great emphasis on social cognition and the increasing interest of social psychologists such as McGuire (1984; McGuire et al 1986) and Markus (1987) in self-concepts and self-schemas has indicated that what was once thought to be a fuzzy area of personality has become increasingly central to the understanding of interpersonal and group behavior as well as to the organization of personality.

Further reason for optimism lies in the recent development by the MacArthur Foundation of a program for the study of conscious and unconscious mental processes and mental health that is currently centered at the Langley Porter Clinic of the University of California San Francisco Medical School under the direction of Mardi Horowitz. This program brings together cognitive, social, and personality psychologists, psychiatrists, and psychoanalysts with the intent of reexamining many of the basic processes of self-schemas, defenses, and neurotic symptoms that may emerge differentially as a function of relative conscious or unconscious representation. Studies combining experimental and personological approaches in the Murray tradition are under way in this program.

Recent Personality Textbooks: How Should the Subject Be Taught?

The emergence of a number of recent textbooks in the psychology of personality highlights the issues that persist regarding how the field ought to be taught and emphasizes a major discrepancy between traditional approaches to the subject and current research in the field. On the one hand, a majority of courses continue to adopt the "theories of personality" orientation. The recent new edition of the classic Hall and Lindzey text continues its original orientation, although with some updating, many more pictures reflecting the impact of the television age, and greater inclusion of current research studies (Hall et al 1985). Simplified copy-cat versions of this text arrive regularly, thus reflecting the widespread use of this model. On the other hand, a number of recent texts have approached the field somewhat differently. These include works by Feshbach & Weiner (1986), Mischel (1986), Babladelis (1984), Phares (1984), and Singer (1984a). This group, while paying some attention to the traditional theories, devotes most of the text's content to major problem areas of the field such as altruism, cognition, sex-role differences, perceived control, the emotions and their relation to cognition and to private experience, etc. One continues to wonder why personality is still so widely taught as a "procession through the graveyard" in the pungent phrase of a prominent personality researcher. It is true that the lives and insights of Freud, Jung, Adler, Sullivan, Rogers, Maslow, etc, make extremely interesting reading and their historical contributions highlight some of the issues of human relationships that must continue at the center of personality research. But we may well ask why no one teaches cognition, social psychology, developmental psychology, or abnormal psychology by using the views of famous people as the centerpiece for the entire course. As Stewart (1985) has pointed out in a review of some of the recent personality texts that primarily focus on current areas of research and problems rather than on individual theories, they "bear witness to the vitality and intellectual fertility of the field of personality" (Stewart 1985, p. 705).

Perhaps one of the signs of maturity of a scientific discipline is that we begin to know too much to organize it all under a few grand encompassing theories. We need more modest theoretical structures that are closely tied to theory developments in the subfields of psychology from which personality must draw its knowledge. By subfields we mean cognition, emotion, motivation, developmental and social processes, and recent developments in brain-behavior relationships, etc. It would appear that the task of personality researchers would be to indicate how individual variation develops in relation to all of the fundamental human processes about which we have so much more information than was available to Freud or Jung or Maslow. We need to find better units of measurement for the variables of intrinsic interest in personality. There is increased excitement over notions of schemas and scripts, long ago foreshadowed by Tomkins (1962) but revived in more sophisticated form recently by Tomkins (1979), Carlson (1981), and Schank & Abelson (1977). The utility of person schemas or Kelly's (1955) Personal Constructs has been identified in studies of the self (Kihlstrom & Cantor 1984; Markus 1985; Singer & Salovey 1985) and in phenomena such as the transference in psychoanalysis (Singer 1985c). These reviews and the research using schemas, prototypes, and scripts demonstrate that personality can be organized in a way compatible with major theoretical units now being employed in basic research and computer science, cognition, social psychology, and developmental psychology. One can only hope (without disrespect for the great historical figures and their contributions to the field) that personality texts will begin to reflect the excitement and the breaking of new ground that characterizes so much of the current research effort.

Towards the Reemergence of the Private Personality as a Central Feature of Personality Research

As suggested by the increased interest in emotion, fantasy and imagination, organized beliefs about self, and schemas and scripts concerning personal as well as other more social interactions, we find in this convergence of social cognition research and personality psychology an increased emphasis on private experience. In personality psychology and in social psychology we see an increased confluence of interest in the interactions between cognition and emotion. In Tomkins' felicitous phrasing (1981b, p. 448):

> Cognition without affect is weak; affect without cognition is blind. Together they enable a viable organism. Freud was surely mistaken in supposing they had evolved in serious mismatch with each other. It is also now clear that *both* the innately endowed cognitive and affective mechanisms have very great (if not unlimited) degrees of freedom built into their

very structures, which made possible the extraordinary plasticity required for the varieties of social and cultural life which have occurred at different historical periods.

Before going on to our review of the current research literature on consciousness, self, and the interface between cognition and emotion in the private personality, we must keep in mind an important caveat that Tomkins has wisely suggested. Changes in historical trends, in broad social expectations that characterize subcultures and indeed even national cultures at different periods of history evoke different integrations of cognition and affect. Whereas fundamental principles of cognition or the fundamental operations of an affect system may be biologically given, their very interaction reflects social experience, which in itself is a reflection of a broader, temporally related context. Organized beliefs about self and others, which may be termed schemas, or constructs about action sequences, which may be called scripts, are units that personality researchers may find especially valuable for integrating the innate nature of affects with the current information processing of the individual. These constructs may be employed in a way that reflects the historical forces that shape personality variations in different generations or cohorts.

THE PRIVATE PERSONALITY: CONSCIOUSNESS AND BELIEFS ABOUT SELF AND OTHERS

An exciting recent review of William James' life and thought by Myers (1986) reminds us how much of modern psychology's agenda was laid out a century ago by America's first and perhaps greatest psychologist. The new book contains chapters on consciousness, memory and the unconscious, emotions, thought, and the self. All of these issues are currently objects of empirical examination, a state of affairs we believe would have excited James the scientist. Of particular relevance for this chapter, however, is the fact that James, except in his studies of abnormal phenomena, seemed less interested in individual variations and subtle and unique aspects of the self or of emotion. Perhaps he left the exploration of such individualized phenomena to the prolific literary exploration of this brother Henry. William James' introduction of the concept of a stream of consciousness, so stimulating to several generations of writers—from his own student Gertrude Stein to James Joyce, Virginia Woolf, William Faulkner, and Saul Bellow—was largely ignored by psychologists for almost 60 years of this century. More recently, however, as personality researchers and specialists in social cognition attempt to examine the major dimensions of the individual that account for beliefs about self or others and for attitudes that may govern overt behavior, they find increasing interest in the return to introspection and reports of consciousness (Lieberman 1979; Sabini & Silver 1981; Singer 1984a,b). Brain researchers, students of artificial intelligence, psychophysiologists, and investigators of the neural and autonomic concomitants of sleep are considerably intrigued by the necessity for studying personal "scripts," ongoing images, fantasies, and interior monologues (Arkin et al 1978; Schank & Abelson 1977; Schwartz et al 1981; Sperry 1976).

Social psychologists are finding increasingly that more extensive samplings of individuals' conscious beliefs and expectations can lead to rather good predictions of how people will behave in specific settings or in response to naturally occurring events (Fishbein & Ajzen 1975; Kreitler & Kreitler 1976, 1982; Sabini & Silver 1981; McGuire 1984). Although one must always keep in mind the limitations of using introspective reports for ascertaining causality sequences in overt behavior as proposed by Nisbett & Ross (1980), the analyses of Natsoulas (1984), Baars (1987), and Singer (1984a) all point to the rich range of information about beliefs and attitudes that emerges from introspective accounts even from relatively less articulate subjects (Pope 1978).

As the Kreitlers (1982) have argued, the ways in which beliefs based on self-report by individuals can lead to predictions of overt actions by these same individuals depend on the relationships between domains in which such beliefs fall. Thus by separately tapping beliefs about personal goals, personal traits, and social norms or general knowledge about a situation to be encountered, one can on the basis of self-reports predict overt action in a variety of situations. Not obvious to the respondent is the connection between the belief domains, and it is this connection that may be unconscious. Indeed it is quite possible that inadequate sampling of private expectations, knowledge, and beliefs about self and others has often led to the poor match of attitude research and overt behavior.

Self-knowledge or self-awareness as a special feature of personality or as a variable that has implications for interpersonal behavior has recently been the subject of a series of reviews of empirical studies by Markus (1983), Andersen (1984), Andersen & Ross (1984), Andersen & Williams (1985). Much of this research, however, still does not address as fully as one might hope the issue of variations in self-knowledge as a personality or individual difference dimension.

Self-consciousness: Implications for Behavior and Health

A greater body of research has emerged in the field of self-consciousness. Here the focus is not so much on what might be called the capacity for introspection in itself or the "validity" of self-knowledge but rather the trait-like characteristics of a personal style involving considerable attention to self-generated thoughts, images, and expectations. The last two or three years have witnessed almost an explosion of studies of various facets of self-consciousness from this perspective. Carver et al (1985) investigated the role of dispositional self-consciousness as a moderator variable of people's tendencies to filter out and to avoid information that would be diagnostic of their specific intellectual abilities. Franzoi (1983), has conducted a series of studies looking at the way in which one's self-concept varies as a function of private self-consciousness. He demonstrated a defensive role represented by a consistent inattention to one's own private thoughts and feelings. Persons scoring low on private self-consciousness measures managed to maintain higher self-concepts in certain domains even in the face of discrepancies with what significant others thought about them. An initial clue about the process of this defensive style was suggested in a subsequent study by Franzoi & Brewer (1984). They found that persons scoring low on private self-consciousness engage in a more selective type of attention to their own personal activities or thoughts when put into a situation of private self-awareness. By contrast, persons scoring higher on such a self-consciousness scale are less selective and engage in much more free-floating and varied forms of self-attention.

Two recent studies by Franzoi & Davis (1985) and Franzoi et al (1985) considered private self-consciousness and self-disclosure; in these studies greater private self-consciousness was associated with greater willingness for self-disclosure of an intimate kind to others. A special feature of such disclosure was that it was linked to increased satisfaction in relationship with others. Lloyd et al (1983) also found evidence that private self-consciousness as a trait led to more positive response from others in "get acquainted" situations.

Can we relate the self-consciousness scales to other approaches to estimating self-awareness and perhaps also denial or avoidance of self-conscious thought? The work of Weinberger has led to a measure tentatively called "repressive defensiveness," which is derived from respondents who show low scores on standard questionnaire scales of anxiety but high scores on measures of social desirability or defensiveness, usually estimated from the Crowne-Marlowe scale. In contrast with true low-anxious respondents (who do not show such defensiveness) the defensive low-anxious respondents or repressors also show a high level of physiological response comparable to that obtained in measurements of non-defensive high-anxious respondents (Bonanno & Singer 1986; Weinberger et al 1979; Qualls 1983; Weinberger 1983). Davis & Schwartz (1986) have found evidence that such a repressive defensive style is associated with the recall of fewer memories about activities of the self when compared with memories reported by other groups. To what extent is this repressive-defensive style related to the low private self-consciousness reported by Franzoi and his co-workers?

We need considerably more research to explore a variety of possible links of self-consciousness (*a*) to the field-dependent cognitive style so extensively studied by Witkin and his collaborators (Witkin & Goodenough 1981; Witkin 1965), (*b*) to the demonstrations that low self-complexity is associated with greater mood fluctuation (Linville 1982), and (*c*) to the extremely important research findings on the repressive style and its relation to physical health. For example, Jensen (1984), in an important study of women with malignant breast cancer, found that independent psychological measures of conscious feelings of helplessness and hopelessness as well as repressive-defensiveness and escapist daydreaming all entered significantly into a regression analysis predicting the outcome of the neoplastic disease. Thus, unawareness of bodily feeling, denial of anxiety, within that denial the persistent experience of helplessness, and, finally, escape into positive fantasy all characterized women whose malignancies later spread despite treatment. What are the implications of a personality style in which someone systematically seems to be inattentive to ongoing thought, to mental confrontations with the risks and dangers of a concurrent serious illness? Perhaps we need more research on the ongoing conscious or unconscious processes by which denial or repression are evident.

In contrast to repressively oriented individuals are those who show a pattern described by Kobasa et al (1982b) and Kobasa et al (1982a) as hardiness, a willingness to confront problems, to reshape them through flexible appraisal and imaginativeness, or to commit oneself to active coping. Hardiness predicts less subsequent physical illness even when stress occurs in the interim. Individuals with low hardiness, low private self-consciousness, or low self-complexity seem to be putting themselves at risk even as they sustain a sense of comfort in conscious awareness. Are such "repressors" actively avoiding spinning out extended sequences of thought about the possible consequences of pain or illnesses? Are they failing to react to such thoughts through some commitment to action by a decision-exploration use of fantasy rather than by pure escape into soothing but perhaps irrelevant daydreams? Are such individuals completely avoiding self-generated consciousness by distracting themselves through routine actions or immersions in a medium such as television? More extended thought sampling or related techniques (see below) may be useful to explore such possibilities more fully.

Another approach to the area of self-consciousness involves not simply the trait aspects but also the implications of an enforced self-awareness. Thus Gibbons et al (1985) found that self-focused attention produces an increase in perceived intensity of affect and also an accuracy of self-reports using techniques such as the mirror method. Several studies also found that self-focused attention might actually enhance depression but at the same time increase accuracy of self-report (Brockner et al 1985; Ingram & Smith 1984; Pyszczynski & Greenberg 1985). Plant & Ryan (1985) found that both the trait-like aspects of self-consciousness as measured by the Public Self-consciousness Scale and also the enforced awareness to the public self tended to reduce intrinsic motivational tendencies. Private self-consciousness as a trait was not related, in their studies, to intrinsic motivation, however.

An important distinction must be made between self-consciousness as a form of monitoring one's own private thoughts and self-consciousness as a monitoring of one's overt actions by excessive attention to how one may appear in public. The latter dimension of personality yields what Greenwald (1981) called an egocentricity bias. Research by Fenigstein (1984), Fenigstein & Levine (1984), and Zuckerman et al (1983) indicates how concern over self-evaluation in public situations may yield biases of assuming greater personal causality for events. Considerable work being done with Snyder's (1979) self-monitoring scale has led to attempts to refine the instrument (Lennox & Wolfe 1984). It is important to note that Snyder's use of the term "self-monitoring" reflects an extraverted self-presentational or social manipulative orientation (Gangestad & Snyder 1985; Snyder & Gangestad 1986); it is in practice perhaps more like public self-consciousness than private self-consciousness. One wonders why more attempts have not been made to link this phenomenon of self-monitoring to the many cognitive style correlates of field dependence reviewed by Witkin & Goodenough (1981) and to the studies of the emotion of shame as developed in the work of Lewis (1971, 1981, 1983). Or is self-monitoring better viewed as a class variable more akin to impression management and Machiavellianism? (See Ickes, Reidhead & Patterson 1986 for a comparison of the dimensions of self-monitoring and Machiavellianism.)

Extensive work continues on the dimension of shyness and its relationship to public or private self-consciousness, as suggested by a thoughtful, theoretical analysis and literature review by Buss (1986). The work of Cheek & Briggs (1982) indicated important differences between the two kinds of self-consciousness: Each of the two kinds of self-consciousness correlated with particular aspects of identity so that private self-consciousness was more related to personal features of self and public self-consciousness was linked more with overt displays or to impression management (Cheek & Briggs 1982). Several studies of shyness reported by Buss (1986) indicated that a shy person is typically fearful, low in self-esteem, above average in public self-consciousness, and low in sociability. Indeed a recent volume edited by Jones et al (1986) goes a long way to clarifying both the theory and measurement of shyness. It identifies the frequent confusion between introversion as a major form of heightened interest and priority assigned to self-generated thoughts, images, and emotions, on the one hand, and the high self-monitoring in social situations as well as fearfulness that characterizes shyness, on the other (Briggs & Smith 1986). Buss (1986), reviewing the literature and formulating the theory of shyness, further supports the distinction between private self-consciousness and shyness. Shyness can be viewed as performed behavior characterized more by public self-consciousness or fear of novelty.

In summary, studies of heightened self-consciousness in terms of attention to one's thoughts and fantasies (private) or in terms of observed or anticipated social behaviors (public) as a personality trait continues to yield intriguing networks or correlations. In addition, using the process of public self-awareness as an experimental intervention also provides significant information on the effect of such processes on self-esteem, mood variability, and shyness. The literature on depression and learned helplessness studied from an attributional standpoint suggests that normal nondepressed individuals persist in an illusion of control. Depressives or persons exposed to heightened public self-awareness tend to show an increase in negative affect or a realistic awareness of lack of control, a result confirmed by studies such as those of Gibbons et al (1985). At least in our society it seems likely that we sustain positive emotional states and a consequent tendency towards relatively effective day-to-day action through a pattern of illusory hopefulness.

RESEARCH STRATEGIES IN THE STUDY OF THE PRIVATE PERSONALITY

We concur with Pervin (1985) that the psychology of personality is undergoing an exciting period of increased novelty and variety in research strategies. This is especially evident in the efforts to assess continuing private experience as well as to estimate ongoing public actions as David Buss (Buss & Craik 1983) has demonstrated. We have already noticed the effective use of questionnaire measures of private and public self-consciousness or efforts to identify a repressive-defensive personality style through questionnaire approaches, and we can also cite the usefulness of questionnaires for assessing patterns of daydreaming (Segal 1980; Gold & Gold 1982; Gold & Reilly 1986; Huba et al 1981, 1983; Starker & Jolin 1982, 1983; Huba & Tanaka 1983–84; Golding & Singer 1983; Giambra 1980a,b; Giambra & Stone 1982). These reports using questionnaires all converge in suggesting that people can generally provide reasonably valid and reliable indices of their own differential patterns of ongoing inner thought through relatively short questionnaires. One must, of course, be alert in the use of such questionnaires to continuing problems of confounding and circular reasoning as Lazarus et al (1985) have pointed out in relation to some of the work on stress measurement. Nicholls et al (1982) have also called attention to the risk that occurs when researchers fail to identify actual item overlap between measures. In looking at several measures of a presumed underlying construct, it is important for investigators to be sure that overlapping items are either eliminated or examined separately from a statistical standpoint to avoid spurious indications of correlations between two questionnaire or interview measures (Nicholls et al 1982; Segal et al 1980; Golding & Singer 1983; Demo 1985).

Although studies are not yet numerous in this area, we are seeing an increase in efforts to employ aggregated case studies, psychobiographical analyses using personal documents, and archival data as resources for personality research. In addition, autobiographical memory is increasingly a focus of interest. Thus Howe (1982) has pointed out the special value of biographical evidence for identifying effects of timing and sequencing of events in a person's life. Helson et al (1984) have similarly explored this issue longitudinally, and Reinke et al (1985) and Frieze et al (1985) have also looked at psychosocial changes in women's lives. Runyan (1981–1983) has contributed considerable evidence to issues related to psychobiographic and idiographic methods in "the study of lives," and Wrightsman (1981) has provided a rationale for the utility of personal documents as data in personality research. Cantor & Kihlstrom (1985) have pointed toward the potential usefulness of self-descriptions of perceived event-goal relationships, and Pervin (1983) has provided considerable evidence of the value of a combined idiographic and nomothetic approach to the study of personal goals. Reflecting this combined approach, Singer (1987) compared within subjects' and between subjects' data to show a relatively strong correspondence between the affects associated with autobiographical memories and their relevance to the attainment and nonattainment of life goals. The special advantages and limitations of idiographic measurement strategies and the necessity for continued application of classical nomothetic principles in prediction research have been reviewed by Paunonen & Jackson (1985). The value of combined approaches and an interactional methodology has also been effectively signaled by Palys & Little (1983) and Lamiell (1981). A study by Rappaport et al (1985) demonstrated how projections across time obtained from an individual could be employed to establish a sense of ego identity. The work of Lamiell et al (1983) and of Little (1983) also provide some support for using combinations of idiographic measurement and personal projection system approaches.

Thought and Experience Sampling

An important development within the past decade has been the emergence of efforts to sample ongoing thought or continuing experience both in the laboratory and in the ordinary course of daily life. Much as the data on the person-situation controversy has led to an increased awareness that we must engage in more extensive continuous sampling of behaviors across time and situations (Epstein 1983; Mischel & Peake 1982), one might argue that to obtain estimates of the private personality we need greater frequency of measures of spontaneous thought across time. Such techniques were developed in a series of laboratory studies by Antrobus & Singer using vigilance tasks or signal detection procedures in the early 1960s and were then extended to more daily life situations by the work of Csikszentmihalyi (1975) and by Hurlburt (1978), Klinger (1978), and Singer (1978). Although, as we shall note, some of the laboratory approaches continue to be employed, there is an increasing interest in the sampling of daily life through these procedures because of improvements in so-called "beeper" technology (see Hormuth 1986 for an excellent review of this technology).

Thought-sampling methods include (a) requiring participants to talk out loud over a period of time while in a controlled environment, perhaps even while processing signals in a vigilance experiment (Antrobus & Singer 1964), and then scoring verbalizations along empirically or theoretically derived categories; (b) allowing the respondent to sit, recline, or stand quietly for a period of time either while processing signals or simply during the period of no assigned activity, followed by periodic interruptions for reports of thought or of perceptual activities; (c) requiring the person to signal by means of a button press whenever a new train of thought begins and then to report verbally in retrospect or to fill out a prepared rating form characterizing various possible features of ongoing thought (Singer 1978, 1985a).

Experimental Intervention and Thought Sampling

Some social and personality implications of thought sampling during a signal detection task were demonstrated in a study by Algom & Singer (1984). It was shown that the interpersonal situation confronting the subject (for example, same or opposite sex experimenter presenting the instruction) actually influenced the frequency and type of task-irrelevant thought and imagery that characterized responses when the subject was interrupted during processing of auditory signals. A series of experiments by Klinger and various associates employed the talking-out-loud or interruption techniques with assigned tasks of various kinds to provide support for the distinction Klinger has proposed between operant thought processes (directed or task-oriented thought) and respondent processes (spontaneous daydreams or undirected thought) (Klinger 1977a,b, 1978, 1981). Klinger et al (1981) also demonstrated by thought-sampling procedures the considerable importance of current concerns as determinants of the material that emerges in the stream of consciousness. Current concerns generally reflect intentions that have been undertaken but not yet fulfilled. These may reflect relatively recent and even fairly minor intentions such as remembering to buy milk on the way home from work or more long-standing and psychologically powerful intentions as yet unfulfilled such as educational or career ambitions, fantasies of power or intimacy, etc.

Differential effects of age, gender, and difficulty of task performance upon the occurrence of problem-solving thoughts were further explored by Parks et al (1985). Recently Mueller & Dyer (1985a,b) have used ongoing thought samples as a basis for proposing a computer simulation of daydreaming.

In a complex experiment by Klos & Singer (1981), an effort was made to ascertain the relative role of long-standing interpersonal stress with parents along with different types of simulated parent-child interactions to predict what thoughts would occur in consciousness during a period of thought sampling. The evidence indicated that long-standing unresolved parental conflicts amplified the effect of more recent simulated parental conflicts that were unresolved. The pure Zeigarnick effect of mental repetition of incompleted tasks entered much more modestly although significantly as a determinant of contents of consciousness for a group of young adults.

Thought and Experience Sampling in Daily Life

Adequate methodology for assessment of spontaneous thoughts in more natural environments has been improving as suggested above (Stone & Neale 1982). Hurlburt & Sipprelle (1978) and Hurlburt (1980) have demonstrated effective use of this approach. For example, Hurlburt et al (1984) carried out extensive idiographic as well as nomothetic studies of individuals sampled both in natural and semi-structured environments and demonstrated considerable stability of certain characteristics of ongoing thought and mood. The application of this method to individual differences required larger subject samples than were available in these studies, but one can anticipate such possibilities in the future. Klinger (1984) used a consciousness-sampling methodology to examine the relationship between test anxiety and test performance. An intriguing implication of his work was the finding that, at least in the naturalistic setting, anxiety is more evident as an effect rather than as a cause of later poor performance.

Some of the most important and imaginative uses of thought sampling have been carried out by Csikszentmihalyi and his colleagues at the University of Chicago. In an important contribution to the study of adolescent personality, Csikszentmihalyi & Larson (1984) followed a large group of adolescents who carried "beepers" that signaled them periodically to report over a period of several weeks. This is the largest scale study yet available of the method, and the results are impressive in indicating that it is possible to test particular predictions about mood, fantasy, and overt activity of teenagers as they go about their business of school, entertainment, or simply doing nothing. Other studies reported by Csikszentmihalyi (1982), Larson & Csikszentmihalyi (1978), and Larson et al (1981) further demonstrate the value of such an approach. Recently, Csikszentmihalyi & Kubey (1981) have been able to show how different patterns of ongoing thought and emotion are related to specific daily activities ranging from direct work efforts through the more passive experience of watching television.

A study of special importance because of its tighter theoretical structure and test of specific predictions based on Thematic Apperception Test (TAT) scores was carried out by McAdams & Constantian (1983). They found that those subjects whose TAT scores indicated a greater motivation for intimacy also revealed more interpersonal thoughts and more positive emotional responses in interpersonal situations on a regular basis during the day than did participants whose responses on the TAT had revealed low intimacy. This data was based on a weekly accumulation of seven daily reports. McAdams has used work of this kind as well as longitudinal studies of TAT responses to indicate the relative importance of both power or autonomy motivation on the one hand and intimacy or affiliative motivation on the other as major dimensions of human experience (McAdams 1985). Other studies involving this technology included those of Franzoi & Brewer (1984), who investigated self-awareness and self-consciousness by utilizing an experiential sampling method during daily activity.

Demo (1985) sought to use such a method in connection with a study of the convergent validity of eight measures of self-esteem. He found, however, that thought sampling in itself was not useful for this purpose because most of the sampled thought did not specifically indicate self-esteem-like responses. Participants reported positive or negative emotions and fantasies of one kind or another, but their thought samples did not yield information that was specifically relevant to drawing a conclusion about self-esteem. Other studies examining the relationships between positive and negative emotions using daily and momentary mood reports were carried out by Diener & Emmons (1984), Diener et al (1985), and Emmons & Diener (1986b). Similarly Hedges et al (1985) showed that daily summary reports of mood yield comparable data to momentary mood reports.

While the use of the "beepers" method has some advantages, other investigators have simply required participants to carry logs or activity sheets that can be checked off. Johnson & Larson (1982) employed such an experience-sampling method with bulimic and non-bulimic individuals. They demonstrated that bulimics show more dysphoric moods and greater mood variability. The bulimics experienced greater loneliness at home and were more likely to engage in overeating and purging there, whereas they seemed relatively more comfortable in social situations at work or school.

Brandstatter (1983) also employed a time-sampling diary method by which he investigated participants' emotional responses to other persons in their everyday life situations. He found that attributions of the causes of moods in various settings could be ascertained and related to personality characteristics of the respondent as well as to the social demand character of situations.

Wheeler et al (1983) investigated the relationship between loneliness and social behavior by sampling actual social interactions and behaviors over a period of weeks. They sought to determine what was the best predictor of loneliness from such data. It turned out that interaction meaningfulness or meaninglessness was a critical variable in determining whether individuals reported recurrent feelings of loneliness.

Starker & Jolin (1983) carried this method into the study of the occurrence and vividness of auditory and visual imagery in thought samples of schizophrenic and nonschizophrenic patients. They found that auditory imagery in general was observed more frequently among schizophrenics who also reported hallucinations. This was not true for those schizophrenics who did not hallucinate. Sewitch & Kirsch (1984) attempted to capture the circumstances surrounding the direct experience of anxiety by using a free response format in which the participants' thoughts were also sampled naturally. They had hypothesized that the experience of anxiety would be preceded by thoughts that had a content of personal threat or danger. This clearly proved to be correct and suggested that anxiety, rather than emerging suddenly as is often thought to be the case clinically, can be linked to specific prior cognitive content if adequate sampling of the stream of consciousness is carried out.

The method of sampling thought through continuous "thinking out loud" has been extensively explored for diagnostic and clinical therapeutic purposes by cognitive behavior therapists (Davison et al 1983; Genest & Turk 1981; Ickes et al 1986; Turk et al 1983). Wherever possible, verbalizations are recorded on audio tape for subsequent evaluation either by the therapist or by the therapist in conjunction with the patient. Most recently Blackwell et al (1985) compared the nature of data generated by "think aloud" instructions when the subjects were actually engaged in problem-solving and by "thought listing" after the subjects had completed each problem. They found interesting differences in the utility of thinking-aloud and follow-up thought-listing procedures, with the former revealing twice as many thoughts based on categorization of sequences while the latter produced more indications of positive problem-solving evaluations and more positive self-evaluations.

In summary, there seem to be valuable uses for a variety of approaches to estimating ongoing thought both in the laboratory under fairly controlled circumstances and in daily life situations. Davison et al (1983) have pointed out the limitations of the method: It sacrifices control over or direct knowledge about what subjects are actually responding to, and it imposes particularly brief intervals on reports because subjects are engaged in their normal business. Nevertheless, it is clear that the approach has considerable potential not only as a means of studying the nature of consciousness but as a way of identifying individual differences in ongoing thought patterns in a systematic fashion. The use of trained raters to score thought samples has a long and established history and can be very effective. The thought-sampling method has also been applied to scoring mentation reports obtained for night dreaming and comparing these with waking thought (Antrobus & Saul 1980; Arkin et al 1978). These studies provide interesting evidence of continuities between the reports obtained in Rapid Eye Movement, Stage 1 EEG sleep, and ongoing thought during relaxed moments in a stimulation environment. Similar continuities between ongoing thought patterns, daydreams, and hypnosis have emerged in studies by Crawford (1982), by Pekala & Levine (1982), and in several studies by Kunzendorf (1985a,b).

A COGNITIVE-AFFECTIVE PERSPECTIVE

Discussions of the relative primacy of affect and cognition in human experience continue to lace the personality literature (Lazarus 1984; Plutchik 1985; Rachman 1984; Zajonc 1984). Recent studies and theory suggest that the two systems are inextricably intertwined and that both must be studied in order to do true justice to the complexity of human personality. Recognition of our need for an integrative theory of cognition, affect, and action can be traced back as far as early Greek philosophy (Broadbent 1958; Singer 1984a,b; Tomkins 1962, 1963, 1980). To understand the complex dynamics of thought, feeling, and behavior is to grasp one of the most central and enduring mysteries of human experience and life itself (Mahoney 1984). Yet, as Iran-Nejad et al (1984) have pointed out, most dominant theories of cognition and comprehension have been slow in incorporating the research on affect in a functional fashion into their theoretical frameworks. Our ways of knowing the world are intrinsically bound up with our ways of feeling (Rychlak 1977, 1981; Tomkins 1962, 1963; Zajonc 1984). Indeed, our emotional system is closely linked to our cognitive system so that it is almost impossible to identify situations in which information processing does not evoke the experience of an affect or of a valuing response (Singer 1985c). Studies of the relationships between cognition and emotions, mood, or affective states have proliferated in recent years. In this literature, however, the terms affect, mood, and emotion are often used interchangeably. Consistent emotional patterns are also components of long-term temperament (Buss & Plomin 1984). Without entering into a definitional debate, the following presentation generally classifies studies in the same manner as the investigators themselves labeled their work.

Affect and Emotion

Even a perfunctory review of the literature confirms the fact that social psychology and behavioral psychology have rediscovered affect (Isen 1984; Lang 1984; Mandler 1984; Zajonc & Markus 1984). Indeed, this recent explosion of research has led Tomkins (1981a, p. 314) to declare that "the next decade or so belongs to affect." With his script formulation of personality, Tomkins (1979) has been an outspoken advocate of a theory of personality that highlights cognitive-affective dynamics. Carlson & Carlson (1984), investigated the role of Tomkins' affective amplification and psychological magnification in explaining the interconnectedness and expansion of the thoughts, actions, feelings, and memories that constitute similarities and differences in personality.

Many other recent studies have exemplified the prevalence of this cognitive-affective trend in several domains. For instance, Greenberg & Safran (1984a,b) emphasize the importance of exploring the ways in which "feeling" and "thinking" interact, particularly in clinical and therapeutic settings (Mahoney 1984). Whereas Isen & Daubman (1984) examined the influence of affect on the categorization of information, Zimring (1983) investigated the link between cognition and feeling and found that focusing on feelings facilitated performance on some cognitive tasks. Such work shows that the manner in which we attend to feelings has cognitive consequences that may influence some aspects of performance. In an intriguing series of studies, Andersen and colleagues (Andersen 1984; Andersen & Ross 1984; Andersen & Williams 1985) investigated the notion that in some contexts people may give more weight to their thoughts and feelings than to their behaviors when making inferences about themselves or personal evaluations. Similarly, other investigators (Strack et al 1985) have found that general life satisfaction depends not only on the hedonic quality of life experiences but also on the ways in which people actually think about these experiences. Kirschenbaum et al (1985) looked at the impact of affect induction on cognitive performance; they confirmed the importance of induced affect as a determinant of self-regulated performance. Clearly, the contemporary personality literature reveals that affect plays an important role in life experiences, in self-regulation, and in the evaluation of self.

The necessity of a comprehensive research paradigm for emotion is acknowledged (Epstein 1983). Clearly, any research strategy that attempts to predict behavior will need to rely, at least in part, on information regarding people's emotional make-up, since such information is likely to provide essential motivational clues to behavior (O'Malley & Gillette 1984). Several investigators have explored the relations between emotions and personality traits (Fisher et al 1985; O'Malley & Gillette 1984). This exploration integrates philosophical inquiry, which has had a long-standing concern for the connection between passions (or emotions) and enduring character patterns (or traits), with psychological research that suggests that personality traits can be represented by a circular configuration similar to that of some theories of emotions (Conte & Plutchik 1981). New theories of emotion, such as a perceptual-motor theory (Leventhal 1984) and a quantitative-experiential theory (Price et al 1985), point to innovative ways in which emotions and cognitions may be integrated into a single paradigm or program of research. Similarly, Averill (1983) attempted such an integration when he addressed the utility of using an emotion, like anger, as a paradigm case for the study of the implications of various theories of emotion. Clearly, at any given phase of a stressful encounter, individual differences in emotion, in large part, reflect individual differences in cognitive appraisal and coping (Folkman & Lazarus 1985; Folkman et al 1986). In a more integrative spirit, Buck (1985) has proposed a fascinating general model (or "prime theory") of the interaction between the cognitive and emotional systems, which suggests that it is in the context of such an interaction that complex human motivation and emotion can be best understood (see also Tomkins 1981a; Singer 1985c). A systems approach to personality development, maintenance, and change is indicative of similar trends in other, related fields, such as clinical psychology and psychiatry (Marmor 1983).

Consistent with the burgeoning interest in the development of new theories of emotion and cognition and the interconnections of the two systems, there has been active debate in the recent literature about how emotions are organized or structured in the context of the human personality. One important structural model of emotions, proposed by Tellegen and his associates (Tellegen 1984; Watson 1984; Watson & Tellegen 1985; Zevon & Tellegen 1982), postulates a "consensual" two-dimensional structure, with emotions falling in a simple structure of positive and negative affect, rather than in a circular arrangement or organizational pattern. In their extensive review and reanalysis, Watson & Tellegen (1985) concluded that the consistent emergence of this two-dimensional configuration confirms the basic structure of affect at the general factor level. Some clinical problems may result from the absence of positive affect, whereas others may result from the presence of excessive negative affect. In an important, related paper, Watson & Clark (1984) focused only on this latter pole, that of negative affect or "negative affectivity." Their review documented the existence of the construct of negative affectivity as a mood-dispositional dimension integrating several distinct and segregated literatures that, in various ways, reflect the common disposition to experience aversive emotional states. In addition to contributing to the debate pertaining to the structure of emotions, this work on negative affectivity has important implications for other, related literatures, such as the formation of depressive schemas. Previous investigations of the structural organization of emotions have generally yielded a circumplex or circular ordering of affect around a limited number of core dimensions (Russell 1980; Russell & Steiger 1982), whereas still other investigations have proposed a different shape of emotion, such as a conical model (Daly et al 1983). As part of the effort to validate the generality of the circumplex conceptualization, Russell (1983) investigated the pancultural aspects of such an organization of emotion, as well as the similarity of emotional facial expressions, from preschoolers to adults (Russell & Bullock 1985). In general, we agree with Watson & Tellegen's (1985) suggestion that the emotion assessment literature parallels the intelligence literature where positing one or more general dimensions is quite consistent with the existence of a larger number of more specific aptitudes. Certain kinds of two-dimensional and multifactorial schemes can play useful explanatory roles and stimulate affect-relevant research in areas (e.g. depression) often unrelated in previous research to the structural organization of emotions.

Mood

The long-term search for causal relationships between mood and personality (Underwood et al 1980) and the debate over the proper role of mood in contemporary models of information processing (Blaney 1986; Singer & Salovey 1987) continue. There is now ample experimental evidence that cognitions, especially in the form of ruminations about affectively toned events, may powerfully influence mood states and overt behaviors. Yet the hypothesis that mood and emotional content influence cognition and memory is not novel; it can be traced to philosophers such as Descartes, Kant, and Hume (Rappaport 1942; Thompson 1985).

Many research investigations are demonstrating the robust effects of mood on cognition, particularly on memory. For instance, Bower and colleagues have investigated many aspects of the interface between mood and cognitive systems (Bower 1981; Bower & Cohen 1982; Gilligan & Bower 1985; see Blaney 1986 and Singer & Salovey 1987, for reviews and evaluations of this literature); their work has demonstrated the influence of mood on such processes as memory retrieval, selective learning, perceptual organization, and cognitive biases (Pervin 1985). In his "network theory of affect," Bower has proposed that "emotions are central units in an associative network which have strong linkages to other aspects of the network—behaviors, beliefs, events, and themes" (Singer & Salovey 1987, p. 3). In this framework, an emotion serves as an active site in memory that spreads its activation to other mood-associated concepts and events, thereby creating greater availability of those mood-associated concepts (Isen et al 1978). As Blaney (1986) suggested, network theory is most closely related to Tomkins' (1980) view of affect as "amplification." In Tomkins' view, the affect of distress heightens current levels of aversive stimulation and this, in turn, evokes amplifying responses, such as "retrieved memories" and "constructed thoughts" (Tomkins 1980, p. 153). Bower's model has fostered a voluminous experimental literature that attempts to operationalize the many ways in which mood states influence cognitive and memorial processes. Network theory has also been linked to theories involving the impact of positive and negative moods on efficacy judgments concerning a wide variety of activities (Kavanagh & Bower 1985), as well as to theories of the informative and directive functions of affectives states on mood, misattributions, and judgments of well-being (Schwarz & Clore 1983).

Much of this work supports the notion that moods are organized responses that influence many psychological subsystems, including the cognitive subsystem; this work generally concludes that moods broadly influence cognitive responses over considerable portions of an individual's lifespan (Isen 1984; Mayer & Bremer 1985; Mayer & Volanth 1985). With respect to learning, recent investigators have found that intense negative (e.g. sad) moods tend to inhibit the learning and recall of any material (Ellis 1985; Ellis et al 1984, 1985). Hewett (1986) in two studies where children were exposed to frightening films used signal detection methodology to show poorer recall of content (d') and greater false-positive bias; they were more likely to report content not previously shown as having appeared in the films (β). Other researchers have examined mood-state dependent retention—that is, the notion that when affective states accompanying learning and remembering are the same, information will be retained better than when they differ (Bower & Mayer 1985; Mecklenbräuker & Hager 1984; Schare et al 1984; see Clark et al 1983 for a study of arousal-state dependent learning). Additional investigations of mood and memory include selective memory about the self (Natale & Hantas 1982), memory of positive, negative, and neutral events (Robinson 1980), memory of unique personal events (Thompson 1985), impact of "bonuses" and "bribes" on mood and memory (Boggiano & Hertel 1983), and constraints on the relationships between mood and memory (Clark & Teasdale 1985). If nothing else, this growing and diverse body of research will provide testimony to our claim that inquiry into the relationships between cognition and affect across psychological domains should be the major issue for the current decade of personality research (Pervin 1985).

Finally, several other studies of the mood and personality interface reflect the diverse nature of current research and represent a departure from traditional personality theory and research (Pervin 1984, 1985). For instance, attention has been given to such varied issues as the impact of chronic and acute stressors on daily reports of mood (Eckenrode 1984), the meaning of daily mood assessments (Stone et al 1985), mood reports of the "blue Monday" phenomenon (Hedges et al 1985), and the impact of negative air ions on mood, memory, and aggression among Type A and Type B individuals (Baron et al 1985). Furthermore, there is some evidence for the influence of mood on perceptions of social behavior and social interactions (Clark & Isen 1982; Forgas et al 1984), on sleep patterns in aging women (Berry & Webb

1985), on Type A behavior patterns (Strube & Lott 1985), and on cognitive models of depression (Clark & Teasdale 1982; Teasdale 1983). Among other things, this diversified surge of theory and research on the role of cognition and affect in private personality processes may represent the development of a new state of affairs, giving the field a "new look" and thus bringing it closer to its conceptualization as a "personality science" (Duke 1986; Duke & Nowicki 1986).

Well-being

Related to more positive aspects of psychological health, the relationship between "subjective well-being" and the emotions has become an area of widespread scientific interest to personality psychologists in recent years (see Diener & Griffin 1984 for a comprehensive bibliography). The many components of affect have come under the microscope of the personality researcher. Although personality psychologists have paid considerable attention to both single-session tests or surveys of global well-being and the structure of momentary affective states, until recently there has been a dearth of empirical work that examined the structure of affect within individuals over time (Diener et al 1985; Linville 1982). Clearly, a complete understanding of the ongoing aspects of subjective well-being necessitates not just a momentary sampling of affect but rather the sampling of affect within the lives of people over a relatively long period of time. In this vein, Diener and his associates have investigated many aspects of subjective well-being, including happiness, life satisfaction, and positive affect, across persons and over time (Diener 1984; Diener & Emmons 1984; Diener et al 1985; Emmons & Diener 1985; Emmons & Diener 1986a). Support has been found for the existence of two dimensions of personal affective structure: frequency of positive and negative affect and intensity of affect (Diener et al 1985). Both intensity and frequency are dimensions that underlie positive and negative affect; further research may help to shed light on the particular circumstances under which these dimensions are differentially dependent and independent of each other.

In addition to the intensity dimension, the temporal dimensions of subjective well-being and its affective consequences have been recently examined in the personality literature. Unquestionably, our subjective experiences carry us beyond the present to the past and to the anticipated future. Time or temporal perspectives are a common, everyday influence on current actions, future plans, and immediate feelings of well-being (Caplan et al 1985). Caplan and his associates investigated the effects of indicators of well-being from the temporal perspective of the person-environment fit (Caplan 1983, 1985). As expected, all time perspectives are not equally salient, although each makes unique contributions to well-being, on the one hand, and to ill-being, on the other hand. Importantly, such work links subjective current, retrospective, and anticipated person-environment fit to positive and negative affect and somatic complaints. Other research suggests that the relation between positive and negative affect differs greatly depending on the time frame, with the strongest negative correlation between the two affects occurring during acute emotional times and the relative independence of the two affects over longer periods (Diener & Emmons 1984). Along with studies of dream content, recurrent dreams, and well-being (Brown & Donderi 1986), personality variables that may influence subjective well-being have been investigated; support was found for a model postulating two different sets of personality traits that influence positive and negative affect separately (Emmons & Diener 1985). Interpersonal competencies related most strongly to positive affect, whereas internal emotional states related most strongly to negative affect. As indicated above, Kobasa and colleagues have examined a personality composite of positive well-being, or "hardiness," as a characterological mediator between life stress and health (Kobasa 1979; Kobasa et al 1981). More recently, Holahan & Moos (1985, 1986) have investigated "hardiness-like" tendencies, or the personality characteristics of people who adapt to life stress with little physical or psychological strain (see Monat & Lazarus 1985 for a recent anthology of stress and coping research).

COGNITIVE PROCESSES, STYLES, AND INFORMATION PROCESSING: THE ROLE OF SCHEMAS,[1] SCRIPTS, AND PROTOTYPES IN THE STRUCTURE OF PRIVATE EXPERIENCE

The major paradigm shift in psychology that has characterized the period since the 1960s has reflected a move away from stimulus-response units toward a recognition that human beings bring meaning and organization into almost every new encounter in the physical or social environment. Whereas most cognitive theories tend to emphasize consciousness and organized meaning structures such as schemas and scripts as a private feature of personality, they do not preclude the possibility that many of our plans and anticipations have become so automatic that they unroll too rapidly for us to notice them in the flurry of events (Singer 1984b).

Freud's discovery of the transference phenomenon was perhaps one of the greatest insights derived from the psychoanalytic method and also serves as a useful vehicle through which psychoanalytic and cognitive perspectives of personality can be meaningfully linked. A critical construct such as the transference phenomenon must be interpretable to some degree within the

---

[1]We have chosen, at the suggestion of George Mandler, to use the anglicized plural of schema rather than its awkward-sounding classical form "schemata."

framework of the experimental literature on such areas as how people process information, how they encode material for storage in some form of memory system, how they retrieve such memories, and how their own expectations influence the way they construe the physical and social environment (Singer 1985c). Whatever the ultimate therapeutic effectiveness of specific transference analysis, Freud's identification of this human experience laid the basis for identifying special forms of organized memory structures that are powerful determinants of biased information processing and that may potentially distort everyday social interactions (Singer & Salovey 1985). Such relatively organized meaning structures have been labeled "schemas" by Bartlett (1932), Piaget (1962), and more recently by researchers in social cognition (Fiske & Linville 1980; Showers & Cantor 1985; Taylor & Crocker 1981). The concept of schemas as organizational structures that encapsulate knowledge about the self or the world is traceable to the usage of Piaget, Lewin, Tolman, and Kelly, as well as to the psychoanalytic constructs of unconscious fantasy, object relations, and transference. It is only during the latter part of the last decade, however, that systematic efforts at operationalizing and experimenting with such concepts have proliferated (Hollon & Kriss 1984; Turk & Speers 1983; Singer 1985c).

General Schemas

Schemas, the most generic of all cognitive structures, provide selection criteria for regulating attention and lend a focus to the encoding, storage, and retrieval of information in a domain. More specifically, they allow the perceiver to identify stimuli quickly, to cluster them into manageable units, and to select a strategy for obtaining further information in order to solve a problem or reach a goal (Singer & Salovey 1985; Taylor & Crocker 1981). Schemas represent the starting point for "top-down" or theory-driven information processing, as opposed to "bottom-up" or data-driven processing, as well as the mechanisms underlying the "hidden agendas" that we all bring to each life experience and situation.

Studies of schemas in several domains have been flourishing in the personality literature. Some of this work represents another useful application of personality research to areas of clinical psychology (Hollon & Kriss 1984; Nasby & Kihlstrom 1985). In the clinical domain, Turk & Salovey 1985a,b) discussed the importance of the concept of schemas as knowledge structures that guide cognitive processing in clients (Turk & Salovey 1985a) as well as in clinicians (Turk & Salovey 1985b). They focus on the clinical implications of shortcomings in human judgment—for example, selective attention, confirmatory biases, egocentric biases, availability and representativeness heuristics, and illusory correlation—shortcomings that Nisbett & Ross (1980) have characterized as inevitable products of schematic processing. A clinically important consequence of schematic processing is schema perseverance, especially when it occurs despite conflicting or contradictory evidence. Because the primary function of schemas is to allow general knowledge to be applied to specific cases, it is often more efficient to accept the general case, even if its fit to a specific instance is imperfect. Indeed, the advantages of schematic processing are lost if schemas frequently must be revised in order to account for the details of every new situation that is encountered. In this way, schemas often persist in the face of evidence to the contrary (Fiske & Taylor 1984; Turk & Salovey 1985a). Such schema perseverance can prove particularly problematic to clinicians who may be unaware of their own biases and preconceptions when working therapeutically with clients, clients whose own psychological difficulties may partially stem from misuses of schematic processing. Indeed, these reviewers have demonstrated that neither clients nor clinicians are immune to the potential dangers of biased cognitive and information processing.

Yet, despite these potential dangers across clinical and everyday settings, researchers have demonstrated that the schemas "buy us" quite a bit (Fiske & Linville 1980), particularly with respect to schema-triggered affect and its impact on social perception (Fiske 1982) and, more recently, with respect to the differential accessibility of schema-relevant and schema-irrelevant information for experts and novices (Fiske & Dyer 1985). Insights into the structure and development of social schemas, likewise, have important implications for people's perceptions of a wide range of situations. For instance, Dworkin & Goldfinger (1985) proposed an information-processing approach to investigating individual differences in the cognition of social situations. Information-processing differences may result from individual differences in schemas influencing people's anticipation, perception, and memory of situations (Dworkin & Goldfinger 1985) as well as in the ecological perception of the "social affordances" of situations (McArthur & Baron 1983). Such research on the schemas reflecting people's processing biases and situational constraints may help to clarify the role of cognitive and social schemas in person-situation interactions.

The schema concept has also been used to investigate schemas of gender (Bem 1981, 1985; Crane & Markus 1982; Larsen & Seidman 1986; Markus et al 1982) as well as schemas of knowledge (Reiser et al 1985; Robinson 1980). Most researchers in this area have examined individual differences in the use of gender identity as a cognitive organizing principle. The schematicity of sex-typed individuals is specific to gender (Frable & Bem 1985). Individuals differ in their readiness to search for and to assimilate incoming information in gender-related terms, with sex-typed individuals having a greater readiness than non-sex-typed individuals to encode and organize information on the basis of gender, despite the existence of other dimensions that could serve equally well as organizing principles (Bem 1985). Alternatively, in the realm of more cognitive aspects of the self, the role of knowledge schemas in organizing and retrieving autobiographical experiences (Reiser et al 1985), in performing pragmatic reasoning (Cheng & Holyoak 1985), and in solving a variety of cognitive tasks (Lewis & Anderson 1985) has been investigated. Clearly, within the framework of an information-processing model of personality, the ways in which people attend to, encode, store, and retrieve information are, to a large extent, determined by the nature of their schemas of other people, of situations, of events, and, of course, of themselves.

Schemas of Self and Person-Schemas

Accordingly, as Pervin (1985) suggests, research on the "self-schema" or the schema as a cognitive structure that influences attention, organization, and recall of information or judgments about the self, may be of particular interest to personality psychologists (Fong & Markus 1982; Goldfried & Robins 1983; Markus 1977, 1983; Markus & Sentis 1982; Markus & Smith 1981; Markus et al 1985; see chapter in this volume by Markus & Wurf). A self-schema is a hierarchically organized body of knowledge or beliefs about one's intentions and capacities stored in long-term memory. A major function of the self-schema is anticipatory; that is, it incorporates hypotheses about incoming stimuli, as well as plans for interpreting and gathering schema-relevant information about the self (Singer & Salovey 1985). There is not yet an extensive body of evidence to suggest that schemas about the self are developed or structured in any different pattern than general schemas about the objects, events, and people in one's environment (Kihlstrom & Cantor 1984). Yet there is ample evidence that self-schemas are characterized by different *functional* properties than more general schemas. For instance, Greenwald (1980–1982; Greenwald & Pratkanis 1984) has reviewed extensively the memory material that can be self-linked; he has identified several features—self-generation, self-reference, and ego-involvement effects—of this material that may explain its enhanced memorability. Similarly, the special role that self-schemas play in the accurate recall of self-generated material, as opposed to material provided by others for passive review, has also been explored (Ingram 1984; Klein & Kihlstrom 1986; Wyer & Frey 1983). Indeed, Greenwald's (1980) metaphor of the self as a personal historian that preserves a record of autobiographical memory may prove useful in accounting for self-related increases in accurate memory as well as in explaining self-related biases, such as egocentricity, beneffectance, and cognitive conservatism. Clearly, the self is a very rich structure with many links to other nodes in affective and cognitive systems of one's personality, which may result in the characteristic "uniqueness" (Kihlstrom & Cantor 1984) and eventual automaticity or "unconsciousness" (Singer & Salovey 1985) of schemas about the self.

The distinction between automatic and nonautomatic processing has inspired much empirical study in recent years, in cognitive as well as in personality and social psychology (Bargh 1984), although Smith & Lerner (1986, p. 258) comment that "research on the development of automatism with tasks that are typical of social psychological research has been virtually nonexistent." One of the major challenges to personality psychology posed by anecdotal reports and psychoanalytic theorizing deals with the extent to which major schemas about the self (and significant others) become so automatic that they remain largely outside the individual's consciousness (Marcel 1983). Bowers & Meichenbaum (1984) recently edited a volume of essays that "reconsidered" the relations between conscious and unconscious determinants of behavior and experience from a largely cognitive perspective.

There are, no doubt, various ways in which schemas can be formed and operate automatically without an individual's phenomenal awareness of their existence. Meichenbaum & Gilmore (1984) suggested that "Core Organizing Principles," or general metascripts, function as metacognitive strategies that may be involved in the unconscious processing of information. Similarly, Baars (1983, 1985) made an important distinction between the processing properties of material in easily retrievable or current conscious awareness (i.e. "the global workspace") and the more specialized properties of the less accessible schemas. Bargh and colleagues studied automatic information processing and its relation to person memory (Bargh & Thein 1985), self-relevant information (Bargh 1982), and social information processing (Bargh 1984). In a study of unconscious processing and impression formation, Bargh & Pietromonaco (1982) found that unwitting experimental exposure to words related to a concept like "hostility" led participants to be more responsive to potential hostile qualities in later evaluating an unknown person or to rate that person in a more negative fashion. Other studies of self-schemas and automaticity investigated attitude activation (Fazio et al 1986), social interaction (Pryor & Merluzzi 1985), social judgment (Smith & Lerner 1986), social inference processes (Smith 1984), and expert-novice differences in schema development (Fiske & Dyer 1985). Recently, Logan (1985) put forward a methodological critique that calls for studies of more complex and realistic tasks than those that have been used in investigations of automaticity and self-schemas to date.

Provocative research on self-schemas, self-image, and social information processing has begun to appear. For instance, Lewicki (1984) advocated a "defensive" model of social information processing in which individuals overestimate the importance of their positive attributes and underestimate negative attributes. Other work found that people's self-symbolization or self-definitional needs would hinder their responding to interpersonal aspects of a situation and would lead to the neglect of others' perspectives (Gollwitzer

& Wickland 1985a,b). In sum, small situational changes were capable of producing related changes in the ways individuals process information about others. A wide range of social and clinical experiences also suggests that a special feature of self-schemas may be the recurrence of prototypical images that serve as models, mentors, or defining characteristics of desired appearances or life styles. Such images may represent polar characteristics of non-self, real-self, or ideal-self dimensions in a particular domain of one's network of self-schemas (Higgins et al 1986; Singer & Salovey 1985; Glick & Zigler 1985).

The relation between self-schemas and depression is an important area for exploration. Linking self-schema theory with psychopathological aspects of personality encourages a cross-fertilization of social, clinical, and personality areas of psychology. Clearly, the schema notion appears to offer considerable promise as a way of construing the biasing, as well as the facilitative, effects of organized experience structures in memory. Central to Beck's causality model of depression is the schema construct (Beck et al 1979). Beck and his colleagues describe dysfunctional schemas as stable, underlying assumptions about the world and the self; these are based on past experiences and direct the processing of current information, possibly leading to biased or distorted interpretations (Beck et al 1979). Kuiper and his colleagues (Kuiper & MacDonald 1983; Kuiper 1986; MacDonald & Kuiper 1985) have integrated an information-processing paradigm for assessing self-schemas with Beck's hypotheses.

As an alternative to the causal role of dysfunctional cognitions and self-schemas in depression that Beck hypothesizes, Hammen and colleagues have taken a different perspective, investigating depressive self-schemas and the ways in which they interact with negative life events (Hammen et al 1985a,b, 1986; Hammen & Zupan 1984). In these studies, Hammen and colleagues focused on, among other things, the question of stability or mood dependence of depressive self-schemas. In applying Bower's (1981) associative network model of memory to depressive self-schema theory, Hammen et al (1986) suggested that self-schemas, or accessible information about the self, are mood-state dependent rather than stable and unchanging. This work, though, "requires additional investigation in a longitudinal design using diverse measures of schemas" (Hammen et al 1985a, p. 1148).

Other studies of depressive self-schemas have explored the interplay of both cognitive and affective characteristics. In a recent review of the literature, Ruehlman et al (1985) investigated evaluative schemas and depression and found that severely depressed individuals possess negativistic evaluative tendencies, with this bias most clearly manifested in the area of self-referential or affect-laden thoughts. Ruehlman (1985) also examined depression and affective meaning for "current concerns," or specialized self-schemas that guide thought, emotion, and behavior in the direction of incentive attainment. Predictably, they found that depressed subjects viewed their concerns in a less positive and less active light than nondepressed subjects. Other studies investigated depressive self-schemas and cognitive accessibility (Gotlib & McCann 1984), cognitive capacity (Riskind & Rholes 1984), cognitive style (Carver et al 1986) and pessimistic self-preoccupation (Strack et al 1985). In an intriguing study, Pietromonaco & Markus (1985) investigated the nature and content of the negative thoughts that accompany depression by examining subjects' thoughts about themselves and others during a series of cognitive tasks. Their results suggested that the negativity in thought that accompanies depression is restricted to thoughts about oneself and does not extend to thoughts about others. Furthermore, they proposed that depressives have a negative self-schema that makes the affective nature of their behavior particularly salient, providing additional evidence for the inextricable relationship between the affective and cognitive systems in self-schema formation and personality development.

Scripts, Prototypes, and Cognitive Style

Scripts, or schemas about the appropriate sequence of events in well-known situations, have been proposed as a major unit of social interaction (Abelson 1981; Schank & Abelson 1977; Tomkins 1979, 1981a,b). In accord with the pioneering work of Tomkins, powerful, emotion-laden scripts originating in childhood are magnified throughout adult life. Specific memories of affectively charged events from childhood, called "scenes," are linked together, forming the basis of the dominant themes that guide cognitive processing and social behavior throughout life (Carlson 1981; Carlson & Carlson 1984).

In an intriguing longitudinal study of scripts and personality, Helson et al (1984) examined the life-span script, or "social clock," of a sample of women. The term social clock suggests both a social group's agreement about when certain events ought to occur in life (e.g. marriage before age 30) and one's own personal set of goals or personal script for achieving such states as intimacy, childbearing, or financial security. In the study's twenty-year follow-up of female college graduates, Helson et al (1984) were able to identify those women adhering to a traditional feminine social clock, those willing to postpone but not give up such expectations of marriage and childbearing, and those women who eschewed such a script early in life or who, by age 28, had chosen career lines that conformed in the 1960s to a masculine social clock. In sum, this study provided preliminary evidence for the existence of "life-span schemas" that are consistent across individuals and time (Frieze et al 1985).

Other recent research includes studies of how scripts influence the ways in which "peak" and "nadir" collections of memories are retrieved (McAdams 1985), how scripts are organized in the form of action-oriented representations (Trzebinski 1985), and how the existence of cultural scripts may explain general patterns of differences in the social behavior of certain ethnic groups (Triandis et al 1984). Indeed, the script concept is alive and well, demonstrating its efficacy as an organizing principle and explanatory mechanism in both the short-term (e.g. going to a restaurant) and long-term (e.g. planning one's life) information processing of events.

Although prototypes are sometimes confused with schemas in that they are represented as a special case of the person schema (Turk & Salovey 1985a), the prototype has developed its own definition in the person perception literature (Hastie & Kumar 1979; Kuiper & Derry 1981). "Prototypes consist of relatively stable, abstract representations of a large set of more or less associated attributes, trait characteristics, characteristic behaviors performed by a type of person, and even situations commonly associated with people of that type" (Turk & Salovey 1985a, p. 8). Important recent research has extended the application of prototypes to different domains, from person perception to situational constraint. Several recent studies have looked at the relation of personality style to prototypes. Horowitz and colleagues (Horowitz et al 1981a,b) have attempted a clinical application of prototypes by suggesting that psychodiagnostic assessments be based on matching the personality characteristics of clients to cognitive prototypes for various diagnostic categories. Magaro & Ashbrook (1985), on the other hand, described five personality styles that each reflect individual prototypes sharing similar constellations of needs, beliefs, and behaviors. Prototypes have been investigated with respect to implicit personality theories (Schneider & Blankmeyer 1983), personality test construction (Broughton 1984), decision-making strategies (Niedenthal et al 1985), and situational prototypicality (Cantor et al 1982; Schutte et al 1985). As organizing structures that assist people in filling in all known attributes of a person, situation, event, or concept, "even if all the attributes are not directly relevant to category membership" (Fiske & Taylor 1984, p. 147), it is clear that prototype theory, at the very least, will continue to serve as a useful organizational framework for the consolidation of research on information-processing approaches to the study of personality.

What might one predict about the relative rapidity and efficiency of schema, script, and prototype formation in individuals differing along particular cognitive and personality dimensions or styles? Kreitler & Kreitler (1976, 1982) have shown that individual differences in schema formation or automaticity are, at least in part, a function of individual variation in styles of meaning assignment. Previous investigations compared several different approaches to the study of cognitive style and personality (Goldstein & Blackman 1978, 1981), whereas other studies focused on the relation between the dimensions of adaptation and innovation and certain personality characteristics (Goldsmith 1984; Kirton & deCiantis 1986). Dickman (1985) investigated the effects of individual differences in a personality trait, impulsivity, on the processing of cognitive information, such as the integration of global and local dimensions of stimuli. Furthermore, in the area of clinical psychology and the practice of psychotherapy, Horowitz et al (1984) presented an intriguing approach to brief psychotherapy, an approach that carefully attends to the therapeutic process in terms of changes in patients' states of mind, relationships, and particularly, style of information processing and personality type. Several other studies of cognitive style in personality differences focused on the dimension of field-dependence and field-independence (McKenna 1983). This research generally suggested that, compared to field-dependent individuals, field-independent individuals are more efficient at "reality monitoring," or determining whether a memory originated in internal thought processes or external perceptual processes (Durso et al 1985; Johnson & Raye 1981), at isolating and encoding the essential elements of memory tasks (Reardon & Rosen 1984), at automatizing relevant item sequences (Jolly & Reardon 1985; Klatzky 1984), and at cognitive restructuring (Frank & Noble 1984). In sum, such research emphasizes that future information-processing models of personality must account for both individual differences in, and differential effects of, cognitive style on the formation, maintenance, and change of schemas about the self and the world around us.

CONCLUDING COMMENTS

We have sought in this review to highlight some of the areas of increasingly active personality research that focus upon the more private features of individual variation—thoughts, feelings, beliefs about self and others. Clearly much is happening also in the study of more public behaviors. One might suggest that the emphasis on actions in the work of Buss & Craik (1983) reflects an effort to define meaningful public personality structures, neither too molecular nor too molar, that are comparable in heuristic value to the schemas, scripts, prototypes, personal constructs and nuclear scenes that are increasingly used in studying private processes. We foresee no diminution in the investigators' interest in such variables. We expect to see even more use of thought samples, autobiographical memories, personal goals, and their links to emotion as well as to overt action in personality exploration. The controversies about temporal and cross-situational stability of personality that have occurred over the past 15 years have heightened our awareness that we must move well beyond the "one-shot," cross-sectional sampling that has often proven an embarrassment in personality research. We need to conduct research that samples many data points across time and situation and that reflects ongoing thoughts and feelings, shifting or stable goals, and current concerns as well as overt social actions or health behaviors (Emmons & Diener 1986b; Singer 1987).

In a sense, personality research has always been drastically underfunded compared to some other "harder" areas of psychology and certainly compared to the physical sciences and to biomedical research. For most of this century the only group of observers who could do the extensive samplings of thought, emotion, and action that is called for by good personological methodology were the psychoanalysts. That may be why so much personality theory grew up around the inevitably tendentious data emerging in clinical reports. But the terminology of psychoanalysis, from "neutralized energy" to "cathexes" to "object relations," has not led to fruitful scientific empirical inquiry unless translated into more operationally definable terms such as "attachment" or "schemas."

Isn't it time that we begin building our personality models out of the available knowledge in psychology itself, the developments in cognition and information-processing, social cognition, psychophysiology, new research on emotion and motivation and the fine developments in direct observations of infants, children, and families? The identifications of individual variations in schema or script formations provide one major link to the vigorous field of cognition, for example. And ought we not consider writing our textbooks so that personality can be understood as a supraordinate system reflecting unique combinations or systematic variations in psychophysiological patterns, emotional response and experience, cognitive capacity, social and developmental processes? Most importantly, we need to plan and to carry out studies that use "natural" experiences and actions, measured often across time and situations in the public and private forms of human expression.

ACKNOWLEDGMENT

Preparation of this chapter was supported in part by a subcontract from the Program on Conscious and Unconscious Mental Processes, John D. and Catherine T. MacArthur Foundation.

Literature Cited

Abelson, R. P. 1981. Psychological status of the script concept. *Am. Psychol.* 36:715–29

Algom, D., Singer, J. L. 1984. Interpersonal influences on task-irrelevant thought and imagery in a signal detection experiment. *Imagination, Cognit., Pers.* 4:69–83

Andersen, S. M. 1984. Self-knowledge and social inference II: Diagnosticity of cognitive/affective and behavioral data. *J. Pers. Soc. Psychol.* 46:294–307

Andersen, S. M., Ross, L. 1984. Self-knowledge and social inference I: *J. Pers. Soc. Psychol.* 46:280–93

Andersen, S. M., Williams, M. 1985. Cognitive/affective reactions in the improvement of self-esteem: When thoughts and feelings make a difference. *J. Pers. Soc. Psychol.* 49:1086–97

Antrobus, J. S., Saul, H. N. 1980. Sleep onset: Subjective, behavioral, and electroencephalographic comparisons. *Waking Sleeping* 4:259–70

Antrobus, J. S., Singer, J. L. 1964. Visual signal detection as a function of sequential task variability of simultaneous speech. *J. Exp. Psychol.* 68:603–10

Arkin, A. M., Antrobus, J. S., Ellman, S. J., eds. 1978. *The Mind in Sleep: Psychology and Psychophysiology.* Hillsdale, NJ: Erlbaum

Averill, J. R. 1983. Studies on anger and aggression: Implications for theories of emotion. *Am. Psychol.* 38:1145–60

Baars, B. J. 1983. Conscious contents provide the nervous system with coherent, global information. In *Consciousness and Self-regulation,* Vol. 3, ed. R. Davidson, G. Schwartz, D. Shapiro. New York: Plenum

Baars, B. J. 1985. *A Cognitive Theory of Consciousness.* Cambridge: Cambridge Univ. Press

Baars, B. J. 1987. *A Cognitive Theory of Consciousness.* London: Cambridge Univ. Press

Babladelis, G. 1984. *The Study of Personality: Issues and Resolutions.* New York: Holt, Rinehart & Winston

Bargh, J. A. 1982. Attention and automaticity in the processing of self-relevant information. *J. Pers. Soc. Psychol.* 43:425–36

Bargh, J. A. 1984. Automatic and conscious processing of social information. In *Handbook of Social Cognition,* ed. R. S. Wyer, T. K. Skull, 3:1–44. Hillsdale, NJ: Erlbaum

Bargh, J. A., Pietromonaco, P. 1982. Automatic information processing and social perception: The influence of trait information presented outside conscious awareness on impression formation. *J. Pers. Soc. Psychol.* 43:437–49

Bargh, J. A., Thein, R. D. 1985. Individual construct accessibility, person memory, and the recall-judgment link: The case of information overload. *J. Pers. Soc. Psychol.* 49:1129–46

Baron, R. A., Russell, G. W., Arms, R. L. 1985. Negative ions and behavior: Impact on mood, memory, and aggression among Type A and Type B persons. *J. Pers. Soc. Psychol.* 48:746–54

Bartlett, F. C. 1932. *Remembering: A Study in Experimental and Social Psychology.* Cambridge: Cambridge Univ. Press

Beck, A. T., Rush, A. J., Shaw, B. F., Emery, G. 1979. *Cognitive Therapy of Depression.* New York: Guilford

Bem, S. L. 1981. Gender schema theory: A cognitive account of sex typing. *Psychol. Rev.* 88:354–64

Bem, S. L. 1985. Androgyny and gender schema theory: A conceptual and empirical integration. In *Nebraska Symposium on Motivation: Psychology and Gender,* ed. T. B. Sonderegger, pp. 179–226. Lincoln: Univ. Nebraska Press

Berry, D. T. R., Webb, W. B. 1985. Mood and sleep in aging women. *J. Pers. Soc. Psychol.* 49:1724–27

Blackwell, R. T., Galassi, J. P., Galassi, M. D., Watson, T. E. 1985. Are cognitive

assessment methods equal? A comparison of think aloud and thought listening. *Cogn. Ther. Res.* 9:399–413

Blaney, P. H. 1986. Affect and memory: A review. *Psychol. Bull.* 99:229–46

Blass, T. 1984. Social psychology and personality: Toward a convergence. *J. Pers. Soc. Psychol.* 47:1013–27

Block, J. H., Block, J. 1980. The role of ego control and ego resiliency in the organization of behavior. *Minn. Symp. Child Dev.* 13:39–101

Boggiano, A. K., Hertel, P. T. 1983. Bonuses and bribes: Mood effects in memory. *Soc. Cognit.* 2:49–61

Bonanno, G. A., Singer, J. L. 1986. *Defensive denial or repressive personality style: Theoretical and methodological implications for health and pathology.* Yale Univ. Unpublished

Bower, G. H. 1981. Mood and memory. *Am. Psychol.* 36:129–48

Bower, G. H., Cohen, P. R. 1982. Emotional influences in memory and thinking: Data and theory. In *Affect and Cognition: The 17th Annual Carnegie Symposium on Cognition,* ed. M. S. Clark, S. T. Fiske. Hillsdale, NJ: Erlbaum

Bower, G. H., Mayer, J. D. 1985. Failure to replicate mood-dependent retrieval. *Bull. Psychon. Soc.* 23:39–42

Bowers, K. S., Meichenbaum, D., eds. 1984. *The Unconscious Reconsidered.* New York: Wiley

Brandstatter, H. 1983. Emotional responses to other persons in everyday life situations. *J. Pers. Soc. Psychol.* 45:871–83

Briggs, J. M., Smith, T. G. 1986. The measurement of shyness. See Jones et al 1986

Broadbent, D. 1958. *Perception and Communication.* London: Pergamon

Brockner, J., Hjelle, L., Plant, R. W. 1985. Self-focused attention, self-esteem, and the experience of state depression. *J. Pers.* 53:425–34

Broughton, R. 1984. A prototype strategy for construction of personality scales. *J. Pers. Soc. Psychol.* 47:1334–46

Brown, R. J., Donderi, D. C. 1986. Dream content and self-reported well-being among recurrent dreamers, past-recurrent dreamers, and non-recurrent dreamers. *J. Pers. Soc. Psychol.* 50:612–23

Buck, R. 1985. Prime theory: An integrated view of motivation and emotion. *Psychol. Rev.* 92:389–413

Buss, A. H. 1986. A theory of shyness. See Jones et al 1986

Buss, D. M., Craik, K. H. 1983. The act frequency approach to personality. *Psychol. Rev.* 90:105–26

Buss, A. H., Plomin, R. 1984. *Temperament:*

Early Developing Personality Traits. Hillsdale, NJ: Erlbaum

Cantor, N., Kihlstrom, J. 1985. Social intelligence: The cognitive basis of personality. *Rev. Pers. Soc. Psychol.* 6:

Cantor, N., Mischel, W., Schwartz, J. 1982. A prototype analysis of psychological situation. *Cogn. Psychol.* 14:45–77

Caplan, R. D. 1983. Person-environment fit: Past, present, and future. In *Stress Research: Where do we go from here?*, ed. C. Cooper. London: Wiley

Caplan, R. D., Tripathi, R. C., Naidu, R. K. 1985. Subjective past, present, and future fit: Effects on anxiety, depression, and other indicators of well-being. *J. Pers. Soc. Psychol.* 48:180–97

Carlson, L., Carlson, R. 1984. Affect and psychological magnification: Derivations from Tomkins' script theory. *J. Pers.* 52:36–45

Carlson, R. 1981. Studies in script theory: I. Adult analogs of a childhood nuclear scene. *J. Pers. Soc. Psychol.* 40:501–10

Carlson, R. 1984. What's social about social psychology? Where's the person in personality research? *J. Pers. Soc. Psychol.* 47:1304–9

Carver, C. S., Antoni, M., Scheier, M. 1985. Self-consciousness and self-assessment. *J. Pers. Soc. Psychol.* 48:117–24

Carver, C. S., Ganellen, R. J., Behar-Mitrani, V. 1986. Depression and cognitive style: Comparison between measures. *J. Pers. Soc. Psychol.* In press

Cheng, P. W., Holyoak, K. J. 1985. Pragmatic reasoning schemas. *Cogn. Psychol.* 17:391–416

Cheek, J. M., Briggs, S. R. 1982. Self-consciousness and aspects of identity. *J. Res. Pers.* 16:401–8

Clark, D. M., Teasdale, J. D. 1982. Diurnal variation in clinical depression and accessibility of memories of positive and negative experiences. *J. Abnorm. Psychol.* 91:87–95

Clark, D. M., Teasdale, J. D. 1985. Constraints on the effects of mood on memory. *J. Pers. Soc. Psychol.* 48:1595–1608

Clark, M. S., Isen, A. M. 1982. Toward understanding the relationship between feeling states and social behavior. In *Cognitive Social Psychology*, ed. A. Hastorf, A. Isen. New York: Elsevier North-Holland

Clark, M. S., Milberg, S., Ross, J. 1983. Arousal cues arousal-related material in memory: Implication for understanding effect of mood on memory. *J. Verb. Learn. Verb. Behav.* 22:633–49

Conte, H. R., Plutchik, R. 1981. A circumplex model for interpersonal personality traits. *J. Pers. Soc. Psychol.* 43:443–57

Crane, M., Markus, H. 1982. Gender identity:

The benefits of a self-schema approach. *J. Pers. Soc. Psychol.* 43:1195–97

Crawford, H. J. 1982. Hypnotizability, daydreaming styles, imagery vividness, and absorption: A multidimensional study. *J. Pers. Soc. Psychol.* 42:915–26

Csikszentmihalyi, M. 1975. *Beyond Boredom and Anxiety.* San Francisco: Jossey-Bass

Csikszentmihalyi, M. 1982. Toward a psychology of optimal experience. *Rev. Pers. Soc. Psychol.*, Vol. 3. Beverly Hills, CA: Sage

Csikszentmihalyi, M., Kubey, R. 1981. Television and the rest of life: A systematic comparison of subjective experience. *Public Opin. Q.* 45:317–28

Csikszentmihalyi, M., Larson, R. 1984. *Being Adolescent.* New York: Basic

Daly, E. M., Lancee, W. J., Polivy, J. 1983. A conical model for the taxonomy of emotional experience. *J. Pers. Soc. Psychol.* 43:443–57

Davis, P. J., Schwartz, G. 1986. Repression and the inaccessibility of affective memories. *J. Pers. Soc. Psychol.* 49: In press

Davison, G. C., Robins, C., Johnson, M. K. 1983. Articulated thoughts during simulated situations: A paradigm for studying cognition in emotion and behavior. *Cogn. Ther. Res.* 7:17–40

Demo, D. H. 1985. The measurement of self-esteem: Refining our methods. *J. Pers. Soc. Psychol.* 48:1490–1507

Dickman, S. 1985. Impulsivity and perception: Individual differences in the processing of the local and global dimensions of stimuli. *J. Pers. Soc. Psychol.* 48:133–49

Diener, E. 1984. Subjective well-being. *Psychol. Bull.* 95:542–75

Diener, E., Emmons, R. A. 1984. The independence of positive and negative affect. *J. Pers. Soc. Psychol.* 47:1105–17

Diener, E., Griffin, S. 1984. Happiness and life satisfaction: A bibliography. *Psychol. Doc.* 14:11

Diener, E., Larsen, R. J., Levine, S., Emmons, R. A. 1985. Intensity and frequency: Dimensions underlying positive and negative affect. *J. Pers. Soc. Psychol.* 48:1253–65

Duke, M. P. 1986. Personality science: A proposal. *J. Pers. Soc. Psychol.* 50:382–85

Duke, M. P., Nowicki, S. 1986. *Abnormal Psychology: A New Look.* New York: Holt, Rinehart & Winston

Durso, F. T., Reardon, R., Jolly, E. J. 1985. Self-nonself-segregation and reality monitoring. *J. Pers. Soc. Psychol.* 48:447–55

Dworkin, R. H., Goldfinger, S. H. 1985. Processing bias: Individual differences in the cognition of situations. *J. Pers.* 53:480–501

Eckenrode, J. 1984. Impact of chronic and

acute stressors on daily reports of mood. *J. Pers. Soc. Psychol.* 46:907–18

Ellis, H. C. 1985. On the importance of mood intensity and encoding demand in memory: Commentary on Hasher, Rose, Zacks, Sanft, & Doren. *J. Exp. Psychol. Gen.* 114:392–95

Ellis, H. C., Thomas, R. L., McFarland, A. D., Lane, J. W. 1985. Emotional mood states and retrieval in episodic memory. *J. Exp. Psychol.: Learn. Mem. Cognit.* 11:363–70

Ellis, H. C., Thomas, R. L., Rodriguez, I. A. 1984. Emotional mood states and memories: Elaborative encoding, semantic processing, and cognitive effort. *J. Exp. Psychol.: Learn., Mem., Cognit.* 10:470–82

Emmons, R. A., Diener, E. 1985. Personality correlates of subjective well-being. *Pers. Soc. Psychol. Bull.* 11:89–97

Emmons, R. A., Diener, E. 1986a. An interactional approach to the study of personality and emotion. *J. Pers.* 54:371–84

Emmons, R. A., Diener, E. 1986b. Personal strivings: An approach to personality and subjective well-being. *J. Pers. Soc. Psychol.* In press

Epstein, S. 1983. A research paradigm for the study of personality and emotions. *Nebr. Symp. Motiv.*, pp. 91–154. Lincoln: Univ. Nebr. Press

Fazio, R. H., Sanbonmatsu, D. M., Powell, M. C., Kardes, F. R. 1986. On the automatic activation of attitudes. *J. Pers. Soc. Psychol.* 50:229–38

Fenigstein, A. 1984. Self-consciousness and the overperception of self as a target. *J. Pers. Soc. Psychol.* 47:860–70

Fenigstein, A., Levine, M. P. 1984. Self-attention, concept activation, and the causal self. *J. Exp. Soc. Psychol.* 20:231–45

Feshbach, S. 1984. The "personality" of personality theory and research. *Pers. Soc. Psychol. Bull.* 10:446–56

Feshbach, S., Weiner, B. 1986. *Personality.* New York: Health. 2nd ed.

Fishbein, M., Ajzen, I. 1975. *Belief Attitude, Intention, and Behavior: An Introduction to Theory and Research.* Reading, MA: Addison-Wesley

Fisher, G. A., Heise, D. R., Bohrnstedt, G. W., Lucke, J. F. 1985. Evidence for extending the circumplex model of personality trait language to self-reported moods. *J. Pers. Soc. Psychol.* 49:233–42

Fiske, S. T. 1982. Schema-triggered affect: Applications to social perception. In *Affect and Cognition*, ed. M. S. Clark, S. T. Fiske. *17th Ann. Carnegie Symp.* Hillsdale, NJ: Erlbaum

Fiske, S. T., Dyer, L. M. 1985. Structure and development of social schemata: Evidence

from positive and negative transfer effects. *J. Pers. Soc. Psychol.* 48:839–52

Fiske, S. T., Linville, P. W. 1980. What does the schema process buy us? *Pers. Soc. Psychol. Bull.* 6:543–57

Fiske, S. T., Taylor, S. E. 1984. *Social Cognition.* Reading, MA: Addison-Wesley

Folkman, S., Lazarus, R. S. 1985. If it changes it must be a process: Study of emotion and coping during three stages of a college examination. *J. Pers. Soc. Psychol.* 48:150–70

Folkman, S., Lazarus, R. S., Gruen, R. J., DeLongis, A. 1986. Appraisal, coping, health status, and psychological status. *J. Pers. Soc. Psychol.* 50:571–79

Fong, G. T., Markus, H. 1982. Self-schemas and judgment about others. *Soc. Cognit.* 1:191–204

Forgas, J. P., Bower, G. H., Krantz, S. E. 1984. The influence of mood on perceptions of social interactions. *J. Exp. Soc. Psychol.* 20:497–513

Frable, D. E. S., Bem, S. L. 1985. If you are gender schematic, all members of the opposite sex look alike. *J. Pers. Soc. Psychol.* 49:459–68

Frank, B. M., Noble, J. P. 1984. Field independence-dependence and cognitive restructuring. *J. Pers. Soc. Psychol.* 47:1129–35

Franzoi, S. L. 1983. Self-concept differences as a function of private self-consciousness and social anxiety. *J. Res. Pers.* 17:275–87

Franzoi, S. L., Brewer, L. C. 1984. The experience of self-awareness and its relation to level of self-consciousness: An experiential sampling study. *J. Res. Pers.* 18:522–40

Franzoi, S. L., Davis, M. H. 1985. Adolescent self-disclosure and loneliness: Private self-consciousness and parental influences. *J. Pers. Soc. Psychol.* 48:764–76

Franzoi, S. L., Davis, M. H., Young, R. D. 1985. The effects of private self-consciousness and perspective taking on satisfaction in close relationships. *J. Pers. Soc. Psychol.* 48:1584–94

Frieze, I. H., Bailey, S., Mamula, P., Moss, M. 1985. Life scripts and life planning: The role of career scripts in college women's career choices. *Imagination, Cognit. Pers.* 5:59–72

Gangestad, S., Snyder, M. 1985. "To carve nature at its joints": on the existence of discrete classes in personality. *Psychol. Rev.* 92:317–49

Genest, M., Turk, D. C. 1981. Think-aloud approaches to cognitive assessment. In *Cognitive Assessment*, ed. T. V. Merluzzi, C. R. Glass, M. Genest. New York: Guilford

Giambra, L. M. 1980a. A factor analysis of

the items of the Imaginal Processes Inventory. *J. Clin. Psychol.* 36:383–409

Giambra, L. M. 1980b. Sex differences in daydreaming and related mental activity from the late teens to the early nineties. *Int. J. Aging Hum. Dev.* 10:1–34

Giambra, L. M., Stone, B. S. 1982. Australian-American differences in daydreaming, attentional processes, and curiosity: First findings based on retrospective reports. *Imagination, Cognit. Pers.* 2:23–35

Gibbons, F. X., Smith, T. W., Ingram, R. E., Pearce, K., Brehm, S. S., Schroeder, D. J. 1985. Self-awareness and self-confrontation: Effects of self-focused attention on members of a clinical population. *J. Pers. Soc. Psychol.* 48:662–75

Gilligan, S. G., Bower, G. H. 1985. Cognitive consequences of emotional arousal. In *Emotions, Cognition, and Behavior,* ed. C. E. Izard, J. Kagan, R. B. Zajonc. Hillsdale, NJ: Erlbaum

Glick, M., Zigler, E. 1985. Self-image: A cognitive developmental approach. In *The Development of Self,* ed. R. Leahy, pp. 1–53. New York: Academic

Gold, S. R., Gold, R. G. 1982. Actual daydream content and the Imaginal Processes Inventory. *J. Ment. Imagery* 6:169–74

Gold, S. R., Reilly, J. P. 1986. Daydreaming, current concerns, and personality. *Imagination, Cognit. Pers.* 5:117–25

Goldfried, M. R., Robins, C. 1983. Self-schemas, cognitive bias, and the processing of learning experiences. In *Advances in Cognitive-Behavioral Research and Therapy,* Vol. 2, ed. P. C. Kendall. New York: Academic

Golding, J. M., Singer, J. L. 1983. Patterns of inner experience: Daydreaming styles, depressive moods, and sex roles. *J. Pers. Soc. Psychol.* 45:663–75

Goldsmith, R. E. 1984. Personality characteristics: Association with adaptation-innovation. *J. Pers.* 117:159–65

Goldstein, K. M., Blackman, S. 1978. *Cognitive Style: Five Approaches and Relevant Research.* New York: Wiley

Goldstein, K. M., Blackman, S. 1981. Cognitive styles. In *Personality: Theory, Measurements, and Research,* ed. F. Fransella. London: Methuen

Gollwitzer, P. M., Wicklund, R. A. 1985a. The pursuit of self-defining goals. In *Action Control: From Cognition to Behavior,* ed. J. Kuhl, J. Beckmann, pp. 61–85. New York: Springer-Verlag

Gollwitzer, P. M., Wicklund, R. A. 1985b. Self-symbolizing and the neglect of others' perspectives. *J. Pers. Soc. Psychol.* 48:702–15

Gotlib, I. H., McCann, C. D. 1984. Construct accessibility and depression: An examination of cognitive and affective factors. *J. Pers. Soc. Psychol.* 47:427–39

Greenberg, L. S., Safran, J. D. 1984a. Integrating affect and cognition: A perspective on the process of therapeutic change. *Cogn. Ther. Res.* 8:559–78

Greenberg, L. S., Safran, J. D. 1984b. Hot cognition-emotion coming in from the cold: A reply to Rachman and Mahoney. *Cogn. Ther. Res.* 8:591–98

Greenwald, A. G. 1980. The totalitarian ego: Fabrication and revision of personal history. *Am. Psychol.* 35:603–18

Greenwald, A. G. 1981. Self and memory. *Psychol. Learn. Motiv.* 15:202–36

Greenwald, A. G. 1982. Is anyone in charge? Personalysis versus the principle of personal unity. In *Psychological Perspectives on the Self,* ed. J. Suls, Hillsdale, NJ: Erlbaum 1:151–81

Greenwald, A. G., Pratkanis, A. R. 1984. The self. In *Handbook of Social Cognition,* ed. R. S. Wyer, J. K. Srull, 3:129–78 Hillsdale, NJ: Erlbaum

Hall, C. S., Lindzey, G., Loehlin, J. C., Manosevits, M. 1985. *Introduction to Theories of Personality.* New York: Wiley

Hammen, C., Marks, T., deMayo, R., Mayol, A. 1985a. Self-schemas and risk for depression: A prospective study. *J. Pers. Soc. Psychol.* 49:1147–59

Hammen, C., Marks, T., Mayol, A., deMayo, R. 1985b. Depressive self-schemas, life stress, and vulnerability to depression. *J. Abnorm. Psychol.* 94:308–19

Hammen, C., Miklowitz, D., Dyck, D. 1986. Stability and severity parameters of depressive self-schema responding. *J. Soc. Clin. Psychol.* 4:23–45

Hammen, C., Zupan, B. A. 1984. Self-schemas, depression, and the processing of personal information in children. *J. Exp. Child Psychol.* 37:598–608

Hastie, R., Kumar, P. A. 1979. Person memory: Personality traits as organizing principles in memory for behavior. *J. Pers. Soc. Psychol.* 37:25–38

Hedges, S. M., Jandorf, L., Stone, A. A. 1985. Meaning of daily mood assessments. *J. Pers. Soc. Psychol.* 48:428–34

Helson, R., Mitchell, V., Moane, G. 1984. Personality and patterns of adherence and nonadherence to the social clock. *J. Pers. Soc. Psychol.* 46:1079–96

Hewett, K. D. 1986. *Children's memory for emotionally arousing television materials.* PhD thesis. Yale Univ., New Haven, CT. Unpublished

Higgins, E. T., Klein, R., Strauman, T. 1986. Self-concept discrepancy theory: A psychological model for distinguishing among different aspects of depression and anxiety. *Soc. Cognit.* In press

Holahan, C. J., Moos, R. H. 1986. Personality, coping, and family resources in stress resistance: a longitudinal analysis. *J. Pers. Soc. Psychol.* 51:389–95

Holahan, C. J., Moos, R. H. 1985 Life stress and health: Personality, coping, and family support in stress resistance. *J. Pers. Soc. Psychol.* 49:739–47

Hollon, S. D., Kriss, M. 1984. Cognitive factors in clinical research and practice. *Clin. Psychol. Rev.* 4:35–76

Hormuth, S. E. 1980. The sampling of experiences *in situ. J. Pers.* 54:262–93

Horowitz, L. M., Post, D. L., deSales French, R., Wallis, K. D., Siegelman, E. Y. 1981a. The prototype as a construct in abnormal psychology: 2. Clarifying disagreement in psychiatric judgments. *J. Abnorm. Psychol.* 90:575–85

Horowitz, L. M., Wright, J. C., Lowenstein, E., Parad, H. W. 1981b. The prototype as a construct in abnormal psychology: 1. A method for deriving prototypes. *J. Abnorm. Psychol.* 90:568–74

Horowitz, M., Marmar, C., Krupnick, J., Wilner, N., Kaltreider, N., Wallerstein, R. 1984. *Personality Styles and Brief Psychotherapy.* New York: Basic Books

Howe, M. J. A. 1982. Biographical evidence and the development of outstanding individuals. *Am. Psychol.* 37:1071–81

Huba, G. J., Aneshensel, C. S., Singer, J. L. 1981. Development of scales for three second-order factors of inner experience. *Multivar. Behav. Res.* 16:181–206

Huba, G. J., Singer, J. L., Aneshensel, C. S., Antrobus, J. S. 1983. *Short Imaginal Processes Inventory.* Port Huron, MI: Res. Psychol. Press

Huba, G. J., Tanaka, J. S. 1983–84. Confirmatory evidence for three daydreaming factors in the short imaginal processes inventory. *Imagination, Cognit. Pers.* 3:139–47

Hurlburt, R. T. 1978. Random sampling of cognitions in alleviating anxiety attacks. *Cognit. Ther. Res.* 2:165–70

Hurlburt, R. T. 1980. Validation and correlation of thought sampling with retrospective measures. *Cognit. Ther. Res.* 4:235–38

Hurlburt, R. T., Lech, B. C., Saltman, S. 1984. Random sampling of thought and mood. *Cognit. Ther. Res.* 8:263–75

Hurlburt, R. T., Sipprelle, C. N. 1978. Random sampling cognitions in alleviating anxiety attacks. *Cognit. Ther. Res.* 2:165–70

Ickes, W., Reidhead, S., Patterson, M. 1986. Machiavellianism and self-monitoring: as different as "Me" and "You." *Soc. Cogn.* 4:58–74

Ickes, W., Robertson, E., Tooke, W., Teng, G. 1986. Naturalistic social cognition: methodology, assessment, and validation. *J. Pers. Soc. Psychol.* 51:66–82

Ingram, R. E. 1984. Information processing and feedback: Effects of mood information favorability on the cognitive processing of personally relevant information. *Cogn. Ther. Res.* 8:371–86

Ingram, R. E., Smith, T. W. 1984. Depression and internal versus external focus of attention. *Cogn. Ther. Res.* 8:139–52

Iran-Nejad, A., Clore, G. L., Vondruska, R. J. 1984. Affect: A functional perspective. *J. Mind Behav.* 5:279–310

Isen, A. M. 1984. Toward understanding the role of affect in cognition. In *Handbook of Social Cognition,* ed. R. S. Wyer, T. K. Skrull, 3:179–236. Hillsdale, NJ: Erlbaum

Isen, A. M., Daubman, K. A. 1984. The influence of affect on categorization. *J. Pers. Soc. Psychol.* 47:1206–17

Isen, A. M., Shalker, T. E., Clark, M., Karp, L. 1978. Affect, accessibility of material in memory, and behavior: A cognitive loop? *J. Pers. Soc. Psychol.* 36:1–12

Jensen, M. 1984. *Psychobiological factors in the prognosis and treatment of neoplastic disorders.* PhD thesis. Yale Univ., New Haven, CT. Unpublished

Johnson, C., Larson, R. 1982. Bulimia: An analysis of moods and behavior. *Psychosom. Med.* 44:341–51

Johnson, M. K., Raye, C. L. 1981. Reality monitoring. *Psychol. Rev.* 88:67–85

Jolly, E. J., Reardon, R. 1985. Cognitive differentiation, automaticity, and interruptions of automatized behaviors. *Pers. Soc. Psychol. Bull.* 11:301–14

Jones, W. H., Cheek, J. M., Briggs, S. R., eds. 1986. *Shyness: Perspectives on Research and Treatment.* New York: Plenum

Kavanagh, D. J., Bower, G. H. 1985. Mood and self-efficacy: Impact of joy and sadness on perceived capabilities. *Cogn. Ther. Res.* 9:507–25

Kelly, G. A. 1955. *A Theory of Personality: The Psychology of Personal Constructs.* New York: Norton

Kihlstrom, J. F., Cantor, N. 1984. Mental representations of the self. *Adv. Exp. Soc. Psychol.* 17:1–41

Kirschenbaum, D. S., Tomarken, A. J., Humphrey, L. L. 1985. Affect and adult self-regulation. *J. Pers. Soc. Psychol.* 48:509–23

Kirton, M. J., deCiantis, S. M. 1986. Cognitive style and personality: The Kirton-adaptation-innovation and Cattell's sixteen personality factor inventories. *Pers. Individ. Differ.* 7:141–46

Klatzky, R. L. 1984. *Memory and Awareness:*

An Information Processing Prospective. New York: Freeman

Klein, S., Kihlstrom, J. F. 1986. Self-reference, incidental recall, and hypermesia. *J. Exp. Psychol. Gen.* 115:26–38

Klinger, E. 1977a. *Meaning and Void: Inner Experience and the Incentives in People's Lives.* Minneapolis: Univ. Minn. Press

Klinger, E. 1977b. The nature of fantasy and its clinical uses. *Psychotherapy: Ther. Res. Pract.* 14:223–31

Klinger, E. 1978. Modes of normal conscious flow. In *The Stream of Consciousness,* ed. K. S. Pope, J. L. Singer. New York: Plenum

Klinger, E. 1981. The central place of imagery in human functioning. In *Imagery,* Vol. 2: *Concepts, Results, and Applications,* ed. E. Klinger. New York: Plenum

Klinger, E. 1984. A consciousness-sampling analysis of test anxiety and performance. *J. Pers. Soc. Psychol.* 47:1376–90

Klinger, E., Barta, S., Maxeiner, M. 1981. Current concerns: Assessing therapeutically relevant motivation. In *Assessment Strategies for Cognitive-Behavioral Interventions,* ed. P. Kendall, S. Hollon. New York: Academic

Klos, D. S., Singer, J. L. 1981. Determinants of the adolescent's ongoing thought following simulated parental confrontation. *J. Pers. Soc. Psychol.* 41:975–87

Kobasa, S. C. 1979. Stressful life events, personality, and health: An inquiry into hardiness. *J. Pers. Soc. Psychol.* 37:1–11

Kobasa, S. C., Maddi, S., Courington, S. 1981. Personality and constitution as mediators in the stress-illness relationship. *J. Health Soc. Behav.* 22:368–78

Kobasa, S. C., Maddi, S., Kahn, S. 1982a. Hardiness and health: A prospective study. *J. Pers. Soc. Psychol.* 42:168–77

Kobasa, S. C., Maddi, S., Puccetti, M. 1982b. Personality and exercise as buffers in the stress-illness relationship. *J. Behav. Med.* 5:391–404

Kreitler, H., Kreitler, S. 1976. *Cognitive Orientation and Behavior.* New York: Springer-Verlag

Kreitler, H., Kreitler, S. 1982. The theory of cognitive orientation: Widening the scope of behavior prediction. In *Experimental Personality Research,* ed. B. Maher. New York: Springer-Verlag

Kuiper, N. A., Derry, P. A. 1981. The self as a cognitive prototype: An application to person perception and depression. In *Personality, Social Interaction, and Cognition,* ed. N. Cantor, J. F. Kihlstrom. Hillsdale, NJ: Erlbaum

Kuiper, N. A., MacDonald, M. R. 1983. Schematic processing of depression: The self-based consensus bias. *Cogn. Ther. Res.* 7:469–84

Kuiper, N. A., Olinger, L. J., MacDonald, M. R. 1986. Depressive schemata and the processing of personal and social information. In *Cognitive Processes in Depression,* ed. L. B. Alloy. New York: Guilford

Kunzendorf, R. G. 1985a. Repression as the monitoring and censoring of images: An empirical study. *Imagination, Cognit. Pers.* 5:31–40

Kunzendorf, R. G. 1985b. Subconscious percepts as "unmonitored" percepts: An empirical study. *Imagination, Cognit. Pers.* 4:365–73

Lamiell, J. T. 1981. Toward an idiothetic psychology of personality. *Am. Psychol.* 36:276–89

Lamiell, J. T., Foss, N. A., Larsen, R. J., Hempel, A. M. 1983. Studies in the intuitive personology from an idiothetic point of view: Implications for personality theory. *J. Pers.* 51:438–67

Lang, P. J. 1984. Cognition in emotion: Concept and action. In *Emotions, Cognition, and Behavior,* ed. C. E. Izard, J. Kagan, R. B. Zajonc, pp. 192–226. Cambridge: Cambridge Univ. Press

Larsen, R. J., Seidman, E. 1986. Gender schema theory and sex role inventories: Some conceptual and psychometric considerations. *J. Pers. Soc. Psychol.* 50:205–11

Larson, R., Csikszentmihalyi, M. 1978. Experiential correlates of time alone. *J. Pers.* 46:677–93

Larson, R., Csikszentmihalyi, M., Graef, R. 1981. Time alone in daily experience: Loneliness or renewal? In *Loneliness: A Source Book of Current Theory, Research, and Therapy,* ed. L. A. Peplau, D. Perlman. New York: Wiley

Lazarus, R. S. 1984. On the primacy of cognition. *Am. Psychol.* 39:124–29

Lazarus, R. S., DeLongis, A., Folkman, S., Gruen, R. 1985. Stress and adaptational outcomes: The problem of confounded measures. *Am. Psychol.* 40:770–79

Lennox, R. D., Wolfe, R. N. 1984. Revision of the Self-monitoring Scale. *J. Pers. Soc. Psychol.* 46:1349–64

Leventhal, H. 1984. A perceptual-motor theory of emotion. *Adv. Exp. Soc. Psychol.* 17:117–82

Lewicki, P. 1984. Self-schema and social information processing. *J. Pers. Soc. Psychol.* 47:1177–90

Lewis, H. B. 1971. *Shame and Guilt in Neurosis.* New York: Int. Univ.

Lewis, H. B. 1981. *Freud and Modern Psychology,* Vol. 1. New York: Plenum

Lewis, H. B. 1983. *Freud and Modern Psychology,* Vol. 2. New York: Plenum

Lewis, M. W., Anderson, J. R. 1985. Discrimination of operator schemata in problem solving: Learning from examples. *Cogn. Psychol.* 17:26–65

Lieberman, D. A. 1979. Behaviorism and the mind: A (limited) call for a return to introspection. *Am. Psychol.* 34:319–33

Linville, P. W. 1982. Affective consequence of complexity regarding the self and others. In *Affect and Cognition: 17th Ann. Carnegie Symp.,* ed. M. S. Clark, S. T. Fiske. Hillsdale, NJ: Erlbaum

Little, B. 1983. Personal projects: A rationale and method for investigation. *Environ. Behav.* 15:273–309

Lloyd, K., Paulsen, J., Brockner, J. 1983. The effects of self-esteem and self-consciousness on interpersonal attraction. *Pers. Soc. Psychol. Bull.* 9:397–403

Loevinger, J., Knoll, E. 1983. Personality: Stages, traits, and the self. *Ann. Rev. Psychol.* 34:195–222

Logan, G. D. 1985. Skill and automaticity: Relations, implications, and future directions. *Can. J. Psychol.* 39:367–86

MacDonald, M. R., Kuiper, N. A. 1985. Efficiency and automaticity of self-schema processing in clinical depressives. *Motiv. Emotion* 9:171–84

Magaro, P. A., Ashbrook, R. M. 1985. The personality of societal groups. *J. Pers. Soc. Psychol.* 48:1479–89

Mahoney, M. J. 1984. Integrating cognition, affect, and action: A comment. *Cogn. Ther. Res.* 8:585–89

Mandler, G. 1984. *Mind and Body: Psychology of Emotion and Stress.* New York: Norton

Marcel, A. J. 1983. Conscious and unconscious perception: Experiments on visual masking and word recognition. *Cogn. Psychol.* 15:197–233

Markus, H. 1977. Self-schemata and processing information about the self. *J. Pers. Soc. Psychol.* 35:63–78

Markus, H. 1983. Self-knowledge: An expanded view. *J. Pers.* 51:543–65

Markus, H., Wurf, E. 1987. The dynamic self-concept: A social psychological perspective. *Ann. Rev. Psychol.* 38:299

Markus, H., Crane, M., Bernstein, S., Siladi, M. 1982. Self-schemas and gender. *J. Pers. Soc. Psychol.* 42:38–50

Markus, H., Sentis, K. 1982. The self in social information processing. In *Psychological Perspectives on the Self.* ed. J. Suls, 1:41–70 Hillsdale, NJ: Erlbaum

Markus, H., Smith, J. 1981. The influence of self-schemata on the perception of others. In *Personality, Cognition, and Social Interaction,* ed. N. Cantor, J. F. Kihlstrom. Hillsdale, NJ: Erlbaum

Markus, H., Smith, J., Moreland, R. L. 1985. Role of the self-concept in the perception of others. *J. Pers. Soc. Psychol.* 49:1494–1512

Marmor, J. 1983. Systems thinking in psychiatry. *Am. J. Psychiatry* 140:833

Mayer, J. D., Bremer, D. 1985. Assessing mood with affective-sensitive tasks. *J. Pers. Assess.* 49:95–99

Mayer, J. D., Volanth, A. J. 1985. Cognitive involvement in the mood response system. *Motiv. Emotion* 9:261–75

McAdams, D. P. 1985. *Power, Intimacy, and the Life Story: Personological Inquiries into Identity.* Homewood, IL: Dorsey

McAdams, D. P., Constantian, C. A. 1983. Intimacy and affiliation motives in daily living: An experience sampling analysis. *J. Pers. Soc. Psychol.* 45:851–61

McArthur, L. Z., Baron, R. M. 1983. Toward an ecological theory of social perception. *Psychol. Rev.* 90:215–38

McGuire, W. J. 1984. Search for the self: Going beyond self-esteem and the reactive self. In *Personality and the Prediction of Behavior,* ed. R. A. Zucker, J. Aranoff, A. I. Rabin, pp. 73–120. New York: Academic

McGuire, W. J., McGuire, C. V., Cheever, J. 1986. The self in society: Effects on social contexts on the sense of self. *Br. J. Soc. Psychol.* In press

McKenna, F. P. 1983. Field dependence and personality: A re-examination. *Soc. Behav. Pers.* 11:51–55

Mecklenbräuker, S., Hager, W. 1984. Effects of mood on memory: Experimental tests of mood-state-dependent retrieval hypothesis and of a mood-congruity hypothesis. *Psychol. Res.* 46:355–76

Meichenbaum, D., Gilmore, J. B. 1984. The nature of unconscious processes: A cognitive-behavioral perspective. In *The Unconscious Reconsidered,* ed. K. Bowers, D. Meichenbaum. New York: Wiley

Mischel, W. 1986. *Introduction to Personality: A New Look.* New York: Holt, Rinehart & Winston. 4th ed.

Mischel, W., Peake, P. K. 1982. Beyond deja vu in the search for cross-situational consistency. *Psychol. Rev.* 89:730–55

Monat, A., Lazarus, R. S., ed. 1985. *Stress and Coping: An Anthology.* New York: Columbia Univ. Press

Mueller, E. T., Dyer, M. G. 1985a. *Towards a computational theory of human daydreaming.* Techn. Rep., Artif. Intell. Lab., Univ. Calif., Los Angeles, AI-85-9

Mueller, E. T., Dyer, M. G. 1985b. *Daydreaming in humans and computers.* Techn. Rep., Artif. Intell. Lab., Univ. Calif., Los Angeles, AI-85-16

Myers, G. E. 1986. *William James. His Life and Thought.* New Haven: Yale Univ. Press

Nasby, W., Kihlstrom, J. F. 1985. Cognitive assessment of personality and psychopathology. In *Information-Processing Approaches to Psychopathology and Clinical Psychology,* ed. R. E. Ingram. New York: Academic

Natale, M., Hantas, M. 1982. Effect of temporary mood states on selective memory about the self. *J. Pers. Soc. Psychol.* 42:927–34

Natsoulas, T. 1984. The subjective organization of personal consciousness: A concept of conscious personality. *J. Mind Behav.* 5:311–36

Nicholls, J. G., Licht, B. G., Pearl, R. A. 1982. Some dangers of using personality questionnaires to study personality. *Psychol. Bull.* 92:572–80

Niedenthal, P. M., Cantor, N., Kihlstrom, J. F. 1985. Prototype-matching: A strategy for social decision making. *J. Pers. Soc. Psychol.* 48:575–84

Nisbett, R., Ross, L. 1980. *Human Inference: Strategies and Shortcomings of Social Judgment.* Englewood Cliffs, NJ: Prentice-Hall

O'Malley, M. N., Gillette, C. S. 1984. Exploring the relations between traits and emotions. *J. Pers.* 52:274–84

Palys, T. S., Little, B. R. 1983. Perceived life satisfaction and the organization of personal project systems. *J. Pers. Soc. Psychol.* 44:1221–30

Parks, C. W., Klinger, E., Perlmutter, M. 1985. *Properties of thoughts as a function of age, gender, and task difficulty.* Presented at the Proc. Am. Psychol. Assoc., Los Angeles, CA

Paunonen, S. V., Jackson, D. N. 1985. Idiographic measurement strategies for personality and prediction: Some unredeemed promissory notes. *Psychol. Rev.* 92:486–511

Pekala, R., Levine, R. 1982. Quantifying states of consciousness via an empirical-ophenomenological approach. *Imagination, Cognit. Pers.* 2:51–71

Pervin, L. A. 1983. The stasis and flow of behavior: Toward a theory of goals. In *Personality: Current Theory and Research,* ed. M. M. Page. Lincoln: Univ. Nebraska Press

Pervin, L. A. 1984. *Current Controversies and Issues in Personality.* New York: Wiley

Pervin, L. A. 1985. Personality: Current controversies, issues, and directions. *Ann. Rev. Psychol.* 56:83–114

Phares, E. J. 1984. *Introduction to Personality.* Columbus, OH: Merrill

Phares, E. J., Lamiell, J. T. 1977. Personality. *Ann. Rev. Psychol.* 28:113–40

Piaget, J. 1962. *Play, Dreams and Imitation in Childhood.* New York: Norton

Pietromonaco, P. R., Markus, H. 1985. The nature of negative thoughts in depression. *J. Pers. Soc. Psychol.* 48:799–807

Plant, R. W., Ryan, R. M. 1985. Intrinsic motivation and the effects of self-consciousness, self-awareness, and ego-involvement: An investigation of internally controlling styles. *J. Pers.* 53:435–49

Plutchik, R. 1985. On emotion: The chicken-and-egg problem revisited. *Motiv. Emotion* 9:197–200

Pope, K. S. 1978. How gender, solitude, and posture influence the stream of consciousness. In *The Stream of Consciousness,* ed. K. S. Pope, J. L. Singer. New York: Plenum

Price, D. D., Barrell, J. E., Barrell, J. J. 1985. A quantitative-experiential analysis of human emotions. *Motiv. Emotion* 9:19–38

Pryor, J. B., Merluzzi, T. V. 1985. The role of expertise in social interaction scripts. *J. Exp. Soc. Psychol.* 21:362–79

Pyszczynski, T., Greenberg, J. 1985. Depression and preference for self-focusing stimuli after success and failure. *J. Pers. Soc. Psychol.* 49:1066–75

Qualls, P. J. 1983. The physiological measurement of imagery: An overview. *Imagination, Cognit. Pers.* 2:89–101

Rachman, S. 1984. A reassessment of the primacy of affect. *Cogn. Ther. Res.* 8:579–84

Rappaport, D. 1942. *Emotions and Memory.* Baltimore: Williams & Wilkins

Rappaport, H., Enrich, K., Wilson, A. 1985. Relation between ego identity and temporal perspective. *J. Pers. Soc. Psychol.* 48:1609–20

Reardon, R., Rosen, S. 1984. Psychological differentiation and the evaluation of juridic information: Cognitive and affective consequences. *J. Res. Pers.* 18:195–211

Reinke, B. J., Holmes, D. S., Harris, R. L. 1985. The timing of psychosocial changes in women's lives: The years 25 to 45. *J. Pers. Soc. Psychol.* 48:1353–64

Reiser, B. J., Black, J. B., Abelson, R. P. 1985. Knowledge structures in the organization and retrieval of autobiographical memories. *Cogn. Psychol.* 17:89–137

Riskind, J. H., Rholes, W. S. 1984. Cognitive accessibility and the capacity of cognitions to predict future depression: A theoretical note. *Cogn. Therapy Res.* 8:1–12

Robinson, J. A. 1980. Affect and retrieval of personal memories. *Motiv. Emotion* 4:149–74

Ruehlman, L. S. 1985. Depression and affective meaning for current concerns. *Cogn. Ther. Res.* 9:553–60

Ruehlman, L. S., West, S. G., Pasahow, R. J. 1985. Depression and evaluative schemata. *J. Pers.,* 53:46–92

Runyan, W. M. 1981. Why did Van Gogh cut off his ear? The problem of alternative explanations in psychobiology. *J. Pers. Soc. Psychol.* 40:1070–77

Runyan, W. M. 1982. In defense of the case study method. *Am. J. Orthopsychiatry* 52:440–46

Runyan, W. M. 1983. Idiographic goals and methods in the study of lives. *J. Pers.,* 51:413–37

Russell, J. A. 1980. A circumplex model of affect. *J. Pers. Soc. Psychol.* 39:1161–78

Russell, J. A. 1983. Pancultural aspects of the human conceptual organization of emotion. *J. Pers. Soc. Psychol.* 45:1281–88

Russell, J. A., Bullock, M. 1985. Multi-dimensional scaling of emotional facial expressions: Similarity from preschoolers to adults. *J. Pers. Soc. Psychol.* 48:1290–98

Russell, J. A., Steiger, J. H. 1982. The structure in persons' implicit taxonomy of emotions. *J. Res. Pers.* 16:447–69

Rychlak, J. 1977. *The Psychology of Rigorous Humanism.* New York: Wiley

Rychlak, J. 1981. Logical learning theory: Propositions, corollaries, and research evidence. *J. Pers. Soc. Psychol.* 40:731–49

Sabini, J., Silver, M. 1981. Introspection and causal accounts. *J. Pers. Soc. Psychol.* 40:171–79

Schank, R. C., Abelson, R. P. 1977. *Scripts, Plans, Goals, and Understanding: An Inquiry Into Human Knowledge Structures.* Hillsdale, NJ: Erlbaum

Schare, M. L., Lisman, S. A., Spear, N. E. 1984. The effects of mood variation on state-dependent retention. *Cogn. Therapy Res.* 8:387–408

Schneider, D. J., Blankmeyer, B. L. 1983. Prototype salience and implicit personality theories. *J. Pers. Soc. Psychol.* 44:712–22

Schutte, N. S., Kenrick, D. T., Sadalla, E. K. 1985. The search for predictable settings: situational prototypes, constraint, and behavioral variation. *J. Pers. Soc. Psychol.* 48:121–28

Schwartz, G., Weinberger, G., Singer, J. A. 1981. Cardiovascular differentiation of happiness, sadness, anger and fear following imagery and exercise. *Psychosom. Med.* 43:343–64

Schwarz, N., Clore, G. L. 1983. Mood, misattribution, and judgments of well-being: Informative and directive functions of affective states. *J. Pers. Soc. Psychol.* 45:513–23

Sechrest, L. 1976. Personality. *Ann. Rev. Psychol.* 27:1–28

Segal, B., Huba, G. J., Singer, J. L. 1980. *Drugs, Daydreaming, and Personality: A Study of College Youth.* Hillsdale, NJ: Erlbaum

Sewitch, T. S., Kirsch, I. 1984. The cognitive content of anxiety: Naturalistic evidence for the predominance of threat-related thoughts. *Cogn. Ther. Res.* 8:49–58

Showers, C., Cantor, N. 1985. Social cognition: A look at motivated strategies. *Ann. Rev. Psychol.* 36:275–305

Singer, J. A. 1987. *Affective responses to autobiographical memories and their relationship to life goals.* PhD thesis. Yale Univ., New Haven, CT. Unpublished

Singer, J. A., Salovey, P. 1987. Mood and memory: Evaluating the network theory of affect. Unpublished

Singer, J. L. 1984a. *The Human Personality: An Introductory Text.* San Diego, CA: Harcourt, Brace Jovanovich

Singer, J. L. 1984b. The private personality. *Pers. Soc. Psychol. Bull.* 10:7–30

Singer, J. L. 1985a. The conscious and unconscious stream of thought. In *Emerging Syntheses in Science,* ed. D. Pines. Santa Fe, NM: Santa Fe Inst.

Singer, J. L. 1985b. *Private experience and public action: The study of ongoing conscious thought.* Paper read as a Henry A. Murray Lecture, Symp. Personality, Mich. State Univ., April 12–13

Singer, J. L. 1985c. Transference and the human condition: A cognitive-affective perspective. *Psychoanalytic Psychol.* 2:189–219

Singer, J. L. 1978. Experimental studies of daydreaming and the stream of thought. In *The Stream of Consciousness,* ed. K. S. Pope, J. L. Singer. New York: Plenum

Singer, J. L., Salovey, P. 1985. Organized knowledge structures in personality: Schemas, self-schemas, prototypes, and scripts. A review and research agenda. Unpublished

Smith, E. R. 1984. Model of social inference processes. *Psychol. Rev.* 91:392–413

Smith, E. R., Lerner, M. 1986. Development of automatism of social judgments. *J. Pers. Soc. Psychol.* 50:246–59

Snyder, M. 1979. Self-monitoring processes. *Adv. Exp. Soc. Psychol.* 12:85–128

Snyder, M., Gangestad, S. 1986. On the nature of self-monitoring: matters of assessment, matters of validity. *J. Pers. Soc. Psychol.* 51:125–39

Sperry, R. 1976. A unifying approach to mind and brain: Ten year perspective. In *Perspectives in Brain Research,* ed. A. Corner, D. F. Swab. Amsterdam: Elsevier

Starker, S., Jolin, A. 1982. Imagery and fantasy in Vietnam veteran psychiatric inpatients. *Imagination, Cognit. Pers.* 2:15–22

Starker, S., Jolin, A. 1983. Occurrence and vividness of imagery in schizophrenic thought: A thought-sampling approach. *Imagination, Cognit. Pers.* 3:49–60

Stewart, A. V. 1985. Introducing personality. *Contemp. Psychol.* 30:703–5

Stone, A. A., Hedges, S. M., Neale, J. M., Satin, M. S. 1985. Perspectives and cross-sectional mood reports offer no evidence of a "Blue Monday" phenomenon. *J. Pers. Soc. Psychol.* 49:129–34

Stone, A. A., Neale, J. M. 1982. Development of a methodology for assessing daily experiences. In *Advances in Environmental Psychology: Environment and Health*, ed. A. Baum, J. Singer, 4:49–89. New York: Erlbaum

Strack, F., Schwarz, N., Gschneidinger, E. 1985. Happiness and reminiscing: The role of time perspective, affect and mode of thinking. *J. Pers. Soc. Psychol.* 49:1460–69

Strack, S., Blaney, P. H., Ganellen, R. J., Coyne, J. C. 1985. Pessimistic self-preoccupation, performance deficits, and depression. *J. Pers. Soc. Psychol.* 49:1076–85

Strube, M. J., Lott, C. L. 1985. Type A behavior pattern and the judgment of noncontingency: Mediation roles of mood and perspective. *J. Pers. Soc. Psychol.* 49:510–19

Taylor, S. E., Crocker, J. 1981. Schematic bases of social information processing. In *Social Cognition: The Ontario Symposium on Personality and Social Psychology*, ed. E. T. Higgins, C. P. Herman, M. P. Zanna. Hillsdale, NJ: Erlbaum

Teasdale, J. D. 1983. Negative thinking in depression: Cause, effect, or reciprocal relationship? *Adv. Behav. Res. Ther.* 5:3–25

Tellegen, A. 1984. Structures of mood and personality and their relevance to assessing anxiety, with an emphasis on self-report. In *Anxiety and the Anxiety Disorders*, ed. A. H. Tuma, J. D. Masters. Hillsdale, NJ: Erlbaum

Thompson, C. P. 1985. Memory of unique personal events: Effects of pleasantness. *Motiv. Emotion* 9:277–89

Tomkins, S. S. 1962. *Affect, Imagery, Consciousness: Vol. 1. The Positive Affects.* New York: Springer-Verlag

Tomkins, S. S. 1963. *Affect, Imagery, Consciousness: Vol. 2. The Negative Affects.* New York: Springer-Verlag

Tomkins, S. S. 1979. Script theory: Differential magnifications of affects. *Nebr. Symp. Motiv.* 26:201–36

Tomkins, S. S. 1980. Affect as amplification: Some modifications in theory. In *Emotion: Theory, Research, and Experience: Theories of Emotion*, ed. R. Plutchik, H. Kellerman. 1:141–64. New York: Academic

Tomkins, S. S. 1981a. The quest for primary motives: Biography and autobiography of an idea. *J. Pers. Soc. Psychol.* 41:306–29

Tomkins, S. S. 1981b. The rise, fall, and resurrection of the study of personality. *J. Mind Behav.* 2:443–52

Triandis, H. C., Marin, G., Lisansky, J., Betancourt, H. 1984. Simpatia as a cultural script of Hispanics. *J. Pers. Soc. Psychol.* 47:1363–75

Trzebinski, J. 1985. Action-oriented representations of implicit personality theories. *J. Pers. Soc. Psychol.* 48:1266–78

Turk, D. C., Meichenbaum, D., Genest, M. 1983. *Pain and Behavior Medicine: A Cognitive-Behavioral Perspective.* New York: Guilford

Turk, D. C., Salovey, P. 1985a. Cognitive structures, cognitive processes, and cognitive-behavior modification: I. Client issues. *Cognit. Ther. Res.* 9:1–17

Turk, D. C., Salovey, P. 1985b. Cognitive structures, cognitive processes, and cognitive behavior modification: II. Judgment and inferences of the clinician. *Cognit. Ther. Res.* 9:19–33

Turk, D. C., Speers, M. A. 1983. Cognitive schemata and cognitive processes in cognitive-behavioral interventions: Going beyond the information given. In *Advances in Cognitive-Behavioral Research and Therapy*, Vol. 2, ed. P. C. Kendall. New York: Academic

Underwood, B., Froming, W. J., Moore, B. S. 1980. Mood and personality: A search for the causal relationship. *J. Pers.* 48:15–23

Watson, D., Clark, L. A. 1984. Negative affectivity: The disposition to experience aversive emotional states. *Psychol. Bull.* 96:465–90

Watson, D., Clark, L. A., Tellegen, A. 1984. Cross-cultural convergence in the structure of mood: A Japanese replication and comparison with U.S. findings. *J. Pers. Soc. Psychol.* 47:127–44

Watson, D., Tellegen, A. 1985. Toward a consensual structure of mood. *Psychol. Bull.* 98:219–35

Weinberger, D. A. 1983. *Distress, suppression of desire and the classification of personality style.* PhD thesis. Yale Univ., New Haven, CT. Unpublished

Weinberger, D. A., Schwartz, G., Davidson, R. 1979. Low-anxious, high-anxious and repressive coping styles: Psychometric patterns and behavioral and physiological responses to stress. *J. Abnorm. Psychol.* 88:369–80

Wheeler, L., Reis, H., Nezlek, J. 1983. Loneliness, social interaction, and sex roles. *J. Pers. Soc. Psychol.* 45:943–53

Williams, R. B. Jr., Barefoot, J. C., Shekelle, R. B. 1985. The health consequences of hostility. In *Anger, Hostility and Behavioral Medicine*, ed. M. A. Chesney, S. E. Goldston, R. H. Rosenman. New York: Hemisphere

Witkin, H. A. 1965. Psychological differentiation and forms of pathology. *J. Abnorm. Psychol.* 70:317–36

Witkin, H. A., Goodenough, D. 1981. *Cognitive Styles, Essense and Origins: Field Dependence and Field Independence.* New York: Int. Univ. Press

Wrightsman, L. S. 1981. Personal documents as data in conceptualizing adult personality and development. *Pers. Soc. Psychol. Bull.* 7:367–85

Wyer, R. S. Jr., Frey, D. 1983. The effects of feedback about the self and others on recall and judgments of feedback-relevant information. *J. Exp. Soc. Psychol.* 19:540–59

Zajonc, R. B. 1984. On the primacy of affect. *Am. Psychol.* 39:117–23

Zajonc, R. B., Markus, H. 1984. Affect and cognition: The hard interface. In *Emotions, Cognition, and Behavior,* ed. C. E. Izard, J. Kagan, R. B. Zajonc. Cambridge, England: Cambridge Univ. Press

Zevon, M. A., Tellegen, A. 1982. The structure of mood change: An idiographic/nomothetic analysis. *J. Pers. Soc. Psychol.* 43:111–22

Zimring, F. M. 1983. Attending to feeling and cognitive performance. *J. Res. Pers.* 17:288–99

Zuckerman, M., Kernis, M. H., Guarnera, S. M., Murphy, J. F., Rappoport, L. 1983. The egocentric bias: Seeing oneself as cause and target of others' behavior. *J. Pers.* 51:621–30

Ann. Rev. Psychol. 1987. 38:575–630

ATTITUDES AND ATTITUDE CHANGE

Shelly Chaiken and Charles Stangor

Department of Psychology, New York University, New York, New York 10003[1]

CONTENTS

INTRODUCTION

Consistent with the prophesies and observations made in the last three reviews of attitudes published in this series (Eagly & Himmelfarb 1978, Cialdini et al 1981, Cooper & Croyle 1984), research and theorizing on the nature of

[1]Charles Stangor is now at the Department of Psychology, Michigan State University, East Lansing, Michigan 48824

0066-4308/87/0201-0575$02.00

attitudes and attitude change have made a strong comeback from the pessimism and decline of interest that characterized the late 1960s and 70s (see McGuire 1985 and Eagly 1986). This fact is reflected in both the number of articles that we initially uncovered and the number of compromises we were forced to make in selecting topics and articles to review.[1] Preparing even a selective review of the literature given the space allotted to us was at times an overwhelming experience, and it was with severe regret that we condensed interesting topics and findings from pages to sentences in our struggle to meet space limitations.

Our task would have been even more difficult and our concern about omissions more severe were it not for the appearance of several excellent review chapters in the third edition of the *Handbook of Social Psychology* (Lindzey & Aronson 1985). The topic of attitude measurement, which we omit, is well surveyed by Dawes & Smith (1985), and McGuire (1985) has once again provided researchers with an illuminating historical and futuristic overview of attitude theory and research. The impact of the mass media on attitudes is covered in a chapter by Roberts & Maccoby (1985), and Kinder & Sears (1985) have reviewed the interdisciplinary literature on political attitudes and opinions. In addition to these *Handbook* chapters, Cooper & Fazio (1984) have provided a review of dissonance theory, Insko (1984) an analysis of contemporary balance theory perspectives, Fazio (1986b) a retrospective on self-perception theory, and Eagly & Chaiken (1984) a review of contemporary theorizing in persuasion. Finally, the latest volume of the Ontario Symposium series (Zanna et al 1986) devoted itself to an integrative exploration of social influence.

While we have followed the format of previous reviews (e.g. Cooper & Croyle 1984) with the inclusion of major sections on attitude-behavior relations and persuasion, our review departs somewhat from recent tradition by inclusion of a separate section on the broad topic of attitude structure. The most unique aspect of our review, however, is the inclusion of a substantial section on minority (and, to a lesser extent, majority) group influence. Although we believe that recent research in this area will be of considerable interest to attitude change researchers and that readers will share our perception of its centrality to the social psychological literature on attitudes, the topic of minority influence has never received more than passing attention in previous reviews in this series (cf Kiesler & Munson 1975).

---

[1] Our charge was to prepare a selective review of the attitudes literature covering the period January 1, 1983 to December 31, 1985. Articles in press as of January, 1986 and a small number of unpublished manuscripts that we considered particularly noteworthy are also included. In addition to a computer-based search for relevant literature, we also hand-searched the major social psychological journals and solicited papers from over 100 researchers in the field.

Our major focus is on research that has investigated the role of cognitive structure and cognitive processes in attitude organization, formation, and change. Social cognitive approaches have long permeated the study of attitudes (see Eagly & Chaiken 1984, McGuire 1985, Eagly 1986), and so this emphasis on cognition is not so much a bias as it is an accurate representation of the present state of the field. Nevertheless, signaling that interest in motivation is indeed on the upswing (see Cooper & Croyle 1984), a healthy subset of the research we located raised questions regarding motivational and affective issues and (often) their relation to cognition.

ATTITUDE STRUCTURE

Consistent with McGuire's (1985, 1986) prediction that attitude research is entering a new "structural era," the last few years have produced a flurry of research and theorizing about the structure of attitudes and their relation to other cognitive systems. In this section we review this work and in the next provide an update of research on the broader structural issue (McGuire 1985) of the reciprocal relation between attitudes and behavior.

Single Versus Multicomponent Views of Attitude

The traditional question of whether attitudes are unidimensional or multidimensional continues to receive research attention. Whereas the unitary view regards attitudes as affective orientations toward objects (e.g. Fishbein & Ajzen 1975), the multidimensional view takes one of two forms. The tripartite model (e.g. Katz & Stotland 1959) assumes that attitudes have an affective, cognitive, and behavioral component, with each varying on an evaluative dimension. Criticisms that this model obscures the attitude-behavior relation (e.g. McGuire 1969, Fishbein & Ajzen 1975; but see Breckler 1984) have led some researchers to delete the behavioral component and to regard attitude as a two-dimensional construct (e.g. Bagozzi & Burnkrant 1979, Zajonc & Markus 1982).

Using covariance structure analysis, Bagozzi & Burnkrant (1979) reanalyzed data on attitude-behavior relations originally reported by Fishbein & Ajzen (1974) and concluded that an affective-cognitive model of attitude fit the data better than did a one-factor model. Dillon & Kumar (1985) performed a similar reanalysis (using LISREL IV, Joreskog & Sorbom 1978) but reached a different conclusion. They argued that although the affective-cognitive model could not be rejected, rival "two-factor" models that were interpretable as unidimensional attitudes with methods variation partialled out fit the data equally well. In a rejoinder, Bagozzi & Burnkrant (1985) challenged Dillon and Kumar's data interpretation and reported yet another reanalysis using the more powerful LISREL VI (Joreskog & Sorbom 1984). They found that the affective-cognitive model achieved convergent, discriminant, and predictive validity while the one-component model failed to achieve even convergent validity.

Regarding the tripartite model, two data sets originally examined using a multitrait-multimethod approach (Ostrom 1969, Kothandapani 1971) have been reanalyzed twice using structural analysis (Bagozzi 1978, Breckler 1983). Both revealed that Ostrom's (1969) data weakly supported the tripartite model while Kothandapani's (1971) data conformed more to a single-factor model. Breckler (1984) argued that prior tests of the tripartite model lacked sensitivity because they relied on verbal measures of all three components and used symbolic attitude objects. To test his reasoning, Breckler conducted two studies in which the tripartite model was evaluated using LISREL V (Joreskog & Sorbom 1981). The tripartite (but not single-factor) model proved statistically acceptable and provided a good fit to the data from the first study which used nonverbal measures of affect and behavior and had subjects respond to a physically present attitude object (a snake). However, in a second study which utilized verbal measures of these components and had subjects respond to a mental representation of the same attitude object, the tripartite model was rejected.

A definitive judgment on the three- (or two-) versus one-dimensional issue seems premature given that the results of structural analyses sometimes vary with the sophistication of researchers' LISREL programs (and their abilities to generate plausible models). Moreover, Breckler's (1984) research suggests that attitude dimensionality may vary as a function of domain studied, and consequently that there may be no transcendental answer to the unidimensional versus multidimensional question. Breckler studied attitudes toward snakes because he assumed that this domain implicated multiple response systems. However, because people may respond to more abstract objects (e.g. sociopolitical issues) primarily at a conceptual level, attitudes toward these objects might be primarily unidimensional. Finally, we note that a multicomponent view is not antithetical to an expectancy-value model of attitude. In an interesting pair of papers, Bagozzi (1984, 1985) examines the Fishbein & Ajzen (1975) model and shows that this framework is just one of a number of unidimensional and multidimensional expectancy-value formulations that could be used to represent attitudes.

Breckler (1984; see also Greenwald 1982b) views attitude as a hypothetical response to an attitude object and affect, cognition, and behavior as three response classes. Other recent (and compatible) definitions view attitude as a disposition to respond favorably or unfavorably toward an object and affect, cognition, and behavior as three domains in which attitude is expressed in observable responses (Ajzen 1984, Davis & Ostrom 1984). In another recent rendition of the trilocular perspective, Zanna & Rempel (1986) have defined attitudes as evaluative appraisals of objects and propose that affect (i.e. emotion), cognition, and behavior are three classes of *information* on which this evaluative judgment is based. Zanna and Rempel thus regard attitudes as separate cognitive entities [versus latent constructs (Breckler 1984)] which, consequently, may be accessed from memory independent of the (affective, cognitive, or behavioral) information on which they are based (see Lingle & Ostrom 1981, Fazio 1986a).

A notable feature of the Zanna-Rempel model is its attempt to initiate an integration of three views of attitude formation; Fishbein & Ajzen's (1975) expectancy-value formulation which Zanna and Rempel interpret as implying a relatively effortful and reasoned attitude formation process (but see Fishbein & Ajzen 1975, McGuire 1985), Bem's (1972) self-perception model which suggests a simpler, less effortful inference process (Taylor 1975, Chaiken & Baldwin 1981, Wood 1982, Tybout & Scott 1983), and an emerging view fired by the primacy of affect debate (Lazarus 1984, Zajonc 1984) and mere exposure research (e.g. Gordon & Holyoak 1983) which suggests that attitude formation requires little, if any, conscientious cognitive processing. In the Zanna and Rempel framework, these three perspectives are viewed as examples of the psychological processes by which cognitive, behavioral, and affective experience, respectively, determine attitudes. Although in need of testing and refinement (e.g. how do the three sources of information combine and interact to influence overall attitude?), this framework possesses numerous implications for various attitude phenomena (e.g. that "ambivalent" attitudes may arise when two or more sources of information yield conflicting evaluative judgments) and should prove heuristically useful to researchers.

Values, Attitudes, and Cognitive Structure

With notable exceptions (e.g. Scott 1959, Rosenberg 1960, Rokeach 1979), attitude researchers have neglected values, our normative beliefs about desirable goals and modes of conduct (Rokeach 1979). Recent research indicates that this neglect is waning; value measurement is being refined (e.g. Braithwaite & Law 1985) and values are broadening our understanding of intergroup and sociopolitical attitudes (e.g. Ellsworth & Ross 1983, McKirnan et al 1983, Sears 1983, Sears & Lau 1983, Tyler 1984, Kinder & Sears 1985), attitude change (e.g. Ball-Rokeach et al 1984), and ideologically based attitude systems (e.g. Feather 1984, 1985, Tetlock 1983c, 1984, 1986, Drake & Judd 1986).

SYMBOLIC ATTITUDES   Although symbolic attitudes have yet to be defined with precision, they are regarded as involving strong affect, tied to important moral concerns or core values, and as primarily expressive (vs instrumental) in nature (Abelson 1982, Sears 1983, Herek 1986a). "Symbolic racism," the most heavily researched of these variables, has been defined as "a blend of antiblack affect and the kind of traditional American moral values embodied in the Protestant Ethic" (Kinder & Sears 1981, p. 416). Attitudes toward value-laden issues such as capital punishment and abortion have also been termed symbolic by some researchers (Ellsworth & Ross 1983, Sears 1983). Given the paucity of research on symbolic attitudes, it is too early to judge the merit of the symbolic-nonsymbolic distinction.

Research by Sears and Kinder (e.g. Kinder & Sears 1981, Kinder & Rhodebeck 1982, Sears & Lau 1983, Sears & Allen 1984) has shown that whites' race-related political attitudes (e.g. opposition to busing) are better predicted by measures of symbolic racism than by measures of short-term material self-interest. Although not couched in terms of symbolic attitudes, studies by Tyler (1984, Tyler et al 1985a,b) have similarly shown that attitudes toward political leaders and institutions are better predicted by people's concerns about fairness than by the personal outcomes they associate with these attitude objects.

Symbolic racism research has not gone uncriticized. Both Bobo (1983) and Sniderman & Tetlock (1986) argue that the Sears and Kinder studies pitted symbolic racism against an overly narrow definition of self-interest, and Bobo claims that self-interest does predict busing attitudes when its definition is broadened (but see Sears & Kinder's 1985 rejoinder). Sniderman and Tetlock have criticized this research on other grounds as well, perhaps most importantly for failing to clearly define symbolic racism at either the operational or conceptual level. These authors also point out that despite their centrality to the symbolic racism construct, values such as individualism and self-reliance have not been assessed in Sears and Kinder's studies. If constructively received, these critiques should inspire a more precise understanding of symbolic racism and other symbolic attitudes and a clearer idea of what role, if any, values play in infusing these attitudes with their presumed emotional significance.

VALUES AND COGNITIVE STRUCTURE   In a series of content analysis studies of political elites, Tetlock (1983c, 1984; Tetlock et al 1984, 1985) has found that complex reasoning about political and social issues is more characteristic of some ideological groups than of others. Specifically, this research indicates that members of the political right tend to reason in less integratively complex ways than do either moderates or left-wing ideologues. Yet, in addition to this "rigidity-of-the-right" phenomenon, complexity also varies with ideological extremity; in a study of British Parliamentarians, integrative complexity was more common among moderate (vs radical) socialists as well as among moderate (vs extreme) conservatives (Tetlock 1984).

To explain both individual and domain-specific (Tetlock 1984) differences in complexity, Tetlock (1984, 1986) has proposed a value pluralism model which assumes that values underlie political ideologies and that ideologies vary not only in the kinds of values that are assigned high priority but also in the degree to which conflict between values is acknowledged. Whereas "monistic" ideologies (e.g. extreme conservatism) assign high priority to one value or to multiple values that are perceived as consistent, "pluralistic" ideologies give priority to values that may often imply conflicting positions on specific issues. According to the model, complexity is a function of the extent to which two or more important and conflicting values are operative. Tetlock (1986) confirmed this hypothesis in a study that measured subjects' value priorities and their integrative complexity with respect to each of six policy issues that activated value conflict. Complexity was greater to the extent that subjects assigned high and near-equal importance to the two conflicting values that were relevant to each issue.

Although Tetlock (1986) did not test the hypothesis that value conflict may result in attitudinal moderation, other findings from his study (e.g. complexity was negatively related to evaluative consistency of thought) as well as previous ones (Tetlock 1984) suggest that this hypothesis would be confirmed. As such, this research complements other recent work on cognitive structure and both evaluative extremity (Linville 1982, Judd & Lusk 1984) and attitude polarization after thought (Leone & Baldwin 1983, Leone et al 1983, Leone 1984, Chaiken & Yates 1985, Millar & Tesser 1986a, Drake & Judd 1986). For example, Judd & Lusk (1984) assert that judgmental extremity depends on both the number and correlation between attribute dimensions that characterize people's cognitive structures. Compatible with value-pluralism logic, these authors find that when uncorrelated, more dimensions give rise to less extreme attitudinal judgments (see Linville 1982) but when correlated, more dimensions produce more extreme judgments. Recent studies on thought-induced attitude polarization (Chaiken & Yates 1985, Millar & Tesser 1986a) have yielded compatible findings.

Impact of Attitudes on Information Processing

Research investigating whether attitudes exert selective effects on exposure and attention to information and on the perception, learning, and retention of information declined considerably in the 1970s as narrative literature reviews reached possibly overly pessimistic conclusions (see Cooper & Rosenthal 1980, Hedges & Olkin 1985) about the existence of several of these phenomena (e.g. Freedman & Sears 1965, Greenwald 1975). As discerned by Cooper & Croyle (1984), interest in the information processing effects of attitudes is reviving. Whether spurred by or simply paralleling the interest social cognition researchers have shown in similar issues (see Markus &

Zajonc 1985, Higgins & Bargh 1987), attitude researchers are addressing both classic and newer questions about how attitudes influence cognitive processes.

Recent studies on selective exposure (Chaffee & Miyo 1983, Frey & Rosch 1984, Sweeney & Gruber 1984, Frey & Stahlberg 1986) as well as two new reviews (Cotton 1985, Frey 1986) indicate that motivated selectivity effects [versus de facto exposure (see Freedman & Sears 1965)] can be obtained, particularly in nonlaboratory settings where implicit demands for high attention and impartial processing are less likely to operate (see Chaiken 1984, Eagly & Chaiken 1984, Frey 1986). For example, Sweeney & Gruber (1984) analyzed survey data collected during the 1973 Watergate hearings and found support for both the approach and avoidance components of Festinger's (1957) selective exposure hypothesis; while McGovern supporters sought out information about the scandal and hearings, Nixonites actively avoided it. As reviewed by Frey (1986), other research in this area has continued to explore variables (e.g. utility, familiarity, decision reversibility, refutability of information, impartiality norm) that either obscure this classic "congeniality" exposure effect or reverse it.

Like selective exposure, the issue of whether prior attitudes influence the learning and retention of new information is important because of its implications for understanding resistance and persistence processes in social influence. Labelled in the 1970s as an unreliable phenomenon (e.g. Fishbein & Ajzen 1972, Greenwald 1975) the hypothesis that people better remember attitudinally congruent information has been reexamined in a number of recent studies (e.g. Read & Rosson 1982, Bothwell & Brigham 1983, Gilmore et al 1983, Pratkanis 1984, Roberts 1984a,b, Howard-Pitney et al 1986, Hymes 1986) and pronounced real though of small magnitude in a recent meta-analytic review (Roberts 1985). Nevertheless, the attitude-memory relation is more complex than the simple congeniality hypothesis suggests and to date research has progressed little beyond the first generation (Zanna & Fazio 1982) issue of establishing that attitudes can, in fact, influence memory (see Chaiken 1984).

Regarding complexities, attitudinally extreme (vs moderate) information is sometimes better remembered, regardless of its consistency (Judd & Kulik 1980, Pratkanis 1984, Hymes 1986), and a number of results indicate that inconsistent attitudinal information sometimes (and for some people) enjoys a memorial advantage (e.g. Cacioppo & Petty 1979, Zanna & Olson 1982, Gilmore et al 1983). A similar complex of findings has been obtained in person memory research (see Markus & Zajonc 1985, Higgins & Bargh 1987) and attitude researchers have much to gain by consulting that literature for clues regarding the cognitive mechanisms that may underlie congruency and incongruency effects (e.g. Burnstein & Schul 1983, Crocker et al 1983,

Hastie 1981, 1984, O'Sullivan & Durso 1984, Stern et al 1984, Wyer & Gordon 1984, Bargh & Thein 1985). Incongruency effects, for example, may arise when people allocate greater attention to inconsistent information in order to integrate or reconcile such information with their preexisting schemas (or attitudes) or refute such information (e.g. Crocker et al 1983, Fiske et al 1983a, Schul et al 1983, Wyer & Frey 1983, Erber & Fiske 1984, Hastie 1984). While this literature provides important insights regarding cognitive mediation, with few exceptions (e.g. Erber & Fiske 1984), it is less informative about motivational issues. Thus, in pursuing attitude-memory relations, researchers should not lose sight of the motivational perspectives (e.g. dissonance theory, protecting one's opinions) that guided an earlier generation of research on this topic (e.g. Jones & Aneshansel 1956, Jones & Kohler 1958, Spiro & Sherif 1975) or ignore relevant findings from selective exposure and persuasion research (e.g. the impact of involvement on information processing). Methodologically, research testing attentional mechanisms underlying attitude-memory effects should take care to construct experimental settings that do not constrain subjects' levels of attention, and memory measures in this research should be broadened to include those tapping distortions (e.g. intrusions) in addition to the simple accuracy of recall measures that have characterized the vast majority of prior work (see Chaiken 1984, Schmidt & Sherman 1984).

Regarding other research on attitudes and cognitive processes, recent studies have explored assimilation and contrast effects in the perception of others' opinion statements (Judd et al 1983, Romer 1983), and the impact of attitudes on memory for the sources of persuasive messages (Johnson & Judd 1983), recollections of past behavior (Ross et al 1983, Olson & Cal 1984, Lydon et al 1986; see Ross & Conway 1986 for a review), expectancies regarding future events (Granberg & Brent 1983), and evaluations of attitude-relevant information (Vallone et al 1985). While most of these studies have documented congruency effects (e.g. past behaviors are construed to be consistent with current attitudes), incongruency effects have also been obtained (e.g. Vallone et al's "hostile media phenomenon"). As with research on memory for attitude-relevant information, the cognitive and motivational factors that produce these effects are not yet well delineated.

ATTITUDE-BEHAVIOR RELATIONS

Research investigating whether and how attitudes influence behavior continues to proceed along two lines. One concerns the ways that cognitions about a behavior are combined to create attitudes and/or intentions toward that behavior (e.g. Fishbein et al 1986) and relies primarily on correlational methodologies (combinatorial approaches). The other concerns the underlying cognitive processes that influence the attitude-behavior relationship (e.g. Fazio 1986a) and relies primarily on laboratory experiments, but often at the expense of studying important social attitudes (process models). After reviewing examples of each of these approaches, we consider the reciprocal effect of behavior on attitudes.

The Theory of Reasoned Action

Although several combinatorial-type models have been proposed in relation to behavioral prediction (e.g. Davidson & Morrison 1983, Jaccard & Becker 1986) most research has been based upon Fishbein and Ajzen's (1975, Ajzen & Fishbein 1980) "theory of reasoned action." This theory suggests that behavior can be predicted through measurement of the individual's attitude toward the behavioral action (Aact) and social norms (SN) that influence the likelihood of performing the behavior. Evaluative judgments about the salient consequences of a particular behavior are assumed to be combined through an expectancy-value formulation to form Aact, while motivational desires to comply with a set of salient normative beliefs are assumed to be similarly combined to determine SN. Most importantly, both Aact and SN are assumed to influence behavior exclusively through behavioral intentions (BI). From its inception the theory has generated a great deal of research, much of which continues to be conducted in applied settings (e.g. Midden & Ritsema 1983, Budd & Spencer 1984, Shimp & Kavas 1984, Black et al 1985, Hoogstraten et al 1985, Fishbein et al 1986). Validity and measurement issues regarding the original model have remained under investigation (Jaccard & Sheng 1984, Bagozzi 1986), and a number of modifications have been proposed (Liska 1984, Ajzen 1985, Bagozzi & Warshaw 1986).

Originally, Fishbein & Ajzen (1975) argued that if everything could be measured precisely within a reasonable amount of time at the same level of specificity, and if the behavior was under "volitional control," then BI and behavior would be perfectly correlated. However, the now perennial search for variables that have effects on behavior that are *not* mediated by behavioral intentions has continued (Gorsuch & Ortberg 1983, Budd & Spencer 1984, Fisher 1984, Bagozzi & Schnedlitz 1985), and at this point it is quite clear that some variables do exert a direct influence on behavior. Perhaps the most robust of these is past behavior (Fredericks & Dossett 1983, Manstead et al 1983, Ajzen & Madden 1986). In fact, in a study that investigated class attendance, Ajzen & Madden (1986, study 1) found previous behavior to be the best single direct predictor of future behavior.

To account for variables whose behavioral impact may not be mediated through intentions, many researchers have suggested that new components be added to the original model. The extent of these proposed modifications ranges from the addition of a single component [e.g. a measure of "moral obligation" (Gorsuch & Ortberg 1983)] to the inclusion of so many constructs (a total of 14 by Bagozzi & Warshaw 1986) that a virtually different model results.

One of the original developers of the theory of reasoned action has himself conceded the necessity of revision. Because the original theory did not include a construct that explicitly tapped the concept of "volitional control" (i.e. situational or internal obstacles to performing the behavior), Ajzen (1985; Ajzen & Madden 1986) has added such a construct as a third independent predictor and christened the new model a "theory of planned behavior." "Perceived control" is designed to tap the individual's perception of the obstacles that might prevent behavior from occurring and has been shown to have both direct and indirect (via behavioral intentions) effects on behavior. In fact, in a study on weight loss (Schifter & Ajzen 1985) perceived control, in addition to its indirect effects through intentions, had a larger direct relation to behavior than did BI itself.

Other researchers have suggested similar constructs to account for the effects of situational and personal constraints on behavior (Maddux & Rogers 1983, Rogers 1985, Ronis & Kaiser 1985, Warshaw & Davis 1985, Wolf et al 1986). For example, Warshaw & Davis (1985) measured individuals' subjective expectancies that they would actually perform a behavior (a construct that includes both intentions and perceived constraints on one's ability to perform the behavior), and Bagozzi & Warshaw (1986) attempted to differentiate internal (e.g. motivation, ability) from external (situational) factors that affect perceived control by including separate measures of each. How these new measures of personal control differ from, or add to, Bandura's (1977) concept of "self-efficacy" is not clear at this time.

At present, researchers seem preoccupied with adding new components to the theory of reasoned action in their efforts to increase the proportion of variance accounted for in behavior. In doing so, however, the attitude construct itself (i.e. Aact) seems often to have been relegated to secondary status and the distinctive expectancy-value conceptualization underlying the original model seems much less evident in its revisions. It is hoped that subsequent work on behavioral prediction will not lose sight of the role played by attitudinal factors and will continue to provide important theoretical insights regarding the attitude-behavior relationship (see Sherman & Fazio 1983).

Process Models

The second approach to the study of the attitude-behavior relationship has been to investigate the underlying cognitive processes by which attitudes influence behavior. Virtually all the research considered in this section investigates the general question of how the relative activation of an attitude or of particular "elements" of an attitude (e.g. cognitions and feelings) at the time attitudes are expressed or behaviors performed affects the attitude-behavior relationship. Following Higgins et al (1982), we use the term "accessibility" to refer to this activation and reserve the related term "availability" to denote the *existence* of a construct in memory.

ATTITUDE ACCESSIBILITY   In the best-developed program of research on attitude accessibility, Fazio and his colleagues (Fazio & Zanna 1981, Fazio et al 1982, 1983, 1984, 1986, Powell & Fazio 1984, Fazio 1986a, Fazio & Williams 1986, Kardes et al 1986) have investigated under what circumstances an attitude is activated (made accessible) upon exposure to a corresponding attitude object. This activation is assumed to be necessary for a substantial attitude-behavior correlation, because if an object does not activate an associated attitude, then the attitude will be unlikely to influence behavior toward the object. In Fazio's (e.g. 1986a) model, attitude is defined as the association between an object (e.g. Democrats) and an evaluation (e.g. "very good"), and the *strength* of this association determines the degree to which the attitude is activated upon exposure to the object. Attitude strength (i.e. associative strength) is operationalized as reaction time (RT) to evaluative queries about the attitude object. Individuals who can quickly evaluate the attitude object are assumed to have a strong attitude, or object-evaluation association, which causes the attitude to be spontaneously activated in the presence of the object and therefore increases attitude-behavior consistency.

Fazio has demonstrated that attitude strength varies as a function of several factors. For one, the manner of attitude formation is critical. Direct experience with the attitude object, which enhances attitude-behavior correspondence (e.g. Smith & Swinyard 1983, Manstead et al 1983; see Fazio & Zanna 1981), produces a stronger object-evaluation association (Fazio et al 1982). A second factor that influences associative strength is the number of times that the attitude has been expressed. For example, Fazio et al (1982) had subjects copy their attitude toward a given object onto several sheets of paper. Compared to control subjects who did not perform this task, repeated-expression subjects evidenced a stronger object-evaluation association as measured by their response latencies to a subsequent attitude query.

Although the above studies were suggestive, they did not make clear whether manipulations of direct experience or repeated expression actually increase the likelihood that attitudes will be spontaneously activated in the presence of their corresponding attitude objects. Recently, more direct tests of this hypothesis have been conducted (Fazio et al 1983, 1986). For example, in a study on attitudes toward puzzles, Fazio et al (1983) first increased associative strength for experimental subjects through either repeated expression or direct experience, while control subjects did not have their attitudes toward the experimental puzzles "strengthened." Then subjects participated in an "unrelated" experiment where one of the puzzles was presented within a series of drawings. As predicted, for subjects whose attitudes had been strengthened (but not control subjects) this priming manipulation influenced their subsequent ratings of an ambiguous stimulus in the direction of the valence of their attitudes toward the puzzle that had been used as a prime. These findings thus demonstrate that, for people whose attitudes have been strengthened, the mere presence of the corresponding attitude object can indeed activate their attitude. In another study, Fazio & Williams (1986) documented the importance of long-term individual differences in the strength of the object-evaluation association. In this study, the latencies of subjects' responses to a query about their Presidential preferences were predictive of attitude-behavior correspondence such that the attitudes of subjects who responded more quickly were more predictive of subsequent voting behavior.

A study by Lord et al (1984) is also relevant to the attitude accessibility hypothesis. In this study, subjects' behavior toward an individual and their attitudes toward a *group* to which the individual presumably belonged were consistent only when the individual was a prototypic exemplar of the group. This finding is consistent with Fazio's accessibility hypothesis if it is assumed that the prototypic group member, as a "good" example of the attitude object, was able to activate subjects' attitudes toward the group itself.

Fazio et al (1986) have suggested that attitude activation in the presence of an attitude object may occur "automatically"; that is, without any conscious, intentional cognitive processing (see Bargh 1984, Sherman 1986, Higgins & Bargh 1987). To demonstrate this, these authors first selected individuals who manifested fast or slow response times in a preliminary task that assessed their attitudes toward various objects (e.g. music). In a subsequent task, these attitude objects were briefly presented to subjects just before they made evaluative judgments about unrelated adjectives (e.g. appealing). Response times for these latter judgments served as the primary dependent measure. Priming subjects with objects toward which their attitudes matched the evaluative valence of the target adjective facilitated response times with respect to the latter judgments, but only for subjects who were assumed to have a strong object-evaluation association. Moreover, because this priming effect was observed at a very short prime-target interval (.3 sec) and not at a longer interval (1 sec), Fazio et al concluded that the activation of these subjects' attitudes had occurred automatically. It is too early to speculate on what impact this evidence regarding automatic activation will have on our general understanding of the attitude-behavior relationship because the extent to which evaluative responses made within one second after exposure to an attitude object are capable of influencing overt behavior in more realistic settings is, at present, uncertain.

The research of Fazio and his colleagues provides a promising approach to the study of the processes underlying the attitude-behavior relationship. In particular, this approach provides some insights regarding how factors that moderate the attitude-behavior relationship (e.g. direct experience, Fazio & Zanna 1981; self-monitoring, Snyder & Kendzierski 1982; moral reasoning, Rholes & Bailey 1983) may operate. For example, Kardes et al (1986) recently extended past research demonstrating higher attitude-behavior correspondence for low (vs high) self-monitoring subjects by showing that response latencies to an attitude query were faster for low self-monitors.

Nevertheless, in the long run, the attitude strength construct will require further articulation. For one, the primary measure of this construct (response time) is also influenced by attitude extremity (Judd & Kulik 1980, Powell & Fazio 1984, Wyer & Gordon 1984, Fazio & Williams 1986) and the overlap between extremity and strength of the object-evaluation association has not always been controlled for experimentally (but see Fazio & Williams 1986). How the strength of the object-evaluation association relates to other measures of "attitude strength" (e.g. confidence, certainty) is also not yet clear (see Raden 1985). Moreover, the accessibility model does not clearly differentiate individuals for whom the attitude is not activated upon exposure to the object because of the weakness of the object-evaluation association from those for whom the attitude is not activated because the attitude itself is not available (a non-attitude).

ACCESSIBILITY OF UNDERLYING ATTITUDE ELEMENTS   Research conducted by Wilson and his colleagues (Wilson et al 1984, 1986, Wilson & Dunn 1986) has focused, not on the accessibility of attitudes per se, but rather on the relative accessibility of cognitions that influence attitude judgments (see Fishbein & Ajzen 1975). In this research, subjects (whose behavior is subsequently assessed) are asked to consider "why they hold the attitude that they do" before they express their attitude toward a given object. Wilson suggests that this "analyzing reasons" manipulation, through a process called "cognitivization" (Wilson et al 1986), activates a different set of cognitions than those that are normally accessible to the individual (and which presumably guide behavior). Hence, Wilson hypothesizes that the correspondence between attitudes assessed after such an intervention and subsequent behavior will be low.

This hypothesis has been supported in a number of studies (see Wilson et al 1986). For example, in a field setting, Wilson & Dunn (1986) had students who were standing on a cafeteria line participate in a "survey" of soft drink preferences. Just before soliciting their attitudes toward each of six drinks, some subjects were asked to give reasons why they liked or disliked each drink, while others were not. Later, subjects were observed purchasing a given soft drink. Subjects in the "analyzing reasons" (versus control) condition evidenced a lower correlation between their beverage attitudes and behavior, presumably because their expressed attitude after "cognitivation" did not match the attitude that (presumably) later influenced their purchase behavior. On the surface, these findings seem surprising because they appear to contradict other studies demonstrating that increasing people's awareness of their attitudes (by having them consider their feelings about the attitude object or through more general self-awareness manipulations) increases attitude-behavior correspondence (e.g. Snyder & Swann 1976, Carver & Scheier 1981, Wicklund 1982).

In a recent experiment designed to address this paradox, Millar & Tesser (1986b) hypothesized that superficially similar manipulations such as "analyzing reasons" and "focusing" (i.e. considering one's feelings) differentially activate the cognitive and affective components of an attitude, respectively. In their study, an "analyzing reasons" manipulation produced higher attitude behavior correlations when behavior was seen in a cognitive light (the puzzles used as the attitude object were seen as instrumental for success at an upcoming "analytical ability" test), while a "focusing" manipulation led to higher attitude-behavior correspondence when behavior was (assumed to be) more affectively driven. More generally, these findings, which support an affective-cognitive model of attitude, indicate that attitudes will be predictive of behavior only when there is a match between the component that underlies the expressed attitude and the component that influences the behavior (see Abelson 1982, Breckler 1984, Zanna & Rempel 1986).

Kallgren & Wood (1986) have also obtained data relevant to accessibility and the attitude-behavior relation. These authors found that the number of attitude-related beliefs and behaviors subjects listed in a two minute period added to the prediction of subsequent behavior over and above that made by attitude measures alone (see also Davidson et al 1985). Although framed in terms of attitude accessibility, such thought-listing tasks may tap the availability of attitude-relevant information or the ability to elaborate on one's attitude rather than accessibility per se.

In summary, there is growing evidence that variability in attitude accessibility or in the accessibility of various attitude "elements" influences both expressed attitudes and the attitude-behavior relationship. Interesting questions for subsequent research include investigating what attitude elements or components are most influential in determining attitudes and behaviors (see, for example, Fiske et al 1983b), how long an attitude or attitude element made accessible remains accessible, and whether attitudes can be primed out of the awareness of the individual. A test of the latter would probably necessitate less obtrusive accessibility manipulations (see Higgins et al 1977, Srull & Wyer 1979, Bargh & Pietromonaco 1982) than have been used thus far (Fazio et al 1983, 1986). If more subtle manipulations prove to influence expressed attitudes in the same way that impression formation can be influenced by nonobvious manipulations of the relative accessibility of trait terms (e.g. Bargh & Pietromonaco 1982), then evidence for subliminal persuasion may be in hand.

The Impact of Behavior on Attitudes

The attitude change that results from behavior that individuals are induced to perform continues to attract research attention. Several mechanisms now exist to account for such attitude change, including self-perception (Bem 1972), dissonance reduction (Festinger 1957), impression management (e.g. Riess et al 1981) and ego enhancement (Steele & Liu 1983).

SELF PERCEPTION   In the past, dissonance explanations were pitted against self-perception explanations (see Cooper & Fazio 1984, Fazio 1986b). Research by Fazio et al (1977) seems to have put this controversy at least temporarily to rest with evidence that, ceteris paribus, dissonance applies to behaviors outside of the "latitude of acceptance" while self-perception applies to behaviors within this latitude. Perhaps as a result, self-perception theory has not received much recent attention in relation to the induced compliance phenomenon (see Crano & Sivacek 1984 and Fazio et al 1984 for other applications of the theory and Fazio 1986b for a review).

In a program of research that bears surface resemblance to self-perception research, Higgins and his colleagues (Higgins & Rholes 1978, McCann & Hancock 1983, Higgins & McCann 1984) have shown that people's behaviors, in the form of their self-generated verbal or written descriptions of a target person, can influence their attitudes toward the target after a temporal delay. Specifically, subjects in their research have been shown to base their subsequent attitudes toward the target on their earlier descriptions of him or her, without appropriately discounting the context in which the descriptions were made (see Higgins & Stangor 1986 for a formal model of these context-induced judgments). For example, Higgins & McCann (1984) asked subjects to communicate information about a target person to another person who purportedly liked or disliked the target. With no other external inducements, communicator-subjects tailored their message to "please" their audience, especially high authoritarian subjects who communicated to a high status audience (see also Tetlock 1983a). Subjects' attitudes proved to be biased in the direction of the evaluative tone of their original (context-induced) message, especially for those who expressed the attitudes 10–14 days (vs immediately) after writing the message. These findings are important because they provide a rare illustration that attitudes expressed primarily because of strategic concerns (rather than as expressions of true feelings) may eventually become internalized (Kelman 1961).

IMPRESSION MANAGEMENT   Impression management (the idea that individuals change their attitudes after writing a counterattitudinal essay in order to avoid appearing inconsistent to others) has gradually replaced self-perception as dissonance theory's prime competition in the induced compliance paradigm (Riesse et al 1981). Generally, recent research has been more supportive of dissonance explanations, both in studies that have manipulated impression management concerns through the status or attractiveness of the experimenter (Rosenfeld et al 1983, 1984) and in studies where postessay attitudes have been assessed under conditions that presumably minimize self-presentational concerns (Jamieson & Zanna 1982, Stults et al 1984).

Overall, however, it seems likely that both dissonance reduction and impression-management concerns operate to produce attitude change after the performance of counterattitudinal behavior (Rosenfeld et al 1983, Elkin & Leippe 1986; see also Tetlock & Manstead 1985). Supporting the multiple determination idea, Baumeister & Tice (1984) demonstrated that attitudes may change in the induced compliance paradigm even under low choice conditions and, conversely, that perception of free choice can produce attitude change even under conditions of complete privacy. What would seem most useful at this time would be an attempted taxonomy of the relevant situational and individual difference factors that influence which mechanisms prevail, under which conditions, and for which people (see Carver & Scheier 1981, Paulhus 1982, Schlenker 1982, Sorrentino & Hancock 1986).

DISSONANCE IN SOCIAL SETTINGS   Several recent studies have productively extended the induced compliance paradigm into more social settings by showing that the group itself may influence the magnitude of attitude change that results from counterattitudinal behavior. In a particularly interesting study, Zanna & Sande (1986) had subjects write a consequential, counterattitudinal essay either alone or in groups of three. In the group conditions, the three members worked together to write the essay but expressed their pre- and postessay attitudes privately. Attitude change in the "alone" conditions was greater for those who had free choice than for those who did not, replicating the standard induced compliance effect. However, in the group situation, attitude change occurred for low choice groups but not for free choice groups. Indirect measures suggested that, although dissonance was equally high for individuals in the free choice/group condition as it was in the free choice/ alone condition, subjects in the group situation were able to diffuse responsibility for the content of the essay to other group members, thus eliminating the need for attitude change.

In a related study, Cooper & Mackie (1983) found that group membership may serve to prevent attitude change under certain conditions. In this study, subjects who were members of an established pro-Reagan group participated in an experiment where they were asked to write essays. Some wrote an essay that was counter to an issue that defined their group membership (supporting the reelection of Carter), while others wrote an essay that was relevant to, but not defining of, group membership (supporting the extension of government-sponsored health programs). Under free choice conditions, attitude change was observed on the nondefining issue but not on the defining issue, as the latter was presumably prevented by social pressure from the group. Interestingly, individuals in the free choice/definitional condition were observed to reduce their dissonance-produced arousal by devaluing members of a pro-Carter group more than individuals in the other experimental conditions. Recent work by Mackie (1986, Mackie & Cooper 1984) on attitude polarization in groups (see also Hinsz & Davis 1984, Orive 1984, Isenberg 1986) also demonstrates the complicating effects that social settings (e.g. needs for group identity) can have on attitudes and attitude change.

These studies are interesting demonstrations of dissonance in social settings and suggest that the social context may serve to either increase or reduce dissonance, and thus affect attitude change. The effects of social context on dissonance-related attitude change (e.g. Cooper & Mackie 1983, Zanna & Sande 1986) and on self-persuasion (e.g. Higgins & McCann 1984) represents one of the more important recent advances in the study of the effects of behavior on attitudes.

ATTITUDE CHANGE INDUCED BY PERSUASIVE MESSAGES

Although one's own behavior can be an important basis for attitude formation and change, the bulk of the attitude change literature considers how influence results from people's exposure to the opinions of others. In persuasion research, subjects read or hear a verbal message consisting of an overall position and usually one or more supportive arguments. Typically, this message is associated with a single communicator (but see Harkins & Petty 1983). The last section of the chapter reviews research in which subjects, often in group settings, are exposed to either the unelaborated or elaborated statements of minority and/or majority group sources.

Persuasion research continues to manifest its long-standing interest in cognitive processes although, as we shall see, motivational issues are beginning to resurface after a period of neglect (see Cooper & Croyle 1984, Eagly & Chaiken 1984). In Eagly and Chaiken's (1984) review of contemporary theorizing, a convenience distinction (which we adopted in discussing attitude-behavior research) was drawn between "process" theories that provide qualitative descriptions of the mechanisms involved in accepting persuasive messages (e.g. attributional reasoning) and "combinatorial" theories that primarily provide quantitative descriptions of how recipients integrate relevant information to form an overall judgement (e.g. information integration theory). Reflecting most current research, our review focuses on process perspectives. For more comprehensive reviews, we refer readers to the Eagly and Chaiken chapter [which includes discussion of how process theories can be linked to combinatorial theories, especially to Anderson's (e.g. 1981) information-integration model] and to McGuire's (1985) *Handbook* chapter.

Two broad-brush sketches of persuasion are currently fashionable, with one emphasizing and the other de-emphasizing detailed information processing. Attitude change theories epitomizing the first perspective [e.g. cognitive response approach (Petty et al 1981); McGuire's 1972 reception-yielding framework] have been labeled "central routes to persuasion" by Petty & Cacioppo (1981) and "systematic" approaches by Chaiken (1980), two terms we use interchangeably. The second "cognitive miser" (Fiske & Taylor 1984) perspective is reflected in Chaiken's (1980, 1986b) heuristic processing model, Cialdini's (1986) consideration of heuristic principles in compliance settings, and Petty & Cacioppo's (1981, 1986) "peripheral route" perspective.

Regarding heuristic processing and the peripheral route to persuasion, researchers have sometimes confused the terms by equating them (e.g. Kruglanski 1986, Sherman 1986). The heuristic model asserts that persuasion is often mediated by simple decision rules (e.g. "length implies strength") that associate certain persuasion cues (e.g. message length) with message validity (Chaiken 1980, 1986b). In contrast, the peripheral route refers to a family of attitude change theories that specify factors or motives that produce attitude change without engendering active message and issue-relevant thinking (Petty & Cacioppo 1981, 1986). These peripheral routes include cognitive perspectives such as heuristic processing (Chaiken 1980) and attributional reasoning (e.g. Kelley 1967, Bem 1972, Eagly et al 1981). However, the peripheral label is also used to refer to models which specify simple affective mechanisms in attitude change (e.g. classical and operant conditioning; also see Batra & Ray 1985 and Lutz 1985), perceptual models such as social judgment theory (Sherif & Sherif 1967), and social-role perspectives which assert that people often agree (or disagree) with messages for reasons that (presumably) would not necessitate thinking about message content [e.g. to identify with or promote a social relationship with liked communicators or comply with powerful ones (Kelman 1961); to manage a favorable social identity (Schlenker 1980)]. So as not to restrict the term "peripheral processing," or dilute the meaning of "heuristic processing," we suggest that they not be used interchangeably.

Message- and Issue-Relevant Thinking: A Systematic Approach

The central-peripheral framework, also called the Elaboration Likelihood Model (Petty & Cacioppo 1986), postulates that central processing occurs when people are both motivated and able to engage in message- and issue-relevant thinking. These factors are also viewed as key determinants of systematic processing although, regarding their independence, Chaiken (1986b) speculates that some ability-reducing variables (e.g. severe distractions) may also undermine motivation for detailed processing.

Recent research suggests a fairly large number of variables that either motivate or enable recipients to engage in message- and issue-relevant thinking. Situational variables include high (vs low) personal relevance of the message topic (e.g. Petty & Cacioppo 1984, Howard-Pitney et al 1986; also see Harkness et al 1985), high (vs low) match between message content and recipients' functional or schematic predispositions (Cacioppo et al 1982, DeBono 1986), repeated (vs single) exposures to messages (Cacioppo & Petty 1985), written (vs broadcast) messages (Chaiken & Eagly 1983), presenting arguments in rhetorical (vs statement) form (Burnkrant & Howard 1984), and having subjects recline (vs stand) during message exposure (Petty et al 1983b). Individual difference variables include prior knowledge about the message topic (Srull 1983, Wood et al 1985) and need for cognition (Cacioppo et al 1983; for studies implicating other situational and individual difference determinants of this processing mode see Harkins & Petty 1983, Heesacker et al 1983, Pallak et al 1983, Tetlock 1983a,b, McFarland et al 1984, Reardon & Rosen 1984, Yalch & Elmore-Yalch 1984, Jepson & Chaiken 1986, Sorrentino & Hancock 1986, Worth & Mackie 1986).

Systematic processing has been assessed in a variety of ways, including self-report, reading time, and argument recall (e.g. Chaiken 1980), number of message- and issue-relevant cognitions generated on thought-listing tasks (e.g. Burnkrant & Howard 1984, Chaiken 1980), physiological measures (Cacioppo & Petty 1986), and whether subjects are able to discriminate between intrinsically strong versus weak persuasive arguments (e.g. Petty et al 1983a). The latter experiments are particularly important because they confirm the prediction (Chaiken 1980, Chaiken & Eagly 1976, 1983, Petty & Cacioppo 1981) that message variables such as complexity and argument quality influence persuasion primarily to the extent that recipients are able and motivated to attend to and process persuasive argumentation. Strong (vs weak) messages induce greater persuasion, for example, for persons who are higher in need for cognition (Cacioppo et al 1983), when recipients are more knowledgeable about the message topic (Wood et al 1985), and when arguments are presented in rhetorical form (Burnkrant & Howard 1984).

INVOLVEMENT   Subjects led to believe that the message topic (e.g. comprehensive exams) will (vs won't) impact on their own lives have also been shown to be less persuaded by weak messages but more persuaded by strong ones (e.g. Petty & Cacioppo 1979, 1984; Petty et al 1981a, Leippe & Elkin

1986). This view of personal relevance, or "issue-involvement" (Petty & Cacioppo 1986), as a motivator of message- and issue-relevant thinking suggests an image of the systematic information processor as open-minded and unbiased and contrasts sharply with earlier views suggesting that ego-involved persons should be uniformly resistant to counterattitudinal messages (e.g. Sherif & Hovland 1961, Kiesler et al 1969). Several recent studies, however, suggest that some compromise position is necessary. Burnkrant & Howard (1984) failed to replicate the argument quality by personal relevance interaction described above. Moreover, in their study, personal relevance influenced the valence, but not the quantity, of message-relevant thinking. More recently, Howard-Pitney et al (1986) found that while higher personal relevance increased systematic processing, this processing tended to be biased in favor of subjects' initial attitudes.

These sorts of findings have led to the suggestions that at more extreme levels of issue involvement, processing may terminate or become biased (Petty & Cacioppo 1986) and that involvement may have curvilinear effects on persuasion when messages contain strong arguments (Burnkrant & Howard 1984, Cooper & Croyle 1984). Alternatively, we suggest that it may be useful to adopt a multifaceted view of involvement (Greenwald 1982a, Greenwald & Breckler 1984, Greenwald & Leavitt 1984, Greenwald & Pratkanis 1984) and to examine the extent to which different types of involvement differentially impact on information processing and persuasion. The latter may be a fruitful task since involvement-like terms have long been one of the area's major vehicles for representing motivational factors in persuasion.

Although traditionally, issue involvement has been distinguished from "response involvement" recent attempts to define the latter primarily in terms of impression management concerns (e.g. Leippe & Elkin 1986, Petty & Cacioppo 1986) seem too narrow given the variety of ways in which this construct has been operationalized over the years (e.g. Johnson & Scileppi 1969, Chaiken 1980, Leippe & Elkin 1986). There are several other ways of distinguishing involvement that may be more useful to researchers. In addition to issue involvement which, following current usage (Petty & Cacioppo 1986), might be defined as the extent to which the message *topic* is seen as personally relevant or significant, the term "position-involvement" might be defined as the extent to which recipients have a vested interest in (Sivacek & Crano 1982) or are committed to (e.g. Kiesler 1971, Abelson 1986) one side of the issue or the other. Although these two types of involvement may often be highly related [particularly when studied in nonmanipulated form (see Howard-Pitney et al 1986)], they are probably worth distinguishing. For example, it may be that at lower levels of position involvement, higher issue involvement leads, as studies have shown (e.g. Petty & Cacioppo 1984), to more and relatively "objective" processing because people are concerned with "seeking the truth" on a personally important topic (see also Leippe & Elkin 1986). Yet, at higher levels of position involvement, recipients may be more concerned with defending or salvaging the validity of their preferred positions and, thus, may engage in more biased information processing (Abelson 1986). To these, still other terms may be added to capture other senses of involvement. For example, something like "content involvement" may be needed to represent the idea that some messages, perhaps because of their self-relevant content, stimulate greater processing than do other messages (e.g. Cacioppo et al 1982, DeBono 1986; see also Greenwald & Leavitt 1984, McGuire 1985). And something like "accuracy" or "validity" involvement may be needed to reflect the idea that even when topics are low in *personal* relevance, recipients may be more or less motivated to process issue-relevant information carefully because they are made to feel more or less accountable for the accuracy of their judgments (see Chaiken 1980, Tetlock 1983b) or ,perhaps more or less responsible to others for whom the topic may be of extreme importance (e.g. to defendants in judicial settings; also see Kruglanski's 1986 discussion of fear of invalidity). Finally, terms like "relational," or "social-identity," and "self-identity" involvement (see Greenwald 1982a) may be needed to capture the ideas that people in persuasion settings may often be primarily concerned with formulating opinions that will facilitate favorable social impressions and maintain their own self-esteem. Like other types of involvement, variations in these two motivational concerns may also impact on the magnitude and nature of information processing in social influence settings (see McFarland et al 1984, Tetlock 1983a, 1985, Leippe & Elkin 1986).

PERSISTENCE   In addition to other mechanisms that influence attitudinal persistence (e.g. Anderson 1983, Anderson et al 1985; Baumgardner et al 1983), the amount of message- and issue-relevant thinking that recipients engage in is thought to be important. Specifically, attitudes formed on the basis of systematic processing, compared to those formed on the basis of simple decision rules or other peripheral mechanisms, have been postulated to be relatively enduring and predictive of subsequent behavior. Although findings consistent with these hypotheses have been obtained in several published studies (Chaiken 1980, Chaiken & Eagly 1983, Pallak et al 1983, Petty et al 1983a), stronger support, particularly regarding the attitude-behavior link, awaits further research. In addition, these straightforward hypotheses may have to be modified to take account of potentially contingent factors (e.g. temporal salience of peripheral cues; type(s) of involvement operative in setting). Finally, the related idea (see Chaiken 1980) that systematic processing may be a prerequisite for obtaining sleeper effects is consistent with recent research indicating that this effect occurs primarily when discounting cues come after message exposure and when messages are constructed to have a strong initial impact on opinions (Hannah & Sternthal 1984, Pratkanis & Greenwald 1985, Greenwald et al 1986).

ROLE OF RECEPTION PROCESSES   Much (though not all) of the above research has been guided by the cognitive response theory logic (e.g. Petty et al 1981c) that persuasion is a function of the favorability and amount of message- and issue-relevant thinking that occurs in persuasion settings (e.g. Petty & Cacioppo 1984; see Cacioppo et al 1981 for a review of other "cognitive response" categories). From a broader information processing perspective, however, this focus on cognitive appraisal and elaborative thinking tends to ignore other processing steps that have been proposed in relation to persuasion (McGuire 1972, 1985). In particular, recent research has been relatively silent regarding the role that reception processes play in persuasion, despite the fact that at least minimal levels of attention to and comprehension of message content would seem necessary preconditions for cognitive appraisal and elaboration (see Leippe 1979, McGuire 1985, Ratneshwar & Chaiken 1986).

Eagly & Chaiken (1984) trace this neglect of reception—a process featured in McGuire's (e.g. 1972) information processing paradigm—to a number of factors. Perhaps most importantly, they note that researchers have generally failed to appreciate that widely used measures of reception such as argument recall are inherently poor indexes of reception because such "learning" measures reflect not only reception—the encoding of message content—but also the storage of message content in memory and its subsequent retrieval. Consequently, most investigators have equated the reception-persuasion relation with the relation between message learning and attitude change (e.g. Fishbein & Ajzen 1981, Petty & Cacioppo 1981) and, on the basis of numerous studies showing low or nonsignificant correlations between argument recall and attitude change, have concluded that reception is unimportant in accounting for persuasion (e.g. Greenwald 1968, Fishbein & Ajzen 1972, Brock & Shavitt 1983, Gibson 1983; see Eagly & Chaiken 1984 for studies that have yielded support for the reception-as-mediator hypothesis).

In addition to refreshing researchers' memories on the point that even the McGuire (1972) paradigm did not view reception as a general, transituational mediator of persuasion (and hence would not predict uniformly high recall-attitude correlations), Eagly & Chaiken (1984) also argue that low argument recall-persuasion correlations are ambiguous regarding the importance of reception because they may often be attenuated due to methodological factors and, more importantly, because details of message content may be forgotten after they are encoded and an attitude judgement formed. In this regard, it is instructive to mention how social cognition research has dealt with a similar issue, the fact that judgments (e.g. impressions) do not consistently covary with memory for experimentally provided information (e.g. trait adjectives). Rather than assuming that the reception and subsequent memory for such information is "unimportant," researchers have treated the recall-judgment link as an empirical and theoretical issue (e.g. Anderson & Hubert 1963, Dreben et al 1979, Bargh & Thein 1985, Carlston & Skowronski 1986). Recent research indicates, for example, that a strong memory-judgment link may obtain primarily when people do not or cannot form "on-line" (Bargh & Thein 1985, Hastie & Park 1986) impressions during information acquisition. Heavily implicated in these studies is the role of processing objectives or goals (see Srull & Wyer 1986); on-line impression formation is most likely when people have the attentional resources and a judgment goal in mind (Sherman et al 1983, Bargh & Thein 1985). For persuasion, these findings suggest the hypothesis that recall-attitude correlations may be relatively low in experiments in which subjects, because of strong prior attitudes or instructional sets, have the explicit or implicit goal of expressing an opinion judgment. In contrast, such correlations may be somewhat higher in experiments that utilize relatively novel opinion topics and disguise the fact that subjects' opinion judgments will subsequently be solicited.

The assertion that cognitive responses are more important (or, to rephrase things, more proximal) determinants of persuasion than memory for message content (e.g. Greenwald 1968, Petty & Cacioppo 1981), while possibly true, is tangential to the reception issue. Attentional and comprehension processes in persuasion are fundamentally important and deserve greater and more detailed scrutiny (see Eagly & Chaiken 1984, Ratneshwar & Chaiken 1986). Signaling renewed interest in these issues, Schmidt & Sherman (1984) have postulated the existence of generic "position schemas" that influence people's comprehension and miscomprehension of persuasive argumentation and possibly their propensities to generate counterarguments. These authors also suggest that low recall-attitude correlations in past research may have been due in part to the fact that researchers have focused primarily on memory for actually presented arguments and have not adequately addressed the importance of intrusions (see also Loken & Wyer 1983). Finally, we note that the importance of attentional mechanisms in persuasion is reflected in recent research that has applied vividness logic (see Taylor & Thompson 1982) to issues such as the persuasive impact of pictorial information (Kisielius & Sternthal 1984), communication modality (Chaiken & Eagly 1983), and both fear and health messages (Rogers 1983, Sherer & Rogers 1984, Meyerowitz & Chaiken 1986, Robberson & Rogers 1986).

Heuristic Processing and Other Peripheral Modes

Chaiken's (1980, 1982, 1986b) heuristic model proposes that people often use simple decision rules in judging the validity of persuasive messages (e.g.

"length implies strength," "expert's statements can be trusted," "consensus implies correctness"). Consequently, without fully absorbing the semantic content of persuasive argumentation or engaging in cognitive elaboration, people may agree more with messages containing many (vs few) arguments, with expert (vs inexpert) communicators, with messages that most (vs few) others agree with, and so on (see Chaiken 1986b for a discussion of the relation between these rules and the representativeness heuristic). In contrast to Petty & Cacioppo's (e.g. 1986) central vs peripheral framework, which some have interpreted as positing two mutually exclusive routes to persuasion (Stiff 1986), heuristic and systematic processing are viewed as parallel modes of information processing (Chaiken 1982, 1986b, Eagly & Chaiken 1984).

Persuasion cues that are thought to be typically mediated by simple decision rules include a variety of source variables and some message and contextual variables. Consistent with the logic that such cues exert their maximal impact on persuasion when recipients are not processing systematically [because systematic processing often provides recipients with message- and issue-relevant information that contradicts a simple decision rule (Chaiken 1986b)], manipulations of source credibility, likability, physical attractiveness, message length, number of arguments, audience reactions, and consensus information have been shown to have a significant impact on persuasion when motivation or ability for message- and issue-relevant thinking is low but little impact when motivation and ability are high (e.g. Chaiken 1980, 1986a,b, Petty et al 1981a, 1983b, Cacioppo & Petty 1984, Petty & Cacioppo 1984, Yalch & Elmore-Yalch 1984, Wood et al 1985, Haugtvedt et al 1986, Ratneshwar & Chaiken 1986, Axsom et al 1987; see also Borgida & Howard-Pitney 1983). That mood manipulations may exert a greater impact on persuasion for subjects who are not highly knowledgeable about the message topic (Srull 1983) is explicable by the heuristic model only to the extent that a simple decision rule relating mood to message validity (e.g. "If it makes me feel good, it must be reasonable") could be said to underlie this cue's persuasive effectiveness (see also Worth & Mackie 1986). Alternately, the persuasive impact of mood may represent some other peripheral attitude change mechanism such as classical conditioning.

Other research on heuristic processing indicates that increasing the salience or vividness of persuasion cues that are typically processed in heuristic fashion increases their persuasive impact, presumably because making these cues salient increases the accessibility of the simple decision rules that are associated with them (Chaiken & Eagly 1983, Pallak 1983). In addition to indirect evidence that heuristic processing often mediates the persuasive impact of a variety of source, message, and contextual cues (e.g. Chaiken & Eagly 1983, Pallak 1983, Axsom et al 1987, Petty & Cacioppo 1984, Wood et al 1985), recent studies (e.g. Wilson et al 1985; see Chaiken 1986b) have shown that manipulating the accessibility of simple decision rules and/or their perceived reliability through priming tasks increases the likelihood that these rules will be used to evaluate message validity in subsequent persuasion settings.

Under many circumstances, heuristic processing probably represents a self-consciously selected satisficing strategy on the part of message recipients. The extent to which such processing might also proceed, at least in some settings, in a less controlled, "automatic" fashion is presently unclear (Eagly 1986, Sherman 1986). Given that heuristic and systematic processing may often proceed in parallel (Eagly & Chaiken 1984, Chaiken 1986b), the possibility also exists that the presence of heuristic cues (e.g. credibility, message length) in persuasion settings may sometimes bias recipients' evaluation of message- and issue-relevant information. Although this possibility has not been investigated directly, some findings regarding source credibility effects (e.g. Sternthal et al 1978) are suggestive.

Aside from heuristic processing, the only other "peripheral" attitude change mechanism that has received more than passing empirical or theoretical attention is Eagly et al's (1981) attributional analysis of communicator characteristics. As discussed more fully in relation to minority influence, this perspective posits that recipients' judgments of message validity (and, hence, persuasion) are the outcome of their causal analysis of plausible reasons for communicators' stated positions on issues. Labeled as a peripheral approach in Petty & Cacioppo's (1981, 1986) framework because it does not implicate message- and issue-relevant thinking, attributional reasoning represents a processing mode that is presumably less effortful than message- and issue-relevant thinking but more effortful than heuristic processing (see Eagly & Chaiken 1984).

Determinants of Processing Mode and More on Motives

With researchers' increased awareness that multiple modes of processing may operate in persuasion settings has come an increased understanding of the conditions under which recipients employ one mode or another. Although much remains to be learned about the determinants of processing modes and the extent to which these modes represent parallel versus mutually exclusive processes, some principles that govern their usage can be derived from current research (see also Eagly & Chaiken 1984, Eagly 1986).

As suggested by Schmidt & Sherman's (1984) work on generic position schemas and Wood et al's (1985) work on prior issue-relevant knowledge, comprehension and message- and issue-relevant thinking may be highly dependent upon recipients possessing at least marginal levels of prior knowledge about the message topic. Prior learning is also an important determinant of whether recipients utilize the simple decision rules specified by the heuristic model because to use such rules, people must have learned and stored in memory the particular knowledge structures that are relevant to available persuasion cues. Moreover, if available in memory (Higgins et al 1982), such knowledge structures must be activated upon presentation of the persuasion cues that are associated with them. Presumably, situational factors such as cue salience (e.g. Pallak 1983) and the frequency and recency of prior activation (e.g. Wilson et al 1985) influence the accessibility of such structures and, hence, their persuasive impact (see Trope & Ginossar 1986 and Higgins & Bargh 1987 for a similar perspective on the use of statistical versus nonstatistical rules in judgment problems). Another important determinant of processing mode is the amount of effortful thinking which it requires. As demonstrated by much current research, people may prefer less effortful modes of processing unless they are especially motivated to engage in a more effortful process.

In speculating about the determinants of processing mode when recipients are primarily concerned with "truth seeking" or maximizing the validity of their opinions, Eagly & Chaiken (1984) suggested that choice of processing mode might also depend on it's *sufficiency* for determining the validity of a message's overall position. If, for example, a causal analysis of the plausible reasons for a communicator's message did not yield a clear-cut assessment of message validity, another processing mode such as message- and issue-relevant thinking might be invoked (e.g. Wood & Eagly 1981). While the sufficiency principle, in combination with the least effort principle, suggests that people often progress from less effortful to more effortful modes, under some circumstances, the reverse direction may also occur (Eagly & Chaiken 1984).

Because processing occurs in the service of motivational goals (see Higgins 1981, Gerard & Orive 1986, Srull & Wyer 1986), perhaps the most important (but least researched) determinant of processing mode is the recipient's primary goal in a particular setting. For example, when people are more concerned with forming a judgment that will be "correct" in the eyes of others rather than "correct" in a truth-seeking sense, it is unlikely that knowledge structures of primary relevance for judging message validity (e.g. the heuristic model's simple decision rules) would be activated or utilized. Nevertheless, even in these settings, choice of processing mode may depend highly on its effortfulness and sufficiency in meeting processing goals. Tetlock (1983a), for example, has shown that when subjects expect to discuss their opinions with another person, whether that other person's views are known or unknown has an important impact on how much subjects think about the opinion issue. When the other's views were known, subjects seemed to use a simple "acceptability heuristic" (Tetlock 1985) and expressed an opinion that closely matched the other person's viewpoint. When the other's views were un-

known, however, subjects' engaged in more extensive information processing, presumably still in the service of formulating an interpersonally acceptable opinion judgment. An explicit recognition that information processing
occurs in the service of people's intrapersonal and interpersonal goals should
stimulate a closer examination of the motives that are activated in persuasion
settings and that recipients bring with them to these settings and how these
motives impact on information processing and attitude change.

ATTITUDE FUNCTIONS   An explicit interest in the motivational bases of
persuasion is reflected in recent attempts (DeBono 1986; Herek 1986a,b;
Hooper 1983; Shavitt 1986; Shavitt & Brock 1986; Snyder & DeBono 1985,
1986; Spivey et al 1983) to test and elaborate the original functional theories
of attitudes, particularly those of Katz (1960) and Smith et al (1956). Most of
this work has focused on the a priori identification of functions, a perennial
stumbling block to research in this area (see Kiesler et al 1969, Himmelfarb &
Eagly 1974, Lutz 1981).

In harmony with the strategy followed in much initial work on functions
(e.g. Katz et al 1956, McClintock 1958), Snyder & DeBono (1986) suggest
that individual differences in attitude functions can be assessed indirectly via
personality measures such as self-monitoring (Snyder 1974), machiavellianism (Christie & Geis 1970), authoritarianism (Adorno et al 1950), and need
for approval (Crowne & Marlowe 1964). In their empirical work, Snyder and
DeBono have shown that the attitudes of high self-monitors may often serve a
social adjustive function (Smith et al 1956), whereas the attitudes of low
self-monitors may often serve a value-expressive function (Katz 1960). For
example, in three studies in which subjects were exposed to product advertisements that were either image-oriented or quality-oriented (presumed to appeal
to social adjustive versus value-expressive concerns, respectively), high self-
monitoring subjects were more influenced by image-oriented than by quality-
oriented ads while the reverse was true for low self-monitoring subjects
(Snyder & DeBono 1985). DeBono (1986) obtained similar findings in a
study on attitudes toward mental illness, and further showed that functionally
relevant messages were processed more systematically (see above).

Given the success of Snyder and DeBono's experiments, subsequent research might pursue their suggestion that personality measures other than
self-monitoring might serve as reasonably good indicators of attitude function. Nevertheless, because this strategy assesses variation in function only
across individuals and not across attitude objects or situations, other measurement strategies are also needed. To address this need, several researchers
have explored the utility of open-ended techniques for measuring functions
directly. Herek (1986a,b), for example, asks subjects to explain their attitudes
toward some topic and these written protocols are content-analyzed to identify
the predominant functions that the attitude object serves. In analyzing

essays on the topic of homosexuality, Herek found evidence for three major functions that corresponded roughly to Katz's value-expressive, ego-defensive, and instrumental functions. A similar thought-listing task has been used by Shavitt & Brock (1986; Shavitt 1986) to explore the hypotheses that different attitude objects may activate different functional concerns and that messages that match an object's functional profile are more persuasive than those that don't.

The further development of these and other (more easily scored) direct measures of function is important for several reasons. First, as shown by Herek's (1986a) research, such measures can be used to validate the existence of postulated functions such as those originally proposed by Katz and Smith et al. Also, as suggested by Shavitt & Brock's (1986) work, such measures can be used to examine variation in attitude functions across attitude objects and domains. They might be used, for example, to substantiate the claim that "symbolic" attitudes primarily serve an expressive rather than instrumental function (e.g. Ellsworth & Ross 1983, Sears 1983; see Attitude Structure section). Finally, direct measures of function may facilitate research on the more subtle functional hypothesis (Smith et al 1956, Herek, 1986a) that attitude functions may vary in their importance as a basis for attitude formation and change across situations. For example, whereas social adjustive concerns may be most likely to guide attitude expression in situations where important reference groups are present, value-expressive concerns no doubt guide attitude expression in situations in which people are forced to confront their values (Rokeach 1985).

Critics of a functional approach might argue that the perspective boils down to Fishbein & Ajzen's (1972, 1975) point that to be persuasive, a message must address a person's salient beliefs. The task of measuring functions, in other words, could be viewed as an attempt to discover the salient (instrumental, value-expressive, social adjustive, etc) beliefs that underlie individuals' attitudes toward various objects in various situations. While this argument has some merit, particularly for practitioners of persuasion, for advancing our understanding of persuasion, the functional approach possesses unique heuristic and predictive value because of its explicit focus on the motivational underpinnings of attitude formation and change.

MINORITY AND MAJORITY GROUP INFLUENCE

In 1969, Moscovici, Lage, and Naffrechoux initiated a corrective to the conformity literature whose "functionalist" perspective, Moscovici (1976) later argued, emphasized the submission of minorities to the neglect of their role as agents of social change or innovation. In a mirror-image rendition of the Asch (1951) paradigm, groups of four subjects and two confederates judged the color of slides that were unambiguously blue. In a consistent minority condition, the confederates claimed to see "green" on each of 36 trials while in an inconsistent condition, the confederates saw "green" on 24 trials and "blue" on 12. Although small in magnitude, the results were clear: "Green" responses were made 8.42 percent of the time by subjects faced with a consistent minority, 1.25 percent of the time by subjects exposed to the inconsistent minority, and only .25 percent of the time by control subjects whose judgments were made in the absence of confederates. Thus, a minority—albeit only a consistent one—could indeed exert influence.

Since this demonstration, a moderate sized literature has accumulated. While the scant attention to minority influence in previous reviews in this series might be said to mirror American social psychology's general neglect of group research (see Maass & Clark 1984, Steiner 1986), it is likely that the literature itself contributed. Like many conformity studies that served as their springboard, numerous minority influence studies have utilized measures and tasks (e.g. perceptual and aesthetic judgments; perceptual and decision making tasks) that appear quite different from those that mark the attitudes literature. Nevertheless, more recent research has broadened to include studies utilizing more explicit attitudinal measures and tasks. As such, the relevance of this literature to the attitudes area is now quite apparent (see Eagly 1986, Zanna et al 1986). Our review focuses on what we perceive to be this literature's major issues and most promising directions. For more comprehensive reviews, we recommend two recent literature reviews (Maass & Clark 1984, Tanford & Penrod 1984) and Moscovici's (1985b) *Handbook* chapter.

Behavioral Consistency and Attribution Theory

As indicated by Moscovici et al (1969), minority consistency seems a key factor in successful innovation. Although Moscovici (1976) discussed several other "behavioral styles" (e.g. fairness, investment) of successful minorities, consistency—the stable, systematic, or patterned responses of a minority over time (Tanford & Penrod 1984)—has been the most heavily researched of these variables.

With occasional exceptions (e.g. Wolf 1985), the hypothesis that a minority's consistency increases its influence has received widespread support (e.g. Nemeth et al 1974, Moscovici & Personnaz 1980, Mugny & Papastamou 1980, Bray et al 1982, Mugny 1982, Richardson & Cialdini 1986). But why? Moscovici and Nemeth (Moscovici & Faucheux 1972, Moscovici & Nemeth 1974) proposed that the minority's consistency (along with their distinctiveness) led perceivers to regard the minority as certain and confident about their position and that it was this "dispositional" attribution that was the more proximal determinant of successful innovation.

While Moscovici and Nemeth's attributional account of consistency has been widely accepted, as Maass & Clark (1984) note, it has rarely been subjected to the stringent testing that has been imposed on mediational hypotheses in other areas (e.g. Batson 1975, Wood & Eagly 1981) and some correlational findings (e.g. Richardson & Cialdini 1986) are not congenial to the idea. Further, Maass & Clark (1984) have criticized the Moscovici and Nemeth formulation conceptually (e.g. for "automatically" assuming that consistency fosters attributions of certainty rather than inferences such as "craziness and dogmatism," p. 438) as well as for failing to account for several empirical findings, including the inhibiting effect of behaviorally "rigid" minorities (e.g. Mugny 1975, Mugny & Papastamou 1980; see Mugny 1982) and a few demonstrations that "double minorities" (i.e. both social and numerical minorities) are sometimes less influential than "single" (i.e. numerical) minorities (Maass & Clark 1982, Maass et al 1982, Mugny et al 1983 as cited in Maass & Clark 1984; but see Nemeth & Wachtler 1973).

In their own analysis of consistency, Maass & Clark (1984) make use of Kelley's (1967) cube model and his augmentation and discounting principles (Kelley 1972). In their analysis (impartial or majority) perceivers process consensus and consistency information but not distinctiveness information because of its unavailability in the typical innovation experiment (where only one entity or issue is discussed). Because the minority disagrees with the majority, perceivers infer low group consensus, and if the minority behaves consistently, they will infer high consistency. This pattern of low consensus/ high consistency lead Maass and Clark to agree with Moscovici and Nemeth that perceivers will make dispositional attributions about consistent minorities (see Orvis et al 1975). Moreover, they argue that this attribution (which they implicitly assume is often certainty and confidence, p. 437) will be augmented because social pressure from the majority constitutes a plausible inhibitory cause for the minority's deviance. But more important, to explain when certainty attributions will prevail versus other types of (person?) attributions, the discounting principle is invoked. Maass and Clark argue that the dispositional attribution of certainty will tend to be discounted to the extent that other plausible (and also facilitative) causes for the minority's consistent behavior are available. For example, in accounting for the reduced effectiveness of rigid minorities and double minorities, Maass and Clark suggest that alternative plausible causes for the minority's consistent behavior such as dogmatism and self-interest respectively may have led subjects to discount certainty and confidence.

Although Maass & Clark's (1984) analysis represents a needed extension of Moscovici & Nemeth's (1974) theorizing, as this year's unpaid critics of the literature, we suggest that a different attributional perspective be taken. Our main criticism of both of the above analyses is their focus on perceivers' attributions regarding the *minority's underlying dispositions* (e.g. their certainty). Curiously, this focus seems more in harmony with correspondent inference theory (Jones & Davis 1965) than with the theorizing that presumably inspired both formulations. In Kelley's (1967, 1972) analyses, the perceiver's central task was not inferring the communicator's (or minority's) dispositions, but rather inferring the causes for the communicator's *message*. In his ANOVA account of persuasion, Kelley (1967) used the term "entity" attribution to refer to perceivers' tendencies to attribute the communicator's message to the environment under discussion. This attribution (which was maximized by a pattern of high consensus, consistency, and distinctiveness) increased persuasiveness because it implied that the communicator's message provided a truthful description of external reality. And in his subsequent multiple plausible causes framework [which features the augmentation and discounting principles (Kelley 1972)], perceivers were viewed as scanning available information for possible causes of the communicator's message and taking into account whether there were one or more causes that seemed plausible and whether these causes would be facilitative or inhibitory in relation to the position stated in the message.

The implications for persuasion of Kelley's multiple plausible causes framework have been developed and successfully tested in several experiments by Eagly and her colleagues (see Eagly et al 1981). Attesting to the greater viability of their perspective, which focuses on attributions about message validity, the Eagly et al research has shown that inferences about communicators' dispositions bear, at best, an indirect relation to persuasion. Regarding Kelley's ANOVA model, Eagly & Chaiken (1984) noted that it has received only limited testing in social influence settings despite its considerable explanatory power. In spelling out the theory's relevance, these authors argued that even in settings that do not provide all information necessary for building the complete Persons X Occasions X Entities matrix, the theory remains useful since various cues in such settings may enable perceivers to make reasonable guesses about how such a matrix might be completed (see also Orvis et al 1975). As noted earlier, for example, Maass & Clark (1984) do not consider distinctiveness information because most experiments deal with only one entity or opinion topic. Yet it is possible that information relevant to this dimension might sometimes stem from other cues, such as the minority's claim that their position was distinctive to the issue under discussion (see Eagly & Chaiken 1984).

Researchers have much to gain by exploring the utility of attribution theory. Nevertheless, as discussed below, attributional reasoning is not the only mode of processing that occurs in group influence settings. Further, current analyses would have to be expanded in order to capture the unique complexities of many of these settings where, for example, perceivers may often be faced with the simultaneous task of inferring the causes of both the minority's and majority's message. Moreover, because attributional approaches assume that perceivers are oriented toward maximizing the validity of their opinions (see Kelley 1967, Eagly & Chaiken 1984), unless informed by other perspectives, such approaches may have limited utility in settings (see below) in which motives such as social approval are paramount.

Minority Versus Majority Influence: Dual Process Views

Building on his earlier theorizing, Moscovici (1980, 1985a) has argued that minority and majority influence are qualitatively different. Majorities instigate a "comparison" process in which the individual's attention focuses on the majority while minorities, if consistent, induce a "validation" process in which the individual's attention focuses more on the stimulus or topic under discussion. These processing differences, which resemble the peripheral-systematic distinction, lead to the prediction that minority influence will be deeper and more enduring. In addition, motivational forces conspire to encourage public agreement with the majority (to gain social approval) and public disagreement with the minority [to avoid rejection and, perhaps, viewing the self as an outgroup member (Mugny 1982)]. Thus, Moscovici concludes that majorities induce "compliance" in which change is publicly expressed but tends to remain only at a "manifest," direct level, whereas minorities induce "conversion" in which change occurs at a "latent," indirect level.

The compliance-conversion distinction embraces the traditional distinction between surface compliance and private acceptance (Kelman 1961). However, Moscovici's notion of "latent" influence, and no doubt his recognition that conformity can produce genuine opinion change (e.g. Insko et al 1983, 1985; Jennings & George 1984; see also Allen 1965, 1975) led him to a broader distinction. In essence, even when majorities induce genuine change, this change should be ephemeral and detectable only on (public or private) measures that relate directly to the issue under discussion. In contrast, minority-induced changes should be more detectable at the private and latent level.

The major research strategy for evaluating this dual process model has involved comparing majority and minority sources to see if they affect differential amounts of public versus private influence, direct versus indirect influence, or differential levels of persistence. Our reading of this research leads to the following observations. Majority influence does seem to be greater than minority influence on public measures (e.g. Mugny 1976, Maass & Clark 1983). And though it often occurs publicly and not privately (e.g. Moscovici & Lage 1976), majority influence is not restricted entirely to the public level since majority source effects are sometimes found on private direct measures (e.g. Wolf 1985) and occasionally on private indirect measures (e.g. Mugny 1984, Mackie 1985). Minority influence, on the other hand, is rarely manifested publicly but is observed with some regularity on private, direct measures of acceptance (e.g. Nemeth & Wachtler 1974, Wolf 1979, Maass & Clark 1983) and often [but not always (Wolf 1985)] on private, indirect measures (e.g. Wolf 1979, Papastamous 1983, Aebischer et al 1984). On the differential persistence issue, the results are equivocal, with one study (Moscovici et al, reported in Moscovici 1980) reporting greater persistence for minority sources and another (Mackie 1985) giving the edge to majority sources.

While this research generally supports dual process expectations, more is needed, particularly regarding latent influence. Different researchers have operationalized this construct in different ways (e.g. Aebischer et al 1984, Wolf 1985), and the degree to which these operationalizations tap one construct is not yet clear (see Wolf 1986). More research is also needed on the understudied persistence issue and perhaps on the additional hypothesis (suggested by research on systematic processing) that attitudes induced by minority, sources might be more predictive of subsequent behavior.

As suggested by current persuasion research, a second strategy for evaluating the dual process model would be to track the cognitive processes that underlie minority versus majority influence. Although only a handful of such results are available, this strategy promises to become a growing trend among researchers. Tesser et al (1983) examined how much attention subjects paid to stimuli (noises) they were asked to judge after learning about the judgments of either one or three ostensibly present other subjects. Consistent with Moscovici's validation process, subjects in the minority (vs majority) conditions evidenced marginally greater attention to the experimental stimuli. Supplementary analyses, however, led to the more refined observation that attention was bimodal in the majority conditions, with some subjects paying little attention to the stimuli (as Moscovici would predict) and others paying much attention (see also Campbell et al 1986).

Consistent with the idea that individuals more carefully process information in the minority paradigm, Moscovici et al (reported in Moscovici 1980) found that subjects recalled more of a persuasive message when it stemmed from a minority (vs majority) source. Nevertheless, three experiments that have assessed cognitive responding have yielded equivocal results (Maass & Clark 1983, Exp. 2; Mackie 1985, Exp. 1 and 2). In these studies, subjects were simultaneously exposed to messages from majority and minority sources [e.g. pro vs con gay rights (Maass & Clark 1983)] and listed their thoughts about "both the majority and minority position" (Maass & Clark 1983) or their "feelings and reactions to the discussion" (Mackie 1985). Subsequently, these thoughts were classified as pertaining to either the majority's or minority's position and as favorable or unfavorable to that position. Although some significant results were obtained, none of the three studies found that subjects generated more message/issue relevant thoughts about the minority's position. Because of their within-subjects designs, however, while these studies are revealing about the favorability and *target* of subjects' thought (i.e. minority vs majority) they do not directly address the question of whether minorities (vs majorities) *stimulate* greater or lesser amounts of thinking (e.g. even if minority sources did instigate greater issue-relevant thinking, such thinking could be targeted toward the minority's message, the majority's, or the issue more generally). To obtain clearer information on this issue, future research should turn to between-subjects designs in which subjects are exposed to messages from either majority or minority sources. In addition, we urge researchers to appreciate both the richness and problems of thought-listing tasks (see Miller & Colman 1981, Eagly & Chaiken 1984). Subsequent research could employ more elaborate coding schemes that more fully captured the nuances of Moscovici's theorizing [e.g. by coding for both message-oriented and source-oriented thoughts (see Chaiken & Eagly 1983)] and should avoid thought-listing directions (e.g. Maass & Clark 1983) that may place demands on subjects to list only one type of thought.

MINORITIES INDUCE DIVERGENT THINKING   Other evidence bearing on the dual-process perspective stems from Nemeth's (1985, 1986a,b) research on group problem solving. Although Nemeth's theoretical view is similar to Moscovici's in some respects, there are important differences.

Like Moscovici, Nemeth asserts that in majority influence settings, attention and thought focuses on the majority's position. However, while Moscovici elaborated little on this comparison process, Nemeth contends that the stressfulness of such situations (e.g. Nemeth 1976) and perhaps other factors [e.g. an assumption that the majority is correct (see Chaiken 1986b, Cialdini 1986, and Axsom et al 1987 for discussions of the "consensus" and "social validation" heuristics)], leads to superficial processing where people's attention and thought converge on the majority's stated position and does not extend to a full consideration of the issue. In contrast, minority sources are postulated to stimulate a greater amount of thinking, and this thinking tends to be more divergent.

For Nemeth, the consequences of these postulated processing differences are much broader than those implied by Moscovici's model which deals primarily with movement toward the specific positions advocated by majority and minority sources. In contrast to this "prevailing" notion of influence, which she aligns more with majorities, Nemeth argues that the unique social influence value of minorities derives from their stimulating the sort of thinking that leads to creative, high quality decisions and judgments.

Support for Nemeth's views come from a series of studies on group problem solving (Nemeth & Wachtler 1983, Nemeth & Kwan 1985, 1986).

For example, Nemeth and Wachtler (1983) asked subjects to detect "standard" figures that were embedded in one or more of six "comparison" figures. On each trial, the standard was easily seen in one comparison but not in the remaining five. Subjects made their judgments in groups of six in which either 2 or 4 confederates claimed to see the standard in both the easy comparison figure (a correct response) and in one other figure (a correct or incorrect response, depending on condition). Consistent with much past research, majorities (regardless of their correctness) elicited greater compliance. More important, however, subjects exposed to minority (vs majority) sources were more likely to find novel correct solutions. Similar findings have been obtained in other studies in this series (see Nemeth 1986a,b) and compatible results suggesting that minorities stimulate high quality decision making were obtained in a study on jury deliberation (Cowan et al 1984).

MULTIPLE MOTIVES AND PROCESSING MODES   The dual-process perspective implicates two motivational bases for majority influence [normative and informational (Deutsch & Gerard 1955)] and one for minority influence (informational). Moreover, even when motivational base is held constant at the informational level, this perspective views majorities as inducing temporary (albeit genuine) opinion shifts while minorities are seen as effecting deeper, more permanent changes. In essence the dual-process perspective associates peripheral attitude change mechanisms with majority influence and systematic mechanisms with minority influence. Yet this "two-process" account is probably an overly simplistic view of the variety of motives and modes of processing that operate in group influence settings.

Regarding motivation, Kelman's (1961) distinctions between compliance and identification (two normative modes) and internalization (an informational mode) indicate that three (vs two) motives often spur agreement with majorities: the desire to gain/avoid social approval/disapproval (compliance), the desire to identify with liked others by genuinely adopting their opinions (identification), and the desire to hold valid opinions (internalization). Although creative researchers might conjure up situations in which the former two motives impact on minority influence, it seems likely that the prime basis for minority influence is informational.

On the cognitive front, we suggest the following complications. First, although it may often be true that the genuine opinion changes induced by majorities are fleeting because they reflect some peripheral attitude change route such as source identification (Petty & Cacioppo 1981) or heuristic processing (Chaiken 1986b, Cialdini 1986), persuasion research suggests that this view is too limited. For example, because high issue-involvement often facilitates central processing, individuals confronted with majorities advocating positions on issues of considerable personal relevance may—more than

Moscovici or Nemeth predict—engage in the kind of message- and issue-relevant thinking that often confers greater persistence. Similarly, we might predict that high need for cognition individuals (Cacioppo et al 1983) will process a majority's message just as systematically as they might process a minority's message. Also, communicating public agreement with majorities may ultimately result in internalized attitude change because of motivational forces such as dissonance reduction (see Himmelfarb & Eagly 1974, Maass & Clark 1984) or because of the delayed cognitive consequences that such goal-directed social communications often have for communicators' own attitudes (e.g. Higgins & McCann 1984; see Attitude-behavior section). Further, the genuine, albeit somewhat shallow (Kelman 1961) attitude change that might result from individuals' desires to identify with an attractive majority group may well persist if (unlike most laboratory experiments) the group continues to be a source of social identity for the individual as time goes by (see Levine & Moreland 1985).

Paralleling persuasion research, across both majority and minority settings at least three processing modes are implicated: heuristic processing, attributional reasoning, and message- and issue-relevant thinking. As discussed earlier (see Persuasion section), researchers still lack a thorough understanding of when these modes [and perhaps more sophisticated ones such as divergent thinking (Nemeth 1986a)] operate and how they may impact upon one another. Nevertheless, at the mode of processing level, *multiple* cognitive processes are likely to underlie both majority and minority influence.

Minority Versus Majority Influence: A Unitary View

Several mathematically formulated social influence models pose an apparent challenge to the dual process perspective. Most notably, both social impact theory (Latané 1981, Latané & Wolf 1981) and Tanford & Penrod's (1984) social influence model treat majority and minority influence within a common theoretical framework and view both influence forms as part of a single process.

Latané's (1981, Latané & Wolf 1981, Wolf & Latané 1985, Wolf 1986) social impact theory asserts that the degree to which individuals are influenced is a multiplicative function of the number of sources, their strength (e.g. expertise), and their immediacy (e.g. proximity). The latter two factors are the theory's vehicle for representing important distal influence variables [e.g. behavioral style and group cohesiveness (see Wolf 1986)]. Nevertheless, with few exceptions (e.g. Wolf & Latané 1983, Wolf 1985), most tests of the theory's predictive power in relation to majority and minority situations have focused on the group size factor (Latané & Wolf 1981, Tanford & Penrod 1984; see also Mullen 1985, 1986 and Jackson 1986 for discussions of research findings regarding strength and immediacy). Social impact theory assumes that a negatively accelerating positive power function relates group size to observed influence; the first source exerts the greatest impact and each additional source a progressively smaller impact. Latane & Wolf (1981) fit power functions to a handful of conformity and minority influence studies in which number of influence sources had been manipulated and found that their model was able to account for a substantial portion of influence variance in both domains.

Tanford & Penrod (1984) have developed a more elaborate Social Influence Model (SIM) which differs from social impact theory (SIT) in some respects yet still focuses primarily on (majority and minority) group size. The most important difference between models is that, in contrast to SIT's group size function, the SIM posits an S-shaped "Gompertz" growth function; whereas the second and third influence sources are expected to exert a greater impact than the first, after this (inflection) point, each additional source exerts a progressively lesser impact. Other notable differences include the fact that the SIM features parameters such as individual differences in persuasibility, type of task and response mode, and source consistency that SIT either does not address or represents via its strength and immediacy variables (for more detailed comparisons, see Tanford & Penrod 1984 and Wolf 1986). On the basis of a meta-analysis of a large number of studies on conformity, minority influence, and deviate rejection, Tanford and Penrod found that the SIM provided a somewhat better fit to existing data than did SIT. More important, however, regression analyses indicated that the amount of influence observed in these studies was largely a function of the number of influence sources and targets. Although the finding that power lies primarily in numbers may not be worldshaking, the fact that group size (transformed by the growth function) accounted for 51% of the variance in influenceability (regardless of whether it was induced by majority or minority sources) is impressive, considering that the second most important predictor of influence, source consistency, accounted for only 10% of the variance and several other variables (e.g. public vs private response mode) did not significantly predict influence. It should be noted, however, that the issue of whether group size interacts with variables such as consistency or response mode was not addressed by Tanford and Penrod, who included no relevant interaction terms in their regression analyses.

On the basis of these results, Tanford & Penrod (1984) concluded that majority and minority influence are part of a "single process" (p. 221), a view shared by Latane and Wolf (e.g. Wolf & Latane 1985), who claim further that the differences between majority and minority influence are merely quantitative. On the surface, such claims seem odd since both of these models are silent with respect to underlying psychological mechanisms (see below). In contrast to these models, Mullen's (1983) recent model of group size does attempt a more process-oriented account of influence. In brief, Mullen argues that in groups with two or more subgroups, individuals' levels of self-attention increase as the relative size of their subgroup decreases and that increased self-attention heightens motivation to match salient behavioral standards (see Carver & Scheier 1981). Thus, in conformity situations (in which the majority's position is assumed to be the standard), Mullen argues and provides evidence that self-attention and conformity covary and that both increase with majority size. Although promising, Mullen's model has not yet been applied to minority influence and in such settings the terms behavioral standard (defined presently as "group norm") and self-attention [which currently refers to public rather than private self-attention (see Carver & Scheier 1981)] will probably require broadening.

Single Versus Dual Process Views: A Resolution and Conclusions

For arguments favoring the dual process over single process viewpoint and vice versa, we refer readers to articles by proponents of each (Maass & Clark 1984, Wolf 1986; also see Doms 1984). Here we offer our own simple-minded resolution: Both camps have been right and both have been wrong.

Regarding the number of processes issue, it appears that single process and dual process theorists have been using the same term differently. Specifically, Latane and Wolf's and Tanford and Penrod's use of "process" seems to refer to the predictive power of their models and/or to their models' functional principles (e.g. SIT's multiplicative function). In contrast, dual process theorists seem to use this term in its more usual sense to refer to psychological processes such as attributional reasoning or issue-relevant thinking. While we prefer the latter usage, it may well be the case, as the single process theorists contend, that the influence impact of both majorities and minorities can be predicted accurately by the equations of social impact theory and the social influence model. However, in contrast to the single or two- process view, our earlier discussion of multiple motives and processing modes gave away our conclusion that multiple psychological processes are operative in both majority and minority influence settings.

A related issue concerns whether differences between majority and minority influence are of a qualitative nature, as dual-process theorists see it (e.g. Moscovici 1980, 1985b, Nemeth 1986a), or merely quantitative, as single process theorists have argued (e.g. Wolf & Latane 1985). Here again it seems that both positions bear some truth. If the term qualitatively different is reserved for attitude change processes that reflect different motivational goals (e.g. seeking social approval versus valid opinions), we think there is merit to the view that some processes operative in majority settings (e.g. compliance, identification) are qualitatively different from those operating in minority settings (e.g. causal reasoning about message validity). Yet, when similar motivational goals (e.g. seeking veridical opinions) underlie both forms of influence, the qualitative-quantitative distinction loses meaning. As we argued earlier, although current dual-process theorizing aligns systematic information processing primarily with minority influence, such processing may well occur in majority settings for certain people (e.g. those high in need for cognition) or under certain circumstances (e.g. involving issues). Similarly, although attributional reasoning has been discussed almost exclusively in the context of minority influence, there is little doubt that this mode of processing also occurs in majority influence settings (e.g. Ross et al 1976). Whether these modes occur to a greater or lesser degree in majority versus minority settings would seem to be primarily a quantitative issue.

In summary, differences between majority and minority influence may sometimes be qualitative (when different motives operate) and other times quantitative (when similar motives operate). As noted in relation to persuasion, group influence researchers need to attain a better understanding of the motives or goals that are aroused in group influence settings [and also individual differences in motivational goals (e.g. Sorrentino & Hancock 1986)], how these goals impact on modes of processing, and how different modes of processing may interact.

We expect that the information processing trend in recent minority influence research will continue and that criticisms of this area's lack of process-oriented methodologies (Maass & Clark 1984) will become obsolete. Nevertheless, in pursuing cognitive accounts of minority (and majority) influence, researchers must not lose sight of important motivational issues by focusing excessively on cognition or by utilizing paradigms that are impoverished in terms of their motivational aspects. As others (e.g. Maass & Clark 1984, Levine & Moreland 1985) have noted, much research on minority and majority influence has studied "minimal" groups with no history and no future. In reading the literature we came across still other studies in which "majority" and "minority" sources were neither physically nor temporally present in the influence setting (e.g. Maass & Clark 1983, Mackie 1985). Although we do not minimize its difficulties, the investigation of real groups with real histories and futures interacting over a length of time may be required to fully understand the complexities of both social control and innovation (see Allen 1985, Levine & Moreland 1985). Finally, although central to much of Moscovici's (1976) initial theorizing, few investigators have studied the impact of social (vs numerical) minorities on innovation (e.g. Maass et al 1982, Kitayama 1983, Aebischer et al 1984). We are hopeful that the next few years will reveal increased attention to this important question as well as increased attention to relevant group process perspectives such as social categorization (Tajfel 1978, Turner 1982, 1985).

CONCLUSION

In the last review, Cooper & Croyle (1984) predicted that the dominance of cognitive approaches in the attitudes area would begin to recede as motivational issues returned to the forefront. Although progress on the motivational front cannot be described as rampant, there are healthy signs in the literature that motivational and affective issues, once a central focus of theorizing and research in the area, are again being raised. Such signs are evident, for example, in recent conceptualizations of attitudes which attempt to distinguish affect, or emotion, from "mere" evaluation (e.g. Breckler 1984, Zanna & Rempel 1986), in research that has attempted to link values to attitudes (e.g. symbolic racism research), in discussions of the conditions under which people are likely to form attitudes (Fazio 1986b), in the renewed empirical interest in attitude functions (e.g. Snyder & DeBono 1986), and in persuasion and group influence researchers' growing awareness that information processing in influence settings occurs in the service of motivational goals (e.g. Eagly & Chaiken 1984, Tetlock 1985, Howard-Pitney et al 1986, Nemeth 1986a).

The fact that attitude researchers are beginning to readdress fundamental issues of motivation does not mean, however, that interest in cognition is waning. Rather, as in other areas of social psychology (see Sorrentino & Higgins 1986), the theme we see emerging in the literature is that cognition cannot be studied in isolation from motivation and that a firm and explicit knowledge of the latter is a prerequisite for fully understanding the cognitive processes underlying attitude organization, formation, and change. We are hopeful that the next several years will reveal significant progress toward this theme's realization and greater articulation.

Our review has paid little attention to methodological issues. With the exception of some research on attitude-behavior relations, which has been conducted in field settings, most research on attitudes is still heavily laboratory-oriented and reliant on the college student as research subject. The attitudes area, like social psychology in general, has clearly survived earlier critiques (e.g. Elms 1975) that these features limited the validity of experimentation. Yet the extent to which research has actually changed very much is debatable. In fact, Sears (1986) claims that social psychological research has steadily increased its reliance on college students and laboratory settings.

Although we do not wish to argue that another "crisis" is imminent and that laboratory experimentation with college subjects be abandoned, researchers do need to be more sensitive to its liabilities. For example, the verbally skilled nature of this subject population in combination with the verbal environment of many laboratory settings and their implicit demands for high attention and "impartial" processing (Frey 1986) may have contributed to researchers' underestimating the importance of reception processes in persuasion (Eagly & Chaiken 1984) and drawing pessimistic conclusions about phenomena such as selective exposure and selective retention (Chaiken 1984, Frey 1986). In addition to these liabilities, Sears (1986), Eagly (1986, 1987), and Levine & Moreland (1985) have suggested that the typical laboratory experiment, because of its impoverished and somewhat detached social environment, may also underestimate the extent to which group norms, social roles, and social identity affect social influence. While we feel that many of these liabilities could be addressed creatively within laboratory settings (see Levine & Moreland 1985), more research on social influence in natural settings (e.g. Cialdini 1986) and on what people report about naturalistic social influence strategies (e.g. Offermann & Schrier 1985, Rule et al 1985, Steffen & Eagly 1985, Howard et al 1986, Rule & Bisanz 1986) would be desirable complements to our laboratory-based knowledge of attitudes.

Our impression of recent research is a relatively optimistic one. Rather than appearing as collections of diverse findings unified only by labels (e.g. persuasion, attitude-behavior relations), some of the subareas we have reviewed reveal a considerable amount of conceptual coherence. When consistency of findings is evaluated only at the phenotypic level of the impact of particular independent variables (e.g. issue-involvement or distraction in persuasion, direct experience or thinking about one's attitudes in the attitude-behavior area), this coherence may not seem so evident. Yet, when viewed at the genotypic level of the impact of the cognitive processes (e.g. message- and issue-relevant thinking in persuasion; attitude accessibility in the attitude-behavior area) that are often influenced by such independent variables (see Eagly & Chaiken 1984), the case for conceptual coherence improves considerably. In this regard, we should also note that although meta-analytic review techniques have often been applied primarily at the phenotypic level (e.g. Tanford & Penrod 1984, Roberts 1985), such techniques are beginning to be used more frequently to test mediational hypotheses and to examine the consistency of research findings at the genotypic level (see, for example, Mullen 1985, Eagly 1987, Isenberg 1986). The continued development of these quantitative reviewing procedures (e.g. Hedges & Olkin 1985) and the likelihood that they will be increasingly applied to attitudinal phenomena should prove to be a boon to subsequent reviewers of the field.

ACKNOWLEDGMENTS

Preparation of this chapter was facilitated by a grant to the senior author from the National Science Foundation (BNS-8309159) and funds from the New York University Psychology Department. We are grateful to the following persons for their comments on a preliminary draft of the chapter: Danny Axsom, John Bargh, Gene Borgida, Alice Eagly, Russ Fazio, Tory Higgins, Beth Meyerowitz, Charlan Nemeth, Richard Petty, Tim Wilson, Wendy Wood, and Mark Zanna.

Literature Cited

Abelson, R. P. 1982. Three modes of attitude-behavior consistency. See Zanna et al 1982, pp. 131–46

Abelson, R. P. 1986. Beliefs are possessions. *J. Theory Soc. Behav.* In press

Adorno, T. W., Frenkel-Brunswik, E., Levinson, D. J., Sanford, R. N. 1950. *The Authoritarian Personality.* New York: Harper

Aebischer, V., Hewstone, M., Henderson, M. 1984. Minority influence and musical preference: Innovation by conversion not coercion. *Eur. J. Soc. Psychol.* 14:23–33

Ajzen, I. 1984. Attitudes. In *Wiley Encyclopedia of Psychology,* ed. R. J. Corsini, 1:99–100. New York: Wiley

Ajzen, I. 1985. From intentions to actions: A theory of planned behavior. In *Action-Control: From Cognition to Behavior,* ed. J. Kuhl, J. Beckmann, pp. 11–39. Heidelberg:Springer.

Ajzen, I., Fishbein, M. 1980. *Understanding Attitudes and Predicting Social Behavior.* Englewood Cliffs, NJ: Prentice-Hall. 278 pp.

Ajzen, I., Madden, T. J. 1986. Prediction of goal-directed behavior: The role of intention, perceived control, and prior behavior. *J. Exp. Soc. Psychol.* In press

Allen, V. L. 1965. Situational factors in conformity. *Adv. Exp. Soc. Psychol.* 2:133–75

Allen, V. L. 1975. Social support for nonconformity. *Adv. Exp. Soc. Psychol.* 8:1–43

Allen, V. L. 1985. Infra-group, intra-group and inter-group: Construing levels of organization in social influence. See Moscovici et al 1985

Alwitt, L. F., Mitchell, A. A., eds. 1985. *Psychological Processes and Advertising Effects.* Hillsdale, NJ: Erlbaum. 305 pp.

Anderson, C. A. 1983. Abstract and concrete data in the perseverance of social theories: When weak data lead to unshakeable beliefs. *J. Exp. Soc. Psychol.* 19:93–108

Anderson, C. A., New, B. L., Speer, J. R. 1985. Argument availability as a mediator of social theory perseverance. *Soc. Cognit.* 3:235–49

Anderson, N. H. 1981. *Foundations of Information Integration Theory.* New York: Academic

Anderson, N. H., Hubert, S. 1963. Effects of concomitant verbal recall on order effects in personality impression formation. *J. Verb. Learn. Verb. Behav.* 2:379–91

Asch, S. E. 1951. Effects of group pressure upon the modification and distortion of judgments. In *Groups, Leadership and Men,* ed. H. Guetzkow. Pittsburgh: Carnegie Press

Axsom, D., Yates, S., Chaiken, S. 1987. *Audience response as a heuristic cue in persuasion. J. Pers. Soc. Psychol.* In press

Bagozzi, R. P. 1978. The construct validity of the affective, behavioral, and cognitive components of attitude by analysis of covariance structures. *Multivar. Behav. Res.* 13:9–31

Bagozzi, R. P. 1984. Expectancy-value attitude models: An analysis of critical theoretical issues. *Int. J. Res. Market.* 1:295–310

Bagozzi, R. P. 1985. Expectancy-value attitude models: An analysis of critical measurement issues. *Int. J. Res. Market.* 2:43–60

Bagozzi, R. P. 1986. Attitude formation under the theory of reasoned action and a purposeful behavior reformulation. *Br. J. Soc. Psychol.* 25:95–107

Bagozzi, R. P., Burnkrant, R. E. 1979. Attitude organization and the attitude-behavior relationship. *J. Pers. Soc. Psychol.* 37:913–29

Bagozzi, R. P., Burnkrant, R. E. 1985. Attitude organization and the attitude-behavior relation: A reply to Dillon and Kumar. *J. Pers. Soc. Psychol.* 49:47–57

Bagozzi, R. P., Schnedlitz, P. 1985. Social contingencies in the attitude model: A test of certain interaction hypotheses. *Soc. Psychol. Q.* 48:366–73

Bagozzi, R. P., Warshaw, P. R. 1986. A theory of goal directed behaviors and outcomes. Univ. Mich. Unpublished ms

Ball-Rokeach, S. J., Rokeach, M., Grube, J. W. 1984. *The Great American Values Test: Influencing Behavior and Belief through Television.* New York: Free Press

Bandura, A. 1977. Self-efficacy: Toward a unifying theory of behavioral change. *Psychol. Rev.* 84:191–215

Bargh, J. A. 1984. Automatic and conscious processing of social information. In *Handbook of Social Cognition,* ed. R. S. Wyer,

Jr., T. K. Srull, 3:1–43. Hillsdale, NJ: Erlbaum

Bargh, J. A., Pietromonaco, P. 1982. Automatic information processing and social perception: The influence of trait information presented outside of conscious awareness on impression formation. J. Pers. Soc. Psychol. 43:437–49

Bargh, J. A., Thein, R. D. 1985. Individual construct accessibility, person memory, and the recall-judgment link: The case of information overload. J. Pers. Soc. Psychol. 49:1129–46

Bar-Tal, D., Kruglanski, A. W., eds. 1986. Social Psychology of Knowledge. New York: Cambridge Univ. Press. In press

Batra, R., Ray, M. L. 1985. How advertising works at contact. See Alwitt & Mitchell 1985, pp. 13–43

Batson, C. D. 1975. Attribution as a mediator of bias in helping. J. Pers. Soc. Psychol. 32:455–66

Baumeister, R. F., Tice, D. M. 1984. Role of self-presentation and choice in cognitive dissonance under forced compliance: Necessary or sufficient causes? J. Pers. Soc. Psychol. 46:5–13

Baumgardner, M. H., Leippe, M. R., Ronis, D. L., Greenwald, A. G. 1983. In search of reliable persuasion effects: II. Associative interference and persistence of persuasion in a message-dense environment. J. Pers. Soc. Psychol. 45:524–37

Bem, D. J. 1972. Self-perception theory. Adv. Exp. Soc. Psychol. 6:1–62

Black, J. S., Stern, P. C., Elworth, J. T. 1985. Personal and contextual influences on household energy adaptations. J. Appl. Psychol. 70:3–21

Bobo, L. 1983. Whites' opposition to busing: Symbolic racism or realistic group conflict? J. Pers. Soc. Psychol. 45:1196–1210

Borgida, E., Howard-Pitney, B. 1983. Personal involvement and the robustness of perceptual salience effects. J. Pers. Soc. Psychol. 45:560–70

Bothwell, R. K., Brigham, J. C. 1983. Selective evaluation and recall during the 1980 Reagan-Carter debate. J. Appl. Soc. Psychol. 13:427–42

Braithwaite, V. A., Law, H. G. 1985. Structure of human values: Testing the adequacy of the Rokeach value survey. J. Pers. Soc. Psychol. 49:250–63

Bray, R. M., Johnson, D., Chilstrom, J. T. 1982. Social influence by group members with minority opinions: A comparison of Hollander and Moscovici. J. Pers. Soc. Psychol. 43:78–88

Breckler, S. J. 1983. Validation of affect, behavior, and cognition as distinct components of attitude. PhD thesis. Ohio State Univ., Columbus

Breckler, S. J. 1984. Empirical validation of affect, behavior, and cognition as distinct components of attitude. J. Pers. Soc. Psychol. 47:1191–1205

Brock, T. C., Shavitt, S. 1983. Cognitive-response analysis in advertising. In Advertising and Consumer Psychology, ed. L. Percy, A. G. Woodside, pp. 91–116. Lexington, MA/Toronto: D. C. Heath

Budd, R., Spencer, C. 1984. Latitude of rejection, centrality and certainty: Variables affecting the relationship between attitudes, norms and behavioural intentions. Br. J. Soc. Psychol. 23:1–8

Burnkrant, R. E., Howard, D. J. 1984. Effects of the use of introductory rhetorical questions versus statements on information processing. J. Pers. Soc. Psychol. 47:1218–30

Burnstein, E., Schul, Y. 1983. The informational basis of social judgments: Memory for integrated and nonintegrated trait descriptions. J. Exp. Soc. Psychol. 19:49–57

Cacioppo, J. T., Harkins, S. G., Petty, R. E. 1981. The nature of attitudes and cognitive responses and their relationships to behavior. See Petty et al 1981b, pp. 31–54

Cacioppo, J. T., Petty, R. E. 1979. Effects of message repetition and position on cognitive response, recall and persuasion. J. Pers. Soc. Psychol. 37:97–109

Cacioppo, J. T., Petty, R. E. 1984. The need for cognition: Relationship to attitudinal processes. In Social Perception in Clinical and Counseling Psychology, ed. R. P. McGlynn, J. E. Maddux, C. D. Stoltenberg, J. H. Harvey, pp. 113–39. Lubbock: Texas Tech Press

Cacioppo, J. T., Petty, R. E. 1985. Central and peripheral routes to persuasion: The role of message repetition. See Alwitt & Mitchell 1985, pp. 91–111

Cacioppo, J. T., Petty, R. E. 1986. Stalking rudimentary processes of social influence: A psychophysiological approach. See Zanna et al 1986

Cacioppo, J. T., Petty, R. E., Morris, K. J. 1983. Effects of need for cognition on message evaluation, recall, and persuasion. J. Pers. Soc. Psychol. 45:805–18

Cacioppo, J. T., Petty, R. E., Sidera, J. A. 1982. The effects of a salient self-schema on the evaluation of proattitudinal editorials: Top-down versus bottom-up message processing. J. Exp. Soc. Psychol. 18:324–38

Campbell, J. D., Tesser, A., Fairey, P. J. 1986. Conformity and attention to the stimulus: Some temporal and contextual dynamics. J. Pers. Soc. Psychol. 51:315–24

Carlston, D. E., Skowronski, J. J. 1986. Trait memory and behavior memory: The effects of alternative pathways on impression judgment response times. *J. Pers. Soc. Psychol.* 50:5–13

Carver, C. S., Scheier, M. F. 1981. *Attention and Self-regulation: A Control-Theory Approach to Human Behavior.* New York: Springer-Verlag

Chaffee, S. H., Miyo, Y. 1983. Selective exposure and the reinforcement hypothesis: An intergenerational panel study of the 1980 presidential campaign. *Commun. Res.* 10:3–36

Chaiken, S. 1980. Heuristic versus systematic information processing and the use of source versus message cues in persuasion. *J. Pers. Soc. Psychol.* 39:752–66

Chaiken, S. 1982. *The heuristic/systematic processing distinction in persuasion.* Presented at Society Exp. Soc. Psychol., Nashville, IN

Chaiken, S. 1984. *Memory for attitudinally consistent versus inconsistent information.* Presented at Ann. Meet. Am. Psychol. Assoc., Toronto

Chaiken, S. 1986a. Physical appearance and social influence. In *Physical Appearance, Stigma, and Social Behavior: The Ontario Symposium,* ed. C. P. Herman, M. P. Zanna, E. T. Higgins, 3:143–77. Hillsdale, NJ: Erlbaum

Chaiken, S. 1986b. The heuristic model of persuasion. See Zanna et al 1986

Chaiken, S., Baldwin, M. W. 1981. Affective-cognitive consistency and the effect of salient behavioral information on the self-perception of attitudes. *J. Pers. Soc. Psychol.* 41:1–12

Chaiken, S., Eagly, A. H. 1976. Communication modality as a determinant of message persuasiveness and message comprehensibility. *J. Pers. Soc. Psychol.* 34:605–14

Chaiken, S., Eagly, A. H. 1983. Communication modality as a determinant of persuasion: The role of communicator salience. *J. Pers. Soc. Psychol.* 45:241–56

Chaiken, S., Yates, S. 1985. Affective-cognitive consistency and thought-induced attitude polarization. *J. Pers. Soc. Psychol.* 49:1470–81

Christie, R., Geis, F. L., eds. 1970. *Studies in Machiavellianism.* New York: Academic

Cialdini, R. B. 1986. Compliance principles of compliance professionals: Psychologists of necessity. See Zanna et al 1986

Cialdini, R. B., Petty, R. E., Caccioppo, J. T. 1981. Attitude and attitude change. *Ann. Rev. Psychol.* 32:357–404

Cooper, H. M., Rosenthal, R. 1980. Statistical versus traditional procedures for summarizing research findings. *Psychol. Bull.* 87:422–49

Cooper, J., Croyle, R. T. 1984. Attitudes and attitude change. *Ann. Rev. Psychol.* 35:395–426

Cooper, J., Fazio, R. H. 1984. A new look at dissonance theory. *Adv. Exp. Soc. Psychol.* 17:229–65

Cooper, J., Mackie, D. 1983. Cognitive dissonance in an intergroup context. *J. Pers. Soc. Psychol.* 44:536–44

Cotton, J. L. 1985. Cognitive dissonance in selective exposure. In *Selective Exposure to Communication,* ed. D. Zillman, J. Bryant, pp. 11–33. Hillsdale, NJ: Erlbaum. 251 pp.

Cowan, C., Thompson, W., Ellsworth, P. 1984. The effects of death qualification on jurors' predisposition to convict and on the quality of deliberation. *Law Hum. Behav.* 8:53–79

Crano, W. D., Sivacek, J. 1984. The influence of incentive-aroused ambivalence on overjustification effects in attitude change. *J. Exp. Soc. Psychol.* 20:137–58

Crocker, J., Hanna, D. B., Weber, R. 1983. Person memory and causal attributions. *J. Pers. Soc. Psychol.* 44:55–66

Crowne, D. P., Marlowe, D. 1964. *The Approval Motive: Studies in Evaluative Dependence.* New York: Wiley

Davidson, A. R., Morrison, D. M. 1983. Predicting contraceptive behavior from attitudes: A comparison of within- versus across-subjects procedures. *J. Pers. Soc. Psychol.* 45:997–1009

Davidson, A. R., Yantis, S., Norwood, M., Montano, D. E. 1985. Amount of information about the attitude object and attitude-behavior consistency. *J. Pers. Soc. Psychol.* 49:1184–98

Davis, D., Ostrom, T. M. 1984. Attitude measurement. See Ajzen 1984, pp. 97–99

Dawes, R. M., Smith, T. L. 1985. Attitude and opinion measurement. See Lindzey & Aronson 1985, 1:509–66

DeBono, K. 1986. Investigating the social adjustive and value expressive functions of attitudes: Implications for persuasion processes. *J. Pers. Soc. Psychol.* In press

Deutsch, M., Gerard, H. B. 1955. A study of normative and informational social influences upon individual judgment. *J. Abnorm. Soc. Psychol.* 51:629–36

Dillon, W. R., Kumar, A. 1985. Attitude organization and the attitude-behavior relation: A critique of Bagozzi and Burnkrant's reanalysis of Fishbein and Ajzen. *J. Pers. Soc. Psychol.* 49:33–46

Doms, M. 1984. The minority influence effect: An alternative approach. In *Current Issues in European Social Psychology,* ed. S. Moscovici, W. Doise, pp. 1–31. Cambridge: Cambridge Univ. Press

Drake, R. A., Judd, C. M. 1986. Extremity shifts on ideologically linked attitude issues: Further evidence for attitude structure. Univ. Colo. Unpublished ms

Dreben, E. K., Fiske, S. T., Hastie, R. 1979.

The independence of item and evaluative information: Impression and recall order effects in behavior-based impression formation. *J. Pers. Soc. Psychol.* 37:1758–68

Eagly, A. H. 1986. Social influence research: New approaches to enduring issues. See Zanna et al 1986

Eagly, A. H. 1987. *Sex Differences in Social Behavior: A Social-role Interpretation.* Hillsdale, NJ: Erlbaum. In press

Eagly, A. H., Chaiken, S. 1984. Cognitive theories of persuasion. *Adv. Exp. Soc. Psychol.* 17:268–359

Eagly, A. H., Chaiken, S., Wood, W. 1981. An attribution analysis of persuasion. In *New Directions in Attribution Research*, ed. J. H. Harvey, W. J. Ickes, R. F. Kidd, 3:37–62. Hillsdale, NJ: Erlbaum

Eagly, A. H., Himmelfarb, S. 1978. Attitudes and opinions. *Ann. Rev. Psychol.* 29:517–54

Elkin, R. A., Leippe, M. R. 1986. Physiological arousal dissonance, and attitude change: Evidence for a dissonance–arousal link and a "Don't remind me" effect. *J. Pers. Soc. Psychol.* 51:55–65

Ellsworth, P. C., Ross, L. 1983. Public opinion and capital punishment: A close examination of the views of abolitionists and retentionists. *Crime & Delinquency* 29:116–69

Elms, A. C. 1975. The crisis of confidence in social psychology. *Am. Psychol.* 30:967–76

Erber, R., Fiske, S. T. 1984. Outcome dependency and attention to inconsistent information. *J. Pers. Soc. Psychol.* 47:709–26

Fazio, R. H. 1986a. How do attitudes guide behavior? See Sorrentino & Higgins 1986

Fazio, R. H. 1986b. Self-perception theory: A current perspective. See Zanna et al 1986

Fazio, R. H., Chen, J., McDonel, E. C., Sherman, S. J. 1982. Attitude accessibility, attitude-behavior consistency, and the strength of the object-evaluation association. *J. Exp. Soc. Psychol.* 18:339–57

Fazio, R. H., Herr, P. M., Olney, T. J. 1984. Attitude accessibility following a self-perception process. *J. Pers. Soc. Psychol.* 47:277–86

Fazio, R. H., Powell, M. C., Herr, P. M. 1983. Toward a process model of the attitude-behavior relation: Accessing one's attitude upon mere observation of the attitude object. *J. Pers. Soc. Psychol.* 44:723–35

Fazio, R. H., Sanbonmatsu, D. M., Powell, M. C., Kardes, F. R. 1986. On the automatic activation of attitudes. *J. Pers. Soc. Psychol.* 50:229–38

Fazio, R. H., Williams, C. J. 1986. Attitude accessibility as a moderator of the attitude-perception and attitude-behavior relations:

An investigation of the 1984 presidential election. *J. Pers. Soc. Psychol.* In press

Fazio, R. H., Zanna, M. P. 1981. Direct experience and attitude-behavior consistency. *Adv. Exp. Soc. Psychol.* 14:161–202

Fazio, R. H., Zanna, M. P., Cooper, J. 1977. Dissonance and self-perception: An integrative view of each theory's proper domain of application. *J. Exp. Soc. Psychol.* 13:464–79

Feather, N. T. 1984. Protestant ethic, conservatism, and values. *J. Pers. Soc. Psychol.* 46:1132–41

Feather, N. T. 1985. Attitudes, values, and attributions: Explanations of unemployment. *J. Pers. Soc. Psychol.* 48:876–89

Festinger, L. 1957. *A Theory of Cognitive Dissonance.* Stanford, CA: Stanford Univ. Press

Fishbein, M., Ajzen, I. 1972. Attitudes and opinions. *Ann. Rev. Psychol.* 23:487–544

Fishbein, M., Ajzen, I. 1974. Attitudes toward objects as predictors of single and multiple behavioral criteria. *Psychol. Rev.* 81:59–74

Fishbein, M., Ajzen, I. 1975. *Belief, Attitude, Intention and Behavior: An Introduction to Theory and Research.* Reading, MA: Addison-Wesley. 578 pp.

Fishbein, M., Ajzen, I. 1981. Acceptance, yielding, and impact: Cognitive processes in persuasion. See Petty et al 1981b, pp. 339–59

Fishbein, M., Middlestadt, S. E., Chung, J. 1986. Predicting participation and choice among first time voters in U.S. partisan elections. In *Mass Media and Political Thoughts: An Information Processing Approach*, ed. S. Kraus, R. Perloff. New York: Sage. In press

Fisher, W. A. 1984. Predicting contraceptive behavior among university men: The role of emotions and behavioral intentions. *J. Appl. Soc. Psychol.* 14:104–23

Fiske, S. T., Kinder, D. R., Larter, W. M. 1983a. The novice and the expert: Knowledge-based strategies in political cognition. *J. Exp. Soc. Psychol.* 19:381–400

Fiske, S. T., Pratto, F., Pavelchak, M. A. 1983b. Citizens' images of nuclear war: Content and consequences. *J. Soc. Issues* 39:41–65

Fiske, S. T., Taylor, S. E. 1984. *Social Cognition.* Reading, MA: Addison-Wesley. 508 pp.

Fredricks, A. J., Dossett, D. L. 1983. Attitude-behavior relations: A comparison of the Fishbein-Ajzen and the Bentler-Speckart models. *J. Pers. Soc. Psychol.* 45:501–12

Freedman, J. L., Sears, D. O. 1965. Selective exposure. *Adv. Exp. Soc. Psychol.* 2:57–97

Frey, D. 1986. Recent research on selective

exposure to information. *Adv. Exp. Soc. Psychol.* 19:41–80

Frey, D., Rosch, M. 1984. Information seeking after decisions: The roles of novelty of information and decision reversibility. *Pers. Soc. Psychol. Bull.* 10:91–98

Frey, D., Stahlberg, D. 1986. Selection of information after receiving more or less reliable self-threatening information. *Pers. Soc. Psychol. Bull.* In press

Gerard, H. B., Orive, R. 1986. The dynamics of opinion formation. *Adv. Exp. Soc. Psychol.* 20: In press

Gibson, L. D. 1983. If the question is copy testing, the answer is . . . "Not Recall." *J. Advert. Res.* 23:39–46

Gilmore, R. F., Axsom, D., Chaiken, S. 1983. *Attitudinal qualities related to the attitude-memory relationship.* Presented at Ann. Meet. Am. Psychol. Assoc., Anaheim

Gordon, P. C., Holyoak, K. J. 1983. Implicit learning and generalization of the "Mere Exposure" effect. *J. Pers. Soc. Psychol.* 45:492–500

Gorsuch, R. L., Ortberg, J. 1983. Moral obligation and attitudes: Their relation to behavioral intentions. *J. Pers. Soc. Psychol.* 44:1025–28

Granberg, D., Brent, E. 1983. When prophecy bends: The preference-expectation link in U.S. presidential elections, 1952–1980. *J. Pers. Soc. Psychol.* 45:477–91

Greenwald, A. G. 1968. Cognitive learning, cognitive response to persuasion, and attitude change. In *Psychological Foundations of Attitudes*, ed. A. G. Greenwald, T. C. Brock, T. M. Ostrom, pp. 147–70. New York: Academic

Greenwald, A. G. 1975. Consequences of prejudice against the null hypothesis. *Psychol. Bull.* 82:1–20

Greenwald, A. G. 1982a. Ego task analysis: An integration of research on ego-involvement and self-awareness. In *Cognitive Social Psychology*, ed. A. H. Hastorf, A. M. Isen, pp. 109–47. New York: Elsevier/North Holland

Greenwald, A. G. 1982b. Is anyone in charge? Personalysis versus the principle of personal unity. In *Psychological Perspectives on the Self*, ed. J. Suls, 1:151–81. Hillsdale, NJ: Erlbaum

Greenwald, A. G., Breckler, S. J. 1984. To whom is the self presented? In *The Self and Social Life*, ed. B. R. Schlenker, pp. 126–45. New York: McGraw-Hill

Greenwald, A. G., Leavitt, C. 1984. Audience involvement in advertising: Four levels. *J. Consum. Res.* 11:581–92

Greenwald, A. G., Pratkanis, A. R. 1984. The self. See Wyer & Srull 1984, pp. 129–78

Greenwald, A. G., Pratkanis, A. R., Leippe, M. R., Baumgardner, M. H. 1986. Under

what conditions does theory obstruct research progress? *Psychol. Rev.* 93:216–29

Hannah, D. B., Sternthal, B. 1984. Detecting and explaining the sleeper effect. *J. Consum. Res.* 11:632–42

Harkins, S. G., Petty, R. E. 1983. Social context effects in persuasion: The effects of multiple sources and multiple targets. In *Basic Group Processes*, ed. P. Paulus. New York: Springer-Verlag

Harkness, A. R., DeBono, K. G., Borgida, E. 1985. Personal involvement and strategies for making contingency judgments: A stake in the dating game makes a difference. *J. Pers. Soc. Psychol.* 49:22–32

Hastie, R. 1981. Schematic principles in human memory. In *Social Cognition: The Ontario Symposium*, ed. E. T. Higgins, C. P. Herman, M. P. Zanna, 1:39–88. Hillsdale, NJ: Erlbaum

Hastie, R. 1984. Causes and effects of causal attribution. *J. Pers. Soc. Psychol.* 46:44–56

Hastie, R., Park, B. 1986. The relationship between memory and judgment depends on whether the judgment task is memory-based or on-line. *Psychol. Rev.* 93:258–68

Haugtvedt, C., Petty, R. E., Cacioppo, J. T. 1986. *Need for cognition and the use of peripheral persuasion cues.* Presented at Ann. Meet. Midwest. Psychol. Assoc., Chicago

Hedges, L. V., Olkin, I. 1985. *Statistical Methods for Meta-Analysis.* New York: Academic. 369 pp.

Heesacker, M., Petty, R. E., Cacioppo, J. T. 1983. Field dependence and attitude change: Source credibility can alter persuasion by affecting message-relevant thinking. *J. Pers.* 51:653–66

Herek, G. M. 1986a. The instrumentality of ideologies: Toward a neofunctional theory of attitudes and behavior. *J. Soc. Issues.* In press

Herek, G. M. 1986b. Can functions be measured? A new perspective on the functional approach to attitudes. Yale Univ. Unpublished ms

Higgins, E. T. 1981. The "Communication game": Implications for social cognition and persuasion. In *Social Cognition: The Ontario Symposium*, ed. E. T. Higgins, C. P. Herman, M. P. Zanna, 1:343–92. Hillsdale, NJ: Erlbaum

Higgins, E. T., Bargh, J. A. 1987. Social cognition and social perception. *Ann. Rev. Psychol.* 38:In press

Higgins, E. T., King, G. A., Mavin, G. H. 1982. Individual construct accessibility and subjective impressions and recall. *J. Pers. Soc. Psychol.* 43:35–47

Higgins, E. T., McCann, C. D. 1984. Social encoding and subsequent attitudes, impressions, and memory: "Context-driven" and motivational aspects of processing. *J. Pers. Soc. Psychol.* 47:26–39

Higgins, E. T., Rholes, W. S. 1978. "Saying is believing": Effects of message modification on memory and liking for the person described. *J. Exp. Soc. Psychol.* 14:363–78

Higgins, E. T., Rholes, W. S., Jones, C. R. 1977. Category accessibility and impression formation. *J. Exp. Soc. Psychol.* 13:141–54

Higgins, E. T., Stangor, C. 1986. Context-driven social judgment and memory: When "behavior engulfs the field" in reconstructive memory. See Bar-Tal & Kruglanski 1986

Himmelfarb, S., Eagly, A. H., eds. 1974. *Readings in Attitude Change.* New York: Wiley

Hinsz, V. B., Davis, J. H. 1984. Persuasive arguments theory, group polarization, and choice shifts. *Pers. Soc. Psychol. Bull.* 10:260–68

Hoogstraten, J., De Haan, W., Ter Horst, G. 1985. Stimulating the demand for dental care: An application of Ajzen and Fishbein's theory of reasoned action. *Eur. J. Soc. Psychol.* 15:401–14

Hooper, M. 1983. The motivational bases of political behavior: A new concept and measurement procedure. *Public Opin. Q.* 47:497–515

Howard, J. A., Blumstein, P., Schwartz, P. 1986. Sex, power, and influence tactics in intimate relationships. *J. Pers. Soc. Psychol.* 51:102–9

Howard-Pitney, B., Borgida, E., Omoto, A. M. 1986. Personal involvement: An examination of processing differences. *Soc. Cognit.* 4:39–57

Hymes, R. W. 1986. Political attitudes as social categories: A new look at selective memory. *J. Pers. Soc. Psychol.* 51:233–41

Insko, C. A. 1984. Balance theory, the Jordan paradigm, and the Wiest tetrahedron. *Adv. Exp. Soc. Psychol.* 18:89–140

Insko, C. A., Drenan, S., Solomon, M. R., Smith, R., Wade, T. J. 1983. Conformity as a function of the consistency of positive self-evaluation with being liked and being right. *J. Exp. Soc. Psychol.* 19:341–58

Insko, C. A., Smith, R. H., Alicke, M. D., Wade, J., Taylor, S. 1985. Conformity and group size: The concern with being right and the concern with being liked. *Pers. Soc. Psychol. Bull.* 11:41–50

Isenberg, D. J. 1986. Group polarization: A critical review and meta-analysis. *J. Pers. Soc. Psychol.* 50:1141–51

Jaccard, J., Becker, M. A. 1986. Attitudes and behavior: An information integration perspective. *J. Exp. Soc. Psychol.* In press

Jaccard, J., Sheng, D. 1984. A comparison of six methods for assessing the importance of perceived consequences in behavioral decisions: Applications from attitude research. *J. Exp. Soc. Psychol.* 20:1–28

Jackson, J. M. 1986. In defense of social impact theory: Comment on Mullen. *J. Pers. Soc. Psychol.* 50:511–13

Jamieson, D. W., Zanna, M. P. 1982. *Attitude change under threat of lie detection in the forced compliance paradigm: A dissonance or impression management phenomenon?* Presented at Ann. Meet. Am. Psychol. Assoc., Washington, DC

Jennings, L. B., George, S. G. 1984. Group-induced distortion of visually perceived linear extent: The Asch effect revisited. *Psychol. Rec.* 34:133–48

Jepson, C., Chaiken, S. 1986. *The effect of anxiety on systematic processing of persuasive communications.* Presented at Ann. Meet. Am. Psychol. Assoc., Washington, DC

Johnson, H. H., Scileppi, J. A. 1969. Effects of ego-involvement conditions on attitude change to high and low credibility communicators. *J. Pers. Soc. Psychol.* 13:31–36

Johnson, J. T., Judd, C. M. 1983. Overlooking the incongruent: Categorization biases in the identification of political statements. *J. Pers. Soc. Psychol.* 45:978–96

Jones, E. E., Aneshansel, J. 1956. The learning and utilization of contravaluant material. *J. Abnorm. Soc. Psychol.* 53:27–33

Jones, E. E., Davis, K. E. 1965. From acts to dispositions: The attribution process in person perception. *Adv. Exp. Soc. Psychol.* 2:219–66

Jones, E. E., Kohler, R. 1958. The effects of plausibility on the learning of controversial statements. *J. Abnorm. Soc. Psychol.* 57:315–20

Joreskog, K. G., Sorbom, D. 1978. *LISREL: Analysis of linear structural relationships by the method of maximum likelihood.* Chicago: Natl. Educ. Resour.

Joreskog, K. G., Sorbom, D. 1981. *LISREL V.* Chicago: Natl. Educ. Resour.

Joreskog, K. G., Sorbom, D. 1984. *LISREL VI: Analysis of linear structural relationships by the method of maximum likelihood.* Mooresville, IN: Scientific Software

Judd, C. M., Kenny, D. A., Krosnick, J. A. 1983. Judging the positions of political candidates: Models of assimilation and contrast. *J. Pers. Soc. Psychol.* 44:952–63

Judd, C. M., Kulik, J. A. 1980. Schematic effects of social attitudes on information processing and recall. *J. Pers. Soc. Psychol.* 38:569–78

Judd, C. M., Lusk, C. M. 1984. Knowledge structures and evaluative judgments: Effects of structural variables on judgmental extremity. *J. Pers. Soc. Psychol.* 46:1193–1207

Kallgren, C. A., Wood, W. 1986. Access to attitude-relevant information in memory as a determinant of attitude-behavior consistency. *J. Exp. Soc. Psychol.* In press

Kardes, F. R., Sanbonmatsu, D. M., Voss, R. T., Fazio, R. H. 1986. Self-monitoring and attitude accessibility. *Pers. Soc. Psychol. Bull.* In press

Katz, D. 1960. The functional approach to the study of attitudes. *Public Opin. Q.* 24:163–204

Katz, D., Sarnoff, D., McClintock, C. 1956. Ego-defense and attitude change. *Hum. Relat.* 9:27–45

Katz, D., Stotland, E. 1959. A preliminary statement to a theory of attitude structure and change. In *Psychology: A Study of a Science,* ed. S. Koch, 3:423–75. New York: McGraw-Hill

Kelley, H. H. 1967. Attribution theory in social psychology. *Nebr. Symp. Motiv.* 15:192–241

Kelley, H. H. 1972. Attribution in social interaction. In *Attribution: Perceiving the Causes of Behavior,* ed. E. E. Jones, D. E. Kanouse, H. H. Kelley, R. E. Nisbett, S. Valins, B. Weiner. Morristown, NJ: General Learning Press

Kelman, H. C. 1961. Processes of opinion change. *Public Opin. Q.* 25:57–78

Kiesler, C. A. 1971. *The Psychology of Commitment: Experiments Linking Behavior to Belief.* New York: Academic

Kiesler, C. A., Collins, B. E., Miller, N. 1969. *Attitude Change: A Critical Analysis of Theoretical Approaches.* New York: Wiley

Kiesler, C. A., Munson, P. A. 1975. Attitudes and opinions. *Ann. Rev. Psychol.* 26:415–56

Kinder, D. R., Rhodebeck, L. A. 1982. Continuities in support for racial equality, 1972 to 1976. *Public Opin. Q.* 46:195–215

Kinder, D. R., Sears, D. O. 1981. Prejudice and politics: Symbolic racism versus racial threats to the good life. *J. Pers. Soc. Psychol.* 40:414–31

Kinder, D. R., Sears, D. O. 1985. Public opinion and political action. See Lindzey & Aronson 1985, 2:659–741

Kisielius, J., Sternthal, B. 1984. Detecting and explaining vividness effects in attitudinal judgments. *J. Market. Res.* 21:54–64

Kitayama, S. 1983. Majority-minority relations in a changing context. *Jpn. Psychol. Res.* 25:164–69

Kothandapani, V. 1971. Validation of feeling, belief, and intention to act as three components of attitude and their contribution to prediction of contraceptive behavior. *J. Pers. Soc. Psychol.* 19:321–33

Kruglanski, A. W. 1986. *Basic Processes in Social Cognition: A Theory of Lay Epistemology.* New York: Plenum. In press

Latané, B. 1981. The psychology of social impact. *Am. Psychol.* 36:343–56

Latané, B., Wolf, S. 1981. The social impact of majorities and minorities. *Psychol. Rev.* 88:438–53

Lazarus, R. S. 1984. On the primacy of cognition. *Am. Psychol.* 39:124–29

Leippe, M. R. 1979. *Message exposure duration and attitude change: An information processing analysis of persuasion.* PhD thesis. Ohio State Univ., Columbus

Leippe, M. R., Elkin, R. A. 1986. When motives clash: Issue involvement and response involvement as determinants of persuasion. *J. Pers. Soc. Psychol.* In press

Leone, C. 1984. Thought-induced change in phobic beliefs: Sometimes it helps, sometimes it hurts. *J. Clin. Psychol.* 40:68–71

Leone, C., Baldwin, R. T. 1983. Thought-induced changes in fear: Thinking sometimes makes it so. *J. Soc. Clin. Psychol.* 1:272–83

Leone, C., Minor, S. W., Baltimore, M. L. 1983. A comparison of cognitive and performance-based treatment analogues: Constrained though versus performance accomplishments. *Cognit. Ther. Res.* 7:445–54

Levine, J. M., Moreland, R. L. 1985. Innovation and socialization in small groups. See Moscovici et al 1985, pp. 143–69

Lindzey, G., Aronson, E., eds. 1985. *The Handbook of Social Psychology,* Vols. 1, 2. New York: Random House. 816 pp., 1120 pp. 3rd ed.

Lingle, J. H., Ostrom, T. M. 1981. Principles of memory and cognition in attitude formation. See Petty et al 1981b, pp. 399–420

Linville, P. W. 1982. The complexity-extremity effect and age-based stereotyping. *J. Pers. Soc. Psychol.* 42:193–211

Liska, A. E. 1984. A critical examination of the causal structure of the Fishbein/Ajzen attitude-behavior model. *Soc. Psychol. Q.* 47:61–74

Loken, B., Wyer, R. S. Jr. 1983. Effects of reporting beliefs in syllogistically related propositions on the recognition of unmentioned propositions. *J. Pers. Soc. Psychol.* 45:306–22

Lord, C. G., Lepper, M. R., Mackie, D. 1984. Attitude prototypes as determinants of attitude-behavior consistency. *J. Pers. Soc. Psychol.* 46:1254–66

Lutz, R. 1981. A reconceptualization of the functional approach to attitudes. *Res. Market.* 5:165–210

Lutz, R. 1985. Affective and cognitive antecedents of attitude toward the ad: A conceptual framework. See Alwitt & Mitchell 1985, pp. 45–63

Lydon, J., Zanna, M. P., Ross, M. 1986.

Persistence and selective recall: More evidence that behavior recall produces commitment to attitude change. Univ. Waterloo, Unpublished ms

Maass, A., Clark, R. D. III. 1982. *Minority influence theory: Is it applicable only to majorities?* Presented at Ann. Meet. Ger. Psychol. Assoc., 33rd, Mainz, West Germany

Maass, A., Clark, R. D. III. 1983. Internalization versus compliance: Differential processes underlying minority influence and conformity. *Eur. J. Soc. Psychol.* 13:197–215

Maass, A., Clark, R. D. III. 1984. Hidden impact of minorities: Fifteen years of minority influence research. *Psychol. Bull.* 95:428–50

Maass, A., Clark, R. D. III, Haberkorn, G. 1982. The effects of differential ascribed category membership and norms on minority influence. *Eur. J. Soc. Psychol.* 12:89–104

Mackie, D. M. 1985. *Systematic and nonsystematic processing of majority and minority persuasive communications.* Presented at Ann. Meet. Am. Psychol. Assoc., Los Angeles

Mackie, D. M. 1986. Social identification effects in group polarization. *J. Pers. Soc. Psychol.* 50:720–28

Mackie, D. M., Cooper, J. 1984. Attitude polarization: The effects of group membership. *J. Pers. Soc. Psychol.* 46:575–85

Maddux, J. E., Rogers, R. W. 1983. Protection motivation and self-efficacy: A revised theory of fear appeals and attitude change. *J. Exp. Soc. Psychol.* 19:469–79

Manstead, A. S. R., Proffitt, C., Smart, J. L. 1983. Predicting and understanding mothers' infant-feeding intentions and behavior: Testing the theory of reasoned action. *J. Pers. Soc. Psychol.* 44:657–71

Markus, H., Zajonc, R. B. 1985. The cognitive perspective in social psychology. See Lindzey & Aronson 1985, 1:137–230

McCann, D., Hancock, R. D. 1983. Self-monitoring in communicative interactions: Social-cognitive consequences of goal-directed message modification. *J. Exp. Soc. Psychol.* 19:109–21

McClintock, C. G. 1958. Personality syndromes and attitude change. *J. Pers.* 26:479–93

McFarland, C., Ross, M., Conway, M. 1984. Self-persuasion and self-presentation as mediators of anticipatory attitude change. *J. Pers. Soc. Psychol.* 46:529–40

McGuire, W. J. 1969. The nature of attitudes and attitude change. In *The Handbook of Social Psychology,* ed. G. Lindzey, E. Aronson, 3:136–314. Reading, MA: Addison-Wesley. 2nd ed.

McGuire, W. J. 1972. Attitude change: The information-processing paradigm. In *Experimental Social Psychology,* ed. C. G. McClintock, pp. 108–41. New York: Holt, Rinehart & Winston

McGuire, W. J. 1985. Attitudes and attitude change. See Lindzey & Aronson 1985, 2:223–346

McGuire, W. J. 1986. The vicissitudes of attitudes and similar representational constructs in twentieth century psychology. *Eur. J. Soc. Psychol.* In press

McKirnan, D. J., Smith, C. E., Hamayan, E. V. 1983. A sociolinguistic approach to the belief-similarity model of racial attitudes. *J. Exp. Soc. Psychol.* 19:434–47

Meyerowitz, B. E., Chaiken, S. 1986. The effect of message framing on breast self-examination attitudes, intentions, and behavior. *J. Pers. Soc. Psychol.* In press

Midden, C. J. H., Ritsema, B. S. M. 1983. The meaning of normative processes for energy conservation. *J. Econ. Psychol.* 4:37–55

Millar, M. G., Tesser, A. 1986a. Thought-induced attitude change: The effects of schema complexity and commitment. *J. Pers. Soc. Psychol.* 51:259–69

Millar, M. G., Tesser, A. 1986b. Effects of affective and cognitive focus on the attitude-behavior relationship. *J. Pers. Soc. Psychol.* 51:270–76

Miller, N., Colman, D. E. 1981. Methodological issues in analyzing the cognitive mediation of persuasion. See Petty et al 1981b, pp. 105–25

Moscovici, S. 1976. *Social Influence and Social Change.* London: Academic

Moscovici, S. 1980. Toward a theory of conversion behavior. *Adv. Exp. Soc. Psychol.* 13:209–39

Moscovici, S. 1985a. Innovation and minority influence. See Moscovici et al 1985, pp. 201–15

Moscovici, S. 1985b. Social influence and conformity. See Lindzey & Aronson 1985, 2:347–412

Moscovici, S., Faucheux, C. 1972. Social influence, conformity bias, and the study of active minorities. *Adv. Exp. Soc. Psychol.* 6:149–202

Moscovici, S., Lage, E. 1976. Studies in social influence III: Majority versus minority influence in a group. *Eur. J. Soc. Psychol.* 6:149–74

Moscovici, S., Lage, E., Naffrechoux, M. 1969. Influence of a consistent minority on the responses of a majority in a color perception task. *Sociometry* 32:365–80

Moscovici, S., Mugny, G., Van Avermaet, E., eds. 1985. *Perspectives on Minority Influence.* Cambridge: Cambridge Univ. Press

Moscovici, S., Nemeth, C. 1974. Social influence II: Minority influence. In *Social Psychology: Classic and Contemporary Integrations*, ed. C. Nemeth, pp. 217–49. Chicago: Rand McNally

Moscovici, S., Personnaz, B. 1980. Studies in social influence II: Instrumental and symbolic behavior. *Eur. J. Soc. Psychol.* 3:461–74

Mugny, G. 1975. Negotiations, image of the other and the process of minority influence. *Eur. J. Soc. Psychol.* 5:209–29

Mugny, G. 1976. Quelle influence majoritaire? Quelle influence minoritaire? *Rev. Suisse Psychol.* 4:255–68

Mugny, G. 1982. *The Power of Minorities*. London: Academic

Mugny, G. 1984. Compliance, conversion and the Asch paradigm. *Eur. J. Soc. Psychol.* 14:353–68

Mugny, G., Kaiser, L., Papastamou, S. 1983. Etude esperimentale autour d'une rotation: Les mechanismes de l'influence des minorites. Univ. Geneve. Unpublished ms

Mugny, G., Papastamou, S. 1980. When rigidity does not fail: Individualization and psychologization as resistances to the diffusion of minority innovations. *Eur. J. Soc. Psychol.* 10:43–62

Mullen, B. 1983. Operationalizing the effect of the group on the individual: A self-attention perspective. *J. Exp. Soc. Psychol.* 19:295–322

Mullen, B. 1985. Strength and immediacy of sources: A meta-analytic evaluation of the forgotten elements of social impact theory. *J. Pers. Soc. Psychol.* 48:1458–66

Mullen, B. 1986. Effects of strength and immediacy in group contexts: Reply to Jackson. *J. Pers. Soc. Psychol.* 50:514–16

Nemeth, C. J. 1976. *A comparison between conformity and minority influence.* Presented to Int. Congr. Psychol., Paris, France

Nemeth, C. J. 1985. Dissent, group process and creativity: The contribution of minority influence. In *Advances in Group Processes*, ed. J. E. Lawler, 2:57–75. Greenwich, CT: JAI Press

Nemeth, C. J. 1986a. Differential contributions of majority and minority influence. *Psychol. Rev.* 93:1–10

Nemeth, C. J. 1986b. Influence processes, problem solving and creativity. See Zanna et al 1986

Nemeth, C., Kwan, J. 1985. Originality of word associations as a function of majority vs. minority influence processes. *Soc. Psychol. Q.* 48:277–82

Nemeth, C., Kwan, J. 1986. Minority influence, divergent thinking and detection of correct solutions. *J. Appl. Soc. Psychol.* In press

Nemeth, C., Swedlund, M., Kanki, B. 1974. Patterning of the minority's responses and their influence on the majority. *Eur. J. Soc. Psychol.* 4:53–64

Nemeth, C., Wachtler, J. 1973. Consistency and modification of judgment. *J. Exp. Soc. Psychol.* 9:65–79

Nemeth, C., Wachtler, J. 1974. Creating the perceptions of consistency and confidence: A necessary condition for minority influence. *Sociometry* 37:529–40

Nemeth, C., Wachtler, J. 1983. Creative problem solving as a result of majority vs. minority influence. *Eur. J. Soc. Psychol.* 13:45–55

Offermann, L. R., Schrier, P. E. 1985. Social influence strategies: The impact of sex, role, and attitudes toward power. *Pers. Soc. Psychol. Bull.* 11:286–300

Olson, J. M., Cal, A. V. 1984. Source credibility, attitudes, and the recall of past behaviours. *Eur. J. Soc. Psychol.* 14:203–10

Orive, R. 1984. Group similarity, public self-awareness, and opinion extremity: A social projection explanation of deindividuation effects. *J. Pers. Soc. Psychol.* 47:727–37

Orvis, B. R., Cunningham, J. D., Kelley, H. H. 1975. A closer examination of causal inference: The roles of consensus, distinctiveness, and consistency information. *J. Pers. Soc. Psychol.* 32:605–16

Ostrom, T. M. 1969. The relationship between the affective, behavioral and cognitive components of attitude. *J. Exp. Soc. Psychol.* 5:12–30

O'Sullivan, C. S., Durso, F. T. 1984. Effect of schema-incongruent information on memory for stereotypical attributes. *J. Pers. Soc. Psychol.* 47:55–70

Pallak, S. R. 1983. Salience of a communicator's physical attractiveness and persuasion: A heuristic versus systematic processing interpretation. *Soc. Cognit.* 2:158–70

Pallak, S. R., Murroni, E., Koch, J. 1983. Communicator attractiveness and expertise, emotional versus rational appeals, and persuasion: A heuristic versus systematic processing interpretation. *Soc. Cognit.* 2:122–41

Papastamou, S. 1983. Strategies of minority and majority influence. In *Current Issues in European Social Psychology*, ed. W. Doise, S. Moscovici, 1:33–83. Cambridge: Cambridge Univ. Press

Paulhus, D. 1982. Individual differences, self-presentation, and cognitive dissonance: Their concurrent operation in forced compliance. *J. Pers. Soc. Psychol.* 43:838–52

Petty, R. E., Cacioppo, J. T. 1979. Issue-involvement can increase or decrease persuasion by enhancing message-relevant cognitive responses. *J. Pers. Soc. Psychol.* 37:1915–26

Petty, R. E., Cacioppo, J. T. 1981. *Attitudes and Persuasion: Classic and Contemporary Approaches.* Dubuque, IA: Brown. 314 pp.

Petty, R. E., Cacioppo, J. T. 1983. Central and peripheral routes to persuasion: Application to advertising. See Brock & Shavitt 1983, pp. 3–23

Petty, R. E., Cacioppo, J. T. 1984. The effects of involvement on responses to argument quantity and quality: Central and peripheral routes to persuasion. *J. Pers. Soc. Psychol.* 46:69–81

Petty, R. E., Cacioppo, J. T. 1986. The elaboration likelihood model of persuasion. *Adv. Exp. Soc. Psychol.* 19:123–205

Petty, R. E., Cacioppo, J. T., Goldman, R. 1981a. Personal involvement as a determinant of argument-based persuasion. *J. Pers. Soc. Psychol.* 41:847–55

Petty, R. E., Cacioppo, J. T., Schumann, D. 1983a. Central and peripheral routes to advertising effectiveness: The moderating role of involvement. *J. Consum. Res.* 10:135–46

Petty, R. E., Ostrom, T. M., Brock, T. C., eds. 1981b. *Cognitive Responses in Persuasion.* Hillsdale, NJ: Erlbaum. 476 pp.

Petty, R. E., Ostrom, T. M., Brock, T. C. 1981c. Historical foundations of the cognitive response approach to attitudes and persuasion. See Petty et al 1981b, pp. 5–29

Petty, R. E., Wells, G. L., Heesacker, M., Brock, T. C., Cacioppo, J. T. 1983b. The effects of recipient posture on persuasion: A cognitive response analysis. *Pers. Soc. Psychol. Bull.* 9:209–22

Powell, M. C., Fazio, R. H. 1984. Attitude accessibility as a function of repeated attitudinal expression. *Pers. Soc. Psychol. Bull.* 10:139–48

Pratkanis, A. R. 1984. *Attitude structure and selective learning.* Presented at Ann. Meet. Am. Psychol. Assoc., Toronto

Pratkanis, A. R., Greenwald, A. G. 1985. A reliable sleeper effect in persuasion: Implications for opinion change theory and research. See Alwitt & Mitchell 1985, pp. 157–73

Raden, D. 1985. Strength-related attitude dimensions. *Soc. Psychol. Q.* 48:312–30

Ratneshwar, S., Chaiken, S. 1986. When is the expert source more persuasive? A heuristic processing analysis. In *American Marketing Association Summer Marketing Educators' Conference Proceedings,* ed. T. A. Shimp, S. Sharma, et al. Chicago: AMA

Read, S. J., Rosson, M. B. 1982. Rewriting history: The biasing effects of attitudes on memory. *Soc. Cognit.* 3:240–55

Reardon, R., Rosen, S. 1984. Psychological differentiation and the evaluation of juridic

information: Cognitive and affective consequences. *J. Res. Pers.* 18:195–211

Rholes, W. S., Bailey, S. 1983. The effects of level of moral reasoning on consistency between moral attitudes and related behaviors. *Soc. Cognit.* 2:32–48

Richardson, K. D., Cialdini, R. B. 1986. Factors related to social change: Shifts in group judgments induced by deviant minorities. Ariz. State Univ. Unpublished ms

Riess, M., Kalle, R. J., Tedeschi, J. T. 1981. Bogus pipeline attitude assessment, impression management, and misattribution in induced compliance settings. *J. Soc. Psychol.* 115:247–58

Robberson, M. R., Rogers, R. W. 1986. Beyond fear appeals: Negative and positive persuasive appeals to health and self-esteem. *J. Appl. Soc. Psychol.* In press

Roberts, D. F., Maccoby, N. 1985. Effects of mass communication. See Lindzey & Aronson 1985, 2:539–98

Roberts, J. V. 1984a. Public opinion and capital punishment: The effects of attitudes upon memory. *Can. J. Criminol.* 26:283–91

Roberts, J. V. 1984b. Selective recall for personally relevant communications. *Can. J. Behav. Sci.* 16:208–15

Roberts, J. V. 1985. The attitude-memory relationship after 40 years: A meta-analysis of the literature. *Basic Appl. Soc. Psychol.* 6:221–41

Rogers, R. W. 1983. Cognitive and physiological processes in fear appeals and attitude change: A revised theory of protection motivation. In *Social Psychophysiology,* ed. J. T. Cacioppo, R. E. Petty, pp. 153–76. New York: Guilford

Rogers, R. W. 1985. Attitude change and information integration in fear appeals. *Psychol. Rep.* 56:179–82

Rokeach, M., ed. 1979. *Understanding Human Values: Individual and Societal.* New York: Free Press

Rokeach, M. 1985. Inducing change and stability in belief systems and personality structures. *J. Soc. Issues* 41:153–71

Romer, D. 1983. Effects of own attitude on polarization of judgment. *J. Pers. Soc. Psychol.* 44:273–84

Ronis, D. L., Kaiser, M. K. 1985. *Correlates of breast self-examination in a sample of college women: Analyses of linear structural relations.* Presented at Ann. Meet. Am. Psychol. Assoc., Los Angeles

Rosenberg, M. J. 1960. A structural theory of attitude dynamics. *Public Opin. Q.* 24:319–41

Rosenfeld, P., Giacalone, R. A., Tedeschi, J. T. 1983. Cognitive dissonance vs. impression management. *J. Soc. Psychol.* 120:203–11

Rosenfeld, P., Giacalone, R. A., Tedeschi, J. T. 1984. Cognitive dissonance and impression management explanations for effort justification. *Pers. Soc. Psychol. Bull.* 10: 394–401

Ross, L., Bierbrauer, G., Hoffman, S. 1976. The role of attribution processes in conformity and dissent: Revisiting the Asch situation. *Am. Psychol.* 31:148–57

Ross, M., Conway, M. 1986. Remembering one's own past: The construction of personal histories. See Sorrentino & Higgins 1986, pp. 122–44

Ross, M., McFarland, C., Conway, M., Zanna, M. P. 1983. Reciprocal relation between attitudes and behavior recall: Committing people to newly formed attitudes. *J. Pers. Soc. Psychol.* 45:257–67

Rule, B. G., Bisanz, G. L. 1986. Schema for goals and strategies for persuasion. See Zanna et al 1986

Rule, B. G., Bisanz, G. L., Kohn, M. 1985. Anatomy of a persuasion schema: Targets, goals, and strategies. *J. Pers. Soc. Psychol.* 48:1127–40

Schifter, D. E., Ajzen, I. 1985. Intention, perceived control, and weight loss: An application of the theory of planned behavior. *J. Pers. Soc. Psychol.* 49:843–51

Schlenker, B. R. 1980. *Impression Management: The Self-concept, Social Identity, and Interpersonal Relations.* Monterey, CA: Brooks/Cole

Schlenker, B. R. 1982. Translating actions into attitudes: An identity analytic approach to the explanation of social conduct. *Adv. Exp. Soc. Psychol.* 15:193–247

Schmidt, D. F., Sherman, R. C. 1984. Memory for persuasive messages: A test of a schema-copy-plus-tag model. *J. Pers. Soc. Psychol.* 47:17–25

Schul, Y., Burnstein, E., Martinez, J. 1983. The informational basis of social judgments: Under what conditions are inconsistent trait descriptions processed as easily as consistent ones? *Eur. J. Soc. Psychol.* 13: 1–9

Scott, W. A. 1959. Empirical assessment of values and ideologies. *Am. Sociol. Rev.* 24:299–310

Sears, D. O. 1983. The persistence of early political predispositions: The roles of attitude object and life stage. In *Review of Personality and Social Psychology,* ed. L. Wheeler, P. Shaver, pp. 79–116. Beverly Hills: Sage

Sears, D. O. 1986. College students in the laboratory: Influence of a narrow data base on social psychology's view of human nature. *J. Pers. Soc. Psychol.* In press

Sears, D. O., Allen, H. M. 1984. The trajectory of local desegregation controversies and whites' opposition to busing. In *Groups*

in Contact: The Psychology of Desegregation, ed. N. Miller, M. Brewer, pp. 123–51. Orlando, FL: Academic

Sears, D. O., Kinder, D. R. 1985. Whites' opposition to busing: On conceptualizing and operationalizing group conflict. *J. Pers. Soc. Psychol.* 48:1141–47

Sears, D. O., Lau, R. R. 1983. Inducing apparently self-interested political preferences. *Am. J. Pol. Sci.* 27:223–52

Shavitt, S. 1986. Attitude functions affect informational bases of attitudes. Presented at Ann. Meet. Midwest. Psychol. Assoc., Chicago

Shavitt, S., Brock, T. C. 1986. Attitude functions affect persuasiveness of appeals. Presented at Ann. Meet. Midwest. Psychol. Assoc., Chicago

Sherer, M., Rogers, R. W. 1984. The role of vivid information in fear appeals and attitude change. *J. Res. Pers.* 18:321–34

Sherif, M., Hovland, C. I. 1961. *Social Judgment: Assimilation and Contrast Effects in Communication and Attitude Change.* New Haven: Yale Univ. Press

Sherif, M., Sherif, C. W. 1967. Attitude as the individual's own categories: The social judgment-involvement approach to attitude and attitude change. In *Attitude, Ego-involvement, and Change,* ed. C. W. Sherif, M. Sherif. New York: Wiley

Sherman, S. J. 1986. Cognitive processes in the formation, change, and expression of attitudes. See Zanna et al 1986

Sherman, S. J., Fazio, R. H. 1983. Parallels between attitudes and traits as predictors of behavior. *J. Pers.* 51:308–45

Sherman, S. J., Zehner, K. S., Johnson, J., Hirt, E. R. 1983. Social explanation: The role of timing, set, and recall on subjective likelihood estimates. *J. Pers. Soc. Psychol.* 44:1127–43

Shimp, T. A., Kavas, A. 1984. The theory of reasoned action applied to coupon usage. *J. Consum. Res.* 11:795–809

Sivacek, J., Crano, W. D. 1982. Vested interest as a moderator of attitude-behavior consistency. *J. Pers. Soc. Psychol.* 43:210–21

Smith, M. B., Bruner, J. S., White, R. W. 1956. *Opinions and Personality.* New York: Wiley

Smith, R. E., Swinyard, W. R. 1983. Attitude-behavior consistency: The impact of product trial versus advertising. *J. Market. Res.* 20:257–67

Sniderman, P. M., Tetlock, P. E. 1986. Symbolic racism: Problems of motive attribution in political debate. *J. Soc. Issues.* In press

Snyder, M. 1974. The self-monitoring of expressive behavior. *J. Pers. Soc. Psychol.* 30:526–37

Snyder, M., DeBono, K. G. 1985. Appeals to image and claims about quality: Understanding the psychology of advertising. *J. Pers. Soc. Psychol.* 49:586–97

Snyder, M., DeBono, K. G. 1986. A functional approach to attitudes and persuasion. See Zanna et al 1986

Snyder, M., Kendzierski, D. 1982. Acting on one's attitudes: Procedures for linking attitudes and behavior. *J. Exp. Soc. Psychol.* 18:165–83

Snyder, M., Swann, W. B. Jr. 1976. When actions reflect attitudes: The politics of impression management. *J. Pers. Soc. Psychol.* 34:1034–42

Sorrentino, R. M., Hancock, R. D. 1986. Information and affective value: A case for the study of individual differences and social influence. See Zanna et al 1986

Sorrentino, R. M., Higgins, E. T., eds. 1986. *The Handbook of Motivation and Cognition: Foundations of Social Behavior.* New York: Guilford

Spiro, R. J., Sherif, C. W. 1975. Consistency and relativity in selective recall with differing ego-involvement. *Br. J. Soc. Clin. Psychol.* 14:351–61

Spivey, W. A., Munson, J. M., Locander, W. B. 1983. Improving the effectiveness of persuasive communications: Matching message with functional profile. *J. Bus. Res.* 11:257–69

Srull, T. K. 1983. The role of prior knowledge in the acquisition, retention, and use of new information. *Adv. Consum. Res.* 10:572–76

Srull, T. K., Wyer, R. S. Jr. 1979. The role of category accessibility in the interpretation of information about persons: Some determinants and implications. *J. Pers. Soc. Psychol.* 37:1660–72

Srull, T. K., Wyer, R. S. Jr. 1986. The role of chronic and temporary goals in social information processing. See Sorrentino & Higgins 1986, pp. 503–49

Steele, C. M., Liu, T. J. 1983. Dissonance processes as self-affirmation. *J. Pers. Soc. Psychol.* 45:5–19

Steffen, V. J., Eagly, A. H. 1985. Implicit theories about influence style. *Pers. Soc. Psychol. Bull.* 11:191–205

Steiner, I. D. 1986. Paradigms and groups. *Adv. Exp. Soc. Psychol.* 19:251–89

Stern, L. D., Marrs, S., Millar, M. G., Cole, E. 1984. Processing time and the recall of inconsistent and consistent behaviors of individuals and groups. *J. Pers. Soc. Psychol.* 47:253–62

Sternthal, B., Dholakia, R., Leavitt, C. 1978. The persuasive effect of source credibility: Tests of cognitive response. *J. Consum. Res.* 4:252–60

Stiff, J. B. 1986. Cognitive processing of persuasive message cues: A meta-analytic review of the effects of supporting informa-

tion on attitudes. *Commun. Monogr.* 53:75–89

Stults, D. M., Messe, L. A., Kerr, N. L. 1984. Belief discrepant behavior and the bogus pipeline: Impression management or arousal attribution. *J. Exp. Soc. Psychol.* 20:47–54

Sweeney, P. D., Gruber, K. L. 1984. Selective exposure: Voter information preferences and the Watergate affair. *J. Pers. Soc. Psychol.* 46:1208–21

Tajfel, H. 1978. Social categorization, social identity, and social comparison. In *Differentiation Between Social Groups,* ed. H. Tajfel, pp. 61–76. London: Academic

Tanford, S., Penrod, S. 1984. Social influence model: A formal integration of research on majority and minority influence processes. *Psychol. Bull.* 95:189–225

Taylor, S. E. 1975. On inferring one's own attitudes from one's behavior: Some delimiting conditions. *J. Pers. Soc. Psychol.* 31:126–31

Taylor, S. E., Thompson, S. C. 1982. Stalking the elusive "vividness" effect. *Psychol. Rev.* 89:155–81

Tesser, A., Campbell, J., Mickler, S. 1983. The role of social pressure, attention to the stimulus, and self-doubt in conformity. *Eur. J. Soc. Psychol.* 13:217–33

Tetlock, P. E. 1983a. Accountability and complexity of thought. *J. Pers. Soc. Psychol.* 45:74–83

Tetlock, P. E. 1983b. Accountability and the perseverance of first impressions. *Soc. Psychol. Q.* 46:285–92

Tetlock, P. E. 1983c. Cognitive style and political ideology. *J. Pers. Soc. Psychol.* 45:118–26

Tetlock, P. E. 1984. Cognitive style and political belief systems in the British House of Commons. *J. Pers. Soc. Psychol.* 46:365–75

Tetlock, P. E. 1985. Accountability: The neglected social context of judgment and choice. In *Research in Organizational Behavior,* ed. B. M. Staw, Z. Cummings, 7:297–332. Greenwich, CT: JAI Press

Tetlock, P. E. 1986. A value pluralism model of ideological reasoning. *J. Pers. Soc. Psychol.* 50:819–27

Tetlock, P. E., Bernzweig, J., Gallant, J. L. 1985. Supreme Court decision making: Cognitive style as a predictor of ideological consistency of voting. *J. Pers. Soc. Psychol.* 48:1227–39

Tetlock, P. E., Hannum, K. A., Micheletti, P. M. 1984. Stability and change in the complexity of senatorial debate: Testing the cognitive versus rhetorical style hypotheses. *J. Pers. Soc. Psychol.* 46:979–90

Tetlock, P. E., Manstead, A. S. R. 1985.

Impression management versus interpsychic explanations in social psychology: A useful dichotomy? *Psychol. Rev.* 92:59–77

Trope, Y., Ginossar, Z. 1986. On the use of statistical and nonstatistical knowledge: A problem-solving approach. See Bar-Tal & Kruglanski 1986

Turner, J. C. 1982. Toward a cognitive redefinition of the social group. In *Social Identity and Intergroup Relations*, ed. H. Tajfel. Cambridge: Cambridge Univ. Press

Turner, J. C. 1985. Social categorization and the self-concept: A social cognitive theory of group behavior. See Nemeth 1985, pp. 76–97

Tybout, A. M., Scott, C. A. 1983. Availability of well-defined internal knowledge and the attitude formation process: Information aggregation versus self-perception. *J. Pers. Soc. Psychol.* 44:474–91

Tyler, T. R. 1984. The role of perceived injustice in defendants' evaluations of their courtroom experience. *Law Soc. Rev.* 18: 51–74

Tyler, T. R., Rasinski, K. A., McGraw, K. M. 1985a. The influence of perceived injustice on support for political authorities. *J. Appl. Soc. Psychol.* 15:700–25

Tyler, T. R., Rasinski, K. A., Spodick, N. 1985b. The influence of voice on satisfaction with leaders: Exploring the meaning of process control. *J. Pers. Soc. Psychol.* 48:72–81

Vallone, R. P., Ross, L., Lepper, M. R. 1985. The hostile media phenomenon: Biased perception and perceptions of media bias in coverage of the Beirut massacre. *J. Pers. Soc. Psychol.* 49:577–85

Warshaw, P. R., Davis, F. D. 1985. Disentangling behavioral intention and behavioral expectation. *J. Exp. Soc. Psychol.* 21:213–28

Wicklund, R. A. 1982. Self-focused attention and the validity of self-reports. See Zanna et al 1982, pp. 149–72

Wilson, D. K., Axsom, D., Lee, M., Chaiken, S. 1985. *Evidence for heuristic processing of persuasive messages.* Presented at Ann. Meet. Am. Psychol. Assoc., Los Angeles

Wilson, T. D., Dunn, D. S. 1986. Effects of introspection on attitude-behavior consistency: Analyzing reasons versus focusing on feelings. *J. Exp. Soc. Psychol.* In press

Wilson, T. D., Dunn, D. S., Bybee, J. A., Hyman, D. B., Rotondo, J. A. 1984. Effects of analyzing reasons on attitude-behavior consistency. *J. Pers. Soc. Psychol.* 47:5–16

Wilson, T. D., Dunn, D. S., Kraft, D., Lisle, D. J. 1986. Introspection and attitude-behavior consistency: The disruptive effects of explaining why we feel the way we do. Univ. VA. Unpublished ms

Wolf, S. 1979. Behavioral style and group cohesiveness as sources of minority influence. *Eur. J. Soc. Psychol.* 9:381–95

Wolf, S. 1985. The manifest and latent influence of majorities and minorities. *J. Pers. Soc. Psychol.* 48:899–908

Wolf, S. 1986. Majority and minority influence: A social impact analysis. See Zanna et al 1986

Wolf, S., Gregory, W. L., Stephan, W. G. 1986. Protection motivation theory: Prediction of intentions to engage in anti-nuclear war behaviors. *J. Appl. Abnorm. Soc. Psychol.* In press

Wolf, S., Latané, B. 1983. Majority and minority influence on restaurant preferences. *J. Pers. Soc. Psychol.* 45:282–92

Wolf, S., Latané, B. 1985. Conformity, innovation and the psychosocial law. See Moscovici et al 1985, pp. 201–15

Wood, W. 1982. Retrieval of attitude-relevant information from memory: Effects on susceptibility to persuasion and on intrinsic motivation. *J. Pers. Soc. Psychol.* 42:798–810

Wood, W., Eagly, A. H. 1981. Stages in the analysis of persuasive messages: The role of causal attributions and message comprehension. *J. Pers. Soc. Psychol.* 40:246–59

Wood, W., Kallgren, C. A., Preisler, R. M. 1985. Access to attitude-relevant information in memory as a determinant of persuasion: The role of message attributes. *J. Exp. Soc. Psychol.* 21:73–85

Worth, L. T., Mackie, D. M. 1986. *Cognitive mediation of positive affect in persuasion.* Presented at Ann. Meet. West. Psychol. Assoc., Seattle, WA

Wyer, R. S. Jr., Frey, D. 1983. The effects of feedback about self and others on the recall and judgments of feedback-relevant information. *J. Exp. Soc. Psychol.* 19:540–59

Wyer, R. S. Jr., Gordon, S. E. 1984. The cognitive representation of social information. See Wyer & Srull 1984, 3:73–150

Wyer, R. S. Jr., Srull, T. K., eds. 1984. *Handbook of Social Cognition*, Vol. 3. Hillsdale, NJ: Erlbaum

Yalch, R. F., Elmore-Yalch, R. 1984. The effect of numbers on the route to persuasion. *J. Consum. Res.* 11:522–27

Zajonc, R. B. 1984. On the primacy of affect. *Am. Psychol.* 39:117–23

Zajonc, R. B., Markus, H. 1982. Affective and cognitive factors in preferences. *J. Consum. Res.* 9:123–31

Zanna, M. P., Fazio, R. H. 1982. The attitude behavior relation: Moving toward a third generation of research. See Zanna et al 1982, pp. 283–301

Zanna, M. P., Higgins, E. T., Herman, C. P., eds. 1982. *Consistency in Social Behavior: The Ontario Symposium*, Vol. 2. Hillsdale, NJ: Erlbaum. 314 pp.

Zanna, M. P., Olson, J. M., Herman, C. P., eds. 1986. *Social Influence: The Ontario Symposium*, Vol. 5. Hillsdale, NJ: Erlbaum. In press

Zanna, M. P., Olson, J. M. 1982. Individual differences in attitudinal relations. See Zanna et al 1982, pp. 75–104

Zanna, M. P., Rempel, J. K. 1986. Attitudes: A new look at an old concept. See Bar-Tal & Kruglanski 1986

Zanna, M. P., Sande, G. N. 1986. The effects of collective actions on the attitudes of individual group members: A dissonance analysis. See Zanna et al 1986

Zimbardo, P. G. 1960. Involvement and communication discrepancy as determinants of opinion conformity. *J. Abnorm. Soc. Psychol.* 60:86–94

Ann. Rev. Psychol. 1987. 38:631–68

HUMAN LEARNING AND MEMORY

Marcia K. Johnson

Department of Psychology, Princeton University, Princeton, New Jersey 08544

Lynn Hasher

Department of Psychology, Temple University, Philadelphia, Pennsylvania 19122[1]

CONTENTS

We consider four general topics in this review of recent work in human memory: the representation of knowledge, relations among memory measures, unconscious and nonstrategic processing, and constraints on acquisi-

---

[1]L. Hasher is now at Department of Psychology, Duke University, Durham, North Carolina.

0066-4308/87/0201-0631$02.00

tion and remembering. In a final section, we also discuss examples of the expanded domains of research on human memory. Together, these research areas illustrate a number of important and interrelated themes and issues.

The issue of the relation between generic and specific knowledge appears in several contexts and remains a challenging theoretical question. Following earlier efforts to carve up memory into components, investigators continue to look for evidence of functional subsystems of memory. Findings from work on memory deficits have become central to this pursuit. Also important in this regard is the increasing variety of topics investigated. Each year, research in learning and memory comes closer to reflecting the wide range of functions that memory serves. Acquisition and forgetting are studied with direct measures of memory such as recall, recognition, frequency judgments, and source discrimination, as well as with indirect measures such as lexical decision, perceptual identification, and word completion tasks. Explaining the pattern of differences among these measures is currently a major concern. Research on such difficult topics as text processing, spatial cognition, affect and memory, and autobiographical memory also highlights the complexity and flexibility of memory. Memory theories are not likely to capture this complexity and flexibility fully in the near future but should do so sooner as a consequence of current efforts from these many directions.

THE REPRESENTATION OF KNOWLEDGE

This section provides an overview of work in four areas (lexical access, semantic decisions, concepts, and schemas) that grew from the assumption of a semantic system or generic knowledge with properties different from those of episodic memories (e.g. Tulving 1983). Recent work raises two major questions: (a) How abstracted is the representation of generic information, and (b) is there a context-free, relatively stable (transituational) set of relations among elements in a generic memory system? Substantial methodological or conceptual problems have also arisen in each area in recent years.

Lexical Access

An important subset of our knowledge is our understanding of words. Work on word recognition is directed at characterizing both the "lexicon," including the relations among its units, and the process by which a presented word makes contact with its representation. The literature is somewhat confusing because the term lexicon is used to refer sometimes to a set of entries specified by their orthographic, phonetic, or morphophonemic characteristics (Taft 1984), sometimes to a set of associative relations (e.g. Fodor 1983; Kintsch & Mross 1985), and sometimes to a set of more extensive semantic relations among lexical units (e.g. Kiger & Glass 1983; Seidenberg et al 1984). We focus here on studies of access to word meaning.

Researchers agree on the importance of three facts: (*a*) Relatively stable differences exist in availability among units—differences tied to frequency of occurrence in the language, or, more specifically, in the subject's experience (Gernsbacher 1984); (*b*) a recent presentation may temporarily increase a unit's availability by activating or priming it (repetition priming); and (*c*) a unit may be primed by the activation of related units (semantic priming). There is less agreement on how to characterize the lexicon on the basis of these findings (see the review by Simpson 1984).

The appropriate interpretation of both repetition and associative priming effects has been a focus of recent debate. One issue is whether repetition-priming effects come exclusively from activation of semantic memory or whether they reflect episodic traces as well (Feustel et al 1983; Salasoo et al 1985; J. C. Johnston et al 1985; Ratcliff et al 1985).

Another controversy surrounds the role of context in semantic priming. Does the occurrence of a word prime all its direct associates (e.g., Kintsch & Mross 1985; Oden & Spira 1983; Onifer & Swinney 1981; Whitney et al 1985) or only those that fit within the current semantic context (Glucksberg et al 1986)? According to the "modularity" hypothesis advanced by Fodor (1983), the lexical system is "encapsulated" and so should be immune to external influences; it is assumed that associative relations are in the lexicon and semantic ones are outside it. Thus, the issue is whether context effects come exclusively from within the lexical system itself (e.g. from associates) or can also come from other levels of language processing—e.g. syntactic constraints, or thematic levels of meaning (Glucksberg et al 1986; Kintsch & Mross 1985; Sanocki et al 1985; Seidenberg et al 1982; Stanovich & West 1983a,b; Tanenhaus & Donnenwerth-Nolan 1984; Wright & Garrett 1984). Interpreting results from such studies depends on whether or not one accepts the notion that associative and semantic relations differ in kind rather than in history.

Underlying much work on lexical access is the assumption that certain tasks (e.g. lexical decision, word naming, Stroop color naming) provide indexes of automatic activation processes within the lexical system that are un-contaminated by subjects' strategies or episodic memories. If this assumption (currently being challenged) is valid, the duration and spread of priming would give a picture of the organization of the lexicon. One problem is that tasks that should all reflect lexical access do not necessarily respond the same way to manipulations of the same variables. Word frequency has a large effect on lexical decisions and a negligible effect on a category verification task (Balota & Chumbley 1984), and it may or may not have an effect on naming, depending on whether words are presented alone or mixed with pseudo-words (Hudson & Bergman 1985); syntactic relations between words produce prim-ing in the lexical decision task but not in the naming task (Seidenberg et al 1984); unassociated but semantically related words produce priming in a lexical decision task but not in the naming task (Huttenlocher & Kubicek 1983; Lupker 1984; but see Seidenberg et al 1984); increasing the proportion of related stimuli in a list increases the associative priming effect in lexical decisions (den Heyer et al 1983; Tweedy et al 1977; Tweedy & Lapinski 1981) but not in naming (Seidenberg et al 1984); and backward associations between the target and the prime affect lexical decisions but not naming (Kiger & Glass 1983; Seidenberg et al 1984).

A potential explanation of this complexity in patterns of findings is that some effects reflect the operation of postlexical, strategic factors that take time to emerge. One way to decrease strategic effects is to restrict the time available for processing the prime. The technique of varying the interval between the onset of the prime and the onset of the target (stimulus onset asynchrony, or SOA) is directed at discovering the relative roles of automatic (lexical access) and attention-demanding (postlexical) processes in context effects (de Groot 1984; den Heyer et al 1983; Onifer & Swinney 1981; Simpson & Burgess 1985; also see Seidenberg et al 1982). Lexical decisions that are made after very brief prime-target intervals (< 200 msec) may reflect automatic activation processes. Another way to reduce strategic effects is to use a methodology of masking the prime to eliminate conscious processing of possible relations between the prime and the target (de Groot 1983; Forster & Davis 1984; also see Henik et al 1983).

In any event, the most commonly used task, lexical decision, is so much more complicated than it first appeared that it might more appropriately be thought of as a complex decision task than as a simple lexical-access task (Hudson & Bergman 1985; Balota & Chumbley 1984; Chumbley & Balota 1984; Lupker 1984; Gordon 1985). As the lexical-decision task appears increasingly complex it becomes tempting to begin to rely on other, seemingly simpler tasks to explore lexical organization—e.g. naming, or perhaps perceptual identification. However, the more we use tasks the more we discover their complexity. In fact, there is already some evidence that naming, too, is not a pure index of lexical-access processes (Balota & Chumbley 1985).

Nor is it clear when the additive-factors logic (Sternberg 1969) is appropriate for isolating the stage (e.g. lexical access) at which a variable has an effect. The rationale for inferring that two variables interact when they affect the same process and do not interact when they affect different processes depends on assuming that the processes in question occur in a discrete serial order. If a later process can begin before a prior one ends (in cascade), then an interaction need not imply that two variables affect the same processes (McClelland 1979; Shoben 1982). Even assuming a stage model, the pattern of results (additive and interactive factors) across different experiments presents a more complex picture than was once assumed. For example, in lexical decisions, visual degradation interacts with semantic relatedness of primes (Becker & Killion 1977) and with stimulus repetitions (Norris 1984). According to additive-factors logic, if all three variables affect the same stage of processing, semantic relatedness and repetitions should interact as well; but they do not (den Heyer et al 1985). At the least, these results imply that one (or more) of these variables affects more than one stage of processing.

Semantic Decisions

If one assumes that semantic memory is a distinct system, it is reasonable to attempt to specify its structure and the processes that operate on that structure. Through the 1970s, the most influential models characterized semantic structure either as a network of nodes connected by labeled links specifying relations or as sets of features (see Chang 1986 for a review). These models helped to generate interest in the difficult problem of the representation of knowledge. However, reservations have been expressed about both the methodology and the underlying conceptualization of semantic memory that guides much of the work in this area (Kintsch 1980; Johnson-Laird et al 1984; Shoben 1982).

Several problems arise from the inherently correlational nature of the designs used to investigate semantic decisions, such as verifying the statement that *A robin is a bird*. For example, the controversy over which factor determines response time (i.e. category size, nesting relationship, semantic similarity between exemplar and category, or familiarity) is unresolved because it is impossible to control all relevant aspects of natural language stimuli except the one of immediate interest (Shoben 1982; also see Chumbley 1986). Furthermore, as Shoben notes, researchers cannot agree on what must be controlled (but see Chang 1986).

Investigations of semantic memory rely heavily on response time as a direct measure of the duration of mental processes. There are drawbacks in this practice. Because a subject's speed-vs-accuracy criterion may vary from item to item or with experimental conditions, response latency may not only be an unsatisfactory measure of absolute duration of a mental process, it may give an inaccurate picture of the relative duration of mental processes engaged by two conditions or tasks. A response-signal, speed-accuracy trade-off method might solve this problem (Dosher 1984a; Pachella et al 1978; Ratcliff & McKoon 1982; Reed 1973; Wickelgren 1977). The function relating accuracy (e.g. d') to amount of processing time before a signal to respond should yield a picture of the continuously accruing information necessary for a task. Like variations in prime-target interval (SOA) used in lexical access research, the response-signal method can be used to explore potential differences between early and late components in activation and/or decision making. Although the prospect of being able to track the revival of a memory is exciting, speed-accuracy functions do not yield unambiguous information (Meyer & Irwin 1981; Wickelgren 1977), and Meyer & Irwin's (1981) further modification of the speed-accuracy trade-off technique ("speed-accuracy decomposition") may prove useful.

Work on semantic decisions has been criticized on conceptual grounds as well (Johnson-Laird et al 1984). Johnson-Laird et al point out that semantic networks (and feature-set theories) are largely concerned with the relations among words (intentional relations) rather than with the relations between words and their referents (extensional relations). Disambiguation cannot be explained solely by selection restrictions operating within a sentence; for example, in "He planted them on the island," disambiguating "them" requires information that is outside the sentence. As Johnson-Laird et al also point out, it is inconceivable that all potential relations (e.g. tomatoes are more squashable than potatoes, except if potatoes are cooked and mashed and tomatoes are frozen solid) are represented within a network of labeled links.

Semantic networks were initially compelling ways to represent knowledge because they provided a mechanism for inference generation. Even if never told that canaries breathe, we can deduce the fact by traversing links in the network—canaries are birds, birds are animals, animals breathe; therefore, canaries breathe. The traversal of links is a formal mechanism that does not need to "know" what any of the words refer to. But, if we are talking about ceramic canaries, then canaries do not breathe. Thus, an inferential system needs to know what is being referred to in order to make appropriate inferences.

Concepts

In the 1970s, new views about abstraction processes involved in category representation helped to stimulate interest in semantic memory. According to such views, processes of feature averaging or feature counting result in the abstraction of typical characteristics of category exemplars; these are represented as a schema or prototype (Medin & Smith 1984; Mervis & Rosch 1981; Smith & Medin 1981). Current alternatives to the abstractionist approach emphasize the importance of specific event information (exemplars) for categorical information (Brooks 1978; Jacoby & Brooks 1984; Hintzman 1986; Medin & Schaffer 1978). At issue here is whether abstract concepts are directly represented in memory (associated as well with some corresponding loss of information for individual events) or whether abstract knowledge is derived when needed from memory representations of unique events. If the latter, there may be no need to postulate a semantic storage system separate from an episodic storage system.

In exemplar models, classification is based on the retrieval of information about exemplars in memory. Category judgments are made by analogy to a similar known exemplar or are based on a number of exemplars weighted according to their similarity to the stimulus. For example, in Hintzman's (1986) theory, each event, represented as a feature list, is copied into memory. Similarity of any two events is determined by the number of features they have in common. When a probe event occurs, each trace in memory is activated, in parallel, by an amount related to its similarity to the probe. The activated traces, in concert, create an "echo." The intensity of the echo, related to the total amount of activation to the probe event, can be used as a discriminative cue for recognition (cf Gillund & Shiffrin 1984) or frequency judgments. The content of the echo can be used to categorize the probe. Hintzman uses a series of computer simulations to demonstrate that a number of phenomena usually taken as support for schema-abstraction can be accounted for by a multiple-trace exemplar theory. Hintzman's paper is a particularly readable example of the growing trend toward evaluating a theory by computer simulation.

A related development is the increasing popularity of distributed-memory models (Knapp & Anderson 1984; McClelland & Rumelhart 1985; also see Eich 1982, 1985; Murdock 1982, 1983; Pike 1984; and chapters in Hinton & Anderson 1981). As in Hintzman's model, the Knapp & Anderson and McClelland & Rumelhart models do not require a separate semantic memory. In distributed-memory models, traces consist of patterns of excitation across units representing features in memory. A given event (pattern of activation) changes the strength of the connections among units which co-occur. Because a particular unit may be involved in many events, the memory for an event does not have a location, or separate existence, but is distributed across feature units. Retrieval is the partial reinstatement of a pattern of activation, using a cue that is a fragment of the original pattern of activation. Concepts or prototype-like patterns develop through the "superimposition" of many similar activation patterns during acquisition: The resulting change in values of connections between units creates a composite trace that functions like an abstraction. These models are similar in many ways to Hintzman's, but the abstraction takes place at retrieval in Hintzman's model and at storage in McClelland & Rumelhart's.

Distributed-memory models represent a sort of middle-ground between prototype theories and Hintzman's multiple-trace theory in that some exemplar information is preserved and recoverable (with sufficiently specific cues). Some information is simply lost ("washed out") in the creation of the composite trace. Both distributed-memory and exemplar models account for the flexibility of meaning that characterizes human behavior by making context part of the probe that determines which traces (or patterns of units) are activated. This flexibility of meaning is harder to capture in a fixed-network or feature-list representation of semantic structure. It is presumably gained at some cost in processing efficiency compared to models in which abstractions are directly represented.

Similarity is a problem at the center of exemplar and distributed-memory (and other) models. A probe activates traces with the same features or one event activates some of the same "units" as another; hence similarity is a function of the number of features or units events have in common. What are these features or units? In both experiments and simulations, similarity is made tractable by using artificial stimuli such as dot patterns or feature lists where each feature has a binary value. This is a reasonable strategy for concretizing certain ideas (such as the echo) or demonstrating the viability of certain general approaches (such as a system without semantic memory). The success of these theories as psychological models will depend on whether they can successfully be applied to memory for natural, complex events.

The sufficiency of similarity for holding together the members of a category is questioned in a recent paper by Murphy & Medin (1985). They point out that similarity depends largely on what is assumed to be a relevant attribute (Tversky 1977) and that this in turn is determined by people's interests, needs, and goals. Thus, things seem similar because a person has a theory that relates them. Murphy & Medin's (1985) ideas here resemble those of other investigators (e.g. Bransford & Johnson 1973, Clark & Gerrig 1983, Johnson-Laird 1983; van Dijk & Kintsch 1983) who emphasize the importance of whether subjects are able to build sensible stories out of the elements of their experience.

Murphy & Medin emphasize another (and possibly prior) problem for determining similarity based on feature overlap. Because we do not know what to count as a feature, attribute, or property in the first place, we cannot define the variables that should enter into the analysis or computation of similarity. In judging the similarity between plums and lawn mowers, what attributes are relevant? Both weigh less than 10,000 kg, cannot hear, can be dropped, take up space, etc.) Models that are based entirely on attribute matching usually do not deal in any detail with the problem of what counts as an attribute (but see Nelson 1984).

Schemas and Scripts

Schema theory is another example of the ongoing tension in cognitive psychology between the specific and the general. Schema-based theories emphasize the general, typically proposing that memory for a particular event is guided at encoding and retrieval by organized clusters of generic knowledge relevant to the immediate situation. In some schematic views, any particular episode will leave little mark on memory except for its theme, a few salient and/or atypical details, and the activation of the generic schema (see Alba & Hasher 1983; Brewer & Nakamura 1984; Thorndyke 1984, for reviews).

One line of work in prose memory suggests that subjects abstract meaning from the flow of verbal information and store only a general representation of that meaning (Alba & Hasher 1983). However, there is now increasing evidence that such surface-structure details as syntax, lexical items, and orthography are not necessarily lost to memory (e.g. Kolers & Roediger 1984; Levelt & Kelter 1982; Masson 1984; but see Brewer & Hay 1984) and that memory for thematic and specific information depends on type of initial processing (Hunt et al 1986). Furthermore, a full picture of memory for prose cannot be had by simply using a recall test; variables that influence recall may not influence recognition (Kintsch & Young 1984). Indeed, performance on recall and recognition tasks, even in combination, may not provide a complete picture of the representations that result from encoding processes (see Locksley et al 1984). For such a picture, especially for one that eliminates strategic components, as Seifert et al (1986) argue, speeded decisions may also be required.

Script theory (Schank & Abelson 1977) is a particularly popular variant of schema theory that asserts the existence of highly structured underlying representations of familiar events (e.g. eating in a restaurant). It continues to stimulate research (Barsalou & Sewell 1985; Abbott et al 1985), and modifications of the original theory have been proposed and explored (e.g. Graesser & Nakamura 1982; Nakamura et al 1985; Schank 1982). It now seems unlikely that an entire scripted representation is activated whenever a script is relevant (Walker & Yekovich 1984), and subjects may fail to spontaneously recognize the thematic similarities across stories (Seifert et al 1986; see also Spencer & Weisberg 1986). Also, the presumably invariant underlying units can be altered by changes in such surface-structure details as punctuation in passages that activate scripts (Mandler & Murphy 1983). Prior knowledge even for such highly familiar categories of experience as scripted activities may be a good deal more flexible in its application to new events (Abbott et al 1985) than was once believed. Schema theory is adapting to such findings by placing more emphasis on specific-event memory as well as on higher-order organizing structures that help create scripts as needed out of lower-order components or "scenes" (e.g. Schank 1982). Other issues that were especially important for schema theories, e.g. inferences, have become active research areas and are described below.

The Episodic-Semantic Distinction Reconsidered

Recent attempts to test directly the proposition that episodic and semantic memories represent isolable systems (e.g. Dosher 1984b; McKoon et al 1985; Neely & Durgunoglu 1985; also see Watkins & Kerkar 1985) have largely not supported the distinction. Criticisms of the semantic-episodic distinction can be found in the commentaries in *Behavioral and Brain Sciences* (Tulving

1984) on Tulving's recent book (1983), in McKoon et al (1986), and in Ratcliff & McKoon (1986). To address some of these issues, Tulving (1984, 1985a,b) has proposed a modified framework in which episodic memory is a subsystem of semantic memory (also see Tulving 1986).

Conclusions

Studies of lexical access, semantic decisions, schemas and scripts, and concepts have independently generated many important facts. Unfortunately, these results have not converged to yield a common picture of semantic memory, except of the most general sort. The solution may be more sophisticated paradigms (e.g. speed-accuracy decomposition) or more careful controls over processes operating in particular tasks (e.g. Glucksberg et al 1986). Another possibility is that the format in which generic knowledge is represented varies with particular knowledge domains; if so, we should not expect a unified solution to the problem of the representation of and access to generic information.

Semantic networks may characterize a subset of basic knowledge, but networks (like associations) are still much too limited to account for the range of cognitive functions that knowledge serves. If there is a theoretical role for a stable semantic structure that is separate from the representation of events, we need to specify how the elements (e.g. entries in a lexicon, nodes in a semantic network) of this structure are acquired and how they articulate with new events. On the other hand, there simply may be limitations upon what we can learn about the representation of knowledge by starting with the pre-theoretical assumption of a separate semantic system. Distributed-memory and exemplar models provide an alternative approach. Ultimately, the value of these models will depend on whether they contribute to uncovering new facts or organizing a larger body of data than previous models. In this regard, it is encouraging that both exemplar models (e.g. Jacoby & Brooks 1984; Hintzman 1986) and distributed-memory models (e.g. McClelland & Rummelhart 1985), like earlier abstraction models, reach beyond categorization data to the domains of memory and perception for support, and that they, in turn, are useful to efforts to analyze other psychological phenomena such as surprise and social judgments (Kahneman & Miller 1986).

The idea that there is a single separate generic memory system and the idea that there is no generic memory are two extremes of a continuum. Characteristics of conceptual knowledge may vary with age of subject (e.g. Nelson 1984) or stage of learning. It is also possible that some types of knowledge may be better characterized in terms of abstractions (or symbols) and other types in terms of exemplars (or distributed connections among elements). Alternatively, task and situation demands may influence the particular type of representation that is generated and/or selected. Increased interest in mixed prototype and exemplar models (Busemeyer et al 1984; Fried & Holyoak 1984; Homa et al 1981; Lingle et al 1984; Medin et al 1984; Nakamura 1985) and in ad hoc or goal-defined categories (Barsalou 1983, 1985) reflects a growing recognition of such possibilities.

RELATIONS AMONG MEMORY MEASURES

How the relationships among different memory tasks should be characterized is currently a central question. Do various tasks tap different memory systems, draw on different aspects of the same trace, and/or represent different combinations of various processes?

Direct vs Indirect Measures

Striking differences have been reported recently between direct and indirect measures of the memory performance of both normal and amnesic subjects. *Direct* memory tasks (free recall, cued recall, recognition) require conscious expressions of remembering; *indirect* memory tasks (e.g. perceptual identification, homophone spelling, word completion, skill learning) do not. An illustrative example and a surprising new finding is Cohen's (1984) report of normal learning of the Tower of Hanoi problem by amnesics who fail to remember having seen the materials before. There is also some evidence that the pattern may be reversed; Martone et al (1984) found that patients with Huntington's disease were disrupted in acquiring the skill of mirror-reading, but not in recognition of repeated items.

Considerable effort has been focused on indirect measures in verbal tasks. Subjects who have recently been exposed to a word are more likely than under control conditions (*a*) to identify it when its presentation is degraded, (*b*) to produce it when asked to complete a word from partial letter cues (e.g. def-?), and (*c*) to have their spelling of a homophone influenced by the prior context in which the word was presented aloud (e.g. taxi *fare*). It is especially noteworthy that subjects may show "memory" for items on indirect tasks that is uncorrelated with their ability to recall or recognize the same items (Eich 1984; Graf et al 1982; Jacoby & Dallas 1981; Jacoby & Witherspoon 1982; Tulving et al 1982). In addition, decrements in performance as a consequence of alcohol ingestion (Hashtroudi et al 1984), aging (Light et al 1986), or posthypnotic amnesia (Kihlstrom 1985) occur on direct tests even though intoxicated, older, or previously hypnotized subjects may perform normally on indirect tests. Finally, whereas direct measures of memory are likely to be influenced by meaningful vs nonmeaningful orienting tasks, indirect measures are less subject to orienting task effects (Graf et al 1982; Graf & Mandler 1984; Jacoby & Dallas 1981; but see Graf & Schacter 1985 for results indicating that orienting tasks may influence whether context effects are observed in word-completion tests).

The view that there is a fundamental difference between memorial information assessed by direct and indirect tasks receives further support from
research with amnesics. In perceptual-identification and word-completion
tasks, amnesics show prior-exposure effects that are comparable to controls',
even though their recognition, cued recall, or free recall of the same words
may be disrupted (Graf et al 1984; Graf et al 1985; Jacoby & Witherspoon
1982; Squire et al 1985). Positive effects of prior exposure on indirect tasks is
not limited to single words; pre-experimental associations between words
(e.g. idioms such as *small potatoes,* or associates such as *stove–hot*) also
benefit from prior exposure (Schacter 1985; Shimamura & Squire 1984).

One explanation for exposure effects is that presentation of a word temporarily activates an abstract lexical or semantic representation of that word (or
other pre-experimental unit), making recently exposed items more accessible.
Consistent with this is the finding that amnesics do not show an exposure
effect in a perceptual-identification task for pseudowords, items for which
there are presumably no lexical entries (Cermak et al 1985). However, several
facts argue against the idea of temporary activation of a lexical entry as the
only source of exposure effects: For normals, the benefit from prior exposure
lasts from under two hours to seven days, depending on the task (Graf et al
1984; Jacoby 1983a; Shimamura & Squire 1984; Tulving et al 1982; Jacoby &
Dallas 1981). The longevity of the effect might be explained by assuming
that, in addition to experiencing lexical priming, normals engage in conscious
recall in these tasks. However, amnesics, who presumably fail at conscious
recall, also show benefits from prior exposure that last between ten minutes
and two hours (Shimamura & Squire 1984), which is beyond the presumed
duration of the temporary and purely lexical activation component of repetition or associative priming (Forster & Davis 1984; Ratcliff et al 1985). More
important, amnesics can learn new associations between unrelated words,
given an indirect test of what they have learned [(Graf & Schacter 1985;
Moscovitch et al 1986); it is possible that only patients with milder forms of
amnesia learn new associations (Schacter 1985)]. That amnesics learn new
associations, and that their disruption on direct tasks is not uniform [recall is
more disrupted than is recognition (Hirst et al 1986)], argues against
characterizing amnesia in terms of disrupted episodic (Tulving 1983) or
declarative (Cohen 1984) memory. The broader impact of these findings on
theoretical approaches to memory is discussed below.

Recognition

Following earlier efforts to distinguish the mechanisms of recognition from
those of recall, investigators continue to search for ways to characterize this
seemingly simple task. Understanding recognition will certainly fit a major
piece into the puzzle of the relations among memory tasks. Various sugges-

tions are currently under consideration. Tulving (1982, 1983) has proposed that recognition and recall include the same type of "ecphoric" process but can be distinguished in the amount of "ecphoric information" required for the task. Two-process approaches to recognition remain influential (e.g. Atkinson & Juola 1973; Mandler 1980; Jacoby & Dallas 1981; W. A. Johnston et al 1985). In these theories it is assumed that a rapid, direct-access familiarity response (based on trace strength, perceptual integration, or perceptual fluency, depending on the model) is separate from a slower recall or search process based on associative or elaborative processing. Gillund & Shiffrin (1984) suggest that the search factor in two-process theories may have been overemphasized. They propose that familiarity responses underlying recognition are affected by the strength of inter-item associative relations and associations between items and context (cf Anderson & Bower 1972, 1974). In effect, they propose that the activation level of an item is determined by the amount of simultaneous activation of episodic traces (which Gillund & Shiffrin call "images"), a suggestion similar to Hintzman's (1986) that recognition is based on "echo" intensity.

Subsystems of Memory?

The patterns of relations among memory measures, along with the performance of amnesics, have been instrumental in the development of recent approaches to human memory which are organized around the idea of separable, functional subsystems. These are components of memory that deal with different types of information or involve different processes, are mediated by different underlying neural mechanisms, and may have different evolutionary histories (e.g. Cohen 1984; Johnson 1983; Squire 1982; Squire & Cohen 1984; Tulving 1985a; Warrington & Weiskrantz 1982; also see chapters in Cermak 1982). Animal-memory researchers have made similar suggestions (Olton et al 1979; Mishkin et al 1984; O'Keefe & Nadel 1978; and see chapters in Squire & Butters 1984; Lynch et al 1984).

A critical issue here is determining the criteria for inferring subsystems. Is it sufficient that two tasks respond differently to the same variable or does valid inference require stochastic independence on the same items tested differently (e.g. Hintzman 1980; Tulving 1985a)? A related question is how dissociations between two tasks should be interpreted if the tasks are presumed to tap the same system or subsystem (e.g. Roediger 1984). Although dissociations between tasks are often interpreted as evidence that task A engages one subsystem and task B engages another (e.g. Cohen 1984), dissociations might also be interpreted as evidence that task A engages processes from two or more subsystems and task B engages a somewhat different combination of processes from the same subsystems (e.g. Johnson 1983). Arguments against the need to infer subsystems have been made; such approaches emphasize the importance of task demands (e.g. Jacoby 1983b; Moscovitch 1984; Moscovitch et al 1986; Roediger & Blaxton 1986). At the least, we will have a better understanding of memory once we have understood the relations among various memory tasks. Characterizing task demands is clearly a first step, whether or not it is motivated by the belief that task demands and, hence, processes may eventually be grouped into classes according to the subsystems they draw upon.

UNCONSCIOUS AND NONSTRATEGIC PROCESSING

A growing interest in nonconscious cognitive processes can be seen in research in perception, attention, social cognition, and memory. In the field of learning and memory, one manifestation of this trend has been a switch in research emphasis from voluntary, strategic mental activities (e.g. organization, mnemonics, elaborative processing) to less effortful, involuntary, automatic, and even unaware or unconscious processes. Generally speaking, two questions have been asked: Are there long-term effects of unconscious processing of stimuli? What do people learn without strategic effort?

Effects of Unconscious Processing

The intriguing question of whether unconscious stimuli influence thought and behavior surfaces periodically in psychology (e.g., Dixon 1971; Erdelyi 1984, 1985; Kihlstrom 1984). Dramatic demonstrations of meaningful processing of unconscious stimuli have been reported (Marcel 1983; Fowler et al 1981; McCauley et al 1980). Lexical decisions concerning suprathreshold words are facilitated by prior exposure of the subject to related, masked subthreshold words. While the results of Marcel (1983) and Fowler et al (1981) may be startling in their implications about how much processing can be initiated by minimal perceptual stimuli, the idea that much perceptual processing proceeds without awareness has long been well accepted.

Do such unconsciously experienced stimuli produce effects that last more than a few seconds? If so, the effects do not appear to be tapped by direct tests of memory (recall, recognition). In contrast, indirect tests do seem to reveal long-lasting consequences of unconscious processing. For example, Eich (1984) found that subjects' spelling of homophones was consistent with an interpretation previously implied in the unattended ear while subjects followed (shadowed) speech in the other ear, even though subjects did not show reliable recognition of the homophones. Consistent with this are recent replications of earlier reports by Kunst-Wilson & Zajonc (1980) showing that exposure durations (2–8 msec) too brief to produce above-chance recognition increase preferences for visual stimuli (Seamon et al 1983, 1984; though see Mandler & Sheebo 1983). Similarly, Lewicki (1986a) reported that subjects can learn to use stimuli they cannot consciously identify to guide visual search.

Memory Without Strategic Processing

Investigators have also been interested in the fate of stimuli that are consciously perceived but not accorded elaborative, effortful, or strategic processing. Early statements of the levels-of-processing framework (Craik & Lockhart 1972) implied that non-elaborative "maintenance" rehearsal should keep information temporarily active without producing long-term memory traces. It is now relatively clear that incidental rote rehearsal of words promotes long-term recognition memory (Glenberg & Adams 1978; Glenberg et al 1977; Naveh-Benjamin & Jonides 1984a,b).

Another illustration of interest in nonstrategic learning is the Hasher & Zacks (1979, 1984) proposal concerning the automatic encoding of such fundamental information as the frequency with which events occur. According to this view, automatic processes code some attributes of consciously experienced stimuli whether or not the person is trying to code that attribute. By definition, automatic processes do not get better with practice or feedback, do not show individual differences or age differences, and are not disrupted by stress or other simultaneous processing demands. Hasher & Zacks (1979, 1984; Hasher et al 1986) showed that frequency judgments are remarkably stable across a range of such variables. These claims have not gone unchallenged. One alternative interpretation of the absence of developmental trends and of improvement with practice is that necessary skills are acquired rapidly; another is that subjects find it difficult to discover test-appropriate strategies (Postman 1982). Furthermore, frequency judgments may vary as a function of age (Kausler et al 1984; Warren & Mitchell 1980), incidental vs intentional instructions (Greene 1984; Williams & Durso 1986), and with competing demands (Fisk & Schneider 1984; Naveh-Benjamin & Jonides 1986). Although the automaticity issue is unresolved, the data show that subjects are sensitive to differences in frequency of occurrence. This sensitivity can be used by people to acquire knowledge of their environment (Hasher & Zacks 1984) and can be exploited by investigators to answer questions about a range of human abilities (Hock et al 1986; Marshall et al 1986).

It has also been proposed that many of the complex rules underlying perception, language, and social conventions are learned nonstrategically. Having studied the acquisition of artificial grammars, Reber and colleagues (e.g. Reber 1976; Reber et al 1980; also see Broadbent et al 1986; McAndrews & Moscovitch 1985) emphasized the importance of implicit learning. When stimuli are complex and the patterns of invariance in stimuli are not obvious, subjects may acquire a better abstract representation of the structure of a language if they do not consciously try to discover rules. Recently,

Carlson & Dulany (1985; Dulany et al 1985) argued against the idea of implicit learning and suggested that subjects consciously learn informal grammars; these are not equivalent to the formal grammars that generated the language items but nevertheless provide a basis for making judgments about the appropriateness of new items. Along with Anderson (1983a), Carlson & Dulany emphasize that once-conscious knowledge can become automatic with practice, but this phenomenon does not mean that the original learning was unconscious (see reply by Reber et al 1985; also see Lewicki 1986b). Whether this alternative characterization of a conscious-to-automatic transition in knowledge is appropriate for the wide range of apparently implicitly learned rules (e.g. natural grammars, social conventions) is not clear.

Some of the controversies in this general area stem from the fact that terms such as consciousness, awareness, effort, attention, capacity, resource, and controlled processes are not used consistently. There is some consensus that automatic processes are involuntary, do not draw on general resources, are not interfered with by attended activities, and do not interfere with attended activities or with other automatic processes (Kahneman & Treisman 1984; but see Shiffrin 1986; Navon 1984; Hirst 1986). The relation between automatic processes and consciousness is less clear. In spite of these definitional and conceptual problems, the general issue of what type of initial processing is necessary for what type of memory test provides a productive focus for future research.

CONSTRAINTS ON ACQUISITION AND REMEMBERING

In this next section we focus particularly on limitations upon inferences made during initial processing and limitations produced by mechanisms of forgetting.

Text Processing

WORKING MEMORY   Working memory can be conceived of as a limited resource system that allocates capacity between two major components, a central executive responsible for the processing of ongoing information and a buffer that briefly maintains information (Baddeley & Hitch 1974; Baddeley 1981, 1983; Hitch 1980). This view seems to meet the requirements of discourse processing, which is widely believed to require ongoing analysis (e.g. pattern recognition, word identification, sentence parsing, and so on) as well as integration of the products of this analysis with preceding text information and with general knowledge. Both sources of information are thought of as being held in a state of heightened accessibility by the buffer component of working memory. Thus it is not surprising that many views of text processing (e.g. Aaronson & Ferres 1984; Ackerman 1984; Bock & Brewer 1985; Spilich 1983; van Dijk & Kintsch 1983; also see Glanzer et al 1984) have at their core the assumption of a limited-capacity working-memory system.

The view that working-memory capacity constrains text processing is strengthened by the development of a measure that assesses the joint operation of storage and processing components of working memory (Daneman & Carpenter 1980; see also Daneman & Green 1986). Strong correlations exist between this measure and performance on text processing and memory tasks (Baddeley et al 1985; Daneman & Carpenter 1980, 1983; Daneman & Green 1986; Masson & Miller 1983; although see Light & Anderson 1985).

Constraints related to working-memory capacity [or efficient utilization of that capacity (Case et al 1982)] have also been invoked by investigators interested in cognitive development across the lifespan (Brainerd 1983b; Smith et al 1983; Wingfield & Butterworth 1984; Zacks & Hasher 1986). Verbal ability—which may be associated with variations in capacity—makes a major contribution to age differences in prose memory (Dixon et al 1984; Hultsch & Dixon 1984; Mandel & Johnson 1984), as do processing demands made at the time of testing (Reder et al 1986).

INFERENCES: TAXONOMY AND MEASUREMENT   Since few texts make all necessary information explicit, another set of constraints on text processing— at least for comprehension—involves the capability of forming inferences. Insofar as inferences require that previously acquired information (whether from the text or elsewhere) be available for integration with text information, working-memory capacity has a role to play.

Research on working-memory constraints on inference generation joins with other work to reveal that making inferences is not nearly so reliable as 1970s schema theories supposed (see Barclay et al 1984; Corbett & Dosher 1978; Singer 1981, Singer & Ferreira 1983). Such findings helped to trigger an intense examination of inference making by memory psychologists who joined in pursuit of this issue with others interested in reading comprehension and language processes.

Consensus has not yet been reached on how to categorize inferences (see, e.g., McKoon & Ratcliff 1986; Seifert et al 1985; Singer & Ferreira 1983). Nor do researchers agree about which measure (or combination of measures) is best for detecting the formation of an inference and determining when it was made. One set of procedures tests for the existence of inferences after subjects read a text. Such measures assess the rate of false recognition of implicit information (Seifert et al 1985); the usefulness of an inferred word as a retrieval cue (McKoon & Ratcliff 1986); the accuracy and speed with which subjects answer questions (Singer & Ferreira 1983); and most recently, speeded item recognition comparing primed with unprimed targets (Guindon & Kintsch 1984; McKoon & Ratcliff 1986).

Other procedures test for the formation of an inference during reading. These procedures include such measures as word-by-word or sentence-by-sentence reading or comprehension times (Corbett 1984; Haberlandt & Graesser 1985; Lorch et al 1985; Murphy 1984) and detection of spelling errors during reading (Garrod & Sanford 1985). As well, speeded recognition tasks have been embedded in ongoing reading tasks (Dell et al 1983). A consensus seems to be emerging that multiple measures are required for a complete picture (e.g. Keenan et al 1984; O'Brien & Myers 1985).

Inference making is not an obligatory consequence of text comprehension processes. A number of task variables affect the probability of drawing an inference—e.g. backward vs forward referents (Singer & Ferreira 1983), the distance between a referent and its antecedent (Murphy 1984), the degree of causal relation between events (Keenan et al 1984), and the likelihood that information is in working memory (Malt 1985). Subject variables such as expertise (Arkes & Freedman 1984), age, and verbal ability (Hultsch & Dixon 1984) are also implicated. Whether or not constraints on working-memory capacity alone can accommodate these findings remains to be seen.

MORE THAN ONE TEXT REPRESENTATION?   One framework for describing discourse comprehension and memory (van Dijk & Kintsch 1983) proposes that two independent representations of a text are formed: (a) a text memory that includes both specific detailed text-level information and summary information; and (b) a situation model that integrates information from the text with existing world knowledge. This view is similar to Johnson-Laird's (1983) proposal that subjects create a mental model in addition to a representation close to the perceptual experience. In addition, Anderson (1983a) has added two types of memory representations—temporal strings and spatial images—to his model, a departure from his previous proposal that information is represented only in terms of abstract propositions. Again, we see the trend to posit multiple records of experience and, especially, to represent specific information in memory theories. By contrast with some characterizations of text representation, such models distinguish text-presented information from subject-generated information at least some of the time. They raise the issue of the functions of multiple representations and the conditions under which one representation might be mistaken for another ["reality monitoring" errors (Johnson & Raye 1981)].

Remembering

SOURCE DISCRIMINATION   Confusion between inferred and stated information in text-processing studies is an example of the more general problem of source discrimination in remembering. People confuse self-generated information with perceived information, thoughts with actions, and information from one external source with that from another (Anderson 1984; Johnson & Foley 1984; Johnson et al 1984). Individual differences in source confusion are a function of age (Foley & Johnson 1985; Mitchell et al 1986; but see Kausler et al 1985), expertise (Arkes & Freedman 1984), personality (Durso et al 1985), clinical diagnosis (Harvey 1985), and memory disorder (Schacter et al 1984). Furthermore, source discrimination and recall or recognition may draw on different aspects of memories (Anderson 1984; Johnson & Raye 1981).

OVERWRITING   According to one view of memory, new, inconsistent information will replace originally stored information—an effect called overwriting (Loftus & Loftus 1980). In keeping with earlier research on the interference theory of forgetting (Postman & Underwood 1973), recent evidence suggests that rather than replacing original information, new, contradictory information can coexist in memory with original information (Alba 1984; Bekerian & Bowers 1983; Christiaansen & Ochalek 1983; Morton et al 1985; Pirolli & Mitterer 1984; Shaughnessy & Mand 1982). Other evidence suggests that the procedures used to demonstrate overwriting (e.g. Loftus et al 1978) may be missing a critical control (McCloskey & Zaragoza 1985). An alternative account of memory errors produced by misleading information can be framed in terms of source confusion (Lindsay & Johnson 1986); subjects may misattribute information from one source to another. The determination of the circumstances in which either overwriting or source confusion occurs is critical not only for theoretical models of forgetting, but also for such applied issues as the validity of eyewitness testimony (Loftus 1979; see also McCloskey & Egeth 1983) and decision making (Fischhoff 1977).

INTERFERENCE   One consequence of the coexistence in memory of two or more sources of highly related information is an increase in the difficulty of remembering either (McGeoch 1942). This can be seen throughout the earlier literature on interference theories of forgetting and in recent demonstrations that similarity in meaning (Dempster 1985; Underwood 1983b), in input modalities (Glenberg 1984), and within the acoustic modality (Underwood 1983a) all disrupt retrieval. Parallel findings may be seen in the fan effect (e.g. Pirolli & Anderson 1985), where retrieval difficulty is indexed by an increase in time to recognize list items (see Nelson et al 1985). Work on the fan effect is guided by Anderson's model of spreading activation, the most recent version of which, ACT* (1983a,b), predicts a variety of important memory effects such as those related to distribution of practice, learning to learn, and interference. Furthermore, the potency of interference is demonstrated by evidence that some interference effects may not be eliminated even with substantial practice (Pirolli & Anderson 1985). By contrast with the strong evidence that multiple responses to the same cue disrupt memory, evidence continues to be weak (Postman & Knecht 1983; Toppino & Gracen 1985) for the widespread belief that multiple cues for the same response facilitate retrieval.

CHANGES IN CONTEXT   There have been several recent experiments on context changes and retention (Dolinsky & Zabrucky 1983; Eich 1986; Fernandez & Glenberg 1985; Saufley et al 1985; Smith 1982; also see Riccio et al 1984). By contrast with the well-established effects of meaning-based stimulus change, environmental changes in context appear to have a smaller effect on performance than might have been assumed (Fernandez & Glenberg 1985; Saufley et al 1985). Eich (1986) found that unless to-be-remembered items had been actively related to elements of the environmental context, change in environmental context between acquisition and a recall test had little effect. Underwood (1983b), too, has recently questioned the relative importance of contextual cues. Eich proposed that the underlying mechanism for apparent environmental context effects may be changes in internal state associated with different contexts. Although this is an interesting possibility, changes in at least one internal state, mood, may have limited effects on retrieval (see below).

EXPANDED RESEARCH DOMAINS

Learning and memory researchers are tackling an ever-wider range of problems—e.g. comprehension of and memory for metaphor (Gerrig & Healy 1983; Gildea & Glucksberg 1983; Marschark & Hunt 1985), creativity (Weisberg 1986), acquisition of skills or "procedural knowledge" (Anderson 1983a; Kolers & Roediger 1984; Ross 1984), educational (Glaser 1984; Lesgold 1984) and therapeutic applications (Wilson & Moffat 1984), developmental aspects of eyewitness testimony (Ceci et al 1986; Goodman 1984), decision making (Busemeyer 1985; Hoch 1984), metamemory (Bransford et al 1982; Lovelace 1984; Maki & Berry 1984; Metcalfe 1986; Nelson et al 1986), music (Halpern 1984; Serafine et al 1986), and the characteristics and timing of neural events that occur during learning and memory as reflected in event-related brain potentials (e.g. R. Johnson et al 1985; Neville et al 1986; Warren & Wideman 1983). By way of illustration, we review three areas that have grown substantially in recent years: affect and memory, spatial memory, and autobiographical memory.

Affect

Based on evidence that changes in the affective valence of words can produce release from proactive interference in the Brown-Petersons task (Wickens &

Clark 1968), Underwood (1983c) included an affective component in his listing of the attributes of memory. Bower (1981), too, proposed that emotional responses can be a component of memory, here conceived of as an associative network that represents an event (see also Clark & Isen 1982; Tyler & Voss 1982). Feeling states can serve as retrieval cues for events associated with that state. At least two related predictions have been explored: (a) Mood will be associated with state-dependency effects such that retrieval will be best if a person is in the same mood as at initial encoding; and (b) mood will give rise to "congruency" or "selectivity" effects such that elements of ongoing events that match a person's current mood will have a higher probability of being encoded than other elements.

Both predictions have been explored (see Blaney 1986 for a review). State-dependency effects tend to be small (Bower et al 1978; Gage & Safer 1985; Schare et al 1984) and are sometimes not found (Bower & Mayer 1985; Wetzler 1985). Selectivity effects are more consistently reported, but there are exceptions here as well (e.g. Bower 1981; Bower et al 1981; Hasher et al 1985). Positive and negative affect do not have symmetrical effects on performance; those associated with positive affect seem to be more systematic (Isen 1984). Negative affect is not without consequence. For example, it can alter people's perception of the risk associated with various sources of morbidity (Johnson & Tversky 1983).

The impact of depression on cognitive function has also received attention from investigators working within the framework of general-capacity models (Ellis et al 1984, 1985; Hasher et al 1985; see Craik & Byrd 1982; and Rabinowitz et al 1982 for an extension of a similar model to memory deficits with age). The basic notion is that depression reduces capacity or causes its reallocation away from learning and memory tasks, resulting in disrupted performance. Confirming evidence comes from the study of clinically depressed patients (Cohen et al 1982), college students (Ellis et al 1984, 1985; although see Hasher et al 1985), and school-aged children (Goldstein & Dundon 1986; Goldstein et al 1985).

Other aspects of the relationship between affect and cognition have been studied, including reflective and nonreflectively-based affect (M. K. Johnson et al 1985), arousal (Clark et al 1983; d'Ydewalle et al 1985), emotion (Mandler 1984; Stein & Levine 1986), stress (Jacobs & Nadel 1985), and consumer behavior (Gardner 1986). Contemporary cognitive psychology can no longer be accused of ignoring affect (Zajonc 1980, p. 152).

Spatial Cognition

Spatial cognition has attracted the interest of investigators in human memory, in part because it allows an exploration of naturalistic memory phenomena in a nonverbal domain (Byrne 1982). We review two lines of research here. One pursues the notion that location information has a special status in memory, possibly as an obligatory code established as a byproduct of visual experience with objects (Hasher & Zacks 1979; Mandler et al 1977). There is evidence of good incidental memory for location, but there is contradictory data on the question of whether intention to store location information improves performance (Cooper & Marshall 1985; Light & Zelinski 1983; McCormack 1982; Park et al 1982). As well, age differences are often found (e.g. Acredolo et al 1975; Light & Zelinski 1983). For text material, memory for location has proven to be an effective cue for content information and vice versa (Lovelace & Southall 1983). Similarly, there is a relation between object recall and location recall (Hazen & Volk-Hudson 1985).

Another line of work is concerned with identifying the underlying organization of spatial information. Research suggests that there are systematic distortions in memory for spatial arrays; for example, what is near in physical space is not necessarily what is near in conceptual space (e.g. Hirtle & Jonides 1985; McNamara et al 1984; see also Stevens & Coupe 1978; Tversky 1981). Spatial information may be organized into hierarchically ordered chunks created by perceived or imagined boundaries; spatial knowledge is different for objects that share a boundary than for objects that cross one (Acredolo & Boulter 1984; Hirtle & Jonides 1985; Maki 1981; McNamara 1986; Newcombe & Liben 1982).

Spatial cognition, an area of increasing concern to investigators in human learning and memory, is also studied by those interested in cognitive development (see e.g. Mandler 1983 for a review), animal behavior (see Kamil & Roitblat 1985; Menzel 1978), and the differences among individuals and between groups of individuals (Caplan et al 1985; Cooper & Mumaw 1985; Just & Carpenter 1985; Strelow 1985). Many methods are available to determine what people learn and remember about spatial information. Investigators have monitored subjects' navigation through space and the search strategies used to find missing objects (DeLoache & Brown 1983; Lockman 1984; Wellman et al 1984). They have asked subjects to make judgments of distance, orientation, and/or direction using either direct (e.g. drawings) or indirect (e.g. triangulation) measures (e.g. Bartlett et al 1983; Enns & Girgus 1985; Hanley & Levine 1983; Moar & Bower 1983; Presson & Hazelrigg 1984; Reed et al 1983). Finally, recognition, drawing, reconstruction and, most recently, reaction time have also been used as response measures (e.g. Dirks & Neisser 1977; Herman 1980; Light & Humphreys 1981; McNamara et al 1984). As is the case for item memory, alternative methods do not necessarily reveal the same patterns of effects across independent variables. Thus a complete picture of what people learn and remember about space will require (at least) a systematic analysis of tasks and measurement methods (see Newcombe 1985). The danger of underestimating the contribution of task variables to performance in spatial (as in other) tasks should not be ignored (Newcombe 1985; Presson & Somerville 1985).

Autobiographical Memory

Because investigators have begun to see the complexity of the underlying representations and/or processes supporting memory for naturally occurring events as a challenge rather than an obstacle, they are currently engaged in a lively exploration of issues, methods, and topics in autobiographical memory.

Like other workers discussed above, investigators of autobiographical memory must grapple with the relationship between general knowledge (e.g. of an airport) and event-specific information (e.g. a particular trip to the airport) (Bahrick & Karis 1982; Linton 1982; Neisser 1984; Reiser et al 1985). For example, Bahrick has studied several types of naturally acquired knowledge: recognition of college classmates, recognition by professors of names and faces of former students, learning and retention of the streets and buildings of a college town, and retention of Spanish learned in high school or college (Bahrick 1983, 1984a,b). Bahrick (1984b) suggests that as level of learning increases, some portion of this type of knowledge becomes permanent [perhaps partly through organizational restructuring (Bahrick 1984c)] and will be indefinitely maintained, even in the absence of further rehearsals, and regardless of potential interference encountered during the retention interval. (See Neisser 1984 for an alternative interpretation, and Slamecka & McElree 1983 for work on the retention of laboratory-learned lists as a function of degree of learning.) This, along with Salasoo et al's (1985) suggestion that letter strings become "codified" after a certain number of repetitions, indicates that the idea of a fundamental difference between stable knowledge domains and episodic memories continues to be compelling.

Schema theory interpretations of autobiographical memory also are relevant to the issue of the relationship between generic and specific information (Kolodner 1983; Nakamura et al 1985; Reiser et al 1985, 1986). For example, Reiser et al (1985) propose that script-like activities (e.g. going to restaurants, going shopping) are a major encoding level for memory. [Similar ideas include basic level concepts (Rosch 1978), basic level situations (Cantor et al 1982), and basic level scenes (Tversky & Hemenway 1983).] Reiser et al suggest that autobiographical events are represented by specific traces with "pointers" from the activity scripts used to encode them. Retrieval of a particular event involves first accessing the relevant activity script and using information in that structure that points to the specific experience.

Issues similar to those that have emerged from laboratory studies include: the problem of defining events or other units of experience (Linton 1986; Neisser 1986), remembering as active problem solving (Baddeley 1982; Reiser et al 1985, 1986), and possible multiple entries representing different kinds of information (Johnson 1983, 1985; Neisser 1986).

Recent papers (especially see Bahrick & Karis 1982 and edited collections by Gruneberg et al 1978; Harris & Morris 1984; Neisser 1982; Rubin 1986) illustrate the growing range of topics and methods in the area of naturally occurring memories—e.g. field studies of daily events (Thompson 1982) and dreams (Johnson et al 1984), single-subject studies (Wagenaar 1986), vivid memories (Rubin & Kozin 1984), remembering to do things ["prospective" memory (Harris 1984; Levy & Loftus 1984)], diary studies of tip-of-the-tongue states (Reason & Lucas 1984), commonplace slips and lapses or "absent-mindedness" (Reason 1984), and the general relation between attention and cognitive failures (Martin & Jones 1984). Questionnaires have been developed for assessing memory of public and private events and for assessing beliefs about memory (see Herrmann 1984 for a list; Morris 1984 for problems; Martin & Jones 1984). In addition, there have been attempts to systematically explore phenomenal qualities of remembered events (Johnson et al 1984; Johnson 1985; Nigro & Neisser 1983).

A major problem in studying autobiographical memory lies in verifying the accuracy and the age of memories. This perhaps partially accounts for the continued interest in memory for public events (for example, the assassination of President Kennedy) for which at least the retention interval is known (e.g. Winograd & Killinger 1983). Public events have been used to study temporal dating processes. The evidence suggests that temporal information is not directly retrieved: People use inferential processes in combination with other knowledge to date specific events. For example, the accessibility of information about an event is useful for dating because we tend to remember less about events as time passes. The result is a systematic bias: People tend to underestimate the time that has passed since events they know more about and overestimate the time since events they know less about (Brown et al 1985). People use personal experiences that happened around the same time to help date public events as well as general knowledge about when certain types of events typically occur (Friedman & Wilkins 1985); they can also use public events to increase their accuracy in dating personal events (Loftus & Marburger 1983). [For recent temporal order studies involving personal memories or laboratory events, see Barclay & Wellman 1986; Winograd & Soloway 1985; Zacks et al 1984; also see Glenberg & Swanson 1986.]

SUMMARY AND CONCLUSIONS

There have been several notable recent trends in the area of learning and memory. Problems with the episodic/semantic distinction have become more apparent, and new efforts have been made (exemplar models, distributed-memory models) to represent general knowledge without assuming a separate semantic system. Less emphasis is being placed on stable, prestored prototypes and more emphasis on a flexible memory system that provides the basis for a multitude of categories or frames of reference, derived on the spot as tasks demand.

There is increasing acceptance of the idea that mental models are constructed and stored in memory in addition to, rather than instead of, memorial representations that are more closely tied to perceptions. This gives rise to questions concerning the conditions that permit inferences to be drawn and mental models to be constructed, and to questions concerning the similarities and differences in the nature of the representations in memory of perceived and generated information and in their functions.

There has also been a swing from interest in deliberate strategies to interest in automatic, unconscious (even mechanistic!) processes, reflecting an appreciation that certain situations (e.g. recognition, frequency judgments, savings in indirect tasks, aspects of skill acquisition, etc) seem not to depend much on the products of strategic, effortful or reflective processes.

There is a lively interest in relations among memory measures and attempts to characterize memory representations and/or processes that could give rise to dissociations among measures. Whether the pattern of results reflects the operation of functional subsystems of memory and, if so, what the "modules" are is far from clear. This issue has been fueled by work with amnesics and has contributed to a revival of interaction between researchers studying learning and memory in humans and those studying learning and memory in animals. Thus, neuroscience rivals computer science as a source of interdisciplinary stimulation.

Research on topics such as memory for spatial location, the relation between memory and affect, and autobiographical memory reminds us that general theories of memory based on studies of verbal materials alone are limited. Investigating how people remember complex natural events should provide us with a larger set of memory phenomena to explain and consequently insight into a wider range of memory principles or a deeper understanding of the ones we already accept (e.g. the role of repetition, encoding specificity), including their functional significance for human behavior.

The major danger that we see for the field is a proliferation of paradigms, none of which is well understood. The studies reviewed here show that even the simplest task may involve a number of processes. Theoretical ideas based on incomplete task analyses are likely to be wrong. At the same time, a single task (no matter how completely understood) cannot reflect the astounding range of memory's capability. Rigid adherence to any standardized research technique is dangerous. Achievements in understanding human learning and memory in the last 100 years (Gorfein & Hoffman 1986; Klix & Hagendorf 1986) have not come from any single approach. There is hope in our collective eclecticism (Baddeley & Wilkins 1984; Bahrick 1984d; Postman 1968).

ACKNOWLEDGMENT

Preparation of this paper was supported by National Science Foundation Grant BNS-8510633, and National Institute of Aging Grant AG04306. Special thanks to Marlene Levine and Janice Seifrid for help in preparing the manuscript.

Literature Cited

Aaronson, D., Ferres, S. 1984. Reading strategies for children and adults: Some empirical evidence. *J. Verb. Learn. Verb. Behav.* 23:189–220

Abbott, V., Black, J. B., Smith, E. E. 1985. The representation of scripts in memory. *J. Mem. Lang.* 24:179–99

Ackerman, B. P. 1984. The effects of storage and processing complexity on comprehension repair in children and adults. *J. Exp. Child. Psychol.* 37:303–34

Acredolo, L. P., Boulter, L. T. 1984. Effects of hierarchical organization on children's judgments of distance and direction. *J. Exp. Child. Psychol.* 37:409–25

Acredolo, L. P., Pick, H. L. Jr., Olson, M. G. 1975. Environmental differentiation and familiarity as determinants of children's memory for spatial location. *Dev. Psychol.* 11:495–501

Alba, J. W. 1984. Nature of inference representation. *Am. J. Psychol.* 97:215–33

Alba, J. W., Hasher, L. 1983. Is memory schematic? *Psychol. Bull.* 93:203–31

Anderson, J. R. 1983a. *The Architecture of Cognition.* Cambridge, MA: Harvard Univ. Press

Anderson, J. R. 1983b. A spreading activation theory of memory. *J. Verb. Learn. Verb. Behav.* 22:261–95

Anderson, J. R., Bower, G. H. 1972. Recognition and retrieval processes in free recall. *Psychol. Rev.* 79:97–123

Anderson, J. R., Bower, G. H. 1974. A propositional theory of recognition memory. *Mem. Cognit.* 2:406–12

Anderson, J. R., Kosslyn, S., eds. 1984. *Tutorials in Learning and Memory: Essays in Honor of Gordon Bower.* San Francisco: Freeman

Anderson, R. E. 1984. Did I do it or did I only imagine doing it? *J. Exp. Psychol: Gen.* 113:594–613

Arkes, H. R., Freedman, M. R. 1984. A demonstration of the costs and benefits of expertise in recognition memory. *Mem. Cognit.* 12:84–89

Atkinson, R. C., Juola, J. F. 1973. Factors influencing speed and accuracy of word recognition. See Kornblum 1973, pp. 583–612

Atkinson, R. C., Herrnstein, R. J., Lindzey, G., Luce, R. D., eds. 1986. *Steven's Handbook of Experimental Psychology.* New York: Wiley. In press. 2nd ed.

Baddeley, A. 1981. The concept of working memory: A view of its current state and probable future development. *Cognition* 10:17–23

Baddeley, A. 1982. Amnesia: A minimal model and an interpretation. See Cermak 1982, pp. 305–36

Baddeley, A. D. 1983. Working memory. *Philos. Trans. R. Soc. London Ser. B* 302:311–24

Baddeley, A. D., Hitch, G. J. 1974. Working memory. See Bower 1974, pp. 47–89

Baddeley, A. D., Logie, R., Nimmo-Smith, I., Brereton, N. 1985. Components of fluent reading. *J. Mem. Lang.* 24:119–31

Baddeley, A. D., Wilkins, A. 1984. Taking memory out of the laboratory. See Harris & Morris 1984, pp. 1–17

Bahrick, H. P. 1983. The cognitive map of a city: Fifty years of learning and memory. See Bower 1983, pp. 125–63

Bahrick, H. P. 1984a. Memory for people. See Harris & Morris 1984, pp. 19–34

Bahrick, H. P. 1984b. Semantic memory content in permastore: Fifty years of memory for Spanish learned in school. *J. Exp. Psychol: Gen.* 113:1–29

Bahrick, H. P. 1984c. Associations and organization in cognitive psychology: A reply to Neisser. *J. Exp. Psychol: Gen.* 113:36–37

Bahrick, H. P. 1984d. Invited Symposium. Long-term memories: How durable, and how enduring? Replicative, constructive, and reconstructive aspects of memory: Implications for human and animal research. *Physiol. Psychol.* 12:53–58

Bahrick, H. P., Karis, D. 1982. Long-term ecological memory. See Puff 1982, pp. 427–65

Balota, D. A., Chumbley, J. I. 1984. Are lexical decisions a good measure of lexical access? The role of word frequency in the neglected decision stage. *J. Exp. Psychol: Hum. Percept. Perform.* 10:340–57

Balota, D. A., Chumbley, J. I. 1985. The locus of word-frequency effects in the pronunciation task: Lexical access and/or production? *J. Mem. Lang.* 24:89–106

Baltes, P. B., Brim, O. G. Jr., eds. 1984. *Life-Span Development and Behavior,* Vol. 6. New York: Academic

Barclay, C. R., Toglia, M. P., Chevalier, D. S. 1984. Pragmatic inferences and type of processing. *Am. J. Psychol.* 97:285–96

Barclay, C. R., Wellman, H. M. 1986. Accuracies and inaccuracies in autobiographical memories. *J. Mem. Lang.* 25:93–103

Barsalou, L. W. 1983. Ad hoc categories. *Mem. Cognit.* 11:211–27

Barsalou, L. W. 1985. Ideals, central tendency, and frequency of instantiation as determinants of graded structure in categories. *J. Exp. Psychol: Learn. Mem. Cognit.* 11:629–54

Barsalou, L. W., Sewell, D. R. 1985. Contrasting the representation of scripts and categories. *J. Mem. Lang.* 24:646–65

Bartlett, J. C., Till, R. E., Gernsbacher, M., Gorman, W. 1983. Age-related differences in memory for lateral orientation of pictures. *J. Gerontol.* 38:439–46

Becker, C. A., Killion, T. H. 1977. Interaction of visual and cognitive effects in word recognition. *J. Exp. Psychol: Hum. Percept. Perform.* 3:389–401

Bekerian, D. A., Bowers, J. M. 1983. Eyewitness testimony: Were we mislead? *J. Exp. Psychol: Learn. Mem. Cognit.* 9:139–45

Blaney, P. H. 1986. Affect and memory: A review. *Psychol. Bull.* 99:229–46

Bock, J. K., Brewer, W. F. 1985. Discourse structure and mental models. See Carr 1985, pp. 55–75

Bouma, H., Bouwhuis, D. G., eds. 1984. *Attention and Performance,* Vol. 10, *Control of Language Processes.* Hillsdale, NJ: Erlbaum

Bower, G. H. 1974. *The Psychology of Learning and Motivation,* Vol. 8. New York: Academic

Bower, G. H. 1981. Mood and memory. *Am. Psychol.* 36:129–48

Bower, G. H. 1982. *The Psychology of Learning and Motivation,* Vol. 16. New York: Academic

Bower, G. H. 1983. *The Psychology of Learning and Motivation,* Vol. 17. New York: Academic

Bower, G. H. 1984. *Psychology of Learning and Motivation,* Vol. 18. New York: Academic

Bower, G. H., Gilligan, S. G., Monteiro, K. P. 1981. Selectivity of learning caused by emotional states. *J. Exp. Psychol: Gen.* 110:451–73

Bower, G. H., Mayer, J. D. 1985. Failure to replicate mood-dependent retrieval. *Bull. Psychon. Soc.* 23:39–42

Bower, G. H., Monteiro, K. P., Gilligan, S. G. 1978. Emotional mood as a context of learning and recall. *J. Verb. Learn. Verb. Behav.* 17:573–85

Bowers, K. S., Meichenbaum, D. 1984. *The Unconscious Reconsidered.* New York: Wiley

Brainerd, C. J., ed. 1983a. *Recent Advances in Cognitive-Developmental Theory: Progress in Cognitive Developmental Research.* New York: Springer-Verlag

Brainerd, C. J. 1983b. Working-memory systems and cognitive development. See Brainerd 1983a, pp. 167–236

Bransford, J. D., Johnson, M. K. 1973. Considerations of some problems of comprehension. See Chase 1973, pp. 383–438

Bransford, J. D., Stein, B. S., Vye, N. J., Franks, J. J., Auble, P. M., et al. 1982. Differences in approaches to learning: An overview. *J. Exp. Psychol: Gen.* 111:390–98

Brewer, W. F., Hay, A. E. 1984. Reconstructive recall of linguistic style. *J. Verb. Learn. Verb. Behav.* 23:237–49

Brewer, W. F., Nakamura, G. V. 1984. The nature and functions of schemas. See Wyer & Srull 1984a, pp. 119–60

Broadbent, D. E., Fitzgerald, P., Broadbent, M. H. P. 1986. Implicit and explicit knowledge in the control of complex systems. *Br. J. Psychol.* 77:33–50

Brooks, L. 1978. Nonanalytic concept formation and memory for instances. See Rosch & Lloyd 1978, pp. 170–211

Brown, N. R., Rips, L. J., Shevell, S. K. 1985. The subjective dates of natural events in very-long-term memory. *Cognit. Psychol.* 17:139–77

Busemeyer, J. R. 1985. Decision making under uncertainty: A comparison of simple scalability, fixed-sample, and sequential-sampling models. *J. Exp. Psychol: Learn. Mem. Cognit.* 11:538–64

Busemeyer, J. R., Dewey, G. I., Medin, D. L. 1984. Evaluation of exemplar-based generalization and the abstraction of categorical information. *J. Exp. Psychol: Learn. Mem. Cognit.* 10:638–48

Byrne, R. W. 1982. Geographical knowledge and orientation. See Ellis 1982, pp. 239–64

Cantor, N., Mischel, W., Schwartz, J. C. 1982. A prototype analysis of psychological situations. *Cognit. Psychol.* 14:45–77

Caplan, P. J., MacPherson, G. M., Tobin, P. 1985. Do sex-related differences in spatial abilities exist? A multi-level critique with new data. *Am. Psychol.* 40:786–99

Carlson, R. A., Dulany, D. E. 1985. Conscious attention and abstraction in concept learning. *J. Exp. Psychol: Learn. Mem. Cognit.* 11:45–58

Carr, T. H., ed. 1985. *The Development of Reading Skills.* San Francisco: Jossey-Bass

Case, R., Kurland, D. M., Goldberg, J. 1982. Operational efficiency and the growth of short-term memory span. *J. Exp. Child Psychol.* 33:386–404

Castellan, N. J., Restle, F., eds. 1978. *Cognitive Theory,* Vol. 3. Hillsdale, NJ: Erlbaum

Ceci, S. J., ed. 1986. *Handbook of Cognitive, Social and Neuropsychological Aspects of Learning Disabilities.* Hillsdale, NJ: Erlbaum. In press

Ceci, S. J., Toglia, M. P., Ross, D. F., eds. 1986. *Children's Eyewitness Memory.* New York: Springer-Verlag. In press

Cermak, L. S., ed. 1982. *Human Memory and Amnesia.* Hillsdale, NJ: Erlbaum

Cermak, L. S., Talbot, N., Chandler, K., Wolbarst, L. R. 1985. The perceptual priming phenomenon in amnesia. *Neuropsychologia* 23:615–22

Chang, T. M. 1986. Semantic memory: Facts and models. *Psychol. Bull.* 99:199–220

Chase, W. G. 1973. *Visual Information Processing.* New York: Academic

Christiaansen, R. E., Ochalek, K. 1983. Editing misleading information from memory: Evidence for the coexistence of original and postevent information. *Mem. Cognit.* 11:467–75

Chumbley, J. I. 1986. The roles of typicality, instance dominance, and category dominance in verifying category membership. *J. Exp. Psychol: Learn. Mem. Cognit.* 12:257–67

Chumbley, J. I., Balota, D. A. 1984. A word's meaning affects the decision in lexical decision. *Mem. Cognit.* 6:590–606

Clark, H. H., Gerrig, R. J. 1983. Understanding old words with new meanings. *J. Verb. Learn. Verb. Behav.* 22:591–608

Clark, M. S., Isen, A. M. 1982. Toward understanding the relationship between feeling states and social behavior. See Hastorf & Isen 1982, pp. 73–108

Clark, M. S., Milberg, S., Ross, J. 1983. Arousal cues arousal-related material in memory: Implications for understanding effects of mood on memory. *J. Verb. Learn. Verb. Behav.* 22:633–49

Claxton, G., ed. 1980. *Cognitive Psychology: New Directions.* London: Routledge & Kegan Paul

Cohen, N. J. 1984. Preserved learning capacity in amnesia: Evidence for multiple memory systems. See Squire & Butters 1984, pp. 83–103

Cohen, R., ed. 1985. *The Development of Spatial Cognition.* Hillsdale, NJ: Erlbaum

Cohen, R. M., Weingartner, H., Smallberg, S. A., Pickar, D., Murphy, D. L. 1982. Effort and cognition in depression. *Arch. Gen. Psychiatry* 39:593–97

Cooper, A., Marshall, P. H. 1985. Spatial location judgments as a function of intention to learn and mood state: An evaluation of an alleged automatic encoding operation. *Am. J. Psychol.* 98:261–69

Cooper, L. A., Mumaw, R. J. 1985. Spatial aptitude. See Dillon 1985, pp. 67–94

Corbett, A. T. 1984. Pronominal adjectives and the disambiguation of anaphoric nouns. *J. Verb. Learn. Verb. Behav.* 23:683–95

Corbett, A. T., Dosher, B. A. 1978. Instrument inferences in sentence encoding. *J. Verb. Learn. Verb. Behav.* 17:479–91

Craik, F. I. M., Byrd, M. 1982. Aging and cognitive deficits. See Craik & Trehub 1982, pp. 191–211

Craik, F. I. M., Lockhart, R. S. 1972. Levels of processing: A framework for memory research. *J. Verb. Learn. Verb. Behav.* 11:671–84

Craik, F. I. M., Trehub, H. S., eds. 1982. *Aging and Cognitive Processes.* New York: Plenum

Daneman, M., Carpenter, P. A. 1980. Individual differences in working memory and reading. *J. Verb. Learn. Verb. Behav.* 19:450–66

Daneman, M., Carpenter, P. A. 1983. Individual differences in integrating information between and within sentences. *J. Exp. Psychol: Learn. Mem. Cognit.* 9: 561–84

Daneman, M., Green, I. 1986. Individual differences in comprehending and producing words in context. *J. Mem. Lang.* 25:1–18

de Groot, A. M. B. 1983. The range of automatic spreading activation in word priming. *J. Verb. Learn. Verb. Behav.* 22:417–36

de Groot, A. M. B. 1984. Primed lexical decision: Combined effects of the proportion of related prime-target pairs and the stimulus-onset asynchrony of prime and target. *Q. J. Exp. Psychol.* 36A:253–80

Dell, G. S., McKoon, G., Ratcliff, R. 1983. The activation of antecedent information during the processing of anaphoric reference in reading. *J. Verb. Learn. Verb. Behav.* 22:121–32

DeLoache, J. S., Brown, A. L. 1983. Very young children's memory for the location of objects in a large-scale environment. *Child Dev.* 54:888–97

Dempster, F. N. 1985. Proactive interference in sentence recall: Topic-similarity effects and individual differences. *Mem. Cognit.* 13:81–89

den Heyer, K., Briand, K., Dannenberg, G. L. 1983. Strategic factors in a lexical-decision task: Evidence for automatic and attention-driven processes. *Mem. Cognit.* 11:374–81

den Heyer, K., Goring, A., Dannenbring, G. L. 1985. Semantic priming and word repetition: The two effects are additive. *J. Mem. Lang.* 24:699–716

Dillon, R. F., ed. 1985. *Individual Differences in Cognition,* Vol. 2. Orlando, FL: Academic

Dirks, J., Neisser, U. 1977. Memory for objects in real scenes: The development of recognition and recall. *J. Exp. Child Psychol.* 23:315–28

Dixon, N. F. 1971. *Subliminal Perception: The Nature of a Controversy.* London: McGraw-Hill

Dixon, R. A., Hultsch, D. F., Simon, E. W., von Eye, A. 1984. Verbal ability and text structure effects on adult age differences in text recall. *J. Verb. Learn. Verb. Behav.* 23:569–78

Dolinsky, R., Zabrucky, K. 1983. Effects of environmental context changes on memory. *Bull. Psychon. Soc.* 21:423–26

Dosher, B. A. 1984a. Degree of learning and retrieval speed: Study time and multiple exposures. *J. Exp. Psychol: Learn. Mem. Cognit.* 10:541–74

Dosher, B. A. 1984b. Discriminating pre-experimental (semantic) from learned (episodic) associations: A speed-accuracy study. *Cognit. Psychol.* 16:519–55

Dulany, D. E., Carlson, R. A., Dewey, G. I. 1985. On consciousness in syntactic learning and judgment: A reply to Reber, Allen, and Regan. *J. Exp. Psychol: Gen.* 114:25–32

Durso, F. T., Reardon, R., Jolly, E. 1985. Self-nonself segregation and reality monitoring. *J. Pers. Soc. Psychol.* 48:447–55

d'Ydewalle, G., Ferson, R., Swerts, A. 1985. Expectancy, arousal, and individual differences in free recall. *J. Mem. Lang.* 24:519–25

Eich, E. 1984. Memory for unattended events: Remembering with and without awareness. *Mem. Cognit.* 12:105–11

Eich, E. 1985. Context, memory, and integrated item/context imagery. *J. Exp. Psychol: Learn. Mem. Cognit.* 11:764–70

Eich, J. M. 1982. A composite holograph associative recall model. *Psychol. Rev.* 89:627–61

Eich, J. M. 1985. Levels of processing, encoding specificity, elaboration, and CHARM. *Psychol. Rev.* 92:1–38

Ellis, A. W. 1982. *Normality and Pathology in Cognitive Functions.* New York: Academic

Ellis, H. C., Thomas, R. L., McFarland, A. D., Lane, J. W. 1985. Emotional mood states and retrieval in episodic memory. *J. Exp. Psychol: Learn. Mem. Cognit.* 11:363–70

Ellis, H. C., Thomas, R. L., Rodriguez, I. A. 1984. Emotional mood states and memory: Elaborative encoding, semantic processing, and cognitive effort. *J. Exp. Psychol: Learn. Mem. Cognit.* 10:470–82

Enns, J. T., Girgus, J. S. 1985. Perceptual grouping and spatial distortion: A developmental study. *Dev. Psychol.* 21:241–46

Erdelyi, M. 1984. The recovery of unconscious (inaccessible) memories: Laboratory studies of hypermnesia. See Bower 1984, pp. 95–127

Erdelyi, M. H. 1985. *Psychoanalysis: Freud's Cognitive Psychology.* New York: Freeman

Fernandez, A., Glenberg, A. M. 1985. Changing environmental context does not reliably affect memory. *Mem. Cognit.* 13:333–45

Feustel, T. C., Shiffrin, R. M., Salasoo, A. 1983. Episodic and lexical contributions to the repetition effect in word identification. *J. Exp. Psychol: Gen.* 112:309–46

Fischhoff, B. 1977. Perceived informativeness of facts. *J. Exp. Psychol: Hum. Percept. Perform.* 3:349–58

Fisk, A. D., Schneider, W. 1984. Memory as a function of attention, level of processing, and automatization. *J. Exp. Psychol: Learn. Mem. Cognit.* 10:181–97

Flavell, J. H., Markman, E. M., eds. 1983. *Cognitive Development,* Vol. 3, *Handbook of Child Psychology,* ed. P. Mussen. New York: Wiley

Fodor, J. A. 1983. *Modularity of Mind: An Essay on Faculty Psychology.* Cambridge, MA: MIT Press

Foley, M. A., Johnson, M. K. 1985. Confusion between memories for performed and imagined actions. *Child Dev.* 56:1145–55

Forster, K. I., Davis, C. 1984. Repetition priming and frequency attenuation in lexical access. *J. Exp. Psychol: Learn. Mem. Cognit.* 10:680–98

Fowler, C. A., Wolford, G., Slade, R., Tassinary, L. 1981. Lexical access with and without awareness. *J. Exp. Psychol: Gen.* 110:341–62

Fried, L. S., Holyoak, K. J. 1984. Induction of category distributions: A framework for classification learning. *J. Exp. Psychol: Learn. Mem. Cognit.* 10:234–57

Friedman, W. J., Wilkins, A. J. 1985. Scale effects in memory for the time of events. *Mem. Cognit.* 13:168–75

Gage, D. F., Safer, M. A. 1985. Hemisphere

differences in the mood state–dependent effect for recognition of emotional faces. *J. Exp. Psychol: Learn. Mem. Cognit.* 11: 752–63

Gardner, M. P. 1986. Mood states and consumer behavior: A critical review. *J. Consum. Behav.* In press

Garrod, S., Sanford, A. J. 1985. On the realtime character of interpretation during reading. *Lang. Cognit. Process.* 1:43–59

Gernsbacher, M. A. 1984. Resolving 20 years of inconsistent interactions between lexical familiarity and orthography, concreteness, and polysemy. *J. Exp. Psychol: Gen.* 113:256–81

Gerrig, R. J., Healy, A. F. 1983. Dual processes in metaphor understanding: Comprehension and appreciation. *J. Exp. Psychol: Learn. Mem. Cognit.* 9:667–75

Gildea, P., Glucksberg, S. 1983. On understanding metaphor: The role of context. *J. Verb. Learn. Verb. Behav.* 22:577–90

Gillund, G., Shiffrin, R. M. 1984. A retrieval model for both recognition and recall. *Psychol. Rev.* 91:1–67

Glanzer, M., Fischer, B., Dorfman, D. 1984. Short-term storage in reading. *J. Verb. Learn. Verb. Behav.* 23:467–86

Glaser, R. 1984. Education and thinking: The role of knowledge. *Am. Psychol.* 39:93–104

Glenberg, A. M. 1984. A retrieval account of the long-term modality effect. *J. Exp. Psychol: Learn. Mem. Cognit.* 10:16–31

Glenberg, A., Adams, F. 1978. Type I rehearsal and recognition. *J. Verb. Learn. Verb. Behav.* 17:455–63

Glenberg, A., Smith, S. M., Green, C. 1977. Type I rehearsal: Maintenance and more. *J. Verb. Learn. Verb. Behav.* 16:339–52

Glenberg, A. M., Swanson, N. G. 1986. A temporal distinctiveness theory of recency and modality effects. *J. Exp. Psychol: Learn. Mem. Cognit.* 12:3–15

Glucksberg, S., Kreuz, R. J., Rho, S. 1986. Context can constrain lexical access: Implications for models of language comprehension. *J. Exp. Psychol: Learn. Mem. Cognit.* 12:323–35

Goldstein, D., Dundon, W. D. 1986. Affect and cognition in learning disabilities. See Ceci 1986

Goldstein, D., Paul, G. G., Sanfilippo-Cohn, S. 1985. Depression and achievement in subgroups of children with learning disabilities. *J. Appl. Dev. Psychol.* 6:263–75

Goodman, G. S., ed. 1984. The child witness. *J. Soc. Issues,* Vol. 40, No. 2

Gordon, B. 1985. Subjective frequency and the lexical decision latency function: Implications for mechanisms of lexical access. *J. Mem. Lang.* 24:631–645

Gorfein, D. S., Hoffman, R. R., eds. 1986. *Memory and Cognitive Processes: The*

Ebbinghaus Centennial Conference. Hillsdale, NJ: Erlbaum

Graesser, A. C., Nakamura, G. V. 1982. The impact of a schema on comprehension and memory. See Bower 1982, pp. 59–109

Graf, P., Mandler, G. 1984. Activation makes words more accessible, but not necessarily more retrievable. *J. Verb. Learn. Verb. Behav.* 23:553–68

Graf, P., Mandler, G., Haden, P. E. 1982. Simulating amnesic symptoms in normals. *Science* 218:1243–44

Graf, P., Schacter, D. L. 1985. Implicit and explicit memory for new associations in normal and amnesic subjects. *J. Exp. Psychol: Learn. Mem. Cognit.* 11:501–18

Graf, P., Shimamura, A. P., Squire, L. R. 1985. Priming across modalities and priming across category levels: Extending the domain of preserved function in amnesia. *J. Exp. Psychol: Learn. Mem. Cognit.* 11: 386–96

Graf, P., Squire, L. R., Mandler, G. 1984. The information that amnesic patients do not forget. *J. Exp. Psychol: Learn. Mem. Cognit.* 10:164–78

Greene, R. L. 1984. Incidental learning of event frequency. *Mem. Cognit.* 12:90–95

Gruneberg, M. M., Morris, P. E., Sykes, R. N. 1978. *Practical Aspects of Memory.* New York: Academic

Guindon, R., Kintsch, W. 1984. Priming macropropositions: Evidence for the primacy of macropropositions in the memory for text. *J. Verb. Learn. Verb. Behav.* 23:508–18

Haberlandt, K. F., Graesser, A. C. 1985. Component processes in text comprehension and some of their interactions. *J. Exp. Psychol: Gen.* 114:357–74

Halpern, A. R. 1984. Organization in memory for familiar songs. *J. Exp. Psychol: Learn. Mem. Cognit.* 10:496–512

Hanley, G. L., Levine, M. 1983. Spatial problem solving: The integration of independently learned cognitive maps. *Mem. Cognit.* 11:415–22

Harris, J. E. 1984. Remembering to do things: a forgotten topic. See Harris & Morris 1984, pp. 71–92

Harris, J. E., Morris, P. E., eds. 1984. *Everyday Memory, Actions and Absent-Mindedness.* London: Academic

Harvey, P. D. 1985. Reality monitoring in mania and schizophrenia. *J. Nerv. Ment. Dis.* 173:67–73

Hasher, L., Rose, K. C., Zacks, R. T., Sanft, H., Doren, B. 1985. Mood, recall, and selectivity effects in normal college students. *J. Exp. Psychol: Gen.* 114:104–18

Hasher, L., Zacks, R. T. 1979. Automatic and effortful processes in memory. *J. Exp. Psychol: Gen.* 108:356–88

Hasher, L., Zacks, R. T. 1984. Automatic processing of fundamental information: The case of frequency of occurrence. *Am. Psychol.* 39:1372–88

Hasher, L., Zacks, R. T., Rose, K. C., Sanft, H. 1986. Truly incidental encoding of frequency information. *Am. J. Psychol.* In press

Hashtroudi, S., Parker, E. S., DeLisi, L. E., Wyatt, R. J., Mutter, S. A. 1984. Intact retention in acute alcohol amnesia. *J. Exp. Psychol: Learn. Mem. Cognit.* 10:156–63

Hastorf, A. H., Isen, A. M., eds. 1982. *Cognitive Social Psychology.* New York: Elsevier

Hazen, N. L., Volk-Hudson, S. 1985. The effect of spatial context on young children's recall. *Child Dev.* 55:1835–44

Henik, A., Friedrich, F. J., Kellogg, W. A. 1983. The dependence of semantic relatedness effects upon prime processing. *Mem. Cognit.* 11:366–73

Herman, J. F. 1980. Children's cognitive maps of larger-scale spaces: Effects of exploration, direction, and repeated experience. *J. Exp. Child Psychol.* 29:126–43

Herrmann, D. J. 1984. Questionnaires about memory. See Harris & Morris 1984, pp. 133–51

Hinton, G. E., Anderson, J. A., eds. 1981. *Parallel Models of Associative Memory.* Hillsdale, NJ: Erlbaum

Hintzman, D. L. 1980. Simpson's paradox and the analysis of memory retrieval. *Psychol. Rev.* 87:398–410

Hintzman, D. L. 1986. "Schema abstraction" in a multiple-trace memory model. *Psychol. Rev.* In press

Hirst, W. 1986. Aspects of divided and selective attention. See LeDoux & Hirst 1986, pp. 105–41

Hirst, W., Johnson, M. K., Kim, J. K., Phelps, E. A., Risse, G., et al. 1986. Recognition and recall in amnesics. *J. Exp. Psychol: Learn. Mem. Cognit.* 12:445–51

Hirtle, S. C., Jonides, J. 1985. Evidence of hierarchies in cognitive maps. *Mem. Cognit.* 13:208–17

Hitch, G. J. 1980. Developing the concept of working memory. See Claxton 1980, pp. 154–96

Hoch, S. J. 1984. Availability and interference in predictive judgment. *J. Exp. Psychol: Learn. Mem. Cognit.* 10:649–62

Hock, H. S., Malcus, L., Hasher, L. 1986. Frequency discrimination: Assessing global-level and element-level units in memory. *J. Exp. Psychol: Learn. Mem. Cognit.* 12:232–40

Homa, D., Sterling, S., Trepel, L. 1981. Limitations of exemplar-based generalization and the abstraction of categorical in-formation. *J. Exp. Psychol: Hum. Learn. Mem.* 7:418–39

Hudson, P. T. W., Bergman, M. W. 1985. Lexical knowledge in word recognition: Word length and word frequency in naming and lexical decision tasks. *J. Mem. Lang.* 24:46–58

Hulse, S. H., Fowler, H., Honig, W. K. 1978. *Cognitive Processes in Animal Behavior.* Hillsdale, NJ: Erlbaum

Hultsch, D. F., Dixon, R. A. 1984. Memory for text materials in adulthood. See Baltes & Brim 1984, pp. 77–108

Hunt, R. R., Ausley, J. A., Schultz, E. E. Jr. 1986. Shared and item-specified information in memory for event descriptions. *Mem. Cognit.* 14:49–54

Huttenlocher, J., Kubicek, L. F. 1983. The source of relatedness effects on naming latency. *J. Exp. Psychol: Learn. Mem. Cognit.* 9:486–96

Isen, A. M. 1984. Toward understanding the role of affect in cognition. See Wyer & Srull 1984b, pp. 179–236

Jacobs, W. J., Nadel, L. 1985. Stress induced recovery of fears and phobias. *Psychol. Rev.* 92:512–31

Jacoby, L. L. 1983a. Perceptual enhancement: Persistent effects of an experience. *J. Exp. Psychol: Learn. Mem. Cognit.* 9:21–38

Jacoby, L. L. 1983b. Remembering the data: Analyzing interactive processes in reading. *J. Verb. Learn. Verb. Behav.* 22:485–508

Jacoby, L. L., Brooks, L. R. 1984. Nonanalytic cognition: Memory, perception, and concept learning. See Bower 1984, pp. 1–47

Jacoby, L. L., Dallas, M. 1981. On the relationship between autobiographical memory and perceptual learning. *J. Exp. Psychol: Gen.* 110:306–40

Jacoby, L. L., Witherspoon, D. 1982. Remembering without awareness. *Can. J. Psychol.* 36:300–24

Johnson, E., Tversky, A. 1983. Affect, generalization, and the perception of risk. *J. Pers. Soc. Psychol.* 45:20–31

Johnson, M. K. 1983. A multiple-entry, modular memory system. See Bower 1983, pp. 81–123

Johnson, M. K. 1985. The origin of memories. See Kendall 1985, pp. 1–27

Johnson, M. K., Foley, M. A. 1984. Differentiating fact from fantasy: The reliability of children's memory. *J. Soc. Issues* 40:33–50

Johnson, M. K., Kahan, T. L., Raye, C. L. 1984. Dreams and reality monitoring. *J. Exp. Psychol: Gen.* 113:329–44

Johnson, M. K., Kim, J. K., Risse, G. 1985. Do alcoholic Korsakoff syndrome patients acquire affective reactions? *J. Exp. Psychol: Learn. Mem. Cognit.* 11:22–36

Johnson, M. K., Raye, C. L. 1981. Reality monitoring. *Psychol. Rev.* 88:67–85

Johnson, R. Jr., Pfefferman, A., Kopell, B. S. 1985. P300 and long-term memory: Latency predicts recognition performance. *Psychophysiology* 22:497–507

Johnson-Laird, P. N. 1983. *Mental Models: Towards a Cognitive Science of Language, Inference, and Consciousness.* Cambridge, MA: Harvard Univ. Press

Johnson-Laird, P. N., Herrmann, D. J., Chaffin, R. 1984. Only connections: A critique of semantic networks. *Psychol. Bull.* 96:292–315

Johnston, J. C., van Santen, J. P. H., Hale, B. L. 1985. Repetition effects in word and pseudoword identification: Comment on Salasoo, Shiffrin, and Feustel. *J. Exp. Psychol: Gen.* 114:498–508

Johnston, W. A., Dark, V. J., Jacoby, L. L. 1985. Perceptual fluency and recognition judgments. *J. Exp. Psychol: Learn. Mem. Cognit.* 11:3–11

Just, M. A., Carpenter, P. A. 1985. Cognitive coordinate systems: Accounts of mental rotation and individual differences in spatial ability. *Psychol. Rev.* 92:137–72

Kahneman, D., Miller, D. T. 1986. Norm theory: Comparing reality to its alternatives. *Psychol. Rev.* 93:136–53

Kahneman, D., Treisman, A. 1984. Changing views of attention and automaticity. See Parasuraman & Davies 1984, pp. 29–61

Kamil, A. C., Roitblat, H. L. 1985. The ecology of foraging behavior: Implications for animal learning and memory. *Ann. Rev. Psychol.* 36:141–69

Kausler, D. H., Lichty, W., Freund, J. S. 1985. Adult age differences in recognition memory and frequency judgments for planned versus performed activities. *Dev. Psychol.* 21:647–54

Kausler, D. H., Lichty, W., Hakami, M. K. 1984. Frequency judgments for distractor items in a short-term memory task: Instructional variation and adult age differences. *J. Verb. Learn. Verb. Behav.* 23:660–68

Keenan, J. M., Baillet, S. D., Brown, P. 1984. The effects of causal cohesion on comprehension and memory. *J. Verb. Learn. Verb. Behav.* 23:115–26

Kendall, P. C. 1985. *Advances in Cognitive-Behavioral Research and Therapy*, Vol. 4. New York: Academic

Kiger, J. I., Glass, A. L. 1983. The facilitation of lexical decisions by a prime occurring after the target. *Mem. Cognit.* 11:356–65

Kihlstrom, J. F. 1984. Conscious, subconscious, unconscious: A cognitive perspective. See Bowers 1984, pp. 149–211

Kihlstrom, J. F. 1985. Posthypnotic amnesia

and the dissociation of memory. *Psychol. Learn. Motiv.* 19:131–78

Kintsch, W. 1980. Semantic memory: A tutorial. See Nickerson 1980, pp. 595–620

Kintsch, W., Mross, E. F. 1985. Context effects in word identification. *J. Mem. Lang.* 24:336–49

Kintsch, W., Young, S. R. 1984. Selective recall of decision-relevant information from texts. *Mem. Cognit.* 12:112–17

Klix, F., Hagendorf, H., eds. 1986. *Human Memory and Cognitive Capabilities, Symp. in Memoriam Hermann Ebbinghaus*, Vols. 1, 2. Amsterdam: Elsevier Science

Knapp, A. G., Anderson, J. A. 1984. Theory of categorization based on distributed memory storage. *J. Exp. Psychol: Learn. Mem. Cognit.* 10:616–37

Kolers, P. A., Roediger, H. L. III. 1984. Procedures of mind. *J. Verb. Learn. Verb. Behav.* 23:425–49

Kolodner, J. L. 1983. Reconstructive memory: A computer model. *Cognit. Sci.* 7:281–328

Kornblum, S., ed. 1973. *Attention and Performance*, Vol. 4. New York: Academic

Kunst-Wilson, W. R., Zajonc, R. B. 1980. Affective discrimination of stimuli that cannot be recognized. *Science* 207:557–58

LeDoux, J. E., Hirst, W., eds. 1986. *Mind and Brain: Dialogues in Cognitive Neuroscience.* New York: Cambridge Univ. Press

Lesgold, A. M. 1984. Acquiring expertise. See Anderson & Kosslyn 1984, pp. 31–60

Levelt, W. J. M., Kelter, S. 1982. Surface form and memory in question answering. *Cognit. Psychol.* 14:78–106

Levy, R. L., Loftus, G. R. 1984. Compliance and memory. See Harris & Morris 1984, pp. 93–112

Lewicki, P. 1986a. *Nonconscious Social Information Processing.* Orlando, FL: Academic

Lewicki, P. 1986b. Processing information about covariations that cannot be articulated. *J. Exp. Psychol: Learn. Mem. Cognit.* 12:135–46

Light, L. L., Anderson, P. A. 1985. Working-memory capacity, age, and memory for discourse. *J. Gerontol.* 40:737–47

Light, L. L., Burke, D. 1986. *Language, Memory, and Aging.* New York: Cambridge Univ. Press. In press

Light, L. L., Singh, A., Capps, J. L. 1986. Dissociation of memory and awareness in young and older adults. *J. Clin. Exp. Neuropsychol.* 8:62–74

Light, L. L., Zelinski, E. M. 1983. Memory for spatial information in young and old adults. *Dev. Psychol.* 19:901–6

Light, P. H., Humphreys, J. 1981. Internal spatial relationships in young children's drawings. *J. Exp. Child Psychol.* 31:521–30

Lindsay, D. S., Johnson, M. K. 1986. Reality monitoring and suggestibility: Children's ability to discriminate among memories from different sources. See Ceci 1986

Lingle, J. H., Alton, M. W., Medin, D. L. 1984. Of cabbages and kings: Assessing the extendability of natural object concept models to social things. See Wyer & Srull 1984a, pp. 71–117

Linton, M. 1982. Transformations of memory in everyday life. See Neisser 1982, pp. 77–91

Linton, M. 1986. Ways of searching and the contents of memory. See Rubin 1986

Lockman, J. J. 1984. The development of detour ability during infancy. *Child Dev.* 55:482–91

Locksley, A., Stangor, C., Hepburn, C., Grosovsky, E., Hochstrasser, M. 1984. The ambiguity of recognition memory tests of schema theories. *Cognit. Psychol.* 16:421–48

Loftus, E. F. 1979. *Eyewitness Testimony.* Cambridge, MA: Harvard Univ. Press

Loftus, E. F., Loftus, G. R. 1980. On the permanence of stored information in the human brain. *Am. Psychol.* 35:409–20

Loftus, E. F., Marburger, W. 1983. Since the eruption of Mt. St. Helens, has anyone beaten you up? Improving the accuracy of retrospective reports with landmark events. *Mem. Cognit.* 11:114–20

Loftus, E. F., Miller, D. G., Burns, H. J. 1978. Semantic integration of verbal information into a visual memory. *J. Exp. Psychol: Hum. Learn. Mem.* 4:19–31

Lorch, R. F. Jr., Lorch, E. P., Matthews, P. D. 1985. On-line processing of the topic structure of a text. *J. Mem. Lang.* 24:350–62

Lovelace, E. A. 1984. Metamemory: Monitoring future recallability during study. *J. Exp. Psychol: Learn. Mem. Cognit.* 10:756–66

Lovelace, E. A., Southall, S. D. 1983. Memory for words in prose and their locations on the page. *Mem. Cognit.* 11:429–34

Lupker, S. J. 1984. Semantic priming without association: A second look. *J. Verb. Learn. Verb. Behav.* 23:709–33

Lynch, G., McGaugh, J. L., Weinberger, N. M., eds. 1984. *Neurobiology of Learning and Memory.* New York: Guilford

Maki, R. H. 1981. Categorization and distance effects with spatial linear orders. *J. Exp. Psychol: Hum. Learn. Mem.* 7:15–32

Maki, R. H., Berry, S. L. 1984. Metacomprehension of text material. *J. Exp. Psychol: Learn. Mem. Cognit.* 10:663–79

Malt, B. C. 1985. The role of discourse structure in understanding anaphora. *J. Mem. Lang.* 24:271–89

Mandel, R. G., Johnson, N. S. 1984. A developmental analysis of story recall and comprehension in adulthood. *J. Verb. Learn. Verb. Behav.* 23:643–59

Mandler, G. 1980. Recognizing: The judgment of previous occurrence. *Psychol. Rev.* 87:252–71

Mandler, G. 1984. *Mind and Body: Psychology of Emotion and Stress.* New York: Norton

Mandler, G., Sheebo, B. J. 1983. Knowing and liking. *Motiv. Emotion* 7:125–44

Mandler, J. M. 1983. Representation. See Flavell & Markman 1983, pp. 420–94

Mandler, J. M., Murphy, C. M. 1983. Subjective judgments of script structure. *J. Exp. Psychol: Learn. Mem. Cognit.* 9:534–43

Mandler, J. M., Seegmiller, D., Day, J. 1977. On the coding of spatial information. *Mem. Cognit.* 5:10–16

Marcel, A. J. 1983. Conscious and unconscious perception: Experiments on visual masking and word recognition. *Cognit. Psychol.* 15:197–237

Marschark, M., Hunt, R. 1985. On memory for metaphor. *Mem. Cognit.* 13:413–24

Marshall, P. H., Pruitt, M. P., Gonzalez, A. 1986. The encoding of frequency of linear positioning motor responses as a function of intention and discriminability. *J. Hum. Movement Stud.* 12:27–33

Martin, M., Jones, G. V. 1984. Cognitive failures in everyday life. See Harris & Morris 1984, pp. 173–90

Martone, M., Butters, N., Payne, M., Becker, J. T., Sax, D. S. 1984. Dissociations between skill learning and verbal recognition in amnesia and dementia. *Arch. Neurol.* 41:965–70

Masson, M. E. J. 1984. Memory for the surface structure of sentences: Remembering with and without awareness. *J. Verb. Learn. Verb. Behav.* 23:579–92

Masson, M. E. J., Miller, J. A. 1983. Working memory and individual differences in comprehension and memory of text. *J. Educ. Psychol.* 75:314–18

McAndrews, M. P., Moscovitch, M. 1985. Rule-based and exemplar-based classification in artificial grammar learning. *Mem. Cognit.* 13:469–75

McCauley, C., Parmelee, C. M., Sperber, R. D., Carr, T. H. 1980. Early extraction of meaning from pictures and its relation to conscious identification. *J. Exp. Psychol: Hum. Percept. Perform.* 6:265–76

McClelland, J. L. 1979. On the time relations of mental processes: An examination of systems of processes in cascade. *Psychol. Rev.* 86:287–330

McClelland, J. L., Rumelhart, D. E. 1985. Distributed memory and the representation of general and specific information. *J. Exp. Psychol: Gen.* 114:159–88

McCloskey, M., Egeth, H. E. 1983. Eyewitness identification: What can a psychologist tell a jury? *Am. Psychol.* 38:550–63

McCloskey, M., Zaragoza, M. 1985. Misleading postevent information and memory for events: Arguments and evidence against memory impairment hypotheses. *J. Exp. Psychol: Gen.* 114:1–16

McCormack, P. D. 1982. Coding of spatial information by young and elderly adults. *J. Gerontol.* 37:80–86

McGeoch, J. A. 1942. *The Psychology of Human Learning.* New York: Longmans, Green

McKoon, G., Ratcliff, R. 1986. Inferences about predictable events. *J. Exp. Psychol: Learn. Mem. Cognit.* 12:82–91

McKoon, G., Ratcliff, R., Dell, G. S. 1985. The role of semantic information in episodic retrieval. *J. Exp. Psychol: Learn. Mem. Cognit.* 11:742–51

McKoon, G., Ratcliff, R., Dell, G. S. 1986. A critical evaluation of the semantic-episodic distinction. *J. Exp. Psychol: Learn. Mem. Cognit.* 12:295–306

McNamara, T. P. 1986. Mental representations of spatial relations. *Cognit. Psychol.* 18:87–121

McNamara, T. P., Ratcliff, R., McKoon, G. 1984. The mental representation of knowledge acquired from maps. *J. Exp. Psychol: Learn. Mem. Cognit.* 10:723–32

Medin, D. L., Altom, M. W., Murphy, T. D. 1984. Given versus induced category representations: Use of prototype and exemplar information in classification. *J. Exp. Psychol: Learn. Mem. Cognit.* 10:333–52

Medin, D. L., Schaffer, M. M. 1978. Context theory of classification learning. *Psychol. Rev.* 85:207–38

Medin, D. L., Smith, E. E. 1984. Concepts and concept formation. *Ann. Rev. Psychol.* 35:113–38

Menzel, E. W. 1978. Cognitive mapping in chimpanzees. See Hulse et al 1978, pp. 375–442

Mervis, C. B., Rosch, E. 1981. Categorization of natural objects. *Ann. Rev. Psychol.* 32:89–115

Metcalfe, J. 1986. Feeling of knowing in memory and problem solving. *J. Exp. Psychol: Learn. Mem. Cognit.* 12:288–94

Meyer, D. E., Irwin, D. E. 1981. *On the time-course of rapid information processing.* Presented at the Psychonomic Soc. meet., Philadelphia. Reprinted as Univ. Mich. Cognit. Sci. Techn. Rep. No. 43, June, 1982

Mishkin, M., Malamut, B., Bachevalier, J. 1984. Memories and habits: Two neural systems. See Lynch et al 1984, pp. 65–77

Mitchell, D. B., Hunt, R. R., Schmitt, F. A. 1986. The generation effect and reality monitoring: Evidence from dementia and normal aging. *J. Gerontol.* 41:79–84

Moar, I., Bower, G. H. 1983. Inconsistency in spatial knowledge. *Mem. Cognit.* 11:107–13

Morris, P. E. 1984. The validity of subjective reports on memory. See Harris & Morris 1984, pp. 153–72

Morton, J., Hammersley, R. H., Bekerian, D. A. 1985. Headed records: A model for memory and its failures. *Cognition* 20:1–23

Moscovitch, M. 1984. The sufficient conditions for demonstrating preserved memory in amnesia: A task analysis. See Squire & Butters 1984, pp. 104–14

Moscovitch, M., Winocur, G., McLachlan, D. 1986. Memory as assessed by recognition and by reading time of normal and transformed script: Evidence from normal young and old people, and patients with severe memory impairment due to Alzheimer's Disease and other neurological disorders. *J. Exp. Psychol: Gen.* In press

Murdock, B. B. Jr. 1982. A theory for the storage and retrieval of item and associative information. *Psychol. Rev.* 89:609–26

Murdock, B. B. Jr. 1983. A distributed memory model for serial-order information. *Psychol. Rev.* 90:316–38

Murphy, G. L. 1984. Establishing and accessing referents in discourse. *Mem. Cognit.* 12:489–97

Murphy, G. L., Medin, D. L. 1985. The role of theories in conceptual coherence. *Psychol. Rev.* 92:289–316

Nakamura, G. V. 1985. Knowledge-based classification of ill-defined categories. *Mem. Cognit.* 13:377–84

Nakamura, G. V., Graesser, A. C., Zimmerman, J. A., Riha, J. 1985. Script processing in a natural situation. *Mem. Cognit.* 13:140–44

Naveh-Benjamin, M., Jonides, J. 1984a. Cognitive load and maintenance rehearsal. *J. Verb. Learn. Verb. Behav.* 23:494–507

Naveh-Benjamin, M., Jonides, J. 1984b. Maintenance rehearsal: A two-component analysis. *J. Exp. Psychol: Learn. Mem. Cognit.* 10:369–85

Naveh-Benjamin, M., Jonides, J. 1986. On the automaticity of frequency coding: Effects of competing task load, encoding strategy, and intention. *J. Exp. Psychol: Learn. Mem. Cognit.* In press

Navon, D. 1984. Resources—A theoretical soup stone? *Psychol. Rev.* 91:216–34

Neely, J. H., Durgunoglu, A. Y. 1985. Dissociative episodic and semantic priming effects in episodic recognition and lexical decision tasks. *J. Mem. Lang.* 24:466–89

Neisser, U., ed. 1982. *Memory Observed: Remembering in Natural Contexts.* San Francisco: Freeman

Neisser, U. 1984. Interpreting Harry Bahrick's discovery: What confers immunity against forgetting? *J. Exp. Psychol: Gen.* 113:32–35

Neisser, U. 1986. Nested structure in autobiographical memory. See Rubin 1986

Nelson, D. G. K. 1984. The effect of intention on what concepts are acquired. *J. Verb. Learn. Verb. Behav.* 23:734–59

Nelson, D. L., Bajo, M. T., Casanueva, D. 1985. Prior knowledge and memory: The influence of natural category size as a function of intention and distraction. *J. Exp. Psychol: Learn. Mem. Cognit.* 11:94–105

Nelson, T. O., Leonesio, J., Landwehr, R. S., Narens, L. 1986. A comparison of three predictors of an individual's memory performance: The individual's feeling of knowing versus the normative feeling of knowing versus base-rate item difficulty. *J. Exp. Psychol: Learn. Mem. Cognit.* 12:279–87

Neville, H. J., Kutas, M., Chesney, G., Schmidt, A. L. 1986. Event-related brain potentials during initial encoding and recognition memory of congruous and incongruous words. *J. Mem. Lang.* 25:75–92

Newcombe, N. 1985. Methods for the study of spatial cognition. See Cohen 1985, pp. 277–300

Newcombe, N., Liben, L. S. 1982. Barrier effects in the cognitive maps of children and adults. *J. Exp. Child. Psychol.* 34:46–58

Nickerson, R. S., ed. 1980. *Attention and Performance,* Vol. 8. Hillsdale, NJ: Erlbaum

Nigro, G., Neisser, U. 1983. Point of view in personal memories. *Cognit. Psychol.* 15:467–82

Norris, D. 1984. The effects of frequency, repetition and stimulus quality in visual word recognition. *Q. J. Exp. Psychol.* 36A:507–18

O'Brien, E. J., Myers, J. L. 1985. When comprehension difficulty improves memory for text. *J. Exp. Psychol: Learn. Mem. Cognit.* 11:12–21

Oden, G. C., Spira, J. L. 1983. Influence of context on the activation and selection of ambiguous word senses. *Q. J. Exp. Psychol.* 35A:51–64

O'Keefe, J., Nadel, L. 1978. *The Hippocampus as a Cognitive Map.* London: Oxford Univ. Press

Olton, D. S., Becker, J. T., Handelmann, G. E. 1979. Hippocampus, space, and memory. *Behav. Brain Sci.* 2:313–65

Onifer, W., Swinney, D. A. 1981. Accessing lexical ambiguities during sentence comprehension: Effects of frequency of meaning and contextual bias. *Mem. Cognit.* 9:225–36

Pachella, R. G., Smith, J. E. K., Stanovich, K. E. 1978. Qualitative error analysis and speeded classification. See Castellan & Restle 1978, pp. 169–98

Parasuraman, R., Davies, D. R., eds. 1984. *Varieties of Attention.* Orlando, FL: Academic

Park, D. C., Puglisi, J. T., Lutz, R. 1982. Spatial memory in older adults: Effects of intentionality. *J. Gerontol.* 37:330–35

Pike, R. 1984. Comparison of convolution and matrix distributed memory systems for associative recall and recognition. *Psychol. Rev.* 91:281–94

Pirolli, P. L., Anderson, J. R. 1985. The role of practice in fact retrieval. *J. Exp. Psychol: Learn. Mem. Cognit.* 11:136–53

Pirolli, P. L., Mitterer, J. O. 1984. The effect of leading questions on prior memory: Evidence for the coexistence of inconsistent memory traces. *Can. J. Psychol.* 38:135–41

Postman, L. 1968. Hermann Ebbinghaus. *Am. Psychol.* 23:149–57

Postman, L. 1982. An examination of practice effects in recognition. *Mem. Cognit.* 10:333–40

Postman, L., Knecht, K. 1983. Encoding variability and retention. *J. Verb. Learn. Verb. Behav.* 22:133–52

Postman, L., Underwood, B. J. 1973. Critical issues in interference theory, *Mem. Cognit.* 1:19–40

Presson, C. C., Hazelrigg, M. D. 1984. Building spatial representations through primary and secondary learning. *J. Exp. Psychol: Learn. Mem. Cognit.* 10:716–22

Presson, C. C., Somerville, S. C. 1985. Beyond egocentrism: A new look at the beginnings of spatial representation. See Wellman 1985, pp. 1–26

Puff, R., ed. 1982. *Handbook of Research Methods in Human Memory and Cognition.* New York: Academic

Rabinowitz, J. C., Craik, F. I., Ackerman, B. P. 1982. A processing resource account of age differences in recall. *Can. J. Psychol.* 36:325–44

Ratcliff, R., Hockley, W., McKoon, G. 1985. Components of activation: Repetition and priming effects in lexical decision and recognition. *J. Exp. Psychol: Gen.* 114:435–50

Ratcliff, R., McKoon, G. 1982. Speed and accuracy in the processing of false statements about semantic information. *J. Exp. Psychol: Learn. Mem. Cognit.* 8:16–36

Ratcliff, R., McKoon, G. 1986. More on the distinction between episodic and semantic memories. *J. Exp. Psychol: Learn. Mem. Cognit.* 12:312–13

Reason, J. 1984. Absent-mindedness and cognitive control. See Harris & Morris 1984, pp. 113–32

Reason, J., Lucas, D. 1984. Using cognitive diaries to investigate naturally occurring memory blocks. See Harris & Morris 1984, pp. 53–70

Reber, A. S. 1976. Implicit learning of synthetic languages: The role of instructional set. *J. Exp. Psychol: Hum. Learn. Mem.* 2:88–94

Reber, A. S., Allen, R., Regan, S. 1985. Syntactical learning and judgment, still unconscious and still abstract: Comment on Dulany, Carlson, and Dewey. *J. Exp. Psychol: Gen.* 114:17–24

Reber, A. S., Kassin, S. M., Lewis, S., Cantor, G. 1980. On the relationship between implicit and explicit modes in the learning of a complex rule structure. *J. Exp. Psychol: Hum. Learn. Mem.* 6:492–502

Reder, L. M., Wible, C., Martin, J. 1986. Differential memory changes with age: Exact retrieval versus plausible inference. *J. Exp. Psychol: Learn. Mem. Cognit.* 12:72–81

Reed, A. V. 1973. Speed-accuracy trade-off in recognition memory. *Science* 181:574–76

Reed, S. K., Hock, H. S., Lockhead, G. R. 1983. Tacit knowledge and the effect of pattern configuration on mental scanning. *Mem. Cognit.* 11:137–43

Reiser, B. J., Black, J. B., Abelson, R. P. 1985. Knowledge structures in the organization and retrieval of autobiographical memories. *Cognit. Psychol.* 17:89–137

Reiser, B. J., Black, J. B., Kalamarides, P. 1986. Strategic memory search processes. See Rubin 1986

Riccio, D. C., Richardson, R., Ebner, D. L. 1984. Memory retrieval deficits based upon altered contextual cues: A paradox. *Psychol. Bull.* 96:152–65

Roediger, H. L. III. 1984. Does current evidence from dissociation experiments favor the episodic/semantic distinction? *Behav. Brain Sci.* 7:223–68

Roediger, H. L. III, Blaxton, T. A. 1986. Retrieval modes produce dissociations in memory for surface information. See Gorfein & Hoffman 1986

Rosch, E. 1978. Principles of categorization. See Rosch & Lloyd 1978, pp. 27–48

Rosch, E., Lloyd, B. B. 1978. *Cognition and Categorization.* Hillsdale, NJ: Erlbaum

Ross, B. H. 1984. Remindings and their effect in learning a cognitive skill. *Cognit. Psychol.* 16:371–416

Rubin, D. 1986. *Autobiographical Memory.*
New York: Cambridge Univ. Press. In press

Rubin, D. C., Kozin, M. 1984. Vivid memories. *Cognition* 16:1–15

Salasoo, A., Shiffrin, R. M., Feustel, T. C. 1985. Building permanent memory codes: Codification and repetition effects in word identification. *J. Exp. Psychol: Gen.* 114:50–77

Sanocki, T., Goldman, K., Waltz, J., Cook, C., Epstein, W., et al. 1985. Interaction of stimulus and contextual information during reading: Identifying words within sentences. *Mem. Cognit.* 13:145–57

Saufley, W. H. Jr., Otaka, S. R., Bavaresco, J. L. 1985. Context effects: Classroom tests and context independence. *Mem. Cognit.* 13:522–28

Schacter, D. L. 1985. Multiple forms of memory in humans and animals. See Weinberger et al 1985, pp. 351–79

Schacter, D. L., Harbluk, J. L., McLachlan, D. R. 1984. Retrieval without recollection: An experimental analysis of source amnesia. *J. Verb. Learn. Verb. Behav.* 23:593–611

Schank, R. C. 1982. *Dynamic Memory: A Theory of Reminding and Learning in Computers and People.* New York: Cambridge Univ. Press

Schank, R. C., Abelson, R. P. 1977. *Scripts, Plans, Goals and Understanding.* Hillsdale, NJ: Erlbaum

Schare, M. L., Lisman, S. A., Spear, N. E. 1984. The effects of mood variation on state-dependent retention. *Cognit. Ther. Res.* 8:387–408

Seamon, J. G., Brody, N., Kauff, D. M. 1983. Affective discrimination of stimuli that are not recognized: Effects of shadowing, masking, and cerebral laterality. *J. Exp. Psychol: Learn. Mem. Cognit.* 9:544–55

Seamon, J. G., Marsh, R. L., Brody, N. 1984. Critical importance of exposure duration for affective discrimination of stimuli that are not recognized. *J. Exp. Psychol: Learn. Mem. Cognit.* 10:465–69

Seidenberg, M. S., Tanenhaus, M. K., Leiman, J. M., Bienkowski, M. 1982. Automatic access of the meanings of ambiguous words in context: Some limitations of knowledge-based processing. *Cognit. Psychol.* 14:489–537

Seidenberg, M. S., Waters, G. S., Sanders, M., Langer, P. 1984. Pre- and postlexical loci of contextual effects on word recognition. *Mem. Cognit.* 12:315–28

Seifert, C. M., McKoon, G., Abelson, R. P., Ratcliff, R. 1986. Memory connections between thematically similar episodes. *J. Exp. Psychol: Learn. Mem. Cognit.* 12:220–31

Seifert, C. M., Robertson, S. P., Black, J. B.

1985. Types of inferences generated during reading. *J. Mem. Lang.* 24:405–22

Serafine, M. L., Davidson, J., Crowder, R. G., Repp, B. H. 1986. On the nature of melody-text integration in memory for songs. *J. Mem. Lang.* 25:123–35

Shaughnessy, J. J., Mand, J. L. 1982. How permanent are memories for real life events? *Am. J. Psychol.* 95:51–65

Shiffrin, R. M. 1986. Attention. See Atkinson et al 1986

Shimamura, A. P., Squire, L. R. 1984. Paired-associate learning and priming effects in amnesia: A neuropsychological study. *J. Exp. Psychol: Gen.* 113:556–70

Shoben, E. J. 1982. Semantic and lexical decisions. See Puff 1982, pp. 287–314

Simpson, G. B. 1984. Lexical ambiguity and its role in models of word recognition. *Psychol. Bull.* 96:316–40

Simpson, G. B., Burgess, C. 1985. Activation and selection processes in the recognition of ambiguous words. *J. Exp. Psychol: Hum. Percept. Perform.* 11:28–39

Singer, M. 1981. Verifying the assertions and implications of language. *J. Verb. Learn. Verb. Behav.* 20:46–60

Singer, M., Ferreira, F. 1983. Inferring consequences in story comprehension. *J. Verb. Learn. Verb. Behav.* 22:437–48

Slamecka, N. J., McElree, B. 1983. Normal forgetting of verbal lists as a function of their degree of learning. *J. Exp. Psychol: Learn. Mem. Cognit.* 9:384–97

Smith, E. E., Medin, D. L. 1981. *Categories and Concepts.* Cambridge, MA: Harvard Univ. Press

Smith, S. M. 1982. Enhancement of recall using multiple environmental contexts during learning. *Mem. Cognit.* 10:405–12

Smith, S. W., Rebok, G. W., Smith, W. R., Hall, S. E., Alvin, M. 1983. Adult age differences in the use of story structure in delayed free recall. *Exp. Aging Res.* 9:191–95

Snow, R. E., Farr, M., eds. 1986. *Aptitude, Learning, and Instruction,* Vol. 3: *Cognition, Conation, and Affect.* Hillsdale, NJ: Erlbaum

Spencer, R. M., Weisberg, R. W. 1986. The role of context in facilitating analogical transfer during problem solving. *Mem. Cognit.* In press

Spilich, G. J. 1983. Life-span components of text-processing: Structural and procedural differences. *J. Verb. Learn. Verb. Behav.* 22:231–44

Squire, L. R. 1982. The neuropsychology of human memory. *Ann. Rev. Neurosci.* 5:241–73

Squire, L. R., Butters, N. 1984. *Neuropsychology of Memory.* New York: Guilford

Squire, L. R., Cohen, N. J. 1984. Human memory and amnesia. See Lynch et al 1984, pp. 3–64

Squire, L. R., Shimamura, A. P., Graf, P. 1985. Independence of recognition memory and priming affects: A neuropsychological analysis. *J. Exp. Psychol: Learn. Mem. Cognit.* 11:37–44

Stanovich, K. E., West, R. F. 1983a. On priming by a sentence context. *J. Exp. Psychol: Gen.* 112:1–36

Stanovich, K. E., West, R. F. 1983b. The generalizability of context effects on word recognition: A reconsideration of the roles of parafoveal priming and sentence context. *Mem. Cognit.* 11:49–58

Stein, N. L., Levine, L. J. 1986. Thinking about feelings: The development and organization of emotional knowledge. See Snow & Farr 1986

Sternberg, S. 1969. The discovery of processing stages: Extensions of Donders' method. *Acta Psychol.* 30:276–315

Stevens, A., Coupe, P. 1978. Distortions in judged spatial relations. *Cognit. Psychol.* 10:422–37

Strelow, E. R. 1985. What is needed for a theory of mobility: Direct perception and cognitive maps—lessons from the blind. *Psychol. Rev.* 92:226–48

Taft, M. 1984. Evidence for an abstract lexical representation of word structure. *Mem. Cognit.* 12:264–69

Tanenhaus, M. K., Donnenwerth-Nolan, S. 1984. Syntactic context and lexical access. *Q. J. Exp. Psychol.* 36A:649–61

Thompson, C. P. 1982. Memory for unique personal events: The roommate study. *Mem. Cognit.* 10:324–32

Thorndyke, P. W. 1984. Applications of schema theory in cognitive research. See Anderson & Kosslyn 1984, pp. 167–91

Toppino, T. C., Gracen, T. F. 1985. The lag effect and differential organization theory: Nine failures to replicate. *J. Exp. Psychol: Learn. Mem. Cognit.* 11:185–91

Tulving, E. 1982. Synergistic ecphory in recall and recognition. *Can. J. Psychol.* 36:130–47

Tulving, E. 1983. *Elements of Episodic Memory.* New York: Oxford Univ. Press

Tulving, E. 1984. Precis of *Elements of Episodic Memory* (and following commentaries). *Behav. Brain Sci.* 7:223–68

Tulving, E. 1985a. How many memory systems are there? *Am. Psychol.* 40:385–98

Tulving, E. 1985b. Memory and conciousness. *Can. Psychol.* 26:1–12

Tulving, E. 1986. What kind of a hypothesis is the distinction between episodic and semantic memory? *J. Exp. Psychol: Learn. Mem. Cognit.* 12:307–311

Tulving, E., Schacter, D. L., Stark, H. A.

1982. Priming effects in word-fragment completion are independent of recognition memory. *J. Exp. Psychol: Learn. Mem. Cognit.* 8:336–42

Tversky, A. 1977. Features of similarity. *Psychol. Rev.* 84:327–52

Tversky, B. 1981. Distortion in memory for maps. *Cognit. Psychol.* 13:407–33

Tversky, B., Hemenway, K. 1983. Categories of environmental scenes. *Cognit. Psychol.* 15:121–49

Tweedy, J. R., Lapinski, R. H. 1981. Facilitating word recognition: Evidence for strategic and automatic factors. *Q. J. Exp. Psychol.* 33A:51–59

Tweedy, J. R., Lapinski, R. H., Schvaneveldt, R. W. 1977. Semantic-context effects on word recognition: Influence of varying the proportion of items presented in an appropriate context. *Mem. Cognit.* 5:84–89

Tyler, S. W., Voss, J. F. 1982. Attitude and knowledge effects in prose processing. *J. Verb. Learn. Verb. Behav.* 21:524–38

Underwood, B. J. 1983a. Interference in memory produced by the acoustic attribute. *Am. J. Psychol.* 96:113–25

Underwood, B. J. 1983b. "Conceptual" similarity and cumulative proactive inhibition. *J. Exp. Psychol: Learn. Mem. Cognit.* 9:456–61

Underwood, B. J. 1983c. *Attributes of memory.* Glenview, IL: Scott, Foresman

van Dijk, T. A., Kintsch, W. 1983. *Strategies of Discourse Comprehension.* New York: Academic

Wagenaar, W. A. 1986. My memory: A study of autobiographical memory over six years. *Cognit. Psychol.* 18:225–52

Walker, C. H., Yekovich, F. R. 1984. Script-based inferences: Effects of text and knowledge variables on recognition memory. *J. Verb. Learn. Verb. Behav.* 23:357–70

Warren, L. R., Mitchell, S. A. 1980. Age differences in judging the frequency of events. *Dev. Psychol.* 16:116–20

Warren, L. R., Wideman, S. S. 1983. Event-related potentials to match and mismatch letters in an immediate item recognition task. *Int. J. Neurosci.* 18:191–98

Warrington, E. K., Weiskrantz, L. 1982. Amnesia: A disconnection syndrome? *Neuropsychologia* 20:233–48

Watkins, M. J., Kerkar, S. P. 1985. Recall of a twice-presented item without recall of either presentation: Generic memory for events. *J. Mem. Lang.* 24:666–78

Weinberger, N. M., McGaugh, J. L., Lynch, G., eds. 1985. *Memory Systems of the Brain: Animal and Human Cognitive Processes.* New York: Guilford

Weisberg, R. W. 1986. *Creativity: Genius and Other Myths.* New York: Freeman

Wellman, H. M., ed. 1985. *Children's Searching: The Development of Search Skill and Spatial Representation.* Hillsdale, NJ: Erlbaum

Wellman, H. M., Somerville, S. C., Revelle, G. L., Hakke, R. J., Sophian, C. 1984. The development of comprehensive search skills. *Child Dev.* 55:472–81

Wetzler, S. 1985. Mood state-dependent retrieval: A failure to replicate. *Psychol. Rep.* 56:759–65

Whitney, P., McKay, T., Kellas, G., Emerson, W. A. Jr. 1985. Semantic activation of noun concepts in context. *J. Exp. Psychol: Learn. Mem. Cognit.* 11:126–35

Wickelgren, W. A. 1977. Speed-accuracy tradeoff and information processing dynamics. *Acta Psychol.* 41:67–85

Wickens, D. D., Clark, S. 1968. Osgood dimensions as an encoding class in short-term memory. *J. Exp. Psychol.* 78:580–84

Williams, K. W., Durso, F. T. 1986. Judging category frequency: automaticity or availability? *J. Exp. Psychol: Learn. Mem. Cognit.* In press

Wilson, B. A., Moffat, N. 1984. *Clinical Management of Memory Problems.* Rockville, MD: Aspen Systems Corp.

Wingfield, A., Butterworth, B. 1984. Running memory for sentences and parts of sentences: Syntactic parsing as a control function in working memory. See Bouma & Bouwhuis 1984, pp. 351–63

Winograd, E., Killinger, W. A. Jr. 1983. Relating age at encoding in early childhood to adult recall: Development of flashbulb memories. *J. Exp. Psychol: Gen.* 112:413–22

Winograd, E., Soloway, R. M. 1985. Reminding as a basis for temporal judgments. *J. Exp. Psychol: Learn. Mem. Cognit.* 11:262–71

Wright, B., Garrett, M. 1984. Lexical decision in sentences: Effects of syntactic structure. *Mem. Cognit.* 12:31–45

Wyer, R. S. Jr., Srull, T. K., eds. 1984a. *Handbook of Social Cognition,* Vol. 1. Hillsdale, NJ: Erlbaum

Wyer, R. S. Jr., Srull, T. K., eds. 1984b. *Handbook of Social Cognition,* Vol. 3. Hillsdale, NJ: Erlbaum

Zacks, R. T., Hasher, L. 1986. Capacity theory and the processing of inference. See Light & Burke 1986

Zacks, R. T., Hasher, L., Alba, J. W., Sanft, H., Rose, K. C. 1984. Is temporal order encoded automatically? *Mem. Cognit.* 12:387–94

Zajonc, R. B. 1980. Feeling and thinking: Preferences need no inferences. *Am. Psychol.* 35:151–75

Ann. Rev. Psychol. 1987. 38:669–718

ORGANIZATIONAL BEHAVIOR:
Some New Directions for I/O Psychology

Robert J. House and Jitendra V. Singh

Faculty of Management Studies, University of Toronto, Toronto, Ontario, Canada M5S 1V4

CONTENTS

0066-4308/87/0201-0669$02.00

INTRODUCTION

In recent years, four comprehensive and insightful reviews of the field of organizational behavior have appeared in the *Annual Review of Psychology*. This review chapter is the fifth in the series. Mitchell (1979) focused on personality and individual differences, job attitudes, motivation, and leadership. Cummings (1982) concentrated on task design, feedback, organizational structure, organizational control and technology, emerging trends in organizational effectiveness, stress, and satisfaction. Staw (1984) reviewed job satisfaction, absenteeism, turnover, and motivation and performance. Most recently, Schneider (1985) directed his attention to motivation, job satisfaction, leadership, groups, organizational climate and productivity, with special emphasis on level of analysis issues. Thus, four reviews of the field have appeared in six years.

One advantage of the frequency of these reviews is that the various authors have had the opportunity to take somewhat different perspectives on the field, since they were not unduly constrained by having to summarize many years of research in one review. Despite these differences, however, if the distinction between the macro (more sociological) and micro (more psychological) sides of the field (Staw 1984) is considered, most of the reviews have concentrated more on the micro side of the field, and appropriately so. Only Cummings (1982) emphasized some of the macro aspects of organizational behavior, such as structure, technology, and control in a significant and explicit way.

Consistent with the approaches taken by the previous authors, we cover a somewhat different territory in this review. Given space limitations, we were forced to be selective, so two main criteria guided our selection of topic areas to be reviewed. First, we review new topic areas here, most of which, with the exception of leadership, have not been significantly addressed in the previous reviews. The four substantive areas chosen are power, leadership, management succession, and decision making. In recent years, new and exciting theories and research findings have accumulated in these areas, and we believe that a review emphasizing these topic areas would be more informative for the field at this time. The earlier reviews have already done an outstanding job of addressing research in more mainstream areas of organizational behavior such as motivation, absenteeism, job design, satisfaction, and productivity. Secondly, we emphasize the interaction of individual and organizational variables in every one of the four topics reviewed. Such an emphasis on cross-level effects (Mossholder & Bedeian 1983, Rousseau 1985) eschews the predominantly individual focus of micro organizational behavior and the predominantly organizational focus of macro organizational behavior, and instead chooses a middle ground. In our reviews of management succession and decision making, the focus on cross-level effects is relatively explicit, but for the particular aspects of the power and leadership literatures reviewed here, there currently does not exist a significant body of work dealing with cross-level effects. We make some suggestions about what such research directions might be and call for cross-level research.

In addition to selectively reviewing research not substantially covered in earlier reviews, our effort has a second more speculative emphasis. Traditionally, the general thrust of most research in organizational behavior has been to attempt to answer *why* certain empirical regularities are observed in organizations. For example, why are some leadership styles more effective under specific circumstances, or why are some jobs more motivating to specific kinds of employees? We raise a different question more rooted in the historical context by asking *how* these empirical regularities got to be that way. We present some preliminary speculations about what may be gained in our understanding of organizational behavior by attempting to answer this question. This view emphasizes a historical, evolutionary study of organizational behavior.

The remainder of this chapter is organized into five sections. In the first section we review the literature on power. In recent years, the dominant approach to the study of power in organizations has been structural. We, however, examine the role individual differences in the power motive may play in organizational behavior. Although there is a wealth of findings from other subdisciplines of psychology, this area has not attracted much attention in organizational behavior. In the second section, we initially review the leadership research on established theories that appeared in 1984 and 1985. In addition, we review some significant new shifts in conceptualizing leadership behavior and its effects—an information processing approach, and theories of charismatic leadership. In the third section, we review research on management succession. Although this literature has relationships with and interesting implications for leadership, and we believe this work should be of interest to industrial/organizational psychologists, it has not been reviewed here earlier. There has been a substantial accumulation of theoretical and empirical work on this topic. We review some of the historical works in this area and use them as a framework for interpretation of more recent studies. In the fourth section we review the literature on decision making. In recent years, some exciting work has been done in the area of individual decision making, particularly by Kahneman and Tversky (Tversky & Kahneman 1974, 1981), and an excellent, comprehensive review of individual decision making has just appeared (Abelson & Levi 1985). We concentrate more on the interaction of organizational variables with decision making in organizations. Finally, we attempt to put some of the work on leadership, power, management succession, and decision making in an evolutionary context. We explore how empirical regularities in organizational behavior may have evolved over time.

We discuss how an examination of processes of selection, imitation and learning, and institutionalization may enhance our understanding of organizational behavior.

POWER MOTIVE

During the 1970s and early 1980s there was an emergence of theoretical and empirical work on the acquisition and exercise of power in complex organizations. This research focused primarily on structural and environmental factors affecting the distribution of power in organizations (Pfeffer 1981a). As a result of this research it has become rather well established that the distribution of power within complex organizations usually reflects the degree to which organizational members cope with critical demands facing the organization, and the degree to which members control critical resources or critical information on which others must depend (Hinings et al 1974, Pfeffer 1981a). This theory and research focuses on dyadic relationships between individuals or on dyadic relationships between organizational subunits and is primarily structural in nature. That is, power is seen to accrue to positions that control critical contingencies derived either from the environment or the technology of the organization. Until recently, little research or theory has been devoted to the more psychological determinants of individual acquisition of power (see Megargee et al 1966, Kipnis 1976, Mowday 1978, 1980 for exceptions to this statement).

More recently David McClelland (1985) has argued that the power motive is especially relevant to the practice of management and to the field of organizational behavior. Further, several studies of the relationship between the power motive and leadership performance and executive success have recently been reported in the psychological literature. In this section we review the research evidence relevant to the power motive and its implications for OB and I/O psychology.

The Power Motive Construct

According to McClelland (1985), there are several classes of natural incentives that are potentially motivating for all humans. These incentives are natural in the sense that they innately give rise to different types of positive or negative emotions. With respect to the power motive, it has been shown that humans learn that having an impact on one's environment or on other people is a source of positive affect. This positive affect occurs as a result of activation of the sympathetic nervous system and is evidenced by an increase in the production of catecholamines: adrenaline, epinephrine, norepinephrine, endorphins, and dopamine. These catecholamines, when released, have been found to increase anger and aggression as well as feelings of pleasure in humans (Berlyne 1967). Further, it is established that catecholamines are essential for many forms of aggressive behavior. Moreover, sex differences are related to differences in catecholamine functioning and assertiveness. The catecholamine system is more responsive to emotional stimuli in males than females and males are more aggressive than females (see McClelland 1985, p. 151). Catecholamine release has been shown to be correlated with arousal of the power motive and with the exercise of power. These findings indicate that the satisfaction one receives from exercising power is derived from catecholamine release. According to McClelland, when humans learn that the exercise of power results in the experience of positive affect, one is said to have learned the power motive or the need for power. Thus, according to McClelland (1985), the need for power is a socially learned set of associations between the arousal or exercise of power and the experience of positive affect.

Correlates of the Power Motive

McClelland and his associates have conducted a substantial number of studies on the power motive construct, approaching 100 at our last count. These studies provide convincing evidence of the validity of the need for power as a theoretical construct and both the construct and predictive validity of the power motive measure. For example, it has been shown that after the power motive has been aroused by showing subjects inspirational speeches such as Churchill's speech at Dunkirk or Henry V's speeches in Shakespeare's *Life of Henry V,* there is a marked gain in norepinephrine excretion in the subjects' urine and in subjects' physiological activation (Steele 1973, 1977). Further, the gain in norepinephrine is positively correlated ($r = .66$, $p < .01$) to the amount of power imagery in stories written after inspirational speeches were heard.

Subjects high on the need for power react more sensitively to power-related stimuli than to neutral stimuli, as evidenced by findings assessing the electrical responsivity of the brain to various stimuli (McClelland et al, unpublished manuscript, 1979; Davidson et al 1980). Individuals high in the need for power recall more "peak" experiences that are described in power terms (McAdams 1982) and more power-related facts relative to neutral facts than do low or neutral power subjects (McAdams & McClelland, unpublished manuscript, 1983). Individuals high in the power motive also respond to several experimental treatments differently than individuals low in the power motive.

For example, Fodor & Farrow (1979) demonstrated experimentally that individuals high in the need for power show partiality toward ingratiating followers. In another study, high power motivated individuals were found to inhibit group discussion more than low power-motivated individuals. As a consequence, the number of alternatives considered were fewer and the quality of decisions lower for groups led by high power-motivated individuals (Fodor & Smith 1982). High power motivated individuals become more highly activated when supervising others than low power individuals. Activation was found to be highest when high power individuals were in an experimental condition in which productivity was stressed and rewarded but attempts by the high powered individuals to gain control of the situation and increase productivity were thwarted (Fodor 1984). Finally, high power males report that they have more arguments, play competitive sports more, have less stable interpersonal relations, favor more assertive foreign policies, experience more emotional problems, and are more impulsively aggressive than low power males (McClelland 1985).

Gender Similarities

Females respond to power-arousing stimuli in a manner similar to males. Specifically, females have been found to respond to a hypnosis demonstration or to an inspirational speech, as evidenced by their responses to the Thematic Apperception Test, to approximately the same extent as men (Stewart & Winter 1976, Steele 1977). Female activation arousal in response to inspirational speeches is also not significantly different from males' (Steele 1977).

Several studies have shown that the behavior of high power motivated males and females are similar to each other and yet different from their low power counterparts. High power males and females, as compared to others low in power motivation, report holding more offices, having prestigious possessions, and even having a preference for the colors red and black (Winter 1973). High power motivated males and females with full time careers pursue the same occupations—occupations that allow the individual to exert significant influence over others. High power motivated individuals choose such occupations as teaching, psychology, business, journalism, or organizational positions of influence. Low power motivated individuals choose positions in other occupations that allow less opportunities to influence others. Further, power motivation is related to a history of heavy drinking for both males and females. The amount consumed in an experimental setting was roughly equivalent for men and women (Wilsnack 1974).

However, in one study females high in power were found to be less overtly assertive and competitive than men (McClelland 1975). McClelland suggests that this finding is likely traceable to the fact that women may inhibit their impulses to be assertive because of stereotypic sex-role expectations. This speculation is consistent with findings of a prior study in which it was found that females who are "self-defining" behave in ways similar to males whereas among "socially defining" females, power motivation predicts behaviors that are congruent with the stereotypic female role (Winter & Stewart 1978).

The Need for Power and Managerial Performance

The combination of high leader achievement motivation and high leader power motivation has been shown to be associated with managerial success (Cummin 1967), with the performance of research and development companies (Wainer & Rubin 1969), and with effectiveness of scientists, engineers, and executives (Varga 1975).

This combination of motives is associated with a number of predicted dependent variables including ratings of managerial performance, managerial promotion rate and choice of managerial occupations (Stahl 1983). No difference between males and females or between races was found on Stahl's measures of achievement and power motivation. Stahl's findings are based on multiple tests over a broad range of occupations. Based on an objectively scored measure of motivation, they are not tied to the use of the Thematic Apperception Test generally used by McClelland and his associates. However, these findings are based on analysis of concurrent relationships. Longitudinal research using both the TAT and Stahl's scale is required to establish the construct validity of that scale.

The Leadership Motive Pattern

In a discussion of leadership, McClelland (1985) argues that high power motive, in combination with low affiliative motive and high activity inhibition, predisposes individuals to be effective leaders. McClelland refers to this motive pattern as the imperialistic motive pattern or the leadership motive pattern. Activity inhibition is measured by simply counting the number of times the word "not" appears in the stories written by subjects in response to TAT stimulus material. McClelland interprets this to be a measure of the degree of restraint one feels with respect to the use of power impulsively, coercively, or manipulatively. McClelland et al (1972), found that men's expressions of the power motive in TAT scores varied qualitatively, depending on whether the individual was high or low in activity inhibition. Men low in activity inhibition had power thoughts much more focused on personal dominance or winning at someone else's expense. However, for men scoring high on activity inhibition, power imagery was more often stated in terms of doing good for others, for humanity, or for some good cause.

According to McClelland (1985), individuals who are high on the need for power and also high on activity inhibition should make more effective managers, especially if the need for power is greater than the need for affiliation. McClelland reasons that the need for power is an appropriate motive for meeting the role demands of positions of influence such as those found in large complex organizations. He also argues that the leadership motive pattern allows an individual to remain socially distant from subordinates and therefore to be more objective with respect to resource allocation, delegation, and discipline. Further, McClelland argues that individuals with the leadership motive pattern enjoy work involving the exercise of power because it enables them to be in control.

There is some evidence for this assertion. In one study both males and females with high inhibited power and need for power greater than the need for affiliation reported behaviors that appeared to reflect respect for institutional authority, discipline, and self-control, caring for others, altruism, and concern for a just world (McClelland 1975). McClelland computed an index consisting of need for power minus the need for affiliation score. This index correlated significantly with indicators of the above variables for subjects high in activity inhibition. For these subjects the correlations ranged from .23 to .48. In contrast, for subjects with low activity inhibition the correlations were either negative or insignificant, ranging from .07 to −.35. The pattern of correlations was similar for males and females.

Further, McClelland & Burnham (1976) found that high level managers with the leadership motive syndrome had work units with higher morale than managers with other motive patterns. Winter (1979, cited in McClelland & Boyatzis 1982) argued that success in leadership is not solely dependent on this motive pattern but is also heavily dependent on other contingencies such as job requirements. In a study of officers in the U.S. Navy, Winter found that the leadership motive syndrome was only predictive of success among nontechnically oriented managerial positions. Success for other high-ranking officers who held their post on the basis of technical or skill requirements was not associated with the leadership motivation pattern.

McClelland & Boyatzis (1982) examined whether the leadership motive pattern is predictive of long-term managerial success. Subjects were entry level managers (all male) at AT & T who completed the TAT from 1956 to 1960. In an effort to verify Winter's (1979) results, each manager's job was classified as technical or nontechnical. The major difference between these two groups was that the technical managers possessed skills required via training or experience that enabled them to understand and work with equipment. Chi square analyses were performed comparing those managers who did and those who did not possess the leadership motive pattern at the original time of testing and at 8 and 16 years later. Results indicated that managers who possessed the leadership motive pattern had significantly higher levels of advancement after 8 and 16 years of experience than those that did not possess this pattern. However, this finding held only for those managers in nontechnical jobs. No such association between the leader motive pattern and promotion was found for "technical" managers. Need for achievement was associated with managerial success for lower level technical jobs. It is suggested that at these levels, promotions are heavily dependent on individual contributions. At higher levels, need for achievement is not associated with success as is the leadership motive pattern. These findings confirm Winter's (1979) earlier findings in that managerial motives had low predictive power with respect to success of technical managers. Perhaps some combination other than the leadership motive pattern might have higher predictive utility. Since technical supervisors constitute a substantial proportion of managers, research concerning the motivational determinants of success among technical managers is called for.

Health Implications

These findings have a number of implications for the health of organizational members. Individuals high on the power motive report that they feel more assertive-rebellious, resentful, sulky (Gough & Heilbrun 1975) and that they have more emotional problems (McClelland 1975). High need for power men also tend to be heavy drinkers, especially if they score low on activity inhibition. McClelland (1979) found in two different samples that individuals with the leadership motive pattern had significantly higher blood pressure, indicating a strain on the cardiovascular system. One study sampled the power imagery of men at the age of 30 and measured their diastolic blood pressure at ages between 51 and 53. This study clearly showed that the inhibited power motive is strongly predictive of long-term susceptibility to hypersensitivity. In other studies it was found that under conditions of stress individuals with the inhibited power motive reported illnesses that were significantly more severe than other motive combination groups, including those low in the need for power and high in power stress. In two studies it was found that men high in the need for power who reported an above median number of power stresses also reported more severe illnesses (McClelland & Jemmott 1980, McClelland et al 1982). Furthermore, those in the high power motive-high stressed group had impaired immune functioning leading to the inference that stressed high power individuals experience damage to their immune function, which makes them more susceptible to diseases (McClelland 1982; McClelland et al, unpublished manuscript, 1982). All of the above findings concerning physiological functions are based on studies of men. There is some preliminary indication that the relationship may not hold in the same way for women (McClelland & Kirshnit, unpublished manuscript, 1982).

Conclusions: The Power Motive

The results of the studies of managers are consistent with the findings of Miner (1978) and his associates based on 25 years of research including 33 predictive studies. Miner also uses a projective measure of motivation: the Miner Sentence Completion Scale (MSCS). This scale has been shown to have predictive validity in bureaucratic organizations. However, it does not predict success in small nonbureaucratic organizations or positions requiring technical ability such as R & D organizations or lower level managerial jobs where managers are primarily concerned with the technical or physical operations of the organization. Thus, the findings by McClelland & Boyatzis (1982), by Winter (1979), and also by Miner and his associates (1978) suggest that the power motive and the leadership motive pattern are more predictive of managerial success only under conditions in which the assertion of social influence is critical and technical expertise is not critical to performance. The above findings with respect to managerial motive patterns and organizational role requirements suggest the need for cross-level research in which leader role demands are measured and leader behavior or leader motives are assessed in terms of such demands.

Research clearly shows that certain stimuli arouse the power motive. Such stimuli as experiencing threat from another, viewing the exercise of power or engaging in the exercise of power are all power arousing. Further, hierarchical stratification, social distance, and the use of status symbols such as titles, uniforms, and attire that distinguishes leaders from subordinates all disinhibit the use of power, especially coercive power (Zimbardo 1970). Taken together, the research on the need for power and the research on de-individuation suggest that organizations can be designed either to facilitate or to inhibit the arousal and exercise of power.

The above review suggests several issues for future research. First, additional research on gender differences or similarities is needed, as is cross-level research. Such research could be directed at relating contextual variables to power arousal, power-related behavior and its effects on both power holders and targets. The research on the power motive and leader motivation pattern has implications not only for leadership and organizational effectiveness but also is of relevance to the health and welfare of leaders and followers.

LEADERSHIP

In this section, after a brief review of three studies concerned with established theories of leadership, we describe and evaluate four recently advanced theories. As will be seen, each of these new theories shows significant promise and represents an important advancement in the leadership literature.

Established Theories

There was relatively little research on established theories during 1984 and 1985. The four most cited theories in 1983, the year for which Schneider (1985) reviewed leadership, were Fiedler's (1978) contingency theory, the vertical dyadic linkage (VDL) theory (Graen & Cashman 1975), Vroom-Yetton's (1973) situational decision theory, and House's (1971) path-goal theory of leadership. Since 1984, four studies were concerned with VDL theory, and a meta-analysis of contingency theory was also reported.

VERTICAL DYADIC LINKAGE THEORY   A field study experiment was conducted by Graen et al (1982). In this experiment managers of information processing technicians were trained (experimental condition) or not trained (placebo control condition) in the theory and procedures of the role-making model on which the VDL theory is based. During the 26 weeks of the experiment, the managers were trained to use the model specifically with their members. They were required to meet with each of their members individually and complete a script that they had role-played many times in training. By the end of the 14th week, all individual role-making interviews were completed for the experimental group, and the treatment was in effect from week 15 to week 26.

The results of this field experiment supported the predictive validity of the leader-member exchange (LMX) model. Compared to the placebo control condition, the experimental group (those under the LMX role-making condition) demonstrated large improvements in all areas tested from the 14 weeks before the treatment to the 12 weeks after the treatment. The areas tested for change from before to after the treatment were (*a*) hard productivity (quantity and quality or work produced on the computer), (*b*) work itself measures (motivating potential of the job, preferred work load, role conflict, role ambiguity and career relevance of the job), (*c*) role-making (leader-member exchange from both points of view, dyadic loyalty, and superior support), and (*d*) job satisfaction (overall and facets: leader, work, pay, social and security). All of the above measures demonstrated significant improvements for the experimental over the control group with the exception of the satisfaction measures, which only showed significant gains for overall and security satisfaction. Satisfaction with the manager (liking) did not differ significantly between the two groups. Hence, it appears that satisfaction with the manager is different from the quality of the LMX.

Another question Graen et al (1982) investigated in their study was whether individual motivation would moderate the effects of the LMX treatment. Employing Hackman & Oldham's (1976) measure of growth need strength (GNS), they found that GNS moderated the effect of the treatment for productivity and preferred work load as hypothesized. The one third of the trained group with the highest GNS scores showed a 52% improvement in hard productivity attributable to the training.

This moderating effect of GNS on the LMX treatment was replicated in a field experiment on a comparable sample of employees conducted by Graen et al (1986). In this field experiment, the higher-GNS group again showed an outstanding 54% improvement in hard productivity and the lower and medium GNS groups demonstrated no significant improvements. In addition, quality of production improved in this study following the training as documented by decreases in the number of errors per weekly caseload.

Given that this model, when followed properly, can produce such desirable results, the question becomes whether or not this training will benefit members having initially lower-quality LMXs (i.e. out-group members) by offering the opportunity for a higher-quality LMX. This question was researched by Scandura & Graen (1984). Controlling for regression effects, these investigators found that those initially lower in the quality of their LMX improved their productivity more than did those who had initially higher LMXs. Again, these improvements in hard productivity were not at the expense of quality or job attitudes.

Another question that arises concerns the longer-term implications of LMX theory and the possible moderating effects of members' career relevant abilities. This question was the focus of a study by Graen & Wakabayashi (1986). In this seven-year panel study of all of the college graduates who joined one large Japanese corporation, they found that ability assessment taken before entry moderated the predictive relationship between quality of LMX taken during the first three years of employment and career progress measures taken after the seventh year. Specifically, they found that both speed of promotion and size of seventh-year bonus were moderated by ability. In what appeared to be a compensatory fashion, those young managers who were higher on either or both quality of LMX or ability showed faster promotions and higher bonuses than those who were lower on both. Hence, there appear to be two separate paths to career success—high ability or high-quality LMX.

Vecchio & Gobdel (1984) tested the VDL theory by examining the relationships between 45 managers and their subordinates in a multiple branch bank. Once again the theory was confirmed by showing that subordinates who enjoyed "in-group" status had higher performance ratings, lower propensity to quit, and higher satisfaction with supervision than those who were members of "out-groups." However, "in-group" status was not associated with objective measures of productivity. Vecchio & Gobdel point out that objective performance may only be predictable from constructs associated with leader-member relations when leaders are able to affect the actual performance of subordinates directly in specific situations. Such situations would be those in which the leader can directly remove obstacles to performance or offer advice or encouragement. Vecchio & Gobdel call for the incorporation of moderator variables which take such situational constraints into account. Further, these authors call attention to the need for further conceptualization and measurement of "in-group" status and suggest that subgroup status should be discarded in favor of a continuous undimensional construct.

CONTINGENCY THEORY   The other established theory to receive attention during the 1984/85 period was Fiedler's contingency theory of leadership. Peters et al (1985) conducted three meta-analyses and several subanalyses of the results of contingency theory research to date. The first was a meta-analysis of the 11 studies that led to the specification of the theory. This analysis resulted in the conclusion that the theory was appropriately induced from studies on which it was based. The second analysis was based on 12 laboratory experiments conducted after the theory was formulated. This analysis demonstrated that the experimental data are consistent with the theory in all octants except octant II. The third meta-analysis was based on 12 field tests of the theory. This analysis showed that the correlations in all octants were in the predicted direction. However, the correlations for octants I, II, III, IV, and VIII did not reach significance. Thus the theory was found to be relatively predictive under the controlled conditions of the laboratory. Under less controlled conditions the theory has predictive validity beyond chance expectancies, but only in three of the eight octants. The authors suggest that additional variables need to be specified to more fully account for variance within octants I, II, III, IV, and VIII.

Thus, there continues to be supportive evidence with respect to these two established theories. Further, the specific behaviors that are implied by the leader–member exchange construct need to be further explicated. Specifically, the leader behaviors associated with the measure of this construct are not as yet clearly established.

New Theories

In addition to the above research, Fiedler (1986), Lord (1985), and Bass (1985) have advanced new and promising theories of leadership.

COGNITIVE RESOURCE UTILIZATION THEORY   Fiedler (1986) has advanced a cognitive resources utilization theory of leadership that is intended to specify the conditions under which leader intelligence and task-related abilities are predictive of subunit or follower performance. The theory is induced from a large number of prior research findings produced by Fiedler and others.

Essentially the cognitive utilization theory attempts to explain the conditions under which leader-cognitive resources such as intelligence, technical competence, or job-relevant knowledge will be employed effectively by the leader. Specifically, the theory predicts that when leaders employ directive leader behavior, are not under stress, enjoy the support of followers, and possess task-relevant knowledge they will make most effective use of whatever cognitive resources they possess.

The theory is consistent with a substantial amount of prior research and provides a framework with which to understand the interaction between leader abilities and degree of leader directiveness. In a forthcoming book Fiedler & Garcia (in press) report the results of numerous studies designed to test the theory. Overall, these studies demonstrated support for the theory, with correlations consistently in the hypothesized direction, often ranging well above .50. Further, the Cognitive Resource Theory helps to unravel the conditions for optimum use of leader abilities. Specifically the theory and supporting evidence demonstrate that when under stress, due to problematic relationships with their superiors or group members, leaders rely on prior experience and do not make effective use of their intelligence. In fact, under such conditions intelligence is either unrelated or inversely related to work group effectiveness, while prior relevant experience is positively related to group effectiveness. These findings are of significance to the practice of leadership since stress is a variable that can be effectively managed. Thus, through the management of stress it is possible to increase the application of intelligence by leaders and to relax one of the major limits to bounded rationality in organizations (Simon 1976). Finally, the theory is linked to Fiedler's earlier Contingency Theory of Leadership (Fiedler 1964). This prior theory specifies the conditions under which leaders will be either directive or nondirective. Leader directive behavior is a function of the interaction of the leader's LPC score and the favorableness of the leader's situation. The more recent Cognitive Resource Theory specifies the conditions under which directive behavior will result in effective utilization of the leader's intelligence.

A major implication of the Cognitive Resource Theory of interest to industrial psychologists concerns leader selection. Traditionally selection procedures usually assume that the more intelligent and experienced an individual the more that individual will be effective. The evidence presented by Fiedler & Garcia demonstrates that, with respect to leaders, this assumption holds true only under limited conditions. Thus selection is likely to be improved if the conditions are specified under which intelligence or experience is required. The Cognitive Resource Theory specifies such conditions.

There have been many calls for leadership theories that combine situational and personality variables. Fiedler's Contingency Theory and his Cognitive Resource Theory are the first to accomplish this combination and to be empirically demonstrated to have predictive validity. The theory not only specifies the leader behavior required for effective use of cognitive abilities and the conditions required for the effective use of such abilities, but also the conditions predictive of effective leader behavior.

SOCIAL INFORMATION PROCESSING THEORY   An important theoretical contribution to the leadership literature has been made by Robert Lord (1985) and his associates. (Lord et al 1978, 1982, 1986; Lord & Smith 1983). These researches have reported a number of studies concerned with how individuals form perceptions and evaluations of leaders as well as attributions about leadership behavior and effects. The literature on leadership perceptions and measurement of leader behavior is analyzed within an information processing model consisting of five steps: selective attention, comprehension, encoding, storage and retention, and information retrieval and judgment. Lord (1985) has summarized both the theory and evidence in an extensive and impressive review of the relevant literature. The prior research that he reviews demonstrates rather clearly that perceptions of leaders are largely based on spontaneous recognition, that leadership is a cognitive category that is hierarchically organized, that there are widely held expectations of the attributes and behavior of leaders, and that experimental treatments designed to change the perceptions of leaders and attributions about them directly affect leadership ratings (Fraser & Lord, unpublished manuscript, 1983; Lord et al 1986).

Based on theory and supporting research, Lord (1985) advanced a number of recommendations for improving the accuracy of leadership ratings and leadership descriptions. Lord's theory successfully explains and predicts how perceptions and ratings of leaders and attributions about them become distorted as a result of systematic biases in information processing. Lord suggests several recommendations to minimize such biases when doing leadership research. These fall into two general categories. One calls for observers to use a more controlled information processing approach when describing leaders. This involves teaching raters different strategies to employ at each of the five stages described in the information processing model. The second involves designing experimental interventions and measurements to be script-based rather than person-based. Since it has been found that raters prefer script-based encoding and retrieval, script-based interventions and measurements are less likely to burden the information processing capabilities of observers. Using scripts also focuses retrieval on specific, concrete events in which the logical, temporal ordering of events facilitates accurate retrieval.

In conclusion, we see this theory as a major contribution to the leadership literature. It points out serious problems of measurement concerning leader behavior and suggests significant implications and prescriptions for the study of leadership.

CHARISMATIC AND TRANSFORMATIONAL THEORIES   There has also been an emergence of a new genre of leadership theories. These theories extend Weber's (1947) conceptualization of charisma and Burns's (1978) conceptualization of transformational leadership.

In contrast to traditional theories of leadership which take as their dependent variables the performance, satisfaction, and cognitions of subordinates, charismatic or transformational leadership theories take as their dependent variables followers' emotional responses to work-related stimuli; followers' self-esteem, trust, and confidence in the leaders; follower values and follower motivation to perform above and beyond the call of duty.

Further, in contrast to traditional leadership theories which describe leaders in terms of task- and person-oriented leader behavior, these newer theories describe leaders in terms of articulating and focusing a vision and mission, creating and maintaining a positive image in the minds of followers, setting challenging expectations for followers, showing confidence in and respect for followers, and behaving in a manner that reinforces the vision and the mission. Theories of this kind have been advanced by Berlew (1974), House (1977), Burns (1978), Bennis & Nanus (1985), Sashkin & Fulmer (1985), and Bass (1985). All of these theories describe charismatic or transformational leaders as individuals who provide for their followers a vision of the future that promises a better and more meaningful life. Studies of charismatic and/or transformational leadership have been reported by Smith (1982), Howell (1985), House (1985), Yukl & Van Fleet (1982), Bass (1985), Waldman et al (1985), and Avolio & Bass (1985).

Smith (1982) found strong support for the proposition that leaders who have reputations for being charismatic have significantly different effects on followers than effective but noncharismatic leaders. Followers of reputed charismatic leaders were more self-assured, experienced more meaningfulness in their work, reported more back-up from their leaders, reported working longer hours, saw their leaders as more dynamic, and had higher performance ratings than the followers of the noncharismatic but effective leaders.

Howell (1985) conducted a laboratory experiment in which both leader behavior and group norms were varied. The effects of charismatic leader behavior on followers were compared with the effects of structuring or considerate leader behavior. Both the leader behavior manipulation and the productivity norm manipulation were checked and were shown to be effectively instantiated as planned. The findings showed that charismatic leader behavior specified by prior theory (House 1977) had a significantly stronger and more positive influence on the performance, satisfaction, and adjustment of the subjects.

Perhaps most interestingly, it was only the charismatic leaders who were able to overcome the negative effects of the low productivity norm condition. That is, regardless of whether the subjects were in the high or low productivity norm condition, those working under charismatic leaders had higher general satisfaction, higher specific task satisfaction, and less role conflict than individuals working under structuring or considerate leaders. Under these latter kinds of leaders, the negative effects of the low productivity norm treatment persisted.

House (1985) conducted an investigation of the behavior and motivation of U.S. presidents. House asked eight political historians to classify U.S. presidents as charismatic or noncharismatic with respect to their cabinet members. A charismatic leader was defined as one who induced a high degree of loyalty, commitment, and devotion to the leader; identification with the leader and the leader's mission; emulation of the leader's values, goals, and behavior; inspiration; a sense of self-esteem from relationships with the leader and his mission; and an exceptionally high degree of trust in the leader and the correctness of his beliefs.

Seven of the nine historians agreed on the classification of six charismatic and six noncharismatic U.S. presidents. Biographies of these presidents and of their cabinet members were content analyzed to determine differences between charismatic leaders and noncharismatic leaders with respect to their effects on followers. In addition, the inaugural addresses of the presidents were content analyzed to determine whether charismatic presidents evidenced different motives than noncharismatic presidents. The achievement, power, and affiliation motives were coded according to the major theme statements following Donley & Winter (1970).

All six charismatic presidents were either reelected or assassinated during their first term. Only one of the six noncharismatics was reelected. The biographies of cabinet members reporting to charismatic presidents were found to have significantly more frequent expressions of positive affect toward the president.

Using previously collected opinions of political historians toward presidents (Maranell 1970), it was shown that charismatic presidents are viewed by political historians as engaging in significantly stronger actions, being more prestigious, more active, more flexible, and having accomplished more in their administrations. Further, the content analysis of the inaugural addresses of the presidents clearly demonstrated that charismatic presidents have a consistent motive pattern that distinguishes them from noncharismatic presidents. Specifically, the charismatic leaders were, as a group, significantly higher on *both* the need for achievement and the need for power as reflected in the inaugural addresses.

Another empirical study relevant to charismatic theory is presented by Yukl & Van Fleet (1982). These authors found in four separate studies that "inspirational leadership" was significantly related to leader effectiveness and high levels of follower motivation. The measures of inspirational leadership consisted of several of the behaviors theoretically characteristic of charismatic leaders (House 1977). Thus, studies of charismatic leaders, or in the case of Yukl & Van Fleet's study, inspirational leaders, demonstrated that the behaviors specified in prior theory (House 1977) rather consistently have the effects predicted by that theory.

A second theory of the same genre is the transformational leadership theory advanced by James MacGregor Burns (1978). Burns contrasted transactional leadership with transformational leadership. For Burns, transactional leadership is based on a bargain struck by both parties to the exchange. Transactional leaders induce followers to behave in ways desired by the leader in exchange for some good desired by the follower. Such relationships usually endure only as long as the mutual need of the leader and follower can be satisfied by continuing exchanges of goods for services. As Burns points out, transactional leadership is based on the exchange of goods which are usually specific, tangible, and calculable. Vertical dyadic linkage theory (Scandura & Graen 1984) and path-goal theory of leadership (House & Mitchell 1974) are examples of what Burns would refer to as transactional theories of leadership.

Bass (1985) and Avolio & Bass (1985) argue that transactional leadership has several limitations, but it is essential to leading others. Specifically, they argue that transactional skills are necessary but not sufficient for transformational leadership to have its theoretical effects.

According to Burns (1978), transformational leadership occurs ". . . when one or more persons *engage* (emphasis original) with others in such a way that leaders and followers raise one another to higher levels of motivation and morality" (page 20). Accordingly, transformational leaders address themselves to followers' ". . . wants, needs and other motivations, as well as their own and thus they serve as an *independent force in changing the make-up of followers' motive base through gratifying their motives*" (emphasis original, page 20).

Burns (1978) argues that transformational leadership in its most effective form appeals to the higher, more general, and comprehensive values that express followers' more fundamental and enduring needs. The values influenced by such leaders are the end values of equality, freedom, a world of beauty, and the instrumental value of self-control.

Bass (1985) found that managers who were seen by their followers as transformational leaders could be characterized by three behavioral dimensions. The first dimension describes charismatic leadership. Factor analyses showed that this dimension accounted for 66% of the response variance. This factor is concerned with faith in the leader, respect for the leader, and inspiration and encouragement provided by his or her presence. The remaining two dimensions associated with transformational leadership were individualized consideration and intellectual stimulation, accounting for 6.0% and 6.3% of the response variance respectively. The two factors associated with transactional leadership were management by exception and contingent reward, accounting for 3.1% and 7.2% of the response variance respectively.

In another study Bass (1985) found the three theoretical transformational leader behavior scales to be more characteristic of transformational leaders and the two transactional leader behaviors to be more characteristic of transactional leaders as classified by expert observers. In a third study Bass (1985) found that biographies of "world class leaders" described such leaders as more charismatic than transactional.

Waldman et al (1985) computed an hierarchical regression analysis of transactional and transformational leadership on self-reported effort and performance measures for two samples of U.S. Army officers and one sample of industrial managers. By entering the two transactional leadership scales into the regression equation first, and following with the transformational leadership scales, they were able to demonstrate that transformational leadership has an incremental effect over and above transactional leadership. This effect on the R^2 ranged from .09 to .48 depending on the sample and criterion variable used. For both criterion variables, in all three samples, transformational leadership had a significant effect over and above transactional leadership.

In another study it was found that high-potential managers were rated significantly higher by followers on all these transformational leadership factors and were also seen as displaying contingent reward leadership more often (Avolio & Bass 1985) than managers rated as having less potential.

Finally, Avolio & Bass (unpublished manuscript, 1985) investigated the association between team performance in a realistic management simulation and postgame ratings of leaders. Teams with leaders having higher ratings of transformational leadership had significantly higher performance, higher levels of satisfaction with the leader, and greater effectiveness as leaders. However, as pointed out by Avolio & Bass (1985), it is possible that by virtue of their successful performance, leaders of high performing teams were described as more transformational than those of low performing teams. That is, because of the teams' successful performance team members may have erroneously attributed transformational qualities to their leaders.

Taken collectively, the studies reviewed above are very encouraging. With the exception of the management game study and the study of the high management potential group, the studies by Bass and his associates might be criticized on the grounds that all of the data are obtained from a common source. That is, followers provided descriptions of both the leaders' behavior and their reactions to the leaders' behavior. Consequently, there is likely to be a fairly high degree of common method bias reflected in these findings. With respect to the management game teams, it is possible that the respondents were reacting to team performance more than to leader behavior. This could occur because the respondents knew the performance of their team prior to completing the leadership description questionnaire. Thus, responses to the questionnaire may reflect attributions òf leadership based on group performance rather than actual leader behavior.

We are not especially concerned with this attributional error problem at this time in the development of the theory because the study of the high management potential group and the studies conducted by Smith (1982) and Howell (1985) are free of this bias and produced constructually similar results to the other studies by Bass and his associates. The design of Smith's study eliminated the possibility of attributional error since the leaders were classified as charismatic or noncharismatic by one source, the nominators, and reactions to the leader were described independently by followers. The study by Howell eliminated attributional error by experimental control.

We now turn to the major research issues and conclusions suggested by the above research and theory.

Conclusions

Leadership research and theory have enjoyed a renewed concern among organizational behavior scholars over the last 15 years. Several theories now exist and continue to be tested and refined. The major refinements have been in the form of moderator variables based on cross-level research. Fiedler's cognitive resource utilization theory is one such example. In many ways the field appears to be calling for cross-level research based on a taxonomy of leadership situations and/or a taxonomy of leader substitutes (Kerr & Jermier 1978). If exhaustive, or nearly so, such taxonomies would allow researchers to determine the kinds of leader behavior and leader motivation most appropriate for each situational category. Those interested in developing such taxonomies might do well to examine the arousal, constraining and rewarding effects of roles, of technology, of norms, and of organizational characteristics such as formalization, standardization, and decentralization.

For example, Comstock & Scott (1977) have shown that task predictibility reduces the qualifications required of staff members with respect to their level of training and continuing professional activities. Further, they found that predictable work flow at the subunit level increases the bureaucratization and centralization of the control system at the next higher organizational level. A similar study might be conducted using subunit technology and control systems to predict leader behavior.

Contingency theory (Fiedler 1978), vertical dyadic linkage theory (Graen & Cashman 1975), path-goal theory (House 1971), as well as cognitive resource utilization theory (Fiedler 1986), all invoke the concept of "substitutes for, or neutralizers of, leadership" as moderator variables. For Fiedler's contingency theory the relevant moderator is situational favorableness. For Fiedler's cognitive resource utilization theory the moderators are group member support and sources of stress on the leader from environmental factors. For Graen the relevant moderator is role orientation. For House the relevant moderators are environmental factors and task characteristics that increase the predictability of demands on individuals. Perhaps it is time to search for generic, and therefore generalizable, properties of substitutes or moderator variables. For example, it is not clear why situational favorableness has the moderating effect it has on the relationship between the least preferred coworker measure and subunit performance. Does lack of situational favorableness induce stress which in some way differentially affects the way high and low LPC leaders utilize their cognitive resources? Similar questions can be raised about the psychological processes underlying the moderator effects of task structure, role orientation, and other substitutes for leadership. Knowledge of the psychological processes underlying the operation of the moderator variables would allow more precise interventions to improve leadership or to improve the match of leaders to situational demands. Fiedler's cognitive resource utilization theory is illustrative of one such theory. This theory articulates the psychological processes by which situational stress interacts with leader behavior to produce effects on subunit or follower performance. Theories concerning the psychological processes that cause followers to respond to different leader behaviors in different situations are also called for. The work of Lord (1985) and his associates is an illustration of one such theory. We believe this line of theory and research has already proved useful in understanding the processes by which followers respond to, characterize, and describe leader behavior and leader effectiveness. Using this theory as a guide, it would be interesting to infer the effects of different situational factors on each of the five stages of information processing when followers describe or evaluate leaders. Do situational-organizational variables induce systematic biases in the various stages of information processing? Do such biases have implications for the attribution, acceptance, and evaluation of leaders.

The newly emerged charismatic and transformational theories also raise several questions. First, one might ask whether or not charismatic theory or transformational theory are overly humanistically biased. Are leaders being characterized more by the desires of researchers than by reality? Can transformational leaders indeed cause followers to elevate their motivation and preferences above their own self-interests? Do they? Or did the leaders identified as charismatic or transformational in the above studies cause followers to pursue a different set of self-interested outcomes rather than dominantly collective or altruistic outcomes?

There are historical accounts of both totalitarian and egalitarian charismatic leaders. Hitler, Mussolini, and James Jones are examples of the former. Martin Luther King, Mahatma Gandhi, John F. Kennedy, and Franklin D. Roosevelt are examples of the latter. What psychological processes and what situational pressures result in the emergence of such leaders? What motives and behaviors differentiate totalitarian from more egalitarian leaders?

Charismatic leaders are hypothesized by House (1977) to cause followers to be unquestioningly obedient and highly trusting. In contrast, transformational leaders are hypothesized by Burns (1978) and Bass (1985) to cause followers to become more autonomous, self-directed, self-actualizing, and altruistic. Are charismatic and transformational leaders indeed qualitatively different?

Do they engage in qualitatively different behaviors? Undoubtedly there are situations that call for charismatic leaders who are able to command voluntary obedience and unquestioning compliance. There are also other situations that call for autonomy, self-direction, and altruism on the part of followers. The more authoritarian charismatic may be appropriate for combat situations, situations which impose short-term unpredicted time pressures, situations which require unusual physical and emotional exertion, and crisis situations. The transformational leader may be most appropriate for situations requiring creativity, adaptability to changing conditions and uncertain environments, and extraordinarily high initiative and personal assumption of responsibility on the part of followers.

While these speculations seem plausible, the current evidence does not support the distinction between the two kinds of leaders. In studying transformational leaders, Bass used factor analysis to derive a measurement scale for charisma. He hypothesized charisma to be one component of transformational leadership. Bass also developed four other scales, two of which are theoretically associated with transformational leadership. Since the charismatic scale accounted for 66% of the response variance, and since this scale is strongly related to the attribution of transformational leadership by followers, it is not at all clear that charismatic leaders and transformational leaders engage in qualitatively different behaviors.

It may be that intellectual stimulation on the part of the leader is a behavior that differentiates totalitarian leaders from egalitarian leaders. Avolio & Bass (1985) argue that the transformational leader, through intellectual stimulation, instills in followers the ability and will to question not only established views but eventually those espoused by the leader. Theoretically, such leaders rely more heavily on rational intellectual persuasion and coaching to encourage followers to think on their own and to develop new ventures which will further their goals while also developing the subordinate in his or her own right.

Graham (1986) sees intellectual stimulation as the pump that primes the well of subordinate independence and autonomy and prevents "habituated followership." She argues that habituated followership is characterized by blind unquestioning trust and obedience such as House describes as one of the charismatic effects. However, Smith (1982) found that his nominated charismatic leaders did not command unquestioning trust and blind obedience, suggesting that contrary to House's theory, habituated followership is not one of the charismatic follower effects.

Howell (1985), while not in disagreement with Graham, speculates that the two kinds of leaders are differentiated by their activity inhibition (activity inhibition is discussed above in the section on the Power Motive). That is, she hypothesizes that charismatic leaders or transformational leaders have extraordinarily high needs for power and at the same time feel inhibited in the use of power for their personal gain. This inhibition theoretically causes such individuals to express and satisfy their need for power in socially constructive and egalitarian behaviors. Howell hypothesizes that, in contrast, those low in activity inhibition will express their need for power in self-interested authoritarian behaviors. What in fact distinguishes egalitarian from totalitarian charismatic or transformational leaders, in terms of psychological make-up and behavior, remains to be established.

One might also ask whether charismatic or transformational leaders have differential appeal and acceptance, depending on the characteristics of the followers. One argument is that followers with high self-esteem, internal locus of control, and high need for autonomy are less likely to respond to charisma than individuals low on these characteristics. The counter argument is that there are indeed some leaders in some situations who by virtue of their leadership and personal abilities are able to establish charismatic relationships with followers, regardless of the followers' personal characteristics. According to this argument, these are the leaders who are generally agreed to be charismatic.

Finally, there is a need to specify the conditions under which charismatic or transformational leadership will be more effective than transactional leadership. Etzioni (1961) argues that charismatic leadership is most appropriate and effective to the extent that (a) moral persuasion is required for follower compliance, (b) followers are required to accept decisions about ends as well as means, and (c) followers are required to accept guidance on matters of morality and ideology.

House (1977) argues that charismatic leadership is appropriate when the task of followers has a significant ideological component. That is, when follower's efforts are directed toward implementation of ideological goals and values, or when their efforts are directed toward creating or delivering some social good, charismatic or transformational leadership which appeals to higher order needs and collective rather than individual values will be more motivational for followers and therefore more effective than transactional leadership.

Conclusions: Leadership

In conclusion, we see the field of leadership as having been significantly advanced over the past several years. New theories and new insights have emerged. Empirical studies have demonstrated, to some extent, the predictive validity of both established and newer theories. Finally, the newer theories and recent studies of leadership raise several important and interesting questions to be answered by future researchers.

EXECUTIVE SUCCESSION

Executive Succession (ES) and executive tenure longevity have been the subject of over 100 studies, most of which were conducted by sociologists or sociologically oriented organizational theorists (Brady & Helmich 1984). Despite the importance of the psychological considerations of the causes and effects of ES, little attention has been given to this topic by psychologists. Following is a selective review of the ES literature. While the results of the vast number of studies on executive succession are mixed, there is substantial agreement with respect to the relationship of several classes of variables to ES. In this section we restrict our review to studies that have yielded relatively consistent results and to those issues of primary concern to psychologists.

We begin with a review of the literature concerned with the causes of ES. Here we consider the causes of both voluntary and nonvoluntary ES. We advance several speculations concerning psychological characteristics associated with ES. We then turn to a discussion of the effects of ES on organization performance and survival. Finally, we discuss the power of executives as it relates to tenure longevity of executives and the effect that succeeding executives have on the postsuccession performance of the organizations they manage.

ES is important to the field of organizational behavior and to I/O psychology for several reasons. First, according to conventional wisdom, the chief executive officer (CEO) is the major holder and distributor of power throughout the organization. He or she plays one of the most important roles in goal and strategy formulation, design of the organizational structure and of the organizational control and reward systems. Further, the CEO plays a major role in keeping the organization aligned with its environment and in implementing and directing major organizational change (Thompson 1967, Pfeffer & Salancik 1978). Succession events also have symbolic significance and are frequently focal points of political processes in organizations (Pfeffer 1981). In addition, CEO succession occurs in all organizations and therefore is a universal variable with respect to the study of organizational behavior.

Causes of Executive Succession

VOLUNTARY SUCCESSION   Voluntary ES may be caused by voluntary retirement, resignation, or death. Such events, when not anticipated by the organization, are disruptive and frequently result in significant organizational problems and threats to survival. There are at least three aspects of voluntary ES that are of interest to psychologists. The first concerns the health of CEOs. As we shall document later, the CEO's position is a precarious one. CEOs are likely to experience frequent periods of very high stress. Little is known about the health implications of CEO role demands. An important question for students of organizational behavior concerns the search for individual differences that permit some CEOs to cope with the stress of their roles. Such differences, if they exist, cause executives to be less prone to health problems that eventually lead to resignation, early retirement, or death. Kobasa (1979) has shown that middle and upper level executives who are psychologically hardy incur less illness under conditions of stress than executives who are not hardy. Individuals who are psychologically hardy approach major life changes with an optimistic and active orientation. They have a clear sense of values, goals, and capabilities, a belief in their importance (commitment to rather than alienation from self), and a strong tendency toward active involvement with their progress (vigorousness rather than vegetativeness). Further, they view impending changes as opportunities for development and as challenges rather than threats. Psychologically hardy executives who suffered high stress reported significantly less subsequent illness than psychologically nonhardy executives who had experienced similar levels of stress (Kobasa 1979).

Other characteristics that are likely to facilitate CEO performance and health are the need for achievement (McClelland 1985) and the need for power (Miner 1978, McClelland 1985). However, as McClelland notes, the need for power is likely to be correlated significantly with the type A behavior syndrome which is strongly implicated in the incidence of coronary disease (Friedman & Rosenman 1974). It is likely that there are selection processes (self-selection and selection by others) that favor high need for power and/or type A personality characteristics. These characteristics put the selected individual at a higher risk of coronary disease and of other psychological disorders reviewed above in the section on the power motive. If selection processes favor executives high in the power motive, it is of significant interest to psychologists to understand how CEOs cope with stressful issues, especially power issues. Psychologists can make a significant contribution to this area of inquiry by studying the behaviors and personal characteristics implicated in effectively coping with such role demands.

The second issue of significance to psychologists concerns the personality characteristics that predispose executives to volunteer for early retirement or voluntarily leave the organization. Early voluntary termination may result from health problems. Voluntary termination may also result from inability to cope with the stresses of the executive role, especially in times of problematic environments and failing organizational performance. The causes and frequency of voluntary termination are not well understood and are of significance to succession planning and selection as well as health management. One form of voluntary termination is early retirement. Health issues associated with early retirement are especially critical given the trend in North

America toward early executive retirement (*Business Week* 1985). Early retirement policies are likely to result in improved morale for lower level managers since such retirements make higher level positions available. Further, early retirement relieves the organization of substantial salary obligations to older managers who can be replaced by younger managers who usually command lower salaries.

The third issue concerns individual differences that are characteristic of highly mobile executives who voluntarily change positions often in their careers. Jennings (1967) referred to such executives as mobiocentric. Kriesberg (1962) referred to executive careers as itinerant or home guard. Itinerant careers are those characterized by frequent progress through the ranks and a high degree of mobility. Such careers are usually associated with shorter tenures and mobility across organizations. In contrast, home-guard careers are usually associated with longer tenures and an upward mobility within, rather than across, organizations. There has been little research, to the best of our knowledge, concerning the personality characteristics of highly mobile executives. One might speculate that highly mobile executives are more "cosmopolitan" as described by Gouldner (1957) than less mobile executives. Cosmopolitans are less loyal to their employing organizations, committed to the specialized role of their professions, and influenced by outside reference groups more than the employing organizations. However, no research has been conducted to validate this speculation empirically. To date little is known about the psychological characteristics of highly mobile executives.

NONVOLUNTARY SUCCESSION   In addition to voluntary ES, there is substantial research suggesting that ES occurs as an organizational response to poor organizational performance or problematic environments. This research is concerned with rates of ES or length of executive tenure as dependent variables. Since this research shows ES or tenure longevity to be predicted from organizational performance or from problematic environments, it is likely that much CEO turnover is involuntary. ES and executive tenure have been shown to be higher among failing firms than nonfailing firms (Schwartz & Menon 1985). Higher rates of ES are also associated with increases in debt/equity ratios, an indicator of solvency problems (Pfeffer & Leblebici 1973, Helmich 1978); with decreases in return on investment (Grusky 1960, Osborn et al 1981, James & Soref 1981, Schwartz & Menon 1985, Tushman et al, unpublished manuscript 1985, Virany et al, unpublished manuscript 1985); with decreases or volatility in profit performance (Gamson & Scotch 1964, Grusky 1960, Eitzen & Yetman 1972, McEachern 1975, Schendel et al 1976, Osborn et al 1981, Brown 1982, Lubatkin & Chung 1985); and with percentage of losing games among sports teams (Grusky 1960, Eitzen & Yetman 1972).

In addition to poor prior organizational performance, ES is predicted by factors that make organizations difficult to manage. For example, Helmich (1978) found ES to be associated with new acquisitions and dispersed operations. Volatility in prior profit, in financial strategy, in merger strategy, in socioeconomic environment, and in supplier and owner relationships have also been found to be predictive of ES (Osborn et al 1981).

ES has also been shown to be predicted by problematic environments. Specifically poor quality relationships with the local and business community (Pfeffer & Salancik 1977), highly competitive funding environments (Pfeffer & Salancik 1977), highly turbulent environments (Weschler 1984), and resource-scarce environments (Salancik et al 1980) are all predictive of ES.

While there are a few exceptions to these findings in the research literature, when taken collectively the above evidence clearly indicates that the role of the CEO is one of negotiating with and adapting to the external environment and inducing internal change to adapt the organization to uncertain, changing and problematic environments. Further, this evidence suggests that the position of CEO is frequently a precarious one which often guarantees little or no job security.

INDIVIDUAL DIFFERENCES   The above findings suggest that effective CEOs are likely to be pro-active with respect to either their environments or the organizations they manage. Therefore, it is reasonable to speculate that such CEOs will have internal loci of control. Further, the overwhelming complexity of changing and uncertain environments suggests that CEOs who are cognitively complex are likely to be more effective than cognitively simple CEOs.

One would also expect that CEOs with well-developed and refined influence skills would be most effective. It would be of significant theoretical as well as practical interest to know whether the need for power (McClelland 1985), dominance (Gough 1968), and machiavellianism (Christie & Geis 1970) are characteristic of effective CEOs. We expect these personality traits to have their strongest effects on CEO behavior in problematic and changing environments. Such environments require the use of influence to negotiate effectively with environmental sectors and also with internal managers. Individuals who have these personality traits are more likely to have well developed and refined influence skills. We also expect personality traits to be most predictive of behavior under organizational arrangements in which the CEO's role is relatively unconstrained by the board of directors, policies, role definitions or other bureaucratic or technological constraints.

Psychologists can potentially make significant contributions to organizational behavior theory by identifying the role demands of CEOs and the psychological characteristics of executives necessary to meet these demands. Stated in another way, some of the psychological questions concerning ES are those related to the match or fit of succeeding executives to their environment and to their organization.

Effects of Executive Succession on Organizational Performance

Finally, there have been a substantial number of studies on the effects of ES on subsequent organizational performance. Overall the findings are mixed. Collectively these studies suggest that the mean effect of ES on postsuccession performance is minimal but that the variance is high. Fortunately, it has been possible to identify some of the moderators of the relationship between ES and subsequent organizational performance. Following are some of the moderators indicated by prior research.

Succeeding executives have a higher probability of having positive effects on organizational performance if the predecessor is a nondominant individual and if the predecessor leaves the organization (Carroll 1984b). Inside successors have been shown to be associated with slow growth (Helmich 1974). Succession patterns with one or more outside successions are associated with more organizational growth (Helmich 1974). As organizations age, they seek proportionately more insiders. Consequently, young organizations have more outside successions than older organizations (Helmich 1975).

The probability of the succeeding CEO having a positive impact on subsequent organizational performance is also associated with the characteristics of the CEO. When the CEO has the ability to cope with organizational uncertainties (Pfeffer & Salancik 1977), has a history of competence (Smith et al 1984), when the attributes of the successor match the demands of the organization (Helmich 1976), and when the successor possesses relevant knowledge and external influence (Shetty & Peary 1976), ES is more likely to lead to effectiveness than when the successor does not have these characteristics.

The effects of ES are also moderated by organizational rigidity. Pfeffer & Moore (1980) found that the tenure of academic department heads was significantly longer in those disciplines in which the paradigm was more highly developed and therefore more rigid. Further, Grusky (1960) found that the closer the personal ties between members of an organization the greater the instability caused by succession. Grusky also found that the less bureaucratic the organization the greater the impact of succession.

Finally, the effects of ES on organizational performance are more positive when the succession is orderly and planned than when the succession is not foreseen and the selection of the new CEO is made under time pressure (Trow 1961).

Inside Versus Outside Succession

In times of poor organizational performance CEOs are more likely to be selected from outside the organization (Schwartz & Menon 1985). The effects of CEOs selected from inside as compared to outside are different. Inside successions provide for more continuity of existing programs and management practices and therefore more organizational stability. Outside successors, in times of poor performance or problematic environments, are more likely to make strategic internal changes and to be more effective in implementing successful turnarounds (Helmich & Brown 1972, Helmich 1974, Reinganum 1985, Samuelson et al 1985). Tushman et al (unpublished manuscript 1985) found that outside successors with a mandate for change will induce improved organizational performance if they make significant strategic changes, especially if such changes include replacement of members of the top management team.

The view that outside successions are the key to organizational turnarounds, a popularly held view (Schendel et al 1976), depends on two further assumptions: first, that outsiders can change organizational policies; second, that acceptable successors are available. However, extremely poorly performing organizations have trouble recruiting good candidates. Further, to the extent that the board of directors is composed of inside managers, they will not be inclined to select outsiders because outsiders are likely to jeopardize their positions (Dalton & Kesner 1985). The consequence of these considerations is that there is a curvilinear relationship between prior firm performance and outside selection. Under conditions of prior effective performance, inside successors are likely to be chosen. Under conditions of extremely poor performance inside successors are also likely to be selected because outsiders will be less willing to join the organization. Under conditions of moderate to moderately low performance outside successors are likely to be selected and also to be willing to accept such positions.

Executive Succession and Power

As indicated by the above review, the position of the CEO can be highly precarious in certain circumstances. First there are several forces that threaten the CEO's job security. Environmental turbulence has been estimated to have caused the mean number of annual voluntary resignations to double from 1974 to 1984 (Weschler 1984). During such times one might expect that anticipated or actual shifts in the environment redistributes power such that CEOs, at that time, anticipate or experience loss of power to their positions and thus voluntarily move on to other organizations. Further, volatility in organizational performance and poor organizational performance are also likely to lead to executive turnover (Osborn et al 1981). Chief executives of large organizations are more likely to have shorter tenure because replacements are more likely to be available and because formalization of the CEO's position together with succession planning makes replacements less disruptive to the organization (Pfeffer & Moore 1980). Finally, organizations operating with less developed paradigms are more likely to lack internal consensus and consequently have more internal conflict. Such conflict is found to lead to more executive turnover (Pfeffer & Moore 1980).

Outside ES is more precarious than inside ES (Helmich 1976). This is most likely because outside ES occurs more for poorly performing firms. Therefore, outside successors inherit a higher initial risk than insiders who more frequently become the CEOs of successfully performing organizations.

Recall that outside succession for failing firms is most effective when coupled with strategic reorientation, redistribution of power, and replacement of key executives (Tushman et al, unpublished manuscript 1985). Consequently, outside successors are much more likely to become embroiled in political processes and conflict with members of the management team than insiders who take over stable, well-performing organizations.

Given that the CEO's job is largely one of social influence, it is reasonable to expect that the CEO's power relative to the board of directors or to other managers will be a significant determinant of his or her job security. This is what the evidence demonstrates. Virany et al (unpublished manuscript 1985) found that the greater the external control of the firm's management the greater was the frequency of succession events. Specifically they found that the control configuration of the organization accounted for 21.2% of the variance in ES. CEOs who held as little as 1% of the outstanding stock had significantly longer organizational tenures (Allen 1981a,b; Allen & Panian 1982). Further, McEachern (1975) and Salancik & Pfeffer (1980) found that tenure of CEOs of owner-managed firms was three times as long as executives of other firms. However, James & Soref (1981) found little effect of control configuration, suggesting that even when in a powerful position, some CEO positions are not entirely secure. Further, a study by Helmich (1976) demonstrated that the tenure of insiders is almost twice as long as the tenure of outsiders. This finding likely reflects the difficulties that outsiders are likely to have when introducing changes and power redistribution.

From the above findings it is clear that a CEO's relative power is a significant determinant of executive tenure and ES rates. It is also suggested by the studies conducted by Tushman and his associates that for failing or low-performing firms ES coupled with strategic change and change in the executive team leads to increasing organizational performance. However, we know little about the political behavior of CEOs and we know little about how they use the control structure to redistribute power, replace key executives, protect their position, and implement such strategic changes.

Conclusions: Executive Succession

In conclusion, it is clear that prior performance downturns or problematic environments are predictive of ES. Further, it is relatively clear that the match between successor characteristics, organizational environment, and organizational characteristics is critical to the postsuccession performance of organizations. It is also clear that the CEO position is a very precarious one, especially for outside successors. Finally, it can be concluded that the relative power of CEOs has much to do with their job longevity.

These conclusions suggest that there are three important potential contributions for psychologists to make to the organizational behavior and I/O psychology literature. The first concerns individual differences which facilitate effective performance and coping with stress. The second concerns the environment-CEO-organization match. The third concerns the postsuccession behavior of CEOs. Little attention has been given to the CEO's leader behavior and the CEO's use of power with respect to other managers and boards of directors as determinants of either organizational effectiveness or postsuccession longevity.

DECISION MAKING IN ORGANIZATIONS

In this section, we review decision making in organizations. Our emphasis on organizations is deliberate, in keeping with one focus of this paper, the interaction of organizational variables with behavior in organizations. Although there exists a rich and insightful literature on individual decision making (see, for example, Allison 1971, Nisbett & Ross 1980, Kahneman et al 1982), we choose not to review that work here. The main reason for our choice is the availability of a long series of comprehensive reviews of individual decision making (Rapoport & Wallsten 1972), behavioral decision theory (Edwards 1961, Becker & McClintock 1967, Slovic et al 1977, Einhorn & Hogarth 1981) and decision making and problem solving (Mac-Crimmon & Taylor 1976) in the literature. More recently, a detailed and complete review of decision making has appeared in the Lindzey and Aronson *Handbook of Social Psychology* (Abelson & Levi 1985).

Our brief review of decision making in organizations has three significant features. First, it draws upon and emphasizes the work on decision making in organizations carried out by March and his colleagues. Beginning with March & Simon (1958), with their emphasis on the cognitive limitations of human decision makers and satisficing in organizations, this perspective has examined behavioral approaches to firm decision making (Cyert & March

1963), decision making in organized anarchies, organizations with ambiguous goals and technologies and fluid participation (Cohen et al 1972), decision making by college presidents (Cohen & March 1974, 1986), decision making under conditions of ambiguity (March & Olsen 1976), the use of information in decision making (Feldman & March 1981), the relationship between behavioral and organizational approaches to decision making (March & Shapira 1982) and military decision making (March & Weissinger-Baylon 1986). We discuss how significant parts of the research on decision making in organizations may be appropriately seen as a successive relaxation of the usual assumptions of rational choice, which are shown by descriptions of decision making to be problematic (March & Olsen 1986). Secondly, we specifically review research on garbage-can models of decision making (Cohen et al 1972, March & Olsen 1976, March & Weissinger-Baylon 1986). Garbage-can decision processes are characterized by independent streams of problems, solutions, decision makers, and choice opportunities which have a temporal rather than a consequential ordering. In recent years, garbage-can processes have been extended beyond decision making in universities and other educational organizations to also apply to Weberian bureaucracy (Padgett 1980), the research process (Martin 1982), planning activities (Bromiley 1986), defense resource allocations (Crecine 1986), and naval warfare (Hughes 1986, Weissinger-Baylon 1986). Thirdly, we briefly review some recent research trends in decision making in organizations, and conclude with some implications of this work for organizational behavior.

Rational Choice and Empirical Observations of Decision Making in Organizations

Classical approaches to decision making presume that decisions in organizations are made intentionally based upon expectations about the future consequences of current actions. Choices depend upon a knowledge of alternatives, a knowledge of the consequences, a consistent preference ordering, and a decision rule. Decision makers are assumed to have an unambiguous set of alternatives that are defined by the situation, plus their associated consequences or their probability distributions. Decision makers are also assumed to have preference orderings by which the alternative consequences of actions can be compared in terms of their subjective values. Finally, decision makers are assumed to have rules by which to choose the best alternative. In such a framework, which underlies much thinking in economics, decision theory, and management science, specific organizational processes cannot affect decisions because, subject only to variations in preferences, such theories assume that choices are dictated by environmental conditions alone (March 1978, 1981a; March & Olsen 1986).

In addition to expectations about the future consequences of current actions, theories of rational choice make assumptions about future preferences for the consequences of those actions. Decision makers are assumed to have preferences that are absolute, i.e. decision makers cannot make choices among alternative preferences; preferences that are stable over time; preferences that are consistent, precise, and unambiguous; and preferences that are exogenous, i.e. the preferences are not affected by the decision processes themselves (March 1978, 1982).

Yet empirical observations of decision making in organizations have proved to be inconsistent with the rational choice theory outlined above (Simon 1978). Three broad criticisms have been made of the rational choice approach. First, the theory makes extraordinary time and information demands on organizations and individuals (Simon 1955, Miller 1956, March & Simon 1958), and information and time are implicitly assumed to be freely available resources. Secondly, the theory assumes that preferences of organizations are unproblematic, that decision makers in organizations either have identical preferences or that conflicts among their preferences can be resolved or managed through some process of agreement or coalition building (March 1962, Cyert & March 1963). Empirical studies, on the other hand, show that conflict is pervasive in organizations and does not appear to be settled by prior agreements (Pfeffer 1981a). Thirdly, not only are organizational goals and preferences problematic, even individual preferences do not have the characteristics assumed by rational choice theory. Decision makers do not follow expressed preferences, and their preferences are unstable. Preferences are inconsistent, imprecise, and are often discovered during processes of decision making (March 1978, March & Olsen 1986). Yet decisions are routinely made in organizations despite these problems.

In addition to limited rationality, conflict, and ambiguity of preferences, empirical studies have uncovered many other problems with decision making in organizations, adding to the complexity and disorder associated with decisions. For example, individuals fight to participate in decisions but do not fully exercise that right (Olsen 1976). Organizations consistently seek more information than is needed and then ignore the new information (Feldman & March 1981, March & Sevon 1983). Decision maker attitudes and commitment may be created retrospectively through processes of rationalization and justification (Staw 1980, O'Rielly & Caldwell 1981) rather than attitudes and preferences prospectively leading to the decisions. Decision makers develop strong preferences for certain organizational outcomes because of goals and incentive and control systems in organizations and are also susceptible to biases in selecting and processing information (O'Rielly 1983). Consequently, the link in organizations between problems and solutions is often tenuous, decision processes are solution centered and consider limited numbers of alternatives (Nutt 1984). Finally, organizations are appropriately seen as loosely coupled systems (Weick 1976) in which changes occur routinely but rarely in a predicted manner, and action is loosely coupled to intentions and preferences (March 1981b).

Based on the above, it may be argued that empirical observations of decision making suggest that most assumptions of rational choice theory are frequently violated in practice. The cognitive and information processing demands placed on decision makers by organizational decisions far exceed their limited cognitive capacities. Alternatives and their consequences are frequently unclear *ex ante* and are discovered through search activity in the process of decision making (March 1981a). Organizations frequently do not have consistent preference orderings. Instead, conflicting preferences lead to political action and the use of power in organizations (March 1981a, Pfeffer 1981a). Also, rules by which to choose the best alternative too often are discovered during the process of decision making instead of guiding decision making (Weick 1979a, Staw 1980), and often rules are instituted for symbolic rather than instrumental reasons (Meyer & Rowan 1977). Thus, empirical research on decision making in organizations may be seen as a process of relaxation of the usual assumptions of rational choice theory.

Garbage-Can Models of Decision Making in Organizations[1]

Against this background of empirical observations of decision making which were generally inconsistent with rational choice theory, the garbage-can model (Cohen et al 1972, March & Olsen 1976) explored whether there was any order in the confusion and complexity of decision making in organizations. A uniquely original approach, it substituted the conventional consequential order assumed in rational approaches to decision making by a temporal order (March & Olsen 1986). Thus, decision making in organizations did not appear to make much sense when the rationality of decisions was examined in terms of their consequences. But if decision making was viewed as the confluence of independent streams of problems, solutions, decision makers, and choice opportunities, with problems being solved when problem streams and solution streams come together, and a decision being made when the decision maker and choice opportunity streams were temporally simultaneous, it was easier to understand decisions in organizations. The problem lay less in the observations of decision making than in the theoretical ideas being used to order those observations. Garbage-can processes occur in all organizations sometimes, but were most likely to be observed in organized anarchies,

[1]This section draws heavily upon March & Olsen 1986.

organizations with ambiguous goals and technologies and fluid participation.

The pure form of the garbage-can model assumes that problems, solutions, decision makers, and choice opportunities are independent streams that are linked determined by their arrival and departure times and the structural constraints that may exist within an organization on the access of problems, solutions, and decision makers to choice opportunities. If there are no structural constraints, problems, solutions, decision makers and choice opportunities are linked mainly by their temporal ordering. The Cohen et al (1972) simulation study showed that in such a garbage-can process with an unsegmented structure, problem resolution is not a common model of decision making. Decisions by flight and oversight are more common (Cohen et al 1972). Garbage-can processes are very sensitive to problem loads in the system. As the load of the relative number of problems increases, problems are less likely to be solved, choices take longer to make, and decision makers move around between decisions more frequently. Overall, the process is sharply interactive, and the outcomes produced are usually the result of the timing of choices, problems, and participants in the decision making. An interesting feature of garbage-can decision process is that they are not dominated by the preferences of decision makers. The decision process and the process outcomes do not appear closely related to intentions. Decision making is highly context dependent, and intentionality gets submerged in the flows of problems, solutions, participants, and choice opportunities. Although it may seem that decision making in such systems will be completely chaotic, important problems are more likely to be solved than unimportant ones, and some decisions do get made in the course of time, although it is difficult to predict *a priori* which decisions they would be. As described below, empirical studies have demonstrated that such decision processes do exist in organizations (March & Olsen 1976). More generally, garbage-can processes may have specific access structures, the relation between problems or solutions and choice opportunities specifying which problems/solutions have access to which choice opportunities, and decision structures, the relation between decision makers and choice opportunities specifying which decision makers have access to which choice opportunities in organizations. These access and decision structures may take any arbitrary configuration, such as being specialized or hierarchical (March & Olsen 1986).

Several studies have examined how garbage-can processes are affected by structural features of organizations. Rommetveit (1976) studied the decision making processes that led to the location of Norway's third medical school as one example of decision making when standard operating procedures are challenged. Although Trondheim had initially been the dominant alternative, moving the decision from one arena to another with different structural features led to the eventual choice of Tromso as the location. Weiner (1976), in a study of decision making on desegregation in the San Francisco Unified School District, explored how deadlines affected garbage-can processes. Deadlines caused resistance to the entrance of new problems and participants in the choice process, a dramatic increase in the energy devoted to the choice by active participants, and led to either partial withdrawal of some participants or the ejection of some problems. Enderud (1976) studied perceptions of power in collegial assemblies at the Technical University of Denmark and found that study respondents inferred decision making power from participation and formal status rather than signs of decision making satisfaction with the decision process or outcomes. Olsen (1976), in a study of the participation of departmental faculty at the University of Oslo, examined a garbage-can process in which participation is viewed as a choice rather than as automatic. The study underlined the need to view participation both as something attractive and as a sacrifice. Attitudes toward increased participation were not explained by hierarchical position, and the complexity of influence processes in a university was evident. March & Romelaer (1976) studied instances of change in a medium size American university using four case studies. They found that the orderly drift of garbage-can decisions is not random but occurs in a context of beliefs, norms, and institutions that produce systematic biases in it. Powell (1978), in a study of publishing decisions, found that timing, the structure of company traditions, the academic status of the author, and whether the initiative was taken by the author or the publisher were important to the outcome. In a simulation study, Anderson & Fischer (1986) introduced solutions explicitly into garbage-can processes, joined problems and solutions with decision makers, and changed the allocation of decision makers to choices to reflect problems important to individuals. Their results were similar to the original study (Cohen et al 1972), except that decision makers were more evenly spread across choice opportunities. Carley (1986), in a theoretical analysis, has suggested conditions for the relative efficiency of garbage-can processes. Some other work has examined the relationship between the flexibility needs of an adaptive system and garbage-can processes (Cohen 1986) and shown the advantages of ambiguity for organizational efficiency (Cohen & Axelrod 1984).

Recent Research Trends

Several other interesting studies have been done on decision making in organizations in recent years. Among the questions asked, there have been examinations of top management decision making (Donaldson & Lorsch 1983, Hickson et al 1986); the applicability of decision making models to administration (Lutz 1982), and the role decision makers' assumptions might play in limiting their applicability (Shrivastava & Mitroff 1984); the use of verbal protocols (Schweiger 1983), participant recollection (Schwenk 1985) and historical case studies (Anderson 1983) to study decision making; and budgetary decision making (Bromiley 1981, Padgett 1980, 1981). Thus, research on decision making continues to attract scholars with a wide variety of substantive and methodological orientations.

Additionally, several themes can be discerned in recent decision making research which are discussed briefly below. First, there is a growing body of research on decision making which argues that instead of being prospectively rational, decision making behavior is strongly affected by processes of *rationalization and justification* in organizations (Staw 1980, 1981), and is often retrospectively rational (Weick 1979a). Research on the escalation of commitment to decisions (Staw 1976, Staw & Fox 1977, Staw & Ross 1978, 1980) has demonstrated some unanticipated consequences of these processes of consistency and justification. O'Rielly & Caldwell (1981) examined the effects of postdecisional justifications on the satisfaction and commitment of new employees and found results consistent with this retrospective rationality view.

Second, decision making in organizations is seen to be the result of *political processes* (Pfeffer 1977, 1981a). Decisions result from the interaction of competing political actors with different preferences (Allison 1971), depending on the power differences among the actors. Pfeffer (1982:chapter 2) has comprehensively reviewed this perspective earlier. Some of the recent studies on this theme have examined the allocation of budgets (Pfeffer & Salancik 1974, Pfeffer et al 1976, Pfeffer & Leong 1977, Hills & Mahoney 1978), curriculum changes (Baldridge 1971), authority-task problems (Hawley & Nichols 1982) and interorganizational decision making in Norwegian oil insurance (Heimer 1985). These studies all suggest that instead of being rational, decision making in organizations frequently is influenced by the use of political processes and power.

Third, important *symbolic* consequences are associated with decisions in organizations. Pfeffer (1981b) sees the main role of management in organizations as symbolic with substantive outcomes being determined more by external constraints than by managerial action. Organizations consistently seek out more information than they require, but ignore the new information in decision making (Feldman & March 1981, March & Sevon 1983), because the activity of information acquisition and search itself has important signalling and symbolic consequences. Organizations even change their formal structure in order to symbolically communicate their priorities to their environments and signal their competence and fit with social values (Meyer & Rowan 1977, Meyer 1980). Organizations sometimes establish consumer affairs departments, providing symbolic evidence that demands of external interest groups are being dealt with by them (Fornell 1976). The use of symbols is also one of the most effective, though often overlooked, ways of bringing about change in organizations (Peters 1978).

Fourth, there is a large and influential literature on *cognitive and information processing* views of decision making in organizations. Although a cognitive approach to decision making dates back at least to March & Simon (1958), and Simon's (1976) approach to administrative behavior was also essentially a cognitive theory, this theme has gained a considerable following in recent years. Weick (1979a,b) proposed that organizations are bodies of thought, causal schemata, and embody specific thinking practices. Axelrod (1976) used archival data to construct causal maps of foreign policy decisions and suggested that such maps could be used to predict future decisions and to improve decision making by examination of implicit causal assumptions. Bougon, et al (1977) analyzed cause maps in a jazz orchestra and assessed the extent to which members shared causal schemata, representing their understanding of the organization and its processes, and how they might react in different situations. O'Rielly (1980) studied the effects of information overload on decision maker performance and also found that the frequency of information use by decision makers is related to the accessibility of information (O'Rielly 1982). Decision makers in organizations are susceptible to biases in the acquisition and processing of information and selectively perceive and use information (O'Rielly 1983). Ungson et al (1981) used an information processing approach to review managerial decision making and specifically examined how managerial problems can be described and the cognitive processes used in managerial contexts. They argued that managerial problems are often ill-structured, and that managers often use causal models, a set of conceptual heuristic operations, in decision making. Kiesler & Sprouil (1982) suggested that managerial problem sensing, a precondition for adaptive decision making, is comprised of the processes of noticing, interpreting, and incorporating stimuli. These processes operate in systematic ways that make some kinds of problem sensing behavior and errors more likely. Harrison & March (1984) argued that the structure of intelligent choice itself creates a systematic bias in the distribution of postdecision surprises. This is most characteristic of decision situations where a large number of alternatives is considered, the true values of alternatives are close, and there is high ambiguity of evaluation. But Goiten (1984) has pointed out that "hindsight bias" (Slovic & Fischhoff 1977) may actually reduce the disappointment decision makers might feel about decision outcomes. Decision strategies of managers have been examined in terms of left-to-right brain hemisphere dominance (Taggart & Robey 1981), and a cognitive simplification perspective has been applied to ill-structured business problems like acquisition and divestment decisions (Duhaime & Schwenk 1985), showing how certain cognitive biases arise in ill-structured decision situations. Thus the cognitive and information processing approach has emphasized how systematic biases occur in managerial decision making, and it has been used to study the cognitive processes that underlie managerial problem solving in ill-structured situations.

Finally, an important stream of research on decision making is perhaps best described as comprised of *context dependent approaches*. Leblebici & Salancik (1981) studied the effects of environmental uncertainty on the structure and decision making of loan departments in banks and found that the normal operations procedures used by banks varied with the diversity of the environment, the source of uncertainty that can be anticipated, but not with volatility, the uncertainty that cannot be anticipated. Meyer (1982) examined the adaptation by organizations to environmental jolts, and found that ideological and strategic variables predict adaptation better than structural variables and organizational slack. Grandori (1984) proposed a prescriptive view on which decision making strategies, on a continuum from optimizing to random, would be appropriate under conditions of uncertainty and conflict of interest. Mintzberg & McHugh (1985) studied the formation of organizational strategies in an "adhocracy," and argued that strategies can emerge from initially thin streams of activity, from the precedents set by individuals, and from the simultaneous convergence of behaviors of various actors. Staw, et al (1981) proposed a multilevel theory of threat rigidity effects in organizations in response to threat that lead to a restriction of information processing and tightening of control in organizations. Using a management game simulation, Gladstein & Reilly (1985) found support for the restriction of information processing in response to threat, though centralization of influence did not change. Singh (1986), in a study of the relationship between performance and risk taking in organizations, found that poor performance led to greater centralization of control, but also found that firms threatened by poor performance are more likely to make riskier decisions, which seems generally to contradict the Staw et al thesis. This theme suggests that the types of decision making processes that are, and sometimes should be, used in organizations strongly depend on the organizational context.

Conclusions: Decision Making

In this section, we selectively reviewed the literature on decision making in organizations. Much of the empirical work on decision making suggests that decisions are made in much less rational ways than specified by rational choice theory. In practice, most of the assumptions of rational choice theory are violated by decision makers. We specifically reviewed work on the garbage-can approach, a descriptive theory of decision making in organizations under conditions of fluid participation, and ambiguous goals and technology. There is considerable support for the position that in many different kinds of organizations, some decisions are appropriately described by this theory. Finally, a review of recent trends in decision making research revealed how rich, new bodies of work are emerging that discuss the impact of rationalization, political, cognitive, symbolic, and contextual processes on decision making in organizations.

ORGANIZATIONAL BEHAVIOR IN AN EVOLUTIONARY CONTEXT

In this section we present some observations on how our understanding of organizational behavior may be improved by an explicit and systematic examination of the processes that affect the evolution of organizational behavior. Historically, students of organizational behavior have usually tried to understand *why* specific empirical regularities relating to, say, job satisfaction or leadership behavior are observed in organizations. Instead, we ask here *how* these empirical regularities got to be that way. Such a view stresses a more historical and evolutionary view of organizational behavior than has traditionally been the case. Our observations are informed by some recent developments in macro-organization theory and are somewhat speculative, since not much theoretical and empirical work has been done in this area. Specifically, we examine briefly processes of selection, imitation and learning, and institutionalization and their impact on patterns of organizational behavior. Given the constraints of this review, it is not possible for us to develop the implications of this evolutionary view fully for each one of the four topic areas reviewed here. Instead, we develop the argument mainly in the context of decision making and power in organizations. Another reason for our choice is that leadership, power, and management succession are related topics. The succession of top managers in organizations is one important mechanism by which power distributions in organizations are altered (Salancik & Pfeffer 1977), and the choice of successor also specifies the leadership style and the achievement and power motives of the leader.

Selection

In recent years, the selection perspective has emerged as a significant theoretical approach to the study of organizational change. One version of the selection argument has argued that populations of organizations change more from processes of selection leading to differential birth and death rates of different organizational forms (Hannan & Freeman 1977, 1984, Aldrich 1979) than processes of adaptation. The mounting empirical evidence suggests that such selection processes indeed operate in organizational populations (see, for example, Carroll 1984a, Singh et al 1986b). Whereas the previous approach focuses at the population level of analysis, a second selection argument examines actions within organizations. It is argued that behavior in organizations reflects rule following, and a significant part of organizational behavior is governed by these rules and standard operating procedures (March 1981a, Nelson & Winter 1982). Thus, the evolution of organizational behavior results from the changing mix of rules and procedures in an organization's repertoire, which may itself result from some adaptive learning processes.

Such selection processes play quite an important role in how decision making behavior and power distributions in organizations change over time. The strategic contingencies theory of intraorganizational power (Hickson et al 1971, Salancik & Pfeffer 1977, Pfeffer 1981a) argues that power in organizations accrues to those individuals or subunits that successfully deal with the critical demands or contingencies facing the organization. As the environment changes, and with it the critical contingencies, the power distribution changes (institutionalization of power, an exception to this, is discussed later), and this is an important mechanism by which organizations adapt to their environments. Such change in power distribution is also normatively appropriate, and organizations whose power distribution changes too little, or inappropriately, become misaligned with their environment and are eventually selected out. Such a selection process would lead to organizations with adapted power distributions outsurviving maladapted organizations.

March (1986) has argued that selection is also an important alternative mechanism for studying decision making behavior in organizations. Considering that the empirical study of decision making in organizations has showed that the usual assumptions of rational choice theory are often violated, it may be appropriate to examine the utility of alternative processes in understanding decision making behavior. One version of this selection argument suggests that decision making behavior is based on the observance of standard operating procedures and rules. Selection processes operate on these rules, systematically selecting out organizations with inappropriate rules, and leading to the survival of appropriate rules and organizations.

Imitation and Learning

Another important process by which changes in organizational behavior may be explained deals with imitation and learning mechanisms. The basic imitation argument is that organizations copy other similar organizations, particularly successful ones (March 1981a; DiMaggio & Powell 1983, p. 152). When organizational technologies are poorly understood and when goals are ambiguous (March & Olsen 1976), the uncertainty causes organizations to model themselves after other organizations, imitating their decision-making practices and structural arrangements. A related argument is that learning in organizations occurs through modifications in rules (March 1981a) and routines (Nelson & Winter 1982) based on feedback from the environment. In an evolutionary sense, surviving organizations are systematically those organizations that develop the appropriate rules and routines, whether through intentional learning or imitation, given the environmental contingencies.

It is plausible that these imitation and learning models underlie some decision making behavior and distribution of power in organizations. Organizations may learn to alter their decision making behavior and power distributions based on environmental feedback. Changes in decision making behavior and distributions of power may also follow imitation mechanisms, particularly under conditions of uncertainty. Provided the environment does not change dramatically, thereby breaking the learning link with past actions, such imitation and learning processes can enhance the survival of organizations (Singh et al 1986a).

Institutionalization

A third process deals with institutionalization in organizations. The institutional perspective (Meyer & Rowan 1977, DiMaggio & Powell 1983, Meyer & Scott 1983, Zucker 1983) suggests that changes in organizational features often occur in response to the changing environment of rationalized myths and the structuration of the organizational field. Isomorphism with the institutional environment enhances the legitimacy of organizations, easing selection pressures on the one hand, and leading to greater spread of institutionalized organizational features on the other. It has been found that the support of the institutional environment reduces death rates in voluntary organizations (Singh et al 1986b). Studies have also shown that when changes in formal organization structure are institutionalized, they are adopted more frequently (Tolbert & Zucker 1983). Thus, institutional processes have an impact on both selection and imitation processes.

Viewed in this light, the traditional emphasis on rational approaches to decision making in organizations is best understood as a reflection of rationality as a dominant social value. Further, decision making behaviors and rules that fit with the institutional environment, or are institutionalized, will outsurvive other decision making behaviors and be imitated more frequently. The institutionalization of power distributions in organizations has important implications for selection as well. Processes of institutionalization lead to organizational power distributions not changing enough or appropriately as the critical contingencies in the environment change. This leads to organizations gradually becoming misaligned with their environments, and eventually some organizations are selected out.

SUMMARY

In this review we covered several new areas of research that have relevance for organizational behavior. Although leadership has been reviewed earlier, power, executive succession, and decision making in organizations have received less attention in prior reviews. Wherever possible, we drew attention to cross-level effects, the interaction of organizational variables and individual behavior, or called for such research. We concluded with some preliminary speculations about how greater attention to processes of selection, imitation and learning, and institutionalization may enhance our understanding of the evolution of organizational behavior.

ACKNOWLEDGMENTS

We are grateful to Jim March for several discussions about the ideas contained in this paper. Many thanks also to Martin G. Evans for his critical review and to Joel Baum and Alan Saks for research assistance.

This paper was made possible by grant #410-84-0095-R2 from the Social Sciences and Humanities Research Council of Canada.

Literature Cited

Abelson, R. P., Levi, A. 1985. Decision making and decision theory. In *The Handbook of Social Psychology*, ed. G. Lindzey, E. Aronson, 1:231–390. New York: Random House. 3rd ed.

Aldrich, H. E. 1979. *Organizations and Environments*. Englewood Cliffs, NJ: Prentice-Hall

Allen, M. P. 1981a. Power and privilege in the large corporation: Corporate control and managerial compensation. *Am. J. Sociol.* 86:1112–23

Allen, M. P. 1981b. Managerial power and tenure in the large corporation. *Soc. Forc.* 60:482–94

Allen, M. P., Panian, S. K. 1982. Power, performance and succession in the large corporation. *Admin. Sci. Q.* 27:538–47

Allison, G. T. 1971. *Essence of Decision*. Boston: Little, Brown

Anderson, P. A. 1983. Decision making by objection and the Cuban missile crisis. *Admin. Sci. Q.* 28:201–22

Anderson, P. A., Fischer, G. W. 1986. A Monte Carlo model of a garbage can decision process. See March & Weissinger-Baylon 1986, pp. 40–64

Avolio, B. J., Bass, B. M. 1985. *Charisma and beyond*. Presented at Ann. Meet. Acad. Manage., San Diego

Axelrod, R. 1976. *Structure of Decision: The Cognitive Maps of Political Elites*. Princeton, NJ: Princeton Univ. Press

Baldridge, J. V. 1971. *Power and Conflict in the University*. New York: Wiley

Bass, B. M. 1985. *Leadership and Performance Beyond Expectations*. New York: Free Press

Becker, G. M., McClintock, C. G. 1967. Value: Behavioral decision theory. *Ann. Rev. Psychol.* 18:239–86

Bennis, W. G., Nanus, G. 1985. *Leaders*. New York: Harper & Row

Berlew, D. E. 1974. Leadership and organizational excitement. In *Organizational Psychology: A Book of Readings*, ed. D. A. Kolb, I. M. Rubin, J. M. McIntyre. Englewood Cliffs, NJ: Prentice-Hall. 2nd ed.

Berlyne, D. E. 1967. Arousal and reinforcement. In *Nebraska Symposium on Motivation: 1967*, ed. D. Levine. Lincoln: Univ. Nebraska Press

Bougon, M., Weick, K. E., Binkhorst, D. 1977. Cognition in organizations: An analysis of the Utrecht jazz orchestra. *Admin. Sci. Q.* 22:606–31

Brady, G. F., Helmich, D. L. 1984. *Executive Succession*. Englewood Cliffs, NJ: Prentice-Hall

Bromiley, P. 1981. Task environments and

budgetary decision making. *Acad. Manage. Rev.* 6:277–88

Bromiley, P. 1986. Planning systems in large organizations: A garbage can approach with application to defense PPBS. See March & Weissinger-Baylon 1986, pp. 120–39

Brown, M. C. 1982. Administrative succession and organizational performance: The succession effect. *Admin. Sci. Q.* 29:245–73

Burns, J. M. 1978. *Leadership*. New York: Harper & Row

Business Week. 1985. Putting mandatory retirement to pasture, pp. 104–5

Carley, K. 1986. Efficiency in a garbage can: Implications for crisis management. See March & Weissinger-Baylon 1986, pp. 195–231

Carroll, G. R. 1984a. Organizational ecology. *Ann. Rev. Sociol.* 10:71–93

Carroll, G. R. 1984b. Dynamics of publisher succession in newspaper organizations. *Admin. Sci. Q.* 29:245–73

Christie, R., Geis, F. L. 1970. *Studies in Machiavellianism*. New York: Academic

Cohen, M. D. 1986. Artificial intelligence and the dynamic performance of organizational designs. See March & Weissinger-Baylon 1986, pp. 53–71

Cohen, M. D., Axelrod, R. 1984. Coping with complexity: The adaptive value of changing utility. *Am. Econ. Rev.* 74:30–42

Cohen, M. D., March, J. G. 1974. *Leadership and Ambiguity: The American College President*. New York: McGraw-Hill

Cohen, M. D., March, J. G. 1986. *Leadership and Ambiguity: The American College President*. Cambridge, MA: Harvard Bus. Sch. Press 2nd ed.

Cohen, M. D., March, J. G., Olsen, J. P. 1972. A garbage can model of organizational choice. *Admin. Sci. Q.* 17:1–25

Comstock, D. E., Scott, W. R. 1977. Technology and structure of subunits: Distinguishing individual and work effects. *Admin. Sci. Q.* 22:177–202

Crecine, J. P. 1986. Defense resource allocation: Garbage can analysis of C3 procurement. See March & Weissinger-Baylon 1986, pp. 72–119

Cummin, P. 1967. TAT correlates of executive performance. *J. Appl. Psychol.* 51:78–81

Cummings, L. L. 1982. Organizational behavior. *Ann. Rev. Psychol.* 33:541–79

Cyert, R. M., March, J. G. 1963. *A Behavioral Theory of the Firm*. Englewood Cliffs, NJ: Prentice-Hall

Dalton, D. R., Kesner, I. F. 1985. Organizational performance as an antecedent of inside/outside chief executive succession: An empirical assessment. *Am. Manage.* 28(4):749–62

Davidson, R. J., Saron, C., McClelland, D. C. 1980. Effects of personality and semantic content of stimuli on augmenting and reducing in the event-related potential. *Biol. Psychol.* 11:249–55

DiMaggio, P. J., Powell, W. W. 1983. The iron cage revisited: Institutional isomorphism and collective rationality in organizational fields. *Am. Sociol. Rev.* 48:147–60

Donaldson, G., Lorsch, J. W. 1983. *Decision Making at the Top*. New York: Basic Books

Donley, R. E., Winter, D. G. 1970. Measuring the motives of public officials at distance: An exploratory study of American Presidents. *Behav. Sci.* 15:227–36

Duhaime, I., Schwenk, C. R. 1985. Conjectures on cognitive simplification in acquisition and divestment decision making. *Acad. Manage. Rev.* 10:287–95

Edwards, W. 1961. Behavioral decision theory. *Ann. Rev. Psychol.* 12:473–98

Einhorn, H. J., Hogarth, R. M. 1981. Behavioral decision theory: *Processes of judgement and choice. Ann. Rev. Psychol.* 32:53–88

Eitzen, D. S., Yetman, N. R. 1972. Managerial change, longevity and organizational effectiveness. *Admin. Sci. Q.* 17(1):110–16

Enderud, H. 1976. The perception of power. See March & Olsen 1976, pp. 386–96

Etzioni, A. 1961. *A Comparative Analysis of Complex Organizations*. New York: Free Press

Feldman, M. S., March, J. G. 1981. Information in organizations as signal and symbol. *Admin. Sci. Q.* 26:171–86

Fiedler, F. E. 1964. A contingency model of leadership effectiveness. In *Advances in Experimental Social Psychology*, ed. L. Berkowitz. New York: Academic

Fiedler, F. 1978. The contingency model and the dynamics of the leadership process. In *Advances in Experimental Social Psychology*, ed. L. Berkowitz. pp. 59–112. New York: Academic

Fiedler, F. E. 1986. The contribution of cognitive resources and behavior to leadership performance. In *Changing Conceptions of Leadership*, ed. Graumann & Moseovici. New York: Springer-Verlag

Fiedler, F. E., Garcia, J. E. 1987. *New Approaches to Leadership: Cognitive Resources and Organizational Performance*. New York: Wiley

Fodor, E. M. 1984. The power motive and reactivity to power stresses. *J. Pers. Sociol. Psychol.* 47:853–59

Fodor, E. M., Farrow, D. L. 1979. The power motive as an influence on the use of power. *J. Pers. Soc. Psychol.* 37:2091–97

Fodor, E. M., Smith, T. 1982. The power motive as an influence on group decision making. *J. Pers. Soc. Psychol.* 42:178–85

Fornell, C. 1976. *Consumer Input for Marketing Decisions: A Study of Corporate Departments for Consumer Affairs*. New York: Praeger

Friedman, M., Rosenman, R. H. 1974. *Type A Behavior and Your Heart*. New York: Fawcett

Gamson, W. A., Scotch, N. A. 1964. Scapegoating in baseball. *Am. J. Sociol.* 70:69–72

Gladstein, D. L., Reilly, N. P. 1985. Group decision making under threat: The Tycoon game. *Acad. Manage. J.* 28:613–27

Goiten, B. 1984. The danger of disappearing post-decision surprise: Comment on Harrison and March, "Decision making and post decision surprises". *Admin. Sci. Q.* 29:410–13

Gough, H. G. 1968. *California Psychology Inventory: An Interpreter's Syllabus*. Palo Alto, CA: Consulting Psychologists Press

Gough, H. G., Heilbrun, A. B. Jr. 1975. *The Adjective Checklist Manual*. Palo Alto, CA: Consulting Psychologists Press

Gouldner, A. W. 1957. Cosmopolitans and locals: Toward an analysis of latent social roles—I and II. *Admin. Sci. Q.* 2:281–306

Graen, G., Cashman, J. F. 1975. A role-making model of leadership in formal organizations: A developmental approach. In *Leadership Frontiers*, ed. J. G. Hunt, L. L. Larson, pp. 143–65. Kent, OH: Kent State Univ. Press

Graen, G. B., Wakabayashi, M. 1986. The Japanese career progress study: a 7-year follow-up, *J. Appl. Psychol.* 69: 603–14

Graen, G., Novak, M., Sommerkamp, P. 1982. The effects of leader-member exchange and job design on productivity and satisfaction: Testing a dual attachment model. *Organ. Behav. Hum. Perform.* 30:109–31

Graen, G. B., Scandura, T. A., Graen, M. R. 1986. A field experimental test of the moderating effects of growth need strength on productivity. *J. Appl. Psychol.* 71:484–91

Graham, J. W. 1986. The essence of leadership: Fostering follower autonomy, *not* automatic followership. In *Emerging Leadership Vistas*, ed. J. G. Hunt. Elmsford, NY: Pergamon. In press

Grandori, A. 1984. A prescriptive contingency view of organizational decision making. *Admin. Sci. Q.* 29:192–209

Grusky, O. 1960. Administrative succession in formal organizations. *Soc. Forc.* 39:105–15

Grusky, O. 1963. Managerial succession and organizational effectiveness. *Am. J. Sociol.* 69:21–31

Hannan, M. T., Freeman, J. 1977. The population ecology of organizations. *Am. J. Sociol.* 82:929–64

Hannan, M. T., Freeman, J. 1984. Structural inertia and organizational change. *Am. Sociol. Rev.* 49:149–64

Harrison, J. R., March, J. G. 1984. Decision making and post decision surprises. *Admin. Sci. Q.* 29:26–42

Hawley, K. E., Nichols, M. L. 1982. A contextual approach to modeling the decision to participate in a "political" issue. *Admin. Sci. Q.* 27:105–19

Heimer, C. A. 1985. Allocating information costs in a negotiated information order: Interorganizational constraints on decision making in Norwegian oil insurance. *Admin. Sci. Q.* 30:395–417

Helmich, D. L. 1974. Organizational growth and succession patterns. *Acad. Manage. J.* 4(17):771–75

Helmich, D. L. 1975. Corporate succession: An examination. *Acad. Manage. J.* 18:429–41

Helmich, D. L. 1976. Succession: A longitudinal look. *J. Bus. Res.* 4:335–64

Helmich, D. L. 1978. Leader flows and organizational process. *Acad. Manage. J.* 21:463–78

Helmich, D. L., Brown, W. B. 1972. Successor type and organizational change in the corporate enterprise. *Admin. Sci. Q.* 17:371–81

Hickson, D. J., Butler, R. J., Cray, D., Mallory, G. R., Wilson, D. C. 1986. *Top Decisions: Strategic Decision Making in Organizations*. San Francisco: Jossey–Bass

Hickson, D. J., Hinings, C. R., Lee, C. A., Schneck, R. E., Pennings, J. M. 1971. A strategic contingencies theory of intraorganizational power. *Admin. Sci. Q.* 16:216–29

Hills, F. S., Mahoney, T. A. 1978. University budgets and organizational decision making. *Admin. Sci. Q.* 23:454–65

Hinings, C. R., Hickson, D. J., Pennings, J. M., Schneck, R. E. 1974. Structural conditions of intra-organizational power. *Admin. Sci. Q.* 19:22–44

House, R. J. 1971. A path-goal theory of leader effectiveness. *Admin. Sci. Q.* 16:321–38

House, R. J. 1977. A 1976 theory of charismatic leadership. In *Leadership: The Cutting Edge*, ed. J. G. Hunt, L. L. Larson, pp. 189–207. Carbondale: South. Ill. Univ. Press

House, R. J. 1985. *Research contrasting the behavior and effect of reputed charismatic versus reputed non-charismatic U. S. Presidents*. Presented at Ann. Meet. Admin. Sci. Assoc., Can. Montreal

House, R. J., Mitchell, T. R. 1974. Path-goal theory of leadership. *J. Contemp. Bus.* 3(4):81–97

Howell, J. M. 1985. *A laboratory study of*

charismatic leadership. Presented at Ann. Meet. Acad. Manage. San Diego

Hughes, W. P. 1986. Garbage cans at sea. See March & Weissinger-Baylon 1986, pp. 249–57

James, D. R., Soref, M. 1981. Profit constraints on managerial autonomy: Managerial theory and the unmaking of the corporation president. *Am. Sociol. Rev.* 46:1–18

Jennings, E. 1967. *The Mobile Manager.* Bur. Bus. Res., Mich. State Univ. Press

Kahneman, D., Slovic, P., Tversky, A. 1982. *Judgment under Uncertainty: Heurisitics and Biases.* Cambridge: Cambridge Univ. Press

Kerr, S., Jermier, J. M. 1978. Substitutes for leadership: Their meaning and measurement *Organ. Behav. Hum. Perform.* 22:375–403

Kiesler, S., Sproull, L. 1982. Managerial response to changing environments: Perspectives on problem sensing from social cognition. *Admin. Sci. Q.* 27:548–70

Kipnis, D. 1976. *The Powerholders.* Chicago: The Univ. Chicago Press

Kobasa, S. C. 1979. Stressful life events, personality and health: An inquiry into hardiness. *J. Pers. Soc. Psychol.* 37:1–11

Kriesberg, L. 1962. Organizational size and succession. *Am. J. Sociol.* 68:355–59

Leblebici, H., Salancik, G. R. 1981. Effects of environmental uncertainty on information and decision processes in banks. *Admin. Sci. Q.* 26:578–96

Lord, R. G. 1985. An information processing approach to social perceptions, leadership and behavioral measurement in organizations. *Res. Organ. Behav.* 7:87–128

Lord, R. G., Binning, J. F., Rush, M. C., Thomas, J. C. 1978. The effect of performance cues and leader behavior on questionnaire ratings of leadership behavior. *Organ. Behav. Hum. Perform.* 21:27–39

Lord, R. G., Foti, R. J., De Vader, D. 1986. A test of leadership categorization theory: Internal structure information processing, and leadership perceptions. *Organ. Behav. Hum. Perform.* In press

Lord, R. G., Foti, R. J., Phillips, J. S. 1982. A theory of leadership categorization. In *Leadership: Beyond Establishment Views,* ed. J. G. Hunt, U. Sekaran, C. Schriesheim. Carbondale: South. Ill. Univ.

Lord, R. G., Smith, J. E. 1983. Theoretical, information processing and situational factors affecting attribution theory models of organizational behavior. *Acad. Manage. Rev.* 8:50–60

Lubatkin, M., Chung, K. 1985. Leadership origin and organizational performance in prosperous and declining firms. *Acad. Manage. Proc.*

Lutz, F. W. 1982. Tightening up loose coupling in organizations of higher education. *Admin. Sci. Q.* 27:653–69

MacCrimmon, K. R., Taylor, R. N. 1976. Decision making and problem solving. In *Handbook of Industrial and Organizational Psychology* ed. M. D. Dunnette, pp. 1397–1454. Chicago: Rand-McNally

Maranell, G. M. 1970. The evaluation of presidents: An extension of the Schlesinger polls. *J. Am. Hist.* 57:104–13

March, J. G. 1962. The business firm as a political coalition. *J. Polit.* 24:662–78

March, J. G. 1978. Bounded rationality, ambiguity, and the engineering of choice. *Bell J. Econ.* 9:587–608

March, J. G. 1981a. Decisions in organizations and theories of choice. In *Perspectives on Organization Design and Behavior,* ed. A. H. Van de Ven, W. Joyce, pp. 205–44. New York: Wiley

March, J. G. 1981b. Footnotes to organizational change. *Admin. Sci. Q.* 26:563–77

March, J. G. 1982. Theories of choice and making decisions. *Trans./Soc.* 20:29–39

March, J. G. 1986. *The pursuit of intelligence in decision making.* Grad. Sch. Bus., Stanford Univ. Unpublished ms

March, J. G., Olsen, J. P., eds. 1976. *Ambiguity and Choice in Organizations.* Bergen, Norway: Universitetsforlaget

March, J. G., Olsen, J. P. 1986. Garbage can models of decision making in organizations. See March & Weissinger-Baylon 1986, pp. 11–35

March, J. G., Romelaer, P. 1976. Position and presence in the drift of decisions. In *Ambiguity and Choice in Organizations,* ed. J. G. March, J. P. Olsen, pp. 251–76. Bergen, Norway: Universitetsforlaget

March, J. G., Sevon, G. 1983. Gossip, information, and decision making. In *Advances in Information Processing in Organizations,* ed. L. S. Sproull, P. D. Larkey, pp. 95–107. Greenwich, CT: JAI Press

March, J. G., Shapira, Z. 1982. Behavioral decision theory and organizational decision theory. In *Decision Making: An Interdisciplinary Inquiry,* ed. G. R. Ungson, D. N. Braustein, pp. 92–115. Boston: Kent

March, J. G., Simon, H. A. 1958. *Organizations.* New York: Wiley

March, J. G., Weissinger-Baylon, R., eds. 1986. *Ambiguity and Command: Organizational Perspectives on Military Decision Making.* Cambridge, MA: Ballinger

Martin, J. 1982. A garbage can model of the research process. In *Judgment Calls in Research,* ed. J. E. McGrath, J. Martin, R. A. Kulka, pp. 17–39. Beverly Hills, CA: Sage

McAdams, D. P. 1982. Experiences of intimacy and power: Relationships between social motives and autobiographical memory. *J. Pers. Soc. Psychol.* 42:292–302

McClelland, D. C. 1975. *Power: The Inner Experience.* New York: Irvington

McClelland, D. C. 1979. Inhibited power motivation and high blood pressure in men. *J. Abnorm. Psychol.* 88:182–90

McClelland, D. C. 1982. The need for power, sympathetic activation, and illness. *Motiv. Emotion* 6:31–41

McClelland, D. C. 1985. *Human Motivation.* Glenview, IL: Scott, Foresman

McClelland, D. C., Alexander, C., Marks, E. 1982. The need for power: stress, immune function, and illness among male prisoners. *J. Abnorm. Psychol.* 91:61–70

McClelland, D. C., Boyatzis, R. E. 1982. Leadership motive pattern and long term success in management. *J. Appl. Psychol.* 67:737–43

McClelland, D. C., Burnham, D. H. 1976. Power is the great motivator. *Harv. Bus. Rev.* 54(2):100–10, 159–66

McClelland, D. C., Davis, W. N., Kalin, R., Warner, R. 1972. *The Drinking Man.* New York: Free Press

McClelland, D. C., Jemmott, J. B. III. 1980. Power motivation, stress and physical illness. *J. Hum. Stress* 4:6–15

McEachern, W. A. 1975. *Managerial Control and Performance.* Lexington, MA: Heath

Megargee, E. I., Bogart, P., Anderson, B. J. 1966. Prediction of leadership in a simulated industrial task. *J. Appl. Psychol.* 50:292–95

Meyer, A. D. 1982. Adapting to environmental jolts. *Admin. Sci. Q.* 27:515–37

Meyer, J. W., Rowan, B. 1977. Institutionalized organizations: Formal structure as myth and ceremony. *Am. J. Sociol.* 83:340–63

Meyer, J. W., Scott, W. R. 1983. *Organizational Environments: Ritual and Rationality.* Beverly Hills, CA: Sage

Meyer, M. W. 1980. Organizational structure as signaling. *Pac. Sociol. Rev.* 22:481–500

Miller, G. A. 1956. The magical number seven plus or minus two: Some limits on our capacity for processing information. *Psychol. Rev.* 63:61–97

Miner, J. B. 1978. Twenty years of research on role motivation theory of managerial effectiveness. *Personnel Psychol.* 31:739–60

Mintzberg, H., McHugh, A. 1985. Strategy formation in an adhocracy. *Admin. Sci. Q.* 30:160–097

Mitchell, T. R. 1979. Organizational behavior. *Ann. Rev. Psychol.* 3:243–81

Mossholder, K. W., Bedeian, A. G. 1983. Cross-level inference and organizational research: Perspectives on interpretation and application. *Acad. Manage. Rev.* 8:486–500

Mowday, R. 1978. The exercise of upward influence in organizations. *Admin. Sci. Q.* 23:137–56

Mowday, R. 1980. Leader characteristics, self-confidence, and methods of upward influence in organization decision situations. *Acad. Manage. J.* 44:709–24

Nelson, R. R., Winter, S. G. 1982. *An Evolutionary Theory of Economic Change.* Cambridge, MA: Belknap Press of Harvard Univ. Press

Nisbett, R., Ross, L. 1980. *Human Inference: Strategies and Shortcomings of Social Judgment.* Englewood Cliffs, NJ: Prentice-Hall

Nutt, P. C. 1984. Types of organizational decision processes. *Admin. Sci. Q.* 29:414–50

Olsen, J. P. 1976. University governance: Non-participation as exclusion or choice. See March & Olsen 1976, pp. 277–313

O'Reilly, C. 1980. Individuals and information overload in organizations: Is more necessarily better? *Acad. Manage. J.* 23: 684–96

O'Reilly, C. 1982. Variations in decision makers' use of information sources: The impact of quality and accessibility of information. *Acad. Manage. J.* 25:756–71

O'Reilly, C. A. 1983. The use of information in organizational decision making: A model and some propositions. *Res. Organ. Behav.* 5:103–39

O'Reilly, C. A., Caldwell, D. F. 1981. The commitment and job tenure of new employees: Some evidence of post decisional justification. *Admin. Sci. Q.* 26:597–616

Osborn, R. N., Jauch, L. R., Martin, T. N., Glueck, W. F. 1981. The event of CEO succession, performance, and environmental conditions. *Acad. Manage. J.* 24(1): 183–91

Padgett, J. F. 1980. Managing garbage can hierarchies. *Admin. Sci. Q.* 25:583–604

Padgett, J. F. 1981. Hierarchy and ecological control in federal budgetary decision making. *Am. J. Sociol.* 87:75–129

Peters, L. H., Hartke, D. D., Pohlmann, J. T. 1985. Fiedler's contingency theory of leadership: An application of the meta-analysis procedures of Schmidt and Hunter. *Psychol. Bull.* 97(2):274–85

Peters, T. J. 1978. Symbols, patterns, and settings: An optimistic case for getting things done. *Organ. Dyn.* 7:3–33

Pfeffer, J. 1977. Power and resource allocation in organizations. In *New Directions in Organizational Behavior,* ed. B. M. Staw, G. R. Salancik, pp. 235–65. Chicago: St. Clair

Pfeffer, J. 1981. *Power in Organizations.* Marshfield, MA: Pitman

Pfeffer, J. 1982. *Organizations and Organization Theory.* Marshfield, MA: Pitman

Pfeffer, J., Leblebici, H. 1973. Executive Recruitment and the development of interfirm organizations. *Admin. Sci. Q.* 18:449–61

Pfeffer, J., Leong, A. 1977. Resource allocations in United Funds: Examinations of power and dependence. *Soc. Forc.* 55:775–90

Pfeffer, J., Moore, W. L. 1980. Average tenure of academic department heads: The effects of paradigm, size and departmental demography. *Admin. Sci. Q.* 25:387–406

Pfeffer, J., Salancik, G. R. 1974. Organizational decision making as a political process: The case of a university budget. *Admin. Sci. Q.* 19:135–51

Pfeffer, J., Salancik, G. R. 1977. Organizational context and the characteristics and tenure of hospital administrators. *Acad. Manage. J.* 20:74–88

Pfeffer, J., Salancik, G. R. 1978. *The external control of organizations: A resource dependence perspective.* New York: Harper & Row

Pfeffer, J., Salancik, G. R., Leblebici, H. 1976. The effect of uncertainty on the use of social influence in organizational decision making. *Admin. Sci. Q.* 21:227–45

Powell, W. W. 1978. Publishers' decision-making: What criteria do they use in deciding which books to publish? *Soc. Res.* 45:227–52

Rapoport, A., Wallsten, T. W. 1972. Individual decision behavior. *Ann. Rev. Psychol.* 23:131–75

Reinganum, M. R. 1985. The effect of executive succession on stockholder wealth. *Admin. Sci. Q.* 30:46–60

Rommetveit, K. 1976. Decision making under changing norms. See March & Olsen 1976, pp. 140–55

Rousseau, D. M. 1985. Issues of level in organizational research: Multi-level and cross-level perspectives. *Res. Organ. Behav.* 7:1–37

Salancik, G. R., Pfeffer, J. 1977. Who gets power—and how they hold onto it: A strategic contingency model of power. *Organ. Dynam.* 5:3–21

Salancik, G. R., Pfeffer, J. 1980. Effects of ownership and performance on executive "tenure" in U.S. Corporations. *Acad. Manage. J.* 23:653–64

Salancik, G. R., Staw, B. M., Pondy L. R. 1980. Administrative turnover as a response to unmanaged organizational interdependence. *Acad. Manage. J.* 23:422–37

Samuelson, B. A., Galbraith, C. S., McGuire, J. W. 1985. Organizational performance and top-management turnover. *Organ. Stud.* 6/3:275–91

Sashkin, M., Fulmer, R. M. 1985. *Toward an organizational leadership theory.* Presented at Bienn. Leadership Symp., Texas Tech Univ.

Scandura, T. A., Graen, G. B. 1984. Moderating effects of initial leader-member exchange status on the effects of leadership intervention. *J. Appl. Psychol.* 69:428–36

Schendel, D., Patton, G. R., Riggs, J. 1976. Corporate turnaround strategies: A study of profit decline and recovery. *J. Gen. Manage.* 3(3):3–11

Schneider, B. 1985. Organizational behavior. *Ann. Rev. Psychol.* 36:573–611

Schwartz, K. B., Menon, K. 1985. Executive succession in failing firms. *Acad. Manage. J.* 28(3):680–86

Schweiger, D. M. 1983. Is the simultaneous verbal protocol a viable method for studying managerial problem solving and decision making? *Acad. Manage. J.* 26:185–92

Schwenk, C. R. 1985. The use of participant recollection in the modeling of organizational decision processes. *Acad. Manage. Rev.* 10:496–503

Shetty, Y. K., Peary, N. S. 1976. Are top executives transferable across companies? *Bus. Horiz.* 19:23–28

Shrivastava, P., Mitroff, I. I. 1984. Enhancing organizational research utilization: The role of decision makers' assumptions. *Acad. Manage. Rev.* 9:18–26

Simon, H. A. 1955. A behavioral model of rational choice. *Q. J. Econ.* 69:99–118

Simon, H. A. 1976. *Administrative Behavior.* New York: Free Press. 3rd ed.

Simon, H. A. 1978. Rational decision making in business organizations. *Am. Econ. Rev.* 69:493–514

Singh, J. V. 1986. Performance, slack, and risk taking in organizational decision making. *Acad. Manage. J.* 29:562–85

Singh, J. V., House, R. J., Tucker, D. J. 1986a. *Organizational change and organizational mortality.* Fac. Manage. Stud., Univ. Toronto. Unpublished ms

Singh, J. V., Tucker, D. J., House, R. J. 1986b. *Organizational legitimacy and the liability of newness. Admin. Sci. Q.* 31:171–93

Slovic, P., Fischhoff, B. 1977. On the psychology of experimental surprises. *J. Exp. Psychol: Hum. Percep. Perform.* 3:544–51

Slovic, P., Fischhoff, B., Lichtenstein, S. 1977. Behavioral decision theory. *Ann. Rev. Psychol.* 28:1–39

Smith, B. J. 1982. *An initial test of a theory of charismatic leadership based on responses of subordinates.* PhD thesis. Univ. Toronto. Unpublished

Smith, J. E., Carson, K. P., Alexander, R. A. 1984. Leadership: It can make a difference. *Acad. Manage. J.* 27(4):765–76

Stahl, M. J. 1983. Achievement, power and managerial motivation: Selecting managerial talent with the job choice exercise. *Personnel Psychol.* 36:775–89

Staw, B. M. 1976. Knee deep in the big muddy: A study of escalating commitment to a course of action. *Organ. Behav. Hum. Perform.* 16:27–44

Staw, B. M. 1980. Rationality and justification in organizational life. In *Research in Organizational Behavior,* ed. B. M. Staw, L. L. Cummings, 2:45–80. Greenwich, CT: JAI Press

Staw, B. M. 1981. The escalation of commitment to a course of action. *Acad. Manage. Rev.* 5:577–87

Staw, B. M. 1984. Organizational behavior: A review and reformulation of the field's outcome variables. *Ann. Rev. Psychol.* 35: 627–66

Staw, B. M., Fox, F. V. 1977. Escalation: Some determinants of commitment to a previously chosen course of action. *Hum. Relat.* 30:431–50

Staw, B. M., Ross, J. 1978. Commitment to a policy decision: A multi-theoretical perspective. *Admin. Sci. Q.* 23:40–64

Staw, B. M., Ross, J. 1980. Commitment in an experimenting society: A study of the attribution of leadership from administrative seminars. *J. Appl. Psychol.* 65:249–60

Staw, B. M., Sandelands, L. E., Dutton, J. E. 1981. Threat-rigidity effects in organizational behavior: A multilevel analysis. *Admin. Sci. Q.* 26:501–24

Steele, R. S. 1973. *The psychological concomitants of psychogenic motive arousal in college males.* PhD thesis. Harvard Univ. Unpublished

Steele, R. S. 1977. Power motivation, activation, and inspirational speeches. *J. Pers.* 45:53–64

Stewart, A. J., Winter, D. G. 1976. Arousal of the power motive in women. *J. Consul. Clin. Psychol.* 44:495–96

Taggart, W., Robey, D. 1981. Minds and managers: On the dual nature of human information processing and management. *Acad. Manage. Rev.* 6:187–95

Thompson, J. D. 1967. *Organizations in Action.* New York: McGraw-Hill

Tolbert, P. S., Zucker, L. G. 1983. Institutional sources of change in the formal structure of organizations: The diffusion of civil service reform, 1880–1935. *Admin. Sci. Q.* 28:22–39

Trow, D. B. 1961. Executive Succession in small companies. *Admin. Sci. Q.* 228–39

Tushman, M., Varany, B., Romanelli, E. 1985. Effects of CEO and executive team succession: a longitudinal analysis. Unpubl. pap., Columbia Univ.

Tversky, A., Kahneman, D. 1974. Judgment under uncertainty: Heuristics and biases. *Science* 185:1124–31

Tversky, A., Kahneman, D. 1981. The framing of decisions and the psychology of choice. *Science* 211:453–58

Ungson, G. R., Braunstein, D. N., Hall, P. D. 1981. Managerial information processing: A research review. *Admin. Sci. Q.* 26:116–34

Varga, K. 1975. N Achievement, n power and effectiveness of research development. *Hum. Relat.* 28:571–90

Vecchio, R. P., Gobdel, B. C. 1984. The vertical dyad linkage model of leadership: Problems and prospects. *Organ. Behav. Hum. Perform.* 34:5–20

Virany, B., Tushman, M., Romanelli, E. 1985. A longitudinal study on determinants of executive succession. Unpublished working pap., Columbia Univ.

Vroom, V. H., Yetton, P. W. 1973. *Leadership and Decision-Making.* Pittsburgh: Univ. Pittsburgh Press

Wainer, H. A., Rubin, I. M. 1969. Motivation of research and development entrepreneurs: Determinants of company success. *J. Appl. Psychol.* 53:178–84

Waldman, D. A., Bass, B. M., Einstein, W. O. 1985. Effort, performance and transformational leadership in industrial and military settings. Sch. Manage., State Univ. N.Y., working pap. 84–78

Weber, M. 1947. In *The Theory of Social and Economic Organization,* ed. T. Parsons. Transl. A. M. Henderson, T. Parsons. New York: The Free Press of Glencoe

Weick, K. E. 1976. Educational organizations as loosely coupled systems. *Admin. Sci. Q.* 21:1–19

Weick, K. E. 1979a. *The Social Psychology of Organizations.* Reading, MA: Addison-Wesley. 2nd ed.

Weick, K. E. 1979b. Cognitive processes in organizations. In *Research in Organizational Behavior,* ed. B. M. Staw, 1:41–74. Greenwich, CT: JAI Press

Weiner, S. S. 1976. Participation, deadlines, and choice. See March & Olsen 1976, pp. 225–50

Weissinger-Baylon, R. 1986. Garbage can decision processes in naval warfare. See March & Weissinger-Baylon 1986, pp. 36–52

Weschler, P. 1984. The long haul to the top. *Dun's Bus. Month.* 123:52–71

Wilsnack, S. 1974. The effects of social drinking on women's fantasy. *J. Pers.* 42:43–61

Winter, D. G. 1973. *The Power Motive.* New York: Free Press

Winter, D. G. 1979. *Navy Leadership and Management Competencies: Convergence Among Tests, Interviews and Performance Ratings.* Boston: McBer

Winter, D. G., Stewart, A. J. 1978. Power motivation. In *Dimensions of Personality,* ed. H. London, J. Exner. New York: Wiley

Yukl, G. A., Van Fleet, D. D. 1982. Cross-situational multi-method research on military leader effectiveness. *Organ. Behav. Hum. Perform.* 30:87–108

Zimbardo, P. G. 1970. The human choice: Individuation, reason, and order versus deindividuation, impulse, and chaos. In *Nebraska Symposium on Motivation: 1969,* ed. W. J. Arnold, D. Levine. Lincoln: Univ. Nebraska Press

Zucker, L. G. 1983. Organizations as institutions. In *Research in the Sociology of Organizations,* ed. S. B. Bacharach, 2:1–47. Greenwich, CT: JAI Press

AUTHOR INDEX

(Names appearing in capital letters indicate authors of chapters in this volume.)

736 AUTHOR INDEX

738　AUTHOR INDEX

SUBJECT INDEX

A

Ablation-behavior studies
  and cortical organization,
  133–34
Abnormal behavior
  in childhood
    see Childhood psy-
    chopathology
Absent-mindedness
  and memory studies, 654
Abstract reasoning
  in adult cognition paradigms,
  167
Academic achievement
  poor
    and attention deficit dis-
    order, 498
Academic employment
  sex discrimination in
    and contributions of women
    to psychology, 282,
    290
Access
  to word meaning
    in memory research, 632–
    35
Accessibility
  attitude
    activation mechanisms, 586
  of knowledge
    in social perception and
    cognition, 407–8, 409
  of social construct information
    in memory, 374–75, 378–
    79, 407, 410, 413–14
  of social knowledge
    and hypothesis testing, 402
Accidents
  prevention of
    behavioral community
    approach to, 444–45
Accuracy
  of hypothesis testing
    in social motivation studies,
    470–74
  of memory
    and belief change, 386–87,
    414
Achievement
  need for
    in executives, 693
    and self-concept, 309–10
Achievement motivation
  and adult personality, 161
  and information seeking
    strategies, 404

Achievement theory
  and control theory
    in social motivation, 477
Acoustics
  ecological
    and perceptual information
    studies, 77
Acquisition
  of knowledge and memory
    constraints on, 646–50
ACTeRS scale
  see Tests and scales
Action psychology
  and career development, 265
Action science
  need for
    in organization develop-
    ment, 344, 362
Active negatives
  as politician types, 232
Activity
  patterning of
    and postnatal behavioral de-
    velopment, 102–6
Activity inhibition
  and power motive studies,
  675–76, 690–91
ACT model
  and self-concept, 301
Adaptation
  and aging, 163
  to movement
    and visual perception stud-
    ies, 10–24
Adaptive responses
  early, 109–15
    getting fed, 111–13
    keeping warm, 110–11
    plasticity in early adaptive
    response systems,
    113–15
Additive-factors logic
  in memory research, 634–35
Additive models
  of information and perception,
  78
Administration
  of organizations
    and decision making stud-
    ies, 704, 706
Adolescence
  depression in, 518–24
Adolescent perceptions
  of nuclear stalemate, 249
Adolescent psychopathology
  and socialized conduct dis-
    order, 507

Adolescents
  social support groups for,
  438
  thought-sampling in
    and personality theory,
    545
Adult development
  and aging, 153–77
    cognitive development,
    165–70
    demography, 170–73
    in the family context, 156–
    60
    gray America and public
    policy, 173–76
    growth and regression in
    adult cognition, 165–
    68
    introduction to, 153–54
    learning and the life cycle,
    171–73
    methodological heresies,
    154–56
    new frontiers in the sociol-
    ogy of knowledge,
    176–77
    personality development,
    160–65
    social cognition, 168–70
Affect
  and cognition theories
    social motivation studies,
    474–83
  cognitive-affective dynamics
    in personality theory, 548–
    51
  and memory research, 650–51
  regulation of
    and self-concept, 317–20
  role in self-concept, 303–4,
    309
Affective disorders
  in adults, 518
    and children, 518–24
  primary prevention of, 430
Affiliation
  need for
    and power motive research,
    676
Affluence
  effects on political psycholo-
    gy, 233, 239, 242
Age differences
  in memory research, 645,
  647–49, 652
Age entitlement programs
  effects of, 175–76

Meta-analysis
  of outcome assessments
    in community interventions,
      450
Metacognitive knowledge
  and self-regulation, 310–11
Metamemory
  recent research in, 650
Metaphor
  comprehension of
    and memory for, 650
Metaphorical language
  in autism, 509
Metascripts
  as core organizing principles
    in private personality, 558
Mexican-American children
  and community intervention
    programs, 431
Microelectrode mapping
  methods
    in cortical research, 132, 136
Micronesians
  navigation skills of
    and mental models, 218
Migration
  and group ties
    in political participation
      studies, 239
Military
  decision making by, 700
Military service
  effects on political behavior,
    242
Milner, Brenda
  contributions to psychology,
    285–86
Miner Sentence Completion
  Scale
  see Tests and scales
Minimum detectable gap length
  (MDG)
  in auditory psychophysics,
    186–88
Minority groups
  community interventions
    among, 447–48
  group influence
    in attitudinal change, 603–
      14
Minority women
  contributions to psychology
    of, 283, 288, 292
Mirror method
  and self-report
    in personality studies, 540
Misperception
  patterns of
    in international conflict
      studies, 245
Mob rule
  political psychological studies
    of, 230

Modes of processing approach
  to information utilization
    in social perception,
      407
Monkeys
  cortical organization of
    comparative studies, 133,
      137–44, 147
Mood
  and causal relationship to per-
    sonality, 551–53
  fluctuation
    and repressive personality
      style, 540
  states
    and information processing,
      475
  variability
    relations to thoughts and
      fantasies, 542
  see also Affect
Morphological differences
  in defining cortical fields,
    132
Motion
  perception of
    and information structuring,
      68–69, 72–74
    and perception of stable en-
      vironment, 1–26
  visual perception of
    and information constraints,
      65–66
Motion parallax
  in perceptual information
    studies, 73
Motivation
  and personality theory re-
    search, 536
  and self-concept mediation,
    321–22
  social
    see Social motivation
  to truth-seeking
    in social perception studies,
      397, 404, 409–10, 414
Motives
  in goal selection
    and self-regulation of be-
      havior, 309–10
  of political leaders, 232–33
Motor behavior
  prenatal
    comparative studies, 95–98,
      117
Motor coordination
  and behavioral subcomponents
    of postnatal behavior, 106–
      9
Motor Excess Scale
  see Tests and scales
Müller-Lyer illusion
  and information use, 78

Multiple comparison procedures
  in variance analysis, 35–42
  applying after significant F
    test, 36
  choosing a multiple com-
    parison procedure, 37–
      39
  disordinal interactions, 41–
    42
  two-way models and linear
    contrasts, 39–41
Multiple-trace exemplar theory
  of memory for concepts, 637
Music
  and memory studies, 650
  perception
    and frequency of informa-
      tion occurrence, 64
  tonality and rhythm, 67, 77
  skills
    in autistic children, 511
Mutual help groups
  as social intervention, 441–43
Mythmaking
  and adaptation
    adult personality studies,
      163
Mythos
  as intuitive thinking mode, 168
Myths
  role in political behavior, 234
My Vocational Identity Scale
  see Tests and scales

N

Naming tasks
  in memory research, 633–34
National Council of Women
  Psychologists
  history of, 294
National health insurance
  and public opinion studies,
    235
National Self-Help Clearinghouse
  for support groups and net-
    works, 441
Native American women
  contributions to psychology,
    283
Naturally acquired knowledge
  memory for, 653–55
Naval warfare
  decision making in
    and garbage-can models,
      700
Navigating
  and mental models, 218
Needs
  of executives
    and succession studies,
      693, 695

CUMULATIVE INDEXES

CONTRIBUTING AUTHORS, VOLUMES 34–38

A

Achenbach, T. M., 35:227–56
Alkon, D. L., 36:419–93
Amir, Y., 37:17–41
Anastasi, A., 37:1–15
Asher, S. R., 34:465–509

B

Bargh, J. A., 38:369–425
Baum, A., 36:349–83
Beer, M., 38:339–67
Ben–Ari, R., 37:17–41
Bettman, J. R., 37:257–89
Birren, J. E., 34:543–75
Borgen, F. H., 35:579–604
Brewer, M. B., 36:219–43
Brislin, R. W., 34:363–400
Browne, M. A., 35:605–25
Brugge, J. F., 36:245–74
Buchsbaum, M. S., 34:401–30

C

Cairns, R. B., 35:553–77
Cantor, N., 36:275–305
Cascio, W. F., 35:461–518
Chaiken, S., 38:575–630
Clark, E. V., 34:325–49
Cohn, T. E., 37:495–521
Cook, T. D., 37:193–232
Cooper, J., 35:395–426
Cross, D. R., 37:611–51
Croyle, R. T., 35:395–426
Cunningham, W. R., 34:543–75
Cutting, J. E., 38:61–90

D

Dark, V. J., 37:43–75
Datan, N., 38:153–80
Deaux, K., 36:49–81
de Boer, E., 38:181–202
Denmark, F., 38:279–98
Diaz-Guerrero, R., 35:83–112
Dick, W., 34:261–95
Dreschler, W. A., 38:181–202
Duncan, C. C., 37:291–319

E

Edelbrock, C. S., 35:227–56
Eysenck, H. J., 34:167–93

F

Farley, J., 36:419–93
Feder, H. H., 35:165–200
Fischer, K. W., 36:613–48
Fraisse, P., 35:1–36
Friedman, A. F., 34:167–93

G

Gagné, R. M., 34:261–95
Gesten, E. L., 38:427–60
Gould, J. L., 37:163–92
Green, B. F., 35:37–53
Grunberg, N. E., 36:349–83

H

Haier, R. J., 34:351–80
Hakel, M. D., 37:135–61
Hall, J. A., 35:37–53
Hall, W. G., 38:91–128
Harris, L. C., 35:333–60
Harvey, J. H., 35:427–59
Hasher, L., 38:631–68
Hastie, R., 34:511–42
Hay, D. F., 37:135–61
Hecht, B. F., 34:325–49
Heller, J. F., 38:461–89
Helzer, J. E., 37:409–32
Hendersen, R. W., 36:495–529
Higgins, E. T., 38:369–425
Hillyard, S. A. 34:33–61
Holahan, C. J., 37:381–407
Honzik, M. P., 35:309–31
Horton, D. L., 35:361–94
House, R., 38:669–718
Hughes, F., 38:153–80

I

Iscoe, I., 35:333–60

J

Jason, L. A., 38:427–60
Johnson, M. K., 38:631–68
Johnston, W. A., 37:43–75

K

Kamil, A. C., 36:141–69
Kaas, J. H., 38:129–51
Keesey, R. E., 37:109–33
Kessler, R. C., 36:531–72
Kihlstrom, J. F., 36:385–418
Klaber, M., 36:115–40
Knoll, E., 34:195–222
Kolers, P. A., 34:129–66
Kolligian, J., Jr., 38:533–74
Kozma, R. B., 37:611–51
Kramer, A., 36:307–48
Kramer, R. M., 36:219–43
Krantz, D. S., 36:349–83
Kutas, M., 34:33–61

L

Lam, Y. R., 36:19–48
Lanyon, R. I., 35:667–701
Lasley, D. J., 37:495–521
Leventhal, H., 37:565–610
Loevinger, J., 34:195–222
London, P., 37:321–49

M

Mahoney, M. J., 35:605–25
Markus, H., 38:299–337
Marshall, J. F., 35:277–308
McFadden, D., 34:95–128
McGaugh, J. L., 34:297–323
McKeachie, W. J., 37:611–51
Medin, D. L., 35:113–38
Miller, D. T., 37:291–319
Miller, N. E., 34:1–31
Mills, C. B., 35:361–94
Mineka, S., 36:495–529
Mirsky, A. F., 37:291–319

771

CHAPTER TITLES, VOLUMES 34–38

nnual Reviews Inc.

NONPROFIT SCIENTIFIC PUBLISHER

4139 El Camino Way
P.O. Box 10139
Palo Alto, CA 94303-0897 • USA

ORDER FORM

Now you can order
TOLL FREE
1-800-523-8635
(except California)

ual Reviews Inc. publications may be ordered directly from our office by mail or use our Toll Free phone line (for orders paid by credit card or purchase order, and customer service calls only); ugh booksellers and subscription agents, worldwide; and through participating professional eties. Prices subject to change without notice.   ARI Federal I.D. #94-1156476

Individuals: Prepayment required on new accounts by check or money order (in U.S. dollars, check drawn on U.S. bank) or charge to credit card — American Express, VISA, MasterCard.

Institutional buyers: Please include purchase order number.

Students: $10.00 discount from retail price, per volume. Prepayment required. Proof of student status must be provided (photocopy of student I.D. or signature of department secretary is acceptable). Students must end orders direct to Annual Reviews. Orders received through bookstores and institutions requesting student ates will be returned.

Professional Society Members: Members of professional societies that have a contractual arrangement with Annual Reviews may order books through their society at a reduced rate. Check with your society for information.

Toll Free Telephone orders: Call 1-800-523-8635 (except from California) for orders paid by credit card or urchase order and customer service calls only. California customers and all other business calls use 415-493-4400 (not toll free). Hours: 8:00 AM to 4:00 PM, Monday-Friday, Pacific Time.

ular orders: Please list the volumes you wish to order by volume number.

ding orders: New volume in the series will be sent to you automatically each year upon publication. Cancel-n may be made at any time. Please indicate volume number to begin standing order.

ublication orders: Volumes not yet published will be shipped in month and year indicated.

fornia orders: Add applicable sales tax.

tage paid (4th class bookrate/surface mail) by **Annual Reviews Inc.** Airmail postage or UPS, extra.

NNUAL REVIEWS SERIES		Prices Postpaid per volume USA/elsewhere	Regular Order Please send:	Standing Order Begin with:
			Vol. number	Vol. number
ual Review of ANTHROPOLOGY				
Vols. 1-14	(1972-1985)	$27.00/$30.00		
Vol. 15	(1986)	$31.00/$34.00		
Vol. 16	(avail. Oct. 1987)	$31.00/$34.00	Vol(s). _____	Vol. _____
ual Review of ASTRONOMY AND ASTROPHYSICS				
Vols. 1-2, 4-20	(1963-1964; 1966-1982)	$27.00/$30.00		
Vols. 21-24	(1983-1986)	$44.00/$47.00		
Vol. 25	(avail. Sept. 1987)	$44.00/$47.00	Vol(s). _____	Vol. _____
ual Review of BIOCHEMISTRY				
Vols. 30-34, 36-54	(1961-1965; 1967-1985)	$29.00/$32.00		
Vol. 55	(1986)	$33.00/$36.00		
Vol. 56	(avail. July 1987)	$33.00/$36.00	Vol(s). _____	Vol. _____
ual Review of BIOPHYSICS AND BIOPHYSICAL CHEMISTRY				
Vols. 1-11	(1972-1982)	$27.00/$30.00		
Vols. 12-15	(1983-1986)	$47.00/$50.00		
Vol. 16	(avail. June 1987)	$47.00/$50.00	Vol(s). _____	Vol. _____
ual Review of CELL BIOLOGY				
Vol. 1	(1985)	$27.00/$30.00		
Vol. 2	(1986)	$31.00/$34.00		
Vol. 3	(avail. Nov. 1987)	$31.00/$34.00	Vol(s). _____	Vol. _____

ANNUAL REVIEWS SERIES		Prices Postpaid per volume USA/elsewhere	Regular Order Please send:	Standing Or Begin with
			Vol. number	Vol. numbe

Annual Review of **COMPUTER SCIENCE**
| Vol. 1 | (1986) . . . . | $39.00/$42.00 | | |
| Vol. 2 | (avail. Nov. 1987) . . . . | $39.00/$42.00 | Vol(s). _____ | Vol. _____ |

Annual Review of **EARTH AND PLANETARY SCIENCES**
Vols. 1-10	(1973-1982)	$27.00/$30.00		
Vols. 11-14	(1983-1986)	$44.00/$47.00		
Vol. 15	(avail. May 1987)	$44.00/$47.00	Vol(s). _____	Vol. _____

Annual Review of **ECOLOGY AND SYSTEMATICS**
Vols. 1-16	(1970-1985)	$27.00/$30.00		
Vol. 17	(1986)	$31.00/$34.00		
Vol. 18	(avail. Nov. 1987)	$31.00/$34.00	Vol(s). _____	Vol. _____

Annual Review of **ENERGY**
Vols. 1-7	(1976-1982)	$27.00/$30.00		
Vols. 8-11	(1983-1986)	$56.00/$59.00		
Vol. 12	(avail. Oct. 1987)	$56.00/$59.00	Vol(s). _____	Vol. _____

Annual Review of **ENTOMOLOGY**
Vols. 10-16, 18-30	(1965-1971, 1973-1985)	$27.00/$30.00		
Vol. 31	(1986)	$31.00/$34.00		
Vol. 32	(avail. Jan. 1987)	$31.00/$34.00	Vol(s). _____	Vol. _____

Annual Review of **FLUID MECHANICS**
Vols. 1-4, 7-17	(1969-1972, 1975-1985)	$28.00/$31.00		
Vol. 18	(1986)	$32.00/$35.00		
Vol. 19	(avail. Jan. 1987)	$32.00/$35.00	Vol(s). _____	Vol. _____

Annual Review of **GENETICS**
Vols. 1-19	(1967-1985)	$27.00/$30.00		
Vol. 20	(1986)	$31.00/$34.00		
Vol. 21	(avail. Dec. 1987)	$31.00/$34.00	Vol(s). _____	Vol. _____

Annual Review of **IMMUNOLOGY**
Vols. 1-3	(1983-1985)	$27.00/$30.00		
Vol. 4	(1986)	$31.00/$34.00		
Vol. 5	(avail. April 1987)	$31.00/$34.00	Vol(s). _____	Vol. _____

Annual Review of **MATERIALS SCIENCE**
Vols. 1, 3-12	(1971, 1973-1982)	$27.00/$30.00		
Vols. 13-16	(1983-1986)	$64.00/$67.00		
Vol. 17	(avail. August 1987)	$64.00/$67.00	Vol(s). _____	Vol. _____

Annual Review of **MEDICINE**
Vols. 1-3, 6, 8-9	(1950-1952, 1955, 1957-1958			
11-15, 17-36	1960-1964, 1966-1985)	$27.00/$30.00		
Vol. 37	(1986)	$31.00/$34.00		
Vol. 38	(avail. April 1987)	$31.00/$34.00	Vol(s). _____	Vol. _____

Annual Review of **MICROBIOLOGY**
Vols. 18-39	(1964-1985)	$27.00/$30.00		
Vol. 40	(1986)	$31.00/$34.00		
Vol. 41	(avail. Oct. 1987)	$31.00/$34.00	Vol(s). _____	Vol. _____